THE CAMBRIDGE HANDBOOK OF INTERNATIONAL AND COMPARATIVE TRADEMARK LAW

Trade in goods and service has historically resisted territorial confinement, but trademark protection remains territorial, albeit within an increasingly important framework of multilateral treaties. Trademark law therefore demands that practitioners, policy makers, and academics understand principles of international and comparative law. This handbook assists in that endeavor, with chapters describing and critically analyzing international and regional frameworks, and providing comparative perspectives on the substantive issues in trademark law and related fields, such as geographic indications, advertising law, and domain names. Chapters contrast common law and civil law approaches while focusing on the US and EU trademark systems in light of the role these systems have played in the development of trademark laws. Additionally, this handbook covers other jurisdictions, both common law and civil law, on the Asia-Pacific, African, and South American continents. This work should be read by anyone seeking a better understanding of trademark law around the world.

IRENE CALBOLI is Professor of Law at Texas A&M University School of Law, Academic Fellow at the University of Geneva, and Visiting Professor at Nanyang Technological University. She is an elected member of the American Law Institute and serves on the editorial boards of the *Oxford Journal of IP Law and Practice*, the *Queen Mary Journal of Intellectual Property*, and the WIPO–WTO Colloquium Papers.

JANE C. GINSBURG is the Morton L. Janklow Professor of Literary and Artistic Property Law at Columbia Law School. She is a member of the American Philosophical Society and the American Academy of Arts and Sciences, Corresponding Fellow of the British Academy, and an honorary fellow of Emmanuel College, University of Cambridge.

The Cambridge Handbook of International and Comparative Trademark Law

Edited by

IRENE CALBOLI
Texas A&M University School of Law

JANE C. GINSBURG
Columbia Law School

CAMBRIDGE
UNIVERSITY PRESS

CAMBRIDGE
UNIVERSITY PRESS

Shaftesbury Road, Cambridge CB2 8EA, United Kingdom

One Liberty Plaza, 20th Floor, New York, NY 10006, USA

477 Williamstown Road, Port Melbourne, VIC 3207, Australia

314–321, 3rd Floor, Plot 3, Splendor Forum, Jasola District Centre, New Delhi – 110025, India

103 Penang Road, #05–06/07, Visioncrest Commercial, Singapore 238467

Cambridge University Press is part of Cambridge University Press & Assessment, a department of the University of Cambridge.

We share the University's mission to contribute to society through the pursuit of education, learning and research at the highest international levels of excellence.

www.cambridge.org
Information on this title: www.cambridge.org/9781009293136

DOI: 10.1017/9781108399456

First published 2020
First paperback edition 2023

A catalogue record for this publication is available from the British Library

Library of Congress Cataloging-in-Publication data
NAMES: Calboli, Irene, editor. | Ginsburg, Jane C., editor.
TITLE: The Cambridge handbook of international and comparative trademark law / edited by Irene Calboli, Texas A&M School of Law [and] Jane C. Ginsburg, Columbia University School of Law
DESCRIPTION: Cambridge, United Kingdom ; New York, NY, USA : Cambridge University Press, 2020. |
SERIES: Cambridge law handbooks | Includes bibliographical references and index.
IDENTIFIERS: LCCN 2020010217 (print) | LCCN 2020010218 (ebook) | ISBN 9781108423090 (hardback) | ISBN 9781108399456 (ebook)
SUBJECTS: LCSH: Trademarks–Law and legislation. | Trademarks (International law)
CLASSIFICATION: LCC K1555 .C36 2020 (print) | LCC K1555 (ebook) | DDC 346.04/88–dc23
LC record available at https://lccn.loc.gov/2020010217
LC ebook record available at https://lccn.loc.gov/2020010218

ISBN 978-1-108-42309-0 Hardback
ISBN 978-1-009-29313-6 Paperback

Contents

Editors and Contributors

Graeme W. Austin, Victoria University of Wellington, BA(Hons), LLB, LLM; Columbia University, LLM, JSD; Burton Fellow in Intellectual Property, Columbia University 1997; Chair of Private Law and Associate Dean (Learning & Teaching); Victoria University of Wellington; Professor of Law, Melbourne University; Barrister of the High Court of New Zealand. He has taught courses in Copyright, Trademarks, Human Rights and Intellectual Property, and International Intellectual Property in the United States, Australia, Canada, People's Republic of China, and Singapore. He is the author and editor of numerous books and articles in these fields. He is an elected member of the American Law Institute and an Associate of the New Zealand Centre for Public Law.

Lionel Bently is Herchel Smith Professor of Intellectual Property at the University of Cambridge, Co-director of the Centre for Intellectual Property Law in the Faculty of Law, and a Professorial Fellow of Emmanuel College, Cambridge. With Professor Martin Kretschmer, he co-manages the website "Primary Sources on Copyright," at copyrighthistory.org. He is currently undertaking a project on the history of trademark law in the United Kingdom.

Nicolas Binctin is Professor in the Faculty of Law of the University of Poitiers, where he manages a postgraduate program on Research and Innovation Development Law and a postgraduate program on Intellectual Property (IP) Law. He teaches IP Law in its various components, at the universities of Poitiers and Paris XII-UPEC, and at the School of Law and Management of the University Paris II Assas-Panthéon. Since 2015 he has been an invited professor at the Academy of Organisation Africaine de la propriété intellectuelle (OAPI) in Yaoundé, Cameroun, and since 2017 has been a visiting professor at Bocconi University. His thesis is entitled *Le Capital intellectuel*, and he has published many articles in French and English, as well as a monograph on corporate strategy and IP law. The sixth edition of his book on IP law was published in September 2020 by Lextenso-LGDJ. He acts as expert or arbiter in different fields of IP and business law.

Robert Burrell is Professor of Intellectual Property and Information Technology Law at the University of Oxford and Professor of Law at Melbourne Law School. His previous academic positions include posts at the Australian National University and King's College London. He has been a Herbert Smith Freehills Visiting Fellow at the University of Cambridge and a visiting professor at the Benjamin N. Cardozo School of Law in New York. Burrell teaches and researches across all areas of intellectual property law. He is the author, with Allison Coleman, of *Copyright Exceptions: The Digital Impact* (Cambridge University Press, 2005) and, with Michael Handler, of *Australian Trade Mark Law* (Oxford University Press, 2010, 2nd ed. 2016). Outside academia, Burrell has spent many years working as a consultant to boutique Australian firms and, in particular, has substantial experience in litigation before the Australian Trade Marks Office.

Irene Calboli is Professor of Law at Texas A&M University School of Law; Academic Fellow at the School of Law, University of Geneva; and Visiting Professor at Nanyang Business School, Nanyang Technological University. She is a member of the editorial board of the *Queen Mary Journal of Intellectual Property* and the WIPO–WTO Colloquium Papers, and a past member of the editorial board of the *Trademark Reporter*. An elected member of the American Law Institute and associate member of the Singapore Academy of Law, she currently serves as a member of the Council of the International Law Association (Singapore Branch); the Board of the European Policy for Intellectual Property Law Association (EPIP); and the Legislation and Regulation Committee of the International Trademark Association (INTA). She has held visiting positions in several universities in Europe, Asia, and the Americas. She is currently a Fulbright Specialist Scholar.

Margaret Chon is the Donald & Lynda Horowitz Professor for the Pursuit of Justice, and formerly Associate Dean for Research at Seattle University School of Law. She is the author of numerous articles, books, book chapters, and review essays on intellectual property, as well as race and law. Her recent coedited volume, *The Cambridge Handbook of Public-Private Partnerships, Intellectual Property Governance, and Sustainable Development* (Cambridge University Press, 2018), focuses on the relationship of global intellectual property institutions to human and sustainable development goals. An alumna of the University of Michigan (MHSA and JD) and Cornell University (AB), she clerked for both the Honorable A. Leon Higginbotham and the Honorable Dolores J. Sloviter of the US Court of Appeals for the Third Circuit. Chon is a member of the American Law Institute and the American Bar Foundation.

Apostolos G. Chronopoulos is Senior Lecturer in Intellectual Property Law at the Centre for Commercial Law Studies, Queen Mary University of London. His research interests span the broader field of intellectual property and competition law. His latest publications include *Strict Liability and Negligence in Copyright Law: Fair Use as Regulation of Activity Levels*, 97 NEBRASKA L. REV. 384–468 (2018).

Jennifer Davis is Emeritus Fellow of Wolfson College and a member of the Centre for Intellectual Property and Information Law, Faculty of Law, University of Cambridge. She has also practiced as a solicitor. She is Chair of the Humanities Society, Wolfson College and has served on the Ethics Committee of the Alan Turing Institute, London. Her work is primarily focused on trademarks and unfair competition but she is also interested in history and linguistics as they relate to intellectual property law. She was part of the collective that produced *Keywords for Today*, published by Oxford University Press (2018). She has also published a number of articles on trademarks and linguistics with Professor Alan Durant of the University of Middlesex. She has authored textbooks on Intellectual Property (IP) and currently, with Professor Tanya Aplin, is the author of *Intellectual Property: Cases and Materials* for Oxford University Press.

Estelle Derclaye is Professor of Intellectual Property Law at the University of Nottingham. She is the author and editor of several books and articles in the field of Intellectual Property (IP) law and has done expert work for the UK Intellectual Property Office, the European Commission, and national and foreign law firms. She was a senior visiting scholar at the University of California, Berkeley in 2010 and at Melbourne Law School in 2013 and a visiting professor at the National University of Singapore in 2015, and regularly gives guest lectures in European universities. Her main areas of research are copyright and designs, the protection of databases, IP overlaps, IP and climate change, and IP and well-being. She is President-Elect of the European Copyright Society, a group of academics aiming to influence policy-making.

Graeme B. Dinwoodie is Global Professor of Intellectual Property Law at Chicago-Kent College of Law, and Visiting Professor at the University of Oxford (where he held the Chair in IP from 2009 to 2018). Dinwoodie holds an LLB (Hons.) degree from the University of Glasgow, an LLM degree from Harvard Law School (where he was a John F. Kennedy Scholar), and a JSD degree from Columbia Law School (where he was a Burton Fellow). In 2008, the International Trademark Association awarded Dinwoodie the Pattishall Medal for Teaching Excellence in Trademark Law. He is the author of five casebooks including *Trademarks and Unfair Competition: Law and Policy* (5th ed. 2018; with Mark D. Janis). His scholarship has appeared in several leading law journals and is widely cited by scholars in Europe, the United States, and elsewhere. He was elected as a member of the American Law Institute in 2003.

Stacey Dogan is Associate Dean for Academic Affairs and Professor of Law at Boston University School of Law, where she teaches courses related to property, intellectual property, and technology law. She is one of the leaders of the Boston University Cyber Alliance – an interdisciplinary group of scholars in law, computer science, philosophy, economics, and other disciplines who are interested in legal and ethical questions raised by the Internet and other new technologies – and is a member of the Steering Committee for the Hariri Institute for Computing and Computational Sciences. She has previously served as the coeditor-in-chief of the *Journal of the Copyright Society* (USA) and Chair of the Intellectual Property Section of the Association of American Law Schools.

Christine Haight Farley is Professor of Law at American University Washington College of Law, where she teaches courses on intellectual property, advertising law, and art law. Her main areas of research are international trademark law, design protection, and art law. She serves as Faculty Director of the Program on Information Justice and Intellectual Property and previously served as Associate Dean for Faculty and Academic Affairs. She has been a visiting professor at the University of Paris West, the University of Puerto Rico, the University of Havana, Monash University, and the National Law University in Lucknow, India. She serves on the Board of Directors for the Center for Inter-American Legal Education and has been a Fulbright Specialist for intellectual property law.

Susy Frankel, FRSNZ, is Professor of Law, holds the Chair in Intellectual Property and International Trade, and is Director of the New Zealand Centre of International Economic Law, at Victoria University of Wellington, New Zealand. Since 2008 Frankel has been Chair of the Copyright Tribunal (NZ). She was the President of the International Association for the Advancement of Teaching and Research in Intellectual Property (ATRIP) from 2015 to 2017. She is a member of the editorial boards of the *Journal of World Intellectual Property Law* and the *Queen Mary Journal of Intellectual Property*. She teaches copyright, trademarks, patents, international intellectual property and international trade law. Her scholarship focuses on international intellectual property and its nexus with international trade, particularly treaty interpretation and the protection of indigenous peoples' knowledge and innovation. In 2018 Susy was elected Fellow of the Royal Society of New Zealand.

Dev S. Gangjee is Professor of Intellectual Property Law at the University of Oxford. Gangjee's research focuses on Intellectual Property (IP), with a special emphasis on branding and trademarks, geographical indications and copyright law. Gangjee is a member of the European Communities Trade Mark Association GI committee. He has most recently co-authored *The Confusion Test in European Trade Mark Law* (Oxford University Press, 2019). Gangjee has acted in an advisory capacity for national governments, law firms, international organizations and the European Commission on IP issues. He is a member of the Editorial Boards of the *Modern Law Review* and *the Indian Law Review*.

Daniel J. Gervais the Milton R. Underwood Chair in Law at Vanderbilt University and Director of the Vanderbilt Intellectual Property Program. Prior to joining Vanderbilt, he was the Acting Dean at the Faculty of Law of the University of Ottawa (Common Law Section). Before he joined the Academy, Professor Gervais was Legal Officer at the GATT (now WTO); Head of Section at WIPO; and Vice-President of Copyright Clearance Center, Inc. (CCC). In 2012, he was elected to the Academy of Europe. He is a member of the American Law Institute.

Jane C. Ginsburg, University of Chicago, BA 1976, MA 1977; Harvard, JD 1980; Université de Paris II, Diplôme d'études approfondies 1985 (Fulbright Scholar), Doctorat en droit 1995, is the Morton L. Janklow Professor of Literary and Artistic Property Law at Columbia University School of Law, and Faculty Director of its Kernochan Center for Law, Media and the Arts. She teaches legal methods, copyright law, international copyright law, and trademark law, and is the author or co-author of casebooks in all four subjects, as well as of many articles and book chapters on domestic and international copyright and trademark law. She is a member of the American Law Institute (and co-reporter of its project on Principles of Intellectual Property and Transnational Litigation, an international Vice President of the Association Littéraire et Artistique Internationale (ALAI)); a corresponding fellow of the British Academy, a member of the American Philosophical Society, a member of the American Academy of Arts and Sciences, an honorary fellow of Emmanuel College, University of Cambridge, and was an affiliated fellow and a resident at the American Academy in Rome.

Michael Handler is Professor in the Faculty of Law, University of New South Wales, Australia, and a member of the Intellectual Property Committee of the Law Council of Australia. He has published numerous books, journal articles, and book chapters on trademark law, and is the co-author, with Robert Burrell, of the Oxford University Press treatise *Australian Trade Mark Law* (2d ed. 2016).

Anselm Kamperman Sanders is Professor of Intellectual Property Law, Director of the Advanced Masters IP Law and Knowledge Management (IPKM LLM/MSc), and Academic Director of the Institute for Globalization and International Regulation at Maastricht University in the Netherlands, co-director of the Annual IP Law School and IP Seminar of the Institute for European Studies of Macau (IEEM), and Adjunct Professor at Jinan University Law School, Guangzhou, China. He is Deputy Judge in the Court of Appeal The Hague. Anselm holds a PhD from Queen Mary University of London, where he worked as Marie Skłodowska Curie Fellow. He is a contributor to the UN World Economic and Social Survey 2018 on Frontier Technologies for Sustainable Development. He coordinates the European IP Institutes Network-Innovation Society, a Horizon 2020 Marie Skłodowska Curie ITN-EJD Action.

Annette Kur is Affiliated Research Fellow at the Max-Planck-Institute for Innovation and Competition, Munich and an honorary professor at Ludwig-Maximilians-University, Munich.

Jyh-An Lee is Associate Professor at Faculty of Law of the Chinese University of Hong Kong, where he currently serves as the Assistant Dean for Undergraduate Studies and the Director of the LLB Programme. He was the legal lead and co-lead of Creative Commons Taiwan and an advisory committee member for Copyright Amendment at the Taiwan Intellectual Property Office (TIPO) at the Ministry of Economic Affairs. He has been the legal lead of the Creative Commons Hong Kong Chapter since October 2018. He is a member of the European Center for E-Commerce & Internet Law advisory board, which is affiliated with the University of Vienna. In 2016, he was appointed as a domain name dispute resolution panelist by the Asian Domain Name Dispute Resolution Centre (ADNDRC) and continues to serve in this capacity. Before starting his academic career, he was a practicing lawyer in Taiwan, specializing in technology and business transactions.

David Lefranc is a French lawyer specializing in intellectual property and IT law. He obtained his doctorate in law in 2003. His thesis addressed legal consequences of fame in copyright and trademark law and rights of personality. As an “avocat,” David Lefranc founded the “Laropoin” legal office. He continues his research through the publication of numerous articles. In 2017, the French Constitutional Court awarded him the legal practice book prize for his *Droit des Applications Connectées* (Larcier). He is also a lecturer at the University of Douai, France.

Susanna H. S. Leong, LLB (Hons) National University of Singapore, LLM (with Merit) University College London, is Professor of Law and Vice Provost (Lifelong Education) at the National University of Singapore. Susanna teaches business-related law modules such as contract, sale of goods and intellectual property to undergraduate and graduate business students in English and Chinese. Susanna’s research interests are in intellectual property and technology-related laws. She has published in international and local academic journals. She is the author of *Intellectual Property Law of Singapore*, published as part of the Law Practice Series by Academy Publishing. She is a member of the World Intellectual Property Organization (WIPO) Arbitration and Mediation Centre’s Domain Name Panel, the Regional Centre for Arbitration, Kuala Lumpur (RCAKL) Panel, and the Asian Domain Name Dispute Resolution Centre (Hong Kong). She is also a member of the Singapore Copyright Tribunal.

Jacqueline D. Lipton, LLB Hons (Melb), LLM/PhD (Cantab) is a visiting professor of law at the University of Pittsburgh where she teaches domestic and international commercial and intellectual property law, with an emphasis on the impact of digital technology and the law. She also teaches online courses in these areas for Seton Hall University and the University of New Hampshire. She is the co-author of leading casebooks on cyberspace law, and the criminal law of information and intellectual property, as well as the sole author of a number of monographs on the law relating to digital technology. She has published widely in the United States, the United Kingdom, and Australia in these areas, and currently divides her time between law teaching and working in the publishing industry, where she represents and consults for authors and artists.

Spyros M. Maniatis is Director of the British Institute of International and Comparative Law and Honorary Professor at the Centre for Commercial Law Studies, Queen Mary University of London. His research interests cover the interface between intellectual property, competition and trade, the regulation of artificial intelligence, and intellectual property in Asia.

Frederick Mostert is Professor of Practice at Dickson Poon School of Law, King's College, London, Research Fellow at the Oxford Intellectual Property Research Centre, University of Oxford, and Research Fellow at the Research Center for Intellectual Property of Tsinghua University School of Law, Beijing. Frederick is the principal author and editor of *Famous and Well-Known Marks – An International Analysis*. He serves on the Editorial Board of the Journal of Intellectual Property Law and Practice. He is Past President of the International Trademark Association and was inducted into the Intellectual Property Hall of Fame.

Ng-Loy Wee Loon is Professor of Law at the National University of Singapore. She is also a member of Singapore's Copyright Tribunal and of the Singapore Domain Name Dispute Resolution Policy Panel. In 2013, she was conferred the "Singapore Law Merit Award" by the Singapore Academy of Law in recognition of her contributions to the development and advancement of Singapore law. In 2016, she was appointed "Senior Counsel *(honoris causa)*" by the Singapore Court of Appeal for her contributions to the legal profession, in particular her assistance to the Court in her role as *amicus curiae*.

Ansgar Ohly holds the Chair of Private Law, Intellectual Property and Competition Law at the Ludwig Maximilian University of Munich. He is also Visiting Professor at the University of Oxford, Visiting Senior Member of St Peter's College, Oxford, and Honorary Bencher of the Middle Temple in London. Prior to joining the Munich Faculty of Law, he was a senior researcher at the Max Planck Institute for Innovation and Competition and, subsequently, a professor at the University of Bayreuth. His main fields of academic interest are all areas of intellectual property law and unfair competition law, with a special emphasis on European developments and on the comparison of civil law and common law systems. He is the co-editor of *GRUR*, the leading German intellectual property journal.

Miquel Peguera is Associate Professor of Law at Universitat Oberta de Catalunya (UOC) (Barcelona, Spain). He holds a PhD in Law from the University of Barcelona (2006), with a doctoral dissertation on the liability of internet intermediary service providers. He has been Affiliate Scholar at Stanford Center for Internet & Society since 2014, co-editor of the *Journal of Intellectual Property, Information Technology and E-Commerce Law* (jipitec.eu) since 2011, and was Visiting Scholar at Columbia University School of Law (2007–2008). His research focuses on the legal aspects of the Internet, particularly regarding copyright, trademarks, privacy, and intermediary liability. He has published extensively on those fields from both an EU and US perspective. He is a consultant with the Spanish law firm Cuatrecasas.

Lisa P. Ramsey is Professor of Law at the University of San Diego School of Law, where she is a founding member of the Center for Intellectual Property Law and Markets. She teaches intellectual property and international intellectual property classes and is an expert on trademark law. Her scholarship focuses on non-traditional trademarks and the potential conflicts between trademark laws and the right to freedom of expression. She has given presentations on trademark law to attorneys, professors, and students throughout the United States and around the world. Professor Ramsey is also an active member of the International Trademark Association and has served on several INTA committees. Before joining the USD law faculty, she was an intellectual property litigator at Gray Cary Ware & Freidenrich and served as a judicial law clerk for the Honorable Rebecca Beach Smith in the United States District Court for the Eastern District of Virginia.

Sam Ricketson, BA, LLB (Melbourne), LLM, LLD (London), is Emeritus Professor in the Melbourne Law School, Australia, where he was previously a professor (2000–2019). Prior to his

Melbourne appointment, Sam was a professor at Monash University, Victoria (1991–2000); before this, he held academic and research positions at the University of Melbourne and Queen Mary College, London. During his career, Sam has written, taught and practised (as a barrister and consultant) in all areas of intellectual property law, at both the national (Australian) and international levels. He is Fellow of the Academy of Social Sciences of Australia and the Australian Academy of Law.

Sandra L. Rierson, University of North Carolina at Chapel Hill, BA 1989; Yale Law School, JD 1992, is an associate professor and the co-Director for the Center for Law and Intellectual Property at Thomas Jefferson School of Law. After graduating from law school, where she was the symposium editor of the *Yale Law Journal*, Professor Rierson clerked for the Honorable Richard A. Gadbois, in the US District Court in Los Angeles, California. Professor Rierson subsequently practiced law with Quinn Emanuel Urquhart & Sullivan, also in Los Angeles, where she became a partner in 1998. Her litigation practice focused on intellectual property and employment law, government contracts, and general business disputes. Professor Rierson's scholarship is in the areas of trademark law, legal history, and women's history. She teaches civil procedure, legal writing I, and trademark and unfair competition law.

Thomas Riis, LLD, PhD, is Professor at the University of Copenhagen, Centre for Information and Innovation Law (CIIR). He has published a large number of books and articles, primarily in the fields of intellectual property law and marketing practice law. Amongst other things, he is the national editor of the *Nordic Journal of Intellectual Property Law Review* (*Nordiskt Immateriellt Rättsskydd*), chairman of the Committee for Good Scientific Practice at the University of Copenhagen and chairman of the Danish Media Board.

Jennifer E. Rothman is William G. Coskran Professor of Law at Loyola Law School, at Loyola Marymount University, Los Angeles. She is an elected member of the American Law Institute and an affiliated fellow of the Yale Information Society Project at Yale Law School. Professor Rothman writes and teaches in the areas of intellectual property and constitutional law. Rothman received her AB from Princeton University, where she won the Asher Hinds Book Prize and the Grace May Tilton Prize. Rothman received her JD from UCLA, where she graduated first in her class. She also has an MFA from the University of Southern California's School of Cinematic Arts. Rothman's book, *The Right of Publicity: Privacy Reimagined for a Public World*, was published in 2018 by Harvard University Press. She is also the founder of the website, *Rothman's Roadmap to the Right of Publicity*, rightofpublicityroadmap.com.

Jens Schovsbo, LLD, PhD, is Professor at the University of Copenhagen, Centre for Information and Innovation Law (CIIR). He has published extensively in Danish, Scandinavian and international law journals primarily on intellectual property law. Amongst other things he is the President of the International Association for the Advancement of Teaching and Research in Intellectual Property (ATRIP) (2019–2021) and a member of the Scientific Advisory Board for the Max Planck Institute for Innovation.

Martin Senftleben is Professor of Intellectual Property Law and Director, Institute for Information Law (IViR), University of Amsterdam. His activities focus on the reconciliation of private intellectual property rights with competing public interests of a social, cultural or economic nature. He is an advisor to the Dutch Ministry of Justice in copyright matters, President of the European Copyright Society, President of the Trademark Law Institute and a member of the

Executive Committees of ALAI and ATRIP. He previously worked as Professor of Intellectual Property at the Vrije Universiteit Amsterdam and Of Counsel at Bird & Bird, The Hague. From 2004 to 2007, he was a legal officer in the trademarks department of WIPO. Besides various articles in leading European and US law journals, his publications include *Copyright, Limitations and the Three-Step Test* (Kluwer Law International 2004) and *European Trade Mark Law – A Commentary* (with Annette Kur, Oxford University Press 2017).

Jeremy N. Sheff is Professor of Law at St. John's University School of Law and the founding Faculty Director of the St. John's Intellectual Property Law Center. He teaches property, introduction to intellectual property, patent law, trademark law, international intellectual property, and First Amendment law. His recent and forthcoming publications include *Jefferson's Taper*, 73 SMU L. REV. (in press); *Legal Sets*, 40 CARDOZO L. REV. 2029 (2019); and *Marks, Morals, and Markets*, 65 STAN. L. REV. 761 (2013); he is also a co-author of the free, open-source Property Law casebook *Open-Source Property*. His forthcoming book, *Valuing Progress: A Pluralist Account of Knowledge Governance*, is under contract with Cambridge University Press.

David Tan, University of Melbourne, BCom 1995, LLB 1995, PhD 2010; Harvard, LLM 1999, is Professor and Vice Dean (Academic Affairs) at Faculty of Law, National University of Singapore (NUS Law). At NUS Law, David pioneered courses in entertainment law, freedom of speech and privacy & data protection law. His areas of research cover personality rights, copyright, trademarks, freedom of expression and tort law. He has published over fifty articles, comments, book chapters and review essays since joining NUS Law in 2008. His publications have appeared in a wide range of journals that include *Yale Journal of International Law, Harvard Journal of Sports & Entertainment Law, Law Quarterly Review* and *Sydney Law Review*. His monograph *The Commercial Appropriation of Fame: A Cultural Analysis of the Right of Publicity and Passing Off* was published by Cambridge University Press in both hardback (2017) and paperback (2018).

Edouard Treppoz is Professor at the University Paris 1 Panthéon-Sorbonne. He is the author of numerous articles dedicated to copyright law, private international law and European intellectual property law, the co-editor of two books on those issues and the co-author of a casebook dedicated to *International Copyright Law – US and EU Perspectives* (ed. Edward Elgar Publisher with Jane C. Ginsburg as a co-author). He served as Visiting Professor of Law at Columbia Law School (spring 2014).

Rebecca Tushnet is the inaugural Frank Stanton Professor of First Amendment Law at Harvard Law School. Her work focuses on copyright, trademark, and false advertising law. Her publications include, *Registering Disagreement: Registration in Modern American Trademark Law* (HARVARD L. REV. 2017); *Worth a Thousand Words: The Images of Copyright Law* (HARVARD L. REV. 2012); and *Copy This Essay: How Fair Use Doctrine Harms Free Speech and How Copying Serves It* (YALE L.J. 2004). She helped found the Organization for Transformative Works, a nonprofit dedicated to supporting and promoting fanworks. Her blog, tushnet.blogspot.com, is one of the top intellectual property blogs. She is also an expert on the law of engagement rings.

Coenraad Visser is Professor of Intellectual Property Law at the University of South Africa, Pretoria, where he specializes in international intellectual property law with special emphasis on developing countries. He is a former editor-in-chief of the *Annual Survey of South African Law*, and the editor of the *South African Mercantile Law Journal*. He was a member of the international advisory board of *Computer Law Review International*. He was a special adviser to the president of the World Bank on Civic Engagement, Empowerment, and Respect for Diversity and one of the contributors to the Scenarios for the Future Project of the European Patent Office. He was a consultant to the Secretariat of the African Union and to the International Association of Library Associations and Institutions on copyright treaty proposals. He is the Founding President of the South African Association of Intellectual Property Law and Information Technology Law Teachers and Researchers.

Kimberlee Weatherall is Professor of Law at the University of Sydney Law School. Kimberlee has published extensively on issues ranging from digital copyright, and bilateral and multilateral trade agreements and IP, to the conception of the consumer in trademark law in the *Modern Law Review*. Her recent funded research projects include an interdisciplinary project on the conception of consumers in trademark law (in conjunction with Australia's Trademarks Office, IP Australia) and on the availability and use of ebooks in Australian public libraries (with a range of state and public libraries and library associations). She is a past member of the Australian Government's Advisory Council on IP and the Advisory Committee to the Australian Law Reform Commission Inquiry into *Copyright and the Digital Economy*. She is currently a member of the Australian Computer Society's Technical Advisory Board and Committee on Artificial Intelligence Ethics.

Jacques de Werra is Professor of Contract Law and Intellectual Property Law at the Law School of the University of Geneva, Switzerland. He holds a PhD in copyright law from the University of Lausanne and an LLM from Columbia Law School. He was a faculty fellow/faculty associate at the now Berkman Klein Center for Internet and Society at Harvard University and has held visiting professor positions at various universities including Stanford Law School, Nagoya University and City University of Hong Kong. He has published in leading law reviews (including the *Harvard Journal of Law and Technology* and the *Columbia Journal of Law and the Arts*) and has authored and edited various books and publications of reference including the *Research Handbook on Intellectual Property Licensing* (Edward Elgar 2013) and the *Law and Practice of Trademark Transactions* (Edward Elgar 2016, with Irene Calboli).

Foreword

Trade mark law is a paradoxical subject. When it is first encountered, one is likely to think that it seems reasonably straightforward. Most people have some notion of what a trade mark is, and the idea that the proprietor of a trade mark should be able to stop the use of signs which are likely to cause confusion has an intuitive appeal. Equally, it is not difficult to see why, for example, registration of signs as trade marks should only be permitted if they are either inherently distinctive for the relevant goods and/or services or have acquired distinctiveness through use. The more one learns about trade mark law, however, the more one comes to understand how difficult it really is. This is partly due to the ever-increasing sophistication of branding practices, the effects of changes in technology and business models and the broader rights which modern legislation tends to confer upon trade mark proprietors. More fundamentally, however, it is because even the most basic concepts turn out to be remarkably slippery. What is (and is not) a trade mark? What amounts to acquired distinctiveness, and is it sufficient that consumers recognise the sign and associate with the applicant's products? What do we mean when we speak of confusion, and does it include such things as initial-interest confusion, post-sale confusion and downstream confusion? Furthermore, experience has taught us that trade marks raise issues concerning such matters as economics (for example, when it comes to exhaustion of rights) and freedom of expression (for example, in regulating what marks may be registered). Trade marks also pose challenges when it comes to questions such as choice of law and accessory liability. For these and other reasons, trade mark law needs to be viewed holistically. For example, in considering the requirement in European law that the use of an identical sign in relation to identical goods or services must affect, or be liable to affect, one of the functions of the trade mark if the use is to infringe that trade mark, it is necessary to consider (among other things) the circumstances in which use of the sign in relation to the proprietor's own goods may infringe, the defence of honest concurrent use, the territorial scope of injunctions, the law with respect to keyword advertising and who bears the burden of proof on this issue.[1]

In this volume Irene Calboli and Jane Ginsburg have assembled a distinguished team of scholars whose contributions explore contemporary trade mark law by first placing it in its public international context and then applying the comparative law method. In the first part, we find eight chapters considering the international dimension. In the second part, we find fifteen pairs of chapters, each of which considers an aspect of trade mark law from both a common law and a

[1] Richard Arnold, *Infringement under Article 10(2)(a) Trade Marks Directive (Recast)/Article 9(2)(a) European Union Trade Mark Regulation and Effect on the Functions of the Trade Mark*. GRUR Int. 884 (2016).

civil law perspective. These perspectives are revealing because common law systems place more emphasis on the rights acquired by the use of a trade mark, while civil law systems place more emphasis on the rights acquired by registration. Moreover, the global spread of the contributors provides insights from a diversity of laws which resemble each other, but differ in subtle yet significant ways. Between them, these chapters consider almost every aspect of trade mark law, including its important boundaries with areas such as advertising law, the right of publicity, unfair competition law and designs. The authors all have something fresh to say about the topics they address, as well as recapping the known law. The volume thus represents a valuable contribution to the scholarly literature, and is more than the sum of its very considerable parts.

Richard Arnold
Royal Courts of Justice, London

Preface

INTERNATIONAL AND COMPARATIVE TRADEMARK LAW: A COMPREHENSIVE APPROACH

Trade in trademark-bearing goods and services resists territorial confinement; sales of goods and performance of services have long traversed borders, and internet commerce has vastly augmented trademarks' yearning for ubiquity. Today, trademarks amount to one of the most economically valuable intangible assets for multinationals and corporate portfolios. The recent rise of Louis Vuitton Moët Hennessy's chairman Bernard Arnault to the second position in the rank of the world's richest persons exemplifies the power of trademarks as best-sellers of products. Yet trademark protection remains territorial; national laws define its subject matter and scope, albeit within an increasingly important framework of multilateral treaties. A few examples (though we could cite many more) illustrate the interplay of multinational commerce and national norms. Nestlé, the Swiss producer of the four-fingers-shaped Kit Kat chocolate bar, has in recent years undertaken multiple legal proceedings to register its trade dress as a shape mark, with different results, in the United Kingdom (with respect to a national trademark), the European Union (with respect to an EU-wide trademark), Singapore, and South Africa. The trademark infringement actions by Christian Louboutin, the French designer of the famed red-sole shoes, encountered a similar fate. In some countries, national offices and courts have found the red sole to be protectable as a mark, while others rejected the claim or canceled Louboutin's registration. The American chain McDonald's has also been the protagonist of multiple legal proceedings across the world to protect its marks against similar names, or names using its famous "Mc" prefix or variations such as "Mac," for products related and unrelated to hamburgers and fast food. Here again, the outcomes of these proceedings have alternated in favor of and against McDonald's. And of course, worldwide litigation involving many of the trademarks that have so enriched Mr. Arnault has resulted in very variable outcomes, including regarding the use of the Louis Vuitton marks in parodies and artistic works.

Trademark law today therefore demands that its practitioners, exponents, and policy makers master (or at least remain alert to) principles of international and comparative law. This book aims to assist that endeavor. Its chapters describe and critically analyze the international and regional frameworks, and then provide comparative law perspectives on the principal substantive issues in trademark law and related fields, such as geographic indications, advertising law, domain names, and licensing. It is the first of its kind to address these topics systematically and comparatively in one comprehensive collection. The book contrasts common law and civil law approaches, and focuses on the US and EU trademark systems. The book accords these systems particular prominence in light of the role they have had, historically, in the development of trademark laws internationally and, in turn, the impact that the principles, rules, and doctrines originating from these two systems have had on the national laws of a large number of jurisdictions worldwide. But it also takes into account other jurisdictions, both common law and civil law, on the Asia-Pacific, African, and South American continents.

METHODOLOGY AND STRUCTURE OF THE BOOK

The book is structured in two main parts. Part One focuses on the trademark law developments at the international level, while Part Two comparatively analyzes the theoretical and practical evolution of trademark law in national and regional systems in the United States. and the European Union and across common law and civil law jurisdictions. In addition to their individual content, the two parts and the chapters within each part remain closely interlinked; the critical reflections that bear on one topic often illuminate the analysis of other subjects.

In particular, Part One addresses the trademark provisions in the international agreements under both the framework of the World Intellectual Property Organization (WIPO) and of the World Trade Organization (WTO). This part includes chapters focusing, specifically, on: the Paris Convention for the Protection of Industrial Property; the Agreement on Trade-Related Aspects of Intellectual Property Rights (TRIPS); the international registration system administered by WIPO through the Madrid Agreement and Protocol, and the more recent Trademark Law Treaty and Singapore Agreement on trademarks. It also includes a chapter addressing the protection of well-known marks under international trademark law, with particular focus on the WIPO Guidelines in this area. Part One also addresses the developments in international trademark law outside the fora of WIPO and the WTO; it includes a chapter focusing on the analysis of the trademark provisions in the post-TRIPS bilateral and plurilateral trade agreements. Similarly, Part One features a chapter comparing the systems of trademark harmonization in several regional organizations: the European Union, the Organisation Africaine de la Proprieté Intellectuelle (OAPI), the African Regional Intellectual Property Organization (ARIPO), the Association of South East Asian Nations (ASEAN), and the Mercado Común del Sur (MERCOSUR). Part One concludes with two chapters focusing, respectively, on conflicts of law related to adjudications of transnational trademark disputes and on the application of alternative dispute resolution mechanisms to trademark disputes across jurisdictions.

Building upon the analysis in Part One, Part Two of the book addresses legislation and judicial doctrines in trademark law from a comparative perspective. This part primarily, but not exclusively, features the EU and US approaches in this area. It highlights the still-existing differences, but also the convergences, between common law and civil law countries. This part is subdivided into fifteen specific areas of inquiry; each topic pairs authors (or joint authors) offering an EU or US perspective, or a common law or civil law perspective. The topics are: the nature and function of trademarks; the types of signs that can be protected as trademarks; the public policy limitations of protectable trademark subject matter; the relationship between trademarks and geographical indications of origin; the concept and treatment of certification and collective marks; the relationship between trademark law and advertising law; the relationship between trademark law and the right of publicity; the relationship between trademarks and domain names and relevant dispute resolution systems; overlapping rights between trademark protection and other intellectual property rights; theories underlying the standards for trademark infringement; trademark protection beyond confusion-based theories, notably trademark dilution; the doctrines related to secondary trademark liability; trademark defenses; the principle of exhaustion of trademark rights; and trademark transactions.

Together, Parts One and Two of the book provide a comprehensive survey of the existing trademark rules and general doctrines that have evolved over the course of the past century at the international level and how these rules (that originated from a variety of national systems subsequently molded into international agreements through international diplomacy) have later been implemented at the national level. These multilateral efforts have produced a largely harmonized trademark system worldwide. Still, the book highlights that, despite this process of harmonization and convergence of national and regional laws, some differences in national trademark laws persist. Moreover, the national application of harmonized principles has led, at times, to different results in adjudication of similar cases across different countries, and the book provides a useful resource also in this respect.

ACKNOWLEDGMENTS

As with all collective works, this book is the result of the joint efforts of many people. We have been fortunate to count on a stellar list of colleagues who have collaborated with us from many regions in the world and have contributed the various chapters in the book. We want to express our gratitude to these distinguished scholars and practitioners. We have no doubt that the readers will enjoy the wealth of information and appreciate the depth of analysis presented in every chapter of the book. This collection also offers an important example of international collaboration of authors from across different jurisdictions and legal traditions. The result is a book that reflects both differences and similarities in national and regional laws, as well as in the views of the contributors.

Our research assistants have been working closely with us throughout the editing process, before the manuscript was delivered to the publisher. We are very grateful to Lee Chedister, Victoria Gonzalez, Megan Pharis, and Elizabeth Ramey for their excellent work, dedication, and patience for many months, and for their reviews of the many drafts of the chapters of the book. We also would like to thank Cambridge University Press, in particular Matt Gallaway for his support during the development of this project from the book proposal to final publication, and Cameron Daddis for editorial assistance. We are grateful as well to our universities, Columbia Law School and Texas A&M University School of Law, for providing us with research support in order to complete the book.

Irene Calboli and Jane C. Ginsburg

April 2020

PART ONE

International Aspects of Trademark Protection

Historical Perspectives and Current Developments

1

The Trademark Provisions in the Paris Convention for the Protection of Industrial Property

*Sam Ricketson**

I INTRODUCTION

Of all the subjects of industrial property falling under the umbrella of the Paris Convention for the Protection of Industrial Property (the Paris Convention), those dealing with trademarks are the most extensive, although many matters of substance are not touched upon. This chapter analyses the scope of these provisions, beginning with a brief account of their history and inclusion in the Convention over the course of successive revisions.

II PRIOR TO THE PARIS CONVENTION

The Paris Convention of 1883 was the first multilateral convention dealing with industrial property.[1] Prior to this, the only international protection for such rights arose in a piecemeal way through a network of bilateral treaties and agreements that had been entered into between many of the industrialized and industrializing countries of Europe and the Americas. In his 1929 treatise, later revised in 1975, Stephen Ladas identified "no less than sixty-nine such acts, divided very unequally between the different countries."[2] These all dealt with trademarks, and, prior to 1865, were generally included as provisions in broader treaties of commerce between countries, rather than subject-specific treaties or agreements. It was only after this date that more subject-specific agreements occurred; as stated, these invariably dealt with trademarks, but about a third or more covered designs and models as well,[3] while only a handful dealt specifically with patents.[4] By contrast with the more detailed provisions found in the comparable bilateral treaties

* Emeritus Professor of Law, Melbourne Law School, University of Melbourne, Australia.

[1] The following section draws on material appearing in SAM RICKETSON, THE PARIS CONVENTION FOR THE PROTECTION OF INDUSTRIAL PROPERTY: A COMMENTARY, Chs. 1–2 (2015) (RICKETSON).

[2] STEPHEN P. LADAS, PATENTS, TRADEMARKS, AND RELATED RIGHTS: NATIONAL AND INTERNATIONAL PROTECTION 43 (2d ed. 1975).

[3] *Id.* at 43.

[4] In this regard, Ladas notes that there was a reciprocal arrangement between Austria-Hungary and Germany made in 1881: Germany and Austria-Hungary Treaty of Commerce, art. 20, 23 May 1881 (*British and Foreign State Papers*, LXXV, 859). There was also a UK agreement with Italy in 1883 which made specific reference to patents for inventions: *Treaty of Commerce and Navigation between Her Majesty and the King of Italy*, 15 June 1883, art. XVII, reproduced in *Commercial No. 12 (1888) (Trade Marks), Extracts from Treaties and Declarations now in force between Great Britain and Foreign Powers relating to Trade Marks, Designs, and Industrial Property*, August 1888, C-5554, London, HMSO, 1888, p. 4.

dealing with literary and artistic works, these agreements were of a limited character, being based essentially on principles of formal, rather than material, reciprocity that were directed at achieving "national treatment" for rights owners in each other's country – in other words, acquiring access to the other country's national system and ensuring that, once there, they were treated in the same way as locals.[5] However, the subject matter covered differed from agreement to agreement, as did the conditions for acquiring protection, which usually required the taking of some formal step such as registration or deposit, either in the country of origin or in the country where protection was claimed (or both).

Moves toward the adoption of a multilateral agreement on trademarks did not begin until the end of the 1870s: prior to this, legal and policy discussion at national and international levels was largely focused on patents, with a significant milestone being the International Patent Congress of 1873, which was held in conjunction with the international exhibition in Vienna that year.[6] The latter did not deal with trademarks, but these were the subject of discussion in the International Congress on Industrial Property that was held during the universal exhibition of Paris in 1878. This Congress passed a series of resolutions covering a wide range of industrial property rights, including twenty-three directed at trademarks.[7] Among these were resolutions on requirements for use and the need for a priority system for filing and recognition in other countries following first filing. Most significantly, the Congress expressed the wish "that the requirement for registration of trademarks should be subject to an international regulation, under which it would be possible for a person possessing a mark to make a single filing/ registration in one state to thereby assure protection of that mark in all other contracting states."[8]

III THE ADOPTION OF THE PARIS CONVENTION AND ITS SUBSEQUENT REVISIONS

The 1878 Paris Congress was the catalyst for the convening of an international conference of states, under the auspices of the French Government, to consider the adoption of a multilateral agreement on the protection of industrial property including trademarks.[9] This meeting was held in 1880 in Paris and, after extensive debates between delegates, resulted in the adoption of a draft text that provided for the establishment of a "Union for the protection of industrial property." This instrument enshrined the principle of national treatment (subject to the need to comply with formalities and conditions imposed by the domestic laws of each state), inaugurated a system of priority periods for filing in other member states of the Union, and included a number of provisions touching on trademark recognition and enforcement.[10] After minor

[5] *See generally* Sam Ricketson and Jane C. Ginsburg, The International Copyright and Neighbouring Rights: The Berne Convention and Beyond, Ch. 2 (2006).

[6] *See also* Thomas Webster, MA, FRS, Report on the International Patent Congress, 1873, *in* Reports on the Vienna Universal Exhibition of 1873, 1874 [C.1072-IV] House of Commons Parliamentary Papers Online. This Congress adopted a series of wide-ranging resolutions calling for procedural and substantive reform in relation to patents at both the national and international levels.

[7] *See also Congrès international de la Propriété Industrielle tenu à Paris du 5 au 17 septembre 1878, Compte-rendu sténographiques, No. 24 de la série* 1879, Paris imprimerie nationale.

[8] Ministry of Agriculture and Trade, Congrès international de la Propriété Industrielle tenu à Paris du 5 au 17 septembre 1878, Résolution No. 23 de la serie, 434 (1879).

[9] On this history generally, *see* Ricketson, *supra* note 1, Chs. 3 and 4.

[10] *See also Conférence internationale pour la protection de la propriété industrielle*, Ministère des Affaires étrangères, Paris, 1880 (Actes 1880).

amendments, this text was formally adopted by a second diplomatic conference in 1883,[11] entering into force on 7 July 1884 with an initial membership of fourteen states,[12] including, shortly afterward, the United States.[13] In its early years, however, a significant number of states remained outside, including Germany, Russia and Japan.[14]

In its original form, the Paris Act of the Convention (the Paris Act 1883) was a limited instrument with few substantive obligations extending beyond its system of priorities and obligation of national treatment. Nonetheless, it was intended by its founders to be a dynamic agreement that would be augmented through successive revisions, and, unlike previous bilateral agreements, it was a multilateral instrument open to any state to join, without any other qualification, geographic, linguistic, economic or otherwise, for admission. For its first seventy-five years, this membership tended to be weighted toward Europe and North America and to countries that were industrialized or industrializing, rather than developing.[15] In addition, any aspirations toward the adoption of a universal law of industrial property (such as a global patent or trademark), were only faintly echoed in its text, if at all (in contrast with the more idealistic resolutions of the 1873 and 1878 Congresses). Nonetheless, it provided, for the first time, a basic platform for obtaining protection of industrial property rights in other member states of the newly established Paris Union, and this was a significant achievement in its own right. No guidance was provided in its text as to the content and extent of the rights to be protected in each member state – indeed, no definition even was to be found of the rights themselves – but the hope was that such matters might be filled out in the process of future revisions. By contrast with the Berne Convention for the Protection of Literary and Artistic Works of 1886, this has not proved to be the case; although trademarks represent the one area where the Convention has achieved the most progress. The chronology of revisions since 1883 speaks for itself:

- Two initial revision conferences in Rome 1886[16] and Madrid 1890[17] came to nothing, the first because it was too soon after the coming into force of the Convention in 1884 and the second because too ambitious a programme of proposals touching on trademarks resulted in the adoption of two ancillary agreements to be entered into by those Paris Union members that desired to do so, but without effecting changes to the Paris text itself.[18]

[11] *See also Conférence internationale pour la protection de la propriété industrielle*, Ministère des Affaires étrangère, Paris, 1883 (Actes 1883).

[12] Belgium, Brazil, Spain, France, Guatemala, Italy, Netherlands, Portugal, El Salvador, Serbia, Switzerland, the United Kingdom, Tunisia, and Ecuador. A number of these members, such as the United Kingdom, France, Spain, and the Netherlands, had extensive colonial possessions to whose territories the Convention was also generally extended.

[13] The United States acceded in 1887.

[14] Of these, Germany joined in 1903, Japan in 1899, and Russia not until 1965 (as the former Soviet Union).

[15] Exceptions to this were Brazil and Tunisia, as well as Ecuador and El Salvador, which soon denounced the Convention after their joining on the ground of their lack of development, not re-joining until the end of the twentieth century: *see also* http://wipo.int/export/sites/www/treaties/en/documents/pdf/paris.pdf.

[16] *Conférence de l'Union pour la Protection de la Propriété Industrielle*, Ministère de l'agriculture, de l'industrie et du commerce, Imprimerie Héritiers Botta, Rome 1886 (Actes 1886).

[17] *See also Procès-Verbaux de la Conférence de Madrid de la Union pour la protection de la Propriété industrielle*, Imprimerie Jent et Reinert, Berne 1892.

[18] These were the Madrid Agreement Concerning the International Registration of Marks, Apr. 14, 1891, 828 UNTS 389, and the Madrid Agreement for the Repression of False or Deceptive Indications of Source on Goods art. 1(1), Apr. 14, 1891, 828 UNTS 389.

- Two revision conferences in Brussels 1897 and 1900, which resulted in some tidying up of the original text.[19]
- A more substantive revision conference in Washington in 1911, which continued this process and added some further provisions.[20]
- A further revision conference in The Hague in 1925, which was notable for including substantive provisions dealing with the repression of unfair competition and the protection of state emblems.[21]
- A further revision conference in London in 1934, which did more of the same.[22]
- A more substantive revision conference in Lisbon in 1958, which made further incremental and "tidying up" changes, but which proved to be the last substantive revision of the Convention.[23]
- The extensive machinery and procedural changes that were made as part of the Stockholm Revision Conference of 1967, but made no change to the substantive provisions of the Convention (with several minor exceptions).
- A prolonged and tragically ineffective series of revision conferences held between 1980 and 1984 in Geneva and Nairobi, which failed even to get down to substantive discussion because of differences between developed and developing countries over the issues of working and compulsory licences of patents. Proposals for further changes with respect to trademarks fell by the way here.[24]

The result is that, as of 2020, notwithstanding its almost universal membership of 177 states, the binding provisions of the Paris Convention are those in the Lisbon text of 1958, as supplemented by the machinery and procedural changes made in the Stockholm Revision of 1967. While a good number of these are concerned with trademarks, more substantive international obligations dealing with the content and scope of such rights have had to await their inclusion in trade-related measures, such as in the Agreement on Trade Related Intellectual Property Rights (TRIPS Agreement; the subject of Chapter 2 in this volume). So far as procedural aspects of trademark protection are concerned, effective international agreements have occurred in the form of special agreements as allowed under Article 19 of the Paris Convention; in particular, the Madrid Trade Marks Registration Treaty 1891, Madrid Protocol 1989, Nice International Classification Agreement 1957, and the more recent World Intellectual Property Organization (WIPO) treaties.[25] Having said this, the Paris Convention remains the starting point for trademark owners seeking protection for their marks in countries other than their own, and this is the subject of the remainder of this chapter.

[19] *See also Actes de la Conférence de Bruxelles, première et deuxième sessions 1897–1900*, Bureau international de l'union, Berne, 1901 (Actes 1897–1900).

[20] *See also Actes de la Conférence réunie à Washington du 15 mai au 2 juin 1911*, Bureau international de l'Union, Berne 1911 (Actes 1911).

[21] *See also Actes de la Conférence réunie à La Haye du 8 octobre au 6 novembre 1925*, Bureau international de l'Union, Berne 1926 (Actes 1925).

[22] *See also Actes de la Conférence réunie à Londres, du 1 mai au 2 juin 1934*, Bureau international de l'Union pour la protection de la propriété industrielle, Berne 1934 (Actes 1934).

[23] *See also* Union internationale pour la protection de la propriété industrielle, *Actes de la Conférence réunie á Lisbonne, du 6 au 31 octobre 1958*, Bureau international de l'Union pour la protection de la propriété industrielle, Geneva 1963 (Actes 1958). For ease of reference in the text above, the following abbreviations will be used to refer to the versions of the Convention adopted by successive revision conference: Paris Act 1883, Brussels Additional Act 1900, Washington Act 1911, Hague Act 1925, London Act 1934, Lisbon Act 1958 and Stockholm Act 1967.

[24] *See also* RICKETSON, *supra* note 1, Ch. 5, 5.02.

[25] Notably the Trademark Law Treaty, Oct. 27, 1994, S. Treaty Doc. No. 105-35, 2037 UNTS 35, and the Singapore Treaty on the Law of Trademarks, Mar. 27, 2006, S. Treaty Doc. No. 110–12.

IV THE PRINCIPAL PARIS CONVENTION PROVISIONS DEALING WITH TRADEMARKS[26]

A *Gaining Protection in the First Place – National Treatment and Priority Periods*

1 *National Treatment*

As in the cases of patents and designs, trademarks are the subject of the national treatment obligation under Article 2(1), and this has been the position since the Paris Act of 1883.[27] The scope of this obligation has not changed, with its requirement that nationals of any country of the Union shall, "as regard[ing] the protection of industrial property, enjoy in all other countries of the Union the advantages that their respective laws now grant, or may hereafter grant to nationals."[28] Since the Hague Act of 1925, this has been "without prejudice to the rights specially granted by this Convention," although, as will be seen, these are relatively few in number. The consequence of according national treatment is then spelt out in the second sentence of Article 2(1): nationals of any Union country are to have the "same protection" in any other Union country as is granted to nationals, and "the same legal remedy against infringement of their rights, provided that the conditions and formalities imposed upon nationals are complied with."[29] No requirement as to domicile or establishment in the country where protection is claimed may be imposed, but certain matters are expressly reserved to the laws of such countries where specific measures concerned with claimants under the Convention will be permissible, including provisions relating to judicial and administrative procedure and jurisdiction, and the designation of an address for service or the appointment of an agent.[30] As with patents, industrial designs and utility models, however, there is no definition of "trademark," leaving this as a matter for the national law of each Union country. Several points may be made here:

(a) As a matter of history, lack of definition may not have been a problem, as "trademark" was generally understood as referring to some kind of visible sign used in relation to goods so as to indicate their source. Accordingly, there may have been a de facto harmony of approach among Paris Union countries, at least at the outset, as to what constituted a "trademark," even if today a range of non-traditional signs, such as sounds and smells, are recognized as marks under many national laws.

(b) The term "trade mark" or "trademark" (to use the American spelling which is adopted in WIPO publications), so far as the Paris Convention is concerned, refers to marks used in relation to goods, rather than to goods and services. Marks for services, or "service marks," are referred to separately under Article 6*sexies*, which was added only at the Lisbon Revision Conference in 1958 (see further below). These may receive lesser protection under the Paris Convention, as they are not included in the priority period provisions contained in Article 4, but they are listed as one of the objects of the protection of "industrial property" under Article 1(2) and must therefore receive the benefit of national

[26] The following discussion draws on more detailed treatment that is to be found in Ricketson, *supra* note 1, Chs. 10 and 12. Further commentaries are to be found in George H. C. Bodenhausen, Guide to the Application of the Paris Convention for the Protection of Industrial Property as Revised at Stockholm in 1967, 67–137 (1968), and Stephen P. Ladas, Patents, Trademarks, and Related Rights: National and International Protection Vol. II, Chs. 30–34 (2d ed. 1975).

[27] Paris Convention for the Protection of Industrial Property, Mar. 20, 1888, as revised at the Stockholm Revision Conference, July 14, 1967, 21 UST 1538, TIAS No. 6903, 828 UNTS 305, art. 2. [hereinafter Paris Convention].

[28] *Id.*, art. 1(2), "trademarks" are included as one of the objects of the "protection of industrial property."

[29] *Id.*, as revised at Stockholm 1967, art. 2(2).

[30] *Id.*, art. 2(3).

treatment under Article 2(1), together with trademarks. The protection of service marks is also now enhanced under the provisions of the TRIPS Agreement.

(c) "Collective marks," or marks owned by groups or associations, are likewise the subject of a separate provision requiring protection (Article 7*bis*), which was introduced to the Convention in the Washington Revision of 1911 (see further below). However, there is no reference to collective marks in the definition of "industrial property" in Article 1(2), which means that they are excluded from national treatment under Article 2(1). The only basis on which national treatment could be required for such marks would be if they could be regarded as falling nonetheless within the scope of the expression "trademark," which would be a stretch, given that such marks are, by definition, collectively rather than individually owned (as in the case of trademarks) and their treatment in the Convention differs from the case of service marks (which are specifically included within the definition of "industrial property").[31]

2 *Right of Priority*

Important as receiving national treatment in each Union country may be, once a foreign trademark owner has arrived there, gaining access to that country in order to be able to enjoy the benefits of that protection is an obvious prior step. In this regard, trademarks enjoy a right of priority for six months in each Union member from the date of filing of the first application, so long as it is a "regular national filing" under the domestic law of any country of the Union.[32] As with patents and industrial designs, trademarks have enjoyed a right of priority since the Paris Act of 1883,[33] and this has been for a period of six months since the Hague Act of 1925.[34] This priority period is fundamental in obtaining trademark protection in other Union countries during this period, as the validity of any subsequent filing in those countries will not be affected by reason of any acts that occur in this period, including use of the mark or third party acts or filings.[35] Until the widespread adoption of the Madrid Protocol in 1989, which enables multiple filings on the basis of an application in one state, Paris priority provided the only route into other national systems for trademark owners.

B Independence of Protection and Recognition of Marks Duly Registered in Other Union Countries

Two important obligations fall for consideration here: first, the requirement under Article 6(3) that Union countries must accord independence of protection to trademarks once registered there, without regard to events or circumstances that have occurred elsewhere, and, secondly, the requirement that Union countries should recognize and protect, subject to certain conditions, trademarks that have been duly registered in another Union country (Article 6*quinquies*). Each

[31] This requirement also applies under the Agreement on Trade-Related Aspects of Intellectual Property Rights, Apr. 15, 1994, Marrakesh Agreement Establishing the World Trade Organization, Annex 1C, 1869 UNTS 299, 33 ILM 1197, art. 2.1 (1994) [hereinafter TRIPS Agreement].

[32] Paris Convention, *supra* note 27, as revised at Stockholm 1967, arts. 4.A(1) and (2) and 4.C(1). "Regular national filing" means any filing that is adequate to establish the date on which the application was filed in the country concerned, "whatever may be the subsequent fate of the application," that is, whether it was subsequently withdrawn or rejected in that country. Art. 4.A(3).

[33] Paris Convention, *supra* note 27, art. 4, § 3.

[34] *Id.*, as revised at The Hague, art 4.C. There were unsuccessful attempts at later revision conferences to increase this period to twelve months: *supra* note 22 at 169, 172, 362–63; *supra* note 23 at 538–42.

[35] Paris Convention, *supra* note 27, as revised at Stockholm 1967, art. 4.B.

obligation came into the Convention at different times and went through various iterations before assuming their present form under the Lisbon Act of the Convention.[36]

1 *Independence of Protection*

The obligation of independence of protection under Article 6(3) for trademarks, once registered in a Union country, is buttressed by two further provisions in Article 6(1) and (2), which deal with the situation prior to registration.[37]

(a) *At filing and thereafter*: Under Article 6(1), the conditions for the filing and registration of trademarks are to be determined in each country of the Union by its domestic legislation. On its face, this is an unexceptional application of the general national treatment principle in Article 2(1). Article 6(1) strictly deals only with trademarks, not service marks, but the latter are entitled to national treatment in any event because service marks are included within the concept of "industrial property" under Article 1(2) and are therefore within the scope of the obligation to accord national treatment under Article 2(1). In general, this also implies independence of protection in that it implicitly excludes reference back to any national law with which the applicant or trademark may previously have been associated.

(b) *No reference to filing, registration or renewal in country of origin*: Independence of protection becomes more evident in the rule applied under Article 6(2), which provides that, where an application for registration of a mark is filed by a national of a country of the Union, registration may not be refused, or any registration so granted invalidated, "on the ground that filing, registration or renewal, has not been effected in the country of origin."[38] Although not stated, it must be assumed that the filing, registration or renewal in the country of origin is of the same mark or something substantially the same – otherwise, the provision is obviously unnecessary. The term "country of origin" is also undefined, but, in the absence of any contrary direction, some guidance may be derived from Article 6*quinquies*(2), where it is defined as the country of the Union where the applicant has a real and effective industrial establishment, or if he has no such establishment, the country of the Union where he has his domicile or of which he is a national (if he has no domicile within the Union).[39] Therefore, the general effect of Article 6(2) is that a Union country in which protection is sought cannot refuse or nullify protection by reference to the fact that there is no protection for the mark in its country of origin. The language used here is quite general: the terms "filing, registration or renewal" are each discrete stages in the gaining and maintenance of protection, and may not have occurred in the country of origin for a variety of reasons – for example, where is a failure of the mark to satisfy the various substantive and/or procedural requirements of the law of the country of origin or simply because of failure on the part of the applicant to initiate and complete one or other of these steps. Article 6(2) applies in any and all of these circumstances. Oddly enough, however, the prohibition here is limited to what has *not* happened in the country of origin (that is, that there has been no filing, registration or

[36] For more detailed treatment, *see* Ricketson, *supra* note 1, Ch. 12, 12.06.

[37] A similar obligation applies with respect to patents under the Paris Convention, *supra* note 27, as revised at Stockholm 1967, art. 4*bis*(1)–(3).

[38] Under art. 3, the phrase "national of a country of the Union" includes nationals of non-Union countries who are domiciled in a Union country or who have "real and effective industrial establishments" in a Union country.

[39] First exploitation of the mark in that country, without anything further, is not included in this definition.

renewal of the corresponding mark), and it makes no mention of the position in any other country. This gives rise to the theoretical possibility that the protecting country could have regard to an applicant's failure to obtain protection in a country other than the country of origin.[40]

(c) *Position after registration*: Notwithstanding anything in Article 6(2), once a mark is "duly registered in a country of the Union," Article 6(3) provides for full independence of protection of that mark, namely that it is to be regarded as "independent of marks registered in other countries of the Union, including the country of origin," underlining the territorial character of the right granted. Again, the reference to "marks registered in other countries" must mean the same or a substantially similar mark, and it is clear that protection is to be unaffected by whatever happens to these marks, whether or not this is in their country of origin.[41] The phrase "duly registered" should be understood as a reference to the law of the protecting country, meaning that the registration has taken place in accord with the conditions imposed under that law.

By way of conclusion, the principle of independence contained in Article 6(3) underlines and reinforces the territorial character of the trademark rights obtained under the Convention, which will then be determined under the laws of the protecting country by reason of the requirement of national treatment under Article 2(1).[42] This interplay between national treatment and independence of protection has important practical and legal implications, particularly with respect to issues of enforcement and exhaustion of rights, if the concept of independence of protection is interpreted as extending beyond the criteria for registration in the protecting country. While there is nothing in the Convention dealing with the exclusive rights to be accorded to trademark owners (this is also the case for patentees and design owners), if these rights, by virtue of the principle of national treatment, extend to the use of protected trademarks on imported goods, then the adoption of a domestic rule of international exhaustion in relation to imported goods bearing marks applied in another country with the authorization of the trademark owner (parallel importations) will potentially cut across the requirement of independence of protection in Article 6(3). Whether the rights of the trademark owner in the country of importation extend to such importations will depend upon what has happened in the country of origin of those goods, or indeed in any other country where the marked goods have been sold, and whether this has occurred with the authorization of the trademark owner (assuming the trademark owner is the same or a related entity in both countries). Such a reference to the legal position in the country of origin of the goods will therefore be inconsistent with the requirement of independence of protection under Article 6(3), leading to the conclusion that international exhaustion of rights is implicitly prohibited under that article.[43] This may be a somewhat bold conclusion to draw, and it must be said that there is no guidance in Article 6(3) as to how far the concept of independence is to be taken once the mark has been registered.

[40] In this regard, it should be noted that Bodenhausen appears to treat art. 6(2) as having a wider effect, namely that the filing and registration of a trademark in each country is "independent of analogous acts regarding the same trademark in other countries, even such acts in the country of origin of the trademark as defined in Article 6quinquiesA(2)"; BODENHAUSEN, *supra* note 26, at 88, § d. This appears to be a generous reading of art. 6(2), and not in accordance with its strict wording.

[41] BODENHAUSEN, *supra* note 26, at 88, § e.

[42] *See also* NUNO PIRES DE CARVALHO, THE TRIPS REGIME OF TRADEMARKS AND DESIGNS, 82, § 2.22 (2011).

[43] *Id.* at 139–40, § 6.38. Note that issues of exhaustion are not addressed one way or the other under art. 6 of the TRIPS Agreement. *See also id.* at 132.

2 *Recognition of Marks Registered in Country of Origin (Dependence of Protection)*

The other side of the coin to independence of protection is the notion that a mark duly registered in its country of origin should be recognized, and therefore entitled to protection, in other countries of the Union. The provisions concerned with this are now contained in Article 6*quinquies*, which was put into its present form at the Lisbon Revision Conference, following a more widely formulated (and subsequently revised) provision that was contained in the original Paris Act 1883.[44] The distinction drawn here by the Lisbon Conference was between "ordinary marks" or marks in general (the subject of Article 6) and marks "as they are" (the subject of Article 6*quinquies*).[45] While this distinction may seem nebulous, it is in fact pointing to a specific and limited situation; namely, where a mark is already registered in one Union country and protection for it is sought in other Union countries. In such a case, it can be argued that international trade and commerce will be facilitated if there is ready acceptance and recognition of the same mark in other Union countries where the trademark owner wishes to do business. On the other hand, any obligation to accord recognition needs to be tempered by reservations to national laws that allow for the withholding of protection in specified circumstances.

The starting point: The circumstances in which recognition must occur are set out in Article 6*quinquies*A(1), which provides that every trademark "duly registered in its country of origin shall be accepted for filing and protected 'as is' (*telle quelle*) in the other countries of the Union, subject to the reservations indicated in this Article." The requirement that the mark must be "duly registered" in its country of origin means that the mere filing of an application in that country is not enough (as under the original Paris Act of 1883),[46] and certainly not just use of the mark as might suffice for protection of an unregistered mark under unfair competition law.[47] The expression "country of origin" is defined in some detail in Article 6*quinquies*A(2) (see above).

Scope of protection to be granted: Under Article 6*quinquies*A(1), marks fulfilling the above conditions are to be "accepted for filing and protected as is in the other countries of the Union." The phrase "as is" (*telle quelle* in the authentic French text)[48] receives no further clarification in the text, apart from the phrase which immediately follows: "subject to the reservations indicated in this Article" (this is a reference to the exceptions set out in Article 6*quinquies*B and C, which are discussed below). In the Paris Act of 1883, it was made clear that the requirement of recognition under Article 6 of that Act was a reference to the "form of the mark" as it had been filed in the country of origin and nothing else.[49] This interpretation was not included in later

[44] *See* Paris Convention, *supra* note 27, art. 6 and, in particular, the subsequent revisions made to art 6 in the Washington Act 1911, *supra* note 20.

[45] Actes 1958, *supra* note 23, at 750.

[46] Paris Convention, *supra* note 27, § 1.

[47] BODENHAUSEN, *supra* note 26, at 105, § c.

[48] It may be noted that in the unofficial BIRPI translations of earlier Acts of the Convention (*see* Washington Act 1911, *supra* note 20, art. 6, and *see also* the Hague Act 1925, *supra* note 23, art. 6, and *see also* Lisbon Act 1958, *supra* note 23, art. 6*quinquies*), the phrase *telle quelle* was rendered as "in its original form" rather than "as is," as in the established English text of the Paris Convention, *supra* note 27, as revised at Stockholm 1967. As will be seen in the discussion in the principal text, the phrase "in its original form" was undoubtedly a clearer indication of what was intended here, but was far from a literal translation of the words "*telle quelle*."

[49] Thus, the following interpretation in para. 4 of the Final Protocol to that Act stated that art. 6, para. 1, was to be understood:

> in the sense that no trade mark may be excluded from protection in one of the States of the Union for the sole reason that it does not comply, *with regard to the signs of which it is composed*, with the conditions of the laws of that State, provided it complies on this point with the laws of the country of origin and that it has been properly filed there. Subject to this exception, which concerns only the form of the mark, and subject to the provisions of the other Articles of the Convention, each State shall apply its domestic law.
>
> Paris Convention, *supra* note 27, as revised at Stockholm 1967, § 4

Acts of the Convention, leaving uncertainty as to its scope, in particular whether this required country A to recognize and protect a mark registered in country B, where this would not otherwise have qualified as a trademark under the law of country A. Examples were such things as three-dimensional shapes, even the shape of the article itself, and, more recently, sounds and smells. This was an issue raised by the British delegation to Washington in 1911, noting that while agreeing to the text of what is now Article 6*quinquies*A(1), one could not disregard the fact that in many of the countries of the Union there were diverging interpretations of the expression "trademark" ("marque de fabrique").[50] Indeed, it was only on the basis of statements by other delegates in committee that it was open to each country to decide for itself what may or may not be admitted as a trademark that the British delegates felt able to agree to the wording of the provision.[51]

As this issue was never clarified in subsequent revisions of Article 6*quinquies*A(1) or its predecessors, some uncertainty arises as to the scope of recognition required under that provision.[52] Thus, if the words "as is" mean the form of the mark, as registered in its country of origin, does this require recognition in a case where the alleged trademark meets the substantive requirements of the law of its country of origin but not of the country in which recognition and protection is now sought (as in the case of shape marks, the example raised by the UK delegation in Washington in 1911)? What if the laws of both countries potentially protect the same elements as a trademark (for example, words or devices which have long been accepted as registrable signs in most national laws) but the law of the country where recognition is sought denies protection on the basis of a particular rule of the forum that certain kinds of words (for example, descriptive or geographical words, are not protected under its law)?[53] A full-blooded application of the recognition principle would imply that all marks, regardless of these differences, should be protected in the event that they are registered in their country of origin, even if this leads to disparities between the positions of locals and foreigners in the country where recognition is sought. Such an interpretation, however, may place too much emphasis on the words "as is" in Article 6*quinquies*A(1) rather than on the words "trademark" which precede it and which do seem to presuppose that a mark will have to be a "trademark" in the protecting country before recognition of its country of origin registration can be required. This was a matter that the programme for the Lisbon Revision Conference sought to address in a somewhat radical proposal that the word "signs" should be substituted for "trademark" in Article 6*quinquies*A(1), so as to read: "[A]ny sign regularly registered as a trade mark in the country of origin shall be accepted."[54] This proposal, however, was defeated in the third committee of the Conference, largely due to the fears of many countries, such as the United Kingdom, that this would have required giving protection to signs that were not protected under domestic law at the time (this, indeed, would have been the effect of the amendment).[55] A decisive majority favoured retention

[50] Actes 1911, *supra* note 20, at 252 (third plenary session).

[51] Report of the British Delegates to the Washington Conference, Cmnd, p. 98. These "comments" do not appear to be recorded in the Actes 1911, *supra* note 20.

[52] *See also* BODENHAUSEN, *supra* note 26, at 110–11.

[53] The programme proposals of the International Bureau at the Lisbon Revision Conference cited several instances in French and Austrian law to support these last examples, where registration had been accepted of words that were protected in their countries of origin, but which would not have otherwise been protected under their domestic laws, apart from the obligation of recognition under what was then art. 6A of the London Act: *see* Actes 1958, *supra* note 23, at 573–74.

[54] Actes 1958, *supra* note 23, at 576.

[55] *Id.* at 601. It was lost decisively in the Third Committee with twenty-two against, seven in favour and six abstentions.

of the present provision, notwithstanding the difficulties of interpretation it raised.[56] But while the resulting uncertainty is unsatisfactory from the perspective of anyone desiring clarity in international agreements, this may not be a problem in practice, when regard is had to the following matters:

(a) The definition of "trademark" under most national laws has now extended to include the kinds of subject matter that were problematic in earlier times, such as the shape of goods, packaging, sounds and smells. Accordingly, the burden of having to recognize something as a trademark that is not protected as such under one's own law may not often arise.
(b) The exceptions reserved to national laws under Article 6*quinquies*B and C may operate to deny protection in specific cases, without necessarily engaging the wider question of whether recognition is required in the first place. These exceptions, which are listed below, have been augmented over time, and do much to temper the absolute character of any obligation of recognition otherwise applying under Article 6*quinquies*A.
(c) If Article 6*quinquies*A(1) is concerned only with the "form of the mark," this must mean that protecting countries remain free to apply restrictions on protection that do not relate to these matters.[57] One such matter might be a requirement of prior use of the mark or a condition that applicant must possess an industrial or commercial enterprise.[58] A further one would be requirements as to ownership.[59]
(d) Finally, it goes without saying that the problems discussed here would not arise if the Convention contained a definition of the subject matter – trademarks – that are to be protected. This, of course, is a problem that bedevils the Convention in other areas such as patents and industrial designs – and is now, to some extent, addressed in the provisions of the TRIPS Agreement.

3 *Exceptions to the Obligation of Recognition in Article 6quinquies*A(1)

These exceptions are contained in Article 6*quinquies*B, which provides that trademarks covered by Article 6*quinquies*A(1) may be "neither denied registration nor invalidated" (the principle of recognition), except in the following circumstances:

(a) when they are of such a nature as to infringe rights acquired by third parties in the country where protection is obtained;
(b) when they are devoid of any distinctive character, or consist exclusively of signs or indications which may serve, in trade, to designate the kind, quality, quantity, intended

[56] *Id.* There were twenty-seven in favour and five against, with no abstentions.

[57] Note here the view of the World Trade Organization Appellate Body in United States – Section 211 Omnibus Appropriations Act of 1998, WT/DS176/ABB/R, §§ 122–48 (Feb. 1, 2002).

[58] Bodenhausen, *supra* note 26, at 111, § e.

[59] *See also* the decision of the World Trade Organization Appellate Body, *supra* note 57, §§ 122–48 concerning such a requirement in § 211 of the United States Omnibus Appropriations Act 1998 law with respect to the recognition of ownership claims regarding confiscated (Cuban) trademarks. And, in another recent proceeding, the WTO Panel said, in relation to the word "protected" in Article 6*quinquies*A(1): "In our view, the text suggests that the term 'protected' refers to the protection that flows from the registration of a sign as a trademark in that jurisdiction where the registration is obtained pursuant to the requirements of Article 6*quinquies* A(1). We note that the term 'protected' in Article 6*quinquies* A(1) in itself does not provide any guidance as to what the protection flowing from the registration under the domestic law should consist of." Australia – Certain Measures Concerning Trademarks, Geographical Indications and Other Plain Packaging Requirements Applicable to Tobacco Products and Packaging, Reports of the Panels, WT/DS435/R, WT/DS441/R WT/DS458/R, WT/DS467/R, 28 June 2018, para. 7.1765 and see further 7.1766–7.1775. No issue as to the interpretation of Article 6*quinquies*A was appealed to the Appellate Body in its decision of 9 June 2020: WT/DSB435/AB/R, and WT/DSB441/AB/R, par 6.544, n 1444, and see also par 6.649.

purpose, value, place of origin of the goods, or the time of production, or have become customary in the current language or in the bona fide and established practices of the trade of the country where protection is claimed;

(c) when they are contrary to morality or public order and, in particular, of such a nature as to deceive the public;

(d) a final proviso makes Article 6*quinquies*B subject to the application of Article 10*bis* which deals with acts of unfair competition (an instance would be where the use of the mark sought to be registered would be of such a nature as to mislead or create confusion as to the nature or characteristics of the goods to which it is to be applied, as provided for in Article 10*bis*(3)(c)).

While limited to marks falling within Article 6*quinquies*A(1), the exceptions listed in Article 6*quinquies*B can be seen as reflecting guidelines as to substantive standards for the registration of marks that Union members might wish to adopt in their national laws generally and which could therefore become the basis for substantive norms to be embodied in another international instrument, such as the TRIPS Agreement, a special WIPO treaty or even a revised version of Paris itself (if this ever proved possible).

Further provisions in Article 6*quinquies* elaborate upon its field of application and include the following: (a) there is no need for there to be exact identity between marks which differ from the registration in the country of origin of the mark only in relation to "elements that do not alter the distinctive character and do not affect the identity of the marks in the form in which these have been registered in the said country of origin" (Article 6*quinquies*C(2)); (b) no person is to benefit from its provisions if the mark for which protection is claimed is not registered in the country of origin – that is, if registration in the country of origin has lapsed for some reason, such as through non-renewal, forfeiture, or nullification (Article 6*quinqies*D);[60] (c) no obligation to renew arises on the part of any other country in which the mark has been registered pursuant to Article 6*quinquies*A, where renewal has been effected in its country of origin, meaning therefore that it is left to the rightholder to seek renewal in these other countries in the normal way (Article 6*quinquies*E); and (d) the benefits of priority under Article 4 are to be accorded to applications for registration of marks filed within the priority period fixed by Article 4C (six months), even when registration in the country of origin does not occur until after the expiration of such period – in other words, applications falling within the circumstances outlined in Article 6*quinquies*A will still have the same priority rights as other applications (Article 6*quinquies*F) and will not be prejudiced by delays occurring in the registration system of the country of origin – for example, where there have been protracted pre-grant opposition proceedings.

C *Service Marks*

From its inception, the provisions of the Paris Convention dealt only with trademarks for manufactured goods. Recognition that marks could be equally important in relation to the provision of services was slow in coming, and received only grudging and limited acceptance in Article 6*sexies*, which was added as late as at the Lisbon Act of 1958, together with their inclusion as a subject for national treatment under the definition of "industrial property" in Article 1(2).

[60] In such a case, the principle of independence of protection should ensure the validity of any registration in the protecting country.

Article 6*sexies* was a compromise provision that provides simply that: "The countries of the Union undertake to protect service marks. They shall not be required to provide for the registration of such marks." The obligation here is in similar terms to that for industrial designs under Article 5*quinquies*, albeit even more clearly expressed in that it is stipulated that no registration system is required. In this regard, the General Report to the Conference emphasized that the "modalities" of this protection were for member countries to determine for themselves; for example, that they might do so through the application of domestic unfair competition laws.[61] As a matter of practice, it now seems the case that most Union countries have adopted registration systems for service marks, and this, in turn, is reflected in the Nice classification system which provides for classes of services as well as goods. So far as the Paris Convention itself is concerned, apart from the obligation to give protection under Article 6*sexies* and the general obligation to accord national treatment under Article 2(1), none of the other provisions of the Paris Convention relating to trademarks apply to service marks. In particular, this excludes the priority system established under Article 4, the obligations with respect to well-known marks under Article 6*bis*, the prohibitions on state emblems, flags and the like under Article 6*ter*, the application of Article 6*quater* on assignments, and the obligation of recognition of marks registered and protected "as is" in their country of origin under Article 6*quinquies*. To the extent that service marks are assimilated to trademarks under the domestic laws of a Union country, such provisions will be extended to the service marks of nationals of other Union countries under the principle of national treatment, but not otherwise. Accordingly, while a protecting country with a registered service mark system might well accord priority to service marks which have been first filed in another Union country, there is no obligation for them to do so under Article 4 of the Paris Convention. This last-mentioned lacuna is now addressed in Article 62.3 of the TRIPS Agreement, which provides that WTO members are to apply Article 4 of the Paris Convention *mutatis mutandis* to service marks.

D Well-Known Marks

The protection of well-known marks under the international conventions is the subject of a separate chapter in this work, so will only be touched upon lightly here. The relevant provision of the Paris Convention is found in Article 6*bis*, which has been supplemented by subsequent international agreements, such as the TRIPS Agreement, as well as by developments in national laws. Article 6*bis* was adopted at the Hague Revision Conference,[62] and appears to have received considerable impetus from the work of the Economic Committee of the League of Nations, which had prepared draft articles relating to the prevention of unfair competition and other practices, including the protection of foreign marks where confusion was caused to local consumers.[63] It was refined further at later revision conferences, and the form and content of the present provision in Article 6*bis* of the Stockholm Act is the same as that adopted at Lisbon.[64] In essence, it allows the owners of well-known marks (for goods) to object to the registration by a third party of a corresponding mark that is a reproduction, imitation or translation liable to create confusion with the well-known mark, or to seek its invalidation within a specified period (five years) other than in cases where the mark has been registered or used in bad faith. The

[61] Actes 1958, *supra* note 23, at 118.

[62] Actes 1925, *supra* note 21, at 241–42, 246, 341–42, 453–56, 523, 543–44, 577.

[63] League of Nations, Economic Committee, Conference of Experts, Geneva (5 May 1924).

[64] *See also* Actes 1934, *supra* note 22, at 187, 275–76, 398–400, 464, 516, and Actes 1958, *supra* note 23, at 637–40, 640–56, 656–66, 757–59, 666–68, 101–02, 117.

requirements here are multi-layered, and embody a carefully limited set of international norms with respect to the protection of well-known marks which are now supplemented under Article 16 of the TRIPS Agreement.[65]

E State Emblems, Armorial Bearings, Flags and the Like

Emblems of sovereignty, governance and public institutions, such as coats of arms and similar symbols, have a considerable history of use in most countries, particularly in Europe. Traders have long recognized the market advantages that may flow from incorporating such elements into their marks and brands. These matters have been the subject of detailed regulation under the Paris Convention from the Hague Act onwards,[66] but had been dealt with to some extent in the Final Protocol of the Paris Act of 1883 in relation to marks that might be refused registration as being contrary to public order where these involved the "use of public armorial bearings and decorations."[67] The present provision in Article 6*ter* is a complicated one which includes a facilitative mechanism[68] for member states to communicate, through the medium of WIPO, relevant "armorial bearings, flags and other State emblems" which each member will undertake to recognize and prevent from being incorporated in trademark registrations applied for by third parties, as well as prohibiting the actual use of marks incorporating such elements.[69] This obligation extends to "official signs and hall-marks,"[70] as well as to the bearings, flags, emblems, abbreviations and names of international organizations.[71] The obligations imposed under Article 6*ter* are the most specific to be found in the Convention, and reflect an early concern of Paris Union countries to protect each state's emblems against unauthorized exploitation by traders and manufacturers within their jurisdiction. In general, the protection required here applies regardless of whether confusion or deception results from their use in third-party trademarks,[72] and such protection extends to the use of "imitations" of such emblems,[73] with the curious qualification that this only applies to imitations "from a heraldic point of view."[74] There

65 Chapter 5 in this volume addresses TRIPS's treatment of well-known marks.

66 Actes 1925, *supra* note 21, art. 6*ter*. Significant proposals here emanated from preliminary documents prepared for the League of Nations, Economic Committee, Conference of Experts on Unfair Competition, *Consideration of an International Draft Convention*, to be held in Geneva, May 5, 1924, dated Oct. 15, 1923 (document in Australian Archives, A432/80, 1938/555, Part 1, No. 2).

67 Paris Convention, *supra* note 27, Final Protocol, § 4.

68 Paris Convention, *supra* note 27, as revised at Stockholm 1967, art. 6*ter*(3) and (4).

69 *Id.* art. 6*ter*(1)(a).

70 *Id.*

71 *Id.* art. 6*ter*(1)(b). This excludes armorial bearings, flags, other emblems, abbreviations and names that are already protected under other international agreements; an example of such an agreement is the Convention (I) for the Amelioration of the Condition of the Wounded and Sick in Armed Forces in the Field, art. 44, Geneva (Aug. 12, 1949), covering the use of the Red Cross emblem and flag.

72 This underlines the different functions played by state insignia and privately owned trademarks.

73 Paris Convention, *supra* note 27, as revised at Stockholm 1967, art. 6*ter*(1)(a).

74 The following explanation of the scope of the "heraldic imitation" offered in a recent WIPO document may be of assistance here as to what the qualification intends:

> This qualification effectively narrows down the scope of the impermissible imitation beyond what would normally be considered unacceptable in trademark law. As State emblems frequently comprise common symbols, such as a lion, an eagle or the sun, imitations are forbidden only if they reproduce the heraldic characteristics of the State sign concerned. In consequence, the symbol as such remains free and may be used in the composition of trademarks.
>
> WIPO Standing Committee on the Law of Trademarks, Industrial Designs and Geographical Indications, Fifteenth Session, "Article 6*ter* of the Paris Convention: Legal and Administrative Aspects," Geneva, 28 November–2 December 2005, SCT/15/3 (Oct. 14, 2005).

is also a provision for countries to object to the protection required under the article within twelve months from the receipt of notification from WIPO,[75] although no grounds for objection are indicated.[76] There is no mechanism for resolving disputes between the country making the notification and the country objecting, apart from the theoretical possibility of seeking a determination from the International Court of Justice under Article 28 (if both countries accept the jurisdiction of that body). In the absence of resolution, therefore, the result of objection will be that the country objecting is not bound to comply with Article 6*ter*(1), although countries not objecting clearly will be. More detailed guidance on the practical operation of Article 6*ter* is to be found on the WIPO website.[77]

F Assignments of Trademarks without Accompanying Goodwill

From its inception, the Paris Convention has not sought to regulate the way in which the private rights protected under its regime are dealt with by their owners; for example, through assignment or licensing. In the case of trademarks, however, a particular problem arose where marks were assigned without the business enterprise with which they were associated.[78] In some countries this was permissible, although issues of consumer confusion might then arise where the mark was used by the assignee. On the other hand, in many other countries this was not allowed. This, in turn, gave rise to problems where trademarks were owned in several countries and the owner assigned the mark in one country without the accompanying business, for example, to a local distributor that was otherwise unconnected with it: did this lead to the invalidity of the registration of marks registered in those countries where this was not possible? Under some national laws, it was established that assignment of the accompanying business or enterprise referred to the business or enterprise as a whole and wherever located, meaning that assignment of the mark for particular territories would not be possible in the absence of transfer of the business as a whole. The principle of independence of protection, however, would suggest that the requirements for assignments should be limited to each territory, making irrelevant what might happen elsewhere.

It was against this background of national differences that Article 6*quater*, which has remained essentially unchanged in later revisions, was adopted in the London Revision Conference in 1934.[79] Article 6*quater*(1) does not attempt to seek to regulate the way in which assignments of trademarks should be dealt with under national laws, but simply provides that the position in other countries should not affect the validity of registration of marks in any particular Union country, so long as the law of that country on assignments has been complied with. This is a limited provision that has no implications for countries which allow assignment of marks without accompanying business or goodwill, but it imposes a modest limitation in the case of countries with the opposite rule, namely that this is confined to what happens in those countries

[75] Paris Convention, *supra* note 27, as revised at Stockholm 1967, art. 6*ter*(4).

[76] For a summary of possible objections, see the advisory document prepared for the WIPO Standing Committee on the Law of Trademarks, Industrial Designs and Geographical Indications, Fifteenth Session, "Article 6*ter* of the Paris Convention: Legal and Administrative Aspects," Geneva, 28 November–2 December 2005, SCT/15/3 (Oct. 14, 2005), § 28.

[77] *See* http://wipo.int/article6ter/en/.; *see also* the discussion in RICKETSON, *supra* note 1, at 12.41–12.56.

[78] For a detailed review of this in the United States, *see* Irene Calboli, *Trademark Assignment "With Goodwill": A Concept Whose Time Has Come*, 57 FLA. L. REV. 772, 777–97 (2005) and, for a more general review of national laws, *see* STEPHEN P. LADAS, THE INTERNATIONAL PROTECTION OF LITERARY AND ARTISTIC PROPERTY, VOL. II, 1303–05 (1938).

[79] Actes 1934, *supra* note 22, at 189–91, 400–05, 466–67, 517.

and should not take account of what may have happened elsewhere. In this regard, it can be seen as simply underlining the territorial nature of trademark protection under the Convention, allowing businesses with trademark registrations in a number of Union countries to assign these marks separately, so long as this is accompanied by the business or goodwill associated with the trademark in each country where this is required. A qualification to this is then contained in Article 6*quater*(2), namely that Article 6*quater*(1) does not impose on Union countries "any obligation to regard as valid the assignment of any mark the use of which by the assignee would, in fact, be of such a nature as to mislead the public, particularly as regards the origin, nature or material qualities of the goods to which the mark is applied." This would certainly cover the situation where a trademark has been assigned only with respect to some of the goods for which it is registered, and is then continued to be used by the assignor in respect of other similar goods not covered by the assignment.[80]

G Nature of the Goods to Which Trademark Is to Be Applied

The origins of this article can be traced back to the Paris Act of 1883, where it was provided that the "nature of the goods to which the trade mark is to be applied shall in no case form an obstacle to the filing of the mark."[81] With one important amendment – the substitution of the term "registration" for the term "filing" – it has remained unchanged in subsequent revisions, and the principle involved is a salutary one, namely that the goods for which a mark is registered are quite distinct from the mark itself and should not prove an obstacle to registration in the case of products that require lengthy health or safety assessments before they can be safely marketed, as in the case of pharmaceuticals.[82] It is only "obstacles" to the registration of such marks on the ground of the nature of the goods that are prohibited under Article 7: registration, of course, could be refused on other grounds, such as lack of distinctiveness or if the registration would be liable to cause deception or confusion. Furthermore, the prohibition here applies only to marks of nationals of other Union countries, meaning that it would be open to a Union member to impose such a limitation in relation to its own nationals. There is also nothing in the wording of Article 7 that excludes the possibility of other restrictions being placed on the use of a trademark by its proprietor, once registered – an issue that has become relevant in current discussions about plain packaging restrictions on the use of trademarks on tobacco products.[83] Finally, Article 7 does not extend to service marks; accordingly, it would be open to domestic laws to prohibit the registration of marks for gambling or prostitution services, notwithstanding that these activities may otherwise be lawful in the jurisdiction concerned.[84]

H Collective Marks

Marks, whether for goods or services, usually identify the provenance of those goods or services with a particular source, such as the manufacturer or provider. Equally, however, marks may be

[80] *Id.* at 517 (example raised by the Hungarian delegate).

[81] Paris Convention, *supra* note 27, art. 7.

[82] The example of pharmaceutical products was given by Charles Jagerschmidt in the initial discussions on this provision: Actes 1880, *supra* note 10, at 89 (fifth session, 10 November 1880).

[83] *See also* TRIPS Agreement, *supra* note 31, art. 20; *See also*, at the national level, *Tobacco Plain Packaging Act 2011*, § 28 (Austrl.); *See also* Sam Ricketson, *Plain Packaging Legislation for Tobacco Products and Trade Marks in the High Court of Australia*, 3 Queen Mary J. Intell. Prop. 224–40 (2013).

[84] This possibility is now excluded under TRIPS Agreement, *supra* note 31, art. 15.4.

used by an association or group of producers to indicate that goods or services emanate from members of that association or group and that they therefore share particular characteristics associated with those producers; for example, a common geographic location, compliance with a particular mode of production or quality standard and so on. It is also possible that such "certification" may be provided by some public or governmental entity. In each of these instances, the application of the association or group mark will provide extra value in the marketing of those goods or services, in addition to the identification with the particular manufacturer or provider that may be provided by the latter's own mark.

Carefully limited obligations to protect marks of this kind – called "collective marks" – have been in the Paris Convention since the Washington Revision Act of 1911. The principal obligation now contained in Article 7*bis*(1) requires:

> (1) The countries of the Union undertake to accept for filing and to protect collective marks belonging to associations the existence of which is not contrary to the law of the country of origin, even if such associations do not possess an industrial or commercial establishment.

The term "collective marks" is not defined, but it is clear from the words that follow ("belonging to associations") that these are marks of a collective or group of traders or manufacturers, as distinct from the individual marks that each may have and apply on their own behalf. The function of the "collective mark" is also not indicated in the provision, but the expression appears to cover two distinct kinds of functions, namely that of certification (that goods possess a particular characteristic or set of characteristics), and of collective production (that they have been made by a member of a particular group of producers).[85] These two functions may overlap in many instances, but conceptually are distinct and in some jurisdictions may be classified as "certification" marks on the one hand and collective or association marks on the other.[86]

While Article 7*bis*(1) refers to the need for the marks to belong to "associations," there is no specific requirement that these should be bodies that are incorporated or recognized in any particular way under the law of the country of origin: all that is prescribed is that the existence of the associations is not to be "contrary to the law of the country of origin." This relieves a foreign association from having to prove affirmatively that it complies with the laws of the country of origin while reserving the right to the country where protection is sought of refusing protection where the existence of the association is shown to be contrary to those laws. Furthermore, such associations do not need to possess an industrial or commercial establishment of their own, meaning that while they may control who uses the mark and how this is done, they do not have to use it themselves with respect to any goods that they may make and market (an unlikely situation in any event with respect to such associations, but a possibility that is not excluded by the terms of Article 7*bis*(1)). It also appears that, while the word "associations" as used in Article 7*bis*(1) does not specifically exclude governmental or other public bodies that carry out certification functions, it seems clear from Conference records that it was intended to be limited to non-governmental associations of traders or manufacturers, as proposals at the Hague Revision Conference to extend this term more widely to cover marks of such governmental or other public associations were not adopted.[87] Having said this, even if foreign national and regional collective marks lie outside the scope of Article 7*bis*(1), they may be entitled to protection by virtue of the principle of national treatment under Article 2(1) where such protection is available

[85] This seems to have been contemplated in the London Conference programme: *See* Actes 1934, *supra* note 22, at 193.

[86] *See, e.g.*, *Trade Marks Act* 1995, Pts 15 (collective marks) and 16 (certification marks) (Austrl.); Trade Marks Act 1994, §§ 49 (collective marks) and 50 (certification marks) (UK).

[87] Actes 1925, *supra* note 21, at 248, 467–68, 545, 577.

under the domestic law of the protecting country, while separate protection for "official" emblems, flags and official hallmarks is available, in any event, under Article *6ter*.[88]

So long as the obligation to protect under Article *7bis*(1) is accorded, there is complete flexibility for Union members under Article *7bis*(2) as to how this is done by the protecting country (each country is to be "the judge of the particular conditions under which a collective mark shall be protected"), including the discretion to "refuse protection if the mark is contrary to the public interest." As to particular conditions that might be applied here by domestic laws, examples given in the report to the plenary committee of the Washington Revision Conference (1911) included conditions as to the character of the association seeking protection and the character of the mark itself,[89] conditions precluding the association itself from making or selling products to which the mark is applied,[90] or prohibitions on assignment.[91] While it is most likely that these conditions will be applied at the time of filing, it would be open for Union countries to impose further conditions at the stage of enforcement. The discretion allowed to Union countries to refuse protection of a foreign collective mark where this is "contrary to the public interest" is also wide-ranging and undefined.[92]

Article *7bis*(3) supplements the undertaking contained in Article *7bis*(1) by providing that protecting countries are not to refuse protection to the marks of any association "the existence of which is not contrary to the law of the country of origin, on the ground that such association is not established in the country where protection is sought or is not constituted according to the law of the latter country." While the first part of this paragraph concerning establishment in the protecting country is strictly unnecessary in view of Article 2(2), the second part deals with the question of recognition where the foreign association has no legal counterpart in the protecting country and can be seen as consistent with the general requirement under international law that there should be recognition of bodies regularly constituted under the law of another country.[93]

I Use of Trademarks

Provisions concerning the use of trademarks for which protection is claimed under the Convention are contained in Article 5C. These apply only to trademarks, but Union countries may obviously extend them to apply to service marks, at their own discretion.

(a) *Where use of a registered trademark is required under national law*: While nothing under the Paris Convention mandates use of a registered trademark as a condition of continued validity of the registration, where this is required under national law Article 5C(1) provides that the registration is to be cancelled "only after a reasonable period" and then only if the person concerned does not "justify his inaction." It is clear from the debates at The Hague Revision Conference,[94] where this provision was first proposed and approved, that there

[88] *See also* Bodenhausen, *supra* note 26, at 130, § d.
[89] Actes1911, *supra* note 20, at 309.
[90] Actes 1934, *supra* note 22, at 517 (declaration in second plenary session by British delegate and acknowledged by the president of the session).
[91] Example given in the programme for the London Revision Conference: *id.* at 1994.
[92] Compare here the more restricted language used in art. *6quinquies*B(3) which refers to "contrary to public order," and seems limited to contravention of some particular rule of the legal or social order of the protecting country – for example, that it is racist, pornographic or liable to deceive the public in that country (the example given in art. *6quinquies*B(3)). "Contrary to the public interest" in art. *7bis*(2), by contrast, suggests that issues of wider concern to the protecting country might be taken into account in refusing protection.
[93] Actes 1934, *supra* note 22, at 194 (Conference programme).
[94] Actes 1925, *supra* note 21, at 339–42, 520, 541, 576.

was no desire to impose any positive requirement of "working" in Union countries (as in the case of patents), but only to provide procedural safeguards in relation to cancellation where this was so. The provision is limited to "registered" marks, so it does not touch upon the situation where a national law requires use of the mark as a prerequisite for registration in the first place – such countries remain free to impose such a requirement without any restriction. The determination of what is a "reasonable period" of non-use before cancellation can occur is also left as a matter for national laws.[95] What constitutes "use" of a mark is likewise left to national laws to determine, but there is a comment in the report of the Hague drafting committee that this was understood as meaning that there had been goods bearing the mark on sale in the country where protection was claimed.[96] Finally, no indication is provided in the provision as to what justifications for inaction may be accepted – again a matter left to national laws to determine. Natural disaster, war and the like are obvious candidates; the suggestion by the Hague drafting committee of "special circumstances of trade" would allow for a more generous range of possibilities here.[97]

(b) *Use of a trademark in a different form*: Article 5C(2) deals with the situation where use of a trademark is required, but the proprietor has used a variation of the mark as registered. Added at the London Revision Conference, this paragraph provides that use of a trademark "in a form differing in elements that do not alter the distinctive character of the mark in the form in which it was registered in one of the countries of the Union" is not to lead to its invalidation or to "diminish the protection granted to the mark."[98] Particular situations contemplated in the London programme as falling within the scope of this provision were uses of a trademark with translated words where the language in use in the country where goods were being sold was different, or where there were other slight differences in the mark that were made in order to adapt it to the circumstances of the country in question.[99] The obvious intention was to avoid too strict or rigid an application of any rule requiring that the form of the trademark actually used must be the same as the one that was registered.[100] Any differences, however, must be only those that do not alter the distinctive character of the mark, recognizing that this is a far from precise standard that will depend upon the circumstances of each case and the judgement of the judicial or administrative authorities of each country. The provision applies in two distinct contexts. The first is clear enough: use of the altered mark should not lead to invalidation of the registration of the mark in jurisdictions where use is a condition for continued registration. The second – that it should not be used as a way of "diminishing the protection granted to the mark" – goes to the rights granted to the proprietor of the mark under national law, which is not something otherwise addressed by the Paris Convention (unlike in Article 16 of the TRIPS Agreement). Thus, if the mark is used in this altered

95 While there was a majority in the third subcommittee of the Hague Revision Conference in favour of specifying a period of three years, there was no unanimity on this point and the expression "reasonable period" ("*une délai équitable*") was adopted by the drafting committee as being "less categoric": *id.* at 520 (report of general committee) and 541 (report of drafting committee). The minimum three-year period now appears in the TRIPS Agreement, *supra* note 31, art. 19.1.

96 Actes 1925, *supra* note 21, at 541.

97 *Id.* (also suggested by the UK delegate at p. 441).

98 Actes 1934, *supra* note 22, at 178–79, 264–65, 387–88, 460, 515.

99 *Id.* at 178.

100 *Id.*

form by a third party without authority, it is to be regarded as much as an infringement as would use of the mark in its original form.

(c) *Concurrent uses of trademark*: Article 5C(3), which was adopted at the London Revision Conference in 1934, deals with only one particular, and limited, instance of concurrent use of "the same mark on identical or similar goods" by industrial or commercial establishments that are considered to be co-proprietors of the mark under the domestic law of the country where protection is claimed.[101] In such circumstances, this is not to prevent registration of the mark or "to diminish in any way the protection granted to the said mark in any country of the Union" (subject to the rider that such use does not mislead the public and is not contrary to the public interest). The restriction here to co-proprietors is a narrow one, leaving national laws free to legislate how they wish with respect to other situations in which concurrent use of a mark might occur.

J Seizure on Importation and "Appropriate Legal Remedies"

The Paris Convention touches only lightly upon the enforcement within Union countries of the industrial property rights that they undertake to protect under the Convention: in general, the matter of remedies for infringement of these rights is a matter for national treatment under Article 2(1).[102] Limited exceptions to this general approach are to be found in Article 9, which deals with the seizure on importation of goods unlawfully bearing protected trademarks and trade names, Article 10, which extends this protection to goods bearing false indications of source, and Article 10*ter*, which requires Union countries to provide "appropriate legal remedies" to repress all the acts referred to in the preceding articles (including also Article 10*bis* on unfair competition). Both Articles 9 and 10 can be traced back to the original 1883 Paris Act. Although framed in apparently stringent terms, on closer inspection it will be seen that they ultimately require little of national laws. The following discussion deals only with Articles 9 and 10*ter*, which are concerned with trademarks and trade names (the other provisions, Articles 10 and 10*bis*, being concerned with indications of source and unfair competition, respectively).

The basic obligation under Article 9(1) requires that "all goods unlawfully bearing a trademark or trade name shall be seized on importation into those countries of the Union where such mark or trade name is entitled to legal protection." Article 9(3) then provides that seizure is to take place "at the request of the public prosecutor, or any other competent authority, or any interested party, whether a natural person or a legal entity, in conformity with the domestic legislation of each country" and, in an interesting gloss, Article 9(2) provides that such seizure is "likewise to be effected in the country where the unlawful affixation occurred or in the country into which the goods were imported." This last provision, inserted in the Washington Revision Conference, has remained unchanged since this time, and it is noteworthy that, unlike other Paris Convention provisions, it imposes obligations on both the country of importation and the country from which the goods emanate and where the mark was applied unlawfully.[103] Nonetheless, these obligations are not as stringent as might be thought on a first reading. First, under Article 9(4), the seizure obligation under Article 9(1) does not extend to goods that are in transit, although authorities are free under this provision to seize them if domestic law so

[101] Actes 1934, *supra* note 22, at 460–01, 515, and *see also* Actes 1958, *supra* note 23, at 544–46, 546–64, 746–50.
[102] Subject to the express reservation to national laws under art. 2(3) of provisions relating to judicial and administrative procedures and jurisdiction, and the designation of an address for service or appointment of an agent.
[103] Actes 1911, *supra* note 20, at 301–02, 309, 254–55.

provides.[104] Secondly, Article 9(5) and (6) contain a sliding scale of lesser alternative measures that Union countries may adopt at their discretion in lieu of seizure. Under Article 9(5), if the domestic law of the importing country does not permit seizure on importation, seizure "shall be replaced by prohibition of importation or by seizure inside the country."[105] However, the imperative character of this direction is qualified by Article 9(6), which provides that if domestic law permits neither seizure on importation nor prohibition of importation nor seizure inside the country, "then, until such time as the legislation is modified accordingly, these measures shall be replaced by the actions and remedies available in such cases to nationals under the law of such country." The mandatory aspects of Article 9(1) and (5) therefore come into play only after implementing domestic legislation is in place; up until that time, national treatment of foreign trademark owners is all that can be expected or required. Furthermore, the words "until such time as the legislation is modified accordingly" in Article 9(6), added in the Hague Revision Conference, do not impose any obligation on Union countries to move to the adoption of seizure or importation prohibition measures at some finite time; rather, they are to be seen as a "simple invitation addressed to countries of the Union which creates no commitment, even moral, for them [to adopt such measures]."[106]

Further aspects of Article 9 that call for comment are:

(a) *Meaning of "unlawfully applied"*: This applies to both trademarks and trade names which must have been "unlawfully applied" to goods. It is not stated under which law the issue of unlawfulness is to be determined, but it must be assumed that this must at least be the country where the application has occurred (usually the country of export). Support for this conclusion is to be found in the reference to the "country where the unlawful affixation occurred" in Article 9(2), but the further question arises as to whether the unlawfulness must arise under the law of the country of importation as well. The answer to this second question must then be found in Article 9(1) which posits that the trademark or trade name must be entitled to legal protection in the Union country into which such importation occurs. The most likely scenario in which the downwardly cascading obligations contained in Article 9(1), (5) and (6) will be activated in the country of importation will be where the trademarks in question are registered in both that country and the country of affixation and has been applied without authorization in the latter. Such a scenario will usually require that the owner of the trademark is the same in both countries or that they are linked in some other way, for example as part of a larger corporate group or through contractual ties. Other scenarios where the marks are unregistered may also be possible, but will depend on how such protection is applied in both countries, and the same will be true of trade names that are unlawfully applied to goods. For most practical purposes, however, the positive obligations under Article 9 have a restricted scope, and will have no application, apart from the overall national treatment obligation, if the country in question has not yet adopted the required seizure or importation measures in accordance with Article 9(6). On the other hand, if it is accepted (as suggested above) that international exhaustion of rights is inconsistent with the principle of independence of protection embodied in Article 6(3), it would follow that some form of relief, if not seizure, should be provided, even in relation

[104] It appears that this exclusion does not apply to the warehousing of goods while they are in transit: Bureau International de l'Union, *Actes de la Conférence Réunie à Paris 1880–1883*, p. 88 and see further pp. 27 and 97.

[105] Adopted at the Brussels Revision Conference: Actes 1897–1900, *supra* note 19, at 45–46, 246–49, 255–56, 311–12.

[106] Actes 1925, *supra* note 21, at 470 (report of fourth subcommittee, statement by the French delegate in response to concerns expressed by the Swiss delegate), 525 (repeated in the general report) and 545 (drafting committee).

to the parallel importation of goods bearing marks that have been applied with the authorization of the trademark owner in the country of affixation.

(b) *Seizure in the country of unlawful application*: This alternative, referred to in Article 9(2), poses practical difficulties of detection and proof, given that there is no trigger point such as importation as in the case of the country of importation where such procedures can be more readily activated at the point of entry into the country. Taken literally, Article 9(2) compels the result that the country of unlawful affixation should have such procedures available at the time the unlawful affixation occurs. In practice, of course, this obligation may be deferred by reason of Article 9(6), so long as the foreign trademark owner can avail itself of the same actions and remedies that are available to nationals of that country.

(c) *Seizure on importation and seizure inside the country*: From a trademark owner's perspective, seizure at the point of entry into the importing country is obviously the most efficacious, thereby preventing the objectionable goods entering into the marketplace in that country, and this is the primary obligation imposed under Article 9(1). However, the options of prohibiting importation altogether or providing for seizure within the country (after importation) are available under Article 9(5). In practice, these options may be more difficult to implement, and Article 9(5) provides no further direction as to how they are to be activated or by whom, e.g., at the request of the public prosecutor, other competent authority or "interested party," as under Article 9(3). Accordingly, it must be assumed that this will be a matter for domestic laws to determine, with the further option under Article 9(6) of leaving this entirely as a matter for national treatment in the event that these laws do not provide for any of the procedures referred to in Article 9(1) or (5). At the same time, it should be noted that if prohibition or internal seizure procedures (however described) are provided under domestic laws, Article 9(5) obviously requires that these should be available to trademark and business name owners from other Union countries.

1 *Appropriate Legal Remedies*

This was adopted at The Hague Revision Conference, on the basis of proposals originally formulated by the League of Nations' Economic Committee.[107] On its face, Article 10*ter*(1) provides an intriguing set of largely unexplored undertakings by Union countries to "assure" to the nationals of other Union countries "appropriate legal remedies effectively to repress all the acts referred to in Articles 9, 10 and 10bis." Questions of standing with respect to associations and federations of industrialists, producers, or merchants are then addressed in Article 10*ter*(2).

So far as trademarks and trade names are concerned, the relevant "acts" referred to are those in Article 9, namely the importation of goods bearing trademarks or trade names unlawfully applied. Given that the default position under Article 9(6) is national treatment, Article 10*ter*(1) appears to mean that something additional is still required by way of provision of "appropriate legal remedies" in order "effectively to repress" the activities proscribed in that Article. However, in view of the specific mention of seizure procedures and importation measures in Article 9(1) and (5), and the default national treatment provision in Article 9(6), these measures could not in themselves be made a requirement through the back door under Article 10*ter*(1). What else, then, may be required under that article by way of legal remedies? The answer may well be supplied by application of national treatment under Article 2(1), where the country in question already has a wide range of remedial relief available to local claimants. On the other hand,

[107] *Id.* at 93 (proposals made by the Economic Committee, League of Nations, 5 May 1924) and 271 (programme proposals).

national treatment carries with it no prescription as to content, only the requirement that there should be no discrimination against foreigners. It therefore follows that Article 10*ter* embodies a more substantive requirement of a minimum of remedies that should be available to foreign rightholders, even in the unlikely event that these are not enjoyed by locals. What kinds of measures, then, would constitute "appropriate legal remedies to repress" the activities proscribed by Article 9 (and Articles 10 and 10*bis*), notwithstanding the generality of this formulation that leaves considerable discretion to each Union country?

Some pointers on these matters are to be found in the records of the Hague Conference at which Article 10*ter* was adopted.[108] The first is that "appropriate legal remedies" do not extend to the imposition of penal sanctions.[109] Secondly, notwithstanding its generality, there are comments in the report of the fourth subcommittee to the Hague Conference indicating that the minimum kind of civil remedies that might be expected to be available would include: (1) injunctions or orders to cease; (2) damages and interest; (3) punishment, though presumably not of a penal kind, of tortious acts with a preventative as well as a compensatory aim.[110] While there may be some uncertainty about the third of these suggestions, the first two fall squarely within the range of civil remedies ordinarily available in most domestic legal systems, although it cannot be presumed that they will necessarily be available in each country with respect to the various acts specified in Articles 9, 10 and 10*bis*. Accordingly, a strong case can be made that in these instances, at least, remedies such as injunctions and damages are required to be available under Article 10*ter*. Even in the case of the third, there may be other potential forms of relief that will serve a preventative as well as compensatory purpose – for example, awards of exemplary or additional damages, orders for an account of profit that strip a defendant of ill-gotten gains, orders for delivery up of dies or moulds used for the unlawful application of trademarks, removal or erasure of offending signs, etc.[111] While considerable discretion is left to domestic laws as to how they give effect to the obligations under Article 10*ter*, the ultimate goal must be to "repress" or eliminate the kinds of unlawful acts specified in the preceding three articles, and this means something more than reflexive reliance upon whatever remedies may already be available under national treatment.

K Miscellaneous Provisions

Other provisions of the Paris Convention that touch on trademarks and related topics should be briefly noted here.[112]

(a) *Grace periods for payment of maintenance fees*: No less than six months should be allowed for the payment of fees prescribed for the maintenance of rights, subject to the payment of a surcharge if prescribed by domestic legislation: Article 5*bis*(1).

(b) *No marking of goods*: No mention or indication of the registration of the trademark on goods can be required as a condition of the right to protection: Article 5D.

108 *See also id.* at 349–51, 478–80, 525–6, 547 (report of drafting committee).

109 It appears that the US delegates were strongly opposed to their inclusion, as originally proposed in the Conference programme: *See also id.* at 252–55, 271, 457, 470, 478–80. *See also id.* at 525–26 (report of general committee), 547 (report of drafting committee) and 581 (adoption in second plenary session).

110 *Id.* at 479.

111 *See, e.g.*, Trade Marks Act 1994, §§ 41(2), 15 and 16 (UK).

112 For the sake of completeness, several other provisions of the Convention touching on trademarks should be noted: art. 6*septies* (measures to be taken where local agents or representatives register the mark of an overseas owner without the latter's permission) and art. 11 ("temporary protection" to be given to patentable inventions, utility models, industrial designs and trademarks in respect of goods exhibited at "official or officially recognized international exhibitions" held in the territory of any Union country). *See also* Ricketson, *supra* note 1, Chs. 12, 12.63 and 12.98.

(c) *Protection of trade names*: Under Article 8, Paris Union countries are required to protect trade names, that is, the names used by traders in relation to their businesses as distinct from marks used in relation to goods or services. This protection is to be without any obligation of filing or registration and is to be given regardless of whether the name forms part of a trademark. This is a positive obligation which leaves considerable discretion to Union countries as to how they accord protection, but goes beyond what might otherwise be required under national treatment (which might be satisfied by providing no protection at all, so long as this was also the case for local claimants).[113]

V CONCLUDING REMARKS

It is easy to dismiss the provisions of the Paris Convention dealing with trademarks as being of limited significance. Thus, they contain little by way of substantive norms as to what is to be protected, how this is to be done, the length of that protection, or the permissible exceptions that may be made to it. Nor do they deal, other than in minor ways, with the procedural or administrative aspects of obtaining and maintaining protection. Such initiatives at the international level have occurred in the arena of trade-related rights through the TRIPS Agreement, through regional instruments, such as in the EU, and through the development of separate WIPO treaties. On the other hand, the priority system to enable foreign traders to access the legal systems of other countries and the national treatment requirement that applies once they have arrived provide a solid platform on which further protections can be built and have underpinned the international system of trademark protection for nearly 140 years. And, as we have seen, there are some other important, if limited, obligations that apply to Paris Union countries, not the least of which is the independence of protection requirement under Article 6, the recognition of marks already registered under Article 6*quinquies*, and the somewhat idiosyncratic provisions with respect to state flags and emblems under Article 6*ter*. Other matters may be only of marginal significance, representing works in progress that have never progressed to completion, such as the provisions on well-known marks, assignments, agents and seizure on importation. Nonetheless, the important thing about platforms is that they represent starting points for future development, and this is the central and historic role played by the Paris Convention.

[113] *See also* RICKETSON, *supra* note 1, Chs. 12, 12.81, and 12.82.

2

A Look at the Trademark Provisions in the TRIPS Agreement

*Daniel J. Gervais**

I STRUCTURAL OVERVIEW

A *The Paris Convention as Backdrop*

The World Trade Organization's (WTO) Agreement on Trade-Related Aspects of Intellectual Property Rights (TRIPS Agreement) was signed (as an annex to the agreement establishing the WTO) on 15 April 1994 and entered into force on 1 January 1995.[1] Leaving aside systems specifically designed to facilitate international registration of trademarks, the multilateral instrument containing substantive trademark law that preceded TRIPS was the Paris Convention.[2]

The Paris Convention played a foundational role in the development of international trademark law.[3] However, it contains little substantive trademark law. In its *Guide to the Paris Convention*, the former Director General of the United International Bureaux for the Protection of Intellectual Property (BIRPI), the predecessor organization of the World Intellectual Property Organization (WIPO), Professor G. H. C. Bodenhausen underscores only the following ones as trademark-specific, non-administrative provisions: Article 6*bis*, concerning well-known marks, Article 6*septies*, allowing states to impose time limits to exercise certain rights in respect of well-known marks, Article 9 on enforcement (seizure) of goods bearing an unlawful trademark, and Article 10*bis*, which is relevant to trademark law even though its focus is on unfair competition.[4] Other provisions are relevant in any overview of the Convention's substantive trademark law provisions, even though they are essentially administrative in nature: priority date, acceptance of

* Milton R. Underwood Chair in Law, Vanderbilt Law School. The Author was a consultant in two WTO cases discussed in this Chapter, namely Australia- Plain Packaging (Appellate Body level only, see note 45) and Saudi Arabia-Measures concerning the protection of intellectual property rights (see note ___).

[1] TRIPS: Agreement on Trade-Related Aspects of Intellectual Property Rights, Apr. 15, 1994, Marrakesh Agreement Establishing the World Trade Organization, Annex 1C, 1869 UNTS 299, 33 ILM 1197 (1994) [hereinafter TRIPS Agreement].

[2] Paris Convention for the Protection of Industrial Property, Mar. 20 1883, last revised July 14, 1967, 21 UST 1583, 828 UNTS 303 [hereinafter Paris Convention]; Trademark Law Treaty, Oct. 27, 1994, in WIPO, Industrial Property and Copyright, Industrial Property Laws and Treaties, Multilateral Treaties 1 (Jan. 1995), http://wipo.int/edocs/lexdocs/treaties/en/tlt/trt_tlt_001en.pdf. The Trademark Law Treaty (TLT) was signed on Oct. 27, 1994, therefore between the signing of the Agreement Establishing the World Trade Organization and its entry into force. The TLT entered into force on Aug. 1, 1996. It contains very little substantive trademark law and is mostly meant to simplify and harmonize national registration procedures.

[3] *See* Chapter 1 in this volume, authored by Professor Sam Ricketson.

[4] G. H. C. Bodenhausen, Guide to the Paris Convention for the Protection of Industrial Property, 11–13 (1969).

TABLE 2.1 *Differences between the Paris Convention and the TRIPS Agreement*

Paris Convention	TRIPS Agreement
No definition of a trademark	Defined in art. 15
Use requirement implicit (art. 5C &6*bis*)	Possibility of use requirement explicit (art. 15.3). Paris provisions also covered by incorporation of Convention into TRIPS (art. 2.1)
Protection of trade names (art. 8)	Covered by incorporation of Convention into TRIPS (art. 2.1)
Protection of well-known marks on goods (art. 6*bis*)	Protection of well-known marks on goods and services (arts. 16.2 and 16.3). Paris provisions also covered by incorporation
Protection of State emblems, armorial bearings, flags, and the like (art. 6*ter*)	Covered by incorporation
Exclusion of nature of goods as obstacle to registration (art. 7)	Exclusion of nature of goods or services as obstacle to registration (art. 15.4)
Marks belonging to associations/ collective marks (art. 7*bis*)	Covered by incorporation
National treatment (art. 2)	National treatment (art. 3) and most-favored nation (art. 4). Paris provisions also covered by incorporation
Goods, with possible extension to services (art. 6*sexies*)	Goods and services
Right of priority (art. 4C(1))	Covered by incorporation
Applications directly (art. 6) or "as is" through pre-existing registration (art. 6*quinquiès*)	Covered by incorporation
Independence of protection (art. 6)	Covered by incorporation
Protection against unfair competition (art. 10*bis*)	Covered by incorporation
	Rights of trademark owners (art. 16)
	Limit on exceptions to rights (art. 17)
	Minimum term of initial registration and renewals (art. 18)
Minimum period of non-use to cancel (art. 5C(1))	Minimum period of non-use to cancel, and partial definition of use (art. 19). Paris provision also covered by incorporation
Use in different form (art. 5C(2))	Covered by incorporation
Concurrent use (art. 5C(3)	Covered by incorporation
	Obligation to not unjustifiably encumber use of a trademark in course of trade (art. 20)
Limited provision on assignment of marks (art. 6*quater*)	Prohibition on compulsory licensing and right of assignment without business (art. 21)
Seizure (art.9) subject to domestic law & appropriate remedies (art. 10*ter*)	Specific border measures, dames, injunctions, provisional measures, and criminal remedies (counterfeiting), Part III of TRIPS. Paris provision also covered by incorporation
Dispute-settlement option, International Court of Justice (art. 28)	Binding dispute-settlement (art. 64 and Dispute-Settlement Understanding, Annex 2 to the Agreement Establishing the WTO)

foreign marks for registration, protection of state emblems, prohibition on refusing registration due to the nature of the goods, and the obligation on states to register and protect collective marks.[5] National treatment should also be on the list.

Table 2.1 may be useful to understand the differences between the Paris Convention and the TRIPS Agreement.

[5] Paris Convention, *supra* note 2, arts. 6*ter*, 7 and 7*bis* respectively.

Let us now turn to an analysis of the trademark provisions in Part II of the TRIPS Agreement, that is, leaving aside for this purpose a full analysis of the enforcement and dispute-settlement provisions.[6]

B The Structure of the TRIPS Trademark Provisions

The TRIPS Agreement is expressly linked to the Paris Convention: WTO members must "comply with Articles 1 through 12, and Article 19, of the Paris Convention (1967)."[7] Moreover, WTO members cannot make reservations to any of the provisions of TRIPS. The Agreement, in other words, is meant to continue painting the international trademark law canvas on which Paris was first inscribed. In many ways, TRIPS fills gaps left untouched by Paris, many of which will likely strike the reader as rather fundamental: defining what constitutes a trademark, and specifying what rights a trademark owner has, how long such rights last, and what exceptions can be made to such rights, all matters absent from Paris with the few minor exceptions mentioned above. TRIPS vastly expands the bare-bones enforcement provisions of the Convention and adds state-to-state dispute settlement.[8] Where there was already "Paris paint" on the canvas, however, the TRIPS negotiators did relatively little. There is an overlap on national treatment protected under both instruments, for instance, to which TRIPS adds most-favored-nation treatment (MFN).[9]

The TRIPS provisions other than the incorporated provisions from the Paris Convention are thus, if one excepts the limited overlap, a complement and in some ways the inverse of Paris and subsequent WIPO-administered instruments, including the Trademark Law Treaty (TLT) and the Singapore Treaty.[10] Whereas the WIPO-administered instruments are heavy on registration but very light on substantive trademark law and enforcement, TRIPS is heavy on substantive trademark law and enforcement but very light on registration and administrative issues. Indeed, the "administrative" part of the TRIPS Agreement (Part IV of the Agreement) contains only modest obligational content, including that registration procedures and formalities be "reasonable" and effected "within a reasonable period of time."[11]

C Is TRIPS Common Law or Civil Law?

It is well known that there are two different worldviews when it comes to trademark law, which one could broadly describe as civil law and common law approaches. Painting with a very broad

6 *See* TRIPS Agreement, *supra* note 1, arts. 41–61 and 64.

7 *Id.*, arts. 72 and 2.1.

8 *Id.*, arts. 41–61 and 64.

9 National treatment obligations are contained in the Paris Convention, *supra* note 2, art. 3 and the TRIPS Agreement, *supra* note 1, art. 3. The former is also incorporated by reference into TRIPS, as noted in the previous note. MFN obligations are contained in art. 4 of TRIPS. One interesting issue that is not addressed here is that the Convention is only "authentic" in French, though official versions exist in English, German, Italian, Portuguese, Russian and Spanish. This rule is contained in art. 29(1), which was not incorporated into TRIPS.

10 On the TLT, *supra* note 2; Singapore Treaty on the Law of Trademarks, Mar. 27, 2006, S. Treaty Doc. No. 110–12, http://wipo.int/edocs/lexdocs/treaties/en/singapore/trt_singapore_001en.pdf [hereinafter Singapore Treaty] entered into force Mar. 16, 2009. The Singapore Treaty builds on the TLT by addressing the use of newer communication technologies to register trademarks. It does, however, contain more substantive provisions such as the recognition of so-called non-traditional marks such as "holograms, three-dimensional marks, color, position and movement marks, as well as non-visible marks such as sound, olfactory or taste and feel marks." *See* WIPO, Summary of the Singapore Treaty, http://wipo.int/treaties/en/ip/singapore/summary_singapore.html.

11 TRIPS Agreement, *supra* note 1, art. 62.1 and 62.2.

brush, one could say that, in common law jurisdictions, trademark law is derived from the tort of "passing off." The original tort of "passing off" prevented a merchant from putting another's mark on their wares.[12] Hence, rights in a trademark typically stemmed from use in commerce of a symbol to distinguish goods or services from one undertaking from those of a competitor.[13] Common law would then prevent, under tort doctrines, the use of a confusing mark by a competitor. Unregistered marks are protected at common law, typically only in the geographic area in which they were used and then only against later users.[14]

As just noted, at common law the existence of protection depended on use in commerce by the plaintiff.[15] Yet modern trademark theory acknowledges that trademarks are meant not only to protect the owners of marks but also to benefit consumers, notably by reducing search costs.[16] Trademarks allow consumers to identify lawful products they wish to purchase and to expect a certain quality they associate with a given trademark. This is an incentive for the trademark owner to maintain their "brand."

Various statutes and legal doctrines have added to the arsenal of common law trademark holders over the years, including notions such as "dilution" in the US trademark law or protection of well-known marks outside the area of commercial activity in which a trademark is actually used.[17] In spite of the add-ons, however, the notion that basic trademark rights arise from use, not from an act of government, remains central to common law systems. Consequently, in most common law jurisdictions obtaining registration of a trademark that is not in use in commerce is not possible.[18] One may *apply* for registration but may not complete the registration process without providing adequate evidence of use.

In civil law systems, by contrast, one may apply and obtain registration of a trademark that is not (yet) in use. Trademark rights arise from the administrative act of registration of the trademark.[19] Unregistered marks are not protected *as such*, although remedies are often available under general rules concerning unfair or parasitic competition.[20] This ex ante approach in the role of government in civil law systems is in marked contrast to the approach in common law jurisdictions where the government intervenes ex post – that is, after use in commerce has begun. The registration process in common law jurisdictions thus recognizes a trademark that is already in existence and use.

[12] Xuan-Thao N. Nguyen, *The Digital Trademark Right: A Troubling New Extraterritorial Reach of United States Law*, 81 NORTH CAROLINA L. REV. 483, 542–43 (2003).

[13] This typically means one or (generally) more arm's-length commercial transactions on a product or service in which the mark is featured as a distinctive symbol identifying the supplier or origin of the product or service. For the United States, *see* Lanham Act § 45, 15 USC § 1127 (1946), which defines "[u]se in Commerce" as "the bona fide use of a mark in the ordinary course of trade, and not made merely to reserve a right in a mark."

[14] CHRISTOPHER WADLOW, THE LAW OF PASSING-OFF (2004) at 6–12.

[15] *See* Aneta Ferguson, *The Trademark Filing Trap*, 49 IDEA 197, 224 (2009).

[16] WILLIAM M. LANDES & RICHARD A. POSNER, THE ECONOMIC STRUCTURE OF INTELLECTUAL PROPERTY LAW (2003) at 185–86.

[17] J. THOMAS MCCARTHY, MCCARTHY ON TRADEMARKS AND UNFAIR COMPETITION vol. 4, § 24:67 (Clark Boardman Callaghan ed., 4th ed. 2014). For example, registration of a trademark at the United States Patent and Trademark office provides protection throughout the United States even if the mark is not actually used in all fifty states. § 26:31. Consonant with common law principles, however, registration is only possible after use in commerce and, for federal registration, use in interstate commerce. § 25:56.

[18] *Id.*

[19] It is true, however, that if a trademark is not used, it will be usually possible to obtain its removal from the register after a certain number of years.

[20] In France, such protection is based upon art. 1382 of the Code Civil. For Germany, *see* Christian Schertz & Susanne Bergmann, *Germany*, *in* CHARACTER MERCHANDISING IN EUROPE, 136–37 (Heijo Ruijsenaars ed., 2003).

That said, it is worth noting that the purpose of the registration of trademarks is typically not simply for the sake of registration itself. It is thus unlike, say, a driver's license that can be used by someone who never drives a car (as a form of identification, for example). A trademark registration has but one purpose: protect the owner against use in commerce by a third party. Simply put, trademarks are typically registered so that they can be used.[21] It is relevant, therefore, in any analysis guided by the object and purpose of the TRIPS Agreement as directed by the application of the Vienna Convention on the Law of Treaties (VCLT)[22] to ask *why* the TRIPS Agreement gives trademark owners a right to access a registration system and rights against use by third parties – in addition to a right against state-imposed unjustified encumbrances on use in Article 20.

Linking this debate to the previous sections comparing TRIPS and the Paris Convention, the Convention appears more as a reflection of the civil law approach to trademark protection in its emphasis on registration and its absence of provisions on rights acquired by use, the latter factor being mitigated, however, by an almost complete absence of *any* rights for trademark holders in the Convention. The Convention date of priority regime presupposes that a trademark holder will have registered their trademark in country A (typically the country of origin) and then apply for registration in other jurisdictions party to the Paris Convention. Common law jurisdictions had to adapt to this system in a variety of ways. For example, US trademark holders sometimes use the Supplemental Register to register trademarks that are not used in the United States so that they can be "exported" to other countries under the Paris Convention Article 6*quinquies* system.[23]

Seen in this light, the TRIPS Agreement looks like a compromise between the major legal systems, as it expressly embraces both use-based and registration-based systems. In a further attempt at compromise, Article 15 of the TRIPS Agreement, which provides that WTO members may make registrability dependent on use,[24] expressly recognizes common law systems' use requirement, and Article 15 makes it clear that actual use of a trademark is not a condition for *filing an application* for registration. Where signs are not inherently capable of distinguishing the relevant goods or services (e.g., the shape or packaging of certain products), registrability *may be made* dependent on distinctiveness acquired through use. This adds to, but is consonant with, the Paris Convention system described above in that it allows for registration of distinctive signs if registered in their country of origin, but also reflects the flexibility left to WTO and Paris Union members to calibrate rules concerning the distinctiveness of trademarks.[25]

In comparing the TRIPS Agreement with Article 6*quinquies*(B) of the Paris Convention, a mark registered in another WTO member and for which an application for registration has been filed should be examined on its individual merits and proper instructions given accordingly to examiners (particularly regarding countries not party to the Paris Convention that are or will

[21] Trademarks are occasionally registered in some jurisdictions for other so-called defensive purposes, but those instances are minimal and also subject to challenge for non-use. *See* Yasuhiro H. Suzuki, *Navigating the "Land of Harmony" and Finding "Harmonization" for Foreign Trademark Applicants and Owners: A Japanese Practitioner's Perspective*, 103 TRADEMARK REP. 519, 562 (2013).

[22] Vienna Convention on the Law of Treaties, May 23, 1969, 1155 UNTS 331 (entered into force Jan. 27, 1980) [hereinafter VCLT].

[23] MCCARTHY, *supra* note 17, vol. 4 at § 19:33.

[24] This applies also to inherently distinctive marks and thus should not be confused with use leading to the acquisition of distinctiveness/secondary meaning of otherwise descriptive marks.

[25] Art. 6*quinquies*(B)(ii) of the Paris Convention, *supra* note 2, permits denial of registration or invalidated when a mark is devoid of any distinctive character.

become WTO members). This is reinforced by Article 6*quinquies*(C) of the Paris Convention, which requires that all factual circumstances be taken into consideration.[26]

The adaptation of the TRIPS Agreement to the common law when compared to the Convention world is not limited to the explicit recognition of the validity of a requirement of use. The definition contained in the first sentence of Article 15.1 of the TRIPS Agreement, discussed below, is not limited to registrable marks.[27] Thus, especially when read in conjunction with Article 16.1[28] *in fine*, also discussed below, the TRIPS Agreement also contemplates rights (e.g., the common law tort of "passing off") in respect of unregistered marks and provides a framework for such protection but without mandating their protection in all WTO members.

The requirement of use and consequences of non-use are also impacted by Article 19, discussed below, which limits cancellation for non-use after an "uninterrupted period of at least three years" if

> valid reasons based on the existence of obstacles to such use are shown by the trademark owner. Circumstances arising independently of the will of the owner of the trademark which constitute an obstacle to the use of the trademark, such as import restrictions on or other government requirements for goods or services protected by the trademark, shall be recognized as valid reasons for non-use.[29]

II THE TRADEMARK PROVISIONS IN THE TRIPS AGREEMENT

The chapter now turns to the individual trademark provisions contained in section 2 of part II the TRIPS Agreement.[30]

A *Article 15*

The TRIPS Agreement does not provide a full trademark code. Rather it fills a number of perceived gaps in the previous set of international rules, including of course those contained in the Paris Convention. If read as an entire document, however, and taking its object and purpose into account, TRIPS does provide clear guidance as to WTO members' shared understandings of the policies and norms relevant to trademarks.[31] The function of trademarks, for example, can be readily understood by reference to the TRIPS Agreement Article 15.1, especially its first sentence, which refers to distinguishing goods and services of undertakings in the course of trade. By defining what constitutes a trademark, this provision limits the ability of WTO members in their flexibility to define protectable subject matter or of what constitutes a trademark.

26 *Id.* at art. 6*quinquies*(C). There are two ways in which an applicant may use the Paris Convention, namely art. 6, where a foreign applicant would register as a national applicant under the national treatment principle, and art. 6*quinquies*, which allows applications based on a foreign registration, in which case the mark must be accepted "as is." *See* US – Section 211 Omnibus Appropriations Act, Appellate Body report, WTO doc. WT/DS176/AB/R, Jan. 2, 2002, at §§ 130–34 [hereinafter US Appropriations Act].

27 TRIPS Agreement, *supra* note 1, art. 15.1.

28 *Id.*, art. 16.1.

29 *Id.*, art. 19.

30 A detailed look at each provision is beyond the scope of this chapter. I invite the reader to consult published commentaries on the TRIPS Agreement, including DANIEL GERVAIS, THE TRIPS AGREEMENT: DRAFTING HISTORY AND ANALYSIS (4th ed. 2013); and Irene Calboli & Christine Haight Farley, *The Trademark Provisions in the TRIPS Agreement*, *in* INTELLECTUAL PROPERTY AND INTERNATIONAL TRADE: THE TRIPS AGREEMENT, 157–92 (Carlos Correa & Abdulqawi Yusuf eds., 2016).

31 WTO members' shared understanding might also be described as the intention of the parties to the agreement.

The Appellate Body noted that "in terms of eligibility for registration, the norm is the presentation of signs that are 'inherently' distinctive. It is only in situations when a sign is not inherently distinctive that the 'distinctiveness acquired through use' becomes relevant.[32] Article 15 allows members to deny registration or impose conditions on filing and registration grounds mentioned in either the TRIPS Agreement or the Paris Convention at grounds not inconsistent with the Convention or Article 15.1.[33]

Article 6*quinquies* of the Paris Convention, incorporated by reference into TRIPS, requires that Paris Union and WTO Members protect a foreign registered mark "as is" in their jurisdiction.[34] Because the Convention contains few obligations concerning substantive rights of trademark holders, this obligation was interpreted in a 2018 panel report that protection was whatever was available under national law, as the panel found no "support in the language of Article 6*quinquies* A(1) for a substantive minimum standard of rights that WTO Members would be obliged to make available to the owner of a trademark that has been registered pursuant to the requirements of Article 6*quinquies* A(1)."[35] Article 15.2 of TRIPS, like Article 6*quinquies*, limits the grounds on which a foreign mark can be refused registration.

Article 15.4 came under special scrutiny in the Australia plain packaging case.[36] In that case, complainants (a group of tobacco-producing countries that brought a case supported by a number of tobacco companies) argued that "the fact that non-word signs are prohibited from being used on tobacco products and packaging means that new non-word signs that are not inherently distinctive have no opportunity to acquire distinctiveness through use on such products, and therefore face obstacles to registration based on the nature of the goods as tobacco products, in violation of Article 15.4."[37] The argument was rejected by the panels as there is no obstacle to the registration because Article 15.4 applies only to the "registration of a sign, or combination of signs, that is otherwise capable of constituting a trademark, and thus eligible for registration, within the meaning of Article 15.1."[38] A trademark that has not acquired distinctiveness would then not be eligible so that the obstacle to registration stems from non-use. The fact that the use of the mark (which might have led to acquired distinctiveness) is prohibited because of the nature of the product was an interesting argument but it was also plainly rejected by the panels.[39]

B *Article 16*

Article 16.1 fills a gap in the Paris Convention in that it provides minimum rights to trademark owners.[40] It provides in part that owners of *registered* trademarks "shall have exclusive right to

[32] World Trade Organization, Australia – Certain measures concerning trademarks, geographical indications and other plain packaging requirements applicable to tobacco products and packaging, Appellate Body Report, doc. WT/DS435/AB/R WT/DS441/AB/R, 9 June 2020, at para 6.579 (hereinafter Appellate Body Report, Australia).

[33] *See* US Appropriations Act, *supra* note 26, §§ 156, 165, 177, and 178.

[34] Singapore Treaty, *supra* note 10 and U.S. Appropriations Act *supra* note 26; "Paris Union" members are states party to the Paris Convention.

[35] Panel Report, *Australia – Certain measures concerning trademarks, geographical indications and other plain packaging requirements applicable to tobacco products and packaging*, WTO doc. WT/DS435/R, WT/DS441/R, WT/DS458/R, WT/DS467/R, June 28, 2018, at § 7.1765 [hereinafter the Australian Plain Packaging Report]. See also the Appellate Body report in the case, infra note 45, and the discussion under Article 20.

[36] *Id.*

[37] Australian Plain Packaging Report, *supra* note 34, § 7.1816. Art. 15.4 parallels art. 7 of the Paris Convention and states that the nature of the goods or services shall not constitute an obstacle to registration.

[38] *Id.* § 7.1856.

[39] *Tobacco Plain Packaging Act 2011* (Cth) art. 28(3)–(4) (Austl.). As for marks already registered whose use of prohibited signs such as logos and other non-word marks, the Australian legislation protects them from deregistration due to non-use.

[40] Under the Paris Convention, as mentioned above, there are very few substantive rights. In the case of trademarks, art. 10*bis*(3) provides some protection. *See* Paris Convention, *supra* note 2.

prevent all third parties not having the owner's consent from using in the course of trade identical or similar signs for goods or services which are identical or similar to those in respect of which the trademark is registered where such use would result in a likelihood of confusion." It requires WTO members to grant the owner of the mark the exclusive right to prevent third parties from using signs identical or similar to the mark in the course of trade for goods or services that are identical or similar to those in respect of which the mark is registered, where such use would result in a likelihood of confusion. The provision adds a presumption of likelihood of confusion when an identical sign is used for identical goods or services. The presumption is helpful especially for provisional measures because the use of an identical sign for identical goods or services normally will result in a very high likelihood of confusion; indeed, one hardly sees how a defendant could succeed in proving the contrary.

Article 16.2 requires that Article 6*bis* of the Paris Convention, dealing with well-known marks, be applied to services.[41]

Article 16.3 deals with the use of certain (well-known) marks in relation to goods or services other than those for which the mark is registered, subject to two cumulative conditions: (a) that a link be made to the owner of the well-known mark and (b) that there be likely damage to the interests of the owner of the well-known mark.

The TRIPS Agreement does not specify who, under national law, must be recognized as the owner of a mark. It certainly does not have to be the owner of a *registration*, as in several countries rights stem from use and exist even without registration.[42]

A most interesting debate about Article 16 is the so-called negative right issue. Do trademark owners have only a negative right to prevent others from using their mark and no positive right to use the mark, and is this a binary situation? In support of the proposition that Article 16 provides for only negative rights, one can cite the panel in the case concerning European geographical indications, which declared that "Article 16.1 of the TRIPS Agreement only provides for a negative right to prevent all third parties from using signs in certain circumstances."[43]

In an article co-authored with Susy Frankel (author of Chapter 4 in this volume), we dispute this interpretation as ignoring "a wealth of literature and theory about the nature of property, the meaning of ownership, the meaning of rights to exclude, and even the specific notion of negative rights."[44] We argued instead that it is the essence of trademarks that they be used in trade and suggested, using Hohfeldian terminology, that the right should be seen as a combination of both exclusion and privilege if one is to understand its veritable purpose, and that trademark owners have a relevant interest in using their marks which is relevant as matter of law.[45] This approach is also consonant with Article 20's limited prohibition (discussed below) on encumbrances to the use of a trademark, which at least implicitly recognizes that trademarks are meant to be used in the course of trade – even absent a "right to use."

Bearing Article 31(1) of the Vienna Convention in mind, Article 20 should inform the interpretation of other articles in the trademark section of Part II of the TRIPS Agreement, just

[41] *See also* art. 15 of the TLT, *supra* note 2.

[42] *See* US Appropriations Act, *supra* note 26, at § 199.

[43] Panel Report, *European Communities – Protection of Trademarks and Geographical Indications for Agricultural Products and Foodstuffs*, WTO doc. WT/DS290/R, Mar. 15, 2005, at fn. 564 [hereinafter European Communities – Protection of Trademarks and Geographical Indications].

[44] Susy Frankel & Daniel Gervais, *Plain Packaging and the Interpretation of the TRIPS Agreement*, 46 Vand. J. Transnat'l L. 1149, 1187–88 (2014).

[45] *Id.* at 1189.

as other articles in that section inform the interpretation of Article 20.[46] Though that position has been taken by a number of scholars, to say that a trademark owner has no "right to use" thus does not, in this author's view, end the discussion, for two interrelated reasons.[47] First, a right to exclude makes sense mostly if and when both the owner and an unauthorized third party are using the same mark (or confusingly similar marks) in commerce, for reasons explained above. Second, the right to exclude is typically based on a likelihood of confusion, which in turn does not follow from whether the mark is registered (consumers are not expected to search the register) or not but from whether consumers know the mark, and, therefore, from whether it is used in commerce.

The Appellate Body found that there was no positive "right to use", just an "exclusive right to prevent" third parties from using a mark, acknowledging however that trademark owners had a legitimate interest in using their mark and in "preserving the distinctiveness, or capacity to distinguish". The exact scope and role of those legitimate interests (discussed below) are mostly relevant under Article 17.[48]

A specific constraint that a use prohibition entails is the inability to acquire or the risk of losing well-known mark status under TRIPS Article 16.3. This argument made by the complainants in the Australia case was brushed aside by the panels, which found that compliance with Article 16.3 was "independent of the actual occurrence" of the factual conditions to obtain that status in the market, so that "a reduction in the factual occurrence in the marketplace of the situations that would trigger well-known trademark protection [does not] constitute a reduction in the availability of such protection."[49]

C *Article 17*

This article allows WTO members to make limited exceptions to trademark rights. An example is given: namely, fair use of descriptive terms. Its wording is inspired from the three-step test found in Article 13 of TRIPS concerning exceptions and limitations to copyright rights, which itself comes from Article 9(2) of the Berne Convention for the Protection of Literary and Artistic Works. To be compatible with this provision, an exception in national law must be limited and "take account of the legitimate interests of the owner of the trademark and of third parties."[50]

To decide whether an exception is limited, one must not look at the number of trademarks to which it may apply but instead to "whether the exception to the rights conferred by a trademark is narrow."[51]

Use in the TRIPS Agreement of the notion of legitimate interests reaffirms the need to factor in interests beyond the rights expressly provided in the TRIPS Agreement minimum set of rights.[52] "Legitimate interests" is a broader notion than positive rights: "a right is a legitimate

[46] *See* Australia Appellate Body Report, para. 6.609.

[47] *See* Mark Davison, *The Legitimacy of Plain Packaging under International Intellectual Property Law: Why There Is No Right to Use a Trademark under either the Paris Convention or the TRIPS Agreement*, *in* Public Health and Plain Packaging of Cigarettes: Legal Issues 81, 94–95 (Tania Voon et al. eds., 2012).

[48] Appellate Body report, Australia, paras. 6.587. 6.588 and 6.650.

[49] *Id.* at § 7.2116.

[50] TRIPS Agreement, *supra* note 1, art. 17.

[51] EC – Protection of Trademarks and Geographical Indications, *supra* note 42, at §§ 7-65–7.651.

[52] Minimum because art. 1.1 of the TRIPS Agreement provides in part that WTO members "may, but shall not be obliged to, implement in their law more extensive protection than is required by this Agreement"; *see* TRIPS Agreement, *supra* note 1.

interest, but not all legitimate interests are rights."[53] A relevant case in this context is the European GI case at the WTO concerning the extra hurdles that applicants had to jump over to protect non-European GIs in the EU. The panel in that case noted that TRIPS does not only set out "standards for legal rights, it also provides guidance as to WTO Members' shared understandings of the policies and norms relevant to trademarks and, hence, what might be the legitimate interests of trademark owners."[54] Part of the owner's legitimate interest lies "in preserving the distinctiveness, or capacity to distinguish, of its trademark so that it can perform that function. This includes its interest in using its own trademark in connection with the relevant goods and services of its own and authorized undertakings."[55] This provides relevant context in interpreting other articles of the trademark section of the TRIPS Agreement, including Article 20, as the Australia panels noted.[56]

D *Article 18*

This article provides that "[i]nitial registration, and each renewal of registration, of a trademark shall be for a term of no less than seven years. The registration of a trademark shall be renewable indefinitely."[57]

This provision establishes a minimum term for the validity of the initial registration of a mark and indefinite renewals thereof: seven years. Under WIPO-administered instruments, the duration of the initial registration and renewals is set at ten years.[58] Typically, a registration can be renewed as long as the mark continues to be a distinctive sign, e.g., was not abandoned (non-use) or rendered generic.

E *Article 19*

Article 19 fills a gap left by the 1958 International Patent and Trademark Conference in Lisbon, Portugal (Lisbon Conference), which was able to deal effectively only with concurrent use by enterprises that are co-proprietors of a mark (and not licensor and licensee, a much more common situation).

Article 19.1 sets the condition imposed on WTO members which requires use to maintain a trademark registration. It may be considered as a more precise version of Article 5C(1) of the Paris Convention, which allows cancellation after a "reasonable period" defined by national legislation. A minimum of three uninterrupted years is required, and the owner of the mark must be given an opportunity to show that there may have been obstacles to such use, including circumstances arising independently of the owner's will, such as import restrictions or other government requirements. Approval (or renewal thereof) necessary to market a product (e.g., an agri-food or pharmaceutical compound) would constitute such an obstacle.[59] In other words, non-use must result from a failure attributable to the owner of the trademark or their

53 Frankel & Gervais, *supra* note 43, at 1190.

54 EC – Protection of Trademarks and Geographical Indications, *supra* note 42, at § 7.664. This paragraph was cited with apparent approval by the Appellate Body in the Australia case, supra, at § 6.650.

55 *Id.*

56 Australia Plain Packaging Report, *supra* note 34, at § 7.2561.

57 TRIPS Agreement, *supra* note 1, art. 18.

58 Protocol Relating to the Madrid Agreement Concerning the International Registration of Marks, of June 27, 1989 (as amended on Nov. 12, 2007), art. 6(1); TLT, *supra* note 2, art. 13(7).

59 Unfortunately, the Appellate Body apparently conflated the "right to use" a mark issue with the right to sell a product or offer a service. These are distinct legal issues in trade law. See Appellate Body report, supra, at § 6.607.

representatives and not, e.g., a government-imposed prohibition (such as a ban on the product or a measure preventing the use of a mark, such as the Australian ban on logos on cigarette packs).

Article 19.2 implies that a WTO member must also accept use by a person other than the owner but subject to their control as use that qualifies to maintain the trademark.[60] Control is often effected by a licensing arrangement enumerating specific conditions under which the mark may be used by the licensee. This puts the spotlight on the control that can and perhaps should be effected by the trademark owner in any licensing transaction and the key role of the specifications (or "*cahier des charges*") that a complete trademark license, including franchising arrangement, should comprise. Under Article 19.2 of the TRIPS Agreement, WTO members have flexibility to require control of the licensee's use by the trademark owner.

While the existence of an optional recordation system for licenses and transfers seems acceptable under the TRIPS Agreement rules, there is some disagreement about whether WTO members may *require* that a license be registered or "recorded." Such registration or recordation may be required under applicable corporate or business licensing laws, tax laws, or other financial regulations not related to intellectual property. Would a WTO member be allowed *not* to consider use by an authorized licensee under control of the trademark owner as sufficient to maintain registration? The text of Article 19.2 of the TRIPS Agreement does not seem to support this conclusion, making it clear that such use "shall be recognized" for that purpose.

The matter was debated during the TRIPS negotiations – that is, prior to the adoption of the TRIPS Agreement text. A need to "control" the use of foreign trademarks by local licensees was felt and justified during the negotiations.[61] This control was affected by a number of countries using "registered user" requirements. As India noted: "The mere authorisation of the use of the trademark by a third party through a private sanction, without the third party being registered as a 'Registered User', shall not constitute use."[62] The fact that this was raised during the negotiations and that no provision was made in the TRIPS Agreement for the survival of this requirement as a condition to maintain registration is an argument against the compatibility of a mandatory requirement to register. This does not mean that registration or recordation of licenses would not be desirable and cannot be effected through other means, however. What it does mean is that sanctions for failure to do so should likely focus not on the validity of the registration or license per se but rather be in the form of administrative measures or adequate fines.

F *Article 20*

Article 20 of the TRIPS Agreement was at the heart of the recent WTO report on Australia's plain packaging legislation and it is, therefore, subject to somewhat more extensive scrutiny in this chapter. An analysis of Article 20 must take account of the fact that some Complainants did not appeal the panels' report, and Australia did not cross-appeal on the issues on which the panels found against it. Hence this Section will refer both to the panels' report and the Appellate

[60] TRIPS Agreement, *supra* note 1, art. 19.2.

[61] GATT Secretariat, *Standards and Principles Concerning the Availability Scope and Use of Trade-Related Intellectual Property Rights: Communication from India*, § 32, GATT Doc. MTN.GNG/NG11/W/37 (July 10, 1989).

[62] *Id.* at 42. Brazil also made the point around the same time that a "licensing agreement per se is not evidence of the use of a mark." GATT Secretariat, *Communication from Brazil*, WTO doc. MTN.GNG/NG11/W/57 (Dec. 11, 1989), at 43. As stated, that seems right, but use by the licensee under the control of the owner would be evidence of use. Brazil also insisted that "evidence of use by third parties requires the registration with the relevant government authority of the license granted by the owner of the mark."

Body's.[63] The plain packaging measure at issue prohibited non-word marks entirely and limited the use, format and size of word marks on cigarette packs.

Article 20 reflects the function of trademarks in the course of trade, a concept well known in common law trademark doctrines. When interpreting Article 20, the domestic law traditions of any one party to the TRIPS Agreement will not necessarily be determinative. State practice, however, may be relevant to determining the ordinary meaning of terms incorporated in the Agreement when those terms were known to have an agreed meaning, and even an object and purpose, reflective of domestic law.[64]

The forced combination of a trademark with another by government regulation was examined in an early WTO dispute-settlement panel report: in *Indonesia – Certain Measures Affecting the Automobile Industry* case,[65] the United States claimed, inter alia, on the basis of Article 20 that Indonesia had violated its TRIPS Agreement obligations by imposing an obligation to use marks associated with its National Car Programme. Its first argument was that: "[A] foreign company that enters into an arrangement with a Pioneer company would be encumbered in using the trademark that it used elsewhere for the model that was adopted by the National Car Programme."[66] The Panel did not accept this argument for the reason that foreign companies voluntarily entered the agreements imposing the use of the second mark.[67] The negotiating history suggests that for at least some of the demanders, part of the target of Article 20 was precisely the forced use of a local mark (on products such as tobacco, incidentally), as the second sentence of the article makes clear. In this case, however, because participating in the National Car Programme was seen as voluntary – and hence, trademark owners arguably "accepted" use of the imposed Indonesian mark – the encroachment upon trademark owners' rights was considered not to violate Article 20. This means that the issue of forced use of one trademark with another (imposed by regulation) has not been fully explored by a dispute-settlement panel. One may venture that, if the function of the trademark was encumbered as a result, a WTO member may have to defend its measure under the justifiability test contained in Article 20.[68] It is also worth noting that at the meeting of the dispute-settlement body discussing adoption of the Panel report, the United States did not object to the adoption (having obtained a favorable ruling on other aspects), but it found the Panel's conclusions on Article 20 "disturbing" and incorrect.[69]

Article 20 was at the heart of the Australia plain packaging case. Australia raised several arguments to oppose the application of Article 20 to its plain packaging legislation, including by arguing that "Article 20 is best interpreted as imposing a discipline on how a Member may encumber the use of a trademark in the course of trade when its domestic laws and regulations otherwise do not prohibit the use of that trademark."[70] In other words, Australia argued that a ban is not an impediment because it is, in a way, more than an encumbrance. This puzzling interpretation of Article 20 was set aside by the panels, which agreed with complainants that "it would be 'counterintuitive' to consider that a measure that restricts the use of a trademark would

[63] This section is based in part on Frankel & Gervais, *supra* note 43.
[64] VCLT, *supra* note 22, art. 31.3(b).
[65] WTO Panel Report, *Indonesia – Certain Measures Affecting the Automobile Industry*, WTO doc. WT/DS54/R (July 2, 1998).
[66] *Id.* at § 14.277.
[67] *Id.* at § 14.278 (emphasis added).
[68] *Id.*
[69] *See* Dispute Settlement Body, *Minutes of Meeting Held on 23 July 1998*, p. 13, WT/DSB/M/47 (Sept. 18, 1998).
[70] Australia Plain Packaging Report, note 34 at § 7.2188 (referring to Australia's first written submission, § 342).

be subject to the disciplines of Article 20 while a more far-reaching measure to prohibit such use would not."[71]

The plain packaging measure at issue was thus found to be a special requirement: a prohibition on use and use in a special form were "requirements" that trademark owners must follow.[72] Indeed, use in a special form is specifically mentioned in Article 20 as an example. Then a special requirement is one that applies to the "use of a trademark in the course of trade."[73] The panels also found – correctly in this author's view – that the use of the phrase "in the course of trade" implied commercial activities.[74]

As to the type of use that is subject to the prohibition on encumbrances by special requirement, the panels continued in the same vein and found that use was use in the course of commercial activities and thus rejected Australia's argument that such use was "limited to the use of a trademark for the specific purpose of distinguishing the goods or services of one undertaking from those of other undertakings."[75]

The key point on appeal was the interpretation of "unjustifiably." Article 20 provides that, to be incompatible with TRIPS, the plain packaging legislation which was found to be a special requirement must encumber "unjustifiably." The panels found for Australia, noting, first, that it was the complainants' duty to prove that the encumbrance was unjustified,[76] even though it acknowledged that a respondent member, "as the Member having taken the measures, may be in a privileged position to explain, in response to a possible prima facie demonstration of violation, why a specific encumbrance is justifiable."[77] This position is understandable as when other tests to justify an impugned measure are included in an obligation provision, the burden of proof is often on the complaining party.[78] Having shifted the burden to complainants, the panel had to find that they had made a prima facie case, which the respondent (Australia) would then have to rebut. The Appellate Body found that it was "the complainant's burden to establish a *prima facie* case of inconsistency with Article 20."[79] This is a logical conclusion from the finding that Article 20, unlike Article 17, is not an exception.

An interesting implied question was whether the justification should be in some way proportional to the nature of the encumbrance. Put differently, would a higher level of encumbrance (such as a total ban) be more fully justifiable? When the text of Article 20 states that the member's obligation is not to "unjustifiably encumber," one could make a logical argument that a higher degree of encumbrance requires a stronger justification. The panels decided otherwise and applied the same standard of review to complete bans as to any other encumbrances by special requirement.[80] The panels devised a multi-factor test, however, that did seem to include some degree of proportionality, namely "the nature and *extent* of the encumbrance arising from the special requirements at issue, the reasons for which these requirements are applied, and whether these reasons sufficiently support them."[81] But the panels muddied the

71 *Id.* at § 7.2238.
72 *Id.* at §§ 7.2231–7.2232.
73 *Id.* at § 7.2231.
74 *Id.* at §§ 7.2261–7.2263.
75 *Id.* at §§ 7.2282 and 7.2284.
76 *Id.* at §§ 7.2164–7.2165.
77 *Id.* at § 7.2167.
78 *See* WTO Secretariat, "Necessity Tests" in the WTO, Note by the Secretariat, WTO doc. S/WPDR/W/27/Add.1, at § 6 (Jan. 18, 2011) [hereinafter Necessity Tests].
79 Appellate Body report, supra, para. 6.643.
80 Australia Plain Packaging Report, *supra* note 34, § 7.2442.
81 *Id.* at § 7.2441.

waters by referring to "good reasons" as sufficient to justify, and then discussing whether a mere rational connection between an encumbrance (including an extreme measure such as a ban) and a stated policy objective might suffice (meaning that, in light of the burden of proof, a complainant would have to prove a complete absence of even a mere rational connection).

The panels had no qualms about the severity of the Australian measure:

> We note that by disallowing the use of design features of trademarks, the [plain packaging] measures prevent a trademark owner from using such features to convey any messages about the product, whether functional or intangible, and deriving any economic value from the use of such features. *Therefore, the [plain packaging] measures prevent a trademark owner from extracting economic value from any design features of its trademark through its use in the course of trade.* In principle, therefore, the [plain packaging] measures' prohibitions on the use of figurative trademarks on tobacco retail packaging and products, as well as of the figurative and stylized elements of composite and word marks, are far-reaching in terms of the trademark owner's expected possibilities to extract economic value from the use of such features.[82]

The Appellate Body clarified the panels' findings, noting, first, that "the language that the Panel used in referring to the expected degree of contribution of the alternative measures in its analysis under Article 20 of the TRIPS Agreement was inconsistent", and added that the "various meanings attributed to the concept of justifiability thus indicate that 'unjustifiable' connotes "something that is fair and capable of being reasonably explained," thus hewing close to the panels' "good reasons."[83]. In the Appellate Body's view the term "reflects the degree of regulatory autonomy that Members enjoy."[84]

Another set of arguments discussed by the panels was the nature and scope of the "justification." There is no doubt, as noted in the above-mentioned joint article, that public health is a valid policy area, one in which a policy measure can be justified by a WTO member.[85] This is, simply put, not a matter of serious debate. In fact, the reason to adopt a policy measure is rarely the debate before WTO panels. Public health is an easy case. It is reflected in Article 8.1 of the TRIPS Agreement, and in the Doha Declaration on TRIPS and Public Health.

Australia relied rather heavily on its implementation of the Framework Convention on Tobacco Control (FCTC). Guidelines to the FCTC suggest that countries "*consider* adopting measures to restrict or prohibit the use of logos, colors, brand images or promotional information on packaging other than brand names and product names displayed in a standard color and font style (plain packaging)."[86] The use of the FCTC and its guidelines is a striking aspect of the report. There is a very considerable body of literature on the interplay between WTO and non-WTO norms in the WTO dispute-settlement process. Here it is obvious that the FCTC has a broad membership (181 parties as of this writing), but a majority of the complainants were not party to the Convention. Second, plain packaging is only a recommendation in the guidelines. Yet the panels took the Convention and its guidelines on board with little discussion about the doctrinal path required to do so.[87] Though the FCTC is mentioned over 1,000 times in the

[82] *Id.* at § 7.2569 (emphasis added).

[83] Appellate Body report, supra paras. 6.645.

[84] *Id.* at 6.647.

[85] Frankel & Gervais, *supra* note 43.

[86] World Health Organization, Framework Convention on Tobacco Control, Guidelines for Implementation of art. 11, at § 46.

[87] The FCTC plays a central role in the panels' discussion of the Technical Barriers to Trade (TBT) arguments made by the complainants, especially under art. 2.5 TBT. In the case of TRIPS, and specifically art. 20, it seems accepted as the justification for the plain packaging measures. *See* Australia Plain Packaging Report, *supra* note 34, at § 7.2596.

panels' report, the Appellate Body did not use this opportunity to clarify the relationship between WTO law and non WTO norms, noting only that "the Panel referred to Articles 11 and 13 of the FCTC Guidelines as additional factual support to its previous conclusion[s]."[88] The Appellate Body also punted (as the US third party submission had suggested) on the role of the 2001 Doha Declaration, noting "regardless of the legal status of the Doha Declaration... the reliance on the Doha Declaration [by the panel] was not of decisive importance for the Panel's reasoning."[89]

There are several known tests in trade law for a WTO member to justify a measure not otherwise compatible with its commitments under WTO instruments, including several shades of the necessity test. Indeed, the WTO itself refers now to necessity tests (plural).[90] These are exceptions of course, but a comparison is nonetheless informative.

The scope of "outs" meant to allow regulatory flexibility other than the necessity test is sometimes unclear, such as the current debates on whether invoking national security provides an automatic, unconditional exception for any measure is a correct interpretation of GATT Article XXI and similar provisions, including TRIPS Article 73. Two panel reports have now found that this broadest exception was not a carte blanche but that in application of the venerable principle of good faith application of treaties a WTO member invoking national security had to demonstrate a "minimum requirement of plausibility in relation to the proffered essential security interests."[91] In the Saudi Arabia case, Qatar alleged that Saudi Arabia had failed to provide either civil or criminal remedies for a massive violation of broadcast signals containing. professional sports and other copyright programs. The panel essentially agreed on both counts. Interestingly, it accepted Saudi Arabia's national security defense, but only for civil remedies, in part because Saudi Arabia adopted "anti-sympathy" measures against Qatar and it was "not implausible that Saudi Arabia might take other measures to prevent Qatari nationals from having access to courts, tribunals and other institutions in Saudi Arabia."[92] However, in what seems a first in the history of both the WTO and the GATT, the panel rejected the defense to justify the application of criminal remedies required under TRIPS Article 61, because "the Saudi authorities" non-application of criminal procedures and penalties to beoutQ is so remote ... as to make it implausible that Saudi Arabia implemented these measures for the protection of its "essential security interests."[93]

Another test is that of rational connection, meaning that a measure otherwise incompatible with a trade commitment would be found to be in compliance with WTO obligations if the measure has a "rational connection to its stated policy objective. This was the test proposed by Australia under to pass the Article 20 justifiability threshold. Canada in its third-party brief noted that "Australia's proposed test of requiring a complainant to establish that there is no rational connection between the requirement and a legitimate public policy objective in order to demonstrate that the requirement is 'unjustifiable' would establish an extremely onerous burden to establish a violation of Article 20."

88 Appellate Body Report, supra, para 6.707.

89 *Id.* at paras 6.657–6.658.

90 *See* Necessity Tests, *supra* note 77.

91 Panel Report, Russia – Measures Concerning Traffic in Transit, WT/DS512/R and Add.1, adopted 26 April 2019 apara 7.531.

92 Saudi Arabia – Measures concerning the protection of intellectual property rights, WT/DS567/R (16 June 2020), a para 7.286.

93 *Id.* para 7.293.

Since public health was invoked as the legitimate policy objective behind the plain packaging measure, the term "necessary" in Article 8 could have been interpreted as suggesting a necessity test. In several cases, the Appellate Body made it clear that "necessity"/ "necessary" did not actually mean "necessary." Rational connection and proportionality were found sufficient to pass necessity tests and were seen as the lowest thresholds (other than the above-mentioned national security cases using "plausibility") to justify a measure otherwise inconsistent with a trade commitment.[94] However, in those cases the respondent bore the burden of proving "necessity". In the plain packaging context, in contrast, using the Australian proposed test the complainant was tasked with proving something like an absence of rational connection, which seems an almost insurmountable burden.

The rational connection test per se did not survive Appellate Body scrutiny. That said, the end result is very similar. Article 20 as interpreted has very little obligational content short of an arbitrary policy measure. As the asbestos ban arguably was for trade in goods, it may be that tobacco trademark ban will stand as the case where the Appellate Body decided not to limit the scope of Members' regulatory autonomy in any meaningful way. Indeed, taking into account the burden of proof and threshold, functionally it would not be completely unreasonable to compare Articles 20 and 73. It is not easy to see the actual difference between a respondent having to demonstrate some plausibility (under 73) and a complainant having to show that no "reasonable explanation" exists for an impugned measure.

It seems unlikely that another case under Article 20 (unlike cases under Article XX of the GATT or XIV of the GATS) will reach the Appellate Body and allow it to fine-tune the analysis. Indeed, very few TRIPS cases have gone to a panel, and only a subset of those made it to the Appellate Body. Perhaps going back to the purported original intent (of not allowing Members to impose a second (local) mark) could still allow a panel to find a violation of Article 20.

G *Article 21*

The key provision on trademark transactions in the TRIPS Agreement is Article 21. It provides as follows:

> Members may determine conditions on the licensing and assignment of trademarks, it being understood that the compulsory licensing of trademarks shall not be permitted and that the owner of a registered trademark shall have the right to assign the trademark with or without the transfer of the business to which the trademark belongs.[95]

One of the purposes is clear: compulsory licensing of trademarks is prohibited. It is true that, while there are cases where compulsory licensing of patents may be justifiable in the public interest, it is typically not so with trademarks. Why would a WTO member want to allow a third party not authorized by the Coca-Cola Company to sell COKE®? Local consumers would be "fooled" into believing that they are purchasing "the real thing." Any problem with the product could tarnish the Coca-Cola mark (and company). There is, therefore, no welfare gain for the public (or obviously for the trademark owner) in allowing this type of free-riding. Since the purpose of a trademark is its ability to distinguish the goods or services of one undertaking from those of another, letting a third party use that link as identifying the product or service without

94 See Robert Howse, The WTO System: Law, Politics, Legitimacy (Cameron May, 2007), at 206.

95 TRIPS Agreement, *supra* note 1, art. 21.

the consent of (and control by) the trademark owner would be nonsensical. Other matters of possible public interest, such as eliminating unused marks from the register, are dealt with elsewhere. If the use of a patented product is allowed under a compulsory license, use of the trademark of the patent holder as an indication could be misleading.[96]

Under a compulsory licensing regime, how would the licensee not working in cooperation with the trademark owner achieve the level of quality control required to maintain the distinctiveness of the mark? Trademarks perform a distinguishing function from which in many legal systems follows a quality control function: consumers rightly expect consistency of the quality (with variations for items such as food products because the materials used necessarily vary). To say that a trademark compulsory license can or should be issued because a third party (such as a government agency) is regulating the quality of a product ignores the source component of the function. That component is indicated by the direction of Article 15 of the TRIPS Agreement that a mark's purpose is to distinguish the goods or services of one undertaking from those of other undertakings.[97] Even if third-party controls are likely to maintain consistency of the goods, the welfare gains of allowing a product not manufactured by A or with A's consent to be sold as A's product are unclear at best. Consumers can be informed that the product manufactured by B is similar to the product made by A if nominative (or another similar non-confusing fair) use of A's mark is allowed.

The TRIPS Agreement ban on compulsory licensing is arguably reinforced by Article 20's prohibition on use encumbrances by special requirement. If the TRIPS Agreement restricts conditions that would be "detrimental to its capability to distinguish the goods or services of one undertaking from those of other undertakings," one wonders in which cases compulsory licenses would not be so detrimental. Fortunately, very few countries allow compulsory licensing of trademarks.[98]

WTO members retain the right to determine conditions of transfer and assignment. This would include contract provisions requiring, for example, that an assignment be in writing. Can registration or recordation be made mandatory? Not as a condition to maintain registration of the mark, as explained above in relation to the TRIPS Agreement Article 19.2.

As far as enforcement by a licensee is concerned, WIPO notes that whether "a licensee should be allowed to join proceedings initiated by the licensor, or whether it would be entitled to damages resulting from an infringement of the licensed mark,"[99] a matter left to national law, is not the same as asking whether "a licensee has the right under the law of a Member State to join infringement proceedings initiated by the holder and to obtain damages resulting from an infringement of the licensed mark."[100] The answer to the second question is clear: the licensee should be able to exercise those rights independently of whether the license is recorded or registered.

This debate about enforcement by a licensee against unauthorized use by a third party continued after the adoption of the TRIPS Agreement. At a 1999 meeting at WIPO, "[s]everal

96 That would not prevent nominative use of that trademark.

97 TRIPS Agreement, *supra* note 1, art. 15. On that function in US law, *see Glover* v. *Ampak, Inc.*, 74 F.3d 57 (Fed. Cir. 1996).

98 GATT Secretariat, *Existence, Scope and Form of Generally Internationally Accepted and Applied Standards/Norms for the Protection of Intellectual Property – Note Prepared by the International Bureau of* WIPO, MTN.GNG/NG11/W/24/Rev. l, p. 37 (Sept. 15, 1988).

99 WIPO, Simplification and Harmonization of Formalities Concerning the Recordal of Licenses for the Use of Marks; Questions Concerning the Indication of Licenses on Products and Their Packaging or in Connection with the Providing of Services or in Advertising, WIPO document TMLlCEII/2, Annex I, at 12 (Dec. 12, 1996. *See also* Committee of Experts on Trademark Licenses, TML/CE/I/3, 70–4 (Sept. 30, 1999).

100 *Id.*

delegations and the representative of an observer organization . . . held that the rights of third parties could depend on recordal and that the licensee could not join in infringement proceedings unless the license was recorded."[101] Indeed the Notes to the Joint Recommendation mention that the "question whether the non-recorded licensee should have the right to join infringement proceedings initiated by the holder and to recover damages was the subject of an intensive debate."[102]

Subject to other provisions of the TRIPS Agreement, members may also allow nominative uses of protected marks, typically as a reference to describe the product bearing the mark, or for comparative advertising purposes.

It should also be noted that the first part of Article 21 seems to apply to all trademarks (including unregistered marks where they are protected), while the latter part (right to assign) applies only to registered marks.

Article 21 goes beyond Article 6*quater*(1) of the Paris Convention, which deems that, in cases where the goodwill or business to which the mark belongs had to be transferred at the same time as the transfer of the mark, transfer of the portion of the goodwill or business located in the country concerned was sufficient. This was fully justified under the principle of independence of rights in different territories.[103] A number of countries did (some still do) require the transfer of the goodwill or business and in some cases, in spite of Article 6*quater*, require the transfer of the entire business, even if parts of it were located in foreign territories. This is potentially in conflict with the "trend" to develop marks as *brands* with value and existence independently of the goods or services they are associated with.

The TRIPS Agreement seemingly meant to eliminate requirements concerning transfer of the business together with the mark. Business may be defined as "the industrial or commercial establishment," i.e., the material basis of the activities.[104] However, contrary to Article 6*quater* of the Paris Convention, Article 21 does not refer to the "goodwill." Bodenhausen, in the well-known *Guide to the Paris Convention*, defines goodwill as the "customer base."[105] It is difficult to imagine that this element was left out unintentionally. The conclusion that follows from such a choice is that while WTO members are not permitted to require transfer of the business, as regards transfers of the goodwill, only Article 6*quater* of the Paris Convention applies (through Article 2.1 of the TRIPS Agreement, which incorporated the substantive provisions of the Paris Convention, including Article 6*quater*).

This conclusion is reinforced by other expressions used in various texts known to negotiators. For example, Article 5A(4) of the Paris Convention speaks of "enterprise or goodwill," the former probably a synonym of "undertaking," a term also used in Article 31(e) of the TRIPS Agreement.[106] The 1994 Trademark Law Treaty (TLT) is relevant as a contemporaneous instrument negotiated among many of the same parties and concluded only a few months after the signing of the WTO Agreement (and the TRIPS Agreement).[107] Article 11(4)(iv) of the TLT does not allow contracting parties, in determining the requirements to be met to record a change of

[101] Standing Committee on the Law of Trademarks Industrial Designs and Geographical Indications (SCT), *Third Session Geneva, Nov. 8–12, 1999*, 122, SCT/3/10 (Nov. 26, 1999).

[102] WIPO, Draft Provisions on Trademark Licenses. WIPO document SCT/4/2 at 20 (Jan. 12, 2000).

[103] Bodenhausen, *supra* note 4, at 104.

[104] *Id.* at 105.

[105] *Id.*

[106] Paris Convention, *supra* note 2, art. 5A(4).

[107] TLT, *supra* note 2.

ownership in a trademark, to request that evidence be furnished that the business or relevant goodwill has been transferred with the mark.[108]

III CONCLUSION

The TRIPS Agreement impacts national and regional trademark rules by limiting the flexibility of WTO members in defining what constitutes a trademark, prohibiting compulsory licensing, and restricting conditions on transfers and licenses and by limiting encumbrances on the use of marks in the course of trade. The 2018 panels' report on the dispute on plain packaging of tobacco in Australia adds a number of elements to define the exact scope of the obligations imposed on WTO members in that respect. The Appellate Body clarified the test for justifiability under Article 20 which, as it now stands, only prohibits regulatory encumbrances (including bans) that are demonstrably incapable of a reasonable explanation. The Australia case also confirmed that trademark owners had no positive right to use, but failed to articulate precisely their legitimate interest in using and the relationship between such use and the scope of protection. Whether the case will stand as an outlier or instead be used as a beacon to illuminate a broader path for public interest measures that limit intellectual property rights, only time will tell.

108 *Id.*, art. 11(4)(iv).

3

The Internationalisation of Trademark Protection

Mapping and Documenting Twenty-Five Years of (Post-Paris Convention and) Post-TRIPS Trademark Agreements

*Susanna H. S. Leong**

I INTRODUCTION

In a world of globalised commerce, the application of the principle of territoriality in trademark law results in complexities and inconveniences to trademark proprietors who desire legal protection in numerous jurisdictions. The adoption and ratification of several important international intellectual property agreements formed the backbone of a global trademark protection system. In terms of multilateral instruments establishing a normative framework for trademark protection internationally, the oldest of them is the Paris Convention for the Protection of Industrial Property, signed in 1883 (Paris Convention). Two important basic principles of international law contained in the Paris Convention – namely, the national treatment principle[1] and the principle of independence of rights[2] – provided the fundamental terms of engagement between country states in the Paris Union[3] for the protection of trademarks internationally.[4] These two basic principles have been preserved and enhanced in the more recent Agreement on Trade-Related Aspects of Intellectual Property Rights (TRIPS) concluded in April 1994.[5] However, it may be said that the Paris Convention contained limited provisions on substantive trademark law and there remained white spaces which required the international trademark community to continue working on it.

The successful conclusion of TRIPS in 1994 is a significant milestone in the history of building a substantive legal framework for the protection of intellectual property rights internationally. TRIPS provides the minimal standards of protection for all recognised categories of intellectual property and allied rights, including patents, copyright, trademarks, industrial designs, geographical names, confidential information and others. It is also the first international intellectual property agreement which successfully introduced a system of trade sanctions

* Professor and Vice Provost, National University of Singapore.

[1] *See* Paris Convention for the Protection of Industrial Property, art. 2, Mar. 20, 1883, as revised at the Stockholm Revision Conference, July 14, 1967, 21 UST 1538, TIAS No. 6903, 828 UNTS 305 [hereinafter Paris Convention].

[2] *Id.* at art. 6.

[3] *Id.* at art. 1(1) (referencing to a Union is made in respect of the countries to which the Convention applies).

[4] For a discussion on "The Trademark Provisions in the Paris Convention for the Protection of Industrial Property" by Sam Ricketson, see Chapter 1 in this volume.

[5] TRIPS: Agreement on Trade-Related Aspects of Intellectual Property Rights, Apr. 15, 1994, Marrakesh Agreement Establishing the World Trade Organization, Annex 1C, 1869 UNTS 299, 33 ILM 1197, art. 2.1 (1994) [hereinafter TRIPS Agreement].

against member states that fall short of the minimum standards of intellectual property rights protection mandated by its provisions.[6]

It has been observed that the negotiations in the Uruguay Round concerning trademarks were "relatively uncontroversial" as compared to the other parts of TRIPS.[7] In general, there was consensus amongst member states of TRIPS on the utilitarian function of trademarks as badges of trade origins by reducing consumer search costs and the need for laws aimed at eradicating counterfeit goods.[8] Several international trademark treaties have been signed, or have become relevant in practice, post-TRIPS in an ongoing effort to further harmonise the international trademark protection framework as laid out first in the Paris Convention and then in TRIPS to address several issues, including those brought about by developments in digital information technology, such as the Internet.

The objective of this chapter is to examine and document the efforts which the intellectual property community has undertaken thus far towards a system of harmonisation of intellectual property rights, both substantive rights and administrative procedures related to national filings and protection of these rights, specifically in the context of trademark law. It begins with a review of the international trademark agreements that were either signed post-Paris Convention, and brought into force either before or after TRIPS, and those signed and implemented after TRIPS. The agreements which fall within the former category are the Madrid Agreement Concerning the International Registration of Marks[9] and the Protocol Relating to the Madrid Agreement Concerning the International Registration of Marks[10] whilst the agreements which come under the latter category include the Trade Mark Law Treaty[11] and the Singapore Trademark Law Treaty.[12] Collectively, the administration of these post Paris Convention and post TRIPS international trademark agreements formed a substantial and significant part of the work of the World Intellectual Property Organization (WIPO).[13]

This chapter additionally examines the frameworks and guidelines set out in three WIPO Joint Recommendations, concerning, respectively: the Protection of Well-Known Marks; Trademark Licenses; and the Protection of Marks and Other Industrial Property Rights in Signs on the Internet, which were adopted almost two decades ago.[14] In this respect, this chapter pays special

[6] *See* Daniel J. Gervais, "A Look at the Trademark Provisions in the TRIPS Agreement," Chapter 2 in this volume.

[7] *See* Annette Kur, *Marks for Goods or Services (Trademarks), in* Research Handbook on the Protection of Intellectual Property under WTO Rules, 411, 411 (Carlos M. Correa & Edward Elgar eds., 2010).

[8] *See* TRIPS Agreement, *supra* note 5: art. 2 of the TRIPS Agreement preserves the continued application of the Paris Convention which laid down the minimum standards for international protection of trademarks. Part II, Section 2 of the TRIPS Agreement sets up the framework in respect of trademark protection to be accorded by member states. Arts. 15 to 21 provide a comprehensive coverage of the different aspects of trademark protection ranging from registrability of subject matter; exclusive rights and exceptions; duration of protection; trademark use and transactions.

[9] The Madrid Agreement Concerning the International Registration of Marks, Apr. 14, 1891, 828 UNTS 389 [hereinafter Madrid Agreement].

[10] The Protocol Relating to the Madrid Agreement Concerning the International Registration of Marks, June 27, 1989, S. Treaty Doc. No. 106-41, WIPO Administered Treaties, https://wipolex.wipo.int/en/treaties/textdetails/12911 [hereinafter Madrid Protocol].

[11] Trademark Law Treaty, Oct. 27, 1994, S. Treaty Doc. No. 105-35, 2037 UNTS 35 [hereinafter Trademark Law Treaty].

[12] Singapore Treaty on the Law of Trademarks, Mar. 27, 2006, S. Treaty Doc. No. 110-2 [hereinafter Singapore Treaty].

[13] The World Intellectual Property Organization (WIPO) is one the specialised agencies of the United Nations. WIPO was created in 1967 "to encourage creative activity, to promote the protection of intellectual property throughout the world."

[14] The Joint Recommendation are described as "soft law," a term generally used to refer to certain categories of norms, technically non-binding in nature, that states nonetheless follow in practice or to which they at least subscribe. *See* Edward Kwakwa, *Some Comments on Rulemaking at the World Intellectual Property Organisation*, 12 Duke J. Comp. & Int'l L. 179 (2002).

attention to the impact on internationalisation of trademark protection brought about by continued advancements in digital information technology. It concludes with a few thoughts on the way forward as the international trademark community continues with its efforts of building a globalised system of trademark protection in the twenty-first century.

II POST-PARIS CONVENTION AND POST-TRIPS WIPO ADMINISTERED INTERNATIONAL TRADEMARK TREATIES

A *International Registration of Trademarks: The Madrid System*

Registered trademarks are property rights conferred by the governments of sovereign countries and they are jurisdictional in nature. Therefore, applications and registrations are required for each country in which the trademark owner seeks protection. A trademark owner seeking protection globally in more than one country faces the daunting task of fulfilling the national application requirements whilst navigating diversities in language, fees and timelines of the national trademark registries in which protection is being sought. All these pose administrative inconveniences and management complexities for trademark owners wanting to go global with their marks. To alleviate the impediments faced by trademark owners and to better serve the international trademark community, it is necessary to create a system for the international registration of trademarks in the form of a centrally coordinated process for trademark owners simultaneously seeking protection of a trademark in many separate jurisdictions.

Presently, two international treaties – namely, the Madrid Agreement Concerning the International Registration of Marks ("the Madrid Agreement") and the Protocol Relating to the Madrid Agreement ("the Madrid Protocol") – together establish the Madrid Protocol System for the International Registration of Marks (Madrid System). The Madrid System provides a convenient administrative process for a mark to be registered and protected in designated countries which are "Contracting Parties" to either one or two of the treaties through one single filing made with the national trademark offices of the "Contracting Parties." Once registered, the mark will be conferred the same protection in the designated countries as a mark registered pursuant to the national trademark registration systems. Both the Madrid Agreement and the Madrid Protocol are administered by the WIPO, which serves as the central coordinating body in processing the international trademark applications filed under the Madrid System.

Any state that is a party to the Paris Convention may choose to become a party to the Madrid Agreement or the Madrid Protocol or both.

1 *The Madrid Agreement*

The Madrid Agreement was established on 13 July 1892. The objective was to provide a simple and inexpensive administrative mechanism which reduced the complexities faced by trademark owners seeking separate registrations in multiple countries. The Madrid Agreement was a Special Agreement within the scope of Article 19 of the Paris Convention.

Under the Madrid Agreement, a natural person or a legal entity, being a national of, domiciled in or with a real and effective industrial or commercial establishment in a member country may file an "international application" of a trademark with the national trademark office of the member country ("office of origin"), with a single fee (based on the number of member countries in which protection is sought). It is important to note that the trademark must, however, have already been registered in the applicant's country in respect of the goods or services covered by the international application.[15] Thus, a valid registration in the applicant's own country or country of origin is a prerequisite to the international registration application under the Madrid Agreement. The International Bureau at the WIPO does not examine the application but will transmit it expeditiously to the national trademark offices of the member countries in which protection of the mark is sought. Each national trademark office has twelve months to examine the application.[16] The national trademark office may either accept or refuse to register the mark in its country. Once registered, the international registration lasts for twenty years and may be renewed subsequently for additional twenty-year periods.[17]

If within five years from the date of the international registration the registration of the mark is terminated for any reason in the country of origin, the international registration as well as the registrations in all the designated member countries shall cease, regardless of whether the reason for the termination exists in any or all of the other designated member countries. This is known as the "central attack" provision.[18] It is an attack on the foundation upon which the international registration is granted – a valid registration of the mark in the country of origin. After five years, the international registration may be attacked only under the national laws of each of the designated member countries.[19] Changes affecting the international registration of a mark such as assignment, or partial or total cancellation must be notified to the International Bureau at the WIPO for recording in the International Trademark Register.[20]

Despite the administrative convenience and other advantages brought about by the Madrid Agreement, signatories to the Agreement remained limited.[21] Notably absent were major trading countries such as the United States of America, Australia, the United Kingdom, Canada and Japan. These countries typically have many trademark filings at the national level and are interested in exporting their trademarks to foreign emerging markets. At the same time, these countries are also choice destinations by foreign trademark owners who wish to seek protection in these important markets. Given their positions as sizeable trademark exchanges, memberships of these countries were thus considered important to the success of the Madrid System. The criticisms made against the Madrid Agreement were many. The need for valid registrations as pre-requisites to the international trademark filings was considered unduly restrictive. The central attack provision which would allow an objector to terminate a registration in countries where he may have no prior rights or on grounds which do not even exist in the countries comes across as draconian. A mandated limit of a 12-month period for national trade mark offices to decide to refuse or to accept registration is too short for some trade mark offices with large volume of applications and adherence to such a timeline, compels the offices to give precedence to international applications over domestic ones. The French language is the only designated working language for the Madrid Agreement and this poses inconvenience and translation costs for countries whose native language is not French. The fees structure is also considered too low for many national trademark offices to process the international registrations made via the Madrid Agreement. However, it should be noted that these criticisms levied on the Madrid Agreement were primarily made from the national trademark offices' perspectives and they

[15] Madrid Agreement, *supra* note 9, art. 1(2).
[16] *Id.* at art. 5(2).
[17] *Id.* at art. 6(1).
[18] *Id.* at art. 6(3).
[19] *Id.* at art. 6(2).
[20] *Id.* at art. 9(1).
[21] Membership of the Madrid Agreement was mainly limited to European and North African countries, with a small representation from Asia, notably China. The total number of contracting parties to the Madrid Agreement is fifty-five. *See* WIPO-Administered Treaties, http://wipo.int/treaties/en/ShowResults.jsp?lang=en&treaty_id=21.

need not necessarily all be disadvantages if seen from the users', i.e. the trademark owners or applicants, point of view.[22]

2 *The Madrid Protocol*

The Madrid Protocol established on 27 June 1989 seeks to rectify the limitations of the Madrid Agreement. Membership in the Protocol is not predicated upon membership in the Agreement. Countries may choose to be members of either or both of the agreements.

Under the Madrid Protocol, it is no longer necessary to have a registration in the country of origin. In its place is an application in the country of origin ("basic" application) and this can be used as a basis for the international registration.[23] Furthermore, the draconian effect of the "central attack" provision in the Madrid Agreement is significantly mitigated by the provision of a "transformation."[24] Essentially, if the "basic" application is revoked or terminated in the country of origin under its national law, the applicant has the option to transform or re-apply for registration in each of the designated countries. This transformation must be made within three months and the new application will retain the priority date of the original application first filed with the WIPO.[25]

Another important difference between the Madrid Protocol and the Madrid Agreement is that the national trademark office in a member country can extend the time period within which it must respond to an application for international registration. It can also declare the time limit to refuse registration be extended to eighteen months.[26] This may be further extended to allow for refusal resulting from opposition proceedings. In terms of fees chargeable, member countries are allowed to charge an "individual fee" for examination of an international application, provided this fee charged is not higher than the fee charged for a domestic/national application.[27] English is introduced as the official working language of the international registration process. The initial term of protection of trademarks internationally registered under the Madrid Protocol is ten years and renewable after periods of ten years.[28] The reduction from the initial twenty years of protection found in the Madrid Agreement to ten years in the Protocol is in line with the term of protection accorded to registered trademarks under TRIPS.

Like the Madrid Agreement, the Madrid Protocol maintains the objective of creating a simple and inexpensive system of international trademark registration.

As of 15 January 2020, the Madrid Union (which is made up of Contracting Parties to the Madrid Agreement and the Madrid Protocol) has a total of 106 members covering 122 countries.[29] The number of memberships in the Madrid Protocol almost doubles that of the Madrid Agreement.[30] Together, these countries represent more than 80 per cent of world trade.

The total number of applications via the Madrid System has reached an all-time high of 63,719 in 2019, representing an increase of 155 per cent from the number of applications in 2000 (Figure 3.1).

[22] *See* Florent Gevers & Alexander von Muhlendahl, *The Madrid Agreement and the Madrid Protocol – Should the Safeguard Clause (Article 9sexies of the Protocol) Be Maintained?*, ECTA Gazette, Spring 2007.

[23] Madrid Protocol, *supra* note 10, art. 2(1).

[24] *Id.* at art. 9*quinquies*.

[25] *Id.*

[26] *Id.* at art. 5(2)(b)–(c).

[27] *Id.* at art. 8.

[28] *Id.* at art. 6(1).

[29] For the current list of member states, see WIPO, https://wipo.int/madrid/en/members/.

[30] As of 15 October 2018, a total of 55 states have become party to the Madrid Agreement whilst a total of 102 states have become party to the Madrid Protocol. *See* WIPO Members of the Madrid Union, http://wipo.int/madrid/en/members/.

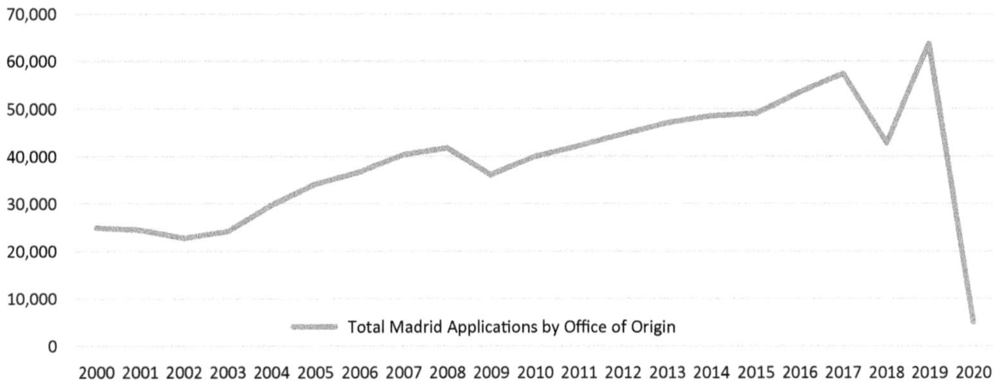

FIGURE 3.1 Total Madrid Applications by Office of Origin (2000–April 2020)

In 2019, the top ten countries with the most filings included the United States of America (10,228,), China (5,583), Germany (4,557), France (4,000), Switzerland (3,465), Japan (3,127), the United Kingdom (2,962), Australia (2,160), Turkey (1,997) and the Russian Federation (1,908). After the dip in numbers in 2018, the total number of Madrid applications increased by 48 per cent from 2018 to 2019. This is perhaps reflective of the global business climate. In the five years to 2017, China saw a general upward trend in application numbers with the most significant increase of 67 per cent year on year between 2016 (3,736) to 2017 (6,276), before a decrease in 2018 (6,110) and 2019 (5,583). The spike in China's trademark applications internationally, as well as domestically, is reflective of the rate of growth and pace of globalisation of Chinese firms in recent times.[31] The significant drop in application numbers in 2020 is expected as economies of countries all over the world contract in the wake of COVID-19 pandemic.[32]

The expansion in membership of the Madrid Union as well as the increase in number of applications in the Madrid System highlight the importance of a centrally coordinated process for trademark applications in multiple jurisdictions and the value the Madrid System offers in terms of the facilitation of such registrations. It is also clear that there is an increase in demand for cross-border registration of trademarks as more and more trademark proprietors take their businesses beyond their own domestic markets. This in turn supports the argument that it is useful to attain harmonisation of not only the substantive trademark law, but also the administrative procedures associated with registration across countries.

B Trademark Registration Formalities: The Trademark Law Treaty 1994 and the Singapore Treaty on the Law of Trademarks 2006

1 The Trademark Law Treaty 1994

Whilst the Madrid System creates a centrally coordinated process for trademark applications in multiple jurisdictions, the search, examination, publication, opposition and grant procedures in trademark registration remain the sole purview of the national and regional trademark offices.

[31] It was reported that China's trademark applications exceeded 5.7 million in 2017, an increase of 55.7 per cent year on year. *See* Chengcheng, *China's Trademark Applications Hit Record High in 2017*, Jan. 20, 2018, XINHUA, http://xinhuanet.com/english/2018-01/20/c_136911172.htm.

[32] The COVID-19 pandemic is an ongoing pandemic caused by a new coronavirus (SARS-CoV-2) that results in severe acute respiratory syndrome. The outbreak first occurred in Wuhan, China in December 2019. The World Health Organization recognised it as a pandemic on 11 March 2020. See https://en.wikipedia.org/wiki/2019%E2%80%9320_coronavirus_pandemic

This is thus another area in the overall framework of international trademark protection which requires standardisation. The Trademark Law Treaty (TLT 1994) was established on 27 October 1994 with objectives to reduce the complexities in the multitude of registration procedures and to increase predictability of application outcomes. This was done through simplification and harmonisation of certain features of these trademark registration procedures and formalities.

The TLT 1994 sets out the rules governing the different phases in a trademark application ranging from application to registration, changes after registration to duration and renewal of registration. These rules are constructed to clearly define the requirements, maximum or permitted, for a trademark application. For example, in the application phase, contracting parties to the TLT 1994 may require, as a maximum, that an application contain the indications stated in Article 3(1)(a)(i) to (xvii) which include a request; the name and address and other indications of the applicant and the representative; various statements concerning the mark (colour, three-dimensional marks, transliteration and translation of the mark, number of representations or reproductions); the goods and services for which registration is sought classified in the relevant class of the Nice Classification; and various declarations of priority and intention to use the mark.

It is further provided that contracting parties to the TLT 1994 must allow for a single application for goods and/or services in several classes of the Nice Classification. At the same time, the rules as set out in the TLT 1994 are exhaustive in that contracting parties are prohibited from demanding further requirements beyond those which are contained in Articles 3(1) to (4) and Article 3(6). Rules are also made pertaining to changes after registration and other matters such as duration of protection and renewals of trademark registrations. All these provisions help standardise and streamline trademark application procedures across regional and national trademark registries and offices.

Since its conclusion, the TLT 1994 has served the international trademark community well by harmonising and simplifying trademark registration procedures which are applicable to countries party to this treaty. However, technological innovations and advancements such as the Internet quickened the pace at which the TLT 1994 needs to be revised as its provisions took no account of the impact of these innovations since they were little known in 1994. For example, at the time the TLT 1994 was adopted, communications with trademark offices were mainly made via post and/or fax machines and the provisions did not extend to electronic communication such as email and other internet-based services. Furthermore, it became possible post-TRIPS for non-conventional types of trademarks such as shapes, colours, holograms and non-visually perceptible types such as sounds to be registered. The TLT 1994 made no provisions for the registration of non-visible trademarks.

To ensure that the rules in the TLT 1994 are kept abreast with technological developments that may have a critical impact on trademark application and administration issues, the original idea was to allow an Assembly of the Contracting Parties to be able to amend the Regulations to the TLT 1994. Unfortunately, the TLT 1994 was adopted without the creation of an Assembly, making it impossible to change the Regulations after their adoption.[33] The TLT 1994 was also deficient in that it did not provide procedures for the recording of trademark licences, or for relief measures when time limits in respect of applications or registrations are not adhered to by trademark holders.[34]

[33] Trademark Law Treaty, *supra* note 11. The TLT 1994 has a two-tier structure. Procedural matters are dealt with under the Regulations.

[34] Singapore Treaty, *supra* note 12, at art. 14, introducing appropriate relief measures in case of failure to comply with time limits in respect of applications or registrations.

These gaps in the TLT 1994 set the stage for the ratification of a new treaty – the Singapore Treaty on the Law of Trademarks 2006 (Singapore Treaty 2006).

2 *The Singapore Treaty 2006*

The Singapore Treaty 2006 was adopted by WIPO member states on 27 March 2006 and it introduces several important revisions to the TLT 1994. Compared to the TLT 1994, the Singapore Treaty 2006 is more comprehensive in scope.

Contracting Parties of the Singapore Treaty 2006 may apply the provisions of the Treaty to marks consisting of signs that can be registered as marks under their national trademark laws, excluding collective marks, certification marks and guarantee marks.[35] Of significance is the inclusion of provisions on the filing of non-conventional marks covering both visually perceptible marks such as three-dimensional, hologram, motion, colour, position and non-visually perceptible marks like sound and others. Specifically, Rule 3 of the Regulations under the Singapore Treaty 2006 spells out the ways each of these different types of mark may be represented in the application. Although the Singapore Treaty 2006 is the first international treaty to recognise the registration of non-conventional trademarks, it does not oblige Contracting Parties to enact substantive domestic laws to register these marks in their countries.[36]

The Singapore Treaty 2006 is a comprehensive international instrument that covers procedures related to the filing of applications; the grant of a filing date; the division of applications or registrations; the recording of changes in names or addresses; the recording of changes in ownership of applications or registrations; the correction of a mistake; the renewal of registrations; and the recording of licences.

For each of these procedures, the Singapore Treaty 2006 defines the maximum list of formal requirements that the trademark offices or registries of a Contracting Party may require from the applicants. By adhering to the same set of harmonised and simplified formalities, applicants from Contracting Parties will find it easier to register trademarks and to maintain their registrations in the jurisdictions of the Contracting Parties. Besides defining with certainty and clarity the maximum list of formalities, the Singapore Treaty 2006 also prohibits certain other requirements, for example, the attestation, notarisation or legalisation of requisite signatures in a communication on paper.[37] Again, this has the beneficial effect of rendering the requisite formalities less cumbersome and costly for trademark applicants and are welcomed.

The objectives of the Singapore Treaty 2006 are to help standardised trademark office procedures and prepare trademark offices to meet future challenges in an effective and efficient manner.[38] Indeed, it has closed the gaps between the old paper-based system of communication and the modern world of electronic transmission of information files in the context of a globalised network of trademark offices or registries. It has further provided the international trademark community with some degree of clarity and certainty in the registration of novel types of trademarks including non-visible signs. With the successful creation of the Assembly of

[35] *Id.* at art. 2(2).

[36] Resolution by the Diplomatic Conference Supplementary to the Singapore Treaty, Mar. 2006, § 3.

[37] Singapore Treaty, *supra* note 12, at art. 8(6) (Communications); *see also* general provisions on "Prohibition of Other Requirements" in art. 3(4) (Application); art. 4(5) (Representation; Address for Service); art. 5(5) (Filing Date); art. 10(4) (Changes in Names or Addresses); art. 11(3) (Change in Ownership); art. 12(3) (Correction of a Mistake); art. 13(2) (Duration and Renewal of Registration); art. 14(5) (Relief Measures in Case of Failure to Comply with Time Limits); art. 17(4) (Request for Recordation of a Licence).

[38] *See The New Singapore Treaty on the Law of Trademarks – What Does It Change?*, WIPO MAGAZINE, June 3, 2006, https://wipo.int/wipo_magazine/en/2006/03/article_0002.html.

Contracting Parties, the Singapore Treaty 2006 can be adapted to address future impacts on trademark registration, maintenance procedures and practices as a result of an ever-changing technological landscape.

This is all well and good from the perspective of trademark offices, as well as trademark owners, since the TLT 1994 and the Singapore Treaty 2006 have greatly facilitated the expansion of the *types* of signs registrable as trademarks post-TRIPS by harmonising the registration formalities. Indeed, for countries in which enforceable trademark rights arise from use without registration, such as under the common law of passing off, the facilitation of registration of marks by treaties like the TLT 1994 and the Singapore Treaty 2006 has the positive effect of encouraging registration of trademarks leading to a more comprehensive and searchable public record of rights.

However, from a normative process point of view, both the TLT 1994 and the Singapore Treaty 2006 are heavy on the administrative or procedural aspects but light in terms of substantive law. From a purely policy perspective, it is also unclear whether the facilitation of more trademarks being registered, in particular the registration of many "limping trademarks," is necessarily a positive trend to be encouraged.[39] The Singapore Court of Appeal in *Société des Produits Nestlé SA* v. *Petra Foods Ltd* explained "limping" trademarks refer to marks "that have never been used as the sole means of identifying trade origin, but have instead always been used alongside other trademarks" that serve as "crutches."[40] Trademark offices must take on the role of effective gate-keepers of the grant of exclusive rights to trademark owners, and this is not merely administrative in nature.

C *The WIPO Joint Recommendation Concerning Provisions on the Protection of Well-Known Marks*

As detailed in Chapter 5 in this volume, because of TRIPS, a more expansive recognition of trademark subject matter, particularly in the protection of well-known marks as a separate and distinct category that warrants greater and wider protection, has become the norm in the intellectual property laws of WTO member countries.[41] In particular, Article 16.3 of TRIPS states that the protection conferred on well-known marks extends to use in relation to goods or services which are not similar to those in respect of which the trademark is registered, provided (a) such use would indicate a connection between those goods or services and the owner of the registered trademark and (b) that the interests of the owner of the registered trademark are likely to be damaged by such use.[42] Under Article 16.2, this protection extends to both trademarks and service marks.[43]

The international protection of well-known marks has its origins in Article 6*bis* of the Paris Convention. As highlighted in Chapter 2, this provision clearly lays down the grounds for infringement and the sanctions in respect of illegitimate use of a well-known mark. However, under Article 6*bis*, it is clear that protection of a well-known mark is conditional on the defendant's use of a mark which is "liable to create confusion" whilst under TRIPS and

[39] For an example of a "limping" trademark, *see Chocolaterie Guylian NV* v. *Registrar of Trade Marks* [2009] FCA 891 (Austl.).

[40] *Société des Produits Nestlé SA* v. *Petra Foods Ltd* [2016] SGCA 64 at [59] (Sing.).

[41] *See* Daniel J Gervais, "A Look at the Trademark Provisions in the TRIPS Agreement," Chapter 2 in this volume.

[42] *See* Paris Convention, *supra* note 1, art. 6*bis*, and TRIPS Agreement, *supra* note 5, art. 16.3.

[43] *See* Paris Convention, *supra* note 1, art. 6*bis*, and TRIPS Agreement, *supra* note 5, art. 16.2.

specifically in respect of the use of well-known marks in relation to dissimilar goods or services; an indication of connection resulting in interests of the registered trademark owner likely to be damaged by such use and not "a likelihood of confusion" would be sufficient. Still, neither the Paris Convention nor TRIPS define or state what constitutes a well-known mark.

In the absence of a clear definition, it did not come as a surprise that legislators and courts across the world struggled in finding consistency in defining the concept of well-known marks.[44] Also, the terminologies used to refer to this special category of marks are not consistent in the substantive laws of the countries party to TRIPS. Under the US Lanham Act, reference is made to "famous marks" whilst the European Directive[45] speaks of marks that have a reputation in the member state.[46] Elsewhere in the Singapore Trade Marks Act, the legislators adopted the term "well-known marks" used in the Paris Convention. Questions as to what actually constitutes a "well-known" mark were also asked within the framework of WIPO. This led, as is recounted in Chapter 5 in this volume, to the adoption of a Joint Recommendation Concerning Provisions on the Protection of Well-Known Marks (Joint Recommendation of Well-Known Marks), which was adopted at the 34th Series of Meetings of the Assemblies of the Member States of WIPO in September 1999, which provided further guidance on the determination of well-known marks and the scope of protection to be accorded to this special category of marks. The Joint Recommendation of Well-Known Marks and the specific criteria to establish whether a mark is well-known are dealt with comprehensively in Chapter 5 and the reader is invited to cross-reference to the extensive and in-depth discussions therein.[47] The paragraphs below serve to highlight and discuss summarily the salient points in Joint Recommendation of Well-Known Marks.

In determining whether a mark is a well-known mark, Article 2(a) of the Joint Recommendation of Well-Known Marks states that the relevant factors (which are not exhaustive) the competent authority in a member state shall consider include:

1 the degree of knowledge or recognition of the mark in the relevant sector of the public;
2 the duration, extent and geographical area of any use of the mark;
3 the duration, extent and geographical area of any promotion of the mark, including advertising or publicity and the presentation, at fairs or exhibitions, of the goods and/or services to which the mark applies;
4 the duration and geographical area of any registrations, and/or any applications for registration, of the mark, to the extent that they reflect use or recognition of the mark;
5 The record of successful enforcement of rights in the mark, in particular, the extent to which the mark was recognized as well-known by competent authorities;
6 the value associated with the mark.

A few observations and comments may be made about these factors. First, these factors are mere guidelines to assist the competent authority to determine whether the mark is a well-known mark

[44] *See* C-375/97, *General Motors Corporation* v. *Yplon (Chevy)*, [1999] I-05421, where the European Court of Justice stated that "reputation" involved some kind of knowledge threshold. Therefore, "a mark would have a reputation where it was known by a significant part of the public concerned by the products or services covered by the trademark."

[45] EU Directive 2015/2436 of the European Parliament and of the Council, art. 10(2)(c), 2015 OJ (L 336) (EC).

[46] *See* Frederick W. Mostert, *Well-Known and Famous Marks: Is Harmony Possible in the Global Village*, 86 TRADEMARK REP. (Mar.–Apr. 1996) at 103–41; *see also* Annette Kur, *Well-Known Marks, Highly Renowned Marks and Marks Having a (High) Reputation – What's It About?*, 23 INT'L REV. INTELL. PROP. & COMPETITION L. 218 (1992).

[47] See Chapter 5 in this volume, authored by Frederick W. Mostert.

and they do not constitute preconditions for reaching that determination.[48] Another observation that may be made about the list of factors in Article 2(a) of the Joint Recommendation is that it encompasses both national and international recognition of a mark as factors in determining whether the mark is well-known or not in a member state. These factors from sections 2(7)(a) to 2(7)(e) also appear equally weighted.[49]

It is worth noting that the Joint Recommendation on Well-Known Marks, in fleshing out the concept of "well-knownness" of a mark, recognises the concept of "niche fame" in that, as regards the knowledge of a given mark by the public, this knowledge may exist in relevant sectors of the public instead of the public at large.[50] Therefore, the recognition of a mark nationally is not limited to the retail or consumer market in the member state, but also extends to persons involved in distribution channels and to business or corporate circles. One final point to note is that the Joint Recommendation on Well-Known Marks stipulates that a member state shall not require, as a condition for determining whether a mark is a well-known mark, factors such as whether the mark has been used in, or that the mark has been registered or that an application for registration of the mark has been filed in or in respect of the member state or in respect of any jurisdiction other than the member state or that the mark is well-known by the public at large in the member state. This is significant as it effectively addresses the "foreign business problem" and the issue of "business within jurisdiction" in relation to the protection of well-known marks, particularly under the common law action of passing off.[51]

In terms of the protection to be accorded to well-known marks, Article 3(1) of the Joint Recommendation of Well-Known Marks states that a member state shall give protection against conflicting marks, business identifiers and domain names, at least with effect from the time when the mark has become well-known in the member state. Article 4 of the Joint Recommendation on Well-Known Marks sets out the conditions to be satisfied in a general framework of what constitutes conflicting marks, which in turn form the basis of upon which remedies such as opposition, invalidation and prohibition of use shall be meted out to the proprietor of a well-known trademark.

[48] *Joint Recommendation Concerning Provisions on the Protection of Well Known Marks*, art. 2(c), Sept. 20–29, 1999, WIPO General Assembly, https://wipo.int/edocs/pubdocs/en/marks/833/pub833.pdf. [hereinafter Joint Recommendation on Well Known Marks] (further stating that the determination in each case will depend upon the particular circumstances of that case and whether all, some or none of the factors mentioned in art. 2(a) are applicable is similarly a function of the factual matrix of the case at hand).

[49] *Id.* In Singapore, the Court of Appeal in *The Amanusa* has identified the degree of knowledge or recognition of the mark in the relevant sector of the public as arguably the most crucial factor when determining whether a trademark is well-known in Singapore as a result of a deeming provision in the Singapore Trademarks Act 1998. In fact, the Court of Appeal went so far as to say that "it appears that all the other relevant factors listed in s 2(7) are irrelevant once it is determined that the trade mark in question is well-known to *any relevant sector of the public in Singapore*" (emphasis added).

[50] Joint Recommendation on Well-Known Marks, *supra* note 48, at art. 2(a), iterates three relevant sectors which are of an illustrative nature only:

(i) actual and/or potential consumers of the type of goods and/or services to which the mark applies;
(ii) persons involved in channels of distribution of the type of goods and/or services to which the mark applies;
(iii) business circles dealing with the type of goods and/or services to which the mark applies.

It is further stated in art. 2(b), that "where a mark is determined to be well-known in at least one relevant sector of the public in a Member State, the mark *shall* be considered by the Member State to be a well-known mark" (emphasis added).

[51] Under the common law of passing off, goodwill cannot subsist independently by itself. It must be attached to some trade, business or calling. As such, goodwill is territorial in nature and trade outside of the jurisdiction cannot constitute goodwill. This particular attribute of locality in goodwill has given rise to the "foreign business problem" – do foreign businesses need to engage in trading activities or do business within the jurisdiction in order to enjoy goodwill so as to pursue an action of passing off or can they merely rely on the reputation they may enjoy within the jurisdiction in the absence of actual "business within jurisdiction"?

A similar set of conditions are laid down in Article 5 of the Joint Recommendation on Well-Known Marks under which business identifiers shall be deemed to be conflict with a well-known mark. A "business identifier" means any sign used to identify a business or a natural person, a legal person, an organisation or an association. Finally, Article 6 of the Joint Recommendation on Well-Known Marks makes provision for the situation where a domain name shall be deemed to be in conflict with a well-known mark at least where the domain name, or an essential part thereof, constitutes a reproduction, an imitation, a translation or a transliteration of the well-known mark, and the domain name has been registered or used in bad faith.

In a way, the adoption of the Joint Recommendation on Well-Known Marks by member states of the WIPO signalled a shift in substantive trademark law from a protection model based solely on consumer confusion of the trademarks to one that also takes into consideration the damage suffered by trademark proprietors and the distinctiveness of their marks. However, it should be noted that the implementation of the protection of well-known marks in the national laws of member states has been fraught with difficulties as courts struggle with relatively novel concepts such as "damaging interests connections"; "dilution in an unfair manner"; and "taking unfair advantage of the distinctive character of a mark," which are not found in a traditional trademark protection framework based primarily on consumer confusion.[52] In this regard, the Joint Recommendation on Well-Known Marks has provided useful guidance in the determination of well-known marks and the scope of their protection.

D The WIPO Joint Recommendation Concerning Provisions on the Protection of Marks, and Other Industrial Property Rights in Signs on the Internet

Innovative technology such as the Internet is disrupting all aspects of human society. In the past two decades, the Internet has not only altered the way information is distributed and consumed, but also dramatically transformed and continues to transform business practices all over the world by providing an alternative marketplace for goods and services that transcends national borders. As the functionality of the Internet evolves over time, trademark owners are confronted with new challenges, in particular the use (or misuse) of their trademarks to influence consumers' choices. One important area concerns online trademark use in relation to the establishment of goodwill or reputation and what constitutes use of the mark within jurisdiction; and trademark infringements.

It should be noted that when TRIPS was negotiated and concluded in 1994, little was known about these issues brought about by the Internet. Recognising the challenges posed to trademark proprietors as a result of the growth of electronic commerce on the Internet, the international trademark community, under the leadership of WIPO, initiated discussions on these challenges at the turn of the millennium which culminated in the adoption of the WIPO Joint Recommendation Concerning Provisions on the Protection of Marks, and Other Industrial Property Rights in Signs on the Internet (Joint Recommendation on Marks and Signs on the Internet) in September 2001.[53] The objectives of the Joint Recommendation on Marks and Signs on the Internet are to provide a clear legal framework for trademark owners who wish to use their marks on the Internet and to participate in the development of electronic commerce.

[52] *See Novelty Pte Ltd* v. *Amanresorts Ltd* [2009] 3 SLR(R) 216 (Sing.).

[53] *Joint Recommendation Concerning Provisions on the Protection of Marks, and other Industrial Property Rights in Signs on the Internet* (Sept. 24–Oct. 3, 2001), WIPO General Assembly, https://wipo.int/edocs/pubdocs/en/marks/845/pub845.pdf. [hereinafter Joint Recommendation on Marks and Signs].

The following paragraphs examine the guidance offered by the Joint Recommendation on Marks and Signs on the Internet on issues such as: whether, under applicable laws, use of a sign on the Internet has contributed to the acquisition, maintenance or infringement of a mark or other industrial rights, or whether such use constitutes an act of unfair competition; to enable owners of conflicting rights in identical or similar signs to use these signs concurrently on the Internet; and to determine remedies.

1 Use of a Sign on the Internet

The Internet is borderless unless national barriers are introduced artificially (such as via the so-called Great Firewall of China).[54] One of the issues which rightholders must deal with is demonstrating "use" of the mark when they offer goods and services online. The question of whether use of a sign on the Internet can be considered use within a jurisdiction is important in the determination of whether the user of the sign has acquired, maintained or infringed a trademark or any other intellectual property right that is protected by the national laws of a country. Within the framework of the Joint Recommendation on Marks and Signs on the Internet, only use of a sign on the Internet that has "commercial effect" in a given member state can be treated as having taken place in that member state.[55] Therefore, not every use of a sign on the Internet should be treated as use within a jurisdiction even though the use might be accessible to internet users based in that country.

Article 3 of the Joint Recommendation on Marks and Signs on the Internet provides a list of factors which may be relevant in determining whether use of a sign on the Internet has a commercial effect in a member state. One important factor evidencing a commercial effect resulting from the use of a sign on the Internet relates to the user of the sign doing business in a member state or undertaking significant plans to do business in the member state in relation to goods or services which are identical or similar to those for which the sign is used on the Internet.[56] The concept of "business within jurisdiction" is a general principle relied upon in trademark law to find trademark use or goodwill in a jurisdiction. Another factor relates to the level and character of commercial activity of the user in relation to the member state. Here the competent authority is invited to consider evidence of commercial activities such as whether the user is actually serving customers located in the member state; whether the user is relying on a territorial disclaimer of non-delivery of goods or services on their website; whether the user offers post-sales activities such as warranty or service in the member state; whether the user undertakes further commercial activities in the member state which are related to the use of the sign on the Internet but which are not carried out over the Internet.[57] The use of a sign on the Internet can also create a commercial effect if the evidence supports a connection of an offer of goods or services on the Internet with the member state, such as the example of an advertisement

[54] *See* Measures for the Administration of Internet Information Services (promulgated by Premier Zhu Rongji on Sept. 25, 2000, adopted at the thirty-first regular meeting of the State Council), http://china.org.cn/business/2010-01/20/content_19274704.htm. (China); Measures on the Administration of Internet Information Services 2001 (promulgated by Premier Zhu Rongji on Sept. 25, 2000, adopted at the thirty-first regular meeting of the State Council), http://china.org.cn/business/2010-01/20/content_19274704.htm. (China); Interim Regulations on the Administration of Internet Publishing 2002 (promulgated by the director of the GAPP Shi Zongyuan, and the Minister of the MII Wu Jichuan on June 27, 2002 to take effect as of Aug. 1, 2002), http://china.org.cn/business/2010-01/20/content_19275637.htm; Internet Society of China, Public Pledge on Self-Discipline for China Internet Industry (promulgated jointly by the State Administration of Press and Publishing and the Ministry of Information Technology, effective Aug. 1, 2002).

[55] Joint Recommendation on Marks and Signs, *supra* note 53, at art. 2.

[56] *Id.* at art. 3(1)(a).

[57] *Id.* at art. 3(1)(b). *See also id.* at Explanatory Notes [3.03] to [3.08].

targeted at a particular member state. Relevant evidence would include whether the goods or services offered can be lawfully delivered in the member state and whether the prices are shown in the official currency of the member state.[58] There are many novel ways in which a sign can be used on the Internet to refer to a trademark owner's mark, such as in emails, in internet banners, in an internet domain name, in a meta-tag, in a link on the internet or through framing. Thus, another factor provided by the Joint Recommendation on Marks and Signs on the Internet to determine commercial effect involves the connection of the manner of use of the sign on the Internet with the member state. Here the competent authority is invited to look at evidence establishing a link between the use of the sign and the member state such as use of the sign in connection with an address, telephone number or other contact within the member state or with a domain name referring to the member state.[59] The last factor mentioned in Article 3 of the Joint Recommendation on Marks and Signs on the Internet pertains to the relation of the use of the sign on the Internet with a right in that sign in the member state. The link between the sign used on the Internet and the subject of a right protected under the law of a member state is strong evidence of a commercial effect in a member state as the rightsowner can be assumed to engage in or has intention to engage in commercial activities within jurisdiction through the exercise of the exclusive right conferred on them.[60]

2 *Acquisition and Maintenance of Rights in Signs*

In the determination of whether rights in the sign have been acquired or maintained through use in a member state, Article 5 of the Joint Recommendation on Marks and Signs on the Internet confirms that use of a sign on the Internet is a relevant factor to be taken into consideration. However, the provision does not specify the legal requirements for acquiring or maintaining a right in a sign through its use or how this is to be calibrated vis-à-vis the use of the sign on the Internet. The determination of such issues remains the sole purview of the applicable national law. An example is the acquisition or maintenance of a right in an unregistered mark under the common law tort of passing off. Indeed, in the context of passing off and in ascertaining whether goodwill is established, courts are cognisant that the invention of the internet, which is borderless and over-arching in its reach, has created new issues as to how goodwill of businesses with a cyberspace presence ought to be assessed.[61]

The issues of what constitutes use within a jurisdiction and the establishment of goodwill in a passing off action, especially in respect to the use of a sign on the Internet, have seen a divide in the approaches taken by the courts. The hard line[62] or soft line[63] approaches are well documented

58 *Id.* at art. 3(1)(c). *See also id.* at Explanatory Notes [3.09] to [3.11].

59 *Id.* at art. 3(1)(d). *See also id.* at Explanatory Notes [3.12] to [3.15].

60 *Id.* at art. 3(1)(e). *See also id.* at Explanatory Notes [3.16].

61 *See 1–800 Flowers Inc.* v. *Phonenames Ltd* [2001] EWCA Civ. (721) (Eng.); *see also Hotel Cipriani SrL* v. *Cipriani (Grosvenor Street) Ltd* [2010] EWCA Civ 110 (Eng.); *see also Euromarket Designs Inc.* v. *Peters* [2001] FSR 288 (Eng.); *see also Amanresorts Ltd* v. *Novelty Pte Ltd* [2009] 3 SLR(R) 216 (*The Amanusa*) (Sing.).

62 Cases that have taken the traditional "hardline" approach have held that to claim for passing off, foreign businesses must actually do business within the jurisdiction. It is a requirement in law to assert goodwill within the jurisdiction and, accordingly, the plaintiffs, i.e. the foreign businesses, must necessarily carry on business within the jurisdiction. *See Alain Bernardin et Cie* v. *Pavilion Properties Ltd* [1967] FSR 341 (Eng.) (CRAZY HORSE Trademark); *see also Star Industrial Co. Ltd* v. *Yap Kwee Kor* [1974–76] SLR(R) 581 (Sing.); *see also The Athletes' Foot Marketing Associates Inc.* v. *Cobra Sports Ltd* [1980] RPC 343 (Eng.); *see also Anheuser-Busch Inc.* v. *Budejovicky Budvar NP* [1984] FSR 413 (Eng.).

63 The "soft line" cases have adopted a less traditional and a more liberal stance which is that the existence and extent of the goodwill acquired by virtue of a trader's business is essentially a question of fact and degree and depending on the facts of the case, a foreign business can still assert goodwill in a jurisdiction if it has acquired substantial reputation

and analysed in the recent Singapore Court of Appeal Decision of *Staywell Hospitality* v. *Starwood Hotels*.[64] The mere existence of domain names and websites featuring the name or mark in which goodwill is asserted would not per se be sufficient proof that the name or the mark has gained the requisite exposure for a conclusion that there is use of the mark within jurisdiction and that goodwill in fact subsists.[65] Some active steps beyond merely facilitating or enabling others to have access to the name or mark concerned are necessary to establish the existence of an identifiable and sizeable customer base on the Internet. A simple and straightforward test suggested is to ascertain the number of "hits" the domain name or website has received and of these "hits" how many originated from internet users situated in the jurisdiction in which goodwill is asserted.[66] In the final analysis, these "hits" should translate into evidence of actual exposure and awareness of the name or mark amongst the relevant public in a jurisdiction which could take the form of direct encouragement or advertisement by the trademark owner which led consumers to the website featuring the mark in question. It should also be appreciated that it would be easier to prove that the website was directed at the customers of a particular jurisdiction if products or services had actually been purchased by customers in that jurisdiction.

3 *Infringement and Liability*

The doctrine of territoriality which is well entrenched in all branches of intellectual property law dictates that any alleged infringement of registered trademark rights must be committed within a jurisdiction for it to be actionable. Essentially, this means there must be "use" of the mark within a jurisdiction to find infringement.

Consistent with the approach taken throughout the provisions in the Joint Recommendation on Marks and Signs on the Internet, the provision on "Use of a Sign on the Internet, Infringement of Rights and Acts of Unfair Competition" in Article 6 merely confirms that use of a sign on the Internet shall be taken into consideration under the laws of a member state in the determination of issues such as infringement and unfair competition if such use has a commercial effect and can thus be deemed to have taken place in that member state. Nothing is said about the substantive criteria for determining that use of a sign on the Internet constitutes an act of infringement or an act of unfair competition which remains the purview of the applicable national law. However, the wording in Article 6 is sufficiently wide to cover new forms of use of a sign on the Internet, including those that might be possible in the future, and member states are obliged to protect rights in marks and other signs in these situations.[67] In general, courts have demonstrated flexibility in their approaches towards the question – what constitutes use of a trademark on the Internet. Judicial sentiments appear to support the following proposition – the mere display of a mark on a website is usually insufficient to show use.[68] What is required is a demonstration of a *connection, nexus or even interactivity* between the trademark holders

even though it has no actual business presence within that jurisdiction. *See Sheraton Corp. of America* v. *Sheraton Motels Ltd* [1964] RPC 202 (Eng.); *see also Maxim's Ltd* v. *Dye* [1977] 1 WLR 1155 (Eng.); *see also Baskin-Robbins Ice Cream Co.* v. *Gutman* [1976] FSR 545 (Eng.); *see also My Kinda Bones Ltd* v. *Dr Pepper's Stove Co. Ltd* [1984] FSR 289 (Eng.).

64 *Staywell Hospitality* v. *Starwood Hotels* [2014] 1 SLR 911 at 131–7 (Sing.).

65 *The Amanusa*, at 54, *per* VK Rajah JA.

66 *Id. See also 800-Flowers TM* [2002] FSR 12 at 138, *per* Buxton LJ.

67 *See* Joint Recommendation on Marks and Signs, *supra* note 53, at Explanatory Notes 6.03. Unusual forms of use of a sign include "such as use of signs in banner advertisements, sale or purchase of signs as keywords for search engines, use as metatags, use in Uniform Resource Locators (URLs), use as search terms, or any other 'new' forms of use that might be possible in the future."

68 *1–800 Flowers Inc.* v. *Phonenames Ltd* [2001] EWCA Civ (721) (Eng.); *see also Euromarket Designs Inc.* v. *Peter & Another* [2000] ETMR 1025 (Eng.).

and the consumers in the jurisdiction within which the rightholders are asserting their trademark rights.

Shortly after the turn of the Millennium when the Joint Recommendation on Marks and Signs on the Internet was adopted, bad faith registration of trademarks as domain names was one of the earliest issues causing great tensions between trademark owners and internet users. The principles provided by the Joint Recommendation on Marks and Signs on the Internet were thus timely and useful in an attempt to address those issues at that time.

However, the world is a very different place two decades on and it is a fair assessment that the normative process on trademark protection on the Internet has not kept up to speed with the rapid developments in this particular area. Indeed, as new and innovative business models emerge on the Internet, trademark owners find that there are new ways in which their trademarks are being referred to and used by third parties. Some of the new uses of trademarks on the Internet include use within listings for non-genuine goods on auction sites;[69] use as keywords by search engine operators;[70] and use on virtual objects that are traded in virtual worlds like "Second Life" and social media such as Facebook and Twitter.[71] These "new" uses of trademarks on the Internet continue to add to the complexities with which trademark owners must grapple in a digitised business environment, and liabilities of Internet intermediaries have become an important issue in the enforcement of trademark rights.

As more and new ways for businesses and individuals to refer to a trademark owner's mark on the Internet continue to emerge, it is appropriate and necessary to examine whether the principles articulated in the Joint Recommendation on Marks and Signs on the Internet remain relevant and adequate to address these issues. At its twenty-fourth session, held in Geneva from 1 to 4 November 2010, the WIPO's Standing Committee on the Law of Trademark, Industrial Designs and Geographical Indications (SCT) requested that the WIPO secretariat examine the Joint Recommendation on Marks and Signs on the Internet with a view of determining, in particular, whether the new ways in which trademarks can be used on the Internet are adequately addressed by the Joint Recommendation.[72] The WIPO Secretariat in response to the WIPO SCT's request prepared and presented a report entitled "Trademarks and the Internet" ("WIPO Secretariat Report on Trademarks and the Internet") at the twenty-fifth session in March 2011. Considering some of the new uses of trademarks on the Internet which are made possible by technological advances, the WIPO Secretariat Report on Trademarks and the Internet concluded that the general principles such as the concept of commercial effect articulated in the Joint Recommendation on Marks and Signs on the Internet remain relevant.[73] However, certain specific legal issues such as the conditions for the determination of an infringement and the liability of internet intermediaries fall outside the scope of the provisions of the Joint Recommendation on Marks and Signs on the Internet.[74]

The Joint Recommendation on Marks and Signs on the Internet was adopted almost two decades ago and the macro-environment has changed dramatically since then. The world is told that humanity is at the advent of the Fourth Industrial Revolution and it is perhaps timely for

[69] See *L'Oreal SA* v. *eBay International AG* [2011] ETMR 52.

[70] See *Google France SARL* v. *Louis Vuitton Malletier SA* [2010] RPC 19; *Interflora Inc.* v. *Marks & Spencer plc* [2012] ETMR 1.

[71] See *Taser Int'l, Inc.* v. *Linden Res., Inc.*, 2:09-CV-00811-ROS (D. Ariz. Apr. 17, 2009).

[72] *See* World Intellectual Property Organization, Standing Committee on the Law of Trademarks, Industrial Designs and Geographic Indicators, SCT/24/4 (Nov. 1–4, 2010).

[73] *See* World Intellectual Property Organization, Standing Committee on the Law of Trademarks, Industrial Designs and Geographic Indicators, at 66, SCT/25/3 (Mar. 28–Apr. 1, 2011).

[74] *See id.* at 59.

an updated version of the Joint Recommendation on Marks and Signs on the Internet or a multilateral international agreement on trademark use and the Internet be discussed and adopted.[75] The challenge is the approach to be undertaken in the normative process. It is made more difficult in light of the rapid pace of technological developments which may have the effect of rendering suggested solutions obsolete very quickly.[76] The resolution of legal issues brought about by the Internet require the development of agreed standards with respect to the determination of liabilities across countries and the prospect of multilateral consensus building is not an optimistic one given the prevailing international geopolitical climate.

E The WIPO Joint Recommendation Concerning Provisions on Trademark Licenses

Commercialisation of a trademark generally takes the form of either an assignment or a licence of the mark by the trademark proprietor. With globalised movements of goods and services, it is useful that the formalities associated with these instruments of trademark commercialisation are harmonised across jurisdictions.

The WIPO Joint Recommendation Concerning Provisions on Trademark Licenses (Joint Recommendation on Trademark Licenses) were adopted by member states at the Thirty-Fifth Series of Meetings of the Assemblies of the Member States of WIPO in September 2000 with the objective of harmonising and simplifying the formal requirements for the recordation of trademark licences and thereby supplementing the Trademark Law Treaty 1994.

Article 2(1) to (6) of the Joint Recommendation on Trademark Licenses sets out the maximum list of elements or indications which can be required by member states in relation to requests for recordation of a licence. Furthermore, Article 7 lists certain formal requirements which cannot be required as part of a request for the recordation of a licence, such as the furnishing of the registration certificate of the mark which is the subject of the licence; the furnishing of the licence contract or a translation of it; and an indication of the financial terms of the licence contract. A similar maximum list of elements or indications and prohibition of additional requirements are applicable to requests concerning the amendment or cancellation of the recordation of a licence.[77]

The Joint Recommendation on Trademark Licenses also provide a prescription of legal effects flowing from the non-recordation of a licence. Essentially, the non-recordation of a licence with the trademark office in member states shall not affect the validity of the registration of the mark which is the subject of the licence or the protection of that mark. Similarly, the recordation of a licence cannot be made a condition for any right that a trademark licensee may have under the national law of member states to join infringement proceedings initiated by the holder or to obtain damages resulting from an infringement of the mark which is the subject of the licence.

The normative framework as laid down in the Joint Recommendation on Trademark Licenses serves as the foundation upon which the subsequent provisions of the Singapore Treaty 2006 in relation to administrative requirements concerning the recordation of trademark licences and legal effects attached to the recordation (or non-recordation) of licences are based.[78]

75 KLAUS SCHWAB, THE FOURTH INDUSTRIAL REVOLUTION (2016).

76 See World Intellectual Property Organization, Standing Committee on the Law of Trademarks, Industrial Designs and Geographic Indicators, at 69, SCT/25/3 (Mar. 28–Apr. 1, 2011).

77 *See* Joint Recommendation on Trademark Licenses, at art. 3.

78 Singapore Treaty, *supra* note 12, at arts. 17–20. For a detailed discussion of the development of international norms in trademark transactions, *see* Marcus Hopperger, *Trademark Transactions and the Normative Framework of the World*

Like the TLT 1994 and the Singapore Treaty 2006, the Joint Recommendation on Trademark Licenses focuses predominantly on the formalities associated with the instruments such as licences and assignments used in trademark transactions and encourages dealings in trademarks as personal property. This is consistent with an observable trend that trademarks are increasingly considered as valuable assets of a firm for its role in building brand image and securing brand loyalty.[79] The growing acceptance of the advertising and investment functions of trademarks, over and beyond the function of trademarks being indicators of origin, will continue to fuel the current expansionist trend in the types of marks registrable and the scope of protection. This may not necessarily be a welcome prospect, especially when there is a lack of clarity whether such a development in the law will bring about greater consumer welfare.

III CONCLUSION

It has been twenty-five years since the conclusion of TRIPS and the world has changed dramatically over the last two decades, whether in the technological, political, social or economic arena. In a greater part, the acceleration of change has been propelled by advancements in technology taking place at a breakneck speed which have had knock-on effects on almost every aspect of human existence. Countries are in a technology race against each other and intellectual property issues are at the forefront of all major trade negotiations and free-trade agreements. At the same time, recent governmental actions such as the imposition of tariffs on imports from China, Canada, Mexico and the European Union by the US Trump Administration and retaliation actions from these respective countries have cast long shadows on the future of international norm-setting processes in a rule-based trade system set up by the World Trade Organization (WTO).

This chapter has endeavoured to map out the journey taken, and the efforts expended thus far in the rule-making process of trademark protection twenty-five years post-TRIPS. The normative process has been made more complex as a result of uncertainties brought about by technological advancements and developments in the geopolitical, social and economic environments. In this regard, the international agreements discussed in this chapter that were signed post-Paris Convention, and brought into force either before or after TRIPS, and those signed and implemented after TRIPS have attempted to address novel issues in the protection of trademarks internationally brought forth by these modalities. Yet these agreements have focused predominantly on formalities and administrative procedures of trademark filings and dealings, and are thin on substantive law. More needs to be done in relation to the development of substantive trademark law to not only address the "technology-related issues" referred to in this chapter but also to address tensions in other interfaces, such as fair use of trademarks in parodies and satires as forms of expression. In a climate of pro-trademark protection that is manifested by an ever-increasing range of trademarks registrable and the expansion in the scope of protection for certain category of (well-known) marks, the need for "exceptions and limitations to trademark

Intellectual Property Organisation, *in* THE LAW AND PRACTICE OF TRADEMARK TRANSACTIONS – A GLOBAL AND LOCAL OUTLOOK 29–50 (Irene Calboli & Jacques De Werra eds., 2016).

[79] *See* Jonathan E. Schroeder, *Brand Culture: Trademarks, Marketing and Consumption*, *in* TRADE MARKS AND BRANDS: AN INTERDISCIPLINARY CRITIQUE 161–76 (Lionel Bently, Jennifer Davis & Jane C. Ginsburg eds., 2008). *See also* David Vaver, *"Brand Culture: Trademarks, Marketing and Consumption" – Responding Legally to Professor Schroeder's Paper*, *in* TRADE MARKS AND BRANDS: AN INTERDISCIPLINARY CRITIQUE 177–98 (Lionel Bently, Jennifer Davis & Jane C. Ginsburg eds., 2008).

rights" cannot be ignored.[80] Unfortunately, it may be said that normative developments in this area have been slow and greater efforts must be expended in the future.

With protectionism currently threatening the international trade system, a look back in history to where we have come from and how much has been achieved as an international community could serve as an encouragement for countries to come together in a collaborative and concerted manner, in spite of the recent geopolitical uncertainties, to make progress in the normative area that might result in a more balanced and equitable system for all stakeholders in the global trademark community.

[80] *See* Irene Calboli & Christine Haight Farley, *The Trademark Provisions in the TRIPS Agreement, in* Intellectual Property and International Trade – The TRIPS Agreement 157–92 at 5.04 (Carlos M. Correa & Abdulqawi A. Yusuf eds., 3d ed. 2016).

4

The Trademark Provisions in Post-TRIPS Mega-Regional Trade Agreements

*Susy Frankel**

I INTRODUCTION

Those nations that seek more extensive protection for trademarks, beyond the levels of protection that are the required minimum standards of the Agreement on Trade-Related Aspects of Intellectual Property Rights (TRIPS Agreement)[1] and the Paris Convention for the Protection of Industrial Property,[2] utilise free trade agreements (FTAs) to achieve these goals. The TRIPS Agreement anticipated that some members would provide more extensive protection, both because many already did provide a higher standard of protection, even at the time the TRIPS Agreement was signed, and because the United States openly stated that it intended to continue to negotiate for more extensive intellectual property standards in bilateral trade agreements post-TRIPS.[3] The wording of the TRIPS Agreement invites this relentless pursuit of increased standards as it provides that: "Members may, but shall not be obliged to, implement in their law more extensive protection than is required by this Agreement, provided that such protection does not contravene the provisions of this Agreement."[4] The use of FTAs for more extensive intellectual property standards is controversial because the overall amount of increased protection has been very extensive since the TRIPS Agreement came into force.[5] The framework of the international system means that post-TRIPS developments are almost always increasing levels of protection and this creates a one-way ratchet, meaning that protection can increase but not

* FRSNZ, Professor of Law, Chair in Intellectual Property and International Trade, Faculty of Law, Victoria University of Wellington.

[1] Agreement on Trade-Related Aspects of Intellectual Property Rights, Apr. 15, 1994, Marrakesh Agreement Establishing the World Trade Organizations, Annex 1C, 1869 UNTS 299, 33 ILM 1197 [hereinafter TRIPS Agreement].

[2] Paris Convention for the Protection of Industrial Property, 828 UNTS 305 (Mar. 20, 1883) [hereinafter Paris Convention].

[3] *See generally* Peter Drahos, *BITS and BIPS Bilateralism in Intellectual Property*, 4 J. World Intell. Prop. 791 (2011).

[4] TRIPS Agreement, *supra* note 1, at art. 1.1. The Paris Convention, art. 19, similarly provides: "It is understood that the countries of the Union reserve the right to make separately between themselves special agreements for the protection of industrial property, in so far as these agreements do not contravene the provisions of this Convention." Paris Convention, supra note 2, at art. 19.

[5] *See generally* Graeme B. Dinwoodie & Rochelle C. Dreyfuss, A Neofederalist Vision of TRIPS: The Resilience of the International Intellectual Property Regime (2012); Annette Kur, *International Norm Making in the Field of Intellectual Property – A Shift Towards Maximum Rules*, 1 World Intell. Prop. Org. (WIPO) J. 27 (2009); Susy Frankel, *The Legitimacy and Purpose of Intellectual Property Chapters in FTAs*, *in* Challenges to Multilateral Trade: The Impact of Bilateral, Preferential and Regional Agreements (Ross Buckley, Vai Io Lo & Laurence Boulle eds., 2008); Susan K Sell, *TRIPS Was Never Enough: Vertical Forum Shifting, FTAS, ACTA, and TPP*, 18 J. Intell. Prop. L. 447, 451 (2011).

decrease.[6] Much of the debate about the effects of increased protection has focused on provisions other than those that relate to the subject matter of trademarks, such as patents and their impact on the availability of medicines. While trademarks have not been in the limelight of this debate, their treatment in post-TRIPS FTAs raises several concerns about their ever-increasing scope in terms of subject matter, the detail and availability of actionable rights for owners of so-called well-known marks, requirements for increased enforcement in both civil and criminal proceedings, and trademarks' relationship with investment chapters in FTAs.

The increases to trademark protection have occurred by means of both bilateral and plurilateral FTAs. These FTAs are sometimes described as "mega-regional" because of the volume of trade that the whole agreement covers (intellectual property is only one part of such agreements). Examples of such mega-regionals include the Trans-Atlantic Trade and Investment Partnership (TTIP)[7] bilateral negotiations, which at this writing are "obsolete" but may develop again;[8] the Regional Economic Cooperation Partnership[9] (RCEP) plurilateral, which is under negotiation at the time of writing; and the completed Trans-Pacific Partnership[10] (TPP), which is not in force as first agreed with the United States, but is in force as the Comprehensive and Progressive Trans-Pacific Partnership (CPTPP) without the United States.[11] Other regional agreements are not so "mega" in trade coverage terms, but are significant regional endeavours, such as the New Zealand and Australia trade agreement, also known as Single Economic Market.[12] While other bilateral trade agreements (not based on region) are significant, such as the United States–Australia Agreement (AUSFTA)[13] and the EU–Singapore Agreement,[14] they do not cover volumes of trade that make them "mega." In some instances, countries are part of multiple overlapping bilateral and even plurilateral agreements. Singapore and New Zealand, for example, not only have a bilateral agreement between them,[15] they both are also part of the CPTPP, the RCEP negotiations, and the Association of Southeast Asian Nations (ASEAN), Australia and New Zealand Free Trade Agreement.[16]

6 Peter Drahos, *The Global Ratchet for Intellectual Property Rights: Why It Fails as Policy and What Should Be Done about It*, Austr. Nat'l Univ. (2003), https://anu.edu.au/fellows/pdrahos/reports/pdfs/2003globalipratchet.pdf.

7 See *Negotiations and Agreements, The Transatlantic Trade and Investment Partnership*, European Commission, http://ec.europa.eu/trade/policy/in-focus/ttip/ [hereinafter TTIP].

8 *Id.*, Council of European Union, Apr. 9, 2019, art. 3 (authorising new negotiations with the United States, making TTIP "obsolete").

9 *Regional Comprehensive Economic Partnership*, Association of Southeast Asian Nations (ASEAN), http://asean.org/?static_post=rcep-regional-comprehensive-economic-partnership [hereinafter RCEP].

10 *Trans-Pacific Partnership Agreement*, Office of the United States Trade Representative, https://ustr.gov/trade-agreements/free-trade-agreements/trans-pacific-partnership (entered into Feb. 4, 2016, not in force) [hereinafter TPP].

11 *Comprehensive and Progressive Trans-Pacific Partnership*, New Zealand Foreign Affairs and Trade (2018), https://mfat.govt.nz/assets/CPTPP/Comprehensive-and-Progressive-Agreement-for-Trans-Pacific-Partnership-CPTPP-English.pdf [hereinafter CPTPP].

12 *See Single Economic Market*, New Zealand Foreign Affairs and Trade, https://mfat.govt.nz/en/countries-and-regions/australia/new-zealand-high-commission/single-economic-market/.

13 The Australia–United States Free Trade Agreement (May 18, 2004, 43 ILM 1248) [hereinafter AUSFTA].

14 *The European Union–Singapore Free Trade Agreement*, Ministry of Trade and Industry, https://mti.gov.sg/Improving-Trade/Free-Trade-Agreements/EUSFTA [hereinafter EUSFTA].

15 *NZ–Singapore Closer Economic Partnership*, New Zealand Foreign Affairs and Trade (2001), https://mfat.govt.nz/en/trade/free-trade-agreements/free-trade-agreements-in-force/nz-singapore-closer-economic-partnership/; *see also CEP Overview*, New Zealand Foreign Affairs and Trade, https://mfat.govt.nz/en/trade/free-trade-agreements/free-trade-agreements-in-force/nz-singapore-closer-economic-partnership/cep-overview/.

16 *ASEAN, Australia and New Zealand Free Trade Agreement (AANZFTA)*, New Zealand Foreign Affairs and Trade, https://mfat.govt.nz/en/trade/free-trade-agreements/free-trade-agreements-in-force/asean-australia-new-zealand-free-trade-agreement-aanzfta/aanzfta-text/#text.

Section II of this chapter uses illustrative examples of FTAs (focusing on some key mega-regionals) to outline the kinds of more extensive protection that have been negotiated and sometimes agreed for trademarks. That more extensive protection predominantly relates to the increased range of the subject matter of trademarks (including smells and scents); more extensive protection for well-known trademarks; the relationship between trademarks and geographical indications; and requirements relating to civil and criminal enforcement measures. All of these sorts of protection are extensions of existing obligations found in the TRIPS Agreement and, therefore, are TRIPS-plus. When an FTA provides for more extensive protection, relating to a matter that TRIPS covers, then members of the World Trade Organization (WTO) must apply that provision on a national treatment basis because the TRIPS Agreement provides: "Each Member shall accord to the nationals of other Members treatment no less favourable than that it accords to its own nationals with regard to the protection[3] of intellectual property."[17] There are a few exceptions to the application of national treatment. Those exceptions relate to existing treaties incorporated into the TRIPS Agreement, but none of those exceptions is of direct relevance to the subject of this chapter.[18] Consequently, when additional trademark-related protections are enacted in domestic laws, they should apply to others on a national treatment basis.[19] In some instances, this may mean that foreigners make better use of intellectual property rights than nationals do, such as when a country imports more trademarked goods than it exports. As a result of continuous increases in the level of protection, some countries have attempted to use FTAs to push back against increasing protection of foreign intellectual property. This pushback, in the trademark context, is evident in relation to rules about exhaustion of rights and parallel importation of trademarked goods, and provisions to address the protection of traditional knowledge. These sorts of FTA provisions are also discussed in Section II.

Section III of this chapter will take a closer look at some of the increased protections and discusses the trade-related effects of those increases. In particular, this section examines first the protection afforded to well-known marks and the adverse effects that these protections can have and, second, the successes and failures of requiring increased enforcement standards.

Other chapters in FTAs, in addition to intellectual property chapters, include obligations that impact the international norms relating to trademarks and intellectual property generally. One of these is investment chapters. Section IV will discuss investment chapters and how they apply to trademarks and relevant investment-related disputes about those chapters. Overall, the pressure to provide more extensive protection for trademarks in FTAs is likely to continue to increase rather than decrease given that multilateral negotiations are facing extensive challenges with increasingly more negotiation taking place outside of the multilateral environment thus diverting resources,[20] and the United States' blocking the appointment of Appellate Body

[17] TRIPS Agreement, *supra* note 1, at art. 1.1, n. 3 following "protection" provides: "For the purposes of Articles 3 and 4 'protection' shall include matters affecting the availability, acquisition, scope, maintenance and enforcement of intellectual property rights as well as those matters affecting the use of intellectual property rights specifically addressed in this Agreement."

[18] TRIPS Agreement, *supra* note 1, at art. 3.1, incorporates the exceptions to national treatment found in treaties that WIPO administers, including the Paris Convention, *supra* note 2. The Paris Convention includes a limited exception relating to judicial and administrative process. *See* Sam Ricketson, The Paris Convention for the Protection of Industrial Property (2015) at 9.25 (discussing the exception).

[19] TRIPS Agreement, *supra* note 1, at art. 3.1.

[20] FTAs are used to create multiple obligations that increase levels of protection and thus progressively increase the extent of protection globally. *See* Frankel, *supra* note 5.

members resulting in the system ceasing to fully function.[21] Whether providing more extensive protection achieves the purposes of both the TRIPS Agreement and trademark law at international level is debatable, as the Concluding Thoughts section of this chapter discusses.

II INCREASES IN PROTECTION AND PUSHBACKS IN POST-TRIPS FREE TRADE AGREEMENTS

Following the TRIPS Agreement, many WTO members have entered into bilateral and plurilateral FTAs, and other agreements continue to be negotiated, that both confirm the level of protection TRIPS requires and also extend trademark protection beyond that detailed in the TRIPS Agreement. With the trade-related multilateral forum not functioning as it ought,[22] bilateral and plurilateral fora are likely to continue to dominate norm-making in the field of trademarks, short of any new World Intellectual Property Organization (WIPO) initiatives. The differences found in trademark laws around the world can be characterised as important because they recognise local interests and are framed to encourage local businesses. In other words, while the international framework sets certain minimum standards, the plurality of approaches possible within that framework has benefits. Others hold the opposite view, that further harmonisation of the minimum standards is required as the plurality of approaches is bad for business, especially for those who trade across borders.[23] Both views carry some weight. It may well be possible to harmonise some aspects of trademark law beyond the levels of protection provided in the TRIPS Agreement, without undercutting (unreasonably) local initiatives and diversity of interests. However, some sorts of protection pose threats to local cultural interests and concerns about global diversity and are consequently problematic.[24] Detailed requirements for the protection of well-known marks and the impact on small and local businesses are a part of those concerns. Another is that the protection of well-known marks continues to grow and simultaneously there is an unjustified failure to protect the traditional knowledge of the less well-known. This situation is, to some, a form of corporate colonialism, especially when the well-known take without consent or compensation from traditional knowledge holders.[25]

A Region and Free Trade Agreements

Some post-TRIPS FTAs are regional in nature and others are not. This is important because trade law has often sought to distinguish FTAs on the basis of region as a justification for

[21] *See, e.g.*, Jennifer Hillman, *A Reset of the World Trade Organization's Appellate Body*, Greenberg Center for Geoeconomic Studies (Jan. 2020), https://cfr.org/report/reset-world-trade-organizations-appellate-body.

[22] It is well-known that negotiating in bilateral and plurilateral groups detracts from commitments to negotiating in the multilateral sphere. While the WTO system recognises that bilaterals can serve to further liberalise trade, that is not always the result, *see* JAGDISH BHAGWATI, LIKE TERMITES IN THE TRADING SYSTEM: HOW PREFERENTIAL AGREEMENTS UNDERMINE FREE TRADE (2008). In the intellectual property context, more extensive protection is permitted under the TRIPS Agreement, art. 1.1. There is a question as to whether that ought to be limitless. I have elsewhere proposed that the goals of the TRIPS Agreement place limits on its expansion, as, after all, more extensive protection under TRIPS 1.1 requires that it is in compliance with the agreement. *See* Susy Frankel, *Challenging TRIPS – Plus FTAs – the Potential Utility of Non-Violation Complaints*, 12(4) J. INT'L EURO. L. 1023 (2009).

[23] *See, e.g.*, Marshall A. Leaffer, *The New World of Intellectual Trademark Law*, 2 MARQ. INTELL. PROP. L. REV. 1, 9 (1998) (stating "territoriality, when applied to intellectual property, ignores basic reality because informational products cannot be located at a particular spot on the globe").

[24] *See infra*, Section III, regarding well-known marks and the effects on small businesses and on traditional knowledge claimants.

[25] *See infra*, Section III.

preferential trade.[26] Mega-regional trade agreements, which can be either plurilateral or bilateral, do not necessary involve regional boundaries. USMCA is regional as Mexico, the United States and Canada are collectively the northernmost parts of North America.[27] This sort of regional FTA is constituted differently from the EU, which includes a regional customs union. A Trans-Atlantic agreement would not be regional in the same way as USMCA. Another example is RCEP, which involves the ASEAN nations (which are regional), plus New Zealand, Australia, India, China, South Korea and Japan.[28] This negotiation involves multiple interrelated regions and is quite expansive.

The mega-regional agreements and negotiations are revealing of the kinds of issues that are currently debated. Region is not, however, a very useful indicator for understanding the substantive types of intellectual property protection that are more extensive than TRIPS, found in such agreements. Region is often important where nations in a region agree to procedural, rather than only substantive norms, to create a regional registration system, such as the EU[29] and African Intellectual Property Organization.[30] Where a regional registration system creates one registration for the region, such regional registrations may coexist with national registrations or may substitute for them. A lesser form of regional integration is found in agreements where there is mutual recognition of some kind.[31] Mutual recognition allows for trademark registration offices to recognise and use examination and registration decisions of another such office, with each office retaining independent registration systems, rather than creating one registration for the region.

B More Extensive Protection

One of the most extensive plurilateral agreements, both in term of its substantive provisions and the volume of world trade it covered, was the TPP.[32] The TPP was finalised but before it was ratified (and thus capable of coming into force) the United States withdrew following an election promise of the then newly elected President Trump. This meant that the TPP did not go ahead in its final form, but rather the remaining eleven parties negotiated to complete the agreement and, in doing so, suspended provisions that had been negotiated by and for the United States.[33] Most of these suspended provisions relate to intellectual property and more specifically provide more extensive protection in patent and copyright law. None of them relate to trademarks. The CPTPP remains open to join, by negotiation, should any country that is not a member wish to so

[26] *See Ch. 10, Regional Trade Exceptions, in* Peter Van Den Bossche and Werner Zdouc, The Law and Policy of the World Trade Organization (4th ed. 2017).

[27] United States–Mexico–Canada Agreement, Office of the United States Trade Representative (Nov. 30, 2018), https://ustr.gov/trade-agreements/free-trade-agreements/united-states-mexico-canada-agreement [hereinafter USMCA].

[28] RCEP, *supra* note 9. At the time of writing India is not longer participating in the negotiations.

[29] *See* European Union Intellectual Property Office, https://euipo.europa.eu [hereinafter EUIPO].

[30] Organisation Africaine de la Propriété Intellectuelle, a group of some French-speaking African nations enables applicants to file a single application for protection of a trademark in designated countries, http://oapi.int [hereinafter OAPI].

[31] An example is the Andean Pact (which includes Bolivia, Colombia, Ecuador and Peru). These sorts of integration mechanisms also may not be successfully negotiated, as was the case with Australia and New Zealand. *See* Susy Frankel and Megan Richardson, *Trans-Tasman Intellectual Property Coordination, in* Learning from the Past, Adapting for the Future: Regulatory Reform in New Zealand 527–53 (Susy Frankel ed., 2011).

[32] TPP, *supra* note 10; *see also* C. L. Lim, Deborah K. Elms, Patrick Low, The Trans-Pacific Partnership (2012).

[33] CPTPP, *supra* note 11. For an explanation of what provisions are suspended, *see CPTPP* v *TPP*, Ministry of Foreign Affairs and Trade, https://mfat.govt.nz/en/trade/free-trade-agreements/free-trade-agreements-in-force/cptpp/understanding-cptpp/tpp-and-cptpp-the-differences-explained.

negotiate. In fact, the TPP began as a development of an agreement among New Zealand, Singapore, Brunei and Chile, which was known as P4. P4 had open-accession provisions, as an enticement to other countries, and particularly the United States, to join.[34]

Under the CPTPP (and the TPP), several articles provide minimum standards in relation to trademark protection and flexibilities. The CPTPP's trademark commitments include procedural and substantive obligations which are illustrative of the types of more extensive protection emerging in mega-regional and some bilateral FTAs.

The CPTPP's main procedural obligation is a requirement that parties either ratify or accede to the Madrid Protocol or the Singapore Treaty on the Law of Trademarks.[35] There is a requirement for parties to adopt the Nice Classification system of classes of goods and services, in relation to which trademarks are registered.[36] This is necessary in order to effectively use the Madrid Protocol as, in any event, the Madrid registration system uses the Nice classifications.[37] Also, parties must provide electronic means for trademark applications and a publicly available electronic register.[38]

As to substantive obligations, the CPTPP addresses trademark subject matter by specifying that parties cannot require that signs be visually perceptible as a condition of registration. In effect, this means that member countries must provide for the possibility of registration for sound, smell, taste and scent marks (as they are variously known).[39] Specifically, the agreement requires that "parties shall make best efforts to register scent marks."[40] The agreement also provides that registration cannot be refused on the ground that "that the sign of which it is composed is a sound."[41]

Related to trademark subject matter, the CPTPP also requires that parties provide for registration of both collective and certification trademarks. Certification trademarks do not have to be a separate category.[42] These provisions point to the link between certification trademarks and geographical indications. The CPTPP requires that each party provide that signs which are geographical indications are capable of protection under its trademark system.[43] The agreement between the United States and Korea (KORUS) goes further and includes provisions for cancellation of geographical indications which may cause confusion with trademarks.[44]

[34] Trans-Pacific Strategic Economic Partnership (P4), NEW ZEALAND FOREIGN AFFAIRS AND TRADE (2006), https://mfat.govt.nz/en/trade/free-trade-agreements/free-trade-agreements-in-force/p4/.

[35] CPPTP, *supra* note 11 at art. 18.72, n. 1. The Madrid Protocol must be ratified under the Free Trade Agreement between the United States of America and the Republic of Korea; *see US–Korea Free Trade Agreement*, OFFICE OF THE UNITED STATES TRADE REPRESENTATIVE (2012), art. 18.1.3(e), https://ustr.gov/trade-agreements/free-trade-agreements/korus-fta/final-text [hereinafter KORUS]; *see also id.* at art. 18.1.3(h) and 18.1.4(c) (Trade Mark Law Treaty must be ratified. Parties "shall make reasonable efforts to ratify or accede" to the Singapore Treaty on the Law of Trade Marks); *see also* USMCA, *supra* note 27, at art. 20.7(2). For a detailed review of the Madrid Protocol and the Singapore Treaty, see Chapter 3 in this volume.

[36] CPTPP, *supra* note 11, at art. 18; *see also* KORUS, *supra* note 35, at art. 18.2.11.

[37] *See* Madrid Goods & Services Manager Aligned with Latest Nice Classification Edition, WIPO (2017), https://wipo.int/madrid/en/news/2017/news_0001.html.

[38] KORUS, *supra* note 35, at art. 18.2.10.

[39] CPTPP, *supra* note 11, at art. 18.18; *see also* KORUS, *supra* note 35, at art. 18.2.1; *see also* USMCA, *supra* note 27, at art. 20.17.

[40] CPTPP, *supra* note 11, at art. 18.18.

[41] *Id.*

[42] CPTPP, *supra* note 11, at art. 18.9, *see also* KORUS, *supra* note 35, at art. 18.2.2; *see also* USMCA, *supra* note 27, at art. 20.18.

[43] CPTPP, *supra* note 11, at art. 18.19, *see also* KORUS, *supra* note 35, at art. 18.2.4.

[44] KORUS, *supra* note 35, at art. 18.2.15 (a).

The United States, Mexico and Canada entered into an agreement known as NAFTA, which came into force in 1994.[45] NAFTA, when entered into, was in most aspects the same as the TRIPS Agreement. Developments under NAFTA are significant when it comes to developing international norms, not only because of the similarity with TRIPS, but also because of the influence the United States has had on norm development. NAFTA has been partially renegotiated as USMCA, which contains mostly the same provisions as the TPP in relation to trademarks. In contrast, the EU–Canada Agreement (CETA) has relatively few trademark provisions.[46] CETA requires "reasonable efforts" to comply with the Singapore Treaty on the Law of Trademarks and the Madrid Protocol.[47] In order to align its laws with trading partners Canada has acceded to the Madrid Protocol and the Nice Classification system. More substantively Canada is moving from the requirement to identify first use for registration to registration with intention to use.[48]

What is perhaps most striking about CETA and its trademark norms is its trademark exceptions clause. The exceptions clause differs from TRIPS in that it *requires* parties to provide for "the fair use of descriptive terms," whereas TRIPS frames this as optional.[49] CETA's approach amounts to a mandatory exception, which is rather unusual in the context of FTAs.[50] Although framed in mandatory terms, the exception is not necessarily more far-reaching than much existing law in many countries. As trademarks must be distinctive to be registered, in many jurisdictions the law does not require a specific exception to infringement in order for the principle of fair use of descriptive terms to prevail. This is because even where a registered trademark involves descriptive terms, the registration does not give exclusive use over those terms. A trademark registration for HAPPY SHOES, for example, would not give the owner exclusive rights to the use of the word "shoes" in relation to trade in shoes. Other entities can also use descriptive terms in their trademarks. In these ways, the notion of fair use of descriptive terms is part of the law governing the scope of trademark registrations that include descriptive terms. For this principle to operate, an exception is not required. In some jurisdictions there is a defence to infringement on the basis of honest practices, where the practice is use of a descriptive term.[51] Where trademarks composed of descriptive terms that have acquired distinctiveness through use (that is a secondary meaning over and above a primary descriptive meaning),

45 North American Free Trade Agreement, Canada–Mexico–US, Dec. 17, 1992, 32 ILM 289 (1993) [hereinafter NAFTA].

46 Comprehensive Economic and Trade Agreement (CETA) between Canada and the European Union, http://ec.europa.eu/trade/policy/in-focus/ceta/ceta-chapter-by-chapter/ [hereinafter CETA].

47 CETA, *supra* note 46, at art. 20.1.13.

48 Trademarks Act, RSC 1985, c. T-13, as amended (Can.). The amendments came into force on June 17, 2019. For an overview, *see The Date Is Set: June 17, 2019 – Canada's New Trademark Law Will Be in Force*, SMART & BIGGAR (Nov. 14, 2018), http://smart-biggar.ca/en/articles_detail.cfm?news_id=1491.

49 CETA, *supra* note 46, at art. 20.15 (providing "Each Party shall provide for the fair use of descriptive terms, including terms descriptive of geographical origin, as a limited exception to the rights conferred by a trademark. In determining what constitutes fair use, account shall be taken of the legitimate interests of the owner of the trademark and of third parties. Each Party may provide other limited exceptions, provided that these exceptions take account of the legitimate interests of the owner of the trademark and of third parties").

50 Mandatory exceptions have been extensively debated outside of trademark law and in particularly in the context of the development of the Marrakesh Treaty to Facilitate Access to Published Works for Persons Who Are Blind, Visually Impaired, or Otherwise Print Disabled. *See* Marrakesh Treaty to Facilitate Access to Published Works for Persons Who Are Blind, Visually Impaired, or Otherwise Print Disabled, June 27, 2013, 52 ILM 1312 (2013) [hereinafter Marrakesh Treaty]. *See also* Lionel Bently & Tanya Aplin, *Whatever Became of Global, Mandatory, Fair Use? A Case Study in Dysfunctional Pluralism, in* IS INTELLECTUAL PROPERTY PLURALISM FUNCTIONAL?, 8 (Susy Frankel ed., 2019).

51 Many common law jurisdictions have these exceptions. *See, e.g.*, Trade Marks Act 1994, c. 26, § 11(2), (UK); Trade Marks Act 1998, § 28 (Sing.); Trade Marks Act 2002, § 94 (NZ); Trade Marks Act 1968, a122 (b) and (c) (Austr.) (referring to "good faith" rather than "honest practices").

however, a guarantee of fair use of descriptive terms provides more certainty than if such guarantee is not on the face of it available and may have to be enforced via litigation.

The exclusive rights that must be available for owners of all trademarks to enjoy, required under the CPTPP and USMCA, include the equivalent of those found under the TRIPS Agreement,[52] but with the notable addition that they must extend to "subsequent geographical indications."[53] The CPTPP exceptions provision is identical to that found in TRIPS.[54] There are also requirements for well-known mark protection, which are discussed in Section III.

The consequences for domestic law will vary depending on whether such provisions are for more extensive protection than what is provided for in the TRIPS Agreement or are about something that falls outside of the coverage of the TRIPS Agreement.[55] The former are accurately described as TRIPS-plus and so any domestic laws made pursuant to the FTA obligation must because of the TRIPS obligation be applied on a national treatment basis.[56] For FTA obligations that fall outside of the TRIPS Agreement, national treatment would not apply as a consequence of the TRIPS Agreement, but it might apply under a national treatment provision in the relevant FTA.

C *Pushing Back against Increases in Protection*

In addition to negotiating the text of provisions providing for more extensive protection, FTAs and negotiations for them reveal attempts to ameliorate the effects of greater protection for trademark subject matter and rights in at least two ways. These attempts at some pushback are evident first in negotiation around the exhaustion of rights and legitimising greater parallel importing, and second in attempts to increase the protection for traditional knowledge.

FTA provisions relating to parallel importing are TRIPS-plus, as TRIPS leaves exhaustion rules as something that members may choose and frame for their own national regimes.[57] Some countries try to encourage international exhaustion and thereby also encourage more parallel importing. The leaked TTP negotiating text reveals that the encouragement of exhaustion has been directed explicitly to trademark law and parallel imports. The relevant clause from the leaked text is below and includes all of the relevant detail that shows both the countries that introduced the clause to the negotiations and those countries that opposed it:[58]

> International Exhaustion of Rights [CL/NZ/SG/VN/PE/MY/BN/AU/CA/MX propose; US/JP oppose]:
>
> The Parties are encouraged to establish international exhaustion of trademark rights. For this purpose, the registration of a trademark shall not entitle the proprietor to prohibit its use in relation to goods which have been put on the market in any country under that trademark by the proprietor or with his consent.

[52] TRIPS Agreement, *supra* note 1, at art. 16.3 and 3.

[53] CPTPP, *supra* note 11, at art. 18.20; *see also* KORUS, *supra* note 35, at art. 18.2.5.

[54] CPTPP, *supra* note 11, at art. 18.21.

[55] TRIPS Agreement, *supra* note 1, at art. 1.2 indicates the coverage of the agreement as all categories of intellectual property referred to in the agreement.

[56] TRIPS Agreement, *supra* note 1, at art. 3; *See also supra* notes 17–18; *see also* Appellate Body Report, *United States – Section 211 Omnibus Appropriations Act of 1998*, § 268, WTO Doc. WT/DS176/AB/R (adopted Jan. 2, 2002) (finding that the US law creating extra steps for non-nationals to use certain trademarks was a national treatment violation).

[57] TRIPS Agreement, *supra* note 1, at art. 6.

[58] *Secret Trans-Pacific Partnership Agreement (TPP) – IP Chapter*, art. QQ.C.11, WIKILEAKS (Nov. 13, 2013), https://wikileaks.org/tpp/ [hereinafter Leaked TTP text]. There are similar proposals regarding copyright and patents.

The United States tried to include in the TPP additional special requirements for border enforcement measures, including that border measures apply not just in relation to counterfeit goods but also "confusingly similar" trademarked goods. The relevant negotiator's note that appears in the leaked text stated, "[t]he scope of border measures in this section will be confined to counterfeit trademark goods, pirated copyright goods. The U.S. proposal for inclusion of, confusingly similar trademark goods is still under negotiation and Parties have different views on this proposal."[59]

In part, this proposal was a counter-move against widening the ambit of exhaustion and related parallel importing. Tightening borders to inspect confusingly similar marks will mean tightening borders to stop parallel imports (which may or may not involve issues of confusing similarity). The negotiating text does not reveal which proposal came first, but the timing is not crucial to understanding how these proposals were, in all probability, incompatible as a practical matter and how they will likely be in dispute in future negotiations. Particularly as in the final text of the TPP and the CPTPP neither of these proposed clauses are present.

Another conflict which has emerged because of growth in global trade, is increased misuses of traditional knowledge and the culture of developing countries and indigenous communities, in particular. As Peter Drahos and I have noted:

> The intersection of indigenous knowledge and IP comes about because of a number of factors, including the creation by indigenous people of global political networks in the second half of the twentieth century, the recognition of the economic value of indigenous knowledge and the increasing activism of developing countries around international IP rights.[60]

Around the world companies use words and symbols from these "exotic" cultures to sell products and to create trademarks. Traditional knowledge is a matter outside of the coverage of the TRIPS Agreement, in the sense that while TRIPS impacts the protection of traditional knowledge, it has no minimum standards requiring its protection.[61] As a matter outside of the TRIPS Agreement, any protection need not be on a national treatment basis unless another agreement requires it. The CPTPP includes the following relevant to traditional knowledge: "Subject to each Party's international obligations, each Party may establish appropriate measures to respect, preserve and promote traditional knowledge and traditional cultural expressions."[62] The best way to understand the relationship between this provision and trademark provisions is to examine the trade effects of well-known mark protection on small businesses and communities that may not be well-known, such as traditional knowledge holders.

III THE TRADE EFFECTS OF MORE EXTENSIVE TRADEMARK PROTECTION

A *Well-Known Marks and Global Imbalance*

The TRIPS Agreement and mega-regional FTAs (such as the CPTPP and USMCA) and some bilateral FTAs (such as AUSFTA and KORUS) require that Article 6*bis* of the Paris Convention apply *mutatis mutandis* (which means that countries may make necessary alterations to fit their

[59] *Id.* at art. QQ.H.6, Special Requirements Related to Border Enforcement, 218 Negotiators Note.

[60] Peter Drahos & Susy Frankel, *Indigenous Peoples' Innovation and Intellectual Property: The Issues*, *in* Indigenous Peoples' Innovation: Intellectual Property Pathways to Development 1–2 (Peter Drahos & Susy Frankel eds., 2012).

[61] *See generally*, Susy Frankel, *Traditional Knowledge, Indigenous Peoples, and Local Communities*, *in* The Oxford Handbook of Intellectual Property Law (Rochelle Dreyfuss & Justine Pila eds., 2018).

[62] CPTPP, *supra* note 11, at art. 29.8.

law while not affecting the main point at issue).[63] The relevant substantive obligation of the Paris Convention requires member states:

> to refuse or to cancel the registration, and to prohibit the use, of a trademark which constitutes a reproduction, an imitation, or a translation, liable to create confusion, of a mark considered by the competent authority of the country of registration or use to be *well known in that country* as being already the mark of a person entitled to the benefits of this Convention and used for identical or similar goods. These provisions shall also apply when the essential part of the mark constitutes a reproduction of any such well-known mark or an imitation liable to create confusion therewith.[64]

The Paris Convention does not define "well-known," so the first step that led to an increased level of protection for well-known marks was the TRIPS Agreement which provides: "In determining whether a trademark is well-known, Members shall take account of the knowledge of the trademark in the relevant sector of the public, including knowledge in the Member concerned which has been obtained as a result of the promotion of the trademark."[65] Providing for increased protection of trademarks is often thought of as a harmonising measure that reduces transaction costs and makes it easier for businesses to trade across borders. Indeed, this is true for many large businesses and others involved in exporting their trademarked goods and services. The implications, however, for other sizes of business (such as medium and small) is not always a reduction in transaction costs; rather it might be a creation of new barriers.

Large business interests lobby their governments to deploy FTAs to increase the level of trademark-related protection in export markets. For example, parties to the CPTPP and to USMCA have included several grounds that are framed as ways that the parties cannot refuse to provide protection for well-known marks. These grounds include that the mark must be registered in the party providing the protection; registered in another jurisdiction; or that it is given recognition as a well-known trademark.[66] Also, parties must allow for the refusal of registration of third-party well-known trademarks.[67] This last obligation presumably is to deal with situations where the owner of the so-called well-known trademark has not registered it and a local business seizes the opportunity to trade under that name or logo. In many common law jurisdictions, but not all, that sort of local business initiative may also be actionable under the tort of passing off.[68] Registration may provide greater protection in some jurisdictions where passing off is not actionable on the basis of mere reputation, but for a plaintiff to succeed there must be actual goodwill, such as local paying customers.[69] This distinction between the protection of registered and unregistered well-known marks is not apparent in many FTAs. The CPTPP, AUSFTA and KORUS, for example, all require that members provide well-known mark protection whether the mark is registered or not.[70]

63 CPTPP, *supra* note 11, at art. 18.22.2; *see also* KORUS, *supra* note 35, at art. 18.2.7.

64 Paris Convention, *supra* note 2, at art. 6*bis* (emphasis added). The relevant provisions are incorporated into the TRIPS Agreement, art. 2.1.

65 TRIPS Agreement, *supra* note 1, at art. 16.2, see Chapter 5 in this volume.

66 CPTPP, *supra* note 11, at art. 18.22.1; *see also* USMCA, *supra* note 27, at art. 20.21(1). *See also* KORUS, *supra* note 35, at art. 18.2.6.

67 CPTPP, *supra* note 11, at art. 18.22.4, USMCA, *supra* note 27, at art. 20.21(4).

68 *See, e.g.*, *Wineworths Grp. Ltd.* v. *Comite Interprofessionel du Vin de Champagne* [1992] NZLR 327 (CA).

69 In the United Kingdom, localised goodwill in the form of customers in the jurisdiction is required. *See Starbucks (HK) Ltd.* v. *British Sky Broad. Grp.* (No. 2) [2015] UKSC 31 (UK). In general, on the protection of well-known marks, see also Chapter 5 in this volume.

70 CPTPP, *supra* note 11, at art. 19.22.2; AUSFTA, *supra* note 13, at art. 17.2.6; KORUS, *supra* note 35, at art. 18.2.7.

In the CPTPP and USMCA, "well-known" is not fully defined. The members of those FTAs agree to "recognise the importance" of WIPO's Joint Recommendations Concerning Provisions on the Protection of Well-Known Marks.[71] That Joint Recommendation details criteria that are applicable to determining matters such as what is well-known.[72] Recognising the importance of the Joint Recommendation is aspirational and not a binding obligation as such, although the United States attempted but failed to negotiate it as a binding obligation in the TPP. In contrast, the Singapore–United States Agreement does require adoption of the Joint Recommendation's standards.[73]

Burton Ong has noted that not all FTAs with the United States include this enhanced well-known mark protection, but that its inclusion in the Singapore–US FTA may be particularly advantageous for US businesses, as the main language of commerce in Singapore is English.[74] As pointed out elsewhere:

> In small market economies the definition of well-known and the increased level of trade mark protection are likely to create an imbalance between such economies and larger ones. Marks which are well-known and originate from the large economies of the world are protected in small market economies, but the converse of well-known in small economies and so therefore protected in large economies is rarely likely to be true. A mark which is well-known in New Zealand, Israel or Singapore may not be well-known in the large economies such as the US and EU. Thus, size and scale creates an imbalance which the Joint Recommendation serves to exacerbate.[75]

As noted, well-known mark protection in a global setting is controversial because such protection tends to favour the multinational businesses of large and developed nations whose cultures dominate much of the globe. This problem is not just a small market economy problem; it is even true for large economies whose global presence may be limited because of language barriers. Local marks well-known in China, for example, will have a large, even though almost exclusively Chinese, audience primarily because of language barriers. Many well-known Chinese trademarks are not well-known in Europe, the Americas and the other non-Chinese-speaking

[71] *Joint Recommendation Concerning Provisions on the Protection of Well-Known Marks*, art. 2, World Intellectual Property Organization, WIPO Doc. 833(E) (Sep. 29, 1999), https://wipo.int/edocs/pubdocs/en/marks/833/pub833.pdf [hereinafter *Joint Recommendation*].

[72] *Id.* at art. 2 provides the following that are relevant to whether a mark is well-known:

1 the degree of knowledge or recognition of the mark in the relevant sector of the public;
2 the duration, extent and geographical area of any use of the mark;
3 the duration, extent and geographical area of any promotion of the mark, including advertising or publicity and the presentation, at fairs or exhibitions, of the goods and/or services to which the mark applies;
4 the duration and geographical area of any registrations, and/or any applications for registration, of the mark, to the extent that they reflect use or recognition of the mark;
5 the record of successful enforcement of rights in the mark, in particular, the extent to which the mark was recognized as well known by competent authorities;
6 the value associated with the mark.

"Relevant sector of the public" is then expansively defined so that it includes small segments of business sectors rather than a requirement for general public awareness. Joint Recommendation, *supra* note 71, at art. 3.

[73] *US–Singapore Free Trade Agreement*, Sing.–US, Enterprise Singapore (2004), https://enterprisesg.gov.sg/non-financial-assistance/for-singapore-companies/free-trade-agreements/ftas/singapore-ftas/-/media//ESG/Files/Non-Financial-Assistance/For-Companies/Free-Trade-Agreements/US-Singapore-FTA/Legal-Text/United20StatesSingapore20FTA20Legal20Text [hereinafter USSFTA].

[74] Burton Ong, *The Trade Mark Law Provisions of Bilateral Free Trade Agreements*, *in* Trade Mark Law and Theory 247 (Graeme B. Dinwoodie & Mark D. Janis eds., 2008).

[75] Susy Frankel, Test Tubes for Global Intellectual Property Issues 156 (2015).

nations of the world. The converse is, however, not necessarily true. Some American and European trademarks are well-known in many parts of the world. It is possible that this is changing over time as large developing economies grow and are becoming more globalised.

Other parts of the Joint Recommendation that address infringement suggest that trademark owners have exclusive rights against most types of dilution, including blurring, tarnishment and more generally free-riding.[76] The Joint Recommendation makes it clear that dilution includes types of dilution that are not anchored in preventing confusion and deception. This seems to be necessary to avoid the interpretation that damage caused by confusion is not just lost sales but also dilution of the reputation of the mark. This expansion and its details were not fully agreed upon when the Joint Recommendation was drafted at WIPO. While there was some kind of consensus around the definition of "well-known," that consensus was not present for the infringement-related recommendations.[77]

The asserted reason for well-known marks protection is the concern that free-riding should be limited so that "people should not reap where they have not sown, that bad faith should be punished, that people who sidle up to their well-known marks are guilty of dishonest commercial practice."[78] As Vaver points out, these are criticisms that "lead nowhere." One might as well say that the well-known mark owner is reaping where it has not sown when it stops a trader in a geographic or market field remote from the owner's fields from using the same or a similar mark uncompetitively.[79] Of course, trademark owners may not agree with this characterisation of some of their offshore activities. Unsurprisingly, those who seek to maximise exploitation of their trademarks do not focus on other effects such as the impact of global markets on new market entrants and small businesses. As explained by Greenhalgh: "there is also a conundrum in global markets, where the need for successful domestic brands to engage in worldwide competition in order to retain profits and jobs in the economy has to be balanced against the promotion of new firms within the domestic economy."[80] The recognition of protection of famous marks pivots on definitions of "well-known." If the mark is not well-known, then at first blush it seems quite justified that it should not get expanded protection, but the matter is not so simple. Why should entities be able to borrow (or indeed misappropriate) symbols and images, for example from indigenous peoples, just because in one part of the world the images appear to be exotic and not well-known (or not well-known as trademarks)? This is what large businesses often do.[81]

In fact, trademark law, and intellectual property law more broadly, encourage these sorts of extractive uses.[82] Trademark law encourages the use of symbols and words that may initially be unrelated to the products they apply to and thus they have distinctive character.[83] Consequently,

[76] Joint Recommendation, *supra* note 71, at art. 4.

[77] Dinwoodie and Dreyfuss note that the definition of well-known in the Joint Recommendation was adopted by consensus but the infringement dilution related extensions were not. *See* Dinwoodie & Dreyfuss, *supra* note 5, at 165.

[78] David Vaver, *Unconventional and Well-Known Trade Marks*, Sing. J. Legal Stud. 1, 16 (2015).

[79] *Id.*

[80] Christine Greenhalgh, Mark Rogers, Philipp Schautschick & Vania Sena, *Trade Mark Incentives, Intellectual Property Office Research Report* (2011), https://pure.mpg.de/pubman/faces/ViewItemOverviewPage.jsp?itemId=item_1351588.

[81] *See* Frankel, *supra* note 61.

[82] For a discussion of the extractive nature of intellectual property, *see* Peter Drahos, Intellectual Property, Indigenous People and their Knowledge 1–14 (2014).

[83] Something that is descriptive of the character or quality of goods cannot usually be a trademark, except where it has acquired a secondary meaning that is distinct from the descriptive meaning. The details of the law around this principle vary between jurisdictions, but the broad principle is enshrined in international intellectual property. The TRIPS Agreement, art. 15, for example, requires that "Any sign, or any combination of signs, capable of distinguishing

in international negotiations relating to intellectual property (and also biodiversity and human rights), there has been a confluence of the absence of protection of traditional knowledge and intellectual property's use of that knowledge. Trademark examples include the Lego Company borrowing Māori and other Pacifica names for its Bioncle toy range; the Ford Motor Company has used Māori insignia to decorate a vehicle so it looks "powerful"; and Sony has appropriated Pacifica images for X Box games.[84] Businesses of this scale also benefit from well-known mark protection. These examples illustrate some of the concerns that have led to the WIPO treaty negotiations for the protection of traditional knowledge.[85] Notably, the law concerning well-known trademarks (and rights of publicity where they exist) requires commercial fame, however defined. The normative underpinnings of these expansive rights are questioned by many.[86]

In contrast, traditional knowledge receives little protection and may well have stronger normative underpinnings than well-known mark protection.[87] The claims of traditional knowledge owners include concerns about impact on culture and identity.[88] These concerns perhaps strike less of a chord with those setting the norms of the international trademark regimes than do the concerns of large corporate export interests and disgruntled celebrities. The protection of traditional knowledge is, of course, not wholly a trademark matter, but it is relevant to international trademark protection and post-TRIPS mega-regional and other FTAs.[89] As standards for protection of largely western trademarks increase, those who seek a different kind of global protection for words and symbols have even greater motivation to do so. New Zealand, for example, does not intend that its FTA obligations to interfere with its ability to protect its indigenous people's rights. Accordingly, and somewhat uniquely, the CPTPP provides that "nothing in this Agreement shall preclude the adoption by New Zealand of measures it deems necessary to accord more favourable treatment to Māori in respect of matters covered by this Agreement."[90]

B More Extensive Trademark Enforcement Provisions

The TRIPS Agreement was the first multilateral intellectual property agreement to set out minimum standards relating to civil and criminal enforcement provisions.[91] For those developed countries seeking stronger enforcement provisions, the TRIPS Agreement was never enough

the goods or services of one undertaking from those of other undertakings, shall be capable of constituting a trademark .... Where signs are not inherently capable of distinguishing the relevant goods or services, Members may make registrability depend on distinctiveness acquired through use." *See also* Darrell A. Posey & Graham Dutfield, Beyond Intellectual Property 86 (Int'l. Dev. Res. Ctr., 1996) (The Quick and Easy Way to Own a Rainforest," describing The Body Shop's "rainforest" trademark).

[84] All of these examples are discussed in *Ko Aotearoa Tēnei: A Report into Claims Concerning New Zealand Law and Policy Affecting Māori Culture and Identity*, Waitangi Tribunal, ch. 1 (2011), http://waitangi-tribunal.govt.nz/news/media/wai262.asp.

[85] *See generally, Traditional Knowledge*, WIPO, https://wipo.int/tk/en.

[86] Stacey L. Dogan, Haelean Laboratories *v.* Topps Chewing Gum: *Publicity as a Legal Right, in* Intellectual Property at the Edge: The Contested Contours of IP (Rochelle Cooper Dreyfuss & Jane C. Ginsburg eds., 2014); *see also* Stacey L. Dogan, *The Right of Publicity: A Cautionary Tale from the US, in* The Internet and the Emerging Importance of New Forms of Intellectual Property (Susy Frankel & Daniel Gervais eds., 2016).

[87] *Id.*; for further discussion of the political and normative claims for the protection of traditional knowledge, *see* Frankel, *supra* note 61.

[88] Many traditional knowledge owners emphasise that they are collective owners with those who share their traditions and are guardians of the knowledge for future generations rather than owners for their own immediate gain.

[89] *See* Susy Frankel, *Trademarks and Traditional Knowledge and Cultural Intellectual Property Rights, in* Dinwoodie & Janis, *supra* note 74.

[90] CPTPP, *supra* note 11, at art. 29.6. Similar clauses are found in other New Zealand trade agreements.

[91] TRIPS Agreement, *supra* note 1, at part III.

and so post-TRIPS there have been several attempts to build on its minimum standards.[92] One of the more controversial mega-intellectual property trade-related agreements was the negotiations among New Zealand, Australia, the United States, the European Union, Canada, Switzerland and Japan to conclude an agreement addressing the enforcement of intellectual property rights. This agreement was known as the Anti-Counterfeiting Trade Agreement (ACTA) and it never came into force. For some time, the details of the negotiations and draft agreement were secret, but in 2010 the text was revealed. ACTA was widely opposed in many countries and, particularly as a result of the EU Parliament voting against its implementation, it never came into force.[93]

One of the significant features of the TRIPS Agreement is its requirement that members have enforcement procedures (both civil and criminal) in their domestic laws.[94] ACTA aimed to expand on those minimum standards for enforcement of intellectual property rights in considerably more detail than the TRIPS Agreement. The scope of, for example, criminal liability and remedies for wilful trademark infringement was an area over which there was little international agreement when the TRIPS Agreement was negotiated. The disagreement is well illustrated by the enforcement battles between the United States and China.

For a number of years the United States and China have been in discussions over enforcement of intellectual property rights in China and other trade concerns. These discussions did not initially result in an agreement about enforcement standards and the United States requested the establishment of a WTO dispute settlement panel. The panel was formed and the United States challenged China's enforcement regime in relation to both trademarks and copyright.[95] The details of the dispute are complex but, in short, the United States challenged whether China's approach of having thresholds of numbers of infringing products, which must be reached before criminal proceedings could be initiated against infringer, complied with the TRIPS Agreement. The United States was not successful in its challenge, which would have obliged China to have a different trademark enforcement regime from what it already had. This was, in part, because the provisions of the TRIPS Agreement did not expressly state the kind of specificity that the United States argued should be found in an enforcement regime. In order to resolve the issue, the WTO Panel interpreted the TRIPS requirement for criminal procedures and penalties in cases of wilful trademark counterfeiting or copyright piracy "on a commercial scale."[96] The Panel found that "commercial scale" was a matter for members to determine and, in the case of China, its authorities had the discretion to use a minimum quantitative threshold below which no prosecutions would be required. The panel provided a kind of qualification of this finding by adding that the product and market in question would need to be taken into account when setting such thresholds. On the evidence, the United States was not able to establish that China had not taken these conditions into account.[97]

ACTA existed independently of this dispute but, undoubtedly, the failure of the United States to achieve strict enforcement measures through the WTO dispute settlement process fuelled the perceived need both for ACTA and for more extensive enforcement procedures in the US's FTAs. Some increases in enforcement standards have been achieved but there have also been

[92] *See* Sell, *supra* note 5.

[93] *See Everything You Need to Know about ACTA*, European Parliament, http://europarl.europa.eu/sides/getDoc.do?type=IM-PRESS&reference=20120220FCS38611&format=XML&language=EN; *see also* Kimberlee Weatherall, *ACTA as a New Kind of International IP Lawmaking*, 26(3) Am. Univ. Int'l L.J. 839–901 (2011).

[94] TRIPS Agreement, *supra* note 1, at part III.

[95] Panel Report, *China – Measures Affecting the Protection and Enforcement of Intellectual Property Rights*, WTO DOC WT/DS362/R (adopted Jan. 26, 2009) [hereinafter Panel Report].

[96] TRIPS Agreement, *supra* note 1, at art. 61.

[97] Panel Report, *supra* note 93.

some limitations. In the TPP, there was a definition of commercial scale relating to copyright but not "wilful trademark counterfeiting" and this continues in the CPTPP.[98] Under the CPTPP such activities must be subject to criminal procedures and penalties.[99] Disagreement over intellectual property rights has continued apace between the United States and China. In early 2020 the two countries came to a deal. The agreement addresses several taademark-related issues, including enforcement at markets and bad faith trademark registrations.[100]

IV TRADEMARKS AND INVESTMENT

In addition to intellectual property chapters in FTAs, such agreements also include investment chapters that incorporate protection for intellectual property (including trademarks) as investment assets. These agreements then provide "investors" with rights against host investment states for expropriation of, and for fair and equitable treatment of, their investment assets.[101] In many FTAs, private investors have rights of private arbitration action against states in which they have invested. This is known as investor-state dispute settlement (ISDS).

Investment obligations in relation to trademarks are not particularly new, but they have only relatively recently been subject to (ISDS) in ways that raised concerns about how trademarks are treated in an investmentframework. The availability of ISDS for foreign but not local interests, more generally, has been hotly debated and calls for governments not to agree to investment obligations that include ISDS have taken place in many countries. Such objections have arisen for several reasons, including that ISDS enables private investors to bring actions against sovereign governments; that the claims are often for exorbitant sums; and the tribunals that hear the claims are not subject to any appellate review.[102]

Investment agreements include trademarks in their coverage as intellectual property features in definitions of "investment." The CPTPP, for example, provides:[103]

> investment means every asset that an investor owns or controls, directly or indirectly, that has the characteristics of an investment, including such characteristics as the commitment of capital or other resources, the expectation of gain or profit, or the assumption of risk. Forms that an investment may take include ... (f) intellectual property rights.

This definition does not explain what the necessary characteristics of an intellectual property investment, or indeed a trademark investment, are. Discussion about the characteristics of investments, more broadly than what it means in the trademark context, are found in investment cases and the rules of the arbitral organisations that hear investment disputes.[104] Although those

[98] CPTPP, *supra* note 11, at art. 18.77.1.

[99] CPTPP, *supra* note 11, at art. 18.77.2. *See also* CPTPP, art. 8.77.3 about trademarks on packaging. KORUS has even stronger enforcement provisions, *see* KORUS, *supra* note 35, at art. 18.10 and *Comparison of ACTA and KORUS FTA Internet Provisions*, INFOJUSTICE.ORG, http://infojustice.org/archives/919; *see also* USMCA, *supra* note 27, at art. 20.85.

[100] Economic and Trade Agreement between the Government of the United States of America and the Government of the People's Republic of China (Jan. 15, 2020), https://ustr.gov/countries-regions/china-mongolia-taiwan/peoples-republic-china/phase-one-trade-agreement/text.

[101] For a general discussion about the extent of the actions of expropriation and fair and equitable treatment, *see* JESWALD W. SALACUSE, THE LAW OF INVESTMENT TREATIES (2d ed. 2015).

[102] Susan D. Franck, *The Legitimacy Crisis in Investment Treaty Arbitration: Privatizing Public International Law through Inconsistent Decisions*, 73 FORDHAM L. REV. 1521 (2005); *see also* Cynthia M. Ho, *Sovereignty under Siege: Corporate Challenges to Domestic Intellectual Property Decisions*, 30 BERK. TECH. L.J. 213, 234 (2015).

[103] CPTPP, *supra* note 11, at art. 9.1.

[104] The main arbitral rules are those of either ICSTID or UNCITRAL. Investment decisions are not formally reported in one place but are often available online.

dispute do not conclude there is a definitive list of such characteristics, they do focus primarily on the principle of an economic contribution to the relevant state economy.[105] The question then arises, for the purposes of this chapter, what is a trademark-related investment?

The global system of trademark registration means that in some parts of the world there is not an economic contribution other than imports made in relation to the trademark registration. Production may be in one place where there is likely to be an investment beyond the trademark, such as making the goods or providing the service to which the trademark is applied. Where there is simply the registration of the trademark, which gives rise to certain exclusive rights for the trademark owner to control sales of imported goods, there is no economic contribution. After all, the purpose of providing trademark standards in the Paris Convention and in the TRIPS Agreement is that global protection can be achieved through the ability to register in foreign countries. Registration does not create the obligation to make the trademarked products in all jurisdictions in which the trademark is registered.[106]

The approach of simply adding intellectual property rights to the definition of an investment in investment agreements does not make intellectual property rights an actionable investment. Professor Dreyfuss and I have shown that a standalone intellectual property right should not be treated as an investment unless it is accompanied by in-state investment, as this is consistent with the goals of both intellectual property, particularly innovation incentives, and those of investment law.[107] As we noted, this approach also finds support in domestic law where, for example, Justice Brandeis in his opinion about the registrability of "Shredded Wheat," noted that the trademark right was something distinct from any financial investment in it and marketing of the product to which the trademark was applied. The trademark applicant, in that case, argued they should be entitled to registration because they had invested $17,000,000 in the descriptive mark. Brandeis said, "[t]hose facts are without legal significance."[108] If investment tribunals hearing ISDS disputes do not recognise the position at domestic law that a naked intellectual property right is not an investment, then those tribunals are progressively reconceptualising international intellectual property law and its underpinnings.[109]

Although there have been few investment disputes involving intellectual property; of the three main ones that have been fully argued and final arbitral awards made, two of them are about trademarks. [110] The first was a dispute over the regulation of trademarks on tobacco products that Philip Morris brought against the government of Uruguay.[111] The relevant impact from the trademark owner's perspective, of Uruguay's regulatory activity was to reduce the available space on the packaging for trademarks in order to emphasise and accommodate health warnings.[112]

105 *Salini Costruttori S.p.A. v. Kingdom of Morocco*, ICSID Case No. ARB/00/4, Decision on Jurisdiction, § 52 (July 23, 2001), 6 ICSID Rep. 398 (2004); *see also* Julian Davis Mortenson, *The Meaning of "Investment": ICSID's Travaux and the Domain of International Investment Law*, 51 HARV. INT'L L.J. 257, 272 n. 55 (2010); *see also* Brigitte Stern, *The Contours of the Notion of Protected Investment*, 24 ICSID REV. 534, 536 (2009).

106 This is a basic function of international trademark law and of comparative advantage, which underpins the economic rationales of the WTO and its agreements.

107 Rochelle Dreyfuss & Susy Frankel, *Reconceptualizing ISDS: When Is IP an Investment and How Much Can States Regulate It?*, 21(2) VAND. J. ENT. & TECH L., 377–415 (2018).

108 *Kellogg Co. v. Natl Biscuit Co.*, 305 US 111, 119 (1938). *See also* Rochelle Dreyfuss & Susy Frankel, *From Incentive to Commodity to Asset: How International Law Is Reconceptualizing Intellectual Property*, 36 MICH. J. INT'L. 101, 115 (2015).

109 Dreyfuss & Frankel, *supra* note 108.

110 *Philip Morris Brand Sarl (Switzerland), Philip Morris Products S.A. (Switzerland) and Abal Hermanos S.A. (Uruguay) v. Oriental Republic of Uruguay*, ICSID Case No. ARB/10/7, Final Award (July 8, 2016).

111 *Id.*

112 *See* Dreyfuss & Frankel, *supra* note 108, at 111–13.

Philip Morris had, as a matter of fact, invested in relevant local business not just the trademarks. Thus, there was less need to discuss about the characteristics of an investment than there might have been had there only been a trademark registration without any accompanying in-state economic investment.

The Tribunal stated that while the features of an investment often include matters such as in-state economic investment, that was not a mandatory legal requirement, but rather described typical features of an investment.[113] From a trademark perspective, that does not provide much guidance for future cases and the approach of the Tribunal fell short of affirmatively stating that registration alone could not amount to an investment, as the facts before it included more than mere registration.

The focus of an ISDS tribunal is on property, but not all property is identical or has the same economic characteristics or rationales for the existence of those property rights. Further, the nature and the rationales for trademarks are not just those that relate directly to property, but include, for example, avoiding consumer confusion. Registration alone should not be an investment of the kind under ISDS because it potentially gives a much greater right to trademark owners than the purposes of trademark law justifies, including its information signalling function, protecting consumers from deceptive uses and allowing for the orderly flow of trademark-related commerce.[114] As Dreyfuss and I state:

> [T]he better way to evaluate the sufficiency of an investment is through reference to article 31 of the [Vienna Convention on the Law of Treaties], which requires that a treaty term be given its ordinary meaning in context, which includes "any relevant rules of international law applicable in the relations between the parties." Under either the ordinary meaning step or via context, tribunals should refer not only to the goals of investment agreements, but also to the objectives of the relevant international IP agreements.[115]

The approach of the *Philip Morris* v. *Uruguay* Tribunal can be contrasted with the position in a later trademark-related investment dispute, *Bridgestone* v. *Panama*.[116] The *Bridgestone* Tribunal discussed the characteristics of trademarks as investments and concluded that the mere registration of a trademark is not an investment, nor are mere sales of trademarked goods.[117] The Tribunal said:

> The picture is, however, transformed if the trademark is exploited. A trademark is exploited by the manufacture, promotion and sale of goods that bear the mark. The exploitation accords to the trademark, by the activities to which the trademark is central, the characteristics of an investment. It will involve devotion of resources, both to the production of the articles sold bearing the trademark, and to the promotion and support of those sales. It is likely also to involve after-sales servicing and guarantees. This exploitation will also be beneficial to the development of the home State. The activities involved in promoting and supporting sales will benefit the host economy, as will taxation levied on sales. Furthermore, it will normally be beneficial for

[113] *See Philip Morris* v. *Uruguay*, Decision on Jurisdiction, §§ 204–10 (July 2, 2013). *See also* Julian Davis Mortenson, *The Meaning of "Investment": ICSID's Travaux and the Domain of International Investment Law*, 51 HARV. INT'L. L.J. 257, 272 (2010).

[114] For discussion of trademark function, *see* Richard A. Posner & William M. Landes, *The Economics of Trademark Law*, 78 TRADEMARK REPORTER 267 (1988); and Annette Kur, *Trademarks Function Don't They? CJEU Jurisprudence and Unfair Competition Principles*, 45 IIC 434 (2014).

[115] Dreyfuss & Frankel, *supra* note 108, at 131.

[116] *Bridgestone Licensing Servs. Inc.* v. *Republic of Pan.*, ICSID Case No. ARB/16/34, Decision on Expedited Objections, §§ 60–61 (Dec. 13, 2017).

[117] *Id.* at 171, 175–76.

> products that incorporate the features that consumers find desirable to be available to consumers in the host country.[118]

This ought to bode well for having the goals of trademark law meaningfully followed in investment-related disputes. However, as the tribunals do not bind each other and there is no appellate level, the possibility of a less trademark-purpose-focused approach remains. This might be described as the chill that more extensive investment protection causes.[119] This has also resulted in many calling for the reform of the system and using FTAs to achieve that.

In the CETA negotiations, for example, debates about ISDS caused particular concern (also in the now defunct TTIP). A case was heard before the Court of Justice of the European Union challenging the EU's competence to enter into such agreements. The challenge did not succeed.[120]

Some of the provisions in the CPTPP, which changed when the TPP transitioned to the CPTPP, relate to investment obligations, but not to the intersection of intellectual property including trademarks and investment, except in as far as they concern tobacco-related investments.[121] Under the CPTPP a party can deny the benefits of the investment chapter where the issues involve tobacco control measures.[122] And in particular, such a claim shall not be submitted to ISDS.[123]

V CONCLUDING COMMENTS

The very words "trade mark" in English and in American English "trademark" are revealing. Unlike other areas of intellectual property, the nomenclature explicitly indicates a trade-related objective. Thus, the inclusion of trademarks in the TRIPS Agreement was, in many ways, straightforward. The trade-related objective of protecting trademarks for the orderly flow of commerce is far from a hidden purpose of trademark law. It is perhaps the most obviously trade-related intellectual property right.

The inclusion of intellectual property in the WTO also infuses intellectual property with trade-related purposes. Those purposes are about providing enough protection and enforcement to protect the use of trademarks in the markets where products are sold and that includes export interests. Before the advent of the TRIPS Agreement, the GATT agreement recognised that trademarks could be used to inhibit, rather than enhance, trade and that was why GATT characterised intellectual property protection as a potential trade barrier.[124]

While the TRIPS Agreement allows the protection of intellectual property and provides a more extensive protection framework, that framework must take into account that more extensive protection has limits. Article 1.1, cited at the beginning of this chapter, shows those limits by the inclusion of the words "provided that such protection does not contravene the provisions

118 *Id.* at 172.

119 Brook K. Baker & Katrina Geddes, *The Incredible Shrinking Victory: Eli Lilly v. Canada, Success, Judicial Reversal, and Continuing Threats from Pharmaceutical ISDS*, 49 Loy. Univ. Chi. L.J. 479, 481 (2017).

120 Opinion C-1/17, pursuant to art. 218(11) TFEU, ECLI:EU:C:2019:341, http://curia.europa.eu/juris/document/document.jsf?text=&docid=213502&pageIndex=0&doclang=en&mode=req&dir=&occ=first&part=1&cid=7850026

121 *TPP Tobacco Exception Proves the New Rule in Trade*, Council on Foreign Relations Global Health Program, https://cfr.org/expert-brief/tpp-tobacco-exception-proves-new-rule-trade.

122 CPTPP, *supra* note 11, at art. 29.5.

123 *Id.*

124 General Agreement on Tariffs and Trade (GATT), art. XX(d), Oct. 30, 1947, 55 UNTS 194 (providing that intellectual property rights for "the protection of patents, trade marks and copyrights, and the prevention of deceptive practices" are an exception to GATT obligations, provided certain criteria are fulfilled).

of this Agreement."[125] Also, as the TRIPS preamble records, the parties desire that "measures and procedures to enforce intellectual property rights do not themselves become barriers to legitimate trade."

Ironically, the ever-increasing protection of trademarks through FTAs may very well distort the purpose of existing agreed international minimum standards of trademark protection. The protection of well-known marks in places where there is little, if any, trade under that trademark seems contrary to the fundamental requirement that trademarks distinguish the goods or services of actual traders. The protection of trademarks as investments, if that is construed too widely so as treat a mere registration as an investment, is another way in which increased protection does not necessarily reflect the goals of trademark law.

The use of mega-regional trade agreements (and other FTAs) to increase the standards of international trademark protection overall seems set to continue, at least until trade rules are once again primarily negotiated in a multilateral forum.

[125] TRIPS Agreement, *supra* note 1, at art. 1.1.

5

The Protection of Well-Known Marks under International Intellectual Property Law

*Frederick Mostert**

I INTRODUCTION

Advertising and the way it functions on social media platforms, such as Instagram and Facebook, is changing the way brands spend their marketing budgets away from traditional media towards social media to promote their famous and well-known marks.[1] The Internet provides increasing opportunities for us to purchase internationally famous branded goods and services. In fact, brands are usually preceded by their reputations. Branded goods or services are often pre-advertised and presold even though they are not yet physically present in the market of any particular country.[2] Against the reality of this background, there is certainly no doubt in the minds of businesspeople that the reputation and goodwill attached to their famous brands have become detached from national and local borders.[3]

Brand owners are thus confronted with the need to protect their well-known trademarks on a global basis. Such a need for protection is particularly significant if one keeps in mind that brands such as "Apple," "Google," and "Microsoft" have been estimated to be worth US$184 billion, US$141 billion, and US$80 billion respectively as intellectual property assets.[4] It is, therefore, not surprising that the appropriate protection of well-known marks has become a significant factor in the trading relations between nations. Not only are the equities and the economic concerns of trademark owners at stake, but also the international standards of fair play and comity between nations. China has reformed its intellectual property laws several times in

* Professor of Practice, The Dickson Poon School of Law, King's College London; Research Fellow, Oxford Intellectual Property Research Centre; and Research Fellow at the Research Center for Intellectual Property, Tsinghua University School of Law. This chapter is substantially drawn (with significant updates to 2018) from my book, FAMOUS AND WELL-KNOWN MARKS: AN INTERNATIONAL ANALYSIS. I wish to express my gratitude to Meagan Ryan (LLB Bond University, LLM King's College London) for her tremendously helpful research and substantial contribution to this chapter.

[1] Felix Richter, 25 *Percent of Global Ad Spend Goes to Google or Facebook*, STATISTA (Dec. 7, 2017), https://statista.com/chart/12179/google-and-facebook-share-of-ad-revenue/.

[2] *Austria Sup. Ct. May 29, 2001 Infringement on the Internet – Question of Jurisdiction – 4 Ob 110/01 – "Boss Cigarettes,* 34 INT'L REV. INTELL. PROP. & COMPETITION L. 97 (2002).

[3] Frederick Mostert, *Is Goodwill Territorial or International? Protection of the Reputation of a Famous Trade Mark Which Has Not Been Used in the Local Jurisdiction*, 12 EUR. INTELL. PROP. REV. 440 (1989). *See also* Graeme Austin, *The Story of Steele v. Bulova: Trademarks on the Line, in* INTELL. PROP. STORIES 395 (Jane C. Ginsburg & Rochelle C. Dreyfuss eds., 2006).

[4] *Best Global Brands 2017 Rankings*, INTERBRAND, https://interbrand.com/best-brands/best-global-brands/2017/ranking/.

the past decade in recognition of the importance of intellectual property in the global market.[5] Similarly, in the online sphere, social media companies[6] and e-commerce platforms such as Alibaba[7] have implemented automated systems to help users protect their intellectual property rights. The protection of the global trading system through the prevention of piracy and unfair exploitation of well-known marks has become essential.

As Professor McCarthy illustrates:

> The well-known marks doctrine is a concept that is required to be available in all nations . . . that are members of the Paris Convention. In many nations of the world, a mark is not protected from an infringing use or registration by another unless it is registered in that nation for those particular goods. . . . The well-known marks doctrine is an exception to that rule. Even in those nations, a trademark or service mark is protected if it is well-known in that nation even though the mark is not actually used or registered in that nation. One common use of the doctrine is to fight trademark pirates who rush to register a well-known mark on goods on which it has not yet been registered in a nation by the legitimate foreign owner. For example, assume hypothetically that construction equipment maker CATERPILLAR has registered its mark for construction equipment in the (hypothetical) nation of Ruritania, but not for wearing apparel. A pirate may register that mark for wearing apparel in Ruritania and then offer to sell that registration to Caterpillar Inc.[8]

Having to extend the general tenets of the law on the one hand, while dealing with conflicts of traditional principles of trademark law on the other, brings a certain provocative element to this area of law. For instance, the concept of "well-known" marks in accordance with Article 6*bis* of the Paris Convention typically provides for protection across borders against trademark pirates in "reputation-without-use" case scenarios. This often seems in contravention of the well-recognised principle of "territoriality" of trademarks. Not only has the notion of the expansion of legal principles beyond the traditional concepts of trademark law been acknowledged in international treaties and national law, but it has also become apparent in case law and in the practice of trademark professionals and lawyers throughout the world. On factual grounds though, and as a matter of evidence, whether a mark is well-known or not is a matter of fact to be assessed by the trier of fact. Classic cases, especially in the so-called reputation-without-use scenarios, would typically rely on factors such as spillover advertising via magazines or television and films, as well as tourist and business travel. But with the advent of the World Wide Web and social media, determining the factual footprint of a trademark via the Internet in the local jurisdiction has assisted the fact-finding mission significantly.

The global village does, however, provide ever-increasing temptations to locally based enterprises to trade on the reputation of globally famous trademarks. Brand-owning companies which own well-known trademarks frequently find that they have not yet been in a position to expand their business activities under those marks and have not obtained registrations for their marks in

[5] The Supreme People's Court, *Outline of the Judicial Protection of Intellectual Property in China (2016–2020)*, China Just. Observer (Apr. 20, 2017), https://chinajusticeobserver.com/outline-of-the-judicial-protection-of-intellectual-property-in-china-2016-2020.

[6] Todd Spangler, *Facebook Connects Video Copyright-Flagging System to Third-Party Tools*, Variety (Oct. 3, 2017), http://variety.com/2017/digital/news/facebook-rights-manager-copyright-videos-third-party-1202578122/; Todd Spangler, *Instagram Now Lets Content Owners Scan for and Block Copyright-Infringing Video*, Variety (Feb. 8, 2018), http://variety.com/2018/digital/news/instagram-block-copyright-infringement-video-1202692290/.

[7] Chris Dawson, *Alibaba Intellectual Property Rights Owners Day*, Tamebay (Jan. 18, 2018), https://tamebay.com/2018/01/alibaba-intellectual-property-rights-owners-day.html.

[8] J. Thomas McCarthy, McCarthy on Trade Marks and Unfair Competition § 25:61 (Thomas Reuters ed., 5th ed. 2015).

all jurisdictions. Even the most famous marks are not used everywhere, and it is not possible to register and maintain trademark registrations in all international classes in all jurisdictions. Similarly, there are often instances where the owner has filed an application to register the mark, but is caught by the lengthy official process that is involved before the mark can be registered. Meanwhile, a potential infringer may have stolen a march on the owner by being the first to use an identical mark. In the event of such a preemption, the question is simply whether the company whose mark's reputation extends to the particular country should be afforded protection, or whether the local enterprise – which intercepted the owner and first used or registered the well-known trademark in the local jurisdiction – should be permitted to do so. For instance, if Starbucks had not yet commenced business activities under its well-known service mark in Russia, should a local enterprise be allowed to file for the Starbucks trade mark in Russia?[9] Should a business in China be permitted to register or use the Fortnum & Mason's trademark with respect to tea without authorisation?[10] If Pizza Hut had not yet commenced business activities under its well-known service mark in Cyprus, should a local entity be allowed to open a Pizza Hut restaurant and sell frozen pizza pies in Cyprus?

Further considerations arising from potential infringers include whether or not the local enterprise that registers the well-known trademark without an intention to use the well-known mark, but an intention to sell the trademark back to the owner, should be permitted to do so. This type of registration is known as "bad faith" registration, and the process for invalidating or removing the registration will depend on the jurisdiction. In an example of one such infringement type case, it was found that multiple bad faith trademark applications were present when 233 "foreign well-known" trademarks were registered without authorisation in China.[11]

Consequently, for businesses that trade in the commercial trenches of the modern international marketplace, a strict adherence to the more traditional territorial concept of trademarks has become an economic concern of global proportions. In addition, it should be noted that the recognition and protection of well-known marks differ from country to country: the definitions and criteria in this area of trademark law remain elusive. Responding to the need for clarity, a list of factors that can act as guidelines for the assessment of whether a mark is well-known were laid out in the WIPO Joint Recommendations Concerning Provisions on the Protection of Well-Known Marks of 1999.[12]

It is apparent that clear guidelines and a universal approach based on common principles are required to protect well-known marks throughout the world.[13] Therefore, keeping in mind national nuances and the differences between legal systems, common principles will be explored in keeping with a harmonised global approach as to the recognition and protection of famous and well-known marks in conformity with the needs of contemporary commerce, including ecommerce. The rationale for the protection of well-known marks internationally is primarily and

[9] Andrew Kramer, *He Doesn't Make Coffee, but He Controls "Starbucks" in Russia*, New York Times (Oct. 12, 2005), https://nytimes.com/2005/10/12/business/worldbusiness/he-doesnt-make-coffee-but-he-controls-starbucks-in.html.

[10] Frederick Mostert & Gloria Wu, *The Importance of the Element of Bad Faith in International Trade Mark Law and Its Relevance Under the New Chinese Trade Mark Law Provisions*, 12 J. Intell. Prop. L. & Prac. 650 (2017).

[11] Christoph Antons & Kui Hua Wang, *Well-Known Trade Marks and Foreign Investment and Local Industry: A Comparison of China and Indonesia*, 20 Deakin L. Rev. 185, 212 (2015).

[12] World Intellectual Property Organization, Joint Recommendation Concerning Provisions on the Protection of Well-Known Marks, WIPO Doc. 833(E), art. 2 (1999), http://wipo.int/edocs/pubdocs/en/marks/833/pub833.pdf [hereinafter WIPO Joint Recommendation].

[13] Theresa Corneau & Sheila Jennings Linehan, *Such Great Names as These: Protection of Famous Trade Marks under the Canadian Trade Marks Act*, 11 Eur. Intell. Prop. Rev. 531, 535 (1995).

equally, as in trademark and unfair competition law, predicated upon the premise of consumer protection – and protecting the trademark owner's interest and fairness in competition.

II SUPRANATIONAL LAW

The law providing protection for well-known marks is rooted in Article 6*bis* of the Paris Convention and supplemented by a series of international agreements including the Agreement on Trade-Related Aspects of Intellectual Property Rights (TRIPS Agreement) and various Free Trade Agreements.

A *ius gentium*, or universal body of law, on well-known marks finds its roots in Article 6*bis* of the Paris Convention, which reads:

> (1) The *countries* of the Union *undertake*, *ex officio* if their legislation so permits, or at the request of an interested party, *to refuse or to cancel the registration, and to prohibit the use, of a trademark which constitutes a reproduction, an imitation, or a translation, liable to create confusion, of a mark considered* by the competent authority of the country of registration or use to be *well-known* in that country as being already the mark of a person entitled to the benefits of this Convention and used for identical or similar goods. These provisions shall also apply when the essential part of the mark constitutes a reproduction of any such well-known mark or an imitation liable to create confusion therewith (italics added).
>
> (2) A period of at least five years from the date of registration shall be allowed for requesting the cancellation of such a mark. The countries of the Union may provide for a period within which the prohibition of use must be requested.
>
> (3) No time limit shall be fixed for requesting the cancellation or the prohibition of the use of marks registered or used in bad faith.

The first recognition of the concept of a well-known mark is embodied in Article 6*bis*, which still serves as a basis for universal application.[14] Clear standards of infringement and legal sanction in respect of the unauthorised registration or use of a well-known mark are demarcated in Article 6*bis*. The Paris Convention does not, however, provide any definitions or criteria for establishing which trademarks qualify as well-known. Some signposts that can aid in clarifying this aspect are included in Articles 16(2) and (3) of the TRIPS Agreement, which state:

> 16(2) Article 6*bis* of the Paris Convention (1967) shall apply, *mutatis mutandis*, to services. In determining whether a trademark is well-known, Members shall take account of the knowledge of the trademark in the relevant sector of the public, including knowledge in the Member concerned which has been obtained as a result of the promotion of the trademark.
>
> 16(3) Article 6*bis* of the Paris Convention (1967) shall apply, *mutatis mutandis*, to goods or services which are not similar to those in respect of which a trademark is registered, provided that use of that trademark in relation to those goods or services would indicate a connection between those goods or services and the owner of the registered trademark and provided that the interests of the owner of the registered trademark are likely to be damaged by such use.[15]

[14] The term "well-known" was first incorporated into the Paris Convention (in the form of Article 6*bis*) as early as 1925. *See* G. H. C. Bodenhausen, ed., Guide to the Application of the Paris Convention for the Protection of Industrial Property 89 (1967).

[15] Articles 9(5) and 9(6) of the Protocol on Harmonization of Intellectual Property Norms in MERCOSUR in the Field of Trademarks, Indications of Source & Appellations of Origin also include provisions similar to those of arts. 16(2) and 16(3) of the TRIPS Agreement.

The TRIPS Agreement thus provides an important element which is to be taken into consideration in determining whether a mark is well-known. Account shall be taken of "the knowledge of the trademark in the relevant sector of the public, including ... as a result of the promotion of the trademark." In other words, awareness of the mark may be gauged by reference to the relevant universe of people in the marketplace who are exposed to the mark through advertising.[16] In addition, the TRIPS Agreement, in effect, expands the reach of Article 6*bis* and makes a legal basis available for the protection of well-known marks on non-competing goods.[17] The TRIPS Agreement, therefore, provides additional legal standards for the recognition and protection of well-known marks. It establishes where to seek evidence of such status but still leaves open the question as to what factors are to be considered in determining when a mark qualifies as well-known.

Some countries have used Free Trade Agreements (FTAs)[18] to enforce stricter intellectual property protection than required by the TRIPS Agreement (known as TRIPS plus).[19] Strict intellectual property protection has been criticised by developing countries because FTAs are seen as reducing the flexibility inherent in the TRIPS Agreement.[20] On the converse side of the argument, developed countries value intellectual property protections in FTAs, including those that try to prevent infringers in emerging economies.[21] By way of example, Article 1708(6) of the North American Free Trade Agreement (NAFTA); Articles 16.1(2)(b)(i) and 16.2(4) of the US–Singapore Free Trade Agreement;[22] Article 4(1)(a) of the US–Jordan Free Trade Agreement;[23] and Article 17.2(9) of the US–Chile Free Trade Agreement[24] contain protections of well-known marks similar to Article 6*bis* and Article 16 of the TRIPS Agreement.[25]

There has been a recent extension of "trademark" protection for trademarks which are "unconventional" or "non-traditional," such as three-dimensional shapes, colours, tastes, sounds, and smells.[26] The application of Article 6*quinquies* of the Paris Convention arguably requires that such trademarks be protected even in countries which do not allow for the registration of such marks.[27]

III THE CRITERIA: WHEN IS A MARK "FAMOUS" AND "WELL-KNOWN"?

Absolute rights are unreasonable and unrealistic.[28] This notion very much holds true for the extended protection afforded to well-known marks – the protection is very limited and has

[16] Frederick Mostert, Famous and Well-Known Marks (2d ed. 2004), at IV, nn. 94–103.

[17] *Id.* at VI.

[18] *See WIPO-Administered Treaties*, WIPO, http://wipo.int/treaties/en/.

[19] Olasupo Owoeye & Oluwabusayo Owoeye, *Intellectual Property, Access to Medicines and Universal Health Coverage through a Health Rights Lens*, 40 Eur. Intell. Prop. Rev. 49, 50 (2018).

[20] Anke Moerland, *Do Developing Countries Have a Say? Bilateral and Regional Intellectual Property Negotiations with the EU*, 48 Int'l Rev. Intell. Prop. & Competition L. 760–83 (2017); Owoeye & Owoeye, *supra* note 19.

[21] Antons & Wang, *supra* note 11.

[22] Free Trade Agreement, US–Sing., arts. 16.1(2)(b)(i) & 16.2(4), May 6, 2003, 42 ILM 1026.

[23] Free Trade Agreement, US–Jordan, art. 4(1)(a), Oct. 24, 2000, 2000 UST LEXIS 160.

[24] Free Trade Agreement, US–Chile, art. 17.2(9), June 6, 2003, 42 ILM 1026.

[25] Lee Ann W. Lockridge, *Honoring International Obligations in US Trademark Law: How the Lanham Act Protects Well-Known Foreign Marks (and Why the Second Circuit Was Wrong)*, 84 John's L. Rev. 1347 (2010). *See also* Evaristus Oshionebo, *The Protection of Famous and Well-Known Trade-Marks in the Context of Non-Competing Use: Has Canada Done Enough*, 13 Asper Rev. Int'l Bus. & Trade L. 27, 28 (2013).

[26] Qian Zhan, *The International Registration of Non-traditional Trademarks: Compliance with the TRIPS Agreement and the Paris Convention*, 16 World Trade Rev. 111–40 (2017).

[27] *Id.* at 130.

[28] Melville B. Nimmer, *Does Copyright Abridge the First Amendment Guarantees of Free Speech and Press?*, 17 UCLA L. Rev. 1180, 1184–93 (1970).

specific boundaries. In fact, this section should be prefaced with a big neon sign – "only truly 'well-known' marks need apply for special protection." Too often, the owners of marks with an ordinary reputation apply for "well-known marks" status and protection akin to the analogous situation in dilution cases. Every Tom, Dick, and Harry claims to be "well-known" or "famous" when the facts clearly do not bear this out.

Well-known marks are afforded special protection and this privileged protection is correspondingly limited to specific circumstances. The factual inquiry in each case boils down to this: has the mark in question acquired sufficient fame or well-known status among the public to warrant the extended protection to the particular territory? It is accordingly suggested that a mark is well-known if it is known to a substantial segment of the relevant public. While terms such as "substantial segment of the relevant public" cannot be defined with mathematical precision, it should be assessed in accordance with underlying tenets of trademark law: by providing such privileged protection, are consumers being protected against possible confusion, and are the owners of the specific mark being safeguarded against likely injury? It is important to avoid abuse because over-protectionism, as a blunt tool for anti-competitive behaviour, does a disservice to the public interest. Moreover, the owners of truly famous and well-known marks lose out in the long run because overzealous claims create a monster that returns to haunt all trademark owners in the inevitable curtailment of existing rights.[29]

In the interest of all trademark owners, sound judgement, balance, and common sense should prevail when formulating claims to establish well-known status. So often does one find in practice that Justice Stewart's remarks aptly apply to determine whether a mark is famous or well-known: "I know it when I see it."[30] However, should this not be the case, a careful application of the below-mentioned criteria to determine whether a specific mark is famous or well-known should serve as a useful guide.

Moreover, most well-known marks cases typically are limited to a "reproduction or imitation" of the mark usually in relation to "identical goods" – akin to counterfeiting – against the background of the Article 6*bis* framing of the benchmark for judging a conflict.

As most well-known cases involve use of imitation marks on identical goods, justified copying on the basis of "fair use" or "due cause" do not typically arise in well-known marks cases (in contrast to famous marks dilution scenarios). In principle, though, the overriding social policies fostering free speech may require newsworthy items to include depictions of well-known marks. Equally, considerations underlying commercial speech in promoting the free flow of information in respect of the price, quality, and other characteristics of products or services in order for consumers to be in the best position to make informed decisions, may also be relevant. The non-commercial use of well-known marks in literary or other artistic works including motion pictures, particularly in works such as parodies or satires, may also be justified. The freedom of speech interest in self-expression and symbolic speech requires artists to refer to real-life examples including well-known marks.

How, though, is a determination made on whether a mark is "well-known"? Sets of guidelines which can assist trademark authorities and courts in determining whether a mark is famous or well-known have emerged in regional and national legislation, case law, and trademark office procedures. For instance, section 43(c) of the US Lanham Act;[31]

[29] Mostert, *supra* note 16, at 1–42.

[30] *Jacobellis* v. *Ohio*, 378 US 184 (1964).

[31] Trademark Law Revision Act of 1988, Pub. L. No. 100-667, § 98–99 (1989) [hereinafter TLRA].

the Cartagena Agreement;[32] the Industrial Property Code of Brazil;[33] the Canadian Trade-Marks Act;[34] cases in Colombia,[35] France,[36] Mexico,[37] Peru,[38] Turkey,[39] the United Kingdom,[40] and before the European Court of Justice;[41] regulations of the Trademark Office in China[42] and Japan;[43] the WIPO Joint Recommendation Concerning Provisions on the Protection of Well-Known Marks;[44] and the Resolution of the International Trademark Association[45] all set forth factors that can serve as useful guidelines. An analysis and comparison of these guidelines points to the following common set of factors that has evolved. These factors are listed below along with the six factors which the WIPO Joint Recommendation Concerning Provisions on the Protection of Well-Known Marks sets out in Article 2(1)(b) as non-exhaustive criteria that a competent authority should consider when inferring that a mark is, or is not, well-known.

A The Distinction between Reputation and "Well-Known Marks"

Some provisions of EU law refer to "well-known marks."[46] The term is referenced in Article 6*bis* of the Paris Convention, for example. However, other provisions refer to marks with "a reputation," such as in Article 4(3) of the EU Directive.[47]

It is still unclear if there is a substantive difference between "well-known marks" and "marks with a reputation." The European Court of Justice (ECJ) has provided guidance on the latter term, holding that a trademark must "be known by a significant part of the public concerned in a substantial part of that territory" to be considered a mark with a reputation.[48] A court should be mindful of the market share of the mark; the presence of "spillover" advertising in the

[32] *Andean Community: Decision No. 344 Establishing the Common Industrial Property Regime*, WIPO (Oct. 21, 1993), http://wipo.int/wipolex/en/details.jsp?id=9454.

[33] Peter Dirk Siemsen & Rodrigo Borges Carneiro, *Brazil*, *in* MOSTERT, FAMOUS AND WELL-KNOWN MARKS, *supra* note 16, at Ch. 3, pt. V.

[34] Daniel R. Bereskin, *Canada*, *in* MOSTERT, FAMOUS AND WELL-KNOWN MARKS, *supra* note 16, at Ch. 3, pt. V.

[35] The *Nautica* case, Res. 1612 (Superintendency, Colombia, Nov. 1, 1995), *reported by* Germán Cavelier, INFOLEX (Jan. 1996).

[36] Andre R. Bertrand, *French Trade Mark Law: From the Well-Known Brand to the Famous Brand*, 4 EUR. INTELL. PROP. REV. 142, 143–44 (1993).

[37] Abraham Diaz & Adrian Martinez Olivares, *Trademarks in Mexico*, LEXOLOGY (Sept. 6, 2017), https://lexology.com/library/detail.aspx?g=c0359736-1c79-42e2-b9a5-af5391680203.

[38] Peru Trademark Office, No. 003040-96-Indecopi/Osd (May 8, 1996).

[39] *Valentino Globe B.V.* v. *Turkish Patent Inst.*, No. 1998/805-2000/457 (1st Commercial Ct. of Ankara, Oct. 12, 2000).

[40] The *Panashiba* case, Application by Balbir Singh Singhani for Panashiba in Class 9 and Opposition thereto by Shiba Electronics Ltd (Trade Marks Registry, UK, May 13, 1996).

[41] Case C-375/97, *General Motors Corporation* v. *Yplon SA*, 1999 ECR I-05421.

[42] Xuemin Chen, *China*, *in* MOSTERT, FAMOUS AND WELL-KNOWN MARKS, *supra* note 16, at Ch. 3, pt. V.

[43] Teruo Doi, *Japan*, *in* MOSTERT, FAMOUS AND WELL-KNOWN MARKS, *supra* note 16, at Ch. 3, pt. V.

[44] WIPO Joint Recommendation, *supra* note 12.

[45] International Trademark Association, *Board Resolutions Well-Known Marks Protection*, INTA (Sept. 18, 1996), http://inta.org/Advocacy/Pages/WellKnownMarksProtection.aspx.

[46] First Council Directive to Approximate the Laws of the Member States Relating to Trade Marks, No. 89/104/EEC, art. 4(2)(d) (Dec. 21, 1988) [hereinafter EU Directive]; Council Regulation on the Community Trade Mark, No. 4/94, art. 8(2)(c) (Dec. 20, 1993) [hereinafter EU Regulation]. These concern conflicting earlier rights in relation to oppositions and invalidations. Under these provisions, an "earlier right" involves a "well-known mark" in the sense of art. 6*bis*.

[47] EU Directive, *supra* note 46, at arts. 4(3), 4(4)(a) & 5(2); EU Regulation, *supra* note 46, at arts. 8(5) & 9(1)(c). These provide that marks with "a reputation" can be protected against the use or registration of similar marks for non-similar goods.

[48] Case C-375/97, *General Motors Corporation* v. *Yplon SA*, 1999 ECR I-05421.

absence of market share; the intensity, geographical extent, and duration of its use; and the level of investment made in its promotion.

B The Degree of Knowledge or Recognition of the Mark in the Relevant Sector of the Public

The best evidence to prove such recognition is probably represented by unsolicited requests from potential licensees, manufacturers, distributors, importers, retailers, and consumers of the goods or services that bear the mark. As such, it constitutes direct evidence of recognition by third parties from the relevant sector of the public.[49] A more indirect proof of recognition is available through survey evidence.[50]

The recognition of the mark lies at the core of establishing famous or well-known status and may be demonstrated by various means.[51] The following additional factors are a non-exhaustive set of guidelines that have emerged to assist with assessing the degree of recognition acquired by the mark in question.[52]

C The Duration, Extent, and Geographical Area in Which the Mark Is Used

The volume of sales and the depth of market penetration within the particular product segment should assist in proving fame.[53] In particular, the recognition of the mark as reflected in the market share of the goods or services for which the mark is used will have significant probative value.[54]

D The Duration, Extent, and Geographical Area of Promotion of the Mark, Including Advertising and Publicity Accorded to the Mark

A mark may become famous and well-known almost overnight through modern advertising and advanced technology, especially social media. More frequently, a mark will become well-known with the passage of time by dint of the continued expense of resources, time, and effort.[55] In those instances where the mark has not yet been used in the local jurisdiction, "spillover advertising" in the form of social media, web platforms, television exposure, circulation of international magazines, travel statistics of people who were probably exposed to the mark, and exhibitions to the trade and public at international trade fairs will be of importance. Advertising can expand the reputation of a famous or well-known mark not only beyond the territory in which the goods or services are actually sold but also beyond the specific goods or

[49] *See* WIPO Joint Recommendation, *supra* note 12, at art. 2(2), for example of what is meant by the relevant sector of the public.

[50] Ruth E. Annand & Helen E. Norman, Blackstone's Guide to the Trade Marks Act 31 (1994).

[51] Wolfgang Buscher, Hans Peter Kunz-Hallstein & Roberto Kunz-Hallstein, *Germany, in* Mostert, Famous and Well-Known Marks, *supra* note 16, at Ch. 3, pt. IV.E.

[52] These guidelines enumerated in Frederick Mostert, Famous and Well-Known Marks (1st ed. 1997), have now in large measure been reflected in the WIPO Joint Recommendation, *supra* note 12, at art. 2(1)(b).

[53] *See* TLRA, *supra* note 31, at 100.

[54] *See* WIPO Joint Recommendation, *supra* note 12; Memorandum from the Int'l Bureau (WIPO), Protection of Well-Known Marks: Committee of Experts on Well-Known Marks (Second Session, Geneva, Oct. 28–31, 1996) at 2 [hereinafter WIPO Memorandum on Well-Known Marks (Second Session)].

[55] *UMBRO*, No. O-112871-96 (Czech Office of Industrial Property, Oct. 6, 1998).

services in relation to which the mark is used. The more effective the advertising, the longer the shadow cast by the famous or well-known mark.

E The Duration and Geographical Area of Any Registrations, and/or Any Applications for Registration of the Mark, to the Extent That They Reflect Use or Recognition of the Mark

A mark may often have a high degree of recognition or use in one location or a lesser degree of recognition or use in a number of locations across the jurisdiction. In other words, the mark may enjoy local or regional fame and well-known status but not necessarily be recognised throughout the whole jurisdiction.[56] The ECJ has also considered the issue of well-known marks in the context of Article 4(2)(d) of the EU Directive, and set a requirement that a mark must be well-known in "a substantial part of the territory" to be considered a "well-known mark." Having a local reputation is insufficient, but the mark need not be well-known throughout the relevant territory.[57] Additionally, use of the mark not in the jurisdiction concerned but in geographic areas that are closely aligned may be particularly relevant – especially if the respective jurisdictions share the same language, are exposed to the same media, enjoy close trading relations, or are neighbouring countries.[58] In fact, not only is the local or regional exposure to the mark relevant, but the scope of the mark's reach throughout the world may also be significant. A recognised presence of the mark in the global village will often cause some spillover exposure to the mark in the local jurisdiction. Significant international recognition is bound to have an effect in the region concerned.[59]

F The Degree of Successful Enforcement and Registration of the Mark and the Degree of Recognition of the Mark by Competent Authorities

The owner's effort to enforce and register the mark worldwide could also serve as an indication of the mark's reputation. Proof of the successful enforcement of the particular mark in the relevant jurisdictions as well as the extent to which the mark has been recognised as being well-known by the appropriate authority may be useful in assessing the mark's reputation.[60]

Although the efficiency of the scope of registration as a test, insofar as it may be limited to the geographical scope of registration only, may be questioned (if it is applied pro forma and in isolation), it may nonetheless serve as a valid indicator of the expansion of a mark's reputation when applied in conjunction with evidence of enforcement, use, and advertising.[61]

G The Value Associated with the Mark

In some instances, the asset value ascribed to the mark by financial institutions could be reflective of its reputation and fame.[62]

[56] MOSTERT, *supra* note 16, at § IV, n. 118.

[57] Case C-328/06, *Alfredo Nieto Nuno* v. *Leonci Monlleo Franquet*, 2007 ECR I-10095.

[58] "WIPO Memorandum on Well-Known Marks (Second Session)," *supra* note 54, at 4–Annex.

[59] WIPO Joint Recommendation, *supra* note 12, at art. 2 (notes).

[60] Mothercare (UK) Limited *v.* Shaheen International Operations Company, 86 TRADEMARK REP. 943 (1996).

[61] *7th Court of Appeal in Civil and Commercial and Other Matters of Caracas*, 86 TRADEMARK REP. 1028 (June 12, 1996).

[62] Memorandum from the International Bureau (WIPO) Committee of Experts on Well-Known Marks, *Protection of Well-Known Marks: Results of the Study by the International Bureau and Prospects for Improvement of the Existing Situation* 36, 7–8 (Geneva, Nov. 13–16, 1995).

H The Degree of Inherent or Acquired Distinctiveness of the Mark

A high degree of acquired distinctiveness would seem to be more probative of fame than mere inherent distinctiveness. The demonstration of distinctiveness can assist in supporting a broader scope of protection for the mark on non-competing goods.[63] Insofar as the distinctiveness of the mark is dependent upon its exclusivity, such determination coincides with the next factor to be considered.

I The Degree of Exclusivity of the Mark and the Nature and Extent of Use of the Same or a Similar Mark by Third Parties

Multiple uses by several parties of the same mark is likely to indicate that wide reputation or fame does not attach to any one of them, except perhaps in a narrow field of use within a specific market. This factor will be of particular significance in a dilution action. The less exclusive a particular mark, the more unlikely that it will become even more diluted by third-party use on non-competing goods.[64]

J The Nature of the Goods or Services and the Channels of Trade for the Goods or Services That Bear the Mark

Insofar as protection on non-competing goods is concerned, the nature of the goods or services will, to a large extent, determine how large a segment of the public has been exposed to the mark.[65] If the mark circulates in multiple channels of trade, this will tend to indicate that a broad reputation among the public may be present that in turn could warrant a correspondingly wider scope of protection on non-competing goods.[66] Conversely, if the use of the mark is limited to a narrow market or specialised channel of trade, such confined use may point to a more limited scope of protection in relation to non-competing goods.[67] In other words, market-specific factors, which may tend to broaden or narrow the exposure of the consuming public to the mark, could have a bearing on the corresponding protection afforded to non-competing goods or services.[68]

K The Degree to Which the Reputation of the Mark Symbolised Quality Goods

The fact that a mark symbolises a specific quality may be particularly relevant in dilution cases where "tarnishing" is involved.[69]

[63] TLRA, *supra* note 31, at 100.

[64] Eastman Photographic Materials Co. Ltd v. John Griffiths Cycle Corp. Ltd, 15 Rep. Patent, Design & Trade Mark Cases 105 (1898). *Cf. Quality Inns Int'l* v. *McDonalds Corp.*, 695 F. Supp. 198 (D. Md. 1988), where McDonald's was able to prevent the registration of "McSleep Inn" for low-range, simple and standard accommodation on the basis that McDonald's was "entitled to enforce its family of marks that are characterised by the combination of the prefix 'Mc' with a generic word."

[65] *See* Mostert, *supra* note 16, at n. 96.

[66] *See* TLRA, *supra* note 31, at 101.

[67] Miles J. Alexander & Michael K. Heilbronner, *Dilution under Section 43(c) of the Lanham Act*, 59 Law & Contemp. Probs. 93, 111 (1996).

[68] *Id.* at 112.

[69] Mostert, *supra* note 16, at § VI, n. 244. In German law, for instance, "Wertschatzung" or the repute, esteem, and positive association that a mark enjoys among consumers, is taken into account in a dilution action. *See* Jurgen Ernst-Moll, *Die beruhmte und die bekannte Marke*, GRUR 8, 11 (1993); Baumbach/Hefermehl, *Warenzeichenrecht und Internationales Wettbewerbs- und Zeichenrecht* 982 (1985).

In the practical application of these criteria, the various factors can be assessed along the following lines. Whether a mark is famous or well-known or not is a question of fact. A case-by-case approach should be adopted as each case will depend upon its own special circumstances. The variances between industries, product and service sectors, as well as the complexity of the extended international marketplace require a list of factors to be considered. It is unlikely that any one of them will be determinative. The circumstances of a given case may dictate that a certain group of factors may be more important for consideration than others. Strong evidence in respect to some factors may, for instance, compensate for a weak showing with respect to other factors.

In sum, the overall picture that emerges from the totality of the evidence will determine whether a mark is considered famous or well-known in the marketplace. The probative value of the evidence presented by either side on each of these factors, which are susceptible to evidentiary disputes, will depend on the quality and quantity offered to the factfinder.[70] The abovementioned criteria accordingly contain a non-exhaustive list of significant factors which serves as a guideline in the application of Article 6*bis* of the Paris Convention, Article 16(2) and (3) of the TRIPS Agreement, and their corresponding provisions in national law.

IV REGISTERS OF WELL-KNOWN MARKS

Some jurisdictions, such as Armenia, Belarus, Brazil, Finland, India, Mexico, Russia, Turkey, and Ukraine, have introduced national registers for well-known marks.[71] The creation of these registries is an interesting development, and there are both advantages and disadvantages to maintaining national well-known trademark registers.

The Brazilian National Institute of Industrial Property (INPI) examines and determines applications for when a mark is famous.[72] The current legislation was introduced in March 2015 and relies on survey evidence of the mark's reputation to the Brazilian general public. The first mark recognised as renowned was Volkswagen's FUSCA.[73] A mark does not have to be internationally renowned to be recognised by the INPI as a famous mark.[74] Prior to the current legislation, Brazil had a system of recognising famous marks when a trademark dispute arose and where the marks were proven to be notorious within Brazil.[75]

China does not maintain a register of well-known trademarks per se. Instead, when a trademark dispute occurs, trademark owners may apply under Article 14 of the Trademark Law of the People's Republic of China for recognition of well-known status.[76] Hermes has brought a number of actions in China seeking recognition as a well-known mark.[77] In the case of *Hermes* v. *Dafeng*, the Beijing High Court considered whether or not the trademark "Hermes" and its Chinese translation were well-known trademarks in 1995, the year that the

[70] Alexander & Heilbronner, *supra* note 67, at 104–14.

[71] INT'L TRADEMARK ASS'N, https://inta.org.

[72] Ana Lucia de Sousa Borda, *Brazil: Highly Renowned Status Granted to Trademark FUSCA*, INTA BULLETIN 70(9) (May 15, 2015).

[73] *Id.*

[74] Guilherme de Mattos Abrantes, *Brazil: INPI Grants Famous Status to VIVO in Controversial Decision*, INTA BULLETIN 72(4) (Mar. 1, 2017).

[75] Peter Dirk Siemsen & Rodrigo Borges Carneiro, *Brazil*, *in* MOSTERT, FAMOUS AND WELL-KNOWN MARKS, *supra* note 16, at Ch. 3, pt. V.

[76] Haochen Sun, *Hermes in the Lost (Luxury) Paradise: How to Secure Enhanced Well-Known Trademark Protection in China*, 38(2) EUR. INTELL. PROP. REV. 104 (2016).

[77] *Id.* at 101–8.

Chinese defendant, Dafeng, registered the Chinese translation of "Hermes" as a trademark.[78] Hermes was unable to produce sufficient evidence to show "Hermes" and its Chinese translation were well-known in mainland China at the time.[79] However in *Hermes* v. *Hermes-Epitek*, the Beijing High Court found that "Hermes" was a well-known trademark at the relevant time, 2004, and there was sufficient evidence of the mark being well-known in mainland China.[80]

In addition to recognising foreign well-known marks which have been proven to be well-known in China, some provinces in China have also recognised certain domestic trademarks as having acquired status as a well-known mark.[81] The determination of whether a mark is well-known led to unfair competition issues in some provinces in China.[82] The competitive advantage associated with being recognised as a well-known trademark also led some local governments to pay companies incentives for becoming well-known.[83] These factors have led to reports of cases where facts of trademark infringement cases were falsified in order for a mark to be declared well-known[84] and filing of trademark applications by third parties in bad faith.[85] Under previous versions of the Trademark Law of the People's Republic of China (2001), a list of well-known marks was published.[86] To address the issues arising from the elevated status of "well-known trademarks," the 2014 amendments to the Trademark Law of the People's Republic of China introduced a prohibition on using the words "well-known trademark" in advertising of goods or services[87] as well as the discontinuance of publishing a list of well-known marks.[88]

In Armenia, the Intellectual Property Agency maintains a list of Well-Known Trademarks.[89] This list currently contains fifty-nine marks, some of which are registered in Armenian using Armenian script whilst others are registered in English using the English alphabet.[90] The National Board of Patents and Registration of Finland maintain a List of Trademarks with a Reputation, as defined under section 6(2) of the Finnish Trademarks Act.[91] This List was introduced in June 2007 and is available at a charge to the public.[92]

The Indian register of well-known marks is maintained by the Indian Intellectual Property Office and contains eighty-one marks including Google, Sony, and Vogue.[93]

78 *Id.*
79 *Id.*
80 *Id.*
81 Paul Kossof, *Chinese National Well-Known Trademarks and Local Famous Trademarks in Light of the 2013 Trademark Law: Status, Effect and Adequacy*, 13 J. Marshall Rev. Intell. Prop. L. [vii] 244 (2013).
82 Antons & Wang, *supra* note 11, at 214.
83 *Id.*
84 Ai Guo Zhang, *The Judicial Determination and Protection of Well-Known Marks in China in the 21st Century*, 48 Univ. Louisville L. Rev. 959, 965 (2010) (citing *Kanwan Fine Chemical Industry Co. Ltd* v. *Li Chaofang*, No. 3 Civil Opinion (Xuancheng City Interim People's Ct. 2006); Antons & Wang, *supra* note 11, at 215.
85 Weijun Zhang, Lizhou Wei & Yanbing Li, *The Third Revision of Chinese Trademark Law – Analysis and Comment*, 45(5) Int'l Rev. Intell. Prop. & Competition L. 556–86 (2014).
86 Kaiyu Xiao, Clause Barrett Christiansen & Matthew J. Elsmore, *The New Legal Framework for Acquiring Well-Known Status in China: Signalling a More Coherent Phase of Enhanced Trade Mark Protection?*, 48(3) Int'l Rev. Intell. Prop. & Competition L. 305–30 (2017).
87 *Id.* at 312.
88 *Id.* at 305–30.
89 Ministry of Economic Development and Investments of the Republic of Armenia, *Intellectual Property Agency: Well-Known Trademarks*, Intell. Prop. Agency, http://aipa.am/en/well-tm/.
90 *Id.*
91 *List of Trademarks with a Reputation*, Finnish Patent & Registration Off., https://prh.fi/en/tavaramerkit/tavaramerkkitietokannat/ltm_tietokanta.html.
92 *Id.*
93 *Well-Known Marks*, Intell. Prop. India, http://ipindiaonline.gov.in/tmrpublicsearch/wellknownmarks.aspx.

The Russian well-known marks register contains 191 registrations.[94] These registrations include word marks in Cyrillic.[95] Extensive evidence of the intensive use of a mark, such as survey evidence, is required to obtain registration on the well-known marks register.[96] Russia has a specialised IP Court, the Intellectual Property Rights Court, which was introduced in July 2013.[97]

Turkey has a register for well-known trademarks maintained by the Turkish Patent Institute.[98] This register has more than 600 registrations.[99] Interesting features of registration on Turkey's Well-Known Trademarks Register include that registration is via application by the trademark owner, assessment is based on evidence that certain criteria are met, the criteria is based on the WIPO Joint Recommendation on Protection of Well-Known Marks' criteria, registration is permanent and not subject to renewal, and registration may be used as evidence in court proceedings of a trademark's reputation but is not indisputable evidence.[100]

Advantages of national well-known marks registers is that there is a centralised reference point of well-known marks which should reduce conflicts at the initial filing stage between potential trademark squatters and the actual owners of the mark. Registers create certainty. Registers may also serve an evidentiary function in trademark infringement actions by replacing the need to collect evidence that the mark is famous in the relevant jurisdiction. This is compared to nations that do not have registers of well-known marks which instead rely on determinations that a mark is well-known. For example, the State Intellectual Property Office of the People's Republic of China (PRC) does not maintain a register of well-known marks; however, it may make individual case determinations that a mark is a famous mark.[101]

Potential disadvantages of national well-known marks registers include that these registers need to be appropriately maintained and that there is a divergence between national registers of well-known marks as to what qualifies for registration as a well-known mark. Other potential disadvantages include the need for the jurisdiction with the register to have a sufficient system of administrative review as the decision to register a mark on such a register is an administrative function which may not be subject to appeal before a court. Further, given the relative ease of brands to become well-known via social media or on the web, and the short time frame associated with the accession or descension of brands as well-known, registers of well-known marks must be subject to periodic review as they will otherwise quickly become outdated.[102] The registries essentially represent a snapshot in time on whether a mark is well-known or not.

[94] *Latest News*, FED. INST. INDUS. PROP., http://fips.ru/wps/wcm/connect/content_en/en/main/.

[95] Irina Filippova & Petr Filippov, *How to Protect Well-Known Marks in Russia*, 241 MANAGING INTELL. PROP. 48 (2014).

[96] *Id.*

[97] Tatiana Petrova, *Russia: Specialized IP Court Now Functioning*, INTA BULLETIN 68(14) (Aug. 1, 2013).

[98] Isik Ozdogan, *Turkey: Requirements for Registering a Well-Known Mark*, INTA BULLETIN 60(6) (Mar. 15, 2005).

[99] Ersin Dereligil, *The System for Well-Known Marks in Turkey*, WORLD TRADEMARK REV. (June/July 2014), http://worldtrademarkreview.com/Magazine/Issue/49/Country-correspondents/Turkey-Destek-Patent-Inc.

[100] Daniel Matthews & Mine Guner, *Turkey: Turkey's Well-Known Trademarks Registry*, MONDAQ (Jan. 16, 2015), http://mondaq.com/turkey/x/367076/Trademark/Turkeys+WellKnown+Trademarks+Registry.

[101] Clark W. Lackert & Maren C. Perry, *Global: Protecting Well-Known and Famous Marks: A Global Perspective*, KING SPALDING LLP (2008), http://buildingipvalue.com/08_global/63-66KingSpalding.pdf.

[102] Peter Dirk Siemsen & Rodrigo Borges Carneiro, *Brazil*, *in* MOSTERT, FAMOUS AND WELL-KNOWN MARKS, *supra* note 16, at Ch. 3, pt. V.

V PROTECTION OF FAMOUS AND WELL-KNOWN MARKS AND THE ELEMENT OF BAD FAITH

A *Bad Faith and Problems Arising from the Growth of Social Media*

Social media platforms have amplified the challenges at present in protecting well-known marks over and above the already existing issues encountered in respect to online marketplaces. These challenges include the use of famous and well-known marks for social media accounts, hashtags, and ad words, as well as in relation to counterfeit goods. In response to these challenges, the outsourcing of management of intellectual property rights, particularly in relation to infringement on social media, is an expanding industry.[103] The sheer volume and capacity for trademark infringement on social media platforms requires increasingly innovative solutions for identifying, preventing, and removing infringing content. For example, in one year, 22,500 videos on YouTube were reported as containing IP infringements,[104] and more than 13,000 complaints were made about infringing content on WeChat.[105]

Some of the factors which enable bad actors to facilitate the sale of illegal content online, including selling counterfeit goods, is the ease of access in social media, anonymity on the Internet, the lack of verification of social media accounts, and the ability to buy products immediately.[106] A further factor contributing to the online sale of counterfeit goods is the normalisation of counterfeit goods amongst social media users.[107]

Commentators have made several suggestions for trademark reform to reduce bad faith registrations; these are starting to see consideration and traction in some jurisdictions. Such reform ideas include the following five suggested reforms:

1 Recognizing bad faith as an independent ground for the refusal, opposition and revocation of a trade mark;
2 Incorporating an element of bad faith [into the relevant national trade mark law];
3 Allowing for default judgment in trade mark opposition and repeal proceedings;
4 Reversing the balance of proof in certain trade mark cases;
5 Establishing a blacklist of parties known to register trade marks in bad faith.[108]

As Bodenhausen indicates: "Bad faith will normally exist when the person who registers or uses the conflicting mark knew of the well-known mark and presumably intended to profit from the possible confusion between that mark and the one he has registered or used."[109] Bad faith as a subjective state of mind presents inherent evidential challenges: it will more often than not have to be inferred from the circumstantial evidence than be proven by direct evidence. One way of relying on these provisions is to argue that the mark in question has become so well-known that it is inconceivable that an applicant was unaware of the mark and that there is a likelihood

[103] *See, e.g.*, BRANDBASTION, https://brandbastion.com/; MARKMONITOR, https://markmonitor.com/.

[104] *Case Study: How a Global Gaming Company Fights IP Infringement on Youtube*, BRANDBASTION, https://blog.brandbastion.com/hubfs/IP%20Bastion%20-%20How%20a%20global%20gaming%20company%20fights%20IP%20infringements%20on%20Youtube.pdf.

[105] He Fang, *How to Prevent Copyright Infringement: Four Things You Shouldn't Do on an Enterprise Social Media Account in China*, KMW (July 19, 2017), http://kwm.com/en/cn/knowledge/insights/attention-to-those-infringement-traps-on-social-media-20170719#id-here.

[106] Jenny Wolfram, BrandBastion, Lecture at King's College London (Dec. 13, 2017).

[107] *Id.*

[108] Mostert & Wu, *supra* note 10, at 650–59.

[109] BODENHAUSEN, *supra* note 14, at 97.

that confusion or association might ensue from adopting a similar mark. An inference may, therefore, be drawn in such instances that the defendant acted with the intent to trade upon the reputation of a famous or well-known mark by adopting an identical mark.

In countries such as China, where a common "business irritant" is bad-faith in trademark applications,[110] a blacklist could work well to reduce such practice. The "blacklist" concept would complement national legislation and would contain a list of applicants who have been found in trademark infringement actions to have registered a mark in bad faith.[111] The list could then be used to reverse the onus of proof.[112]

The concept of increased online platform responsibility for illegality online has been detailed by the European Commission in a 2017 communication titled "Tackling Illegal Content Online: Towards an Enhanced Responsibility of Online Platforms."[113] This communication encourages online platforms to make use of technology to automatically detect and filter content, to use "trusted flaggers" who identify illegal content for removal, and to "take measures which dissuade users from repeatedly uploading illegal content of the same nature and aim to effectively disrupt the dissemination of such illegal content."[114]

B The Element of Bad Faith in Proceedings for the Refusal of an Application or for the Cancellation of Registration and for Injunctive Relief

It is important to note that Article 6*bis*(3) of the Paris Convention specifically stipulates that there shall be no time limit on cancelling a mark that has been registered in bad faith. As Bodenhausen indicates: "Bad faith will normally exist when the person who registers or uses the conflicting mark knew of the well-known mark and presumably intended to profit from the possible confusion between that mark and the one he has registered or used."[115]

Bad faith as a subjective state of mind will more often than not have to be inferred from the circumstantial evidence than be proven by direct evidence. In foreseeing this possibility, the Mercosur Protocol, for instance, specifically contains a provision not only for cancelling trademark registrations that were obtained in bad faith, but also for refusing applications when "the applicant evidently could not claim ignorance of (a mark) as belonging to an owner established or domiciled in any of the Member States and likely to cause therewith confusion or association."[116] One way of relying on these provisions is to argue that the mark in question has become so well-known that it is inconceivable that an applicant was unaware of the mark and that there is a likelihood that confusion or association might ensue from adopting a similar mark.[117] An inference may, therefore, be drawn in such instances that the defendant acted with the intent to trade upon the reputation of a famous or well-known mark by adopting a similar mark.

[110] UK Intellectual Property Office, *Bad-Faith Trade Marks in China*, UKIPO (Sept. 2017), https://gov.uk/government/uploads/system/uploads/attachment_data/file/645337/Bad-faith_Trade_Marks_in_China_factsheet_-_Sep_2017.pdf.

[111] Mostert & Wu, *supra* note 10.

[112] *Id.*

[113] European Commission, Communication from the Commission to the European Parliament, the Council, the European Economic and Social Committee and the Committee of the Regions, *Tackling Illegal Content Online: Towards an Enhanced Responsibility of Online Platforms*, COM(2017) 555 final (Brussels, Sept. 28, 2017).

[114] *Id.*

[115] Bodenhausen, *supra* note 14, at 93.

[116] Mercosur Protocol, art. 9(4), http://ipiba.org/1403-2/.

[117] Industria De Diseno Textile SA *v.* Oriental Cuisines Pvt Ltd and Ors, INTA Bulletin (Sept. 1, 2015).

Equally, during proceedings for injunctive relief the courts will, under the "balance of convenience test," usually examine not only such factors as the damage that may result from the likelihood of confusion or dilution but also the presence of bad faith.[118] Judges are frequently confronted with the relevance of the element of "bad faith" in weighing the equities under the "balance of convenience test." What role should the factor of bad faith play in determining which of the two parties has the better right to the mark,[119] i.e., the owner of the well-known mark who wishes to extend its business under its mark to a particular jurisdiction, or the local "enterprising entrepreneur" who intercepted the owner by first using or registering a similar mark?

C The Element of Bad Faith

Predatory intent or bad faith refers to the intent of the defendant to trade upon the reputation of a famous or well-known mark by adopting a similar mark.[120]

Although the presence of bad faith may constitute an important factor in weighing the competing interests of the parties concerned, this concept should be distinguished from the presence of bad faith as a requirement in an action for trademark infringement, passing-off, or unfair competition. The better view is that bad faith should not be required to establish infringement under either the likelihood of confusion or likelihood of dilution standards.[121]

The significance of bad faith in weighing the competing interests of the parties concerned was eloquently described in the landmark *Orkin* decision[122] in Canada. In this case, an action for passing-off was brought against the background of a reputation-without-use situation. The plaintiff had established a well-known business under the "Orkin" mark in the United States for pest-control services. After the defendant commenced using the "Orkin" mark in Ontario in relation to identical services, the plaintiff sought injunctive relief. Justice Morden approached the matter by weighing the "affected interests." According to the judge, these include the defendant's and the public's interests in the absence of unreasonable restraints on freedom of trade, the plaintiff's right to the protection of its valuable name, and the right of the community to be protected against deception.[123] The judge opined that the possibility of Orkin having a monopoly in Ontario on its name and distinctive logo was considerably less troubling than the deceptive use of its name and symbol by another.[124] He went on to place strong emphasis on the defendant's bad faith and indicated that although bad faith alone will not convey a cause of action to a foreign plaintiff, it is a relevant factor that should be taken into account when weighing competing interests. He concluded that "the public are entitled to be protected from such deliberate deception and Orkin, which has laboured long and hard and made substantial expenditures to create the reputation which it now has … is entitled to the protection of its name from misappropriation."[125]

118 *O Kavli AS* v. *Synnove Finden ASA*, Lovdata LB-2000-02398 (Norwegian Appeal Court Borgarting Lagmannsrett, Aug. 24, 2000).

119 Report of the First Session of WIPO's Committee of Experts (Geneva, Nov. 13–16, 1995), 14, § 61; *id.* at 15, § 69; *id.* at 16, § 73.

120 *Person's Co. Ltd* v. *Christman*, 900 F.2d 1565, 1569–70, 14 USPQ2d 1477 (Fed. Cir. 1990), *aff'g* 9 USPQ2d 1477, 1480 (TTAB 1988), *on reconsid.* 10 USPQ2d 1634 (TTAB 1989).

121 Alexander and Heilbronner, *supra* note 67, at 114.

122 *Orkin Exterminating Co. Inc.* v. *Pestco Co. of Canada Ltd*, 50 OR (2d) 726, 19 DLR (4th) 90, 5 CPR (3d) 433 (Ont CA) (1985).

123 *Id.* at 447–8.

124 *Id.* at 448.

125 *Id.*

In contrast to *Orkin*, the United States Court of Appeals for the Second Circuit emphasised in the *Bukhara Grill* case the principle of territoriality and the requirement of domestic use over bad faith for a mark to enjoy protection under US trademark law.[126] The Court held that "absent some use of its mark in the United States, a foreign mark holder generally may not assert priority rights under federal law, even if a United States competitor has knowingly appropriated that mark for his own use."[127]

In contrast, in the *Ten-Ichi* case[128] in Hong Kong, the court expressed the following sentiments about the presence of bad faith:

> All the plaintiffs wish to do is to exploit their legitimate business interests which have been accumulated over the years and which have achieved a high standard of international reputation. They therefore would be prevented from opening a restaurant here apparently on the basis that the defendants have quite deliberately stolen their name and their description; in my judgement, it defies common sense for me to say that the genuine interest of the plaintiff should be prejudiced in that way.[129]

The element of bad faith was also considered to be a significant factor in court decisions in jurisdictions such as the Benelux,[130] Brazil,[131] France,[132] Germany,[133] Hong Kong,[134] India,[135] Israel,[136] Peru,[137] Singapore,[138] the United Kingdom,[139] Venezuela,[140], Zimbabwe,[141] and Turkey.[142] In recent decisions in China, "bad faith" has been indirectly considered in the application of the current Trademark Law of the People's Republic of China for consistency with international trademark norms.[143] Furthermore, bad faith registration and use of another's earlier trade or service mark as a domain name are necessary factors that must be shown before a domain name will be cancelled, transferred, or changed under the Universal Domain Name Dispute Resolution Policy.[144]

[126] *ITC Ltd* v. *Punchgini, Inc.*, 482 F.3d 135, 155 (2d Cir. 2007).

[127] *See also Person's Co.* v. *Christman*, 900 F.2d 1565, 1569–70 (1990) (holding that foreign use is not sufficient to establish priority rights even over a US competitor who took the mark in bad faith).

[128] *Ten-Ichi Co. Ltd* v. *Jancar Ltd*, FSR 151 (1990), 2 HKC 330 (1989).

[129] *Id.* at 157–8.

[130] *Ben & Jerry* (The Hague District Court, Sept. 20, 1995), *reported in* INTA BULLETIN (Feb. 12, 1996), at 4.

[131] *Uno a Erre Italia Spa* v. *the INPI AC*, Judicial Register DJ-II (Mar. 19, 1991), at 19304.

[132] *Corona* (Bordeaux Court of Appeal, Feb. 28, 1994); *Aldi Marche* (Caen Court of Appeal, Jan. 4, 1990).

[133] *Dimple*, GRUR 550 (1985), 17 INT'L REV. INTELL. PROP. & COMPETITION L. 271 (1986) (German Federal Supreme Court, Nov. 29, 1984).

[134] *Re Omega*, 2 HKC 473, 478–79 (Hong Kong High Court, Apr. 21, 1995).

[135] *N.R. Dongre* v. *Whirlpool Corp.*, 300 AIR Delhi 38 (Civil Appellate Jurisdiction, High Court of Delhi, Mar. 21, 1995) (affirmed by the Supreme Court of India, Aug. 30, 1996).

[136] *City Central Ltd* v. *Chanel* (French Société Anonyme) (Tel Aviv–Jaffa District Court, Feb. 7, 1995).

[137] *Reebok*, No. 003040-96-Indeco-pi/Osd (Peru Trademark Office, May 8, 1996).

[138] *RH Macy & Co. Inc.* v. *Trade Accents*, 1 SLR 581 (Singapore High Court, June 27, 1991).

[139] *Harrods Ltd* v. *R. Harrod Ltd*, 41 REP. PATENT, DESIGN & TRADE MARK CASES 74 (1924); *John Walker & Sons Ltd* v. *Henry Ost & Co. Ltd*, 1970 REP. PATENT, DESIGN & TRADE MARK CASES 489 (1970).

[140] *Galerias Lafayette SA* (Supreme Court of Justice, Venezuela, Mar. 10, 1994).

[141] *Marks and Spencer (Southern Rhodesia) Ltd* v. *Greaterman Stores (Rhodesia) Ltd* (Patents Tribunal for the Federation of Rhodesia and Nyasaland, Aug. 16, 1961).

[142] Bestway Inflatables & Material Corp. Inc. *v.* Burak Ithalat ve Ihracat dis Ticared Ltd Sti, 2012 EUR. TRADE MARK REP. 28 (Asliye Hukuk Mahkemesi Turkey, Nov. 15, 2011).

[143] Yang Yang, *Comment on "Haitang Bay": Has the Law Provided for Full Protection against Trade Mark Registrations in Bad Faith? An Interpretation of the Supreme People's Court of China in Li v. Trademark Review and Adjudication Board*, 46(4) INT'L REV. INTELL. PROP. & COMPETITION L. 491, 497 (2015).

[144] *See* MOSTERT, *supra* note 16, § VI, 2.

As Professor McCarthy notes in a similar context of trademark law, where there is hard evidence present of the defendant's intent to obtain a free ride on the coattails of the plaintiff's reputation, courts will not refrain from highlighting the underlying equities:

> Even though actual copying or intent to ride on another's good will and reputation is not necessary, its presence may turn the scales in a close case. Obviously, a judge is less inclined to leniency for an infringer who knew well what he was doing than he would be for an alleged infringer who acted innocently, albeit foolishly or negligently.[145]

McCarthy proceeds to refer to the following dictum: "Where as here it plainly appears that there is a purpose to reap where one has not sown, to gather where one has not planted, to build upon the work and reputation of another, the use of the advertising or trade name or distinguishing mark of another, is in its nature fraudulent and will be enjoined."[146]

How does one prove the presence of an intent to trade on the reputation of a famous or well-known mark? Because intent is a subjective state of mind, it will more likely be inferred from circumstantial evidence than shown by direct evidence.[147]

Direct evidence may, nonetheless, be present in some instances by way of prior written or oral statements by the defendant or in the form of instructions given by the defendant to a designer or printer.

Such direct evidence is normally not readily available,[148] so intent is usually inferred from the conduct of the defendant. Circumstantial evidence upon which the courts have tended to focus includes the access the defendant had to the famous or well-known mark or the substantial similarity between the well-known mark and defendant's mark.[149]

In circumstances where the defendant knew or clearly must have known of the famous or well-known mark,[150] and/or where there is a substantial similarity between the plaintiff's and defendant's respective marks,[151] a wrongful intent should easily be inferred. The inference drawn from such circumstances is even more compelling when the defendant had the freedom to choose from a wide variety of other possible marks but "'just happened' to choose a mark confusingly similar to plaintiff's mark."[152] For instance, the adoption of a foreign-language word in the local jurisdiction that happens to be identical to a foreign well-known mark will require some explanation.[153] Accordingly, many brands entering a foreign market seek to register the brand in roman characters and in the foreign country's native characters.[154] However, even where the trademark includes local-language words or characters, there may still be infringement of a trademark if the registration was not by the owner of the original trademark in roman

[145] McCarthy, *supra* note 8, at § 23:110.

[146] *Aetna Casualty & Surety Co.* v. *Aetna Auto Finance Inc.*, 123 F.2d 582, 584, 51 USPQ 435, 437–38 (5th Cir. 1941), *cert. denied*, 315 US 824, 62 S. Ct. 917, 86 L. Ed. 1220, 52 USPQ 644 (1942).

[147] *See generally*, James A. Carney, *Setting Sights on Trademark Piracy: The Need for Greater Protection against Imitation of Foreign Trademarks*, 81 Trademark Rep. 30, 41 (1991); *id.* at 55–56.

[148] *Id.*

[149] Team Lotus Ventures Ltd's Application; Opposition of Group Lotus Ltd, 1999 Eur. Trade Mark Rep. 669 (UK Trade Marks Registry, Oct. 23, 1998).

[150] McCarthy, *supra* note 8, at § 23:115.

[151] Carney, *supra* note 148, at 55; McCarthy, *supra* note 8, at § 23:119.

[152] McCarthy, *supra* note 8, at § 23:115.

[153] *Apple Computer Inc.* v. *Apple Leasing & Industries*, 1992(1) Arbitration L. Rep. 93, 128 (Delhi High Court, May 4, 1991).

[154] Win Yan Lam, *Chinese Character Marks in the Eyes of the European Public*, 39(12) Eur. Intell. Prop. Rev. 764 (2017).

characters, as was considered in the *Michael Jordan* case.[155] Wrongful intent is also particularly apparent when the defendant's explanation of why it chose a mark that is very similar to the famous or well-known mark defies all credulity–the elaborate epics one so often encounters in practice.[156] In essence, if the defendant's adaptation of a mark similar to the famous or well-known mark is not merely "coincidental," predatory intent should be proven.

The "coincidental" adoption by a defendant of inherently distinctive marks which are arbitrary, fanciful, or coined such as, for example, "Google," "Viagra," or "Pepsi" is almost always without credibility.[157] The evidence may be equally compelling when it is shown that other truly distinctive elements, such as unique devices, original stylistic script, foreign-language words, or unique colour combinations, design features, and shapes were copied.[158] The same principle applies to marks that are not inherently distinctive but have acquired distinctiveness. For instance, one does not chance upon a bright idea in the middle of the night to adopt "Kentucky Fried Chicken" for fast-food outlets. In this context, Lord Denning's remark aptly applies: "The arm of coincidence may be long but it does not stretch to infinity."[159]

VI CONCLUSION

Well-known marks are protected under the Paris Convention, TRIPS Agreement, and various FTA provisions. The WIPO Joint Recommendation Concerning Provision on the Protection of Well-Known Marks identifies factors to be considered when determining whether a mark is "well-known." The expanding global marketplace, particularly enabled by the Internet and social media, means that the protection of famous marks and well-known marks has become increasingly significant. The approach of national jurisdictions as to the protection of famous and well-known marks continues to be varied, with some nations introducing national registers of famous and well-known marks. The element of bad faith is more often recognised by registrars and courts as a crucial factor in protecting well-known marks from trademark infringers.

[155] Mostert & Wu, *supra* note 10.

[156] *RH Macy & Co. Inc.* v. *Trade Accents*, 1992(1) SLR 581, 589 (Singapore High Court, June 27, 1991).

[157] Peru Trademark Office, No. 003040-96-Indecopi/Osd (May 8, 1996).

[158] Reebok International Limited *v.* Demitrios Tsikatos, No. 18508, 86 Trademark Rep. 923 (Greek Administrative Court, Nov. 8, 1995).

[159] The State of the Netherlands *v.* Iam Humlum, 2002 Eur. Trade Mark Rep. 98. (WIPO Arbitration & Mediation Center, June 17, 2002).

6

Regional Trademark Protection

Comparing Regional Organizations in Europe, Africa, South East Asia, and South America

Irene Calboli and Coenraad Visser***

I INTRODUCTION

This chapter addresses the harmonization of trademark laws, both substantive law and administrative procedures, within different regional organizations. The topic of regional harmonization and procedural integration of laws is relevant in today's geopolitical and economic framework considering the importance of trademarks for regional trade as well as the relevance of regional organizations as alternative fora for advancing trade and intellectual property (IP)-related negotiations instead of (or in addition to) multilateral negotiations at the World Trade Organization (WTO) and the World Intellectual Property Organization (WIPO). In particular, this chapter compares four distinct regional organizations in order to highlight different levels of regional harmonization and cooperation in these areas – from full harmonization, including the establishment of supranational rights and supranational institutions ruling on the interpretation of national and regional laws, to less integrated approaches based on the cooperation of national or regional offices regarding trademark registrations, and related administrative procedures.

In particular, this chapter analyzes the following organizations: (1) the European Union (EU) – the first regional organization, which has both harmonized national trademark laws and established a supranational regional right, the EU Trademark (previously the Community Trademark, CTM);[1] (2) the Organisation Africaine de la Proprieté Intellectuelle (OAPI), which also operates a unitary registration system, and the African Regional Intellectual Property Organization (ARIPO), which operates a regional registration office cooperating with the national registration offices of the contracting states;[2] (3) the Association of South East Asian Nations (ASEAN), whose members are discussing the feasibility of a unitary ASEAN trademark right, but still concentrate regional cooperation on the harmonization of national filings and

* Professor of Law, Texas A&M University School of Law; Academic Fellow, School of Law, University of Geneva.

** Professor of Intellectual Property Law, University of South Africa. We would like to thank Jane Ginsburg for comments on an earlier draft, Martha Chikowore for assistance with the sources related to Section III of the chapter, and Victoria Gonzalez and Megan Pharis for research and editorial assistance.

[1] *See* discussion *infra* Section II. This chapter does not address the implications of the future separation of the UK from the EU regarding the status of the current EU trademarks that currently include, under the territory covered by the unitary right, the UK. For an overview of the impact of "Brexit" on intellectual property rights in the UK, *see* Richard Arnold, Lionel A. F. Bently, Estelle Derclaye & Graeme B. Dinwoodie, *The Legal Consequences of Brexit through the Lens of IP Law*, 101 JUDICATURE 65 (2017).

[2] *See* discussion *infra* Section III. This section also briefly refers to the recent creation of the Pan-African Intellectual Property Organization (PAIPO), a specialized agency of the African Union, created by the Union's Assembly in 2016.

other procedures;[3] and (4) the Mercado Común del Sur (MERCOSUR), whose member states have not consistently ratified the regional Protocol focusing on trademarks and have simply harmonized national laws based on their international obligations, despite the initial objective of pursuing a stronger level of harmonization and cooperation between members.[4] Almost all the members of these organizations are signatories to the Agreement on Trade Related Aspect of Intellectual Property Rights (TRIPS),[5] the Paris Convention for the Protection of Industrial Property, and several other WIPO treaties.[6]

From the comparison, we note that today different regional organizations follow different levels of harmonization and cooperation, due to a variety of regional and national circumstances, which are at times similar across regional organizations and at times are unique to the specific organizations. Still, we also note that most regional organizations show a consistent trend toward an increase in cooperation between their members, in particular regarding the administrative procedures of registration, opposition, and cancellation of trademarks. This increase in regional cooperation does not necessarily aim at creating a unitary trademark right in the organization at issue, such as the one implemented in the EU and OAPI, even though it may result in the creation of unitary rights at a later stage, as proved by the renewed discussion about the creation of regional unitary rights in ASEAN akin to those in the EU and OAPI. Hence, cooperation amongst members of regional organizations can also prove challenging and less successful in practice than originally planned, as is indicated by lower than expected cooperation between the members of MERCOSUR. Ultimately, the examples examined in this chapter provide us with a comprehensive sample of the opportunities and challenges of the process of harmonization and integration of laws.

II TRADEMARK HARMONIZATION IN THE EUROPEAN UNION: NATIONAL HARMONIZATION AND CREATION OF A UNITARY RIGHT

The main elements of the EU trademark legislation, the EU Trademark Directive,[7] and the EU Trademark Regulation,[8] were designed in the 1970s,[9] even though the harmonization of national trademark laws was recognized as an important aspect for the establishment of the European internal market already with the Treaty of Rome in 1957.[10] In 1976, the European

[3] *See* discussion *infra* Section IV.

[4] *See* discussion *infra* Section V.

[5] *See* Agreement on Trade-Related Aspects of Intellectual Property Rights, Apr. 15, 1994, Marrakesh Agreement Establishing the World Trade Organization, Annex 1C, 1869 UNTS 299, 33 ILM 1197 (1994) [hereinafter TRIPS].

[6] *See* Paris Convention for the Protection of Industrial Property, Mar. 20, 1883, *as revised* July 14, 1967, 21 UST 1583, 828 UNTS 305 [hereinafter Paris Convention]. For current memberships to the various WIPO treaties regarding the protection of trademarks, *see* WIPO Summary Table, https://wipo.int/treaties/en/summary.jsp.

[7] Council Directive 89/104, 1989 OJ (L 40) 1 (EC), replaced by European Parliament and Council Directive 2008/95, 2008 OJ (L 299) 25 (EC) [hereinafter Trademark Directive], and repealed by European Parliament and Council Directive 2015/2436, 2015 OJ (L336) 1 (EU) [hereinafter 2015 Directive].

[8] Council Regulation 40/94 of Dec. 20, 1993, on the Community Trade Mark, 1994 OJ (L 011) 1 (EC), replaced by Council Regulation 207/2009, 2009 OJ (L 78) 1 (EC), and now replaced by EU Trademark Regulation (EU) 2017/1001 of the European Parliament and of the Council of June 14, 2017 on the EU trademark, 2017 OJ (L 154) 1 (EC).

[9] *See generally*, Annette Kur, *Harmonization of the Trademarks Laws in Europe – An Overview*, 28 INT'L REV. INTELL. PROP. COMPETITION L. 1 (1997); Friedrick Karl Beier, *The Development of Trademark Law in the Last Twenty-Five Years*, 26 INT'L REV. INTELL. PROP. COMPETITION L. 769 (1995); Paul Maier, *OHIM's Role in European Trademark Harmonization: Past, Present and Future*, 23 FORDHAM INTELL. PROP. MEDIA & ENT. L.J. 687,689 (2013).

[10] Consolidated Version of the Treaty on the Functioning of the European Union, Mar. 30, 2010, [2010] OJ C83, as amended following the entering into force of the Treaty of Lisbon on Dec. 1, 2009. Treaty of Lisbon, Dec. 13, 2007, [2007] OJ C306 [hereinafter TFEU]. *See* Timothy W. Blakely, *Beyond the International Harmonization of Trademark*

Commission published a Memorandum on the creation of a unitary trademark right[11] based on the observation that, with growing pan-European commercial activities, a unitary right would enable manufacturers and distributors to adapt to the European market more efficiently than would a variety of national systems.[12] Still, aware that national trademark law would continue to apply and differences continue to exist, the Memorandum proposed a two-tier system that called for both the creation of a unitary right, the Community Trade Mark (CTM), and the convergence of national trademark laws through harmonization.[13] As a result of ongoing discussions concerning the location of the office in charge of and the official languages to be used for the CTM, the EU Trademark Directive was adopted a few years earlier than the CTM Regulation. As other chapters in this volume describe, both the EU Directive and CTM Regulation have been important points of reference for the process of international harmonization of trademark law.[14]

Directive 89/104/EEC was approved on 21 December 1988.[15] It harmonized the national provisions related to the law of trademarks that affected the internal market and the free movement of products (effectively all of trademark law). In particular, the Directive encompassed: the definition of what constitutes a mark; absolute and relative grounds for refusal of registration;[16] the scope of rights conferred by a trademark;[17] limitations of the effects of trademarks including fair use,[18] exhaustion,[19] acquiescence,[20] and the requirement of use;[21] basic principles of licensing; grounds for revocation.[22] With respect to these provisions, some (most) provisions were mandatory while others were optional.[23] When an issue of interpretation of the terms of the Directive would arise regarding any of the mandatory provisions, the Court of Justice of the European Union (CJEU, then the European Court of Justice, ECJ) would provide a conclusive interpretation of the harmonized measures, so the national interpretations of the

Law: The Community Trade Mark as a Model of Unitary Transnational Trademark Protection, 149 U. PA. L. REV. 309, 323 (2000).

11 *Commission of the European Communities, Memorandum on the Creation of a EEC Trade Mark*, 7 INT'L REV. INTELL. PROP. COMPETITION L. 367 (1976).

12 Charles Gielen, *Harmonization of Trade Mark Law in Europe: The First Trade Mark Directive of the European Council*, 8 EIPR. 262 (1992).

13 *Id.*

14 In this respect, *see* in particular Chapters 1, 2, and 5 in this volume.

15 The first draft was published in December 1980. The proposal, as modified according to the opinion of the Economic and Social Committee and the amendments of the European Parliament, was submitted to the Council in December 1985. Several member states commented on it, resulting in the new text of October 1986. This in turn was discussed by the Working Group and in December 1987 a new text, strongly influenced by the Dutch delegation, was published and approved by the Council in June 1988. Following the advice of the Economic and Social Committee in October 1988 and the opinion of the European Parliament in December 1988, the Trademark Directive was adopted by the Council on Dec. 21, 1988. *See* Trademark Directive, *supra* note 7.

16 Trademark Directive, *supra* note 7, art. 3(1)(a).

17 *Id.* at art. 5(1)(a).

18 *Id.* at art. 6(2).

19 *Id.* at art. 7(1).

20 *Id.* at art. 9(1).

21 *Id.* at art. 10(1).

22 *Id.* at art. 12(1).

23 On this point *see, e.g.*, Kur, *supra* note 9, at 3. For example, the Trademark Directive did not make mandatory two essential features later adopted in the CTM Regulation: the free assignment of trademarks and protection against their use for dissimilar products. However, the majority of member states adopted all the provisions of the Trademark Directive, including those not mandatory. The only exceptions were Greece, where the implementation law did not allow for the free assignment of trademarks, and Austria, which did not include in its Trademarks Act protection against the use of a reputed trademark for dissimilar goods. The Spanish Trademarks Act also gave rise to some doubts in this respect as well. *See id.*

terms could be reconciled.[24] Soon after the adoption of the Directive, the CJEU started to receive questions of interpretation from national courts. The questions multiplied over time and, in the past three and half decades, the CJEU has issued a long line of decisions relating to the interpretation of the provisions of the EU Trademark Directive.[25]

Nonetheless, supporters of a more comprehensive harmonization process criticized the optional character of some of the Directive's provisions. For example, the Directive did not mandate protection against the use of well-known marks in connection with dissimilar products (even though most countries implemented the relevant provision).[26] Similarly, the Directive was mostly silent regarding non-registered marks or other signs used in the course of trade, such as trade names.[27] Additionally, the Directive left enforcement to national courts.[28] Moreover, the Directive did not touch upon questions of procedure concerning the registration, nullity, and invalidity of trademarks.[29] For example, member states remained free to decide whether a license had to be registered and whether prior rights could be invoked only during registration procedures or before the courts in nullification proceedings, or both.[30] Where national laws provided for the registration of collective or certification marks (not included in the Directive), national laws also provided grounds for nullification or invalidation of these marks other than those provided for in the Directive for the general types of marks.[31] Moreover, the Directive did not address national procedural rules with respect to assessing the likelihood of confusion, such as the burden of proof.[32]

Five years later, in 1993, the CTM Regulation was adopted. The Regulation created a unitary right valid across all EU member states. Notably, applicants could acquire the EU-wide right even if they had not used the mark in every EU member state. On the other hand, a declaration of invalidity in any of the member states would invalidate the CTM for the entire EU.[33] As mentioned, the delay in adopting the CTM Regulation resulted primarily from disagreements related to institutional and procedural matters. Selecting official languages was one bone of great contention. Ultimately, it was decided that the working languages would be German, English, Spanish, French, and Italian. The final draft also recognized national rights as a ground for opposition. Previous drafts were rejected because they did not give sufficient protection to national rights.[34] Ultimately, the 1993 CTM Regulation incorporated most of the substantive provisions included in the Trademark Directive. In addition, the Regulation established the Office of Harmonization in the Internal Market (OHIM, today the European Union Intellectual

[24] TFEU, *supra* note 10, art. 177.

[25] *See, e.g.*, Matthias Leistner, *Harmonization of Intellectual Property Law in Europe: The European Court of Justice's Trade Mark Cases 2004–2007*, 45 Common Mkt. L. Rev. 1, 69–91 (2008); *See also Annual Review of EU Trademark Law*, 107 The Trademark Rep. 2 (Mar.–Apr. 2017); For an updated review of EU trademark law, *see* Annette Kur & Martin Senftleben, European Trademark Law – A Commentary (2017).

[26] *See, e.g.*, Kur, *supra* note 9, at 3.

[27] *Id.*

[28] *Id.*

[29] Trademark Directive, *supra* note 7, 5th Recital.

[30] Gielen, *supra* note 12, at 263.

[31] *Id.*

[32] Trademark Directive, *supra* note 7, 10th Recital.

[33] *See* the summary provided by Lars Meyer, *Much Ado about Nothing – Characteristics, Benefits, and Practical Implications of the European Community Trademark*, 5 Chi.-Kent J. Intell. Prop. 158, 160 (2005–2006); *see also* Michael Fammler & Christopher Aide, *Enforcement of CTMs in the EU: The Real Test of Their Commercial Value*, 86 J. Pat. & Trademark Soc.'y 135, 139 (2004).

[34] *See, e.g.*, David C. Wilkinson, *The Community Trade Mark Regulation and Its Role in European Economic Integration*, 80 Trademark Rep. 107, 122 (1990).

Property Office, EUIPO), which is located in Alicante, Spain. The OHIM/EUIPO is responsible for the examination and granting of the CTMs (now renamed EUTMs).[35] The Regulations also established a system of oppositions based on pre-existing CTMs or national marks.[36] Likewise, it established that examination and opposition decisions are subject to appeal, with a Board of Appeal within the Office, whose decisions can be appealed before the CJEU.[37]

The new CTM system proved immediately very successful. On 1 April 1996 (the first possible filing date), the OHIM received 22,000 CTM applications. By the end of 1996, about 46,000 applications were filed, and an additional 27,000 applications were filed in 1997.[38] Most of the applications filed during the first years of the creation of CTMs came from other members of the EU and from the United States.[39] The CTM system rapidly gained popularity among practitioners and registrants across the world as well.

In 2009, the European Commission decided to review the existing system to further harmonize national trademark laws in the EU, streamline procedures, and facilitate cooperation between member states. The Commission asked the Max Planck Institute for Intellectual Property and Competition Law in Munich to conduct the review.[40] In 2013, following the Max Planck report, the Commission launched a proposal for revision of the existing Directive and the Regulation. After two years of discussions, consultations, and revisions, in December 2015, the European Parliament approved the revised EU trademark reforms.[41] The changes discussed in the package included amendments to the examination, opposition and revocation proceedings, modifications of the grounds for refusal of registration, changes in the description of the marks and the selection of goods and services, and appeal procedures. The reforms were finalized with the adoption of new versions of the Trademark Directive and Regulation. At the outset, all previous reference to "Community" were replaced with European Union. The EU Trademark Directive 2015/2436 was adopted and entered in to force in January 2015; the EU Trademark Regulation 2015/2424 was adopted and entered into force in March 2016. In 2017, additional parts of the reform package came into force with EU Regulation 2017/1001. The OHIM became the EUIPO, and the CTM the EU Trademark (EUTM).[42]

Amongst the most relevant reforms were the following. The requirement to represent a mark graphically, which prescribed that a trademark application include a graphical representation of

35 Regulation 2015/2424 Of the European Parliament and of the Council of Dec. 16, 2015, amending Council Regulation (EC) No. 207/2009 on the Community trade mark and Commission Regulation (EC) No. 2868/95 implementing Council Regulation (EC) No. 40/94 on the Community trademark, and repealing Commission Regulation (EC) No. 2869/95 on the fees payable to the Office for Harmonization in the Internal Market (Trade Marks and Designs) art. 2, OJ (L 341) 21 (EU).

36 *Id.* at art. 8(b)(5).

37 *Id.* at art. 65.

38 Maier, *supra* note 9, at 697.

39 *See* Intellectual Property Rights Statistics: Statistics Explained, https://ec.europa.eu/eurostat/statistics-explained/pdfscache/33899.pdf.

40 Max Planck Institute for Intellectual Property and Competition Law, *Study on the Overall Functioning of the European Trade Mark System*, https://ip.mpg.de/fileadmin/IP/pdf2/mpi_final_report_with_synopsis.pdf.

41 *See Commission Proposal for a Regulation of the European Parliament and of the Council Amending Council Regulation (EC) 207/2009 on the Community Trade Mark*, COM (2013) 161 final (Mar. 27, 2013); *see also* Resolution on the Proposal for a Regulation of the European Parliament and of the Council to Approximate the Laws of the Member States Relating to Trade Marks, PARL. EUR. DOC. P7 TA 0119 (2014) [hereinafter TMD Resolution]; *see* Brussels European Council Press Release, ST 12130/14 (July 23, 2014), http://consilium.europa.eu/uedocs/cms_data/docs/pressdata/en/intm/144127.pdf. The common Council position was formed after the finalization of the manuscript. References to the position of the Council without specifically mentioning the Common Position of 23 July indicate that the position has remained unchanged.

42 For a comprehensive review of all the changes and amendments, *see* Annette Kur, *The EU Trademark Reform Package – (Too) Bold a Step Ahead or Back to Status Quo?*, 19 MARQ. INTELL. PROP. L. REV. 15 (2015).

the mark, no longer applies. Instead, the new text of the Directive provides that a mark should simply be visually perceptible, which facilitates applications of non-traditional marks with the EUIPO and national offices.[43] The new text also states that the class(es) of goods and services for which marks are applied for must be identified with "clarity and precision" based on the "natural and usual meaning of the terms" as part of trademark applications.[44] Absolute grounds for refusal of registrations or cancellation were expanded to now include: (1) "signs which consist exclusively of the shape, *or another characteristic*, which results from the nature of the goods or is necessary to achieve a technical result, or which gives substantial value to the goods";[45] and (2) designations of origin, geographical indications, traditional terms for wine, traditional specialties guaranteed, and plant varieties.[46] Relative grounds that affect the registrability of a sign as a mark now exclude signs that constitute: (1) designation of origin or geographical indications; and (2) signs identical or similar to marks with a reputation also related to similar goods or services.[47] Mandatory refusals and cancellations (such as refusal and cancellations based on the applicant acting in bad faith or when the sign applied for is identical or similar to a sign registered for similar or dissimilar products, which has a reputation in the member states in question for national marks, or in the EU for EUTMs) became mandatory at the level of all EU national offices.[48] Revocation and invalidity proceedings were also streamlined and now can take place before the relevant sections of national offices.[49] By contrast, EUTMs could no longer be filed through national offices.[50] Regarding the EUTMs in particular, the fee structure was changed and a one-fee-per-class-system for trademark applications and renewals now applies.[51]

As for infringement actions, the reform package included the following. Using a registered trademark as a trade or company name (or part of such) became a specific infringement, as is using the mark in packaging, labels, or other materials where there's a risk that these would be used in relation to products which would be infringing.[52] Trademark holders were also granted the right to prohibit goods in transit that would be regarded as counterfeit in the member state where they come under customs inspection, unless the owner of the goods can show that the trademark owner is not entitled to prevent the goods being placed on the market in the country of final destination.[53] The reforms also harmonized the rights of licensees related to infringement and clarified that only *exclusive* licensees can sue if the owner fails to bring an action

[43] *Id.* at 24–25. *See* Commission Implementing Regulation (EU) 2018/626 of Mar. 5, 2018 laying down detailed rules for implementing certain provisions of Regulation (EU) 2017/1001 of the European Parliament and of the Council on the European Union trade mark, and repealing Implementing Regulation (EU) 2017/1431, OJ L 104 (Apr. 24, 2018, 37–56), art. 3(1) stating that "[t]he trade mark shall be represented in any appropriate form using generally available technology, as long as it can be reproduced on the Register in a clear, precise, self-contained, easily accessible, intelligible, durable and objective manner so as to enable the competent authorities and the public to determine with clarity and precision the subject matter of the protection afforded to its proprietor."

[44] *Id.*

[45] *Id.* at 25–28.

[46] *Id.* at 28–30.

[47] *Id.*

[48] *Id.* at 24–25.

[49] *Id.* at 23–4.

[50] *Id.* at art. 30.

[51] Regulation (EU) 2017/1001 of the European Parliament and of the Council of June 14, 2017 on the European Union Trade Mark, 2017 OJ (L 154) 1 (EU), art. 31.

[52] 2015 Directive, *supra* note 7, at art. 9(a); *see also* Regulation (EU) 2017/1001 of the European Parliament and of the Council of June 14, 2017 on the European Union Trade Mark, 2017 OJ (L 154) 1 (EU), art. 10.

[53] Kur, *supra* note 42, at 34–37.

within an appropriate period after she has been given formal notice by the licensee.[54] Last, but not least, the reform packages increased the number of defenses. Notably, the Directive clarifies that the following are lawful unauthorized uses of trademarks: (1) using a mark for reference purposes, notably to identify or refer to the products of the owner of the mark, in particular where the reference is needed to indicate the purpose of the products; (2) using one's own name; and (3) using a mark that has not been in use by its owner for over five years.[55]

As has been the case in the past decades, the EU trademark system continued to grow after the reforms. EUTM applications and registrations, many of which are now coming from Asia and emerging markets, have increased.[56] National offices are also implementing the reform package and the process of harmonization of laws has intensified, as desired by the European Commission. The success of the system is due both to the need to harmonize the functioning of the internal market and the convenience of the unitary right for the applicants. However, as the many decisions of the CJEU have demonstrated, the process of harmonization is lengthy and requires independent institutions and adjudication process, probably the most complex part of the harmonization chain in any regional organization.[57]

III TRADEMARK HARMONIZATION IN AFRICA: TWO CONTRASTING SYSTEMS TO FULFILL DIFFERENT NEEDS OF REGIONAL ORGANIZATIONS

In Africa, intellectual property issues are discussed in several regional fora, such as the Southern African Development Community,[58] the East African Community,[59] and the African Union.[60] In the current context, two African regional trademark systems, OAPI and ARIPO, have been created to provide cost-effective trademark protection by making it possible for trademark owners to obtain protection in a number of countries by means of one application. At the outset, though, three differences between the two systems should be noted. First, the OAPI system is based on the unification of laws, whereas the ARIPO system allows for the harmonization of trademark laws, and for the coexistence of national and ARIPO laws. Second, the official languages of the two organizations reflect the colonial histories of their members – French for OAPI and English for ARIPO – even though Rwanda, a French-speaking country, opted to be a member of ARIPO and is increasingly using English. Both organizations have Portuguese and Spanish-speaking members – Mozambique and São Tomé Príncipe in ARIPO, and Equatorial

[54] 2015 Directive, *supra* note 7, at art. 13(a); *see also* Regulation (EU) 2017/1001 of the European Parliament and of the Council of June 14, 2017 on the European Union Trade Mark, 2017 OJ (L 154) 1 (EU), art. 80.

[55] Kur, *supra* note 42, at 32–34.

[56] European Union Intellectual Property Office (EUIPO), *2018 Annual Report*, https://euipo.europa.eu/tunnel-web/secure/webdav/guest/document_library/contentPdfs/about_euipo/annual_report/annual_report_2018_en.pdf.

[57] *See* Kur & Sentfleben, *supra* note 25 (recounting the most important decisions of the CJEU and the General Court through the past several decades).

[58] *See* Marumo Nkomo, *Regional Integration in the Area of Intellectual Property: The Case for Southern African Development Community Involvement*, 18 L., Democracy and Dev., 317–33 (2014).

[59] *See* Fernandos dos Santos & Patrick Juvet Lowé Gnintedem, *Regional Frameworks for Protection of Intellectual Property in Africa, in* Intellectual Property Law, Practice and Management: Perspectives from Africa 592, 593–94 (Adejoke Oyewunmi et al. eds., 2018).

[60] *See, e.g.*, the African Model Legislation for the Protection of the Rights of Local Communities, Farmers and Breeders, and for the Regulation of Access to Biological Resources (2000). *See* Johnson Ekpere, *African Model Law on the Protection of the Rights of Local Communities, Farmers and Breeders, and for the Regulation of Access to Biological Resources, in* African Perspectives on Genetic Resources: A Handbook on Laws, Policies and Institutions 275 (Kent Nnadozie et al. eds., 2003); Emmanuel Sackey & Glenda Mutasa, *Traditional Knowledge, Expressions of Folklore and Genetic Resources, in* Intellectual Property Law, Practice and Management: Perspectives from Africa 408, 453–54 (Adejoke Oyewunmi et al. eds., 2018).

Guinea (where Spanish, Portuguese, and French are official languages) and Guinea-Bissau in OAPI. Third, the OAPI legislative provisions cover both the substantive and procedural aspects of trademark law, whilst ARIPO addresses only the procedural aspects and leaves the substantive content of trademark rights largely to the national laws of its members.[61] The review below will accordingly show different founding principles of the two organizations – unification in the case of OAPI, along the lines of the EU, and complementarity and cooperation in the case of ARIPO.

A *The Organisation Africaine de la Properté Intellectuelle*

The origin of OAPI dates back to the Libreville Agreement of 13 September 1962, establishing the *Office Africain et Malgache de la Propriété Industrielle* (OAMPI). The withdrawal of Malagasy from OAMPI and the need to expand the range of intellectual property rights covered by the agreement led to the *Accord de Bangui relatif á la création d'une Organisation Africaine de la Properté Intellectuelle, constituant révision de l'Accord relatif á la création d'une Office Africain et Malgache de la Propriété Industrielle*, adopted on 2 March 1977 in Bangui, Central African Republic. The Bangui Agreement entered into force on 8 February 1982, and its text was later revised extensively.[62] OAPI has seventeen members: Benin, Burkina Faso, Cameroon, Central African Republic, Chad, Comoros, Congo, Côte d'Ivoire, Gabon, Guinea, Equatorial Guinea, Mali, Mauritania, Niger, Guinea Bissau, Senegal, and Togo. Its seat is in Yaoundé, Cameroon.

The most relevant feature of the OAPI system for trademarks is that OAPI operates a unitary registration system, similar to the EU, with a special register for trademarks and service marks.[63] Unlike the EU, though, OAPI serves as the national intellectual property office for each of its member states. Accordingly, OAPI member states do not have national industrial property administration offices coexisting with the regional system.[64] However, a unique feature of the OAPI system is that the courts of each OAPI member state are competent to rule on intellectual property infringements taking place in any member state. A final legal decision as to the validity of an intellectual property title rendered by a court in one member state is binding on all other member states, except for decisions based on domestic public policy and morality.[65]

OAPI member states are contracting parties, inter alia, of the Paris Convention,[66] the Lisbon Agreement,[67] the Nairobi Treaty,[68] and the TRIPS Agreement.[69] OAPI, in its own name,

[61] *See* Yeukai Mupangavanhu, The Regional Integration of African Trade Mark Laws: Challenges and Possibilities, unpublished LLD thesis, University of the Western Cape (2013), 162–63 (on file with the authors).

[62] *Accord relatif a la creation d'une Organisation Africaine de la Propriete Intellectuelle, constituant revision de J'Accord relatif a la creation d'un Office Africain et Malgache de la Propriété Industrielle (Bangui (République centrafricaine), le 2 Mars 1977)*, later revised by the *Accord portant révision de l'Accord de Bangui du 2 mars 1977 instituant une Organisation Africaine de la Propriété Intellectuelle (Bangui (République centrafricaine), le 24 février 1999)* [hereinafter Bangui Agreement]. For the official translation of the revised text, see https://wipolex.wipo.int/en/text/181151. On the historical evolution of the organization, *see* Mupangavanhu, *supra* note 61, at 151–52; Caroline B. Ncube, Intellectual Property Policy, Law and Administration in Africa. Exploring Continental and Sub-regional Co-operation 110 (2016); Dos Santos & Gnintedem, *supra* note 59, at 599–600.

[63] *Id.* at art. 13.

[64] *Id.* at art. 2.2.

[65] *Id.* at art. 18. *See* Dos Santos & Gnintedem, *supra* note 59, at 602–03, 625.

[66] *See* Paris Convention, *supra* note 6.

[67] Lisbon Agreement for the Protection of Appellations of Origin and their International Registration (as amended on Sept. 28, 1979), https://wipolex.wipo.int/en/text/285838. For the contracting parties, *see* https://wipo.int/export/sites/www/treaties/en/documents/pdf/lisbon.pdf.

[68] Nairobi Treaty on the Protection of the Olympic Symbol, Sept. 26, 1981, https://wipolex.wipo.int/en/text/287432. For the contracting parties, *see* https://wipo.int/export/sites/www/treaties/en/documents/pdf/nairobi.pdf.

[69] TRIPS, *supra* note 5.

acceded to the Madrid Protocol;[70] it entered into force for OAPI on 5 March 2015.[71] This was controversial, as the Bangui Agreement does not expressly provide for the accession to international instruments by OAPI directly instead of by the respective OAPI member states.[72]

Unlike the Banjul Protocol analyzed below related to ARIPO,[73] Annex III of the Bangui Agreement additionally contains some provisions relating to substantive trademark law.[74]

In terms of the Bangui Protocol,

> any visible sign used or intended to be used and capable of distinguishing the goods or services of any enterprise shall be considered a trademark or service mark, including in particular surnames by themselves or in a distinctive form, special, arbitrary or fanciful designations, the characteristic form of a product or its packaging, labels, wrappers, emblems, prints, stamps, seals, vignettes, borders, combinations or arrangements of colors, drawings, reliefs, letters, numbers, devices and pseudonyms.[75]

According to Article 3 of the Bangui Agreement, the following marks may not be registered: (1) a mark that is devoid of distinctiveness, notably because it consists of signs or matter constituting the necessary or generic designation of the product or its composition; (2) a mark that is identical to a mark that belongs to another owner and is already registered, or the filing or priority date of which is earlier, and which relates to the same, or similar, goods or services, or where it so resembles such a mark that it is liable to mislead or confuse; (3) a mark that is contrary to *l'ordre public*, morality, or the law; (4) a mark that is liable to mislead the public or business circles, notably as to the geographical origin, nature, or characteristics of the relevant goods or services; (5) a mark that reproduces, imitates, or incorporates armorial bearings, flags, or other emblems, the abbreviated name or acronym, or an official sign or hallmark indicating control and warranty of a state or intergovernmental organization established by an international convention, except with the permission of the competent authority, state, or organization.[76]

The owner of a well-known mark[77] may apply to the court for the invalidation, on the national territory of any member state, of the effects of the filing of a mark liable to be confused with its own. Such action may not be taken after a period of five years has expired from the date of the application in so far as the latter was filed in good faith.[78]

Registration of a mark confers on its owner the exclusive right to use the mark, or a sign resembling it, in connection with the goods or services for which it has been registered, and similar goods or services.[79] Registration of the mark likewise confers on the owner the exclusive right to prevent all third parties from using in business without its consent, identical or similar signs for goods or services that are themselves similar to those for which the trademark or service

70 Protocol Relating to the Madrid Agreement Concerning the International Registration of Marks, June 27, 1989, https://wipolex.wipo.int/en/text/283483 [hereinafter Madrid Protocol].

71 Notification No. 203, Accession by the African Intellectual Property Organization, Dec. 5, 2014, https://wipo.int/treaties/en/notifications/madridp-gp/treaty_madridp_gp_203.html.

72 *See* Ncube, *supra* note 62, at 118.

73 Banjul Protocol on Marks within the Framework of the African Regional Intellectual Property Organization, https://wipolex.wipo.int/en/text/345095 [hereinafter Banjul Protocol]. It was adopted by the Administrative Council at Banjul, The Gambia, on Nov. 19, 1993 and last amended on Nov. 25, 2013.

74 *See* Ncube, *supra* note 62, at 120.

75 Bangui Agreement, *supra* note 62, art. 2(1).

76 *Id.* at art. 3.

77 Within the meaning of the Paris Convention, *supra* note 6, art. 6*bis*; TRIPS, supra note 5, art. 16.2.

78 Bangui Agreement, *supra* note 62, art. 6.

79 *Id.* at art. 7(1).

mark has been registered, where such use is liable to cause confusion.[80] Where an identical sign is used for identical goods and services, a risk of confusion shall be presumed to exist.

Registration of the mark does not confer on its owner the right to prohibit a third party from using in good faith their name or address, a pseudonym, a geographical name, or accurate information concerning the nature, quality, quantity, purpose, value, place of origin, or time of production of its goods or rendering of its services in so far as the relevant use is limited to the purpose of mere identification or information, and cannot mislead the public as to the source of the goods or services.[81] Registration of a mark does not confer on its owner the right to prohibit a third party from using the mark in relation to goods that have been lawfully sold under the mark on the national territory of the member state in which the right of prohibition is exercised, on condition that the goods have not undergone any alteration.[82]

As in most other countries, trademarks and service marks are registered for renewable terms of ten years.[83] Hence, at the request of any interested party, a court may order the cancellation of any registered mark which, for an uninterrupted period of five years prior to the request, has not been used on the national territory of one of the member states, except where the registered owner has legitimate reasons for having failed to use it.[84] The cancellation may extend to all or part of the goods or services for which the mark was registered.

At this time, the system created by OAPI seems to be functioning efficiently. Based on the most recent publicly available statistics, in 2011, from 2007 to 2011 trademark applications from OAPI member states hovered around 1,000 applications annually.[85] The total number of trademark applications from all applicants worldwide ranged from 2,548 in 2007 to 3,267 in 2011.[86] The figures for the years 2011–17 seem to reflect a similar increase in the number of trademark applications, ranging between 3,000 and 5,000 annually, even though updated official statistical information is not yet available for this period.[87]

B *The African Regional Intellectual Property Organization*

ARIPO was created on 9 December 1976, by the adoption of the Agreement on the Creation of the African Regional Intellectual Property Organization by the Diplomatic Conference for the adoption of an Agreement on the Creation of an Industrial Property Organization for English-Speaking Africa at Lusaka, Zambia (the Lusaka Agreement).[88] Membership of the organization

80 *Id.* at art. 7(2).
81 *Id.* at art. 7(3).
82 *Id.* at art. 7(4).
83 *Id.* at art. 19.
84 *Id.* at art. 23(1).
85 Hamidou Kone, *The African Intellectual Property Organization (OAPI)*, country report presented at the WIPO Workshop on Measures for Accession to, and Effective Use of, the Madrid System, March 8 to 9, 2012, at Tokyo, Japan (WIPO/TM/TYO/12/Z/OAPI), https://wipo.int/edocs/mdocs/aspac/en/wipo_tm_tyo_12/wipo_tm_tyo_12_z_oapi.pdf.
86 *Id.*
87 This information was provided by the OAPI Head of Service, Operation of Information Systems, Direction of Information Systems and Publication, (unofficial and unpublished table on file with the authors).
88 Agreement on the Creation of the African Regional Intellectual Property Organization by the Diplomatic Conference, https://wipolex.wipo.int/en/text/301376 [hereinafter Lusaka Agreement]. It was subsequently amended by the Administrative Council of ARIPO (on Dec. 10, 1982, Dec. 12, 1986, and Nov. 27, 1996) and the Council of Ministers (on Aug. 13, 2004). On the historical evolution of ARIPO, *see* Mupangavanhu, *supra* note 61, at 151–52; NCUBE, *supra* note 62, at 110; Dos Santos & Gnintedem, *supra* note 59, at 599–600; Martha Kabaira Chikowore & Adejoke Oyewunmi, *General Introduction*, *in* INTELLECTUAL PROPERTY LAW, PRACTICE AND MANAGEMENT: PERSPECTIVES FROM AFRICA 1 (Adejoke Oyewunmi et al. eds., 2019).

is open to the member states of the United Nations Economic Commission for Africa (UNECA) or the African Union.[89] As of 1 March 2015, the organization had nineteen member states: Botswana, The Gambia, Ghana, Kenya, Lesotho, Liberia, Malawi, Mozambique, Namibia, Rwanda, Sào Tomé and Príncipe, Sierra Leone, Somalia, Sudan, Swaziland, Uganda, United Republic of Tanzania, Zambia, and Zimbabwe. The organization has to establish and maintain close and continuous working relationships with the UNECA, the World Intellectual Property Organization, and the African Union.[90] ARIPO may also cooperate with governments of states which are not members of the organization but which want to assist the organization in achieving its objects.[91] Currently, twelve states have observer status in this capacity: Angola, Algeria, Burundi, Egypt, Eritrea, Ethiopia, Libya, Mauritius, Nigeria, Seychelles, South Africa, and Tunisia.

In addition to its constitutive act, ARIPO has four protocols.[92] One of them is the Banjul Protocol, which relates specifically to trademarks.[93] As of 15 May 2020, eleven countries were party to the Banjul Protocol: Botswana, Lesotho, Liberia, Malawi, Mozambique, Namibia, Sào Tomé and Príncipe, Swaziland, Tanzania, Uganda, and Zimbabwe.

However, the Banjul Protocol and its implementing regulations do not provide for substantive trademark law. Any harmonization of substantive trademark law will accordingly flow from the member states' membership of international agreements such as the Paris Convention,[94] and the TRIPS Agreement.[95]

The Protocol merely establishes a regional registration office, entrusted with the registration of marks and their administration on behalf of the contracting states.[96] All applications for registration are examined according to the national law of a designated state;[97] the same applies to the cancellation of a registration, whether for non-use or any other ground.[98]

The most recent annual statistics released by ARIPO show the number of trademark applications in 2018 filed through the national route (26,668), the regional route (ARIPO) (1,671), and the international route (Madrid) (9,145).[99]

[89] Lusaka Agreement, *supra* note 88, at art. IV.

[90] *Id.* at art. V.

[91] *Id.* at art. VI.

[92] Protocol on Patents and Industrial Designs within the Framework of the African Regional Intellectual Property Organization, adopted at Harare, Zimbabwe, on Dec. 10, 1982, https://aripo.org/wp-content/uploads/2018/11/Harare-Protocol-2019.pdf; Protocol on Marks within the Framework of the African Regional Intellectual Property Organization [hereinafter Banjul Protocol], adopted at Banjul, The Gambia, on Nov. 19, 1993, https://aripo.org/wp-content/uploads/2018/11/Banjul-Protocol-2019.pdf; Protocol on the Protection of Traditional Knowledge and Expressions of Folklore within the Framework of the African Regional Intellectual Property Organization, adopted at Swakopmund, Namibia, on Aug. 9, 2010, https://aripo.org/wp-content/uploads/2019/06/Swakopmund-Protocol-on-the-Protection-of-Traditional-Knowledge-and-Expressions-of-Folklore-2019.pdf; Protocol for the Protection of New Varieties of Plants within the Framework of the African Regional Intellectual Property Organization, adopted at Arusha, Tanzania, https://aripo.org/wp-content/uploads/2018/12/Arusha-Protocol_20181.pdf. *See, generally,* Dos Santos & Gnintedem, *supra* note 59, at 605–12.

[93] *Id.*

[94] Paris Convention, *supra* note 6.

[95] TRIPS, *supra* note 5.

[96] Banjul Protocol, *supra* note 92, § 1:1. A detailed set of Administrative Instructions under the Regulations for Implementing the Protocol on Marks within the Framework of the African Regional Intellectual Property Organization, came into effect on Jan. 1, 2018. For the text, *see* Administrative Instructions, https://aripo.org/wp-content/uploads/2000/01/Administrative-Instructions_Banjul-Protocol_2018-Edition.pdf.

[97] *Id.* at § 6:1.

[98] *Id.* at § 8:2.

[99] *See* African Regional Intellectual Property Organization, https://aripo.org/ip-statistics/ (reporting the statistics on trademark filings for 2017 and 2018, even though the information relating to a few members is not available).

An application for the registration of a trademark may be filed either with the ARIPO Office or with the relevant office of a contracting state.[100] The application should indicate the contracting states in which protection is sought.[101] Where an application is filed with a national office, that office must transmit the application to the ARIPO Office within one month of receiving the application.[102] The application should indicate the goods and/or services for which protection is sought, and the corresponding class or classes under the Nice Agreement.[103] The ARIPO Office checks that the applicant has made such an indication and that it is correct. Where the applicant does not give the required indication, or provides an incorrect indication, the ARIPO Office classifies the goods or services in terms of the Nice classification, on payment of a classification fee.[104] Finally, the application must contain a declaration of actual use of the mark or an intention to use the mark, or be accompanied by an application for the registration of a person as a registered user of the mark.[105]

The ARIPO Office checks the application for compliance with the formal requirements,[106] and affords non-compliant applicants an opportunity to rectify their applications, failing which their applications will be refused.[107] An unsuccessful applicant may ask the office to reconsider an application.[108] If, after the office has reconsidered the application, the it still refuses the application, the applicant may lodge an appeal against the decision to the Board of Appeal,[109] or request designated states to consider the application under their national law.[110]

Once an application complies with the formal requirements, the ARIPO Office notifies the relevant offices in the designated states.[111] Within twelve months, each designated state may make a written communication to the office that, if a mark is registered by it, that registration shall have no effect on its territory on the basis of any grounds, both absolute and relative, including the existence of third-party rights.[112] The refusing state should give reasons, based on its national laws, for its refusal.[113] These grounds are communicated to the applicant, who has a right of reply as well as of appeal or review under the relevant national law.[114]

Absent a communication from a designated state that it will not protect a mark, two further steps complete the protection of the mark in designated states. First, the acceptance of the mark is published in the *Marks Journal*.[115] Secondly, after three months have passed, during which opposition proceedings may commence, the mark will be registered and a registration certificate issued.[116] An opposition is decided under the national laws of the designated state concerned.[117]

[100] Banjul Protocol, *supra* note 92, § 2:1.
[101] *Id.* at § 3:1.
[102] *Id.* at § 2:4.
[103] *Id.* at § 3:2. The Nice Agreement Concerning the International Classification of Goods and Services for the Purposes of the Registration of Marks, June 15, 1957, as last amended on Sept. 28, 1979, https://wipolex.wipo.int/en/text/287532 [hereinafter Nice Agreement].
[104] Banjul Protocol, *supra* note 92, § 3:4.
[105] *Id.* at § 3:5.
[106] *Id.* at § 5:1.
[107] *Id.* at § 5:2.
[108] *Id.* at § 5*bis*.1.
[109] *Id.* at § 5*bis*.2.
[110] *Id.* at § 5:4.
[111] *Id.* at § 5:3.
[112] *Id.* at § 6:2.
[113] *Id.* at § 6:3.
[114] *Id.* at § 6:4.
[115] *Id.* at § 6*bis*.1.
[116] *Id.* at § 6*bis*.2.
[117] *Id.* at § 6bis.4.

As under the OAPI system, and most trademark registration systems, trademarks are registered for renewable terms of ten years.[118]

In addition to the problems of economic viability of the ARIPO Office flowing from the modest number of trademark applications filed at the office (considering the number of countries and potential applicants both national and foreign),[119] the International Trade Mark Association (INTA) found that there are disparities in the national laws of member states that may cause difficulties in the operation of the Banjul Protocol.[120] In addition, ARIPO and its member states face these general challenges: limited resources to undertake its objectives and programs; a lack of national and institutional trademark policies; limited knowledge and information relating to trademark law in the national offices; and a limited communication infrastructure.[121]

C The Pan-African Intellectual Property Organization

On 31 January 2016, the assembly of the African Union[122] adopted the statute of the Pan-African Intellectual Property Organization (PAIPO),[123] as a specialized agency of the Union.[124] For the purposes of the statute, the term "intellectual property" includes "symbols, names, images and designs used in commerce."[125] The functions of PAIPO include harmonizing the intellectual property standards "that reflect the needs of the AU, its Member States and RECs; ARIPO and OAPI," facilitating the realization and harmonization of national legislation and regional treaties with continental intellectual property standards, and strengthening existing regional organizations, or such other organizations, as may be necessary.[126]

It appears, then, that PAIPO is a regional organization with modest aims. Its stated preference for harmonization of laws and its focus on strengthening existing regional organizations mean that it is unlikely to be a vehicle for establishing a Pan-African organization with a central trademark registry granting a unitary trademark right.

IV TRADEMARK HARMONIZATION IN THE ASSOCIATION OF SOUTHEAST ASIAN NATIONS: INTEROPERABILITY TO PAVE THE WAY FOR A FUTURE UNITARY RIGHT?

ASEAN was established in 1967 upon the signing of the ASEAN Declaration (or Bangkok Declaration)[127] by five founding members: Indonesia, Malaysia, the Philippines, Singapore,

118 *Id.* at §§ 7:1 and 7:2.

119 *See supra* note 99.

120 *See* Mupangavanhu, *supra* note 61, at 149. For example, some disparities related to the substantive examination which is left to the designated states. While some states examine on absolute and relative grounds, Burundi does not examine on either set of grounds, whilst Lesotho does not examine an application on relative grounds.

121 *Id.* at 150.

122 *See* the Decision on the Specialized Technical Committees, at the 26th Ordinary Session of the Assembly of the African Union, Addis Ababa, Jan. 30–31, 2016 (Assembly/AU/Dec.589(XXVI)), para. 2(x), https://au.int/sites/default/files/decisions/29514-assembly_au_dec_588_-_604_xxvi_e.pdf.

123 Statute of the Pan-African Intellectual Property Organization, https://au.int/sites/default/files/treaties/32549-treaty-0053_-_paipo_e.pdf. On the evolution of PAIPO, *see* Y. Mupangavanhu, *African Union Rising to the Need for Continental IP Protection? The Establishment of the Pan-African Intellectual Property Organization*, 59 J. OF AFR. L., 1–24 (2015).

124 *Id.* at art. 2.

125 *Id.* at art. 1 ("Intellectual Property").

126 *Id.* at art. 4.

127 1967 Association of Southeast Asian Nations Declaration (Bangkok Declaration), Aug. 8, 1967, ILM 1233.

and Thailand. Later, its membership expanded to Brunei Darussalam (1984), Vietnam (1995), Myanmar (1997), Lao PDR (1997), and Cambodia (1999). The initial aim of ASEAN was to promote peace and stability in the region,[128] with a long-term vision to create a regional economic organization.[129] ASEAN members follow the principles of consensus and non-interference with national policies: "the ASEAN Way."[130] ASEAN did not create institutions charged with developing, administering, and ruling on issues related to ASEAN-focused policies. Still, in 1992, ASEAN members signed an Agreement on the Common Effective Preferential Tariff Scheme for the ASEAN Free Trade Area[131] (AFTA) to foster regional economic integration and eliminate tariff and non-tariff barriers.[132] In 2003, they agreed to establish an ASEAN Community and, in 2007, adopted the ASEAN Charter.[133] One of the cornerstones of the ASEAN Community was the creation of the ASEAN Economic Community (AEC), which launched in 2015[134] with the goal to create a single market.[135]

In 1995, ASEAN members also adopted the ASEAN Framework Agreement on Intellectual Property Cooperation[136] (Framework Agreement) with the objective to cooperate in several IP-related areas, including trademarks.[137] To date, this cooperation has focused primarily on administrative matters such as assistance with domestic procedures adopted for trademark searches, as well as the creation of regional databases. Even though ASEAN members have not engaged in legislative harmonization regionally, all have reformed national trademark laws in the past two decades, many very recently, as part of their obligations as members of the WTO and TRIPS,[138] as well as the Paris Convention for the Protection of Industrial Property.[139] As of today, most ASEAN members are members of several other WIPO international agreements related to trademarks, including the Madrid Protocol for international trademark registrations.[140]

In 1996, pursuant to the IP Framework Agreement, ASEAN members established the ASEAN Working Group on Intellectual Property Cooperation (AWGIPC), which serves as a consultative

[128] *Id.*

[129] *Id.*

[130] 1976 Treaty of Amity and Cooperation in Southeast Asia, Feb. 24, 1976.

[131] Agreement on the Common Effective Preferential Tariff (CEPT) Scheme for the ASEAN Free Trade Area (AFTA), art. 5, Jan. 28, 1992, WIPO Lex. No. TRT/AFTA/001 [hereinafter CEPT-AFTA].

[132] ASEAN Trade in Goods Agreement (ATIGA), art. 8(d), Feb. 26, 2009, WIPO Lex. No. TRT/ASEAN/001 (stipulating that the protection and enforcement of IPRs may constitute a general exception to the prohibition to non-tariff barriers within ASEAN; ATIGA replaced the earlier CEPT-AFTA scheme signed in 1992).

[133] 2003 Declaration of ASEAN Concord II (Bali Concord II), Oct. 7, 2003.

[134] Cebu Declaration on the Acceleration of the Establishment of an ASEAN Community by 2015, Jan. 13, 2007: ASEAN members committed to accelerate the establishment of the ASEAN Economic Community in the Cebu Declaration on the Acceleration of the Establishment of an ASEAN Community by 2015. The ASEAN Community consists of the three pillars of the ASEAN Security Community, the ASEAN Economic Community (AEC), and the ASEAN Socio-Cultural Community.

[135] Declaration on the ASEAN Economic Community Blueprint, § 9, 2008 [hereinafter ASEAN AEC Blueprint]. For a detailed analysis of the creation of the AEC, *see* Stefano Inama & Edmund W. Sim, The Foundation of the ASEAN Economic Community: An Institutional and Legal Profile (2015).

[136] ASEAN Framework Agreement on Intellectual Property Cooperation, Dec. 15, 1995, WIPO Lex. No. TRT/ASEAN-IP/001 [hereinafter 1995 ASEAN IP Framework Agreement].

[137] *Id.* at art. 3(1).

[138] *See* TRIPS, *supra* note 5.

[139] Paris Convention, *supra* note 6.

[140] For example, Indonesia, Thailand, Singapore, Malaysia, Philippines, Vietnam, Cambodia, Brunei and Laos are members of the Madrid Protocol; Madrid Protocol Concerning the International Registration of Marks, June 27, 1989, WIPO MM/DC/27 Rev. (1989); Singapore is a member of the Singapore Treaty, Singapore Treaty on the Law of Trademarks, Mar. 27, 2006, S. Treaty Doc. No. 110-2; Indonesia is a contracting party to the Trademark Law Treaty, Trademark Law Treaty, Oct. 27, 1994, S. Treaty Doc. No. 105-35, 2037 UNTS 35.

group and includes the IP offices of the ASEAN members.[141] Various intra-ASEAN IP-related initiatives have been adopted by the AWGIPC, including: the Hanoi Plan of Action;[142] ASEAN Intellectual Property Rights Action Plan 2004–2010;[143] ASEAN Intellectual Property Rights Action Plan 2011–2015;[144] and the ASEAN Intellectual Property Rights Action Plan 2016–2025.[145]

In the early 1990s proposals emerged for a common ASEAN system for trademarks (perhaps following the momentum of the launch of the CTM Regulation in Europe). Notably, the 1995 IP Framework Agreement, in Article 1(5), included a statement saying "Member States shall explore the possibility of setting up of an ASEAN trademark system, including an ASEAN Trademark Office, if feasible, to promote the region-wide protection of trademark bearing in mind developments on regional and international protection of trademarks."[146] At that time, since no ASEAN member was yet a member of the WTO, this statement also meant that any development in this direction had to be in line with the principles set forth by TRIPS and the WIPO treaties, should ASEAN members want to join the international system in the future.[147] Ultimately, due to the challenges in practice, ASEAN members did not pursue this initiative.

Still, the ASEAN Economic Community Blueprint set out various other initiatives leading to greater harmonization among ASEAN members, again focusing primarily on achieving a higher level of technical and procedural convergence.[148] In order to reach this objective, members identified several strategic measures, including: strengthening IP offices and building IP infrastructure; developing regional IP platforms; joining several international treaties related to IP; expanding the ASEAN IP Ecosystem. One of the biggest steps towards procedural harmonization was the implementation, in 2014, of the Common Guidelines for the Substantive Examination of Trademarks in the ASEAN member states.[149] Even though the guidelines seek only to complement current practices being applied by the various ASEAN IP offices, they are an important tool for interoperability within national administrative agencies.

Under the ASEAN IP Portal, ASEAN members also launched ASEAN TMView, a database which was developed with the assistance of the EU. The database represents a link between ASEAN IP offices, applicants, and other stakeholders and offers an avenue to share information, creating interoperability regarding notices, regulations and procedures, data, internet links, and other relevant sources available.[150] In particular, the database allows ASEAN IP offices to share search and examination results among themselves free of charge. It also allows applicants to

[141] ASEAN, *About the AWGIPC*, https://aseanip.org/about.

[142] ASEAN, *Hanoi Plan of Action*, 1997, https://asean.org/?static_post=hanoi-plan-of-action.

[143] ASEAN, *Intellectual Property Rights Action Plan 2004–2010*, https://asean.org/?static_post=asean-intellectual-property-right-action-plan-2004-2010.

[144] ASEAN Secretariat, ASEAN IPR Action Plan 2011–2015, Aug. 11, 2011.

[145] ASEAN Intellectual Property Rights Action Plan 2016–2025, Jan. 1, 2016 [hereinafter ASEAN IP 2016–2025].

[146] 1995 ASEAN IP Framework Agreement, supra note 146, art. 1(5). *See also* Edy Santoso & Martin Roestamy, *ASEAN's Lack of Integration in Trademark Registration Related to ASEAN Economic Community (AEC) by 2015*, 18 J.L. Pol'y & Globalization 15, 20 (2013).

[147] *See* Elizabeth Siew-Kuan Ng, *ASEAN IP Harmonization: Striking the Delicate Balance*, 25 Pace Int'l L. Rev. 129, 137–38 (2013).

[148] ASEAN AEC Blueprint, *supra* note 136. *See also, generally*, Elizabeth Siew-Kuan Ng & Graeme W. Austin (eds.), International Intellectual Property and the ASEAN Way: Pathway to Interoperability (2017).

[149] ASEAN Secretariat, Common Guidelines for the Substantive Examination of Trademarks in the ASEAN Member States (1st ed.), Dec. 2018, https://asean.org/wp-content/uploads/2017/12/35.-November-2017-Common-Guidelines-for-the-Substantive-Examination-of-Trademarks.pdf.

[150] ASEAN TMView has been developed by the IP offices of ASEAN members with the support of the EU-ASEAN Project on the Protection of Intellectual Property Rights (ECAP III Phase II) administered by the EUIPO. The database can be accessed at http://asean-tmview.org.

search for trademark applications and registrations across ASEAN members, that is, national registrations in the separate ASEAN IP offices.[151] In addition, also with the help of the EU, ASEAN members developed the ASEAN TMclass, a database of classified goods and services for the registration of trademarks, which assists applicants with information regarding the terms to be included in a trademark application. ASEAN TMclass gives access to more than 13,800 standard terms and enables users to search for and verify the correct classification of those terms for goods or services in accordance with the criteria established by the Nice Agreement.[152]

Interestingly, in the latest 2016–2025 ASEAN Action Plan, the idea of the creation of a trademark registration system including the whole ASEAN territory resurfaced. Notably, under Initiative 9, titled "Improve service delivery of A[SEAN] M[ember] S[tate]s through connected online services, including patent, trademark, copyright and industrial design search systems, and online filing systems," item 9.2. refers to "[c]onduct[ing] a feasibility study for an ASEAN TM Registration system."[153] This time, the Action Plan refers only to a feasibility study, yet in February 2019, ASEAN members met with representatives of the EU to discuss this point specifically.[154] In particular, the EU will assist ASEAN in carrying out the feasibility study, which "will consider aspects such as legal infrastructure, operational set-up, fee structures, stakeholder interests, and the impact on national trademark systems."[155] According to EU representatives, an ASEAN regional system "would potentially reduce the time for businesses to register their trademarks across all ten ASEAN Member States and create greater certainty on registration procedures, ultimately improving the ease for businesses to operate in the region and fostering new investment."[156] Still, it is too soon to predict the possibility, in practice, that ASEAN members effectively move forward with a proposed pan-ASEAN unitary right in the near future. Certainly, as this chapter has described, regional trademark systems already operate in the EU and OAPI with a differentiated level of institutional harmonization. ASEAN may become the next regional organization to create a unitary right building on the intense cooperation on procedural aspects for national registrations that has taken place in ASEAN in the past years.

V TRADEMARK HARMONIZATION IN THE SOUTHERN COMMON MARKET: STILL A WORK IN PROGRESS

The Mercado Común del Sur (MERCOSUR), or "the Southern Common Market," is a regional trading bloc that seeks to achieve Latin American economic, political, and social integration. In 1991, Argentina, Brazil, Paraguay, and Uruguay signed the Asunción Treaty,[157] thereby founding MERCOSUR.[158] In 2006, Venezuela became a member. However, in August 2017, Venezuela had its membership suspended until "the full restoration of the democratic

[151] *Id.*

[152] ASEAN TMclass has been developed by the IP offices of ASEAN members also with the support of EUIPO's program ECAP III Phase II. The databases can be accessed at http://a.asean-tmclass.org.

[153] ASEAN IP 2016–2025, *supra* note 145, Initiative 9.2.

[154] William New, *ASEAN IP Offices Discuss Regional Trademark System*, IP WATCH, Feb. 18, 2019, https://ip-watch.org/2019/02/18/asean-ip-offices-discuss-regional-trademark-system/.

[155] *Id.*

[156] *Id.*

[157] Tratado para la Constitución de un Mercado Común entre la República Argentina, la República Federativa del Brasil, la República del Paraguay y la República Oriental del Uruguay [hereinafter Asunción Treaty], Asunción, Mar. 26, 1991, https://mercosur.int/documento/tratado-asuncion-constitucion-mercado-comun/.

[158] On the origins and evolution of MERCOSUR, *see* Andrés Malamud, *MERCOSUR Turns 15: Between Rising Talk and Declining Achievement*, 18 CAMBRIDGE REV. INT'L AFF. 421–36 (2005); John A. E. Vervaele, *Mercosur and Regional Integration in South America*, 54 INT'L & COMP. L.Q. 387, 390–91 (2005).

order in the country" is verified.[159] Bolivia started the process of accession in 2015.[160] Chile, Colombia, Ecuador, Guyana, Peru, and Surinam are associated members.[161]

MERCOSUR's main objective is to increase the efficiency and competitiveness of the members' economies by opening markets, promoting economic development in the framework of a globalized world, improving infrastructure and communications, making better use of available resources, preserving the environment, generating industrial complementation, and coordinating macroeconomic policies.[162] The member states worked to achieve this through the establishment of a Common External Tariff (CET)[163] and the undertaking of a common trade policy. It should also be noted that Latin America has made various attempts at integration of economic systems. This includes the creation of organizations like the Asociación Latinoamericana de Libre Comercio (ALALC) and ALADI,[164] which seem to have had little success due to the different economic, political, and social levels of its members.[165]

In the past decades, MERCOSUR members have worked to reach agreements on a substantial number of trade matters and have adopted several resolutions seeking to harmonize their national legal and regulatory systems. Since the beginning, however, the major problem for cooperation, the implementation and expansion of the MERCOSUR agenda has been the absence of both an effective dispute resolution mechanism and effective supranational institutions. In particular, the MERCOSUR structure is based on: the Consejo del Mercado Común (CMC), which consists of the Ministers for Foreign Affairs and the Economy and the Meetings of the Heads of State; the Grupo del Mercado Común (GMC), the executive branch of MERCOSUR, in charge of agricultural matters and harmonization of technical product norms, the environment, financial services, border control, tourism, and the Comisión del Commercio del Mercosur (CCM), which handles specialized economic issues, such as competition, procurement, customs, and consumer protection.[166] The CMC also deals with complaints in these areas from state parties and private parties. All MERCOSUR decisions should be unanimous as they are theoretically binding on the members. Yet no effective implementation control mechanism is in place, which compromises, in practice, the functioning of MERCOSUR as a regional organization.

Regarding the harmonization of trademark laws, in 1995 MERCOSUR adopted a Protocol to harmonize intellectual property norms in the field of trademarks, indications of source, and

159 Decisión sobre la Suspensión de la República Bolivariana de Venezuela en el Mercosur en Aplicación del Protocolo de Ushuaia sobre Compromiso Democrático en el MERCOSUR, Sao Paulo, Aug. 5, 2017, https://mercosur.int/documento/decision-sobre-la-suspension-de-venezuela-en-el-mercosur/.

160 The protocol to admit Bolivia to Mercosur was adopted in 2015 (Protocolo de Adhesion del Estadio Plurinacional de Bolivia al MERCOSUR, Brasilia, July 12, 2015). All MERCOSUR members, except Brazil, have ratified the protocol. In July 2019, Bolivia announced that its president will seek a meeting with his Brazilian counterpart to discuss Brazil's failure to ratify this protocol, https://plenglish.com/index.php?o=rn&id=44469&SEO=bolivias-joining-mercosur-to-strengthen-trade-in-the-region.

161 *See* Mercosur, https://mercosur.int/en/about-mercosur/mercosur-countries/. Associated states are members of the Asociación Latinoamericana de Integración (ALADI) with which MERCOSUR has concluded free trade agreements, and which subsequently requested to be considered as associated states. They may participate in meetings of MERCOSUR bodies that deal with issues of common interest. Similarly, associated members may be countries with which MERCOSUR has concluded limited economic integration agreements under art. 25 of the Montevideo Treaty (Instrumento que instituye la Asociación Latinoamericana de Integración, Montevideo, Aug. 12, 1980).

162 *See About Mercosur*, Merco Press, https://en.mercopress.com/about-mercosur.

163 Asunción Treaty, *supra* note 157, art. 1.

164 *See* Andrés Malamud, *Theories of Regional Integration and the Origins of MERCOSUR*, *in* The Law of MERCOSUR 9, 24 (Marcílio Toscana Franca Filho et al. eds., 2010).

165 Umberto Celli Jr., *Mercosur: An Opportunity for Investment*, 20 Int'l Bus. Law. 480, 481 (1992). ALALC and ALADI comprised the ten Latin American countries of South America plus Mexico and Cuba: *see* Malamud, *supra* note 158, at 23 fn. 73.

166 Asunción Treaty, *supra* note 157, ch. II.

appellations of origin.[167] However, only Paraguay and Uruguay have ratified the Protocol to date,[168] which accordingly still has to enter into force in Argentina and Brazil. The failure of Argentina and Brazil to ratify the Protocol may be attributed, at least in part, to the political turmoil and shifting alliances, and the economic tribulations of the region. Moreover, the Protocol does not purport to achieve total harmonization at the legislative level. Rather, like its contemporary the TRIPS Agreement,[169] it seeks to establish minimum protection standards for certain matters.[170] Notably, the states party to the Protocol oblige themselves[171] to comply with the provisions of the Paris Convention[172] and the TRIPS Agreement.[173]

In particular, the Protocol defines the term "trademark" to connote any sign that is susceptible of distinguishing goods or services in commerce.[174] Trademark protection has to be extended to service and collective marks; the protection of certification marks is optional.[175] A state party may set as a condition of registration that a sign be visually perceptible.[176] A trademark may consist of "fancy words" ("palabras de fantasia"), names, pseudonyms, commercial themes, letters, numbers, monograms, figures, portraits, labels, shields, imprints, trimmings, lines and stripes, combinations and arrangements of colors, and the shape of the products, of their containers or fittings, or of the means or places of sale of the products or services.[177] Motion, scent, and sound marks are clearly excluded from registrability under the Protocol. Trademarks may also consist of national or foreign geographical indications, provided that they are not indications of source ("indicaciones de procedencia") or denominations of origin ("denominaciónes de origen").[178] The states commit themselves reciprocally to protect their indications of sources and denominations of origin.[179]

167 Protocolo de Armonizacion de Normas Sobre Propiedad Intelectual en el MERCOSUR en Materia de Marcas, Indicaciones de Procedencia y Denominaciones de Origen [hereinafter MERCOSUR Trademark Protocol], Asunción, Aug. 5, 1995. For an English translation, *see* Protocol on Harmonization of Intellectual Property Norms in MERCOSUR in the Field of Trademarks, Indications of Source, and Appellations of Origin, http://ipiba.org/1403-2/. On the evolution of the Protocol, *see* Félix Vacas Fernández, *The Protection of Intellectual Property in MERCOSUR in* THE LAW OF MERCOSUR 317, 321 (Marcílio Toscana Franca Filho et al. eds., 2010).

168 On Nov. 15, 1996 and Dec. 14, 1998, respectively. It entered into force on for these countries on Aug. 6, 2000.

169 TRIPS, *supra* note 5.

170 MERCOSUR Trademark Protocol, *supra* note 167, art. 1. Compare the TRIPS Agreement, *supra* note 5, art. 1.1.

171 *Id.* at art. 2(1).

172 Paris Convention, *supra* note 6, arts. 6–7.

173 TRIPS, *supra* note 5, arts. 15–21.

174 MERCOSUR Trademark Protocol, *supra* note 167, art. 5(1) (referring to "qualquier signo que sea susceptible de distinguir en el comercio productos o servicios" (any sign capable of distinguishing goods and services in the course of trade).

175 *Id.* at art. 5(3).

176 *Id.* at art. 5(2) (referring to marks "visualmente perceptible" [visually perceptible]). This requirement derives from Brazilian trademark law: Lei no. 9.279 de 14 de maio de 1996 (Lei da Propriedade Industrial, alterada pela Lei no. 10.196, de 14 de feveiro de 2001), art. 122.

177 *Id.* at art. 6(1). Container marks are not protected by Argentinian trademark law: Carlos Adrian Garaventa and Pablo Wegbrait, *Integration of Intellectual Property in Latin America, in* INTERNATIONAL INTELLECTUAL PROPERTY AND THE ASEAN WAY: PATHWAYS TO INTEROPERABILITY, 291, 296 (Elizabeth Siew-Kuan Ng & Graeme W. Austin eds., 2017).

178 *Id.* at art. 6(2). An "indication of source" is the "geographic name of a country, city, region or place of its territory, known as an extraction, production or manufacturing center of a certain product or rendering of a certain service" (art. 19(2), translated by Garaventa & Wegbrait, *supra* note 177, at 297). A "denomination of origin," in turn, connotes the "the geographic name of a country, city, region or place of its territory, which identifies goods or services whose qualities or characteristics result exclusively or essentially from the geographic medium, including natural and human factors" (art. 19(3), translated by Garaventa & Wegbrait, *supra* note 177, at 297).

179 *Id.* at art. 19(1).

The Protocol does not distinguish between absolute and relative grounds for refusing a trademark registration.[180] It simply states that the following may not be registered as trademarks: (1) descriptive signs, or signs that are generically used to designate products or services, or types of products or services, that the trademark distinguishes; (2) signs that constitute indications of source or denominations of origin; (3) signs that are misleading, contrary to morality, or public order; (4) signs that are susceptible to suggesting falsely a connection to persons living or dead, or to religions; (5) signs that are formed with national symbols or symbols of any country; (6) signs that are susceptible of falsely suggesting a relation with persons living or dead, or with the national symbols of any country, or that offend their value or respectability; (7) signs that imitate or duplicate, partly or completely, a trademark that the applicant evidently could not fail to have recognized as belonging to an owner established or domiciled in any of the party states, or that is susceptible of causing confusion or association.[181] The Protocol also states that a party state must reject an application for the registration of a trademark that has been proven to infringe upon the rights of third parties; a party state must likewise invalidate the registration of trademarks applied for in bad faith that have been proven to infringe upon rights of third parties.[182]

As established also in the TRIPS Agreement, Article 6*bis* of the Paris Convention,[183] on the protection of well-known marks, applies *mutatis mutandis* to services under the Protocol. In this respect, the Protocol offers some guidelines in order to determine the notoriety ("notoriedad") of the trademark. Notably, it states that the knowledge of the sign must be taken into account, including such knowledge in the party state in which protection is requested, which knowledge has been acquired from the publicity ("publicidad") of the sign.[184] The party states must protect trademarks that have become exceptionally well known ("conocimiento excepcional") and that belong to nationals of the party states. Such protection shall be against the duplication or imitation of said trademarks, in any line of activity, provided that there is a possibility of harm.[185]

Still in parallel with the TRIPS Agreement, the Protocol provides that the registration of a trademark grants the owner an exclusive right of use, and the right to prevent any person from performing, without the owner's consent, the following acts: the use, in commerce, of a sign identical or similar to the trademark, for any products or services, when such use may cause confusion or a risk of association with the holder of the registration; unjust economic or commercial damage caused by a dilution of the distinctive force or the commercial value of the trademark; or a risk of an improper use of the prestige of the trademark or of its owner.[186]

In those party states in which there is an obligation to use the trademark, a competent authority may cancel the registration of a trademark when it has not been used in any of the states for five years preceding the date on which the cancellation action was filed. The non-use may be excused when there are reasons that justify the lack of use of the trademark.[187]

Priority for the registration of a trademark is granted to the person who first requests it, unless that right is claimed by a third party who has used the trademark in a public, peaceful way and in

180 Uruguay is the only country to make that distinction: Ley No. 17.011 del 256 de septiembre de 1998, dictanse normas relativas a las marcas, chapter II.
181 *Id.* at art. 9(1), (2) and (4).
182 *Id.* at art. 9(3).
183 Paris Convention, *supra* note 66.
184 MERCOSUR Trademark Protocol, *supra* note 167, art. 9(5).
185 *Id.* at art. 9(6).
186 *Id.* at art. 11.
187 *Id.* at art. 15.

good faith, in any of the party states, for a minimum of six months, provided that upon presentation of their objection, the party also requests the registration of the trademark.[188]

Lastly, party states are obliged to adopt the Nice classification[189] if they have not already done so.[190]

Of the four party states, only Brazil has acceded to the Madrid Protocol.[191] It entered into force for Brazil on 2 October 2019.[192]

In summary, the Protocol establishes minimum standards for the region in line with the Paris Convention and the TRIPS Agreement without adding additional provisions to those already provided in these agreements. As the four MERCOSUR party states are all members of these two instruments, there is a significant degree of harmonization even in the absence of the ratification by all states of the Protocol at this time. In the end, though, the failure to ratify the Protocol, combined with the lack of engagement of states has led commentators to dismiss MERCOSUR as simply another instance of Latin American "grands mots, petits effets."[193]

In addition, MERCOSUR may have been overtaken by a new economic grouping: 2010 marked the creation of the Community of Latin American and Caribbean States (CELAC), a regional bloc of thirty-three states. The integration model of CELAC is completely different from that of its predecessors, and it has very different objectives, such as strengthening the sovereign powers of Latin American states, and promoting development in the region, without neglecting social issues. In September 2015, shortly after Ecuador took over the pro tempore presidency, during the third Meeting of Ministers and Higher Officials in Science, Technology and Innovation of the CELAC, it was made known that the priority of the Ecuadorian presidency would be to "encourage a process towards the definition of common regional policies in areas concerning science, technology and research, within an approach of regional sovereignty."[194] One of the aspects that Ecuador intended to tackle in order to achieve this goal is harmonization of industrial property policies in the region. The CELAC ministers have accordingly been entrusted with developing a new legal framework in line with the goals of the regional bloc. The ministers consider that this initiative differs from the TRIPS Agreement, which they consider to reinforce technological dependence.[195] Yet, nine years later, these promises have also come to naught.

VI CONCLUSION: THE DIFFERENT PATHS (AND POLITICS) OF REGIONAL TRADEMARK PROTECTION

The comparative analysis of the EU, OAPI, ARIPO, ASEAN, and MERCOSUR highlights a variety of paths that can be followed as part of the process of regional harmonization and integration of trademark laws. As was stressed in the introduction, these various paths largely reflect different stages of regional integration as well as regional and national development.

188 *Id.* at art. 8.

189 Nice Agreement, *supra* note 103.

190 MERCOSUR Trademark Protocol, *supra* note 167, art. 18.

191 Madrid Protocol, *supra* note 70.

192 *See* Madrid (Marks) Notification No. 224, https://wipo.int/treaties/en/notifications/madridp-gp/treaty_madridp_gp_224.html.

193 Malamud, *supra* note 158, at 27. Garaventa & Wegbraith similarly conclude that all proposals for intellectual property harmonization in Latin America are "frail" (*supra* note 177, at 291).

194 Garaventa & Wegbrait, *supra* note 177, at 300.

195 *Id.*

In particular, in light of the analysis of the organizations addressed in this chapter, we identify three main levels of harmonization and integration, defined as follows: (1) "hard, or harder, integration and harmonization" in regions that have developed a system of a supranational unitary right such as the system today adopted by the EU and OAPI; (2) "soft, or softer, integration and harmonization" in regions in which nation states have developed a variety of mechanisms for interoperability and cooperation between national offices, as in ARIPO and to a lesser degree in ASEAN, and are currently exploring the possibility of greater integration possibly through the creation of a unitary rights, as in ASEAN; and (3) "minimal substantive integration and harmonization" in regions where administrative regional cooperation regarding trademarks does not seem a priority and discussions on larger integration and creation of unitary rights have not led to reforms, such as MERCOUSUR and most other free trade areas worldwide.

Certainly, members of regional organizations need to share minimum standards of harmonization of national laws in order to promote a minimum level of regional market integration. As mentioned in the introduction, this minimum level of integration is largely achieved today by the fact that most countries worldwide, including the vast majority of members of any regional organization, are signatories to the Paris Convention, the TRIPS Agreement, and several WIPO treaties, including treaties regarding the international registration of marks and related administrative procedures. Still, regional organizations generally go beyond this minimum level of harmonization and integration, even though not all regional organizations can aim today at achieving a full-scale market integration through the creation of unitary trademark rights like the systems currently applied by the EU and OAPI. In particular, as demonstrated by the analysis of existing organizations in this chapter, the establishment of supranational unitary rights requires a level of regional commitment that may not easily be achieved or advisable in some regional organizations at the present time. It also generally requires the creation (and acceptance) of regional institutions, including adjudication bodies. Instead, regional organizations should still follow the type of harmonization and regional integration process that best suits the regional interests of each organization, including the national interests and the level of economic and social development of its members.

For example, a full-scale economic integration was the primary objective of the European project since its inception. Under the design of its founding fathers, the EU has historically been driven by functionalist, and even federalist theories of regional integration. As a result, EU member states were required early on to harmonize their national laws, including on trademarks. The importance of free movement of goods was at the heart of the creation of the CTM Regulation as the original name of the EUIPO indicated – Office for the Harmonization of the Internal Market. Hence, even for the EU, several decades had to pass to reach a fully integrated trademark system. In this respect, the role of the EU institutions (the CJEU and the EU Commission in particular) was crucial for the EU to achieve a full-scale harmonization and integration of trademark law and policies. A similar observation applies to OAPI, except that with OAPI the substructure supporting the integration was almost more cultural (shared strong cultural ties to a former colonial ruler) than economic. Both the EU and OAPI systems are based on the principle of supremacy – as regional integration involves an association of states with different legal systems, the only way to have all members operate according to the same rules is to create a common legal system that outranks the members' domestic legal systems. However, unlike the EU, where the EU trademark system operates in parallel with national trademark laws, OAPI gives effect to the principle of supremacy by creating a supranational trademark law and registry to supplant national trademark systems and laws. Yet the courts of each OAPI member state are competent to rule on any intellectual property infringement, and a final legal decision as to the validity of an intellectual property title rendered by a court in one member state is binding on all other member states, except for decisions based on public policy and morality. This principle diverges from the EU system, in which only the decisions of the CJEU are binding on EU member states.

On the other side, the system of interoperability created by the members of ARIPO represents integration in the weakest sense of all the systems canvassed here. The Banjul Protocol merely establishes a regional registration office, entrusted with the registration of marks and their administration on behalf of the contracting states. An application for registration is examined according to the national law of a designated state. There is no attempt at any harmonization of substantive trademark law. Both OAPI and ARIPO face the problem of inconsistency of judicial rulings, especially in the absence of a supranational court (such as the CJEU in Europe) to hand down definitive judgments. It is an indication of the trade insignificance of the ARIPO trademark system that neither of the continental economic powerhouses (Nigeria and South Africa) have acceded to the system. In any event, as the two most recent protocols adopted by ARIPO show, the focus of the organization has shifted from industrial property to the protection of traditional knowledge and genetic resources.

Somewhat in between the EU, OAPI, and ARIPO sits ASEAN. While ASEAN members aim at integrating their national markets, including the harmonization of laws related to trademarks, ASEAN has adopted "a more flexible IP cooperation model" which "enables its members to move forward collectively, but at varying paces in accordance with their developmental level and capacity." Translated into practice, this reflects a more modest approach towards regional integration which is focused primarily on administrative cooperation and interoperability between national offices rather than a full-scale integration of laws, at least for the time being. Moreover, even though ASEAN members are again considering the creation of a unitary trademark rights, the Achilles heel of the process of ASEAN integration remains the fact that ASEAN never created (and does not seem to desire) strong supranational regional institutions, such as the CJEU or the European Commission. Yet, as the EU experience has demonstrated, institutions are necessary for the long-term and full-scale harmonization of laws, especially regarding the creation and functioning of a unitary regional trademark system.

Finally, MERCOSUR started off auspiciously with an approach in line with contemporary instruments, particularly the TRIPS Agreement – harmonization through setting minimum standards of protection to be enacted by party states. The uptake by the party states has been slow, with the two most important economies (Brazil and Argentina) yet to ratify the Protocol. And twenty-four years later, they are increasingly unlikely to do so, especially with larger and more important regional economic blocs emerging. Compared with the EU, MERCOSUR lacks one of the building blocks of hard integration and harmonization – economic, institutional, and political stability. Compared with OAPI, MERCOSUR lacks the interest to create a unitary supranational system of intellectual property rights; compared with ARIPO and ASEAN, MERCOSUR also seems to lack the desire to create a close system of interoperability between the national offices of its party states. Given the constant flux in political alliances and economic systems in the region, the outlook for meaningful integration and harmonization of trademark systems in MERCOSUR remains quite uncertain.

In conclusion, different regional organizations across the world have chosen a variety of paths to integrate and collaborate in the area of trademark law, regarding the harmonization of laws as well as the administrative procedures of registering trademarks, addressing oppositions and cancellations, and adjudicating legal disputes in this area. These paths span a large spectrum of options, which go from a system based on full integration and the creation of supranational rights to a median solution of seeking administrative interoperability, to a minimum of harmonizing national laws in line with general international agreements. The choice of which path to take is largely dependent on each regional organization and its members based on regional and national interests regarding levels of development – economic and social – political structure, geographical size, and possible interactions of individual members with countries outside the specific regional organizations. The levels of regional integration in the area of trademark law have also evolved within time, as the examples in this chapter indicate, and this has generally led to closer regional cooperation. This trend is clearly visible in the EU, OAPI, ARIPO, and ASEAN. On the other side, the level of cooperation originally envisioned for MERCOSUR has been weaker than expected. This reminds us that, despite the original objective, political, economic, and other circumstances can delay, or negatively affect, the process of integration in individual organizations.

7

Territoriality and Supranationality

Judicial and Legislative Competence in International Trademark Disputes

Edouard Treppoz and Jane C. Ginsburg***

I INTRODUCTION

Well before online shopping, advertising, and infringement, trademarks resisted territorial confinement. Thanks to mail-order deliveries, broadcasting spillovers, tourism, and immigration, marks might be used, or simply known, beyond their countries of registration.[1] The Internet greatly amplifies a preexisting condition of international commerce. As other chapters in this volume detail, trademark law has developed substantive responses to unauthorized supranational exploitation of trademarks.[2] This chapter addresses the phenomenon from a litigation perspective: what national court is competent to adjudicate a multiterritorial trademark dispute, and what law applies? While these questions precede e-commerce, the Internet has vastly multiplied their occurrence, thus augmenting the need for fair and predictable solutions.

This chapter will examine EU and US approaches to judicial competence (which court decides) and to legislative competence (what law applies). Given the more extensive development of these issues in the European Union, the chapter will focus primarily on EU regulations with some comparative glances at the United States. This comparative study is limited to these two jurisdictions since they have developed a rich and mature core of decisions on those complex issues. With respect to the EU perspective, we determined not to address national rules of private international law, but to examine how EU rules of judicial and legislative competence apply to litigations involving the EU-wide trademark title on the one hand and national trademark rights on the other.

II COMPETENCE OF EU COURTS TO DECIDE MULTITERRITORIAL TRADEMARK DISPUTES

Trademark rights in the EU can be both national and community-wide. Trademark owners may register marks with local authorities to secure rights in particular EU member states; they may

* Professor, Faculty of Law, University of Paris 1, Panthéon-Sorbonne.

** Morton L. Janklow Professor of Literary and Artistic Property Law, Columbia Law School, Columbia University. Thanks to Professor Barton Beebe; and for research assistance to Andrew McWhorter, Columbia Law School Class of 2019.

1 *See, e.g.*, Graeme Austin, *The Story of* Steele v. Bulova*: Trademarks on the Line*, *in* Intellectual Property Stories 395 (Jane C. Ginsburg & Rochelle Cooper Dreyfuss eds., 2005); Leah Chan Grinvald, *A Tale of Two Theories of Well-Known Marks*, 13 Vand. J. Ent. & Tech. L. 1 (2010); Alexis Weissberger, *Is Fame Alone Sufficient to Create Priority Rights: An International Perspective on the Viability of the Famous/Well-Known Marks Doctrine*, 24 Cardozo Arts & Ent. L.J. 739 (2006).

2 See Chapters 1, 5, and 6 in this volume.

also obtain an EU-wide title through registration with the European Union Intellectual Property Office (EUIPO). The EU Trade Mark Directive[3] harmonizes national trademark laws; the EU Trade Mark Regulation[4] establishes the existence and scope of protection of the community-wide title.

A *Multilateral Litigations and National Trademarks*

The Brussels I*bis* Regulation determines the competence of EU member state judges to adjudicate claims of infringement.[5] The Regulation, as restrictively interpreted by the Court of Justice of the European Union (CJEU), adopts a territorialist approach unfavorable to plaintiffs seeking multiterritorial relief. We will first lay out the Regulation's general structure and then explain its application to trademark infringement claims.

1 *General Structure*

Article 4 of the Regulation sets forth a general rule designating the forum of the defendant's domicile.[6] The Regulation also provides rules of special competence, particularly with respect to multiple defendants, and regarding tort claims (including trademark infringement). Thus, in the case of multiple defendants, Article 8.1 allows jurisdiction over all codefendants at the domicile of one codefendant on the condition that separate litigations pose a risk of irreconcilable judgments. With respect to tort claims, Article 7.2 permits the courts of the place where the wrongful act has occurred (or, for prospective relief, may occur) to exercise jurisdiction.

Two additional provisions of the Brussels I*bis* Regulation may play an important role in trademark infringement actions. Article 35 permits a court to enter "provisional, including protective, measures" even if that court lacks substantive competence over the merits of the case. And Article 24.4 establishes a rule of exclusive competence in cases challenging the validity of registered rights, including trademarks. In theory, the exclusive competence of the court of the member state of registration does not affect infringement actions. In practice, as we will see, this text often limits the trademark owner's forum-selection options because it governs actions in which challenges to the registration are raised as a defense.

2 *Application to Trademark Infringement Claims*

In theory, a trademark owner may litigate in a forum other than the EU defendant's domicile in three instances. First, if the infringement occurs in a member state other than the defendant's domicile; second, when there are multiple defendants domiciled in different states; third, when the trademark owner seeks provisional remedies such as a temporary restraining order to prevent

[3] Directive 2015/2436, of the European Parliament and of the Council of Dec. 16, 2015, to approximate the laws of the member states relating to trademarks, 2015 OJ (L 336) (EU).

[4] Council Regulation 207/2009 of Feb. 26, 2009, on the Community trademark, 2009 OJ (L 78) (EC), amended by Regulation 2015/2424.

[5] Regulation 1215/2012 of the European Parliament and of the Council of Dec. 12, 2012 on jurisdiction and the recognition and enforcement of judgments in civil and commercial matters (recast), 2012 OJ (L 351) (EU). The Regulation applies to EU member state domiciliary defendants; it does not apply to infringement claims against defendants not domiciled in an EU member state, see art. 4. In matters concerning the registration or validity of an EU national registered right, including trademarks, the Regulation will apply regardless of the defendant's domicile, see art. 24.4.

[6] *See generally* Eva Storskrubb, Civil Procedure and EU Law (2008); Brussels I Regulation (Ulrich Magnus & Peter Mankowski eds., 2d ed. 2012); Samuel P. Baumgartner, *Recent Reforms in EU Law: Recognition and Enforcement of Foreign Judgments*, 97 Judicature 188, 190 (2014).

sales of allegedly infringing goods. In practice, multiple fora may not be available to the trademark owner, but the alleged infringer may effectively engage in forum-shopping.

Article 7.2 provides for jurisdiction "in matters relating to tort, delict or quasi-delict, in the courts for the place where the harmful event occurred or may occur." Article 7(2) of the Brussels I Regulation offers an option to the plaintiff, who can also seize a court of the country in which the infringement occurred. For example, the owner of an Italian trademark infringed by a German competitor can choose between a German court having jurisdiction under Article 4 and an Italian court having jurisdiction under Article 7(2). The choice becomes more complicated if the infringement is spread over several countries, especially in the case of infringement over the Internet. The connecting factor referring to the place of the tort seems useless, for such an infringement is not limited to one country. For infringement of personality rights, the CJEU's solution was to offer a new powerful jurisdictional tool for the victim in order to fight efficiently against these new harms made on the Internet.[7] This tool was the creation of a *forum actoris* at the place of the alleged victim's center of interest, this court having general jurisdiction over all territorial claims. As a matter of fact, the victim could choose between two courts having general jurisdiction – that of the defendant's domicile and that of the victim's center of interest. This *forum actoris* could have been easily and efficiently extended to IP. Nevertheless, the Court decided not to extend it to IP because of the principle of territoriality.[8] Instead, the European Court of Justice has resolved the issue of cyber infringement by deciding that plaintiff could bring its action only "before either the courts of the Member State in which the trade mark is registered or the courts of the Member State of the place of establishment of the advertiser."[9]

As to the place of the damage, the Court subsequently decided in a copyright case "that the occurrence of damage and/or the likelihood of its occurrence arise from the accessibility in the Member State of the referring court."[10] Thus, the jurisdiction of the court may depend on the existence of a local trademark registration and the accessibility in the forum of the potential infringing website, even if the website does not target this specific forum state.[11] While the jurisdiction of the place where the damage occurs is limited to locally-occurring damage, the courts of the place where the event giving rise to the damage possess a general territorial jurisdiction. Therefore, a German court could have jurisdiction over the infringement of an Austrian trademark if the infringement event originated in Germany. Nevertheless, this connecting factor will usually point to the same court as Article 4 (ex Article 2) of the Brussels I*bis* Regulation. In most cases, the place where the harm occurred would be the same place as the defendant's domicile.

Consequently, the only national court with competence over all nationally distinct infringements will be the court of the defendant's domicile. There will in theory be one member state court with jurisdiction over the entire multiterritorial claim. But in reality, the alleged infringer may "torpedo" the trademark owner's ability to consolidate the action in a single forum. It suffices for the defendant to initiate actions challenging the validity of each national registration.

[7] Joined Cases C-509/09 & C-161/10, *eDate Advertising GmbH* v. *Martinez* v. *Société MGN Ltd.*, 2011 ECR I-10269.

[8] "Contrary to the situation of a person who considers that there has been an infringement of his personality rights, which are protected in all Member States, the protection afforded by the registration of a national mark is, in principle, limited to the territory of the Member State in which it is registered, so that, in general, its proprietor cannot rely on that protection outside the territory." Case C-523/10, *Wintersteiger* v. *Prods. 4U Sondermaschinenbau GmbH*, 2012 ECR I-0000, § 25.

[9] *Id.*

[10] Case C-441/13, *Hejduk* v. *EnergieAgentur.NRW GmbH*, ECLI:EU:C:2015:28, § 34.

[11] The fact that the European Court endorses the targeting criterion for the EU trademark might change the analysis when it comes to national trademarks (Case C-172/18, *AMS Neve* v. *Heritage Audio SL*, ECLI:EU:C:2019:674).

Indeed, ever since the 2006 decision in *Roche Nederland BV* v. *Primus* [GAT],[12] now codified at section 4 of Article 24, the courts of the member state of registration have exclusive jurisdiction "irrespective of whether the issue is raised by way of an action or as a defence." As a result, while the forum may have competence over the infringement claim, this competence does not extend to incidental questions going to the validity of each national registration. Thus, if the trademark infringement plaintiff encounters a defense of invalidity of the registration, the claim must be heard in the courts of the member state of registration. As a practical matter, the trademark owner may end up having to anticipate seeing its multiterritorial action thus frustrated, and thus of its own motion litigate locally in each national jurisdiction.

The same observation applies to actions involving multiple codefendants. Suppose a trademark is registered in several EU member states and is allegedly infringed in the same way in each member state of registration – but by different defendants, such as local subsidiaries of the same corporation. Article 8.1 could allow the trademark owner to initiate an action against all defendants in any of the fora in which at least one defendant is domiciled. However, in its *Roche* decision, concerning national patent rights, the CJEU found no risk of inconsistent judgments under Article 8.1.[13] The court ruled that the risk turned on an identity of law and facts, but in that case, the IP title in each country was different (each national patent being independent of the others) and did not present itself because each patent law was territorial to each state. This excessively formalist approach[14] in practice imposes on the trademark owner the obligation to sue each infringer locally even if all the national infringements are interrelated, and even if the national laws are substantively similar. As a result, notwithstanding the right owner's endeavor to consolidate its action before a single forum, the CJEU's caselaw requires fragmentation.[15]

With respect to provisional remedies, the option allowed by Article 31 remains confined, once again, to territorial competence. This result follows from Article 42, which requires for recognition of a provisional measure the production of a certificate attesting to the competence of the court over the substance of the claim. Finally, and even more radically, the CJEU's interpretations subject the right owner to the infringer's forum-shopping. This reversal of the normal course of forum-shopping in favor of the infringer derives from the possibility in national law to initiate an action seeking a declaration of non-infringement. The procedural consequence is that the infringer, in place of the right owner, becomes the plaintiff. Particularly since the CJEU's decision in *The Ship Tatry* issued in 1994,[16] the rightholder may not select its preferred forum to initiate an infringement action. The rightholder will be bound by the infringer's selection of a forum for its declaratory judgment action. The reason for this outcome is simple: EU law recognizes that a negative action, in this case an action for a declaration of non-infringement, has the same cause and the same object as the positive action, that is, the

[12] Case C-539/03, *Roche Nederland BV* v. *Primus*, 2006 ECR I-06535.

[13] *Id.*

[14] For critiques of *Roche*, see, e.g., Horatia Muir-Watt, Brussels I Regulation (Ulrich Magnus & Peter Mankowski eds., 2d ed. 2012), art. 6 A 25 a; *and also* Tristan Azzi, *Les conflits de procédure*, *in* Droit international privé et propriété intellectuelle in Droit international privé et propriété intellectuelle 215 (Cyril Nourrisat & Edouard Treppoz eds., 2010).

[15] Notwithstanding the CJEU's subsequent *Solvay* decision (Case C-616/10, *Solvay SA* v. *Honeywell*, ECLI:EU:C:2012:445), which did uphold a specific application of the interrelated codefendants basis of jurisdiction, the CJEU does not appear inclined to abandon its general approach in *Roche* when each codefendor infringes locally in its domicile's country (see for an implicit confirmation of *Roche* when it comes to national titles: Joined Cases C-24/16 & C-25/16, *Nintendo Co. Ltd.* v. *BigBen Interactive GmbH*, Sept. 27, 2017, ECLI:EU:C:2017:724, §51).

[16] Case C-406/92, *Owners of Ship "Tatry"* v. *Owners of Ship "Maciej Rataj,"* 1994 ECR I-05439.

infringement claim. The concrete consequence pertains to the application of the rules of *lis pendens*, which require that the court subsequently seized by the right owner suspend the action in favor of the court first seized by the infringer. The Italians have self-interestedly called for the development of these so-called torpedo injuctions,[17] through which the infringer brings a declaratory judgment action before a slow-moving court; this forum selection will subsequently oblige the right owner to litigate its infringement claim before the same court. The deleterious effects of this caselaw have been multiplied by the CJEU's judgment in *Folien Fischer*[18] issued in 2012 bringing actions seeking declarations of non-infringement within the scope of Article 7.2 of the Regulation. The effect was to open the way to forum-shopping by the defendant that would be binding on the rightholder, against its will.

The paradox that emerges from this rapid survey of the concrete applications of the Brussels I*bis* Regulation is that the rightholder is compelled to fragment territorially its infringement actions – as if the territoriality of the title imposed a territoriality of litigation, even though this is in fact incorrect – while the infringer benefits from forum-shopping rather than the rightholder. EU procedural rules, therefore, seem to favor the infringer over the rightholder, even though nothing in the substantive or procedural texts requires this outcome.[19]

B Multilateral Litigations and Unitary European Union-Wide Trademarks

Litigations based on EU trademarks are governed by a specific text characterized as a *lex specialis*.[20] This *lex specialis* allows the plaintiff to consolidate the litigation before a single forum that will have a pan-European jurisdiction. In three important decisions, the CJEU enhanced the forum-shopping opportunities that EU rules offer to trademark plaintiffs.

1 *The Pan-European Opening for European Union-Wide Title:* A lex specialis *Consistent with Rightholder Interests*

The arrival of the truly European trademark title[21] (Regulation 207/2009 of 27 February 2009, amended by Regulation 2424/2015) affected the rules on judicial competence respecting infringement claims. Competence no longer derives from the Brussels I*bis* Regulation, but from the rules set out in the regulation on EU-wide trademark title, aptly characterized as *lex specialis*.[22] The goal of these rules is to assure the rightholder that the courts of at least one member state will be competent to hear a trademark infringement claim. Pursuant to Article 97 of Regulation 207/2009, the search for a competent forum proceeds according to successive points of attachment, starting with the courts of the member state on whose territory the defendant is domiciled. Failing that, competence may be based on the member state in which the plaintiff is domiciled, or where the Trademark Office has its seat. For an EU

17 Mario Franzosi, *Worldwide Patent Litigation and the Italian Torpedo*, 7 EIPR 382 (1997).

18 ECJ, Oct. 25, 2012, *Folien Fischer*: Case C-133/11, *Folien Fischer AG* v. *Ritrama SpA*, ECLI:EU:C:2012:664.

19 *See, e.g.*, Dário Moura Vicente, La Propriété Intellectuelle en Droit International Privé 413 (2009); James J. Fawcett & P. Torremans, Intellectual Property and Private International Law (2d ed. 2011). For a comparison with soft law principles that derogate from the EU approach, see Edouard Treppoz, *Etude comparée des principes de l'American Law Institute et du Max Planck Institut sur le droit international privé et la propriété intellectuelle*, *in* Droit international privé et propriété intellectuelle, *supra* note 14, at 271.

20 See Case C-360/12, *Coty Ger. GmbH* v. *First Note Perfumes NV*, ECLI:EU:C:2014:1318, no. 27. This rule means "*lex specialis derogate legi generali.*" Therefore, the specific Regulation 207/2009 derogates from the general Regulation 1215/2012.

21 Regulation 207/2009 of Feb. 27, 2009, amended by Regulation 2424/2015.

22 Case C-360/12, *Coty Ger. GmbH* v. *First Note Perfumes NV*, ECLI:EU:C:2014:1318.

trademark, the Spanish courts thus will always be competent, since the EU Intellectual Property Office is located in Alicante. To these cascading points of attachment Article 97 of the Regulation adds a point of attachment based on the act of infringement or, more precisely, on the place of impact of the infringement. These two points of attachment (domicile of the parties, and place of the infringement) cumulatively offer an option to the rightholder. The choice is nonetheless not equal, since the territorial scope of the court's competence is not the same in the two instances. While the competence of defendant's and plaintiff's fora, or subsidiarily of the EU IPO, extends "to acts of infringement committed on the territory of any [M]ember State," the competence of the forum of the place of infringement will be limited to the acts of infringement committed on the territory of the state where the acts occurred (Article 98 of Regulation 207/2009).[23] In one case, the court will have pan-European jurisdiction, but not in the other.

It is noteworthy that the problems discussed in the context of national trademarks disappear when the action concerns an EU-wide trademark. Moreover, Article 97(5) of the Regulation provides that the court of the place where the infringement occurred is not competent to hear a claim seeking a declaratory judgment of non-infringement, thereby limiting the risks of the infringer's forum-shopping. One may add, by way of comparison, that the forum adjudicating a claim of infringement of an EU-wide trademark remains, in principle, competent to rule on exceptions pertaining to the validity of the mark (Articles 96(d), 100 and 104 of the Regulation). Finally, the EU legislature has not required that the second-seized forum in an EU-wide trademark infringement action suspend its adjudication in favor of a court first seized in an action seeking a declaratory judgment of non-infringement (Article 104 of the Regulation). The Regulation thus acknowledges that the forum-shopping of which the rightholder of a national trademark is deprived remains available to the rightholder of an EU-wide trademark. As we will see, the CJEU has reinforced that interpretation.

2 *Rightholder-Favorable Caselaw*

Three decisions of the CJEU extend the superiority of the rules on judicial competence when an EU-wide trademark rather than a national title is at issue. The combination of the 2011 *DHL* decision, the 2017 *Hummel* decision, and the 2017 *Nintendo* decision clearly extends a plaintiff's forum-shopping options.

First, the important 2011 *DHL* decision[24] endows the EU trademark with "optimal effectiveness on the territory of each [M]ember State."[25] The question in that case concerned the territorial scope of an injunction, specifically a prohibition *sous astreinte* (accompanied by fines for noncompliance) that a French judge ordered in a litigation concerning an EU trademark. The CJEU tied the question of the remedy to the court's competence, but also to that of the scope of the right infringed (point 33). According to the court, the injunction may have a

[23] In a recent decision (Case C-172/18, *AMS Neve* v. *Heritage Audio SL*, ECLI:EU:C:2019:674), the Court of Justice had to determine the expression "the act of infringement has been committed" for a cyber-infringement of an EU trademark. For the Court, the place from which the defendant took decisions and steps is immaterial; the Court focused instead on the place of the public being targeted (Case C-172/18, *AMS Neve* v. *Heritage Audio SL*, ECLI:EU:C:2019:674). Whereas the advocate general (Opinion of Advocate general Szpunar, Case C-172/18, no. 75) clearly established that the endorsement of the targeting criterion for the EU trademark would not affect the accessibility criterion for national trademarks, the decision is more ambiguous concerning the fate of the accessibility criterion for national trademarks (for a more detailed analysis: Edouard Treppoz, Revue Trimestrielle de Droit Européen, 2019, 918).

[24] Case C-235/09, *DHL Express France SAS* v. *Chronopost SA*, 2011 ECR I-02801.

[25] Louis d'Avout, Recueil Dalloz, 2011.2442, Pan. DCI.

pan-EU effect if the forum has a pan-EU competence, and the infringement is localized in the totality of the EU. Thus, the court's competence extends to the maximum territorial zone of the prohibition, a maximum that may be reduced based on the territorial scope of the infringement. We see that the pan-EU scope of protection spills over to the competence of the forum and to the scope of the injunction that it may enter. The effectiveness of the title is usefully extended by the injunctions that protect it.

A second, more recent decision in the 2017 case *Hummel Holding* concerned the interpretation of the term "establishment" in Regulation 207/2009.[26] In the absence of a member state defendant's domicile, the plaintiff may proceed before the courts of one of the defendant's establishments, and these will have EU-wide competence. In that case, the CJEU adopted a broad definition of "establishment," based particularly on the appearance of the "establishment acting as an extension of the parent body" (point 38). Especially, according to the Court, "it is, in principle, irrelevant for the purposes of [a]rticle 97(1) of Regulation No[.] 207/2009 whether the establishment thereby determined has participated in the alleged infringement" (point 40). The taking into account of appearances together with the absence of a link between the litigation and the said establishment leads to a very substantial opening of plaintiff's forum-shopping opportunities. In the *Hummel* case before the CJEU, the rightholder sued in Germany for infringements committed throughout the EU despite the absence of a link between defendant's German subsidiary and the litigation.

The third example of this judicial enlargement is recent and thoroughly illustrates the difference in the rules of judicial competence depending on whether the litigation concerns a national title or an EU-wide title. Notably, the decision in the 2017 *Nintendo* case concerned registered designs rather than trademarks, but the analysis was the same.[27] A Japanese company that produced video game consoles sued a French infringer and its German subsidiary.[28] The rightholder sought to bring the French defendant before the codefendant's domiciliary court, in Germany, so that the German courts would enter a pan-EU remedy against both codefendants. Had a national title been at issue, this consolidation of defendants and remedies would not have been possible, but the EU-wide nature of the title led to an affirmative outcome. The reason is simple, according to the CJEU's reasoning. For national titles, each territorial infringement is distinct, and multiple national adjudications present no risk of irreconcilable judgments (point 46). By contrast, the unitary character of protection of an EU-wide title leads to the conclusion that there is one single legal situation throughout the EU; judgments rendered by multiple national fora do present a risk of irreconcilability (point 48).

In the previously quoted *Hummel* decision, the difference in rules of judicial competence might be explained by the different goals of the texts at issue. While the Brussels I*bis* Regulation seeks connections between the defendant and the forum in order to protect the weaker party, the purpose of regulations creating a single EU-wide title is "to strengthen the protection of EU trade marks, to prevent inconsistent decisions on the part of the courts and to ensure that the unitary character of those trade marks is not undermined" (point 28). EU intellectual property rights alter the rules of procedure, thus establishing their autonomy relative to the Brussels I*bis* Regulation's general rules of judicial competence.[29] On the other hand, when the applicable

[26] Case C-617/15, *Hummel Holding A/S* v. *Nike Inc.*, ECLI:EU:C:2017:390.

[27] Joined Cases C-24/16 & C-25/16, *Nintendo Co. Ltd.*

[28] *Id.*

[29] *See generally*, Edouard Treppoz, *Does Size Matter? A Comparative Study on Jurisdiction Rules Applicable to Domestic and EU IP Titles*, *in* Research Handbook on EU Private International Law 152 (Peter Stone & Youseph Farah eds., 2015).

text is the same, only its interpretations diverge. One is territorialist and unfavorable to trademark owners; the other is pan-European and favorable to rightholders. The justification for this difference resides, for the CJEU, in the national or European scope of the protection conferred. In practice, beyond the forum-shopping that the European title can confer on rightholders, the Trade Mark Regulation's jurisdictional enlargement furnishes a strong argument in favor of obtaining EU-wide titles.

C *Comparison with the United States*

In the United States, trademarks exist at both the federal (nationwide) and state levels. But the impact of the mark's territorial ambit on judicial competence is far less stark than in the EU. The Lanham Federal Trademarks Act contains no sections equivalent to the jurisdictional provisions of the EU Trade Mark Regulation. Moreover, in the United States, judicial competence subdivides into subject matter jurisdiction (competence over the legal claim) and personal jurisdiction (competence over the defendant). While federal courts have subject matter jurisdiction over claims "arising under" federal law, and are specifically competent to hear claims alleging infringement of rights under the Lanham Federal Trademarks Act,[30] the Federal Rules of Civil Procedure defer to the general rules of personal jurisdiction of the state in which the court seized is located.[31] In general, a state court will have competence over a resident defendant with respect to any claim, regardless of its territorial connection to the state (general jurisdiction).

Thus, for example, a New York defendant who allegedly sells goods bearing infringing marks in Colorado may be sued in New York for acts committed outside the state. A state court will also have personal jurisdiction over nonresident defendants who commit wrongful acts within the state, or who commit wrongful acts outside the state, but that cause harm within the state (specific jurisdiction).[32] The court's territorial competence over claims alleging harm within the state will be limited to in-state conduct or effects. Thus, a New York court exercising jurisdiction on the basis of a nonresident's sale of infringing goods in the state should not have authority to enter a nationwide injunction for violation of New York trademark law.[33] By the same token, in

30 *See* 28 USC §§ 1337(a), 1338(a) (2018).

31 *See* Fed. R. Civ. P. 4(k)(1)(A). Fed. R. Civ. P. 4(k)(2) provides for nationwide jurisdiction with respect to federally based rights, but it applies only where the defendant's acts create contacts nationwide, and only in the event that no state court would have had jurisdiction. Trademark infringements are likely to involve sufficient contacts with at least one state to belie the predicate of this basis of federal jurisdiction.

32 To satisfy due process concerns of "fair play and substantial justice" (*Int'l Shoe Co.* v. *Wash., Office of Unemployment Comp. & Placement*, 326 US 310, 316 (1945) (quoting *Milliken* v. *Meyer*, 311 US 457, 463 (1940))), state laws affording a tort-out/impact-in basis of jurisdiction may further require that the impact in the forum have been foreseeable and/or that the defendant derive substantial income from interstate commerce. *See, e.g.*, NY CPLR § 302 (a)(3) (2006), which provides in relevant part:

> [A] court may exercise personal jurisdiction over any non-domiciliary, or his executor or administrator, who in person or through an agent ... commits a tortious act without the state causing injury to person or property within the state ... if he:
>
> (i) regularly does or solicits business, or engages in any other persistent course of conduct, or derives substantial revenue from goods used or consumed or services rendered, in the state, or
>
> (ii) expects or should reasonably expect the act to have consequences in the state and derives substantial revenue from interstate or international commerce.

33 On the context of violations of state antidilution statutes, see David S. Welkowitz, *Preemption, Extraterritoriality, and the Problem of State Antidilution Laws*, 67 Tul. L. Rev. 1, 81–82 (1992) ("a state that prohibits the future commercial activities of a person outside of the state with persons not before the court, based solely on a violation of local law, sets itself up as a national legislature, capable of making policy for other states that either disagree with the policy of the forum state or have not yet made up their minds about the question").

theory, a federal court sitting in New York would on the same facts lack jurisdiction over the nonresident's sale of infringing goods outside New York. In fact, it does not appear that federal courts exercising specific jurisdiction limit the scope of relief for infringement of federal (nationwide) trademark rights to acts committed or impacting within the state in which the court is located.[34]

Questions of specific personal jurisdiction arise when the alleged trademark infringement originates from a website located outside the forum. When consumers in the forum can obtain the goods or services sent from the website into the forum, the analysis should be no different from other instances of transborder infringement, for example by mail order delivery. Website operators who target customers within the forum are "purposefully avail[ing themselves] of the privilege of conducting activities within the forum State, thus invoking the benefits and protections of its laws,"[35] and the forum's exercise of personal jurisdiction would be consistent with norms of due process. But US courts have ruled that a website's mere accessibility in the forum, without more, does not suffice to establish the contacts requisite to the exercise of personal jurisdiction over a nonresident defendant.[36] Thus, for example, where the website did not enable consumers in the forum to order tickets for performances in an allegedly infringingly named nightclub located in another state, and where other indicia pointed to exclusively extra-forum activities, the court dismissed the trademark action for lack of personal jurisdiction.[37] In general, indicia of targeting include:

> shipping goods directly into the forum for sale there; filling orders from the forum; or selling to third parties, knowing the goods will be incorporated into products and distributed in the forum. They also include efforts taken to customize materials for communication to, or use in, the jurisdiction, such as developing content and advertisements of interest to an audience in the forum, or use of the forum's language, currency, or units for measuring size and volume.[38]

If at least some of these indicia are present, the forum will have jurisdiction, at least over claims arising out of the contacts between the offshore website and the forum. It is less clear in practice whether the forum will confine its entry of relief to forum-based harm, particularly if the claim asserts violations of nationwide trademark rights.

III WHAT LAW APPLIES IN MULTITERRITORIAL TRADEMARK DISPUTES?

Confronted with territorially complex infringements, the CJEU has evolved away from a strictly territorialist approach. We will first examine its approach to the application of national

34 *See, e.g.*, *United States* v. *AMC Entm't, Inc.*, 549 F.3d 760, 770 (9th Cir. 2008) ("Once a court has obtained personal jurisdiction over a defendant, the court has the power to enforce the terms of the injunction outside the territorial jurisdiction of the court, including issuing a nationwide injunction"). Courts in the Second Circuit have also endorsed nationwide injunctions on the basis of state laws. *See Deere & Co.* v. *MTD Prods., Inc.*, 41 F.3d 39, 46 (2d Cir. 1994) ("district courts have in other circumstances granted nationwide injunctive relief on trademark dilution claims"); *Stern's Miracle-Gro Prod., Inc.* v. *Shark Prod., Inc.*, 823 F. Supp. 1077, 1095 (SDNY 1993) (granting a nationwide injunction based on state antidilution laws); *Eastman Kodak Co.* v. *Rakow*, 739 F. Supp. 116, 120 n. 3 (WDNY 1989) ("Defendant's contention that the geographic scope of this injunction is limited to New York state is without merit").

35 *Hanson* v. *Denckla*, 357 US 235, 253 (1958).

36 *See, e.g.*, *Zippo Mfg. Co.* v. *Zippo Dot Com, Inc.*, 952 F. Supp. 1119 (WD Pa. 1997).

37 *Bensusan Rest. Corp.* v. *King*, 937 F. Supp. 295 (SDNY 1996). *See also Nat'l K-9, Inc.* v. *Nat'l Canine Assoc.*, 2010 US Dist. LEXIS 65212 (SD Ohio 2010) (trademark infringement claim dismissed for lack of personal jurisdiction when out-of-state website was accessible in-state but was "relatively passive" and had only two in-state registered users).

38 American Law Institute, Intellectual Property: Principles of Principles Governing Jurisdiction, Choice of Law, and Judgments in Transnational Disputes § 204, cmt. C. (2008).

trademark laws, and then will see how, with respect to the EU-wide trademark, the Court has significantly derogated from territorial application of EU law. Turning then to US law, we observe that the approach of US courts tends to be unilateralist – that is, US courts have articulated conditions for the application of US trademark law in transnational infringements but have generally not endeavored to articulate what law applies when US law does not.

A Multilateral Litigations and National Trademarks in the European Union

The 2011 *L'Oréal* case[39] constitutes the initial and seminal decision in which the CJUE answered the tricky question of applicable law concerning cyber trademark infringement. L'Oréal sued eBay for the sale on its online marketplace of allegedly infringing goods not yet put into the EU market. The goods bearing L'Oréal's trademark were located in Hong Kong (China). For the Court, neither the original localization of the goods of the seller outside the EU nor the localization of the platform outside the EU could have the effect of precluding the application of EU member state law (point 61). Following a unilateralist logic, the Court subordinated the application of EU law to the localization of the public targeted by the offers within the EU. The Court's express objective was to preserve the "practical utility" (point 62) and "effectiveness" (point 63) of EU member state intellectual property law. It is clear that making the countries of the offers' origin the point of attachment would have resulted in delocalizing the offers to non-EU countries, thus eluding the mandatory application of EU member state law. Following a logic similar to the principle of territoriality, this decision imposes a fragmentation of applicable law according to the locations of the targeted public, with each law being locally applicable on the basis of acts localized within its borders.

With the application of Rome II Regulation, this seminal decision remains operative. The only change will be to switch from a unilateral approach endorsed by the Court to a bilateral approach retained by the Regulation. Following Article 8 of the Rome II Regulation, the law of the country for which protection is claimed applies. Nevertheless, when the infringement is committed in more than one country, Article 8 is not sufficient to determine the applicable law. A choice has to be made between the law of the infringement's point of origin and the law(s) of the infringement's points of impact. The 2011 *Football Dataco* case shows that the 2011 *L'Oréal* case is still a precedent in order to deepen the connecting factor retained in Article 8.[40] In that case based on the Rome II Regulation, the CJEU ruled UK law applicable because of the targeting of the UK audience. The solution should be the same if the audience targeted is that of a third country.

Recently, EU law has perfected the extraterritorial application of the law of the targeted public in the case of goods in transit. The classic position of European law did not reach goods in transit even though, according to the law of the country through which the goods transited, infringement was clear.[41] Furthermore, proof of infringement in the country for which the goods were destined would not justify their seizure in the country of transit. The reform of EU trademark law permits the rightowner to prohibit the introduction of goods in transit that bear without authorization a national or EU trademark.[42] This prohibition can be overcome if the owner of the goods proves that the affixation of the mark is lawful under the law of the country of final

[39] ECJ, July 12, 2011: Case C-324/09, *L'Oréal SA* v. *eBay Int'l AG*, 2011 ECR I-06011.

[40] Case C-604/10, *Football Dataco Ltd.* v. *Yahoo! UK Ltd.*, ECLI:EU:C:2012:115.

[41] Joined Cases C-446/09 & C-495/09, *Koninklijke Philips Elecs. NV* v. *Lucheng Meijing Indus. Co. Ltd. & Nokia Corp.* v. *Her Majesty's Comm'rs of Revenue & Customs*, 2011 ECR I-12435, § 62.

[42] Directive 2015/2436 of Dec. 16, 2015; Regulation 2015/2424 of Dec. 16, 2015.

destination.[43] The applicable law is a subtle combination of the law of the country where the goods are currently located, albeit in transit, and the law of final destination, where the goods will shortly be. Consistently with the seminal case of *L'Oréal* issued in 2011, the approach to goods in transit shows nevertheless that the system is more complex than a strict territorial approach.[44]

B Multilateral Litigations and EU Trademarks

As we have seen, the EU Trade Mark Regulation creates a unitary title throughout the EU. As a result, there is only one law applicable to infringements occurring within the EU. Nevertheless, the Regulation does not solve all procedural or substantive issues. In the lacunae of the EU Trade Mark Regulation, national laws remain applicable (Articles 101 and 102). Rules on conflicts of laws determine which law is applicable. With the subsequent adoption of the Rome II Regulation, its Article 8 applies, displacing the national conflicts rules in effect at the time of the promulgation of the EU Trade Mark Regulation.

Article 8 of the Rome II Regulation supplies a conflicts rule for intellectual property infringement. The rule distinguishes according to the EU or national source of protection. For national protection, Article 8.1 designates the "law of the country for which protection is claimed." For an EU trademark, Article 8.2 makes the applicable law "the law of the country in which the act of infringement was committed." The difference is radical. In one case, the applicable law is based on protection. In the other, the point of attachment falls back on the place of the harm, and not of protection. The CJEU has recently interpreted this rule.[45] Applying analyses both linguistic (point 95) and teleological (point 96), the Court concluded that the point of attachment could not include multiple countries of impact of the infringement, but must be the country from which the infringement originated. Thus, while in principle the Court applies the laws of the countries of impact in the case of cross-border infringement of national trademarks,[46] it has, by contrast, opted for the application of the law of the country of origin of the infringement in the case of cross-border infringement of EU trademarks. The Court has frequently noted that this localization allows it to assess the conduct of the alleged infringer "in a global manner" (points 103 and 109). The Court has clearly adopted a global approach to the alleged infringement without distinguishing country by country. The designated law thus acquires an extraterritorial application, covering the totality of the infringing conduct, despite multiple localizations of points of impact. There is no doubt that the unitary character of the right influences the localization of the relevant act in the country of origin of the infringement. For an EU-wide protection, the Court has adopted a conflicts rule of extraterritorial and European application.

Two practical questions remain as to determination of the origin of the infringement. First, when it comes to an infringement made over the Internet, the Court has said that:

> In such circumstances, it must be held that the event giving rise to the damage is the conduct by which an operator offers for sale allegedly infringing goods, inter alia by placing an offer for sale on its website. Accordingly, the place where the event giving rise to the damage occurred within

[43] See art. 9.4 of the Regulation 2015/2424 of Dec. 16, 2015, and art. 10.4 of Directive 2015/2436 of Dec. 16, 2015.

[44] For a critical analysis of the reform, see Vincenzo di Cataldo, *Goods in Transit and Trade Mark Law (and Intellectual Property Law?)*, 49 IIC – Int'l Rev. Intell. Prop. & Competition L. 436 (2018).

[45] Joined Cases C-24/16 & C-25/16, *Nintendo Co. Ltd.*

[46] *See supra* Section III.A.

> the meaning of article 8(2) of Regulation No[.] 864/2007 is the place where the process of putting the offer for sale online by that operator on its website was activated.[47]

It is unclear if the connecting factor should be based on the sole process or the people behind the process. Taking into consideration previous caselaw concerning judicial competence,[48] it seems relevant to localize the people in charge of the process and not the sole process, especially given the easy manipulation of the place from which an online offer of sale emanates. Second is a question related to an infringement whose origin is in a third (non-EU) country. Does the 2017 *Nintendo* case mean that if the process of putting the offer for sale occurs in a third country, the law of this third country is applicable? The CJEU does not answer that question; *Nintendo* involved intra-EU infringements. Nevertheless, one could argue that the applicable law has to be the law of an EU member state. When the infringement originates outside the EU, the logic would be to switch from a connecting factor by the origin of the offer to a connecting factor by the impact, as in the 2011 *L'Oreal* case.

C *Comparison with the United States*

Considerations of territoriality simplify the inquiry into the law applicable in US trademark infringement actions. In general, US courts apply US law to infringements impacting in the United States, and refrain from extending US law to acts occurring outside the United States, or from protecting foreign marks not used in the United States. US courts depart from that position in two situations. First, with respect to protection, US courts sometimes protect a well-known foreign mark against usurpation by a local user. Second, regarding infringement, US courts may, in certain circumstances, find acts occurring abroad to violate US trademark law. Note that in both instances, US courts are not inquiring into the applicable foreign law; they are identifying situations in which US law will apply notwithstanding the extraterritorial aspects of the controversy.[49]

1 *Famous Foreign Trademarks*

As discussed elsewhere in this volume,[50] Paris Convention member states incur an obligation to protect foreign marks against acts of unfair competition; these can include a third party's bad faith local registration of a foreign mark well-known, but not yet registered or used, in the jurisdiction. While US courts decline to apply the Paris Convention directly,[51] and some do not

[47] *Nintendo Co. Ltd.*, at § 108.

[48] To localize the place of the event this seminal decision chose the establishment of the publisher and not the act of publishing: "In the case of a libel by a newspaper article distributed in several Contracting States, the place of the event giving rise to the damage, within the meaning of those judgments, can only be the place *where the publisher of the newspaper in question is established*, since that is the place where the harmful event originated and from which the libel was issued and put into circulation." Case C-68/93, *Shevill* v. *Press* All. SA, 1995 ECR I-00415, § 24 (emphasis supplied).

[49] Marketa Trimble has observed that choice of law issues may not arise in US litigations involving transnational conduct because none of the parties has raised the question, and the Court has no *sua sponte* obligation to examine applicable law. *See* Marketa Trimble, *The Territorial Discrepancy between Intellectual Property Rights Infringement Claims and Remedies*, 23 Lewis & Clark L. Rev. 501 (2019). *See also* Erika Marie Brown, *Extraterritorial Application of Trademark Law under the Lanham Act: Recent Decisions from the Second Circuit*, 11 N.Y. Int'l L. Rev. 55, 68 (1998) (criticizing *Les Ballets Trockadero de Monte Carlo, Inc.* v. *Trevino*, 945 F. Supp. 563 (SDNY 1996), in which the court applied US law to trademark infringements allegedly occurring in Japan as "indulging in a somewhat risky gamble that Japanese law would operate as predicted by an American court").

[50] *See* Chapter 1 in this volume.

[51] *See, e.g.*, *Person's Co. Ltd.* v. Christman, 900 F.2d 1565, 1569–70, 14 USPQ.2d 1477 (Fed. Cir. 1990); *Almacenes Exito S.A.* v. *El Gallo Meat Mkt., Inc.*, 381 F. Supp. 2d 324 (SDNY 2005).

formally recognize the doctrine of famous foreign marks, they will protect a foreign mark that has acquired local goodwill.[52] The trademark owner bears the burden of persuasion that its mark is sufficiently well-known within the US. It is not enough that the mark is well-known outside the United States;[53] US courts generally require that the foreign mark be sufficiently recognized in the United States that its use or registration in the United States by an unrelated party would likely confuse US consumers.[54] Four scenarios suggest when a foreign mark owner might be able to establish the requisite recognition. First, the unauthorized US user of the mark may be targeting immigrant consumers familiar with the mark in their home countries, and who would assume a relationship between the US user and the enterprise they knew from home.[55] Second, the mark owner does business near the US border with Mexico or Canada, and that proximity, especially through local border-spillover advertising, or frequent travel back and forth across the border, make US consumers aware of the mark, even though the claimant's goods or services remain on the other side of the border.[56] Third, and a variation on the second theme, US consumers travel abroad and encounter the mark in the countries they visit.[57] Fourth, and in the future most likely, knowledge of a mark and its associated goods or services may spread via the Internet, not only through the producer's generally accessible website, but also through social media and other forms of communication in which consumers as well as producers promote or discuss the mark.[58] In that way, a US consumer may become well-acquainted with the mark even if the goods or services are not yet offered in the United States.

[52] *See, e.g., ITC Ltd.* v. *Punchgini, Inc.*, 518 F.3d 159 (2d Cir. 2008). When a local entrepreneur appears to be making a preemptive strike to register a well-known foreign mark before the trademark owner files its own application, US courts may also generously interpret the doctrine of "use analogous to trademark use" to encompass the foreign mark owner's preparations for marketing in the US. Analogous use may not suffice to create use-based rights in the United States, but can provide a basis for opposing a rival's registration of the mark. *See Aktieselskabet AF 21 Nov. 2001* v. *Fame Jeans Inc.*, 525 F.3d 8 (DC Cir. 2008).

[53] *See, e.g., Person's*, 900 F.2d at 1565 (Japanese department store's name was well-known in Japan, but not in United States); *ITC Ltd.*, 518 F.3d at 159 (Buhkara Grill may be well-known in India and other non-US venues, but there was no evidence that consumers in New York associated the name with the foreign plaintiff's enterprise).

[54] *See, e.g., ITC Ltd.*, 518 F.3d at 159; *Grupo Gigante SA De CV* v. *Dallo & Co.*, 391 F.3d 1088 (9th Cir. 2004).

[55] *See, e.g., Grupo Gigante*, 391 F.3d at 1088; *Almacenes Exito*, 381 F. Supp. 2d at 384; *Industria de Alimentos Zenu S.A.S.* v. *Latinfood U.S. Corp.*, No. CV 16-6576 (KM)(MAH), 2017 WL 6940696 (DNJ, Dec. 29, 2017) (defendant adopted marks well-known in Colombia and Latin America and allegedly targeted Colombian-American consumers; court declined to dismiss Lanham Act claim even though plaintiff's US trademark registrations had lapsed); *Belmora LLC* v. *Bayer Consumer Care AG*, 819 F.3d 697, 710 n. 8 (4th Cir. 2016) ("defendant, as alleged here, has – as a cornerstone of its business – intentionally passed off its goods in the United States as the same product commercially available in foreign markets to influence purchases by American consumers").

[56] *See* 5 McCarthy on Trademarks and Unfair Competition § 29:64 (5th ed.). The alleged deception may affect consumers on both sides of the border. *See, e.g., Belmora* v. *Bayer*, 819 F.3d at 711 ("The complaint alleges Belmora's misleading association with BCC's [the foreign mark owner's] FLANAX has caused BCC customers to buy the Belmora FLANAX in the United States instead of purchasing BCC's FLANAX in Mexico. For example, the complaint alleges that BCC invested heavily in promoting its FLANAX to Mexican citizens or Mexican-Americans in border areas. Those consumers cross into the United States and may purchase Belmora FLANAX here before returning to Mexico. And Mexican-Americans may forgo purchasing the FLANAX they know when they cross the border to visit Mexico because Belmora's alleged deception led them to purchase the Belmora product in the United States").

[57] *See, e.g.*, Leah Chan Grinvald, *A Tale of Two Theories of Well-Known Marks*, 13 Vand. J. Ent. & Tech. L. 1 (2010); Frederick W. Mostert, *Well-Known and Famous Marks: Is Harmony Possible in the Global Village?*, 86 Trademark Rep. 103 (1996).

[58] *See, e.g.*, Shontavia Johnson, *Trademark Territoriality in Cyberspace: An Internet Framework for Common-Law Trademarks*, 29 Berkeley Tech. L.J. 1253 (2014); Stacey L. Dogan & Mark A. Lemley, *Trademarks and Consumer Search Costs on the Internet*, 41 Hous. L. Rev. 777 (2004); Marshall A. Leaffer, *The New World of International Trademark Law*, 2 Marq. Intell. Prop. L. Rev. 1 (1998).

2 *Extraterritorial Violations of US Law*

In *Steele* v. *Bulova Watch Co.*,[59] the US Supreme Court endorsed the extraterritorial reach of the Lanham Act, in a case presenting a close nexus with US commerce.[60] There, the US defendant manufactured and sold false Bulova watches in Mexico. US residents purchased the watches in Mexico, some apparently believing the watches were genuine; when the watches failed, US consumers brought them to US Bulova sellers for repair. The defendant had obtained a Mexican trademark registration for the Bulova mark, but Mexican authorities cancelled the mark before the Supreme Court ruled. *Steele* v. *Bulova*'s facts generated factors that have guided the analysis of subsequent controversies involving extraterritorial conduct allegedly infringing US trademarks. In *Bulova*, (1) defendant was a US citizen (indeed, both parties were US citizens); (2) the defendant appears to have at least in part targeted US consumers, thus affecting US commerce; and (3) defendant had not acquired foreign trademark rights with which the extraterritorial enforcement of US trademark rights would have conflicted.[61] Subsequent caselaw suggests that the defendant's citizenship may be dispositive, at least to the extent that US courts have so far declined to find Lanham Act violations by foreign defendants who act in their home countries and do not target US commerce.[62] For example, in *McBee* v. *Delica*, the First Circuit ruled that the Lanham Act did not apply to a Japanese clothing company's unauthorized appropriation of the name of US jazz musician Cecil McBee as a trademark for a line of clothing for teenage girls. Although the defendant's website was accessible in the United States, the Court concluded that the defendant was not seeking to sell its clothing in the United States because the website was written in Japanese and accepted payments in Japanese yen. The defendant also declined to ship goods into the United States, thus avoiding claims that it was seeking to sell to expatriate Japanese in the United States. The defendant's exploitation of the mark therefore lacked a "substantial effect on United States commerce."[63]

By contrast, the Fifth Circuit entertained a Lanham Act claim regarding one company's alleged imitation of the other's mark where two US-based companies were competing to sell rice in the Saudi Arabian market even though the consumers allegedly misled by the unauthorized use of the mark would have been located in Saudi Arabia. The parties' common US citizenship, and the infringement's impact on plaintiff's US-based business, created a sufficient effect on US commerce.[64] It is worth noting that the court found "some effect" on US commerce,[65] and did not require a "substantial" effect. In fact, US courts appear to disagree over the requisite intensity of the effect on US commerce, with some courts accepting "some effect" even when the defendant is not a US citizen.[66] In those instances, however, courts found a US nexus, for

[59] *Steele* v. *Bulova Watch Co.*, 344 US 280 (1952).

[60] For a detailed examination of *Steele* v. *Bulova*, see Austin, *supra* note 1, at 395.

[61] *See, e.g.*, *Vanity Fair Mills, Inc.* v. *T. Eaton Co.*, 234 F.2d 633, 642 (2d Cir. 1956) requiring (1) the defendant's conduct must have a substantial effect on US commerce; (2) the defendant must be a US citizen; and (3) there must be no conflict with trademark rights established under the foreign law.

[62] *See, e.g.*, *Vanity Fair Mills*, 234 F.2d at 633 (Canadian retailer selling in Canada: "the remedies provided by the Lanham Act ... should not be given an extraterritorial application against foreign citizens acting under presumably valid trade-marks in a foreign country." *Id.* at 643); *McBee* v. *Delica Co.*, 417 F.3d 107, 119 (1st Cir. 2005) (Japanese clothing designer selling in Japan).

[63] *McBee*, 417 F.3d at 120.

[64] *See Am. Rice, Inc.* v. *Arkansas Rice Growers Coop. Ass'n*, 701 F.2d 408 (5th Cir. 1983).

[65] *Id.* at 414 n. 8.

[66] *Compare Trader Joe's Co.* v. *Hallatt*, 835 F.3d 960, 969 (9th Cir. 2016) (requiring only "some effect") *with Nintendo of Am., Inc.* v. *Aeropower Co.*, 34 F.3d 246, 250 (4th Cir. 1994) (requiring a "significant effect") with *Vanity Fair Mills*, 234 F.2d at 641, 642 ("substantial effect").

example, when a foreign defendant allegedly planned in the United States to sell counterfeit Reebok shoes in Mexico, and some of the shoes ended up in the United States.[67] Perhaps more problematically, the Ninth Circuit found "some effect" on US commerce when a foreign US resident defendant purchased Trader Joe's trademarked goods in the United States and sold them in Canada under conditions that could mislead purchasers into believing the Canadian store was an authorized retailer of the US grocery chain. Unlike the trademark owners in *Steele* v. *Bulova* or *Reebok* v. *Marnatech*, however, Trader Joe's did not allege that the defendant's goods (which bore genuine trademarks, but were distributed outside Trader Joe's quality control mechanisms) made their way back to the United States.[68] The Ninth Circuit nonetheless found "some effect" on US commerce through potential harm to Trader Joe's reputation in the United States if word of consumer dissatisfaction with the Canadian imitator spread across the border back into the United States. The origination of the infringing activities in the United States, where the defendant purchased the goods for resale in Canada, and subsequently hired assistants to purchase goods in the United States, also impacted US commerce, the court held.[69] The court further observed that while not a US citizen, the defendant's US legal residence brought him within Congress's regulatory power.[70]

While sometimes vigorously stretched, the *Steele* v. *Bulova* factors (and the circuit courts' variations[71]) enable US courts to determine when it is appropriate to apply US trademark law to allegedly infringing activities occurring outside the United States. The characterization of the requisite impact on US commerce may vary by circuit, but it appears that the "effect" will suffice when the defendant is a US citizen or resident, or when the infringing activities are initiated in or from the United States, or when the defendant has targeted US consumers, or should reasonably anticipate that US consumers shopping abroad, particularly in neighboring countries, will encounter the infringing goods or services. Particularly when the defendant is not a US citizen or resident, the wrongful act is not the foreign sale as such, but its entry into "channels of international communication that lead to the United States."[72]

IV CONCLUSION

Multiterritorial trademark infringements require courts, where rules of jurisdictional competence allow, to adjudicate before a single forum claims arising in multiple territories. That forum typically will be defendant's residence. Consolidation of litigation in a single forum conserves judicial and parties' resources and promotes efficient outcomes (at least, so long as a judgment requiring execution in another forum is in fact recognized and enforced). While in many jurisdictions trademarks are considered registered rights, and as such confined to adjudication in the country of registration, we believe that limiting judicial competence over infringement claims to the courts of the country of registration entails undesirable fragmentation and inefficiency. From this point of view, jurisdictional rules applicable to EU trademarks offer a relevant model. The same efficiency should be given to the owners of national titles as proposed by the

[67] *Reebok Int'l, Ltd.* v. *Marnatech Enters., Inc.*, 970 F.2d 552 (9th Cir. 1992).

[68] The Second Circuit has held that "uses of the [plaintiff's] mark abroad that are likely to make their way to American consumers" can justify finding extraterritorial conduct (sales abroad) to violate the Lanham Act. *Sterling Drug, Inc.* v. *Bayer AG*, 14 F.3d 733, 746 (2d Cir. 1994).

[69] *Trader Joe's*, 835 F.3d at 971.

[70] *Id.* at 972.

[71] *See, e.g.*, *Vanity Fair Mills*, 234 F.2d at 633; *Trader Joe's*, 835 F.3d at 969 (quoting *Love* v. *Associated Newspapers, Ltd.*, 611 F.3d 601, 613 (9th Cir. 2010)).

[72] *Sterling Drug*, 14 F. 3d at 746.

ALI Principles[73] and CLIP Principles[74] of jurisdiction in transnational intellectual property litigation.

Consolidation of applicable law proves more controversial. While US courts unilaterally apply US law to the extraterritorial infringements if the litigation presents sufficient contacts with the United States, for example, all parties are US nationals or residents even though the allegedly infringing acts may be occurring abroad, we believe that distributive application of the laws of the countries whose consumers the alleged infringement misleads is more consistent with the nature of the intellectual property right at stake. That distributive application of the laws of the publics targeted may at first sight appear cumbersome for the commercial actor on the Internet. It is nevertheless the consequence of his choice to target various national publics.

[73] ALI Principles governing Jurisdiction, Choice of Law, and Judgment in Transnational Disputes.

[74] Principles on Conflicts of Laws in Intellectual Property (CLIP).

8

Alternative Dispute Resolution for Trademark Disputes

*Jacques de Werra**

I INTRODUCTION

The challenges and costs of litigating (multi-territorial) trademark (similarly to other intellectual property) disputes before national courts are well-known.[1] This explains the growing importance of alternative dispute resolution (ADR) mechanisms, specifically arbitration, for solving trademark[2] (and other intellectual property) disputes.[3] In an international dispute, ADR can particularly offer the advantage to centralize the dispute resolution process and thus avoid the fragmentation before parallel regional or national courts.[4] The increasing reliance on and trust in ADR systems for solving trademark (and other IP) disputes is not surprising: it mirrors the growing importance of ADR in the general dispute resolution ecosystem. The significance of

* Professor of Intellectual Property Law and Contract Law, School of Law, University of Geneva.

[1] This chapter will focus on trademark disputes, it being noted that similar issues arise with respect to other types of intellectual property rights; it is based on various papers by the author, most particularly Jacques de Werra, *Alternative Dispute Resolution Mechanisms for Solving Trademark Disputes (Mediation, UDRP, Arbitration)*, *in* THE LAW AND PRACTICE OF TRADEMARK TRANSACTIONS 293 (I. Calboli & J. de Werra eds., 2016).

[2] *See* Ashlyn Calhoun, *"It All Started with a Mouse": Resolving International Trademark Disputes Using Arbitration*, 2018 J. DISP. RESOL. 87–101 (2018); James Morrison, *A Turning Tide, Arbitrating International Trademark Disputes and the Importance of the New WIPO Arbitration Rules*, 69 INT'L. TRADEMARK ASSN. BULL. 10 (Nov. 1, 2014), http://inta.org/INTABulletin/Pages/ATurningTideArbitratingInternationalTrademarkDisputesandtheImportanceoftheNewWIPOArbitrationRules.aspx.

[3] *See* Joe Tirado & Alejandro I. Garcia, *Reasons to Arbitrate IP Cases*, INTELL. PROP. MAG. (Dec. 8, 2014), http://intellectualpropertymagazine.com/copyright/reasons-to-arbitrate-ip-cases-105157.htm; Miriam R. Arfin, *The Benefits of Alternative Dispute Resolution in Intellectual Property Disputes*, 17 HASTINGS COMM. & ENT. L.J. 893, 896 (1995); Jacques de Werra, *Can Alternative Dispute Resolution Mechanisms Become the Default Method for Solving International Intellectual Property Disputes?*, 43 CAL. W. INT'L. L.J. 39 (2012); Jacques de Werra, *Arbitrating International Intellectual Property Disputes: Time to Think beyond the Issue of (Non-)Arbitrability*, 3 INT'L BUS. L.J. 299, 311 (2012); Jacques de Werra, *Intellectual Property Arbitration: How to Use It Efficiently?*, SING. L. GAZETTE, Jan. 2012, at 27–30, http://v1.lawgazette.com.sg/2012-01/304.htm.

[4] An interesting recent example is the dispute between Pirelli and its former Spanish trademark licensee Licensing Projects SL, which led to an ICC arbitral award, and to litigation in Spain and in France, in which the arbitral award was annulled on procedural grounds (i.e. because of the principle of access to justice that may require admitting counterclaims that are raised by the defendant, here Licensing Projects SL, even if such party cannot pay the advance on costs as required under the relevant (ICC) arbitration rules). *See* Gómez-Acebo & Pombo Abogados, *Alicante Court Considers Trademark Infringement Stemming from Arbitration*, Lexology (Nov. 14, 2012), http://lexology.com/library/detail.aspx?g=9e7dc57d-6a08-4625-bf7a-f4e2ced6c3b5; Andrea Pinna, *La Confirmation de la Jurisprudence Pirelli par la Cour de Cassation et les Difficultés Pratiques de Garantir au Plaideur Impécunieux l'accès à la Justice Arbitrale*, 2013-2 THE PARIS J. OF INT'L. ARB. 479 (2013).

ADR in trademark disputes is not, however, limited to international multi-territorial disputes; ADR can also be of significant value for national trademark disputes.

One key institutional factor supporting the growing importance of ADR in trademark (and other IP) disputes results from the trend encouraging or even imposing the use of ADR that animates many IP offices around the world in cooperation with the World Intellectual Property Organization (WIPO) Arbitration and Mediation Center, which plays a significant role in this respect.[5] As a result, ADR cannot and should not be considered as an unusual dispute resolution mechanism in trademark disputes: ADR rather constitutes a mainstream component of the trademark dispute resolution ecosystem.[6]

This chapter will distinguish between different ADR mechanisms. It will start by discussing ADR mechanisms outside of arbitration that may be used to solve trademark disputes with a focus on mediation and on the ADR system for internet domain name disputes (Section II). It will then turn to arbitration, which raises specific issues and thus calls for a separate discussion (Section III).

II ALTERNATIVE DISPUTE RESOLUTION FOR TRADEMARK DISPUTES (OUTSIDE OF ARBITRATION)

Trademark disputes can be solved by the submission to various ADR mechanisms outside of courtroom litigation and arbitration. Among various ADR tools, trademark disputes can be submitted to mediation (see Section II.A). Specific types of trademark disputes relating to internet domain names can further be submitted to tailored ADR mechanisms specifically developed for such disputes. This is the case of the now extremely well-established system of the Uniform Domain Name Dispute Resolution Policy which has guided the development of other similar ADR systems for internet domain name disputes (see Section II.B).

A Mediation

Mediation offers the parties in dispute the ability to find an amicable settlement of their dispute by submitting it to a neutral third party who shall assist them in this process (without decision-making power). The advantages of mediation are essentially that it can help find creative, interest-based (i.e. focusing on the business interests of the parties more than on their legal positions), time and cost-effective solutions to certain types of trademark[7] (and other IP) disputes.[8] Many IP offices have promoted the use of mediation for solving trademark (and other IP) disputes. This is particularly the case of the European Union Intellectual Property Office

[5] *See* Joyce A. Tan, *WIPO Guide on Alternative Dispute Resolution (ADR) Options for Intellectual Property Offices and Courts*, WIPO 2018, https://wipo.int/publications/en/details.jsp?id=4342, *see* Ch. IV at p. 37 ("Institutionalizing ADR for Intellectual Property Disputes") and Annex A at p. 51 listing WIPO Arbitration and Mediation Center collaborations with IPOs and courts in multiple countries; *see also* WIPO, *WIPO ADR for IP Office and Courts*, https://wipo.int/amc/en/center/specific-sectors/ipoffices/.

[6] *See* Jacques de Werra, *Specialised Intellectual Property Courts – Issues and Challenges, Global Perspectives for the Intellectual Property System*, Issue No. 2 Ctr. for Int'l Intell. Prop. Studies/Int'l Ctr. for Trade and Sustainable Dev't. 2016, 15–41, https://archive-ouverte.unige.ch/unige:82262.

[7] *See* Manny D. Pokotilow, *Why Mediation for Trademark and Unfair Competition Disputes Should Be Your First Choice of Dispute Resolution*, 72 Disp. Resol. J. 3 (2017); David Bernstein, *A Case for Mediating Trademark Disputes in the Age of Expanding Brands*, 7 Cardozo J. Conflict Resol. 139 (2005); *see also* the dedicated webpage of the International Trademark Association (INTA) on mediation, http://inta.org/mediation/Pages/Mediation.aspx.

[8] *See* Asako Wechs Hatanaka, *Optimising Mediation for Intellectual Property Law – Perspectives from EU, French and UK Law*, 49 Int'l. Rev. Intell. Prop. and Competition L. 384 (May 2018); *see also* Nick Gardner, *Mediation and Its Relevance to Intellectual Property Disputes*, 9 J. of Intell. Prop. L. & Prac. 565 (2014).

(EUIPO; at that time it was still operating under the name Office for Harmonization in the Internal Market, OHIM) which launched intellectual property mediation services in October 2011.[9] The intellectual property mediation services offered by EUIPO initially resulted from a decision of the Presidium of the Board of Appeal of 14 April 2011, on the amicable settlement of disputes.[10] The basic idea was to promote mediation (without excluding other available alternative dispute resolution mechanisms).[11] The mediator must be chosen from a list provided by EUIPO, whereby all the mediators are staff members of EUIPO.[12] Mediation is available only during the course of appeal proceedings and on relative grounds relating to conflicts between the private rights of the litigants.[13] It is consequently not available on grounds of public policy such as absolute grounds for refusal of European trademarks or designs.[14]

Many other intellectual property offices have started to offer diverse forms of mediation services. By way of illustration, the WIPO Arbitration and Mediation Center and the Patent Office of the Republic of Poland recently set up a joint dispute resolution procedure to facilitate the mediation of trademark opposition disputes pending before the Patent Office of the Republic of Poland (PPO) that shall be governed by the WIPO mediation rules.[15] As a rule, these mediation systems are conceived as voluntary-based dispute resolution systems. Some regulations have, however, attempted to make mediation a mandatory step before the initiation of formal court proceedings,[16] but this obligation is uncertain to enforce because it may jeopardize the fundamental right of access to justice.[17]

Given that it is a relatively informal and non-adjudicatory process that does not lead to any binding decision by the mediator (in case of successful mediation, the parties can enter into a binding settlement agreement), the use of mediation for solving trademark disputes does not raise major legal or policy issues.[18]

[9] *See* European Union Intellectual Property Office [hereinafter EUIPO], https://euipo.europa.eu/ohimportal/en/mediation.

[10] Decision 2011-1, of the Presidium of the Boards of Appeal, on the Amicable Settlement of Disputes, https://euipo.europa.eu/tunnel-web/secure/webdav/guest/document_library/contentPdfs/law_and_practice/presidium_boards_appeal/in_force/2011-1_presidium_decision_on_mediation_en.pdf; this decision was replaced by Decision 2013-3 of the Presidium of the Boards of Appeal of July 5, 2013, on the amicable settlement of disputes, https://euipo.europa.eu/tunnel-web/secure/webdav/guest/document_library/contentPdfs/law_and_practice/presidium_boards_appeal/presidium_decision_2013-3_en.pdf [hereinafter Decision on Mediation].

[11] *See id.* at recital 2 ("A friendly settlement should be easier to achieve with recourse to mediation, without prejudice to other alternative dispute resolution mechanism").

[12] "The Office shall maintain a list of qualified members of its staff, who are suitably prepared to intervene in mediation proceedings in the sense of the present decision." *Id.* at art. 7, § 1. For the list of mediators, *see* EUIPO, https://euipo.europa.eu/ohimportal/fr/mediators.

[13] Decision on Mediation, *supra* note 10, at art. 1, § 1. ("The request for mediation proceedings may be presented, by a joint declaration from the parties, at any time following the lodging of an appeal").

[14] *Id.* at art. 1, § 2.

[15] World Intellectual Property Organization, https://wipo.int/amc/en/center/specific-sectors/ipoffices/poland/ [hereinafter WIPO].

[16] For a discussion, *see* Mark Vilenchik, *Expanding the Brand: The Case for Greater Enforcement of Mandatory Mediation in Trademark Disputes*, 12 Cardozo J. Conflict Resol. 281 (2010–2011).

[17] In Greece the compulsory mediation system for IP disputes was successfully challenged, *see* Marina Perraki, *Mandatory Mediation Questioned – Greece* (July 17, 2018), http://trademarkblog.kluweriplaw.com/2018/07/17/mandatory-mediation-questioned-greece/ (indicating that on June 28, 2018, the Greek Supreme Court's administrative plenary panel issued an opinion holding that the mandatory mediation introduced by law 4512/2018 according to which all disputes concerning trademarks, patents and industrial designs initiated before civil courts in Greece are subject to mandatory mediation is contrary to the Greek Constitution and the European Convention on Human Rights).

[18] Even if the use of institutional mediation rules in a mediation, such as the WIPO mediation rules (https://wipo.int/amc/en/mediation/rules/), can offer very valuable guidance and can significantly facilitate and support the mediation process.

B The Uniform Domain Name Dispute Resolution Policy and Other Trademark-Related Internet Domain Name Alternative Dispute Resolution Mechanisms

The Uniform Domain Name Dispute Resolution Policy (UDRP) is probably the best example of a successful global ADR system for solving (international) trademark disputes. The UDRP was adopted by the Internet Corporation for Assigned Names and Numbers (ICANN) on 26 August 1999.[19] ICANN, a "California Nonprofit Public-Benefit Corporation,"[20] is not a public state agency.[21] The UDRP, which was based on policy recommendations prepared under the aegis of the World Intellectual Property Organization (WIPO),[22] has been extremely successful in solving a phenomenal number of internet domain name cybersquatting disputes since its adoption. Its value and importance are clearly evidenced by the record number of cases brought in recent years.[23] In addition to the intrinsic quality of the UDRP's design features, its success and innovation result particularly from the way the UDRP was contractually imposed in the domain name regulatory ecosystem.[24] Among the contractual obligations imposed on all domain name registrars for generic Top Level Domains (gTLD) in order to be accredited with ICANN is the obligation on the registrars to contractually require from their own clients who register domain names to submit to the UDRP.[25] The same obligation applies to cases where the registrars enter into agreements with third-party resellers who ultimately contract with end-customers.[26] Consequently, submission to the UDRP is imposed on all internet domain name holders of gTLD in a hierarchical way, starting from ICANN (top) to the holder of a given domain name (bottom). In other words, a chain of mutual contractual obligations ultimately imposes the UDRP on the relevant domain name holders.

Even if the merits of a complaint under the UDRP depend on the complainant's ability to show ownership or control over a trademark,[27] which generally consists of a registered trademark

[19] *See Internet Corp. for Assigned Names and Numbers, Uniform Domain Name Dispute Resolution Policy* (Oct. 24, 1999), http://icann.org/dndr/udrp/policy.htm [hereinafter UDRP].

[20] ICANN, *Bylaws for Internet Corporation for Assigned Names and Numbers* (as amended June 18, 2018), Internet Corporation for Assigned Names and Numbers, http://icann.org/en/general/bylaws.htm [hereinafter ICANN].

[21] The independence of ICANN was reflected in "the Affirmation of Commitments" between the US Department of Commerce and ICANN dated Sept. 30, 2009. *See ICANN, The Affirmation of Commitments – What It Means* (Sept. 30, 2009), http://icann.org/en/announcements/announcement-30sep09-en.htm#affirmation; ICANN is engaged in a complex multistakeholder process since the expiration of the contract between ICANN and the US Department of Commerce National Telecommunications and Information Administration (NTIA) to perform the Internet Assigned Numbers Authority (IANA) functions on Oct. 1, 2016; on this, *see Stewardship of IANA Functions Transitions to Global Internet Community as Contract with U.S. Government Ends*, https://icann.org/news/announcement-2016-10-01-en and https://icann.org/stewardship-accountability.

[22] WIPO Internet Domain Name Process (1999), http://wipo.int/amc/en/processes/process1/report/finalreport.html.

[23] *See WIPO Cybersquatting Cases Grow by 12% to Reach New Record in 2018* (Geneva, Mar. 15, 2019), https://wipo.int/pressroom/en/articles/2019/article_0003.html.

[24] *See* Nicholas Smith & Erik Wilbers, *The UDRP: Design Elements of an Effective ADR Mechanism*, 15 AM. REV. INT'L ARB. 215, 217–18 (2004).

[25] *See* ICANN, *2013 Registrar Accreditation Agreement*, § 3.8, https://icann.org/resources/pages/approved-with-specs-2013-09-17-en ("During the Term of this Agreement, Registrar shall have in place a policy and procedures for resolution of disputes concerning Registered Names. Until ICANN adopts an alternative Consensus Policy or other Specification or Policy with respect to the resolution of disputes concerning Registered Names, Registrar shall comply with the Uniform Domain Name Dispute Resolution Policy ('UDRP') identified on ICANN's website (https://icann.org/general/consensus-policies.htm), as may be modified from time to time") [hereinafter Registrar Accreditation Agreement].

[26] *See id.* at art. 3.12.2 ("Any registration agreement used by reseller shall include all registration agreement provisions and notices required by the ICANN Registrar Accreditation Agreement and any ICANN Consensus Policies").

[27] UDRP, *supra* note 19, at art. 4a(i) ("[Y]our domain name is identical or confusingly similar to a trademark or service mark in which the complainant has rights").

in at least one country, the UDRP is generally characterized by its delocalized nature, in terms of both geography and legal system.[28] In other words, the UDRP applies regardless of geographic localization factors and does not depend on the country(ies) or region(s) of registration of the relevant trademark(s), on the domicile/seat of the owner of such trademark(s) or on the domicile/seat of the registrant of the dispute domain name. The UDRP is also legally delocalized and essentially independent from any legal system because the substantive criteria the UDRP is based on and on the basis of which decisions are rendered are independent from any national or regional regulation, except for the existence and control of a trademark by the complainant.[29] The substantive criteria of a decision under the UDRP essentially relate to the good or bad faith registration and use of the relevant domain name by its holder.[30] Consequently, the UDRP creates a corpus of autonomous rules for internet-related trademark disputes that constitute a kind of global *lex electronica*.[31]

The adjudicatory power of experts appointed to decide a dispute under the UDRP is narrow in its scope; the decision can only grant the transfer or cancellation of the relevant domain name or, alternatively, reject the UDRP complaint.[32] The UDRP also provides for the automatic enforcement of decisions ordering a transfer or cancellation of the disputed domain name by notifying the registrar. The respondent (the holder of the relevant domain name) may escape this outcome only if it notifies the dispute resolution entity within ten business days of the initiation of a lawsuit in the relevant jurisdiction.[33] The party may notify the dispute resolution entity by filing appropriate evidence establishing the initiation of court proceedings, such as a copy of the complaint file-stamped by the clerk of the court.[34] UDRP decisions (which are

[28] Unregistered trademarks may however suffice. See WIPO Overview of WIPO Panel Views on Selected UDRP Questions, 3rd ed. ("WIPO Jurisprudential Overview 3.0"), § 1.1.1., WIPO, http://wipo.int/amc/en/domains/search/overview3.0/index.html.

[29] This independence from national law may sometimes be challengeable, particularly when the parties in dispute are located in the same country; decisions nevertheless refrain from importing national law into the UDRP. *See* Administrative Panel Decision, *Covance, Inc.* v. *Covance Campaign*, Case No. D2004-0206 (WIPO, Apr. 30, 2004), http://wipo.int/amc/en/domains/decisions/html/2004/d2004-0206.html ("As a matter of principle, this Panel would not have thought that it was appropriate to import unique national legal principles into the interpretation of paragraph 4(c) of the Policy. This is so even if the effect of doing so is desirable in aligning decisions under the Policy with those emerging from the relevant courts and thus avoiding instances of forum shopping"); *see also* Administrative Panel Decision, *Housing Ass'n, Ltd.* v. *Mr. D. Morgan*, Case No. D2007-1461, 1066 (WIPO, Jan. 18, 2008), http://wipo.int/amc/en/domains/decisions/html/2007/d2007-1461.html.

[30] UDRP, *supra* note 19, at art. 4b & c.

[31] *See* Gralf-Peter Calliess, *Reflexive Transnational Law: The Privatisation of Civil Law and the Civilisation of Private Law*, 23 Zeitschrift für Rechtssoziologie 185–216 (2002) (Ger.) (evidencing the structural and conceptual differences between the UDRP and *lex mercatoria*, which applies in the international business context).

[32] UDRP, *supra* note 19, at art. 4(i) ("The remedies available to a complainant pursuant to any proceeding before an Administrative Panel shall be limited to requiring the cancellation of your domain name or the transfer of your domain name registration to the complainant").

[33] UDRP, *supra* note 19, at art. 4(k). The complaint must "[s]tate that Complainant will submit, with respect to any challenges to a decision in the administrative proceeding canceling or transferring the domain name, to the jurisdiction of the courts in at least one specified Mutual Jurisdiction." *See also* ICANN, *Rules for Uniform Domain Name Dispute Resolution Policy*, art. 3(b)(xii), https://icann.org/en/help/dndr/udrp/rules. "Mutual Jurisdiction means a court jurisdiction at the location of either (a) the principal office of the Registrar (provided the domain-name holder has submitted in its Registration Agreement to that jurisdiction for court adjudication of disputes concerning or arising from the use of the domain name) or (b) the domain-name holder's address as shown for the registration of the domain name in Registrar's Whois database at the time the complaint is submitted to the Provider." *Id.* at art. 1.

[34] UDRP, *supra* note 19, art. 4(k) ("We will then implement the decision unless we have received from you during that ten (10) business day period official documentation (such as a copy of a complaint, file-stamped by the clerk of the court) that you have commenced a lawsuit against the complainant in a jurisdiction to which the complainant has submitted under Paragraph 3(b)(xiii) of the Rules of Procedure").

rendered on the basis of the substantive factors of the UDRP) are however not binding on national courts which can decide the dispute *de novo* (on the basis of their national IP law).

The UDRP consequently institutes and provides an autonomous dispute resolution mechanism for victims of unauthorized domain name registrations they consider to infringe upon their trademarks. It is essential to note that the UDRP is not imposed on victims (i.e. the claimants in UDRP proceedings) who have the option to resolve their disputes through domestic courts or other dispute resolution bodies (for instance by arbitration if the parties are bound by a pre-existing agreement with an arbitration clause). The victims may indeed have an interest in submitting their case to domestic courts or to other dispute resolution bodies rather than the UDRP if they wish to claim remedies unavailable under the UDRP,[35] such as damages resulting from online trademark infringement activities.

In contrast, even if the UDRP provides that parties can litigate their domain name disputes in other fora, the holders of disputed domain names – defendants in UDRP proceedings – are *contractually obligated* to submit to the UDRP if a UDRP case is initiated against them by a third-party trademark owner.[36] The contractual obligation derives from the general terms and conditions of the domain name registrar. The registrar is, in turn, obligated to implement the UDRP based on its accreditation agreement with ICANN.[37] This consequently confirms that the UDRP is based on a chain of contracts, which reflects the point that important aspects of the internet governance ecosystem are based on contracts.[38]

As a result of its success,[39] the UDRP has served as a global model for designing dispute resolution mechanisms for various categories of internet domain names with national or regional extensions such as country code Top Level Domain Names (ccTLDs).[40]

This is what was done (among many other examples) for the policy relating to disputes about ".eu" domain names in the EU (the "EU Policy"). The EU Policy, which applies to ".eu" domain names, is essentially based on a 2004 European Commission Regulation which established public policy rules concerning the implementation and functions of the ".eu" Top Level Domain and the principles governing registration.[41] The Commission Regulation 874/2004 will be repealed by Regulation (EU) 2019/517 of 19 March 2019 (Regulation 2019/517) on the

35 *Id.* at art. 4(i) (*see supra* note 32).

36 *See id.* at art. 4(k) ("The mandatory administrative proceeding requirements . . . shall not prevent either you or the complainant from submitting the dispute to a court of competent jurisdiction for independent resolution before such mandatory administrative proceeding is commenced or after such proceeding is concluded").

37 *See* Registrar Accreditation Agreement, *supra* note 25, at art. 3.8.

38 *See* Lee A. Bygrave, Internet Governance by Contract (2015).

39 It must, however, be noted that the UDRP has sometimes been criticized for being too protective of the interests of trademark owners. *See* Michael Geist, *Fair.com? An Examination of the Allegations of Systemic Unfairness in the ICANN UDRP*, 27 Brook. J. Int'l L. 903 (2002) (providing the solution to the forum shopping and bias issues); Michael Geist, *Fundamentally Fair.com? An Update on Bias Allegations and the ICANN UDRP*, http://aix1.uottawa.ca/%7Egeist/fairupdate.pdf (providing a statistical update and reinforcing the solution provided previously).

40 *See* EUIPO, *Comparative Case Study on Alternative Resolution Systems for Domain Name Disputes* (2018), 6 (noting that the domain name dispute resolution systems – except for the Danish Domain Complaints Board (.dk) – reach similar outcomes in selected scenario by comparison to the UDRP), https://euipo.europa.eu/tunnel-web/secure/webdav/guest/document_library/observatory/documents/reports/2019_Comparative_case_study_on_alternative_resolution_systems/Comparative_case_study_on_alternative_resolution_systems_for_domain_name_disputes.pdf.

41 *See* Commission Regulation 874/2004 of Apr. 28, 2004, Laying Down Public Policy Rules Concerning the Implementation and Functions of the .eu Top Level Domain and the Principles Governing Registration, 2004 OJ (L 162) 40 (EC) [hereinafter the Commission Regulation 874/2004]; *see also* Regulation 733/2002 of the European Parliament and of the Council of Apr. 22, 2002, Implementation of the .eu Top Level Domain, art. 1, 2002 OJ (L 113) 5 (EC) (implementing the ".eu" country code Top Level Domain within the community); *see also ADR Rules and Supplemental Rules*, ADR.eu, http://eu.adr.eu/adr/adr_rules/index.php, for ".eu" domain name dispute rules that implemented the ADR system.

implementation and functioning of the ".eu" top-level domain name and amending and repealing Regulation (EC) No. 733/2002 and repealing Commission Regulation (EC) No. 874/2004 that came into effect on 18 April 2019 and will be applicable on 13 October 2022, except for a new right for EU citizens residing in non-EU countries to register .EU domain names, that applies since 19 October 2019 (Article 20).

The Commission Regulation 874/2004 states that "[t]he Registry should provide for an ADR procedure which takes into account the international best practices in this area and in particular the relevant World Intellectual Property Organization (WIPO) recommendations, to ensure that speculative and abusive registrations are avoided as far as possible."[42] Furthermore, it provides that "ADR should respect a minimum of uniform procedural rules, similar to the ones set out in the Uniform Dispute Resolution Policy adopted by the Internet Corporation of Assigned Names and Numbers (ICANN)."[43] These references show that the ADR process must follow "the international best practices" and that the UDRP, as an element of these best practices, provides a valuable guidance in defining the procedural rules adopted under the EU Policy.

Despite the similarities the EU Policy shares with the UDRP, an important element where they noticeably differ is the nature of the rights that can be invoked by a complainant in such proceedings. While, as noted above, the UDRP only applies for the benefit of *trademark* owners, the EU Policy is significantly broader in its scope of protection. The regulation provides for a broad definition of protectable rights and includes "registered national and community trademarks, geographical indications or designations of origin, and, in as far as they are protected under national law in the Member-State where they are held: unregistered trademarks, trade names, business identifiers, company names, family names, and distinctive titles of protected literary and artistic works."[44]

Neither the UDRP nor the other internet domain name dispute resolution systems derived from it can be considered as arbitral proceedings.[45] The decisions rendered under the domain dispute proceedings are not enforceable as arbitral awards (under the New York Convention on the Recognition and Enforcement of Foreign Arbitral Awards of 10 June 1958), and these proceedings are not mandatory.[46] In addition, contrary to the principle of confidentiality that generally applies to ordinary arbitration proceedings, the decisions rendered under these policies are published as a matter of principle.[47]

Beyond these regional or national implementations of the UDRP in various legal systems (such as the EU Policy as discussed above), the development of the internet domain name system has generated new types of trademark disputes and has consequently generated new types of protection mechanisms[48] and new types of ADR systems for solving these disputes.[49]

[42] Commission Regulation 874/2004, *supra* note 41, at recital 16; Regulation 2019/517 similarly provides for the submission of disputes to ADR (art. 4, para. 4) and similarly states that (recital 17) "[t]he alternative dispute resolution (ADR) procedures to be adopted should ... take into account the international best practices in this area and in particular the relevant recommendations of the World Intellectual Property Organization, to ensure that speculative and abusive registrations are avoided as far as possible. Those ADR procedures should respect uniform procedural rules that are in line with those set out in ICANN's Uniform Domain Name Dispute-Resolution Policy."

[43] *Id.* at recital 17.

[44] *Id.* at art. 10.

[45] *See* Philippe Gilliéron, La procédure de résolution en ligne des conflits relatifs aux noms de domaine 26 (2002).

[46] *See* UDRP, *supra* note 19, art. 4(k) entitled "[a]vailability of court proceedings" (under certain conditions).

[47] Commission Regulation 874/2004, art. 22, § 11, 2004 OJ (L 162) 44 (EC).

[48] *See* ICANN's Trademark Clearinghouse, https://newgtlds.icann.org/en/about/trademark-clearinghouse.

[49] A detailed description of these mechanisms would go beyond the scope of this chapter.

The creation by ICANN of new generic top-level domains (new gTLDs) has generated new types of disputes for which ADR mechanisms have been put in place to protect a variety of stakeholders and interests, including trademark owners.[50] The WIPO Arbitration and Mediation Center was appointed by ICANN as the exclusive provider of dispute resolution services for the category of "Legal Rights Objections (LRO)" under ICANN's New gTLD Program.[51] The LRO was particularly designed to protect trademark owners.[52] The LRO leads to independent expert determinations so it constitutes another example of an ADR system for global internet domain name disputes similar to the UDRP even if the LRO is much more limited in its reach.

As the UDRP and its "progeny" clearly show, the digital borderless online environment constitutes a very ADR-friendly environment for solving cross-border trademark-related disputes which could apply beyond domain name disputes.[53]

III ARBITRATION OF (INTERNATIONAL) TRADEMARK DISPUTES

A *Introduction*

Not all types of international trademark disputes can be subject to arbitration (or other ADR mechanisms) because the submission to arbitration (and to other ADR mechanisms) is generally based on the consent of the parties. As a result, disputes relating to large-scale counterfeiting activities are unlikely to be submitted to ADR because the parties to such disputes are unlikely to agree on any consent-based dispute settlement and these activities may call for criminal sanctions which are not reconcilable with ADR.

The recourse to arbitration for solving trademark disputes requires certain conditions to be satisfied.

B *Conditions*

One preliminary question that arises is whether private arbitral tribunals have the power to decide on all trademark law issues and specifically on the validity of trademarks because this may fall under the exclusive jurisdictional power of domestic courts. This raises the issue of the objective arbitrability of the disputes; that is, the ability of certain subject matters to be submitted for decision to arbitration (see Section III.B.1). Even if trademark disputes can be submitted to arbitration, the parties in dispute must duly agree to submit their dispute to arbitration, raising the issue of the arbitration clause's scope (see Section III.B.2). Due attention must also be paid to the choice of the governing law (see Section III.B.3) and to temporary injunctions (see Section III.B.4).

[50] *See* ICANN New Generic Top Level Domains, https://newgtlds.icann.org/en/.

[51] *See* WIPO, *Legal Rights Objections under ICANN's New gTLD Program*, https://wipo.int/amc/en/domains/lro/.

[52] *See* ICANN Applicant Guidebook, § 3.5.2, http://newgtlds.icann.org/en/applicants/agb/objection-procedures-04jun12-en.pdf. The independent panel will determine whether the potential use of the gTLD applied for by the applicant (i) takes unfair advantage of the distinctive character or the reputation of the objector's registered or unregistered trademark or service mark ("mark") or intergovernmental organization (IGO) name or acronym, or (ii) unjustifiably impairs the distinctive character or the reputation of the objector's mark or IGO name or acronym, or (iii) otherwise creates an impermissible likelihood of confusion between the applied-for gTLD and the objector's mark or IGO name or acronym.

[53] On the use of ADR (and specifically arbitration) for trademark disputes in "virtual worlds," *see* Boris Shapiro, *Trademark Arbitration: A First Rate Change for a Second Life Future*, 8 Chi.-Kent J. Intell. Prop. 273 (2009).

1 *Objective Arbitrability of Intellectual Property Disputes*

In order to adjudicate international intellectual property and specifically trademark disputes by arbitration,[54] the parties should have the power to remove these disputes from the court systems.[55] This raises the issue of the objective arbitrability of intellectual property disputes, which has triggered a relatively intensive scholarly debate (which cannot be analyzed in detail in this chapter).[56]

According to a restrictive minority view, certain types of IP disputes raise concerns of public policy to the extent that only national courts should have jurisdiction to decide them, to the exclusion of arbitral tribunals, so that IP disputes would objectively (i.e. because of their very nature) not be arbitrable. This restrictive approach applies particularly to disputes relating to the validity of industrial property rights such as trademarks. It mirrors the rule that frequently applies to national courts, according to which only the courts of the country of registration of the relevant industrial property rights have jurisdictional power to decide on the validity of such rights.

A more liberal view tending to become mainstream considers trademark disputes and, more generally, intellectual property disputes, as arbitrable.[57] One argument supporting this approach is, in essence, that trademarks are rights under the control of their owners over which they can dispose. Many national arbitration regulations define the condition of objective arbitrability by reference to whether the relevant subject matter can be freely disposed of by its owner: if such matter can be disposed of by its owner, the matter is arbitrable.[58] On this basis, given that IP rights and trademark rights are disposable, IP and trademark disputes should as a general rule be objectively arbitrable.[59] One practical way to promote the arbitrability of IP disputes is to limit the jurisdictional powers of arbitral tribunals that would have to assess the validity or nullity of trademarks so the decision shall only be effective between the parties (*inter partes*) and not against third parties (*erga omnes*).[60]

[54] As reflected above, the recourse to mediation or other informal ADR mechanisms including mediation is obviously less problematic to the extent that the neutral third parties (the mediators), which take part in the proceedings to solve disputes, do not have adjudicative power, and thus do not impinge on the power of domestic courts.

[55] *See, e.g.*, Mehmet Polat Kalafatoglu, L'Arbitrabilité en Matière de Propriété Industrielle, Etude en Droit de L'arbitrage International (2018); Bernard Hanotiau, *L'arbitrabilité des litiges de Propriété Intellectuelle*, *in* La Résolution des Litiges de Propriété Intellectuelle [Resolution of Intellectual Property Disputes] 156–74 (Jacques de Werra ed., 2010).

[56] *See generally* Nelson Holzner, Die Objektive Schiedsfähigkeit von Immaterialgüterrechtsstreitigkeiten (2001); Julian D. M. Lew, *Final Report on Intellectual Property Disputes and Arbitration*, 9 ICC Int'l Ct. of Arb. Bull., 41–45 (1998); Stefan Liniger, Immaterialgüterrechtliche Streitigkeiten vor Internationalen Schiedsgerichten mit Sitz in der Schweiz (2002).

[57] *See* Hanotiau, *supra* note 55, for a detailed comparative overview of the issue; *see also* the dissenting opinion in *Scherk v. Alberto-Culver Co.*, 417 US 506, 527 (1974), which objected to the submission to arbitration of securities regulation claims and made the distinction between these non-arbitrable claims and trademark disputes that could be arbitrable ("There has been much support for arbitration of disputes; and it may be the superior way of settling some disagreements. If A and B were quarreling over a trade-mark and there was an arbitration clause in the contract, the policy of Congress in implementing the United Nations Convention on the Recognition and Enforcement of Foreign Arbitral Awards, as it did in 9 U.S.C. § 201 et seq., would prevail").

[58] The liberal Swiss arbitration regime, which is regulated under Chapter XII of the Swiss Act on Private International Law of Dec. 18, 1987, is a good example. *See* François Dessemontet, *Arbitration of Intellectual Property Rights and Licensing Contracts*, *in* Enforcement of Arbitration Agreements and International Arbitration Awards: The New York Convention in Practice 556 (Emmanuel Gaillard & Domenico di Pietro eds., 2008).

[59] *See* Anna P. Mantakou, *Arbitrability and Intellectual Property Disputes*, *in* Arbitrability: International & Comparative Perspectives 263, 266–67 (Loukas A. Mistelis & Stavros L. Brekoulakis eds., 2009).

[60] The positions differ from one country to the other (whereby the position of Swiss law is very liberal in the sense that the validity of national industrial property rights can be decided by arbitral tribunals), for an analysis, *see* Hanotiau, *supra* note 55.

It should, in any event, be emphasized from a practical perspective that in spite of its dogmatic interest, the concerns resulting from the risk of lack of objective arbitrability of IP disputes do not arise frequently in IP arbitration cases.[61]

If the validity of the trademark is not at stake, other types of disputes such as about the ownership, the transfer and/or the infringement of trademarks (for instance in the context of trademark coexistence agreements), are generally considered to be objectively arbitrable.[62]

2 *Consent of the Parties to Submit to Arbitration: The Scope of the Arbitration Clause*

"[A]rbitration is a creature of contract."[63] On this basis, the consent of the parties to submit to arbitration is a key condition to submit a dispute to arbitration. This general principle is of particular importance for trademark (and other intellectual property) arbitration because the risk is that the agreement of the parties to submit a dispute to arbitration (generally in an arbitration clause) may not cover trademark disputes (see Section III.B.2.i). This risk can result from the sometimes misguided desire of the parties to exclude certain types of disputes from the scope of the arbitration clauses by way of carve-out clauses. Parties sometimes do it for IP disputes that shall consequently remain outside of the scope of the arbitration clause and thus be non-arbitrable, which may be complex to handle (see Section III.B.2.ii).

(I) SCOPE OF THE ARBITRATION CLAUSES It is critical to carefully draft the relevant arbitration clauses so these clauses are effective. It is important the clause encompasses not only classical contractual disputes and contractual claims[64] but also covers non-contractual disputes, such as disputes about the relevant trademark (or other intellectual property rights).[65]

61 Defining which law shall govern this issue is complex, *see* TREVOR COOK & ALEJANDRO GARCIA, INTERNATIONAL INTELLECTUAL PROPERTY ARBITRATION (ARBITRATION IN CONTEXT SERIES), ch. 4 at 48 seq. (2010); for a recent and interesting discussion of this issue under Indian law, *see* Saniya Mirani & Mihika Poddar, *Arbitrability of IP Disputes in India – A Blanket Bar?*, KLUWER ARBITRATION BLOG (Mar. 9, 2019), http://arbitrationblog.kluwerarbitration.com/2019/03/09/arbitrability-of-ip-disputes-in-india-a-blanket-bar/.

62 *See* Andrea Mondini & Raphael Meier, *Patentübertragungsklagen vor Internationalen Schiedsgerichten mit Sitz in der Schweiz und die Aussetzung des Patenterteilungsverfahrens*, 5 SIC! 289 (2015).

63 *Steelworkers* v. *Am. Mfg. Co.*, 363 US 564, 569 (1960).

64 *See* Alexander Peukert, *Contractual Jurisdiction Clauses and Intellectual Property*, *in* 24 INTELL. PROP. & PRIVATE INT'L L. 55, 57 (Josef Drexl & Annette Kur eds., 2005), for a similar issue with respect to the drafting of choice of jurisdiction clauses; for a case discussing the scope of a choice of court clause (in a dispute involving contractual claims and non-contractual – i.e. copyright infringement – claims), *see Phillips* v. *Audio Active Ltd.*, 494 F.3d 378 (2nd Cir. 2007); it should also be noted that the trend supporting a growing freedom of parties to choose a court (beyond IP disputes) is confirmed by the case law of the ECJ, *see* Case C-352/13, *Cartel Damages Claims (CDC) Hydrogen Peroxide SA* v. *Akzo Nobel NV et al.*, EURLex 62013CJ0352 (admitting the validity of choice of clause provisions under art. 23(1) of Regulation No. 44/2001 for actions for damages for an infringement of art. 101 TFEU and art. 53 of the Agreement on the European Economic Area of May 2, 1992, in contracts for the supply of goods, even if the effect thereof is a derogation from the rules on international jurisdiction provided for in art. 5(3) and/or art. 6(1) of that regulation, provided that those clauses refer to disputes concerning liability incurred as a result of an infringement of competition law).

65 *See, e.g.*, *Rhône-Poulenc Spécialités Chimiques* v. *SCM Corp.*, 769 F.2d 1569 (Fed. Cir. 1985) (interpreting the scope of an arbitration clause). In the case at hand, the arbitration clause provided that "[a]ny controversy or claim arising out of or relating to this Agreement or the breach thereof, shall, unless amicably adjusted otherwise, be settled by arbitration in Florida in accordance with the rules of the International Chamber of Commerce." *Id.* at 1571. The Federal Circuit determined that "[a]lthough the dispute involves claim interpretation, it arises out of the agreement . . . [and] hold that the determination of the scope and infringement of the '485 patent are the quintessence of the agreement and that the parties intended such central determinations to be included within the scope of its broad arbitration clause." *Id.* at 1572; *see also Simula, Inc.* v. *Autoliv, Inc.*, 175 F.3d 716, 720–21, 723 (9th Cir. 1999) (finding the nondisclosure of trade secrets to be a key part of the relevant agreements and therefore subjecting all claims "arising in connection with" those agreements to arbitration); for a recent example about the scope of an

While this principle sounds simple (or even simplistic), case law confirms this is not always put in practice. It is indeed (unfortunately) not uncommon that disputes arise about the scope of the jurisdictional power of an arbitral tribunal when the arbitration clause is drafted too narrowly, specifically regarding disputes arising after the termination of a trademark (or other IP) license agreement.

Parties should be wary of the risk that arbitral tribunals might be reluctant to admit their jurisdiction for post-contractual disputes relating to the infringement of the previously licensed intellectual property rights on the ground that the arbitration clause would be limited to contractual claims. This was decided in International Chamber of Commerce (ICC) case 4491,[66] where the sole arbitrator held "the Plaintiff's claims for damages and injunctive relief after the termination of the license agreement are not within the scope of the arbitration provisions of the licensing agreement,"[67] noting the arbitration clause had a somewhat unusual wording.[68]

This confirms the tremendous importance of taking all the required measures to avoid, or at least to minimize, the risks of diverging interpretations of the scope of arbitration clauses, which frequently materialize in international intellectual property-related transactions. This is shown by the high-profile dispute between a US group (AMSC) and its former Chinese partner and client (Sinovel), which was ultimately submitted to the Chinese Supreme People's Court. This dispute raised contractual and intellectual property infringement issues (that is, infringement of copyright on computer source code for wind turbines) and led to various parallel judicial and arbitral proceedings in China. The Chinese Supreme Court held the non-contractual claims for copyright infringement were not covered by the relevant arbitration clause and were thus to be submitted to Chinese courts, and not to the Beijing Arbitration Commission as claimed by Sinovel.[69]

This case confirms that the jurisdictional interactions and the risks of conflicts between courts and arbitral tribunals can be complex and that courts and arbitral tribunals should work in a mutually supportive manner as a matter of principle.

(II) INTELLECTUAL PROPERTY CARVE-OUT CLAUSES Parties to an intellectual property (and specifically a trademark) license agreement may be tempted to include sophisticated dispute resolution clauses in their agreement, under which they would carve out certain types of disputes from the scope of the arbitration clause in "intellectual property carve out"[70] provisions.[71] This can lead to intricate difficulties when a dispute arises between the parties since it is frequently complicated to distinguish intellectual property claims (excluded from the scope of the arbitration clause) from contractual claims (covered by the arbitration clause). This lesson

arbitration clause contained in a settlement agreement that followed trademark infringement proceedings, *see Zetor N. Am., Inc.* v. *Rozeboom*, 861 F.3 807 (8th Cir. 2017).

66 As resulting from the excerpts of the award published in the *Journal of International Arbitration*, vol. 75 (1985).

67 *Id.* at 76.

68 *Id.* at 76, stating that "the arbitrator found that the matters to be arbitrated under the licensing agreement are 'possible disagreements between the (Plaintiff) and (the Defendant)' [sic]."

69 For a comment of the dispute, *see* Arthur Dong & Meng Li, *Is an Infringement Claim within the Scope of Arbitration Clause under Laws of PRC?*, KLUWER ARBITRATION BLOG (May 29, 2014), http://kluwerarbitrationblog.com/blog/2014/05/29/is-an-infringement-claim-within-the-scope-of-arbitration-clause-under-laws-of-prc/.

70 As formulated by the District Court, *Oracle Am., Inc.* v. *Myriad Group AG*, No. C-10-05604 SBA, 2011 WL 3862027, *20 (ND Cal., Sept. 1, 2011).

71 Carve-out clauses can (of course) arise in non-IP disputes and can lead to complex challenges, *see, e.g.*, *Lombard N. Cent. PLC* v. *GATX Corp.* [2012] EWHC 1067 (Comm) (UK).

can be learned from the interesting US case *Oracle America Inc.* v. *Myriad Group*.[72] In this case, the dispute resolution clause that had been agreed upon between the parties split the jurisdictional power between arbitration (for breach of contract claims) and court litigation by carving out certain types of disputes (essentially intellectual property infringement claims) from the jurisdictional power of the arbitral tribunal. While the decision addressed only the issue of who gets to decide on the interpretation of the scope and reach of the arbitration clause under US law between the California federal courts or the arbitral tribunal, its relevance is broader to the extent that this decision can (and should) serve as a useful warning/reminder of the risks of carve-out provisions contained in arbitration clauses, which are sometimes included by the parties in their intellectual property (and specifically trademark-related) contracts for the purpose of reserving the power to enforce their intellectual property rights against the other contracting party before state courts.

The Court of Appeals for the Ninth Circuit recognized the power of arbitral tribunals to rule on their own jurisdiction, which is reflected in all major arbitration rules.[73] It further confirmed the arbitration-friendly approach existing under US law (as reflected in case law, particularly in the decision of the US Supreme Court in *Scherk* v. *Alberto-Culver Co.*, relating to an international trademark dispute), which is finding its way globally.[74] The decision is of high practical relevance because it clearly illustrates the risks of "intellectual property carve-out" contained in arbitration clauses. In this dispute, the bifurcation of adjudication powers between the courts and the arbitral tribunal led to a stay of all court and arbitral proceedings for an extended period of time (some eighteen months) which can hardly be considered an adequate method for efficiently solving international commercial intellectual property-related disputes. Parties should, therefore, duly assess the potential consequences and risks of inserting intellectual property carve-out provisions in their intellectual property agreements and, if they opt for such clauses, draft them as precisely as possible.[75] This concern is obviously not limited to intellectual property carve-out clauses, but rather affects all contractual limits to the scope of arbitration clauses. This is clearly expressed in the International Bar Association Guidelines for Drafting International Arbitration Clauses (2010), which indicate that "[a]bsent special circumstances, the parties should not attempt to limit the scope of disputes subject to arbitration and should define this scope broadly."[76] The Guidelines therefore wisely state:

> The parties should bear in mind that, even when drafted carefully, exclusions may not avoid preliminary arguments over whether a given dispute is subject to arbitration. A claim may raise some issues that fall within the scope of the arbitration clause and others that do not . . . a dispute over the ownership or validity of intellectual property rights under a licensing agreement [which would have been carved out] may also involve issues of non-payment, breach and so forth, which

[72] *Oracle Am., Inc.* v. *Myriad Grp.* A.G., 724 F.3d 1069 (9th Cir. 2013); this analysis is derived from Jacques de Werra, *Risks of IP Carve-Out in Arbitration Clauses*, 9 J. Intell. Prop. L. & Practice 184 (2014), http://jiplp.oxfordjournals.org/content/9/3/184.full.

[73] *Id.*; *see, e.g.*, United Nations Commission on International Trade Law, Arbitration Rules, Gen. Assemb. Res. 31/98, at art. 23, § 1 (2010) [hereinafter UNCITRAL Rules], which was applicable in this case and provides that "[t]he arbitral tribunal shall have the power to rule on its own jurisdiction, including any objections with respect to the existence or validity of the arbitration agreement."

[74] *Scherk* v. *Alberto-Culver Co.*, 417 US 506 (1974).

[75] As reflected by Patrick Rohn & Philipp Groz, *Drafting Arbitration Clauses for IP Agreements*, 7 J. Intell. Prop. L. & Practice 652, 654 (2012), who suggest carefully defining the types of disputes to be carved out "in order to avoid future jurisdictional disputes as to whether particular claims or defenses are covered by the clause's scope."

[76] *IBA Guidelines for Drafting International Arbitration Clauses, Guideline* 3, Int'l. Bar Assn., https://ibanet.org/ENews_Archive/IBA_27October_2010_Arbitration_Clauses_Guidelines.aspx.

could give rise to intractable jurisdictional problems in situations where certain disputes have been excluded from arbitration.[77]

If an arbitral tribunal decides on an issue for which it had no jurisdictional power based on the arbitration clause, this can constitute a ground for annulling the award and, in an international setting, for refusing the enforcement and recognition of a foreign award. The enforcement of the foreign award could be refused on the ground the award would exceed the scope of the jurisdictional power the parties have agreed to give to the arbitral tribunal. Article 5, paragraph 1 of the New York Convention of 1958 provides that the

> [r]ecognition and enforcement of the award may be refused, at the request of the party against whom it is invoked, only if that party furnishes to the competent authority where the recognition and enforcement is sought, proof that ... (c) The award deals with a difference not contemplated by or not falling within the terms of the submission to arbitration, or it contains decisions on matters beyond the scope of the submission to arbitration, provided that, if the decisions on matters submitted to arbitration can be separated from those not so submitted, that part of the award which contains decisions on matters submitted to arbitration may be recognized and enforced.

C *Governing Law*

One advantage of arbitration is its flexibility. This can materialize in the broad freedom left to the parties to define the law that shall govern their dispute.[78] This liberty means the parties can be in a position to apply one single law to their international trademark dispute. This can be illustrated by taking the example of a global trademark coexistence agreement giving the right to one contracting party to register and use trademarks provided they do not create any risk of confusion with the other party's trademarks.[79] In such a case, the risk of confusion between conflicting trademarks, which is a standard issue under trademark law, would be governed by the law of each country where the alleged infringement takes place under the traditional rules of conflict of laws, leading to the multiplication of parallel governing laws. This would imply that even if the coexistence agreement were governed by a single law chosen by the contracting parties (as the law governing the coexistence agreement), the existence of a risk of confusion could, depending on the interpretation of the contractual clause at issue, still be governed by multiple national trademark laws in each of the countries where the alleged infringement took place. In order to avoid this consequence, parties involved in international commercial arbitration may prefer to submit all contractual and non-contractual issues to a single national (trademark) law. They could consequently select one law to apply to all issues at stake, particularly on the issue of the risk of confusion, avoiding the disadvantages of applying multiple different national laws that may lead to conflicting results, in spite of the harmonization of international trademark protection standards (in particular, thanks to the TRIPS agreement).[80]

[77] *Id.* at § 16.

[78] *See* Swiss Act on Private International Law, *supra* note 58, at art. 187, § 1.

[79] *See, e.g.*, Tribunal Fédéral [TF] [Swiss Federal Supreme Court], Feb. 17, 2015, 4A_553/2014, decided by the Swiss Supreme Court in a case defining the respective rights to use certain trademarks/corporate names in the framework of a corporate spin-off transaction in the Swiss industrial "von Roll" group; for disputes about trademark coexistence agreements *see Apple Corps. Ltd.* v. *Apple Comput., Inc.* [2006] EWHC 996 (Ch) (UK) and *Omega SA* v. *Omega Eng'g Inc.* [2011] EWCA Civ. 645 (UK).

[80] For additional examples, *see* Trevor Cook & Alejandro Garcia, International Intellectual Property Arbitration, Arbitration in Context Series 87 (2010).

A choice of law clause could also cover issues relating to the validity or enforceability of the relevant trademarks and other intellectual property rights, at least to the extent the award to be rendered shall only have an effect between the parties (that is, *inter partes*). The parties to an international trademark agreement covering several countries should indeed have the power to decide in the arbitration clause of the agreement that the validity or enforceability of trademarks registered in different countries or regions shall not be governed by each and every national trademark law in the relevant countries or regions, but shall rather be analyzed on the basis of one single national (or, for the EU, regional) trademark law.[81] The parties consequently enjoy great freedom in the definition of the governing law (in the agreement itself or in the subsequent arbitration proceedings), whereby the choice of a unique law applying to a global dispute may facilitatie the proceedings (in terms of time and costs). Nevertheless this creates a risk of the "winner takes all," in the sense that if the parties choose to submit the issue of the validity or of the infringement of the relevant trademark to one single law, one answer will be given to this issue which will turn out to be unfavorable to one party.

In any event, it is essential to realize that a choice of law clause, which would relate only to the law governing the contract and which would consequently not cover non-contractual issues, will not be sufficient. The scope of the choice of law clause should therefore be formulated more broadly.[82] One approach could be to mirror the scope of the arbitration clause with the scope of the choice of law clause in the sense that the arbitral tribunal shall have the power to decide all relevant legal issues by application of one single governing law.[83]

This flexibility in the choice of the governing law can be an important advantage of arbitration over state court litigation in many areas of the world. This is particularly the case in the EU because of Article 8 of Regulation 864/2007 (Rome II), which provides that "[t]he law applicable to a non-contractual obligation arising from an infringement of an intellectual property right shall be the law of the country for which protection is claimed" (Article 8, paragraph 1), and that this rule is mandatory (that is, it cannot be overridden by contract pursuant to Article 8, paragraph 3[84]), whereby this provision does not apply in arbitration.[85]

It should be kept in mind that the freedom of the parties to choose the law that shall govern their dispute does not (and cannot) affect the potential application of mandatory legal principles, specifically of competition law. This was confirmed in the landmark *Benetton–EcoSwiss* case, which was a trademark licensing dispute[86] and was submitted to the Court of Justice of the European Union (at that time the Court of Justice of the European Communities).[87] In this case, the Court famously held that "a national court to which application is made for annulment

[81] *Id.*, at 93 sq.; ROHN & GROZ, *supra* note 75, at 655.

[82] See WIPO, *Arbitration and Mediation Center*, http://wipo.int/amc/en/clauses/#4. The standard arbitration clause provides that: "The dispute, controversy or claim shall be decided in accordance with the law of [specify jurisdiction]."

[83] COOK & GARCIA, *supra* note 80, at 130.

[84] "The law applicable under this Article may not be derogated from by an agreement pursuant to Article 14."

[85] An arbitral tribunal having its seat in the European Union will not be bound to apply art. 8 (*see* COOK & GARCIA, *supra* note 80, at 94), even if the application of Regulations Rome I and Rome II by arbitral tribunals is debated in the legal literature: *see* Davor Babić, *Rome I Regulation: Binding Authority for Arbitral Tribunals in the European Union?*, 13 J. PRIVATE INT'L. L. (2017), 71; Burgu Yüksel, *The Relevance of the Rome I Regulation to International Commercial Arbitration in the European Union*, 7 J. PRIVATE INT'L. L. 149 (2011); ROHN & GROZ, *supra* note 75, at 655, leave this issue open.

[86] Benetton granted Eco Swiss the right to manufacture watches and clocks bearing the words "Benetton by Bulova," which could be sold by Eco Swiss and Bulova.

[87] Case C-126/97, *Eco Swiss China Time Ltd* v. *Benetton International NV*, 1999 ECR I-03055.

of an arbitration award must grant that application if it considers that the award in question is in fact contrary to article 81 EC (ex Article 85), where its domestic rules of procedure require it to grant an application for annulment founded on failure to observe national rules of public policy."[88] On this basis, parties to an international trademark agreement should keep a close eye on the potential application of competition law which may affect or even jeopardize the enforceability of their contract (which may prove of strategic interest for the contracting party wishing to escape from its contractual liability and can be of particular relevance for trademark licensees seeking to escape from the obligation to pay royalties under their license agreement). The critical relevance of competition law on intellectual property licensing and on IP arbitration is confirmed by the decision rendered by the CJEU on 7 July 2016 in the patent licensing dispute between Genentech and Hoechst GmbH, Sanofi-Aventis Deutschland GmbH (in the course of which arbitral proceedings took place and arbitral awards were challenged for annulment before French courts, which referred the case to the CJEU). The CJEU decided that Article 81 of the Treaty (now Article 101 TFEU) does not preclude the imposition on the licensee, under a license agreement such as that at issue in the main proceedings, of a requirement to pay a royalty for the use of a patented technology for the entire period that agreement was in effect, in the event of the revocation or non-infringement of a licensed patent, provided the licensee was freely able to terminate that agreement with reasonable notice.[89]

D *Provisional Measures*

Given the necessity of quickly reacting against trademark infringement activities (also because of the risk of irreparable harm and of damage to the reputation of the trademark/brand owner),[90] provisional (interim) measures are of fundamental importance in many trademark disputes.[91] It is thus very important to ensure provisional measures can be obtained from courts.[92] In licensing disputes, the victim who may want to request provisional measures is not only the licensor[93] but sometimes also the licensee.[94]

The submission of a dispute to arbitration in a trademark agreement shall not prevent one of the parties requesting provisional measures from a court, specifically at the place where the damage has occurred or may occur.[95] However, certain courts have adopted a restrictive

88 *Id.*

89 Case C-567/14, *Genentech Inc.* v. *Hoechst GmbH, Sanofi-Aventis Deutschland GmbH*, 2014 EURLex 62014CJ0567.

90 For an example, *see* the decision of the Tribunal Fédéral [TF] [Swiss Federal Supreme Court] Apr. 13, 2010, Arrêts du Tribunal Fédéral Suisse [ATF] 136 III 200, which was rendered upon appeal against a procedural order issued by a sole arbitrator in a WIPO arbitration case which ordered the transfer of the stock of goods from the trademark licensee to the trademark licensor because the licensee was getting rid of the stock at depreciated prices which damaged the brand and the reputation of the licensor; for a comment of this case, *see* Jacques de Werra, *Liquidation d'un Contrat de Licence de Marque et Mesures Provisionnelles: Quelques Observations à la Lumière de l'ATF 136 III 200*, SIC! 662 (2010), https://sic-online.ch/fileadmin/user_upload/Sic-Online/2010/documents/662.pdf.

91 COOK & GARCIA, *supra* note 80, at 221; ROHN & GROZ, *supra* note 75, at 656.

92 One of the reasons is that a procedural order which would be rendered by an arbitral tribunal will not necessarily be enforceable, given that an arbitral tribunal does not have any coercive power to enforce, by contrast to a state court, *see* ROHN & GROZ, *supra* note 75, at 658.

93 *See Performance Unlimited, Inc.* v. *Questar Publishers, Inc.*, 52 F.3d 1373 (6th Cir. 1995).

94 *See Fairchild Semiconductors Corp.* v. *Third Dimension Semiconductor*, 564 F.Supp.2d 63 (D. Maine, Dec. 12, 2008).

95 *See* WIPO, *WIPO Arbitration Rules*, 2020, http://wipo.int/amc/en/arbitration/rules/newrules.html, as follows (art. 48 d): "A request addressed by a party to a judicial authority for interim measures or for security for the claim or counter-claim, or for the implementation of any such measures or orders granted by the Tribunal, shall not be deemed incompatible with the Arbitration Agreement, or deemed to be a waiver of that Agreement."

approach about this,[96] which is not justified because there is no incompatibility between requesting provisional measures before a court and submitting the dispute on the merits to arbitration.[97]

A request for provisional measures can also be obtained from the arbitral tribunal. If the arbitral tribunal has not been constituted, some arbitration rules provide for the appointment of an "emergency arbitrator."[98] This need for quick action in international trademark disputes should also be taken into account by the parties negotiating a trademark agreement and an arbitration clause. They should consequently carefully select arbitration rules that will meet their needs and expectations (and specifically provide for emergency arbitration).[99]

IV CONCLUSION

ADR methods are growing in importance for solving all types of private disputes, including trademark disputes. As shown in this chapter, ADR mechanisms (and specifically mediation, UDRP, and arbitration) can be of significant value for solving international trademark disputes and should consequently be duly considered by trademark owners and by parties negotiating trademark-related agreements.

While the specificities of intellectual property (specifically trademark) ADR and specifically arbitration should not be overestimated,[100] they must not be fully neglected. Contracting parties and their counsel should indeed take all required measures to benefit from the flexibilities ADR mechanisms can offer and should consequently consider their high potential, but also their limits, when drafting dispute resolution clauses in trademark-related agreements.

96 *Simula Inc.* v. *Autoliv Inc.*, 175 F.3d 716 (9th Cir. 1999): "Because the district court correctly concluded that all of Simula's claims were arbitrable and the ICC arbitral tribunal is authorized to grant the equivalent of an injunction pendente lite, it would have been inappropriate for the district court to grant preliminary injunctive relief. Therefore, we affirm the district court's denial of preliminary injunctive relief"; *but see In re Faiveley Transport Malmo AB*, 522 F. Supp. 2d 639 (SDNY 2007) (holding that the arbitration clause: "[a]ny dispute arising out of or in connection with this agreement shall be finally settled by arbitration without recourse to the courts" did not prevent the filing of temporary measures before courts in New York).

97 *Sauer-Getriebe KG* v. *White Hydraulics, Inc.*, 715 F.2d 348 (7th Cir. 1983).

98 *See* WIPO Arbitration rules, *supra* note 95, art. 49; on this issue, *see* Rohn & Groz, *supra* note 75, at 657.

99 *See* ICC, *ICC Intellectual Property Roadmap* 66, 2017, https://iccwbo.org/publication/icc-intellectual-property-roadmap-current-emerging-issues-business-policymakers, holding that "[t]o ensure that injunctive interim or conservatory relief is available even before arbitration commences. To that effect, parties should consider choosing arbitration rules that provide for interim measure to be granted by the arbitral tribunal but also for emergency relief even before the constitution of the tribunal."

100 *See* William W. Park, *Irony in Intellectual Property Arbitration*, 19 Arb. Int'l. 451 (2003) (holding in the introduction that "[o]n scrutiny, the special nature of IP arbitration is not really all that special").

PART TWO

Comparative Perspectives on Trademark Protection

Convergence and (Remaining) Divergence

I

The Nature and Functions of Trademarks

9

Trademark Functions in European Union Law

*Annette Kur**

I INTRODUCTION

Before embarking on a discussion of trademark functions, it is appropriate to briefly explore the meaning of "functions" in Intellectual Property (IP) law. Generally speaking, each IP right has an *essential function* defined by the basic task assigned to it. Thus, patents and copyright incentivize innovation and the creation of new works; trademarks indicate commercial origin. Second, IP rights (IPRs) typically fulfill *economic functions* that are more varied than the essential ones. Thus, for instance, patents can have the economic function to maximize leveraging power on particular markets, or to attract venture capital. Third, the legal or *legally protected functions* are determined by the elements of an IP right that a particular legislature has chosen to protect. While the essential functions usually determine the *core* of the legal protection granted, they do not necessarily confine the scope of the rights conferred. That is, the legal or legally protected functions may go beyond the essential functions, for reasons of policy or convenience. The economic functions typically operate as a catalyst in that process: where a discrepancy is observed between the economic functions and the written law, the legislature or the courts may be motivated to better align the latter with market reality. Of course, that scheme can also be reversed: where the operation of IPRs on the market yields undesirable or detrimental economic effects, legislative steps or judicial practice may be called for in order to bring the legal functions back to basics.

So far, these observations apply to all IP rights alike. For trademark law the issue holds yet another facet. Unlike other IPRs, trademarks are not protected for their intrinsic value, but only in their relation to an object that is necessarily (at least conceptually) separate from them. Furthermore, at least in principle, the object to which the trademark relates is not protected as such, but may be freely copied. This means that while protection in copyright, patent and industrial design law lies on the *object itself* – the invention, the work, the design – trademark law is concerned with the manner in which signs are *used to designate commercial objects*. In other words, protection is not related to what trademarks *are*, but what they *do*; it is a *functions-based*, not an object-based, type of protection. This explains why the issue is much more prominent in the legal discourse in trademark law than in patent or copyright law.

These considerations form the background for the discussion of trademark functions in European Union law in the present chapter. We will first consider in Section II the origins of

* Affiliated Senior Fellow, Max Planck Institute for Innovation and Competition, Munich.

the discussion which started decades before the harmonization within the EU and the Court of Justice of the European Union (CJEU)'s case law construing the EU Trademarks Directive and subsequent Regulation. After a brief presentation of CJEU jurisprudence in Section III, Section IV analyzes the effects on the legal acquis within the EU. This section argues that the CJEU's functions jurisprudence has de facto harmonized a substantial part of business-to-business (B2B) unfair competition law. While the effects are, all in all, predominantly positive, the functions jurisprudence is precarious where the borderlines imposed by the written law are clearly overstepped, and where the reference to functions is turned into a panacea promulgating unfair competition-inspired solutions without a proper legal basis. Section V elaborates on this point, followed by a brief conclusion.

II THE ORIGINS (FROM A GERMAN PERSPECTIVE)

As long as trademarks were treated as a particular variety of protection against unfair competition, there was no need to discuss the trademark functions. The differences vis-à-vis protection of absolute, subjective rights granted to holders of patents and copyright were so obvious that nothing had to be explained about the inherent confinements of such rights. In the infancy of modern trademark protection systems, it was clear and uncontested that protection was granted only where use of the same or a similar mark by others was likely to mislead the public as to the commercial origin of the goods.

However, from the early days, a gradual convergence could be observed of concepts underlying copyright and patents on the one hand, and trademark law on the other. Already in the Paris Convention, patents, utility models and industrial designs were bundled up together with trademarks in the overarching term of "industrial property."[1] Furthermore, by embracing the notion of extended protection of famous marks against even non-confusing uses,[2] many countries set out on a route towards "emancipation" of trademark rights from their original *raison d'être.*[3] Although for many years dilution was considered as an exemption from the general rule and did not trigger a general debate on the foundations of trademark law, it signaled that the commercial interests vested in distinctive signs were too big for protection restricted to indicating origin to cover, and that the law, at least in certain cases, was willing to break away from the narrow scheme so as to offer assistance.

The practical relevance of a functions-oriented approach vis-à-vis property concepts became visible in debates concerning the international dimensions of the exhaustion principle. If it is accepted that trademarks belong to a species of absolute industrial property rights that enjoy an exclusive market position within a given territory, there is no reason to differentiate between patents, designs and trademarks with regard to the proprietor's right to keep goods covered by the right off the domestic market. If, however, the premise is accepted that trademarks are not "just another industrial property right," but that their scope of protection is inherently confined to what

[1] Paris Convention for the Protection of Industrial Property, Mar. 20, 1888, art. 1(2), as revised at the Stockholm Revision Conference, July 14, 1967, 21 UST 1538, TIAS No. 6903, 828 UNTS 305 [hereinafter Paris Convention].

[2] *See* Barton Beebe, *The Suppressed Misappropriation Origins of Trademark Antidilution Law: The Landgericht Elberfeld's Odol Opinion and Frank Schechter's The Rational Basis of Trademark Protection*, *in* INTELLECTUAL PROPERTY AT THE EDGE: THE CONTESTED CONTOURS OF IP 59–80 (Rochelle Cooper Dreyfuss & Jane C. Ginsburg eds., 2013); and Graeme B. Dinwoodie, *Dilution as Unfair Competition: European Echoes*, *in* INTELLECTUAL PROPERTY AT THE EDGE: THE CONTESTED CONTOURS OF IP 81–102 (Rochelle Cooper Dreyfuss & Jane C. Ginsburg eds., 2013).

[3] That process is comprehensively described in Andreas Sattler's thesis: ANDREAS SATTLER, EMANZIPATION UND EXPANSION DES MARKENRECHTS (2015).

they are meant to do, namely to indicate commercial origin, then the result changes: as long as the products to which the mark is attached are genuine in the sense that they originate from the trademark holder, there can be no infringement, irrespective of where they were first released on the market. In other words, whether trademark rights are subject to national or international exhaustion may turn on the question of whether it is taken for granted that the mark's essential function of indicating origin necessarily limits the exercise of the rights conferred.[4]

After controversial discussions, and following earlier decisions from the Netherlands[5] and Switzerland,[6] the latter position was adopted inter alia in Germany by the Federal Court of Justice in the 1960s,[7] with support from scholarly literature.[8] The conflict and its solution proved to be highly influential. For decades to come, major court decisions or academic treatises dealing with trademark law emphasized as a starting point that the origin function[9] defined, mandatorily and exclusively, what could be protected under trademark law.[10] Evidence for the dominance of the origin function was found in a number of features of pre-harmonized law in Germany (and other member states such as Italy, Austria and Greece), such as the restriction of protection to likelihood of confusion, the principle of specialty (no protection against use for dissimilar goods), the prohibition of isolated transfer of marks, etc.

In Italy,[11] Switzerland,[12] and Germany alike, the 1970s and 1980s saw a lively scholarly debate on trademark functions under legal and economic aspects.[13] The one-sided approach towards trademark protection was criticized inter alia for being inconsistent with its own premises,[14] but

[4] This is, of course, not the only way of motivating international versus national exhaustion. The first sale doctrine developed in US jurisprudence rather operates on the basis of implied consent, which does not differentiate per se between the different forms of rights.

[5] *Grundig* v. *Prins*, Hoge Raad (Supreme Court of the Netherlands), Dec. 14, 1956; 1957 GRUR Int. 259; 1957. Bijblad bij de Industriële Eigendom (Bie) 46; 1962 (Neth.).

[6] *Philips AG* v. *Radio Import GmbH*, Bundesgericht, Oct. 4, 1960, 86 (II.) Entscheidungen des Schweizerischen Bundesgerichtes 270 (Swit.).

[7] Bundesgerichtshof (BGH; Federal Court of Justice), Jan. 22, 1964, Gewerblicher Rechtsschutz und Urheberrecht (GRUR), 372. In his comment in the "foreign" part of the journal, *Friedrich-Karl Beier* GRUR AUSLAND, 205 (1964), amply reports on previous jurisprudence of German (appeal) courts, foreign decisions, and the controversies in the German literature.

[8] In particular by Friedrich-Karl Beier. Most influential proved to be Beier's article in Territorialität des Markenrechts und internationaler Wirtschaftsverkehr GRUR 8 (1968) (Friedrich-Karl Beier, *Territoriality of Trademark Law and International Trade*, INT'L REV. INTELL. PROP. COMPETITION L. 48 (1970)) that captured the contents of his (unpublished) dissertation.

[9] Sometimes also tagged as "Unterscheidungsfunktion" (distinction function).

[10] For an overview *see* Friedrich-Karl Beier & Ulrich Krieger, *Wirtschaftliche Bedeutung, Funktion und Zweck der Marke*, GRUR INTERNATIONAL 125 (1976) (report written for AIPPI Q 68, Economic significance, functions and purpose of the trademark); see also FRAUKE HENNING-BODEWIG & ANNETTE KUR, MARKE UND VERBRAUCHER, VOL. I 228 (1988) (with further references).

[11] See Adriano Vanzetti, *Funzione e Natura Giuridica del Marchio*, I RIV. DIR. COMM. 16 (1961). This seems to have been the first publication of its kind in Europe. A slightly abbreviated German translation was published in GRUR AUSLAND, 128 (Part I) and 185 (Part II) (1965). For a view from the early 1980s, *see, e.g.*, Vito Mangini, *Competition and Monopoly in Trademark Law: An EEC Perspective*, INT'L REV. INTELL. PROP. COMPETITION L. 591 (1980), in particular 607 et seq.

[12] In particular by Alois Troller, *Wesen und Unwesen der Marke*, *in* FESTSCHRIFT FÜR PHILIPP MÖHRING 291–314 (Wolfgang Hefermehl, Rudolf Nirk & Harry Westermann eds., 1965).

[13] In addition to the writings by F.-K. Beier, *see, e.g.*, Ludwig Heydt, *Parallelimporte und Warenzeichenrecht*, GRUR 450–67 (1969); Walter Oppenhoff, *Wandel der Markenrechtskonzeption?* GRUR INTERNATIONAL 333–436 (1973); Rolf Sack, *Die Rechtlichen Funktionen des Warenzeichens*, GRUR 402–12 (Part I); 445–53 (Part II) (1972); RUPERT SCHREINER, DIE DIENSTLEISTUNGSMARKE – TYPUS, RECHTSSCHUTZ UND FUNKTION (1983); FRAUKE HENNING-BODEWIG & ANNETTE KUR, MARKE UND VERBRAUCHER VOL. I 227–58 (1988).

[14] That criticism was focused on rather marginal points, for instance on the fact that trademarks do not identify the enterprise from which the goods originate by its proper name, or that products of the same origin may bear different marks, etc.

also because by solely focusing on the origin function a number of other functions were neglected that might be more important economically, thus alienating the law from commercial reality.[15] In the context of that debate, specific terminology was developed in order to characterize the additional economic functions performed by a mark. Those debates coined, inter alia, the now familiar terms of "advertisement," "communication" and "quality" function.[16]

After harmonization and implementation of the First Trade Mark Directive (104/89/EEC) into national law, the discussions became largely moot. Most of the issues previously debated under the aspect of functions had been resolved by positive law. Protection was no longer confined to likelihood of confusion and to use of a mark for identical or similar goods; assignment of marks was permitted without the business or relevant part of business accompanying it; and exhaustion occurred only in the case of goods being released by the trademark proprietor or with their consent within the European Economic Area (EEA). Thus, it seemed that under the new legislation the autarchy of the essential origin function had been conquered by complementing the range of legally protected functions with at least some of the economic functions. This caused the functions debate to ebb for more than a decade, only to become more intense when it was revived by the CJEU.

III JURISPRUDENCE OF THE COURT OF JUSTICE OF THE EUROPEAN UNION: FROM *SILHOUETTE* TO KEYWORD ADVERTISING

The trigger for what became the CJEU's functions jurisprudence lay hidden in the text of the Trade Mark Directive (TMD)[17] and the Trade Mark Regulation (originally CTMR;[18] now EUTMR).[19] More precisely, it was implied in the so-called double identity clause, Article 5(1)(a) TMD 89/104/EEC[20] and Article 9(1)(a) CTMR.[21] Pursuant to the provision, the proprietor of a registered mark is entitled to prevent all third parties not having her consent from using in the course of trade "any sign which is identical with the trade mark in relation to goods or services which are identical with those for which the trade mark is registered." No likelihood of confusion needs to be shown.

It was clear from the beginning that the provision applies to counterfeits. Use of identical marks on identical products not originating from the trademark holder is infringing irrespective

[15] That argument was proffered in particular by Alfons Kraft, *Markenrecht und Markenschutz*, MARKENARTIKEL HEUTE: MARKE, MARKT UND MARKETING 85–109 (1978) (special edition of the journal *Markenartikel*). While most other authors agreed that the advertising (also termed "suggestive" or "attracting") function of a mark was eminently important in practice, the majority opinion held that it should not, or at least not fully, determine the legal scope of the trademark protection granted.

[16] *See, e.g.*, the attempt made by Rolf Sack, *supra* note 13, to sort out the different categories of trademark functions and the nomenclature proposed.

[17] Originally enacted as First Council Directive 89/104/EEC of Dec. 21, 1988, to approximate the laws of the member states relating to trademarks, OJ L 40, 11.2.1989, 1–7; codified as Directive 2008/95/EC of the European Parliament and of the Council of Oct. 22, 2008, to approximate the laws of the member states relating to trademarks, OJ L 299, 8.11.2008, 25–33 [hereinafter TMD 2008]; recast as Directive (EU) 2015/2436 of the European Parliament and of the Council of Dec. 16, 2015 to approximate the laws of the member states relating to trademarks, OJ L 336, 23.12.2015, 1–26 [hereinafter TMD 2015].

[18] Originally enacted as Council Regulation (EC) No. 40/94 of Dec. 20, 1993 on the Community trademark, OJ L 11, 14.1.1994, 1–36; codified as Council Regulation (EC) No. 207/2009 of Feb. 26, 2009 on the Community trademark, OJ L 78, 24.3.2009, 1–42 [hereinafter TMR 2009].

[19] Regulation (EU) 2017/1001 of the European Parliament and of the Council of June 14, 2017, on the European Union trademark, OJ L 154, 16.6.2017, 1–99 [hereinafter EUTMR].

[20] Unchanged in the codified version, TMD 2008, *supra* note 17; now TMD 2015, *supra* note 17, art. 10(2)(a).

[21] Unchanged in the codified version, TMR 2009, *supra* note 18; now EUTMR, *supra* note 19, art. 9(2)(a).

of whether the relevant public can easily recognize that the products are fake – for instance when they are offered for a very low price on street markets.[22] More difficult to decide was whether it also applies to use of the mark by third parties correctly designating goods or services as originating from the trademark holder (referential use). Nothing can be found about that in the *travaux* – the issue was either ignored or deliberately left undecided. The legal position(s) prevailing in the member states at the relevant time were partly unclear and divergent. While in Germany use of a mark for referential purposes was not considered as falling within the ambit of trademark law,[23] France[24] and in particular the uniform Benelux trademark law were more open in that regard: While such uses most often were not considered as infringing, at least they were not excluded from trademark law *ab initio*.[25]

In early decisions by the CJEU interpreting the double identity clause the crucial importance of the issue was not realized, or at least it was not addressed. In *Silhouette*,[26] the CJEU had to decide the questions of whether Article 7 TMD 89/104[27] (now Article 15 TMD 2015/2436) permitted assertions of international exhaustion, and if not, on which legal basis an injunction could be issued against an importer of goods released on the market outside the EU.[28] The CJEU gave a negative answer to the first question and pointed to the double identity clause with regard to the second.[29] Thus, it was taken for granted that the provision applies not only to counterfeits but also to use of the mark for products which, after all, are genuine goods. The same matter-of-course type of approach was reflected in *BMW* v. *Deenik*[30] and *Gilette* v. *LA Laboratories*, where the CJEU endorsed application of the double identity clause although in both cases the marks were used only to refer to goods sold under those marks, without any contention by the alleged infringers that they themselves were the source of goods bearing those marks.[31] Obviously the CJEU did not see any problem here because, similar to exhaustion, the law includes a specific limitation concerning use of a protected sign in order to indicate the purpose of one's goods or services, making it appear logical that use for such purposes must in principle be capable of falling within the ambit of trademark protection.

[22] This follows from the fact that different from art. 16(1) TRIPS the double identity rule in EU law is formulated as an absolute rule and no mere presumption of likelihood of confusion that can be rebutted. Agreement on Trade-Related Aspects of Intellectual Property Rights, Apr. 15, 1994, Marrakesh Agreement Establishing the World Trade Organization, Annex 1C, 1869 UNTS 299, 33 ILM 1197 (1994) [hereinafter TRIPS Agreement].

[23] Even after implementation of the TMD, it was argued by a majority that the sytem had not changed in that regard. *See in particular* Erhard Keller, Schutz Eingetragener Marken Gegen Rufausnutzung Nach Deutschem und Europäischem Recht 12, 75 et seq. (1994).

[24] *See* Georges Bonet, L'Usage e la Marque d'Autrui dans la Publicité 109 et seq. (1991).

[25] Uniform Benelux Law on Marks (of Mar. 19, 1962, as amended on Nov. 10, 1983) art. 13 A(2) (1983).

[26] Case C-355/96, *Silhouette International Schmied* v. *Hartlauer Handelsgesellschaft*, [1998] ECR I-04799, ECLI:EU:C:1998:374.

[27] Same in the codified version, TMD 2008, *supra* note 17. The provision provided that "[t]he trade mark shall not entitle the proprietor to prohibit its use in relation to goods which have been put on the market in the Community under that trade mark by the proprietor or with his consent."

[28] The issue was triggered by the fact that in Austria, art. 5(1)(a) TMD 2008, *supra* note 17, had not been implemented, as the legislature was of the opinion that it only related to counterfeits and was therefore redundant in view of the fact that trade in such goods was prohibited anyhow under the likelihood of confusion clause and also on the basis of § 9 of the Austrian Unfair Competition Code. In case of parallel import of genuine goods which was at stake in *Silhouette*, the national court found, however, that likelihood of confusion could not be established, so that it became necessary to identify a different ground for taking action. See the explanation of the legal background in Case C-355/96, *Silhouette International Schmied* v. *Hartlauer*, [1998] ECR I-04799.

[29] Case C-355/96, *Silhouette*, § 35.

[30] Case C-63/97, *BMW* v. *Karel Deenik*, [1999] ECR I-00905, ECLI:EU:C:1999:82, § 42.

[31] Case C-228/03, *Gillette* v. *L.A. Laboratories*, [2005] ECR I-02337, ECLI:EU:C:2005:177, §28.

A different line of reasoning emerged for the first time in *Hölterhoff*. [32] The CJEU declared that use of a mark to describe the properties of goods sold under the mark did not infringe "any of the interests which [the double identity clause] is intended to protect."[33] No mention was made of trademark functions in that case, but the message was clear: not all uses of marks referring to the product as originating from the proprietor should fall within the double identity clause; some kind of initial filtering was necessary. More explicit argumentation was offered in *Arsenal v. Reed*, where the functions theme was introduced for the first time.[34] The dispute concerned unlicensed use of (the football club) Arsenal London's emblem and logo on fan articles. The referring judge had posed the question whether it was a valid argument against applying the double identity clause that the relevant public did not perceive the signs as a badge of origin of the products on which they appeared, but only as a token of loyalty and affiliation. The CJEU first pointed out that trademark rights constitute an essential element in the system of undistorted competition which the EC Treaty (as it then was) is intended to establish and maintain, and that in that context, "the essential function of a trade mark is to guarantee the identity of origin of the marked goods or services to the consumer or end user by enabling him, without any possibility of confusion, to distinguish the goods or services from others which have another origin."[35] And:

> It follows that the exclusive right under [the double identity clause] was conferred in order to enable the trade mark proprietor to protect his specific interests as proprietor, that is, to ensure that the trade mark can fulfil its functions. The exercise of that right must therefore be reserved to cases *in which a third party's use of the sign affects or is liable to affect the functions of the trade mark*, in particular its essential function of guaranteeing to consumers the origin of the goods.[36]

Regarding the actual dispute, the CJEU remarked that the situation was "fundamentally different" from that in *Hölterhoff*,[37] and that "[h]aving regard to the presentation of the word Arsenal on the goods at issue in the main proceedings ... the use of that sign is such as to create the impression that there is a material link in the course of trade between the goods concerned and the trade mark proprietor,"[38] meaning that use of the mark in the actual case was "liable to jeopardise the guarantee of origin which constitutes the essential function of the mark."[39] Interestingly the opinion of Advocate General Ruiz-Jarabo Colomer in the same case had been much bolder; one might even say "visionary" (if that is not too big a word). The Advocate General observed, inter alia, that it

> Seems ... to be simplistic reductionism to limit the function of the trade mark to an indication of trade origin. The messages it sends out are ... autonomous. A distinctive sign can indicate at the same time trade origin, the reputation of its proprietor and the quality of the goods it represents, but there is nothing to prevent the consumer, unaware of who manufactures the goods or provides the services which bear the trade mark, from acquiring them because he perceives the mark as an emblem of prestige or a guarantee of quality. When I regard the current functioning of the market and the behaviour of the average consumer, I see no reason whatever

32 Case C-2/00, *Hölterhoff* v. *Freiesleben (Sun Spirit and Context Cut)*, [2002] ECR I-04187, ECLI:EU:C:2002:287.
33 *Id.*, at §16.
34 Case C-206/01, *Arsenal* v. *Reed*, [2002] ECR I-10273, ECLI:EU:C:2002:651 § 47.
35 *Id.*, at §48.
36 *Id.*, at §51 (emphasis added).
37 *Id.*, at § 55.
38 *Id.*, at §56.
39 *Id.*, at § 60.

> not to protect those other functions of the trade mark and to safeguard only the function of indicating the trade origin of the goods and services.[40]

In the opinion of the Advocate General it should therefore be sufficient that the products were bought because of the mark appearing on them, whether or not that causes a misconception with regard to origin. As pointed out above, however, the CJEU preferred to base its decision on the origin function, even though, in order to secure the desired result, the findings of the referring court had to be replaced by the CJEU's own evaluation of the impression produced on the relevant public.[41]

The same kind of reasoning was applied – but led to a different result – in *Opel* v. *Autec*, concerning use of Opel's figurative mark ("Opel-Blitz") on scale model toy cars.[42] As the toy manufacturer had clearly indicated its mark on the packages and accessories such as the remote control, the referring court declared that there was no risk for consumers being misled as to the commercial origin of the toy cars. The CJEU thereupon remarked that

> [i]f the referring court intended to emphasise that the relevant public does not perceive the sign identical to the Opel logo appearing on the scale models marketed by Autec as an indication that those products come from Adam Opel or an undertaking economically linked to it, it would have to conclude that the use at issue in the main proceedings does not affect the essential function of the Opel logo as a trade mark registered for toys.[43]

In addition, without having received a question pertaining to that point, the CJEU referred to the option of granting extended protection for marks having a reputation. No mention was made of the possibility to include more and other trademark functions than the essential one of guaranteeing origin into the assessment of protection under the double identity clause.

The *Opel* judgment was widely understood as separating the functions analysis under the double identity clause from that applying to extended protection, to the effect that with regard to the former only the essential function of guaranteeing origin could be taken into account. That understanding was not (yet) disrupted by the first CJEU decision dealing with comparative advertising, *O2 Holdings* v. *Hutchinson*.[44] The sign used by the defendant to refer to the plaintiff's services was only *similar* (i.e. not identical) to the registered mark. The case was therefore not subsumed by the CJEU under the double identity clause but was treated as a case to be assessed for likelihood of confusion.[45] Apart from that, and quite importantly, *O2* v. *Hutchinson* established the principle that use of a mark in comparative advertising cannot be prohibited on the basis of trademark law if it complies with the requirements in the relevant directive (then: Directive 84/450/EEC).[46]

In *L'Oréal* v. *Bellure*,[47] the dispute concerned marketing of so-called smell-alikes. Inter alia, comparative charts were distributed to retailers that juxtaposed a number of valuable brands to

[40] *Id.*, Opinion by Advocate General Ruiz-Jarabo Colomer of June 13, 2002, ECLI:EU:C:2002:373, §§46 and 47.

[41] The referring judge (Laddie J.) therefore refused to follow the CJEU's ruling on the ground that it was *ultra vires*, and rejected Arsenal's infringement claim (*Arsenal Football Club* v. *Matthew Reed*, [2002] All ER (D) 180 (UK)). The decision was however reversed by the Appeal Court (*Arsenal Football Club* v. *Matthew Reed*, [2003] EWCA Civ 696 (UK)).

[42] Case C-48/05, *Adam Opel* v. *Autec*, [2007] ECR I-01017, ECLI:EU:C:2007:55.

[43] *Id.*, at § 24.

[44] Case C-533/06, *O2 Holdings* v. *Hutchinson*, [2008] ECR I-04231, ECLI:EU:C:2008:339.

[45] *Id.*, at §53.

[46] *Id.*, at § 45.

[47] Case C-487/07, *L'Oréal* v. *Bellure*, [2009] ECR I-05185, ECLI:EU:C:2009:378.

the trademarks under which the respective smell-alikes were sold.[48] The situation was different from O2 insofar as the marks used to identify the brands were *identical* to those actually protected for the plaintiffs. The CJEU could therefore not avoid giving an answer to the question whether such use falls within the ambit of the double identity clause, and to explain why that is so in spite of previous contentions suggesting that application of the provision is reserved to uses jeopardizing the origin function. This produced the by now famous phrase that the functions protected under the double identity clause "include not only the essential function of the trade mark, which is to guarantee to consumers the origin of the goods or services, but also its other functions, in particular that of guaranteeing the quality of the goods or services in question and those of communication, investment or advertising."[49]

Since *L'Oréal*, referring to the functions protected by the double identity clause in addition to the essential function of guaranteeing origin has become a staple element in CJEU decisions addressing the double identity clause. Most prominent among those decisions was a wave of cases dealing with use of marks as adwords.[50] Two of those cases, *Google France* v. *Louis Vuitton*[51] and *Interflora* v. *Marks and Spencer*[52] added further boilerplate modules by delivering definitions of the advertising and the investment functions: the advertising function pertains to the trademark holder's use of the mark "for advertising purposes designed to inform and persuade consumers," and it is infringed if use by a third party under the double identity clause "adversely affects the proprietor's use of its mark as a factor in sales promotion or as an instrument of commercial strategy."[53] The investment function concerns use of the mark "by its proprietor to acquire or preserve a reputation capable of attracting consumers and retaining their loyalty," and it may be jeopardized where use of the mark substantially interferes with that kind of use.[54] As the CJEU admits, that definition largely overlaps with the advertising function as defined in *Google France*, however it is said to be "none the less distinct from the latter. Indeed, when the trade mark is used to acquire or preserve a reputation, not only advertising is employed, but also various commercial techniques."[55]

Regarding more concretely the assessment of situations in which the additional trademark functions might be detrimentally affected, the CJEU remains remarkably cautious. Concerning keyword advertising, the CJEU declares that the use of a competitor's mark in order to trigger the

48 In addition to distributing such comparative charts, the smell-alikes were marketed vis-à-vis consumers in containers and packages as well as under trademarks that evoked the precious brands without coming so close as to cause a likelihood of confusion. Only the first of these marketing methods was subject to the CJEU's considerations on the double identity clause

49 Case C-487/07, *L'Oréal* v. *Bellure*, § 58. It is important to note that the final decision was left to the referring court; see § 63: "It is for the referring court to determine whether, in a situation such as that which arises in the main proceedings, the use which is made of the marks belonging to L'Oréal and others is liable to affect one of the functions of those marks, such as, in particular, their functions of communication, investment or advertising." Furthermore, in § 65 the CJEU affirmed the principle that the question of whether such use can be prohibited depends on its compatibility with the requirements set forth in Directive 84/450/EEC. In the excited reactions following the *L'Oréal* decision, those inherent restrictions of the CJEU's findings were often overlooked.

50 See in addition to the cases quoted in the following footnotes: Case C-278/08 *BergSpechte* v. *Guni*, [2010] ECR I-02517, ECLI:EU:C:2010:163; Case C-91/09, *Eis.de* v. *BBY Vertriebsgesells*, [2010] ECR I-00043* ECLI:EU:C:2010:174; Case C-588/08, *Portakabin* v. *Primakabin*, [2010] ECR I-06963, ECLI:EU:C:2010:416; Case C-324/09, *L'Oréal* v. *eBay*, [2011] ECR I-06011, ECLI:EU:C:2011:474.

51 Joined Cases C-236/08 to C-238/08, *Google France* v. *Louis Vuitton et al.*, [2010] ECR I-02417, ECLI:EU:C:2010:159.

52 Case C-323/09, *Interflora* v. *Marks & Spencer*, [2011] ECR I-08625, ECLI:EU:C:2011:604.

53 *Google France*, at §§ 91, 92.

54 *Interflora*, at § 60, 62.

55 *Id.*, at §61.

display of one's own advertising as a "sponsored link" is *not liable* to have an adverse effect on the advertising function of the trademark,[56] inter alia because the proprietor's mark will most likely show up in a high position in the list of natural search results.[57] Regarding the investment function, the CJEU points out that it cannot be accepted that the proprietor of a trademark may – in conditions of fair competition that respect the trademark's function as an indication of origin – prevent a competitor from using a sign identical with that trademark in relation to goods or services identical with those for which the mark is registered, if the only consequence of that use is to oblige the proprietor of that trademark to adapt its efforts to acquire or preserve a reputation capable of attracting consumers and retaining their loyalty. Likewise, the fact that that use may prompt some consumers to switch from goods or services bearing that trademark cannot be successfully relied on by the proprietor of the mark.[58]

The advertisement and investment functions are therefore without much effect insofar as keyword advertisement is concerned. The accent rather lies on the origin function, which is interpreted rather broadly: pursuant to *Google France* and subsequent case law, an adverse effect on the origin function is foundwhere the ad, while not suggesting the existence of an economic link, is vague to such an extent on the origin of the goods or services at issue that normally informed and reasonably attentive internet users are unable to determine, on the basis of the advertising link and the commercial message attached thereto, whether the advertiser is a third party vis-à-vis the proprietor of the trade mark or, on the contrary, economically linked to that proprietor.[59] The origin function is thus detached to some degree from likelihood of confusion – which would have to be established in a positive manner by the trademark proprietor – to be aligned with the transparency requirement imposed by Article 6(a) of the e-commerce directive (31/2000/EC) on all kinds of commercial communication on the Internet.[60]

IV FUNCTIONS AND THE EUROPEAN UNION *ACQUIS*

The CJEU's functions jurisprudence has met with critical reactions,[61] in particular in the direct aftermath of *L'Oréal* v. *Bellure*.[62] There was indeed reason for concern: the development of case

[56] *Google France*, at §98; *Interflora*, at § 59.

[57] *Google France*, at §97.

[58] Case C-323/09, *Interflora* v. *Marks & Spencer*, [2011] ECR I-08625, ECLI:EU:C:2011:604, § 64.

[59] Joined Cases C-236/08 to C-238/08, *Google France* v. *Louis Vuitton et al.*, § 90.

[60] Directive 2000/31/EC of the European Parliament and of the Council of June 8, 2000 on certain legal aspects of information society services, in particular electronic commerce, in the Internal Market, OJ L 178, 17.7.2000, 1–16.

[61] Apart from criticism by courts and scholarly literature, the CJEU's functions jurisprudence was also the target of interventions by the EU Commission. Inter alia the Commission proposed in the framework of the trademark law reform to stipulate that protection under the double identity rule should be confined to cases when the allegedly infringing use "affects or is liable to affect the function of the trade mark to guarantee to consumers the origin of the goods and services." For reasons for and against the change, *see* Martin Senftleben, *Function Theory and International Exhaustion*, Euro. Intell. Prop. Rev. 518–24 (2014) on the one hand, and Annette Kur, *Trade Marks Function, Don't They? CJEU Jurisprudence and Unfair Competition Principles*, 2014 Int'l Rev. Intell. Prop. Competition L. 434–54 (2014) on the other.

[62] Case C-487/07, *L'Oréal* v. *Bellure*. See in particular Jacob LJ, § 30, stating that there is nothing in the legislation about functions, that they are conceptually vague and ill-defined, and lead to overly broad protection. In the same vein, Martin Senftleben, *Trade Mark Protection – A Black Hole in the IP Galaxy (Editorial)*, 4 Int'l Rev. Intell. Prop. Competition L. 383–87 (2011); Martin Senftleben, *Adapting EU Trade Mark Law to New Technologies – Back to Basics?*, *in* Constructing European Intellectual Property: Achievements and New Perspectives (Cristophe Geiger ed., 2013). A critical approach is also taken by Koppensteiner, Markenrecht ch. 2 C III, 52 et seq. (4th ed. 2012); Ansgar Ohly, GRUR 1131 (2011) (commenting on CJEU Case C-323/09 *Interflora* v. *Marks & Spencer*).

law had been unclear and inconsistent,[63] and the CJEU's rather insensitive approach towards the specific situation presented in *L'Oréal* v. *Bellure* – marketing of "smell-alikes" that were legitimate as such[64] – fueled fears that trademark holders would be able to inhibit any use of their marks that they consider as objectionable simply by invoking the advertising, investment or another yet unspecified trademark function.[65]

At least in part, those concerns were soothed in the meantime. In the light of *Google France*[66] and *Interflora* it can hardly be maintained that the functions jurisprudence is overly rightholder-biased.[67] On the contrary, the decisions have scaled back the protection previously granted to trademark holders, for instance in France and in other member states where use of marks as adwords was considered as per se infringing.[68] Contrary to what has been claimed by critics, it is also not correct to say that the CJEU "invented" the additional trademark functions out of the blue; as was shown above (Section II), the notions as well as (most of) the terminology were well-established at least in parts of Europe from the 1960s.[69] It is true that after realizing that a gap had been left by the legislature not specifying whether "absolute protection" in double identity cases was meant to include use of marks for the purpose of designating the proprietor's own products, the CJEU seems to have been wavering at first between an approach limited to encroachment of the origin function[70] and an attitude embracing the full spectrum of economic functions described by Advocate General Ruiz-Jarabo Colomer in his opinion in *Arsenal*.[71] However, the choice ultimately made by the CJEU to adopt, after initial hesitations in *Arsenal* and *Adam Opel*, the second, more generous approach can hardly be condemned as clearly inappropriate[72] or even illegitimate.[73]

63 This concerned in particular *Adam Opel* (supra note 42) – where the CJEU seemed to proclaim that prejudice caused to the essential origin function was a necessary prerequisite for finding infringement under the double identity clause – and *L'Oréal* v. *Bellure* (supra note 47), where the opposite was held.

64 The CJEU took no account of the legitimate interests of consumers to be informed about the specific properties – the smells corresponding to brands – of the products offered by the defendants.

65 That impression was also conveyed by the decision handed down by Lord Justice Jacob in the Appeal Court after the *L'Oréal* case came back from the CJEU, *L'Oréal* v. *Bellure* [2010] EWCA Civ 535 (UK). However, the judge's contention in para. 32 of that decision, that he was forced by the CJEU to decide against the defendants on the basis of the advertising function, is not quite correct; see CJEU *L'Oréal* v. *Bellure* para. 63 (quoted supra, note 47). The problem rather lay in art. 3(1)(h) (now art. 4(1)(g)) MCAD, where the CJEU did not grant leeway for the referring court to arrive at its own conclusions; *id.* para. 76. See Annette Kur, Lionel Bently & Ansgar Ohly, *Sweet Smells and a Sour Taste – The ECJ's L'Oréal Decision*, https://papers.ssrn.com/sol3/papers.cfm?abstract_id=1492032; see also Ansgar Ohly, Chapter 19 (IV.2) in this volume.

66 Joined Cases C-236/08 to C-238/08, *Google France* v. *Louis Vuitton et al.*

67 Case C-323/09, *Interflora* v. *Marks & Spencer*.

68 *See* Tobias Bednarz & Charlotte Waelde, *Search Engines, Keyword Advertising and Trade Marks: Fair Innovation or Free Riding?*, *in* LAW AND THE INTERNET 267, 284–5 (Lilian Edwards & Charlotte Waelde eds., 3d ed. 2009); *see also* Tobias Bednarz, *Keyword Advertising before the French Supreme Court and Beyond – Calm at Last after Turbulent Times for Google and Its Advertising Clients?*, INT'L REV. INTELL. PROP. COMPETITION L. 641 (2011).

69 Such as Jacobs LJ in *L'Oréal* v. *Bellure* [2010] EWCA Civ. 535, § 30.

70 As in Case C-206/01, *Arsenal* v. *Reed*, and Case C-48/05, *Adam Opel* v. *Autec*.

71 *See Arsenal Football Club* v. *Matthew Reed*, [2002] All ER (D) 180 (UK) and the ensuing appeal *Arsenal Football Club* v. *Matthew Reed*, [2003] EWCA Civ 696 (UK).

72 Inter alia the CJEU's decision was backed up by the fact that the function of indicating origin is addressed in the preamble to European trademark legislation in its various versions as representing only one, albeit particularly important, example of protected trademark functions, thereby insinuating that other functions must be protected as well.

73 One argument against the CJEU's functions jurisprudence highlighted in particular by *Martin Senftleben*, [2014] EIPR 2014, 518–24, claims that by granting protection under the double identity clause to the advertising and investment functions the CJEU "has created an avenue for bypassing the EU system of protection against dilution," which is reserved to marks having a reputation and comes with its own system of checks and balances that are lacking under the double identity clause. The argument does not take into account that although there is indeed no need to

Apart from pragmatic, market-oriented considerations that may have motivated the CJEU's findings, the choice made also complies with a general pattern that can be observed in other areas of IP law and maybe beyond.[74] Where two or several options for interpretation present themselves to the CJEU, the Court will typically endorse the one that gives it maximum competence, thereby sometimes risking overstretch in the area covered by the exclusive rights at stake. But once competence has been established, the CJEU, at least in principle, takes a cautious approach, remaining conscious of the need to balance the protection granted against countervailing interests of competitors, users and society as a whole.[75] The functions jurisprudence in trademark law operates in the same way: on the one hand it includes in the realm of trademark law modes of use which do not cause any risk for consumers of being misled as to commercial origin. On the other hand, by requiring that the use must be such as to (potentially) jeopardize the trademark functions, infringement claims are subjected to inherent restrictions complementing the (under the previous law) rather deficient catalogue of written limitations of the rights conferred.[76] And, different from what seemed to be heralded by *L'Oréal* v. *Bellure*, those restrictions can be quite substantial, in particular where use of another person's mark is made with the aim to present competing offers. Under the circumstances given at the relevant time, when national jurisprudence strongly varied on this point and limitations capturing the full breadth of referential use were still lacking, the positive impact of the message thus sent should not be underestimated.

This does not mean that the functions jurisprudence is free from flaws. In particular it is unfortunate that the terminology employed by the CJEU in its definition of the trademark functions forces national courts into a scheme of convoluted reasoning that obscures rather than explains the actual considerations on which the assessment relies. On the other hand, this makes it all the more important for scholars and courts not to focus on the surface covered by awkward language, but to address and reveal the core of the matter lying beneath those words. It must be added that the task has become easier, as the recent trademark law reform[77] has extended the previously rather narrow catalogue of trademark limitations by embracing referential use for any purpose,[78] and by including an express reference to the Misleading and Comparative Advertisement Directive (2006/114/EC; MCAD).[79] As most of the previously problematic cases are thus covered by the new provisions, it should no longer be necessary to engage in void and fruitless discussions about trademark functions and their definitions in order to solve a given dispute.

show "reputation" as a formal requirement under the double identity clause, the prerequisite of identity in regards to marks and products is considerably stricter than what is required for the establishment of a "link" triggering access to extended protection ("dilution"). Furthermore, as the CJEU demonstrated in Joined Cases C-236/08 to C-238/08, *Google France* v. *Louis Vuitton et al.*, and Case C-323/09, *Interflora* v. *Marks & Spencer*, the functions jurisprudence, if properly applied, does come with its own, though unwritten, checks and balances. For more extensive reasoning on the "circumvention" argument by Senftleben and others, *see* Kur, *supra* note 61.

74 This approach can also be observed in copyright; *see* Michael Grünberger, *Bedarf es einer Harmonisierung der Verwertungsrechte und Schranken?*, Zeitschrift für Urheber- und Medienrecht (ZUM), 273, 286 et seq. (2015).

75 *Id.*

76 The previous version of the TMD (TMD 2008, *supra* note 17) as well as the Community Trademark Regulation (CTMR) in its versions TMR 2009, *supra* note 18, and Council Regulation (EC) No. 207/2009 of Feb. 26, 2009, on the Community Trade Mark, OJ No. L 78/1 of Mar. 24, 2009, only contained a rather meagre catalogue of exhaustively formulated limitations that was not able to counterbalance all kinds of referential uses.

77 Directive (EU) 2015/2436 of the European Parliament and of the Council of Dec. 16, 2015, to approximate the laws of the member states relating to trademarks, OJ L 336, 23.12.2015, 1–26 [hereinafter TMD 2015], and EUTMR, *supra* note 19.

78 *See* TMD 2015, *supra* note 77, art. 14(1)(c) and EUTMR, *supra* note 19, art. 14(1)(c).

79 See TMD 2015, *supra* note 77, art. 10(3)(f) and EUTMR, *supra* note 19, art. 9(1)(f).

Anyhow, where such discussions persist, inspiration should be drawn from Advocate General Kokott's opinion in *Viking Gas*, where she basically reasoned that the essence of the functions discussion lies in a thorough assessment of the parties' interests under the leitmotiv of undistorted competition, whatever names the functions are called by.[80]

It has been stated before that this understanding of the functions jurisprudence infuses European trademark law with a heavy portion of continental "unfair competition" type of thinking.[81] Going further than that, it is claimed here that what has happened is indeed a kind of de facto harmonization by jurisprudence, partly absorbing portions of commercial practices that are subject to harmonization under the MCAD and the Unfair Commercial Practices Directive (UCPD), but also pushing into areas that were left non-harmonized by the latter.[82] Modes of trademark use traditionally considered in many European jurisdictions as presenting an issue for unfair competition law, such as use in comparative advertising or use for referential purposes, now form an integrated part of trademark law,[83] thus adding to the growing number of trajectories between trademark legislation and the (in Europe) formally separate area of unfair commercial practices.[84]

The impact on the national level is two-fold. Insofar as claims are based on trademark infringement, national courts are bound to observe the CJEU judgments. Where, on the other hand, claims are raised on the basis of domestic unfair competition law in aspects that are not harmonized by the UCPD and the MCAD, courts are free in principle to arrive at different conclusions.[85] However, where the legal issue presented under trademark and unfair competition law is essentially the same, national courts will most likely try to avoid discrepancies in regard to the outcome, thus broadening the area of de facto synchronized practice.[86] Furthermore, where the use at stake is product-related,[87] primary EU law[88] might pose another obstacle against prohibiting trademark uses that are not objectionable on the basis of the functions jurisprudence.[89]

80 Advocate General Kokott's opinion of Apr. 7, 2011, in Case C-46/10, *Viking Gas* v. *Kosan*, [2011] ECR I-06161, §§ 45 et seq., 55 et seq. It is true that this poses an issue with regard to legal security; see critical remarks by Senftleben and Ohly as well as the more optimistic attitude expressed by Kur, *supra* note 61.

81 Kur, *id.* at 444.

82 Directive 2005/29/EC of the European Parliament and of the Council of May 11, 2005 concerning unfair business-to-consumer commercial practices in the internal market, OJ L 149, 11.6.2005, 22–39 [hereinafter UCPD]. For details see Ansgar Ohly, Chapter 19 (II) in this volume.

83 This is of practical relevance not least with regard to the sanctions imposed: insofar as use falls within the ambit of trademark law, sanctions must comply with the Enforcement Directive (2004/48/EC), while that is not the case for violations of the MCAD or UCPD.

84 For further examples see contribution by Ansgar Ohly, Chapter 19 in this volume.

85 A reservation must be made with regard to the CJEU's tendency to preclude the application of national law, as in its decision of Sept. 19, 2013, Case C-661/11, *Martin Y Paz* v. *Depuydt and Gauquie*, [2013] EURLex 62011CJ)661 ECLI: EU:C:2013:577; *see infra*, Section V.2.

86 For a practical example see the BGH's *Hard Rock Café* judgment reported by Ansgar Ohly, Chapter 19 (III.2), this volume; Bundesgericht [BGH] [Federal Court of Justice] 2013 GRUR 1161, translated in INT'L REV. INTELL. PROP. COMPETITION L. 484 (2014).

87 CJEU jurisprudence distinguishes between product- and marketing-related rules. Only the former are held to form potential obstacles to transborder trade that must be scrutinized under art. 34 TFEU; see CJEU decisions of Nov. 24, 1993, Joined Cases C-267/91 and C-268/91, Keck and Mithouard, [1993] ECR I-6097, ECLI:EU:C:1993:905, §14 et seq.

88 In particular the principle of free trade as embedded in Treaty on the Functioning of the European Union, art. 325(4), art. 34, Oct. 26, 2012, 2012 OJ (C 326) 47 [hereinafter TFEU].

89 If use of a mark is prohibited on the basis of unfair competition law, obstacles resulting therefrom for inter-EU trade can only be justified on the basis of the argument that the prohibition is indispensable to safeguard the interests of legitimate trade (established case law since CJEU decision of Feb. 20, 1979, C-120/1978, *Rewe* v. *Bundesmonopolverwaltung für Branntwein (Cassis de Dijon)*, [1979] ECR 6349, ECLI:EU:C:1979:42). That

In order to make the picture complete it must be added that the final assessment of actual disputes is regularly left to the national courts. If and to the extent that the national courts make use of that freedom, much latitude is left for national traditions and attitudes to prevail in the grey zones between trademark law and unfair competition-based protection. Courts only need to observe the general guidelines spelled out by the CJEU, for example that use of a mark as adword is not infringing per se, but only if the ad triggered thereby is misleading or too vague to rule out misunderstandings. All in all, this combination of general rules developed by CJEU jurisprudence and deference granted to the national courts with regard to assessing the actual conflict offers a broad, but basically workable paradigm for dealing with trademark uses lying at the fringes of traditional infringement scenarios.

V BEYOND THE LIMITS OF HARMONIZATION

A *Mitsubishi*

Apart from focusing on the trademark functions, the CJEU in the case law quoted above has also developed a number of criteria that must be examined and affirmed before the effect on the trademark functions can be addressed.[90] In particular, it must be established that the mark is used, without authorization, in the course of trade. That requirement was further specified as meaning that the use must not be made for purely private purposes,[91] and that it must occur within, or pertain to, the territory where the alleged conflict arises.[92] Furthermore, "use" in this sense was said to mean "use in the alleged infringer's commercial communication."[93]

This was the generally accepted state of the law when the CJEU was seized with the *Mitsubishi* case.[94] The dispute arose when two Belgian firms imported truck lifts with Mitsubishi's wordmark and figurative sign attached to it from a member of the Mitsubishi group outside the EEA, and, while the goods were placed in the customs warehousing procedure, removed the trademarks and replaced them with their own. Mitsubishi claimed that those practices amounted to infringement of its trademark rights. Having doubts in that regard, the Court of Appeals in Brussels referred to the CJEU the following questions:

- whether the removal amounted to trademark infringement under the double identity clause;
- whether it made a difference for the answer whether the person removing the mark affixed their own mark; and
- whether it made a difference for the answer that the consumers, in spite of the marks having been removed and/or replaced, still recognized the products from their shape and appearance as coming from Mitsubishi.

In his opinion of 26 April 2018, Advocate General Campos Sánchez-Bordona declared that a negative answer must be given to all those questions. He emphasized that harmonization of

argument would likely fail if the same conduct is considered as not jeopardizing any of the protected trademark functions.

[90] In particular in Case C-206/01, *Arsenal* v. *Reed*, and Joined Cases C-236/08 to C-238/08, *Google France* v. *Louis Vuitton et al.*

[91] Established case law since *Arsenal* (*id.*), § 40; see also *Google France* (*id.*), § 50 and additional references made there.

[92] Joined Cases C-446/09 and C-495/09, *Nokia* and *Philips*, [2011] ECR I-12435, ECLI:EU:C:2011:796, §§ 55, 56.

[93] Joined Cases C-236/08 to C-238/08, *Google France* v. *Louis Vuitton et al.*, § 56.

[94] CJEU decision of July 25, 2018, Case C-129/17, *Mitsubishi* v. *Duma*, [2018] EURLex 62017CJ0129 ECLI:EU:C:2018:594.

trademark law only pertained to *use* of the mark, leaving it to member states to regulate the consequences of conduct hindering or suppressing such use.[95] Accordingly,

> [i]f it were accepted that non-use can, nevertheless, be interpreted as constituting use for the purposes of the two articles concerned, that would be tantamount to giving EU law a meaning which, in my view, goes beyond the meaning which should be attributed to it under that legislation … *Under the guise of a task of interpretation, this would, in all likelihood, amount instead to the adoption of a legislative solution.*[96]

However, that warning note did not impress the CJEU. The Court duly noted[97] that, contrary to previous cases,[98] the goods did not bear the marks at issue at the time of being released on the market in the EEA,[99] and that the defendants did not in any way use the signs at the relevant time in their commercial communication.[100] Nevertheless, the CJEU declared that removal of the marks "prevents the goods for which that mark is registered from bearing that mark the first time that they are placed on the market in the EEA and, hence, deprives the proprietor of that trade mark *of the benefit of the essential right … to control the initial marketing in the EEA of goods bearing that mark,*" thereby implying that once goods are released on the market outside the EEA, the proprietor of the sign has a vested right to control the import of those goods into the EEA, whether or not the mark is attached to them.[101]

In addition to invoking the rather spurious "right to import control" the CJEU referred to the adverse effect that the defendants' conduct has on the trademark functions. Regarding the origin function, the Court points out that "any act by a third party preventing the proprietor of a registered trade mark … from exercising his right to control the first placing of goods bearing that mark on the market in the EEA, by its very nature undermines that essential function of the trade mark."[102] Concerning the advertising and investment functions, the CJEU reasons that removal and replacement of the mark before import

> precludes the trade mark proprietor from being able to retain customers by virtue of the quality of its goods and affects the functions of investment and advertising of the mark where, as in the present case, the product in question is not still marketed under the trade mark of the proprietor on that market by him or with his consent.[103]

[95] *Id.*, Opinion of Apr. 26, 2018, ECLI:EU:C:2018:292, § 66.

[96] *Id.*, at § 67 (emphasis added).

[97] Case C-129/17, *Mitsubishi* v. *Duma*, § 41.

[98] The closest similarities exist with the CJEU's decision in Case C-379/14. *TOP Logistics* v. *Bacardi*, [2015] EURLex 62014CJ0379 ECLI:EU:C:2015:497, concerning use of a mark on products placed under the duty suspension procedure. The case corresponded to *Mitsubishi* insofar as infringement was found even though in that situation the goods were not (yet) used directly vis-à-vis consumers. However, the situation was fundamentally different insofar as the infringing mark was *on the products* and not removed from them.

[99] This was another difference vis-à-vis the decision in *TOP Logistics* (*id.*). By placing the goods in the duty suspension procedure they were "technically" imported, whereas they remain outside of EU or EEA commerce as long as they are in the customs warehousing procedure, as in *Mitsubishi*.

[100] In that point the situation diverged from CJEU decision Case C-558/08, *Portakabin* v. *Primakabin*, where the allegedly infringed mark had been used in advertisements relating to a product from which the trademark had been removed. The CJEU considered that to constitute use in the course of trade (§ 86). As the referring court's question did not pertain to the removal of the mark as such, the issue was not addressed.

[101] Case C-129/17, *Mitsubishi* v. *Duma*, § 42 (emphasis added).

[102] *Id.*, § 44.

[103] *Id.*, § 46.

And finally the CJEU adds that the defendants' actions are "contrary to the objective of ensuring undistorted competition."[104]

There is not much to say in favor of the CJEU's reasoning. Claiming that removing the mark in the situation at stake must be an infringement because the proprietor "would be deprived of the right" to control import of goods under the mark is nothing but a *petitio principii*. Likewise unconvincing are the CJEU's considerations regarding the origin function. The Court seems to refer to a kind of virtual origin function existing independently of the trademark actually attached to a product in the relevant territory. That is hardly compatible with previous statements by the CJEU that the function of indicating origin only guarantees that use of the mark under which the product is released on the market in the relevant territory is exclusively controlled by the trademark proprietor.[105] Whether a different trademark was attached to the goods *before* they entered the relevant territory, or whether they are identical in terms of quality and origin with goods bearing a different mark, is irrelevant under legal aspects, at least insofar as trademark law and the essential origin function are concerned.

More substance than that can be found in the CJEU's references to the additional trademark functions. It is certainly so that the commercial interests of a trademark holder are negatively affected if by removing the trademark from the goods produced or otherwise put in commerce by them it is made impossible to bring the specific qualities of those goods to the attention of the public so as to benefit from the goodwill thus gained. However, that does not automatically mean that such actions must necessarily be prohibited. As pointed out in the Advocate General's opinion, the fact that only some member states have chosen to include the removal of marks in the catalogue of infringing acts whereas others prefer engaging in a case-by-case assessment on the basis of unfair competition law or not to prohibit such conduct at all shows that the matter can be contentious and more complex than what a brief analysis undertaken from the perspective of trademark holders might yield.

The CJEU obviously chose to neglect those misgivings. One is tempted to assume that the motivation corresponded to what is reported to have been articulated by the Commission in the hearings, namely that "in the absence of harmonisation of the provisions on unfair competition between undertakings in the EU, the rights of trade mark proprietors should be strengthened judicially."[106] It is true that the absence of a common legal solution regarding removal and replacement of trademarks before import or in other situations may appear as unfortunate. However, that does not justify judicial activities where it does not amount only to choosing the broader option of two basically tenable interpretations of the written law, but to "create" harmonized law without a proper mandate. As is rightfully remarked by Advocate General Campos Sánchez-Bordona: "The gradual creation of the internal market necessitates acceptance that, where there are no measures harmonising national laws, differences between those laws are legitimate until such time as that situation is rectified by legislative action on the part of the EU."[107]

[104] *Id.*, § 47.

[105] *See, e.g.*, CJEU decision of Mar. 30, 2006, Case C-259/04, *Elizabeth Emanuel* v. *Continental Shelf*, [2006] ECR I-03089, ECLI:EU:C:2006:215, §§ 44, 45. The same notion is reflected in the CJEU's understanding of a trademark's "specific subject matter"; see CJEU decision of June 22, 1994, Case C-9/93, *IHT Internationale Heiztechnik* v. *Ideal-Standard*, [1994] ECR I-02789, ECLI:EU:C:1994:261, §§ 37, 38.

[106] *Id.*, Reported by Advocate General Campos Sánchez-Bordona, Opinion of Apr. 26, 2018, ECLI:EU:C:2018:292, § 91.

[107] *Id.*

B *Martin Y Paz*

Another example of the CJEU's tendency to overstep the borderlines of harmonization by invoking the functions doctrine is presented by *Martin Y Paz*.[108] The decision has been commented on extensively elsewhere;[109] some brief remarks shall suffice here. The dispute concerned an infringement claim filed by the proprietor of a registered mark against a co-user of that mark. The defendant asserted that the plaintiff had applied for registration of the mark in bad faith, after the mark had been in co-use for many years. As the time period prescribed under national trademark law had lapsed, the defendant could no longer request cancellation. In that situation, national (Belgian) unfair competition law would have granted relief by enjoining the plaintiff from enforcing the unfairly acquired right against the defendant. However, the CJEU precluded any such possibility, declaring that injunctions may be filed only against modes of use that are liable to jeopardize the trademark functions. Thus, the CJEU ignored that the TMD only harmonizes trademark law insofar as registration and cancellation as well as use of registered marks by third parties are concerned, but not regarding allegedly unfair use made of the mark by the trademark proprietor.

VI CONCLUSION

The CJEU did not invent the doctrine of trademark functions or its utilization for motivating results that the written law cannot yield. However, the Court readily and with increasing confidence embraced that concept as the opportunity arose, using it to create a fairly consolidated body of case law combining elements of trademark law and unfair commercial practices. It is true that this has produced uncertainties, and that the terminology as well as the typical brevity of the CJEU's reasoning have impeded rather than promoted a better understanding of the underlying scheme of thoughts. However, considering that the relevant cases are typically outliers in comparison to established categories of trademark infringement, it is inevitable that a certain margin of legal uncertainty persists, especially where new phenomena emerge in the context of digital marketing practices. In that situation it is preferable to have the CJEU expounding the overall guidelines for such practices than to enter in a prolonged phase of divergent national jurisprudence each time a novel issue arises.

However, the overall relatively positive picture is stained where the CJEU utilizes the functions doctrine to preclude application of national law, or to develop on the basis of trademark functions and the notion of undistorted competition an autonomous approach to unfair B2B conduct, without due regard to the limits of legal harmonization that has been achieved so far.

[108] CJEU decision of Sept. 19, 2013, Case C-661/11, *Martin Y Paz* v. *Depuydt and Gauquie*, EURLex 62011CJ0661 ECLI: EU:C:2013:577.

[109] Kur, *supra* note 61, 446–53.

10

The Function of Trademarks in the United States

*Graeme B. Dinwoodie**

I INTRODUCTION

In recent years, as well explained by Annette Kur,[1] an assessment of the function of trademarks has become a direct doctrinal mechanism used by courts in the European Union to determine the scope of trademark protection in a number of contexts. In the United States, no equivalent doctrinal mechanism has developed, at least not in those precise terms; US courts do not speak the language of "functions" as the Court of Justice has now done for two decades. However, features of US trademark law have clearly been shaped with a similar awareness of the importance of the functions of marks. In particular, US courts have for over a century referenced the core function of a trademark to identify the source or origin of the product on which it is affixed. And litigants and scholars seeking to expand the scope of protection have sought to emphasize that marks do much more than identify source, often tendering explanations that hint at the advertising and investment functions of marks (without using those terms).

This chapter explores the functions of trademarks in the United States and the role those functions have played in the development of US trademark law.[2] Section II sets out the classical source-identifying function of trademarks in US law. Section III focuses on the earliest changes in this original understanding of the function of marks and suggests some of the reasons behind this ready evolution. Section IV discusses further contexts in which contemporary US law has arguably moved more extensively beyond the protection of the strict origin function. In particular, I stress that in expanding the scope of confusion-based claims and enacting dilution protection, US courts have implicitly recognized (and protected) additional functions of marks.

* Global Professor of Intellectual Property Law, IIT Chicago-Kent College of Law; Visiting Professor of Law, University of Oxford.

[1] *See* Annette Kur, Chapter 9 in this volume.

[2] The chapter does not address the functions of a trademark registration (as opposed to trademarks). The functions of a trademark registration are grounded in public notice and industrial policy (most notably, the expansion of trade). *See* Graeme B. Dinwoodie, *Trademarks and Territory: Detaching Trademark Law from the Nation-State*, 41 HOUS. L. REV. 885 (2004); *see also* Robert Burrell, *Trade Mark Bureaucracies*, in TRADEMARK LAW & THEORY 95, 95 (Graeme B. Dinwoodie & Mark D. Janis eds., 2008) (noting that justifications for trademark protection do not also justify a registration system).

II MARKS AS SOURCE-IDENTIFIERS

Trademarks are signs that are used by traders to identify their goods or services and distinguish them from the goods or services of others.[3] This is a function that the mark serves for the benefit of both producers and consumers.[4] Producers create goodwill by marking their product in a way that differentiates it from other similar products. This facilitates competition in the marketplace by allowing traders to gain customers through the quality of their products or services. By protecting the connection between producer and product, trademark law "fosters competition ... by securing to the producer the benefits of good reputation."[5] Likewise, a consumer seeing the mark NEW BALANCE emblazoned on a pair of running shoes understands that those shoes come from a particular producer and are different from running shoes bearing the mark NIKE. The integrity of that understanding is protected by trademark law to offer consumers reassurance regarding their purchase. The core function that the trademark serves in this example is to identify the source or origin of particular goods (in this instance, New Balance); hence, marks are often referred to as source-indicators. This "source" or "origin" function remains the basic function of protected marks in the United States, as it does around the world.

In the nineteenth century, this articulation of the function served by trademarks accurately described the role marks played in commerce. It also reflected the function that US courts identified as sufficiently important to warrant legal protection (arguably well beyond the point in time when this was the only function actually performed by marks).[6] Thus, in 1916, the United States declared that "the primary and proper function of a trademark is to identify the origin or ownership of the article to which it is affixed."[7]

Such observations about the function of marks never gave rise to general doctrines declining *in haec verbis* to offer broader protection than necessary to protect against adverse effects on the function of marks, as occurred in the European Union.[8] But the US courts were clearly alert to the relevance of the function of marks to the scope of protection even before the development of comprehensive federal protection. For example, in *Prestonettes, Inc.* v. *Coty*, the US Supreme Court addressed an allegation of trademark infringement arising from Prestonettes' use of the trademark COTY in label information on Prestonettes perfume and powder products.[9] The label

[3] *See* 15 USC § 1125. (The term "trademark" includes "any word, name, symbol, or device, or any combination thereof ... used by a person ... to identify and distinguish his or her goods, including a unique product, from those manufactured or sold by others and to indicate the source of the goods, even if that source is unknown.")

[4] *See* S. Rep. No. 79-1333, at 3 (1946).

[5] *See Park 'N Fly, Inc.* v. *Dollar Park & Fly, Inc.*, 469 US 189, 198 (1985) (citing S. Rep. No. 1333, 79th Cong., 2d Sess., 3–5 (1946) (citations omitted)).

[6] *Cf.* European Commission, Explanatory Memorandum on the Creation of an EEC Trade Mark §68, (SEC 76) 2462 final, July 6, 1976, *Bulletin of the European Communities*, Supplement 8/76 (1976) ("Any regulation of trade mark law depends ultimately on the functions which are attributed to the trade mark").

[7] *See Hanover Star Milling* v. *Metcalf*, 240 US 403, 415 (1916).

[8] *See, e.g.*, *Hölterhoff* v. *Freiesleben*, Case C-2/00, [2002] ETMR 79 at [16] (CJEU 2002); *Arsenal* v. *Reed*, Case C-206/01, [2003] RPC 9 at [51] (CJEU 2002) ("The exercise of that [double-identity] right must therefore be reserved to cases in which a third party's use of the sign affects or is liable to affect the functions of the trade mark, in particular its essential function of guaranteeing to consumers the origin of the goods"). In later cases, the Court of Justice stressed that the functions at stake, even in actions involving marks without a reputation, were plural. *See L'Oréal SA* v. *Bellure*, Case C-487/07, [2009] ETMR 55 at [58] (CJEU 2009) ("These functions [protected in double identity claims] include not only the essential function of the trade mark, which is to guarantee to consumers the origin of the goods or services, but also its other functions, in particular that of guaranteeing the quality of the goods or services in question and those of communication, investment or advertising").

[9] *Prestonettes, Inc.* v. *Coty*, 264 US 359 (1924).

truthfully represented that COTY perfume was an ingredient in Prestonettes' products. Justice Holmes rejected the trademark infringement allegation in these terms:

> [W]hat new rights does the trade mark confer? ... A trade mark only gives the right to prohibit the use of it so far as to protect the owner's good will against the sale of another's product as his ... When the mark is used in a way that does not deceive the public we see no such sanctity in the word as to prevent its being used to tell the truth. It is not taboo.

Restricting the infringement cause of action to such prohibitions as are necessary "to protect the owner's good will against the sale of another's product as his" has clear parallels in contemporary EU case law and in pre-harmonization German law supporting international exhaustion on the basis that the mark accurately denoted the origin of the imported goods.[10] Yet it also contained the seeds for expansion if we come to understand that in different social or commercial circumstances the "owner's goodwill" was imperilled by conduct other than "the sale of another's product as his."

III RECOGNIZING EVOLUTIONS IN THE FUNCTION OF MARKS

With industrial changes in the late nineteenth century, consumers came to rely less on the actual origin (or manufacturer) of goods.[11] The function of trademarks as "identifiers of source" no longer described all that trademarks did in the marketplace. The notion of "source" or "origin" of a good thus changed as economic structures changed. The person who sold the goods under a particular mark may not have been the manufacturer, but someone in a number of possible commercial relationships with the manufacturer: franchisor–franchisee, licensor–licensee, or foreign manufacturer–local distributor.

As these commercial relationships increasingly determined the nature of the goods consumers purchased, the trademark evolved from a term designating the manufacturer as such, to mean rather the commercial actor who "stood behind" or "vouched for" the goods in question. In many ways, this is not much of a move from what went before. It only requires a slightly expanded notion of the "source" of goods to see that this could encompass the person "standing behind," even if not physically making, the goods. As with the traditional conception, trademark law is acting to prevent consumer confusion once consumers are purchasing based upon the guarantor of the goods rather than the actual producer. Consumers came to know that the mark owner did not *make* all the goods or services for which it vouched. Trademarks had become more generally a guarantor of the consistent quality of goods, and of slightly different consumer expectations – even if the development of those expectations ultimately depended in the first place upon the mark identifying the goods of one trader and distinguishing them from the goods of others.[12]

This was, in its first incarnation, hardly a radical shift. The consumer who purchased NEW BALANCE sneakers had some confidence that the next pair of NEW BALANCE sneakers would be of the same quality as the previous pair because they were vouched for by the same producer. And the producer's goodwill is protected by ensuring that the mark is not used on

[10] *See* Kur, *supra* note 1, at 163–164.

[11] *See* Jerre B. Swann, *Dilution Redefined for the Year 2002*, 92 Trademark Rep. 585, 586 (2002) (Swann describes marks identifying the particular manufacturer and nothing more as "manufacturer marks" or "source marks").

[12] *See* European Commission, Explanatory Memorandum on the Creation of an EEC Trade Mark § 68, (SEC 76) 2462 final, July 6, 1976, Bulletin of the European Communities, Supplement 8/76 (1976) ("Both economically and legally the function of the trade mark as an indication of origin is paramount ... From this basic function of the trade mark are derived all the other functions which the trade mark fulfils in economic life").

goods of inconsistent quality. The slight expansion in protected functions thus fitted with the classical dual purposes of trademark law. Consistent quality of goods was one of the expectations protected by trademarks as source-identifiers.[13] For that reason, the so-called quality function is closely related to the source or origin function.[14]

Consequently, US trademark law found it easy and appropriate to expand protection, resulting in liberalization of rules on licensing and assignment of marks that validated these commercial arrangements. But those liberalizations remained grounded in some regard for the core purposes of trademark law. In the United States, assignments had to be accompanied by the goodwill accompanying the mark, which came to be understood as the assignee having the means necessary to make the goods of the same quality as the assignor.[15] And licences were valid only if the use of the mark by the licensee "is controlled by the owner of the mark with respect to the nature and quality of the goods or services on or in connection with which the mark is used."[16] These conditions ensured the consumer expectation of consistent quality – as would historically have been ensured by the goods coming from a single origin – was protected.[17]

But the evolution of trademarks from being indicators of source to indicators of quality does not stop there. Qualities need not be physical. NEW BALANCE sneakers may indeed tell you that the product is that sturdy sneaker that supports your leg muscles. But NEW BALANCE may also convey the image of "luxury", or "athleticism". As Jerre Swann has persuasively written:

> There are still "manufacturer" brands . . .: consumers, for example, buy soup from CAMPBELL'S. That name, however, now connotes more than just one company's liquid consumable – it means (in the consumer's mind) "M'm! M'm! Good!" COKE no longer merely sells cola; COKE sells refreshment. KODAK no longer merely sells film; KODAK sells a "Kodak moment." CAMPBELL'S, COKE and KODAK are promises, not as to a producer, but as to the fulfilment of a perception; strong, singular brands today are trustmarks, not as to source, but as to sensation.[18]

For good or ill, the function that marks serve for both producers and consumers has changed.[19]

[13] *See* American Law Institute, Restatement (Third) of Unfair Competition § 33 cmt. a (1995) ("Emphasis on the quality assurance function of trademarks led modern courts to uphold the validity of trademark licenses when the control retained by the licensor was sufficient under the circumstances to insure that the licensee's goods or services would meet the expectations created by the presence of the trademark").

[14] *See* 1 J. Thomas McCarthy, Trademarks and Unfair Competition § 3:10, at 3–20 (2020) ("the quality function [of a trademark] does not replace the source function: it stands alongside it. In fact, one could accurately state that the quality theory is merely a facet of the older source theory").

[15] *See* 15 USC § 1060. (A mark is "assignable with the goodwill of the business in which the mark is used, or with that part of the goodwill of the business connected with the use of and symbolized by the mark.") In other countries, the requirement that the registered mark be assigned with accompanying goodwill has been eliminated. *See* Lionel Bently, Brad Sherman, Dev Gangjee and Phillip Johnson, Intellectual Property Law 1168 (5th ed. 2018) (discussing UK law, but noting difference with unregistered mark asserted in passing off claim).

[16] *See* 15 USC § 1055, 1127.

[17] Even when the understanding of source had expanded to encompass quality and sponsorship (rather than simply to identify the manufacturer) of the product, US courts recognize that there might be commercial functions served by the mark that were not legally protectable (with a nod to the expansions that had occurred). *See Smith* v. *Chanel, Inc.*, 402 F.2d 562, 566 (9th Cir. 1968) ("the only legally relevant function of a trademark is to impart information as to the source or sponsorship of the product. Appellees argue that protection should also be extended to the trademark's commercially more important function of embodying consumer good will created through extensive, skillful, and costly advertising. The courts, however, have generally confined legal protection to the trademark's source identification function for reasons grounded in the public policy favoring a free, competitive economy").

[18] *See* Swann, *supra* note 11.

[19] The question whether this has been for good or ill has been a matter of ongoing contestation. *See* Ralph S. Brown, Jr., *Advertising and the Public Interest: Legal Protection of Trade Symbols*, 57 Yale L.J. 1165, 1166 (1948); *see also* Naomi Klein, No Logo: Taking Aim at the Brand Bullies (1999).

Reformulation of the purposes of trademark law in economic terms, as occurred in the last two decades of the twentieth century, facilitated this expansion of the protected trademark functions. Drawing on scholarship in the field of law and economics, the Court of Appeals for the Seventh Circuit explained the purpose of trademarks in these terms:

> Trademarks help consumers to select goods. By identifying the source of the goods, they convey valuable information to consumers at lower costs. Easily identified trademarks reduce the costs consumers incur in searching for what they desire, and the lower the costs of search the more competitive the market. A trademark also may induce the supplier of goods to make higher quality products and to adhere to a consistent level of quality.[20]

Reduction of search costs does indeed offer an explanation for protecting the source-identifying function of marks. But consumer search costs can be increased by any number of uses of marks. Once a consumer is looking to make purchasing decisions by reference to an expanded set of variables, such as quality, endorsement, affiliation and the like, uses that interfere with consumer understanding regarding those variables become as problematic under search costs theory as uses that undermine the source signal.[21] Stripping away the economic theory, making consumer expectations and confusion more central to the calculus of infringement, became a vehicle for protecting broader functions of marks as consumers came to use marks for a wider variety of purposes. Thus, when, as a commercial matter, consumers' expectations embodied in the mark were tied to the source or origin of the goods, then expectations-based protection would necessarily be limited to the origin function of marks. But as consumer expectations evolved, this was no longer true.

IV CONTEMPORARY ATTENTION TO EXTENDED FUNCTIONS

A *General*

Scholarly reformulations in terms of search costs, which tended to assimilate empirical functions in the marketplace with legally protectable functions,[22] became a vehicle for justifying broader protection.[23] But they were buttressed by changes trademark owners secured in the language of the Lanham Act in 1962 and 1988. In 1962, Congress amended the infringement provision for registered marks in section 32(1)(a), requiring a likelihood of confusion "as to the source of origin of such goods" by eliminating the final language and requiring only "use [which] is likely to cause confusion, or to cause mistake, or to deceive."[24] This appeared to render actionable the confusion of persons other than purchasers and confusion regarding matters other than the

[20] *Scandia Down Corp.* v. *Euroquilt, Inc.*, 772 F.2d 1423 (7th Cir. 1985).

[21] *See* Andrew Griffiths, A *Law-and-Economics-Perspective on Trade Marks, in* Trade Marks and Brands: An Interdisciplinary Critique 241, 250 (Lionel Bently, Jennifer Davis & Jane Ginsburg eds., 2008) (noting the expansive potential of search costs theory).

[22] *See* Jonathan Aldred, *The Economic Rationale of Trade Marks: An Economist's Critique, in* Trade Marks and Brands: An Interdisciplinary Critique, *supra* note 21 at 267, 268 (noting the elision of the positive and normative in the classic account by Landes and Posner in William M. Landes & Richard Posner, *Trademark Law: An Economic Perspective* 30 J. L. & Econ. 265 (1987)); *see* Kur, *supra* note 1, at 163 (linking scholarly arguments in Europe about providing extended protection with commercial reality).

[23] *See* Mark P. McKenna, *Trademark Use and the Problem of Source*, 2009 U. Ill. L. Rev. 773, 824 (2009) (arguing that "the search costs theory, in its present form, is theoretically and practically incapable of providing a normative basis for limiting the scope of trademark rights").

[24] *Syntex Labs., Inc.* v. *Norwich Pharm. Co.*, 437 F.2d 566, 568 (2d Cir. 1971).

source of origin.[25] In 1988, the unfair competition provision in section 43(a) – which was the formal basis for a federal action for unregistered trademark infringement and which by virtue of the effective merger of trademark and unfair competition law operated in tandem with section 32 to define the range of actionable uses of marks – was amended to make explicitly actionable uses "likely to cause confusion, or to cause mistake, or to deceive as to the affiliation, connection, or association of such person with another person, or as to the origin, sponsorship, or approval of his or her goods, services, or commercial activities by another person."

Courts clearly took into account these changes in statutory language – which seemed to de-emphasise source or origin in 1962 and elevate the role of trademarks in expressing "affiliation, connection, association ... sponsorship, or approval" in 1988 – in expanding the scope of protection offered to marks in the last quarter of the twentieth century.[26] But the expansions in protection were also supported by a sense among courts that trademarks were performing other functions in the marketplace.[27]

B Extended Notions of Actionable Confusion

Thus, from the expanded relationships of licensor–licensee, consumers came to understand that the mark may simply reflect the endorsement by the mark owner of the goods, or some other affiliation or connection between the mark owner and the goods. Protection against use on what came to be known as related goods, upon which the mark owner had not yet used the mark, was another major expansion of protection in the second half of the twentieth century. How can we justify this expansion? It is not hard for a positivist. The structure of business organization evolved such that companies began to diversify their product range. As consumers became aware of that economic reality, consumers expected that the use of a mark on a related good did signal a connection with the first mark owner (perhaps as manufacturer or perhaps through a licence). If that was the consumer's assumption, so the argument went, trademark law should provide consumers with assurance regarding its accuracy.

Merchandizing is very big business, whether pursued by traditional producers of goods distributing promotional goods bearing their mark, by universities raising much-needed additional cash, by sports teams trying to get cash to buy new players (or pay the wages of existing ones), or by celebrities cashing in on these economic realities. Beginning in the 1970s, trademark owners became relatively secure in their ability legally to control the merchandizing of their marks. The early cases sustaining relief for plaintiffs talk primarily of the "commercial value" of the plaintiff's marks as a result of the plaintiff's efforts and the fact that commercial

[25] It is a matter of debate whether Congress intended the extent of expansion that the 1962 amendment has precipitated. *See* Sara Stadler, *The Wages of Ubiquity in Trademark Law*, 88 IOWA. L. REV. 731, 800–01 (2003).

[26] *See Ferrari S.P.A. Esercizio* v. *Roberts*, 944 F.2d 1235 (6th Cir. 1991) (post-sale confusion actionable, citing 1962 reforms); *Syntex Labs., Inc.* v. *Norwich Pharmacal Co.*, 437 F.2d 566 (2d Cir. 1971) (non-competing goods); *Boston Prof'l Hockey Ass'n, Inc.* v. *Dallas Cap & Emblem Mfg.*, 510 F.2d 1004 (5th Cir. 1975) (confusion as to endorsement, citing 1962 broadening of language); *Checkpoint Sys., Inc.* v. *Check Point Software Technologies, Inc.*, 269 F.3d 270, 295 (3d Cir. 2001) (initial interest confusion, citing 1962 language changes). *But see Elec. Design & Sales, Inc.* v. *Elec. Data Sys. Corp.*, 954 F.2d 713 (Fed. Cir. 1992) (drawing narrower significance of language change).

[27] One has to be careful about drawing causal conclusions these motivational lines too firmly. Even if the legal norm had not changed, a similar result might have been achieved over time by an evolution in social norms. For example, consolidation of business in the second half of the twentieth century may have prompted consumers to view the question of "source" more broadly, and if courts acted on that, they may have implemented the same expansion of trademark rights that Congress effected by amendments to § 32 in 1962. But these changes were expedited and embedded by a combination of changes in the legal standards and the social function of marks.

practices had grown up under which trademark owners (in the early cases, sports franchises) had engaged in merchandizing activities.[28] Those cases recognized that the thing of commercial value is the mark itself, over and above the physical goods to which the mark may be affixed, and the mark was thus selling the product as well as indicating its source.

Likewise, in landmark cases opening the door to what were temporally expanded notions of actionable confusion (such as post-sale confusion or initial interest confusion), US courts were clearly alert to expanded functions of marks in the marketplace. For example, in *Ferrari* v. *Roberts*, the Court of Appeals for the Sixth Circuit accepted the doctrine of post-sale confusion.[29] As a result, the plaintiff manufacturer of upscale sports cars with distinctive designs was able to enjoin the defendant's manufacture and sale of fibreglass kits that replicated the exterior design features of those cars. There was no confusion among customers at the point of sale. Production of the plaintiff's cars was intentionally limited to preserve exclusivity, and thus a new car sold for approximately $230,000. Most of the defendant's replicas were sold as kits for about $8,500 and the defendant informed his purchasers that his significantly cheaper cars and kits were not genuine Ferraris. Nevertheless, the majority of the court found that confusion could exist post-sale when individuals later seeing a vehicle bearing the defendant's product might mistakenly believe them to be a genuine Ferrari and refrain from purchasing the real car because they were unimpressed with the quality.

At the doctrinal level, this simply required the court to read the concept of confusion expansively, which the 1962 reforms allowed it to do.[30] But in addition to relying on the statutory language deleting the requirement that confusion be as to source or origin, the Sixth Circuit noted that "this interpretation was necessary to protect against the cheapening and dilution of the genuine product, and to protect the manufacturer's reputation."[31] The court sought to protect against consumers believing that Ferraris had become too commonplace. The defendant's products would interfere with the image of "prestige" that was conveyed by the Ferrari design. The (design) mark arguably "sold" the car, the "prestige" or "uniqueness" being the product.[32]

Similar awareness of the different functions of marks is arguably at play in the development of liability for initial interest confusion. Courts have recognized claims for initial interest (or what

[28] *See Boston Prof'l Hockey Ass'n, Inc.*, 510 F.2d at 1004 ("the sale of a reproduction of the trademark itself on an emblem is an accepted use of such team symbols in connection with the type of activity in which the business of professional sports is engaged"); *see also Bd. of Supervisors for La. State Univ. Agric. & Mech. Coll.* v. *Smack Apparel Co.*, 550 F.3d 465, 485 (5th Cir. 2008) ("it is not unreasonable to conclude, given the degree to which sports emblems are used to advertise teams and endorse products, that a consumer seeing the emblem or name of a team on or associated with a good or service would assume some sort of sponsorship or association between the product's seller and the team"). *Compare* Kur, *supra* note 1, at 163 ("[extended protection] signaled that the commercial interests vested in distinctive signs were too big for protection restricted to indicating origin could cover").

[29] *See Ferrari S.P.A. Esercizio*, 944 F.2d at 1235.

[30] *See* Jeremy Sheff, Chapter 27 in this volume ("this surface dissimilarity [as to the treatment of luxury goods] masks a deeper convergence with respect to conspicuously consumed goods: the American system achieves similar results to the European system through convoluted reasoning regarding consumer psychology"). The construction of a narrative of actionable confusion that extended beyond that occurring at point of sale rather than directly appealing to the extended functions is not unknown in Europe. *See* Kur, *supra* note 1, at 168 (noting that although the Advocate-General in *Arsenal*, *see infra* note 66, had appealed to extended functions, "the CJEU preferred to base its decision on the origin function, even though in order to secure the desired result the findings of the referring court had to be replaced by the CJEU's own evaluation of the impression produced on the relevant public"). Interestingly, the example discussed by Annette Kur (*Arsenal*) is a case that is often cited as an indication of support for a theory of post-sale confusion in the European Union. *See generally* BENTLY ET AL., *supra* note 15, at 1047.

[31] *See Ferrari S.P.A. Esercizio*, 944 F.2d at 1244.

[32] *See* Jeremy Sheff, *Veblen Brands*, 96 MINN. L. REV. 769 (2012); *see also Gen. Motors Corp.* v. *Keystone Auto. Indus.*, 453 F.3d 351, 358 (6th Cir. 2006). For a summary of case law to the same effect, see Sheff, *supra* note 30, at [10]–[16].

might be called "pre-sale") confusion for some time.[33] However, there was a rush of such claims in the early years of commercial exploitation of the Internet. In particular, trademark owners argued that use of their marks by competitors as metatags residing in the code behind websites would cause consumers to be confused into considering the competitors' products, believing them to emanate from the mark owner even if the consumer would be disabused of that confusion prior to consummation of any transaction.[34]

In recent years, US courts have begun to retreat somewhat in their acceptance of initial interest confusion claims. Again, judges in the leading cases effecting this reversal appear informed by not only general policy concerns (such as an evolution in the understanding of the typical internet consumer, and concerns about undue paternalism) but also a sense of what trademark functions ought to be protected. Thus, in *Multi Time Machine, Inc.* v. *Amazon.Com, Inc.*, a divided Ninth Circuit reflected growing scepticism about the appropriateness of such claims.[35] There, the plaintiff manufacturer of a certain military-style wristwatch sought to preserve the exclusivity of its products by ensuring they were not available on the Amazon.com website. Indeed, they were successful in that endeavour. However, a consumer typing the plaintiff's mark into the Amazon internal search engine would be presented with a search list of other brands of military-style watches that Amazon does carry (specifically identified by their brand names) without any indication that Amazon did not sell the plaintiff's brand of watch. This was because the Amazon search engine algorithm used the plaintiff's mark as an indication that the consumer was searching for military-style wristwatches and would thus be amenable to purchasing similar watches from different producers if it could not buy the plaintiff's watch.

The majority of the Ninth Circuit rejected these claims. On one level, the conclusion is unremarkable: "Because Amazon's search results page clearly labels the name and manufacturer of each product offered for sale and even includes photographs of the items, no reasonably prudent consumer accustomed to shopping online would likely be confused as to the source of the products."[36] But this traditional statement of the scope of confusion-based claims was at odds with a series of cases in the Ninth Circuit accepting the theory of initial interest confusion.[37] The plaintiff claimed initial interest confusion might occur because Amazon lists the search term used (the plaintiff's mark) three times at the top of the search page. As a result, the plaintiff argued that Amazon should be required to revise its search results pages, explaining to customers that it did not sell the plaintiff's watches before suggesting alternatives.

The majority rejected that claim, and its reasoning turned on the conviction that "the core element of trademark infringement [is whether the defendant's conduct] is likely to confuse customers about the *source* of the products."[38] That was the only function of a trademark against which the producer was entitled to relief. It reflects a reluctance to allow the trademark owner control over other functions that a mark may perform in online searching or in the provision of

33 *See Mobil Oil Corp.* v. *Pegasus Petroleum Corp.*, 818 F.2d 254 (2d Cir. 1987); *Grotrian, Helfferich, Schulz, Steinweg* v. *Steinway & Sons*, 365 F. Supp. 707 (SDNY 1973) (pre-sale confusion allegedly caused by defendant's use of the Grotrian-Steinway name for pianos), *modified*, 523 F.2d 1331 (2d Cir. 1975).

34 The initial interest confusion doctrine has been the subject of concentrated criticism from its first application to the internet context. *See, e.g.*, Jennifer Rothman, *Initial Interest Confusion: Standing at the Crossroads of Trademark Law*, 27 Card. L. Rev. 105 (2005); Stacey L. Dogan & Mark A. Lemley, *Trademark and Consumer Search Costs on the Internet*, 41 Hous. L. Rev. 777 (2004).

35 *See Multi Time Mach., Inc.* v. *Amazon.Com, Inc.*, 804 F.3d 930, 933 (9th Cir. 2015).

36 *Id.*

37 *See, e.g., Dr. Seuss Enterprises, L.P.* v. *Penguin Books USA, Inc.*, 109 F.3d 1394, 1405 (9th Cir. 1997); *Brookfield Commc'ns, Inc.* v. *West Coast Entm't Corp.*, 174 F.3d 1036, 1062 (9th Cir. 1999); *Playboy Enters., Inc.* v. *Netscape Commc'ns Corp.*, 354 F.3d 1020 (9th Cir. 2004).

38 *See Multi Time Mach., Inc.*, 804 F.3d at 933 (emphasis added).

advertising. The dissenting judge would have allowed a jury to consider whether "users who are confused by the search results are confused as to why [plaintiff's] products are not listed."[39] In positing that users might wonder whether a competitor has acquired the plaintiff or was otherwise affiliated with or approved by the plaintiff, the dissent noted that such a possibility was "especially true as to a brand like [the plaintiff], as many luxury brands with distinct marks are produced by manufacturers of lower-priced, better-known brands – just as Honda manufactures Acura automobiles but sells Acura automobiles under a distinct mark that is marketed to wealthier purchasers, and Timex manufactures watches for luxury fashion houses Versace and Salvatore Ferragamo."[40] The dissenting judge was willing to take into account the actual functions luxury marks play in the marketplace.

C Dilution

Some scholarly and judicial critics of the developments discussed in the section immediately above were quick to point out that courts were extending protection to functions of marks beyond that of source-identification, effectively creating dilution protection.[41] Dilution offered marks protection against non-competitors using marks on dissimilar products without proof of any confusion.[42] And it is arguable that dilution protection consciously *was* intended to protect functions of marks beyond the source or origin function.[43] The justifications for dilution, both modern and historical, emphasize the preservation of the (typically premium) image associated with the mark and the ability of the mark itself to "sell" goods of a type quite different from those to which it was first applied to identify the source. In the parlance of the Court of Justice of the European Union, dilution protection secured the investment and advertising functions of marks.[44]

But protection of these functions under extended confusion claims (such as post-sale confusion or initial interest confusion) was available even to marks that did not pass any higher fame

[39] *See id.* at 943 (Bea J, dissenting).

[40] *See id.*

[41] *See Ferrari S.P.A. Esercizio*, 944 F.2d at 1248 (Kennedy J, dissenting) ("The majority first misconstrues the scope of protection afforded by the Lanham Act by . . . reading an anti-dilution provision into the language of section 43(a)"). The *Ferrari* majority did little to combat that sense in quoting the district court to the effect that "if the country is populated with hundreds, if not thousands, of replicas of rare, distinct, and unique vintage cars, obviously they are no longer unique. Even if a person seeing one of these replicas driving down the road is not confused, Ferrari's exclusive association with this design has been diluted and eroded. If the replica Daytona looks cheap or in disrepair, Ferrari's reputation for rarity and quality could be damaged." 944 F.2d at 1245; *see also* Sheff, *supra* note 30, at 7 ("the equivalent of such [misappropriation-based] liability has long been available [in the United States] through expansive – though still putatively confusion-based – theories of infringement"); *see also* Barton Beebe, *Intellectual Property Law and the Sumptuary Code*, 123 HARV. L. REV. 809, 852 (2010).

[42] *See* 15 USC § 1125(c)(1).

[43] *Cf.* Frank I. Schechter, *Fog and Fiction in Trade-Mark Protection*, 36 COLUM. L. REV. 60, 64 (1936) ("A condition precedent to any intelligible discussion of these problems is the proper appraisal of the functional concept of a trademark today . . . [A] trade-mark . . . is not merely [the producer's] commercial signature but is a creative 'silent salesman'"); *Google France SARL. v. Louis Vuitton Malletier SA*, Cases 236/08–238/08, EU:C:2009:569 at AG [94]–[95] (AG Maduro, 2009) ("The Court has confirmed that this special protection for trade marks which have a reputation does not depend on there being a risk of confusion on the part of consumers. Accordingly, such special protection is independent of the essential function of the trade mark of guaranteeing the origin of the goods or services, and relates to other functions of the trade mark. The Court has stated that such other functions of the trade mark include guaranteeing the quality of goods or services and those of communication, investment or advertising") (citing *L'Oréal SA* v. *Bellure NV*, Case C-487/07, EU:C:2009:378 at [50] (ECJ 2009)).

[44] *See Interflora* v. *Marks & Spencer*, Case C-323/09, EU:C:2011:604 CJEU 2011) (defining "advertising function" and "investment function").

threshold that federal law would impose when Congress eventually enacted federal protection against dilution.[45] In that regard, the dissenting voices in the United States are in line with some of the criticism[46] that the Court of Justice of the European Union attracted after its decision in *L'Oréal SA* v. *Bellure*, in which it expressly extended the so-called double identity cause of action to protect against the communication, advertising and investment functions of marks (as well as the origin function).[47]

Of course, it has never been fully explained why the element of fame or reputation that is statutorily required to make out a federal blurring or tarnishment claim in the United States is theoretically germane to the supposed harm to be remedied by those two claims.[48] Some of the reasoning behind dilution that was advanced by Frank Schechter – the accepted architect of dilution claims – would appear to have turned only on whether a mark was inherently distinctive and some state statutes did not require fame as a precondition to protection.[49] To be sure, the "unfair advantage" variant of a dilution claim does depend upon the mark having some additional notoriety to make the advantage claim plausible, and the greater the notoriety the potentially greater benefit and hence unfairness. But that cause of action is not available in the United States, unlike in the European Union.[50]

However, some of the other background theoretical propositions advanced by Schechter in proposing the cause of action did appear to tie the justification for extended protection to a subset of marks that do more than identify source.[51] In particular, the assertion by Schechter that dilution protection was required because certain marks performed additional functions through "their selling power" and their "advertising" function means that any assessment of the role of functions in US trademark law must thus account for the existence of dilution protection.

1 *Schechter and Functions*

Frank Schechter's article *The Rational Basis of Trademark Protection*, which appeared in the HARVARD LAW REVIEW in 1927, is commonly accepted as providing the intellectual foundation for dilution law in the United States.[52] The conventional characterization of Schechter's theory

45 *See* 15 USC § 1125(c)(1) (offering protection to "the owner of a famous mark that is distinctive"); 15 USC § 1125(c)(2) (defining a mark as famous "if it is widely recognized by the general consuming public of the United States as a designation of source of the goods or services of the mark's owner").

46 *See* Martin Senftleben, *Function Theory and International Exhaustion*, 35 EUR. INTELL. PROP. REV. 518 (2014). Of course, the double identity claim has other limits that the dilution claim does not, such as identity of marks and goods. *See* Annette Kur, *Trade Marks Function, Don't They? CJEU Jurisprudence and Unfair Competition Principles*, 45 I.I.C. 434, 445, n. 56 (2014).

47 *See L'Oréal SA* v. *Bellure NV*, Case C-487/07.

48 In that regard, the European approach to the "reputation" threshold might make more sense (as might the lack of any fame requirement under certain state dilution laws in the United States). It is much easier to be a mark with a reputation under EU law than a famous mark under US law. *See General Motors Corp.* v. *Yplon*, Case C-375/97, [2000] RPC 572 (articulating European standard); *see also Datacard Corp.* v. *Eagle Techs. Ltd* [2011] EWHC 244 (Pat), at § 291 ("reputation . . . is not a particularly onerous requirement"); *Coach Servs.* v. *Triumph Learning LLC*, 668 F.3d 1356, 1373 (Fed. Cir. 2012) ("It is well-established that dilution fame is difficult to prove").

49 *See* N.Y. GEN. BUS. LAW § 360–l (McKinney 2019); *see also Van Praagh* v. *Gratton*, 993 F. Supp. 2d 293, 304 (EDNY 2014).

50 The 2006 reforms of US dilution law made it clear that the blurring and tarnishment causes of action defined in the statute exhaustively demarcated the possible causes of action under § 43(c). *Cf. Ty Inc.* v. *Perryman*, 306 F.3d 509 (7th Cir. 2002) (rejecting theory of dilution pre-2006 based on free-riding). Thus, for example, the US dilution cause of action no longer provides relief against acts of cybersquatting as such, although the same conduct could separately constitute both dilution and cybersquatting.

51 *See infra* text accompanying notes 54–55.

52 *See* Frank I. Schechter, *The Rational Basis for Trademark Protection*, 40 HARV. L. REV. 813 (1927); *Moseley* v. *V Secret Catalogue, Inc.*, 537 US 418, 429 (2003); 141 Cong. Rec. 38559–61 (1995) (remarks of Sen. Hatch).

of dilution is varied. Three accounts dominate. First, Schechter argued that the "preservation of the uniqueness of a trademark constitute[s] the only rational basis for its protection," and a cause of action for dilution would protect the mark's uniqueness.[53] Second, the examples discussed by Schechter in *Rational Basis* might suggest that dilution protection was a reaction to the narrow scope of protection available at that time under US law when the mark was used by the defendant on goods different from those on which the plaintiff used its mark.[54]

Third, and of most relevance for this chapter, some have understood the dilution cause of action as an attempt to protect a function of marks that was not (according to Schechter) protected at that time, namely, the ability of the mark itself to sell the product, rather than merely identify its source.[55] *Rational Basis* stresses that the "selling power" of the mark was its true function, and that required a scope of protection not conferred in 1927, when pre-Lanham Act US trademark law clearly focused on protecting the origin-indication function of marks.[56]

Dilution is a doctrine that has been heavily criticized by scholars and that met substantial resistance from US courts.[57] To some extent this is because, as suggested by this account of Schechter's original proposal, there is no clarity on (let alone acceptance of) its theoretical underpinnings. Schechter's invocation of property rights was often seen by some as an unthinking formalist approach to trademark protection without regard for its purpose. Trademarks were property and producers should thus have full dominion over them.[58]

However, in an important historical reassessment in 2007, Robert Bone challenged the account of Schechter as a formalist who thought that defined protection flowed inevitably from the label of "property."[59] Bone saw Schechter's method as the mark of a legal realist,[60] and argued that "Schechter proposed dilution in the spirit of legal realism. He believed that dilution was the real reason to protect marks because it was the reason that fit the way marks actually functioned in the marketplace."[61] In more recent work, Barton Beebe took issue with the emphasis that Bone placed on Schechter's reference to functions. Tracing the origins of Schechter's work in German case law, Beebe suggested that Schechter consciously sought to

[53] *See* Schechter, *supra* note 52, at 831–32.

[54] The use requirement of US. law, and the doctrine of specialty, confined the scope of US trademark rights far more strictly than would be the case in many other systems. *See, e.g., Borden Ice Cream Co.* v. *Borden's Condensed Milk Co.*, 201 F. 510 (7th Cir. 1912). The case law was beginning to move from the *Borden* approach when Schechter wrote, *see, e.g., Aunt Jemima Mills Co.* v. *Rigney & Co.*, 247 F. 407 (2d Cir. 1917), but this was an ongoing battle in the courts for years to come. *See* Robert G. Bone, *Taking the Confusion out of "Likelihood of Confusion": Toward a More Sensible Approach to Trademark Infringement*, 106 Nw. U. L. Rev. 1307 (2012).

[55] *See* Ilanah Simon Fhima, *Exploring the Roots of European Dilution*, Intell. Prop. Q. 25, 29 (2012) ("Schechter's argument rests on harm to the senior mark's selling power by virtue of harm to the senior mark's distinctiveness").

[56] *See Prestonettes, Inc.* v. *Coty*, 264 US 359, 368 (1924) ("A trade-mark only gives the right to prohibit the use of it so far as to protect the owner's good will against the sale of another's product as his").

[57] *See* Clarisa Long, *Dilution*, 106 Colum. L. Rev. 1029 (2006) (discussing judicial resistance to dilution).

[58] *See* David J. Franklyn, *Debunking Dilution Doctrine: Toward a Coherent Theory of the Anti-Free-Rider Principle in American Trademark Law*, 56 Hastings L.J. 117, 164 (2004) (noting role of property theory in Schechter's justification).

[59] *See* Robert G. Bone. *Schechter's Ideas in Historical Context and Dilution's Rocky Road*, 24 Santa Clara Comput. & High Tech L.J. 469 (2007). Bone invoked Schechter's book of two years before *Rational Basis* to highlight Schechter's opposition to formalistic protection of property. *See id.* at 485, n. 86 (quoting Frank I. Schechter, The Historical Foundations of the Law Relating to Trade-Marks 160 (1925)). Bone instead lays the conceptualization of dilution in terms of "property" rights at the door of Rudolf Callmann, writing a couple of decades after Schechter. *See* Bone, *supra* note 59, at 499.

[60] *See* Bone, *supra* note 59, at 489 ("Schechter's analysis follows a typical realist format: start by explaining how judges are straining formalistic doctrines to implement underlying policies in a modern setting; then expose the policies beneath the formalisms; and conclude by calling for the elimination of formalisms and for decisions based directly on the policies").

[61] *See id.* at 471.

obscure the real formalism of his misappropriation-grounded approach because of the then-growing critique of formalism by the realist school, and that his discussion of the "true functions" of marks was one of the ways by which he did so.[62]

Schechter's reliance on the functions of marks beyond source-identification to justify dilution protection satisfied neither Bone nor Beebe. For Beebe, this was a distraction invented by Schechter to sustain a formalist doctrine in a time of critical or realist thought.[63] For Bone, Schechter's attention to the functions of marks confirmed him as a realist.[64] But Bone found little normatively persuasive in Schechter because, in an act of assimilation not uncommon for many (but not all) realists, Schechter assumed too readily that the descriptive functions of marks provided a normative guidepost.[65] This is the trap into which EU courts have arguably fallen, by assuming that all the functions served by marks should be within the control of the mark owner.[66]

2 *Statutory Implementation*

Of course, despite the recognition by Congress and the US Supreme Court that Shechter and *Rational Basis* provided the theoretical stimulus for dilution, neither federal nor state law in the United States has mapped closely to his academic work. The statutes have several obvious divergences from Schechter's work and courts have recognized as much. For example, one reading of Schechter's theory would allow the mark owner to stop *any* second use of a protected mark.[67] However, embracing that account of the Schechter model would run headlong into other theoretical difficulties, and in particular resistance to trademark rights in gross in a word (rather than the underlying goodwill).[68] Most marks are not unique, and the same sign can function as a mark for a number of different products without affecting the distinctiveness and reputation of the mark.

Despite this distancing from Schechter, the courts have also recognized difficulties when dilution is divorced from Schechter's model.[69] They keep gravitating to some of the formalistic

62 Barton Beebe, *The Suppressed Misappropriation Origins of Trademark Antidilution Law: The Landgericht Elberfeld's* Odol *Decision and Frank Schechter's* The Rational Basis of Trademark Protection, *in* INTELLECTUAL PROPERTY AT THE EDGE: THE CONTESTED CONTOURS OF IP 59, 63 (Rochelle Cooper Dreyfuss & Jane C. Ginsburg eds., 2014) ("Schechter . . . needed somehow to clothe his essentially formalist misappropriation doctrine in the guise of legal realism").

63 *See id.* at 63.

64 *See* Bone, *supra* note 59, at 471.

65 *See id.*, at 487, 506.

66 *See Arsenal* v. *Reed*, Case C-206/01, [2003] ETMR 19 (AG Colomer) at [46] ("It seems to me to be simplistic reductionism to limit the function of the trade mark to an indication of trade origin . . . The trade mark acquires a life of its own, making a statement, as I have suggested, about quality, reputation and even, in certain cases, a way of seeing life"); *see also* Kur, *supra* note 1, at 167 (noting the different approach of the Court in *Arsenal*, which grounded its analysis in confusion and the origin function).

67 *See* ILANAH SIMON FHIMA, TRADEMARK DILUTION IN EUROPE AND THE UNITED STATES 3 (2011); *Ringling Bros.-Barnum & Bailey Combined Shows, Inc.* v. *Utah Div. of Travel Dev.*, 170 F.3d 449, 544–46 (4th Cir. 1999) ("[Schechter's] radical dilution proposal, whose practical effect if fully adopted would be to create as the whole of trademark-protection law property rights in gross in suitably 'unique' marks never has been legislatively adopted by any jurisdiction in anything approaching that extreme form").

68 *See* Sandra L. Rierson, Chapter 29 in this volume, at 1. Rierson notes that Schechter's theory of dilution was not that far removed from the formalist protection afforded technical trademarks at the turn of the twentieth century. *See id.* at 5. This observation suggests that the partial assimilation of dilution protection with double identity claims in the European Union is not without precedent. *Cf.* Senftleben, *supra* note 46, at 518 (critiquing effective circumvention of dilution law by expansion of double identity claims).

69 *See, e.g.*, *Ringling Bros.-Barnum & Bailey Combined Shows, Inc.*, 170 F.3d at 546 ("[T]he cases demonstrate that once the dilution concept is sought to be given any form other than that of Schechter's simple original proposal it begins to lose its coherence as a legally enforceable norm. Specifically, it becomes difficult to identify the legal interest sought to be protected from "dilution," hence the legal harm sought to be prevented").

means by which Schechter sought to implement his theory.[70] But it is not clear in practice how dilution protection in the United States (or indeed elsewhere) effectively protects additional functions of the mark. It is sometimes asserted that control over a product's image and over its use on dissimilar goods has facilitated the creation, development, and extension of brands.[71] As noted above,[72] such extended control would appear to be within the reach of dilution law and thus dilution may be the vehicle allowing for the modern protection of brands and of the communication and investment functions mark owners want to protect.[73]

But legislative and doctrinal implementation of dilution often appears still quite tied to protection of the distinctiveness of the source, which is strongly redolent of origin function. For example, blurring is defined as "association arising from the similarity between a mark or trade name and a famous mark that *impairs the distinctiveness* of the famous mark."[74] And the blurring factors found in the post-2006 legislation bear close resemblance to the factors used by courts to determine whether there is actionable likelihood of confusion.[75] As applied by the courts, these factors seem to depart in only minor respects from a confusion analysis, with some courts even giving weight to surveys testing confusion.[76] In this regard, the blurring test may be little more than a second shot at establishing confusion.[77] Certainly, some courts and scholars see dilution as little more than a different operationalization of the concern for search costs that justifies trademark protection of the origin function.[78] Indeed, even tarnishment – which is defined in terms of effects on reputation, and thus seems closer in conception to protection of

[70] In particular, courts continue to play with presumptions flowing from the use of identical marks. *See, e.g., Savin Corp.* v. *The Savin Group*, 391 F.3d 439, 452–54 (2d Cir. 2004); *cf. Louis Vuitton Malletier SA* v. *Haute Diggity Dog, LLC*, 507 F.3d 252 (4th Cir. 2007); *Visa Int'l* v. *Serv. Ass'n v. JSL Corp.*, 610 F.3d 1088 (9th Cir. 2010). Formally, courts have rejected an identity requirement. *See Levi Strauss & Co.* v. *Abercrombie & Fitch Trading Co.*, 633 F.3d 1158 (9th Cir. 2011).

[71] *See* Mark P. McKenna, *The Normative Foundations of Trade Mark Law*, 82 Notre Dame L. Rev. 1839, 1843 (2007) ("Modern [US] law . . . sees a mark itself as a repository for value and meaning, which may be deployed across a wide range of products and services. [It] amounts to little more than industrial policy intended to increase brand value").

[72] *See supra* text accompanying notes 41–44.

[73] *See* Dev S. Gangjee, *Property in Brands: The Commodification of Conversation, in* Property Concepts in Intellectual Property Law 29, 29 (H. Howe & J. Griffiths eds., 2013) ("Contemporary EU trade mark law . . . protects the more expansive brand dimension associated with a successful trade mark. The [CJEU] has enabled this by recognising not only the origin indication function of marks, but also their advertising, investment and communication functions as well").

[74] *See* 15 USC § 1125(c)(2)(B) (emphasis added); *see also* Rierson, *supra* note 68, at 10–11 (noting connection of blurring to source identifying function).

[75] *See* 15 USC § 1125(c)(2)(B) ("[D]ilution by blurring is association arising from the similarity between a mark or trade name and a famous mark that impairs the distinctiveness of the famous mark. In determining whether a mark or trade name is likely to cause dilution by blurring, the court may consider all relevant factors, including the following: (i) The degree of similarity between the mark or trade name and the famous mark; (ii) The degree of inherent or acquired distinctiveness of the famous mark; (iii) The extent to which the owner of the famous mark is engaging in substantially exclusive use of the mark; (iv) The degree of recognition of the famous mark; (v) Whether the user of the mark or trade name intended to create an association with the famous mark; and (vi) Any actual association between the mark or trade name and the famous mark").

[76] *See Starbucks Corp.* v. *Wolfe's Borough Coffee, Inc.*, 736 F.3d 198 (2d Cir. 2013).

[77] *See* Graeme B. Dinwoodie & Mark D. Janis, *Dilution's (Still) Uncertain Future*, 105 Mich. L. Rev. First Impressions 98 (2006) (predicting that courts may view the statutory blurring test as little more than "confusion analysis with a different paint job"). This prediction is largely borne out by the case law. *See* Barton Beebe, *The Continuing Debacle of U.S. Antidilution Law: Evidence from the First Year of Trademark Dilution Revision Act Case Law*, 24 Santa Clara High Tech. L.J. 449 (2008); Sheff, *supra* note 30, at 7 ("since the passage of the TDRA not a single U.S. Court of Appeals has found – or affirmed a finding – that a defendant was not liable for infringement but was liable for dilution by blurring").

[78] *See Ty Inc.* v. *Perryman*, 306 F.3d 509, 511 (7th Cir. 2002) (Posner J) ("[The] concern [motivating blurring] is that consumer search costs will rise if a trademark becomes associated with a variety of unrelated products"); Stacey L. Dogan & Mark A. Lemley, *What the Right of Publicity Can Learn from Trademark Law*, 58 Stan. L. Rev. 1161, 1197

image[79] – has been explained by some courts as grounded largely on the same theory as blurring.[80] Perhaps this simply affirms that a mark can serve the additional functions recognized by modern trademark law only if it first serves the origin function.[81] And perhaps it is very hard to draw clear lines between the different functions of the mark. Even the Court of Justice, which has clearly recognized that there could be harm to the extended functions without harm to the origin function,[82] has acknowledged that the functions inevitably overlap; and that Court's definition of the conduct that adversely affects each function does not offer any real clarity.[83]

V CONCLUSION

Dilution is the cause of action most commonly understood as an attempt to protect new functions of marks other than source-identification. But in the United States, claims of post-sale confusion and initial interest confusion have developed to protect such additional functions, albeit with only passing acknowledgment of those functions. Moreover, it is not clear that protection of additional functions such as advertising or investment is driving judicial assessment of dilution claims, which appear tied by the language of the legislation to protection of the origin function (beyond perhaps the context of tarnishment claims). As a comparative matter, this might suggest that the approach to the protection of additional functions in Europe makes more sense. Courts in the European Union are arguably more sceptical of post-sale confusion and initial interest confusion claims,[84] making it more likely that claimants seeking to protect exclusivity or image will depend upon the dilution cause of action that is understood in part as intended to protect those additional functions.[85]

(2006) ("[L]ike traditional trademark law, dilution properly understood is targeted at reducing consumer search costs").

79 *See* Rierson, *supra* note 68, at 14 (suggesting that tarnishment is concerned with harm to goodwill rather than distinctiveness).

80 *See Ty Inc.*, 306 F.3d at 511 (Posner J) ("tarnishment" is a second form of dilution [but] analytically it is a subset of blurring, since it reduces the distinctness of the trademark as a signifier of the trademarked product or service").

81 *See* European Commission, Explanatory Memorandum on the Creation of an EEC Trade Mark §68, (SEC 76) 2462 final, July 6, 1976, Bulletin of the European Communities, Supplement 8/76 (1976) ("Any regulation of trade mark law depends ultimately on the functions which are attributed to the trade mark. Both economically and legally the function of the trade mark as an indication of origin is paramount … From this basic function of the trade mark are derived all the other functions which the trade mark fulfils in economic life").

82 *See L'Oréal SA* v. *Bellure*, Case C-487/07, [2009] ETMR 55 at [58] (CJEU 2009).

83 *See Interflora* v. *Marks & Spencer*, Case C-323/09, EU:C:2011:604 at [59] (CJEU 2011) (defining "advertising function" as use of the mark "effectively to inform and win over consumers"); *see also Interflora* v. *Marks & Spencer*, [2013] EWHC 1291 (Ch) at [270]–[274] (defining investment function, which overlaps with advertising function, as "use to acquire or preserve a reputation capable of attracting consumers and retaining their loyalty," which is adversely affected by damage to the image conveyed by the trademark); *see generally* Kur, *supra* note 1, at 169–170 (discussing these functions, but noting that they have played little role in the keyword cases in which they were announced, which have turned on the meaning of the origin function).

84 At the very least, the Court of Justice and leading national courts have been somewhat sceptical of extending the confusion-based claim to encompass initial and post-sale confusion theories. *See generally* Bently et al., *supra* note 15, at 1046–48.

85 Plaintiffs in Europe can also protect those functions using the double-identity cause of action. *See L'Oréal SA* v. *Bellure NV*, Case C-487/07, at [50]. In one sense, that development (requiring identical marks) follows Schechter faithfully, whereas in another (the requirement of identical goods) the development is wholly at odds with Schechter's focus on dissimilar goods.

II

Signs That Can Be Protected as Trademarks

11

Protectable Trademark Subject Matter in Common Law Countries and the Problem with Flexibility

*Lisa P. Ramsey**

I INTRODUCTION

Words, names, and logos used as trademarks can provide consumers with useful information about a product's source or qualities.[1] Examples are BILLABONG for clothing, SINGAPORE AIRLINES for airline travel services, WHITTAKER'S for chocolate, and Starbucks' mermaid logo for coffee. Today some companies are also claiming trademark rights in other subject matter that is non-verbal or non-visual, including the exterior and interior design of buildings, the three-dimensional shape of packaging and products, colors, sounds, scents, textures, and flavors.[2] Examples of such "non-traditional" marks registered in the United States are the design and layout of Apple's retail store; a skull-shaped bottle for alcoholic beverages sold by Globefill, Inc. under the Crystal Head Vodka brand; LEGO's Minifigure shape for toy figures; the color magenta used in advertising for T-Mobile's wireless telecommunication services; the sound of a Zippo cigarette lighter opening, igniting, and closing; the scent of Play-Doh for Hasbro Inc.'s toy modeling compound; and the texture of leather wrapping around the middle surface of a bottle of wine sold by the David Family Group.[3] While companies have applied to register flavors (such as an orange flavor for pharmaceuticals),[4] as of this writing the author has been unable to find a registered flavor mark in the United States or any other country.

* Professor of Law, University of San Diego School of Law. I appreciate the helpful comments on this paper from Rob Batty, Robert Burrell, Irene Calboli, Jane Ginsburg, Michael Handler, Tan Tee Jim, Kayla Jimenez, Ng-Loy Wee Loon, Teresa Scassa, Martin Senftleben, David Tan, Edward Timberlake, Rebecca Tushnet, Genevieve Wilkinson, and the participants at the 38th Annual Congress of the International Association for the Advancement of Teaching and Research in Intellectual Property at Vanderbilt Law School, the University of San Diego School of Law faculty colloquium, the Eighth Annual International Intellectual Property Scholars Roundtable at Florida State University College of Law, and the 2019 Works-in-Progress Intellectual Property Colloquium at the University of Houston Law Center. In addition, Sasha Nuñez and Elizabeth Parker provided excellent editorial assistance.

[1] *See* WIPO COMM. ON DEV. & INTELLECTUAL PROP., *Study on Misappropriation of Signs*, CDIP/9/INF/5 (Martin Senftleben ed., Mar. 14, 2012).

[2] *See id.*; THE PROTECTION OF NON-TRADITIONAL TRADEMARKS: CRITICAL PERSPECTIVES (Irene Calboli & Martin Senftleben eds., 2018) [hereinafter NON-TRADITIONAL TRADEMARKS].

[3] Registration No. 4,277,914 (store design); Registration No. 4,043,730 (bottle design); Registration No. 4,903,968 (Minifigure); Registration No. 3,263,625 (color); Registration No. 5,527,388 (sound); Registration No. 5,467,089 (scent); Registration No. 3,896,100 (texture).

[4] US Trademark Application Serial No. 76,467,774 (filed Nov. 18, 2002; abandoned Sept. 12, 2006).

This chapter evaluates how Australia, New Zealand, Singapore, and the United States determine what subject matter or "signs" are eligible for trademark registration and protection.[5] One important feature of the trademark laws in these common law jurisdictions is flexibility in what types of signs can qualify as a trademark.[6] The broadness of the definition of a "sign" or "trademark" in the laws of these four countries and other World Trade Organization (WTO) members is due, in part, to international obligations to protect trademarks in the Trade-Related Aspects of Intellectual Property (TRIPS) Agreement.[7] TRIPS Article 15(1) provides that "any sign" can qualify as a trademark if it is capable of distinguishing one trader's goods or services from those of others.[8] Article 15(1) also states that "[s]uch signs, in particular words including personal names, letters, numerals, figurative elements and combinations of colours as well as any combination of such signs, shall be eligible for registration as trademarks."[9] As discussed later, allowing flexibility in what can be registered as a trademark can benefit companies seeking to distinguish their brands in new ways.[10]

Yet such flexibility may also stifle fair competition and non-misleading expression.[11] Competitors and others accused of trademark violations may be unable to determine early in a trademark dispute whether certain subject matter claimed as a common law trademark is actually protectable, distinctive, and otherwise valid under trademark law. For example, it is not clear whether a hand gesture is a sign capable of functioning as a trademark in the United States. In 2017, Gene Simmons – the frontman of the rock band Kiss – applied to register the devil's horn hand gesture for entertainment services in the form of live musical performances and personal appearances by a musical artist, but withdrew the application after fellow musicians complained that he was trying to capitalize on a symbol that is part of rock culture.[12] The lack of certainty in what can qualify as a mark may chill the use of certain communicative symbols or product features that were intrinsically expressive, useful, or desirable before they were claimed as trademarks.[13]

[5] This chapter focuses on US law since the author is from this country, but it also includes a discussion of the laws of Australia, New Zealand, and Singapore because the primary language in these countries is English and excellent resources exist on these laws. *See, e.g.*, Robert Burrell & Michael Handler, Australian Trade Mark Law (2d ed. 2016); Susy Frankel, Intellectual Property in New Zealand 489–718 (2d ed. 2011); Tee Jim Tan, Law of Trade Marks and Passing Off in Singapore (3d ed. 2014). For useful information about United States trademark law, *see* J. Thomas McCarthy, McCarthy on Trademarks and Unfair Competition (5th ed. 2019). Other jurisdictions have a similar flexible approach to determining what subject matter may qualify as a trademark, *see, e.g.*, Teresa Scassa, Canadian Trademark Law 65–67 (2d ed. 2015), but a discussion of other laws is not included here due to space limitations.

[6] *See infra* Section II.A.

[7] Agreement on Trade-Related Aspects of Intellectual Property Rights, art. 15(1), Apr. 15, 1994, Marrakesh Agreement Establishing the World Trade Organization, Annex 1C, 1869 UNTS 299, 33 ILM 1197 (1994) [hereinafter TRIPS]. *See* Burrell & Handler, *supra* note 5, at 67; Jacey K. McGrath, *The New Breed of Trade Marks: Sounds, Smells and Tastes*, 32 Victoria U. Wellington L. Rev. 277, 284 (2001); *see also* Irene Calboli & Martin Senftleben, *Introduction*, in Non-Traditional Trademarks, *supra* note 2, at 1–4.

[8] TRIPS, *supra* note 7, art. 15(1).

[9] *Id.*

[10] *See infra* Section III.A.

[11] *See infra* Section III.B; Lisa P. Ramsey, *Free Speech Challenges to Trademark Law after Matal v. Tam*, 56 Hous. L. Rev. 401, 461–69 (2018).

[12] US Trademark Application Serial No. 87,482,739 (filed June 9, 2017; abandoned June 20, 2017) (describing the mark as "a hand gesture with the index and small fingers extended upward and the thumb extended perpendicular"); Ronald Abrams, *Gene Simmons Abandons Hand Gesture Trademark Application*, Forbes (June 21, 2017, 08:44 PM), https://www.forbes.com/sites/legalentertainment/2017/06/21/breaking-gene-simmons-abandons-hand-gesture-trademark-application/#8c326fcfaacf. This gesture also means "I love you" in American Sign Language. *Id.*

[13] Lisa P. Ramsey, *Non-Traditional Trademarks and Inherently Valuable Expression*, in Non-Traditional Trademarks, *supra* note 2, at 337, 352–61; Ramsey, *supra* note 11, at 461–69.

Allowing almost anything to be registered and protected as a trademark will encourage companies to spend time and money promoting and policing weak marks that require proof of acquired distinctiveness for protection. Once a mark is deemed to be distinctive and otherwise valid, its owner obtains the exclusive right to use it in connection with certain products and can sue for infringement and other trademark violations. Larger, well-established brands will likely have an advantage in establishing distinctiveness for non-traditional marks due to higher sales volumes and the ability to spend more on extensive "look for the mark" advertising. They can also spend more money on litigation.

When an accused infringer receives a demand letter or complaint alleging trademark violations, it may be able to successfully challenge the validity of the trademark or defend itself against the infringement claims. But smaller companies and individuals often cannot afford to litigate a trademark dispute or petition to cancel a trademark registration. Even if they would get a favorable result in court or at the trademark office, the time and expense of litigation may cause that competitor to stop use of this communicative symbol or desirable product feature claimed as a trademark by another. The protectable trademark subject matter requirement can serve a critical "gatekeeping" function by encouraging the adoption, use, and registration of the types of marks which are more effective at communicating source-identifying product information and which better promote competition and trademark law's other important goals.[14] Legislators should use this requirement to decide as a matter of public policy exactly what types of signs should be registered and protected, and consider categorically leaving certain types of subject matter in the public domain free for use by everyone in the marketplace.

II REQUIREMENTS FOR TRADEMARK REGISTRATION AND PROTECTION

A *The Types of Signs Eligible for Trademark Registration and Protection*

The federal trademark statute in the United States – also known as the Lanham Act – has a very broad definition of what may qualify as a trademark per the US Supreme Court in *Qualitex*, a case involving the color green-gold used as a mark for dry cleaning press pads.[15] The Lanham Act provides that "[t]he term 'trademark' includes any word, name, symbol, or device, or any combination thereof" that is used to identify and distinguish goods or services and to indicate a product's source, even if that source is unknown.[16] "Since human beings might use as a 'symbol' or 'device' almost anything at all that is capable of carrying meaning," the Court said "this language, read literally, is not restrictive."[17] Per the Court, "[i]t is the source-distinguishing ability of a mark – not its ontological status as color, shape, fragrance, word, or sign – that permits

[14] Ramsey, *supra* note 13, at 352–61; Ramsey, *supra* note 11, at 447–53, 461–69. *See generally* Ann Bartow, *The True Colors of Trademark Law: Greenlighting a Red Tide of Anti Competition Blues*, 97 Ky. L.J. 263 (2009); Glynn S. Lunney Jr., *The Trade Dress Emperor's New Clothes: Why Trade Dress Does Not Belong on the Principal Register*, 51 Hastings L.J. 1131 (2000); Kenneth L. Port, *On Nontraditional Trademarks*, 38 N. Ky. L. Rev. 1 (2011).

[15] *Qualitex Co. v. Jacobson Products, Co.*, 514 US 159, 162–64 (1995). *See* Jane C. Ginsburg, *"See Me, Feel Me, Touch Me, Hea[r] Me" (and Maybe Smell and Taste Me too): I Am a Trademark – A US Perspective*, *in* Trade Marks and Brands: An Interdisciplinary Critique 92, 93–97 (Lionel Bently, Jennifer Davis, & Jane C. Ginsburg eds., 2008); Graeme B. Dinwoodie, *The Death of Ontology: A Teleological Approach to Trademark Law*, 84 Iowa L. Rev. 611, 646–47 (1999). Professor Lunney argues that a close reading of the Trademark Act of 1946 and its accompanying legislative history reveal that Congress did not intend to allow registration of trade dress on the principal register back in the 1940s. Lunney, *supra* note 14, at 1134–36; Glynn S. Lunney Jr., *Trademark Monopolies*, 48 Emory L.J. 367, 373–91 (1999).

[16] 15 USC § 1127 (2012).

[17] *Qualitex*, 514 US at 162.

it to serve" the basic purposes of trademark law.[18] The Lanham Act also states that a distinctive word, name, symbol, or device (or combination of these) cannot be refused registration on the principal trademark register "on account of its nature" unless one of the specific statutory exceptions to registration applies.[19] If a sign is not yet distinctive but is capable of becoming distinctive, the United States Patent and Trademark Office (USPTO) may register the sign on the supplemental trademark register instead of the principal register.[20] The supplemental register does not confer any substantive trademark rights, but it can help a company obtain registration of descriptive terms, colors, and other non-inherently distinctive signs in foreign countries.[21]

Due to a broad definition of the word "sign" in their trademark statutes, almost any type of subject matter can also be eligible for registration in Australia,[22] New Zealand,[23] and Singapore.[24] All three countries explicitly allow registration of marks consisting of a letter, word, name, signature, numeral, device, brand, heading, label, ticket, shape, or color.[25] Other subject matter included on the detailed list of signs that can qualify as a mark are aspects of packaging in Australia and Singapore, sounds and scents/smells in Australia and New Zealand, and tastes in New Zealand.[26]

Importantly, the statutory list of trademark-eligible signs in all of these jurisdictions is inclusive rather than exclusive.[27] That means other types of subject matter not listed in the trademark statutes can qualify as a mark if the sign is capable of distinguishing the source of goods or services and the mark satisfies the other requirements in the trademark law, as discussed next.

B The Distinctiveness Requirement

As noted previously, TRIPS Article 15(1) provides that "[a]ny sign, or any combination of signs, capable of distinguishing the goods or services of one undertaking from those of other undertakings, shall be capable of constituting a trademark" and such signs "shall be eligible for registration as trademarks."[28] However, Article 15(1) also allows WTO members to "make registrability depend on distinctiveness acquired through use" where the sign is "not inherently capable of distinguishing the relevant goods or services."[29] In Australia,[30] New Zealand,[31] Singapore,[32] and the United States,[33] the government requires proof of acquired distinctiveness through use (also known as secondary meaning or factual distinctiveness) before registering certain types of marks

[18] *Id.* at 164.
[19] 15 USC § 1052.
[20] 15 USC § 1091.
[21] McCarthy, *supra* note 5, at § 19.33.
[22] *Trade Marks Act 1995* (Cth) § 6(1) (Austl.).
[23] Trade Marks Act 2002, § 5(1) (NZ).
[24] Trade Marks Act (Cap 332, 2005 rev. ed.) § 2(1) (Sing.).
[25] *See supra* notes 22–24.
[26] *Id.*
[27] Burrell & Handler, *supra* note 5, at 65–66, 72–73 (Austl.); Frankel, *supra* note 5, at 499–501 (NZ); McCarthy, *supra* note 5, at § 7:105 (US); 1 Tan, *supra* note 5, at 56 (Sing.).
[28] TRIPS, *supra* note 7, art. 15(1).
[29] *Id.*
[30] *Trade Marks Act 1995* (Cth) § 41 (Austl.). *See* Burrell & Handler, *supra* note 5, at 85–161.
[31] Trade Marks Act 2002, §§ 5, 18 (NZ). *See* Frankel, supra *note 5, at 504–06, 523–46.*
[32] Trade Marks Act (Cap 332, 2005 rev. ed.) §§ 2(1), 7(1) (Sing.). *See* 1 Tan, *supra* note 5, at 310–12, 324–59.
[33] 15 USC § 1052 (2012); *Abercrombie & Fitch Co. v. Hunting World, Inc.*, 537 F.2d 4, 9–10 (2d Cir. 1976). *See* McCarthy, *supra* note 5, at §§ 11:1–11:72, 15:1–15:73.

that do not automatically serve a source-distinguishing function. Acquired distinctiveness may be established using evidence of extensive sales and advertising of products featuring the mark, lengthy and exclusive use of the sign as a mark for this product, and consumer surveys showing that the primary significance of the sign is to identify the product's origin. Marks that are "inherently distinctive" may be registered without such evidence.

In the United States, examples of inherently distinctive marks include made-up words (such as CLOROX for bleach) and existing words having no connection to the products for sale (such as APPLE for computers) or only suggesting the product's qualities (such as TIDE for laundry detergent). If the mark consists of a personal name (such as MCDONALD'S for restaurant services) or the term is descriptive (such as 24 HOUR FITNESS for health club services) or geographically descriptive (such as AMERICAN AIRLINES for airline travel services) the alleged trademark owner must prove the sign has acquired distinctiveness through use in the United States before it can be registered and protected as a trademark.[34] Generic language that is customarily used by the public to identify the type of product rather than its source (such as SHREDDED WHEAT for biscuits made of shredded wheat or ESCALATOR for a moving stairway) can never be registered or protected as a mark, and any evidence of acquired distinctiveness is irrelevant.[35]

When the alleged mark consists of subject matter that is non-verbal or non-visual, different trademark doctrines may be used to determine if the mark is sufficiently distinctive for registration and protection. For example, in the United States, a logo, two-dimensional design on product packaging, and the décor of a retail establishment may be deemed to be inherently distinctive if it is unique or unusual in that particular field.[36] On the other hand, proof of acquired distinctiveness is usually required if the alleged mark consists of a common basic design or shape (such as a rectangle), is merely a refinement of a commonly adopted and well-known form of ornamentation for this type of product, or is not capable of creating a commercial impression distinct from any accompanying words.[37] If the mark consists of a color or product design (such as a cocktail shaker shaped like a penguin), the company claiming trademark rights must establish that this mark has acquired distinctiveness; such marks can never be inherently distinctive.[38] Moreover, a substantial showing of acquired distinctiveness is generally required before the USPTO will register a color, shape, scent, flavor, or other types of non-traditional marks.[39] One reason is because these things are usually perceived by consumers as a product attribute rather than as a source-identifying mark, and the government wants to be sure that the sign actually functions as a mark.[40]

34 *Id.*; 15 USC § 1052(f); US Patent & Trademark Office, Trademark Manual of Examining Procedure §§ 1209, 1212 (Oct. 2018), https://tmep.uspto.gov/RDMS/TMEP/current [hereinafter TMEP].

35 15 USC §§ 1064(3), 1065(4); TMEP, *supra* note 34, at § 1209.01(c). *See* McCarthy, *supra* note 5, at §§ 12:01–12:64.

36 *Two Pesos, Inc.* v. *Taco Cabana, Inc.*, 505 US 763, 768–76 (1992); *Seabrook Foods, Inc.* v. *Bar-Well Foods Ltd.*, 568 F.2d 1342, 1344 (CCPA 1977).

37 *Seabrook*, 568 F.2d at 1344. *See* McCarthy, *supra* note 5, at §§ 8:13, 11:14.

38 *Wal-Mart Stores, Inc.* v. *Samara Bros., Inc.*, 529 US 205, 212 (2000); *Qualitex Co.* v. *Jacobson Prods. Co., Inc.*, 514 US 159, 162–63 (1995). For the approach in Singapore, see *Société des Produits Nestlé SA* v. *Petra Foods Ltd.*, [2017] 1 SLR 35 at [21–69].

39 TMEP, *supra* note 34, at §§ 1202.13, 1202.03(d), 1202.05(a).

40 *Id.* at § 1202.13; *In re N.V. Organon*, 79 USPQ 2d (BNA) 1639, 1650–51 (TTAB 2006); *cf. Wal-Mart*, 529 US at 213 (noting that for product designs and colors "we think consumer predisposition to equate the feature with the source does not exist" and "[c]onsumers are aware of the reality that, almost invariably, even the most unusual of product designs … is intended not to identify the source, but to render the product itself more useful or more appealing").

C Clear Notice of the Subject Matter Claimed as a Mark Must Be Provided

In addition to being distinctive, trademarks must also be capable of graphic representation or meet other criteria that provides sufficient notice of what subject matter is registered or protected by the trademark law. The TRIPS Agreement gives WTO members the option to deny registration to marks which are not "visually perceptible,"[41] but Australia, New Zealand, Singapore, and the United States have adopted more flexible notice requirements.

For example, in New Zealand, a sign can qualify as a "trade mark" under the New Zealand Trade Marks Act if it is capable of being "represented graphically."[42] Per the Practice Guidelines of the Intellectual Property Office of New Zealand, the trademark applicant must include "a clear graphic representation of the mark in order to obtain a filing date."[43] If an applicant seeks to register a color in New Zealand, it must file a representation of the color of the mark or a description of it using a widely known and readily available color standard, such as the color indexing scheme of the Pantone color system.[44] If the asserted mark is a three-dimensional shape of a product or its packaging, the applicant must file a pictorial representation of that shape in a form that clearly shows all of the features of the mark and a written description that distinguishes the three-dimensional mark from a two-dimensional mark.[45] The graphic representation requirement can be satisfied for a sound mark using musical notation or a written description, such as Unilever's "squeak produced by the friction of the thumb or forefinger on dishware" for its Sunlight brand of dishwashing liquid.[46] Like New Zealand, Australia and Singapore also require marks to be capable of being "represented graphically."[47]

To obtain a registration in the United States, applicants must usually submit a detailed drawing showing the mark sought to be registered, an accurate and concise description of the mark (if the mark is not in standard characters), and a "specimen" showing how the mark is used in commerce (such as a photograph of the product's packaging).[48] If the mark consists only of a sound, scent, flavor, or texture, the applicant must submit a detailed description of the mark in lieu of a drawing and comply with other requirements in the law.[49] For example, for sound marks, the USPTO's Trademark Manual of Examining Procedure (TMEP) states that applicants should submit an audio reproduction of the mark to supplement and clarify the description of the mark.[50] An example of a recent registration is Zippo Manufacturing Company's mark for lighters used by smokers consisting of "the sounds of a windproof lighter opening, igniting, and closing."[51] The USPTO website contains several specimens of use relating to this mark, including a video showing the Zippo lighter making sounds when it opens, ignites, and closes.[52]

[41] TRIPS, *supra* note 7, art. 15(1).

[42] Trade Marks Act 2002, § 5 (NZ).

[43] Intellectual Property Office of New Zealand, Practice Guidelines: Filing Trade Mark Applications § 4.3 (Feb. 25, 2019), https://www.iponz.govt.nz/about-ip/trade-marks/practice-guidelines/current/filing-trade-mark-applications.

[44] *Id.* § 4.3.1.

[45] *Id.* § 4.3.2. The written description of the shape need not be supplied on the date the application is filed. *Id.*

[46] *Id.* § 4.3.3; Registration No. 247,094 (NZ). *See* Frankel, *supra* note 5, at 502, 542.

[47] *Trade Marks Act 1995* (Cth) § 40 (Austl.); Trade Marks Act (Cap 332, 2005 rev. ed.) §§ 2(1), 7(1)(a) (Sing.). *See* Burrell & Handler, *supra* note 5, at 81–84.

[48] TMEP, *supra* note 34, at §§ 807, 808, 808.02, 904. Note, however, that a specimen of use may not be required for certain applications, such as an application to register a mark in the United States based on a foreign registration pursuant to section 44 of the Lanham Act. *Id.* §§ 904, 1009.

[49] *Id.* §§ 807, 807.09, 904.03(m), 1202.13.

[50] *Id.* § 807.09.

[51] Registration No. 5,527,388.

[52] *Id.* ("Specimen" dated Dec. 12, 2016).

For scent or flavor marks, the USPTO requires the applicant to "submit a specimen that contains the scent or flavor and that matches the required description of the scent or flavor" to prove "that the specimen for a scent or flavor mark actually identifies and distinguishes the goods and indicates their source."[53] The examining attorney must be able to smell the scent or taste the flavor. Thus, the specimen will usually consist of the actual goods themselves, but a "scratch and sniff" sticker for a scent mark may also be an acceptable specimen in some cases.[54] Hasbro, Inc. was recently successful in registering the scent of its Play-Doh brand of toy modeling compound described as "a sweet, slightly musky, vanilla fragrance, with slight overtones of cherry, combined with the smell of salted, wheat-based dough."[55] Per the records associated with the registration, Hasbro's attorney sent a container of its Play-Doh product containing this scent to the USPTO.[56]

D Other Grounds for Refusal of Registration and Protection Must Not Apply

There are also similarities and differences with regard to other grounds for refusal of an application to register a trademark in the laws of Australia, New Zealand, Singapore, and the United States. Examples of areas of convergence include laws banning registration of flags and other government symbols, deceptive marks, and marks likely to deceive or cause confusion with a previously registered mark.[57] Moreover, all of these countries have banned registration of marks that are contrary to morality or public order, as they are permitted to do within their international trademark obligations,[58] but the actual language in the statutes varies from nation to nation.[59]

There is significant divergence in the laws of these four nations on whether and how they ban registration and common law protection of functional product features. In Singapore, functionality of a sign is an absolute ground for refusal of a registration, and this rule applies to signs which "consist exclusively of – (a) the shape which results from the nature of the goods themselves; (b) the shape of goods which is necessary to obtain a technical result; or (c) the shape which gives substantial value to the goods."[60] The Singapore Court of Appeal recently applied the "technical result" provision in a trademark dispute involving the four-finger and two-finger shape of the Kit Kat brand of chocolate-coated wafer candy bars.[61] Per the court, the decision-maker must first identify "the essential characteristics of the shape" claimed as a mark from the perspective of the average consumer, and then determine "whether each and every one of the essential characteristics performs a technical function."[62] After examining the rectangular slab shape and the breaking grooves arranged along the length of each bar, the court determined

53 TMEP, *supra* note 34, at § 904.03(m).

54 *Id.*

55 Registration No. 5,467,089.

56 *Id.* ("Specimen" dated Feb. 14, 2017).

57 *Trade Marks Act* 1995 (Cth) §§ 39, 43 (Austl.); Trade Marks Act 2002, §§ 17(1)(a), 24–30 (NZ); Trade Marks Act (Cap 332, 2005 rev. ed.) §§ 7(4)(b), 7(11), 8, 56 (Sing.); 15 USC §§ 1052(a), 1052(b) & 1052(d) (2012). *See* Burrell & Handler, *supra* note 5, at 163–64, 172–80.

58 Paris Convention for the Protection of Industrial Property, art. 6*quinques*(B)(3), Mar. 20, 1883, 21 UST 1583, 828 UNTS 305 (revised July 14, 1967) [hereinafter Paris Convention]; TRIPS, *supra* note 7, art. 15(2).

59 *Trade Marks Act* 1995 (Cth) § 42(a) (Austl.); Trade Marks Act 2002, § 17(1)(c) (NZ); Trade Marks Act (Cap 332, 2005 rev. ed.) § 7(4)(a) (Sing.); 15 USC § 1052(a). *See* Lisa P. Ramsey, *A Free Speech Right to Trademark Protection?*, 106 Trademark Rep. 797 (2016). Note the US Supreme Court recently held that the ban on registration of immoral, scandalous, or potentially disparaging matter in 15 USC § 1052(a) is an unconstitutional regulation of expression in violation of the First Amendment right to free speech. *Iancu* v. *Brunetti*, 139 S.Ct. 2294, 2297–8 (2019); *Matal* v. *Tam*, 137 S.Ct. 1744, 1751 (2017). *See* Ramsey, *supra* note 11, at 410–23.

60 Trade Marks Act (Cap 332, 2005 rev. ed.) § 7(3) (Sing.). *See* 1 Tan, *supra* note 5, at 311.

61 *Société des Produits Nestlé SA* v. *Petra Foods Ltd.* [2017] 1 SLR 35.

62 *Id.* at [81–87].

that each of these essential features is "necessary to obtain a technical result" and affirmed the decision to revoke the registration of the shape on this ground.[63]

The United States trademark statute more broadly bans registration of "any matter that, as a whole, is functional."[64] If the mark is not registered on the principal register, a company asserting trade dress protection in a civil action for infringement must prove "that the matter sought to be protected is not functional."[65] According to the US Supreme Court, "a product feature is functional, and cannot serve as a trademark, if it is essential to the use or purpose of the article or if it affects the cost or quality of the article."[66] A product attribute desired by consumers for aesthetic rather than utilitarian reasons may also be functional under the competitive necessity test if granting exclusive trademark rights to that feature "would put competitors at a significant non-reputation-related disadvantage."[67] The functionality doctrine has been applied in the United States to marks consisting of product designs (such as a dual-spring mechanism that keeps road signs upright),[68] colors (such as black for floral packaging),[69] flavors (such as an orange flavor for medicine),[70] and other types of trade dress for goods and services.[71]

There is no ban on registration of functional product features in Australia and New Zealand.[72] The trademark offices in those countries sometimes reject functional matter on the ground of lack of distinctiveness, but Professors Burrell and Handler convincingly argue that using the distinctiveness requirement to stop registration of functional product features may not sufficiently protect competition.[73] One reason is that such a refusal can always be overcome through evidence that the mark has acquired distinctiveness through its use with the relevant goods or services. Adding a non-functionality requirement to the trademark statutes in Australia and New Zealand will allow more companies to incorporate useful or intrinsically appealing shapes, colors, and other features into their products or packaging, and thereby increase consumer choice and competition in the marketplace.[74]

E Priority through Registration or Use of the Mark

In Australia,[75] New Zealand,[76] Singapore,[77] and the United States,[78] a distinctive sign will be protected under trademark law only if the trademark owner has priority through registration or

[63] *Id.* at [89–115]. *See* David Tan & Stanley Lai Tze Chang SC, *Intellectual Property Law*, 17 SAL Ann. Rev. 504, 555–64 (2016) (providing a useful summary of this decision).

[64] 15 USC § 1052(e)(5) (2012).

[65] 15 USC § 1125(a)(3).

[66] *TrafFix Devices Inc.* v. *Marketing Displays Inc.*, 532 US 23, 32 (2001) (internal quotations omitted); *Qualitex Co.* v. *Jacobson Products Co.*, 514 US 159, 165 (1995).

[67] *TrafFix*, 532 US at 32; *Qualitex*, 514 US at 165.

[68] *TrafFix*, 532 US at 30–35.

[69] *In re Florists' Transworld Delivery, Inc.*, 106 USPQ 2d (BNA) 1784 (TTAB 2013).

[70] *In re N.V. Organon*, 79 USPQ 2d (BNA) 1639 (TTAB 2006).

[71] TMEP, *supra* note 34, at § 1202.02(a)(i)–(viii). *See* McCarthy, *supra* note 5, at §§ 7:63–7:93.

[72] Burrell & Handler, *supra* note 5, at 71; Frankel, *supra* note 5, at 538–41; Rob Batty, *Is New Zealand's Trade Marks Law out of Shape?*, 33(5) Eur. Intell. Prop. Rev. 281 (2011).

[73] Burrell & Handler, *supra* note 5, at 71, 88–93, 158–61.

[74] *Id. See generally* Michael Handler, *Disentangling Functionality, Distinctiveness, and Use in Australian Trade Mark Law*, 42 Melbourne U. L. Rev. 55 (2018) (providing a useful discussion of these laws).

[75] Burrell & Handler, *supra* note 5, at 27–28, 335–66, 457–504.

[76] Frankel, *supra* note 5, at 489–90, 547–52, 564–72, 597–98.

[77] 1 Tan, *supra* note 5, at 209–26; 2 Tan, *supra* note 5, 83–237.

[78] McCarthy, *supra* note 5, at §§ 16:1–16:34, 19:1–19:122. *See generally* Rebecca Tushnet, *Registering Disagreement: Registration in Modern American Trademark Law*, 130 Harv. L. Rev. 867 (2017) (discussing several excellent proposals for reform of trademark registration laws). Trademarks not registered or used within a country but which are well

use of the mark in connection with certain goods or services. Registration of a mark can provide substantial benefits in litigation, including a presumption of ownership and validity of the trademark. Unregistered marks may be protected in actions for passing off or unfair competition as long as the common law mark is distinctive and meets the other requirements in that nation's law. Use of the mark in connection with the goods or services listed in the registration is required to maintain the registration, and will usually be required to pursue a claim for trademark violations, but use may not be required before registration depending on the jurisdiction and the circumstances.

F The Sign Must Be Used or Perceived as a Mark and Not Fail to Function as a Mark

Some jurisdictions have a separate requirement for registration and protection of a mark that is related to the distinctiveness, non-functionality, and use requirements but also different from them: the subject matter must be used, perceived, or function as a source-identifying mark. For example, in the United States the USPTO can reject an application to register a sign on the separate ground that this subject matter fails to function as a mark or is not used as a trademark as required by Sections 1, 2, 3, and 45 of the Lanham Act.[79] Regardless of a company's intent when using a phrase, design, décor, or product attribute in the marketplace, not every word, symbol, or feature placed on or incorporated into packaging or goods, or used in connection with services, necessarily performs a source-distinguishing function."[80]

As explained by the USPTO in the TMEP, certain subject matter may fail to function as a mark due to the sign's "inherent nature or the manner in which it is used."[81] For example, due to its inherent nature, the flavor of medicine or food will usually be perceived as a mere physical attribute of the product rather than as an indicator of its source.[82] It is unlikely that flavor could be effectively used alone – without a brand name or other source-identifying mark – on products or point-of-purchase displays, in advertisements, or in another manner to actually help consumers identify the product's source and not just its flavor. Thus, the inherent qualities of this type of sign may lead to a failure-to-function rejection for the flavor regardless of the manner in which it is used.

Certain two-dimensional designs and words may also fail to function as marks due to their inherent nature, while others may be refused registration due to the manner in which they are used. A failure-to-function refusal is more likely if the proposed mark has a widely recognized non-source-identifying meaning or is commonly used to convey information. Examples include a recycling symbol or "Made in USA" displayed on packaging for a variety of products, "I Love You" for jewelry, and the peace symbol or "I ♥ DC" displayed prominently on the front of

known to the relevant sector of the public in that country may also be protected under trademark or unfair competition law to satisfy international obligations to protect well-known marks under Article 6*bis* of the Paris Convention and Articles 16(2) and 16(3) of the TRIPS Agreement. *See, e.g.*, Burrell & Handler, *supra* note 5, at 246–55; McCarthy, *supra* note 5, at §§ 4:3, 29:4. 29:61–64.

79 TMEP, *supra* note 34, at § 1202 (citing 15 USC §§ 1051, 1052, 1053, 1127).

80 *Id.*

81 *Id.*

82 *In re Pohl-Boskamp GmbH & Co.*, 106 USPQ 2d (BNA) 1042 (TTAB 2013) (peppermint flavor for pharmaceuticals); *In re N.V. Organon*, 79 USPQ 2d (BNA) 1639 (TTAB 2006) (orange flavor for pharmaceuticals); *New York Pizzeria, Inc. v. Syal*, 56 F.Supp.3d 875, 880–82 (SD Tex. 2014) (rejecting claim to common law trademark rights in the flavor of food). *See generally* Nancy L. Clarke, *Issues in Federal Registration of Flavors as Trademarks for Pharmaceuticals*, 1993 U. Ill. L. Rev. 105; Amanda E. Compton, *Acquiring a Flavor for Trademarks: There's No Common Taste in the World*, 8 Nw. J. Tech. & Intell. Prop. 340 (2010); John T. Cross, *Trademark Issues Relating to Digitalized Flavor*, 19 Yale J. L. & Tech. 339 (2017).

clothing. The USPTO will usually refuse registration of these types of signs on the ground that they are merely ornamental or informational matter that fails to function as a mark.[83] On the other hand, if the trademark applicant submits a specimen showing use of the design or words only in a source-identifying manner – such as the Nike swoosh or "Nike" printed on a hangtag or label for clothing – the USPTO will probably conclude that sign functions as a mark for a particular product in that context.[84]

Failure-to-function doctrine is different than the distinctiveness requirement because a phrase, design, or décor may be classified as inherently distinctive when used in connection with certain products, but this sign may still not function as a trademark that identifies and distinguishes the source of goods or services.[85] An example can clarify this. Despite finding the exterior building design of the Rock and Roll Hall of Fame and Museum to be unique, a US appellate court refused to protect common law trademark rights in this design because this subject matter was not used as a mark to identify the source of museum services and it was not perceived as a mark by consumers.[86] If a trademark office or court determines that a certain phrase or trade dress has acquired distinctiveness, that sign also likely functions as a mark. But if the evidence indicates only that consumers associate this term, color, or other product feature with the party claiming trademark rights, and do not perceive it as a source-identifying mark, this matter may fail to function as a trademark.[87]

Failure-to-function doctrine also differs from trademark laws requiring use of a mark in commerce in connection with goods or services. A term, symbol, or product feature may be used by a company in the ordinary course of trade when it advertises and sells its products, and thus satisfy the "use in commerce" requirement for registration in the United States, but still fail to function as a "trademark" or "service mark" because this sign was not used to identify and distinguish the goods or services of the alleged trademark owner or indicate the product's source.[88] Examples include use of a phrase in a descriptive or informational manner in an advertisement for services rendered in commerce (such as "Our Lawyers are Doctors" for legal services) or on the packaging of products sold in commerce (such as "Farm to Table" for wine).

Consumers may be more likely to perceive a product feature as a trademark if they are instructed to "look for" the company's distinctive color or shape, "listen for" its particular sound, or "smell for" its specific scent in the marketplace to identify the product's source. Regardless of whether such advertising is successful, that product feature still cannot be registered or protected under trademark law in the United States if it is functional (or in Singapore if it is a functional product shape).[89] Moreover, a product feature is more likely to fail to function as a mark and be deemed functional under trademark law if the seller's advertising touts that feature as useful or appealing to consumers (such as by noting the pleasant orange taste of a medicine).[90]

83 TMEP, *supra* note 34, §§ 1202.03–1202.04(d), 1202.17(c)(i)(A), 1202.17(e)(ii).

84 For a detailed discussion about failure-to-function doctrine, *see generally* Alexandra J. Roberts, *Trademark Failure to Function*, 104 Iowa L. Rev. 1977 (2019); Lisa P. Ramsey, *Using Failure to Function Doctrine to Protect Free Speech and Competition in Trademark Law*, 104 Iowa L. Rev. Online 70 (2020).

85 *Id.*

86 *Rock & Roll Hall of Fame and Museum, Inc.* v. *Gentile Productions*, 134 F.3d 749, 753–56 (6th Cir. 1998).

87 TMEP, *supra* note 34, at § 1202 (stating that "not everything that is recognized or associated with a party is necessarily a registrable trademark").

88 15 USC § 1127 (2012) (definition of "use in commerce," "trademark," and "service mark"). *See* Ramsey, *supra* note 84, at 85–86.

89 *See supra* Section II.D; Ramsey, *supra* note 84, at 80–81, 99–100.

90 *In re* N.V. *Organon*, 79 USPQ 2d (BNA) 1639 (TTAB 2006).

A sign must also be used or perceived as a mark to maintain a registration in Singapore. For example, the Singapore High Court found that a company's use of the word "LOVE" in a decorative manner on jewelry was insufficient to constitute "genuine use in the course of trade" of its registered LOVE mark as required by Sections 22(1)(a) and 22(1)(b) of Singapore's Trade Marks Act "because consumers were unlikely to perceive the decorative 'LOVE' mark as a trade mark."[91] A similar legal analysis was used by the Singapore Court of Appeal when it determined that the registrations for the shape of Kit Kat chocolate bars should be revoked on the basis that the shapes were not put to "genuine use" as a mark or "badge of origin."[92] The court evaluated the nature of the company's use of the mark along with other evidence relating to use, and noted the products with the registered shapes were not visible through the opaque packaging and the words "Kit Kat" were displayed prominently on the candy and its packaging.[93] The court found "that the manner in which the Registered Shapes were used would have led consumers to believe that these shapes were mere manifestations of Kit Kat chocolate bars rather than indicators of origin."[94] Per the court, the "genuine use" requirement in the Trade Marks Act "should be construed as trade mark use" because a mark serves to indicate a product's source, registration facilitates this function and provides notice of trademark rights, and allowing trademarks not in bona fide use as marks to remain on the register would be deceptive and could harm competition.[95]

When a trademark office or court determines that a certain type of trade dress is perceived as a product attribute rather than a source identifier, this conclusion may be made based on a consumer survey or other evidence about how the sign functions in the marketplace. Yet it may also be based on a general concern about the potential harm to competition and freedom of expression if trademark rights are granted to these types of marks, as discussed later in Section III.B.

III THE ADVANTAGES AND DISADVANTAGES OF FLEXIBILITY IN WHAT SIGNS CAN QUALIFY AS PROTECTABLE TRADEMARK SUBJECT MATTER

A *Advantages of Flexibility: Eligibility for Exclusive Trademark Rights in Almost Anything that is Capable of Distinguishing a Product's Source*

If a sign is distinctive and complies with other requirements of the trademark laws in Australia, New Zealand, Singapore, or the United States, that mark will be eligible for registration and protection against infringement and other trademark violations.[96] Flexibility in what signs can be registered or protected as a mark can benefit companies that use new methods to distinguish themselves in a crowded market.[97] A business may do a better job attracting and retaining

[91] *Love & Co. Pte Ltd* v. *The Carat Club Pte Ltd* [2009] 1 SLR(R) 561 at [122].

[92] *Société des Produits Nestlé SA* v. *Petra Foods Ltd.* [2017] 1 SLR 35 at [116–25].

[93] *Id.* at [122–23].

[94] *Id.* at [124].

[95] *Id.* at [119].

[96] Burrell & Handler, *supra* note 5, at 367–504 (Austl.); Frankel, *supra* note 5, at 559–72 (NZ); McCarthy, *supra* note 5, at 23:1–25:25 (US); 1 Tan, *supra* note 5, at 587–725 (Sing.); 2 Tan, *supra* note 5, at 83–237 (Sing.).

[97] *See, e.g.*, Thomas P. Arden, Protection of Nontraditional Marks: Trademark Rights in Sounds, Scents, Colors, Motions and Product Designs in the U.S. (2000); Anne Gilson LaLonde & Jerome Gilson, *Getting Real with Nontraditional Trademarks: What's Next after Red Oven Knobs, the Sound of Burning Methamphetamine, and Goats on a Grass Roof?*, 101 Trademark Rep. 186 (2011); Jerome Gilson & Anne Gilson LaLonde, *Cinnamon Buns, Marching Ducks and Cherry-Scented Racecar Exhaust: Protecting Nontraditional Trademarks*, 95 Trademark Rep. 773 (2005).

customers if its branding efforts incorporate more than one of the five human senses of sight, sound, smell, taste, and touch.[98] Even if the public is currently more likely to perceive this non-verbal or non-visual subject matter as a mere attribute of the goods or services rather than as a mark, this may change if companies educate consumers about the source-identifying information provided by their non-traditional marks.[99] Moreover, consumers who are blind or visually impaired may benefit if trademark protection of non-visual marks encourages more brands to use three-dimensional shapes, sounds, scents, or textures to identify and distinguish their products in the marketplace.[100]

Thus, in jurisdictions where almost anything capable of carrying source-distinguishing meaning is eligible for registration and protection as a mark, an attorney may reasonably suggest to a client that it consider applying to register all potentially distinctive features of its goods, services, packaging, point-of purchase displays, and store or website designs. It does not matter whether the client originally intended to use this feature to convey source-identifying information, or if this type of subject matter claimed as a mark is listed in the trademark statute. All that matters at the time of the application is whether this sign is capable of becoming distinctive and complies with the other requirements in the law. It is not unreasonable to apply to register everything that could qualify as a mark if the client can afford the attorney and filing fees.

If there is no limit on what signs can qualify as a mark, trademark attorneys will likely do their best to expand the list of what may constitute protectable trademark subject matter to obtain a beneficial result for their clients. Registration will provide clients with an exclusive right to use this subject matter in connection with certain goods or services and it can be used to block the registration by competitors of identical or confusingly similar marks. The registration may also discourage others (including non-competitors) from using a communicative symbol or product feature that is identical or similar to the client's mark. For example, a trademark registration for a particular three-dimensional shape may encourage third parties to not use a three- or two-dimensional version of that exact shape and different variations of that shape. Moreover, since registration is not required for trademark protection and almost anything is eligible for protection as a mark, demand letters and complaints alleging common law trademark rights in non-traditional subject matter not listed in the trademark statute must be taken seriously by anyone accused of trademark violations. This flexibility in what types of subject matter can qualify as a trademark benefits owners of those marks, but it may not promote competition or free expression, as discussed next.

B Disadvantages of Flexibility: Potential Harm to Competition and Free Expression

As discussed elsewhere, current trademark laws harm competition and free expression when they do not give adequate notice of what unauthorized uses of registered language or product features are allowed or prohibited.[101] Thus, a significant problem with allowing flexibility in what subject matter can qualify as a mark is that it can exacerbate the chilling effect of trademark laws which

[98] *See, e.g.*, Martin Lindstrom, Brand Sense: Build Powerful Brands Through Touch, Taste, Smell, Sight, and Sound (2005).

[99] Calboli & Senftleben, *supra* note 7, at 3.

[100] Professor Johnson argues that courts should use a disability perspective in trademark law, but concludes that trademark protection for three-dimensional models of airplanes, cars, and other vehicles could increase prices for these products and thereby disadvantage visually disabled people who use the models for information. Eric E. Johnson, *Intellectual Property's Need for a Disability Perspective*, 20 Geo. Mason U. Civ. Rts. L.J. 181, 204–06 (2010).

[101] Ramsey, *supra* note 13, at 338–39, 352–57; Ramsey, *supra* note 11, at 460–61; Ramsey, *supra* note 59, at 836–44; Lisa P. Ramsey, *Increasing First Amendment Scrutiny of Trademark Law*, 61 SMU L. Rev. 381, 414–57 (2008).

are already vague and broad in scope.[102] Aggressive demand letters or complaints by companies claiming trademark rights in common law marks may encourage small businesses and individuals accused of trademark violations to settle before a trademark office or court can determine if that alleged mark is actually protectable trademark subject matter and complies with all of the requirements for registration or protection. Increasing predictability regarding the types of signs that can qualify as marks and excluding certain types of subject matter from protection by trademark law may better promote fair competition and trademark law's other important goals than solely relying on the distinctiveness requirement and other trademark doctrines currently in the laws of Australia, New Zealand, Singapore, and the United States.

Not only is it unclear whether certain subject matter can qualify as a trademark when it is not explicitly listed in the statutory definition of a sign or mark, but it may also be challenging for trademark litigants to determine the boundaries of non-verbal or non-visual marks that are registered. If the trademark owner provided an accurate description or drawing of the mark in its trademark application, this can convey useful information about the content and scope of the mark and warn competitors that this mark is not available for use. Words, names, logos, and other "traditional" marks can easily satisfy this notice requirement, but it may be more difficult to precisely describe sounds, scents, flavors, and other non-traditional marks.[103] The trademark office may only have a graphic representation of a sound mark on file (instead of an audio reproduction), and certain written descriptions of a sound mark may encompass a range of sounds. For scent or flavor marks, applicants may attempt to describe them using words (such as "freshly cut grass" or "orange") or a chemical formula, but this verbal disclosure may not accurately provide information about the mark's strength or other qualities. Submitting a physical sample of the scent or flavor mark may provide more clarity with regard to the contours of the mark, but not everyone interested in the registration will have easy access to that sample. Moreover, the sample's scent or flavor may degrade or otherwise change over time and thereby no longer provide accurate information about the mark used by the trademark owner to identify and distinguish its goods or services.

If the precise contours of a mark are unclear, competitors and other traders may assume that mark has a broader scope and avoid using marks that are only distantly similar to the mark actually used by the registrant. Thus trademark rights in certain non-traditional trademark subject matter may in effect be broader than rights in word marks and other traditional marks. There is always a chance the party claiming infringement owns a very broad scope of rights in a non-traditional mark since (1) the right of trademark exclusivity extends to marks which are identical *or* similar to the mark – identity of the parties' marks is not required – and (2) courts and juries may deem the mark to encompass a larger range of subject matter than what is actually used by the trademark owner since the registration may not provide clear notice of the boundaries of the mark.[104] Of course there is also uncertainty with regard to the scope of trademark rights for signs consisting of words, but we can clearly identify the exact contours of the word NIKE and we are more familiar with how that type of subject matter conveys source-identifying meaning and non-trademark messages.

[102] *Id. See also* BURRELL & HANDLER, *supra* note 5, at 67–71 (noting the expansion on what can qualify as a mark may harm competition and cause other problems); 1 TAN, *supra* note 5, at 51–54 (discussing the disadvantages of extending the scope of registrable marks to non-traditional marks).

[103] FRANKEL, *supra* note 5, at 502–04; McGrath, *supra* note 7, at 307–13.

[104] Jeanne C. Fromer & Mark P. McKenna, *Claiming Design*, 167 U. PA. L. REV. 123, 146–60 (2018); Mark A. Lemley & Mark P. McKenna, *Scope*, 57 WM. & MARY L. REV. 2197, 2243–59 (2016).

Another point to consider is that identity of the parties' goods or services is also not required for a finding of infringement or other trademark violations. Thus if a company owns a registration for a particular shape for certain goods or services, its trademark rights may extend not only to different variations of the shape used by that company but also to products different than the goods or services listed in the registration or used by the trademark owner. For example, Globefill Inc. recently accused a British couple of trademark infringement when they sold their "Bloody Hell Hot Sauce" brand of hot sauce in a bottle that was similar to the company's registered skull shape used in connection with Crystal Head Vodka.[105] Per the Bloody Hell Hot Sauce website, the hot sauce company is no longer using its skull-shaped bottle design and online purchases were temporarily put on hold in December 2018 because the company was working on the design of its new bottle.[106]

An additional challenge for companies accused of trademark violations in the United States is that the infringement statutes do not explicitly require commercial use of the mark, and neither infringement nor dilution laws require the defendant's use of the mark to be misleading for liability.[107] Moreover, in Australia, New Zealand, and Singapore, a trademark owner can establish infringement without proving that this unauthorized use of its mark is likely to cause confusion in cases of "double identity," where the parties' marks and products are identical.[108] Thus governments cannot justify trademark laws allowing registration and protection of "any sign" capable of becoming distinctive on the basis that these laws only regulate misleading commercial expression.[109]

Existing statutory defenses such as descriptive or nominative fair use do exclude certain beneficial uses of language from trademark protection.[110] In addition, the requirement that another's mark be used as a mark for infringement liability in Australia and New Zealand limits the scope of trademark rights in ways that promote competition and freedom of expression.[111] But these defensive doctrines are primarily useful in disputes involving word marks and are not sufficient to prevent the scope of trademark rights in non-traditional marks from expanding broadly in an anti-competitive manner.

In the United States, there is no trademark use requirement in the infringement statute and no statutory defense for fair use by the defendant of another's registered shape, color, or other product feature in a functional, ornamental, or informational manner. The functionality provision only applies if the plaintiff's mark is functional, and the parties may be selling different goods or services.[112] Failure-to-function doctrine also focuses on the validity of the plaintiff's mark and may not help accused infringers who are using the sign claimed as a mark in a different manner. A trademark applicant may be able to overcome a failure-to-function rejection

[105] Telegraph Reporters, *Dan Ackroyd Threatens to Sue Isle of Wight Hot Sauce Company after Business Pitch Goes Horribly Wrong*, The Telegraph (July 21, 2017 3:03 PM), https://www.telegraph.co.uk/news/2017/07/21/dan-ackroyd-threatens-sueisle-white-hot-sauce-company-business/.

[106] Bloody Hell Hot Sauce, https://www.bloodyhellhotsauce.com/ (screenshot dated Dec. 21, 2018, on file with author).

[107] 15 USC §§ 1114(1), 1125(a)(1)(A), 1125(c) (2012). Infringement laws in the United States only require a likelihood of confusion, and dilution laws apply regardless of whether there is any actual or likely confusion. *Id.*

[108] *Trade Marks Act* 1995 (Cth) § 120(1) (Austl.); Trade Marks Act 2002, § 89(1)(a) (NZ); Trade Marks Act (Cap 332, 2005 rev. ed.) § 27(1) (Sing.).

[109] Ramsey, *supra* note 13, at 338, 343, 354; Ramsey, *supra* note 11, at 407, 429–31, 434–39; Ramsey, *supra* note 59, at 832–45, 873–75; Ramsey, *supra* note 101, at 395–98.

[110] *See, e.g.*, 15 USC §§ 1115(b)(4), 1125(c)(3)(A). *See* Ramsey, *supra* note 13, at 350–51, 356; Ramsey, *supra* note 11, at 468; Ramsey, *supra* note 59, at 839–43.

[111] *Trade Marks Act* 1995 (Cth) § 120 (Austl.); Trade Marks Act 2002, § 89(2) (NZ).

[112] 15 USC § 1052(e)(5); Ramsey, *supra* note 13, at 356–57.

and register its mark by submitting a new specimen showing its source-identifying use of the mark in a manner that is not ornamental or informational. Yet when a competitor uses this same sign only in an ornamental or informational way, the trademark owner may still sue for trademark violations and claim this use of the mark is infringing. The registrant may also submit notice-and-takedown requests to online service providers such as Amazon, Redbubble, Etsy, or CafePress, and demand removal of products that display the registered mark in a non-trademark manner.[113]

Thus not only is it sometimes difficult to determine whether subject matter claimed as a mark is actually protected under a nation's trademark law, but additional uncertainty may be created by the fact that the exact contours of a non-traditional mark are unclear and the scope of rights can extend to marks that are distantly similar, to dissimilar goods or services, and to uses of marks which are non-commercial, not misleading, or used otherwise than as a mark. All of this may lead some accused infringers to settle and self-censor their expression once they receive a demand letter or complaint alleging trademark violations.[114] Of course, they can always argue in litigation that the plaintiff's mark is invalid (because it lacks distinctiveness, is functional, or fails to function as a mark), this unauthorized use of the mark is not infringing or diluting, or a statutory or common law defense applies. But small businesses and individuals may not be able to afford to litigate to a successful result in a trademark dispute and fight for their right to use non-source-identifying product features or other communicative symbols claimed as a mark by another. Such a result is bad for competition and freedom of commercial expression, as it reduces the number of competing products with useful or desirable features in the marketplace.

Trademark laws can promote competition and expressive values by requiring all signs to be distinctive, non-functional, and used as a mark before they are registered and protected. Yet also categorically excluding certain types of subject matter from registration and common law trademark protection may better serve these goals.[115] Product features and other non-traditional marks are often deemed to be weak marks and usually require proof of acquired distinctiveness through use for registration. Consumer surveys and large amounts of money spent on advertising can help prove a color, shape, sound, or scent has acquired distinctiveness, but obtaining such evidence may not be within the budget of a small company. Focusing on the distinctiveness of a mark instead of categorically denying registration to certain types of marks will generally favor larger companies with higher sales volumes and advertising expenditures and may harm competition by disadvantaging start-up companies and individuals. Moreover, our current trademark system encourages trademark owners to police weak marks against unauthorized use by others, as third-party use of the same mark can count against a finding of acquired distinctiveness. Such enforcement efforts can stifle competition and non-misleading expression.

If certain types of non-traditional marks are usually rejected for registration on the grounds of lack of distinctiveness, functionality, or failure to function as a mark, it may better promote

[113] *See* Steve Brachmann, *Taking on Trademark Trolls and Frivolous Marks, Trademark Watch Dawgs Wades into Divisive Waters*, IP WATCH DOG (Apr. 11, 2019), https://www.ipwatchdog.com/2019/04/11/trademark-watch-dawgs-wades-into-divisive-waters-trademark-trolls/id=108151/.

[114] *See generally* James Gibson, *Risk Aversion and Rights Accretion in Intellectual Property Law*, 116 YALE L.J. 882, 907–27 (2007); Leah Chan Grinvald, *Policing the Cease-and-Desist Letter*, 49 U.S.F. L. REV. 411 (2015); Leah Chan Grinvald, *Shaming Trademark Bullies*, 2011 WIS. L. REV. 625; William McGeveran, *Rethinking Trademark Fair Use*, 94 IOWA L. REV. 49 (2008); Kenneth L. Port, *Trademark Extortion: The End of Trademark Law*, 65 WASH & LEE L. REV. 585 (2008).

[115] *See* Caitlin Canahai & Mark P. McKenna, *The Case against Product Configuration Trade Dress*, in TRADEMARK LAW AND THEORY: REFORM OF TRADEMARK LAW (Graeme Dinwoodie & Mark Janis eds., in press 2020), https://ssrn.com/abstract=3336366; Ramsey, *supra* note 13, at 358; Ramsey, *supra* note 11, at 461–69.

competition and be more efficient to categorically deny registration and common law trademark protection to this type of subject matter.[116] Critics of this proposal will note that TRIPS Article 15(1) provides that "any sign" that is "capable of distinguishing the goods or services" of traders "shall be capable of constituting a trademark" and such signs "shall be eligible for registration as trademarks." Yet WTO members could argue that certain categories of subject matter are simply *not* capable of distinguishing goods or services. If certain signs are incapable of ever becoming distinctive because of their inherent nature, then TRIPS does not require them to be capable of constituting a trademark and they need not be eligible for registration. Unless this type of mark is explicitly listed in Article 15(1), such as a combination of colors, WTO members could argue that they have discretion to determine as a matter of law what subject matter can qualify as a sign that is capable of distinguishing goods or services.[117] Arguably the language in Article 15(1) is ambiguous, and this narrow interpretation of the text is consistent with those nations' international obligations under TRIPS because deeming certain signs to be incapable of distinguishing goods or services protects the right to freedom of expression and promotes fair competition.[118] In the United States, functional product features and generic terms are not registered or protected under trademark law regardless of whether they have acquired distinctiveness, so perhaps a similar approach could be used for certain types of subject matter that should remain in the public domain for use by all traders in the marketplace.

IV CONCLUSION

The requirements for trademark registration in Australia, New Zealand, Singapore, and the United States diverge in some ways, but one common feature of these trademark laws is flexibility in what signs are eligible for registration and protection. Trademark offices and judges may not have sufficient information to determine whether a particular expansion of law relating to what qualifies as protectable trademark subject matter is justified and furthers trademark law's goals. Legislatures are in a better position to evaluate the advantages and disadvantages of recognizing new types of subject matter that should be eligible for registration and protection. They should consider revising their trademark laws to increase predictability in what types of signs can qualify as marks, exclude certain signs that usually fail to function as marks from eligibility for registration and protection, and make other changes to their laws that better protect competition and freedom of expression.

116 Ramsey, *supra* note 13, at 352–61; Ramsey, *supra* note 11, at 447–53, 461–69.

117 *Cf.* Ng-Loy Wee Loon, *Absolute Bans on the Registration of Product Shape Marks*, in NON-TRADITIONAL TRADEMARKS, *supra* note 2, at 147–64 (arguing that nations have discretion under TRIPS to exclude functional product shapes from registration regardless of whether they have acquired distinctiveness).

118 *Cf.* Lisa P. Ramsey, *Free Speech and International Obligations to Protect Trademarks*, 35 YALE J. INT'L L. 405, 459–67 (2010) (discussing how WTO members can protect the right to freedom of expression in trademark laws without violating their international obligations to protect trademarks).

12

Signs Eligible for Trademark Protection in the European Union

Dysfunctional Incentives and a Functionality Dilemma

*Martin Senftleben**

I INTRODUCTION

In the European Union, the criteria for determining a sign's eligibility for trademark protection are largely harmonized.[1] On one hand, the trademark legislation and office practices in EU member states must keep within the harmonized legal framework set forth in the EU Trade Mark Directive (TMD).[2] On the other hand, the European Union Trade Mark Regulation (EUTMR)[3] provides for a set of eligibility criteria applying to European Union trademarks (EUTM) with equal effect throughout the EU territory.[4] As the rules in the Regulation are in line with those in the Directive, the two legislative instruments constitute a robust body of harmonized norms informing the decision on the registration of a sign as a trademark. The harmonizing effect is enhanced by the fact that national courts must refer questions relating to the application and interpretation of eligibility criteria to the Court of Justice of the European Union (CJEU).[5]

As in other regions of the world,[6] the criteria applied to determine eligibility for trademark protection are quite flexible in the EU:

* Professor of Intellectual Property Law and Director, Institute for Information Law (IViR), University of Amsterdam.

[1] See the discussion of regional harmonization of trademark law by Irene Calboli and Coenraad Visser in Chapter 6 in this volume.

[2] Directive 2015/2436 of the European Parliament and of the Council of Dec. 16, 2015, to approximate the laws of the member states relating to trademarks, 2015 OJ 2015 (L 336) 1 (EU).

[3] Regulation 2017/1001 of the European Parliament and of the Council of June 14, 2017, on the European Union Trade Mark (codification), 2017 OJ (L 154) 1 (EU).

[4] EUTMs are registered at the European Union Intellectual Property Office (EUIPO, the former Office for Harmonization in the Internal Market (OHIM)). The application of eligibility criteria is thus in the hands of one central institution at the application stage.

[5] With regard to the impact of the CJEU on the harmonization of intellectual property law in the EU, *see* Vincent Cassiers & Alain Strowel, *Intellectual Property Law Made by the Court of Justice of the European Union, in* Christophe Geiger, Craig Nard, & Xavier Seuba, eds., Intellectual Property and the Judiciary 175, 176–83 (2018); Martin Senftleben, *The Perfect Match – Civil Law Judges and Open-Ended Fair Use Provisions*, 33 Am. Univ. Int'l L. Rev. 1 (2017). *See also* Karen Alter & Laurence Helfer, *Nature or Nurture? Judicial Lawmaking in the European Court of Justice and the Andean Tribunal of Justice*, Int'l Org. at 563 (2010).

[6] As to examples of common law trademark systems, *see* Lisa Ramsey, Chapter 11 in this volume. For a broader overview of the approaches taken in the different regions of the world, *see* the contributions to *Study on Misappropriation of Signs* (Martin Senftleben ed.), WIPO Document CDIP/9/INF/5, dated Mar. 14, 2012, http://wipo.int/edocs/mdocs/mdocs/en/cdip_9/cdip_9_inf_5.pdf.

> A trade mark may consist of any signs, in particular words, including personal names, or designs, letters, numerals, colours, the shape of goods or of the packaging of goods, or sounds, provided that such signs are capable of:
>
> (a) distinguishing the goods or services of one undertaking from those of other undertakings; and
>
> (b) being represented on the register in a manner which enables the competent authorities and the public to determine the clear and precise subject matter of the protection afforded to its proprietor.[7]

This definition leaves room for the extension of trademark protection to non-traditional types of marks. Shape, sound and color marks are explicitly mentioned in the provision. Moreover, the enumeration of different types of signs predominantly serves illustrative purposes. As the words "in particular" indicate, the list does not constitute a closed catalogue. In principle, "any signs" that are distinctive and can be represented adequately on the register are eligible for trademark protection in the EU.[8] Under this elastic standard, trademark offices applying EU trademark law have accepted, for instance, abstract colors[9] and color combinations,[10] motion and multimedia marks,[11] melodies and sounds,[12] taste marks,[13] hologram marks[14] and position marks.[15]

The following analysis of the trend to register non-traditional marks in the EU outlines the legal framework the CJEU developed to assess the eligibility of non-traditional types of source identifiers for trademark protection (following Section II). Sections III–VI discuss the objective to safeguard freedom of competition and the legal instruments the CJEU employs for this purpose: the requirement of providing evidence of the acquisition of distinctive character through use in trade, as well as the categorical exclusion of functional signs from trademark protection. In conclusion, it will become apparent that the basic requirement of distinctive

7 First Council Directive 89/104, of the European Parliament and of the Council of Dec. 21, 1988 to Approximate the Laws of the Member States Relating to Trade Marks, 1989 OJ (L 040) 1 (EEC), *repealed by* Directive 2008/95, of the European Parliament and of the Council of Oct. 22, 2008 to Approximate the Laws of the Member States Relating to Trademarks, 2008 OJ (L 299) 25 (EC), art. 3 [hereinafter TMD]; Trademark Regulation of 2017: Regulation (EU) 2017/1001 of the European Parliament and of the Council of June 14, 2017 on the EU trademark, 2017 OJ L 154/1 (EC) [hereinafter EUTMR].

8 As to the discussion about the recognition of non-traditional marks in the EU, *see* Ivo Lewalter and Paul T. Schrader, *Die Fühlmarke*, Gewerblicher Rechtsschutz und Urheberrecht 476 (2005); Felix Hauck, *Aktuelle Entwicklungen bei der Eintragung von Farbmarken*, Gewerblicher Rechtsschutz und Urheberrecht 363 (2005); Annette Kur, *Alles oder Nichts im Formmarkenschutz?*, Gewerblicher Rechtsschutz und Urheberrecht – International Teil 755 (2004); Adrien Bouvel, *QuImporte le Flacon ... Le Droit des Marques Malmené par les Emballages*, Propriétés Intellectuelles 863 (2004); Ruth Arnet, *Markenschutz für Formen*, sic! 829 (2004); Jochen Pagenberg, *Trade Dress and the Three-Dimensional Marks – The Neglected Children of Trademark Law?*, 35 Int'l Rev. Intell. Prop. Competition L. 7 (2004); M. Bölling, *Der EuGH und die abstrakte Farbmarke – Von der bewussten Entwertung einer Markenform*, Markenrecht 384 (2004); S. Bingener, *Das Wesen der Positionsmarke oder Wo die Positionsmarke hingehört*, Markenrecht 377 (2004); Alison Firth, Ellen Gredley, & Spyros Maniatis, *Shapes as Trade Marks: Public Policy, Functional Considerations and Consumer Perception*, 23 European Intel. Prop. Rev. 2 (2001).

9 EUTM Registration No. 000031336 (Milka lilac); EUTM Registration No. 000212787 (Deutsche Telekom magenta); EUTM Registration No. 000962076 (UPS brown). *Cf.* Case C-104/01, *Libertel Groep BV* v. *Benelux Merkenbureau*, (2004) ECR I-3793, § 68.

10 Case C-49/02, Heidelberger Bauchemie Trademark Application, (2004) ECR I-6152, § 35; Joined Cases T-101/15 and T-102/15, *Red Bull* v. *EUIPO-Optimum Mark*, (2017) §§ 3, 12.

11 EUTM Registration Nos. 3429909, 017279712, 017279704, 017350901; Finland Registration No. 229446.

12 Norway Registration No. 226092. *Cf.* Case C-283/01, *Shield Mark BV* v. *Joost Kist h.o.d.n. MEMEX*, (2003) ECR I-14313 § 62.

13 Benelux Registration No. 625971 accompanied by the description "The TM consists of the taste of liquorice applied to goods in class 16."

14 EUTM Registration No. 017579491.

15 Germany Registration No. 302010059754 (Steiff button in ear); Germany Registration No. 30142541, 39504594; Italy Registration No. 00011748533 (Lloyd Shoes red stripe).

character plays an ambiguous role in the regulation of access to trademark protection for non-traditional marks. It is both an obstacle to trademark protection and an incentive for enhanced investment in non-traditional types of marks (Section VII).

II REFINEMENT OF REGISTRATION REQUIREMENTS IN CJEU JURISPRUDENCE

As harmonized EU trademark law explicitly offers room for the registration of non-traditional marks, the CJEU had the opportunity to clarify the statutory registration requirements and delineate the range of signs eligible for protection. The situation in the field of color marks can serve as an example. In *Libertel*, the Court held that color per se may constitute a trademark. At the time of the decision, EU legislation required trademarks to be represented "graphically" on the register.[16] According to the Court, the requirement of graphical representation could be satisfied in the case of an abstract color by indicating an international color identification code.[17] As a result of the 2015 EU trademark law reform, the focus on graphical representation was abandoned[18] in favor of the more elastic requirement that the mark be capable of being represented in a manner enabling the competent authorities and the public to determine "the clear and precise subject matter of the protection afforded to its proprietor."[19] More specifically, current EU legislation allows trademark applicants to represent the mark in any appropriate form using generally available technology – not necessarily graphic means – as long as the representation is "clear, precise, self-contained, easily accessible, intelligible, durable and objective."[20] The latter list of requirements stems from the *Sieckmann* decision, where the CJEU adopted these general criteria for assessing a sign's representation for registration purposes.[21]

The legislative change – from graphical representation to more open-ended criteria of clear and precise representation – does not affect the general acceptance of abstract color marks in the EU. However, it may lead to stricter representation requirements pertaining to color combinations. In *Red Bull/EUIPO (Optimum Mark)*, the CJEU decided on the compliance of Red Bull's representation of a blue and silver color combination with the requirement of sufficient clarity and precision. The question arose because Red Bull had only specified that the ratio of the colors (accompanied by relevant color codes) was "approximately 50%–50%" and the colors would be applied "in equal proportion and juxtaposed to each other."[22] Discussing these indications, the CJEU recalled the landmark decision *Heidelberger Bauchemie*, where it had established that in the case of a mark combining colors per se, those colors had to be represented "in accordance with a specific arrangement or layout, associating the colours in a predetermined and uniform way, in order to prevent numerous different combinations of those colours which would not permit the consumer to perceive and recall a particular combination."[23]

[16] The decision was based on Directive 89/104 of the First Trademark Harmonization of Dec. 21, 1988, to approximate the laws of the member states relating to trademarks, art. 2 1989 OJ (L 40) 1 (EEC), which provided as follows: "A trade mark may consist of any sign *capable of being represented graphically*, particularly words, including personal names, designs, letters, numerals, the shape of goods or of their packaging, provided that such signs are capable of distinguishing the goods or services of one undertaking from those of other undertakings" (emphasis added).

[17] Case C-104/01, *Libertel Groep BV* v. *Benelux Merkenbureau*, § 68.

[18] As to this change of the representation requirement, see ANNETTE KUR & MARTIN SENFTLEBEN, EUROPEAN TRADEMARK LAW – A COMMENTARY, § 4.05 (2017).

[19] EUTMR, *supra* note 7, art. 4(b); TMD, *supra* note 7, art. 3(b).

[20] EUTMR, *supra* note 7, recital 10; TMD, *supra* note 7, recital 13.

[21] Case C-273/00, *Ralf Sieckmann* v. *Deutsches Patent- und Markenamt*, (2002) ECR I-11737, §55.

[22] Case C-124/18P, *Red Bull* v. *EUIPO (Optimum Mark)*, §§ 10, 39–41.

[23] *Id.* at § 38, referring to Case C-49/02, *Heidelberger Bauchemie GmbH*, § 35.

On this basis, the CJEU found that the mere indication of the ratio of the two colors blue and silver allowed for the arrangement of those colors in numerous different combinations and failed to constitute a systematic arrangement associating the colors in a predetermined and uniform way. By contrast, the indications given by Red Bull could lead to different forms of use producing very different overall impressions. Referring to the first instance findings of the General Court of the European Union (GCEU), the CJEU pointed out that the word "approximately" allowed for different arrangements of the colors at issue. The juxtaposition of the colors could take different forms, "giving rise to different images or layouts, while still being in equal proportion."[24] Therefore, the graphic representation at issue, accompanied by a description indicating only the proportions of the two colors, could not be considered sufficiently precise. Red Bull's color combination marks were thus invalid.[25]

Even though the case concerned the previous requirement of graphical representation, the GCEU had seized the opportunity in its first instance decision to comment on the impact of the current requirement of a sufficiently clear and precise representation. In the framework of the proceedings, the argument had been made that the new formula of a representation enabling "the competent authorities and the public to determine the clear and precise subject matter of the protection afforded to its proprietor"[26] indicated a relaxation of the representation requirement in EU trademark law.[27] Rebutting this argument, the GCEU had pointed out that the new wording was intended to reinforce legal certainty and could be deemed more restrictive than the previous graphical representation requirement, insofar as it expressly incorporated the objectives which the CJEU had identified in its decisions in *Sieckmann* and *Heidelberger Bauchemie*.[28] According to the GCEU, it was neither impossible nor disproportionate to require an applicant to provide a clear and precise indication of the systematic spatial arrangement of colors constituting a color combination mark.[29] As explained, the final decision of the CJEU confirms this position.[30]

As to sound marks, the CJEU pointed out in *Shield Mark* that a trademark may also consist of a sign which is not in itself capable of being perceived visually. Sound signs meeting the general protection requirements could constitute trademarks. For a melody, musical notation was sufficient to represent the sign on the register.[31] As the new legislation no longer requires graphical representation, other modes of representation also enter the picture. Arguably, a sound file is even clearer and more precise, easily accessible and intelligible than musical notation.[32]

These decisions show that the CJEU has developed a nuanced approach to the subject matter of trademark protection. In any case, smell remains outside the scope of EU trademark law. In *Sieckmann*, the CJEU held that, for olfactory signs, neither a chemical formula nor a description or smell specimen (or any combination of these means of representation) were sufficient to provide a clear and precise representation of the sign for trademark registration purposes.[33]

[24] *Id.* at §§ 43–45.
[25] *Id.* at § 47.
[26] EUTMR *supra* note 7, art. 4(b); TMD *supra* note 7, art. 3(b).
[27] Joined Cases T-101/15 and T-102/15, *Red Bull* v. *EUIPO(Optimum Mark)*, § 117.
[28] *Id.* at §118.
[29] *Id.* at § 119.
[30] Case C-124/18P, *Red Bull* v. *EUIPO (Optimum Mark)*, §§ 46–48.
[31] Case C-283/01, *Shield Mark BV* v. *Joost Kist h.o.d.n. MEMEX*, § 62.
[32] *Cf.* Kur & Senftleben, *supra* note 18, §§ 4.27–4.29.
[33] Case C-273/00, *Ralf Sieckmann* v. *Deutsches Patent- und Markenamt*, § 73.

III NEED TO KEEP FREE AS A COUNTERWEIGHT

As the described CJEU decisions already indicate, the general recognition of non-traditional types of marks in the EU does not mean that signs in a non-traditional category will automatically find their way into trademark registers on the continent. In addition to the requirement of a clear and precise representation, absolute grounds for refusal in EU trademark law can pose substantial obstacles. Besides the functionality doctrine,[34] the basic requirement of distinctive character plays a crucial role. Signs devoid of distinctive character, descriptive signs that indicate characteristics of goods or services, and signs that have become customary in the current language or established trade practices are not eligible for trademark protection.[35] It should be noted, however, that the exclusionary effect of these grounds for refusal is different. Whereas a finding of functionality cannot be overcome by demonstrating that distinctive character has been acquired as a result of use in trade, the absolute grounds for refusal based on a lack of distinctiveness, descriptiveness or genericness no longer apply when distinctive character has been obtained through use in trade.[36]

Regardless of the different configuration of the exclusionary effect, the functionality doctrine and the grounds for refusal based on insufficient distinctiveness share the same rationale: both recognize the need to keep certain signs free for the public and other traders. This overarching rationale has a deep impact on the acceptance of non-traditional marks in the EU.

A *Lack of Distinctive Character*

Confirming the particular importance of the need to keep free in the context of an assessment of a sign's distinctive character, the CJEU explained in *Windsurfing Chiemsee* that the absolute ground for refusal concerning descriptive signs ensured that "descriptive signs or indications relating to the categories of goods or services in respect of which registration is applied for may be freely used by all, including as collective marks or as part of complex or graphic marks."[37] With regard to geographically descriptive indications, the Court further specified that it was in the public interest that signs in this category remained available, "not least because they may be an indication of the quality and other characteristics of the categories of goods concerned, and may also, in various ways, influence consumer tastes by, for instance, associating the goods with a place that may give rise to a favourable response."[38] When it comes to non-traditional types of marks, the CJEU relies on similar considerations. The Court uses the need to keep free as a central instrument to regulate access to trademark protection. In *Henkel*, the Court pointed out that average consumers were not "in the habit of making assumptions about the origin of goods based on the shape of their packaging, in the absence of any graphic or word element."[39] Therefore, it could prove more difficult to establish distinctive character in the case of product packaging for which trademark protection was sought. Only a trademark which significantly departed from the norm or customs of the sector and thereby fulfilled the function of an

34 TMD *supra* note 7, art. 4(1)(e); EUTMR *supra* note 7, art. 7(1)(e).

35 TMD *supra* note 7, art. 4(1)(b)(c) and (d); EUTMR *supra* note 7, art. 4(1)(b)(c) and (d).

36 TMD *supra* note 7, art. 4(4); EUTMR *supra* note 7, 7(3).

37 Cases C-108/97 and C-109/97, *Windsurfing Chiemsee Produktions- und Vertriebs GmbH (WSC)* v. *Boots- und Segelzubehör Walter Huber and Franz Attenberger*, (1999) ECR I-02779 § 25.

38 *Id.* at § 26.

39 Case C-218/01, *Henkel KGaA*, (2004) ECR I-01725 § 52; Cases C-53/01 to C-55/01, *Linde AG, Winward Industries Inc., and Rado Uhren AG*, (2003) ECR I-03161 § 48; Case C-417/16 P, *August Storck KG* v. *European Union Intellectual Property Office*, (2017) ECLI:EU:C:2017:340 § 34.

indication of commercial origin was not devoid of distinctive character.[40] Similarly, the Court held in *Libertel* with regard to color per se that consumers were not "in the habit of making assumptions about the origin of goods based on their color or the color of the packaging, in the absence of any graphic or word element."[41] Against this background, distinctiveness without any prior use was inconceivable save in exceptional circumstances, and particularly where the number of goods or services for which the mark was claimed was very restricted and the relevant market very specific.[42]

On the basis of this jurisprudence, the shape of products or their packaging, and abstract colors, are likely to be found devoid of distinctive character in the European Union. Trademark rights can only be obtained by showing that distinctive character has been acquired through use in trade. This additional hurdle can be regarded as the result of an effort made by the CJEU to keep standard product packaging and colors per se free for other traders and the public at large.[43] The Court explicitly acknowledged with regard to colors that there was "a public interest in not unduly restricting the availability of colours for the other operators who offer for sale goods or services of the same type as those in respect of which registration is sought."[44]

B Functionality

The need to keep free also constitutes a core argument for refusing trademark rights because of functionality. The functionality doctrine in the EU prevents the registration of signs which consist exclusively of a shape, or another characteristic, which results from the nature of the goods concerned, is necessary to obtain a technical result (utilitarian functionality), or gives substantial value to the goods (aesthetic functionality).[45] In *Philips/Remington*, the CJEU explained that the rationale underlying these grounds for refusal was "to prevent trade mark protection from granting its proprietor a monopoly on technical solutions or functional characteristics of a product which a user is likely to seek in the products of competitors."[46] With regard to technical shapes, the Court added that the refusal of registration pursued an aim which was in the public interest, "namely that a shape whose essential characteristics perform a technical function and were chosen to fulfil that function may be freely used by all."[47]

In *Hauck/Stokke*, the CJEU confirmed the basic rationales underlying the functionality doctrine in the context of aesthetic functionality. The Court referred to the objective to prevent monopolies on essential product characteristics to safeguard undistorted competition, and an

[40] Case C-218/01, *Henkel KGaA*, § 49.

[41] Case C-104/01, *Libertel Groep BV* v. *Benelux Merkenbureau*, § 65.

[42] *Id.* at § 66.

[43] The hurdle to be surmounted, however, need not necessarily be high. *See e.g.* Bundesgerichtshof [BGH][Federal Court of Justice], July 9, 2009, GEWERBLICHER RECHTSSCHUTZ UND URHEBERRECHT 138, 2010, § 43 (Ger.): "In the case of a shape mark having characteristics that depart from the basic shape of the type of goods concerned, there is, as a general rule, no reason to assume that the threshold for acquiring distinctive character is particularly high." Accordingly, the fact that 62 percent of the relevant public recognized the shape mark was deemed sufficient. With regard to color per se, the German Federal Patent Court held that, in a small market segment, a recognition of the color mark by 50 percent of the relevant public is sufficient in light of a considerable market share of the applicant on that particular market. *See* Bundesgerichtshof [BGH] [Federal Court of Justice] Dec. 9, 2008 GEWERBLICHER RECHTSSCHUTZ UND URHEBERRECHT 71, 2010 (Ger.).

[44] Case C-104/01, *Libertel Groep BV*, § 55.

[45] TMD *supra* note 7, art. 4(1)(e); EUTMR *supra* note 7, art. 7(1)(e).

[46] Case C-299/99, *Koninklijke Philips Elecs. NV* v. *Remington Consumer Prods Ltd.*, (2002) ECR I-05475 § 78.

[47] *Id.* at § 80.

artificial perpetuation of intellectual property rights with a limited term of protection, such as copyright, patent rights and rights relating to industrial designs.[48]

Given this recognition of the need to keep free, the CJEU delineates the scope of the respective absolute grounds for refusal rather broadly. With respect to shapes necessary to obtain a technical result, the Court held that the ground for refusal could not be overcome by establishing that competitors could use alternative shapes to achieve the same technical result. The doctrine of utilitarian functionality applied irrespective of whether the shape at issue was the only one capable of obtaining the required technical result, or whether there were several shapes which were functionally equivalent.[49]

Similarly, the absolute ground for refusal relating to shapes and other product characteristics which give substantial value to the goods (aesthetic functionality) applies not only when the value of a given shape is due to its inherent beauty and attractiveness.[50] In *Hauck/Stokke*, the Court developed several factors, namely the presumed perception by the average consumer, the nature of the category of goods concerned, the artistic value of the shape in question, its dissimilarity from other shapes in common use on the market concerned, a substantial price difference in relation to similar products, and the development of a promotion strategy focused on accentuating the aesthetic characteristics of the product in question.[51] Accordingly, a broad range of product features may be deemed functional from an aesthetic perspective.

IV RISK OF DYSFUNCTIONAL INCENTIVES

Assessing the impact of these absolute grounds for refusal, the aforementioned fundamental difference between the provisions must be taken into account: whereas the absolute grounds for refusal relating to functionality cannot be overcome by showing that a shape or other product characteristic has acquired distinctiveness as a result of use in trade,[52] the absolute grounds for refusal relating to non-distinctive, descriptive and generic signs no longer apply when a sign of this nature has become distinctive because of the use made of it in trade.[53] To assess the distinctive character of a mark, the CJEU developed the following factors:

> the market share held by the mark; how intensive, geographically widespread and long-standing use of the mark has been; the amount invested by the undertaking in promoting the mark; the proportion of the relevant class of persons who, because of the mark, identify goods as originating from a particular undertaking; and statements from chambers of commerce and industry or other trade and professional associations.[54]

To establish distinctive character on the basis of these factors, it is sufficient to show that the relevant public, "or at least a significant proportion thereof," perceives the descriptive sign as an indication of commercial origin.[55] If distinctive character can be demonstrated, the scope of

[48] Case C-205/13, *Hauck GmbH & Co. KG* v. *Stokke A/S and Others*, (2014) ECLI:EU:C:2014:322 §§ 18–20.

[49] Case C-299/99, *Koninklijke Philips Elecs. NV*, §§ 81–83; Case C-48/09 P, *Lego Juris A/S* v. *Office for Harmonisation in the Internal Mkt. (Trade Marks and Designs) (OHIM)*, (2010) ECR I-08403 §§ 53–58.

[50] With regard to the exclusion from trademark registration in such cases, *see* Case T-508/08, *Bang & Olufsen A/S* v. *Office for Harmonisation in the Internal Mkt. (Trade Marks and Designs) (OHIM)*, (2011) ECR II-06975, §§ 74–79.

[51] Case C-205/13, *Hauck GmbH & Co. KG*, §§ 34–35.

[52] Case C-299/99, *Koninklijke Philips Elecs. NV*, § 57; Case C-371/06, *Benetton Group SpA* v. *G-Star Int'l BV*, (2007) ECR I-07709, §§ 25–27; Case C-48/09 P, *Lego Juris A/S* § 47.

[53] TMD *supra* note 7, art. 4(4); EUTMR *supra* note 7, art. 7(3).

[54] Cases C-108/97 and C-109/97, *Windsurfing Chiemsee Produktions- und Vertriebs GmbH (WSC)*, § 51.

[55] Case C-108/05, *Bovemij Verzekeringen NV* v. *Benelux-Merkenbureau*, (2006) ECR I-07605 § 28.

protection still depends on the degree to which distinctiveness is attained. For instance, a trademark based on a descriptive indication may remain a weak trademark. Minor deviations from the mark or use modalities that emphasize the descriptive character may already eliminate a likelihood of confusion.[56]

Distinctiveness acquired through use is not relevant exclusively in the context of descriptive signs. It is also necessary to overcome the absolute grounds for refusal relating to signs devoid of distinctive character (which often is invoked in the case of non-traditional source identifiers) and generic signs that have become customary in the current language or established trade practices.[57] As the aforementioned decisions in *Henkel* and *Libertel* show, the CJEU leaves little room for a finding of inherent distinctiveness when it comes to shapes and color per se. Assuming consumers are not in the habit of relying on these kinds of signs to identify the commercial source, shapes and abstract colors will normally be deemed devoid of distinctive character in the EU. To obtain trademark rights, applicants must surmount the additional hurdle of demonstrating the acquisition of distinctiveness in consequence of use in trade.

As discussed in the previous section, it remains to be seen whether this strategy is sufficient to keep shapes and colors in the public domain and ensure free availability for all market participants and the public at large. While this is not intended, the jurisprudence of the CJEU may encourage marketing campaigns based on product packaging or color– marketing efforts that aim at a change in the perception of consumers. The more often the public is confronted with a shape mark or abstract color mark, the more alert it will be to the fact that, besides standard word and figurative marks, shapes and color may also indicate the commercial source of goods and services. In *Libertel*, the CJEU explicitly recognized the option of acquiring distinctive character through use in trade:

> However, even if a colour per se does not initially have any distinctive character within the meaning of Article 3(1)(b) of the Directive, it may acquire such character in relation to the goods or services claimed following the use made of it, pursuant to Article 3(3) of the Directive. That distinctive character may be acquired, inter alia, after the normal process of familiarising the relevant public has taken place.[58]

This ruling testifies to the elasticity of distinctive character as a tool to regulate access to trademark protection. With the focus on consumer perception, a flexible, changeable factor enters the picture. While, according to the Court, color per se is not inherently distinctive, use in trade can change this verdict and lead to the acquisition of trademark rights. On its merits, the decision confirms that substantial investment in educating the public will be rewarded with trademark rights to the color concerned. The moment a trader succeeds in establishing the necessary link between the abstract color sign and their enterprise in the minds of consumers, they will acquire exclusive trademark rights to the color concerned.

Viewed from this perspective, the requirement of demonstrating the acquisition of distinctive character through use in trade is both an obstacle and an incentive. Offering the prospect of trademark rights, the *Libertel* decision can be understood to encourage marketing campaigns

[56] *See e.g.* Oberster Gerichtshof [OGH][Supreme Court], Mar. 23, 2010, Ob 18/09k, Gewerblicher Rechtsschutz und Urheberrecht – Internationaler Teil 82, 2011 (Austria); Bundesgerichtshof [BGH][Federal Court of Justice], Nov. 19, 2009, Gewerblicher Rechtsschutz und Urheberrecht 729, 2010 §§ 27–29 (Ger.).

[57] TMD *supra* note 7, art. 4(4); EUTMR *supra* note 7, art. 7(3). As descriptive indications, these signs fall under an absolute ground for refusal in the absence of acquired distinctive character. *See* TMD *supra* note 7, art. 4(1)(b) and (d); EUTMR *supra* note 7, art. 7(1)(b) and (d).

[58] Case C-104/01, *Libertel Groep BV*, § 67.

based on color.[59] Enterprises may perceive the decision as an incentive to reserve "their" individual color in a particular market segment. If the link between the enterprise and the color becomes well-known, this exclusivity may even be extended to unrelated markets.[60] The owner of an abstract color mark with a reputation may invoke trademark rights even in cases where competing goods and services are not similar to those for which the color mark is registered.[61] At the same time, marketing campaigns based on color per se may gradually change the perception of consumers. As already pointed out, every abstract color mark which consumers learn to perceive as a badge of origin makes them more alert to the fact that, besides standard word and figurative marks, color may also indicate the commercial source of goods and services.[62]

As a result, the CJEU may have to revise its own assumptions about the inherent distinctiveness of color per se and other signs in non-traditional categories – at least if these assumptions must be understood as references to empirical findings. Branding and marketing research offers hardly any support for the assumption that the perception of consumers differs markedly from standard trademarks when it comes to marketing campaigns based on certain non-traditional source identifiers, such as abstract color marks.[63] If empirical evidence of consumers becoming more and more acquainted with color per se as a regular identifier of commercial source is already sufficient to neutralize the "not in the habit" formula of the CJEU, it is hardly possible to uphold the general rule that aside from unusual, exceptional cases, abstract color is not inherently distinctive.[64] The moment empirical evidence shows that today's consumers are "in the habit" of making assumptions about commercial origin on the basis of color – just as they are in the habit of making origin assumptions on the basis of words and logos – inherent distinctive character can hardly be denied, unless there is another reason for doubting the capability to distinguish goods and services, such as a descriptive or generic character. Empirical evidence of a parallel trend in the field of product design and product packaging may support a similar line of reasoning with regard to the inherent distinctive character of shapes. Hence, a focus on empirical findings may frustrate the effort made by the Court to use the requirement of proof of acquired distinctive character as a bulwark against broad access to trademark protection.

To avoid this result, the CJEU could clarify that the assumption of consumers not being "in the habit" of relying on shapes and abstract colors as indications of commercial source is not

59 *Cf.* Lotte Anemaet, *The Public Domain Is under Pressure: Why We Should Not Rely on Empirical Data When Assessing Trademark Distinctiveness*, 47 Int'l. Rev. Intell. Prop. Competition L. 303, 331–32 (2016); Martin Senftleben, *Public Domain Preservation in EU Trademark Law – A Model for Other Regions?*, 103 Trademark Rep. 775, 812–13 (2013); Lisa P. Ramsey, *Descriptive Trademarks and the First Amendment*, 70 Tenn. L. Rev. 1095, 1150 (2003); Robert C. Denicola, *Trademarks as Speech: Constitutional Implications of the Emerging Rationales for the Protection of Trade Symbols*, 158 Wis. L. Rev. 170 (1982).

60 In the case of certain abstract color marks, such as Milka Lilac (EUTM 000031336 of Oct. 27, 1999) and Deutsche Telekom Magenta (EUTM 000212787 of Aug. 3, 2000), it cannot be ruled out that the marks have attained the status of a mark with a reputation in several EU member states. As to the possibility of invoking the enhanced protection for marks with a reputation in these EU member states, *see* Case C-125/14, *Iron & Smith kft* v. *Unilever* NV, (2015) ECLI: EU:C:2015:195, §§ 19–20, 29 and 34.

61 EUTMR *supra* note 7, art. 9(2)(c); TMD *supra* note 7, art. 10(2)(c).

62 This assumption is corroborated by the fact that, from the perspective of marketing psychology, it is doubtful to assume that consumers have more difficulty perceiving a colour as a distinctive sign than traditional types of marks, such as word and figurative marks. By contrast, color is a strong signal for our senses and, accordingly, has a promising potential for use as an identifier of commercial source. The assumption of consumers not being "in the habit" of perceiving color as a distinctive element in the marketing of goods or services can thus be unmasked as a legal fiction from the perspective of marketing psychology. *Cf.* Anemaet, *supra* note 59, 316–20.

63 *See* Anemaet, *supra* note 59, 316–20.

64 Case C-104/01, *Libertel Groep BV*, § 66.

only an empirical consideration but also a normative correction.[65] Emphasizing the need to keep signs in these categories free for other traders and the public, the Court could state that changes of consumer perception in empirical reality do not directly impact the assumptions concerning the capability of shapes and abstract colors to identify the commercial source of goods and services in the sense of trademark law. As it is undesirable to deem shapes and abstract colors inherently distinctive in light of the need to keep signs in these categories free, the Court could point out that the additional hurdle of evidence testifying to the acquisition of distinctive character through use in trade is a normative necessity. For normative reasons – the undesirability of trademark law readily accepting shapes and color per se for registration – it is advisable to limit the impact of empirical changes of consumer perception on the registration analysis. These changes can be factored into the equation when assessing the acquisition of distinctive character as a result of use in trade. However, the changes must not lead to a protection automatism allowing traders to monopolize individual colors and shapes by simply arguing that, because of changed source identification habits of consumers, shapes and colors have become inherently distinctive and must be registered without intensive prior use.

In EU trademark law, it is not unusual to apply an amalgam of empirical facts and normative corrections. In infringement cases requiring the assessment of a likelihood of confusion, for instance, the CJEU has posited that marks with a high distinctive character enjoy enhanced protection.[66] In *Sabèl/Puma*, the Court held that the more distinctive the earlier mark, the greater the likelihood of confusion. It was therefore "not impossible that the conceptual similarity resulting from the fact that two marks use images with analogous semantic content may give rise to a likelihood of confusion where the earlier mark has a particularly distinctive character, either per se or because of the reputation it enjoys with the public."[67] Hence, the more distinctive the trademark, the broader the area of similarity in which the trademark proprietor can obtain protection against confusion. On its merits, this protection privilege for highly distinctive marks is the result of a normative decision. While the Court assumes an enhanced risk of confusion, the consuming public will usually remember very clearly the details of marks that are widely recognized on the market. From an empirical perspective, the public is less likely to be confused when it is confronted with a competing sign resembling a mark with a reputation. The risk of confusion will be higher if the relevant public is only vaguely familiar with the mark.[68] Therefore, the decision to offer proprietors of "strong" trademarks enhanced

65 With regard to the discussion on empirical and normative factors shaping decisions in the field of trademark law, *see* Kimberlee Weatherall, *The Consumer as the Empirical Measure of Trade Mark Law*, 80 MODERN L. REV. 77 (2017); Graeme B. Dinwoodie & Dev S. Gangjee, *The Image of the Consumer in European Trade Mark Law*, *in* THE IMAGE(S) OF THE CONSUMER IN EU LAW 345 (Doroto Leczykiewicz & Stephen Weatherill eds., 2016); Jennifer Davis, *Revisiting the Average Consumer: An Uncertain Presence in European Trade Mark Law*, INTELL. PROP. Q. 15 (2015); Vicki Huang, Kimberlee Weatherall, & Elizabeth Webster, *The Use of Survey Evidence in Australian Trade Mark and Passing Off Cases*, *in* THE LAW OF REPUTATION AND BRANDS IN THE ASIA PACIFIC 181 (Andrew T. Kenyon, Ng-Loy Wee Loon, & Megan Richardson eds., 2012); Laura Heymann, *The Reasonable Person in Trademark Law*, 52 ST. LOUIS UNIV. L.J. 781 (2008); Graeme Dinwoodie, *What Linguistics Can Do for Trademark Law*, *in* TRADE MARKS AND BRANDS: AN INTERDISCIPLINARY CRITIQUE 148 (Lionel Bently, Jennifer Davis, & Jane Ginsburg eds., 2008); Barton Beebe, *An Empirical Study of the Multifactor Tests for Trademark Infringement*, 94 CAL. L. REV. 1581 (2006); Jennifer Davis, *Locating the Average Consumer: His Judicial Origins, Intellectual Influences and Current Role in European Trade Mark Law*, 9 INTELL. PROP. QTLY. 2(005); Graeme W. Austin, *Trademarks and the Burdened Imagination*, 69 BROOKLYN L. REV. 827 (2004).

66 EUTMR *supra* note 7, art. 9(2)(b); TMD *supra* note 7, art. 10(2)(b). For a discussion of empirical and normative impact factors in this context, *see* KUR & SENFTLEBEN, *supra* note 18, §§ 5.165–5.181.

67 Case C-251/95, *SABEL BV* v. *Puma AG, Rudolf Dassler Sport*, (1997) ECR I-06191 § 24; Case C-39/97, *Canon Kabushiki Kaisha* v. *Metro-Goldwyn-Mayer Inc., formerly Pathe Commc'ns Corp.*, (1998) ECR I-05507, § 18.

68 *Cf.* KUR/SENFTLEBEN, *supra* note 18, §§ 5.151–5.155.

protection against confusion rests on normative considerations rather than factual circumstances: it would appear inconsistent to disadvantage owners of marks with a reputation by curtailing protection against confusion on the ground that consumers know every detail of the mark. Instead of punishing brand owners for their success in creating a highly distinctive mark, a mark's particularly high degree of distinctiveness can be invoked to compensate for a lower degree of similarity between the signs or products involved.[69]

This configuration of the infringement analysis leads to a protection reflex that can be qualified as a normative correction of empirical consumer perception. The grant of broader protection against confusion is a legal fiction for highly distinctive trademarks: even though consumers are unlikely to be confused because they recognize even small deviations from the mark with a reputation, the trademark proprietor is nonetheless entitled to bring an anti-confusion claim. The legal fiction of an enhanced risk of confusion covering a broader range of similar signs leads to protection irrespective of whether an empirical analysis would bring to light a risk of confusion.[70]

If normative corrections of empirical findings are possible when assessing the impact of a mark's degree of distinctiveness on the confusion analysis, the CJEU may take a similar step in the context of assessing the distinctive character of non-traditional types of marks, such as shape and abstract color marks, at the registration stage. In *Henkel* and *Libertel*, the Court already recognized the need to keep signs of this nature free for other traders and the public at large. This normative consideration could serve as a basis for positing that the assumption of consumers not being "in the habit" of relying on shape and color as identifiers of commercial source cannot be set aside by empirical findings pointing in the opposite direction.

V CULTIVATION OF ACQUIRED DISTINCTIVENESS AS A GATEKEEPER

However, the Court has not taken this step yet. Instead, it embarked on a further cultivation of the requirement of acquired distinctiveness as a central threshold criterion without clarifying the empirical or normative nature of its approach. In *Nestlé/Mondelez (KitKat)*, the CJEU discussed the evidence necessary to establish the acquisition of distinctive character through use when the applicant seeks to register a shape as an EUTM. The case concerned the shape of the KitKat chocolate bar which Nestlé sought to register at EU level. As an EUTM constitutes a unitary right covering the entire territory of the EU,[71] the Court emphasized that, in order to be accepted for registration as an EUTM, the shape was required to have distinctive character throughout the EU.[72] Regarding the evidence to be produced by the applicant, this implies that the registration of a shape which, *ab initio*, is devoid of distinctive character, only becomes

[69] Case C-108/07P, *Ferrero Deutschland GmbH* v. *Office for Harmonisation in the Internal Mkt. (Trade Marks and Designs) (OHIM)*, (2008) ECR I-0061, § 58; Case C-251/95, *SABEL BV* v. *Puma AG*, § 24; Case 39/97, *Canon Kabushiki Kaisha* v. *Metro-Goldwyn Mayer*, § 18. With regard to similar rules in US law, *see* J. Thomas McCarthy, *Dilution of a Trademark: European and United States Law Compared*, 94 TRADEMARK REP. 1163 (2004).

[70] For a discussion of the trademark owner's interest in enhanced protection against confusion on the basis of the reputation of the mark, see Tobias Cohen Jehoram & Henriette Van Helden, *Bekend, Bekender, Bekendst: Goodwill-Bescherming van Merken*, *in* IN VARIETATE CONCORDIA? NATIONAL AND EUROPEAN TRADEMARKS LIVING APART TOGETHER 111 (Benelux Office for Intellectual Property ed., 2011); Mireille Buydens, *Pouvoir Distinctif de la Marquee et Risque de Confusion: Larvatus Prodeo?*, *in* IN VARIETATE CONCORDIA? NATIONAL AND EUROPEAN TRADEMARKS LIVING APART TOGETHER 33 (Benelux Office for Intellectual Property ed., 2011); A. A. Quaedvlieg, *Verwaterd of Verward, een Kwestie van Bekendheid?*, *in* EEN EIGEN, OORSPRONKELIJK KARAKTER – OPSTELLEN AANGEBODEN AAN PROF. MR. JAAP H. SPOOR 275 (Dirk J. G. Visser & D. W. F. Verkade eds., 2007).

[71] EUTMR *supra* note 7, art. 1(2).

[72] Joined Cases C-84/17 P, C-85/17 P and C-95/17 P, *Société des produits Nestlé SA and Others* v. *Mondelez UK Holdings & Servs. Ltd*, (2018) ECLI:EU:C:2018:266, §§ 67–68.

possible if the applicant succeeds in demonstrating that the shape has acquired distinctive character throughout the EU territory.[73]

This is a strict test that requires evidence with respect to each individual member state. The CJEU made it clear that proof of distinctive character following use in a significant part of the EU was insufficient.[74] If the applicant used the same distribution network for several member states or the mark was recognized across the borders of member states due to a close geographic, cultural or linguistic connection, it was conceivable that evidence provided to establish secondary meaning was relevant regarding several member states, or even the entire EU.[75] Nonetheless, the evidence submitted had to be capable of establishing the acquisition of distinctive character through use in each and every member state.[76] It was not sufficient that "the party with the burden of providing such evidence merely produces evidence of such acquisition that does not cover part of the European Union, even a part consisting of only one Member State."[77]

In *Nestlé/Mondelez (KitKat)*, the Board of Appeal of EUIPO had not addressed whether the KitKat shape had acquired distinctive character in Belgium, Ireland, Greece and Portugal.[78] Against this background, the CJEU concluded that the finding of acquired distinctive character was vitiated by an error of law. For the grant of an EUTM, it was not sufficient to ascertain that the chocolate bar had obtained distinctive character in various other member states and a significant part of the EU. By contrast, it would have been necessary to adjudicate whether the shape also had acquired distinctiveness in Belgium, Ireland, Greece and Portugal.[79] It follows from this decision that if an applicant seeks to register a non-traditional type of mark as an EUTM, it can be particularly difficult to surmount the additional hurdle of proof for the acquisition of distinctive character through use.

VI IMPACT OF AESTHETIC FUNCTIONALITY

Further challenges for applicants filing a non-traditional trademark follow from the interplay between the grounds for refusal relating to a lack of distinctive character and the functionality doctrine in EU trademark law. As explained above, the CJEU delineated the conceptual contours of aesthetic functionality rather broadly in *Hauck/Stokke*. Instead of focusing on attractiveness and artistic value, the Court developed various factors which support a finding of aesthetic functionality, including the dissimilarity of a shape for which trademark protection is sought "from other shapes in common use on the market concerned."[80] This functionality factor calls to mind the condition which the Court established in *Henkel* regarding the assessment of inherent distinctiveness of shapes. As discussed, the Court assumed in *Henkel* that consumers were not in the habit of perceiving shapes as indications of commercial source. Nonetheless, the Court left a loophole for a finding of inherent distinctive character: "a simple departure from the norm or customs of the sector is not sufficient to render inapplicable the ground for refusal given in Article 3(1)(b) of the Directive. In contrast, a trade mark which significantly departs

[73] *Id.* at § 76.
[74] *Id.* at § 78.
[75] *Id.* at §§ 80–82.
[76] *Id.* at § 83.
[77] *Id.* at § 87.
[78] *Id.* at §§ 17–18.
[79] *Id.*. at § 88.
[80] Case C-205/13, *Hauck GmbH & Co. KG*, §§ 34–35.

from the norm or customs of the sector . . . is not devoid of distinctive character."[81] When this criterion for the assumption of inherent distinctiveness is placed in the context of the described aesthetic functionality factor following from *Hauck/Stokke*, it becomes clear that trademark applicants will have to navigate between Scylla and Charybdis: if they emphasize that the shape for which they seek trademark protection departs significantly from the norm or customs in the sector, they risk a finding of aesthetic functionality. On the basis of *Hauck/Stokke*, dissimilarity from other shapes in common use on the relevant market is an indication that the shape may be functional from an aesthetic perspective.

This configuration of the interplay between the test of inherent distinctiveness and the test of aesthetic functionality makes the option of acquiring distinctive character through use in trade even more important. As a showing of inherent distinctiveness on the basis of a significant departure from the norm or customs in a given market segment involves the risk of finding aesthetic functionality, EU trademark law encourages a different rights acquisition strategy: the selection of a less extravagant shape design and the investment in marketing campaigns educating consumers to recognize this shape as an indication of commercial source. As a finding of aesthetic functionality cannot be set aside by demonstrating that distinctive character has been obtained through use in trade, it makes less sense to train consumers to perceive an unusual shape as a source identifier.[82] Even if the investment in the recognition of the shape leads to distinctiveness, the grant of trademark rights may still be denied on the ground that the shape is functional.

Admittedly, this implies that outstanding design is less likely to attract trademark protection in the EU than mediocre design.[83] However, it is an open question whether this result is undesirable. While the denial of trademark protection because of aesthetic functionality will be bad news for the trademark applicant, it may be conducive to follow-on innovation in the cultural sector. If an outstanding shape design is ineligible for trademark protection, the shape will enter the public domain after the expiry of industrial design and/or copyright protection.[84] After a limited period of protection, the design can thus serve as a freely available basis for new creations. Once trademark rights are granted, however, the trademark proprietor can renew the registration indefinitely (as long as the sign is put to genuine use). This, in turn, will thwart the objective to provide entirely free source material for follow-on innovation. To the extent that trademark rights prevent remix and reuse in the cultural domain, the design at issue will not fall into the public domain.[85] From a broader public policy perspective, it can thus be consistent to exclude outstanding product design from trademark protection.

[81] Case C-218/01, *Henkel KGaA*, § 49; Case C-417/16 P, *August Storck KG* v. *European Union Intell. Prop. Office (EUIPO)*, (2017) ECLI:EU:C:2017:340, § 35.

[82] Case C-299/99, *Koninklijke Philips Elecs NV*, § 57; Case C-371/06, *Benetton Gr. SpA* v. *G-Star Int'l. BV.*, §§ 25–27; Case C-48/09 P, *Lego Juris A/S*, § 47.

[83] For a more detailed, critical discussion of this outcome, *see* Annette Kur, *Too Pretty to Protect? Trade Mark Law and the Enigma of Aesthetic Functionality*, *in* Max Planck Institute for Intellectual Property & Competition Law Research Paper No. 11-16, 17-18, 22-11 (Max Planck Institute 2011).

[84] For a detailed discussion of the different approaches to overlapping copyright and specific industrial design protection regimes, *see* the contributions to The Copyright/Design Interface – Past, Present and Future (Estelle Derclaye ed., 2018). With regard to the configuration of cumulative copyright and industrial design protection at EU level, *see* the prejudicial questions which the Portuguese Supreme Court asked in Case C-638/17, *Cofemel* v. *G-Star*, (2017) ECLI:EU:C:2017:93. *Cf.* European Copyright Society, *Opinion of the European Copyright Society in Relation to the Pending Reference before the CJEU in Cofemel v G-Star*, C-683/17, https://europeancopyrightsociety.org/.

[85] For a more detailed assessment of the corrosive effect of trademark rights, *see* Martin Senftleben, *Vigeland and the Status of Cultural Concerns in Trade Mark Law – The EFTA Court Develops More Effective Tools for the Preservation of the Public Domain*, 48 Int'l. Rev. Intell. Prop. & Competition L. 683, 696–705 (2017).

The *Bang & Olufson* case sheds light on this dilemma. In this case, the GCEU explained that, like the concept of utilitarian functionality, the concept of aesthetic functionality served the purpose of preventing the grant of a monopoly relating to industrial design with particular value.[86] More specifically, the invocation of aesthetic functionality as a ground for refusal was necessary where the shape at issue revealed a very specific design that constituted an essential element of its branding and increased the appeal of the product to which it was applied.[87] Regarding the attractive loudspeaker shape which Bang & Olufson sought to register, the Court found that the shape would be perceived "as a kind of pure, slender, timeless sculpture for music reproduction."[88] This positive assessment, however, did not culminate in the grant of trademark rights. Instead, the GCEU held that the aesthetic appearance made the shape an important selling point that had to be kept free to prevent an impediment of competition.[89] On one hand, this decision seems to punish Bang & Olufson for the development of attractive design. Instead of supporting the acquisition of a particularly strong intellectual property portfolio – trademark rights in addition to copyright and industrial design protection – the Court took the outstanding aesthetic qualities of the shape as a starting point to categorically exclude the possibility of a trademark registration. On the other hand, the decision can be expected to enhance free competition and broaden consumer choice. Once the limited term of copyright and industrial design protection expires, competitors enjoy the freedom of copying Bang & Olufson's "pure, slender, timeless sculpture for music reproduction." They can offer consumers comparable product design at a lower price. This erosion of the monopoly position provides an incentive for Bang & Olufson to embark on the development of new, even more attractive loudspeaker design. Hence, the cultural innovation cycle continues to evolve. Freedom of imitation for competitors and the exposure of the former intellectual property owner to the rigors of free competition are likely to stimulate new innovation steps. The denial of trademark rights can thus be deemed desirable from a broader socioeconomic perspective.

While the calibration of the tests of inherent distinctiveness and aesthetic functionality in the EU poses particular challenges to trademark applicants, it would be wrong to paint a black-and-white picture. The acquisition of rights to non-traditional marks, such as shape marks, has not become impossible. As already indicated, the selection of a shape or other product characteristic that does not define the value of the product may lead to the acquisition of trademark rights once consumers have been educated to recognize the selected sign as an identifier of commercial source.

Moreover, it is to be considered that CJEU jurisprudence has also set certain limits to the scope of the functionality doctrine. In *Nestlé/Cadbury* (KitKat), the CJEU confirmed its earlier decision in *Hauck/Stokke* that the three types of functionality in EU trademark law – concerning essential features (1) resulting from the nature of the goods; (2) necessary to obtain a technical result; (3) giving substantial value to the goods[90] – are separate grounds for refusal that operate independently of one another.[91] While it was possible that the essential features of a sign may be covered by one or more functionality grounds, the registration as a trademark could only be

[86] Case T-508/08, *Bang & Olufsen A/S*, § 66.
[87] *Id.* at § 74.
[88] *Id.* at § 75.
[89] *Id.*
[90] EUTMR *supra* note 7, art. 7(1)(e); TMD *supra* note 7, art. 4(1)(e).
[91] Case C-215/14, *Société de Produits Nestlé SA* v. *Cadbury UK Ltd*, (2015) ECLI:EU:C:2015:395, § 46. As to the earlier decision, *see* Case C-205/13, *Hauck GmbH & Co. KG* v. *Stokke A/S and Others*, § 39.

refused where at least one of those grounds was fully applicable to the sign at issue.[92] Hence, the Court rejected the establishment of 100 percent functionality by combining and adding up different functionality grounds that only applied in part to the sign at issue: "An interpretation … which allowed the application of that provision where each of the three grounds for refusal set out was only partially established, would clearly run counter to the public interest objective underlying the application of the three grounds for refusal."[93]

The question of cumulative application of functionality grounds had arisen because the examiner dealing with Nestlé's attempt to register the KitKat shape had identified three specific features: the basic rectangular slab shape; the presence, position and depth of the grooves running along the length of the bar; and the number of grooves, which, together with the width of the bar, determined the number of "fingers."[94] While, according to the examiner, the first of these features resulted from the nature of the goods, the other two were necessary to obtain a technical result. The combination of these arguments led to the conclusion that the shape was functional in its entirety.[95] The CJEU, by contrast, held that, where a shape contained three essential features – one resulting from the nature of the goods and two necessary to obtain a technical result – functionality could only be established where at least one of the grounds for refusal was fully – 100 percent – applicable to the shape.[96]

This approach can offer an important escape route in functionality cases. In *Best-Lock/EUIPO* (Lego), for instance, the CJEU confirmed the lower instance decision that the shape of the Lego mini figure was not dictated in its entirety by the aim to achieve a technical effect. The essential characteristics of the shape – the head, body, arms and legs which are necessary to give the figure a human appearance – did not serve a technical function. The holes under the feet and inside the backs of the legs and hands of the Lego manikin allowed the user to join the figure to other elements, in particular interlocking building blocks. However, these elements could not be deemed essential characteristics.[97] Therefore, the Court dismissed the invalidity claim based on utilitarian functionality.

In theory, a different result could have followed from a combination of functionality grounds. As the Lego mini figure is modelled on the appearance of humans, it could have been stated that, to a large extent, the shape resulted from the nature of toys seeking to imitate the shape of humans (functionality ground 1). In addition, it could have been argued that the non-human holes on the feet, legs and hands were dictated by the technical necessity to enable the connection with toy bricks (functionality ground 2). Adding up these arguments, courts and examiners could have come closer to the verdict of functionality. As explained, however, CJEU jurisprudence precludes this "bricolage" of different functionality grounds. Instead, the shape at issue must fall under one of the functionality grounds in its entirety.

Prior to the 2015 trademark law reform, the shape of goods constituted the only field of application of the EU functionality doctrine. Not surprisingly, functionality case law only concerned attempts to register shapes as trademarks. As a result of the trademark law reform, however, the doctrine's scope has been broadened.[98] Currently, the EU functionality rules cover

[92] Case C-215/14, *Société de Produits Nestlé SA*, (2015) ECLI:EU:C:2015:395, § 48.

[93] *Id.* at § 50.

[94] *Id.* at § 19.

[95] *Id.* at § 20.

[96] *Id.* at § 51.

[97] Case C-452/15 P, *Best-Lock (Europe) Ltd* v. *European Union Intell. Prop. Office (EUIPO)*, (2016) ECLI:EU:C:2016:270, §§ 18–20.

[98] *See* Kur & Senftleben, *supra* note 18, §§ 4.173–4.177.

"the shape, or another characteristic" of goods.[99] Against this background, the question arises how the CJEU will apply the rules stemming from the assessment of shapes to a broader range of product characteristics, including color.

In *Louboutin and Christian Louboutin*, Advocate General Maciej Szpunar gave a foretaste of elastic application. The case concerned the question whether the red sole of Louboutin shoes constituted a valid trademark. Even though the issue had to be adjudicated on the basis of the former functionality doctrine (confined to shapes), the Advocate General saw room for the inclusion of color aspects. In his first opinion, he arrived at the conclusion that the old, shape-centered functionality doctrine could "potentially apply to signs consisting of the shape of the goods which seek protection for a certain color."[100] Color/shape combinations would thus have fallen within the scope of the functionality doctrine. In his second opinion, the Advocate General added that Louboutin could not shield its design feature from scrutiny in the light of functionality by declaring the red sole a position mark. The introduction of the concept of a position mark into the EU legal system did not impact the applicability of functionality considerations to a sign consisting of the shape of the goods and seeking protection for a certain color.[101]

However, the CJEU did not seize the opportunity to clarify the application of the functionality doctrine to color aspects in *Louboutin and Christian Louboutin*. Instead, the Court noted that

> while it is true that the shape of the product or of a part of the product plays a role in creating an outline for the colour, it cannot, however, be held that a sign consists of that shape in the case where the registration of the mark did not seek to protect that shape but sought solely to protect the application of a colour to a specific part of that product.[102]

As this decision concerned the previous functionality doctrine that was confined to the shape of products, it does not offer guidance as to the application of the current, broader functionality doctrine to color features of goods. Instead, the decision in *Louboutin and Christian Louboutin* raises the question whether color aspects that remained under the radar of the previous shape-centered functionality doctrine and made their way into the EU trademark register are exposed to a functionality challenge under the new, broadened functionality doctrine that covers not only shape but also other product characteristics. In *Textilis*, the CJEU denied any retroactive effect of the new legislation "in order to ensure observance of the principles of legal certainty and the protection of legitimate expectations."[103] The Court clarified that the substantive rules of EU law could be applied to situations existing before their entry into force "only in so far as it clearly follows from their terms, objectives or general scheme that such effect must be given to them."[104] In the absence of any such reference points for retroactive effect in the amended EUTMR, the CJEU saw no room in *Textilis* for the application of the broadened functionality doctrine to signs registered before 23 March 2016 – the date of entry into force of the amended legislation.[105] Functional color elements that survived scrutiny and were registered under the former functionality doctrine are thus unlikely to be declared functional and invalid under the current legislation.[106]

99 EUTMR *supra* note 7, art. 7(1)(e); TMD *supra* note 7, art. 4(1)(e).
100 Case C-163/16, *Christian Louboutin SAS* v. *Van Haren Schoenen BV*, (2017) ECLI:EU:C:2017:495, §§ 65–66.
101 *Id.* at §§ 34, 42.
102 Case C-163/16, *Christian Louboutin and Christian Louboutin SAS* v. *van Haren Schoenen BV*, (2018) ECLI:EU:C:2018:64, § 24.
103 Case C-21/18, *Textilis Ltd and Ozgur Keskin* v. *Svenskt Tenn Aktiebolag*, (2019) ECLI:EU:C:2019:199, § 30.
104 *Id.* § 30.
105 *Id.* §§ 31–33.
106 *Id.* § 33.

VII CONCLUSION

In sum, the discussion of the EU approach to non-traditional marks yields mixed results. On one hand, EU trademark law and practice recognize a wide range of non-traditional marks. As an exception to the rule of acceptance, smell signs have not obtained access to EU trademark registers yet. In contrast, shapes, abstract colors, color combinations, motion marks, multimedia marks, melodies, sounds, taste marks, hologram marks and position marks are all registrable. In principle, the doors to trademark protection in the EU are thus wide open.

On the other hand, the CJEU has transformed the basic requirement of distinctive character into a substantial hurdle for trademark applicants. Assuming that consumers are not in the habit of making assumptions about the origin of goods or services on the basis of non-traditional source identifiers, such as shape and color, the Court de facto obliges trademark applicants to acquire distinctive character through use before filing a non-traditional trademark. Proof of acquired distinctive character can be particularly difficult in the case of EUTMs. As the Court requires evidence with respect to each individual EU member state, the burden imposed on trademark applicants is considerable.

When the conceptual elasticity of the EU functionality doctrine – covering shape and other product characteristics after the 2015 trademark law reform – is factored into the equation, the emphasis on acquired distinctive character as a gatekeeper criterion is even enhanced. In line with CJEU jurisprudence, trademark applicants trying to establish inherent distinctiveness by emphasizing the singularity of product features for which they seek protection may be confronted with a finding of aesthetic functionality that leads to a categorical exclusion of trademark rights. Therefore, reliance on less exotic product features and the acquisition of distinctiveness through use over time seems a safer rights acquisition strategy.

It remains to be seen whether the Court's reliance on acquired distinctive character as a central threshold for obtaining trademark rights to non-traditional marks proves to be sustainable. If the assumption of consumers not being in the habit of recognizing non-traditional marks is an empirical finding (instead of a normative assumption), this bulwark against easy access to trademark protection will crumble into dust the moment consumers no longer focus on traditional source identifiers, such as word and figurative marks. Moreover, distinctive character is a volatile regulatory tool.[107] Relying on this requirement, the Court leaves the issue to the ingenuity of marketing specialists. With sufficient investment in marketing campaigns teaching consumers to perceive a shape, color or sound as a trademark, an enterprise seeking to protect its entire brand experience can finally arrive at a multifaceted trademark portfolio.

Hence, the hurdles erected by the CJEU are not only a deterrent but also an incentive. As long as the acquisition of trademark rights remains possible, brand developers may see the requirement of acquired distinctive character as an invitation to invest in the cultivation of non-traditional source identifiers. The final word on the consistency of the threshold requirements for the protection of non-traditional marks in EU trademark law thus depends on whether one finds the protection of non-traditional marks desirable. This overarching policy question, however, goes beyond the scope of the current analysis.[108]

107 For a more detailed discussion of this point, *see* Senftleben, *supra* note 5, § 50, 812–17.

108 For a detailed discussion of the policy questions arising from the protection of non-traditional trademarks, *see* Irene Calboli & Martin Senftleben, The Protection of Non-Traditional Trademarks – Critical Perspectives (2018).

III

Public Policy Limitations of Trademark Subject Matter

13

Public Policy Limitations on Trademark Subject Matter

A US Perspective

Christine Haight Farley[*]

I INTRODUCTION

What public policy objectives are contained in the subject-matter limitations of US trademark law? This question has recently taken on a renewed interest for US legal scholars. The general public policies that animate trademark law – encouraging fair competition and protecting consumers from deceptive practices – can certainly be found in some of the doctrines that constrain trademark subject matter. Some of the specific constraints found in US law, however, do not align with these traditional trademark policy goals. These instances raise fascinating questions, such as what policy goals are being advanced in these provisions, and are these policy goals appropriate within trademark law. These are the questions that lie behind the currently live question of whether the government's denial of registration based on justifications outside the heart of trademark law is a valid restriction on speech.

Rather than explicitly announcing the policy goals of restricting trademarks, US trademark law is somewhat tacit about the reasons behind the rules. For instance, what is the policy reason behind the historical prohibition on the registration of immoral, scandalous, and disparaging marks?[1] Until just a few years ago, commentators would have unthinkingly stated that the bar enables the government to protect the public from harmful marks.[2] That answer would have not only lacked statutory and legislative history support, but it would have failed to account for why harmful marks may still be used and even protected under federal law. While the trademark laws in other jurisdictions may be explicit about their objectives of protecting "morality" and "public order,"[3] US trademark law has never included a reference to public order, and other than the

[*] Professor, American University Washington College of Law. I am grateful to Bianca Petcu for invaluable research assistance.

[1] *See* Trademark (Lanham) Act of 1946, 15 USC § 1052(a)(1) (2018).

[2] *See* Stephen R. Baird, *Moral Intervention in the Trademark Arena: Banning the Registration of Scandalous and Immoral Trademarks*, 83 Trademark Rep. 661, 788 (1993).

[3] Many countries that ratified the Paris Convention implemented its permissive scheme of refusing marks that are "contrary to morality or public order" and, in so doing, adopted that precise language. *See* International Convention for the Protection of Industrial Property, art. 6*quinquies*, as modified at The Hague on Nov. 6, 1925, 47 Stat. 1789, 1804–05, TS 834 and London on June 2, 1934, 53 Stat. 1748, 1776–78, TS 941 (the Paris Convention entered into force as to the United States on May 30, 1887); Colin Manning, *Moral Bars on Trade Mark Registration*, U. C. Cork L. Sch. (Mar. 28, 2017), https://papers.ssrn.com/sol3/papers.cfm?abstract_id=2875687 (recounting the adoption of this provision in several European national laws); Enrico Bonadio, *Brands, Morality and Public Policy: Some Reflections on the Ban on Registration of Controversial Trademarks*, 19 Marq. Intell. Prop. L. Rev. 39, 43 (2015) (reviewing the morality bars in several European jurisdictions and Australia).

presence of the word "immoral," the statute provides no clue as to what concerns animated Congress's reference to morality.[4]

This chapter provides an account of the public policy limitations on trademark subject matter under US law. Section II presents a backdrop to these limitations by explaining the general flexibility as to what constitutes a protectable mark. Section III describes the bars to registration available under Section 2 of the Lanham Act and Section IV explicates the policy rationales behind these bars. Section V reviews the recent Supreme Court decisions in *Matal* v. *Tam* and *Iancu* v. *Brunetti*, which address constitutional constraints on statutory bars to registration. Finally, Section VI considers the implications of these decisions on other public policy-based subject matter limitations.

II ANYTHING CAN BE A TRADEMARK

US trademark law is regulated by the Trademark Act of 1946, commonly known as the "Lanham Act."[5] The Lanham Act provides for federal registration, causes of action for both registered and common-law trademarks, and remedies.[6] In addition to the Lanham Act, trademarks in the United States may be protected under the common law and by state registration.[7] The United States Patent and Trademark Office (USPTO) is instructed by the Lanham Act, but also by the Trademark Manual of Examining Procedure (TMEP).[8] The TMEP, which is regularly updated, offers trademark examining attorneys in the USPTO, trademark applicants, and attorneys and representatives for trademark applicants with "a reference work on the practices and procedures relative to prosecution of applications to register marks in the USPTO."[9]

Although the Lanham Act has been amended several times since 1946,[10] there has been no major amendment dealing with the subject matter of trademark protection.[11] Case law on the subject matter of trademarks has been robust in some areas, such as distinctiveness,[12] and sparse in others, such as the prohibition on the registration of flags and state emblems.[13]

What may be protected as a trademark under US law is extremely broad and flexible. Section 45 of the Lanham Act clearly delineates the various types of protectable marks, including

[4] 15 USC § 1052(a).

[5] *Id.* § 1051 et seq.

[6] *Id.* §§ 1051, 1114, 1116–19, 1124, 1125(a)–(d).

[7] *See* J. Thomas McCarthy, McCarthy on Trademarks and Unfair Competition § 19:3 (5th ed. 2018).

[8] TMEP (8th ed. Oct. 2018).

[9] *Id.*

[10] 15 USC § 1127 (2018).

[11] *Id.* § 1091(c) The few revisions that added "major" changes include the addition of causes of action for dilution and bad faith domain name registration, and the opportunity to apply for registration on an intent to use basis. Although a bar to registration for functional marks was added to § 2 in 1998, it was not a major amendment because this bar had already been a part of common law. *See* Pub. L. No. 105–330, 112 Stat. 3064 (1998); Robert G. Bone, *Trademark Functionality Reexamined* 7 J. Legal Analysis 183 (2015) (describing the history of the functionality bar in US common law). Revisions to § 2 following the North American Free Trade Agreement (NAFTA) and the Agreement on Trade-Related Aspects of Intellectual Property Rights (TRIPS) made the primarily geographically deceptively misdescriptive bar absolute and added a bar to registering a false geographical indication for a wine or spirit. *See* Pub. L. No. 103–82, 107 Stat. 2114 (1993); Pub. L. No. 103–465, 108 Stat. 4809, Title V, Subtitle B, Sec. 522 (1994).

[12] *See Converse* v. *ITC*, 909 F.3d 1110 (Fed. Cir. 2018) (determining distinctiveness of a product configuration); *Royal Crown Co.* v. *Coca-Cola Co.*, 892 F.3d 1358 (Fed. Cir. 2018) (determining distinctiveness of a common word that characterizes a product category).

[13] *See In re McGinley*, 660 F.2d 481 (CCPA 1981); *See also In re Old Glory Condom Corp.*, 26 USPQ 2d 1216, 1217 (TTAB 1993); *See* McCarthy, *supra* note 7, § 19:77. 15 USC § 1127.

trademarks, service marks, certification marks, and collective marks.[14] The definition of what constitutes a trademark is also found in this section:

> The term "trademark" includes any word, name, symbol, or device, or any combination thereof – (1) used by a person, or (2) which a person has a bona fide intention to use in commerce and applies to register on the principal register established by this chapter, to identify and distinguish his or her goods, including a unique product, from those manufactured or sold by others and to indicate the source of the goods, even if that source is unknown.[15]

According to this definition, whether registered or unregistered, to be protected under US trademark law a mark must meet two broad standards: It must be used in commerce, and it must be distinctive.[16] The requirement of use is constitutionally based, addressed in the statute, and further clarified by numerous federal court opinions.[17] The requirement of distinctiveness is not defined in the Act and is the subject of numerous cases that continue to be litigated today.[18]

The subject matter of trademark law has long been addressed by the federal courts. In particular, the Court of Appeals for the Federal Circuit, which decides all appeals dealing with the denial of trademark registration, and the Supreme Court have had a major impact on these rules.

In the mid-1990s, in the space of three years, the Supreme Court decided two cases that significantly expanded trademark subject matter. In *Two Pesos Inc.* v. *Taco Cabana*, the Supreme Court was faced with trade dress – a restaurant's design – that was not registered and lacked secondary meaning.[19] The Court decided that trade dress that is inherently distinctive is entitled to protection despite the absence of proof of secondary meaning. The Court reasoned that only descriptive marks required secondary meaning.[20] The Court was persuaded that nothing in the Lanham Act dictated that either unregistered marks or trade dress be subjected to different standards.[21] A few years later, in *Qualitex Co.* v. *Jacobson Products Co.*, the Supreme

[14] *Id.*

[15] *Id.* The 1946 Lanham Act offered the first statutory definition of a trademark in US law, integrating "technical trademarks" and "trade names." *See* McCarthy, *supra* note 7, § 4:3. The present definition is a result of a 1988 amendment of the original definition, which read: "The term 'trademark,' includes any word, name, symbol, or device or any combination thereof adopted and used by a manufacturer or merchant to identify his goods and distinguish them from those manufactured or sold by others." This definition was no doubt drawn from the Supreme Court's definition in *McLean* v. *Flemming*, 96 US 245 (1878) (stating a "trade-mark may consist of a name, symbol, figure, letter, form or device, if adopted and used by a manufacturer or merchant in order to distinguish the goods he manufactures or sells … from those manufactured or sold by others").

[16] *See* McCarthy, *supra* note 7, § 3.01[1] ("requirements for qualification of a word or symbol as a trademark" are that it be (1) a "symbol," (2) "use[d] … as a mark," (3) "to identify and distinguish the seller's goods from goods made or sold by others," but that it not be "functional").

[17] 15 USC § 1127; *see United Drug Co.* v. *Theodore Rectanus Co.*, 248 US 90, 100 (1918) ("Undoubtedly, the general rule is that, as between conflicting claimants to the right to use the same mark, priority of appropriation determines the question"); *Hana Financial, Inc.* v. *Hana Bank*, 135 S. Ct. 907, 909 (2015) ("Rights in a trademark are determined by the date of the mark's first use in commerce. The party who first uses a mark in commerce is said to have priority over other users"); *B & B Hardware, Inc.* v. *Hargis Industries, Inc.*, 135 S. Ct. 1293, 1299, 1310 (2015) ("One who first uses a distinct mark in commerce thus acquires rights to that mark").

[18] *See Converse* v. *ITC*, 909 F.3d 1110 (Fed. Cir. 2018) (determining distinctiveness of a product configuration); *Royal Crown Co.* v. *Coca-Cola Co.*, 892 F.3d 1358 (Fed. Cir. 2018) (determining distinctiveness of a common word that characterizes a product category).

[19] *Two Pesos Inc.*, 505 US 763.

[20] *Id.* ("Section 2 of the Lanham Act provides that a descriptive mark that otherwise could not be registered under the Act may be registered if it has become distinctive of the applicant's goods in commerce." Citing *Park 'N Fly*).

[21] *Id.* ("There is no persuasive reason to apply to trade dress a general requirement of secondary meaning which is at odds with the principles generally applicable to infringement suits under § 43(a).")

Court was faced with a "trademark that consists, purely and simply, of a color."[22] The Court noted that the "language of the Lanham Act describes that universe [of trademark subject matter] in the broadest of terms."[23] "Since human beings might use as a 'symbol' or 'device' almost anything at all that is capable of carrying meaning," the Court reasoned, "this language, read literally, is not restrictive."[24] The Court pronounced that the doctrine of secondary meaning would afford any symbol – without restriction – the opportunity to become a mark. The Court therefore decided that a single color, like trade dress, is protectable under "ordinary legal trademark requirements."[25]

Following these cases, what constitutes a protectable mark in US trademark law is quite broad and without clear limitations, save a showing of secondary meaning.[26] As a result, US trademark law, as compared with other jurisdictions, has been solicitous of a great variety of non-traditional marks such as trade dress, sound marks, scent marks, tactile marks, and single colors.

III STRICT STATUTORY LIMITS

In contrast to the apparent breadth of what can constitute a protectable mark and the generality of subject matter standards is a set of statutory limitations that come in the form of prohibitions on what can be registered as a mark in the United States. These bars to registration are found in Section 2 of the Lanham Act. According to this section, marks will be refused registration if they include matter that is deceptive, immoral or scandalous, falsely suggestive of a connection with persons, institutions or religions, geographical indication for wine or spirits other than the place of origin of the goods, government insignia, a living person's name, portrait or signature without written consent, likely to cause confusion with an existing mark, merely descriptive, deceptively misdescriptive, primarily geographically descriptive, primarily geographically deceptively misdescriptive, primarily merely a surname, or functional.[27]

The 1905 Trademark Act contained a slightly smaller set of prohibitions on registration that were similar to Section 2 of the Lanham Act. These provisions, in Section 5 of the Act, prohibited the registration of immoral or scandalous matter, flags and state emblems, confusingly similar marks, the name of an individual, firm, corporation, or association, not portrayed in a distinctive manner, descriptive words, merely a geographical name, a portrait of a living individual without consent.[28] In addition to developing and elaborating on some of these bars, the 1946 Lanham Act added bars for disparaging marks and marks that are primarily merely a surname. The bars for geographical indications and functional marks were later added in revisions of the Lanham Act.[29]

The prohibitions on registration set out in Section 2 do not appear to have a great deal in common and, in any event, are not organized into related categories. Some subparagraphs contain a number of unrelated bars, such as Section 2(a), which deals with such unrelated categories as geographical indications and immoral marks,[30] while others contain only a single

[22] *Qualitex Co.*, 514 US 159 (1995).
[23] *Id.* at 162.
[24] *Id.*
[25] *Id.*
[26] *See* The Protection of Non-Traditional Trade Marks: Critical Perspectives (Irene Calboli & Martin Senftleben eds., 2019) (discussing the distinctiveness requirement for non-traditional marks across jurisdictions).
[27] 15 USC §§ 1052(a–e) (2018).
[28] Trademark Act of 1905, Act of Feb. 20, 1905, 33 Stat. 724, 15 USCA §§ 81 et seq. (1905).
[29] *See supra*, note 11.
[30] 15 USC § 1052(a).

bar, such as Section 2(c), which addresses only the registration of the name or portrait of a living person.[31] In addition, the prohibitions do not announce consistent standards. Some bars are absolute,[32] while other bars may be overcome by secondary meaning.[33] Finally, some bars are per se, such as the bar on the registration of flags, while others appear to require proof of deception or likely confusion.[34] In sum, they are quite a hodgepodge of restrictions.[35] Oddly, this is due only in small part to amendments that have occurred since the passage of the act.[36]

Even though bars to registration have been a part of US statutory trademark law since 1905, there now seems to be some uncertainty about the straightforward and fundamental question as to the effect of Section 2 on unregistered common law marks. While both registered and unregistered common law marks are federally protected under the Lanham Act in that both are granted causes of action, the symmetry between the two is elsewhere unclear.[37] It is axiomatic that registration does not give rise to trademark rights, but only grants certain benefits to a trademark owner.[38] That is, under US trademark law, a trademark must be in existence to receive federal registration.[39] Therefore, if registration is cancelled, it follows that common law rights may still subsist. What is less clear is whether corollary common law rules exist for all subject matter limitations. It now appears to be an open question as to what if any effect a refusal of registration, by the USPTO or as declared by a court, would have on the common law rights in a mark.[40] Previously, the Supreme Court has stated that "it is common ground that § 43(a) protects qualifying unregistered trademarks and that the general principles qualifying a mark for registration under § 2 of the Lanham Act are for the most part applicable in determining whether an unregistered mark is entitled to protection under § 43(a)."[41] In 2017, however, the Supreme Court explicitly chose to side-step this question.[42]

31 *Id.* § 1052(c).

32 *In re Hoefflin*, 97 USPQ 2d 1174, 1175 (TTAB 2010) (stating that § 2(c) "absolutely bars the registration of a designation that identifies a particular living individual absent written consent"); TMEP § 1206 (8th ed. Oct. 2018).

33 *See* 15 USC § 1052(f) (2018).

34 *Univ. of Notre Dame du Lac* v. *J.C. Gourmet Food Imps. Co.*, 703 F.2d 1372 (Fed. Cir. 1983) ("the board has applied a more stringent test under Sec. 2(a) requiring not only likelihood of confusion of source but also an intent to trade upon the goodwill of a prior user").

35 *See In re Brunetti*, 877 F.3d 1330, 1340 (Fed. Cir. 2017) ("§ 2(a) contains a hodgepodge of differing prohibitions on registration"); Baird, supra note 2 at 788 ("Section 2(a) is really a hodgepodge [sic] of several distinct statutory bars to federal trademark registration"); *see* Carl J. Minniti III, *The Lanham Act's Unconstitutional Hodgepodge*, 17 Rutgers J. L. & Religion 315 (2016).

36 Only the amendment that added the registration bar on geographical indications to § 2(a) contributed to the disorder of § 2. *See supra* note 11.

37 *See* 15 USC §§ 1114, 1125(a) (2018) (§ 32 grants a cause of action for federally registered marks, while § 43(a) grants a cause of action for unregistered common law marks).

38 *Matal* v. *Tam*, 137 S. Ct. 1744, 1751 (2017) (quoting *B&B Hardware* ("[F]ederal law does not create trademarks")).

39 15 USC § 1051(a)(2) ("The application shall include specification of the applicant's domicile and citizenship, the date of the applicant's first use of the mark, the date of the applicant's first use of the mark in commerce, the goods in connection with which the mark is used, and a drawing of the mark").

40 Dicta in the Federal Circuit's opinion in *In re Tam* called this into question. *In re Tam*, 808 F. 3d 1321, 1344–45, n. 11 (en banc), as corrected (Feb. 11, 2016) ("there is no authority extending §43(a) to marks denied under §2(a)'s disparagement provision").

41 *Two Pesos Inc.* v. *Taco Cabana*, 505 US, 763, 768 (1992).

42 *Matal* v. *Tam*, 137 S. Ct. 1744, 1753 n. 1 (2017)("We need not decide today whether respondent could bring suit under §43(a) if his application for federal registration had been lawfully denied under the disparagement clause").

IV WHY THESE BARS?

What is the public policy behind the hodgepodge of subject matter limitations contained in Section 2? The Lanham Act is not particularly revealing on the policy goals that animate it. At the end of a section of definitions, Section 45, the Act states that

> The intent of this chapter is to regulate commerce within the control of Congress by making actionable the deceptive and misleading use of marks in such commerce; to protect registered marks used in such commerce from interference by State, or territorial legislation; to protect persons engaged in such commerce against unfair competition; to prevent fraud and deception in such commerce by the use of reproductions, copies, counterfeits, or colorable imitations of registered marks; and to provide rights and remedies stipulated by treaties and conventions respecting trademarks, trade names, and unfair competition entered into between the United States and foreign nations.[43]

This language comes the closest to explicitly stating the reasons for Congress's enactment of a trademark act. In this provision, we can see clearly the public policy of protecting consumers against confusion and protecting the goodwill of trademark owners.[44] Congress also makes clear its intention to implement international treaties in the Act.

There is no mention in this provision, however, for any other public policy goal such as protecting the public against marks that could be harmful in any other way. Surprisingly, there is also no more than a hint about the public policy of ensuring free competition.[45]

The majority of the bars contained in Section 2 do not further the goals of the Lanham Act as stated in Section 45.[46] Certainly, the prohibitions on the registration of deceptive marks and

[43] 15 USC § 1127 (2018).

[44] Congressman Lanham, who sponsored the bill that became the Act, and for whom it is named, stated: "The purpose of [the Act] is to protect legitimate business and the consumers of the country." 92 CONG. REC. 7524 (1946). The Senate Report elaborated:

> The purpose underlying any trade-mark statute is twofold. One is to protect the public so it may be confident that, in purchasing a product bearing a particular trade-mark which it favorably knows, it will get the product which it asks for and wants to get. Secondly, where the owner of a trade-mark has spent energy, time, and money in presenting to the public the product, he is protected in his investment from its misappropriation by pirates and cheats. This is the well-established rule of law protecting both the public and the trade-mark owner. (S. REP. NO. 1333, 3 (1946))

In *Park 'N Fly v. Dollar Park & Fly*, the Supreme Court confirms these policy goals: "The Lanham Act provides national protection of trademarks in order to secure to the owner of the mark the goodwill of his business and to protect the ability of consumers to distinguish among competing producers." *Park 'N Fly v. Dollar Park & Fly*, 469 US 189, 198 (1985).

[45] The legislative history does include a reference to competition: "To protect trademarks, therefore, is to protect the public from deceit, to foster fair competition, and to secure to the business community the advantages of reputation and good will by preventing their diversion from those who have created them to those who have not. This is the end to which this bill is directed." S. REP. NO. 1333, 4 (1946) (emphasis added). The meaning of "fair competition" in this passage, however, is not the equivalent of "free competition," but more likely the equivalent of "not unfair competition." This passage also contains this sentence, which clarifies the intended meaning of "competition": "trade-marks, indeed, are the essence of competition, because they make possible a choice between competing articles by enabling the buyer to distinguish one from the other." *Id.*

[46] The Court of Appeals for the Federal Circuit stated the same:

> various provisions of the Lanham Act do not align with this as an exclusive or even a primary policy objective. *See* § 2(e) (prohibiting a mark which "(2) when used on or in connection with the goods of the applicant is primarily geographically descriptive of them ... (4) is primarily merely a surname," or "(5) comprises any matter that, as a whole, is functional"). Therefore, we find it difficult to conclude that the provisions in § 2 of the Lanham Act, including § 2(b), were all intended to protect the public from "pirates and cheats." (*In re City of Houston*, 731 F.3d 1326, 1330 (Fed. Cir. 2013))

marks that make a false connection in Section 2(a), confusingly similar marks in Section 2(d), and deceptively misdescriptive and primarily geographically deceptively misdescriptive marks in Section 2(e) all appear to be related to the goal of preventing consumer confusion. Other registration bars, such as for marks that are merely descriptive, primarily geographically descriptive, primarily merely a surname, relate to the definitional requirement of distinctiveness. Certain other prohibitions, however, seem unrelated to the traditional trademark policy goals of prevention confusion or requiring distinctiveness. Namely, the prohibition on the registration of disparaging, scandalous, immoral, and functional marks all appear to relate to public policy goals that exist beyond the confines of Section 45's stated policy goals. Even the prohibition on registering marks that contain an inaccurate geographical indication for wine or spirits, flags and state emblems, or a non-consenting living person's name, portrait, or signature, are unrelated to preventing confusion since they are not conditioned on the consumer's mistaken beliefs.[47]

The legislative history of the bars on registration in both the 1905 Act and the Lanham Act runs from nonexistent to scant. There was only one exchange during a 1939 hearing in the House of Representatives that sheds light on what Congress was trying to achieve in drafting some of these provisions. In this exchange, it was suggested that any use of the name of any president, living or long dead, should be prohibited in Section 2(c).[48] There was a discussion about not wanting "Abraham Lincoln gin" or "George Washington coffee."[49] One representative stated, however, that while "Abraham Lincoln gin" should be prohibited, "George Washington coffee" should be allowed.[50] It was also stated that the abuses of presidents' names should be taken care of by Section 2(a).[51] These exchanges suggest that Congress was concerned with protecting the reputation of presidents and that it envisioned a variety of means to achieve this goal. Ultimately, this protection was written to endure only during the life of the president and his widow.[52]

Without the aid of legislative intent, courts and commentators have tendered some proposals about the public policy goals behind these prohibitions on registration. For instance, it has been suggested that Section 2(c)'s bar on the registration of the name or portrait of a living person is

Likewise, the Trademark Trial and Appeal Board has stated:

> The prevention of confusion or deception is not the only concern of Trademark Act § 2. That section sets out a number of grounds for refusal of registration that have nothing to do with confusion. For example, Trademark Act § 2(a) prohibits registration of immoral or scandalous matter, and Section 2(e) sets out a variety of subject matter which is not registrable because – for various reasons – it is not considered to be a trademark – at least not without a showing of distinctiveness. (*The Government of the District of Columbia*, 101 USPQ 2d 1588 (TTAB 2012))

47 The inclusion of a bar on registering "a geographical indication which, when used on or in connection with wines or spirits, identifies a place other than the origin of the goods" was intended to implement art. 23 of the TRIPS Agreement, which obligates member states to prohibit the use and registration of geographical indications for wines and spirits not originating in the place indicated even where the use or registration would not be misleading. *See* Agreement on Trade-Related Aspects of Intellectual Property Rights, art. 23, Apr. 15, 1994, Marrakesh Agreement Establishing the World Trade Organization, Annex 1C, Legal Instrument-Results of the Uruguay Round, 33 ILM 1125 (1994) [hereinafter TRIPS].

48 *Hearing on H.R. 4744 Before the Subcommittee on Trade-Marks of the H. Committee on Patents*, 76th Cong. 18 (1939), reprinted in *Univ. of Notre Dame du Lac*, 703 F.2d 1372, 1379.

49 *Id.*

50 *Id.*

51 *Id.*

52 15 USC § 1052(c) (2018) (The text at the time of that hearing did not refer to the identity of a president: "(c) Consists of or comprises the name, portrait, or signature of a living individual unless by his written consent").

animated by a concern for privacy and the right of publicity.[53] In the 1930s when Section 2(c) was drafted and considered, the right to privacy was in its infancy,[54] but could well have inspired this provision. The right of publicity, however, significantly postdates this provision.[55] Whatever the policy goal of Section 2(c) may be, it is definitely not to prevent falsely suggesting a connection with a person since that goal is accomplished in Section 2(a).[56]

Section 2(b) of the Lanham Act prohibits the registration of marks that include a flag, coat of arms, or other insignia (or any simulation thereof) of any government from a municipality to a foreign nation. A similar prohibition first appeared in the 1905 Trademark Act.[57] This prohibition resembles Article 6*ter* of the Paris Convention[58] and may be a result of that international obligation.[59]

Commentary on Article 6*ter* of the Paris Convention indicates that the policy goal is to respect sovereign control of flags and state emblems.[60] Although certain uses of flags and state emblems may cause confusion as to the source of origin of goods, it would appear that this concern is not the reason for either the treaty or statutory prohibition.[61] In the case of the treaty provision, two standards are specified: one for intergovernmental organizations; and one for flags and state emblems. In the case of intergovernmental organizations, member states are only obligated to

53 *In re Hoefflin*, 97 USPQ 2d 1174, 1176 (TTAB 2010) (stating that § 2(c) "is intended to protect the intellectual property right of privacy and publicity that a living person has in his/her identity").

54 Samuel D. Warren & Louis Brandeis, *The Right to Privacy*, 4 HARV. L. REV. 193 (1890) (often credited as spawning the new right to privacy. New York was the first state to enact a privacy law in 1903. This statute prohibits the use of the name, portrait, or picture of any living person without prior consent for "advertising purposes" or "for the purposes of trade").

55 *Haelan Laboratories, Inc.* v. *Topps Chewing Gum, Inc.*, 202 F.2d 866 (2d Cir. 1953). (In his decision, Judge Jerome Frank distinguished the "right of publicity" from the "right of privacy" by focusing on the economic interests involved, rather than the personal interests characteristic of the right of privacy. *Haelan* is also cited as the first articulation of these interests as the "Right of Publicity.")

56 15 USC § 1052(a) (prohibiting the registration of a mark that would "falsely suggest a connection with persons, living or dead").

57 *See* Act of Feb. 20, 1905, ch. 592, § 5(b), 33 Stat. 724, 725–26, *repealed by* Trademark (Lanham) Act of 1946, ch. 540, 60 Stat. 427 (interestingly, the 1905 Act also prohibited the registration of any designation that indicated a fraternal society, institution, organization, club, or society incorporated in the United States).

58 *See* International Convention for the Protection of Industrial Property, as modified at The Hague on Nov. 6, 1925, 47 Stat. 1789, 1804–05, TS 834 and London on June 2, 1934, 53 Stat. 1748, 1776–78, TS 941 (the Paris Convention entered into force as to the United States on May 30, 1887).

59 Article 6*ter* was introduced in 1925, thus before the 1946 Lanham Act, but after the 1905 Act. G. H. C. BODENHAUSEN, GUIDE TO THE APPLICATION OF THE PARIS CONVENTION FOR THE PROTECTION OF INDUSTRIAL PROPERTY 95 (1969). However, the 1883 text of the Paris Convention provided that registration of a mark by a member state "may be refused, if the object, for which it is asked, is considered contrary to morals and to public order." Paris Convention, art. 6 (1883). A protocol accompanying the 1883 convention offered further guidance on art. 6. It stated that "it is understood that the use of public armorial bearings and decorations may be considered contrary to public order, in the sense of the final paragraph of Article 6." Paris Convention, Final Protocol, art. 4 (1883).

60 BODENHAUSEN, *supra* note 59, at 96 ("The reasons for this are that such registration or use would violate the right of the State to control the use of symbols of its sovereignty") (citations omitted). A WIPO report repeats this formulation. WIPO, Article 6*ter* of the Paris Convention: Legal and Administrative Aspects, SCT/15/3 (2005), 4 ("The reason for this exclusion is that registration or use of such emblems would encroach upon the right of the State concerned to control the use of the symbols of its identity and sovereignty") [hereinafter WIPO]. In addition, according to one commentary, delegates had argued that commercial uses were a "profaning" of these signs. See Actes 1911, 298; SAM RICKETSON, THE PARIS CONVENTION FOR THE PROTECTION OF INDUSTRIAL PROPERTY: A COMMENTARY 560 (2015). Moreover, previous to the Hague Act, the Final Protocol of the Paris Act had included marks such as "public armorial bearings and decorations" as marks that may be refused registration as being contrary to public order. *Id.*

61 Bodenhausen states that in addition to the loss of sovereign control, the use of flags and state emblems "might mislead the public with respect to the origin of goods to which such marks would be applied." BODENHAUSEN, *supra* note 59, at 96. In similar fashion, the WIPO report also notes this possibility: "Moreover, use of a State emblem as a trademark by an unrelated or unauthorized person is likely to mislead the public as to the origin or sponsorship of the goods to which the mark is attached." WIPO, *supra* note 60.

protect them when the use or registration would likely cause confusion.[62] In contrast, as Professor Bodenhausen makes clear in his authoritative guide to the Paris Convention, the obligation to protect flags and state emblems "is absolute and may not depend on suggestions of any connection between the trademark and the emblem."[63] Likewise, Section 2(b) of the Lanham Act, as well as Section 5 of the 1905 Act, similarly apply per se, and do not depend on a finding of deception, confusion, or a false suggestion of a connection.[64]

The prohibition on the registration of functional marks should be far more straightforward. This prohibition is relatively new to the statutory scheme, having been enacted only in 1998, but has been a feature of US common law since the late nineteenth century.[65] Nonetheless, commentators disagree about the public policy this limitation on subject matters serves: be it promoting competition, enforcing a natural right to copy, facilitating downstream innovation, or channeling innovation to patent law.[66] In its most recent functionality case, the Supreme Court neglected to elucidate the policy goal behind this doctrine, which may have contributed to the decision's failure to clarify the applicable tests.[67] In the case of the functionality bar, it is not that the animating policy is unaccounted for so much as it is ambiguous. In any event, the public policy behind the functional bar appears to be somewhat peripheral to the objectives of preventing confusion and protecting goodwill stated in Section 45.

V THE GOVERNMENT'S INTEREST IN REGULATING REGISTRATION

Recent litigation in the United States has pointedly raised the question of whether all of the limitations on registration contained in the Lanham Act can withstand constitutional challenge. Two recent cases, *Matal* v. *Tam* and *Iancu* v. *Brunetti*, have directly challenged two of the statutory constraints on what can be registered as a mark in the US.[68] In *Tam*, the Supreme Court ruled that the denial of registration to disparaging marks was an unconstitutional restriction of free speech.[69] As a result, the USPTO may no longer apply this statutory provision.

62 *See* Paris Convention, art. 6*ter*(1)(c)("The countries of the Union shall not be required to apply the said provisions when the use or registration referred to in subparagraph (a), above, is not of such a nature as to suggest to the public that a connection exists between the organization concerned and the armorial bearings, flags, emblems, abbreviations, and names, or if such use or registration is probably not of such a nature as to mislead the public as to the existence of a connection between the user and the organization").

63 *See* Bodenhausen, *supra* note 59, at 98; *see also* Stephen P. Ladas, Patents, Trademarks, and Related Rights: National and International Protection 1246 (1975); Ricketson, *supra* note 60, at 566–68 ("confusion on the part of the public is not required here by the terms of Article 6*ter*"; "it is not conditioned on the presence of confusion as in the case of international government organizations"). Moreover, both Bodenhausen and Ladas state that art. 6*ter* is a self-executing provision.

64 Marks that may suggest a false connection with an institution are barred in § 2(a). The Trademark Trial and Appeal Board makes this point in a recent case:

> In fact, if prevention of confusion were the "central purpose" of Trademark Act § 2(b), it would be superfluous, because registration of marks which would cause confusion is prohibited under Trademark Act § 2(d), and Trademark Act § 2(a) prohibits registration of marks which would be deceptive or falsely suggest a connection with others. To the contrary, rather than simply being a special case of confusion, registration of governmental insignia is prohibited by Trademark Act § 2(b) regardless of whether confusion would result. (*The Government of the District of Columbia*, 101 USPQ 2d 1588 (TTAB 2012) (emphasis added))

65 *See* Pub. L. No. 105–330, 112 Stat. 3064 (1998); Robert G. Bone, *Trademark Functionality Reexamined*, 7 J. Legal Analysis 183 (2015) (describing the history of the functionality bar in US common law).

66 *Id.* at 184.

67 *See TrafFix Devices, Inc.* v. *Marketing Displays, Inc.*, 532 US 23 (2001).

68 *See Matal* v. *Tam*, 137 S. Ct. 1744 (2017); *see In re Brunetti*, 877 F.3d 1335 (Fed. Cir. 2017).

69 *Matal* v. *Tam*, 137 S. Ct. 1744 (2017).

The Supreme Court struck down as unconstitutional a second trademark registration bar. The court ruled in *Iancu* v. *Brunetti*[70] that the government may no longer deny trademark registration to marks that are "scandalous" or "immoral." Thus, as a result of this litigation, the list of limitations on trademark subject matter has recently contracted and may further contract.

In *Matal* v. *Tam* the Supreme Court reviewed the statutory prohibition on the registration of a trademark that "consists of or comprises ... matter which may disparage ... persons, living or dead, institutions, beliefs, or national symbols, or bring them into contempt, or disrepute."[71] The USPTO and the lower courts found that under this provision, the applied-for mark THE SLANTS was disparaging to people of Asian descent and must be denied registration.[72] In addition to challenging this finding, the applicant, Simon Tam, raised a constitutional challenge to the provision. The argument was that even though the provision only denies registration, leaving the mark owner free to use the mark, it nevertheless has a "chilling effect" on free speech because in denying the significant benefits that come with registration, the government is steering mark owners away from certain speech.[73]

In striking down the challenged law in an unanimous decision, the Supreme Court held that the disparaging marks provision of the Lanham Act "offends a bedrock First Amendment principle: Speech may not be banned on the ground that it expresses ideas that offend."[74] The provision violates the First Amendment because it facially discriminates based on viewpoint.[75] Viewpoint discrimination is presumptively unconstitutional and subject to a strict scrutiny analysis.[76] The Court found that the disparagement bar did not survive strict scrutiny because the government's interest in denying registration to disparaging marks was neither compelling nor narrowly tailored.[77]

Writing for four justices,[78] Justice Alito found that the disparaging marks provision also failed the *Central Hudson* test,[79] which dictates an intermediate scrutiny analysis.[80] To survive intermediate scrutiny,[81] the regulation must further an important government interest, and must do so by means that are substantially related to that interest.[82] In this case, the government could not easily identify the government's interest that the provision advances. The question of the government's interest came up in oral arguments both in the Court of Appeals for the Federal Circuit and the Supreme Court. During oral argument in the Supreme Court, Justice Breyer questioned the USPTO's deputy solicitor general about the purpose of the disparagement provision.[83] Surprising most legal commentators, he responded that the provision was consistent with broader trademark policy because disparaging marks were a distraction to the public.[84]

70 588 US ___ (2019).
71 15 USC § 1052.
72 *See In re Tam*, 808 F.3d 1321 (Fed. Cir. 2015).
73 Brief for Respondent, *Matal* v. *Tam*, 137 S. Ct. 1744 (2017), 2017 WL 2621315 at *33.
74 *See id.* at 1751 (Alito J).
75 *See id.* at 1763.
76 *Id.* at 1748.
77 *Id.* at 1749.
78 Although the decision was unanimous, the Court produced two opinions, each representing for justices. Justice Gorsuch did not participate. *See id.* at 1747, 1749.
79 *Id.* at 1749.
80 *See Central Hudson Gas & Electric Corp.* v. *Public Service Commission*, 447 US 557, 566 (1980) (subjecting restrictions on commercial speech to intermediate scrutiny).
81 The Supreme Court created this test in *Craig* v. *Boren*, 429 US 190 (1976).
82 *Craig* v. *Boren*, 429 US 190 (1976).
83 Transcript of Oral Argument at 7–8, *Matal* v. *Tam* 137 S. Ct. 1744 (2017).
84 *Id.* at 8.

The lack of a clearly identifiable rationale for this provision in the legislative history is something addressed in the scholarship.[85]

In his concurring opinion, Justice Kennedy stated that this "case does not present the question of how other provisions of the Lanham Act should be analyzed under the First Amendment."[86] Nonetheless, Justice Kennedy went part way to answer this question by observing that trademark law does not run afoul of the First Amendment when it prohibits the use of confusing and misleading trademarks.[87] Although this statement is only dicta, it explicitly raises the question of exactly when trademark law may runs afoul of the First Amendment when it prohibits the non-misleading use of trademarks or denies registration for other reasons.

While the Supreme Court was deciding *Tam*, another case was waiting in the wings. Within two years of deciding *Tam*, the Supreme Court had before it the precise question anticipated by Justice Kennedy of how another provision of the Lanham Act should be analyzed under the First Amendment. In *Iancu* v. *Brunetti*, at issue was the constitutionality of the Lanham Act's prohibition on the registration of scandalous and immoral marks.[88] The case involved Erik Brunetti's application for the trademark "FUCT" for apparel, which was refused by the USPTO under Section 2(a) of the Lanham Act as scandalous and immoral,[89] and therefore unregistrable.[90]

The main issue in *Brunetti* was whether the registration bar for scandalous and immoral marks is also a regulation of the expression of a viewpoint and thus unconstitutional under *Tam*. According to the majority, this provision disfavors ideas and as such is substantively indistinguishable from the provision in *Tam*.[91] Here, "the Lanham Act allows registration of marks when their messages accord with, but not when their messages defy, society's sense of decency or propriety."[92]

It would appear that no further statutory or doctrinal vulnerabilities emerge from this decision that had not been portended by *Tam*. This decision, however, does pave a path forward for amending the Lanham Act to add a bar to the registration of marks that are "scandalous in their mode of expression," or are "vulgar, lewd, sexually explicit, or profane."

In *Tam*, the justices did not agree on everything. In *Brunetti*, the justices expressed disagreement. Chief Justice Roberts, Justice Breyer, and Justice Sotomayor each filed separate opinions. Although each concurred that the registration bar on marks that are "immoral" amounts to unconstitutional viewpoint discrimination, each believed that the "scandalous" bar could be saved by accepting the government's proposed limiting application of this provision to marks that are "vulgar," "lewd," "sexually explicit or profane."

In addition to these three justices, Justice Alito, the author of the majority opinion in *Tam*, stated in his concurring opinion that the court's opinion would not "prevent Congress from adopting a [] statute that precludes the registration of marks containing vulgar terms that play no real part in the expression of ideas."[93] He went on to note that the mark in question in this

[85] Christine Haight Farley, *Registering Offense: The Prohibition of Slurs as Trademarks*, in Diversity in Intellectual Property: Identities, Interests, and Intersections (Irene Calboli & Srividhya Ragavan eds., 2015); Christine Haight Farley, *Stabilizing Morality in Trademark Law*, 63 Am. U. L. Rev. 101 (2014).

[86] *Matal* v. *Tam*, 137 S. Ct. 1744, 1773–74 (2017) (Kennedy J).

[87] *Id.*

[88] 139 S, Ct. 2294 (2019).

[89] The USPTO has long followed the established precedent of treating the two terms, "scandalous" and "immoral" as a unitary provision. *See In re Brunetti*, 877 F.3d 1330, 1336 (Fed. Cir. 2017).

[90] *Id.* at 1335.

[91] 139 S. Ct. at 2301.

[92] *Id.* at 2300.

[93] *Id.* at 2303.

case – FUCT – "is not needed to express any idea and, in fact, as commonly used today, generally signifies nothing except emotion and a severely limited vocabulary."[94]

In *Brunetti*, it would appear that some Justices have retreated from the idea that a registration refusal is a burden on speech. Justice Breyer flatly stated that "an applicant who seeks to register a mark should not expect complete freedom to say what she wishes, but should instead expect linguistic regulation."[95] Perhaps the most striking rebuttal of registration as speech comes in this passage in Chief Justice Roberts' opinion:

> Whether such marks can be registered does not affect the extent to which their owners may use them in commerce to identify goods. No speech is being restricted; no one is being punished. The owners of such marks are merely denied certain additional benefits associated with federal trademark registration. The Government, meanwhile, has an interest in not associating itself with trademarks whose content is obscene, vulgar, or profane. The First Amendment protects the freedom of speech; it does not require the Government to give aid and comfort to those using obscene, vulgar, and profane modes of expression.[96]

Thus, in *Brunetti*, the court seemed more inclined to endeavor to find the statute constitutional than it did in *Tam*. Perhaps in *Brunetti*, it became clear to the court that at issue was whether the government should be obligated to register a white supremacist's application for the N-word. Even though *Tam* involved a purported racial epithet, the court did not express any unease such as comes through in the opening lines of Justice Sotomayor's opinion: "The Court's decision today will beget unfortunate results. . . . [T]he Government will have no statutory basis to refuse (and thus no choice but to begin) registering marks containing the most vulgar, profane, or obscene words and images imaginable."[97]

Just three cases have caused a recent interest in these trademark registration provisions: first the Redskins case (*Blackhorse* v. *PFI*),[98] then *Tam*, and finally *Brunetti*.[99] On the constitutional issue alone, these three cases have produced seventeen court opinions. Even still, many important questions have been explicitly sidestepped such as to what extent, if any, the commercial speech doctrine plays, whether viewpoint-neutral content discriminatory registration bars pass muster, or whether trademark registration may be considered as a government program or subsidy. For these reasons, perhaps there will be more such cases to come.

Both Supreme Court decisions held that the registration bars were unconstitutional because they were viewpoint-based. Left as an open question is what the appropriate test or standard of scrutiny is when trademark regulations are not viewpoint-based.[100] We will have to wait to learn whether content-based trademark restrictions are also subject to strict scrutiny or, as commercial speech, intermediate scrutiny.

VI RECONSIDERING PUBLIC POLICY LIMITATIONS

The broad reading of the First Amendment in *Tam* and *Brunetti* will likely have an impact beyond these cases. If another court decides that trademark registration bars are subject to either

94 *Id.*.
95 *Id.* at 2306.
96 *Id.* at 2303–34.
97 *Id.* at 2308.
98 112 F. Supp. 3d 439 (ED Va. 2015).
99 Previously, the constitutionality of these provisions was settled by the Court of Customs and Patent Appeals, the predecessor to the Court of Appeals for the Federal Circuit, in *In re McGinley*, 660 F.2d 481 (CCPA 1981).
100 *Matal* v. *Tam*, 137 S. Ct. 1744, 1767–68 (Kennedy J).

strict or intermediate scrutiny, certain other limitations on subject matter contained in the Lanham Act may be vulnerable. In *Tam*, Justice Kennedy stated that "[t]he central purpose of trademark registration is to facilitate source identification," and "[w]hether a mark is disparaging bears no plausible relation to that goal."[101] According to this reasoning, any limitation on the registration of a mark must relate to the public policy facilitating source identification in order to survive constitutional scrutiny.[102]

As a result of *Brunetti*, other public policy limitations on registration may also be in jeopardy. Section 2 of the Lanham Act contains other registration bars that are not directed at facilitating source identification. For instance, Section 2(a) prohibits the registration of inaccurate geographical indications of origin for wine or spirits, Section 2(b) prohibits the registration of flags and state emblems, and Section 2(c) prohibits the registration of the names or portraits of specific living persons absent written consent.[103] While each of these bars may prevent registrations that could be considered false or misleading, significantly these provisions are not aimed at that objective and are not conditioned on such a finding. Would these prohibitions then survive strict or intermediate scrutiny? Would they even survive the lowest level of scrutiny, rational basis, which demands that the law's means be "rationally related" to a conceivable and legitimate state end?[104] The absence of any clear policy behind the bar on disparaging marks caused trouble for the government in *Tam*. These other non-misleading-based bars similarly suffer from not having a clearly identifiable policy rationale.

Many of the subject matter limitations contained in section 2 relate to international treaty obligations. For the most part, the Paris Convention adopted a permissive scheme with regard to the refusal of trademarks. Under Paris Convention Article *6quinquies*, member states may, but are not obligated to, refuse marks that are "contrary to morality or public order."[105] Both the bar on flags and state emblems and the bar on inaccurate geographical indications for wines and spirits, however, are mandatory obligations under the Paris Convention or the TRIPS Agreement.[106] In these instances only, there is a question of whether an international treaty obligation creates a compelling government interest that would satisfy strict scrutiny. The Supreme Court has not yet so held.[107] However, even if it were so inclined, the fact that these bars to registration only partially implement treaty obligations would complicate that analysis.[108]

101 *Id.* at 1768 (Kennedy J).

102 In addition to § 2 bars, the Lanham Act also includes a provision that creates a ground for opposing the registration of a mark based on dilution. *See* 15 USC § 1063(a) ("Any person who believes that he would be damaged by the registration of a mark upon the principal register, including the registration of any mark which would be likely to cause dilution by blurring or dilution by tarnishment under section 1125(c) of this title, may, upon payment of the prescribed fee, file an opposition"). This provision, like certain other registration bars, does not relate to the public policy facilitating source identification.

103 15 USC §§ 1052(a)–(c).

104 *Lochner* v. *New York*, 198 US 45 (1905) (Holmes' dissent is the first mention of rational basis).

105 *See* International Convention for the Protection of Industrial Property art. 6quinquies, as modified at The Hague on Nov. 6, 1925, 47 Stat. 1789, 1804–05, TS 834 and London on June 2, 1934, 53 Stat. 1748, 1776–78, TS 941.

106 *See id.*; TRIPS, *supra* note 47.

107 *See Boos* v. *Barry*, 485 US 312, 322–24 (1988) ("[T]he fact that an interest is recognized in international law does not automatically render the interest 'compelling' for purposes of First Amendment analysis").

108 Article 6*ter* of the Paris Convention obligates member states to both refuse registration and prevent the use of marks that contain flags and state emblems. *See supra* note 57. Section 2(b) only prohibits the registration of such marks. Likewise, art. 23 of TRIPS obligates member states to provide the legal means for interested parties to prevent the use of inaccurate geographical indications for wine and spirits in addition to refusing their registration. *See* TRIPS *supra* note 47. Section 2(a) addresses only the registration bar.

VII CONCLUSION

The Supreme Court's recent decisions in *Tam* and *Brunetti* have provoked a momentary focus on the public policy behind the Lanham Act's diverse subject matter restrictions. Together these cases clarify that the First Amendment constrains what limitations the US government may place on the subject matter of trademarks. As a result of these cases, US trademark law may diverge from other jurisdictions as the constitutional protection of speech has caused an expansion of trademark subject matter. We may now add freedom of expression to the list of public policy concerns that shape trademark subject matter.

14

Public Policy Limitations on Trademark Subject Matter

An EU Perspective

Jens Schovsbo and Thomas Riis***

I INTRODUCTION

The European Union has issued two set of rules on trademarks. The first, the EU Trade Mark Regulation (EUTR), created a single title for protection throughout all of the EU countries (the EU Trade Mark (EUTM)), based on applications to the European Union Intellectual Property Office (EUIPO).[1] The EU Trade Mark Directive (EUTD) harmonized the national trademark laws of the EU countries.[2]

In the following, we focus on some of the general criteria for protecting EUTMs, as that criteria has developed in the case law from the Court of Justice of the EU (CJEU), the General Court of the EU (GCEU) and the Boards of Appeal of the EUIPO (BoA).[3] Over the years, the CJEU played a very active role in developing the EU trademark system, and stressed the societal values and interests in "undistorted competition" within (what eventually became) the EU.[4] In the same vein, the CJEU has emphasized the public interest in not restricting the availability of descriptive signs or indications (*Freihaltebedürfnis*).[5] It has also expressed concern about the risk of over-extending trademark protection: for instance, the Court has made it clear that protection should not by itself confer "an unjustified advantage for a single trader,"[6] and that trademark law offers no protection "against practices inherent in competition."[7] Most recently, the EUTR and EUTD have been amended to now explicitly recognize that trademark rules "should be applied

* Professor, Centre for Information and Innovation Law (CIIR), University of Copenhagen.
** Professor, Centre for Information and Innovation Law (CIIR), University of Copenhagen.

1 Regulation (EU) 2017/1001 on the European Union trademark, of June 16, 2017, 2017 OJ L 154, 1–99. The first Regulation was Council Regulation (EC) No. 40/94 of Dec. 20, 1993 on the Community trademark, of Jan. 14, 1994, 1994 OJ L 11, 1–36.

2 Directive (EU) 2015/2436 of the European Parliament and of the Council of Dec. 16, 2015, to approximate the laws of the member states relating to trademarks, of Dec. 23, 2015, 2015 OJ L 336, 1–26. The Directive should be implemented in national law by Jan. 15, 2019, cf. art. 54.

3 As we focus on case law from the EU system, we will as a general rule not look into national case law.

4 Judgment of the CJEU in Case C-10/89, SA *Cnl-Sucal* NV v. *Hag* GF AG (Hag II), 1990 ECR I-03711, ECLI:EU:C:1990:359, §13.

5 Judgment of the CJEU in Joined Cases C-108/97 and C-109/97, *Windsurfing Chiemsee* v. *Boots- und Segelzubehör Walter Huber and Franz Attenberger*, ECLI:EU:C:1999:230, §25.

6 Judgment of the CJEU in Case C-104/01, *Libertel Groep BV* v. *Benelux Merkenbureau*, 2003 ECR I-03793, ECLI:EU:C:2003:244, § 54.

7 Judgment of the CJEU in Case C-323/09, *Interflora Inc., Interflora British Unit* v. *Marks & Spencer plc.* v. *Flowers Direct Online Ltd.*, 2011 ECR I-08625, ECLI:EU:C:2011:604, § 57.

in a way that ensures full respect for fundamental rights and freedoms, and in particular the freedom of expression."[8]

With these general remarks in mind, we now to turn to the specific issues at hand.

II TRADEMARK SUBJECT MATTER IN EU LAW

In keeping with the international standards,[9] EU law recognizes "any signs" capable of "distinguishing the goods or services of one undertaking from those of other undertakings" and of being "represented" on the Register of the EUIPO as "trade marks."[10]

The scope of trademark protection is thus very wide. However, it is not unlimited. Most importantly for the present purposes, trademark subject matter is delimited by the grounds for refusal in Articles 7 and 8 of the EUTR.[11]

The various grounds for refusal found in those provisions can be divided into two general groups. The first group limits trademark subject matter on the basis of *public policy* concerns.[12] The second group limits trademark subject matter on the basis of the practical circumstance of delimiting trademark rights from conflicting rights.[13]

The first group of grounds for refusal, those which limit trademark subject matter on the basis of public policy concerns, include the following:

- signs which do not conform to the requirements of Article 4 [distinctiveness and clear and precise representation];
- trade marks which are devoid of any distinctive character;
- trade marks which consist exclusively of signs or indications which may serve, in trade, to designate the kind, quality, quantity, intended purpose, value, geographical origin or the time of production of the goods or of rendering of the service, or other characteristics of the goods or service;
- trade marks which consist exclusively of signs or indications which have become customary in the current language or in the bona fide and established practices of the trade;
- trade marks which are contrary to public policy or to accepted principles of morality;
- trade marks which are of such a nature as to deceive the public, for instance as to the nature, quality or geographical origin of the goods or service.[14]

[8] EUTR, *supra* note 1, Point 21; EUTD *supra* note 2, point 27.

[9] TRIPS: Agreement on Trade-Related Aspects of Intellectual Property Rights, Apr. 15, 1994, Marrakesh Agreement Establishing the World Trade Organization, Annex 1C, 1869 UNTS 299, 33 ILM 1197 (1994), art. 15 [hereinafter TRIPS Agreement].

[10] EUTR, *supra* note 1, art. 4.

[11] Some limitations have also been acknowledged in the international intellectual property right (IPR) conventions, *see* most notably TRIPS Agreement, *supra* note 9, art. 15 (excluding descriptive signs) and art. 17 (allowing for limitations for fair use).

[12] It is important to bear in mind that public policy concerns also have an important role to play in respect of the scope of trademark rights and, in particular, regarding the exceptions to the exclusive rights, *see* in particular EUTR *supra* note 1, art. 14. However, in this chapter we address exclusively public policy limitations on trademark subject matter. *See*, for the "broader view," *e.g.* Martin Senftleben, *Free Signs and Free Use: How to Offer Room for Freedom of Expression within the Trademark System*, *in* Research Handbook on Human Rights and Intellectual Property 354–76 (Christophe Geiger ed., 2015).

[13] This group consists of all the so-called relative grounds for refusal in EUTR, *supra* note 1, art. 8 (older trademark rights and geographical indications) and some of the "absolute grounds" for refusal (art. 7(1)(h)–(m): state emblems etc., geographical indications and plant variety denominations).

[14] For the present purposes, the wording of the current provisions do not differ substantially from the wording of the provisions contained in the previous versions of the EUTR and EUTD, *supra* notes 1 and 2. *See further* Annette Kur & Martin Senftleben, European Trade Mark Law (2017) § 4.44 et seq.

The listed limitations all constitute absolute grounds for refusal, and accordingly the EUIPO must refuse an application *ex officio* if it falls within one of these categories.[15] As such, the limitations must be considered essential for the EU trademark system to function.

Three different policy objectives underlie the public policy limitations in Article 7(1):

Safeguarding the public domain (III.A).
Limiting the use of offensive signs (III.B).
Preventing consumer deception (III.C).

The CJEU has explained that the grounds for refusal to register a sign according to Article 7(1) must be interpreted in the light of the underlying (individual) public interests.[16] In the following, we examine those underlying policy objectives and describe how they are pursued in Article 7 EUTR. Furthermore, we assess the relative importance of each objective, identify possible overlaps and discuss possible developments in EU case law regarding evaluation of the objectives. This enables us to identify and understand the general public policy and interests lying behind the EU rules on trademark subject matter and the development of the interrelationship between policy objectives and trademark subject matter.

III PUBLIC POLICY LIMITATIONS OF TRADEMARK SUBJECT MATTER

A *Safeguarding the Public Domain*

Most of the grounds for refusal in EUTR Article 7 that are based on public policy concerns aim to exclude certain signs from protection. In this way, they serve to safeguard the *public domain*.[17] From a practical point of view, the most important grounds for refusal to safeguard the public domain are the provisions on *distinctiveness*, and the exclusion from trademark subject matter of *descriptive* signs in Article 7(1)(b)–(d) of the EUTR. These (to a large extent overlapping) provisions constitute the main gatekeepers to trademark protection as signs which do not pass muster cannot be recognized as trademarks.[18] In the following, we give a brief overview of some main points from the extensive case law from the EU Courts and Boards of Appeals.[19] It is important to note at the outset that according to EUTR Article 7(3), Article 7(1)(b)–(d) shall not apply if the trademark *has become distinctive* in relation to the goods or services for which registration is requested as a consequence of the use which has been made. In this way, these limitations may be overcome through use of a sign for goods or services, and the effect on these efforts in perception of the sign by the "the average consumer."[20] The overall framework for determining whether a sign makes it past the post or not is the principle of undistorted competition.[21]

[15] EUTR, *supra* note 1, arts. 42 and 59; art. 7 may also be relied upon before national courts in invalidity proceeding.

[16] Judgment of the CJEU in Case C-48/11, *Lego Juris A/S* v. *OHIM*, ECLI:EU:C:2010:516, § 43.

[17] As this concept was defined by the Court of Justice of the European Free Trade Association States in *Vigeland*, *see infra* note 61. For 3-D marks and other functional signs, the functionality doctrine in EUTR, *supra* note 1, art. 7(1)(e) excludes functional signs from trademark protection; *see* Ilanah Fhima, *The Public Interest in European Trade Mark Law*, Intell. Prop. Quarterly 311 (2017), at 314.

[18] Kur & Senftleben, *supra* note 14, at § 4.55.

[19] *See* generally *id.*, at para. 4.50 et seq.

[20] Judgment of the CJEU in Case C-342/97, *Lloyd Schuhfabrik Meyer & Co. GmbH* v. *Klijsen Handel BV*, 1999 ECR I-03819, ECLI:EU:C:1999:323 § 26.

[21] Kur & Senftleben, *supra* note 14, at § 4.51 with reference to Judgment of the CJEU in Case C-517/99, *Merz & Krell GmbH & Co.*, 2001 ECR I-06959, ECLI:EU:C:2001:510 § 21.

1 Lack of Distinctive Character

Marks devoid of distinctive character are excluded from registration pursuant to EUTR Article 7(1)(b).[22] According to the CJEU, the public interest underlying Article 7(1)(b) is manifestly inseparable from the essential function of a trademark, which is "to guarantee the identity of the origin of the marked product to the consumer or end-user by enabling him or her, without any possibility of confusion, to distinguish the product or service from others which have another origin."[23] For a trademark to possess distinctive character, it must be able to identify the product or service as originating from a particular undertaking, and to distinguish that product from those of other undertakings.[24] Generally, the CJEU has set the benchmark at a rather low level.[25] The Court has repeatedly stated that the same criteria for assessing distinctiveness apply, no matter the type of the mark.[26] However, in some instances the Court has recognized the need to take special or broader concerns into account. In *Henkel* (concerning the shape of two tablets, i.e. a 3-D trademark), the Court thus held that only trademarks that *depart significantly* from the norm or customs of the industry and thereby fulfil the essential function of indicating origin, are not devoid of any distinctive character for the purposes of that provision.[27] Consequently, signs that conform to or depart only insignificantly from the norm or customs of the industry are left freely available for other enterprises to use. "Distinctive character" is thus delimited by the requirement of availability (*Freihaltebedürfnis*).[28] The requirement of a *significant departure* in this way expands the scope of Article 7(1)(b), and thereby limits the reach of trademark protection for marks where the public interest in free and unrestricted competition is particularly pertinent.[29] On a similar note, the Court noted in *Libertel*[30] (where the issue concerned an orange colour) that in assessing the potential distinctiveness of a given colour as a trademark, regard must be given to the *general interest in not unduly restricting the availability of colours* for other traders offering for sale goods or services of the same type as those for which registration is sought.[31]

[22] The requirement of distinctiveness is also included as part of the ground for refusal in EUTR, *supra* note 1, art. 7(1)(a). On the relationship between art. 7(1)(a) and 7(1)(b)–(d), see Judgment of the CJEU in Case C-299/99, *Koninklijke Philips Electronics NV* v. *Remington Consumer Products Ltd.*, 2002 ECR I-05475, ECLI:EU:C:2002:377, §§ 38–40.

[23] Judgment of the CJEU in Case C-305/14, *Sergiu Lucian Băbăşan* v. *Inspectoratul Judeţean de Poliţie Satu Mare*, 2014 EUR-Lex CELEX 62015CA0200, ECLI:EU:C:2004:532, §§ 27 and 23.

[24] Judgment of the CJEU in Joined Cases C-456/01 P & C-457/01 P, *Henkel KGaA* v. *OHIM*, 2004 ECR I-05089, ECLI:EU:C:2004:258, § 34.

[25] Kur & Senftleben, *supra* note 14, at § 4.53.

[26] Judgment of the CJEU in Joined Cases C-53/01–C-55/01, *Linde AG, Winward Industries Inc. and Rado Uhren AG*, 2003 ECR I-03161, ECLI:EU:C:2003:206, § 42.

[27] Judgment of the CJEU in Joined Cases C-456/01 P & C-457/01 P, *Henkel KGaA* v. *OHIM*, § 39 (concerning the identical provision in art. 3(1)(b) EUTD).

[28] However, according to the GCEU, *Freihaltebedürfnis* does not imply an absolute exclusion of certain signs and therefore single letters – like colours and numbers presented singly – are not excluded per se "as fundamental elements, [that] must remain available to all as a 'general reserve' for the purposes of identification, description or other uses," *see* Judgment of the GCEU in Case T-23/07, *BORCO-Marken-Import Matthiesen GmbH & Co. KG* v. *OHIM*, 2009 ECR II-00887, ECLI:EU:T:2009:126, § 48; *see also* the Judgment of the CJEU in the same case, Case C-265/09 P, *BORCO-Marken-Import Matthiesen GmbH & Co. KG* v. *OHIM*, 2010 ECR I-08265, ECLI:EU:C:2010:508.

[29] *See* Fhima, *supra* note 17, at 318. Naturally, the exclusion effect of these principles depends on where one draws the line between "significant" and "insignificant" differences; *see also* Irene Calboli, *Chocolate, Fashion, Toys and Cabs: The Misunderstood Distinctiveness of Non-Traditional Trademarks*, Int'l rev. Indus. Prop. & Comp. L. 1 (2018); Danny Freidmann, *The Bottle Is the Message: Only the Distinctive Survive as 3-D Community Trade Marks*, GRUR Int'l. 1195 (2014).

[30] *Libertel*, *supra* note 6.

[31] *Id.*, para. 60. *See also* Judgment of the GCEU in Case T-97/08, *KUKA Roboter GmbH* v. *OHIM*, 2010 ECR II-05059, ECLI:EU:T:2010:396, § 44.

2 *Descriptive Signs*

The availability requirement is also essential when it comes to descriptive signs excluded from trademark subject matter under EUTR Article 7(1)(c)–(d). In *Windsurfing Chiemsee*[32] (regarding the name of the geographical location "Chiemsee"), the CJEU stated that it is in the public interest that signs or indications that may serve to designate the geographical origin of goods or services must remain available to all undertakings as indications of the geographical origin of the category of goods or services concerned.[33]

The CJEU has applied an expansive interpretation of EUTR Article 7(1)(c), thereby strengthening the public policy objective of safeguarding the public domain.[34] In *Wrigley* (on the word DOUBLEMINT for chewing gum), the Court held that for the Office for Harmonization in the Internal Market (OHIM) (now EUIPO) to refuse to register a trademark under EUTR Article 7(1)(c), it is not necessary that signs and indications composing the mark be in use at the time of the application in a way that is descriptive of goods or services, such as in relation to which the application is filed, or of characteristics of those goods or services.[35] It is sufficient that such signs and indications *could* be used for such purposes. A sign must therefore be refused registration under that provision, if at least one of its possible meanings designates a characteristic of the goods or services concerned. Accordingly, Article 7(1)(c) is applicable to more signs than those that are "exclusively descriptive."

The ground for refusal in Article 7(1)(c) is applicable even when there are more usual signs or indications for designating the same characteristics, regardless of the number of competitors that may have an interest in using the signs or indications of which the mark consists.[36]

In addition, the CJEU held in *Windsurfing Chiemsee* that the application of the provision similar to EUTR Article 7(1)(c) "does not depend on there being a real, current or serious need to leave a sign or indication free." In the EUIPO Examination Guidelines ("Guidelines"), that statement has been interpreted as implying that the provision does not require a "konkretes (concrete) Freihaltebedürfnis," which must imply that an abstract *Freihaltebedürfnis* suffices.[37] An abstract *Freihaltebedürfnis* must imply that the delimitation of the scope of freely available signs can be based on more general considerations of reasonableness.

Another indication of the expansive interpretation of Article 7(1)(c) favoured by the CJEU relates to neologisms (new words) composed of known words. Such neologisms may have distinctive character, but usually do not pass muster. In *Campina Melkunie*, for example, the applicant applied for registration of the mark BIOMILD for dairy products, and the mark was used for yoghurt with a mild taste.[38] The Court held:

> As a general rule, the mere combination of elements, each of which is descriptive of characteristics of the goods or services in respect of which registration is sought, itself remains descriptive of those characteristics within the meaning of Article 3(1)(c) of the Directive [similar to

[32] *Windsurfing Chiemsee*, *supra* note 5.

[33] *Id.* §§ 26 and 30. Similar in Judgment of the CJEU in Case C-191/01 P, *OHIM* v. *Wm. Wrigley Jr. Company*, 2003 ECR I-12447, ECLI:EU:C:2003:579, § 31; and *Linde supra* note 6, § 74.

[34] Cf. Fhima, *supra* note 17, at 318 (regarding EUTR art. 7(1)(b)).

[35] Judgment of the CJEU in Case C-191/01 P, *OHIM* v. *Wm. Wrigley Jr. Company*.

[36] Philips, *supra* note 22, § 61, and Judgment of the CJEU in Case C-265/00, *Campina Melkunie BV* v. *Benelux-Merkenbureau*, 2004 ECR I-01699, EU:C:2004:87, § 42.

[37] Guidelines for the Examination of European Union Trade Marks and Registered Community Designs, EUIPO, § B.4.1.4.2. (2017), https://euipo.europa.eu/tunnel-web/secure/webdav/guest/document_library/contentPdfs/law_and_practice/designs_practice_manual/WP_1_2017/examination_of_design_invalidity_applications_en.pdf.

[38] Judgment of the CJEU in Case C-265/00, *Campina Melkunie BV*, *supra* note 36, § 42.

> Article 7(1)(c) EUTR] even if the combination creates a neologism. Merely bringing those elements together without introducing any unusual variations, in particular as to syntax or meaning, cannot result in anything other than a mark consisting exclusively of signs or indications which may serve, in trade, to designate characteristics of the goods or services concerned.[39]

According to the Court, if such a word shall escape the exclusion concerning descriptive signs, there must be:

> a perceptible difference between the neologism and the mere sum of its parts: that assumes that, because of the unusual nature of the combination in relation to the goods or services, the word creates an impression which is sufficiently far removed from that produced by the mere combination of meanings lent by the elements of which it is composed, with the result that the word is more than the sum of its parts.[40]

In practice it is nearly impossible to find examples that meet this test.[41] Thus, the effect of the relatively high threshold is to keep most such signs free from trademark protection.[42]

Summing up, the ability of the distinctiveness and non-descriptiveness requirements in serving as gatekeepers to the trademark system depends on where the lines are drawn between signs that can be accepted and those that cannot. If too much is protected, there is a risk that the values associated with the public domain are being undermined.[43] It falls outside of the scope of the current study to discuss the state of the practice in detail. We note, however, as a general point that the focus of the CJEU on the principle of undistorted competition as, in the words of Kur and Senftleben, "the general precept for the examination" regularly applied by the CJEU, and the ability of potential trademark holders to overcome a lack of distinctiveness or the original descriptive nature of a sign, clearly limit the effectiveness of these provisions to serve the general interests in protecting the public domain.[44] As pointed out by *Anemaet*, the current structure may create "dysfunctional incentives" and make it attractive for companies to invest in appropriating descriptive, cultural and non-traditional signs.[45] We discuss in Section IV how the legal framework could be improved to better reflect the general interests in keeping certain signs completely outside of reach of trademark protection.

B Limiting the Use of Offensive Signs

EUTR Article 7(1)(f) excludes from registration trademarks that are contrary to public policy or accepted principles of morality. The provision does not limit the use of the expression, as such, but merely prevents anyone from gaining trademark exclusivity to such marks. For this reason, the GCEU has found[46] that the limitation does not encroach on the right to free expression

[39] *Id.* § 39.

[40] *Id.* § 41. In early cases the threshold was very low, *see* in particular Judgment of the CJEU in Case C-383/99, *Procter & Gamble Company* v. *OHIM*, 2001 ECR I-06251, ECLI:EU:C:2001:461 (accepting BABY-DRY for diapers); for an overview of case law, *see* KUR & SENFTLEBEN, *supra* note 14, at § 4.106 et seq.

[41] *See* Fhima, *supra* note 17, at 319.

[42] *See* also KUR & SENFTLEBEN, *supra* note 14, § 4.107 et seq.

[43] Lotte Anemaet, *The Public Domain Is Under Pressure – Why We Should Not Rely on Empirical Data When Assessing Trademark Distinctiveness*, INT'L REV. INTELL. PROP. &COMPETITION L. 303, 304 (2016).

[44] KUR & SENFTLEBEN, *supra* note 14.

[45] Anemaet, *supra* note 43.

[46] Judgment of the GCEU in Case T-417/10, *Federico Cortés del Valle López* v. *OHIM*, 2012 ECLI:EU:T:2012:120 § 26. In the United States, the situation is different, *see Matal* v. *Tam*, 137 S. Ct. 1744 (2017) (finding the related provision in the Lanham Act, 15 USC §1052(a) and a refusal of theUnited States Patent and Trademark Office (USPTO) to register the trademark "The Slants" (a derogatory term for persons of Asian descent) to violate the First Amendment). *See* on

recognized in the European Convention on Human Rights, Article 10.[47] Even though the rule does not aim to restrict anyone from using certain offensive words, figures etc., it does seek to disincentivize the development and use of such expressions. Also, by not providing such marks with a "government stamp" as part of the registration process, any perception that the expression is in some way "supported" or "accepted" by the state is avoided.

1 *The Traditional Scope of the Provision: Offensive Uses*

"Public policy" and "principles of morality" are inherently vague concepts but refer to principles and standards regarded as a fundamental concern to the state and the whole of society.[48] Examples of types of marks covered by Article 7(1)(f) include words, phrases and signs which, because of their blasphemous, derogatory, racist, discriminatory or other offensive meaning, are perceived as being shocking or offensive. Sometimes the offensive nature is inherent in the word or figure. In other instances, the offensiveness lies in the use of a particular (in other contexts neutral or even positive) word or figure for certain products or services. The test for establishing whether or not a mark is sufficiently shocking is an objective one, and according to EUIPO's Examination Guidelines, "the concept of morality in Article 7(1)(f) EUTMR is not concerned with bad taste or the protection of individuals' feelings."[49] It is only in those rare instances where *public interests* are at stake that the limits have been trespassed. Practically, in order to fall foul of the provision a trademark must be perceived by the relevant public, or at least a significant part of it, as going directly against the basic moral norms of the society. There is no requirement that the expression is illegal in national law.[50] The meaning of the mark is as it is perceived by a reasonable consumer with average sensitivity and tolerance thresholds.[51] The nature of the goods for which the mark is being used matters,[52] but due account should also be given to other persons who, without being concerned by those goods and services, will encounter that sign

this Chapter 13 in this volume. *See* further on the interface to fundamental rights Christophe Geiger & Leonardo Machado Pontes, *Trade Mark Registration, Public Policy, Morality and Fundamental Rights*, *in* 20 YEARS OF THE BOARDS OF APPEAL AT EUIPO, ANNIVERSARY BOOK: CELEBRATING THE PAST, LOOKING FORWARD TO THE FUTURE (2017); Centre for International Intellectual Property Studies (CEIPI) Research Paper No. 2017-01, available at SSRN: https://ssrn.com/abstract=3009170 or http://dx.doi.org/10.2139/ssrn.3009170.

[47] The European Court of Human Rights recently found that Lithuania had violated art. 10 of the European Convention on Human Rights through the banning of a series of commercials that used the expressions "Jesus, what trousers!" and "Dear Mary, what a dress!" (translated from Lithuanian), *see Sekmadienis Ltd.* v. *Lithuania*, 69317 Eur. Ct. HR 14 (2018). The European Convention on Human Rights and case law from the European Court of Human Rights can be found at https://echr.coe.int/Pages/home.aspx?p=basictexts&c=#n1359128122487_pointer.

[48] Judgment of the Court of Justice of the European Free Trade Association States, *infra* note 61, para 94. *See also* Judgment of the GCEU in Case T-1/17, *La Mafia Franchises, SL* v. *European Union Intellectual Property Office (EUIPO)*, 2018 ECLI:EU:T:2018:146 § 25.

[49] Guidelines for the Examination of European Union Trade Marks and Registered Community Designs, EUIPO, § B.4.7.3 (2017).

[50] See *La Mafia*, *supra* note 48 (where the mere fact that the Mafia as an organization is not illegal did not bring the use of the word outside of the exception).

[51] Judgment of the GCEU in Case T-417/10, *Federico Cortés del Valle López*, *supra* note 46, § 21 (on a figurative mark containing the word "Hijoputa" (meaning "motherfucker" in Spanish)) and *La Mafia*, *supra* note 48 (on "Mafia"). *See* also Decision of the BoA R 0495/2005-G, SCREW YOU, point 21: "The Office should not refuse to register a trade mark which is only likely to offend a small minority of exceptionally puritanical citizens. Similarly, it should not allow a trade mark on the register simply because it would not offend the equally small minority at the other end of the spectrum who find even gross obscenity acceptable. Some people are easily offended; others are totally unshockable."

[52] Decision by the BoA R 0495/2005-G (where the BoA noticed that "a person who is sufficiently interested in [sex toys] to notice the trade marks under which they are sold is unlikely to be offended by a term with crude sexual connotations." The mark was accepted for condoms and sex toys). In the same vein, BoA R-111/2002-4, *Dick Lexic Ltd.* v. *OHIM* (accepting DICK & FANNY even though these names may be understood as slang expressions for the male and female sexual organs). *See also* Judgment of the GCEU in Case T-526/09, *PAKI Logistics GmbH* v. *OHIM*,

incidentally in their day-to-day lives.[53] Furthermore, there is an interest in ensuring that children and young people, even if they are not the relevant public of the goods and services in question, do not encounter offensive words in shops accessible to the general public.[54] Not only negative and racist and derogatory terms etc. are covered; the use of signs with a religious meaning, national symbols or symbols with a spiritual and political value may be also excluded.[55]

Since EUTMs enjoy protection within all of the EU countries, the assessment needs to reflect varying national circumstances. According to the GCEU: "the relevant public within the European Union is, by definition, within a Member State and that the signs likely to be perceived as being contrary to public policy or to accepted principles of morality are not the same in all Member States, inter alia for linguistic, historic, social and cultural reasons."[56] For this reason, it is necessary to take account both of the circumstances common to all EU states (such as "the spiritual and moral heritage of the European Union"[57]) and of the particular circumstances of individual member states which are likely to influence the perception of the relevant public within those states.[58] Account may even be taken of certain groups of people within states; for instance, "the average European consumer of Turkish origin."[59]

By way of illustration of the traditional application of the provision, the GCEU recently decided in *La Mafia* that a trademark containing the word element "la Mafia" to designate a restaurant chain and alluding to the *Godfather* series of films, was rightfully considered as "particularly shocking or offensive" and as such, rejected as being in breach of public policy.[60] The Court remarked that the word element "la Mafia" is understood worldwide as referring to a criminal organization originating in Italy, whose activities extend to states other than the Italian Republic, i.e. within the European Union (paragraph 35). The Court takes the view that such criminal activities breach the very values on which the European Union is founded, in particular the values of respect for human dignity and freedom as laid down in Treaty on the Functioning of the European Union (TFEU) Article 2, and Articles 2, 3 and 6 of the Charter of Fundamental Rights of the European Union (paragraph 36). Those values are indivisible and make up "the spiritual and moral heritage of the European Union." Next, the Court turned its attention to Italy in particular and noted how the word element "la Mafia" has deeply negative connotations there, on account of the serious harm done by that criminal organization to the

2011 ECR II-00346, CLI:EU:T:2011:564 § 17; *see* generally on the case law Kur & Senftleben, *supra* note 14, at para. 4.209 and Geiger & Pontes, *supra* note 46.

53 *La Mafia, supra* note 48, and PAKI, *supra* note 52, § 16.

54 Guidelines for the Examination of European Union Trade Marks and Registered Community Designs, EUIPO, § B.4.7.3 (2017).

55 So far, there is no case law from the EU Courts on religious expressions. Inspiration could be found in the case law of the European Court of Human Rights, *see supra* note 47 with reference to *Sekmadienis* (*see* in particular its points 70 et seq.). *See* from the BoA Case R-2613/2011-2 on the trademark ATATURK (which is the name of the founder of the modern Turkey; the mark was refused).

56 *La Mafia, supra* note 48, § 28.

57 *Id.*

58 *Id.* at § 29. *See* Geiger & Pontes, *supra* note 46; see also Judgment of the GCEU in Case T-232/10, *Couture Tech Ltd.* v. *OHIM*, 2011 ECR II-06469, ECLI:EU:T:2011:498 (on a trademark consisting of the coat of arms of the former Union of Soviet Socialist Republics (USSR); the Hungarian Criminal Code had banned certain uses of "symbols of despotism," including the hammer and sickle and the five-point red star).

59 Decision of the BoA Case R-2613/2011-2 – ATATURK, §31; *see* Kur & Senftleben, *supra* note 14, at § 4.210 for more examples including Decision of the BoA R 176/2004-2, *Elektron-Bremen* v. *OHIM* (on BIN LADIN, which was refused).

60 *La Mafia, supra* note 48, in particular § 40. *See* Eleonora Rosati, *General Court Confirms that "La Mafia se Sienta a la Mesa" Cannot Be a Trade Mark on Public Policy Grounds*, 13(6) J. Intell. Prop. L. & Prac. 432 (2018) (pointing out how practices vary).

security of Italy (paragraph 37). On this basis, the Court concluded that the BoA had rightly found that "the word element 'la Mafia' in the contested mark would manifestly bring to mind, for the relevant public, the name of a criminal organisation responsible for particularly serious breaches of public policy."[61]

2 *Post-Vigeland*: Safeguarding the Public Domain

In the recent *Vigeland* decision, the European Free Trade Area (EFTA) Court[62] introduced a completely new perspective on the provision.[63]

The case concerned an application by the municipality of Oslo to register works of art by the Norwegian artist Gustav Vigeland as trademarks. The copyright to the works in question (sculptures and visual works) had lapsed, and the works therefore had passed to the public domain. The Norwegian Patent Office refused most of the applications, partly because of lack of distinctiveness and partly because the marks were found to be descriptive or consisting exclusively of shapes giving substantial value to the goods. On appeal, the Norwegian Board of Appeal for Intellectual Property decided to ask the EFTA Court whether the trademark registration of the works could conflict with the prohibition on public policy or accepted principles of morality. The Court answered in the affirmative. In reaching this conclusion it held:

> registration of a sign as a trade mark may only be refused as contrary to public policy . . . in exceptional circumstances. An artwork may be refused registration, for example, under the circumstances that its registration is regarded as a genuine and serious threat to certain fundamental values or where the need to safeguard the public domain, itself, is considered a fundamental interest of society. It is for the referring body to determine whether those requirements are met, in light of the relevant matters of fact and law.[64]

The Court points out that the rejection of sculptures, etc. as trademarks does not prevent anyone from using the sign in question in the course of trade (paragraph 101). In this way, the Court indicated that it saw the exclusivity offered by trademark law to lie at the heart of the rejection of protection.[65] In other words, it is *trademark protection itself* which is hereby acknowledged as

[61] *La Mafia*, *supra* note 48, § 38. It did not matter that the trademark was intended to allude to the *Godfather* films and not to the criminal organization as such, since the mark would anyway convey "a globally positive image of that organisation and, therefore, trivialises the serious harm done by that organisation to the fundamental values of the European Union" (§ 47). Nor did it matter that several EU and even Italian trademarks contained the word element "Mafia" (§§ 49 and 50).

[62] Judgment of the EFTA Court Case E-05/16, Norwegian Board of Appeal for Industrial Property Rights 2017 (appeal from the Municipality of Oslo, https://report.eftacourt.int/2017/e516/).

[63] For background, *see* Lionel Bentley, *Trade Mark Protection of Public Domain Works: A Comment on the Request for an Advisory Opinion of the Court of Justice of the European Free Trade Association States in Case E-05/16 – Norwegian Board of Appeal for Industrial Property Rights – Appeal from the Municipality of Oslo*, European Copyright Society, Nov. 1, 2016, https://europeancopyrightsociety.org/2016/11/02/515/; Geiger & Pontes, *supra* note 46, at 11 et seq.; Senftleben, *supra* note 12, at 357 et seq. (with references to national case law including from Germany, where the approach taken by the EFTA Court had been rejected). Also both the Comment and Martin Senftleben note that the Judgment of the EFTA Court finds some resonance in the Opinions of the Advocate Generals in Case 299/99, *Koninklijke Philips Electronics NV* v. *Remington Consumer Products Ltd*, 2001 ECLI:EU:C:2001:52 point 31 and Case C-283/01, *Shield Mark BV* v. *Joost Kist h.o.d.n. Memex*, 2003 ECLI:EU:C:2003:197 point 52.

[64] *Vigeland*, *supra* note 62, § 96.

[65] In its decision, the Norwegian Board of Appeal followed the decision of the EFTA Court closely and found that the works in question must be considered to hold "significant cultural value" (point 22) and that protection would be considered as being contrary to ordre public. *See* the decision at https://kfir.no/attachments/6bd29736d2718b937aac81519540b3d207037e52/250-20190315013326599713.pdf and Yann Basire, *Public Domain versus Trade Mark Protection: The Vigeland Case*, 13(6) J. Intell. Prop. L. & Practice 434 (2018).

having the potential to contravene public policy and morality, rather than the use of the sign and the message contained therein.

As pointed out by Senftleben, the decision is remarkable in representing an unusually firm determination to defend the public domain[66] as a fundamental value in trademark law.[67] Currently, the exact scope of the decision is unclear, however. The Court was very careful to cabin the effects of the decisions, and it was clearly indicated that the limitation does not include the use of each and every work of art as a trademark (such use continues to be normally allowed for). It is just in those rare circumstances where trademark law is being relied upon to (as it were) *reclaim* exclusivity in "certain pieces of art [which] ... enjoy a particular status as prominent parts of a nation's cultural heritage, an emblem of sovereignty or of the nation's foundations and values" (paragraph 92, see also paragraph 102) that protection amounts to "a genuine and sufficiently serious threat to a fundamental interest of society" (operative part point 3) and is cut off. Even though this may only happen in few instances, those are arguably important as they would allow individuals to propertize works of general cultural importance.

For the present study, the decision is particularly important because it introduces public policy and principles of morality as a means of safeguarding the public domain. According to such a reading the judgment should (within a very narrow window) be seen as a corrective mechanism that remedies the structural inability of the traditional balancing tools found in trademark law for the purpose of safeguarding the public domain (*see* above Section III.A on distinctiveness etc.). As noted explicitly by the EFTA Court, the "problem" with the traditional principle of distinctiveness in this regard is that it may be *overcome* through the use of the sign by a company (see above Section III.A), and thus leave the use of such signs to the limitation which allows for the use in accordance with honest practices. Even though acquiring distinctiveness might not be possible in practice for all of the works of art in question (fame as a work of art does not suffice), had the Court rejected the works of art because of lack of distinctiveness, it would have opened the door to the municipality of Oslo to claim trademark protection based on the use of the works of art as signs that indicate goods or services originating from the municipality. By opting for the rule on public policy and morality instead of distinctiveness, the Court side-stepped the test of distinctiveness and ruled out that the unilateral actions of the municipality could lead to trademark protection.[68] Naturally, the assessment under Article 7(1)(f) could change over time, but the point of reference would be the public interest and not the consumer conception as created by the marketing efforts of the potential rightholder.[69] The decision in this way reflects both the broad and imprecise nature of the concepts of "public policy and principles of morality" and the strength of the public policy reasons underlying the protection of the public domain; *see* more below, in Section IV.

[66] Defined in § 66 in the following way: "The public domain entails the absence of individual protection for, or exclusive rights to, a work. Once communicated, creative content belongs, as a matter of principle, to the public domain. In other words, the fact that works are part of the public domain is not a consequence of the lapse of copyright protection. Rather, protection is the exception to the rule that creative content becomes part of the public domain once communicated."

[67] Martin Senftleben, *Vigeland and the Status of Cultural Concerns in Trade Mark Law – The EFTA Court Develops More Effective Tools for the Preservation of the Public Domain*, 6 Int'l Rev. Intell. Prop. & Competition L. 683 (2017). *See* on the case also Basire, *supra* note 65.

[68] *See* Basire, *supra* note 65 (criticizing the Court for applying the provision on public policy and morality excessively and suggesting a more traditional approach with a focus on distinctiveness).

[69] *See* in particular Anemaet, *supra* note 43.

C Preventing Consumer Deception

The objective of preventing deception of consumers is primarily served by the Article 7(1)(g) EUTR, according to which trademarks of such a nature as to deceive the public, for instance as to the nature, quality or geographical origin of the goods or service, shall not be registered. The exclusion regarding deceptive marks reflects the general interest in consumer protection.[70] The fact that deceptive trademarks have not generated much case law or scholarly debate may indicate that deception is not an important instrument to delimit trademark subject matter.

The CJEU found in *Elizabeth Emanuel* that "deception" within the meaning of Article 3(1)(g) of the First Trademark Directive (the wording of which is identical to that of EUTR Article 7(1)(g)) presupposes the existence of "actual deceit or a sufficiently serious risk that the consumer will be deceived."[71] In the specific case, the designer Elizabeth Emanuel formed a company called "Elizabeth Emanuel PLC" and assigned to that company her business of designing and selling clothing, and all assets of the business including its goodwill and an application to register the trademark ELIZABETH EMANUEL, registered in 1997. The registered trademark was assigned to another company which filed a new application for registration of the trademark ELIZABETH EMANUEL. The designer Elizabeth Emanuel then lodged an application to revoke the registered trademark "Elizabeth Emanuel" on the grounds that the trademark was deceptive. The Court held that the trademark ELIZABETH EMANUEL would not deceive the public, because it was the name of the designer who originally used the mark but was no longer associated with the trademark owner.[72]

The Court further stated that if the owner of the trademark ELIZABETH EMANUEL has an intention of making consumers believe that Ms Emanuel is still the designer of the goods bearing the mark or that she is involved in their design, that might be fraudulent. However, that would not invalidate a trademark right consisting of the name ELIZABETH EMANUEL on grounds of deception or affect the prospects of such a trademark being registered.[73] Accordingly, a deceptive use of a trade may be fraudulent, but the trademark in itself is not deceptive.[74]

As it follows from the judgment, the threshold ("actual deceit or a sufficiently serious risk that the consumer will be deceived") is high, and the mere fact that a trademark includes information that is not actually correct does not in itself make the mark deceptive. The high threshold for deception can be compared to the main rule for infringement in EUTR Article 9(2)(b), according to which infringement requires "a likelihood of confusion on the part of the public; the likelihood of confusion includes the likelihood of association between the sign and the trade mark." According to established case law, this criterion shall *not* (as in the case of deceptive marks) be interpreted as "actual confusion or a sufficiently serious risk that the consumer will be confused."

Prima facie, it could be argued that "deception" resembles "misleading action" which is harmonized by Article 6 of the Unfair Commercial Practices Directive (UCPD).[75] The UCPD stipulates that

[70] Judgment of the CJEU in Case C-259/04, *Elizabeth Florence Emanuel* v. *Continental Shelf 128 Ltd.*, 2006 ECR I-03089, ECLI:EU:C:2006:215 § 46.

[71] *Id.*, § 47.

[72] *Id.*, § 51.

[73] *Id.*, § 50.

[74] See Ron Moscona, *What Really Matters – The Designer's Name or the Name on the Label?*, 29(4) Euro. Intell. Prop. Reports 152 (2007).

[75] Directive 2005/29/EC of the European Parliament and of the Council of May 11, 2005, concerning unfair business-to-consumer commercial practices in the internal market, OJ L 149, 22.

> a commercial practice shall be regarded as misleading if it contains false information and is therefore untruthful or in any way, including overall presentation, *deceives or is likely to deceive the average consumer*, even if the information is factually correct . . . and in either case causes or is likely to cause him to take a transactional decision that he would not have taken otherwise.[76]

Accordingly, a "misleading action" requires only likelihood to deceive and likelihood that the average consumer will take a transactional decision that they would not have taken otherwise and not, as in the EUTR, actual deceit or a sufficiently serious risk that the consumer will be deceived. The lower threshold of misleading action in the UCPD is in conformity to the statement of the CJEU in the *Elizabeth Emanuel* judgment, where the court recognized that the use of a trademark can be fraudulent (misleading) without invalidating the trademark due to deception.

The high threshold of deception in the EUTR is reflected in the EUIPO Examination Guidelines, with two assumptions. First, there is no reason to assume that a trademark is intentionally applied for in order to deceive customers. No deceptiveness objection should be raised if a non-deceptive usage of the mark is possible vis-à-vis the goods and services specified; i.e. an assumption is made that non-deceptive use of the sign will be made if possible. Second, the average consumer is reasonably attentive and should not be regarded as particularly vulnerable to deception. An objection will generally only be raised where the mark leads to a clear expectation that is patently contradictory to, for instance, the nature or quality or geographical origin of the goods.[77]

There is a delicate interface between the grounds for refusal in EUTR Article 7(1)(c)–(d) on descriptive signs and the ground for refusal in Article 7(1)(g) on deception. A BoA Decision concerned the registration of the term ARCADIA, which was applied for in respect of wines, spirits (beverages) and liqueurs in Class 33.[78] The term was refused registration under Article 7(1)(c) because it was descriptive of the geographical origin of wines: Arcadia is a Greek region known for its wine production. The applicant subsequently offered to limit the specification of goods to exclude wines made in Greece. However, according to the BoA, that would render the trademark deceptive under Article 7(1)(g), since it would convey false information as to the origin of the goods.[79]

An essential difference between the ground for refusal in respect of descriptive signs and the ground for refusal in respect of deceptive signs is that the former is subject to expansive interpretation whereas the latter is subject to restrictive interpretation. This difference indicates that in the interpretation of EU trademark law, the policy objective of preventing deception of consumers appears less important than the objective of safeguarding the public domain.

[76] The concept of "misleading" is clarified by the CJEU in Judgment of the CJEU in Case C-281/12, *Trento Sviluppo srl, Centrale Adriatica Soc. coop. arl* v. *Autorità Garante della Concorrenza e del Mercato*, 2013 ECLI:EU:C:2013:859; and in Judgment of the CJEU in Case C-453/10, *Jana Pereničová, Vladislav Perenič* v. *SOS financ spol. s r.o.*, 2012 ECLI: EU:C:2012:144.

[77] Guidelines for the Examination of European Union Trade Marks and Registered Community Designs, EUIPO, § B.4.8.1.

[78] Decision of the BoA, R 246/1999-1 – ARCADIA (2000).

[79] Guidelines for the Examination of European Union Trade Marks and Registered Community Designs, EUIPO, § B.4.2.7.5.

IV FINAL REMARKS AND CONCLUSION

In our examination of public policy limitations on trademark subject matter, we find that the pertinent limitations are based on one or more of the following three public policy values:

Safeguarding the public domain.
Limiting the use of offensive signs.
Preventing deception of consumers.

Traditionally, the three policy values have been closely connected to specific grounds for refusal. Safeguarding the public domain has been pursued by the provisions on distinctiveness and descriptive sign (EUTR Article 7(1)(a)–(d)), limiting the use of offensive signs by the provision on public policy and principles of morality (EUTR Article 7(1)(f)), and preventing deception of consumer by the provision on deception (EUTR Article 7(1)(g)). The one-to-one relation between public policy values and grounds for refusal in trademark law is flawed, as clearly illustrated by *Vigeland* where the provision on public policy and morality – which typically is used for limiting the use of offensive signs (as in *La Mafia* and *Atatürk*) – instead was used to safeguard the public domain.

Vigeland illustrates the pre-eminent nature of the interest in safeguarding the public domain which runs as an undercurrent in EU trademark law, affecting both the rules and principles we have focused on here and the exceptions found in EUTR Article 14. For this reason, it is both remarkable and regrettable that neither the Regulation nor the Directive explicitly make it clear that the application of the provisions in trademark law should take into account the overall societal interests of all interested stakeholders, including trademark holders, competitors, private users and society in general. As we have shown in our analyses, the current rules and principles leave room for courts to manoeuvre to factor all interests into the analysis. Thus in *Henkel*,[80] the CJEU required that a registrable trademark shall depart *significantly* from the norm or customs of the sector; otherwise, it shall be devoid of any distinctive character. The CJEU used a similar expansive interpretation in respect of neologisms composed of known words.[81] For colours, the competition interest in access should be taken into account.[82] Presently, there is no clear framework in the EU trademark system for courts to develop such notions further.[83]

We finally note that an important vehicle for the future developments in these areas may have been provided in 2015 by the explicit inclusion of *the fundamental rights interests* in the EUTR and EUTD. As pointed out above in Section I, it now follows explicitly from the Recitals that courts should ensure that the trademark rules are applied in a way that ensures full respect for fundamental rights and freedoms. Several commentators have linked the safeguarding of the public domain to free speech. Senftleben, for instance, describes the public domain as offering "a reservoir of unprotected and protected signs that are available for political, artistic and commercial speech."[84] In a similar vein, Anemaet notes that the public domain is "essential

[80] *Henckel*, *supra* note 24.
[81] *Campina*, *supra* note 38.
[82] *Libertel*, *supra* note 6.
[83] Kur & Senftleben, *supra* note 14 at § 4.74 (pointing out that the Trade Mark Study 2016 suggested it should be made clear in the Preamble that due account must be taken of interests of all parties involved – consumers, the general public as well as competitors; *see* the Study, https://ip.mpg.de/fileadmin/IP/pdf2/mpi_final_report_with_synopsis.pdf. However, the proposal was not implemented).
[84] Senftleben, *supra* note 12, at 355. *See* also Rochelle Cooper Dreyfuss, *Reconciling Trademark Rights and Expressive Values: How to Stop Worrying and Learn to Love Ambiguity*, in Trademark Law and Theory – A Handbook of Contemporary Research 261 (Graeme B. Dinwoodie & Mark David Janis eds., 2008). On the "public domain" in

to ensure free and fair competition, freedom of speech and political and artistic freedom of expression" and calls for a more normative application of the test of distinctiveness to protect these interests.[85] As argued elsewhere, it would also seem that the "constitutionalization" would serve to support claims that, for instance, signs of cultural importance should not be protected.[86] To a large extent, these current trends of EU trademark law would not imply a change of the basic and well-known principles of trademark law. It would rather be a reminder of those principles and the policy values underlying them.

trademark law, *see* also Jennifer Davis, *Protecting the Common: Delineating a Public Domain in Trade Mark Law*, in TRADEMARK LAW AND THEORY – A HANDBOOK OF CONTEMPORARY RESEARCH 345 (Graeme B. Dinwoodie & Mark David Janis eds., 2008).

85 Anemaet, *supra* note 43, at 304.

86 Jens Schovsbo, *Mark My Words – Trademarks and Fundamental Rights in the EU*, 8 UC IRVINE LAW REVIEW 555 (2018).

IV

The Relationship between Trademarks and Geographical Indications

15

Sui Generis or Independent Geographical Indications Protection

*Dev S. Gangjee**

I INTRODUCTION

Contemporary newspaper headlines are a constant reminder that a sense of place matters. This sensibility applies to traditional regional foodstuffs, beverages and crafts as well. Provenance matters, since our consumption choices in the aggregate have socioeconomic consequences. Our purchases have an impact on regional economic development, ecological sustainability, global transport systems and the relationship between urban and rural areas.[1] Geographical indications (GI) regimes facilitate the signalling of this provenance. As a form of intellectual property (IP), they protect the collectively generated brand value associated with designations for traditional regional products. Prominent examples include "Scotch" for whisky, "Champagne" for sparkling wines, "Darjeeling" for tea and "Parmigiano Reggiano" for cheese. According to the World Intellectual Property Organization (WIPO), in "certain jurisdictions, GIs may be protected through a system that applies specifically and exclusively to them – a sui generis system of protection. Such systems establish a specific right, a sui generis right, over GIs, separate from a trademark right or any other IP right."[2] Over time, these IP outliers have multiplied and mainstreamed. The time is ripe for an account of their underlying logic and characteristic features. This chapter analyses one of the prominent means adopted internationally to achieve the ends of GI protection.

A GI is a sign that identifies "a good as originating in the territory of a [World Trade Organization (WTO)] Member, or a region or locality in that territory, where a given *quality*, reputation *or other characteristic* of the good is essentially attributable to its geographical origin."[3] It represents a causal link between product and place, depending on local environmental factors and traditional production methods. This causal link is exemplified by the French notion of *terroir*, associated with wine grown in specific regions. In the past, a diverse array of regimes

* Professor, Faculty of Law, University of Oxford.

[1] David Watts, Jo Little, & Brian Ilbery, "*I Am Pleased to Shop Somewhere That Is Fighting the Supermarkets a Little Bit": A Cultural Political Economy of Alternative Food Networks*, 91 Geoforum 21 (2018). *Cf.* Sini Forssell & Leena Lankoski, *The Sustainability Promise of Alternative Food Networks: An Examination through "Alternative" Characteristics*, 32 Agric. & Human Values 63 (2015).

[2] *Geographical Indications: An Introduction*, 28 (WIPO, 2017), https://wipo.int/edocs/pubdocs/en/geographical/952/wipo_pub_952.pdf. *Sui generis* is a Latin expression, literally meaning of its own kind/genus or unique in its characteristics. The expression refers to an entity or concept that could not be included in a wider concept.

[3] Agreement on Trade-Related Aspects of Intellectual Property Rights, Apr. 15, 1994, Marrakesh Agreement Establishing the World Trade Organization, Annex 1C, 1869 UNTS 299, 33 ILM 1197, art. 22.1 (1994) [hereinafter TRIPS Agreement].

regulating origin marking have protected such signs against unauthorised misuses by third parties.[4] The initial regulatory approach consisted of protection against unfair competition: protect signs to preserve their meaning. In this volume, Kimberlee Weatherall makes a compelling case for its continuing relevance and attractive flexibility, if certain adjustments are made.[5] This approach is operationalised via tort (i.e., judge-made) or statutory regimes which grant relief against recognised forms of misconduct. For instance, will the use of Rioja on wine produced outside the eponymous Spanish region mislead consumers? Nevertheless, over the course of the twentieth century, there has been a shift towards registration-based protection. WIPO data for 2018 reveals the existence of approximately 59,500 protected GIs, while China alone had more than 8,500 GIs in force.[6] Protection is possible via trademark registration, where GIs are protected as collective or certification marks.[7] It is also possible via so-called *sui generis* systems, increasingly referred to as independent GI protection systems, as they become more widely adopted. For that reason, "independent" will replace "sui generis" in this chapter. Against the implicit backdrop of trademark law as the comparator, this chapter unpacks independent protection by addressing the following questions: What are we describing when we refer to independent GI protection? What familial features does this phrase conjure up? Why do these features exist and is operational practice congruent with their underlying rationales? These enquiries are worth pursuing, because the architecture of independent registration is built upon the normative foundations of GI protection. This chapter therefore resonates with Weatherall's interest in exploring how platonic concepts are translated into the real world. An independent GI regime can be usefully mined as the site where GI theory is translated into GI practice. The criteria for regulating registrability reflect the underlying justificatory commitments. This chapter identifies tensions and strains as these independent systems strive to live up to these commitments.

The emergence of independent GI protection regimes can be historically traced to *both* the inability of nineteenth-century trademark law to accommodate geographical signs[8] *and* the special interdependence, coordination and verification requirements associated with collectively used geographical brands, which is approached in contemporary social science research through the theoretical lenses of collective action, conventions or governance.[9] Section II selectively

[4] The history is reviewed in Dev Gangjee, Relocating the Law of Geographical Indications (2012).

[5] See Chapter 16 in this volume.

[6] *World Intellectual Property Indicators 2018*, 190–93 (WIPO, 2018), https://wipo.int/edocs/pubdocs/en/wipo_pub_941_2018.pdf. Note that while the majority of records reflect protection under *sui generis* systems (Table 5.4), the data does not comprehensively reflect GIs found within registered trademark systems, so the actual total of protected GIs may be higher.

[7] The case for GI protection via certification and collective marks is considered by Weatherall in Chapter 16. *See also* Daniel Gervais, *A Cognac after Spanish Champagne? Geographical Indications as Certification Marks*, *in* Intellectual Property at the Edge 105 (Rochelle Dreyfuss & Jane Ginsburg eds., 2014); D. Peter Harvey, *Geographical Indications: The United States' Perspective*, 107 Trademark R. 960 (2017); Xinzhe Song, *The Role Played by the Regime of Collective and Certification Marks in the Protection of Geographical Indications – Comparative Study of Law and Practice in France, the EU and China*, 21 J. World Intell. Prop. 437 (2018); Paula Zito, *Australian Laws and Regulations on Regional Branding on Food and Wine Labels: Part 2*, 29 Australian Intell. Prop. J. 127 (2019).

[8] Geographical signs are descriptive and not distinctive. They describe the region of production and consequently cannot distinguish a specific commercial source, which is the foundational requirement for trademark protection. Additionally, these signs are used by a group of producers and incapable of being exclusively claimed by one commercial entity. Both these features led to incompatibility with early trademark registration systems, until collective and certification marks were sufficiently developed as alternatives. *See* Gangjee, *supra* note 4, 60–64; Sam Ricketson, The Paris Convention for the Protection of Industrial Property: A Commentary [12.74]–[12.75] (2015).

[9] On the historical emergence of the influential French wine appellation regimes, *see* Alessando Stanziani, *French Collective Wine Branding in the Nineteenth–Twentieth Centuries*, *in* Research Handbook on Intellectual Property and Geographical Indications 13 (Dev S. Gangjee ed., 2016); Geneviève Teil, *Protecting Appellations of Origin: One Hundred Years of Efforts and Debates*, *in* The Importance of Place: Geographical Indications as

reviews the distinctive features conventionally associated with independent GI protection, which reflect their functional commitments. For instance, if the central claim for GIs is that qualifying products exhibit a distinctive connection to a defined region, then a registration system will have to verify this link and confirm the boundaries of the region. We find these features reflected in existing national and regional GI regimes, bilateral agreements and proposed or existing multilateral registration systems. Section III concludes by emphasising two relatively neglected institutional dimensions of independent systems. As opposed to a trademark registry which "also does" GI registration, specialist registrars are more closely involved with pre- as well as post-registration aspects in the lifecycle of a GI product. Additionally, the design of the representative producer organisation – whom it includes and how decisions are made – is crucial to the success of a GI.

II THE DISTINGUISHING FEATURES OF INDEPENDENT GI PROTECTION

The origins of modern, independent GI protection regimes can be traced to French legislative experimentation with wine protection across the late nineteenth and mid-twentieth centuries.[10] The emergent institutional features were designed in response to rampant wine fraud. The need was to protect designations for authentic regional wines (the *what* question), identify those legitimately entitled to use wine appellations in accordance with appropriate, locally adapted production methods (the *who*, *how* and *where* questions) and develop legal mechanisms to protect regional reputations against misuse (questions relating to *scope* and *institutional design*). The early French regime has parallels in Italy and its key features were eventually adopted by the EU as a template for unitary, pan-European protection.[11] The EU model has in turn proved influential both as the basis for discussions in multilateral fora, as the harmonised regime for twenty-eight countries and in shaping the provisions of free trade agreements with third countries.[12] Since several countries have cultural and developmental reasons for promoting their regional products, technical assistance initiatives supported by the EU are helping the independent GI model to migrate across the globe.[13]

The result is that a growing number of countries have independent GI protection systems. The initial mapping is contained in two studies by WIPO and the WTO.[14] The EU subsequently

A Tool for Local and Regional Development 148 (William van Caenegem & Jen Cleary eds., 2017); For the ongoing significance of coordination mechanisms and collective action, *see* Xiomara F. Quinones-Ruiz et al., *Insights into the Black Box of Collective Efforts for the Registration of Geographical Indications*, 57 Land Use Pol'y 103 (2016).

[10] Gangjee, *supra* note 4, at ch. 3; Stanziani, *supra* note 9.

[11] Andrea Zappalaglio, *The Why of Geographical Indications: The Transformation of the Link between the Product and Its Place of Origin in Europe* 11–141 (2018) (unpublished PhD thesis, University of Oxford) (on file with the Oxford University Research Archive, University of Oxford).

[12] DG AGRI, *Working Document on International Protection of EU Geographical Indications: Objectives, Outcome and Challenges*, 11 (June 25, 2012), https://ec.europa.eu/agriculture/sites/agriculture/files/consultations/advisory-groups/international/2012-06-25/agri-working-doc_en.pdf ("In the new generation of FTAs a satisfactory GI Chapter is a 'must have' for the EU"); Tim Engelhardt, *Geographical Indications under Recent EU Trade Agreements*, 46 Int'l Rev. Intell. Prop. & Competition L. 781 (2015); Masayoshi Omachi, *A Tale of Two Approaches: Analysis of Responses to EU's FTA Initiatives on Geographical Indications (GIs)*, 18 Chic.-Kent J. Intell. Prop. 153 (2019).

[13] Catherine Saez, *EU Makes Push to Facilitate Geographical Indication in ACP Countries*, Intellectual Property Watch (May 16, 2011), https://ip-watch.org/2011/05/16/eu-makes-push-to-facilitate-geographical-indications-in-acp-countries/; for East Asia, the EU–ASEAN Project on the Protection of Intellectual Property Rights (ECAP III) ran until 2017 and resulted in the ASEAN GI database. It has now been replaced by the ASEAN Regional Integration Support from the European Union Plus (ARISE +) project.

[14] WIPO, Standing Committee on the Law of Trademarks, Industrial Designs and Geographical Indications, *Document SCT/6/3 Rev. on Geographical Indications: Historical Background, Nature of Rights, Existing Systems for Protection and Obtaining Protection in Other Countries*, Doc. SCT/8/4 (Apr. 2, 2002) (prepared by the secretariat), https://wipo

commissioned a survey of 160 countries, published in 2007, indicating whether *sui generis* or independent protection is available in a given jurisdiction.[15] The WTO has recently developed a dynamically updated and conveniently searchable database – the E-TRIPS Gateway – allowing users to search for relevant GI laws and regulations that have been notified under Article 63.2 of the TRIPS Agreement.[16] Finally, in order to compile up-to-date operational experience with GI protection, WIPO conducted a survey in 2018–2019 and elicited over fifty national and regional responses, with most respondents referring to *sui generis* systems in their jurisdictions.[17] These replies are available on the Standing Committee on Trade Marks (SCT) Geographical Indications Information Database.[18] There is now a legislative corpus and considerable operational experience to draw on when analysing independent GI registration systems.

A *Justificatory Foundations*

GI regimes protect geographical signs against misuse by unauthorised third parties, but what ought to count as a misuse remains contested. One set of rationales is universally embraced and flows from preserving the informational efficiency of signs. Exclusive rights flowing from registration grant legitimate users control over such geographical signs. Legal remedies are available against those who use identical or similar signs to mislead consumers in relation to origin or quality. Clear signalling facilitates consumer choice as well as honest competition, allowing legitimate producers to reap reputational rewards.[19] Registration-based GI certification systems additionally verify the content of these provenance and quality signals, correcting information asymmetries between producers and consumers. Certification by a public authority converts what might otherwise be credence or experience attributes of goods into search attributes, so that consumers can trust these signs.[20]

However, this logic goes only so far to explain the features of GI regimes. It accounts for rules preventing universally recognised categories of unfair competition (e.g. misleading or confusing uses) as well as certification, including via certification or collective trademark registration. An additional set of rationales is associated with independent GI systems, which have greater public or state involvement, certain mandatory registration requirements and enhanced protection, such as prohibiting not just misrepresentation but misappropriation or pure "free riding." The legal protection of GIs is said to generate a range of desirable public goods, including:

(i) Enabling endogenous or embedded territorial development, by equitably distributing benefits in the form of price premia across the supply chain;[21]

.int/meetings/en/doc_details.jsp?doc_id=2091; WTO, *Review under Article 24.2 of the Application of the Provisions of the Section of the TRIPS Agreement on Geographical Indications* IP/C/W/253/Rev.1 (Nov. 24, 2003).

15 O'Connor & Co., *Geographical Indications and TRIPs: 10 Years Later … Part II – Protection of Geographical Indications in 160 Countries around the World* (Report commissioned for EC (DG Trade) 2007).

16 *See E-TRIPS Gateway*, World Trade Organization (WTO), http://tripsims.wto.org/.

17 *Document SCT/40/5, Compilation of the Replies to Questionnaire I on the National and Regional Systems that can Provide a Certain Protection to Geographical Indications*, Feb. 25, 2019, Annex 14–15 [hereinafter WIPO Compilation].

18 *See SCT Geographical Indications Information Database*, WIPO, https://wipo.int/memberprofilesgeo/#/.

19 Cerkia Bramley et al., *The Economics of Geographical Indications: Towards a Conceptual Framework for Geographical Indication Research in Developing Countries, in* The Economics of Intellectual Property 109 (WIPO ed., 2009). For judicial recognition, *see* Case C-393/16, *Comité Interprofessionnel du Vin de Champagne* v. *Aldi*, EU:C:2017:991, [38].

20 Dev Gangjee, *Proving Provenance? Geographical Indications Certification and Its Ambiguities*, 98 World Dev. 12 (2017).

21 *See* Recital 4 of Regulation (EU) No. 1151/2012 on Quality Schemes for Agricultural Products and Foodstuffs 2012 OJ (L 343) 1 (hereinafter Regulation 1151/2012) (rewarding the efforts of producers to produce a diverse range of quality

(ii) Biodiversity preservation, by favouring locally cultivated flora or fauna;[22]
(iii) Sustaining local or national cultural heritage, where GIs have symbolic cultural value or cultural practices are involved in their production;[23] and
(iv) Providing market-based mechanisms to reward the traditional knowledge, which is reflected in production methods.[24]

These additional justifications are derived from the link between product and place. If the best-known trademarks symbolically represent globalisation – think COKE – then GIs reflect the continuing significance of place and the local. They have the potential to operate as multifunctional instruments, reproducing place and sustaining local identities while simultaneously offering opportunities to participate in global markets.[25] To the extent that independent GI regimes do more than just protect informational efficiency, these supplementary justifications are mobilised to explain the increased regulatory thickness of GI regimes, as well as the greater scope of protection on offer.[26] These additional policy underpinnings translate into distinctive legal and regulatory architectural features. Compared to other forms of GI protection, there is greater public involvement because public goods – such as rural employment and the sustainability of regional landscapes – are being sought as outcomes. This state involvement takes the following forms: compiling inventories of target regional products, catalysing producer group formation, providing support with registration costs, and mediating between conflicting stakeholder interests during the specification-drafting process. Once GIs are registered, government departments or agencies may "own" them, while in some *sui generis* systems, public authorities help to police the GI by pursuing infringements in the marketplace.[27] Empirical research, drawing on social science methods, is used to measure the ability of GI protection systems to actually deliver on these policy goals.[28]

products can benefit the rural economy and is important for disadvantaged areas); *see also* art. 4 of the same Regulation; Leonardo Cei et al., *From Geographical Indications to Rural Development: A Review of the Economic Effects of European Union Policy*, 10 SUSTAINABILITY 3745 (2018); Dominique Barjolle, *Geographical Indications and Protected Designations of Origin: Intellectual Property Tools for Rural Development Objectives, in* RESEARCH HANDBOOK ON INTELLECTUAL PROPERTY AND GEOGRAPHICAL INDICATIONS 440 (Dev S. Gangjee ed., 2016). *Cf.* Justin Hughes, *The Limited Promise of Geographical Indications for Farmers in Developing Countries, in* GEOGRAPHICAL INDICATIONS AT THE CROSSROADS OF TRADE, DEVELOPMENT, AND CULTURE: FOCUS ON ASIA-PACIFIC 61 (Irene Calboli & Ng-Loy Wee Loon eds., 2017).

22 Laurence Bérard & Philippe Marchenay, *Local Products and Geographical Indications: Taking Account of Local Knowledge and Biodiversity*, 58 INT'L SOCIAL SCI. J. 109 (2006).

23 Irene Calboli, *Of Markets, Culture, and Terroir: The Unique Economic and Culture-Related Benefits of Geographical Indications of Origin, in* INTERNATIONAL INTELLECTUAL PROPERTY: A HANDBOOK OF CONTEMPORARY RESEARCH 433 (Daniel Gervais ed., 2015). *See also* GEOGRAPHICAL INDICATIONS AT THE CROSSROADS OF TRADE, DEVELOPMENT, AND CULTURE: FOCUS ON ASIA-PACIFIC (Irene Calboli & Ng-Loy Wee Loon eds., 2017).

24 Teshager Dagne, *The Identity of Geographical Indications and Their Relation to Traditional Knowledge in Intellectual Property Law*, 5 W.I.P.O. J. 137 (2014). *Cf.* Susy Frankel, *The Mismatch of Geographical Indications and Innovative Traditional Knowledge* 29 PROMETHEUS 253 (2011).

25 Rosemary Coombe & Nicole Aylwin, *Bordering Diversity and Desire: Using Intellectual Property to Mark Place-Based Products*, 43 SAGE J. ENV'T & PLAN. A: ECON. & SPACE 2027 (2011).

26 Xiaoyan Wang, *Absolute Protection for Geographical Indications: Protectionism or Justified Rights?*, 8 QUEEN MARY J. INTELL. PROP. 73 (2018); *cf.* Michael Handler, *Rethinking GI Extension, in* RESEARCH HANDBOOK ON INTELLECTUAL PROPERTY AND GEOGRAPHICAL INDICATIONS 146 (Dev S. Gangjee ed., 2016).

27 Gangjee, *supra* note 20, at 13–14.

28 *See Value of Production of Agricultural Products and Foodstuffs, Wines, Aromatised Wines and Spirits Protected by a Geographical Indication (GI)*, AND-INTERNATIONAL (Oct. 2012), https://ec.europa.eu/agriculture/sites/agriculture/files/external-studies/2012/value-gi/final-report_en.pdf; Áron Török & Hazel Moir, *Understanding the Real-World Impact of GIs: A Critical Review of the Empirical Economic Literature*, ANU CENTRE FOR EUROPEAN STUDIES (July 2018), https://politicsir.cass.anu.edu.au/sites/default/files/docs/2018/7/Briefing_Paper_GeographicalIndications_Vol.9_No.3.pdf.

B Subject Matter: Signs for Products

Independent GI regimes protect geographical signs as their subject matter. The sign must convey the message that a specific product originates in a certain place (such as Café de Colombia). These regimes do not protect the underlying production methods. Thus "GIs are about what things can be called. They are about labelling, packaging and marketing. Nothing in GI rules prevents any producer anywhere from using the techniques specified as being associated with the GI name. But they may not use the name to communicate the production techniques they have used."[29] While Champagne is a protected term in many jurisdictions, the *méthode champenoise* has been widely adopted by sparkling wine producers around the world. As for the types of signs envisaged, the international reference point in Article 22.1 of TRIPS refers broadly to indications. Besides geographical place names, these might include symbols or figurative logos (such as the stylised Darjeeling tea picker profile or ducal crown for Parma ham), indirect geographical references (Basmati, Cava or Feta) and even the distinctive shapes of bottles or containers for these traditional regional products.[30] Contemporary systems recognise geographic terms (including entire country names or abbreviations of geographical names), indirect or non-literal geographic names, figurative elements and other elements (such as shapes).[31] However certain national or regional systems, such as the EU's Regulation 1151/2012, will recognise only a subset of these signs. Thus only geographical words (both direct and indirect) can be registered while figurative signs or logos will not be recognised. This explains why these figurative elements are protected via collective or certification marks in the EU.[32] By contrast, the Indian GI registry permits the registration of geographical logos as well as combined word and logo indications.[33]

When it comes to the universe of potential products, Article 22.1 of TRIPS refers broadly to goods. Nevertheless, the historic trajectories of national and regional protection systems serve as a reminder that they have originated in the context of regulating specific economic sectors. Independent systems are often restricted to specific categories of products. Alluding to its origins within the Common Agricultural Policy framework, the EU's regime under Regulation 1151/2012 is "limited to the agricultural products intended for human consumption listed in Annex I to the Treaty [on the Functioning of the European Union] and to a list of products outside the scope of that Annex that are closely linked to agricultural production or to the rural economy."[34] Until recent administrative reforms to consolidate IP agencies, China previously had two independent GI regimes, one of which was reserved for agricultural products.[35] The United States and Australia have independent GI regimes for regulating wine labelling.[36] Wines, spirits,

[29] Hazel Moir, *Geographical Indications: An Assessment of EU Treaty Demands*, *in* Australia, the European Union and the New Trade Agenda 122 (Annmarie Elijah et al. eds., 2017).

[30] Gangjee, *supra* note 4, at 215–16.

[31] WIPO Compilation, *supra* note 17, at Annex 18–22.

[32] Song, *supra* note 7.

[33] Examples include Darjeeling for tea (Serial no. 1), Pokkali for rice (Serial no. 86) and Banaras for saris (Serial no. 193).

[34] Recital 15 of Regulation 1151/2012.

[35] Haiyan Zheng, *A Unique Type of Cocktail: Protection of Geographical Indications in China*, in Geographical Indications at the Crossroads of Trade, Development, and Culture in the Asia-Pacific 380 (Irene Calboli & Wee Loon Ng-Loy eds., 2017); Yuan Fang, *Reforming the Multi-Agency System: A Path to Better Chinese GI Protection*, Berkley Tech. L.J. Blog (Apr. 16, 2019), http://btlj.org/2019/04/reforming-the-multi-agency-system-a-path-to-better-chinese-gi-protection/.

[36] *See American Viticultural Areas Scheme*, Alcohol & Tobacco Tax & Trade Bureau, https://ttb.gov/wine/american-viticultural-area-ava; *Australian Wine GIs Register*, Wine Australia, https://wineaustralia.com/labelling/register-of-protected-gis-and-other-terms.

agricultural products and foodstuffs feature most frequently as protected subject matter. These four categories constitute the vast majority of the 8,127 GIs found within the global database of the Organization for an International Geographical Indications Network (oriGIns).[37] Across the EU, accounting for both regional as well as national-level protection, "GIs in force relating to 'wines and spirits' accounted for 57.1% of the 2017 total, followed by agricultural products and foodstuffs (28.2%)."[38] Newer independent regimes, including those with an interest in non-agricultural GIs such as crafts or textiles, are open to any type of product and have borrowed from trademark law to facilitate this. India adopts the Nice classification for goods, used for trademark registration, where products are divided into thirty-four classes for administrative convenience.[39] Examiners rely on such classification systems when conducting a search to check whether a prior similar sign exists for a similar class of goods, which indicates there will be a conflict between the new application and a prior sign.

The categories of products recognised by a system have more than just administrative significance; they speak to its epistemological foundations. Wines are the archetype for the agricultural products template around which independent GI systems have developed. They form the conceptual core of GIs. These products are associated with a physical geography causal narrative: the soil and climate of a region distinctively influences the quality of the final product.[40] This causal connection is what sets GIs apart as a category of signs. It is reflected within the TRIPS definition of a GI in Article 22.1, where the "quality, reputation or other characteristic of the good is essentially attributable to its geographical origin." As we move from marble extracted from the ground, through grapes and olives grown in distinct regions, to cheeses, charcuterie and eventually textiles and toys, is this physical geography link attenuated to the point of implausibility? Or do alternative or supplementary means exist to connect products to place? These are the issues confronting the EU as it considers whether to expand its agricultural products and foodstuffs regime to incorporate non-agricultural GIs, including crafts and textiles.[41] These issues relating to the nature of the link arguably account for why TRIPS stops at goods, while trademark law extends into services. To be clear, TRIPS does not prohibit services from being recognised as GI and some countries do so. A handful of national systems recognise banking, health services or traditional healing methods.[42] Brazil has recognised "Porto Digital" as a GI for an urban technology park, for software services.[43] Yet skilled

[37] Organization for International Geographic Indications Network, https://origin-gi.com/i-gi-origin-worldwide-gi-compilation-uk.html.

[38] WIPO, *supra* note 6, at 190–91.

[39] *See Classifications of Goods – Name of the Classes*, IP India, http://ipindia.nic.in/writereaddata/images/pdf/classification-of-goods.pdf.

[40] Elizabeth Barham, *"Translating Terroir" Revisited: The Global Challenge of French AOC Labeling*, *in* Research Handbook on Intellectual Property and Geographic Indications 46 (Dev S. Gangjee ed., 2016). *Cf.* Matteo Ferrari, *The Narratives of Geographical Indications*, 10 Int'l J. L. in Context 222 (2014).

[41] *Commission Green Paper on Making the Most Out of Europe's Traditional Know-How: A Possible Extension of Geographical Indication Protection of the European Union to Non-Agricultural Products*, COM (2014) 469 final (July 15, 2014); Delphine Marie-Vivien, *Do Geographical Indications for Handicrafts Deserve a Special Regime? Insights from Worldwide Law and Practice*, *in* The Importance of Place: Geographical Indications as a Tool for Local and Regional Development 221 (William van Caenegem & Jen Cleary eds., 2017).

[42] Irina Kireeva & Bernard O'Connor, *Geographical Indications and the TRIPS Agreement: What Protection Is Provided to Geographical Indications in WTO Members?*, 13 J. World Intell. Prop. 275, 282 (2010); WIPO Compilation, *supra* note 17, at Annex 64–68.

[43] *See Portodigital*, https://portodigital.org/home; Emanoel Querette et al., *Local Institutions, Culture and Competitiveness: Leveraging Porto Digital's Reputation through a Geographical Indication of Software* (IASP 30th Conference on Science and Technology Parks, Recife 2013).

people can relocate and are arguably capable of delivering the same quality of service elsewhere. Can services be anchored to place in the same way that grapes, olives or coffee plantations can be? While services therefore constitute one end of the spectrum, where human factors are predominantly or perhaps solely responsible for the end product, the extent to which an emphasis on human factors (and their mobility) uproots territorial links is debated across certain categories of goods as well.

C *The Link between Product and Place*

The casual link between product and place is what sets a GI apart, as a discrete category within intellectual property law. In this regard, it resembles the crucial subsistence requirement of originality for copyright law or distinctiveness for trademark law. We have seen that Article 22.1 of TRIPS refers to the quality, characteristics or reputation of a product being "essentially attributable" to its geographical origin. The definition of an Appellation of Origin (AO) in Article 2(1)(i) of the Geneva Act of the Lisbon Agreement[44] refers to a geographical denomination "which serves to designate a good as originating in that geographical area, where the quality or characteristics of the good are due exclusively or essentially to the geographical environment, including natural and human factors, and which has given the good its reputation." Independent registration systems require this localising link to be explicitly articulated, to be spelled out in detail, since it relates to the normative basis for GI protection as well as facilitating policy goals such as territorial development. The key elements of this link requirement are (i) that the distinctive features of a product are (ii) causally attributable (iii) to its specific geographical origin, which encompasses both natural and human factors in that region. As WIPO acknowledges:

> The link should be made between the product, its specific and particular features on the one hand, and the geographical name applied for on the other. It will therefore be necessary to explain how the quality, reputation or other characteristics are linked to the geographical area and thus to determine the delimitation criteria and the specifications of the product resulting therefrom.[45]

The role of a registrar is then to verify this link requirement. Applications which do not satisfy this will be unsuccessful. This is confirmed inter alia by Article 8(c)(ii) of EU Regulation 1151/2012 (requiring evidence of the link as an essential part of the application), the recent WIPO survey, and Regulations under the Geneva Act of the Lisbon Agreement.[46]

The link is thus a crucial ingredient in the product specification, also referred to as the qualification document or *cahier des charges* submitted by an applicant. The application "should demonstrate in what way the product's characteristics are due to the geographical area and what the natural, human and other elements are which give its specificity to the product … [it] must describe the specificities of the product and of the geographical area which produces or

[44] World Intellectual Property Organization [WIPO], Geneva Act of the Lisbon Agreement on Appellations of Origin and Geographical Indications and Regulations under the Geneva Act of the Lisbon Agreement on Appellations of Origin and Geographical Indications, WIPO Doc. LI/DC/19 (May 20, 2015).

[45] WIPO Standing Committee on the Law of Trademarks, Industrial Designs and Geographical Indications: Tenth Session (Geneva, Apr. 28–May 2, 2003), Geographical Indications: Document prepared by the Secretariat, WIPO Document SCT/10/4 (Mar. 25, 2003).

[46] *See* WIPO Compilation, *supra* note 17, at Annex 34–6; Regulations under the Geneva Act of the Lisbon Agreement on Appellations of Origin and Geographical Indications, R. 5(3), May 20, 2015.

influences these factors, and how these two are linked."[47] However, registrars assessing this link must confront the following questions. First, TRIPS recognises two broad pathways for linking a product to place: (i) the seemingly more objective qualities or characteristics route, or (ii) the apparently subjective reputation option.[48] The former pathway relates to the physical attributes of a product. "Specific quality means that some characteristics differentiate the product from the other products of the same category and consumers perceive it as such."[49] These distinctive qualities, arising from a combination of natural and human factors specific to the region of origin, are said to give the product its typicity, or a specific form of anchorage to a region. Distinctive features might be the shape or form, texture or organoleptic qualities (relating to flavour or fragrance) of a product. For example, milk production in a mountainous region may be coordinated in order to facilitate cooperative or collective production. Local breeds of cattle feed on alpine meadows, ingesting regionally specific grasses and flora, which manifest in the aroma of the cheese that is produced via a traditional ripening method.[50] Qualities or characteristics may therefore be summarised as distinguishing product features causally attributable to geographic origin. In addition to paper audit trails or livestock tagging, it is increasingly possible to scientifically establish links with a specific region of origin and associated raw materials. Climate, vegetation and latitude all affect naturally occurring isotope composition. Natural abundance isotope ratios can therefore be used to determine provenance since they provide information on plant type or diet as well as geographical origin (since the stable isotope ratios of hydrogen and oxygen are dependent on latitude).[51]

By contrast, the second of these pathways – the reputation option – is far more ambiguous. Reputation is an independent basis for satisfying the link under TRIPS as well as specific national or regional systems, with the EU's Protected Geographical Indication (PGI) being a prominent example. When is a product's reputation "essentially attributable" to its geographical origin? One response may be to draw on historical sources and focus on situated production techniques. As opposed to contemporary commercial reputation (the object of trademark or unfair competition protection), a more GI-specific approach requires the assessment of: (1) the product's contemporary reputation, which can demonstrate continuity with (2) its historic reputation over time, attributable to specific or distinctive features of the product and (3) these features of the product in turn were causally attributable to natural or human factors specific – but not necessarily unique – to the region of origin.[52] Without a coherent approach to reputation as a stand-alone basis for linking products to place, the GI approach runs the risk of collapsing into the trademark approach of merely assessing whether a product currently has a reputation in the marketplace.

[47] *Guide to Applicants for Completion of the Single Document*, European Commission, http://ec.europa.eu/agriculture/quality/schemes/guides/guide-for-applicants_en.pdf.

[48] For the drafting history and interpretative possibilities, *see* Gangjee, *supra* note 4, 223–37.

[49] Emilie Vandecandelaere et al., Linking People, Places and Products: A Guide for Promoting Quality Linked to Geographical Origin and Sustainable Geographical Indications 12 (2d ed. 2009–2010).

[50] Institut National de l'Origine et de La Qualité (INAO), *Guide du demandeur d'une appellation d'origine protégée (AOP) ou d'une indication géographique protégée (IGP)* (Nov. 2017), 24–26.

[51] *See, e.g.*, Emilia Furia et al., *Multielement Fingerprinting as a Tool in Origin Authentication of PGI Food Products: Tropea Red Onion*, 59 J. Agric. & Food Chemistry 8450 (2011); Georgios Danezis et al., *Food Authentication: Techniques, Trends & Emerging Approaches*, 85 Trends in Analytical Chemistry 123 (2016) (describing the full range of analytical techniques including chromatographic techniques, isotopic techniques, spectroscopy and highly sensitive molecular genomics and proteomics).

[52] Dev S. Gangjee, *From Geography to History: Geographical Indications and the Reputational Link, in* Geographical Indications at the Crossroads of Trade, Development, and Culture in the Asia-Pacific 36 (Irene Calboli & Wee Loon Ng-Loy eds., 2017).

Another set of questions relates to the strength of the link between product and place.[53] This is evidenced by the different qualification requirements for the two types of GIs recognised in Article 5 of EU Regulation 1151/2012. The Protected Designation of Origin (PDO) requires all the production steps to take place within the designated region of origin in addition to requiring that the raw materials be sourced from that region.[54] However, the Protected Geographical Indications (PGI) – which is entitled to the same scope of protection and treated equally in all material ways – requires any one of the production steps (production, processing or preparation) to take place in the region, while also permitting raw materials to be sourced from outside the region. The room for manoeuvre that the PGI offers is often welcomed by producers.[55] There may be historic reasons for sourcing raw materials externally – in the case of Stilton cheese, milk quotas in the past led to a decline in local supplies – while for other products, such as Prosciutto di Parma, their growing popularity leads to increasing demand and the need to scale up inputs.[56] Yet an independent registration system which is increasingly permissive of loose linkages undermines its own credibility by diluting the value of the certification signal (guaranteeing origin) to consumers. This debate also implicates the extent to which natural or human factors are responsible for the end quality of the product.[57]

Besides the two forms of linkage to place and the degree of permitted flexibility, one additional aspect being investigated is the extent to which an applicant must specify with a degree of precision which form of linkage is being adopted: quality, characteristics or reputation? Empirical analysis of EU agricultural products and foodstuff registrations suggests that this is often unclear, with applicants and national registries working with a mélange of all three options.[58]

D *Defining the Region of Origin*

Having outlined the link requirement, the need to delimit the region of production is more readily apparent. “The territorial basis for the entitlement of a GI must be closely linked to the specificity of the product and its geographical origin. This is also the main constraint of the system as it excludes all producers outside the territorial delimitation from using the GI.”[59] Regions of origin need to be precisely defined – usually via written descriptions and maps – by resorting to a range of criteria. Inevitably, this is a delicate process and boundary disputes are not uncommon. The GI might refer to a political or administrative unit within a state (a federal unit, district, commune, village etc.) or it might refer to a non-political geographical region, such as a wine-growing area or vineyard. Since wine was the archetypical product, the “criteria for delimiting

[53] WIPO Compilation, *supra* note 17, at Annex 38–39.

[54] There is an exception for raw material consisting of live animals and milk, contained in Article 5(3), provided the external production area is also defined and quality controls are in place.

[55] Matthew Rippon, *Traditional Foods, Territorial Boundaries and the TRIPS Agreement: The Case of the Melton Mowbray Pork Pie*, 16 J. World Intell. Prop. 262 (2013).

[56] *See* Dossier No. UK/PDO/0017/0277; Dossier No. IT/PDO/0117/0067.

[57] Irene Calboli, *In Territorio Veritas: Bringing Geographical Coherence in the Definition of Geographical Indications of Origin under TRIPs*, 6 W.I.P.O. J. 57 (2014); Irene Calboli, *Geographical Indications of Origin at the Crossroads of Local Development, Consumer Protection and Marketing Strategies*, 46 Int'l R. Intell. Prop. & Competition L. 760 (2015). *Cf.* Andrea Zappalaglio, *The Debate between the European Parliament and the Commission on the Definition of Protected Designation of Origin: Why the Parliament Is Right*, 50 Int'l R. Intell. Prop. & Competition L. 595 (2019).

[58] Zappalaglio, *supra* note 11. Andrea Zappalaglio is presently one of the coordinators of a research project at the Max Planck Institute to investigate this point further: Project on the Overall Assessment of the Functioning of EU GIs.

[59] Vandecandelaere et al., *supra* note 49, at 61.

non-political geographic areas, a practice most frequently conducted in the context of wine production, was found to aim at establishing the homogeneity of a production area and its distinctiveness as compared to other such areas."[60] A review of different national approaches indicates that the following are relevant: (i) natural features, such as rivers and contour lines indicating degrees of elevation; (ii) geographical and geological aspects including soil, drainage, climate and irrigation; (iii) human factors such as choices of plant varieties and specific production methods, which are often related to the local socioeconomic, political and cultural context, (iv) the history of production, (v) the location of different stages of processing.[61] This broad range of natural and human causal factors reinforces the point that place is made and not found. Place is not some objective entity that can be defined empirically by geologists or physical geographers in isolation; it is socially constructed.[62] This is true for delineating wine regions as well. A boundary dispute for the appellation for the sweet wine Sauternes took over a decade to resolve.[63] In the *Coonawarra* boundary determination dispute in Australia, while the aim was to identify a discrete and homogenous tract of land (here, the cigar-shaped *terra rossa* tract) based on physical geography attributes, historical criteria relating to the founding and development of the area, the use of the geographical expression to refer to the area and the history of grape wine production were also relevant.[64] Since a range of factors are considered, each delimitation process calls for a bespoke solution in order to balance them.

Many independent systems recognise that production boundaries can expand or possibly even contract over time, which requires a reassessment of these factors.[65] The complexity of the assessment further increases where handicrafts, textiles or so-called recipe-based products (foodstuffs such as pastries, confectionaries or charcuterie) are concerned, since human factors may be more pronounced. A homogenous tract of land with its geological features and climatic factors is simply not relevant as a baseline. Here some registrars prefer an (over)inclusive approach, adopting administrative units – an entire federal state or province – which is hard to justify in terms of the casual link to the product that will have been produced in only parts of that unit.[66] In other situations, the potential for applicants to exclude their competitors by drawing an arbitrary or indefensible geographical boundary, excluding the competitor's site of production, must be borne in mind.[67]

[60] WIPO, Standing Committee on the Law of Trademarks, Industrial Designs and Geographical Indications, *Document SCT/9/4: The Definition of Geographical Indications* (Oct. 1, 2002) (prepared by the secretariat), https://wipo.int/edocs/mdocs/sct/en/sct_9/sct_9_4.pdf.

[61] WTO Review, *supra* note 14, at [32]–[36]; VANDECANDELAERE ET AL., *supra* note 49, at 63–68.

[62] Wei Zhao, *Understanding Classifications: Empirical Evidence from the American and French Wine Industries*, 33 POETICS 179 (2005); Marion Demossier, *Beyond Terroir: Territorial Construction, Hegemonic Discourses, and French Wine Culture*, 17 J. ROYAL ANTHROPOLOGICAL INST. 685 (2011); Warwick Murray & John Overton, *Defining Regions: The Making of Places in the New Zealand Wine Industry*, 42 AUSTRALIAN GEOGRAPHER 419 (2011).

[63] Erica Farmer, *Delicious Enigmas: Legal Geographical Indication Regimes in Bordeaux and the United Kingdom* 142–50 (2013) (unpublished PhD thesis, UCL London) (on file with the UCL Library, UCL London).

[64] *Beringer Blass Wine Estates* v. *Geographical Indications Committee* (2002) 70 ALD 27 (Austl.); Glenn Banks & Scott Sharpe, *Wine, Regions and the Geographic Imperative: The Coonawarra Example*, 62 NEW ZEALAND GEOGRAPHER 173 (2006).

[65] WIPO Compilation, *supra* note 17, at Annex 55–64.

[66] This is the approach adopted by the Indian GI registry for crafts and textiles.

[67] Dev Gangjee, *Melton Mowbray and the GI Pie in the Sky: Exploring Cartographies of Protection*, 3 INTELL. PROP. QUARTERLY 291 (2006); Rippon, *supra* note 55; Sarah Bowen & Kathryn de Master, *New Rural Livelihoods or Museums of Production? Quality Food Initiatives in Practice*, 27 J. RURAL STUD. 73 (2011) (on the potential for powerful extralocal actors to co-opt the specification at the expense of local communities).

E Other Factors Relating to Registration

This chapter is much too modest a canvas for comprehensively reviewing the distinctive features of *sui generis* or independent GI regimes. Additional aspects of registration include whether traditional methods of production must be specified, whether product specifications can be amended over time, whether fees must be paid, whether renewal is required and how lists of registered users of GIs are to be maintained and enforced.[68] Reflecting the additional policy objectives of GI protection, some independent systems are also committed to enhanced or stronger protection, extending coverage to (i) dissimilar products; (ii) in situations where not only misrepresentation but also pure misappropriation is actionable; and (iii) by recognising increasingly indirect mental evocation of the protected GI through purely conceptual association, even when there is no visual or phonetic similarity between signs.[69] Many independent regimes have deeming provisions which insulate a registered GI from subsequently becoming generic, by legal fiat.[70] Both these aspects of stronger protection are controversial and contested, as Weatherall documents in Chapter 16.

With the comprehensiveness disclaimer in place, three final observations will reinforce the central argument presented here: the architecture and operation of an independent protection system relates to its core commitments and normative foundations. First, who ought to be able to apply for a GI? While registration formalities often focus on the legal nature of the applicant (for instance, is the applicant a cooperative which has recognised legal form), the extent to which the applicant must represent the interests of those across the product's supply chain is an important yet overlooked consideration.[71] Many independent systems do not formally require that applicants must represent the supply chain, with Switzerland being a noteworthy counter-example: Swiss law requires that the membership of the applicant group must represent at least half the total volume of production concerned as well as be supported by more than 60 per cent of the operators involved in placing the end product on the market or being involved in one of the key stages of production.[72] The significance of an inclusive and participatory producer organisation is elaborated upon in Section III below. Second, what is the legal nature of the rights obtained upon registration? Unlike certification or collective mark regimes which refer to owners,

[68] See the WIPO and WTO overviews, *supra* note 14; WIPO Compilation, *supra* note 17. Further finessing of these features can be found amidst the 214 queries proposed as the basis for the WIPO Compilation. *See* WIPO, Standing Committee on the Law of Trademarks, Industrial Designs and Geographical Indications, *Document SCT/6/3 Corrignedum to Doc. SCT/39/6/ Rev.* (Mar. 26, 2018), https://wipo.int/edocs/mdocs/sct/en/sct_39/sct_39_www_402617.pdf.

[69] Thus Recital 32 of Regulation 1151/2012 endorses a "high level" of protection. For substantive discussion, *see* Case C-44/17, *The Scotch Whisky Association* v. *Michael Klotz*, EU:C:2018:415 (Can the visually and phonetically dissimilar "Glen Buchenbach" evoke the PDO for Scotch whisky?); Case C-614/17, *Fundación Consejo Regulador de la Denominación de Origen Protegida Queso Manchego* v. *Industrial Quesera Cuquerella SL*, ECLI:EU:C:2019:344 (Can a visual image of the La Mancha region evoke the (word) PDO for Manchego cheese?). This can be contrasted with the limits of unfair competition or registered trademark approaches, outlined by Weatherall in Chapter 16.

[70] *See, e.g.*, Regulation 1151/2012, art. 13(2); WIPO, Geneva Act of the Lisbon Agreement on Appellations of Origin and Geographical Indications, art. 12.

[71] WIPO Compilation, *supra* note 17, at Annex 73–80. In practice, independent GI registrars will often informally assess the extent to which an applicant represents the interests of the supply chain. However, collective or certification marks systems do not have this "representativeness" requirement, instead prioritising the applicant's technical competence to certify and the extent to which certification is open to anyone satisfying the relevant standards. For the latter, *see* Jeffrey Belson, Certification and Collective Marks, Ch 3 (2d ed. 2017).

[72] *See* WTO, *Review under Article 24.2 of the Application of the Provisions of the Section of the TRIPS Agreement on Geographical Indications: Response to the Checklist of Questions – Switzerland*, Feb. 11, 2019 (IP/C/W/117/Add.13/Rev.1/Corr.1). For background, *see* Barbara Abegg, *The Geographical Trade Mark: A Swiss Innovation Worth Copying?* 49 Int'l Rev. Intell. Prop. & Competition L. 565 (2018).

independent registration systems refer to beneficiaries with a right to use the GI, or right-holders.[73] However, the preamble to TRIPS begins by recognising "that intellectual property rights are private rights" which implies that they should be capable of being owned. The awkwardness of the fit with conventional IP rights is thus exposed, since jurisdictions tend to favour their own doctrinal methods for situating GIs within private, public or commons property models, or sometimes even conclude that the use of a GI label is a regulatory permission as opposed to a property right. The point being made is that while GIs are by now well-established as a form of IP, there is no international consensus around the nature of the property interest.

The third observation is this: how actively does an independent regime regulate the accompanying "internal" inspection and control framework that accompanies each GI application? The control framework exists to ensure that members of the GI club don't cut corners or free-ride; each producer must abide by the product specification as part of bargain for being allowed to use the GI. One trend which has been noted is that specialist independent GI registrars, including the influential National Institute of Origin and Quality (INAO) in France, have started to outsource inspection to private certification compliance bodies, leading to a more competitive (or fragmented) compliance landscape.[74] Recent research also indicates that the follow-up inspection systems have wide variations, even within supposedly harmonised regimes (are checks conducted randomly, once a year, or only at the time of joining?),[75] while regulatory structures for some GIs may exist largely on paper.[76] Yet such control mechanisms are fundamental to the quality and provenance guarantee that is being certified by independent GI systems. There is considerable variation at the national and regional level as to whether monitoring compliance with the product specification falls within the purview of the registrar's obligations and whether a public institution or private party conducts these inspections.[77] The extent to which the registrar has ongoing oversight obligations therefore has considerable significance.

III CONCLUSION: INSTITUTIONAL DESIGN FOR SUCCESSFUL GIS

Recent empirical research convincingly suggests that the process of registration and legal recognition is an important step, but just one step, towards establishing successful and sustainable GIs. A dynamic perspective is called for, which tracks the "biography" of a GI both before

[73] WIPO Compilation, *supra* note 17, at Annex 166–69; art. 5 of the Geneva Act of 2015; *see generally* Vadim Mantrov, EU Law on Indications of Geographical Origin: Theory and Practice 67–76 (2014); Delphine Marie-Vivien, The Protection of Geographical Indications in India: A New Perspective on the French and European Experience Part III (2015).

[74] Delphine Marie-Vivien et al., *Are French Geographical Indications Losing Their Soul? Analyzing Recent Developments in the Governance of the Link to the Origin in France*, 98 World Dev. 25 (2017).

[75] *Protection and Control of Geographical Indications for Agricultural Products in the EU Member States*, European Union Intellectual Property Office (EUIPO) 4 (Dec. 2017), https://euipo.europa.eu/tunnel-web/secure/webdav/guest/document_library/observatory/documents/reports/Enforcement_of_GIs/EUIPO_Geographical_Indications_full_report_en.pdf (referring to "the high heterogeneity in the approach the Member States have adopted to implementing controls").

[76] Yogesh Pai & Tania Singla, *"Vanity GIs": India's Legislation on Geographical Indications and the Missing Regulatory Framework*, *in* Geographical Indications at the Crossroads of Trade, Development and Culture 333 (Irene Calboli & Ng-Loy Wee Loon eds., 2017).

[77] WIPO Compilation, *supra* note 17, at Annex 193–202. According to the same survey, the absence of an effective inspection system is not mentioned as the basis for invalidating the GI in many countries (Annex 217–22). However, non-compliance with the conditions of the specification is a ground for cancellation in art. 54 of EU Regulation 1151/2012.

and after registration. Here two sets of institutional arrangements are crucial.[78] The first relates to the role and priorities of the independent registrar. Unlike a patent office or trademark registry, which looks recognisably similar around the world, GI registrars vary considerably across jurisdictions, while different subject matter-specific regimes may exist within a jurisdiction. The registrar may be a specialised wine-regulation body, part of an agricultural ministry with a broader remit or a trademark registry which is also responsible for independent GI registration.[79] The process of registration and its priorities will vary significantly depending on the nature of the registrar. For example, INAO has historically engaged very closely with groups of producers wishing to register GIs, offering expert guidance, maintaining sectoral panels of technical experts and being involved with subsequent inspection structures.[80] By contrast, a trademark-influenced approach to registration will be more light-touch, working with the application-as-submitted and relying largely on an opposition (during registration) or invalidation (after registration) process to draw out differences and identify flaws. These registry-level variations in the rigour of assessment are potentially explained by differing underlying commitments to "state or market" approaches to GIs.[81] These variations have significant consequences when it comes to multilateral registration systems. To what extent can a member of such a multilateral register trust an application submitted by another member, which might be applying different registrability criteria, or be perceived as less demanding?[82] Even amongst those registrars situated within national agricultural ministry hierarchies, there are significant variations: Will applicants interact with local, regional or national government agencies? Then there is the matter of whether the registrar is reacting to top-down signals generated by national government policy, setting GI registration targets to be achieved on paper, as opposed to engaging with requests emerging directly from producer groups.[83] Within the universe of independent systems, the depth of engagement – and the sustainability of the GI – varies considerably depending on the type of registrar and its engagement with collective producer organisations.

If the first set of institutional design questions is specific to independent GI systems, the second is applicable to all registration-based GI systems. How should the rules and practices of the collective producer organisation be designed in order to achieve sustainable production, ensure committed producer participation and attain market success? It is not just about identifying the product with sufficient precision but also identifying processes which enable egalitarian participation across the supply chain and informed debate around product quality. Here a useful analytical lens is collective action, which studies the actions undertaken by groups (or their representatives) in pursuit of their members' perceived shared interests. Of particular

[78] For an excellent comparison of France and Vietnam, highlighting the relevance of institutional differences and the policy context, *see* Barbara Pick, *Empirical Analysis of Geographical Indications in France and Vietnam: Opportunities and Constraints*, London Sch. Econ. (2018), http://etheses.lse.ac.uk/3916/.

[79] London Economics, *Evaluation of the CAP Policy on Protected Designations of Origin (PDO) and Protected Geographical Indications (PGI)* (Report for the European Commission, 2008), 63–66.

[80] Marie-Vivien, *supra* note 74.

[81] Delphine Marie-Vivien & Estelle Biénabe, *The Multifaceted Role of the State in the Protection of Geographical Indications: A Worldwide Review*, 98 World Dev. 1 (2017).

[82] This was reflected in the debate over whether a "home" country registration should be *erga omnes*, having binding legal effects on members, in the context of the (stalled) initiative to establish a WTO Wines and Spirits international register. WTO Secretariat, Side-by-Side Presentation of Proposals, May 4, 2007 (TN/IP/W/12/Add.1), [92]–[116]. In the lead-up to the revised Lisbon Agreement, it was observed that applications should have sufficient information regarding the link, precise geographical area etc., so that members can appropriately evaluate whether definitional requirements are met. WIPO Working Group on the Development of the Lisbon System, Results of the Survey of the Lisbon System, June 18, 2010 (LI/WG/DEV/2/2), Annex at [53]–[58].

[83] Dwijen Rangnekar, *Geographical Indications and Localisation: A Case Study of Feni*, ESRC Rep. (2009).

interest is the role of formal and informal institutions which support and coordinate such action.[84] Creating the conditions for inclusive conversations matters a great deal. The inclusion of diverse and heterogeneous interest groups and a high degree of direct enterprise participation at an early stage during the GI application process can generate benefits such as trust and social cohesion, which then supports the actual use of the GI label and a better implementation of associated quality standards.[85] An additional issue is whether the direct and indirect benefits of participation in the collective outweigh the transaction costs? And can institutional design ensure that these benefits are shared equitably across the supply chain?[86] At the same time, managing heterogenous groups has its own challenges, with pre-existing group structures (a cooperative or trade union) as well as supportive local government institutions playing a positive role.[87]

In conclusion, independent registration systems are increasingly prevalent around the world and reflect the underlying functional commitments and normative foundations of GI protection. They are worth evaluating as useful sites where theory meets operational practice. However, these regimes ought to be assessed dynamically, beyond the core requirement of the formal product specification and the application process. The institutional design issues relating to registrars as well as collective organisations can make all the difference between successful GIs and those which exist only on paper.

[84] Eleanor Ostrom's work is influential. Eleanor Ostrom, *Collective Action Theory*, *in* The Oxford Handbook of Comparative Politics 186 (Carles Boix & Susan Stokes eds., 2007).

[85] Xiomara Quinones-Ruiz et al., *Why Early Collective Action Pays Off: Evidence from Setting Protected Geographical Indications*, Renewable Agriculture & Food Sys. (Apr. 2017), at 179; *Adding Value to Traditional Products of Regional Origin: A Guide to Creating a Quality Consortium*, U.N. Indus. Dev. Org. 31–36 (2010), https://unido.org/sites/default/files/2011-07/ENG_Publication%20ORIGIN_0.pdf.

[86] Vandecandelaere et al., *supra* note 49, at 97–103.

[87] Quinones-Ruiz et al., *supra* note 9. For useful lessons from "failed" GIs, *see* Thanasis Kizos et al., *The Governance of Geographical Indications: Experiences of Practical Implementation of Selected Case Studies in Austria, Italy, Greece and Japan*, Brit. Food J. 2863 (2017).

16

Does the Unfair Competition Approach to Geographical Indications of Origin Have a Future?

*Kimberlee Weatherall**

I INTRODUCTION

There is appeal to the platonic concept of the Geographical Indication of origin (GI): that certain geographical locations may, through natural conditions (climate, soil, water, etc.) and/or localised tradition and artisan know-how, become peculiarly associated with distinctive high-quality produce, and that consumers benefit from understanding and valuing these unique peculiarities from all over the world. Law reflecting this ideal would ensure only local practitioners could invoke that association to attract a premium for their products and prevent misappropriation by unconnected interlopers. In theory at least, such a system could satisfy natural justice by rewarding those who practise and preserve cultural heritage; confer legal rights consistent with more historically Western concerns to provide incentives for investment in quality; and banish deception. The collective nature of these rights, tied to places and peoples rather than individuals, and not purely proprietary in the markets-and-transfer sense,[1] would find support outside Western traditions.

But platonic concepts rarely survive intact during the translation to the mundane – and complex – real world. Geographical terms can carry a plurality of messages, not just one. To consumers of tea, "Darjeeling" can invoke a kind of tea with certain qualities: the "champagne of teas" (irony intended); tea from a region in India; perhaps the romance of women in saris picking tea leaves and not much more. Different meanings may predominate among those from different cultural backgrounds.[2] This complicates the picture for lawmakers. It means deciding whether to privilege one meaning, or accommodate many (and how), deciding between the communicative needs of producers or their competitors, and the understanding or misunderstanding of sophisticated global consumers or dilettantes.

Policymakers' efforts to reconcile these competing interests; decide who/what is in; who/what is out; or what form of rights (and exceptions) are appropriate to achieve our assorted goals are further complicated by deeply political valences and economic conflict. GIs' core territory lies in

* Professor of Law, The University of Sydney. Thanks to the editors for their very useful comments on an earlier draft, and to Dr. Joannes Tandjung for sparking my interest in geographical indications of origin. Thanks also to Professor Dev Gangjee, whose own contribution to this volume better informed the discussion in this chapter.

[1] Dev Gangjee, *Quibbling Siblings: Conflicts between Trademarks and Geographical Indications* 82 CHI.-KENT L. REV. 1253, 1256–58 (2007).

[2] Daniel Gervais, A *Cognac after Spanish Champagne? Geographical Indications as Certification Marks*, *in* INTELLECTUAL PROPERTY AT THE EDGE: THE CONTESTED CONTOURS OF IP 130, 149 (Rochelle Cooper Dreyfuss & Jane C. Ginsburg eds., 2014).

agriculture; they implicate significant global trade and market access interests in this endlessly controversial area of policy. GIs are also part of the Development Agenda in international intellectual property (IP); GIs specifically are promoted by some countries in the developing world as a form of IP where they think they may have a comparative advantage. And the issues are not just economic, but also political and cultural. Lionising tradition, or tying it to economic advantage, is politically charged in a world of emigration and diasporas, empire, and post-colonial hangovers. Not every tradition is exclusive to a single country or region, and some traditions could be actively problematic. To the extent that marketing images of Darjeeling depend on racial and gender stereotypes, and veil economic realities in the tea industry,[3] they confront us with the challenge of promoting tradition, while simultaneously progressing human civil, political, economic, and social rights.

With so many questions and challenges, and a flexible international legal framework, it is not surprising that different countries have adopted widely contrasting approaches to protection. As Gangjee too notes in Chapter 15 in this volume, we are currently in a period where legal protection for GIs in a particular form – through *sui generis* (or, as Gangjee characterises them, "independent") registration systems that grant relatively strong exclusive rights in GIs – is expanding globally via trade agreements and national and regional legal reform: to new kinds of products; to terms hailing from many cultures and languages; and in ambition in terms of the public policies to be served by legal protection. Against this background, this chapter is concerned with the other model for providing legal protection for GIs, via unfair competition and trademark law. This method is most closely associated with common law jurisdictions (such as the United States, New Zealand, South Africa, and Australia), but found elsewhere, for example in Taiwan and, historically, Singapore. This chapter asks whether unfair competition approaches have a future in the midst of these current expansions.[4] The reality is that unfair competition systems, which are, at their core, based on local consumer perceptions, are not likely, without some adjustments, to respond well to the more culturally diverse GIs for which protection is now being sought.

Like a number of commentators writing from within traditions relying on unfair competition,[5] I am sceptical regarding the benefits of *sui generis* registration, at least as it is embodied in certain (often EU-inspired) models and (as outlined below), the Lisbon Agreement for the Protection of Appellations of Origin and their International Registration ("Lisbon Agreement").[6] But interest in protecting traditions linked to place, via some form of GI system, is not confined to Europe. Countries across Asia, Africa, and South America are promoting GIs and GI systems. Some have legitimate cultural and economic interests in securing legal protection for certain terms. As is

[3] Rosemary Coombe & S. Malik, *Rethinking the Work of Geographical Indications in Asia: Addressing Hidden Geographies of Gendered Labor*, *in* Geographical Indications at the Crossroads of Trade, Development, and Culture: Focus on Asia-Pacific 87 (Irene Calboli & Wee Loon Ng-Loy eds., 2017).

[4] Foreshadowing this, *see* Daniel Gervais, *Irreconcilable Differences – The Geneva Act of the Lisbon Agreement and the Common Law*, 53 Hous. L. Rev. 339, 368–71 (2015).

[5] *See, e.g.*, Michael Handler, *Rethinking GI Extension*, *in* Research Handbook on Intellectual Property and Geographical Indications 146 (Dev Gangjee ed., 2016); Mark Davison et al., *In Vino Veritas? The Dubious Legality of the EU's Claims to Exclusive Use of the Term "Prosecco,"* 29 Australian Intell. Prop. J. 110 (2019); Michael Handler & Robert Burrell, *GI Blues: The Global Disagreement over Geographical Indications*, *in* Emerging Challenges in Intellectual Property 163 (Kathy Bowrey et al. eds., 2011); Susy Frankel, *Geographical Indications and Mega-Regional Trade Agreements and Negotiations*, *in* Geographical Indications at the Crossroads of Trade, Development, and Culture: Focus on Asia-Pacific 147 (Irene Calboli & Wee Loon Ng-Loy eds., 2017).

[6] Lisbon Agreement for the Protection of Appellations of Origin and their International Registration, 923 UNTS 205 (Oct. 31, 1958) [hereafter Lisbon Agreement].

argued below, there is a case for common law countries making adjustments to their law, to accommodate those claims better than they presently do.

Common law countries could respond to these shifts by simply expanding *sui generis* registration, which many such countries already have in place for wine and spirits GIs. But, as this chapter argues, there is an alternative. Certain limited but consequential adjustments by common law countries to unfair competition and trademark systems could make their systems more cosmopolitan and accommodating to a much wider range of GIs.[7]

II HOW EXPANDING GEOGRAPHICAL INDICATIONS' TERRITORY CHALLENGES UNFAIR COMPETITION APPROACHES

A *What Are Geographical Indications, and How Are They Protected?*

GIs are defined in the Agreement on Trade-Related Aspects of Intellectual Property Rights (TRIPS) as "indications which identify a good as originating in the territory of a [WTO] Member, or a region or locality in that territory, where a given quality, reputation, or other characteristic of the good is essentially attributable to its geographical origin."[8] The definition covers most obviously geographical terms, like Champagne, but also other signs carrying this particular message, including specially designed logos that incorporate geographical terms; local symbols; and other traditional terms.[9] You can't stick a pin in "Feta" on a map, but according to the Court of Justice for the European Union, feta is a cheese, made *in Greece* from sheep or goat milk, using particular methods: making the term a GI.[10]

TRIPS Article 22 imposes on WTO members an obligation to prevent, in relation to other members' GIs:

(a) the use of any means in the designation or presentation of a good that indicates or suggests that the good in question originates in a geographical area other than the true place of origin in a manner which misleads the public as to the geographical origin of the good; [and]
(b) any use which constitutes an act of unfair competition within the meaning of Article 10*bis* of the Paris Convention (1967).

Article 22 also requires that members refuse or invalidate registrations of trademarks that contain or consist of a GI with respect to goods not originating in the territory indicated, where such use would mislead the public as to the true place of origin (Article 22.3). Thus, the baseline required

[7] Gervais, *supra* note 2, at 154.

[8] Agreement on Trade-Related Aspects of Intellectual Property Rights, Apr. 15, 1994, Marrakesh Agreement Establishing the World Trade Organization, Annex 1C, 1869 UNTS 299, 33 ILM 1197, art. 22.1 (1994) [hereinafter TRIPS Agreement]. The definition is incorporated into national legislation in many countries, World Trade Organization (WTO), *Review under Article 24.2 of the Application of the Provisions of the Section of the TRIPS Agreement on Geographical Indications*, WTO Doc. IP/C/W/253/Rev.1 (Nov. 24, 2003).

[9] *See also* Council Regulation (EEC) 2018/92 of the European Parliament and of the Council of July 14, 1992 on the protection of geographical indications and designations of origin for agricultural products and foodstuffs, art. 2.3, OJ (L 208); Council for Trade-Related Aspects of Intellectual Property Rights, *Review under Article 24.2 of the Application of the Provisions of the Section of the TRIPS Agreement on Geographical Indications: Summary of the Responses to the Checklist of Questions*, WTO Doc. IP/C/W/253/Rev.1 (Nov. 24, 2003).

[10] F.G.R. v. *Comm'n*, 2005 ECR I-09115. Other non-geographical GIs include Basmati (rice, India), Rooibos (tea, South Africa), or Navara/Njavara (rice, India); Delphine Marie-Vivien, *The Protection of Geographical Indications for Handicrafts: How to Apply the Concepts of Natural and Human Factors to all Products*, 4 W.I.P.O. J. 191, 199 (2012).

by TRIPS for GIs is protection against actions that mislead consumers or otherwise constitute unfair competition. In relation to wines and spirits, however, Article 23 requires a more absolute form of protection against the use of a GI on wines/spirits not originating in the place indicated, prohibiting use even where the true origin of the goods is indicated, and even where the GI is used in translation, or accompanied by expressions such as "kind," "type," "style," "imitation," or the like. Registration of trademarks for wines/spirits that contain a GI must also be refused or invalidated, subject to grandfathering of pre-TRIPS registrations.[11]

The TRIPS system represents a (messy) compromise between, broadly, two styles of national legal protection for GIs.[12] Some countries – especially but not exclusively those following the English common law tradition, such as Australia, New Zealand, and the United States, but also, for example, Singapore and Taiwan – have historically provided legal protection for GIs via a combination of unfair competition and trademark registration. Other countries, notably France and Italy, developed extensive *sui generis* systems for protecting GIs, in some cases tied into administrative systems for policing the qualities and characteristics of goods produced and sold under those GIs. Harmonisation at the European Union level extended this kind of *sui generis* registration system across Europe. Of course, from country to country, whichever of these "types" has been adopted, there can be considerable variation, and some degree of overlap. As a result of TRIPS, unfair competition-based systems commonly provide Article 23 protection for wines and spirits via a range of means, including *sui generis* registration systems confined to wines and spirits only.[13] Systems reliant on *sui generis* registration can vary significantly.

The Lisbon Agreement provides a system for multilateral registration of, and international protection of, geographical indications. It requires members to provide protection akin to (although not identical with)[14] TRIPS Article 23 for *all* members' GIs registered under the system (subject to protection for previously existing trademarks).[15] Registration by a member country of a GI under the Lisbon System ensures protection in all Lisbon members, subject to a limited period in which registration can be refused; no maintenance fees are required, and Lisbon GIs

[11] TRIPS includes some exceptions, including grandfathering of existing trademarks and the ability to refuse to protect GIs which are generic, i.e., the common name for a product. *See* TRIPS art. 24.

[12] *See generally* Handler, *supra* note 5.

[13] For example, the United States does so through alcohol labelling regulation. Gervais, *supra* note 4. Australia and New Zealand protect GIs via a *sui generis* registration system confined to wines and spirits: in Australia since 1993 (via amendment to the *Australian Wine and Brandy Corporation Act* 1980 (Cth) (Austl.) (now the *Wine Australia Act* (Cth) (Austl.); New Zealand since July 27, 2017, when the *Geographical Indications (Wine and Spirits) Registration Act Commencement Order 2017* (NZ), brought into effect the *Geographical Indications (Wines and Spirits) Registration Act* (NZ) passed in 2006 (now significantly amended by the *Geographical Indications (Wines and Spirits) Registration Amendment Act 2016* (NZ)). This is not universally true: South Africa instead has utilised a power granted to the Minister under the *Merchandise Marks Act 1941* (South Africa) § 15 to simply prohibit the use of certain terms and signs by notice published in the appropriate Gazette. A long list of EU terms was protected this way following the conclusion of an economic partnership between South Africa and the EU. *See* Estelle Biénabe & Delphine Marie-Vivien, *Institutionalizing Geographical Indications in Southern Countries: Lessons Learned from Basmati and Rooibos*, 98 World Development 68, 63 (2017).

[14] *See* Gervais, *supra* note 4, at 348–50.

[15] The Lisbon Agreement art. 3 requires that members protect GIs against any usurpation or imitation, even if the true origin of the product is indicated or if the appellation is used in translated form or accompanied by terms such as "kind," "type," "make," "imitation," or the like. The Geneva Act (in force in 2020) is more detailed, specifically referring to a dilution form of protection, against use in respect of goods that are not of the same kind, but where use "would indicate or suggest a connection between those goods or services and the beneficiaries of the appellation of origin or the geographical indication, and would be likely to damage their interests, or, where applicable, because of the reputation of the appellation of origin or geographical indication in the Contracting Party concerned, such use would be likely to impair or dilute in an unfair manner, or take unfair advantage of, that reputation" (as well as preventing use on goods of the same kind, including where translated, or accompanied by terms such as "'style,' 'kind,' 'type,' 'make,' 'imitation,' 'method,' 'as produced in,' 'like,' 'similar' or the like."): art. 11.

cannot become generic and hence invalid unless the GI becomes generic in its country of origin. The Lisbon System, in other words, mandates a strong form of protection from and for its members. It is, however, small. The Lisbon Agreement has only 30 Contracting Parties; the EU was not at the time of writing a contracting party although several European countries are (but the EU in late 2019 joined the Geneva Act of the Lisbon Agreement, concluded in 2015, which clarifies and modernises the Agreement).[16] Although formally agnostic as to the method by which GIs are protected, features of the Geneva Act are hostile to unfair competition systems.[17]

B The Expansion of GIs and the Challenge to Unfair Competition Systems

Legal protection for GIs is currently expanding in three ways.

First, the scope of potentially protected terms is expanding to new kinds of products, including non-agricultural products like handicraft. This has been considered at an EU level and implemented in some individual countries in Europe and beyond (for example, Indonesia).[18] GIs of this kind tend to be based less on geographical and natural features and more on human factors, such as local histories and traditions, and on reputation. As Gangjee's chapter in this volume notes (Chapter 15), this expansion is challenging for a number of reasons.[19] One potential issue is that, unmoored from geographical features which influence the qualities of the product, the claim to uniqueness or exclusivity can be harder to support. No one country, for example, can lay exclusive claim to the tradition of batik (fabric made using a wax-resist dyeing technique), but there are certainly countries, including both Malaysia and Indonesia, which assert cultural and historical connections to the art. Identifying the legitimacy of a claim, its scope and boundaries, and how geography is linked, as well as how to manage competing claims to culture, all pose challenges for any system seeking to protect such GIs.

Second, we are seeing an expansion in *ambitions* for GIs, with scholars and policymakers alike emphasising new goals: agricultural and regional development; increasing incomes for marginalised groups; environmental protection and sustainability; the promotion of human rights such as racial, post-colonial and gender equity; diversity and resistance to homogenisation; the preservation and enlivening of culture and heritage.[20] GIs are seen as "vectors of national, regional and

[16] World Intellectual Property Organization (WIPO), *Geneva Act of the Lisbon Agreement on Appellations of Origin and Geographical Indications* (2015), https://wipo.int/treaties/en/text.jsp?file_id=370297. At the time of writing the Geneva Act has 5 Contracting Parties.

[17] *See* Gervais, *supra* note 4.

[18] *Commission Green Paper on Making the Most out of Europe's Traditional Know-How: A Possible Extension of Geographical Indication Protection of the European Union to Non-agricultural Products Text with EEA Relevance*, COM (2014) 469 final (Oct. 6, 2015).

[19] For a strong critique of this trend, in particular for its departure from objective grounds for protection, *see* Irene Calboli, *In Territorio Veritas: Bringing Geographical Coherence in the Definition of Geographical Indications of Origin under TRIPS*, 6 W.I.P.O. J. 57 (2014) [hereinafter Calboli, *Territorio Veritas*]; Irene Calboli, *Geographical Indications between Trade, Development, Culture and Marketing: Framing a Fair(er) System of Protection in the Global Economy?*, *in* Geographical Indications at the Crossroads of Trade, Development, and Culture: Focus on Asia-Pacific 3 (Irene Calboli & Wee Loon Ng-Loy eds., 2017). (hereinafter Calboli, *Framing a Fair(er) System*). For an attempt to make sense of protection based on more human factors, *see* Dev Gangjee, *From Geography to History: Geographical Indications and the Reputational Link*, *in* Geographical Indications at the Crossroads of Trade, Development, and Culture: Focus on Asia-Pacific 36 (Irene Calboli & Wee Loon Ng-Loy eds., 2017).

[20] Tomer Broude, *Taking "Trade and Culture" Seriously: Geographical Indications and Cultural Protection in WTO Law*, 26 Univ. Pennsylvania J. Int'l Econ. L. 623, 651–52 (2005); Rosemary Coombe & Nicole Aylwin, *Marks Indicating Conditions of Origin in Rights-Based Sustainable Development*, 47 Univ. Cal. Davis L. Rev. 753 (2014); Christoph Antons, *Geographical Indications, Heritage, and Decentralization Policies: The Case of Indonesia*, *in* Geographical Indications at the Crossroads of Trade, Development, and Culture: Focus on Asia-Pacific 485 (Irene Calboli & Wee Loon Ng-Loy eds., 2017); Graham Dutfield, *Geographical Indications and Agricultural*

local cultural identities," and a partial answer to long-standing demands within the World Intellectual Property Organization (WIPO) for better legal protection for traditional knowledge and traditional cultural expressions,[21] and for more equal treatment of the cultural contributions of non-Western and developing countries. Major developing country GI proponents include Cuba, India, Jamaica, Kenya, Pakistan, and Sri Lanka. The evidence that GIs are serving any of these goals *well* is, as Frankel notes, mixed, and suggests that success depends on investment, institutional and community support, infrastructure, and marketing.[22] This chapter however is not concerned with the extensive empirical literature on whether GIs work or how to make them work; its chief concern is how unfair competition systems can respond to the expansion.

This is important because, third, *sui generis* GI registration systems are expanding into and out of new countries via a wave of bilateral trade agreements,[23] sector-specific international negotiations, technical assistance, and local initiatives.[24] The EU's pursuit of clawback of European terms is one catalyst,[25] and generates dynamics which implicate a wider circle of new GIs for which protection is sought. By encouraging and assisting its bilateral partners to implement EU-style *sui generis* GI registration,[26] and offering reciprocal protection for submitted lists of GIs,[27] the EU creates incentives for its partners to identify, and promote, local GIs whether currently well-known or not. Japan, South Korea and Vietnam have all negotiated GI "exchanges,"[28] securing EU protection for local GIs, while extending protection in their own markets to a range of EU terms considered generic in many common law countries – like ASIAGO, FONTINA, and FETA.[29] These new monopolies on GI terms affect the ability of agricultural exporters from third countries to use terms which are generic in their home market. In response, some, including for example stakeholders in Australia, are earnestly discussing whether they, too, should push for local GI systems,[30] not least because protection in the country of origin is a

Community Development: Is the European Model Appropriate for Developing Countries?, *in* The Intellectual Property and Food Project: From Rewarding Innovation and Creation to Feeding the World 485 (Charles Lawson & Jay Sanderson eds., 2013); Sarah Bowen, *Development from Within? The Potential for Geographical Indications in the Global South*, 13 J. World Intell. Prop. 231 (2010); Kasturi Das, *Prospects and Challenges of Geographical Indications in India*, 13 J. World Intell. Prop. 148 (2010).

[21] Biénabe & Marie-Vivien, *supra* note 13. *But cf.* Susy Frankel, *The Mismatch of Geographical Indications and Innovative Traditional Knowledge*, 29 Prometheus 253 (2011); Lorraine V. Aragon, *Copyright Culture for the Nation? Intangible Property Nationalism and the Regional Arts of Indonesia* 19 Int'l J. Cultural Prop. 270 (2012).

[22] Frankel, *supra* note 5. *See also* Brad Sherman & Leanne Wiseman, *From Terroir to Pangkarra: Geographical Indications of Origin and Indigenous Knowledge*, *in* Research Handbook on Intellectual Property and Geographical Indications (Dev Gangjee ed., 2016).

[23] Challenges arising from bilateral agreements in this area are not new. *See, e.g.*, Case C-3/91, *Exportur SA v. LOR SA and Confiserie du Tech SA*, 1992 ECR 1-5529 (legality of bilateral agreement re GIs under EU law).

[24] Geographical Indications have been protected by *sui generis* law in Thailand since 2003, in Vietnam since 2005, in Cambodia since 2014, and in the Lao PDR since 2011. Delphine Marie-Vivien & Isabelle Vagneron, *One Size Fits All or Tailor-Made? Building Appropriate Certification Systems for Geographical Indications in Southeast Asia*, 3 World Food Pol'y 105 (2017).

[25] European Commission Press Release IP/03/1178, WTO talks: EU steps up bid for better protection of regional quality products (Aug. 28, 2003). *See* Handler, *supra* note 5; Masayoshi Omachi, *A Tale of Two Approaches: Analysis of Responses to EU's FTA Initiatives on Geographical Indications (GIS)*, 18 Chi.-Kent J. Intell. Prop. 153 (2019).

[26] The EU–Vietnam Free Trade Agreement, for example, in art. 12.24 requires Vietnam to "maintain a system for the registration and protection of geographical indications," and art. 12.25 requires specific protection for a specified list of EU terms. Art. 12.27 provides broad art. 23 TRIPS protection for agricultural GIs generally.

[27] Omachi, *supra* note 25.

[28] Texts of EU trade agreements are available via the EU's website. Notably Singapore did not request protection for any local GIs. European Comm'n, https://ec.europa.eu/trade/policy/countries-and-regions/negotiations-and-agreements/.

[29] These particular terms are sometimes subject to various "grandfathering" clauses, as outlined further below.

[30] William van Caenegem et al., *Provenance of Australian Food Products: Is There a Place for Geographical Indications?*, Rural Industries Res. & Dev. Corp. Australia (July 2015), https://agrifutures.com.au/wp-content/uploads/publica

precondition for protection overseas.[31] Over time, these combined dynamics push towards global expansion of registered GI systems.

Whether or not we are convinced that *sui generis* registration, and/or broad Article 23/Lisbon-style exclusive rights are justified, we may still want to respond to the claim to global distributive justice, and promote cultural heritage.[32] This means trying to address the aspirations of the countries and traditional producers of Asia, Africa, and South America, i.e., claimants beyond those associated with Western "wines, cheese and meats." At the very least, we should arguably try to ensure they do not face unnecessary *barriers* when they seek to reach, educate, and sell to consumers beyond their local audiences. These producers may have years, even centuries of production and tradition, but no global reputation as of yet, and risk being pre-empted in important overseas markets.

Responding to these claims will require legal change within unfair competition systems. The new GIs come from many cultures, countries, and languages, making them less likely to be globally known. Examples (from lists registered with the EU by its trading partners) include Japanese GIs such as Tajima (beef), Yubari Melon, Yame Dentou Hongyokuro (tea); from Vietnam, Phú Quôc (fish extract), Môc Châu (tea), Thanh Hà (lychees); and at least a hundred Chinese GIs,[33] including Anji Bai Cha (Anji White tea), Zaoyuan Da Mi (Zaoyun rice); and Zhengshan Xiao Zhong (Lapsang Souchong tea) (using here the English phonetic representations of GIs that are natively expressed in Chinese characters).[34] Many of these GIs – except perhaps the last – may have a strong reputation only in their place of origin or culturally similar countries; or among a subset of diaspora consumers, meaning that protection predicated on consumer deception, as we see in unfair competition systems, will not protect them, unless representative organisations are quick to register for trademark protection.

In seeking to respond to these claims, we need also to recognise the potential for a range of conflicts that will need to be managed. When "origin" producers (i.e., those from an "indicated" geographical location) seek to register a GI or enter a third-country market, there can be conflict with local traders that are already using a term, descriptively or within trademarks; as Gangjee has noted, this situation is more common than new trademark owners confronting an existing GI.[35] This scenario can give rise to legitimate, competing interests, not readily resolved by a blanket rule in favour of the first registrant ("first in time, first in right").[36] For origin producers entering a new market, trademark or even descriptive use by local traders can be a barrier to truthful communication of origin. If "Kampot" is (or is part of) a registered trademark for

tions/15-060.pdf; Handler, *supra* note 5; *see also* Paula Caroline Zito, *Australian Laws and Regulations on Regional Branding on Food and Wine Labels*, 29 AUSTRALIAN INTELL. PROP. J. 67 (2019); *id.* at 127.

31 TRIPS art. 24(9); Omachi, *supra* note 25, at 200. Although note that protection at home need not necessarily be via a *sui generis* registration system: as earlier noted South Africa has used the simpler method of prohibiting use of certain terms, such as rooibos. *See* Biénabe & Marie-Vivien, *supra* note 13.

32 *See* Broude, *supra* note 20.

33 Protected pursuant to a specific agreement between the EU and China concluded in June 2017. European Commission Press Release IP/17/1507, 100 European geographical indications set to be protected in China (June 2, 2017). The list could well be more extensive over time: as Gangjee notes in Chapter 15 in this volume, there are over 8,000 GIs in force within China: presumably only the most important 100 are listed in China's agreement with the EU.

34 *See also* the list of Asian GIs registered in the EU, reproduced in Christopher Heath, *How Would Geographical Indications from Asia Fare in Europe?*, *in* GEOGRAPHICAL INDICATIONS AT THE CROSSROADS OF TRADE, DEVELOPMENT, AND CULTURE: FOCUS ON ASIA-PACIFIC 87 (Irene Calboli & Wee Loon Ng-Loy eds., 2017).

35 Gangjee, *supra* note 1, at 1262.

36 *Id.*

spices,[37] producers of Kampot pepper from the Cambodian region could have a problem even using the term. If they *are* able to rely on exceptions within trademark law to use it descriptively, they could face an uphill battle educating consumers about the differences between "authentic" Kampot pepper from Cambodia and other products, or developing prestige status for the original.[38] This issue is real. A quick review of Australia's trademarks register reveals that some oft-cited GI success stories of the Asia-Pacific region,[39] such as Kampot (Cambodia, pepper), Nuoc Mam Phú Quôc (Vietnam, fish sauce), and Kobe (beef) have already been included in registered or pending trademarks. On the other hand, the ambitions – and marketing – of origin traders may "de-genericise" a term.[40] GI expansion can thus mean local traders – who may have connections of heritage or tradition to the indicated place, and who might have been using the term in their own branding or to describe products – face loss of trademarks or loss of the exclusivity that trademark rights ordinarily provide, and may legitimately resent origin traders' apparent "free-riding" on their existing local goodwill.[41]

III THE FAST AND THE FAMOUS: GEOGRAPHICAL INDICATIONS WITHIN AN UNFAIR COMPETITION SYSTEM

In unfair competition systems, GIs are protected using a combination of trademarks and broader causes of action in unfair competition and related causes of action.[42] The core organising principle of unfair competition systems is that market misconduct should be prevented, most importantly by ensuring that consumers are not misled. This means, inter alia, protecting the reputation of products and producers, as communicated by signs. This system best protects the *famous*; and the *fast*, i.e., those who proactively register for protection first, regardless of reputation.[43] This will fail to assist some new GI claimants: those in the process of coalescing around GIs – like Kampot (Pepper) or Nuoc Mam Phú Quôc (fish sauce), mentioned above.[44] I focus below on the Australian system, one of those most historically resistant to GIs,[45] in order to highlight the importance of *detail* and the interconnectedness of all the parts that impact on GI protection in an unfair competition system. The lessons are, however, of more general application.

[37] Kampot pepper has some claim to unique qualities. *See generally* Marie-Vivien & Vagneron, *supra* note 24. At the time of writing there were two pending trademark applications in Australia using the term Kampot Pepper, including one for the word mark, "KAMPOT PEPPER AUSTRALIA" (TM application 1954608), although this application received an adverse first examination report and has since been withdrawn.

[38] Gangjee, *supra* note 1, at 1262 (discussing Parma Ham examples that have arisen in a range of countries).

[39] Marie-Vivien & Vagneron, *supra* note 24.

[40] Gervais, *supra* note 2, at 139 (recognising this possibility and citing McCarthy's recognition); *see also* Gervais, *supra* note 4, at 355. Or terms can acquire geographical meaning: *Canary Wharf Group Plc* v. *The Comptroller General of Patents, Designs and Trade Marks* [2015] EWHC 1588 (Ch.); [2015] FSR 34 (Eng.).

[41] The situation for third-country traders is illustrated by the "plight" of Danish feta producers after the CJEU decision on feta. Marie-Vivien, *supra* note 10. *See also Koppamurra Wines Pty Ltd* v. *Mildara Blass Ltd* [1998] FCA 226 (Austl.) (expressing concern over a "deliberate and carefully planned scheme" to "hijack" a trademark in the creation of a GI); *Rothbury Wines Pty Ltd* v. *Murray Tyrrell et al.* [2008] ATMOGI 1 (Austl.) (rejecting proposed GI on objection of registered trademark owner).

[42] In many countries there is also a limited *sui generis* system, not the focus of this chapter, protecting GIs for wine and spirits GIs, as required by TRIPS art. 23, and in some cases specific wine-based agreements with the EU. *See, e.g.*, *Wine Australia Act 2013* (Cth) (Austl.).

[43] *See* Gangjee, *supra* note 1 (discussing "first in time, first in right").

[44] *Id.* at 1275.

[45] For some of the reasons why Australia is resistant, extending beyond legal tradition to consider Australia's approaches to agricultural policy, *see* Handler, *supra* note 5.

A *Protecting Geographical Indications within the Trademark System*

The first and best protection for GIs within most unfair competition-based systems is via registered trademarks. The fit is not perfect. Although they involve protection of a sign that communicates producers' messages to consumers, GIs have at least two inherent features that are antithetical to classical trademark rules: (1) GIs are by definition inherently descriptive terms, which traditional trademark doctrine tends to treat as non-registrable and (2) they are used by multiple traders, where trademarks are generally intended to communicate (a single) origin or trade source.

The second issue is readily addressed through special forms of registered trademarks designed for collective use, found in trademark systems around the world.[46] In the Australian system, certification trademarks (CTMs)[47] are a special category of marks that indicate that goods or services comply with certain quality standards or characteristics.[48] For a CTM to be registrable, a set of rules and standards must be specified, and compliance with those rules must be certified. The CTM is then licensed in a non-discriminatory manner to producers whose goods meet these standards.[49] CTMs overcome several problems with classic trademarks for protecting GIs: they can be used to signal geographical origin and quality rather than a single trade origin; and they can be managed through rules covering the full range of questions that are important for GIs, including the geographical boundaries of origin, inputs/ingredients, production processes, and quality standards.[50] Obtaining registration of a CTM can involve significant bureaucratic hurdles, depending on the jurisdiction, although perhaps no more than apply for registration within *sui generis* GI systems. At the time of writing, CTMs on the Australian register include many GIs that have attracted controversy over the years: Stilton (cheese), Darjeeling (tea), Parma and Parma Ham (processed meat), Tequila (spirit), Solingen (steel and steel instruments), and Scotch Whiskey; Gorgonzola, Asiago, Halloumi (all cheeses), Pisco (spirit), and Basmati (rice) are all pending.[51] Relatively few CTMs from the Asia-Pacific region are registered in Australia. Ceylon Tea (figurative), Thai Hom Mali Rice (rice), and Chinese characters translated as Long

[46] Note that while the basic nature of CTMs is similar across jurisdictions, the specific rules vary. For example, in the United States, Singapore, and New Zealand a CTM cannot be owned by a person or entity that trades in the relevant goods; in Australia the owner may also be a user under the Act. *See, e.g., Trade Marks Act 1995* (Cth) § 169 (Austl.), although rules which allowed use by the certifier would attract scrutiny during examination.

[47] *Trade Marks Act 1995* (Cth) §§ 168–83 (Austl.); *see also* 15 USC § 1054; *Trade Marks Act 1998* Sch. 2 (Sing.); *Trade Marks Act 2002*, §§ 5, 14, 54–56 (NZ). In some cases ordinary trademarks have been used as part of a strategy to develop a geographically based "brand," with one well-known example being Ethiopian coffee. Ramona Teuber, *Geographical Indications of Origin as a Tool of Product Differentiation: The Case of Coffee*, 22 J. Int'l Food & Agribusiness Marketing 277 (2010). For a critique *see* Heath, *supra* note 34. There are also collective trademarks, which denote an association, with the collective mark indicating membership, which could be conditioned, for example, on geographical origin. *See Trade Marks Act 1995* (Cth) pt 15 (Austl.). It is not necessary to register rules governing use of a collective mark; in the EU collective marks have been used for GIs. *See* Heath, *supra* note 34 (citing the example of DARJEELING).

[48] *Trade Marks Act 1995* (Cth) § 169 (Austl.).

[49] *Trade Marks Act 1995* (Cth) § 175 (Austl.); *Trade Marks Regulations 1995* (Cth) reg. 16.6 (Austl.), prescribing that in approving CTM rules, the ACCC must consider principles of competition law, unconscionable conduct, unfair practices, product safety, and product information.

[50] In relation to the United States, *see U.S. Trademark Manual of Examining Procedure* (TMEP) § 1306.06(f)(i), noting that the certification statement with a CTM can refer to characteristics other than geographical origin, e.g., inputs/production methods. For example, the US registration for ROQUEFORT certifies that the cheese "has been manufactured from sheep's milk only, and has been cured in the natural caves of the community of Roquefort, Department of Aveyron, France." US Registration No. 0571798.

[51] Notably as of July 2019 both a word and figurative mark for BASMATI had received an initial adverse report, although the process was far from over.

White Hill People Ginseng are registered; Fuling Zhacai (preserved mustard vegetables), Cambodian Premium Aromatic Rice Malys Angkor (figurative), Xuyilongxia (Lobster), Vietnam Rice (figurative), and Japanese characters representing Yame Tea or Yamecha (a kind of green tea processed in the Fukuoka prefecture) are pending at the time of writing. A range of geographical certification marks are registered in the United States, including various Idaho Potato marks, Roquefort and Stilton (cheese), and Darjeeling (tea).[52]

CTMs do not provide administrative systems or evaluation of GIs akin to that which would be provided by a *sui generis* system based on a European model.[53] The trademark system is not designed to reflect the foundational criteria for GIs, and the trademark officials who assess CTMs are not specialists in product quality standards or the relationship between place and product. But CTM systems can afford some opportunities for considering the "merits" of a GI. In Australia, the rules for applying the CTM are reviewed prior to grant by the Australian Competition and Consumer Commission (ACCC), not only for their consistency with competition principles, but also consumer protection.[54] In deciding whether to approve the proposed rules for using a CTM, the ACCC can solicit external input to supplement its expertise. This enables examination of how the reality behind a CTM matches to consumer understanding, and, where there is a mismatch, CTMs have been rejected. For example, the ACCC rejected a CTM which would have certified as "free range" eggs produced by hens kept at density levels many times the industry's own recommendations.[55] A proposed geographical CTM which allowed a significant proportion of the inputs to be sourced outside the region would likely raise similar concerns. And while the ACCC process is not equivalent to the kind of examination of geographical features and history you would see in a *sui generis* system, the differences may be less than might appear. *Sui generis* registration systems are far from perfect assessors of the historical legitimacy of GIs, or the geographical, natural, and human factors that influence the characteristics of goods.

There are other ways in which protecting GIs within the trademark system departs from *sui generis* models like those of Europe, and the Lisbon system. Like other trademarks, CTMs must be renewed, and can be lost if they are not used in the jurisdiction[56] or if they become generic (something the Lisbon Agreement prevents).[57] CTMs must also be distinctive: they must be

[52] Gervais, *supra* note 4, at 364.

[53] Note however that, as Gangjee mentions in Chapter 15 in this volume, the administrative mechanisms within *sui generis* systems also vary. *See also* Marie-Vivien & Vagneron, *supra* note 24.

[54] A system of this kind is not universal. Taiwan ensures expert input by involving various relevant government departments in examining proposed certification rules. Szu-Yuan Wang, *Protection of Geographical Indications in Taiwan: Turning a Legal Conundrum into a Policy Tool for Development*, *in* GEOGRAPHICAL INDICATIONS AT THE CROSSROADS OF TRADE, DEVELOPMENT, AND CULTURE: FOCUS ON ASIA-PACIFIC 359 (Irene Calboli & Wee Loon Ng-Loy eds., 2017). In New Zealand and Singapore, on the other hand, examination of the rules is by the Trade Marks Office. Rules in both countries require the Registrar to be satisfied that the applicant is "competent to certify the goods or services for which the mark is to be registered," as well as to take into account public interest considerations. But advice on the New Zealand website notes that "the examiner will not get too involved in assessing … technical requirements for authorised use of the mark as the regulations and the registration are open to cancellation or alteration." *Practice Guidelines, Certification Marks*, NEW ZEALAND INTELL. PROP. OFFICE, https://iponz.govt.nz/about-ip/trade-marks/practice-guidelines/current/certification-marks/.

[55] ACCC, Initial Assessment of Certification Trade Mark Application CTM1390450 filed by the Australian Egg Corporation Ltd, Nov. 2, 2012. *Id.* at 543–44. The ACCC received 1,700 submissions. ROBERT G. BURRELL & MICHAEL HANDLER, AUSTRALIAN TRADE MARK LAW 543–44 (2d ed. 2016).

[56] This is true in the United States. *See* Gervais, *supra* note 4, at 367. But not in Australia. *See Trade Marks Act* 1995 (Cth) § 170 (Austl.).

[57] *Trade Marks Act* 1995 (Cth) § 24 (Austl.); *cf.* Lisbon Agreement, *supra* note 6, at art. 6; Geneva Act, *supra* note 16, at art. 12.

capable of distinguishing the certified goods or services from uncertified goods or services.[58] Historically, many trademark systems had rules that prevented descriptive or geographical terms from ever being registrable under this requirement,[59] to prevent monopolies on signs competitors need.[60] But this rule is often relaxed in the case of GIs. The Australian Examiner's Manual notes that geographical descriptiveness is less of a concern with GI CTMs, which allow use by multiple traders from the area who might need access to the descriptive meaning, and are hence less "monopolistic" in nature.[61] US law also provides that a registered certification mark containing a geographic designation that functions to certify regional origin is not considered geographically descriptive.[62] Taiwan's Trademark Act of 2012 goes so far as to waive the requirement of distinctiveness in relation to geographical certification marks and geographical collective marks.[63]

Further, it has become easier to register geographical terms. Today, secondary meaning will make a descriptive term registrable,[64] so determined marketing can commandeer even an obviously geographical word.[65] Australian courts, for example, have become readier to conclude a mark is inherently distinctive and hence immediately registrable, with the High Court in *Cantarella Bros Pty Ltd* v. *Modena Trading Pty Ltd* holding as distinctive the Italian descriptive terms CINQUE STELLE (five stars) and ORO (gold) for coffee products on the basis that the words were not understood as being descriptive by ordinary (English-speaking) Australians.[66] *Cantarella* makes it particularly easy to register foreign language marks, so new GIs from non-English-speaking countries could readily be registered, as or within CTMs or trademarks. In other cases, where distinctiveness remains a challenge, a geographical term can be registered as a figurative or composite mark with minimal additions. There is for example a plethora of

[58] That is, in the "differential distinctiveness" rather than the source distinctiveness sense. Barton Beebe, *Search and Persuasion in Trade Mark Law*, 103 MICH. L. REV. 2020, 2028–31 (2005); *Trade Marks Act* 1995 (Cth) § 177 (Austl.). The usual distinctiveness ground does not apply. *Trade Marks Act* 1995 (Cth) §§ 41 & 170 (Austl.).

[59] For an excellent discussion of the importance of this particular rule, and its development in the United States, *see* Robert Brauneis & Roger E. Schechter, *Geographic Trademarks and the Protection of Competitor Communication* 96 TRADEMARK REPORTER 1, 2 (2006). Indeed, under the 1905 US Act, brands consisting of geographic terms could never be registered as a trademark, on the basis that all place names should remain available for use by all competitors. *Id.* In Australia, *see Trade Marks Act* 1955 (Cth) §§ 24–26 (Austl.); *Clark Equipment Co.* v. *Registrar of Trade Marks* (1964) 111 CLR 511 (Austl.).

[60] *Re W. & G. du Cross Ltd Application* [1913] AC 264 (Eng.); *Canal Co.* v. *Clark* 80 US 13 Wall. 311 (1871); *York Trade Mark* [1894] RPC 231 (Eng.); Case C-109/97, *Windsurfing Chiemsee Produktions* v. *Boots & Attenberger*, 1999 ECR I-2779.

[61] Trade Mark Examination Manual, Part 35, 1.5 (as at June 1, 2019), *but see Parish of Pokolbin Incorporated* [2014] ATMO 98 (Oct. 9, 2014) (Eng.) which took a narrow view of the language in the Manual, arguing that it might be easier to register marks *containing* geographical terms, but not those *consisting of* such terms. *See also* New Zealand Intellectual Property Office, *supra* note 54; *Trade Marks Act* 1998 (Sing.) Sch. 2 Clause 3 (specifically stating that a certification mark can be registered which consists of signs used to designate the geographical origin of goods – but also limiting the exclusive rights in such a mark to allow use of the sign "in accordance with honest practices in industrial or commercial matters").

[62] 15 USC § 1052(e)(2) (barring registration of any mark that is primarily geographically descriptive of goods or services but providing an exception for indications of regional origin).

[63] Wang, *supra* note 54.

[64] *Trade Marks Act* 1995 (Cth) § 41 (Austl.). For a description of similar trends in the United States, *see* Brauneis & Schechter, *supra* note 59.

[65] Burrell & Handler, *supra* note 55, at 103. Australian examples include OREGON (for saws and tools) and SAKATA (a Japanese city; for rice snacks) are both registered trademarks.

[66] *Cantarella Bros Pty Ltd* v. *Modena Trading Pty Ltd* (2014) 254 CLR 337 (Austl.); Burrell & Handler, *supra* note 55, at 98; at 115–17. For similar developments in the United States, *see* Brauneis & Schechter, *supra* note 59, at 29.

Australian logo and figurative mark registrations incorporating the name BAROSSA – a well-known wine and premium Australian food region.[67]

The trend to allow registration of geographical terms can help a GI claimant seeking a CTM – if they are *fast*. The applicant for a foreign term, or the determined marketer *could* be a GI association – or it could be a local trader drawing on a GI tradition, or a trader seeking to free-ride off the reputation of a place.[68]

Strong rules preventing registration of marks that make objectively misleading uses of geographical terms could prevent (some) interlopers from registering GIs and help protect slower GI claimants. But although trademark laws commonly include rules against misleading marks,[69] they may protect only famous geographical terms.[70] In Australian law, for example, having inaccurate geographical terms in a mark does not make it unregistrable: the question is whether consumers will be misled by the use – a *subjective*, not objective test. Registration is only prevented if consumers are aware of the foreign geographical indication, and have some expectation of what it means,[71] that would be frustrated by the registration and use of the mark. This will not help GI claimants lacking a presence in the public consciousness. It is possible in Australia to challenge the registration of a mark that has *become* misleading over time,[72] which might enable a slow GI claimant to educate the public and make a case for removal: the Greek producers of feta could seek to educate Australian consumers that "real" feta comes only from Greece. But there is a discretion *not* to remove a mark that becomes deceptive through no fault of the trademark owner.[73] Attempts by a GI claimant to "educate" the public may therefore succeed in "lifting all boats" – the GI-origin goods and those of any existing trademark owners – assuming such efforts aren't immediately stopped as infringement, and assuming too that the court is inclined to sympathy toward a trademark owner who has stood by while such efforts were undertaken.[74]

67 Paula Zito, *Australian Laws and Regulations on Regional Branding on Food and Wine Labels: Part 2*, 29 AUSTRALIAN INTELL. PROP. J. 127, 130–33 (2019).

68 In some systems, trademarks can become incontestable on descriptiveness grounds five years after registration if unchallenged. 15 USC § 1065.

69 E.g., *Trade Marks Act 1995* (Cth) § 43 (Austl.) (general prohibition on misleading trademarks); *Trade Marks Act 1995* (Cth) § 61 (Austl.) (specific rule where there is an existing GI); *see also* Haiyan Zheng, *A Unique Type of Cocktail: Protection of Geographical Indications in China*, *in* GEOGRAPHICAL INDICATIONS AT THE CROSSROADS OF TRADE, DEVELOPMENT, AND CULTURE: FOCUS ON ASIA-PACIFIC 87 (Irene Calboli & Wee Loon Ng-Loy eds., 2017) (citing a case in China applying rules against misleading trademarks to cancel a geographically misleading mark that interfered with a GI).

70 As Gangjee notes, a critical question can also be timing. In the US Parma case, it was decided that the mark PARMA was not deceptive at the time a trademark was registered, but had the potential to become more deceptive as Italian products entered the market. Unfortunately for the GI claimant, the relevant time was the date of registration under US and Canadian law. Gangjee, *supra* note 1, at 1272–75.

71 *Mount Everest Mineral Water Ltd* v. *Himalayan Spring Mineral Water* [2010] ATMO 85, [13] (Austl.). A similar approach in the United States has been criticised in Brauneis & Schechter, *supra* note 59.

72 *Trade Marks Act 1995* (Cth) § 88(2)(c) (Austl.). The provision has been applied in a case where the owner of a (non-geographical) trademark had allowed another company to use the mark without exercising the necessary quality or financial control to make the second company an authorised user, a state of affairs that was held to create confusion. *Health World Ltd* v. *Shin-Sun Australia Pty Ltd* (2008) 75 IPR 478 (Austl.). A case where a mark has, at the time of registration, no particular geographical or qualitative connotation, but acquires such a connotation over time, is another example of the potential application of § 88(2)(c) given by Burrell & Handler, *supra* note 55, at 324–25.

73 In these circumstances the court has the discretion to refuse rectification of the register. *Trade Marks Act 1995* (Cth) § 89 (Austl.); Burrell & Handler, *supra* note 55, at 331.

74 There is room for debate whether the case where a trademark owner fails to take action against the promotional efforts of a GI claimant, giving rise to potential consumer confusion around the meaning of the term, would be one where the confusion is not the "fault" of the TM owner. Burrell & Handler, *supra* note 55, at 332; *cf.* Europe, where "vigilant

As for whether a geographical term is misleading or confusing, Australian courts have on occasion simultaneously downplayed consumers' overall knowledge of the importance of geography, while taking a relatively robust view of their ability to dissect messages contained within a mark. In the *Bavaria* case, a firm brewing beer in the Netherlands was able to register a figurative mark for beer prominently titled "Bavaria," despite opposition from the Bavarian Brewery Association. The court held that the mark was not misleading, because consumers would not have a sophisticated understanding of the role of geographical location for beer (viewing the beer as "European"), *and* would dissect the mark: inclusion of the word "Holland" in the figurative mark meant that consumers would not think the beer was Bavarian.[75] This thinking is also reflected in the way some marks have proceeded to registration: marks that *would* suggest geographical origin are registered conditionally – but by requiring that if the mark is applied to goods *other than* from the specified region, the packaging will include information to specify the actual place of manufacture. For example, an Australian-registered mark for "Byron Bay Blonde Ale" is subject to the condition "that in instances where the trade mark is used on beer that is not brewed by the applicant or that is not brewed in Byron Bay the product or packaging to which the trade mark is attached will include further information specifying the place of manufacture and/or the company that brewed the beer."[76]

A specific provision in Australian law allows a foreign GI owner to oppose registration of a trademark where it relates to similar goods or would cause confusion.[77] But it only applies to proposed trademarks that *consist of, or contain*, the foreign-recognised GI – not any mark that would *cause confusion with* the foreign GI.[78] Thus it did not apply in the *Bavaria* case where the EU-recognised GI was *Bayerisches Bier*.[79] This limitation is striking when compared to the extraordinarily broad rights of opposition granted to trademark owners to oppose registration of a GI in Australia's (wine and spirits only) *sui generis* regime. A trademark owner can object to registration of a GI where that GI is likely to *cause confusion* with a word, expression or other indication that is, or is contained in, a trademark.[80] Had similar drafting been adopted in the trademark legislation to allow opposition by GI owners as found in the *sui generis* system, owners of the GI could at least have argued that the figurative trademark application in which *Bavaria* was the most prominent feature would likely *cause confusion with* the word "Bayerisches" *contained in* the GI. Notably too, within the Australian *sui generis* system a trademark owner can oppose a GI even if: (a) the mark relates to different goods; or (b) the owner has only an unregistered mark; or (c) even if conditions on the trademark registration disclaim ownership of

conduct" on the part of the trademark owner is required to avoid revocation of a generic mark. Case C-145/05, *Levi-Strauss & Co.* v. *Casucci SpA*, 2006 ECR I-3703, 30–31.

75 *Bavaria NV* v. *Bayerischer Brauerbund eV* (2009) 177 FCR 300, 104 (Austl.); *Scotch Whisky Association* v. *De Witt* (2007) 74 IPR 382 (Austl.) ("Glenn Oakes" would not suggest that the (bourbon) product originated in Scotland); *NV Sumatra Tobacco Trading Co.* v. *Philip Morris Products Inc.* [1998] ATMO 69 (Austl.) ("USA Blend Cigarettes" did not suggest that the goods contained US-grown tobacco).

76 Australian-registered Trade Mark 1252120 ("Byron Bay Blonde Ale," figurative). Trademarks that relate to wine are often registered with a condition that the products must come from the relevant region, consistent with other wine labelling laws. *Wine Australia Act 2013* (Cth) (Austl.).

77 *Trade Marks Act 1995* (Cth) § 61 (Austl.).

78 For discussion and some criticism, *see* Zito, *supra* note 67, at 135–41; Burrell & Handler *supra* note 55, at 175–78.

79 *Bavaria NV* v. *Bayerischer Brauerbund eV* (2009) 177 FCR 300 (Austl.) (this court decision overturned the decision of the trademark office). Regional collectives have used this ground to oppose geographically misdescriptive marks. *See, e.g.*, *K-Swiss Inc.* v. *Federation of the Swiss Watch Industry FH* [2009] ATMO 78; (2009) 83 IPR 635 (Austl.) (K-SWISS for watches not from Switzerland); *Lacheteau SAS* v. *New Zealand Winegrowers* [2009] ATMO 82 (2009) 84 IPR 134 (Austl.) (KIWI CUVEE for wine not from New Zealand).

80 *Wine Australia Act 2013* (Cth) § 40RB (Austl.); *Rothbury Wines Pty Ltd* v. *Tyrrell* [2008] ATMOGI 1 (Austl.).

the term. This discussion highlights the importance of engaging with the details of the legislative system in ascertaining the degree of protection, or non-protection, of GIs.[81]

Finally, the rules in trademark law often favour the *fast* and the *famous* in infringement analysis. In Australia, for example, registered trademark owners have a defence to infringement,[82] and even in the absence of registration, a trader who is using a sign (including a GI) before registration of a CTM may have both a right to register their own mark, and a defence to infringement.[83] And although there is a defence to infringement for good faith descriptive use of a geographical term, it is not clear that use of a GI – which is intended to perform a strong branding function rather than a purely descriptive one – would always count as good faith, descriptive use.

This discussion of trademark law, even though limited in scope, and focused primarily on Australian law, reveals a complex picture for GIs. GIs can be proactively protected through a trademark system, but to receive protection, GI claimants need to be either fast, or famous. It has also highlighted details within the Australian system that increase the chance that trademarks that are objectively misleading about geography will be registered, and actively favour trademark owners and registrants by giving them broader rights of opposition than GI claimants. Targeted interventions in these details may hold out some hope for managing conflicts in our new GI world: a point we will return to below.

B Unfair Competition

Aside from CTMs, the chief legal protection for GIs in an unfair competition-based system lies in actions to prevent the use of signs in ways that will mislead consumers: causes of action we can put under the umbrella of "unfair competition."[84] These include (depending on the jurisdiction) one or more actions in tort (or *delict*), such as passing off; misappropriation/unfair commercial conduct; and statutory consumer protection regimes – for example, actions prohibiting firms from misleading consumers,[85] and specific consumer protection standards dealing with country-of-origin labelling.[86] In the United States, actions to protect collective geographically based goodwill have been recognised under broad common law unfair competition principles[87] and carried forward at the federal level via section 43(a) of the Lanham Act, which

[81] To similar effect, *see* Wang, *supra* note 54 (discussing the repeated amendments of Taiwanese trademark legislation in an attempt to "fit" the protection of GIs).

[82] *Trade Marks Act 1995* (Cth) § 122(1)(e) (Austl.).

[83] *Trade Marks Act 1995* (Cth) § 44(4) (Austl.) (right to registration); *Trade Marks Act 1995* (Cth) § 122(1)(f) & (fa) (Austl.).

[84] As Davis notes, although it is often said that countries like the United Kingdom do not have an action in unfair competition, a wide range of actions under other names – including passing off, examined here – come close to covering the same field. Jennifer Davis, *Why the United Kingdom Should Have a Law against Misappropriation*, 69 CAMBRIDGE L.J. 561, 561 (2010).

[85] *See, e.g., Australia Competition and Consumer Act 2010* (Cth) § 18 (Austl.); 15 USC § 1125(a)(1)(B).

[86] *See, e.g., Australia Competition and Consumer Act 2010* (Cth) Sch. 2, § 29(1) (Austl.) (prohibition on false or misleading representations concerning the place of origin of goods); *Australia Competition and Consumer Act 2010* (Cth) Sch. 2 § 255 ("safe harbour" provisions for certain country-of-origin representations); *see* Paula Zito, *Australian Laws and Regulations on Regional Branding on Food and Wine Labels (Part 1)*, 29 AUSTRALIAN INTELL. PROP. J. 67, 72–76 (2019); *see also* ACCC v. *Kingisland Meatworks & Cellars Pty Ltd* [2012] FCA 859 (Austl.). Also relevant in some cases are standards governing quality and marketing of food. The Australia New Zealand Food Standards Code deals with country-of-origin labelling requirements; compliance with the code is mandatory under state legislation within Australia. *See, e.g., Food Act 2003* (NSW) § 21 (Austl.); *Food Act 2006* (Qld) § 39 (Austl.).

[87] *Pillsbury-Washburn Flour Mills Co.* v. *Eagle*, 86 F. 608 (7th Cir. 1898) (recognising that a group of flourmills could have a collective equity entitling them to prevent use of a term – "Minnesota Patent" – consistently applied to flour produced in a particular way in a particular location, where there was substantial goodwill).

prohibits the use of "any word, term, name, symbol, or device, or any combination thereof, or any false designation of origin, false or misleading description of fact, or false or misleading representation of fact, which … in commercial advertising or promotion, misrepresents the nature, characteristics, qualities, or geographic origin of his or her or another person's goods, services, or commercial activities."[88] This provision protects producers from a particular geographical region from misappropriation of their collective goodwill arising from the fact that products from those regions embody certain qualities and characteristics.[89]

In the United Kingdom and systems deriving from it, the key common law action is passing off: an action in tort that prevents a trader ("the first trader") from misrepresenting to consumers, generally by adoption of some word or other sign peculiarly associated with a second trader, that the first trader's goods are associated with the second trader. The classic action protects a second trader's proprietary interest in their accumulated goodwill: i.e., the good name, reputation and connection of a business.[90] Extended passing off, as it is known, protects collective goodwill associated with signs, including geographical terms, an extended form of the action first recognised in the UK decision in *J Bollinger SA* v. *Costa Brava Wine Co. Ltd.*[91] In that case, an English judge held that the French producers of sparkling wine from the Champagne region were entitled to protection for their shared goodwill in the term "Champagne," understood as indicating (only) wine made from grapes sourced in a particular region in France, according to the méthode champenoise. A series of UK cases have built on this foundation, turning extended passing off into an important form of protection consistent with TRIPS Article 22 for signs that meet the TRIPS definition of a GI.[92] This reasoning has been applied to other geographical terms, such as Sherry (a derivation of Jerez, Spain)[93] and Scotch Whisky,[94] and to non-geographical terms which indicate products made according to particular methods or with certain ingredients, such as Advocaat,[95] or Vodka.[96]

These various causes of action are united by the fact that they are based on abstract proscriptions of market misconduct.[97] Whether (as in some countries, like Australia) confined to uses of signs that *mislead* consumers, or whether extending to even non-confusing use of a sign that takes advantage of existing goodwill (per a more European concept of unfair competition), the

[88] 15 USC § 1125(a).

[89] *Scotch Whiskey Ass'n* v. *Barton Distilling Co.*, 489 F.2d 809 (7th Cir. 1973); *Black Hills Jewellery Mfg. Co.* v. *Gold Rush, Inc.*, 633 F.2d 746 (8th Cir. 1980); *Roquefort* v. *William Faehndrich, Inc.*, 198 F.Supp. 291 (SDNY 1961), *aff'd*, 303 F.2d 494 (2d Cir. 1962); *State of Fla.* v. *Real Juices, Inc.*, 330 F.Supp. 428 (MD Fla. 1971); J. McCarthy, McCarthy on Trademarks and Unfair Competition (4th ed. 2012), § 27:49.

[90] *Fage UK Ltd* v. *Chobani UK Ltd* [2014] EWCA (Civ.) 5 (Eng.).

[91] *J Bollinger SA* v. *Costa Brava Wine Co. Ltd* [1960] Ch. 262. For a detailed discussion *see* Dev Gangjee, *Spanish Champagne: An Unfair Competition Approach to GI Protection*, *in* Intellectual Property at the Edge: The Contested Contours of IP 105 (Jane C. Ginsburg and Rochelle Cooper Dreyfuss eds., 2014).

[92] *Vine Products Ltd* v. *MacKenzie & Co. Ltd* [1969] RPC 1 (Sherry) (Eng.); *John Walker & Sons Ltd* v. *Henry Ost & Co. Ltd* [1970] RPC 489 (Ch.) (Scotch Whiskey) (Eng.); *Taittinger SA* v. *Albev* [1993] FSR 641 (Eng.); *Chocosuisse Union des Fabricants Suisses de Chocolat* v. *Cadbury Ltd* [1998] RPC 117 (Ch.); [1999] RPC 826 (CA) (Eng.); *Fage UK Ltd* v. *Chobani UK Ltd* [2014] EWCA (Civ.) 5 (Eng.); [2014] FSR 29; *Wineworths Group Ltd* v. *Comité Interprofessionel du Vin de Champagne* [1992] 2 NZLR 327 (NZCA); *Institut National des Appellations d'Origine des Vins et Eaux-de-Vie* v. *Andrews Wines Ltd* [1987] CIPR 138 (Can.); *Shaw Brothers (Hong Kong) Ltd* v. *Golden Harvest Ltd* [1972] RPC 559 (Hong Kong); *Scotch Whisky Association* v. *Kyer Meakin Breweries*, 1972 ILR 124 (India).

[93] *Vine Products* v. *MacKenzie & Co. Ltd* [1969] RPC 1 (Ch.) (Eng.).

[94] *John Walker & Sons Ltd* v. *Henry Ost & Co. Ltd* [1970] RPC 489 (Ch.) (Eng.).

[95] *Erven Warnink BV* v. *J. Townend & Sons (Hull) Ltd* [1979] AC 731 (Eng.).

[96] *Diageo North America Inc.* v. *Intercontinental Brands (ICB) Ltd* [2010] EWHC 17; affirmed on appeal [2010] EWCA Civ. 920; [2011] RPC 2 (Eng.).

[97] Gangjee, *supra* note 19, at 45; *see also* World Intellectual Property Organization, International Bureau, Protection against Unfair Competition: Analysis of the Present World Situation 48, 54–60 (2014).

foundation of the action lies in consumer perceptions.[98] Actions of this kind can and do protect GIs – provided they have a local reputation, i.e., fame. Indeed it is crucial to prove, not that given products as a matter of objective fact have certain qualities or characteristics, but that (some proportion of) consumers in the jurisdiction *think* they do.[99] Legal proceedings, brought when an interloper enters or threatens to enter the market,[100] crystallise the local population's knowledge and understanding of the (geographical) sign. Consumers need not necessarily even expect qualities that can be articulated with any precision, provided they are aware of a sign, and *think* that the sign indicates something important.[101] This is consistent with protecting foreign famous GIs – after all, the consumers of New Zealand are not necessarily familiar with all the practices that define a fish sauce from Vietnam, but (some) may appreciate there is (meant to be) something different about it.[102] On the other hand, it means that the reputation that founds a GI need not be "essentially or causally attributable to geographical origin."[103] While some cases, like *Bollinger*, rely extensively on evidence regarding the administrative and regulatory systems supporting a GI term in its place of origin, in the UK case *Fage* v. *Chobani* – the "Greek Yoghurt" case – there was no recognised GI (or any of the underpinning systems for such a GI) in Greece;[104] the case relied entirely on local labelling conventions in the United Kingdom that had built up a consumer expectation that "Greek Yoghurt" came from Greece. *Diageo*, a case exploring whether VODKAT encroached on collective goodwill in "Vodka,"[105] is another non-GI case turning on the fact that consumers expected that Vodka was made in a particular way, from particular ingredients. Unfair competition actions are not, in other words, actions designed to promote GI interests, or reward localised efforts to develop particular, geographically bound qualities or characteristics, and different courts can reach different results on what the sign means,[106] and whether compliance with quality standard is a requirement. And note that again, as with registered trademark systems, it is famous GIs that will benefit.

Even the most globally famous indications will not necessarily receive broad (TRIPS Article 23-style) protection – or indeed protection at all – in unfair competition law. The extent

[98] Although in some cases the impetus for crystallising legal protection may be an action brought in opposition to the registration of a trademark involving the GI, brought by GI claimants asserting an unregistered mark. *See, e.g.*, the US Cognac cases. Gervais, *supra* note 2.

[99] *Chocosuisse Union des Fabricants Suisse de Chocolat* [1998] RPC 117, 128 (Eng.) (stating that it makes no difference to the cause of action "if there is no difference or discernible difference in quality and ingredients between goods sold under or by reference to the term and competing goods"); *Fage UK Ltd* v. *Chobani UK Ltd* [2014] EWCA Civ. 5 [2014] FSR 29 (Eng.).

[100] Actions for passing off can be brought *quia timet*. *Erven Warnink BV* v. *J. Townend & Sons (Hull) Ltd* [1979] AC 731 (Eng.).

[101] *Chocosuisse Union des Fabricants Suisse de Chocolat* v. *Cadbury Ltd* [1998] RPC 117 (Eng.); *Consorzio del Prosciutto di Parma* v. *Marks & Spencer Plc* [1991] RPC 351, 371 (Eng.). US courts also rejected an argument that consumers must understand that the mark communicates that goods are certified (rather than just that the goods have certain qualities or characteristics). *Institut National des Appellations d'Origine* v. *Brown-Forman Corp.*, 47 USPQ 2d 1875 (TTAB 1998); Gervais, *supra* note 2, at 138.

[102] Gervais, *supra* note 4, at 362.

[103] Gangjee, *supra* note 19, at 46.

[104] In fact, in *Fage* the viability of the action depended on there *not* being a protectable GI, since if there were, any action would have to be brought under EU GI laws.

[105] *Diageo North America Inc.* v. *Intercontinental Brands (ICB) Ltd* [2010] EWHC 17; affirmed on appeal [2010] EWCA (Civ.) 920; [2011] RPC 2 (Eng.). *See* Davis, *supra* note 84. This was even hinted in one UK case. *Vine Products* v. *Mackenzie* [1969] RPC 1, 23 (Ch.) (Eng.).

[106] *See, e.g.*, *Chocosuisse Union des Fabricants Suisses de Chocolat* v. *Cadbury Ltd* [1998] RPC 117, 135 (Eng.) (where Laddie J found that "Swiss chocolate" encompassed all chocolate, made in Switzerland in accordance with Swiss Regulations, but the Court of Appeal held that the chocolate would have to have particular qualities). *Chocosuisse Union des Fabricants Suisses de Chocolat* v. *Cadbury Ltd* [1999] RPC 826, 839–40 (Eng.).

of protection provided to GIs by unfair competition actions depends a great deal on where protection is sought. Some differences result from factual or market variations in consumer perceptions.[107] Australia and New Zealand might be very close, but their respective courts came to opposite conclusions on whether "Champagne" was a generic term referring to sparkling wine of a certain style (as it was in Australia, where the local wine industry had extensively used the term for its own products),[108] or only the wine from a particular region in France (as it was in New Zealand, whose wine industry had not done the same).[109]

Other jurisdictional differences arise from different approaches to more general doctrinal questions. Australian courts tend to be more sceptical of the scope of alleged misrepresentations than UK courts, and stricter on remedies. For example, an Australian court rejected an attempt to prevent the use of "the glamour, Frenchness and accoutrements otherwise associated with Champagne wines and the name Champagne,"[110] even for services in the marketing of sparkling wines. French champagne makers brought an action for misleading and deceptive conduct against an individual who operated under an alter ego, "Champagne Jayne," in her capacity as wine educator, consultant, and event manager promoting French champagnes but also other sparkling wines.[111] The initial claim sought to prevent Ms. Powell from using the name at all, or promoting other sparkling wines. The final court order only prevented Powell from using the term "ambassador," or from "referring to wines which are not Champagne Wines without clearly stating that they are not Champagne Wines" in her public communications.[112] Compare this to the German Federal Supreme Court ruling as unacceptable references to "champagne" to suggest the outstanding quality even of *unrelated* goods.[113]

What constitutes actionable damage or harm can also vary. UK courts have recognised a wide range of potential harms, including harm arising from dilution of the exclusiveness of a sign via association, rather than confusion.[114] That is, the kinds of harms protected against extend more generally to a continental conception of "unfair competition" or misappropriation.[115] US decisions also pay attention to the "irreparable harm" that would result from uses that would "diminish the effectiveness of the advertising for which millions of dollars have been spent or are to be spent and dilute the strength or uniqueness" of a (common law or registered)

[107] Burrell & Handler, *supra* note 55, at 538 (noting that outcomes in one jurisdiction may well not be any safe guide when dealing with the same terms in another jurisdiction).

[108] *Comité Interprofessionel du Vin de Champagne* v. *NL Burton Pty Ltd* (1981) 38 ALR 664 (Austl.). Marketing of Australian wines as "champagne" has been forbidden since 2011 as a result of a bilateral treaty with the EU, but understandings of the term still vary within Australia. *See Comité Interprofessionel du Vin de Champagne* v. *Powell* (2015) 330 ALR 67 (Austl.).

[109] *Wineworths Group Ltd* v. *Comité Interprofessionel du Vin de Champagne* [1992] 2 NZLR 327 (NZ). *See also Institut National des Appellations D'Origine* v. *Vintners Int'l Co.*, 954 F.2d 1574 (Fed. Cir. 1992) ("Chablis with a Twist" case, holding that US consumers would see "Chablis" as a generic term for a style of wine).

[110] *Wineworths Group Ltd* [1992] 2 NZLR 327 at [10].

[111] *Comité Interprofessionel du Vin de Champagne* v. *Powell* (2015) 330 ALR 67 (Austl.).

[112] Final order dated Dec. 23, 2015, on file with author.

[113] Annette Kur, *Quibbling Siblings – Comments to Dev Gangjee's Presentation*, 82 CHI.-KENT L. REV. 1317, 1321. *See also Yves Saint Laurent Parfums SA* v. *Institut National des Appellations D'Origine (INAO)* [1994] ECC 385 (Cour d'Appeal, Paris) (action under Consumer Code provision forbidding use of a GI or appellation d'origine that would be liable to appropriate or weaken the renown of the appellation; injunction granted against sale of "Champagne" Perfume by Yves Saint Laurent).

[114] *J. Bollinger SA* v. *Costa Brava Wine Co. Ltd (No. 2)* [1961] 1 WLR 277, 292 (Eng.); *Taittinger SA* v. *Albev Ltd* [1993] FSR 641, 678 (Eng.); *Chocosuisse Union des Fabricants Suisse de Chocolat* v. *Cadbury Ltd* [1998] RPC 117, 143 (Eng.).

[115] *See generally* Davis, *supra* note 84 (arguing that UK decisions that extend the scope of recovery to (unproven) dilution-type harms effectively mean that the United Kingdom has an action against unfair competition).

certification mark.[116] Damage is often assumed, without proof, and rarely calculated.[117] Burrell and Handler, on the other hand, argue from an Australian perspective that "[g]eneralised complaints about the defendant 'diluting' the plaintiff's brand or 'cashing in' on the plaintiff's reputation ought not to trigger liability," and that "it ought . . . to be necessary to identify clearly the adverse economic effects one is seeing to guard against," for example by establishing a change or likely change in consumer behaviour resulting from the confusion of consumers.[118] The *Champagne Jayne* case reflects this thinking.

Who can bring a claim can also vary. In the UK cases, under extended passing off, any affected producer may file a claim in civil courts without first having to show formal control or a government system for regulating produce from a given region.[119] The US courts have sometimes been less liberal.[120] This reflects the characterisation of US claims, in some cases, as based on common law certification marks,[121] bound by requirements of such marks, including for example that, like their registered counterparts, they must be owned by an independent organisation that does not use the mark.[122]

Thus, the picture outside the registered system is again a complex one for GIs operating in an unfair competition system. Passing off and consumer protection laws can be used to prevent conduct that uses well-known GIs inappropriately. But the legal actions discussed in this section are not only dependent on proof of fame; they are even less targeted to the nature of GIs than the trademark law mechanisms discussed earlier, and, as this analysis has sought to draw out, can vary quite significantly between jurisdictions based on details such as the scope of recognised misrepresentations and damage; and judicial attitudes to when consumer confusion is likely to arise.

IV NOT FAST, NOT FAMOUS: MAYBE FLEXIBLE?

As we have seen, registered GI systems are expanding, including, in particular, to GIs hailing from a wide range of languages and cultures. Fast and famous GIs receive significant protection under an unfair competition-based system, taking into account both causes of action at general law and trademark registration. But these systems offer little to localised producers hailing from different cultures; nor, with their limited interest in the underlying reality of GIs, will they promote broader cultural or development ambitions.[123] This means that the new GIs pose a particular challenge for unfair competition systems.

[116] *State of Fla.* v. *Real Juices, Inc.*, 330 F.Supp. 428 (MD Fla. 1971); *see also, e.g.*, *Black Hills Jewelry Mfg. Co.* v. *Gold Rush, Inc.*, 633 F.2d 746, 753 (8th Cir. 1980) (to obtain an injunction under 15 USC §1125(a) (Lanham Act §43(a)) a plaintiff need only show that the falsities complained of had a tendency to deceive).

[117] Davis, *supra* note 84, at 576–77.

[118] Burrell & Handler, *supra* note 55, at 539.

[119] *Erven Warnink Besloten Vennootschap* v. *J. Townend & Sons (Hull) Ltd* [1979] AC 731 (Eng.).

[120] Gervais, *supra* note 2, at 130 & 141 (citing *State of Idaho Potato Com'n* v. *G & T Terminal Packaging, Inc.*, 425 F.3d 708, 721–22 (9th Cir. 2005)).

[121] Gervais, *supra* note 2 (citing *Bureau Nat'l Interprofessionnel du Cognac & Schieffelin & Co.* v. *Int'l Better Drinks Corp.*, 6 USPQ 2d 1610, 1614 (TTAB 1988); *Institut National des Appellations d'Origine* v. *Brown-Forman Corp.*, 47 USPQ 2d 1875 (TTAB 1998)).

[122] *Black Hills Jewelry Mfg. Co.* v. *Gold Rush, Inc.*, 633 F.2d 746 (8th Cir. 1980).

[123] By contrast, registration proponents argue that the very process of developing a GI for ex ante *sui generis* registration can (but will not always) "result in new experiences, capabilities, knowledge acquired by involved actors, improved vertical and horizontal integration, higher or better accepted quality standards." Xiomara F Quinones-Ruiz et al., *Insights into the Black Box of Collective Efforts for the Registration of Geographical Indications*, 57 LAND USE POL'Y 103, 104 (2016).

To date, countries based in unfair competition systems have three main responses to GI expansionism. One is to simply adopt *sui generis* registration to a greater or lesser extent. Singapore, for example, created a new GIs register in 2019 that extends to agricultural foodstuffs, as a result of its free trade agreement with Europe.[124] Notably, the new Singaporean law retains some unfair competition/trademark roots. The new system does not appear to enable Singapore to join the Lisbon system, since it requires that GIs be renewed every ten years;[125] nor does it extend to handicrafts or other products where protection is sought by a number of developing countries. China is another country that has in recent years adopted (more than one system of) *sui generis* registration.[126]

Other countries have so far sought to horse-trade over broad protection for specific terms, or fight the trend.[127] Countries negotiating trade agreements with the EU in particular have engaged in horse-trading, providing protection for a list of key EU terms in return for improved access to the EU market,[128] or as part of comprehensive trade agreements. Under this approach, tailored protection is given to a confined list of terms emerging from a trade agreement, usually by specific legislative or ministerial decree, but no *sui generis* system is adopted and so protection is not secured for GIs from countries not party to the trade agreement. One recent example is the "complicated compromise" whereby Canada, as part of its trade agreement with the EU, extended protection to the EU list of wine and agricultural product GIs.[129] As Handler notes, this kind of trading can be mutually beneficial; market participants, like wine producers, may be entirely happy to "give up" certain generic terms in return for better and easier market access in Europe.[130] But agreements of this kind also add complexity to domestic law and to international trade. These deals often involve – as in the Canada–EU agreement – grandfathering of existing uses,[131] and specific rules for certain key generic terms (for example, allowing use of key generic terms, like "feta," with "like" or "style").[132] A cheese exporter therefore cannot be sure where they can export, say, Fontina cheese without checking the particular rules for certain countries, contained in trade agreement annexes, and even the dates of trademark or GI registration.[133]

The United States and other "new world" countries, on the other hand, have pushed back against the EU approach, via other trade agreements which embed a "trademarks trump GIs" approach. The Comprehensive and Progressive Agreement for Trans-Pacific Partnership

[124] *Geographical Indications Act 2014* (Sing.). Key amendments came into effect in April 2019.

[125] *Geographical Indications Act 2014*, §§ 50–55 (Sing.).

[126] China's system is complicated, involving more than one form of registration. *See* Zheng, *supra* note 69; although, as Gangjee notes in his contribution to this volume (Chapter 15), there has been some recent consolidation of GI administration and protection.

[127] *See* Handler & Burrell, *supra* note 5; Frankel, *supra* note 5.

[128] *See generally* Handler, *supra* note 5; for other examples *see also* Antony Taubman, *Thinking Locally, Acting Globally: How Trade Negotiations Over Geographical Indications Improve "Fair Trade" Rules, in* Research Handbook on Intellectual Property and Geographical Indications 202 (Dev Gangjee ed., 2016).

[129] Frankel, *supra* note 5; Omachi, *supra* note 25 (describing this as a "solution-based" approach – one that seeks solutions for individual GIs during trade negotiations). South Africa adopted a similar approach: see Biénabe & Marie-Vivien, *supra* note 13.

[130] Handler, *supra* note 5.

[131] *See, e.g.*, Trademarks Act, RSC 1985, c. T-13, 11.17(3), (5)–(7) (Can.). Grandfathering of existing uses is also a feature of the South African agreement with the EU: Biénabe & Marie-Vivien, *supra* note 13.

[132] *Trademarks Act*, RSC 1985, c. T-13, § 11.17(4) (Can.) (allowing use of Feta, Gorgonzola, Fontina and Munster with qualifying terms in Canada); Frankel, *supra* note 5, at 156; Omachi, *supra* note 25.

[133] A cynic might suggest that this complexity also serves the interests of EU GI owners, and state proponents of *sui generis* registration, by encouraging traders to move to markings that will be safe across all markets.

(CPTPP),[134] for example, requires: (1) that members grant trademark owners exclusive rights including over later GIs that would be likely to cause consumer confusion and (2) opposition or cancellation of a GI registration where the GI "is likely to cause confusion" with a trademark which is the subject of an existing or pending registration,[135] or where the GI is the common name for the relevant good, i.e., the name is generic.[136] These provisions are expressed to apply to *all* new GIs, including those negotiated internationally – thus the EU attempting clawback with a CPTPP member will have to submit GIs to an opposition (or equivalent) process.[137]

None of this is conducive to a reduction in conflict, whether at the international level or between individual traders, and none of it really helps to build a workable compromise for the long term.[138] "Fight or horse-trade" is a political reality which is unlikely to be supplanted at least in relation to the EU, given its ambitions for specific terms. But this doesn't help non-European GI claimants outside Europe. The Canada–EU trade agreement, for example, did not lead Canada to institute a *sui generis* protection system open to the GI claimants of the Asia-Pacific: it seems that, at least for now, any other country wanting protection will have to engage in its own negotiations with Canada: as Europe did, and South Korea.[139] This will not help our sympathetic, slow GI claimants wanting to build knowledge of their products in overseas markets, and entitled to view current systems as tilted towards certain "old world" Western interests. Their success may turn on whether their country has something to offer Canada, or is prepared to engage in comprehensive trade negotiations. Even Singapore's recent adoption of a *sui generis* registration system will assist only the proactive and fast (and only in relation to agricultural foodstuffs). Slow GI claimants may still find themselves pre-empted by trademarks that already exist, or that are registered between now and when they seek protection in Singapore.

The question, then, is whether there is an alternative: one that does not involve following an EU/Lisbon model of protection; which better serves non-Western cultural and traditional interests; and reduces the risk of future conflicts between trademarks and GIs. It could be possible, by making small, but consequential changes to existing trademark law to make it less unfriendly to the slow or less famous GIs. Such changes could make a real difference to reducing future GI and trademark conflicts and promoting coexistence. The analysis is based on five core intuitions:

1 There is no obvious public policy interest in allowing local firms to register foreign GIs in their trademarks to the exclusion of GI claimants.
2 It is not self-evident that either trademarks, or GIs, ought always to trump the other.[140] In a significant subset of cases, coexistence is both feasible and desirable. Allowing later-entrant

[134] The Comprehensive and Progressive Agreement for Trans-Pacific Partnership (CPTPP) is the successor to the Trans-Pacific Partnership (TPP) originally negotiated among the United States, Brunei, Australia, Canada, Chile, Japan, Malaysia, Mexico, New Zealand, Peru, Singapore, and Vietnam. The United States pulled out of the TPP in 2016, following which the remaining countries renegotiated the agreement now known as the CPTPP. The CPTPP retains many of the original provisions of the TPP, including the GI provisions discussed here (a range of other provisions were suspended, with the potential to be revived should the United States at any stage seek to rejoin). *See* Omachi, *supra* note 25. The authoritative CPTPP text is available at https://mfat.govt.nz/en/trade/free-trade-agreements/free-trade-agreements-in-force/cptpp/comprehensive-and-progressive-agreement-for-trans-pacific-partnership-text-and-resources.

[135] CPTPP 18.32.1(a). *See* Omachi, *supra* note 25, discussing CPTPP.

[136] CPTPP 18.32.1(c); this is based on how consumers understand the term. CPTPP 18.32.2.

[137] For an analysis of how this works, *see* Frankel, *supra* note 5. In August 2019 Australia, which was engaged in trade negotiations with the EU, had just published a list of terms sought by the EU, inviting oppositions.

[138] *See also* Frankel, *supra* note 5, noting the risk of ongoing conflict.

[139] *Trademarks Act*, RSC 1985, c. T-13, §§ 11.11–11.24 (Can.).

[140] Gangjee, *supra* note 1.

GIs to trump trademarks is unjust where traders have built the local market over time. Equally, there is injustice in allowing trademarks to trump "GIs [which] have already done the hard work of building national reputations, often over centuries."[141] The trademark owner's claim is particularly weak where their mark is new, and/or has limited goodwill.

3 Coexistence is feasible because of the natural flexibility of language and human comprehension,[142] and our capacity, as human beings, to comprehend more than one meaning in a term based on context. In ordinary language, *bark*, *nails*, and *jam* all have more than one meaning. A significant proportion of consumers are likely capable of understanding, with appropriate good-faith labelling (by New Zealand firms) and advertising (by Japanese producers), that there is a difference between "New Zealand-grown Wagyu Beef" and meat from Japan;[143]

4 "Consumer confusion" in law is already tolerated in other circumstances where more than one trader has a legitimate interest in a trademark, such as cases of "honest concurrent use";

5 "Consumer confusion" is only loosely tied to empirical proof. In many (though not all) jurisdictions, the question the law asks is whether a *hypothetical* consumer would have some (legally defined) mental state when confronted with a similar mark.[144] Legal rules can define the knowledge, attitude, or capacities of the hypothetical consumer, in particular, by making them globally oriented, cosmopolitan, and even multilingual.

What would a more nuanced response look like? We can illustrate by considering the limited amendments that could render Australian law less hostile to foreign, non-Western GIs, reduce the inequalities between trademarks and GIs, and reduce the incentive for opportunistic local traders to "hijack" traditional or geographical terms in advance of slower GI claimants. We can imagine amendments to trademark law which would:

1 Remove the asymmetry whereby a trademark owner can oppose a GI that causes confusion with *a word or expression contained in* a trademark, but a foreign GI owner can oppose only trademarks that contain or consist of the (exact) registered GI. To promote coexistence, any opposition should consider the whole, not subparts, of the two signs (trademark and GI). This amendment would enable active foreign GI claimants not yet trading locally to prevent pre-emption;

2 Make it harder for non-GI associations to register potential (slow) GIs as trademarks, by:

   a Deeming (geographically) descriptive foreign language signs to be not at all distinctive. CTMs should continue to be exempt from this rule, in order to ensure GI associations' ongoing access to trademark protection. This would not prevent all trademark registrations by third parties of nascent GIs: secondary meaning could still make a sign registrable, as would adding figurative elements. Per point 1 above, the existence of figurative marks including reference to a GI would not (necessarily) preclude later GI registration.

   b Deeming misleading (and so unregistrable) any objectively false use of geographical term (in English or a foreign language) as, or in, a trademark, regardless of consumer

[141] *Id.* at 1268.

[142] Taubman, *supra* note 128, at 203.

[143] *Id. See also* Gangjee, *supra* note 1, noting that US and Italian producers of "Parma ham" were capable of negotiating coexistence with consent (but were overridden by legal rules).

[144] *See generally* Kimberlee Weatherall, *The Consumer as the Empirical Measure of Trade Mark Law* 80 Modern L. Rev. 57 (2017); Graeme Dinwoodie & Dev Gangjee, *The Image of the Consumer in European Trade Mark Law*, *in* The Images of the Consumer in EU Law (Dorota Leczykiewicz & Steven Weatherill eds., 2016).

knowledge, unless the applicant tenders evidence that the relevant location does not and is not likely to be a source of the registered, or similar, goods or services. The sheer number of places with names in the world means this could rule out too many possible marks at least for common goods/services; some size threshold (e.g., towns or regions over a certain population) might be necessary. It could also be objected that this prevents "whimsical" or evocative use of geographically inaccurate terms. It is not clear, however, that the benefits of allowing evocative (but inaccurate) use outweigh the potential costs. Since some geographical terms are also the names of products, there could also be an exception, to allow inclusion in trademarks of common language terms, provided: (i) there is no use or intention to use the term in a misleading way and (ii) there is no claim to exclusivity in the term (noted as a condition on the registration). As an alternative, if a general prohibition on objectively false use of geographical terms is too broad an exclusion, a narrower option would be to deem misleading/unregistrable any objectively false use of a geographical term – in any language – where the geographical term is registered as a GI in at least one other country.[145]

3 To recognise that tweaking the application system will always favour the fast, suitable amendments should be considered for cases where the trademark owner is first, and registers unopposed. This could mean:
   a Guidelines could be drafted for the assessment of confusion in registration or infringement that make it easier for approved use of a recognised foreign GI to be considered non-confusing and so non-infringing. This would allow, say, good faith use of "Kampot" by an authorised GI user from the relevant region in Cambodia, which ought not infringe an Australian- or New Zealand-registered trademark that includes the term KAMPOT. Such rules could, for example, take into account other factors: good faith of the user; aspects of packaging (such as the presence of strong branding); the geographical nature of the indication. In other words, the guidelines could focus on the context which humans use to interpret a sign, rather than presuming confusion from mere presence of a trademark term on an imported good.[146]
   b Considering a special category of "honest concurrent use" for GIs with an extensive (albeit overseas) history of use; and
   c Considering exceptions to infringement, to allow good-faith use of GIs *as GIs* (and not just for their descriptive content) – i.e., for their ability to distinguish certified from non-certified goods or services.

[145] It might also be objected that either approach would create significant work in examination. Some opportunistic applications would be caught by allowing foreign GI owners to oppose registrations, as allowed for in point 1 above. But it is not possible to rely *only* on opposition, if our concern is to protect not only active/fast GI claimants, but more slow/nascent claims. This could be addressed in part by allowing removal of a trademark at any time if it can be shown that a trademark included a false geographical term (the broad prohibition), or a foreign-registered GI existed (the narrower prohibition), at the time the trademark was registered. This would put the onus on the trademark applicant to ensure no GI is included, on pain of losing their mark at a later point. If the Trademark Office were to provide a consolidated list of registered GIs, regularly updated, this could be incorporated into both applicant and office systems with relative ease; as Gangjee has noted in his contribution to this volume (Chapter 15), there are an increasing number of easy ways to search for registered GIs. Rules like this, if generally adopted, would also create incentives for other countries, or the secretariat of the Lisbon Treaty system, to make GI registers readily available, and searchable. This would be consistent too with past suggestions to create a multilateral GI register for notification purposes within TRIPS: *see generally* Taubman, *supra* note 128; Kur, *supra* note 113.

[146] Guidelines of this kind would likely need to be legislated in Australia, at least where the test of confusion focuses narrowly on the mark and not on other aspects of packaging or the market; there is no "global appreciation" test in Australia.

These amendments would seek to reduce the likelihood of conflicting trademarks being registered in the first place, and, in the event of conflicting claims, would encourage coexistence.[147] The WTO has recognised that protection of GIs can be a legitimate qualification on trademark owners' rights, and similar provisions to those interpreted in the WTO case are included in other treaties, including the CPTPP.[148] The thrust of the CPTPP is to require grounds for opposition for cases where confusion is likely, but it cannot and does not dictate the meaning of "confusion" or the law's conception of the consumer, and insofar as these proposals are concerned with updating and refining these core concepts, they lie within domestic discretion to implement IP law. Amendments of this kind could be adopted by countries like Australia, New Zealand, or the United States, which largely retain their unfair competition-based systems, or Canada, as a supplement to the highly specific broad protection it has already incorporated into its trademark legislation, in order to avoid or reduce future conflicts with GIs from other countries. Finding ways to enable coexistence is also consistent with the direction of countries such as Singapore, which has post-CPTPP and following its agreement with the EU created a domestic system "aiming for settlement among concerned parties as much as possible, while abiding by the [first in time, first in right] principle."[149] Singapore, and other countries which choose to adopt a *sui generis* system covering agricultural foodstuffs, might consider whether amendments of this kind would be a useful addition to reduce the risk of future GI–TM conflicts, and to address the claims of non-agricultural GIs, such as handicrafts.

Amendments of this kind would inevitably meet resistance from organisations that consider coexistence an intolerable incursion into exclusive rights in either trademarks, or GIs. It would not be consistent with the Lisbon Treaty system, which demands TRIPS Article 23-style protection of GIs against use by other traders, even qualified by terms like "style" or "like" (e.g., "Basmati-style rice"); nor is it likely to fully satisfy the claims of GI proponents from the non-Western world who wish to see global protection for their products equal to that accorded to wines and spirits, and European meats and cheeses. Stronger Article 23 protection would still be a matter of horse-trading. But that is, perhaps, as it should be: broader protection is costly to competitors, and hence arguably requires an explicit and direct benefit in return. The suggestions here are a compromise proposal, that would adjust, without abandoning, a local unfair competition and trademark-based approach to GIs, and seek to balance competing interests.

It should be noted that these suggestions would not change the fundamentals of the unfair competition approach: the causes of action and systems within such a system are not designed to meet GI objectives. Nor will the suggestions here address every issue. We can still expect some conflicts within and between communities of origin traders. The boundaries of states change over time, and people move and take their culture with them, meaning there could be multiple populations that can lay claim to cultural and agricultural traditions. This is even more of a potential issue with handicrafts than with agricultural products, so these new GIs in particular increase the potential for cross-border conflict. We have also already seen conflict between countries with similar traditions, cultures, and handicrafts, just as we have between the Danish,

[147] As noted earlier, some consumer confusion is commonly tolerated in the trademark system. *See* Beebe, *supra* note 58. For a full discussion of the potential for exceptions and coexistence, *see* Gangjee, *supra* note 1.

[148] Panel Report, *European Communities – Protection of Trademarks and Geographical Indications for Agricultural Products and Foodstuffs, Complaint by the United States* § 7.688; *European Communities – Protection of Trademarks and Geographical Indications for Agricultural Products and Foodstuffs, Complaint by Australia* § 7.644–7.686, WTO Doc WT/DS290/R (Mar. 15, 2005); Gangjee, *supra* note 1; CPTPP art. 18.21.

[149] Omachi, *supra* note 25, at 179–87; Gangjee, *supra* note 1, at 1271, explaining that in the US Parma Ham dispute, law overrode an agreement between the parties to coexist.

Bulgarian, and Greek makers of feta cheese. Pisco (a spirit) is claimed as heritage by both Peru and Chile,[150] and significant public political conflict has occasionally arisen between Malaysia and Indonesia over perceived conflicting claims to important elements of cultural heritage, such as Batik (wax-resist dyed fabric), Pendet (dance) and the folksong Rasa Sayang;[151] between Malaysians and Singaporeans over Yee Sang/Yusheng (a Lunar New Year delicacy) and between South Korea and Japan over Kimchi/Kimuchi.[152] Recognising such claims involves a politically fraught process of identifying a geographical area, beneficiaries, allowable raw materials, and methods of processing or manufacture, and those ruled out or in may contest the characterisation.

Still, the small changes suggested here could make a big difference to conflict between GIs and trademarks, and as such may even offer *more* benefit for slower, more internationally nascent GIs than introduction of a *sui generis* register that implements a first-in-time, first-in-right principle liable to facilitate faster interlopers.

V CONCLUSIONS

This chapter began with a question: do unfair competition approaches have a future? As the chapter has argued, unfair competition-based systems are really quite good at protecting GIs if they are famous, or at least fast. But can they adapt to a world where GI systems are expanding apace, and in particular where the new GIs are from culturally and linguistically diverse backgrounds, and may be neither fast nor famous? There are legitimate claims, by producers in a range of countries, to some protection, at the very least from pre-emption of their historically grounded claims to tradition.

This chapter argues that legal systems all over the world do not have to adopt broad, EU-style protection for every GI, nor adopt the blunt position of "first in time, first in right," or that either trademarks or GIs must always prevail. All too often policymakers and negotiators use a sledgehammer to crack a nut: failing to achieve their goals, and generating unnecessary conflict, because they don't seek to achieve their goals through targeted change.[153] And so this chapter has sought to show an alternative: one where we acknowledge that there are problems with a "pure" unfair competition approach in this new world, but where we leverage the capacities of both language to carry multiple meanings in context, and the human mind to parse those meanings, to find a new accommodation of interests. It is not hopeful that this kind of creativity will prevail: the world where this adaptation is allowed to succeed may be just as "Platonic" as the world of idealised GIs with which this chapter started.

150 Dutfield, *supra* note 20, at 189–90.

151 Jinn Wing Chong, *Mine, Yours, or Ours? The Indonesia-Malaysia Conflicts over Shared Cultural Heritage*, 27 Sojourn: J. of Social Issues in Se. Asia 1 (2012).

152 Kamilia Lahrichi, *7 of the World's Fiercest Food Feuds*, CNN (Oct. 1, 2014), https://cnn.com/travel/article/food-fights/index.html.

153 Robert Burrell & Kimberlee Weatherall, *Exporting Controversy? Reactions to the Copyright Provisions of the US–Australia Free Trade Agreement: Lessons for US Trade Policy*, 2008 U. Ill. J.L., Tech. & Pol'y 259 (2008).

V

Certification and Collective Marks

17

Anglo and EU Frameworks for Certification and Collective Trademarks

*Graeme W. Austin**

I INTRODUCTION

Ordinary trademarks promise consistent quality. This promise is the *quid pro quo* for the trademark proprietor's right to control the goodwill symbolized by the mark. Subject to external regulatory controls (safety standards, truth in labeling laws, etc.), it is largely up to the trademark proprietor to set its own standards. If a firm wants to attach its brand to a chocolate product containing low levels of cocoa butter, that is its prerogative.[1] It will be motivated to do so if consumers signal their approval with purchases. In these days of incessant licensing of trademarks, consumer confidence is grounded as much in the *ability* of trademark proprietors to control quality as in any obligation imposed on trademark proprietors to exercise quality control.[2] In theory, consumer responses will provide the necessary incentive for trademark proprietors to police supply chains and licensees, so as to ensure that products and services bearing the mark live up to the relevant standards. In other words, insofar as trademark law is concerned, market responses largely dictate the level of trademark proprietors' investment in standards, not external controls.

Certification trademarks, in contrast, promise consumers consistency with a predefined set of standards.[3] Well-known examples include "WOOLMARK," "FAIRTRADE," and the leaping-bunny device for cruelty-free products. They promise consumers that there has been compliance with specified standards adopted by the owner of the mark. The characteristics that are typically "certified" include quality, materials, geographical origin,[4] compliance with technical standards, fair labor practices, environmental standards, and safety standards.

Collective marks can also operate as promises to consumers that predetermined standards have been met.[5] Collective marks tell consumers that a trademark is being used by a member of an association or a group. Trademark rights in a collective mark exist because of the mark's

* Chair in Private Law, Victoria University of Wellington; Professor of Law, University of Melbourne. Thanks to Kathleen Henning, LLM candidate, and Miles Sandston, LLB candidate, Victoria University of Wellington, for excellent research assistance. Thanks to Professors Ginsburg and Calboli for the invitation to join this project, and to Professor Michael Handler for insightful comments on an earlier draft.

[1] *See, e.g., Société des Produits Nestlé, SA* v. *Casa Helvetia, Inc.*, 982 F.2d 633, 636 (1st Cir. 1992).

[2] *See Scandecor Dev. AB* v. *Scandecor Mktg. AB*, [2002] FSR 7 (HL) at [38]–[39].

[3] On the legal significance of the distinctions between ordinary trademarks and certification marks, see *Aristoc Ltd.* v. *Rysta Ltd.*, [1945] AC 68 (HL).

[4] *See* Chapters 15 and 16 in this volume.

[5] *See* Miguel Ángel Medina González, *Collective, Guarantee and Certification Marks and GIs: Connections and Dissimilarities*, 7 J. Intell. Prop. L. & Prac. 251, 252 (2012) (discussing the similarities between collective and certification marks).

capacity to distinguish the goods or services of the members of the association which is the proprietor of the mark from those of other undertakings.[6] Collective marks may be owned by associations of manufacturers, suppliers of services, or groups of individual producers and traders. As a result of group ownership, these marks often act as signals as to quality control. As Jeffrey Belson notes, "association implies standardization."[7] Membership of such associations can be, and very often is, conditioned on compliance with specified standards. For example, as with certification marks in the Anglo common law tradition, if membership of the association is conditioned on rules about geographical origin, an association's collective mark can serve as a geographical indicator.[8]

This chapter discusses certification and collective marks in the Anglo tradition. That tradition will be illustrated by the provisions in the UK Trade Marks Act 1994, but reference will be made to the laws of other common law jurisdictions where there are salient distinctions. The chapter also outlines the new European Union framework. It first sets out the legislative provisions. It then discusses some of the important characteristics of these marks, focusing on the application of the distinctiveness standard for certification marks as well as any relevant controls on the administration of this species of trademark. Finally, the chapter briefly considers infringement issues. It concludes with some brief reflections on the social role of certification trademarks as "private governance" vehicles.[9] The US system for protection of certification marks is discussed in Chapter 18 in this volume by Professor Margaret Chon.

Certification marks and collective marks (to the extent they perform similar functions) straddle conventional trademark principles and consumer protection regulation. The goods and services with which they are used are very often "credence goods": their characteristics – for example, whether fabric genuinely is wool – are not necessarily apparent to consumers.[10] The mark serves as a kind of guarantee that the goods or services are what they are claimed to be. Certification marks are often used as a way of signaling compliance with national standards in areas such as health and safety or environmental stipulations. Within the the EU context, for example, there are broad, horizontal requirements for accreditation of Conformity Assessment Bodies.[11] Regulatory objectives are set by government agencies, accompanied by an obligation to test products against compliance standards. In turn, private entities are delegated the task of testing products against specified standards, accompanied by the ability to approve the use of the certified trademarks to goods that comply with those standards.[12] In this sense, certification marks can facilitate public/private partnerships that give specific content

[6] *See, e.g.*, Regulation (EU) 2017/1001 of the European Parliament and of the Council of June 14, 2017 on the European Union Trade Mark OJ L. 154, June 16, 2017. On the history of the recent amendments to EU trademark law, *see* Graeme B. Dinwoodie, *Territorial Overlaps in Trademark Law: The Evolving European Model*, 92 Notre Dame L. Rev. 1669, 1671 n. 7 (2017). EUTMR, art. 74.1 defines a collective mark as a mark that is "capable of distinguishing the goods or services of the members of the association which is the proprietor of the mark from those of other undertakings."

[7] Jeffrey Belson, Certification and Collective Marks: Law & Practice 83 (2017).

[8] *See, e.g.*, *Tea Board* v. *Office for Harmonisation in the Internal Mkt. (Trade Marks and Designs)*, [2015] All ER 311 (DARJEELING mark).

[9] *See* Edward Peter Stringham, Private Governance: Creating Order in Economic & Social Life (2015).

[10] Ariel Katz, *Beyond Search Costs: The Linguistic and Trust Functions of Trademarks*, 2010 BYU L. Rev. 1555, 1562–63 (2010).

[11] *See* European Commission, *Internal Market, Industry, Entrepreneurship and SMEs*, https://ec.europa.eu/growth/single-market/goods/building-blocks/conformity-assessment_en.

[12] In the US context, in contrast, certification marks sometimes operate more by way of private governance mechanisms than by top-down regulation. *See* David Adelman & Graeme W. Austin, *Trademarks and Private Environmental Governance*, 93 Notre Dame L. Rev. 709 (2017).

(setting and enforcing standards) to overarching regulatory goals. Some collective marks also serve this function.[13]

II THE LEGISLATIVE FRAMEWORK AND ITS HISTORY

Certification marks can be registered under the trademark systems of common law countries, and, since 1 October 2017, have been able to be registered under the EU Trade Mark Regulation (EUTMR).[14] As will be seen from the definition below, the EUTMR exempts designations of geographical origin: these are treated in a *sui generis* manner in the EU context.[15] Most common law countries also make provision for collective marks.[16]

The UK Trade Marks Act 1994 defines "certification mark" in section 50 as a mark "which is described as such when the mark is applied for and indicates that the goods or services in connection with which it is used are certified by the proprietor of the mark in respect of origin, material, mode of manufacture of goods or performance of services, quality, accuracy or other characteristics."[17] This Act also made provision for the first time for the registration of collective trademarks. Under the 1994 legislation, a collective mark indicates a connection in trade to the organization that is the owner of the mark. A "collective mark" is now defined as a mark "which is described as such when it is applied for and is capable of distinguishing the goods and services of members of the association which is the proprietor of the mark from those of other undertakings."[18] Marketplace use of collective marks differs from that of ordinary marks in a key respect: by definition, they do not protect or enhance the *individual* goodwill of a single firm.[19] The association is the guardian of the goodwill: the members have a mutual interest in protecting the goodwill, to avoid the collective mark from becoming associated with inferior goods or services.

The legislative framework has a long prehistory. The early trade guilds controlled the marking of products by guild members. The marks served a regulatory function, controlling quality through the exclusive right to attach the guild mark. Guilds typically operated under letters patents and were controlled through local chambers of commerce. They controlled key industries: textiles, masonry, carpentry, wheel making, silverware, etc. For individual artisans and craftspeople, entry to these markets, and the ability to exercise their craft, often depended on guild membership. In turn, guild members were typically required to mark their goods with the guild mark.[20]

The first statutory attempt to define a trademark, the 1862 Merchandise Marks Act (UK), did not include a reference to certification.[21] Specific provision for "certification" as a basis for trademark

[13] This section draws from BELSON, *supra* note 7, at 81–82.

[14] Regulation (EC) No. 207/2009 of the Council of Feb. 26, 2009, last amended by Regulation (EU) No. 2015/2424 of the Parliament and the Council of Dec. 16, 2015.

[15] *See* Chapter 15 in this volume.

[16] Canada is a notable exception. *See* ROGER T. HUGHES ET AL., HALSBURY'S LAWS OF CANADA: TRADE-MARKS, PASSING OFF AND UNFAIR COMPETITION 17 (2016).

[17] Trade Marks Act, 1994, § 50 (UK), as amended by the Trade Marks Regulations 2018 (SI 2018/825)(parentheses deleted).

[18] *Id.* § 49(1), as amended by the Trade Marks Regulations 2018 (SI 2018/825).

[19] BELSON, *supra* note 7, at 160.

[20] FRANK SCHECHTER, THE HISTORICAL FOUNDATIONS OF THE LAW RELATING TO TRADE-MARKS 171 (Faculty of Law of Columbia Univ. eds., 1925).

[21] As Sherman and Bentley recount, the definition of a "trade mark" in the 1862 Act was the first attempt in British law to define a trademark. The definition was problematic and was not carried through in later legislation. *See* BRAD SHERMAN AND LIONEL BENTLEY, THE MAKING OF MODERN INTELLECTUAL PROPERTY LAW: THE BRITISH EXPERIENCE 1760–1911 167–68 (1999).

registration first appeared with the Trade Marks Act of 1905. It defined a "trade mark" as a mark that is "[u]sed or proposed to be used upon or in connexion with goods for the purpose of indicating that they are the goods of the proprietor of such mark by virtue of manufacture, selection, certification, dealing with or offering for sale." The 1905 legislation also provided for the registration of marks that had been certified (described as "special marks" in the statute's marginal notes):

> Where any association or person undertakes the examination of any goods in respect of origin, material, mode of manufacture, quality, accuracy, or other characteristic, and certifies the result of such examination by mark used upon or in connection with such goods, the Board of Trade may, if they shall judge it to be to the public advantage, permit such association or person to register such mark as a trade mark in respect of such goods, whether or not such association or person be a trading association or trader possessed of a goodwill in connection with such examination and certifying. When so registered such trade mark shall be deemed in all respects to be a registered trade mark, and such association or person to be the proprietor thereof, save that such trade mark shall be transmissible or assignable only by permission of the Board of Trade.[22]

A 1919 amendment to this section mandated that the Board of Trade should be satisfied that "such association or person is competent to certify as aforesaid." As is discussed below in Section V, this change took on significance in the case law concerning the level of control required to be exercised by the proprietor of the trademark over authorized users. The phrase "competent to certify" continued with the 1938 Trade Marks Act (UK).

The Trade Marks Act 1994 aligned UK law with the European Council Directive 89/104/EEC and the European Community Trademark system. A major amendment to the latter system came into force as of 1 October 2017: the codification of an EU certification mark. Until this change to the EUTMR, certification marks could not be protected as EU trademarks. The objective of the new system is to provide a bespoke legal framework for protecting EU certification marks.[23]

The recent decision of the Court of Justice of the European Union in *WF Gözze Frottierweberei GmbH, Wolfgang Gözze* v. *Verein Bremmer Baumwollbörse*,[24] underscored the necessity for the new EU system. Among the issues before the Court was whether individual EU trademarks could serve as certification marks. The Court clarified that such marks should not be registered as ordinary trademarks if the marks do not at least fulfill the essential function of the mark as indicating the origin of goods and services. The decision should serve to channel applicants whose use of marks is *only* for the purposes of certification to the new EU certification system.[25]

[22] Trade Marks Act, 1905, § 62 (UK). The relationship between these provisions was discussed by the Chancery Division in *Prorace Ltd.* v. *Le Brasseur*, [1927] 1 Ch. 589. The defendant in a trademark infringement action counterclaimed with the allegation that the plaintiff could only register its mark under the latter section. Without seeking the imprimatur of the Board of Trade, the plaintiff had licensed another party to use its mark on payment of a royalty, while also undertaking to certify each article produced by the licensee. The Court held that the arrangement was not contemplated by the phrase "by virtue of … certification" in the general definition of a trademark largely on the basis that any other approach would render the latter provision redundant.

[23] *See* Regulation 2015/2424, Recital 27.

[24] C-689/15, EU:C:2017:435, June 8, 2017.

[25] *See* Axel Paul Ringelhann, *CJEU Clarifies That EU Individual Marks Cannot Be Used Exclusively as Labels of Quality*, 12 J. Intell. Prop. L. & Prac. 724, 726 (2017).

Article 83(1) of the EUTMR describes a certification mark in the following terms. The list of characteristics that might be certified is non-exhaustive and the definition explicitly excludes geographical indicators:

> An EU certification mark shall be an EU trade mark which is described as such when the mark is applied for and is capable of distinguishing goods or services which are certified by the proprietor of the mark in respect of material, mode of manufacture of goods or performance of services, quality, accuracy or other characteristics, with the exception of geographical origin, from goods and services which are not so certified.

The general provisions of the EUTMR now also apply to EU certification marks, unless the specific provisions in the EUTMR relating to EU certification marks provide otherwise.[26] The owner of a EU certification mark may provide the certification service itself, or control and supervise the certification services of another party. As with certification marks protected under the Anglo tradition, the certification mark cannot be owned by a person running a business involving the supply of the goods and services of the kind certified.[27]

Sitting alongside the Anglo statutory provisions and EU regulations are a number of important international treaty obligations. Collective marks are recognized by Article 7*bis* of the Paris Convention,[28] an amendment adopted at the 1911 Washington Conference of the Convention. This article requires countries of the Paris Union to accept for filing and protect collective marks belonging to associations the existence of which is not contrary to the laws of the country of origin. The association does not need to possess an industrial or commercial establishment; protection needs to be established in the country where protection is sought. Additional disciplines are imposed, albeit indirectly, by the TRIPs Agreement, which expressly requires members to protect geographical indications by legal protections directed at avoiding misleading the public.[29] Stronger protections are afforded to wines and spirits.[30] TRIPS also requires compliance with key substantive provisions of the Paris Convention, including Article 7*bis*. Accordingly, members of the World Trade Organization (WTO) must comply with the substantive protections afforded to collective marks provided by the Paris Convention.[31]

III ANGLO COMMON LAW PROTECTIONS

Anglo common law principles also provide a measure of protection for certification and collective marks. The passing off tort protects a trader against misrepresentation by another firm that seeks unlawfully to appropriate goodwill belonging to the claimant. In a passing off claim,

[26] *See* EUTMR, arts. 83–93.

[27] *See* EUTMR, art. 83(2).

[28] Paris Convention for the Protection of Industrial Property, Mar. 20, 1883, as rev. at Stockholm, July 14, 1967, 21 UST 1583, 828 UNTS 305.

[29] These are defined in Part II of TRIPS as "indications which identify a good as originating in the territory of a member, or a region or locality in that territory, where a given quality, reputation or other characteristic of the good is essentially attributable to its geographical origin."

[30] TRIPS Agreement, art. 23.2. The protections afforded to geographical indications used in the context of wines and spirits are not limited to uses that mislead the public.

[31] Further international disciplines were included in the 2015 Geneva Act of the Lisbon Agreement on Appellations of Origin and Geographical Indications (as adopted on May 20, 2015). This instrument is not well aligned to the prevailing approach of common law countries to protect geographical origins primarily through trademark doctrines. *See* Daniel Gervais, *Irreconcilable Differences? The Geneva Act of the Lisbon Agreement and the Common Law*, 53 HOUS. L. REV. 339 (2015).

it must be established that goodwill or reputation attaches to the goods or services, that the defendant has misrepresented that the goods or services offered are those of the claimant, and that the claimant is likely to suffer damage because of the misrepresentation. Trade associations may protect their goodwill through the passing off tort,[32] and the principle has been extended to unincorporated associations. One case[33] involved an unincorporated association of furniture manufacturing companies that organized a biannual exhibition, known as "The Long Point" exhibition.[34] The defendant company, a former member of the association, applied to register "The Long Point" as a trademark. The defendant resisted the association's claims that the trademark was invalid and that its use would amount to passing off on the basis that as an unincorporated association the plaintiff could not own the goodwill in the name. Deciding for the plaintiff, the court held that the unincorporated association could, through its members, own the goodwill, and was entitled to protect it through the tort of passing off.[35]

The so-called extended form of passing off also shares some common ground with protections afforded to registered certification marks. In these cases,[36] the passing off tort typically protects the "quality" of goods represented by a name, in situations where the plaintiff is not necessarily the only party entitled to use the term.[37] In the leading case of *Erven Warnink BV* v. *J. Townend & Sons (Hull) Ltd.*,[38] the House of Lords upheld a holding of passing off against an English trader that marketed a drink as "Keeling's Old English Advocaat," which had different ingredients to the Dutch admixture of brandewijn (a type of distilled brandy), egg yolks and sugar, marketed under the name "Advocaat." The ingredients of the latter drink were in fact stipulated by Dutch regulations, but this was regarded as largely irrelevant by Lord Diplock, who delivered the leading speech in the case. In his Lordship's analysis, what mattered was whether the term "Advocaat" had a reputation in England as having these ingredients. In some extended passing off cases, individual plaintiffs might well enjoy the exclusive right to use a mark to signal that the product has been made in a specified way or includes specified ingredients.[39] But as the Advocaat case shows, this is not necessary. In such cases, the plaintiffs represent the group of traders (who may or may not be affiliated in any way) whose marketing practices established the "goodwill" in the ingredients and/or processes of manufacture for which they seek protection through the passing off tort.[40]

[32] *See, e.g., Soc'y of Accountants & Auditors* v. *Goodway & London Ass'n of Accountants Ltd.*, [1907] 1 Ch. 489. For a more recent instance, see *Nat'l Guild of Removers & Storers Ltd.* v. *Silveria (t/a CS Movers)*, [2011] FSR 9.

[33] *Artistic Upholstery* v. *Art Form Ltd.* [1994] 4 All ER 227.

[34] Unincorporated associations may own registered collective marks. *See* Alison Firth, *Collectivity, Control and Joint Adventure: Observations on Marks in Multiple Use, in* PERSPECTIVES ON INTELLECTUAL PROPERTY: TRADE MARKS RETROSPECTIVE 174 (N. Dawson & A. Firth eds., 2000). In this essay Professor Firth provides an illuminating discussion of the tensions between the statutory provisions and registry practice in the context of ownership structures adopted by some proprietors of collective trademarks. *See also* TERESA SCASSA, CANADIAN TRADEMARK LAW 60 (2010).

[35] *See also Soc'y of Accountants and Auditors* v. *Goodway & London Ass'n of Accountants Ltd.*, [1907] 1 Ch. 489.

[36] *See, e.g., Chocosuisse Union des fabricants suisses de chocolat* v. *Cadbury Ltd.*, [1999] EWCA Civ. 856.

[37] This is not always done successfully. *See, e.g., Consorzio del Prosciutto di Parma* v. *Marks & Spencer Plc*, [1991] RPC 351, 369 (CA).

[38] *Erven Warnink BV* v. *J. Townend & Sons (Hull) Ltd.*, [1979] AC 731.

[39] *See, e.g., Comité Interprofesional du Vin de Champagne* v. *Wineworths Grp. Ltd.*, [1991] 2 NZLR 432 (HC).

[40] The analogy between passing off and protection of registered certification trademarks is only partial. Typically, proprietors of certification trademarks may not themselves use the trademark for the kinds of goods or services for which the certification is provided. *See* Trade Marks Act, 1994, sched. 2, para. 4 (UK). Also, as was held *in Chocosuisse Union des fabricants suisses de chocolat* v. *Cadbury Ltd.*, [1999] EWCA Civ. 856, passing off actions in this context must be brought by parties who own the goodwill in the mark at issue. The Court of Appeal held that the action could not be brought by a party in a representational capacity.

IV ADAPTATION OF THE DISTINCTIVENESS STANDARD

On its face, the UK Trade Marks Act 1994 does not distinguish between the distinctiveness standard applicable to certification marks and the standard applicable to ordinary trademarks. The 1994 Act simply provides that the general statutory qualification for a trademark – the ability of a trademark to distinguish goods and services of one undertaking from those of another undertaking –"shall be construed as a reference to distinguishing goods or services which are certified from those which are not."[41]

Even so, the distinct functions of certification marks do appear to influence the approach to distinctiveness at the application stage. The UK Trade Mark Examination Manual explains:

> In many cases an objection applicable to an ordinary trade mark will be equally applicable to a certification or collective mark, however, there will also be circumstances where it is not. For example, the mark shown below may not be acceptable as an ordinary trade mark in respect of meat or meat products (it is unlikely that the average consumer will regard it as pointing towards a single trade source for these goods) but would be acceptable as a certification mark as it is capable of performing that particular distinguishing function.[42]

The Intellectual Property Office of Singapore, in the context of similarly worded provisions, explains the distinction with the example of the mark "100% Organic" combined with designs. The Singapore Manual explains that while this would not be acceptable as an ordinary trademark, it might pass muster as a certification mark "if it is capable of identifying goods which are certified from those which are not." According to the Singapore Manual, the simple composite word mark "100% Organic" would not, however, be acceptable, on the basis that it would not be capable in itself of distinguishing certified goods from those that are not. The examination guidelines provided by the New Zealand Intellectual Property office reminds examiners that the special characteristics of certification trademarks can inform the analysis of distinctiveness:

> Certification marks distinguish goods or services certified in respect of origin, material, mode of manufacture, quality, accuracy, performance, or other characteristics. This contrasts to the test for distinctiveness of a standard trade mark, as a standard trade mark must simply be capable of distinguishing the goods and services of a single party from those of another.[43]

These slight variations on the conventional approach to descriptiveness indicate that the most salient information provided by a certification mark is the information the marks convey about the standards themselves. The relevant preferences consumers express through purchasing decisions are not confined to the single source of goods. The distinctive standard serves the latter well – but the former kind of preference may be as, if not more, important for consumers. For this reason, descriptive signaling of the characteristics that are the focus of the consumers' preferences may be more readily tolerated for certification marks than for ordinary trademarks. Most anticompetitive effects of more descriptive marks can be addressed through the use of disclaimers.[44]

[41] *Id.*, sched. 2, para. 2.

[42] Intellectual Property Office (UK), *Manual of Trade Mark Practice*, https://gov.uk/guidance/trade-marks-manual/certification-and-collective-marks.

[43] Ministry of Business, Innovation, and Employment (NZ), *Trade Mark Practice Guidelines*, https://iponz.govt.nz/about-ip/trade-marks/practice-guidelines/current/certification-marks/.

[44] UK Intellectual Property Office [UKIPO], Manual of Trade Marks Practice 49–51 (2009), https://gov.uk/guidance/trade-marks-manual. On the scope for disclaimers the EU context, see *Patent-och registreringsverket v. Hansson*, C-705/17, EU:C:2019:481, June 12, 2019.

While the general provisions of the EUTMR, in particular Article 7, apply to EU certification marks, the EU Trade Mark Examination Guidelines[45] acknowledge the specific characteristics of certification marks: "[w]hen assessing the general grounds of refusal of Article 7(1)(b), (c) and (d) EUTMR, the specific function of certification marks – that is to distinguish goods or services certified by one certifier (i) from those that are not certified at all and (ii) from those certified by another certifier – must always be kept in mind." At the same time, the Guidelines note that when an applicant claims that a mark has acquired distinctiveness: "[A]ny claim of distinctiveness acquired through use will need to be supported by evidence showing that use of the mark has been made, and the mark is in fact recognised on the relevant market as a certification mark."

V REGULATORY CONTROLS

The leading UK case on the obligations of the proprietor of a certification trademark to control its use by authorized users is *South Island Cotton Certification Trade Marks*.[46] The applicant sought to expunge from the register a certification mark that had been cited against it. Sitting in a judicial capacity, Aldous QC, as he then was, rejected the applicant's submission that a certification mark proprietor must be able to ensure that a mark is being correctly used. So holding, Mr. Aldous drew on the legislative history – including the changes between the 1905 and 1919 legislation – noting that following the 1991 amendments, a proprietor of the trademark was no longer required to examine or investigate the goods or take on responsibility for ensuring that an authorized user's goods complied with the regulations. What mattered was whether the proprietor of the mark had the legal and practical ability to certify.[47]

Aldous QC did not consider it appropriate to regard the trademark proprietor as having to "police" the use of the mark. A better analogy was "the committee of a club." The "committee" is "entrusted to vet any applicant to see whether he has the correct qualification to join and can eject any member acting in breach of the clubs' rules." Mr. Aldous continued:

> No analogy is perfect, but the requirement for investigation having been abolished in 1919, I do not believe it right to introduce it by a construction of the word competent in the 1938 Act. Further my view is consistent with the regulations which require the proprietor to satisfy himself that an authorised user is of good standing and agrees to use the mark only upon "proper" goods, but do not impose an obligation upon the proprietor to ensure that the authorised user acts in accordance with the agreement.[48]

Here, the "committee of a club" metaphor anticipates later interest by economists in the "club goods" attributes of certification marks.[49] Certification trademarks are a "club," to the extent that the authorized users collectively invest in the production of a resource: the certification

[45] Guidelines for Examination of European Union Trade Marks European Union Intellectual Property Office (EUIPO) [hereinafter EUIPO Guidelines]. Guidelines adopted by the Executive Director on Sept. 22, 2017 (Decision EX-17-1), which entered into force on Oct. 1, 2017 § 6.

[46] *South Island Cotton Certification Trade Marks*, [1989] RPC 87.

[47] Here, Aldous QC followed *Union Nationale Inter-Syndicate des Marques Collective's Application*, (1922) 39 RPC 97 (applying the 1919 legislation).

[48] *Id.*

[49] Tracey M. Roberts, *Innovations in Governance: A Functional Typology of Private Governance Institutions*, 22 Duke Envtl. L. & Pol'y F. 67, 81 (2011); Graeme Auld, Constructing Private Governance: The Rise and Evolution of Forest, Coffee, and Fisheries Certification 14 (2014).

standards. That resource is in turn rendered "excludable" by a combination of the trademark rights and the right to decide who may use the mark in trade.

An important distinction between ordinary trademarks and certification marks is that the proprietor of a certification mark is typically precluded from using the mark in trade.[50] The UK trademark statute explicitly precludes registration of the mark if the proprietor carries on business involving the supply of goods or services of the kind certified. This requirement protects the public interest in the certification system, by avoiding the possibility that the certifier would relax the standards in the case of its own use of the mark in commerce. Use of the mark by the certifying entity is a ground for revocation.

Proprietors of certification marks are also precluded from denying the use of the mark to any person or entity that complies with the certification standards. This is an important distinction between certification and other kinds of trademarks. In general, proprietors of trademarks may choose to whom to license the use of the marks. In the certification context, the restriction helps to ensure that certification trademarks do not become vehicles for unfair competition.

The Australian Competition and Consumer Commission (ACCC) has taken on a specific role in ensuring that the rules adopted by proprietors (or would-be proprietors) of certification trademarks protect the public interest by ensuring that certification authorities are competent to apply the relevant standards, and that certifying entities' internal rules do not give rise to unfair competition by excluding parties that would qualify to use the mark.[51] Leading Australian commentators Robert Burrell and Michael Handler observe that applicants most often struggle at the ACCC stage,[52] referencing a recent controversy over an application for registration that would have led to the proprietor of the certification mark controlling the labeling of eggs as "free range." The ACCC received over 1,700 public submissions on the application. Following an initial adverse review, the application was withdrawn.[53] The ACCC must also give its consent to assignments of certification marks.[54]

Fees can also be a barrier to entry, especially for smaller firms. Where fees are excessively high, there is a risk that certification marks will be used in an anticompetitive way. Accordingly, the UK Trade Marks Act 1994 provides that fees proposed to be charged must be approved by the Trade Marks Registry.[55]

Another relevant control imposed by the UK Trade Marks Act is the requirement that the Registrar give consent to any assignment or other transmission of a certification mark.[56] That restriction is not imposed on proprietors of ordinary trademarks. As with the original applicant for the mark, the new owner must satisfy the Registrar that it is competent to certify the goods or services and is able to monitor the use of the certification mark by authorized users.

Similar issues relating to the potential for abuse arise in the context of collective marks. Proprietors of collective marks usually adopt rules governing membership of the association. Where membership is conditioned on compliance with rules as to quality or other relevant characteristics of the goods or services to which the mark attaches, these rules act as quality

[50] Australia is an exception. *See Trade Marks Act 1995* § 171 (Austl.).

[51] When a certification trademark application is received by the Australian Registrar of Trade Marks, the application is forwarded to the ACCC for consideration. For further information on the role of the ACCC in Australian trademark law, see https://accc.gov.au/business/exemptions/certification-trade-marks.

[52] Robert Burrell & Michael Handler, Australian Trade Mark Law 543 (2d ed. 2010).

[53] *Id.* at 543–44.

[54] *Id.* at 566. Under Australian law, collective marks are not assignable.

[55] Trade Marks Act, 1994, sched. 2, para. 6(2) (UK).

[56] *Id.* at § 192(2).

control mechanisms. Under Schedule 1 of the Trade Marks Act 1994, these regulations must be submitted to the Registrar, and the rules will be open for inspection.

Despite these specific stipulations in the 1994 Act's schedule, any distinct market or, indeed, legal function of collective marks was called into question in a 2014 decision *The National Guild of Removers and Storers Ltd.* v. *Milner (t/a Intransit Removals and Storage)*[57] in the Intellectual Property Enterprise Court. There, Judge Halcon observed:

> I find it hard to think of a circumstance in which an association entitled to apply for a collective mark could not avoid the cost and inconvenience of those provisions, and indeed evade the safeguards to the public they afford, by applying instead for a trade mark. But whatever the legislative intent at the time of drafting, the view on how a trade mark may be used has been updated and has altered.[58]

On this view, the specific requirements in the Schedule could be avoided by merely registering an ordinary trademark and then achieving the control necessary to maintain the goodwill attached to the mark through licensing it. Drawing on the famous decision of the House of Lords in *Scandecor Development AB* v. *Scandecor Marketing AB*,[59] the court specifically rejected the argument that licensing the mark would jeopardize the goodwill or the entitlement to the mark. There, Lord Nicholls observed:

> For their quality assurance customers rely on the self-interest of the owner. They assume that if a licence has been granted the owner can be expected to have chosen a suitable licensee and imposed suitable terms. They also assume that during the currency of any licence the licensee, as well as the owner, is likely to have an interest in maintaining the value of the brand name. Customers are not to be taken to rely on the protection supposedly afforded by a legal requirement that the proprietor must always retain and exercise an inherently imprecise degree of control over the licensee's activities.[60]

National Guild of Removers and Storers Limited indicates that these general principles can apply to collective marks. Adapted to that context, it might be said that consumers may rely on the collective self-interest of the proprietor.

The EUTMR also requires an applicant for EU certification and collective marks to submit the regulations governing the use of the mark. Under Article 79 of the EUTMR, "[T]he proprietor of an EU collective mark shall submit to the Office any amended regulations governing use." For certification marks, the applicant must file information as to the characteristics of the goods or services to be certified; the conditions governing the use of the certification mark; and the testing and supervision measures (including sanctions) to be applied by the certification mark owner.[61] This information must be submitted within two months of filing the application. The EU system imposes a broad "duty of neutrality": a proprietor of a certification mark is precluded from having any economic (business) interest in the relevant market. This includes being economically linked to the parties using the mark.[62]

[57] *Nat'l Guild of Removers & Storers Ltd.* v. *Milner (t/a Intransit Removals and Storage)*, [2014] FSR 38.
[58] *Id.* at [66].
[59] *Scandecor Dev. AB* v. *Scandecor Mktg. AB*, [2001] UKHL 21.
[60] *Id.* at 39.
[61] EUTMR, art. 84.
[62] EUIPO Guidelines, *supra* note 45, § 4.

VI INFRINGEMENT PRINCIPLES

In the main, the UK trademark legislation applies the same infringement principles to certification marks as are applied to ordinary trademarks. This is given express statutory force in section 1(2) of the Trade Marks Act 1994 (UK), which states that references to a trademark include, unless the context otherwise requires, a certification mark. The same approach is adopted for collective marks.[63] The UK Act adopts a "double identity" approach to infringement: accordingly, the use of an identical mark to the certification mark in respect of the goods or services for which it is registered in itself amounts to infringement.[64] In addition, the United Kingdom adopts the usual likelihood of confusion grounds for infringement: identical mark/similar goods; and similar sign/identical goods.

For the purposes of infringement, an authorized user of a certification mark is treated in the same way as a licensee of an ordinary trademark. The Trade Marks Act 1994 (UK) specifies that the authorized user has the rights of a licensee in the context of unauthorized application of the mark in the context of marketplace activity, orders for the disposal of infringing goods and other material; and importation prohibitions, and customs regulations. A Schedule to the Act also specifies that in infringement actions brought by proprietors of registered certification marks, the loss suffered or likely to be suffered by authorized users shall be taken into account, and the court may require the proceeds of any pecuniary remedy to be held on behalf of such users.[65]

Schedule 1 of the Trade Marks Act 1994 provides for the ability of authorized users of collective marks to require the proprietor to initiate infringement proceedings. If the proprietor refuses to do so, or does not act within two months, the authorized user may initiate proceedings on its own behalf. The proprietor of the mark must be joined as a party but is immunized from costs unless it participates in the proceedings.[66] As with certification marks, in proceedings brought by the proprietor of a collective mark, the effects of the infringement on authorized users must be taken into account by the court.[67]

VII CONCLUSION

From this brief overview of the key legal principles and legislative provisions relating to certification marks, it will be apparent that certification and collective marks are not associated with dominant justifications for trademarks: reducing consumer search costs, so that consumers can find products or services from a single source.[68] The roles they serve are more diverse,

[63] Trade Marks Act, 1994, sched. 1, para. 11 (UK).

[64] *Id.* at § 10(1).

[65] *Id.* at sched. 2.

[66] *Id.* at sched. 1, para. 12.

[67] *Id.* at sched. 1, para. 12(6).

[68] William M. Landes & Richard A. Posner, *The Economic Function of Trademarks*, 30 J.L. & ECON. 265, 270 (1987). In Australia, the distinction between conventional and certification marks took on a constitutional dimension in *Attorney-General of NSW* v. *Brewery Employees' Union*, [1908] HCA 94, where it was held that it was beyond the power of the Australian Commonwealth to legislate for trademark protections for marks that could be registered and used to indicate that goods were made by "an individual Australian worker or association of Australian workers" (in other words, a trade union). As Sam Ricketson explains in his insightful analysis of this case, the constitutional point is no longer relevant as a result of subsequent developments in Australian law. *See* Sam Ricketson, *The* Union Label *Case: An Early Australian IP Story*, *in* LANDMARKS IN AUSTRALIAN INTELLECTUAL PROPERTY LAW 15, 34 (Andrew Kenyon, Megan Richardson, & Sam Ricketson eds., 2009). The *Union Label* case does, however, illustrate some of the conceptual tensions between the functions performed by ordinary trademarks and those performed by certification marks.

including helping to ensure that consumer expectations as to predetermined standards are fulfilled.

Thus, it may be that the most important social, political, and economic functions performed by these kinds of marks are not fully captured by the blackletter law outlined in the earlier sections of this chapter. For example, certification marks can act as a vehicle for forms of "private governance."[69] They can allow consumers to express political preferences – about matters such as environmental regulation or fair labor standards – through their purchasing decisions. In other words, consumers are able to vote with their wallets, with the expectation that these purchasers will encourage individual firms (or, in the case of collective marks, associations) to invest in developing, maintaining, and policing standards.

In the environmental context, for example, the importance of the private governance roles of these kinds of marks is likely to depend on the background political context. Where the state has retreated from environmental regulation – or, perhaps, is even hostile toward environmental protections – consumers' political preferences expressed through purchasing decisions are likely to be more important than in jurisdictions in which citizens can rely on governmental measures. Or, to put it more bluntly, depending on the political regime in place, consumers' ethical purchasing decisions might be all we have.

These kinds of marks advance a conceptual challenge for traditional trademark thinking. Conventional trademark doctrines are directed at serving the single normative end of enhancing competition by ensuring that consumers can find the single source from which they seek to purchase goods. In contrast, certification marks are able to serve different normative ends: environmental justice, prevention of animal cruelty, fair labor standards, product safety, to name a few. For that reason alone, these "underutilized and underappreciated"[70] categories of trademark, as a leading commentator once described them, deserve greater attention than they have so far received.

[69] Adelman & Austin, *supra* note 12.

[70] Dev Gangjee, *The Business End of Collective and Certification Marks, in* Trade Mark Law and Sharing Names: Exploring Use of the Same Mark by Multiple Undertakings 79 (Illana Simon Fhima ed., 2009). Professor Chon collects references to recent scholarly treatments of these categories of marks in Chapter 18 in this volume.

18

Certification and Collective Marks in the United States

*Margaret Chon**

I INTRODUCTION

This chapter will discuss certification (and, to a lesser extent, collective) marks, which comprise an increasingly important proportion of marks in use within interstate and international commerce.[1] Unlike trademarks and service marks, which serve primarily as indicators of source, certification marks have other acknowledged functions in trademark law and policy. For example, certification marks in the United States exist "to certify regional or other origin, material, mode of manufacture, quality, accuracy, or other characteristics of such person's goods or services or that the work or labor on the goods or services was performed by members of a union or other organization."[2] According to the US Patent and Trademark Office (USPTO), "a certification mark … inform[s] purchasers that the goods or services of a person possess certain characteristics or meet certain qualifications or standards established by another person. [It] does not indicate origin in a single commercial or proprietary source the way a trademark or service mark does."[3]

* Donald and Lynda Horowitz Professor for the Pursuit of Justice, Seattle University School of Law. My gratitude to Michelle Smit, who provided valuable feedback at the Trademark Scholarship Symposium of the 2018 INTA Annual Meeting, Jeanna McClellan (class of 2018) and Lauren Sewell (class of 2019) for their helpful research support, Professor Barton Beebe for generously sharing data, as well to the various participants of the International Intellectual Property Roundtable (particularly Professor Lisa Ramsey) for feedback on this scholarly project.

[1] Unpublished data provided to the author by Professors Barton Beebe and Jeanne Fromer indicate that the number of applications for registration of certification marks has increased steadily from 55 in 1985 to 720 in 2008, with a subsequent decline to 369 in 2016. Recent and forthcoming treatments of this topic in the context of the United States include Jorge L. Contreras, *Trademarks, Certification Marks and Technical Standards*, *in* CAMBRIDGE HANDBOOK OF TECHNICAL STANDARDIZATION LAW (Jorge L. Contreras ed., 2019); JEFFREY BELSON, CERTIFICATION AND COLLECTIVE MARKS LAW AND PRACTICE (2017); Jeanne C. Fromer, *The Unregulated Certification Mark(et)*, 69 STAN. L. REV. 121 (2017); Michelle B. Smit, *Note, (Un)Common Law Protection of Certification Marks*, 93 NOTRE DAME L. REV. 419 (2017); Wynn Heh, *Who Certifies the Certifiers?*, 16 VT. J. ENVTL. L. 688 (2015); Jeffrey Young, *Trademark Rights and Their Implementation: The Importance of Idaho Potatoes*, 19 J. CONTEMP. LEGAL ISSUES 241 (2008); *see also* Margaret Chon, *Marks of Rectitude*, 77 FORDHAM L. REV. 2311 (2009); Margaret Chon, *Slow Logo: Brand Citizenship in Global Value Networks*, 47 U.C. DAVIS L. REV. 935 (2014); Margaret Chon, *Tracermarks: A Proposed Information Intervention*, 53 HOUSTON L. REV. 421 (2015); and Margaret Chon, *Trademark Goodwill as a Public Good: Brands and Innovations in Corporate Social Responsibility*, 21 LEWIS AND CLARK L. REV. 277 (2017). In Chapter 17 in this volume, Graeme W. Austin covers various non-US legal regimes governing certification and collective marks. Graeme W. Austin, *Anglo and EU Frameworks for Certification and Collective Trademarks.*

[2] 15 USC § 1127 (2006); *see also* Trademark Manual of Examining Procedure (hereinafter TMEP) § 1306.01 Types of Certification Marks (Oct. 2018).

[3] TMEP § 1306.01(b), Purpose is to Certify, Not to Indicate Source; *see also* USPTO, Certification mark applications, https://uspto.gov/trademarks-getting-started/trademark-basics/certification-mark-applications.

FIGURE 18.1 Examples of geographic certification marks registered with the USPTO[4]

In particular, certification marks can signal characteristics such as geographic origin[5] and/or standards met with respect to quality, materials, or mode of manufacture.[6] Thus, certification marks are used in the United States as the primary "legal means" to protect geographical indications (GIs) under Article 22 of the World Trade Organization Agreement on Trade Related Aspect of Intellectual Property (TRIPS).[7] The Paris Convention Article 7*bis*, incorporated into TRIPS via Article 1(2), mandates the protection of collective marks, which are also occasionally used as "legal means" to indicate regional origin in the United States.[8] This is in direct contrast to EU certification and collective marks, both of which exclude goods and services of geographic origin from their ambit, presumably in deference to the EU's tradition of the *sui generis* GI right.[9]

Figure 18.1 sets forth examples of geographic certification marks that are registered with the USPTO.[10]

As can be seen from these examples, the USPTO has registered geographic certification marks to certify both agricultural and non-agricultural goods and services, so long as they

[4] Serial Number 3499131 ("The certification mark, as used by authorized persons, certifies that the flag has been made in the U.S. of materials that are domestic in origin and that all processes in every step of the U.S. flag's manufacture were completed in U.S. facilities with U.S. labor"); and Registration Number 4221403 ("The certification mark, as used by authorized persons, certifies the regional origin of potatoes grown in the State of Idaho and certifies that those potatoes conform to grade, size, weight, color, shape, cleanliness, variety, internal defect, external defect, maturity and residue level standards promulgated by the certifier").

[5] TMEP § 1306.05, Geographic Certification Marks ("A geographic certification mark may feature a recognized geographic term that identifies the relevant geographic region, as in the marks ROQUEFORT for cheese, DARJEELING for tea, and COLOMBIAN for coffee").

[6] TMEP § 1306.01, Types of Certification Marks ("Certification marks may be used to certify that authorized users' goods or services meet certain standards in relation to quality, materials, or mode of manufacture (e.g., approval by Underwriters Laboratories)").

[7] TRIPS: Agreement on Trade-Related Aspects of Intellectual Property Rights, Apr. 15, 1994, Marrakesh Agreement Establishing the World Trade Organization, Annex 1C, 1869 UNTS 299, 33 ILM 1197 (1994) [hereinafter TRIPS Agreement] (mandating "legal means" for WTO member states to mark "quality, reputation or other characteristic of a good . . . essentially attributable to its geographic origin" via geographical indications). TRIPS Article 22 only requires a minimum level of protection for GIs ("legal means"); it is "silent as to the mechanism of protection and it is understood that each country may fulfill these obligations through its own particular domestic law tools." Justin Hughes, *Champagne, Feta, and Bourbon: The Spirited Debate about Geographical Indications*, 58 Hastings L.J. 299, 314 (2006).

[8] TRIPS Agreement, art. 2(1) (mandating that members "comply with Articles 1 through 12 . . . of the Paris Convention"); Paris Convention for the Protection of Industrial Property, art. 7*bis*, 828 UNTS 305 (Mar. 20, 1883) (mandating that members "accept for filing and protect collective marks belonging to associations"); Belson, *supra* note 1, at 40–41 and 79–80 (describing adoption of art. 7*bis*).

[9] European Trademark Regulation (EUTMR) No. 2015/2424 of Dec. 16, 2015 (OJ L 341/21 24.12.2015 arts. 83 and 74, respectively).

[10] USPTO, Examination Guide 2–14: Geographic Certification Marks (July 2014).

FIGURE 18.2 Examples of certification marks based upon non-geographic environmental and/or labor standards, registered with the USPTO[11]

are associated with a geographic provenance ("regional origin") recognizable as such to the consumer.[12]

In addition to functioning as the legal means to effectuate treaty obligations to protect GIs,[13] as shown by Figure 18.1, certification marks can also indicate conformance to technical standards, safety standards, environmental standards, as well as other characteristics.[14] Figure 18.2 sets forth further examples of certification marks that are premised on environmental or labor standards.

Unlike a certification mark, a collective mark *is* a type of trademark or service mark. But instead of being used by a seller or provider to indicate the source of the goods or services, a collective mark is "used by the members of a cooperative, an association, or other collective group or organization."[15] Figure 18.3 shows some examples of collective marks, which convey the association to which the mark belongs. As discussed above, these can also include associations of agricultural producers attributable to a particular geographic origin.[16] Collective marks can also include collective membership marks, which denote membership within an organization as opposed to membership-based indicators of source.[17]

Both certification and collective marks can convey information about certain qualities of a product that are not immediately apparent to a consumer from a point of purchase examination of a product or experience of a service, but still meaningful to a consumer's purchasing

[11] Serial Numbers 86312698 ("The certification mark, as used or intended to be used by persons authorized by the certifier, certifies or is intended to certify that the goods and/or services provided have been produced, traded, and marketed in accordance with the certifier's certification standards"); 85578135 ("The certification mark, as used by authorized persons, certifies that the operations, enterprises, projects or businesses, or the products or services produced, manufactured, distributed, processed, purchased or sold by such operations, enterprises, projects or businesses, have met criteria or standards established by the certifier or other standard-setting bodies, pertaining to conservation of natural resources, protection of plants and wildlife, reduction of greenhouse gas emissions or climate change mitigation, and contribution to the well-being of local communities"); and 76688528 ("The certification mark, as used by authorized persons, certifies that the work or labor on the said goods was performed by members of the certifier union").

[12] *Swiss Watch Int'l, Inc.* v. *Fed. of the Swiss Watch Indus.* 101 USPQ 2d 1731, 1744 (TTAB 2012) (refusing to cancel the certification "SWISS MADE" on the basis of genericness) ("Even in those situations where a certification mark is used in connection with products having an agricultural origin, there is a recognition that processing of the product, even when that processing does not have an intrinsic connection with the land, can be an element of the certification standards"); *see also* BELSON, *supra* note 1, at 50–51 (listing more examples of geographic certification marks registered with the USPTO).

[13] TRIPS Agreement, art. 22, *supra* note 9.

[14] *See* Contreras, *supra* note 1 for examples.

[15] 15 USC § 1127 (2006).

[16] *See* Belson, *supra* note 1, at 167–68 for other examples.

[17] TMEP § 1306.6.

FIGURE 18.3 Examples of collective marks registered with the USPTO[18]

choices; these qualities are sometimes referred to as credence attributes.[19] From this perspective, the ability of certification marks in particular to guarantee standards regarding "material, mode of manufacture, quality, accuracy, or other characteristics" allow them to act as potential disciplinary mechanisms along cross-border supply chains.[20] Without this work of certification marks, consumers may find it difficult or impossible to determine whether the goods or services have been ethically or sustainably sourced, for example, because global markets rely upon pervasive manufacturing outsourcing. Thus, certification marks can supplement the largely non-verifiable and marketing-driven subjective information conveyed by trademarks. They provide more potentially objective information about the credence attributes of the goods and services to which they are affixed.

In the United States, standard setting is often carried out through public–private partnerships, sometimes, but not always, coordinated by or through federal regulatory agencies.[21] The USPTO recognizes this, stating that the certification mark "standards do not have to be originally created by the applicant. They may be standards established by another party, such as specifications promulgated by a government agency or standards developed through research of a private research organization."[22] An example of a government agency creating and promulgating standards, the US Environmental Protection Agency, has registered certification marks related to its ENERGY STAR program,[23] which it then uses to encourage energy-efficient industry standards that are adopted voluntarily.[24]

These decentralized regulatory functions of certification marks fit uneasily within the dominant modern policy goals of trademark law, which are undergirded by a search cost rationale. The search cost theory posits that the primary work of marks is to provide an efficient signal

[18] Serial Numbers 78886874 and 87811048.

[19] *See* Chon, *Slow Logo*, *supra* note 1, at 946 (quoting Ariel Katz, *Beyond Search Costs: The Linguistic and Trust Functions of Trademarks*, 2010 BYU L. REV. 1555, 1561 (2010) ("[T]he fact that a can of tuna looks like a can of tuna is a search attribute. The fact that the content tastes like tuna is an experience attribute. Whether the content is indeed tuna and not a good imitation, or whether it is safe for consumption, are credence attributes").

[20] Margaret Chon, *Marks and More(s): Certification in Global Value Chains*, *in* TRADEMARK PROTECTION AND TERRITORIALITY CHALLENGES IN A GLOBAL ECONOMY 79, 83 (Irene Calboli & Edward Lee eds., 2014) ("Typically an entity (often a third party) will certify that a good or service conforms to a standard, which can be set privately – through a firm itself, a civil society organization, a trade association, or a combination of some or all of the above. . . . Certification marks can inform . . . end-consumers of product qualities related to the largely opaque steps of the process leading to the product to which they are affixed. These process standards include not only quality assurance standards, which are within the classic trademark mandate, but also a multitude of other process measures").

[21] *See* Belson, *supra* note 1, at 53–56.

[22] TMEP § 1306.03(b).

[23] ENERGY STAR STAR, USPTO Registration No. 3569551 and ENERGY ENERGY STAR, USPTO Registration No. 3575484.

[24] *See* BELSON, *supra* note 1, at 224–25; *see also* ENERGY STAR, https://energy.gov/eere/buildings/energy-star.

for rational consumers to associate a product or service with a particular *origin or source of manufacture* in a market. Sometimes referred to as the trademark's source signal, it assumes that marks serve primarily to decrease consumers' search costs by providing them with a shorthand reference or symbol upon which they can rely repeatedly.[25]

This source function model arguably falls short of fully addressing the so-called trust function of certification marks – that is, informing the consumer of the underlying attributes of goods and services, whether set through public law or private standard-setting activities.[26] As a result, unresolved doctrinal and policy issues exist regarding the relationship of certification marks to trademarks. In addition to the blurring of search and trust functions, these include the inconsistent oversight of the enforcement of certification standards as well as the lack of consumer access to direct information about the standards themselves..

II STATUTORY AND ADMINISTRATIVE REQUIREMENTS

This section highlights statutory and relevant administrative law provisions directly addressing certification marks and (where noted) collective marks. The 1946 Lanham Act defines a "mark" to include "any trademark, service mark, collective mark, or certification mark."[27] Section 4 clarifies that "collective and certification marks ... shall be registrable under this chapter, in the same manner *and with the same effect* as are trademarks."[28] Thus most of the Lanham Act provisions relating to trademarks and service marks also apply to certification and collective marks (indeed, as stated above, the Act defines a collective mark as a specific type of trademark or service mark). Because geographic certification (and collective) marks are often administered through governmental entities, the Lanham Act recognizes that holders of collective and certification marks can include "nations, States, municipalities, and the like ... even though not possessing an industrial or commercial establishment."[29]

While requirements for registration of certification marks are generally the same as those for trademarks, the treatment of distinctiveness is different for geographic certification marks.[30] For example, the Trademark Manual of Examining Procedure (TMEP) states that a geographic certification mark "does not require a secondary meaning in order to qualify for registration as a certification mark.... [A] geographical name may be registered as a certification mark even if it is primarily geographically descriptive."[31] The registration of geographic certification marks is exempt from section 2(e)'s general prohibition on the registration of "primarily geographically descriptive" marks due to its proviso: "except as indications of regional origin ... registrable under section [4]."[32] Sections of the TMEP are devoted to the differentiation of unregistrable

[25] Stacey L. Dogan & Mark A. Lemley, *Trademarks and Consumer Search Costs on the Internet*, 41 Houston L. Rev. 777, 778 (2004); William M. Landes & Richard A. Posner, *Trademark Law: An Economic Perspective*, 30 J. of L. & Economics 265, 275 (1987).

[26] *See* Katz, *supra* note 19, at 1563; *cf.* Dev Gangjee, *The Business End of Collective and Certification Marks*, in Trademark Law and Sharing Names: Exploring Use of the Same Mark by Multiple Undertakings 79, 84–86 (Ilanah Simon Fhima ed., 2009) (discussing different functions of certification marks in the UK context).

[27] 15 USC § 1127 (2006).

[28] *Id.* § 1054 (1999) (emphasis added).

[29] *Id.* § 1054 (1999); this language is consistent with the language of the Paris Convention art. 7*bis*.

[30] 15 USC § 1054 (1999).

[31] TMEP § 1306.02, Certification Marks that Are Origins of Regional Origin (*Community of Roquefort v. William Faehndrich, Inc.*, 303 F.2d 494, 497, 133 USPQ 633, 635 (2d Cir. 1962)).

[32] 15 USC § 1052(e)(2) (2006).

"primarily geographically descriptive" trademarks from registrable geographic certification marks.[33] For example, it states that:

> The issue in determining whether a designation is registrable as a regional certification mark is whether the public understands that goods bearing the mark come only from the region named in the mark, not whether the public is expressly aware of the certification function of the mark per se. If use of the designation in fact is controlled by the certifier and limited to products meeting the certifier's standards of regional origin, and if purchasers understand the designation to refer only to products produced in the particular region and not to products produced elsewhere, then the designation functions as a regional certification mark.[34]

A registration application for certification marks already in use requires a "copy of the certification standards" and a "statement specifying what the applicant is certifying about the goods or services in the application."[35] Any application to the USPTO for a certification mark registration, whether for a geographic or non-geographic mark, must also be accompanied by an assertion "that the applicant is exercising legitimate control over the use of the certification mark in commerce."[36]

The standards represented in the certification statement should be sufficiently detailed to give notice of standards being certified.[37] Once the registration issues, however, neither the USPTO nor any other public agency regularly monitors whether the stated standards continue to be accurate; it is entirely up to a certification holder (or its licensees) to control the quality of these standards.

Section 14(5)(A) of the Lanham Act provides the closest thing to government oversight of standards represented by certification marks: A petition to cancel registration may be "filed . . . by *any person* who believes that he is or will be damaged," if the certification mark owner "does not control, or is not able legitimately to exercise control, over the use of such mark."[38] The question of adequate control is typically raised (if at all) in cancellation proceedings filed by potential competitors, former licensees, or the Federal Trade Commission.[39] The section below on relevant case law reveals that a certification mark holder's lack of control over the use of the mark is only infrequently challenged and even more infrequently used as a basis for cancellation.[40]

[33] TMEP § 1306.02, Certification Marks that Are Indications of Regional Origin.
[34] *Id.*
[35] 37 CFR § 2.45 (a)(4)(i) (2015).
[36] TMEP § 1306.06(f)(iii), Exercise of Control.
[37] TMEP § 1306.06(f)(1), Statement of What the Mark Certifies ("The characteristics or features that the mark certifies should be explained in reasonable detail, so that they are clear. The broad suggestive terms of the statute, such as quality, material, mode of manufacture, are generally not satisfactory by themselves, because they do not accurately reveal the nature of the certification. How specific the statement should be depends in part on the narrowness or breadth of the certification.")
[38] 15 USC § 1064(5) (2006); *see also* TMEP § 1306.01(a), Use is by Person Other than Owner ("The owner of a certification mark does not produce the goods or perform the services in connection with which the mark is used, and thus does not control their nature and quality. Therefore, it is not appropriate to inquire about control over the nature and quality of the goods or services. What the owner of the certification mark does control is use of the mark by others on their goods or services. This control consists of taking steps to ensure that the mark is applied only to goods or services that contain the characteristics or meet the requirements that the certifier/owner has established or adopted for the certification").
[39] 15 USC § 1064 ("[T]he Federal Trade Commission may apply to cancel on the grounds specified in paragraphs (3) and (5) of this section").
[40] For a recent example of an unsuccessful challenge to a certification mark, *see Swiss Watch International, Inc.* v. *Fed. of the Swiss Watch Indus.*, *supra* note 11 (refusing to cancel the certification "SWISS MADE").

While "control" is a key term of art under the Lanham Act, it is not defined by the statute and is therefore subject to a relatively large latitude for judicial interpretation.[41]

Section 14(5)(A) of the Lanham Act sets forth several additional cancellation grounds specific to certification marks. For example, a certification mark owner should not: "(B) engage[] in the production or marketing of any goods or services to which the certification mark is applied, or (C) permit[] the use of the certification mark for purposes other than to certify."[42] In addition, because certification mark holders furthermore are required to certify others who meet the certification standards, section 14(5)(D) has been characterized as a compulsory licensing provision.[43] Trademark holders have autonomy in choosing licensees, whereas certification mark holders are under a legal obligation to license any firm that meets their stated standards. Certification mark holders may not "discriminately refuse[] to certify ... the goods or services of any person who maintains the standards or conditions which such mark certifies,"[44] or else the mark may be subject to cancellation.[45]

Together, these various grounds for cancellation of certification marks indicate legal constraints upon certification mark holders, based upon principles of unfair competition. To allow the certification mark holder to use the certification mark to promote the mark holder's own goods or services would essentially permit a standard setter to have an unfair competitive advantage in the market for goods and services conforming to that standard. However, a certification mark holder is not precluded from using *other* marks so long as they are not the certification mark – a practice sometimes termed co-branding.[46] Nor is a certification mark holder precluded from using the mark to "advertis[e] or promot[e] recognition of the certification program or of the goods or services to which its ... mark is applied."[47] Because marketing synergies can be created between a trademark and any applicable certification marks, co-branding approaches are prevalent, which the USPTO acknowledges.[48]

Finally, the Lanham Act provides for various grounds for cancellation under section 14 that are applicable to all marks, including certification marks, such as cancellations based upon the likelihood of dilution, if filed within five years within the date of registration of the mark.[49] It also provides for cancellation at any time if mark becomes "the generic name for the goods or services ... or is functional, or has been abandoned, or its registration was obtained fraudulently or contrary to the provisions of section [4]."[50] As a result, much of the case law interpreting these provisions of section 14 with regard to trademarks is potentially applicable to certification marks as well. Like all other kinds of marks sought to be registered federally, certification marks are subject to administrative procedures for registration, opposition, and cancellation within

[41] For a comprehensive and updated critique of the concept of "control" related to trademark transactions, notably trademark assignment and licensing, *see* Irene Calboli, *Trademark Transactions in the United States: Towards De Facto Trading in Gross?*, *in* The Law and Practice of Trademark Transactions: A Global and Local Outlook 439 (Irene Calboli & Jacques de Werra eds., 2016).

[42] 15 USC § 1064 (2006).

[43] *See also* 3 McCarthy on Trademarks and Unfair Competition § 19:92 (4th ed. 2008) ("This obligation distinguishes a certification mark from a trademark and creates a kind of compulsory licensing") (cited by *Idaho Potato Comm'n* v. *M&M Produce Farm & Sales*, 335 F.3d 130, 138 (2d Cir. 2003)).

[44] 15 USC § 1064(5)(D) (2006).

[45] *Id.* § 1064.

[46] An example of co-branding is the use of a fair trade certification mark along with a specific trademark applied to food, such as coffee. *See also* TMEP § 1306.06(c), Relation Between Certification Mark and Trademark or Service Mark on Specimens.

[47] 15 USC § 1064 (2006).

[48] TMEP 1306.06(c), Relation Between Certification Mark and Trademark or Service Mark on Specimens.

[49] *Id.* § 1064(1) (2006).

[50] *Id.* § 1064(3) (2006).

the USPTO.[51] Appeals from the Trademark Trial and Appeal Board (TTAB) can be taken to the US Court of Appeals for the Federal Circuit or the party can opt to file a civil action in a US district court.[52]

III RELEVANT CASE LAW

Summarized in this section are significant judicial and administrative interpretations pertaining to certification marks, followed by those regarding collective marks. Because both types of marks are to be given the "same effect as are trademarks,"[53] they are subject to many of the same defenses to infringement such as aesthetic functionality,[54] nominative fair use,[55] and the first sale doctrine.[56] However, this section will focus on the differences, rather than similarities, between these marks and trademarks.

A *Certification Marks*

The Second Circuit has emphasized the public policy rationales underlying certification marks as follows:

> [T]he certification mark regime protects a further public interest in free and open competition among producers and distributors of the certified product. It protects the market players from the influence of the certification mark owner. … [T]his interest is akin to the public interest in the "full and free use of ideas in the public domain" embodied in the patent laws.[57]

Based on these fundamental principles, the court found a substantial public interest in preventing licensee estoppel between certification mark holders and their licensees, compared to trademark contexts where they have been occasionally upheld.[58] The court permitted a distributor whose license had been terminated by the certification mark holder to challenge whether the latter wielded adequate control over its mark despite a no-challenge clause in the license. To do otherwise, the court indicated, would be to sanction "a non-quality-control related restriction on the sellers of the certified product and other licensees that benefits the mark owner in contravention of the mark owner's obligation not to interfere with a free market for products meeting the certification criteria."[59]

In addition, courts and the USPTO have consistently found that common law rights can inhere in certification marks, just as they can with trademarks, although this recognition has

51 *Trademark Trial and Appeal Board,* USPTO, https://uspto.gov/about-us/organizational-offices/trademark-trial-and-appeal-board.

52 Trademark Trial and Appeal Board Manual of Procedure (TBMP) § 901, https://tbmp.uspto.gov/RDMS/TBMP/current (June 2019).

53 15 USC § 1054 (1999).

54 *Int'l Order of Job's Daughters* v. *Lindeburg & Co.*, 633 F.2d 912 (9th Cir. 1980) (aesthetic functionality doctrine applied to registered collective mark).

55 *Int'l Info. Sys. Sec. Certification Consortium* v. *Sec. Univ., LLC,* 823 F.3d 153 (2d Cir. 2016) (nominative fair use doctrine applied to registered certification mark).

56 *Sebastian Int'l, Inc.* v. *Longs Drug Stores Corp.*, 53 F.3d 1073 (9th Cir. 1995) (first sale doctrine applied to registered collective mark).

57 *Idaho Potato Comm'n* v. *M&M Produce Farm, supra* note 43, at 138–39 (citing *Lear* v. *Adkins*); *accord Nat'l Board for Certification in Occupational Therapy* v. *American Occupational Therapy Ass'n*, 24 F. Supp. 2d 494 (D. Md 1998). This quote also suggests that the free flow of truthful commercial speech may also be important in this area of trademark law.

58 *Idaho Potato, supra,* note 57.

59 *Id.* at 139.

been limited so far to certification marks indicating regional origin.[60] While obviously not subject to cancellation from the federal register, common law rights to marks can be litigated within the same basic statutory framework as registered marks, under the aegis of section 43(a).[61]

As noted above, section 14(3) of the Lanham Act provides numerous bases for cancellation of marks, even when incontestable,[62] and section 14(5) provides additional bases for cancellation of certification marks.[63] The interpretation of these provisions constitutes the richest area of decisional law on certification marks, particularly the question whether the certification mark holder has exerted sufficient control over the mark. A recent precedential opinion of the TTAB summarized the extant case law involving control:

> The statute does not define "control." Case law has interpreted this provision in two ways. One is that the owner of the mark has, implicitly or explicitly, given permission to others to use the mark without ensuring that their products or services meet the certification mark owner's standards. … The second interpretation of this provision is akin to the mark becoming generic, i.e., that the certification mark owner has failed to control use by third parties to the extent that the mark no longer acts as an indicator of source, or more particularly, as an indicator of certification of the products or services. …
>
> The question is whether the control is adequate[, that is,] "the owner must take reasonable steps, under all the circumstances of the case, to prevent the public from being misled."[64]

As explained by the Federal Circuit, the issue of reasonable control is highly fact-dependent, and "is entirely consistent with the precedent of this court, which speaks in terms of 'adequate control' … as well as 'sufficient control[,]' [which] are, in effect, shorthand expressions to denote a flexible standard of reasonableness based on the totality of the facts and circumstances."[65] And as the court also recognized, "[i]n the case of a certification mark registrant, the risk of misleading the public may be even greater because a certification mark registration sets forth specific representations about the manufacture and characteristics of the goods to which the mark is applied."[66]

A second basis for finding lack of control by the certification mark holder is genericism, which is also a basis for cancellation for all types of marks regardless of incontestable status[67] as a well as a basis for denying initial registration of a mark.[68] A recent district court decision elaborated upon the genericism test specific to the context of certification marks: "A certification term … is

60 *Black Hills Jewelry Mfg. Co.* v. *Gold Rush, Inc.*, 633 F.2d 746 (8th Cir. 1980); *Fla.* v. *Real Juices, Inc.*, 330 F. Supp. 428 (MD Fla. 1971); *Inst. Nat'l Des Appellations d'Origine* v. *Brown-Forman Corp.*, 47 USPQ 2d 1875, 1885 (TTAB 1998); *Pillsbury-Washburn Flour Mills Co.* v. *Eagle*, 86 Fed. Rep. 608, 618 (7th Cir. 1898) (cited by Belson, *supra* note 1, at 23); *see also* 3 McCarthy on Trademarks and Unfair Competition § 19:90 (4th ed. 2008); Restatement (Third) of Unfair Competition § 11 (1995)); *but see* Smit, *supra* note 1 (arguing against recognition); *see also Syndicat des Proprietaires Viticulteurs de Chateauneuf-du-Pape* v. *Pasquier desVignes*, 107 USPQ 2D 1930 (Trademark Trial & App. Bd. June 14, 2013) (finding lack of evidence to support common law rights).

61 15 USC § 1125(a) (2012).

62 *Id.* § 1064(3) (2006).

63 *Id.* § 1064(4) (2006).

64 *Swiss Watch Int'l, Inc.* v. *Fed. of the Swiss Watch Indust.*, *supra* note 11, at 1739–40 (citing *Tea Board of India* v. *Republic of Tea Inc.*; *Midwest Plastic Fabricators*; and *Engineered Mechanical Services, Inc.* v. *Applied Mechanical Technology, Inc.*, 584 F. Supp. 1149, 223 USPQ 324 (MD La. 1984) ("The owner of a mark is not required to constantly monitor every nook and cranny of the entire nation and to fire both barrels of his shotgun instantly upon spotting a possible infringer")).

65 *Midwest Plastic Fabricators, Inc.* v. *Underwriters Labs. Inc.*, 906 F.2d 1568, 1572–73 (Fed. Cir. 1990).

66 *Id.* at 1572.

67 15 USC § 1065 (2010).

68 *Id.* § 1052(e) (2006).

generic when customers do not associate it with a particular certifying entity's standard, but rather an entire class of certifying entities' standards."[69]

The question of genericism of geographic certification marks has been somewhat fraught because section 2(e) embodies an inherent tension: on the one hand, it prohibits registration of "primarily geographically descriptive" marks but, on the other hand, it allows "indications of regional origin" as a nod to treaty obligations to protect GIs.[70] In upholding an injunction against an importer of cheese labeled as "Roquefort" that was not in fact produced in the Roquefort region of France, the Second Circuit found no genuine issue of fact "concerning the existence of generic meaning, i.e., whether the term 'Roquefort' has acquired principal significance as a description of blue-mold sheep's milk regardless of its origin and without reference to the method of curing employed in the limestone caves of Roquefort, France." In doing so, it asserted:

> [A] geographical name registered as a certification mark must continue to indicate the regional origin, mode of manufacture, etc. of the goods upon which it is used, just as a trade-mark must continue to identify a producer. . . .
>
> When the meaning of a mark that had previously served as an indication of origin changes so that its principal significance to purchasers is that of indicating the nature or class of goods and its function as an indication of origin is subservient thereto, it is no longer a mark but rather is a generic term.[71]

For certification marks, as with trademarks, the "test for determining whether a mark is generic is its primary significance to the relevant public."[72] Determining the "relevant public" is similar to that for trademarks – that is, the public that consumes the identified products. Nonetheless, this determination can have a spin specific to geographic certification marks. In a precedential opinion involving a French wine appellation of origin, the TTAB stated:

> [T]he issue is not whether the public is expressly aware of the certification function of the mark or the certification process underlying use of the mark, but rather is whether the public understands that goods bearing the mark come only from the region named in the mark. If use of the designation in fact is controlled by the certifier and limited to products meeting the certifier's standards of regional origin, and if purchasers understand the designation to refer only to products which are produced in the particular region, and not to products produced elsewhere, then the designation functions as a regional certification mark. *Neither the statute nor the case law requires that purchasers also be expressly aware of the term's certification function, per se.*[73]

Finally, recent case law suggests that the infringement test for certification marks may differ from the test for trademarks, contrary to some prior precedent.[74] The Second Circuit recently found

[69] *Basel Action Network* v. *Int'l Ass'n of Elecs. Recyclers*, 793 F.Supp. 2d 1200, 1204 (WD Wa 2011).

[70] 15 USC § 1052(e) (2006).

[71] *Cmty. of Roquefort* v. *William Faehndrich, Inc.*, 303 F.2d 494, 497 (2d Cir. 1962) (emphasis added); *accord Luxco, Inc.* v. *Consejo Regulador del Tequila*, AC, 2017 TTAB LEXIS 174 (TTAB 2017) ("a certification mark identifying geographic origin will not be deemed to be a generic term if it retains its ability to designate geographic source").

[72] *Tea Bd. of India* v. *Republic of Tea, Inc.*, 80 USPQ 2D (BNA) 1881 (TTAB 2006).

[73] *Institut Nat'l des Appellations d'Origine* v. *Brown-Forman Corp.*, 47 USPQ 2d 1875, 1885 (TTAB 1998) (emphasis added). *See also Consorzio del Prosciutto di Parma* v. *Parma Sausage Prods.*, 23 USPQ 2D 1894 (TTAB 1992) (establishing a bright-line test for the timing of the consuming public's awareness of the regional origin of a geographic certification mark, that is, the date of registration); *In re Cooperativa Produttori Latte E Fontina Valle D'Acosta*, 230 USPQ 131 (TTAB 1986) (holding that a type of cheese is generic because non-certified producers outside that region use the term to identify non-certified cheeses).

[74] *In re Fla. Citrus Comm'n*, 1968 TTAB LEXIS 198, 160 USPQ (BNA) 495 (TTAB 1968) ("There is nothing in the language of Section 2(d) which mandates or warrants application of one level of likelihood of confusion analysis

that the determination of likelihood of confusion under section 32[75] has a potentially broader ambit for certification marks: "As is plain from this statutory text, the Act's protection against infringement is not limited to any particular type of consumer confusion, much less exclusively to confusion as to source. Rather, the Lanham Act protects against numerous types of confusion, including confusion regarding affiliation or sponsorship."[76] The Court went on to state that a certification mark can be infringed by the use of the mark on services or goods that have not in fact been certified, as well as the incorporation of a certification mark into a composite trademark, which might be likely to cause confusion as to sponsorship, affiliation or connection.[77]

In summary, although certification marks are subject to the same overall legal framework in the United States as trademarks, distinct differences exist in the judicial treatment of each type of mark.

B *Collective Marks*

Certification marks are often grouped together with collective marks because both types of marks denote characteristics related to being part of a group. However, unlike certification marks, collective marks are either trademarks or service marks, in which the underlying product or service is affiliated with "members of a cooperative, an association, or other collective group or organization,"[78] such as a union, rather than an individual mark holder. As described in detail in the TMEP, a "collective trademark or collective service mark indicates origin of goods or services in the members of a group. A collective membership mark indicates membership in an organization. A certification mark certifies characteristics or features of goods or services."[79]

Some confusion surrounds the distinction between collective and certification marks because both marks may communicate something "group-like" about the quality of the goods or services. Collective marks *primarily* indicate that the source of the goods or services is an organization or a member of the organization that owns the collective mark. By virtue of such organizations mandating certain standards for membership, collective marks may *secondarily* communicate certain information about the quality of the goods or services. In contrast, certification marks may be used by anybody within a group providing a particular type of goods or services so long as these comply with the standards established by the owner of the certification mark; thus certification marks *primarily* communicate that the goods or services satisfy those certification standards.

Only a handful of cases address collective marks. The Federal Circuit, speaking through Judge Rich, reinforced that individual (as opposed to associational) proprietary ownership of collective marks is impermissible according to the terms of the Lanham Act, whereas this proscription does not apply to certification marks.[80] Furthermore, the District of New Jersey

(i.e., the du Pont analysis) in cases where the plaintiff's mark is a trademark or service mark, but a different and more limited likelihood of confusion analysis in cases where the plaintiff's mark is a certification mark"); *accord Inst. Nat'l Des Appellations D'Origine* v. *Brown-Forman Corp.*, 1998 TTAB LEXIS 122, 47 USPQ 2D (BNA) 1875 (TTAB 1998).

[75] 15 USC § 1114 (2005).

[76] *Int'l Info. Sys. Sec. Certification Consortium* v. *Sec. Univ.*, LLC, 823 F.3d 153, 163 (2d Cir. 2016); Sandra Edelman, *How to Infringe a Certification Mark*, THE TMCA (June 16, 2006), https://thetmca.com/how-to-infringe-a-certification-mark-the-second-circuit-counts-the-ways/.

[77] *Id.*

[78] 15 USC § 1127 (2006).

[79] TMEP § 1306.09(a), Distinction Between Certification Mark and Collective Mark.

[80] *F.R. Lepage Bakery, Inc.* v. *Roush Bakery Prods. Co.*, 851 F.2d 351, 354 (Fed. Cir. 1988) ("A collective mark is said to be 'a trademark or service mark used by the members of a cooperative, an association or other group or organization.' It follows logically that only such an organization as is indicated by the statutory definition can become the owner of a collective mark and as a corollary only such an organization, after acquiring ownership by use, can obtain a collective

recently stated that "a collective trademark or service mark is an indication of the specific commercial source of the goods or services,"[81] albeit a source that is a collective.

The TTAB has also stated that the so-called anti-use-by-ownership rule applicable to certification marks does not apply to collective marks, and therefore true collective mark owners can use and license collective marks on their own goods and services.[82] This makes sense as a policy matter, since the anti-competition concerns relevant to certification marks are not as significant for collective marks that are used primarily to signal membership within an organization that produces goods or services, such as membership within a union, for example. Indeed, the owner of a collective mark may exclude others from using a mark even if they have the same characteristics as the mark owners.[83]

Thus collective and certification marks are mutually exclusive; a mark cannot be both a collective and certification mark, because the certification mark holder is prohibited by section 14(5) from using the mark as an indication of its own goods or services, whereas the organization that owns a collective mark may use the collective mark on its own goods or services.[84] As Belson points out, some of the conflation of collective with certification marks stem from the close relationships between association and standardization.[85] The boundary between collective marks and certification marks is challenged where, for example, a membership association may be using the collective mark as a certification of a uniform standard provided by its members.[86] However, such hybrid use does not provide a basis for challenging an otherwise incontestable collective mark on the basis of inadequate control.[87]

IV POLICY ISSUES AND CONCLUSION

As stated earlier, certification marks and trademarks coexist somewhat awkwardly within the US legal framework, which has evolved from the tort of passing off to "the twin objectives of minimizing consumer search costs ... and preserving market competition."[88] The primary

mark registration. For the group or organization to part with such a mark or its registration by assignment creates an anomalous situation if attempted to be made to a non-organization type of corporation or to an individual").

[81] *Opticians Ass'n of Am.* v. *Indep. Opticians of Am., Inc.*, 734 F. Supp. 1171, 2027 (DNJ 1990).

[82] *Roush Bakery Prods. Co.* v. *F. R. Lepage Bakery, Inc.*, 13 USPQ 2D 1045, 1051 (TTAB 1989).

[83] *Opticians Ass'n of Am.* v. *Indep. Opticians of Am.*, 920 F.2d 187, 195 (3d Cir. 1990).

[84] 15 USC § 1064(5)(B); *see also* TMEP 1306.06(a), Distinction Between Certification Mark and Collective Mark; *In re Fla. Citrus Comm'n*, 1968 TTAB LEXIS 198, 160 USPQ (BNA) 495 (TTAB 1968) ("A reading of the legislature hearings leading to the enactment of the Lanham Act reveals an intent to preclude the owner of a certification mark from producing or selling goods or services in connection with which the certification mark is to be used. That is, to prevent a party from certifying his own goods or services. It also appears therefrom that there was a continuing deep concern on the part of the framers of the Statute over the possible use of the certification mark as weapon to create a monopoly in a particular field and to perpetuate a fraud upon the purchasing public; and that they attempted through the proscriptive language in Sections 4 and 14(e) (2) to preclude the possibility of such fraudulent misuse occurring through the sanction of a Federal registration").

[85] *See* BELSON, *supra* note 1, at 83.

[86] *Opticians Ass'n of Am.* v. *Indep. Opticians of Am., Inc.*, 734 F. Supp. 1171, 1179) (DNJ 1990); ("purported collective membership mark must lose qualities of a collective membership mark and assume qualities of a certification mark before its designation will be deemed improper"); *see also* Am. Speech-Language-Hearing Ass'n, 1984 TTAB LEXIS 19, 224 USPQ (BNA) 798 (TTAB 1984).

[87] *Opticians*, *supra* note 83, at 194 ("section 14(5) defenses are only available when a challenged mark was *registered* as a certification mark. The ... marks were not registered as certification marks, and must therefore be classified according to their actual registrations for the purposes of applying section 14").

[88] David E. Adelman & Graham W. Austin, *Trademarks & Private Environmental Governance*, 93 NOTRE DAME L. REV. (2017), https://ssrn.com/abstract=3036611 or http://dx.doi.org/10.2139/ssrn.3036611; *see also* BELSON, *supra* note 1, at 213–42 (discussing eco-labels).

reliance on the source-signaling of trademarks to effectuate these dual policy aims overlooks the trust-signaling roles of certification marks. Certification marks can promote the free flow of commercial information by allowing companies to provide consumers with potentially accurate information about their products (e.g., location, style of manufacture). Thus certification marks have the potential to increase social welfare through consumer choices of goods or services representing higher levels of food safety, health, and environment (e.g., organic labels and certifications), labor conditions (e.g., fair trade), general safety (e.g., Underwriters Laboratories), compliance with religious practices (e.g., halal or kosher), or other market-relevant characteristics that consumers cannot assess easily or immediately on the face of these goods or services.

A market-based approach to regulation relies heavily on the role of marks such as these to accurately convey product qualities, which are often aligned with standards applicable across borders. Yet the global regulatory governance system is not adequately incorporated into the dominant US legal framework surveyed in this chapter. In the EU, by contrast, some progress has been made to centralize some of the standards signifying high safety, health, and environmental requirements via "CE marking," for example.[89]

As more weight is being placed on marks to ensure robustness of standards associated with credence attributes of goods and services, adequate legal oversight of the trust functions of marks is underdeveloped relative to that of trademarks. Three major issues stand out: (1) the primary legal doctrines in many legal regimes including the United States focus either on consumer confusion or erosion of business goodwill, without recognizing the critical importance of compliance with the producers' stated or implied process standards; (2) relatedly, these types of marks cannot be differentiated from the more predominant trademark functions as signals of source or origin of manufacturing; and (3) as a result, firms and producers are not often optimally incentivized to rigorously ensure the process qualities of these products.[90] Enforcement of standards in the United States is horizontally driven by market competitors through the Lanham Act's control requirements. As the previous section demonstrates, these statutory requirements have not resulted in the cancellation of many (if any) registered certification marks, due to lack of enforcement. And at least one court has found that inadequate control may not be used as a defense to infringement.[91] Because of these omissions, commentators have suggested various ways to increase the robustness of standards enforcement as well as transparency of standards to the consumers. Their suggestions include (but are not limited to) strengthening the government's gatekeeping and enforcement roles, increasing incentives for more rigorous private standard-setting, and liberalizing standing so that private parties other than narrowly drawn categories of competitors can challenge misleading certification marks.[92]

Other factors, however, may discourage the emergence of legal reforms associated with certification marks. Liability issues exist in the form of breach of warranty and strict products

89 European Commission, CE Marking, https://ec.europa.eu/growth/single-market/ce-marking_en ("The letters 'CE' appear on many products traded on the extended Single Market in the European Economic Area (EEA). They signify that products sold in the EEA have been assessed to meet high safety, health, and environmental protection requirements"); *see also* Mehmet Cetik, *Do Europe's Product Labels Converge? The Case of EU Ecolabel, EU Energy Label and CE Marking* (Oct. 25, 2011). TILEC Discussion Paper No. 2011-048, https://ssrn.com/abstract=1949080 or http://dx.doi.org/10.2139/ssrn.1949080.

90 Adelman & Austin, *supra* note 88, at 4–5 ("Most importantly, legal doctrines that allow conventional trademarks to proliferate undermine the efficacy of certification marks when they cause consumers to become overwhelmed by competing standards and technical information even if they are not confused about the sources of goods or services").

91 *Opticians Ass'n of Am. v. Indep. Opticians of Am.*, 920 F.2d 187, 194 (3d Cir. 1990) ("Even if we assume arguendo that the district court correctly found the ... marks to be certification marks by reason of their use, section 14(5) remains inapplicable [because they were not registered as such]").

92 *See, e.g.*, Fromer, *supra* note 1; Chon, *supra* note 1, Adelman & Austin, *supra* note 88.

liability claims, for instance.[93] Moreover, vigilant certification mark holders could be subject to claims of negligent misrepresentation,[94] false advertising, and/or other reputation-based torts by non-certified producers. Simultaneously, however, environmentally and health-conscious consumers increasingly make decisions based on certification marks and would prefer more information than is currently available.[95] Thus the benefits of market differentiation and increased market share driven by these types of marks could outweigh their possible drawbacks. Another set of unresolved issues relates to digital marking of products and services.[96] While these issues are beyond the scope of this chapter, it is important to note the increasing pervasiveness of digital commerce along with the challenges for far-flung consumers and producers of goods and services to assess and/or guarantee authenticity.

Although resting somewhat uneasily within the applicable legal framework within the United States, certification and collective marks are potentially useful tools for addressing the complexity of cross-border trade and digital commerce. As a result, it will be intriguing to see how these types of marks continue to evolve to meet newer versions of these ancient functions.[97]

[93] Belson, *supra* note 1, at 86–142 (summarizing multiple bases for product certifier liability).

[94] *Water & Sanitation Health, Inc.* v. *Rainforest All., Inc.*, 2015 US Dist. LEXIS 182334 (WD Wa. 2015); *Handsome Brook Farm* v. *Human Farm Animal Care*, 700 Fed. Appx. 251 (4th Cir. 2017) (unpublished opinion).

[95] *See, e.g.*, Organic Foods and Beverages Market Analysis by Product (Fruits & Vegetables, Meat, Fish & Poultry, Dairy Products, Frozen & Processed Food), Organic Beverages (Non-Dairy, Coffee & Tea, Beer & Wine)), and Segment Forecasts, 2018–2025, GRAND VIEW RESEARCH, at https://grandviewresearch.com/industry-analysis/organic-foods-beverages-market (Apr. 2017).

[96] *See* BELSON, *supra* note 1, at 243–63.

[97] *See id.*, at 9–14 (describing the regulatory origins of certification and collective marks in guilds beginning in the eleventh century).

VI

The Relationship between Trademark Law and Advertising Law

19

Trademark Law and Advertising Law in the European Union: Conflicts and Convergence

*Ansgar Ohly**

I TRADEMARK LAW AND UNFAIR COMPETITION LAW IN THE EUROPEAN UNION: A TALE OF TWO REALMS

Trademark law and unfair competition law share common purposes. Causing a likelihood of confusion with another trader's mark is the classical and typical case of trademark infringement. At the same time, creating confusion is one of the examples of unfair competition listed in Article 10*bis* of the Paris Convention for the Protection of Industrial Property (Paris Convention). In recent decades, trademark law has extended beyond this core area. In both the United States and the European Union, well-known marks are now protected against dilution, and in the EU well-known marks are also protected against misappropriation. Before trademark law entered this field, protection against denigration and misappropriation was mainly provided via unfair competition law, although national laws differ in this respect, particularly as regards misappropriation. It thus comes as no surprise that US law considers both fields of law as closely related.[1] They both protect traders and consumers, and the Lanham Act not only protects registered trademarks but also prohibits misleading advertising and acts which are likely to cause confusion.[2] Some of the leading treatises cover both trademark and unfair competition law.[3]

In the EU, there is a wider gulf between both fields of law. There are four reasons for this. First, the law of registered trademarks has been fully harmonised, whereas unfair competition law remained almost entirely domestic until the turn of the millennium. While the Unfair Commercial Practices Directive of 2005 (UCPD)[4] harmonised national provisions on unfair practices in relations between businesses and consumers (B2C), and while the Directive on Misleading and Comparative Advertising of 1997, re-enacted in 2006 (MCAD),[5] introduced common European provisions on comparative advertising, significant areas of substantive law and remedies against

* Professor of Private Law, Intellectual Property and Competition Law at the Ludwig Maximilian University of Munich, Visiting Professor at the University of Oxford.

[1] *See* Chapter 20 by Rebecca Tushnet in this volume.

[2] 15 USC § 1125(a)(1) (2012).

[3] *See* J. Thomas McCarthy, McCarthy on Trademarks and Unfair Competition (5th ed. 2017); Louis Altman & Malla Pollack, Callmann on Unfair Competition, Trademarks and Monopolies (2016).

[4] Directive 2005/29/EC of the European Parliament and of the Council of May 11, 2005 concerning unfair business-to-consumer commercial practices in the internal market and amending Council Directive 84/450/EEC, Directives 97/7/EC, 98/27/EC and 2002/65/EC of the European Parliament and of the Council and Regulation (EC) No. 2006/2004 of the European Parliament and of the Council, 2005 OJ (L 149) 22.

[5] Directive 2006/114/EC of the European Parliament and of the Council of Dec. 12, 2006 concerning misleading and comparative advertising, 2006 OJ (L 376) 21.

unfair commercial practices remain unharmonised. The links between trademark law and unfair competition law were not least severed because the Court of Justice of the European Union (CJEU), in its role as chief interpreter of EU law, shaped an autonomous European trademark policy, whereas the national approaches to unfair competition law in general and to misleading practices in particular still differ considerably.[6] Second, this difference is mirrored by institutional competences in the EU. While trademark law, as a part of intellectual property law, falls within the competence of the Directorate-General GROW (Internal Market, Industry, Entrepreneurship and SMEs), the UCPD follows the logic of EU consumer protection law, which, in the European Commission, is administered by the Directorate-General JUST (Justice and Consumers). Third, EU trademark law has, for better or worse, gone through a process of "emancipation and expansion."[7] EU trademark law has developed into a full intellectual property right. This has impacted the scope of trademark rights as well as remedies. Consumer protection is advanced as a purpose of trademark law to a lesser extent in the EU than in the United States. Some continental European jurisdictions have a long tradition of protecting goodwill against misappropriation, whereas the economic analysis of the law, in particular the search cost rationale, has only recently received attention in Europe. Fourth, one important connection between both areas, namely provisions which protect traders against passing off, is missing in EU law. Despite some similarities in principle, there are significant differences in detail between the common law tort of passing off, the French notion of "confusion" and the German tort of causing confusion by sale of imitated articles.[8]

This chapter will give an outline of how EU trademark law and unfair competition law have developed and how this development has, at first, led to an estrangement between both areas (Section II). But it will also try to show that there has been a significant recent trend towards convergence. Analysis of trademark confusion has arguably become less formal and more context-sensitive and has, hence, adopted some characteristics of unfair competition methodology (Section III). Comparative advertising is governed by the MCAD, which set out to liberalise the law of comparative advertising. But for reasons explored below, this attempt backfired, and the MCAD became unduly protective of the reputation of luxury goods. The directive has had a strong impact on trademark law, such that both areas of law have converged in this respect (Section IV).

II THE PIONEER AND THE LATECOMER OF HARMONISATION

Trademark law is one of the pioneers of European harmonisation. The Trade Mark Directive of 1988,[9] meanwhile newly enacted in 2015 (TMD),[10] is the first directive which harmonised substantial parts of intellectual property law; the Community Trade Mark Regulation of 1993,[11]

[6] *E.g.*, Case C-661/11, *Martin Y Paz Diffusion SA* v. *Depuydt*, 2013 ECR I-577, §§ 54–62, where defendant was prevented from relying on national doctrines of unfair competition against claim for trademark infringement.

[7] As Andreas Sattler shows in his historical analysis. *See generally*, ANDREAS SATTLER, EMANZIPATION UND EXPANSION DES MARKENRECHTS (2015).

[8] *See* Ansgar Ohly, *The Freedom of Imitation and Its Limits – A European Perspective*, 41 INT'L REV. OF INTELL. PROP. & COMPETITION LAW 506 (2010).

[9] First Council Directive 89/104/EEC of Dec. 21, 1988 to approximate the laws of the member states relating to trademarks, 1998 OJ (L 40) 1.

[10] Directive 2015/2436 of the European Parliament and of the Council of Dec. 16, 2015 to approximate the laws of the member states relating to trademarks, 2015 OJ (L 336) 1.

[11] Council Regulation 40/94 of Dec. 20, 1993 on the Community trademark, 1993 OJ (L 011) 1 (EC) [hereinafter TMR 1993].

re-enacted in 2017 as the EU Trade Mark Regulation (EUTMR),[12] created the Office for Harmonisation in the Internal Market, now renamed the EU Intellectual Property Office, which grants EU-wide trademarks. The TMD and the EUTMR influence each other. The infringement provisions in both instruments are worded almost identically, and they are interpreted similarly by the CJEU.[13] The TMD aims at full harmonisation. Thus, the conditions of infringement, in particular, are the same in all member states.

Unfair competition law, on the other hand, was the orphan on EU harmonisation for a long time. There are several reasons why harmonisation in this area proved to be more difficult than in intellectual property law. First, the systematic approaches between the member states differ significantly.[14] Some states, for example Germany, Spain and Sweden, follow a monistic approach. They have enacted single-market practices or unfair competition acts which protect competitors, consumers and the general public. Other states, for example France and Italy, have dualist models in that they distinguish between consumer protection law and unfair competition law.[15] The former has been consolidated in consumer protection acts, whereas the latter is a part of general civil responsibility. In the common law countries, of which now only Ireland remains in the EU, "unfair competition" is not commonly used as a technical term.[16] Economic torts such as passing off protect traders and separate legislation protects consumers, but self-regulation of advertising practices plays a stronger role than in most continental European states. Second, and relatedly, the means of enforcement differ. German law largely relies on enforcement through competitors, trade and consumer organisations, which are provided with a civil right of action by the Act against Unfair Competition. In consequence, unfair competition law is a practically important branch of commercial law, and there is much litigation. In 2017, the German Federal Supreme Court decided forty-four unfair competition cases. In contrast, in France consumer protection law is largely implemented by means of criminal sanctions. In the common law countries self-regulation plays an important role; many cases of misleading or comparative advertising which would trigger litigation in Germany are dealt with by the self-regulatory bodies. Third, unfair competition law is closely related to general tort law, which has not been harmonised in the EU. Fourth, legal policies as to the right amount of judicial intervention into market processes differ significantly between countries with a high level of market regulation and more liberal systems. In short, European unfair competition law is a fascinating field of research for comparative lawyers, but a nightmare for harmonisation. Due to prevailing differences between member states, European unfair competition law lacks the teleological coherence that advertising law has in the United States and in other common law countries.

Nevertheless, important progress was made in the early millennium years. In 2005, the Directive on Unfair Commercial Practices (UCPD)[17] was passed. The UCPD is limited to B2C relations and protects consumers from misleading and aggressive practices. This subcategory of unfair competition law will be referred to as "unfair commercial practices law."

[12] Regulation 2017/1001 of the European Parliament and of the Council of June 14, 2017 on the European Union trademark, 2017 OJ (L 154) 1.

[13] *See* Graeme B. Dinwoodie, *The Europeanization of Trade Mark Law*, in THE EUROPEANIZATION OF INTELLECTUAL PROPERTY LAW 75, 86–90 (Ansgar Ohly & Justine Pila eds., 2013).

[14] *See* Ansgar Ohly, *Unfair Competition (Basic Principles)*, in MAX PLANCK ENCYCLOPEDIA OF EUROPEAN PRIVATE LAW, VOL. II, at 1712–15 (Jürgen Basedow, Klaus J. Hopt, Reinhard Zimmermann & Andreas Stier eds., 2012).

[15] *See* Sylvie Nérisson, *France*, in INTERNATIONAL HANDBOOK ON UNFAIR COMPETITION, § 11, paras. 5, 24–51 (Frauke Henning-Bodewig ed., 2013).

[16] *See generally* Richard Arnold, *English Unfair Competition Law*, 44 INT'L REV. OF INTELL. PROP. AND COMPETITION LAW 63 (2013).

[17] MCCARTHY, *supra* note 3.

At its heart is what could be called a "three-step test."[18] A practice is unfair under Article 5 UCPD when it is (1) proscribed by a "black list" of thirty-one cases, (2) misleading or aggressive as defined in Articles 6 to 9 UCPD or (3) unfair according to the general prohibition of unfair practices, defined as acts which are contrary to the requirements of professional diligence and materially distort the economic behaviour of consumers.[19] Conditions of unfairness are fully harmonised. Member states are precluded from setting either lower or higher standards.[20] But the UCPD leaves it to the member states to decide about the means of enforcement. They can choose between criminal and administrative enforcement or private remedies, or combine the two.[21]

The other important directive, the Directive on Misleading Advertising of 1984, was amended in 1997 to encompass comparative advertising. In 2006 it was re-enacted as the Directive on Misleading and Comparative Advertising.[22] Its initial purpose was the protection of traders, consumers and the public, but since the enactment of the UCPD, EU law has rather followed the French model and distinguished between consumer protection and protection of traders, to which the MCAD was reduced in 2005. While the MCAD only sets a minimum standard with respect to misleading advertising, the conditions of comparative advertising, analysed in more detail below, have fully harmonised.

III TRADEMARK LAW AND MISLEADING PRACTICES

A *The Statutory Framework*

The infringement provisions in the EUTMR and the TMD are similar. According to Articles 9(2) EUTMR, 10(2) TMD, there are three kinds of infringement: (a) the use of a sign which is identical with the trademark for identical goods or services ("double identity"), (b) the use of a sign which is identical with or similar to the trademark for at least similar goods or services where such use causes a likelihood of confusion ("likelihood of confusion"), and (c) the use of a sign which is identical with or similar to the trademark for any kinds of goods or services where such use takes unfair advantage or causes detriment to the reputation or the distinctiveness of the trademark ("dilution and misappropriation").

In unfair commercial practices law, Article 6 UCPD prohibits misleading practices, defined as commercial practices "which either contain false information or which are likely to deceive the average consumer, even if the information is factually correct, and which are likely to cause consumers to take a transactional decision that they would not have taken otherwise."

According to Article 6(2) UCPD, creating confusion is also regarded as a misleading practice. So, at first sight, both areas of law seem to live in perfect harmony, as they both prohibit causing a likelihood of confusion. But a closer analysis discloses significant differences, which harbour potential for conflicts. First, the UCPD does not provide for any defences. It is inspired by the goal of strong consumer protection and does not take scenarios into account in which some degree of consumer confusion may be inevitable. Thus, in countries which allow enforcement by civil actions, trademark owners who fail to enforce their right may be tempted

[18] This author has, of course, misappropriated this term from international copyright law.

[19] UCPD, *supra* note 4, art. 5.

[20] Case C-261/07 and C-299/07, *VTB VAB NV* v. *Total Belgium NV*, 2009 ECR I-244, § 52; Case C-304/08, *Zentrale zur Bekämpfung des unlauteren Wettbewerbs eV* v. *Plus Warenhandelsgesellschaft mbH*, 2010 ECR 12, § 41.

[21] UCPD, *supra* note 4, art. 11.

[22] *Supra*, note 5.

to rely on the provisions against misleading practices to avoid trademark exceptions. This can result in conflicts with trademark policy, as the German *Hard Rock Café* case, discussed below at Section III.2, illustrates. Second, the classical test of trademark confusion is rather formal and strongly reminiscent of the determination of scope in other areas of intellectual property law. The unfair competition analysis is more fact-sensitive. A court will look at all the circumstances of the case. Both perspectives can lead to different results, although there are indications that the CJEU is moving toward a more competition- or market-oriented assessment of trademark confusion, as the *Google France* and *Specsavers* cases, discussed below at Section III.3, indicate.

B Hard Rock Café: *Conflicting Policies*

Until recently[23] there was a Hard Rock Café in the main pedestrian zone of Heidelberg, which was not a member of the Hard Rock Group and which used the Hard Rock name and logo without a licence from the trademark owner. This is surprising, given that Germany is not exactly known as a counterfeiters' haven. The reason is that the Heidelberg café was opened at a time when the Hard Rock Café in London was the only one in Europe, and long before the name "Hard Rock Café" was registered as a trademark in Germany or, for that matter, became internationally well-known. Since the UK trademark was territorially restricted, the Heidelberg café owner had the earlier rights for Germany. The conflict is evident. Under the logic of trademark law, the owner of the earlier rights prevails. Moreover, since the Hard Rock Group had not taken any action for a long time, the doctrine of laches also worked in the café owner's favour. Consumer protection law, on the other hand, is ahistorical. It does not look at the genesis of the marks unless consumers know about it. Heidelberg being one of Germany's top tourist destinations, most visitors, many of them from the United States or Asia, did not know about the café's history and tended to think that it was genuine.[24] Thus consumer policy militated in favour of granting a remedy.

This conflict is difficult to solve, mainly because the UCPD does not take account of the fact that the advertiser may have a justification for engaging in misleading conduct. The German Federal Supreme Court first acknowledged a parallel application of trademark law and unfair competition law, thereby giving up its earlier theory that trademark law took precedence over advertising law when the claim was based on a likelihood of confusion. Second, the court applied the trademark law doctrine of laches and extended it to unfair competition law.[25] On this basis, the court allowed the defendant to continue operating the restaurant, but held that unfair competition law imposed a duty on him to inform consumers by disclaimers on its website and in its offline advertising about the fact that the establishment was not related to the trademark owner, in order to dispel confusion as effectively as possible without closing down the restaurant.[26]

[23] After a settlement with the Hard Rock Group, the café closed in March 2017.

[24] The ratings at www.tripadvisor.com provide anecdotal evidence. When I checked the website on Nov. 23, 2018, headlines of some of the first posts were: "Not a Real HRC"; "Fake!! Bad service, poor quality food, long waiting time"; "Americans, you agree that this terrible place be called HRC?!?"

[25] Bundesgerichtshof [BGH] [Federal Court of Justice], Aug. 15, 2013, I ZR 188/11, translated in 45 Int'l Rev. of Intell. Prop. and Competition Law 484 (2014). *See also* Birgit Clark, *Between a Rock and a Hard Place? Bundesgerichtshof Decides Hard Rock Café Trade Mark Dispute*, 9 J. Intell. Prop. L. & Prac. 544 (2014).

[26] The Federal Supreme Court distinguished between operation of the restaurant, which it considered to be a single, ongoing infringement, and sale of merchandise, with respect to which the court considered each sale to be a separate infringing act. Thus, the doctrine of laches applied with respect to operation of the restaurant, whereas the sale of merchandise was found to be infringing. Several commentators have criticised this distinction. *See* Michael

The *Hard Rock* case illustrates why the internal logics of both areas differ in some respects. Modern EU trademark law has many of the hallmarks of intellectual property law. First, it mainly serves the trademark owner's interests, whereas competitor and consumer interests in the free use of signs only enter the equation as limiting factors. Second, it is historical in the sense that priority is one of the main criteria for resolving collisions between two signs. Thirdly, in bilateral relations between the trademark owner and the potential infringer it seems fair to apply a doctrine of laches: the right owner can be expected to enforce their rights within a reasonable time, and after that period the interests of the potential infringer in using the sign may prevail. EU unfair commercial practices law, on the other hand, is informed by the logic of consumer protection law. It mainly protects consumers, although Recital 8 to the UCPD acknowledges that it may indirectly also benefit competitors. Second, the main benchmark for resolving disputes is the perception of the average consumer at the time at which the offer is made. Considerations of priority are immaterial, as long as they do not have an impact on how the consumer understands a particular advertisement. Thirdly, the doctrine of laches makes much less sense in multi-person scenarios. While the Hard Rock Group can be blamed for not having sued the Heidelberg publican earlier, American, Chinese or Japanese tourists who are deceived about the affiliation of the Heidelberg café cannot.

The law is called upon to create a reasonable equilibrium between all interests. To borrow a phrase from German constitutional law, "practical concordance" should be achieved between trademark law and unfair practices law. The German Federal Supreme Court's judgment at least partly achieves this goal. While its reasoning on the doctrine of laches can be criticised, the result makes sense: the owner can continue operating the café, as dictated by trademark law logic, whereas he must take all reasonable steps to inform consumers about his lack of a commercial connection with the Hard Rock Group, as the logic or consumer protection law requires.

C Google France *and* Specsavers: *From an IP to an Unfair Competition Approach?*

The traditional approach to assessing the likelihood of confusion in EU trademark law is rather formal. The court will look at the similarity of signs, the similarity of goods or services, and the distinctiveness of the mark. These three criteria form a flexible system in which the strength of one criterion can compensate the weakness of another one.[27] Assessment of confusion is thus mainly an abstract and normative exercise,[28] which is reminiscent of the methodology in other areas of intellectual property, where one of the key elements of the infringement analysis is the determination of scope. When the sign is highly similar to the registered trademark, the court is likely to find infringement. What is more, Articles 9(2)(a) EUTMR, 10(2)(a) TMD prohibit the use of an identical sign for identical goods and services per se; proof of a likelihood of confusion is not required.

This can be illustrated by the *Arsenal* case. A trader had sold fan articles which bore the name and the logo of the English Premier League football club FC Arsenal. The name and the logo had been registered as trademarks by the club. The trader made it sufficiently clear that he was

Goldmann, *Zur Verwirkung nach § 242 BGB beim Schutz geschäftlicher Bezeichnungen und im Lauterkeitsrecht*, in 119 Gewerblicher Rechtsschutz und Urheberrecht 657 (2017).

[27] Case C-39/97, *Canon Kabushiki Kaisha* v. *Metro-Goldwyn-Mayer Inc.*, 1998 ECR I-5507; Annette Kur & Martin Senftleben, European Trade Mark Law, §§ 4.328–29, 5.106 (2017).

[28] *See* Kur & Senftleben, *supra* note 27, §§ 5.165–65.181; Ilanah Fhima, *Introducing Reality into Trade Mark Law*, 9 J. Intell. Prop. L. & Prac. 684, 686 (2014).

not selling any official merchandise. Laddie J thought that the name and the logo were not used as trademarks but as "badges of support" and asked the CJEU whether the offer of the fan articles amounted to trademark infringement. The CJEU applied Article 9(2)(a) TMD and held that there was infringement because the signs and the goods were identical.[29] Because of the "double identity" provision, the court did not even have to discuss whether there was a doctrine of "post-sale confusion" in EU law.[30] An unfair competition analysis may well have led to a different result. Consumers knew what they were buying and did not care whether their scarves or shirts had been officially authorised.

Recently, however, there have been signs of convergence. The first group of cases where this tendency can be observed are the keyword advertising cases. They present a challenge because both the advertiser who registers a third person's trademark as a keyword and the search engine operator who sells it use the trademark in an atypical way. Thus, courts on both sides of the Atlantic had to modify their infringement tests in order to factor in context of the use.[31] The CJEU mitigated the rigour of the double identity infringement provision by adding the unwritten requirement that the use must interfere with the functions of the trademark. According to the Court, the main function is the origin function, but other functions such as the advertising, investment, communication and quality function are protected as well.[32] In its leading keyword advertising judgment of 2010, *Google France*, the CJEU thus enquired whether keyword advertising had a negative impact on the origin function, and thus essentially introduced a likelihood of confusion analysis. However, the court did not apply the traditional criteria, but rather drew on transparency obligations,[33] which are set up by the EU Directive on electronic commerce[34] and which are a part of advertising and media law rather than trademark law. On this basis, the CJEU held that the origin function was affected when either the advertisement misled consumers as to a commercial relation between the advertiser and the trademark owner or was unclear and did not allow the consumer to determine whether such a relation existed.[35]

There are several reasons why this approach can be criticised: the transparency obligations on the advertiser are possibly too strict, the CJEU did not provide sufficient guidance to the national courts, and national courts have since reached starkly divergent judgments.[36] But the *Google France* case shows a departure from a formalist approach to a more

[29] Case C-206/01, *Arsenal Football Club plc* v. *Reed*, 2002 ECR I-10273.

[30] There is no well-entrenched or established doctrine of post-sale confusion in EU trademark law. *See* Case C-361/04 P, *Ruiz-Picasso* v. *OHIM*, 2006 ECR 25; Kur & Senftleben, *supra* note 27, §§ 5.131–35.146; Ansgar Ohly, *Post-Sale Confusion?*, in Marktkommunikation zwischen Geistigem Eigentum und Verbraucherschutz, Festschrift für Karl-Heinz Fezer zum 70. Geburtstag 603, 607–09 (Wolfgang Büscher et al. eds., 2016).

[31] *See 1-800 Contacts, Inc.* v. *Lens.com, Inc.*, 722 F.3d 1229, 1242, 1244–45 (10th Cir. 2013); Stacey Dogan, *Principled Standards vs. Boundless Discretion: A Tale of Two Approaches to Intermediary Trademark Liability Online*, 37 Colum. J.L. & Arts 503, 521–22 (2014).

[32] Case C-487/07, *L'Oréal SA* v. *Bellure NV*, 2009 ECR I-5158, § 58. For a critical analysis of the "functions theory," *see* Annette Kur, *Trade Marks Function, Don't They? CJEU Jurisprudence and Unfair Competition Practices*, 45 Int'l Rev. of Intell. Prop. and Competition Law 434 (2014); Martin Senftleben, *Function Theory and International Exhaustion: Why It Is Wise to Confine the Double Identity Rule in EU Trade Mark Law to Cases Affecting the Origin Function*, Euro. Intell. Prop. Rev. 518 (2014).

[33] Case C-236/08 and C-238/08, *Google France SARL* v. *Louis Vuitton Malletier SA*, 2010 ECR I-02417 159, § 86.

[34] Directive 2000/31/EC, of the European Parliament and of the Council of June 8, 2000 on certain legal aspects of information society services, in particular electronic commerce, in the Internal Market ("Directive on electronic commerce"), art. 6, 2000 OJ (L 178) 1.

[35] Case C-236/08 and C-238/08, *Google France SARL* v. *Louis Vuitton Malletier SA*, §§ 89–90.

[36] Unlike the French Cour de cassation in *Google France* v. *CNRRH* (*see* Cour de cassation [Cass.] [supreme court for judicial matters] 1e civ., July 13, 2010, *Google France* v. *CNRRH* (Fr.), translated in 42 Int'l Rev. of Intell. Prop. and Competition Law 737 (2011)) the German courts have repeatedly held that the origin function is not affected when the advertisements displayed on the Google website are clearly labelled as such. *See* BGH, Dec. 12, 2012,

fact-sensitive and consumer information-oriented approach, albeit for an unusual category of trademark uses, namely the use in algorithms. Another example is a recent German decision in an action brought against Amazon, which is reminiscent of the judgment of the Ninth Circuit in *Multi-Time Machine* v. *Amazon*.[37] When users entered the claimant's trademark into the Amazon search engine, the list of results also contained advertisements for competing products. The Munich Court of Appeal had considered this practice as trademark use and had given judgment for the claimant on the basis of the fact that both the signs and the products were identical.[38] The Federal Supreme Court, however, applied the *Google France* criteria. It referred the case back to the Court of Appeal but ordered it to take into account the perspective of an average internet user who is familiar with search engines and capable of detecting the differences between clearly labelled products.[39]

Another tendency becomes apparent in the *Specsavers* case. The claimant was a UK company which sells glasses and operates under the name "Specsavers." It was the owner of a word mark, but also of a device mark which consisted of a stylised pair of glasses, consisting of nothing more than two white oval shapes on a black ground. The claimant used this logo in a green colour with the word "Specsavers" superimposed on it. The defendants were a chain of retail shops which also sold glasses. They used a similar shape in green and white with the word "ASDA" superimposed. Under traditional trademark law principles, a court could have asked whether the claimants had used their logo "as a trade mark" and might have compared the trademark as registered, i.e. in black and white and without any writing, with the defendant's sign. The CJEU in its judgment of 2013, however, pointed out that all circumstances of the case had to be taken into account for the analysis of confusion and that the court had to compare the mark in the colour in which it was actually used with the defendant's sign,[40] thereby factoring market reality into the analysis of confusion.[41] This approach is in line with the speech of Kitchin LJ, as he then was, in his reference to the CJEU, in which he advocated a context-specific approach.[42] Both in the reference and in the final decision, which largely concerned the question of "genuine use," Kitchin LJ attached importance to factors such as the quantity of use of the logo by the claimant, logos used by other competitors, the fact that defendants had deliberately adopted a similar logo, and witness statements that confirmed consumers relied on the device to identify the claimant.[43]

Is the pendulum swinging back from an intellectual property approach to an unfair competition approach, and toward analysing trademark confusion? It is probably too early to tell. The algorithm cases are very specific, because the trademarks are used in an atypical way. If judges applied traditional criteria, they would almost always find infringement, as the sign used in the algorithm is identical to the trademark for technical reasons. This result would conflict with trademark policy, as consumers can often tell the difference and benefit from information

I ZR 217/10 – Most-Pralinen ["Most" chocolates], 115 GEWERBLICHER RECHTSSCHUTZ UND URHEBERRECHT 290 §§ 26–30 (2013).

[37] *Multi-Time Machine, Inc.* v. *Amazon.com, Inc.*, 804 F.3d 930 (9th Cir. 2015).

[38] OLG München, May 12, 2016, 29 U 3500/15 – Ortlieb, 16 GEWERBLICHER RECHTSSCHUTZ UND URHEBERRECHT-RECHTSPRECHUNGS-REPORT 403 (2016).

[39] BGH, Feb. 15, I ZR 138/16 – Ortlieb I, 120 GEWERBLICHER RECHTSSCHUTZ UND URHEBERRECHT, 924 (2018).

[40] Case C-252/12, *Specsavers International Healthcare Ltd.* v. *Asda Stores Ltd.*, 2013 ECR 497, §§ 34–41.

[41] KUR & SENFTLEBEN, *supra* note 27, § 5.117.

[42] GRAEME B. DINWOODIE & DEV S. GANGJEE, *The Image of the Consumer in EU Trade Mark Law*, in THE IMAGES OF THE CONSUMER IN EU LAW 359–60 (Dorota Leczykiewicz & Stephen Weatherill eds., 2016); ILANAH FHIMA & DEV S. GANGJEE, THE CONFUSION TEST IN EUROPEAN TRADE MARK LAW, 188–194 (2019).

[43] *Specsavers Int'l Healthcare Ltd.* v. *Asda Stores Ltd*, [2014] EWCA Civ. 1294, §§ 23–37.

about competing products, which in turn enhances competition. Trademark law can either take account of these policy concerns by making the analysis of likelihood of confusion more fact-specific or by providing a robust defence of referential use. The *Specsavers* scenario is closer to classical trademark cases, but it can also be explained on the basis of traditional doctrine. In many jurisdictions, the registration of a sign in black and white is considered to cover all types of colours, which allows taking the colour in which the owner uses the sign in practice into account. And even the traditional analysis of conflicts between signs composed of a logo and a word has been more fact-specific, as the CJEU has always advised the national courts to look at the overall impression of both signs from a consumers' perspective.[44] Also, a context-specific analysis of both signs may turn out to be too narrow, as trademark registration gives the owner the right to use the sign in different contexts. Indeed, pursuant to Articles 16 TMD and 18 EUTMR, the sign does not need to be used right away, but only within a period of five years. So even use of a sign that has not been used at all may be infringing. At least in classical cases where the infringer attaches a sign to products or uses the sign in their own advertising, parts of the context will always have to be left out of account. Probably, the question of which facts beyond mere comparison of the registered mark and the sign as used by the infringer will remain to be decided by courts and discussed in legal literature for years to come.

IV TRADEMARKS AND COMPARATIVE ADVERTISING

A *Of European Legacy and of Anti-Parasitism Protection through the Back Door*

Whereas free speech concerns played an instrumental role in shaping US law's treatment of comparative advertising,[45] there is a tradition of granting protection against misappropriation in general and against comparative advertising in particular in several continental European states.[46] Unsurprisingly, for a country home to some of the world's most cherished luxury goods, French unfair competition law has traditionally granted strong protection against misappropriation of reputation or, in French legal terminology, against "parasitisme."[47] The German Supreme Court held in 1931 that comparative advertising amounted to unfair competition.[48] The court advanced two reasons for this decision. First, "nobody could be a judge in his own cause": comparative advertising was notoriously unreliable and therefore potentially misleading. Second, no trader had to accept being instrumentalised for a competitor's advertising efforts. This second argument is essentially a misappropriation argument that blends into a line of unfair competition cases which at that time protected well-known marks against dilution[49] and which provided protection against slavish imitation. Even UK law was less permissive than its reluctance against the notion of unfair competition might suggest. While, unlike in Germany, there is

44 Case C-120/04, *Medion AG* v. *Thomson GmbH*, 2005 ECR I-8551, § 28.

45 *See* Chapter 20 in this volume, by Rebecca Tushnet.

46 *See* opinion of Advocate General Léger in Case C-112/99, *Toshiba Europe GmbH* v. *Katun Germany GmbH*, 2001 ECR 80, § 1: "The concept of comparative advertising is new to Community law. For a long time the Member States were hostile to it. Only recently, following the adoption of Directive 97/55/EC, (2) was the introduction of comparative advertising into the national legal systems accepted as a matter of principle, but only subject to very strict conditions as to the circumstances in which it is permitted."

47 *See* Philippe Le Tourneau, Le Parasitisme (1998); André Lucas, Agnes Lucas-Schloetter & Carine Bernault, Traité de la propriété littéraire et artistique, § 21 (5th ed. 2017).

48 Reichsgericht (German Supreme Court until 1945), Oct. 6, 1931, II 493/30 – Hellegold, 36 Gewerblicher Rechtsschutz und Urheberrecht, 1299, 1301 (1931).

49 *See* Andreas Sattler, *Dilution of Well-Known Trademarks – An Analysis of Its Foundations in Germany and the European Union*, 3 Zeitschrift fur geistiges Eingentum 304 (2011).

no unfair competition law remedy against truthful and non-confusing comparative advertising, Section 4(1) of Trade Marks Act 1938, which was repealed in 1994, protected marks registered in Part A of the bipartite UK register against "importing a reference," which essentially meant that the use of such a mark in a comparison amounted to a trademark infringement.[50] This is not to say that these national approaches are correct in principle, but it helps to explain why EU law developed against a backdrop of scepticism toward comparative advertising.

The directive of 1997 is nevertheless a puzzling piece of legislation, because it is a prime example of a compromise solution which cloaked a fundamental dispute. The express purpose of the directive is to liberalise comparative advertising, which at that time was still prohibited in several Member States, inter alia in France and Germany.[51] Recital 2 stresses the positive impacts of comparative advertising on consumer information and on competition.[52] In this vein, Article 4 MCAD provides that comparative advertising, which is defined in broad terms by Article 2(c) MCAD "shall be permitted" under eight conditions.[53] These conditions combine the model of rational consumer decision making and the principle of proportionality. Comparative advertising is permitted if it provides reasonable information to consumers and if it does not interfere with the interests of the competitor that is identified in the advertisement to a greater extent than necessary for the purpose of informing consumers.[54] Read from this perspective, the eight conditions stated in Article 4 MCAD are coherent. First, comparative advertising is permitted when it (a) is not misleading, (b) compares products intended for the same purpose, and (c) objectively compares material, relevant, verifiable and representative features. When this is the case, a comparison provides useful information, whereas comparisons between unrelated products, subjective comparisons, or unrepresentative comparisons are at best neutral from the consumer's perspective. Comparisons that (d) discredit the competitor, (f) take unfair advantage of the reputation, or (h) create confusion, interfere with the competitor's interests more than necessary. Even from this perspective, however, conditions (e) according to which products with designations of origin may only be compared to products with identical designations, and (g) according to which products must not be presented as imitations, are hard to justify. As far as can be gleaned from the genesis of the directive, these conditions were not part of the initial proposal, but were later inserted as the result of national lobbying in favour of the wine and the perfume industries.[55]

Had Article 4 MCAD been interpreted in this purely permissive way, it would have allowed more liberal approaches while initiating a liberalisation in countries like Germany. But it seems that there was no consensus between the member states about the flipside, namely about the question of whether comparisons would be prohibited which did not meet the criteria. This question was left open, although some recitals support interpretation of Article 4 as not only liberalising but also proscriptive.[56] Soon after the directive's entry in force, the CJEU indeed

[50] *Bismag Ltd.* v. *Amblins (Chemists) Ltd.*, 57 RPC 209 (1940); Ansgar Ohly & Michael Spence, The Law of Comparative Advertising, 18–22 (2000).

[51] *See* Ohly & Spence, *supra* note 50, at 42.

[52] Recital 2 to TMR 1997, *supra* note 11; Recitals to the consolidated version are shorter and address comparative advertising in much less detail.

[53] "Any advertising which explicitly or by implication identifies a competitor or goods or services offered by a competitor." This definition is odd, because it does not even require a comparison. The CJEU has never decided whether there is an unwritten requirement that the advertisement be "comparative," although some national courts have done so. *See BGH – Coaching-Newsletter*, Gewerblicher Rechtsschutz und Urheberrecht 74 (2012).

[54] Ohly & Spence, *supra* note 50, at 57–59.

[55] *Id.* at 44.

[56] *See* Recitals 7–9, 11, 15 of TMR 1997, *supra* note 11.

held that Article 4 aimed at full harmonisation[57] and that comparative advertising was permitted only if all conditions were met.[58] The result is far from satisfactory, mainly because neutral comparisons, i.e. comparisons that do not serve consumers' information interests, are prohibited even if they do not have a negative impact on the competitor's interests.

This can be illustrated by an example which never went to court, but which nicely demonstrates the point. The Royal Albert Hall Proms end with the Last Night of the Proms, which is both a musical spectacle and a friendly celebration of Britishness. Some pieces are played every year, most importantly Henry Wood's "Fantasia on British Sea-Songs" and Edward Elgar's "Pomp and Circumstance." An advertisement published in a Prom programme of the 1990s shows a Jaguar on a German motorway while passing a sign towards Munich and Stuttgart, the homes of Jaguar's main competitors, BMW and Mercedes. The caption says: "'Why a Jaguar?' I asked. 'Because' he said, 'I've always preferred Elgar to Wagner.'" This is a purely subjective comparison, which falls foul of Article 4(c) MCAD, but neither harms consumers nor seriously affects BMW and Mercedes, which can happily point out that Wagner is the more famous composer and that the comparison between elegant playfulness (Elgar and Jaguar) and power (Wagner and Mercedes) may not even be far-fetched. For both reasons, the comparison may even work in the German producers' favour. Most importantly, both the average European consumer and the average European trader can be expected to read this friendly allusion to different national characters with a sense of humour.[59] The reason for this unsatisfactory outcome is that Article 4(c) MCAD aptly circumscribes advertisements which benefit consumers, but that the corresponding ban on neutral advertisements is hard to justify.

B L'Oréal v. Bellure: *Trademark Law and Comparative Advertising Law Synchronised*

The MCAD is a comparative advertising directive. It is not a part of trademark law. So for some time after its enactment, its relationship to trademark law remained unclear. German courts in particular, at that time, applied a narrow concept of trademark use which required the infringer to use the trademark as a designation of origin for their own products. This is usually not the case with comparisons, since their entire point is to distinguish clearly between the advertised product and the referenced product. In those EU member states providing civil law remedies against unfair competition, the question does not matter much. In Germany, for example, traders can sue competitors for unfair comparative advertising under unfair competition law and obtain injunctions and damages. But in UK law the issue is more relevant, as the statutory instrument implementing the MCAD into UK law does not provide for civil remedies.[60] Hence the only way of enforcing the MCAD in a civil court is by means of a claim for trademark infringement.

This is how the leading case on the relationship between trademark and unfair competition law reached the CJEU. L'Oréal and other perfume houses sued producers of lookalike and smell-alike perfumes for trademark infringement. The packaging of the lookalikes alluded to the well-known brands, but the names were sufficiently different. Resellers, however, were provided with a table which listed the respective trademarks and which compared smells of brand

[57] Case C-44/01, *Pippig Augenoptik GmbH & Co.* v. *Hartlauer Handelsgesellschaft mbH*, 2003 ECR I-3095, § 44.

[58] Case C-487/07, *L'Oréal SA* v. *Bellure NV*, 2009 ECR I-5158, § 67.

[59] Although of course, this may change in times of increasing nationalism.

[60] The Business Protection from Misleading Marketing Regulations 2008, SI 2008 No. 1276, only provides for enforcement by the Office of Fair Trading and the local weights and measures authorities. With the closure of the OFT, these powers passed on to the Competition and Markets Authority.

perfumes with imitations. The CJEU held that use of a trademark in comparative advertising was a potential infringement but that Article 4 MCAD effectively provided a defence in the case of permitted comparisons.[61] Since Article 4(g) prohibits the presentation of goods as imitations, the tables of correspondence amounted to infringements.[62] When the case returned to the Court of Appeal, Jacob LJ did not mince words and strongly criticised the judgment as overprotective and preventative of truthful advertising.[63]

But systematically the judgment makes perfect sense, as far as the relationship between trademark law and the MCAD is concerned. It is entirely consistent with the broad notion of use, which the CJEU applies, to regard use of a competitor's mark in a comparison as potentially infringing. And once the CJEU had interpreted Article 4 MCAD as prohibiting comparisons which do not meet the criteria, it follows consistently that use of a competitor's mark which falls foul of the conditions amounts to an infringement.

The crux is that Article 4(g) MCAD is a misguided piece of legislation at odds with intellectual property policy: when IP law prohibits imitations it provides sufficient remedies, but when IP law allows the imitation, both the interest of consumer information and the freedom of expression militate in favour of allowing the information. The CJEU implemented the legislative intent faithfully. The CJEU's only alternative would have been to rebel against a bad provision and to restrict it to narrow circumstances, for example by requiring an explicit claim of imitation as opposed to the implicit information in the comparative list, although there was evidence that Article 4(g) MCAD specifically targeted comparative lists in the perfume business. The real damage occurred when the EU Council and Parliament passed Article 4(g) MCAD without sufficient consideration of the consequences.[64] It remains to be seen what the CJEU will do if it ever has to decide a trademark action brought by the owner of a trademark for drugs against a manufacturer of generics after the term of patent protection has expired. Arguably an advertisement for a generic drug which points out the therapeutic equivalence with the original product would be a "claim of imitation," but prohibiting the information would undermine the policy of patent protection and seriously interfere with health policy. The CJEU would probably find ways of distinguishing, but a drugs case would plainly expose the flaws of Article 4(g) MCAD.

Meanwhile, the approach the CJEU adopted has been codified in EU trademark law. Articles 9(3)(f) EUTMR and 10(3)(f) TMD provide that the trademark owner can prohibit use of their trademark if the comparison is unfair according to the criteria of the MCAD. It follows a contrario that the use of the trademark in "fair" comparisons is justified. It should be added that the CJEU also applies the criteria of Article 4 MCAD when applying the fair use exceptions of EU trademark law. Article 14 TMD and EUTMR allow use of non-distinctive or descriptive elements as well as referential use, but the use must comply with honest practices. The CJEU has repeatedly held that a practice is dishonest when it is misleading, when it denigrates a competitor, or when it takes unfair advantage of a competitor's reputation.[65]

[61] Case C-487/07, *L'Oréal SA* v. *Bellure NV*, § 54, referring to Case C-533/06, *O2 Holdings Ltd.* v. *Hutchison 3G UK Ltd.*, 2008 ECR I-04231, § 45.

[62] Case C-487/07, *L'Oréal SA* v. *Bellure NV*, §§ 53, 75–79.

[63] *L'Oréal* v. *Bellure* [2010] EWCA (Civ.) 535 [14]–[20] (Eng.).

[64] *See* Annette Kur, Lionel A. F. Bently & Ansgar Ohly, *Sweet Smells and a Sour Taste – The ECJ's L'Oréal Decision* (Nov. 30, 2009), https://papers.ssrn.com/sol3/papers.cfm?abstract_id=1492032.

[65] Case C-228/03, *Gillette Co.* v. *LA-Laboratories Ltd.*, 2005 ECR 2363, §§ 42–9; Kur & Senftleben, *supra* note 27, § 6.72.

C Siemens *and* Swirl: *Consumer Information Trumping Misappropriation*

L'Oréal v. *Bellure* is an unusual case because Article 4(g) MCAD is cast in such specific terms that the hands of the CJEU ware arguably tied. The more general provision of Article 4(f) MCAD gives the courts more room to balance the conflicting interests. It provides that comparative advertising is only permitted when "it does not take unfair advantage of the reputation of a trade mark, trade name or other distinguishing marks of a competitor."

This provision is not easy to apply because, arguably, in a comparison of the "A is as good as B" type, A always takes advantage of B's reputation where B is better known than A. Since the directive aims at allowing comparative advertising to provide consumers with reasonable information, the consumer interest must be taken into account when applying the "unfairness" proviso. In this context, the principle of proportionality, which was initially developed in constitutional law, is helpful. Under this principle, a state interference with fundamental rights is proportionate, when (1) it serves a legitimate purpose, (2) does not interfere with the citizen's right to a greater extent than necessary, and (3) is reasonable in the light of the respective weight of the public interest and of the citizen's right. Applied to comparative advertising, interference with the competitor's reputation is justified when (1) comparison provides consumers with truthful information, (2) comparison does not interfere with the competitor's reputation to a greater extent than necessary to inform consumers, and (3) damage done to the competitor is not out of proportion to the information interest.

Although the CJEU has never expressly applied this test, most of its judgments are in line with these elements. The *Siemens* judgment of 2007 is an example in point. The defendant manufactured computer components which were exchangeable with the original Siemens components. Defendant not only distributed lists of comparison but also adopted serial numbers including those serial numbers of Siemens components. So the component equivalent to "Siemens 928-3UB21" would be sold under the serial number "VIPA 928-3UB21." The CJEU held that this practice did not amount to unfair comparative advertising. First, the relevant consumers were traders who knew the difference between original parts and defendant's parts. Secondly, there was no unfair misappropriation. Serial numbers are weak carriers of reputation anyway, but the defendant's use of serial numbers was also the most efficient way of informing consumers that both products were interchangeable. In the same vein, the German Federal Supreme Court allowed an online shop to advertise vacuum cleaner bags by reference to the market leader "Swirl" and to offer its own bags with the reference "like Swirl M50."[66]

At first sight, these judgments seem difficult to reconcile with the *L'Oréal* case. The only distinguishing factor seems to be that perfumes enjoy a cachet of luxury while vacuum cleaner bags do not. But the deeper reason is that Article 4(g) MCAD is a protectionist exception from the more general rule of Article 4(f) MCAD.[67] Under Article 4(f) MCAD, consumer interest in information arguably could have justified the comparative list of smells.

[66] BGH, Apr. 2, 2015, I ZR 167/13 – Staubsaugerbeutel im Internet [Vacuum cleaner bags on the Internet], 117 Gewerblicher Rechtsschutz und Urheberrecht, 1136 (2015).

[67] It should be acknowledged, though, that the CJEU also found the comparative perfume tables to have fallen foul of MCAD, art. 4(f). This conclusion is understandable, given that art. 4(g) is a special case of misappropriation, and it would have been difficult methodologically to find infringement under the special rule while denying infringement under its generalisation. Without art. 4(g), the result may well have been different, although this is, of course, a speculation.

V CONCLUSION: CONVERGENCE, CONSUMER INFORMATION AND THE ALLURE OF UPMARKET PERFUME

EU trademark law and unfair competition law are converging. When assessing a likelihood of confusion, the CJEU is arguably moving from a formal, scope-oriented approach to a more context-sensitive approach where the perception of the average consumer plays a stronger role. The CJEU relies on EU law of comparative advertising when determining scope of trademark protection and when interpreting EU fair use exceptions. Meanwhile, both the TMD and the EUTMR explicitly provide that use of a trademark in unfair comparative advertising amounts to a trademark infringement, which also means that, in contrast, use of a trademark in comparisons permissible under Article 4 MCAD does not infringe.

From a methodological standpoint and with the aim of an effective implementation of EU law ("effet utile") in mind, the CJEU's attempt to construe EU law as a coherent whole makes perfect sense. But it also increases the importance of the MCAD, which is partly over-protective and, with respect to Article 4(g) MCAD, openly annoying. Article 5 MCAD gives considerable discretion to member states when choosing the method of enforcement. In particular, member states are not under an obligation to provide for a civil action. While Germany, in line with its tradition, incorporated the directive into the Act against Unfair Competition – which is enforced by competitors, trade associations and consumer organisations – the United Kingdom did not provide for civil law claims against unfair comparative advertising. Practically, UK provisions implementing the MCAD have had very limited effect. The United Kingdom's attempt to "restrict the harm" done by MCAD was thwarted when the CJEU incorporated the directive into trademark law. The United Kingdom may be able to solve this problem by abolishing the Business Protection from Misleading Marketing Regulations after Brexit, depending of course on the extent to which the United Kingdom will still be bound by EU law in its future relations with the EU. The remaining EU member states should muster the strength to revise Article 4 MCAD, although politically, the EU law's protectionist trend may not diminish after the withdrawal of the United Kingdom.

20

The False Advertising/Trademark Law Interface at Common Law

*Rebecca Tushnet**

I INTRODUCTION

Both trademark infringement and false advertising are understandable as species of unfair competition, related in that both operate to protect consumers and competitors against distortion in the market caused by misleading information. But they have differing subject matter and often different tests for liability for the same type of claim. In particular, advertisers often want to make comparative claims identifying a particular competitor, whether by name or by some other recognizable characteristic. If these claims are false, no separate principle of trademark law is required to conclude that they should be banned, even if they are neither confusing in the trademark sense nor disparaging. For example, if ads falsely claim the advertiser's product is as good on some specific measure as the trademark owner's product while clearly indicating the separate source, false advertising law prohibits the claim. However, if claims such as "cheaper than Brand X, but just as effective" are not false or misleading, then general advertising law allows them – unless trademark law has some separate force in controlling advertising claims that aren't about the source or sponsorship of the advertiser's product.

The United States has taken the most aggressive position that general advertising law's permissiveness toward non-false claims should control in such situations, while other common law countries are more ambivalent. This chapter focuses on the US approach and contrasts it to other common law jurisdictions that give somewhat more solicitude to trademark owners, though always uneasily and without much clarity on the boundaries. In each jurisdiction, trademark law has the potential to complicate an otherwise straightforward advertising law issue centered on the presence or absence of factual falsity. In general, a focus on protecting consumers' access to useful information would be both simpler and likely more beneficial to society at large than an approach that allows trademark rights to interfere with nondeceptive information.

II FALSE ADVERTISING LAW AND COMPARATIVE ADVERTISING IN THE UNITED STATES

General false advertising law regulates factual claims of all kinds in advertising, including comparative claims. The legal landscape in the US allows many sources of potential liability: federal and state regulators can sue businesses for deceptive advertising under the Federal Trade

* Frank Stanton Professor of First Amendment Law, Harvard Law School.

Commission Act and similar state "little FTC" acts; businesses can sue other businesses under the federal Lanham Act, which covers both trademark infringement and general false advertising; and consumers can bring state-law claims under consumer protection laws specifically barring deceptive trade practices.[1] This proliferation of laws has led to many doctrinal flourishes and epicycles. For example, this chapter uses "falsity" to encompass both literal falsity and misleadingness. Although both are actionable, US courts in Lanham Act cases have distinguished the two by reasoning that "misleadingness" occurs when consumers receive a false factual message from a literally true or potentially ambiguous advertisement. When a message is not literally false (or "false by necessary implication," where a message is not practically ambiguous despite the theoretical possibility of a truthful reading), a plaintiff in a Lanham Act case must provide extrinsic evidence to show that a misleading message has actually been received by consumers.[2] Outside the United States, and in non-Lanham Act US cases, this distinction is not generally made. Courts instead use common sense and other evidence to determine whether a claim is false or misleading and do not distinguish between the two concepts in imposing liability. Nor is the distinction particularly significant to the subject of this chapter. The core question of false advertising law is whether a false claim has been made to a substantial number of consumers, regardless of the semantic form in which it has been communicated.

In all its modern forms, false advertising is generally strict liability. As with trademark infringement, no showing of wrongful intent is required as long as consumers are likely to be deceived by a statement.[3] As a result, if a comparative claim is factually false, it is wrongful and actionable regardless of trademark law and regardless of the related specialized branch of "unfair competition" law aimed at protecting non-trademark sales symbols against uses that confuse as to the source or sponsorship of a product.[4] If a comparative claim is true, by contrast, it is encouraged by advertising law.

In the United States, the Federal Trade Commission (FTC) regulates competition, both against monopolistic practices and against false advertising that disrupts competition on the merits. For many decades, the FTC has explicitly promoted comparative advertising[5] and considers restrictions on such advertising to be anticompetitive restrictions on trade. Groups of advertisers or trade groups may violate antitrust law if they agree to avoid comparative advertising or even to avoid "disparaging" but non-false comparative advertising.[6] Defending the integrity or reputation of a brand is no excuse for anticompetitive agreements that go beyond protection

[1] *See generally* Eric Goldman & Rebecca Tushnet, Advertising & Marketing Law: Cases and Materials, Ch. 3 (4th ed. 2018) (providing an overview of the varying sources of regulatory authority).

[2] *See, e.g., United Indus. Corp.* v. *Clorox Co.*, 140 F.3d 1175 (8th Cir. 1998) (explaining the general rule); *Clorox Co. PR* v. *Proctor & Gamble Com. Co.*, 228 F.3d 24 (1st Cir. 2000) (adding the concept of necessary implication).

[3] *See, e.g., SharkNinja Operating LLC* v. *Dyson Inc.*, 200 F. Supp. 3d 281, 287 (D. Mass. 2016) ("The language of the statute is compulsory, and it includes no exceptions for cases in which a manufacturer undertakes good faith, commercially reasonable efforts to remove a false claim from the marketplace upon learning of its falsity. Good faith is simply not a defense to a false advertising claim under the Lanham Act"); *cf. Fitzgerald Publ'g Co.* v. *Baylor Publ'g Co.*, 807 F.2d 1110, 1113 (2d Cir. 1986) (stating general US rule that trademark infringement is strict liability, and intent is not an element).

[4] *See* Paris Convention for the Protection of Industrial Property, Mar. 20, 1888, as revised at the Stockholm Revision Conference, July 14, 1967, 21 UST 1538, TIAS No. 6903, 828 UNTS 305, art. 10*bis*.

[5] *See* 16 CFR §14.15(c) ("Comparative advertising, when truthful and nondeceptive, is a source of important information to consumers and assists them in making rational purchase decisions. Comparative advertising encourages product improvement and innovation, and can lead to lower prices in the marketplace").

[6] *See, e.g., In re Mass. Bd. of Registration in Optometry*, 1988 FTC LEXIS 34, at *15 (1988) ("Restraints on truthful advertising for professional services are inherently likely to produce anticompetitive effects. '[T]he nature or character of these restrictions is sufficient alone to establish their anticompetitive quality'").

against confusion about source or sponsorship – and comparative advertising is rarely confusing in that sense.

So far, so good. But in some situations, comparative statements are neither true nor false. Such nonfactual claims are known in advertising law as "puffery": vague statements that cannot be proven true or false or statements that are so unbelievable that reasonable consumers wouldn't rely on them. In theory, no information would be lost to consumers from a ban on puffery. Yet false advertising law in common law regimes has historically been uninterested in regulating puffery (at least where not compelled by adherence to EU requirements, as discussed below).[7] By allowing puffery, the law provides advertisers with breathing space – they need not fear losing a false advertising case over claims that consumers wouldn't take as making specific promises. Puffery also provides advertisers with an opportunity to attract consumers with clever or creative advertising which, among other things, allows them to build brands – not just indicators of source, but repositories of meaning for consumers whose favorable associations can prompt sales even when product characteristics are interchangeable. Thus, it is not surprising that trademark owners want to be able to use puffery; self-interest means that proponents of strong trademark rights are also proponents of fairly limited advertising law.

Traditionally, the US approach has not changed very much for trademark-specific claims. This is one manifestation of the extremely speech-protective orientation of US law: the presence of a specific target that might rather obviously be harmed by denigration by a competitor triggers no special concern. When consumers are unlikely to be materially deceived, US law prefers the parties fight their battles in the marketplace, not in the courts. The advertiser certainly has an incentive to cherry-pick comparisons, touting its price superiority where performance is not so much in its favor or vice versa, but consumers are presumed to understand this up to the point at which the comparison becomes affirmatively misleading or false.

Comparisons can also be particularly useful to smaller or newer competitors, who might otherwise have trouble letting consumers know about their competing offerings. An explicit comparison means consumers don't have to remember lots of specific product details and statistics, which they are unlikely to do. Direct comparison can also be a uniquely effective sales tactic by drawing the attention of consumers and cutting through the clutter of other, less relevant advertising. Yet false advertising law doesn't care very much whether the competitor is identified or whether the claim is of superiority over all others, except insofar as specificity contributes to making a claim sufficiently factual and verifiable to be falsifiable and not a mere puff.[8]

In the United States, then, companies generally can't interfere with the free play of competition merely to "protect their trademarks" in the absence of confusion. Recently, for example, the FTC succeeded in its antitrust proceeding against 1-800-Contacts, which sued numerous

[7] So much so, in the United States at least, that there is some concern not to regulate falsity so aggressively that advertisers are deterred from making true but hard-to-verify claims. *See, e.g., Rhone-Poulenc Rorer Pharms., Inc.* v. *Marion Merrell Dow, Inc.*, 93 F.3d 511, 515 (8th Cir. 1996) ("To ensure vigorous competition and to protect legitimate commercial speech, courts [evaluating whether tests are sufficiently reliable to support an advertiser's claim] should give advertisers a fair amount of leeway, at least in the absence of a clear intent to deceive or substantial consumer confusion"). The result is that competing advertisers may be able to make contradictory claims, and neither may be able to prove the other's false. *See Proctor & Gamble Co.* v. *Chesebrough-Pond's, Inc.*, 747 F.2d 114 (2d Cir. 1984).

[8] *See, e.g., August Storck K.G.* v. *Nabisco, Inc.*, 59 F.3d 616 (1995) ("A use of a rival's mark that does not engender confusion about origin or quality is therefore permissible. The use is not just permissible in the sense that one firm is entitled to do everything within legal bounds to undermine a rival; it is beneficial to consumers. They learn at a glance what kind of product is for sale and how it differs from a known benchmark").

competitors for buying search engine ads that would display when someone searched for "1-800-Contacts." 1-800-Contacts, through lawsuits and threats of lawsuits, extracted numerous agreements from competitors to prevent any such ads, even when the competitors' ads appeared only because the searcher's query included the generic word "contacts." The FTC successfully argued that competitors who bought "1-800-Contacts," "1-800-Contacts coupons," and the like as keywords to trigger ads were promoting price competition (which was especially important as contacts are essentially a commodity product – all resellers buy from the same manufacturers). 1-800-Contacts had advertised heavily, so consumers were more likely to know about it than the alternatives, and it correspondingly charged higher prices than its competitors. Consistent with the theory supporting comparative advertising as a sales technique, competitors' ads shown to consumers who searched for 1-800-Contacts were more likely than ads shown in response to other searches to result in clicks and sales. Thus, 1-800-Contacts's threats and agreements suppressed advertising that was especially likely to guide consumers to cheaper products.[9]

1-800-Contacts argued that it was merely protecting its trademark rights. The administrative judge hearing the case succinctly rejected this defense because it wrongly assumed that displaying an ad in response to a search for 1-800-Contacts was trademark infringement, which in the absence of confusing text (e.g., an ad falsely claiming to be an ad for 1-800-Contacts) it is not.[10] The judge pointed to empirical evidence that consumers who enter a trademark as a search term are often interested in competing alternatives, rather than definitively seeking to transact only with the trademark owner.[11] Even if consumers did begin with the intent to seek out 1-800 Contacts, it is not wrongful to persuade them to do otherwise by nondeceptive means. The full Commission agreed with the judge's reasoning and affirmed the decision.[12]

III THE TRADEMARK INTERFACE IN THE UNITED STATES

Although 1-800-Contacts' claim to be defending its trademark rights failed, and although similar lawsuits against keyword advertising have uniformly failed on the merits when the ad text itself doesn't use the asserted trademark, the very existence of such lawsuits suggests the potential for using trademark law to suppress comparative advertising. When the alleged falsity is a misrepresentation of a connection with a trademark owner, a trademark claim has some benefits over false advertising claims. It's simple for a trademark owner to plausibly claim that it is specifically harmed by trademark infringement, thus providing it with standing to sue. Moreover, modern trademark law has largely dispensed with a requirement of materiality. Whether or not consumers *care* about source, sponsorship, or affiliation, the trademark owner can regularly prevail if

[9] *In re 1-800 Contacts, Inc.*, No. 9372, slip op. at 98 (FTC, Oct. 30, 2017) ("The advertising restrictions contained in the Settlement Agreements significantly impair competition for selling online contact lenses by prohibiting a type of advertising that is especially important for price competition among online sellers of contact lenses and for potential new entrants").

[10] *Id.* at 170.

[11] *Id.* at 181 (citing David J. Franklin & David A. Hyman, *Trademarks as Search Engine Keywords: Much Ado about Something?* 26 HARV. J.L. & TECH. 481, 532 (2013) (when asked, in the abstract, what consumers wished to see in response to a brand search, almost half responded that they wanted to see information relating to other brands)); Eric Goldman, *Brand Spillovers*, 22 HARV. J.L. & TECH. 381, 411–12 (2009) ("many consumers entering a trademarked search term may not be looking for the trademark owner's goods or services").

[12] *In the Matter of 1-800 Contacts, Inc.*, No. 9372, 2018 WL 6078349, at *26 (FTC, Nov. 7, 2018) ("When an agreement limits truthful price advertising on the basis of trademark protection, it must be narrowly tailored to protecting the asserted trademark right. The agreements here are not – they restrict advertising regardless of whether the ads are likely to be confusing and, apparently, regardless of whether competitors actually use the trademark term (requiring negative keywords)").

consumers are likely to be mistaken about the relationship between the trademark owner and the defendant. This is in contrast to the materiality requirement in general false advertising law, in which even blatant falsehoods aren't actionable if they wouldn't affect reasonable consumers' decisions.[13]

Thus, while trademark owners are certainly willing to litigate false advertising claims against competitors who make factual statements, they may well prefer to raise trademark-specific arguments. This means that intellectual property interests may conflict with a general right to engage in truthful, or at least nonmisleading, advertising. The standard US approach has been to let general false advertising principles prevail, finding trademark owners' proprietary interests insufficient to override an advertiser's freedom to choose persuasive, non-false tactics.

A classic statement of this freedom can be found in *Smith* v. *Chanel*, a case about purportedly "smell-alike" perfumes, which strongly protected "use of another's trademark to identify the trademark owner's product, absent misrepresentation regarding the products or confusion as to their source or sponsorship." The idea that the trademark "embod[ied]" goodwill developed by the trademark owner did not put it off-limits for others' use; the legal protection of trademarks was limited to protecting their "source identification function," and this was so because of "public policy favoring a free, competitive economy." In particular, competitors had a right to copy unpatented articles such as Chanel's perfume, and the public also had a strong interest in that copying taking place so that different entities could compete on price (and perhaps on other features) to provide the unpatented scent. Given the right to make the underlying product, it followed that there was an equal right to communicate the availability of that product in non-Chanel hands. Indeed, the benefit of price competition might easily be lost if the competitor couldn't make equivalence claims. And the most effective way – "and, where complex chemical compositions sold under trade names are involved, often the only practical way" – to make such claims was to use the trademark in advertising. (Later, this reasoning would be called "nominative fair use," but to the mid-twentieth-century courts, no such specific label was required.) Assuming that the comparative claim of equivalence was true, a rule of law preventing the comparison would encourage perpetual monopoly, in contrast to the time-limited patent and copyright monopolies, and lead to overcharging of consumers who only wanted the underlying product without caring whether it came from Chanel.[14]

Smith states the general US rule. As one prominent trademark treatise summarizes, "it is neither trademark infringement nor unfair competition to truthfully compare competing products in advertising, and in doing so, to identify by trademark, the competitor's goods."[15] (A skeptic of the value of comparative advertising might note that, in fact, the advertiser in *Smith* was found to have engaged in false advertising on remand – it apparently could not deliver on its promise.[16])

In recent years, however, matters have been complicated in the United States by a kind of doctrinal overgrowth that can make the pro-competitive background principles harder to see. This is not just a matter of aggressive marketers pushing the lines – indeed, in some of the

[13] *See, e.g., Nat'l Basketball Ass'n* v. *Motorola, Inc.*, 105 F.3d 841, 855 (2d Cir. 1997) (literally false claim to provide sports scores "from the arena" was immaterial since consumers wanted timely, accurate score reports and didn't care if reporters were actually present in the arena); Rebecca Tushnet, *Running the Gamut from A to B: Federal Trademark and False Advertising Law*, 159 U. PENN. L. REV. 1305, 1344–73 (2011) (discussing the materiality divide between trademark and advertising law).

[14] *Smith* v. *Chanel, Inc.*, 402 F.2d 562 (9th Cir. 1968).

[15] 4 J. THOMAS MCCARTHY, MCCARTHY ON TRADEMARKS AND UNFAIR COMPETITION § 25:52 at 171 (4th ed. 2013).

[16] *Chanel, Inc.* v. *Smith*, 528 F.2d 284 (9th Cir. 1976).

closest-to-the-line cases, such as retailers' imitation of national brands' trade dresses for their house-branded competing versions, the test that courts apply is no different than in other standard confusion cases.[17] Rather, the doctrine has often gotten messier and more unpredictable in situations where one party identifies another using its word mark or is otherwise not making a standard trademark use.

A Doctrinal Proliferation within US Trademark Law

The *Chanel* court was confident that truthful comparative advertising was beneficial and thus wasted little time on whether it was confusing.[18] Other courts relied on the idea that credibly comparative advertising can't be infringing, since consumers will easily know that the advertiser is not affiliated with the producer whose product is being unfavorably compared.[19] But, perhaps because the passage of time encourages doctrinal complexity, in recent decades some courts have crystallized the protection for comparative advertising into a larger category known as "nominative use."[20] Nominative use, also known as nominative fair use, purports to provide a bright line protecting some communications that include the trademark as a reference point but don't inherently use the trademark as an indicator of the speaker's own identity.

The Ninth Circuit has the most succinct and useful definition of nominative use in its *New Kids* test, and it's often used by district courts in circuits that have yet to opine definitively on the matter. In the Ninth Circuit, a nominative fair use occurs when (1) the plaintiff's product is not readily identifiable without using the trademark; (2) the defendant uses the plaintiff's trademark only as reasonably necessary to identify the plaintiff's product, and (3) the defendant does nothing else to suggest plaintiff's sponsorship or endorsement.[21] This kind of use is conclusively presumed to be nonconfusing – it simply isn't the kind of "trademark use" with which the law is concerned – even though most US courts impose no formal "use as a mark" requirement in trademark infringement cases generally.

Most notably, this test has no place for evidence of actual consumer confusion, whether anecdotal or survey-based, meaning that any such evidence should be disregarded. This exclusion makes sense, given the context – the *New Kids* litigation was over whether the trademark owner had the right to authorize newspaper polls, and free speech principles counsel against giving a trademark owner such rights. Additionally, asking consumers whether they think trademark owners must (or do) give permission for newspaper polls about themselves is unlikely to produce relevant answers. It's just not the kind of thing consumers think or care about unless prodded by a surveyor to do so. Thus, there was both a strong normative reason to define nominative fair uses as outside the trademark owner's legitimate rights and a strong practical reason to doubt the evidentiary value of any supposed confusion evidence.

Unfortunately, there are several variations in definitions of nominative fair use. In the Third Circuit, for example, nominative fair use is defined more narrowly. Rather than being merely a use that is necessary to identify the trademark as a subject of discussion, the use must also be one

[17] E.g., *McNeil Nutritionals, LLC* v. *Heartland Sweeteners, LLC*, 511 F.3d 350 (3d Cir. 2007).

[18] *See also Lindy Pen Co., Inc.* v. *Bic Pen Corp.*, 725 F.2d 1240, 1248 (9th Cir. 1984) (court "recognized that liability for infringement may not be imposed for using a registered trademark in connection with truthful comparative advertising").

[19] *Sen* v. *Amazon.com, Inc.*, No. 16-CV-01486-JAH-JLB, 2018 WL 4680018 (SD Cal. Sept. 28, 2018) (finding that the suggestion of "monumentally cheaper" competitors wasn't plausibly confusing as to source or affiliation).

[20] *Beachbody, LLC* v. *Universal Nutrients, LLC*, No. CV 16-02015-R, 2016 WL 3912014119 (CD Cal. July 18, 2016).

[21] *New Kids on the Block* v. *News Am. Pub., Inc.*, 971 F.2d 302 (9th Cir. 2002).

that's necessary for the *speaker* to explain who or what it is (e.g., that it is staffed by people who gained their experience working for plaintiff or that it makes spare parts compatible with plaintiff's products).[22] This formulation would not cover most comparative advertising, which needs to be protected for some other reason, perhaps just by the intuition that comparative advertising isn't confusing as to source or sponsorship. The Sixth Circuit has questioned whether the nominative use defense should be recognized at all while also holding that infringement requires "use in a trademark way," an idea that protects defendants' discursive uses of others' marks and therefore replicates much of what nominative fair use does.[23]

Worst of all, the Second Circuit has held that the nominative fair use factors are simply to be added to the usual multifactor confusion test as additional considerations in appropriate cases.[24] These new factors are somehow to be weighed against the other traditional factors in assessing likely confusion. But the standard infringement factors were developed mainly to assess the likelihood of confusion where the parties' marks and/or goods were similar but not necessarily the same.[25] Those factors are deeply ill-suited for evaluating informative uses of trademarks. For example, the stronger the plaintiff's mark, the more likely the usual test is to find infringement, but useful comparisons often require reference to dominant brands. The more closely related the parties' goods are, the more likely the usual test is to find infringement, but comparisons to a direct competitor are usually the most useful. The more similar the parties' marks are, the more likely the usual test is to find infringement, but comparisons require identical replication of at least the verbal elements of the plaintiff's mark. Indeed, mechanical application of the usual confusion factors would find "Pepsi tastes better than Coke" to be likely to cause confusion between Coke and Pepsi.[26]

The *New Kids* test ought to permit many comparative advertising usages, but that's not always the case. Even aside from the doctrinal conflicts detailed above, sometimes courts interpret factor three – whether the defendant did anything else, other than use the plaintiff's mark, to cause confusion – as meaning that the use of the plaintiff's mark must not be confusing.[27] Such courts must then either replicate a confusion analysis that nominative fair use was supposed to obviate or simply announce a conclusion about confusion.

These doctrinal epicycles came about because, once US courts started looking at confusion as the sum and substance of trademark law, there was a pressure to formalize the intuition that comparative advertising isn't confusing. But courts wanted to add a caveat that *confusing* (unsuccessful) comparative advertising, or perhaps infringing advertising pretending to be

22 *Century 21 Real Estate Corp.* v. *Lendingtree, Inc.*, 425 F.3d 211 (3d Cir. 2005).

23 *Hensley Mfg.* v. *ProPride, Inc.*, 579 F.3d 603 (6th Cir. 2009).

24 *Int'l Info. Sys. Sec. Certification Consortium, Inc.* v. *Sec. Univ., LLC*, 823 F.3d 153 (9th Cir. 2016).

25 *See, e.g., Polaroid Corp.* v. *Polarad Elecs Corp.*, 287 F.2d 492 (2d Cir. 1961) (similar but not identical marks and related but not identical goods). The names of the factors vary from court to court, but they are highly similar in practice, focusing on (1) the strength of the plaintiff's mark, (2) the similarity of the parties' marks, (3) the relatedness of the parties' goods and/or services and the likelihood the plaintiff would expand into providing the goods/services of the defendant, (4) the parties' marketing channels, (5) any evidence of actual confusion, and (6) the defendant's intent in adopting its mark.

26 There are various workarounds to reimpose common sense into the test. Although US courts have generally rejected a requirement that the defendant's use of the plaintiff's mark must be understandable as use *as a mark identifying the defendant* – the simplest way to avoid the Pepsi/Coke problem – it is possible to tweak factors such as the sophistication of the relevant consumers to incorporate not just their ability to distinguish between marks (identical in the comparative advertising case) but also their understanding of the practice of comparative advertising. But *New Kids* was a concrete way of formalizing the intuition that applying the standard likely confusion factors to informational and communicative uses of a mark produces mostly nonsense, and is far more trouble than it's worth.

27 *See, e.g., Estate of Fuller* v. *Maxfield & Oberton Holdings, LLC*, 906 F. Supp. 2d 997, 1012 (ND Cal. 2012) (applying this reasoning).

comparative, was still actionable.[28] The underlying problem is that a test that looks only at what the defendant did and not at evidence of consumer reactions to that behavior doesn't fit comfortably in a trademark system that purports to turn on consumer protection and perceptions. Because plaintiffs have an incentive to suppress competition, they have reason to assert claims against even truthful competitors.[29] As long as trademark law's defense of comparative advertising holds out the confusion caveat, trademark owners will continue to assert that every defendant is deliberately confusing and not comparing.

In response to this incentive to sue too often, courts often simply consult their own intuitive sense of confusion (or its absence), creating uncertainty and the risk of error. The risk of false positives – nonconfusing advertising suppressed despite its lack of deceptiveness – seems to outweigh the benefits of conducting a standardless mini-confusion inquiry. The original *New Kids* formulation of factor three, by contrast, calls back to basic unfair competition principles, asking whether the defendant did anything, other than use the plaintiff's mark to refer to the plaintiff, that is likely to cause confusion. By excluding the nominative use itself from the inquiry, this test is more formalist than the "does the use cause confusion?" version, but it is nonetheless easier for courts to apply, making it more likely to end anticompetitive, information-suppressing suits quickly and cheaply. And given how unlikely it is that consumers will be confused about source or sponsorship by comparative advertising and other informational uses, the mix of information in the market is likely to be better for them under such a rule.[30]

If doctrinal overgrowth cannot be entirely avoided, it can perhaps be made more predictable and easer to resolve on a limited set of facts. US and other courts should look to the original *New Kids* test for a test that protects truthful speech with a simpler, quicker test than a costly, necessarily imperfect assessment of all theoretically relevant facts.

B Dilution and Other Nonconfusion Protection

Perhaps unsurprisingly given the American history of all-but-unfettered market competition, American courts were initially not very receptive to the idea that valuable trademarks deserved special protection, beyond protection against confusing uses, because they were valuable.[31] *Smith* v. *Chanel* again gave the classic American position, beginning with the idea that "[a] large expenditure of money does not in itself create legally protectable rights" – even though the trademark owner created the public's desire for an unpatented product "at great

[28] *G. D. Searle & Co.* v. *Hudson Pharm. Corp.*, 715 F.2d 837, 841 (3d Cir. 1983) ("The use of a competitor's trademark for purposes of comparative advertising is not trademark infringement so long as it does not contain misrepresentations or create a reasonable likelihood that consumers will be confused as to the source, identity, or sponsorship of the advertiser's product"); *Calvin Klein Cosm. Corp.* v. *Lenox Labs., Inc.*, 815 F.2d 500, 503–04 (8th Cir.1987); *August Storck KG* v. *Nabisco, Inc.*, 59 F.3d 616, 618 (7th Cir. 1995) ("A use of a rival's mark that does not engender confusion about origin or quality is therefore permissible"); *SSP Agric. Equip., Inc.* v. *Orchard-Rite Ltd.*, 592 F.2d 1096, 1103 (9th Cir. 1979) ("The use of a competitor's trademark for purposes of comparative advertising is not trademark infringement so long as it does not contain misrepresentations or create a reasonable likelihood that purchasers will be confused as to the source, identity, or sponsorship of the advertiser's product").

[29] See Glynn Lunney, *Trademark's Judicial De-evolution: Why Courts Get Trademark Cases Wrong Repeatedly*, 106 Cal. L. Rev. 1195 (2018).

[30] For example, the evidence discussed in *1-800-Contacts* indicates that keyword advertising increases price competition and does not confuse consumers about the source of goods or services or the existence of an affiliation between the advertiser and its target (though they may be confused about other things, such as the difference between organic and sponsored search results). *See supra* notes 9 and 12.

[31] *See* Thomas R. Lee, *Demystifying Dilution*, 84 B.U. L. Rev. 859, 868–69 (2004).

effort and expense," it could not monopolize that market.[32] We may disapprove of copying, but it serves an important public interest by creating price competition. Furthermore, because it was clear that the advertised product was from someone other than Chanel, Chanel received all the protection for its reputation that it was due. If the defendants' product was in fact inferior to Chanel's, consumers would punish the defendants for that failure.[33] Rational consumers should not think less of Chanel for having imitators, as long as the imitators were clear about their lack of connection to Chanel.

As dilution entered American law, matters could have changed for comparative advertising. American courts failed to fully conceptualize dilution – sometimes it was characterized as protection for the uniqueness of a mark,[34] for example, and other times as protection of a mark's "selling power,"[35] but those are very different things, implying different subsets of trademarks to be protected and different harms to protect them against. The lack of a coherent concept for dilution other than "uses trademark owners didn't like" created substantial uncertainty[36] and opened dilution as a potential pathway for trademark owners to suppress nondeceptive comparative advertising.

This potential was strikingly, albeit briefly, realized in the 1994 *Deere* v. *MTD* case.[37] The Second Circuit evaluated an ad for a lawnmower that, among other things, mocked the well-known deer trademark of its competitor by presenting the noble deer as frightened of a tiny dog, accentuated with humorous "boink" sounds as the animated avatar ran away. The court of appeals concluded that this mockery constituted actionable dilution under New York state law because of the alteration in the trademark. Moreover, it contemplated that this kind of claim was "likely to recur with increasing frequency in this era of head-to-head comparative advertising."[38]

In *Deere*, some combination of alteration plus direct competition tipped the balance against the comparative advertiser:

> Sellers of commercial products who wish to attract attention to their commercials or products and thereby increase sales by poking fun at widely recognized marks of noncompeting products risk diluting the selling power of the mark that is made fun of. When this occurs, not for worthy purposes of expression, but simply to sell products, that purpose can easily be achieved in other ways. The potentially diluting effect is even less deserving of protection when the object of the joke is the mark of a directly competing product.[39]

However, the court of appeals specifically stated that its holding "imposes no restriction on truthful advertising properly comparing specific products and their 'objectively measurable attributes.'"[40] In other words, for comparisons made by altering trademarks, the general US rule allowing puffery and negative puffery in advertising was reversed by dilution law, but not the general US rule allowing truthful claims, no matter how unflattering.

32 *Smith*, 402 F.2d at 568.

33 Nor was the copyist in *Smith* using the trademark as a generic word: "[t]he slight tendency to carry the mark into the common language which even this use may have been outweighed by the substantial value of such use in the maintenance of effective competition." *See id.*

34 *See, e.g., Pignons SA de Mecanique de Precision* v. *Polaroid Corp.*, 657 F.2d 482, 495 (1st Cir. 1981).

35 *See, e.g., Allied Maint.* v. *Allied Mech.*, 369 NE 2d 1162, 1164 (NY 1977).

36 *See* Barton Beebe, *Intellectual Property Law and the Sumptuary Code*, 123 Harv. L. Rev. 809 (2010); Sara Stadler Nelson, *The Wages of Ubiquity in Trademark Law*, 88 Iowa L. Rev. 731 (2003); *Gone in 60 Milliseconds: Trademark Law and Cognitive Science*, 86 Tex. L. Rev. 507 (2008).

37 *Deere & Co.* v. *MTD Prods., Inc.*, 41 F.3d 39 (2d Cir. 1994).

38 *Id.* at 40.

39 *Id.* at 45.

40 *Id.*

The *Deere* court seemed to believe that it was announcing an important rule for the age of comparative advertising, but in fact its rule collapsed almost immediately. Had it survived, courts would have needed to ask whether negative puffery without alteration of the targeted mark was actionable. In addition, they would have needed to evaluate what kinds of alterations were sufficient to be diluting – for example, removing a well-known font from a word mark in a comparative ad probably decreases the likelihood of any confusion about source, but might be an "alteration" from the usual presentation and might make the trademark less attractive, if we believe (as designers do) that fonts can be used to improve goodwill. Instead, a subsequent case brought under New York law established that the Muppets could make fun of the meat product Spam in the movie *Muppet Treasure Island* without violating the *Deere* rule because of the lack of direct competition and the lighthearted nature of the Muppets' alteration (from Spam to a wild boar character, Spa'am).[41]

Moreover, in 1995, Congress enacted a federal dilution law that exempted comparative advertising from the scope of dilution protection, without any reference to alteration or the lack thereof.[42] When the federal dilution law was subsequently revised, its protection for comparative advertising was untouched.[43] After the federal dilution law arrived, courts declined to do two separate dilution analyses when considering defenses, and reasoned as if state dilution regimes had the same exceptions as the federal law, and so *Deere* passed into well-deserved desuetude.

More recently, the Supreme Court in *Matal* v. *Tam* invalidated prohibitions on the registration of "disparaging" marks on the grounds that the First Amendment's free speech guarantee protected applicants against such viewpoint discrimination.[44] Even without deliberate exceptions for comparative advertising, it is hard to imagine that *Deere*-style dilution would fare any better against a First Amendment challenge than the "disparagement" ban, so it is unlikely that the United States will soon see more attempts to suppress comparative advertising on trademark-specific grounds.[45]

IV THE UNITED KINGDOM MEETS THE EUROPEAN UNION

These US developments can be contrasted to changes driven in the United Kingdom by the need to transpose the EU's directive on comparative advertising to English law. It remains to be seen whether Brexit will lead to the resurrection of the traditional English solicitude for comparative advertising, which was far more accepting than the Continental approach.

Like the United States, the United Kingdom historically took a relatively permissive approach to comparative advertising. The House of Lords initially read the United Kingdom's Trade Marks Act of 1905 with an eye toward protecting competition. If the law's ban on unauthorized use by another of a registered trademark on goods identical to those of the trademark owner were read without implying some kind of limit on actionable uses, comparative advertising would be made difficult or impossible, and that result could not be tolerated.[46] Although the UK courts

[41] *Hormel Foods Corp.* v. *Jim Henson Prods., Inc.*, 73 F.3d 497 (2d Cir. 1996).

[42] Trademark Amendments Act of 1999, 1999 Enacted S. 1259, 106 Enacted S. 1259, 113 Stat. 218, codified at 15 USC § 1125(c).

[43] Trademark Dilution Revision Act of 2006, 109 PL 312, 120 Stat. 1730, codified at 15 USC §1125(c).

[44] *Matal* v. *Tam*, 137 S.Ct. 1744 (2017).

[45] *See Am. Freedom Def. Initiative, et al.* v. *King Cty.* (9th Cir. Sept. 27, 2018) (striking down rule for advertising on public transit that prohibited "demeaning" ads, following *Matal*).

[46] 102 *Irving's Yeast-Vite Ltd.* v. *F. A. Horsenail* (1934), 51 RPC 110 (HL) (interpreting Trade Marks Act 1905 § 39, 5 Edw. 7, c. 15: "The registration of a person as proprietor of a trade mark shall, if valid, give to such person the exclusive right to the use of such trade mark upon or in connection with the goods in respect of which it is

allowed some remedies for nonconfusing but putatively damaging uses of a mark,[47] they did not welcome a general anti-free-riding principle.[48]

However, as a result of both trademark and advertising directives attempting to harmonize the rules across the European Union, comparative advertising is practically quite difficult under EU rules. Under the directive specific to comparative advertising, such advertising is permitted only if all of the following are true:

(a) it is not misleading;
(b) it compares goods or services meeting the same needs or intended for the same purpose;
(c) it objectively compares one or more material, relevant, verifiable and representative features of those goods or services, which may include price;
(d) it does not create confusion in the marketplace between the advertiser and a competitor;
(e) it does not discredit or denigrate the trademarks, trade names or other distinguishing signs of a competitor;
(f) for products with a designation of origin, it relates to products with the same designation;
(g) it does not take unfair advantage of the trademark or other distinguishing sign of a competitor;
(h) it does not present goods or services as imitations or replicas of goods or services bearing a protected trademark or trade name.[49]

Section (c) requires comparison of objectively verifiable qualities, indicating that comparative puffery may be unlawful even if – or perhaps because – consumers wouldn't receive any factual message about the parties. Section (e) tracks the idea of trademark tarnishment (indicating that the *Deere* ad discussed above would likely be unlawful under EU law). Section (g) appears even broader because it does not indicate what constitutes "unfair" advantage – presumably the adjective has some purpose, but it is hard to see the limiting principle, and trademark owners are likely to see unfairness in any referential use.[50] Section (h) would specifically preclude the ad at issue in the *Chanel* case, which involved claims to have made a successful copy. Despite all this, the directive appears to contemplate the existence of *some* legitimate comparative advertising. If the directive is to have any meaning at all – and not work as a flat ban – there must be some way to determine *fair* free-riding/advantage-taking.

Although the comparative advertising directive is supposed to be consistent with trademark law, the earlier trademark directive provides another source of EU law that had to be honored;[51] perhaps it could be used to measure unfairness. In *Boehringer Ingelheim Ltd.* v. *Vetplus Ltd.*, the Court of Appeal assessed use of another's trademark in comparative advertising about the relative

registered"). *Trade Marks Act* 1995 § 122(1)(d) (Austl.) states that "a person does not infringe a registered trade mark when: . . . the person uses the trade mark for the purposes of comparative advertising."

[47] Ilanah Simon Fhima, *Exploring the Roots of European Dilution*, INTELL. PROP. Q., 2012, at 25.

[48] *See Barclays Bank* v. *RBS Advanta*, [1996] EIPR 368 (UK) (denying a preliminary injunction against an ad comparing credit card providers' terms); *Vodafone Grp., PLC* v. *Orange Pers. Comms. Serv., Ltd.*, FSR 34 (1996) (UK) (dismissing claim against ad that said a cellphone provider's customers "on average ... save £20 a month" over the competition).

[49] *See* Council Directive 2006/114 (EC). In India, courts similarly require comparisons to be of material, relevant, verifiable and representative features, and comparisons may not compare a product with one designation of origin to another with a different designation of origin. *Havells India Ltd. & Anr.* v. *Amritanshu Khaitan & Ors.*, DelHC CS (OS) 107/2015 (India).

[50] Mark Lemley has observed that plaintiffs often litigate as if the term "unfair competition" is redundant. Mark A. Lemley, *The Surprising Virtues of Treating Trade Secrets as IP Rights*, 61 STAN. L. REV. 311, 322 (2008); *cf.* Mark A. Lemley & Mark P. McKenna, *Unfair Disruption*, https://papers.ssrn.com/sol3/papers.cfm?abstract_id=3344605 (developing the argument at length).

[51] Council Directive 104/89/EEC (EU).

amounts of a desirable ingredient in a canine nutritional supplement. The key question was whether the comparison fell within the "honest practices" exception of the trademark directive.[52] In particular, the existence of a valid trademark doesn't allow its owner

> to prohibit a third party from using, in the course of trade, ... (b) indications concerning the kind, quality, quantity, intended purpose, value, geographical origin, the time of production of goods or of rendering of the service, or other characteristics of goods or services; (c) the trade mark where it is necessary to indicate the intended purpose of a product or service, in particular as accessories or spare parts; provided he uses them in accordance with honest practices in industrial or commercial matters.

The Court of Appeals applied an objective standard for "honesty" and concluded that a truthful comparative claim would be allowed as an honest practice.[53] This was consistent with the relatively pro-comparative advertising position of prior English courts. Under this formulation, there remains a question of whether puffery, which is neither true nor false, is "honest" – which could be resolved in different ways, depending on whether the baseline is to encourage non-false advertising or to prohibit all unauthorized uses of a mark unless they are sufficiently well-justified. Given that British courts have tolerated a fair amount of puffing, the rule most consistent with the rest of ordinary advertising practice would be to allow trademark-related puffery as well, as long as it wasn't misleading or confusing.[54]

Under the EU rules, however, UK courts were forced to limit comparative advertising beyond the preferences of domestic law, despite their "strong predilection, free from the opinion of the ECJ, ... to hold that trade mark law did not prevent traders from making honest statements about their products where those products are themselves lawful."[55] The European Court of Justice held that certain comparative advertising, in particular "smell-alike" advertising for perfumes, was not allowed.[56] As critics supporting the prior English approach have recognized, this suppression of truthful information harms consumers (especially those who don't have the money to buy the original, but perhaps also those of us who have to smell them).[57]

After Brexit, judges or the legislature may decide to restore the former British toleration for unauthorized, nondeceptive uses of trademarks in comparative advertising. As Graeme Dinwoodie and Rochelle Dreyfuss have noted, it will be easier to re-implement a British comparative advertising regime specifically than to reinstate pre-EU trademark rules in general because,

[52] Trademark Act 1994, § 10(6) (UK) (providing an honest practices exemption generally: "Nothing in the preceding provisions of this section shall be construed as preventing the use of a registered trade mark by any person for the purpose of identifying goods or services as those of the proprietor or a licensee. But any such use otherwise than in accordance with honest practices in industrial or commercial matters shall be treated as infringing the registered trade mark if the use without due cause takes unfair advantage of, or is detrimental to, the distinctive character or repute of the trade mark").

[53] *Boehringer Ingelheim & Ors* v. *Vetplus Ltd.* [2007] EWCA Civ. 661 (UK).

[54] *Cable & Wireless plc* v. *British Telecomms plc*, [1998] FSR 383 (UK) (holding that the standard was whether the public would say that the ad was dishonest; the general public expects "hyperbole" from advertisers and the law is not "puritanical" where the public is not likely to be fooled); CAP News, *A Quick Guide to Comparative Advertising* (Feb. 28, 2019), https://asa.org.uk/news/a-quick-guide-to-comparative-advertising.html (guidance provided by British advertising regulatory authority indicating that, though "obvious[] 'puffery'" would be understood as the advertiser's subjective opinion, comparative claims that consumers would understand as objective would need substantiation).

[55] *L'Oréal SA* v. *Bellure NV* [2007] EWCA 968 Civ.; Case C-487/07, *L'Oréal SA* v. *Bellure NV*, [2009] ECR I-5185; *L'Oréal SA* v. *Bellure NV* [2010] EWCA Civ. 535 (Jacob J) (UK).

[56] Case C-87/07, *L'Oreal SA* v. *Bellure NV*, 2009 ECR I-518, 65 (UK).

[57] Carys J. Craig, *Perfume by Any Other Name May Smell as Sweet ... But Who Can Say? A Comment on L'Oreal v. Bellure*, 22 Intell. Prop. J. 321 (2010); Robert Burrel & Dev Gangjee, *Trade Marks and Freedom of Expression: A Call for Caution*, 41 Int'l Rev. Intell. Prop. & Competition L. 544, 559–61 (2010).

though ad campaigns often cross borders, it is still relatively easy to limit ads within specified geographic boundaries.[58] Though an advertiser may want marks, slogans, package shapes and logos to cross oceans and languages, it can and often must be more localized about other, purportedly informational ad content, which is precisely where comparative advertising occurs. Thus, a defense for comparative advertising, whether framed as a matter of the scope of the trademark owner's rights or in some other way, is easier to vary nationally than matters like registration or perhaps even exhaustion.

V OTHER COMMON LAW VARIANTS

Common law jurisdictions vary in how thoroughly trademark exceptionalism has overridden general advertising law principles that otherwise allow truthful and non-false (puffing) claims. In Canada, for example, the Canadian Trade-Marks Act bars unauthorized uses of a mark that depreciate the value of that mark.[59] This could be read as removing protection for truthful, nondeceptive comparative advertising.[60] The first court to interpret this provision did so when Clairol sued Revlon for putting Clairol marks on Revlon's packaging and brochures in the context of a comparison color chart designed to show that the parties' hair color products were equivalent.[61] There were no allegations of false or misleading claims. However, the court nonetheless found that the use on the packaging reduced Clairol's business advantage and thus unlawfully depreciated the goodwill of the marks. The use in brochures didn't count as a regulated "use" of the mark on the goods, according to Canada's definition,[62] so it may also have depreciated the goodwill of the marks but that didn't matter. By contrast, "use" on services includes use in advertising, so brochures and posters comparing *services* would apparently be unlawful regardless of their truth.[63]

Other Canadian courts have prohibited comparative advertising under the depreciation provision only where a defendant falsely implies a connection between the parties.[64] Still others have tried to reconcile the case law by setting up an evanescent distinction between illegitimate comparative advertising that touts the similarities between the parties' products, which supposedly appropriates the plaintiff's goodwill, and legitimate comparative advertising that stresses the differences, distancing itself from the plaintiff's goodwill.[65] Of course, falsely implying a connection is very different from touting the similarities between products – for one thing, absent further information, the touting of the similarities may be completely true, not false.

[58] Graeme B. Dinwoodie & Rochelle Cooper Dreyfuss, *Brexit and IP: The Great Unraveling?*, 39 CARDOZO L. REV. 967 (2018).

[59] Trade-Marks Act, RSC 2010, c. T-13, §22(1) ("No person shall use a trade-mark registered by another person in a manner that is likely to have the effect of depreciating the value of the goodwill attaching thereto").

[60] Norman Siebrasse, , *Comparative Advertising, Dilution, and Section 22 of the Trade-Marks Act*, 18 CAN INTELL. PROP. REV. 276, 280 (2001).

[61] *Clairol In'l Corp. et al.* v. *Thomas Supply & Equip. Co.* (1968), 55 CPR 176 (Can. Ex. Ct.) (Can.). This decision has been criticized for its inconsistent results for goods and services as well as its overextension to uses that don't attempt to use the mark as an indicator of source for the defendant's goods or services).

[62] *See also Syntex Inc.* v. *Apotex Inc.*, (1987) 1 CPR (3d) 145 (Fed.Ct. App.) (Can.) (use on advertising flyer for goods wasn't actionable use on goods).

[63] Mirko Bibic & Vicky Eatrides, *Would Victoria's Secret Be Protected North of the Border? A Revealing Look at Trade-Mark Infringement and Depreciation of Goodwill in Canada*, 93 TRADEMARK REP. 904, 926 (2003).

[64] *Nintendo of America. Inc.* v. *Camerica Corp.* (1991), 34 CPR (3d) 193 (Fed. TD) at 205–06 (Can.).

[65] *Future Shop Ltd.* v. *A. & B. Sound Ltd.* (1994), 55 CPR (3d) 182 (Sup. Ct. Br. Col.) (Can.); *see* David S. Welkowitz, *Protection against Trademark Dilution in the U.K. and Canada: Inexorable Trend or Will Tradition Triumph?*, 24 HASTINGS INT'L & COMP. L. REV. 63, 107 (2000) (pointing out that it's hard to say a price comparison doesn't stress non-price similarities as an inherent part of its appeal, so that *Future Shop*'s distinction is hard to maintain).

It would be better to limit the idea of "appropriating" goodwill to cases of confusing use, not cases of referential use. Otherwise, what constitutes a covered "use" of a mark can dominate the analysis rather than the truth or falsity of the ad in which the mark appears and the resulting benefit or harm to consumers.

New Zealand's limited recent case law is closer to the American model, though it begins with formalist definitions of trademark "use" that more closely resemble Canada's. *Mitre 10 (NZ) Ltd.* v. *Benchmark Building Supplies Ltd.*[66] began after Benchmark posted its competitor Mitre 10's advertising brochures outside its shops with its own lower prices written on stickers that were then stuck over Mitre 10's prices. The brochures had originally been created by Mitre 10 and delivered to houses; Benchmark made no copies of its own. The question was whether this constituted trademark (or copyright) infringement. The Court of Appeal easily saw a prima facie case of trademark infringement. In the brochures, the marks were used to distinguish Mitre 10's goods and services from others' and so Benchmark was using the marks in the same way Mitre 10 did – to perform a trademark function. (One could plausibly say that Benchmark wasn't using Mitre 10's marks to identify Benchmark's *own* goods and services, which is the core trademark function. Instead, it was using the marks to identify the subject matter of its advertising claim. Only if it had been using Mitre 10's marks to identify *itself* would those two things have been the same.)

However, the New Zealand court then examined comparative advertising as a defense. The Trade Marks Act 2002 had removed a longstanding prohibition against comparative advertising. Section 94 now specifies:

> A registered trade-mark is not infringed by the use of the registered trade-mark for the purposes of comparative advertising, but any such use otherwise than in accordance with honest practices in industrial or commercial matters must be treated as infringing the registered trade-mark if the use, without due cause, takes unfair advantage of, or is detrimental to, the distinctive character or the repute of the trade-mark.

The Court of Appeal ruled that the defense should not be construed narrowly. In particular, the use at bar would not be detrimental to the marks' "distinctive character" because Benchmark was using the marks to identify and distinguish Mitre 10's goods – which a court in the United States might have called nominative use. This rather unusual advertising method nonetheless took no more advantage than more conventional forms of comparative advertising and was not unfair.

The New Zealand Court of Appeal explicitly referred to British precedent, specifically Jacob J's decision in *Cable & Wireless plc* v. *British Telecommunications plc*,[67] which interpreted the United Kingdom's highly similar honest practices requirement. In assessing honesty, the Court of Appeal agreed, courts should take into account that members of the public are used to advertising tactics, including the use of hyperbole; by contrast, "[a]n advertisement which is significantly misleading is not honest." The use of the qualifier "significantly," which might be analogized to "materially" in US jargon, indicates that perfect accuracy is not required as long as the gist or sting of the comparison is true. Thus, despite finding prima facie infringement, the ultimate outcome in *Mitre 10* was very similar to that in the United States: truthful, nonmisleading advertising is protected even when it uses another's trademark without permission.

66 *Benchmark Bldg. Supplies Ltd.* v. *Mitre 10 Ltd.* [2004] 1 NZLR 26 (CA) (NZ); Alexandra Sims, *Shop Wars: Copyright, Moral Rights, and Comparative Advertising*, 10 N.Z. Bus. L. Q. 9 (2004).

67 *Cable & Wireless plc* v. *British Telecomms. plc* [1998] FSR 383 (UK).

VI CONCLUSION: SOME COMPARISONS

Advertising law in the United States has a strong pro-comparative advertising tilt. Trademark law has the potential to interfere with that policy, even after the clear exclusion of comparative advertising from dilution liability. The current US approach often relies on judges' intuitions that blatant comparisons aren't confusing, or in the alternative uses a test for noninfringement that tries to formalize that intuition. The strong version of the Ninth Circuit nominative use test does the best at shutting down anticompetitive lawsuits by allowing most comparative uses to be set outside the scope of trademark law and committed to the jurisdiction of false advertising law without detailed inquiry.

However, not all bright-line rules are the same. For example, the Canadian approach seems overcommitted to a formal definition of "use as a mark" that produces conflicting results for goods versus for services, which can have no justification in utility or morality. Moreover, where there is "use," protecting marks against denigration can mean prohibiting truthful comparative advertising. This interferes with consumers' decision making and provides the trademark owner with an unfair advantage of its own – protection against competition from an alternative that the consumer might prefer, as in the *Clairol* case.

The UK approach first asks whether the use is confusing, and seems to protect clear comparisons as nonconfusing, without intricate doctrinal maneuvering.[68] The next step, allowing comparative advertising consistent with honest practices, leaves much room for debate; what *other* than false advertising could be inconsistent with honest practices? But if, as Jacob J suggested, honesty and lack of falsehood or misleadingness are coextensive, then the UK rule has much to recommend it.

Fundamentally, false advertising law has a much more sensible approach to comparative advertising. We should be asking what's true and what's false, and we should only ban the latter. That still requires a rule for when comparative advertising is neither true nor false – as in the *Deere* case, where the challenged use of a plaintiff's mark is in the service of mere negative puffery. The target of brand mockery now might seem less attractive for unquantifiable, emotional reasons. Many trademark owners believe that, even if they acquired their reputations through puffery and unfalsifiable claims, they should not be exposed to losing their reputations through others' similar tactics. This seems like unwillingness to allow competitors to play by the same rules of non-factual reputation-shaping. True, the law in its majesty allows unknowns to puff themselves up as they please just as the big players do, but for a new entrant, that technique often isn't nearly as helpful as it was for an earlier market participant, nor is it as effective as gaining attention with a reference to a better-known competitor. Truthful and unfalsifiable comparative advertising encourages competition, whether it is on prices or even just on the ability to build an attractive image for consumers. Trademark law should do its best not to interfere with this dynamic.

[68] O2 v. *Hutchison* 3G (C-533/06) [2008] ETMR 853 (UK).

VII

The Relationship between Trademark Law and the Right of Publicity

21

Commercial Exploitation of the Human Persona in the United States

Who Needs Trademarks When You Have the Right of Publicity?

*David Tan**

I INTRODUCTION

This chapter explores the overlap between the right of publicity and trademark laws in the protection of the commercial value of the human persona against unauthorized exploitation. It discusses the ambit of trademark registration for the indicia of identity of well-known individuals and interrogates whether it would even be necessary for celebrities, in light of the availability of the right of publicity in a majority of state jurisdictions in the United States, to seek trademark registration for distinctive aspects of their personae.

It has been pointed out that there is much in common between the right of publicity and trademark law: "The right of publicity protects a celebrity's interest in her name and likeness, much as trademark law protects a business's name. Both areas of law give rights-holders some measure of control over the meaning of their identities by permitting them to control the use of associated symbols."[1] Indeed, over a decade ago Stacey Dogan and Mark Lemley argued that the right of publicity should be reconceived as a trademark-like right in order to better comprehend and cabin the expansive scope of the right of publicity.[2] However, their clarion call has fallen on deaf ears as the right of publicity continues its victorious march to protect against the unauthorized commercial uses of celebrities' likenesses from greeting cards to video games.[3]

In the twenty-first century, celebrities, like trademarks, have become common points of reference for millions of individuals who may be total strangers but share a collective transnational consumer culture.[4] In the United States, the judicial recognition of an expansive list of actionable indicia of identity in the common law right-of-publicity cases is supported by a generous statutory framework in states like California and Illinois. The right of publicity, broadly defined as the "inherent right of every human being to control the commercial use of his or her identity,"[5] has been well-established in the United States for over six

* Professor and Vice Dean (Academic Affairs), Faculty of Law, National University of Singapore; Director (Intellectual Property), EW Barker Centre for Law & Business.

[1] Stacey L. Dogan & Mark A. Lemley, *What the Right of Publicity Can Learn from Trademark Law*, 58 STAN. L. REV. 1161, 1164 (2006).

[2] *Id.* at 1165–66.

[3] *E.g.*, *Hilton* v. *Hallmark Cards*, 599 F.3d 894 (9th Cir. 2010); *Hart* v. *Elec. Arts, Inc.*, 717 F.3d 141 (3d Cir. 2013); *Keller* v. *Elec. Arts, Inc. (In re NCAA Student-Athlete Name & Likeness Licensing Litig.)*, 724 F.3d 1268 (9th Cir. 2013); *Davis* v. *Elec. Arts, Inc.*, 775 F.3d 1172 (9th Cir. 2015).

[4] DAVID TAN, THE COMMERCIAL APPROPRIATION OF FAME: A CULTURAL ANALYSIS OF THE RIGHT OF PUBLICITY AND PASSING OFF 27 (2017).

[5] J. THOMAS MCCARTHY, THE RIGHTS OF PUBLICITY AND PRIVACY § 3:1 (2d ed. 2000) (Apr. 2018 update).

decades.[6] It is not a trademark right, but it protects the "associative value" that celebrities bring to products and services.[7] It does not require one to prove a likelihood of confusion, but it requires a proof of fame. It exists not for the furtherance of the interests of consumers or for the progress of the arts and sciences, but for the economic benefit of the famous individual. Generally perceived to be a property right akin to an intangible or intellectual property right, the right of publicity has been invoked mainly by celebrities to monetize their identity and to prevent unauthorized commercial uses of various aspects of their persona.

Section II provides an overview of the nature and scope of the right of publicity in its protection of the human persona as it is commonly understood in the United States. Section III discusses the obstacles one may encounter in attempting to register the human persona as a trademark, focusing on the requirements of distinctiveness and source-identifying function. Section IV concludes that in light of the expansive reach of the right of publicity, there is no compelling reason to extend trademark protection to the human persona in the United States.

II THE SCOPE OF THE RIGHT OF PUBLICITY

A *Overview of the Right of Publicity*

Despite its controversial nature and lack of acceptance in virtually all the common law jurisdictions outside of the United States, Thomas McCarthy, one of the foremost authorities on the right of publicity, remarks, "the initial phase of questioning what the right of publicity is, and whether it should exist at all, has passed into history."[8] Dogan and Lemley have identified the rationales as belonging to three categories: "the moral or natural rights story; the exhaustion or allocative-efficiency account; and the incentive-based rationale."[9] These theoretical justifications have all been subject to numerous criticisms,[10] but there is no doubt that the right of publicity is firmly entrenched in American jurisprudence and provides the fundamental protection for the commercial value of the celebrity identity in the United States.

To establish a prima face case, a plaintiff must usually prove that their identity has been used, that is, a "more than de minimis number of ordinary viewers of [the] defendant's use identify the plaintiff."[11] Each of the US states that recognize the right of publicity has a different definition of identity. There exists a cornucopia of common law and statutory publicity right regimes in over thirty states.[12]

The Ninth Circuit has pointed out that "[i]dentifiability ... is a central element of a right of publicity claim."[13] Unlike in Lanham Act section 43(a) claims in the United States and passing-off claims in Commonwealth common law jurisdictions such as the United Kingdom and

[6] It was first recognized by the Second Circuit in 1953 that baseball players had a "right of publicity" in their images. *Haelan Labs., Inc.* v. *Topps Chewing Gum, Inc.*, 202 F.2d 866, 868 (2d Cir. 1953). In the only right-of-publicity case ever to reach the US Supreme Court, the Court affirmed the recognition of such an actionable right. *Zacchini* v. *Scripps-Howard Broad. Co.*, 433 US 562 (1977) ("*Zacchini*").

[7] Tan, *supra* note 4, at 2.

[8] McCarthy, *supra* note 5, at § 1:34.

[9] Dogan & Lemley, *supra* note 1, at 1180 (footnotes omitted).

[10] For a summary of these criticisms, see Tan, *supra* note 4, at 45–62.

[11] McCarthy, *supra* note 5, at § 3:17.

[12] In 2018, thirty-three states had provided their citizens with a remedy for infringement of the right of publicity. Twenty-one states recognize publicity rights by way of common law, and of those, eight also have statutory provisions broad enough to encompass the right of publicity. McCarthy, *supra* note 5, at § 6:2.

[13] *Waits* v. *Frito-Lay, Inc.*, 978 F.2d 1093, 1102 (9th Cir. 1992) ("*Waits*"). *See also White* v. *Samsung Elecs. Am., Inc.*, 971 F.2d 1395, 1398–99 (9th Cir. 1992) ("*White*").

Australia, in a right-of-publicity claim, there is no need to prove likelihood of confusion as to source or endorsement or misleading conduct. The classic definition of identity in a common law claim is usually "name and likeness," with a number of states recognizing "persona" as a broader concept encompassing all aspects of identity, while the definition in a statutory cause of action tends to enumerate specific actionable aspects of identity like "name, voice, signature, photograph or likeness."[14] These indicia of identity would be relevant for the purposes of possible trademark registration.[15] It is important to appreciate that an expansive interpretation of what constitutes actionable aspects of identity does not equate liability for the defendant. Theoretically, once the plaintiff is identified from the defendant's use, one should proceed to consider if the commercial value of that identity has been appropriated by the defendant. In the final and most significant hurdle, the right of publicity, whether common law or statutory in nature, must be weighed against the preeminent position of the freedoms of speech and press guaranteed in the First Amendment. In articulating the First Amendment defense, the conflict between free speech values and the plaintiff's proprietary right of publicity presents a significant challenge for courts attempting to formulate different balancing tests to resolve this issue, but the transformative elements/use test appear to have gained support from a majority of Circuit Courts.[16] This test draws from the first factor of the fair use doctrine in copyright law: an unauthorized use of celebrity identity would be permitted if it was "transformative." Transformativeness, according to this approach, protects creative works when their market value is derived primarily from the creativity added by the artist rather than from the celebrity's fame.[17]

B *An Expansive Protection of Actionable Indicia of Identity*

Since the landmark recognition of publicity rights in *Haelan Laboratories, Inc.* v. *Topps Chewing Gum, Inc.*,[18] courts have had difficulty determining the extent to which a use must evoke a celebrity's persona before the use violates their right of publicity. Courts have used the term "persona" as an all-encompassing label for all those elements which identify a person. The state jurisdiction of California, as well as the Sixth and Ninth Circuits,[19] have extended the actionable indicia of identity to any distinctive aspect of a celebrity's public personality. The *Restatement (Third)* has also chosen the California approach as its model code in allowing claims for the unauthorized use of "name, likeness, or other indicia of identity."[20] It has been said that the right of publicity is no longer limited to "the name and likeness of an individual, but

[14] E.g., CAL. CIVIL CODE § 3344 (West 2018); N.Y. CIV. RIGHTS LAW §§ 50–51 (2018); TENN. CODE ANN. § 47-25-1101 to 1108 (2018). Illinois extends protection to all aspects of the human persona. Illinois Right of Publicity Act 1999, 765 ILL. COMP. STAT. ANN. 1075/5 (2018).

[15] Lanham Act, 15 USC § 1127 (2006) ("any word, name, symbol, or device" is registrable).

[16] E.g., *Cardtoons, LC* v. *Major League Baseball Players Ass'n*, 95 F.3d 959, 969–76 (10th Cir. 1996); *ETW Corp.* v. *Jireh Publ'g, Inc.*, 332 F.3d 915, 922 (6th Cir. 2003) ("*ETW Corp.*"); *Hilton* v. *Hallmark Cards*, 599 F.3d 894 (9th Cir. 2010); *Hart* v. *Elec. Arts, Inc.*, 717 F.3d 141 (3d Cir. 2013).

[17] For a discussion of this test, see TAN, *supra* note 4, at 167–76. The key question for courts adopting the transformative use test is "whether the depiction or imitation of the celebrity is the very sum and substance of the work in question" (in which case the defendant is liable for commercial appropriation of identity) or "whether a product containing a celebrity's likeness is so transformed that it has become primarily the defendant's own expression rather than the celebrity's likeness" (in which case the First Amendment trumps the plaintiff's claim).

[18] *Haelan Labs., Inc.* v. *Topps Chewing Gum, Inc.*, 202 F.2d 866 (2d Cir. 1953).

[19] E.g., *Carson* v. *Here's Johnny Portable Toilets, Inc.*, 698 F.2d 831 (6th Cir. 1983) ("*Carson*"); *Midler* v. *Ford Motor Co.*, 849 F.2d 460 (9th Cir. 1988); *White*, 971 F.2d 1395 (9th Cir. 1992); *Wendt* v. *Host Int'l, Inc.*, 125 F.3d 806 (9th Cir. 1997).

[20] RESTATEMENT OF THE LAW (THIRD) OF UNFAIR COMPETITION § 46 (1995).

now extends to a person's nickname, signature, physical pose, characterization, singing style, vocal characteristics, body parts, frequently used phrases, car, performance style, mannerisms, and gestures, provided that these are distinctive and publicly identified with the person claiming the right."[21] The use of "name" has been widely accepted to include a plaintiff's real name, nickname, stage name or fictitious name. The touchstone for identification appears to be that the "name" must identify the plaintiff *as the celebrity* that the consuming public is familiar with. But the plaintiff's name has to be used as a symbol of identity to obtain a commercial advantage and not as a mere name. Thus, the use of his real name "John William Carson," which does not identify Johnny Carson the celebrity, would not satisfy the identifiability requirement in a right-of-publicity claim.[22] The courts have made it clear that mere name-sameness of a fictional character is not sufficient identifiability to satisfy a right-of-publicity claim; the courts will consider "plus factors"[23] like whether the defendant intentionally named a character after the plaintiff and whether the target audience for the defendant's product was the same as the plaintiff's audience.

"Likeness" is a generic label used, particularly in a common law publicity claim, to encompass two- and three-dimensional visual representations that portray the plaintiff's persona through their physical appearance. Examples of "likeness" include picture, portrait, image and photograph in a variety of media like painting, drawing and sculpture, where the facial characteristics of the plaintiff are recognizable.[24] In *Newcombe* v. *Adolf Coors Co.*, the drawing of a baseball player depicting him in a distinctive windup stance was held to be readily identifiable as the plaintiff by the public.[25] In *Allen* v. *National Video*[26] and *Onassis* v. *Christian Dior-New York*,[27] both Woody Allen and Jacqueline Kennedy Onassis succeeded in obtaining injunctions against the use of pictures featuring their lookalikes in advertisements. Even where the likeness has been altered, for example in a video game or comic book character[28] or in a digitally manipulated photograph,[29] the celebrity still may be identified in light of the factual circumstances.

The word "evoke" generally means "to call forth," "to conjure up," or "to bring to mind or recollection." Presently, all the other indicia of identity outside of "name" and "likeness" which are recognized by the courts fall into three broad categories, united by their ability to – either singularly or in various combinations – "evoke" the celebrity in the minds of the audience in a manner that readily identifies the plaintiff. These three categories are: (i) a distinctive voice that evokes the celebrity (as represented by the typical sound-alike imitation cases); (ii) a role or character that is evocative of the plaintiff (as represented by the typical use of a film or television

[21] Rosemary J. Coombe, *Author/izing the Celebrity: Publicity Rights, Postmodern Politics, and Unauthorized Genders*, 10 CARDOZO ARTS & ENTM'T L.J. 365, 367 (1992).

[22] *Carson*, 698 F.2d at 837.

[23] MCCARTHY, *supra* note 5, at § 4:48. When Lew Alcindor converted to Islam and adopted the Muslim name Kareem Abdul-Jabbar, the Ninth Circuit held that the unauthorized use of the plaintiff's little-known birth name "Lew Alcindor" together with other factual information of his basketball victories in an advertisement nevertheless may sufficiently enable the audience to identify the celebrity Kareem Abdul-Jabbar. *Abdul-Jabbar* v. *Gen. Motors Corp.*, 85 F.3d 407, 416 (9th Cir. 1996).

[24] E.g., *Wendt* v. *Host Int'l, Inc.*, 125 F.3d 806 (9th Cir. 1997).

[25] *Newcombe* v. *Adolf Coors Co.*, 157 F.3d 686, 692 (9th Cir. 1998).

[26] *Allen* v. *Nat'l Video, Inc.*, 610 F.Supp. 612 (SDNY 1985).

[27] *Onassis* v. *Christian Dior-New York, Inc.*, 472 NYS 2d 254 (1984).

[28] E.g., *Kirby* v. *Sega of Am., Inc.*, 144 Cal. App. 4th 47 (2006) ("*Kirby*"); *Winter* v. *DC Comics*, 30 Cal. 4th 881 (2003) ("*Winter*"); *Doe* v. *TCI Cablevision*, 110 SW 3d 363, 369 (Mo. 2003) ("*Doe*").

[29] E.g., *Hoffman* v. *Capital Cities/ABC, Inc.*, 255 F.3d 1180 (9th Cir. 2001); *Grant* v. *Esquire, Inc.*, 367 F.Supp. 876 (SDNY 1973).

character popularized by the plaintiff); (iii) other indicia that evoke the celebrity (as seen in the more difficult cases where the defendant may have used a combination of objects, dress, makeup, performing style, music, set design, etc.).

The Ninth Circuit decisions for the state of California have expanded the meaning of identity in a common law publicity claim to include virtually any attribute associated with a celebrity individual.[30] Even where the use of a robot that was identified with Vanna White probably did not constitute a likeness of the celebrity, the Ninth Circuit held that it may nonetheless be an appropriation of her identity under a common law claim and remanded the case for trial.[31] Similarly, the Third Circuit, in interpreting New Jersey law, extends a generous reading of identity to any "defining trait that becomes associated with a person when he [or she] gains notoriety or fame."[32] Such an expansive and charitable reading of actionable indicia of identity for a common law right-of-publicity claim finds no parallel in trademark law.

The Ninth Circuit's decision in *White* v. *Samsung* has "probably gone the farthest in any case in any court in the [United States]"[33] in protecting publicity rights. The expansive approach in *White* may have a considerable influence in other state jurisdictions because of the deference that Ninth Circuit decisions are usually given in cases concerning publicity rights.[34] Refusing to "permit the evisceration of the common law right of publicity,"[35] the Ninth Circuit majority held that the identifiability of the plaintiff in a common law right-of-publicity action extended beyond name and likeness to anything that evoked the plaintiff's personality.[36] Thus, like a name, likeness, voice or fictitious character, different combinations of objects, symbols, gestures, words, music and other indicia can also trigger the public's recognition of the plaintiff.[37]

In summary, the identity requirement so broadly construed can include any characteristic that is clearly evocative of a particular celebrity in the minds of the audience,[38] rendering the right of publicity a powerful weapon to prevent unauthorized commercial appropriation of the human persona. As Jennifer Rothman remarked, "once the Supreme Court in *Zacchini* officially placed the right of publicity in the pantheon of IP, it began to expand . . . far beyond what its underlying justifications merited."[39]

[30] *E.g.*, *White*, 971 F.2d 1395 (9th Cir. 1992); *Waits*, 978 F.2d 1093 (9th Cir. 1992); *Midler*, 849 F.2d 460 (9th Cir. 1988); *Motschenbacher* v. *R. J. Reynolds Tobacco Co.*, 498 F.2d 821 (9th Cir. 1974).

[31] *White*, 971 F.2d at 1399.

[32] *McFarland* v. *Miller*, 14 F.3d 912, 923 (3d Cir. 1994). In this case, the court held that it was a triable issue of fact to whether George McFarland had become so inextricably identified with Spanky – a character the deceased actor portrayed in the "Our Gang" comedy series – that his own identity would be invoked by the name "Spanky."

[33] Steven C. Clay, *Starstruck: The Overextension of Celebrity Publicity Rights in State and Federal Courts*, 79 MINN. L. REV. 485, 486 (1994).

[34] Arlen W. Langvardt, *The Troubling Implications of a Right of Publicity "Wheel" Spun out of Control*, 45 UNIV. KAN. L. REV. 329, 330–31 (1997). While *White* was decided over twenty-five years ago, it is still being cited today as an authority, together with *Zacchini*, for upholding the right of publicity in a variety of situations where the defendant has appropriated the economic value that the plaintiff has built in an identity or performance. *E.g.*, *Sarver* v. *Chartier*, 813 F.3d 891 (9th Cir. 2016).

[35] *White*, 971 F.2d 1395, 1399 (9th Cir. 1992).

[36] *Id.* at 1398–99. The majority referred to *Motschenbacher*, *Midler* and *Carson* with approval.

[37] In *Jordan* v. *Jewel Food Stores, Inc.*, the Seventh Circuit held that Jewel's ad, depicting a pair of basketball shoes which bore on the tongue of each shoe the number "23," which Michael Jordan wore for most of his tenure with the Chicago Bulls, was a misappropriation of his identity. *See Jordan* v. *Jewel Food Stores, Inc.*, 743 F.3d 509 (7th Cir. 2014).

[38] Unsurprisingly, this expansive scope of actionable indicia of identity has been criticized by a number of scholars. *E.g.*, Daniel Gervais & Martin L. Holmes, *Fame, Property, and Identity: The Scope and Purpose of the Right of Publicity*, 25 FORDHAM INTELL. PROP., MEDIA & ENTERTAINMENT L.J. 181, 221–23 (2014).

[39] JENNIFER E. ROTHMAN, THE RIGHT OF PUBLICITY: PRIVACY REIMAGINED FOR A PUBLIC WORLD 87 (2018). *See also id.* at 67–86.

III THE HUMAN PERSONA QUALIFYING AS A TRADEMARK

A *Overview of Trademark Registration*

In US law, a trademark is defined to include "any word, name, symbol, or device, or any combination thereof – used by a person … to identify and distinguish his or her goods … from those manufactured or sold by others and to indicate the *source of the goods*."[40] The terms "symbol" or "device" would seem appropriate for natural attributes of the human persona such as likeness or voice, and should encompass other evocative aspects of identity such as inanimate objects in line with the more generous right-of-publicity laws in certain state jurisdictions. Recent developments of the law suggest that these terms would cover a wide kaleidoscope of subject matter, and exclude only subject matter specifically listed as unregistrable under the Lanham Act.[41]

However, there are still a couple of significant obstacles. In order to register a trademark, the dual requirements of distinctiveness and source identifier must be satisfied.[42]

1 *Distinctiveness*

The US Lanham Act does not define "descriptive," but it prohibits the registration of marks that are "merely descriptive" of the goods or services for which the marks are sought to be registered.[43]

Registration always requires that an applicant prove the mark is distinctive.[44] The courts have interpreted this requirement to be satisfied by showing the mark (i) is either inherently distinctive, or has acquired distinctiveness through secondary meaning and (ii) is not functional.[45] Depending on a mark's eligibility for trademark registration, an owner of a mark may seek federal protection under either the principal or supplemental register.[46] Section 43(a) of the Lanham Act also provides a federal cause of action for infringement of an unregistered trademark which affords such marks essentially the same protection as those that are registered.[47] The broadly phrased false designation of origin provision provides a civil remedy to litigants whose indicia of identity have been used in a commercial context.[48]

Under the current interpretation of the Lanham Act, celebrities may receive trademark protection for their name if their name has acquired secondary meaning by becoming associated

[40] Lanham Act, 15 USC § 1127 (2006) (emphasis added).

[41] *Id.* § 1052.

[42] *E.g.*, *Viacom Int'l, Inc.* v. *IJR Capital Invs., LLC*, 891 F.3d 178 (5th Cir. 2018).

[43] Lanham Act, 15 USC § 1052 (e)(1), (f).

[44] *Id.* § 1052.

[45] *E.g.*, *Qualitex Co.* v. *Jacobsen Prods. Co.*, 514 US 159, 165 (1995); *Two Pesos, Inc.* v. *Taco Cabana, Inc.*, 505 US 763, 768 (1992); *Inwood Labs., Inc.* v. *Ives Labs., Inc.*, 456 US 844, 851 n. 11 (1982); *Christian Louboutin SA* v. *Yves Saint Laurent America Holding, Inc.*, 696 F.3d 206, 216–28 (2d Cir. 2012).

[46] *See* J. Thomas McCarthy, McCarthy on Trademarks and Unfair Competition § 19.36 (4th ed. 2013) (June 2018 update). A supplemental registration confers no benefits of validity beyond those gained at common law. Principal registration receives the strongest federal trademark protection providing "prima facie evidence of the validity of the registered mark … and of the owner's exclusive right to use the registered mark." 15 USC § 1057(b). *See also* § 1091(c).

[47] *Two Pesos, Inc.* v. *Taco Cabana, Inc.*, 505 US 763, 768 (1992). When Colonel David Randolph Scott, a retired astronaut and the mission commander for NASA's 1971 Apollo 15 voyage, best known for being the seventh man to walk on the moon, sued Bulova for using his identity in various forms in the advertisements and promotional materials for the commemorative Lunar Pilot Chronograph (the Moon Watch) based on the original chronograph that Scott wore to the moon, the court held that one does not need to have a registered trademark for products that he is marketing or selling in order to proceed with a false endorsement claim. *Scott* v. *Citizen Watch Co. of Am., Inc.*, 2018 WL 1626773 at *9 (ND Cal. 2018).

[48] 15 USC § 1125 (a)(1)(A).

in the minds of consumers with a particular source.[49] A number of celebrities in the United States have succeeded in registering their names as a trademark.[50] For example, Johnny Carson's name was found by the Trademark Appeal Board to have acquired secondary meaning as the source of particular television "monologues, comedy routines and the hosting of guest appearances of others."[51] Likewise, a single image which contains the likeness of a celebrity can also be registered as a trademark if it has acquired secondary meaning, such as a distinctive "Elvis Pose" where Elvis Presley was "dressed in one of his characteristic jumpsuits and holding a microphone in a singing pose."[52] However, the court cautioned that not all images or likenesses of Elvis Presley would qualify for trademark protection, but only those with featured the specific "Elvis Pose." Unlike the right of publicity, which may protect the general likeness of a well-known individual, a celebrity is unable to secure a trademark in their overall likeness. The Sixth Circuit also confirmed that the right of publicity and trademark laws function differently, holding that Tiger Woods could not prohibit the sale of paintings and lithographs by Rick Rush depicting his likeness:

> Images and likenesses of Woods are not protectable as a trademark because they do not perform the trademark function of designation. They do not distinguish and identify the source of goods. They cannot function as a trademark because there are undoubtedly thousands of images and likenesses of Woods taken by countless photographers, and drawn, sketched, or painted by numerous artists, which have been published in many forms of media, and sold and distributed throughout the world. No reasonable person could believe that merely because these photographs or paintings contain Woods's likeness or image, they all originated with Woods.[53]

In urging the United States Patent and Trademark Office (USPTO) to restructure its registration requirements to accommodate a spectrum of celebrity likenesses as trademarks, it has been argued that a celebrity persona "surely has the capacity to operate as an identifying source or origin of any goods or services associated with the celebrity."[54] While a celebrity individual may be readily identified or recognized from uses of myriad indicia of identity in a commercial context, this does not inevitably equate to the public identifying the particular celebrity as the *source or origin* of the goods or services depicting that celebrity. Courts across the common law world have repeatedly emphasized this point in both trademark infringement and passing-off claims.

To qualify as a trademark, a persona mark has to satisfy all three requirements: (i) the mark exists in a tangible form as a word, name, symbol, device or any combination of these, and is distinctive; (ii) the particular aspect of persona is adopted and used as a mark by a manufacturer or seller of goods or services; and (iii) it identifies and distinguishes the seller's good or services from those made or sold by others.[55] The primary rationales for trademark protection have been well-canvassed by the courts and scholars and will not be revisited here.[56] The essence of

49 Secondary meaning may be proven through factors such as survey evidence, testimony of consumers, exclusivity, the manner and length of the use. *E.g.*, *Filipino Yellow Pages, Inc.* v. *Asian J. Publ'n, Inc.*, 198 F.3d 1143, 1151 (9th Cir. 1999).

50 A name, portrait, or signature identifying a particular living individual may only be registered with the "written consent" of that individual. 15 USC § 1052 (c).

51 *In re Carson*, 197 USPQ (BNA) 554, 555 (TTAB 1977). In contrast, Carson gets a broader protection for his persona under the right of publicity where it was found that the phrase "Here's Johnny" was a protectable indicia of identity. *Carson*, 698 F.2d 831 (6th Cir. 1983).

52 *Estate of Presley* v. *Russen*, 513 F. Supp. 1339, 1364 (DNJ 1981)

53 *ETW Corp.*, 332 F.3d 915, 922 (6th Cir. 2003).

54 Ann Olivier McGeehan, *Trademark Registration of a Celebrity Persona*, 87 Trademark Rep. 351, 361 (1997).

55 J. Thomas McCarthy, McCarthy on Trademarks and Unfair Competition § 3.1 (2002).

56 *E.g.*, *Mishawaka Rubber & Woolen Mfg. Co.* v. *S. S. Kresge Co.*, 316 US 203, 205 (1942); *Park 'n Fly* v. *Dollar Park & Fly*, 469 US 189, 198 (1985). The Supreme Court has commented: "[T]rademark law, by preventing others from

trademark law, at least traditionally, is "to prevent competitors from diverting consumers who, had they not been deceived, would have purchased from the trademark owner."[57]

The human persona is not expressly barred from registration as a trademark. However, as a general rule, a person's image or likeness cannot function as a trademark,[58] *unless* a particular likeness had acquired secondary meaning capable of accomplishing a source-identifying function. In particular, a significant difficulty lies in proving that a celebrity's likeness has acquired a meaning beyond identifying the individual.[59] The celebrity individual must demonstrate that the likeness – or any persona mark sought to be registered – identifies and *distinguishes* their goods from those of others.[60] This acquired distinctiveness requirement is intertwined with the source-identifying function, which will be discussed in the next section.

Secondary meaning arises when a descriptive – or otherwise unprotectable – word or phrase has been used in such a manner, for a sufficient duration and frequency, that it becomes uniquely identified with the user and/or the user's product.[61] While it appears that a plethora of indicia of identity may be registered as a trademark, a celebrity is unable to own an "amorphous" trademark in their likeness or overall appearance,[62] although a right of publicity may subsist in one's likeness. Ann McGeehan observes that the narrow drawing requirement for trademark application fails to accommodate the entire celebrity persona to be protected as it protects only a singular visual expression of a celebrity's likeness; she notes that unauthorized users can easily find another angle, pose or costume which clearly invokes a mental impression of the celebrity.[63] The Sixth Circuit Court of Appeals has held that the likeness "of a human being, unlike a portrait of a fanciful cartoon character, is not inherently 'distinctive' in the trademark sense of tending to indicate origin."[64] However, Circuit Courts have also recognized the likeness of celebrity – including other indicia of identity – as if it is an *unregistered trademark* for the purposes of a false endorsement claim under Lanham Act section 43(a). Mark Lee commented that these quasi-trademark decisions effectively hold that "virtually any indicia of a celebrity in an advertisement or on merchandise could be 'unfair' if it misleads an appreciable portion of the consuming public into believing the celebrity recognizable by the indicia used endorsed the product."[65] Indeed the recognition of evocative aspects of identity (i.e., beyond the natural attributes of the human persona) as actionable in a right-of-publicity claim in the number of US

copying a source-identifying mark, reduces the customer's costs of shopping and making purchasing decisions, for it quickly and easily assures a potential customer that *this* item – the item with this mark – is made by the same producer as other similarly marked items that he or she liked (or disliked) in the past." *Qualitex Co.* v. *Jacobsen Prods. Co.*, 514 US 159, 163–64 (1995).

57 Mark A. Lemley & Mark McKenna, *Irrelevant Confusion*, 62 Stan. L. Rev. 413, 422 (2010).

58 *ETW Corp.*, 332 F.3d 915, 922 (6th Cir. 2003); *Pirone* v. *MacMillan, Inc.*, 894 F.2d 579, 583 (2d Cir. 1990).

59 This rule extends to the general use of likenesses. Commenting that "a designation may serve both ornamental and source-identifying purposes," the Sixth Circuit held that Museum's disparate uses of several different perspectives of its building design failed to "create a consistent and distinct commercial impression as an indicator of a single source of origin or sponsorship." *Rock & Roll Hall of Fame & Museum, Inc.* v. *Gentile Prods.*, 134 F.3d 749, 755 (6th Cir. 1998).

60 *See* Naeha Prakash, *Stars in Their Eyes: The Dominance of the Celebrity Brand and Intellectual Property Norms Protection through Fan Goodwill*, 35 Hastings Comm. & Ent. L.J. 247, 259 (2013). *See also* Justin F. McNaughton, Ryan Kairalla, Leslie José Zigel & Armando Christian Perez, *EEEEEEEYOOOOOO!: Reflections on Protecting Pitbull's Famous* Grito, 9 N.Y.U. J. Intell. Prop. & Ent. L. 179 (2020).

61 Restatement (Third) of Unfair Competition § 13, cmt. e (1993); Anthony L. Fletcher, *Separating Descriptive Sheep from Generic Goats*, 103 Trademark Rep. 487, 487 (2013).

62 McCarthy, *supra* note 46, at § 10.39 ("While a certain image of a person can certainly serve as a good trademark or service mark, there cannot be such a thing as a trademark that consists of any and all images of a person").

63 McGeehan, *supra* note 54, at 353.

64 *ETW Corp.*, 332 F.3d 915, 922 (6th Cir. 2003).

65 Mark S. Lee, Entertainment and Intellectual Property Law § 13:7 (2013).

state jurisdictions such as California and Illinois may also be persuasive in a Lanham Act false endorsement claim that such distinctive and commercially valuable aspects of a celebrity's identity should also be regarded as "marks"; false endorsement claims were advanced with right-of-publicity claims in cases such as *White*, *Wendt*, and *Carson*.

2 *Source-Identifying Function*

Whether one views it as a trademark registration requirement or as a consideration in an infringement claim, the "use as a mark" requirement to identify the source of goods or services can be a key impediment to the success of celebrities enforcing persona marks. It has been argued that since contemporary trademark law has advanced to protect a kaleidoscope of distinctive source identifiers that span the spectrum of colors, scents, sounds, fictional characters and various indicia of a celebrity's personality, the overall likeness of a celebrity should be accepted for trademark registration so long as it can serve the same source-identifying function.[66]

In response to criticisms that a celebrity's likeness is always changing and hence should not be recognized as a trademark, Matt Whibley points out that "trademark law protects morphing marks as long as they create the same commercial impression."[67] He further explains: "[E]ach image of a person is different – a different camera angle, different lighting, exposure, or different artistic medium all together. Yet these images, in whatever manner they appear, create the same commercial impression – the recognizable identity of the celebrity."[68] Even if one accepts Whibley's contention that general likeness is prima facie registrable because changes in a celebrity's appearance nonetheless convey the same commercial impression,[69] it is still difficult to overcome the objection that a celebrity's likeness is *not* a source identifier. However, celebrities can nonetheless fall back on a Lanham Act section 43(a) false endorsement claim.

Goods bearing a celebrity's likeness – for instance, memorabilia depicting Princess Diana,[70] calendars featuring Babe Ruth,[71] or paintings using Tiger Woods' likeness[72] – are *about* that celebrity, not *originating from* that celebrity. In *Pirone* v. *MacMillan*, the Second Circuit emphasized: "Such use is not a trademark use and not an infringement ... the photographs ... indicate the contents of the calendar, not its source."[73] Even without the benefit of a registered-likeness trademark, celebrities may nonetheless avail themselves of a false endorsement claim under section 43(a) of the Lanham Act as if an unauthorized commercial use of their likeness was an infringement of an unregistered mark, as clearly indicated by the Ninth Circuit in *Downing* v. *Abercrombie & Fitch*.[74]

[66] Matt Whibley, *Celebrity and Trademarks: Why Courts Should Recognize a Celebrity-Likeness Mark*, 43 Sw. L. Rev. 121, 131–44 (2013).

[67] *Id.* at 139 (citing *Qualitex Co.* v. *Jacobsen Prods. Co.*, 514 US 159, 164 (1995)).

[68] *Id.*

[69] *Contra Rock & Roll Hall of Fame & Museum, Inc.* v. *Gentile Prods.*, 134 F.3d 749, 755 (6th Cir. 1998).

[70] *Cairns* v. *Franklin Mint Co.*, 107 F.Supp.2d 1212, 1216 (CD Cal. 2000).

[71] *Pirone* v. *MacMillan, Inc.*, 894 F.2d 579, 584 (2d Cir. 1990).

[72] *ETW Corp.*, 332 F.3d 915, 922 (6th Cir. 2003).

[73] *Pirone* v. *MacMillan, Inc.*, 894 F.2d 579, 584 (2d Cir. 1990).

[74] *Downing* v. *Abercrombie & Fitch*, 265 F.3d 994 (9th Cir. 2001) ("*Downing*"). In *Downing*, the plaintiff surfers alleged that fashion retailers Abercrombie & Fitch (A&F) misappropriated their names and likenesses in violation of California's statutory and common law protections against commercial misappropriation, and that the publication of the photograph in A&F's fashion catalog, *The Quarterly*, violated the Lanham Act. *The Quarterly* accounts for approximately 80 percent of A&F's overall advertising budget. The primary purpose of *The Quarterly* is to build brand awareness and increase sales. The Ninth Circuit held that neither the California state law claim nor the Lanham Act claim were precluded by the First Amendment and remanded the case for trial.

B The United States Lanham Act and the Celebrity False Endorsement Claim

In *White* v. *Samsung*, the Ninth Circuit Court of Appeals commented that Vanna White owned a "mark" in her distinctive appearance for the purposes of false endorsement. In *Downing*, the Ninth Circuit again noted that the term "mark" applies to the celebrity's persona in respect of a false endorsement claim under section 43(a) of the Lanham Act, 15 USC § 1125(a), adapting the *Sleekcraft* factors employed for evaluating likelihood of confusion in a trademark infringement claim so as to be applicable to the celebrity cases. Under the law of false endorsement, likelihood of customer confusion is the determinative issue.[75] The relevance of these factors and their importance vary from case to case, and the likelihood of confusion standard is predominantly factual in nature. These eight *Downing* factors for celebrity false endorsement mimic the eight *Sleekcraft* factors for trademark infringement:

1 the level of recognition that the plaintiff has among the segment of the society for which the defendant's product is intended;
2 the relatedness of the fame or success of the plaintiff to the defendant's product;
3 the similarity of the likeness used by the defendant to the actual plaintiff;
4 evidence of actual confusion;
5 marketing channels used;
6 likely degree of purchaser care;
7 defendant's intent on selecting the plaintiff; and
8 likelihood of expansion of the product lines.[76]

Hence it appears that – as least for a living celebrity – it may not matter so much to them that the celebrity is not able to secure trademark registration for their likeness.

Courts have frequently referred to the nominative fair use doctrine when evaluating trademark infringement claims. Different Circuit Courts use different variations of the nominative fair use test.[77] When the trustees of the Diana Princess of Wales Memorial Fund and the executors of the Estate of Diana, Princess of Wales attempted to enjoin Franklin Mint's use of the name and likeness of the late Princess Diana on commercially sold jewelry, plates, and dolls, and in advertisements for these products, the Ninth Circuit held that there was no likelihood of confusion as to the origin of Franklin Mint's Diana-related products in respect of the Lanham Act's false endorsement claim,[78] and in addition, it was a permissible nominative fair

[75] Famous tennis player Anna Kournikova sued *Penthouse* magazine for publishing semi-nude photos of another woman resembling her, but the court found that Kournikova failed to prove that the average reader believed that she voluntarily associated herself with the adult magazine or otherwise approved the use of her name and likeness. *Kournikova* v. *Gen. Media Commc'ns, Inc.*, 278 F.Supp.2d 1111, 1129–30 (CD Cal. 2003). On the other hand, singer-songwriter Tom Waits succeeded in his false endorsement claim against Frito-Lay for having an imitator sing in a commercial as actual consumer confusion had occurred, and the court concluded that consumers were likely to be misled into believing that Waits was endorsing the product. *Waits* v. *Frito-Lay, Inc.*, 978 F.2d 1093, 1111 (9th Cir. 1992).

[76] *Downing*, 265 F.3d 994, 1007–08 (9th Cir. 2001). The *Sleekcraft* factors are: (i) strength of the plaintiff's mark; (ii) relatedness of the goods; (iii) similarity of the marks; (iv) evidence of actual confusion; (v) marketing channels used; (vi) likely degree of purchaser care; (vii) defendant's intent in selecting the mark; and (viii) likelihood of expansion of the product lines. *AMF, Inc.* v. *Sleekcraft Boats*, 599 F.2d 341, 348–49 (9th Cir.1979).

[77] *E.g.*, *Int'l Info. Sys. Sec. Certification Consortium, Inc.* v. *Sec. Univ., LLC*, 823 F.3d 153 (2d Cir. 2016); *Universal Commc'n Sys., Inc.* v. *Lycos, Inc.*, 478 F.3d 413 (1st Cir. 2007); *Century 21 Real Estate Corp.* v. *Lendingtree, Inc.*, 425 F.3d 211 (3d Cir. 2005); *Cairns* v. *Franklin Mint Co.*, 292 F.3d 1139 (9th Cir. 2002) ("*Cairns*"). In the Ninth Circuit, nominative fair use is not an affirmative defense because it does not protect a defendant from liability if there is, in fact, a likelihood of consumer confusion. The Third Circuit treats nominative fair use as an affirmative defense that may be asserted by the defendant despite a likelihood of consumer confusion.

[78] 15 USC § 1125(a)(1).

use.[79] Essentially, nominative fair use of a mark lies outside the strictures of trademark law because it does not implicate the source-identification function that is the purpose of trademark. The Ninth Circuit clarified that in a nominative fair use context, the defendant has "used the plaintiff's mark to describe the *plaintiff*'s product for the purpose of, for example, comparison to the defendant's product" and that the "nominative fair use analysis *replaces* the *Sleekcraft* analysis" for likelihood of confusion.[80]

The nominative fair use analysis is appropriate where a defendant has used the plaintiff's mark to describe the plaintiff's product, *even if the defendant's ultimate goal is to describe his own product.* For instance, this defense would apply to the unauthorized use of a celebrity's name or likeness in merchandising by a trader to describe the goods offered by the trader so long as there is no misleading conduct as to endorsement or sponsorship. In *New Kids on the Block* v. *News America Publishing*, it was held that the newspapers permissibly used the trademark "The New Kids" to describe the *plaintiff*'s product, i.e., the band "The New Kids on the Block," even though the ultimate goal was to describe the newspapers' telephone polls about the band. Similarly, in *Cairns* v. *Franklin Mint Co.* it was permissible nominative fair use for Franklin Mint to use Princess Diana's name and likeness to describe Princess Diana, although Franklin Mint's ultimate goal was to describe its own Diana-related products. In the United Kingdom, the courts have also distinguished character merchandising from advertising claims, holding that selling any memorabilia or garment with a recognizable image of a famous individual is *not*, in and of itself, an act of passing off.[81]

IV CONCLUSION

Writings in cultural studies suggest that a contemporary celebrity is any individual who is widely recognized by the public, and therefore the distinctive characteristics of a particular celebrity have the capacity to trigger instant recognition amongst the public. Daniel Boorstin's definition of a celebrity as "a person who is known for his well-knownness"[82] has been widely adopted as a starting point for a broad definition of a contemporary celebrity based on a ubiquitous media presence and public recognition. It is because a celebrity is characterized by their well-knownness in society that their commercial value may be easily captured without an obvious reference to name or likeness as the celebrity can be evoked by many other means familiar to the consuming public.[83]

The "whole structure of celebrity is built on the construction of the individuated personality" and, in practice, the famous individual has a widely circulated "highly identifiable, even iconic, physical image"[84] that is "imbued with euphoric values."[85] In exploiting their fame, advertisements featuring celebrities often aim to produce an audience desire to resemble physically the idealized image or to identify with the celebrity personality through the consumption of

[79] *Cairns*, 292 F.3d at 1155. To establish a nominative fair use defense, a defendant must prove the following three elements: first, the plaintiff's product or service in question must be one not readily identifiable without use of the trademark, second, only so much of the mark or marks may be used as is reasonably necessary to identify the plaintiff's product or service, and third, the user must do nothing that would, in conjunction with the mark, suggest sponsorship or endorsement by the trademark holder. Lanham Act, 15 USC § 1115(b).

[80] *Cairns*, 292 F.3d at 1150 (referring to *New Kids on the Block* v. *News Am. Publ'g, Inc.*, 971 F.2d 302, 308 (9th Cir.1992)) (internal citations omitted).

[81] *E.g.*, *Irvine* v. *Talksport* [2002] 1 WLR 2355 (Ch.); *Fenty* v. *Arcadia Grp. Brands Ltd. (t/a Topshop)* [2015] EWCA Civ. 3 [2015] 1 WLR 3291.

[82] Daniel J Boorstin, The Image: A Guide to Pseudo-Events in America 57 (1961). *See also* Tan, *supra* note 4, at 22, 89–90.

[83] This was noted in passing reference by the *White* majority. *White*, 971 F.2d 1395, 1399 (9th Cir. 1992).

[84] Graeme Turner, Understanding Celebrity 39 (2d ed. 2014).

[85] Roland Barthes, *The Rhetoric of the Image*, *in* Image-Music-Text 32, 35 (Stephen Heath trans., 1977).

products associated with the celebrity. I have previously argued that the right of publicity does not protect identity as property per se, but protects against an unauthorized commercial exploitation of that *associative economic value*.[86] In a way, the celebrity persona can function in much the same manner as trademarks in communicating information and enhancing the appeal of brands and marketability of products.

Increasingly, it seems that any readily recognizable characteristic that is distinctive of a celebrity is likely to be construed by the courts to possess a pecuniary value by which an unauthorized appropriation is actionable under the common law right of publicity in many US state jurisdictions. Although Dogan and Lemley are firmly in favor of restricting the scope of the right of publicity by adopting aspects of trademark doctrine in a modified form, they rightly point out that: "Because most publicity cases will involve associational uses rather than source-indicating uses, the type of connection between product and celebrity identity *differs* somewhat from the typical connection between product and trademark in Lanham Act infringement suits."[87] One of the most interesting aspects of celebrity is the intensifying degree to which the celebrity has been incorporated into our daily lives. The cultural and social pervasiveness of the celebrity suggest that members of the public can identify a particular celebrity by more than just a mention of name or a photograph in the newspapers. The celebrity, "as a social phenomenon and economic juggernaut, hinges essentially on the public's awareness of consequential interest in particular individuals."[88] Moreover, the study of entertainment celebrities have also shown that "[e]ach industry produces a range of celebrity types that not only are constructed to have distinctive qualities when compared with other celebrities within that industry, but are differentiated from the production of celebrities in each of the *other* domains of the entertainment industry."[89] These distinctive qualities may be "a complex configuration of visual, verbal and aural signs."[90] Insofar as the cases hold that a celebrity may be identified by any distinctive attribute or a combination of elements beyond name and likeness, they are supportable by observations and research in cultural studies on the contemporary celebrity.

Although it has been argued by some that more generous trademark protection ought to be granted to celebrities to reward the time, energy and financial resources devoted to building the celebrity brand, and to address free-riding concerns,[91] there are perhaps more compelling arguments *against* extending trademark rights to celebrities who already have the dubious benefit of an expanding right of publicity to vindicate unauthorized commercial exploitation of the associative value of their identity.[92]

86 TAN, *supra* note 4, at 108–10, 114–16.

87 Dogan & Lemley, *supra* note 1, at 1215 (emphasis added).

88 ELIZABETH CURRID-HALKETT, STARSTRUCK: THE BUSINESS OF CELEBRITY 221 (2010).

89 P. DAVID MARSHALL, CELEBRITY AND POWER: FAME IN CONTEMPORARY CULTURE 186 (1997). Marshall's seminal work outlines how the film, television and pop music industries have organized their production of celebrities around particular characteristics.

90 RICHARD DYER, HEAVENLY BODIES: FILM STARS AND SOCIETIES 38 (2d ed. 2004).

91 *E.g.*, Whibley, *supra* note 66, at 134–44. Others have advanced a more doctrinal argument suggesting that recognizing a persona mark is not an attempt to expand the definition of a trademark but to accommodate what has already been granted protection. *E.g.*, McGeehan, *supra* note 54, at 362–65.

92 While space constraints here prevent a discussion of how celebrities in a number of Commonwealth common law jurisdictions where the right of publicity is not recognized – such as the United Kingdom, Australia, Hong Kong and Singapore – resort to the passing-off action that is akin to the Lanham Act false endorsement claim, I have undertaken a comprehensive analysis of this elsewhere. My conclusion is that not only is the extended passing-off claim adequate in protecting against such unauthorized exploitation, it is also able to consider, in a more holistic manner than in a right-of-publicity claim, the interests of the different constituents of the celebrity trinity which comprises the celebrity individual, the producers and the audience. TAN, *supra* note 4, at 199–245.

22

Commercial Exploitation of the Human Persona in European and French Law

Who Needs Trademarks When You Have Personality Rights?

*David Lefranc**

I INTRODUCTION

Celebrities' commercial interests seem well – and even very well – protected in US law. One can even wonder if there is not an excess of protection. Chapter 21 in this volume, authored by David Tan, is entitled: "Who Needs Trademarks When You Have the Right of Publicity?" The critical scope of this question seduces the civil law specialist, who indeed wonders whether US law has not gone too far in protecting celebrities. The civil law specialist is very surprised to learn that in the United States, a celebrity can control the commercial use of their physical postures, of body parts or even of their car! Viewed from the other side of the Atlantic, it seems that in the United States it is easier to acquire a right of publicity than an intellectual property right.

In European and French laws, personality rights, which protect the moral interests of the person, cover both rights of privacy and right to individuals' names and images. Case law is very well established on this point. With regard to protection against commercial exploitation of fame, it is generally accepted that rights of personality may also offer judicial remedies. However, the legal basis for these remedies is not very clear, probably because statutory text is silent on this point. One thing is certain: personality rights do not offer as much protection as the American right of publicity.

That is why this study will endeavour to answer the question asked in Chapter 21: "who needs trademarks when you have personality rights?" In his chapter, which complements this study from a common law perspective, David Tan showed that celebrities were using three legal bases to exploit the commercial value of their fame: the right of publicity, registered trademarks and unregistered trademarks, through the action of false endorsement. This chapter will inquire if there are equivalent legal bases in European and French laws for protection of the interests secured by the right of publicity.

II PERSONALITY RIGHTS AND EXPLOITATION OF FAME UNDER EUROPEAN AND FRENCH LAW

The right of publicity does not exist under that name in European and French laws. The only equivalent of the right of publicity may be found in personality rights. But European law has

* Avocat, Cabinet LAROPOIN, Lecturer at the Faculty of Law of Douai (France). The author would like to thank Amandine Quenton for the excellent work of translation and Sébastien Oddos for his careful review of the chapter. The author would also like to thank Professor Ginsburg for the additional reviews of the various drafts of this chapter.

never harmonised personality rights through member states. There is no European directive, no regulation about the commercial exploitation of the name and the image of individuals. The only texts mentioning the name and the image of people in an indirect way are the specific texts in trademark law, as we shall see hereinafter.

The same is true in French law. There is no general law about the commercial exploitation of the name and the image of individuals. The law recognises only the protection of private life. Article 9 of the French Civil Code constitutes the entirety of legislation on this issue since 1970, and states that "Everyone has the right to respect for his private life."[1] Originally, the purpose of this text was to condemn the moral damage of an individual, information about whose private life has been published without their authorisation. The fame of the individual is irrelevant for the application of this text. The case law is very clear on that point: "the description of the relations existing between a mother and her daughter, the story of the complicity which exists between them, the recounting of their feelings, their common tastes, their common activities are of the domain of the family life of a person, which, no matter her fame, is exactly a matter of her private life."[2] Saying that fame is irrelevant for the protection of private life means that famous people have the same rights as any other individual. The rule cautions that celebrities retain their privacy, even though journalists might claim that celebrities' lives should be a matter of public record.

Case law construing Article 9 of the French Civil Code has condemned the moral damage caused by the non-consensual use of someone's image. Most of the time, it is a question of condemning the publication of an image that violates privacy. This is why some decisions affirm that neither the right to respect of one's private life nor rights in one's image depend on the fame of the individual. The solution derives from the principle of the equality of citizens as a matter of human rights: "Considering that articles 9 of the civil code and 8-1 of the European Convention for the Protection of Human Rights and Fundamental Freedoms, guarantee to every person, whatever his or her fame, fortune or functions, the right to the respect for his/her private life and for his/her image."[3]

In the absence of legislation, it is up to the courts to go beyond privacy to protect the commercial interests of famous people.[4] In an earlier study, we pointed out that in French law, case law does not treat the exploitation of the name and the exploitation of the image in the same way.[5] The Court of Cassation (France's highest private law court) recognises the existence of a genuine property right in the name. Head Chef Alain Ducasse was allowed to prohibit the filing by an unrelated company of a trademark application composed of the name "Ducasse."[6] By contrast, the Court of Cassation has not devised an equivalent protection for the image of famous people. The only court decisions on this subject are from courts of appeal.

[1] CODE CIVIL [C. CIV.] [CIVIL CODE] art. 9 (Fr.).

[2] *Point de vue* v. *Caroline Grimaldi*: *Juris-Data*, Cour d'appel [CA] [regional court of appeal] Versailles, civ., Feb. 15, 2001, no. 2001-183105; *see also* Cour de cassation [Cass.] [supreme court for judicial matters] 1st civ. ch., May 31, 2007, appeal no. 06-13008.

[3] *Lagardère Digital France* v. X: *Juris-Data*, Cour d'appel [CA] [regional court of appeal] Versailles, civ., Feb. 2, 2018, no. 2018-001390.

[4] There is a specific law about the image of professional athletes: CODE DU SPORT [C. SP.] [CODE OF SPORT] art. L. 222-2-10-1. This text forces sport associations to specify the image agreements signed with athletes, and notably "the extent of the commercial exploitation of the image, the name or the voice of the sportsman or the professional trainer, in particular the duration, the object, the context, the media and the geographical zone of this commercial exploitation."

[5] D. Lefranc, *Do the French Have Their Own "Haelan" Case? The Droit à l'Image as an Emerging Intellectual Property Right*, *in* INTELLECTUAL PROPERTY AT THE EDGE 39 (R. Cooper Dreyfus & Jane C. Ginsburg eds., 2014).

[6] Cour de cassation [Cass.] [supreme court for judicial matters] comm. ch., May 6, 2003, appeal no. 00-18192.

A 2005 ruling of the Court of Appeal of Versailles adopts a solution leading to a result similar to the outcome under the American right of publicity.[7] In this case, Universal Music was assignee of the image right of a famous singer, Johnny Halliday. Universal succeeded in prohibiting the reproduction of the artist's image on calendars.

Another case concerns another French musical celebrity of the 1970s, Michel Polnareff. This person always cultivated a very specific physical appearance, just like David Bowie or Elton John. Polnareff is known for his shoulder-length blond, curly hair. One of his distinctive signs is a pair of rectangular glasses with white edges. Cetelem, a credit agency, made a commercial in which some celebrities' bad-quality doubles are filmed. Doubles of Marilyn Monroe and Michael Jackson also appear. Polnareff did not appreciate the advertisement and filed a claim against Cetelem. He won, even though the public did not confuse the double with the real character at all. "[T]he appropriation of Michel Polnareff's attributes – plentiful blonde and curly hair and dark glasses with white frames – implies ... the appropriation of the celebrity and the image of the plaintiff, even though there would be no actual confusion between the character in the advertisements and Michel Polnareff."[8] With this "Polnareff" case, French case law comes close to the American *Vanna White* case.[9] The exploitation of the celebrity's fame gives rise to liability, no matter if the name of the celebrity is cited or their image is reproduced. If the disputed likeness clearly evokes the celebrity's character in the public's mind, liability is justified.

To the best of our knowledge, the Court of Cassation's review has never been sought in such a case. Therefore, case law does not present a unified trend. Another court could have invoked the absence of confusion between the bad-quality double and the real singer to reject Michel Polnareff's claim. Even among lower courts' decisions, there is almost no equivalent to the Polnareff case, except for the following two cases.

Jo-Wilfried Tsonga and Gaël Monfils are two famous French tennis players. Invoking their personality rights, these two athletes filed a claim against Matmut, a French insurance company. Matmut produced a radio advertisement in which two comedians were playing word games in order to evoke the family names of Monfils and Tsonga. Another word game concerned the French word "racket," which means *extortion*, but is pronounced like the word "raquette," meaning *tennis racket*. Background sounds of a tennis game could be heard on the advertisement's soundtrack. Through the soundtrack and puns, the promotional recording evoked the public characters of the two sportsmen. The judge ruled that Matmut had abusively exploited the fame of the athletes: "It appears in the case in point, that on the pretext of plays on words, the defendant used free of charge the fame of the appellants. This abuse constitutes a tort."[10]

This decision reinforces the *Polnareff* ruling. But there is another more recent decision. The famous American songwriter Tom Waits brought an action in France against Bartabas, a French artist specialised in equestrian shows. In his show titled "We indeed Finish off the Angels (Elegies)," Bartabas claimed that he aimed to "pay a tribute" to Tom Waits. He included songs from Waits on the show's soundtrack, and, most importantly, reproduced Waits's portrait on the press kit and imitated the appearance of his "hobo" character. Waits alleged this was all done

[7] *Calendriers Jean Lavigne* v. *Universal Music*: *Juris-Data*, Cour d'appel [CA] [regional court of appeal] Versailles, 12th ch., Sept. 22, 2005, no. 2005-288693.

[8] *Michel Polnareff* v. *BNP Paribas*, Tribunal de grande instance [TGI] [court of original jurisdiction] Paris, 17th ch., June 22, 2016, RG no. 15/05541.

[9] *White* v. *Samsung Electronics America Inc.*, 971 F.2d 1395, 1398–99 (9th Cir. 1992).

[10] *Gaël Monfils and Jo-Wilfried Tsonga* v. *Matmut*, Cour d'appel [CA] [regional court of appeal] Paris, Pole 2, 7th ch., Dec. 14, 2016, , RG no. 15/15470: *Juris-Data* no. 2016-029278.

without his permission. In February 2019, the Paris court ruled in part against Bartabas.[11] The judges considered that Bartabas's admiration of Waits did not justify that the American author be deprived of "means of expression that participate in his identification and are personal."[12] Thus, Waits's personality rights enabled him to prohibit the reuse of the visual elements that made him famous. But, as often in French law, the legal basis of this ruling is not very clear.

We have already said that Article 9 of the French Civil Code is the only tool left by the legislator in judges' hands to protect the image of individuals. But this article evokes only "privacy." In addition, it is not at all clear that it is adapted to the protection of an artist's character. The image of the "hobo" is a creation necessarily different from the genuine image of Waits, especially when he receives his friends in his living room. Article 9 of the Civil Code was not originally designed to protect the artistic identity of a person. Instead, it was designed to protect individuals' real identity in their social life. We therefore have the impression that the French judge sometimes agrees to protect the same interests as the ones covered by the American *right of publicity*. But French case law does not permit us to affirm the existence of a genuine property right in someone's image. Celebrities win their lawsuits because judges recognise the existence of an offence engaging the responsibility of the defendant, who has exploited their fame. In other words, French courts appear to focus more on the free-riding commercial defendant than on the existence or scope of any property rights of the plaintiff.

If any *a contrario* interpretation may be relevant, the Court of Cassation's case law seems to confirm indirectly this analysis. Henri Salvador was a famous French singer. During his lifetime, he filed a case against a producer of phonograms who had reproduced his portrait on CD compilations of his performances without his authorisation. The Court of Cassation upheld his claim:

> But since everyone has the right to prevent the reproduction of his/her image except in the context of freedom of expression, the Court of Appeal correctly decided that the reproduction of the photograph of the artist on the cover of a compilation, which constitutes an act of commercial exploitation and not the exercise of the person's freedom of expression, was subject to prior authorization and, in the absence of the relevant person's authorization, this reproduction was illicit and infringed the right to his image.[13]

Henri Salvador died in 2008. After his death, his widow wanted to file a similar claim against another producer of CD compilations. This time she lost, even at the Court of Cassation, which, in January 2018, responded: "the right to one's image, which is an attribute of personality, is extinguished with the individual's death and is not transmissible to his heirs."[14]

So how to explain the different outcome between the two rulings? Certainly, by the death of the holder of the personality rights, Henri Salvador. If the right to one's image was a property right, Salvador's widow would have won her case because under French law a property right is always transmissible to someone's heirs. It confirms that French law protects image rights only as a personal, non-property, right under general tort law theories.

[11] *Thomas Waits (AKA Tom Waits), Kathleen Brennan & others* v. *Zingaro & Bartabas*, Tribunal de grande instance [TGI] [court of original jurisdiction] Paris, 3rd ch., 2d sect., Feb. 8, 2019, RG no. 16/09059. The court found that Waits had authorised acts, such as incorporation of his music on the soundtrack, that would otherwise have constituted copyright infringement.

[12] *Id.*

[13] *Henri Salvador*, Cour de cassation [Cass.] [supreme court for judicial matters] 1st civ. ch., Sept. 24, 2009, appeal no. 08-11112.

[14] Cour de cassation [Cass.] [supreme court for judicial matters], 1st civ. ch., Jan. 31, 2018, appeal no. 16-23591.

III PERSONALITY RIGHTS AND TRADEMARK RIGHTS

To exploit their fame, celebrities can also apply for a trademark consisting of their distinctive signs. Celebrities may register national trademarks (French, Italian, German, etc.) or also European Union trademarks.[15] Since the latter are protected everywhere in Europe, they are frequently used in practice. Applicable right to these two types of trademarks is roughly the same, since the laws of European Union member states have been harmonised by directives.[16] This is the case in particular for French law. European and French laws have similar definitions for trademarks: a trademark must enable the public to recognise the origin of products or services.[17] Therefore, the following question arises: can a celebrity's name (Section III.A) or image (Section III.B) fulfil this function of guaranteeing the origin of products or services?

A *Trademarks Consisting of a Family Name*

Can a family name be registered as a trademark under European law and French law? The answer is affirmative (Section III.A.1). Trademarks consisting of a name enjoy the same protection as granted to the other trademarks, so long as they are distinctive of the goods or services in connection with which they are to be used (Section III.A.2). Conversely, personal names are protected against a third party's filing as a trademark (Section III.A.3).

1 *Application for a Trademark Consisting of a Name*

There is no doubt that someone's name can fulfil a function that is very close to that of a trademark. Indeed, the general public associates an individual with their media, political, artistic or commercial activities because of their name. But individuals' names are often used as trademarks. Article L.711-1 of the *French Intellectual Property Code* (IPC) refers to the family name and the pseudonym as signs a trademark may consist of.[18] Article 4 of the European Union Trade Mark Regulation (EUTMR) also mentions "personal names."[19]

Therefore, names are expressly mentioned by law as signs that can be used in a trademark application. That is why EU member states cannot discriminate against any such trademark applications. The European Court of Justice made such a reproach to the British Register of

[15] Regulation (EU) 2017/1001 of the European Parliament and of the Council of June 14, 2017 on the EU trademark, 2017 OJ L 154/1 (EC) [hereinafter EUTMR]. This regulation repealed Regulation 207/2009 of Feb. 26, 2009 on the EU trademark, which codified and amended Council Regulation 40/94 of Dec. 20, 1993 on the Community Trade Mark, 1994 OJ L11/1 (EC).

[16] Council Directive 89/104/EEC to approximate the laws of the member states relating to trademarks, 1989 OJ L 40/1 (EC); Directive 2008/95/EC of the European Parliament and of the Council of Oct. 22, 2008 on the Community Trade Mark [codifying First Council Directive 89/104/EEC of Dec. 21, 1988 to Approximate the Laws of Member States Relating to Trademarks, 1988 OJ (L 40) 1, as amended]; Council Directive 2015/2436 of the European Parliament and of the Council of Dec. 16, 2015 to approximate the laws of the member states relating to trade marks, 2015 OJ L 336/1. French national provisions are not yet adopted according to the 2015 directive.

[17] Case 119/75, *Société Terrapin (Overseas) Ltd.* v. *Société Terranova Industrie CA Kapferer & Co.* (1976) EURLex 61975CJ0119 (CJEC): "the basic function of the trademark to guarantee to consumers that the product has the same origin"; *See also*, "the essential function of a trade mark is to guarantee the identity of origin of the marked goods or services to the consumer or end user by enabling him, without any possibility of confusion, to distinguish the goods or services from others which have another origin. For the trade mark to be able to fulfil its essential role in the system of undistorted competition which the Treaty seeks to establish and maintain, it must offer a guarantee that all the goods or services bearing it have been manufactured or supplied under the control of a single undertaking which is responsible for their quality." Case C-206/01, *Arsenal Football Club plc* v. *Matthew Reed*, (2002) ECR I-10273 (CJEC).

[18] Code de la Propriété Intellectuelle [C. ip.] [Intellectual Property Code] art. L711-1.

[19] EUTMR, *supra* note 15, art. 4.

Trademarks. Nichols PLC had applied for the registration of the trademark "Nichols" in the United Kingdom. The office rejected the application by objecting that the family name "Nichols" was very common in the territory. The Chancery Division of the High Court of Justice (England & Wales) submitted a question for a preliminary ruling to the Court of Justice of the European Union in order to determine whether it is possible to reject the trademark registration of a common family name. The Court of Justice of the European Union answered that European law strictly prohibits any such restrictions. Trademark registration conditions are the same for any type of trademarks, without any exception for family names:

> 25. The criteria for assessment of the distinctive character of trademarks constituted by a personal name are therefore the same as those applicable to the other categories of trade mark.
>
> 26. Stricter general criteria of assessment based, for example, on:
>
> – a predetermined number of persons with the same name, above which that name may be regarded as devoid of distinctive character,
> – the number of undertakings providing products or services of the type covered by the application for registration, or
> – the prevalence or otherwise of the use of surnames in the relevant trade, cannot be applied to such trademarks.[20]

Since European law widely admits family names as trademarks, there are numerous examples. For instance, Paul McCartney, former bass player and songwriter of The Beatles, applied for the registration of his name as a trademark with the EUIPO through his music editor MPL Music Publishing.[21]

Belgian musician Paul Van Haver registered his pseudonym "Stromae" with the EUIPO.[22] Thanks to the European Union right of priority, this trademark has been extended to the American territory by the WIPO under the Madrid Agreement.[23] Indeed, Stromae became famous to American audiences by playing at Madison Square Garden, and by collaborating with the famous rapper Kanye West. The USPTO first refused registration of the "Stromae" trademark, since it was not clearly indicated in the application whether the trademark was identifying an individual: "Applicant must clarify whether the name in the mark identifies a particular living individual."[24] On 11 February 2011, Paul Van Haver signed an affidavit in order to regularise his American application. Since then, the "Stromae" American trademark (No. 4162827) has been registered in the United States from 26 June 2012.

In the case of Stromae, the difference in registration procedure between Europe and tUnited States is interesting. Admittedly, American and European laws prohibit the filing of a name without the consent of the person concerned. But European law, unlike US law, does not provide for administrative verification at the filing stage. EU Regulation distinguishes absolute and relative grounds for refusal of a trademark application. Absolute grounds for refusal include cases where the sign applied for is incapable of becoming a genuine mark.[25] Relative grounds for refusal include cases where the sign applied for infringes the rights of third parties.[26] Respect for the rights of personality is of course a relative ground for refusal. At the time of filing, the law

[20] Case C-404/02, *Nichols PLC* v. *Registrar of Trade Marks*, (2004) ECR I-08499 (CJEC, 2nd ch., aff.).
[21] PAUL MCCARTNEY, European Union Trademark, Registration No. 000907972, filed on Oct. 29, 1999.
[22] STROMAE, European Union Trademark, Registration No. 009145939, filed on the June 1, 2010.
[23] STROMAE, International Trademark No. 1055787, registered on Sept. 21, 2010.
[24] STROMAE, USPTO Application Serial No. 79089026, Refusal Note, Jan. 11, 2011.
[25] EUTMR, *supra* note 15, art. 7.
[26] *Id.*, art. 8.

obliges EUIPO only to verify the absolute grounds for refusal.[27] French law is essentially identical.[28] Conversely, section 1052 of the US Lanham Act states that: "No trademark by which the goods of the applicant may be distinguished from the goods of others shall be refused registration on the principal register on account of its nature unless it … (c) Consists of or comprises a name, portrait, or signature identifying a particular living individual except by his written consent."[29]

Thus, American law seems to be more protective of individuals' names than European and French laws. This is why Stromae had to confirm his agreement with the USPTO to allow the Mosaert SPRL company to file the artist's name as a trademark.

2 *Protection of a Trademark Consisting of a Name*

Trademarks consisting of a name have the same protection as any other kind of trademark. A few case law examples will illustrate it.

A famous French tennis player, René Lacoste, turned his name into a very famous clothing trademark.[30] This trademark is still protected today by French courts. For instance, in 2004 New Lady Company was held liable for infringement of the "Lacoste" trademark after selling "Lacote" T-shirts without the letter "s."[31]

Famous French couturier Jean-Paul Gaultier filed an application for registration of his name as a trademark to sell clothes and also perfume.[32] An advertising TV clip promoting one of his perfumes used a melody of the composer Bellini, taken from his opera *La Norma*. EMI France, a record producer, published a compilation of tunes used in advertising clips. The Bellini piece was part of the compilation. The compilation record cover mentioned the name of "Jean-Paul Gaultier" to remind the public of the advertising clip. EMI France was condemned for counterfeiting the "Jean-Paul Gaultier" trademark.[33]

3 *Protection of Names against Illicit Filing as a Trademark*

Since names can generally become trademarks, it is normal that holders of names can oppose the application for registration of a trademark which would reproduce any such names. Article 60 EUTMR allows the cancellation of a trademark which would infringe a "right to a name."[34] Article L. 711-4 French IPC obliges anyone who applies for a trademark registration to respect the "personality rights of another person, particularly his surname, pseudonym."[35]

Case law invalidates a trademark that infringes a right on a name, when there is a risk of confusion between the name and the trademark. To establish this risk of confusion, judges examine whether the name is known or not. For example, the singer Charles Aznavour enjoyed fame beyond the borders of France. During summer 2017, his name was even engraved on the Hollywood Boulevard's Walk of Fame in Los Angeles. This artist agreed to chair a charitable society helping Armenians suffering from a violent earthquake. A member of this association

[27] *Id.*, art. 42.

[28] Code de la Propriété Intellectuelle [C. ip.] [Intellectual Property Code] art. R. 712-10.

[29] Lanham Act, 15 USC § 1052.

[30] LACOSTE, French Trademark No. 1033587, filed on Nov. 21, 1977.

[31] *La Chemise Lacoste* v. *New Lady*, Tribunal de grande instance [TGI] [court of original jurisdiction] Paris, 3rd ch., 1st sect., Feb. 18, 2004, case no. M20040127, https://inpi.fr/fr/base-jurisprudence.

[32] JEAN PAUL GAULTIER, French Trademark No. 1641732, filed on July 20, 1989.

[33] *Jean-Paul Gaultier & Alii* v. *EMI France & Alii*, Tribunal de grande instance [TGI] [court of original jurisdiction] Paris, 3rd ch., Jan. 15, 2003, case no. M20030016, https://inpi.fr/fr/base-jurisprudence.

[34] EUTMR, *supra* note 15, art. 60.

[35] Code de la Propriété Intellectuelle [C. ip.] [Intellectual Property Code], art. L.711-4.

filed an application for the trademark "Aznavour pour l'Arménie" [Aznavour for Armenia] without his authorisation. The trademark was invalidated:

> Considering that the identical appropriation, by the registration of the disputed trademark, of the surname "Aznavour" which is well known and associated with Charles Aznavour can, by creating a risk of confusion, infringe the prior personality rights of this performer of international fame, at the sense of provisions of the article L. 711-4 of the Code of Intellectual Property.[36]

However, non-famous people cannot prohibit the use of their name as a trademark. An Irano-Swiss actor named Karim Kadjar filed a lawsuit against the carmaker Renault, which had named one of its cars "Kadjar." The actor claimed that he was the descendant of the "Kadjar" Turkmen dynasty. But the Court said that the celebrity of the dynasty did not matter. What mattered was to prove the existence of some degree of personal fame. Karim Kadjar was not sufficiently well known by the French public to obtain the invalidity of the "Kadjar" trademarks registered by Renault:

> Mr. Karim Kadjar does not demonstrate that he would enjoy personally, as a result of his activity as an actor, such fame which would have benefited his surname; the production of his portfolio, which mentions undisclosed productions, and existence of future broadcasts of a television film and a motion picture being insufficient to inform the court of the public's knowledge of his performances and, through them, his name.[37]

Another similar case confirms that people who are unknown by the public cannot prevent the registration of their name as a trademark. Coca-Cola sold a drink called "Coca-Cola light sango." Mr. Abdel Sango filed a lawsuit against Coca-Cola to ask for the invalidity of the Coca-Cola Company's trademarks. He lost since he could not demonstrate some degree of personal fame attached to his name. The Court of Appeal judged as follow:

> Abdel Sango in no way demonstrates that with respect to normally informed and reasonably attentive and intelligent French consumers or motion picture or broadcasting professionals, the patronymic Sango would have acquired a certain fame attached to the personality of Abdel Sango, while it results, on the contrary, from extracts of the "Yellow Pages" obtained by means of the Google search engine that this name is widespread in particular in the department of Hauts-de-Seine; considering that consequently, it has not been demonstrated that the patronymic Sango enjoyed such fame in civil or artistic life so that the choice of this name as a trademark would lead to a risk of confusion susceptible to infringe the personality rights of Abdel Sango.[38]

This decision was later confirmed by the Court of Cassation.[39]

French case law is harmonised with European case law, as can be seen in the "Becker" case. Mrs. Barbara Becker, who was famous in Germany, asked for the registration of a trademark composed of her full name: "Barbara Becker." The owner of a previous "BECKER" trademark opposed her request for registration. The Court admitted the existence of a risk of confusion between both signs, since the family name "Becker" would be predominant for the public. Therefore, the Court refused Mrs. Becker's request. But the Court of Justice of the European Union (CJEU) rejected this solution.

[36] *Lévon S* v. *Charles Aznavour*, Cour d'appel [CA] [regional court of appeal] Versailles, 12th ch., Feb. 16, 2016, case no. M20160075, https://inpi.fr/fr/base-jurisprudence.

[37] *Karim Kadjar* v. *Renault*: *Juris-Data*, Tribunal de grande instance [TGI] [court of original jurisdiction] Paris, 3rd ch., 1st sect., June 9, 2016, case no. 2016-024034.

[38] *Sango* v. *Coca-Cola Services France*, Cour d'appel [CA] [regional court of appeal] Versailles, 12th ch., 1st sect., Feb. 25, 2010, *Juris-Data* case no. 2010-001356.

[39] Cour de cassation [Cass.] [supreme court for judicial matters] 1st civ. ch., Apr. 10, 2013, appeal no. 12-14525.

According to the CJEU, the German court's reasoning was purely theoretical since it was not based on a concrete analysis of all the case's factual circumstances. The name "Becker" was very common in Germany. Furthermore, the full name of Barbara Becker had gained some notoriety for the public. Thus, the German court was wrong in pretending that the added first name was not material in assessing the existence of a risk of confusion.

> 36. Although it is possible that, in a part of the European Union, surnames have, as a general rule, a more distinctive character than forenames, it is appropriate, however, to take account of factors specific to the case and, in particular, the fact that the surname concerned is unusual or, on the contrary, very common, which is likely to have an effect on that distinctive character. That is true of the surname "Becker" which the Board of Appeal noted is common.
>
> 37. Account must also be taken of whether the person who requests that his first name and surname, taken together, be registered as a trade mark is well known, since that factor may obviously influence the perception of the mark by the relevant public.
>
> 38. Furthermore, it must be held that, in a composite mark, a surname does not retain an independent distinctive role in every case solely because it will be perceived as a surname. The finding with respect to such a role may be based only on an examination of all the relevant factors of each case.[40]

A subsequent *Fiorucci* decision further establishes that famous people are protected against a third party's exploitation of their name as a trademark. Fiorucci was a famous stylist in his home country, Italy, and all around the world. His New York shop allowed him to meet Andy Warhol. He remained famous for having designed the clothes of the 1970s disco era. In 1990, he sold his "creative heritage" to a Japanese company, Edwin Co. Ltd. This company became the transferee of trademarks reproducing the stylist's family name. In 1999, Edwin Co. attempted to apply for registration of a new trademark "Elio Fiorucci" with the EUIPO. Fiorucci filed an action for invalidity, since he did not authorise this new registration application. The EUTMR indeed states that a European trademark can be declared invalid if it infringes "a right to a name." Edwin claimed that Fiorucci could use this text only to prohibit a trademark damaging his personality but not his commercial interests. This argument was rejected by the Court:

> 33. … it should be noted that the words "right to a name" do not provide any support for the restrictive interpretation proposed by the appellant, to the effect that the provision concerns only that right as an attribute of personality and does not cover commercial exploitation of a name. …
>
> 36. It follows that, contrary to what the appellant maintains, the wording and structure of Article 52(2) of Regulation No 40/94 do not, where a right to a name is asserted, allow application of that provision to be restricted merely to situations where the registration of a Community trade mark [called today "European Union trademark"] conflicts with a right intended exclusively to protect a name as an attribute of the personality of the person concerned.[41]

According to this decision, European trademark law respects all the kinds of rights in the name that member states can grant to their citizens. In this case, the ECJ agreed to consider that Italian law permits celebrities to control the commercial use of their name. Therefore, Elio Fiorucci could obtain the invalidity of the trademark applied for by the Edwin company.

[40] Case C-51/09, *Barbara Becker* v. *Harman International Industries Inc. & EUIPO*, (2010) ECR I-05805 (ECJ, 4th ch.).

[41] Case C-263/09, *Edwin Co. Ltd.* v. *EUIPO & Elio Fiorucci*, (2011) ECR I-05853 (ECJ, grand ch.); on this case, see Lefranc, *supra* note 5, at 41.

FIGURE 22.1 Paul Wight, a.k.a. "Big Show"

B Trademarks Composed of an Individual's Portrait

Can someone's portrait be registered as a trademark? The question arises less frequently than for family names (Section III.B.1). Protection of a portrait by a trademark certainly has specificities (Section III.B.2).

1 Application for the Registration of a Portrait as a Trademark

The portrait or the silhouette of an individual are not mentioned by the texts as examples of signs commonly used as trademarks. In the same way, photographs are not mentioned either. Article L. 711-1 French IPC authorises applications for signs such as: "Figurative signs such as: devices, labels, seals, selvedges, reliefs, holograms, logos, synthesized images; shapes, particularly those of a product or its packaging, or those that identify a service; arrangements, combinations or shades of color."[42] Article 4 of the EUTMR evokes the "designs," "colours" and "shape of goods or of the packaging of goods."[43] The physical appearance of an individual is not mentioned.

Yet the face of an individual allows their identification without any doubt during their activities. Indeed, a face concentrates the facial characteristics by which someone is recognised by the public – in the street or on the packaging of a product. In the field of wrestling, the World Wrestling Entertainment, Inc. filed applications for European trademarks consisting of several portraits of famous wrestlers (Figure 22.1).[44]

[42] Code de la Propriété Intellectuelle [C. ip.] [Intellectual Property Code] art. L 711-1.

[43] EUTMR, *supra* note 15, art. 4.

[44] The mark consists of a black and white photograph of a man's face, European Trademark No. 010004943, filed on May 27, 2011.

Sometimes, the mere silhouette of someone can be directly recognisable by the public. But being recognised as an individual is not necessarily the same thing as being recognised as a trademark.

Why did the legislator not mention individuals' portraits among the signs able to compose a trademark? Of course, the aforementioned lists of possible signs are neither exhaustive nor mandatory. An individual's photographic portrait is certainly able to become a trademark. If the legislation does not specify a portrait as an example of trademark subject matter, that does not mean that it is forbidden to file an application for this kind of visual sign. More likely, the absence of portraits from the relevant legal rules simply means that it is less obvious for a portrait to be perceived as a trademark by the public.

We may suggest two reasons for the omission of portraits: a legal one (b) and an economic one (a).

(I) ECONOMIC REASON FOR THE OMISSION OF PORTRAITS With regard to the economic reason, filling a person's portrait as a trademark can be risky, when this person is famous. When the person is not famous, their portrait can become an autonomous distinctive sign. The public then associates the portrait with the products or services of the company without developing interest in the actual person. When the person is famous, it is much more difficult to break the link between a portrait used as a mark and the face of the real person. Fundamentally, a mark must indicate a unique origin for the goods and services it covers. If a company exploits the portrait of a famous person who subsequently parts ways with the company, it runs the risk that this portrait indicates two commercial origins: its own and that of the activities of the still living famous person. Even if the famous person does not offer competing activities on the market, this forces the public to recognise two different original functions on the same face. It is a real source of dilution of the distinctive power of a brand. Thus, there is an economic risk to build a company's economic success on the face of a famous person who can leave the company or even disapprove of it.

Companies in the field of mass consumption sometimes make the choice to celebrate the person of their founder. For instance, *Kentucky Fried Chicken* exploits the image of its founder, Colonel Sanders (Figure 22.2).[45]

This marketing decision may backfire if the relations between the founder and the company deteriorate. Even though the company may enjoy trademark rights in a particular, often stylised, image of the founder, the founder's subsequent disapproval of the company's goods or services can prove embarrassing. In his lifetime, Sanders lamented a loss of quality of the food in KFC's restaurants after he sold his business. His criticisms were so strong that he was sued for defamation by his former company. However, the Supreme Court of Kentucky rejected the claim.[46] In this story, Sanders's face communicated conflicting information to the public. The KFC company used it to convey a positive image of the products covered by the brand, while the person of Sanders conveyed a negative image of these same products.

By contrast, McDonald's corporation would not encounter similar difficulties with the clown character of "Ronald McDonald." Since this character is a work of visual art, it is not likely to criticise the owner. As stated in the filing of the 1967 word trademark "Ronald McDonald," this

[45] The mark consists of a black and white, stylised face of Colonel Sanders, French Trademark No. 96608837, filed on Feb. 2, 1996 (this trademark is now expired, since KFC uses a new design of its founder's portrait: the mark consists of a black and white, stylised face of Colonel Sanders, European Trademark No. 17935090, filed on July 25, 2018).

[46] *Kentucky Fried Chicken of Bowling Green, Inc.* v. *Sanders*, 563 SW 2d 8 (1978).

FIGURE 22.2 Kentucky Fried Chicken's founder, Colonel Sanders, used in the French figurative trademark

name is not intended to identify any particular living individual.[47] When McDonald's registered the whole design of the character as a trademark, no one could claim any opposing right of publicity or personality (Figure 22.3)[48]

Thus, McDonald's brand policy appears less risky than KFC's. Certainly, in time, Sanders eventually died. But a conflict between a company and its "mascot" can be fatal when launching a business.

(II) LEGAL REASON FOR THE OMISSION OF PORTRAITS A legal reason may also explain why it is not obvious to turn a living person's portrait into a trademark. When a trademark is composed of a copyrighted work (a drawing, for instance), the trademark owner may become the assignee of the entire monopoly of exploitation on it. They will then be entitled to forbid any reuse of the creation by the author. When a firm owns a trademark composed of a name, it is entitled by contract to forbid the physical person from exploiting this name in relation with identical or similar goods or services.[49] In most cases, the contract will effectively cut the link between the natural person and the brand composed of a sign associated with their personality. By contrast, it is not so easy to reach this goal with trademarks composed of a portrait.

47 RONALD MCDONALD, US Registration No. 0874861.

48 The mark consists of a drawing of the Ronald McDonald character, US Registration No. 5039734.

49 *Pierre Bordas*, Cour de cassation [Cass.] [supreme court for judicial matters] comm. ch., Mar. 12, 1985, appeal no. 84-17163; on this case, see Lefranc, *supra* note 5, at 43.

FIGURE 22.3 McDonald's trademark clown character

The real problem with a person's portrait lies in its nature. Any person can make a change of name for an economic activity, while it is harder to change a face.[50] When a company files a trademark consisting of a portrait of a famous person, the transaction is hazardous for both parties. The operation is risky for the famous person: because a mark is protected against the reproduction not only of identical but of similar images used as commercial signs, the mark gives the power to its owner to prohibit exploitation of a modified form of the photograph filed, whenever there is a likelihood of confusion.[51] This means that such a mark still expropriates the person of some of the rights they hold on their own face. The transaction is also risky for the company that owns such a brand. A famous face will often escape the company that wants to exploit it for commercial purposes. A contract which would generally prohibit a person from using their face to carry on business would certainly be considered illegal under French law, even limited to one single kind of activity. The only acceptable prohibition should concern the specific photograph that would be filed as a trademark, without affecting all aspects of the person's face. Unfortunately, to our knowledge there is no case law on this issue. Nonetheless, we believe that individual freedom suffers more from a brand consisting of a portrait than a brand consisting of a name. It's easier to buy a name than to buy a face, because it is easier to disassociate a person's name than their portrait.

Cases of trademarks consisting of a portrait have never really been debated in EU community or national courts. To the best of our knowledge, only a recent decision exists on this question. Maartje Verhoef was an international model. She worked, in particular, for Calvin Klein, Giorgio Armani, Dior, Chanel, etc. In 2015, she applied for the registration of her portrait as a European trademark with the EUIPO (Figure 22.4).

The office partly refused the registration because it considered that this trademark would have been descriptive. Adopting a rather sexist reasoning, the examiner said that a female's portrait reflects the audience to whom some products are sold, such as cosmetics, jewellery and bags. On appeal, the EUIPO disapproved of such reasoning. The office did not dispute the difficulties

[50] A person can change their face through makeup, but this change is ephemeral. Only cosmetic surgery can permanently change someone's face. However, apart from criminals, very few individuals seek to become unrecognisable. Cosmetic surgery is mainly used to fight against ageing or repair the consequences of an accident.

[51] EUTMR, *supra* note 15, art. 9(2)(b); Code de la Propriété Intellectuelle [C. ip.] [Intellectual Property Code] art. L. 713-3.

FIGURE 22.4 Portrait of Maartje Verhoef

raised by the application of portraits for registration as trademarks, but refused to block their registration on principle. It is true that often packaging includes a portrait of individuals in order to indicate the intended public. However, those individuals represent the public in general. The portrait of Maartje Verhoef did not have such function. The following shows the main ground for accepting the registration of this trademark:

> 37. A photo of a person's face, in the form of a passport photo, is a unique representation of that person, including his/her specific external features. Besides elements including a person's first name and last name, a depiction of a person's face in the form of a passport photo serves to identify that person and therefore to distinguish him/her from others. In the Board's opinion, the image at issue is therefore capable of fulfilling the essential function of a trade mark, namely distinguishing the goods and services in respect of which registration is sought from those with a different origin.[52]

The same trademark had been registered in the United States,[53] even if Maartje Verhoef – just like Stromae before her – had to confirm her authorisation[54] in writing after a provisional refusal.[55]

In European and French laws, as in US law, it is not possible to apply for the registration of a portrait of a living person without their authorisation. Indeed, the right to prevent exploitation of

52 Case R 2063/2016-4, *Giraffen houden van Wodka* v. *EUIPO* (2017), https://euipo.europa.eu/eSearchCLW/#basic/*///number/2063%2F2016-4 (EUIPO, 4th Board of Appeal); the mark consists of a photo of a woman's head, European Trademark Registration No. 014679351, filed on Oct. 14, 2015.

53 The mark consists of a photo of a woman's head, US Registration No. 5097855.

54 Lanham Act, 15 USC § 1052(c).

55 The mark consists of a photo of a woman's head, USPTO Application Serial No. 79181070, Refusal Note, Feb. 11, 2016.

one's image right is, just like the right over one's name, a prior right which can be opposed to the registration of a trademark. Article L. 711-4 IPC states that: "Signs may not be adopted as marks where they infringe earlier rights, particularly: ... g) The personality rights of another person, particularly his ... likeness."[56] In a similar way, Article 60(2) of the EUTMR considers the invalidity of a European trademark that would infringe personality rights predating the filing.[57]

2 *Protection of Trademarks Composed of a Portrait*

At the beginning of this study, we saw that European and French laws were not sufficiently protecting the economic value of fame. Celebrities could be tempted to apply for the registration of their portraits as trademarks, thinking that they would acquire equivalent rights to the American right of publicity. This may be an error. A right on a trademark is limited by both the registered graphic representation (a) and by the categories of products and services covered (b).

(I) LIMITATION BY THE REPRESENTATION OF THE TRADEMARK The scope of the trademark right is strictly limited to the image as represented in the registration application. But an individual's appearance can be affixed to millions of images, according to their age, hairdo, makeup, weight, health, the light, etc. No trademark will be able, through one single portrait, to protect the thousands of representations of an individual during their lifetime. Besides, it is forbidden to modify the registration of a trademark except for a change of holder or address.[58] Indeed, a trademark must be used as it appears in the application. Otherwise, the trademark could be revoked for non-use.[59] In the case of a trademark consisting of a portrait, it means that this portrait in particular has to be reproduced on packaging or on the products themselves.

Personality rights are not so limited: the individual can prohibit the reproduction of their image under any past, present or future form. Parents can prohibit the reproduction of their baby's image, even if their face will be very different as an adult.[60] In contrast, the protection of someone's face through trademark law would imply sequential applications. But with what frequency: every one year, five years, ten years? Roman Opalka, a conceptual artist, throughout his lifetime, made photographic self-portraits on a regular basis to document the effects of time on the appearance of his face.[61] In contrast to a name which is an intangible series of letters, someone's image is elusive. A name has an inert form, while a face has a living form. It is not feasible to file all aspects of a person's portrait: at birth, at three, six, ten, fifteen, twenty, thirty, etc. The trademark fixes the individual's portrait for the whole time of the registration.

(II) LIMITATION OF PRODUCTS AND SERVICES The extent of a trademark's right is furthermore limited by the claimed products and services. By contrast, personality rights do not

[56] CODE DE LA PROPRIÉTÉ INTELLECTUELLE [C. IP.] [INTELLECTUAL PROPERTY CODE] art. L. 711-4.

[57] EUTMR, *supra* note 15, art. 60(2): "An EU trade mark shall also be declared invalid on application to the Office or on the basis of a counterclaim in infringement proceedings where the use of such trade mark may be prohibited pursuant to another earlier right under the Union legislation or national law governing its protection, and in particular: (a) a right to a name; (b) a right of personal portrayal."

[58] EUTMR, *supra* note 15, art. 49: "An EU trade mark application may be amended, upon request of the applicant, only by correcting the name and address of the applicant, errors of wording or of copying, or obvious mistakes, provided that such correction does not substantially change the trade mark or extend the list of goods or services"; *id.*, art. 54: "The EU trade mark shall not be altered in the Register during the period of registration or on renewal thereof."

[59] EUTMR, *supra* note 15, art. 58.

[60] Cour de cassation [Cass.] [supreme court for judicial matters] 2nd civ. ch., Feb. 19, 2004, appeal no. 02-12742.

[61] "Autoportraits" may be seen on Roman Opalka's official website: http://opalka1965.com/fr/autoportraits.php?lang=en. The artist described his work like this: "what I call my self-portrait is made of thousands of working days. Each one corresponds to a number and to a precise moment in which I stopped painting."

encounter this limitation. The individual can invoke their image right to complain about the use of their appearance with respect to any unauthorised commercial activities.

IV PERSONALITY RIGHTS AND DECEPTIVE MARKETING PRACTICES

French and European trademark laws do not contain any rule similar to Article §1125(a) (section 43(a)) of the Lanham Act. There is nothing like it in the EUTMR, in directives harmonising the national rights and in the French Intellectual Property Code. A similar rule does exist, but it is not expressly included in intellectual property law. A European Directive of 2005 obliged member states to condemn *misleading commercial practices*.[62] Before that text, French law regulated only misleading advertising. The directive has been implemented in French law since a 2008 statute.[63] Today, Article L. 121-1 of the French consumer Code prohibits the creation of confusion in the public's mind, notably regarding the origin of goods or services.[64]

But, as far as we know, celebrities do not seem to use that legal basis to fight against the unlawful exploitation of their fame. We only found one French decision. François Théron was an ice-cream maker since 1977. In 1992, he started to collaborate with the Picard Company, a distribution chain of frozen food. He assigned to Picard "the exclusive rights for the exploitation of his family name . . . in order to register it as a trademark." Picard filed several applications for trademarks consisting of the name "François Théron." The parties' relationship subsequently deteriorated. In 2008, Théron sued for the restitution of the trademarks using his name. He claimed:

> the conditions of marketing of products carrying the mark "François Théron" are unmistakably likely to mislead the public as far as the packaging contains mentions appearing as being written by his hand, under his signature, accompanied by an "advice of tasting" appearing as a personal recommendation from him; that he so sees himself wrongly attributed in the eyes of the consumers a role in the creation of products marketed by SA Picard Surgelés, and guarantor of their quality, which is not anymore the case.[65]

Théron was also claiming – just like in *Sanders* v. KFC – that the quality had worsened since he left. The Paris Court of Appeal rejected this argument. According to the judges, a trademark was not, under French law, a guarantee of quality. The trademark is only a guarantee of origin of the goods. "[T]he mark composed of the surname and first name of a natural person is not, for the consumer, the guarantee of a determined quality, supposed to be associated with the personality of whom it borrows the name."[66] Therefore, consumers are not led to believe that Théron was effectively participating in the creation of the recipes. Théron's action for misleading commercial practices was therefore rejected.

[62] Directive 2005/29/EC of the European Parliament and of the Council of May 11, 2005 concerning unfair business-to-consumer commercial practices in the internal market and amending Council Directive 84/450/EEC, Directives 97/7/EC, 98/27/EC and 2002/65/EC of the European Parliament and of the Council and Regulation (EC) No. 2006/2004 of the European Parliament and of the Council (OJ L 149, June 11, 2005, 22).

[63] Loi 2008-3 du 3 janvier 2008, pour le développement de la concurrence au service des consommateurs [Law 2008-3 of Jan. 3, 2008, for the development of the competition at the service of the customers], https://legifrance.gouv.fr/affichTexte.do?cidTexte=JORFTEXT000017785995#LEGISCTA000017795968.

[64] CODE DE LA CONSUMMATION [C. CON.] [CONSUMER CODE] art. L. 121-1.

[65] *François Théron* v. *SAS Picard Surgelés*, Cour d'appel [CA] [regional court of appeal] Paris, Pole 5, ch. 1, Apr. 9, 2014, case no. 12/18387, http://lexisnexis.fr.

[66] *Id.*

In the same vein, fashion designers tried to get their name back after assigning it. Just like François Théron, they refused to endorse the quality of the goods made by the assignee. Instead of denouncing some misleading commercial practices, they tried to obtain the invalidity of the trademarks that reproduce their name. Their claims were rejected, for the same reason as the one used against Théron: the trademark is not a guarantee of quality, but a guarantee of origin. In European law, the Court of Justice reminded Elizabeth Emanuel of this. Elizabeth Emanuel was a famous British fashion designer who designed the wedding dress of Princess Diana:

> 48. In the present case, even if the average consumer might be influenced in his act of purchasing a garment bearing the trade mark "ELIZABETH EMANUEL" by imagining that the appellant in the main proceedings was involved in the design of that garment, the characteristics and the qualities of that garment remain guaranteed by the undertaking which owns the trade mark.
>
> 49. Consequently, the name Elizabeth Emanuel cannot be regarded in itself as being of such a nature as to deceive the public as to the nature, quality or geographical origin of the product it designates.[67]

Under French law, judges come to the same solution. There is an emblematic case adopting this point of view. In 1991, the fashion designer Inès de la Fressange assigned trademarks made of her name and the right to have others registered to a company. In 1999, that company dismissed her for misconduct. Like Elizabeth Emanuel, she tried to invalidate the trademarks consisting of her name. The Paris Court of Appeal accepted her claim by considering that the public would continue to believe that the products were supervised by Mrs. de la Fressange.[68] The Court of Cassation invalidated this analysis.[69] In its opinion, the fashion designer could not contest the property of trademarks that she assigned herself.

V CONCLUSION

The question "who needs trademarks when you have personality rights?" can be answered. In European and French law, trademark law is not being overtaken by personality rights. The main reason is certainly that celebrities are not as well protected as in the United States. The commercial exploitation of an individual's fame is always treated by torts, without any recognition of some real property right. Furthermore, it seems that all the legal tools are not exploited to protect fame. In particular, the legal action against misleading commercial practice is rarely used. Finally, personality and trademark rights still remain complementary, without supplanting each other.

[67] Case C-259/04, *Elizabeth Florence Emanuel* v. *Continental Shelf 128, Ltd.*, (2006) ECR I-03089 (ECJ, 3rd ch.).

[68] *SA Inès de la Fressange* v. *Mrs. Inès Seignard de la Fressange*, Cour d'appel [CA] [regional court of appeal] Paris, 4th ch., sect. A, Dec. 15, 2004, *Juris-Data* no. 2004-258939.

[69] *SA Inès de la Fressange* v. *Mrs. Inès Seignard de la Fressange*, Cour de cassation [Cass.] [supreme court for judicial matters] comm. ch., Jan. 31, 2006, appeal no. 05-10116.

VIII

Trademarks and Domain Names

23

Legal Regulation of Internet Domain Names in North America

*Jacqueline D. Lipton**

I INTRODUCTION

The regulation of internet domain names in North America, and at the international level, is fairly closely intertwined with trademark law, largely because trademark holders were the first big losers in the domain space. In the mid-to-late 1990s, when domain names first came into existence, cybersquatters took advantage of trademark holders' unfamiliarity with the Internet by registering domain names corresponding with their marks in order to profit from either selling the names back to the "rightful" markholders, or to their competitors, or perhaps to others who may want to use the name for some other purpose, such as for a consumer gripe site.[1] In the absence of laws specific to the domain name system, and because the main concerns about apparently wrongful uses of domain names came from trademark holders, it was trademark law that dealt with the first spate of domain name disputes in national courts. Markholders brought infringement[2] and dilution actions[3] against cybersquatters who, they claimed, had wrongfully registered and used their trademarks in corresponding domain names. These wrongful registrations came in many forms including (a) basic cybersquatting – registering a domain name corresponding with a mark in the hopes of extorting money for transfer of the mark to the trademark holder; (b) typosquatting – registering a misspelling of a mark as a domain name for similar purposes, with hopes that the name would be worth something to the trademark holder because of the risk an internet user would mistype the mark and end up on the registrant's website; (c) registering a domain name corresponding with a trademark in the hopes of directing traffic away from a legitimate trademark holder's website; and (d) registering a domain name corresponding with a trademark in order to lure an internet user to a "clickfarm" website where the user would be "mousetrapped" into clicking on advertising in attempts to escape the website.

Traditional trademark laws were not always a good fit for these kinds of problems. However, for the most part, the American judiciary was able to find creative ways to interpret trademark laws to hold the domain name registrants liable for trademark infringement or dilution, at least

* Visiting Professor of Law, University of Pittsburgh; Director, Authography LLC.

[1] Jacqueline Lipton, Internet Domain Names, Trademarks and Free Speech 25 (2010) (explaining the nature of gripe sites relating to disaffected consumers and employees who wish to complain about a trademark holder).

[2] *See, e.g., Planned Parenthood Fed'n of Am., Inc.* v. *Bucci*, 1997 US Dist. LEXIS 3338 (SDNY 1997).

[3] *Id. See also Panavision Int'l, LP* v. *Toeppen*, 141 F.3d 1316 (9th Cir., 1998).

where the courts found some form of bad faith conduct on the part of the domain name registrant in situations such as those listed above.[4]

There were some areas for which trademark law, as it existed in the 1990s, was nevertheless problematic in the domain space. These areas included situations where the domain name in question corresponded to, say, a famous person's name (e.g., Julia Roberts) or a cultural, geographic, or religious term (e.g., Madonna, Amazon, Ubuntu). Many of these words and phrases could not properly be described as trademarks under domestic law, at least in the United States, whose trademark law requires a person claiming a trademark in a personal name or other descriptive term to establish "secondary meaning."[5]

The secondary meaning requirement basically asks the plaintiff to establish that consumers actually do associate the word or phrase with a particular product or service.[6] The rationale behind the requirement is that trademarks are defined as words, logos, symbols, etc. that serve as *source identifiers*, distinguishing the products or services of one undertaking from those of another.[7] Where a word or phrase, like a person's name or place name, doesn't serve that function, it is not a trademark. Of course, some personal names do, in fact, operate as trademarks. For example, "Madonna" is a registered trademark in the entertainment field.[8] However, many prominent people, including politicians who increasingly conduct business and communications online, are unlikely to be able to establish trademarks in their personal names.[9]

Another respect in which traditional trademark law proved problematic in the context of domain name disputes involved jurisdictional concerns. Trademarks are generally geographically bounded. For example, in the United States it is possible to have a federally registered mark and/or marks registered for particular states. However, there is really no such thing as an "international" mark,[10] although there are systems that allow markholders to simultaneously register their marks in multiple countries.[11] Domain names, on the other hand, are effectively international in scope. Wherever you physically register the name, you basically hold the domain name for the Internet at large. Unlike trademarks, which can coexist in different jurisdictions and in different product and service markets simultaneously, there is only one "trademark.com" version of the name and only one person can register it at a time.

This has led to scarcity problems involving domain names, which the Internet Corporation for Assigned Names and Numbers (ICANN) has tried to remedy by increasing the number of

4 *See infra* Sections I and II.

5 J. Thomas McCarthy, McCarthy on Trademarks and Unfair Competition § 13.2 (5th ed. 2018) ("Personal names are placed by the common law into that category of noninherently distinctive terms which require proof of secondary meaning for protection. Under the traditional rule, personal names are regarded as in the same category as descriptive terms. This mans [sic] that they can be protected as trademarks only upon proof that through usage, they have acquired distinctiveness and secondary meaning").

6 *Id.*

7 *Id.* at § 3.1

8 *MADONNA – Trademark Details*, JUSTIA Trademarks, https://trademarks.justia.com/735/72/madonna-73572121.html.

9 For example, Uniform Domain Name Dispute Resolution (UDRP) arbitrators have cast doubt on whether politician Kathleen Kennedy Townsend or singer Bruce Springsteen can effectively claim a trademark in their respective personal names. *See* WIPO Arbitration and Mediation Center, Administrative Panel Decision, *Kathleen Kennedy Townsend* v. *B. G. Birt*, No. D2002–0030 (Apr. 11, 2002), https://wipo.int/amc/en/domains/decisions/html/2002/d2002-0030.html; WIPO Arbitration and Mediation Center, Administrative Panel Decision, *Bruce Springsteen* v. *Jeff Burgar*, No. D2000–1532 (Jan. 25, 2001), https://wipo.int/amc/en/domains/decisions/html/2000/d2000-1532.html.

10 McCarthy, *supra* note 5, at § 29.1 ("Under the territoriality doctrine, a trademark is recognized as having a separate existence in each sovereign territory in which it is registered or legally recognized as a mark").

11 *Madrid Protocol*, United States Patent and Trademark Office (USPTO), https://uspto.gov/trademark/laws-regulations/madrid-protocol (explaining the international trademark filing system).

generic top-level domains (gTLDs) in recent years.[12] Multiple trademark holders often vie with each other, and with cybersquatters and other domain name speculators, for ownership of a particular name. For whatever reason, the "trademark.com" gTLDs remain the most desirable, despite all the options.

The differing jurisdictional reach of domain names versus trademarks also puts pressure on domestic trademark systems to deal effectively with disputes where the litigants are typically in different countries. It can be difficult, or even impossible, for a domestic American court to exercise personal jurisdiction over a foreign defendant in some situations. Whatever the rules of procedure may say in a particular court about foreign defendants, speculative cybersquatters living in other countries are unlikely to appear in American courts to fight over a domain name. If the court rules against them on an ex parte basis, many of them are happy to lose the domain name to the extent they're playing a numbers game. If they register multiple domain names corresponding with others' marks and lose one or two domestic proceedings in which they do not both appear, the cost is much less for them than attempting to defend each proceeding that may arise. Meanwhile, the markholder has to choose between paying the cybersquatter for return of the name privately or filing a complaint in court for which they will pay all the costs even if the defendant cybersquatter does not appear and the markholder ultimately wins the name.

From the late 1990s onwards, a number of initiatives were implemented in American trademark law, and by ICANN at the international level, to address these challenges. As a result, traditional trademark law as an avenue for redressing domain name disputes has now been augmented by provisions of the Anti-Cybersquatting Consumer Protection Act (ACPA) in the United States, which includes a substantive provision against cybersquatting,[13] as well as an *in rem* provision that was intended to assist with at least some jurisdictional questions.[14] Congress also enacted a specific cybersquatting prohibition relating to personal names[15] outside the trademark context. Some United States state legislatures have gone further and have created specific statutes for particular wrongful conduct involving domain names, such as misuse of domain names in the political process.[16]

Meanwhile, ICANN implemented the Uniform Domain Name Dispute Resolution Policy (UDRP),[17] which was formally adopted in 1999. This policy is incorporated into domain name registration agreements for the most prevalent and desirable gTLDs and some country-code top-level domains (ccTLDs).[18] All domain name registrants subject to this policy agree to submit to a mandatory, but also fast, inexpensive, online, dispute resolution procedure in the event that a trademark holder complains about the registration.[19] Like the ACPA, this policy is focused on protecting trademark holders against cybersquatters. More recently, and in light of its new gTLD program launched in 2012, ICANN also released a Uniform Rapid Suspension System (URS),[20] which is similar to the UDRP but can result in an order suspending the domain name

[12] A "gTLD" is a string of characters "to the right of the dot" in a domain name.

[13] 15 USC § 1125(d)(1)(A) (2018).

[14] *Id.* §1125(d)(2).

[15] *Id.* § 8131 (2018).

[16] For a survey of some of these laws, see Lipton, *supra* note 1, at 43–51.

[17] *Uniform Domain Name Dispute Resolution Policy*, ICANN, https://icann.org/resources/pages/help/dndr/udrp-en.

[18] These are the two-letter strings to the right of the dot containing codes identifying particular countries, e.g., ".ca" for Canada, ".au" for Australia, and ".uk" for the United Kingdom.

[19] *See* UDRP, cl. 4(a).

[20] *Uniform Rapid Suspension*, ICANN, https://icann.org/resources/pages/urs-2014-01-09-en.

registration,[21] rather than a cancellation or transfer order, which is the remedial measure contemplated under the UDRP.[22]

This chapter will examine each of these measures that regulate domain name disputes with a focus on North American trademark law and comparisons, where appropriate, with the UDRP and the URS. At the outset, it is important to note that the UDRP has been astronomically successful in dealing with domain name disputes, making it cheaper, easier and faster to resolve disputes than domestic litigation. The UDRP also elegantly sidesteps the jurisdictional issues that arise in domestic litigation because it relies on an arbitration contract, a contract made initially between the domain name registrant and the relevant domain name registry. In terms of the applicability and effectiveness of a UDRP arbitration, it is irrelevant where the complainant, the domain name registrant, and the registry are located. They might all be in the same, or different, jurisdictions and the policy would be equally applicable.

Thus, it must be borne in mind when examining the North American law relating to domain names that, after 1999, the amount of disputes litigated in domestic courts decreased dramatically. As a result, domain name disputes have not created a rich or nuanced jurisprudence in the United States. The ACPA, in particular, has not been often used since it was enacted at the same time ICANN adopted the UDRP. It has simply been cheaper for trademark holders to rely on the UDRP, and in some later cases the URS, than to test the waters with the ACPA.

II TRADEMARK INFRINGEMENT AND EARLY DOMAIN NAME DISPUTES

The trademark infringement action was one of the first avenues of legal recourse for markholders concerned about registration of domain names corresponding with their marks. It remains an available option although costs and jurisdictional concerns lead disputants to prefer recourse to the UDRP or the URS, where available. The trademark legislation in the United States is the Lanham Act, which includes the basic trademark infringement action as well as actions for trademark dilution, discussed in the next section, and cybersquatting, discussed in the section after that.

The basic trademark infringement action revolves around the markholder establishing the following elements: (1) that it has a valid mark, whether registered or unregistered; (2) that the defendant has used the mark, or a similar mark, commercially; and (3) the mark has been used in a manner that creates a likelihood of consumer confusion about the source of a particular product or service.[23] Outside of jurisdictional concerns, the main practical problems with early cybersquatting disputes argued as trademark infringement actions included questions as to whether the defendant domain name registrant was using the plaintiff's mark *in commerce* as contemplated by the Act. There were also questions as to whether certain uses of marks in the domain space would be likely to confuse consumers.

With respect to the "commercial use" issue, the infringement actions relating to both registered and unregistered marks, require the defendant to have used the plaintiff's mark (or a facsimile of the mark) "in commerce." Early domain name registrants argued that the use of someone else's mark in a domain name was not necessarily a use in commerce, depending on what the relevant website was used for. For example, in the *Planned Parenthood*[24] litigation, a

[21] *See* URS, cls. 4, 10.

[22] *See* UDRP, cl. 4(i).

[23] 15 USC §§1114(1), 1125(a) (2018).

[24] *Planned Parenthood Fed'n of Am., Inc.* v. *Bucci*, 1997 US Dist. LEXIS 3338 (SDNY 1997).

defendant who had registered "plannedparenthood.com" for a website critical of the plaintiff, argued that its use of the domain name was not "in commerce" as contemplated by the Lanham Act. The argument failed. The court effectively held that activities taking place over the Internet as a commercial communications medium were commercial activities almost by default.[25] The court further held that because the domain name registrant used the website to promote sales of a book antithetical to the plaintiff's views on family planning, even though the book was written by a third party not involved in the litigation, there was sufficient evidence of the use of the domain name "in commerce" for Lanham Act purposes.[26]

Planned Parenthood is obviously not a typical cybersquatting case because the domain name had not been registered with the intention of making a profit from selling it to the trademark holder or a competitor. Rather, it had been registered to promote views antithetical to those of Planned Parenthood. The plaintiff likely would not have had the opportunity to negotiate a transfer of the domain name absent the possibility of a legal remedy. The defendant wanted to keep the name for himself.

The question of "likelihood of consumer confusion" has arguably been a little more difficult for markholders to establish in domain name-based infringement actions. However, courts seem to have deferred as much as they can to the interests of trademark holders in the cybersquatting, and similar, contexts. In the *Planned Parenthood* case, consumers would not likely have been confused as to source or affiliation of the website. A consumer searching for Planned Parenthood online and ending up on a website espousing views that challenge those of Planned Parenthood would be unlikely to believe they had found an authorized or affiliated Planned Parenthood website.

However, the court found that consumers might be deterred from searching for the plaintiff's actual website after happening across the defendant's website.[27] This basis for finding likelihood of consumer confusion has come to be identified as a digital species of the traditional "initial interest confusion" doctrine in trademark law.[28] That doctrine basically allows for a trademark infringement action to be successfully established where the plaintiff shows that, while consumers may not have been confused at the time of making a final purchasing decision, they may have been initially confused about the source or affiliation of a product or service.[29] In other words, they may know they are buying Brand Y instead of Brand X, but they would never have thought to purchase Brand Y if not for their initial interest confusion. An example of this is where a retailer prominently displays Brand Y in confusingly similar packaging right beside Brand X in the store.

A similar decision on consumer confusion was made in the case of *Brookfield Communications* v. *West Coast Entertainment Corporation*.[30] Here, the Ninth Circuit held that the use of another's trademarks in meta-tags on a website to facilitate search engines prioritizing the defendant video rental company's website over the plaintiff's could amount to initial interest confusion, even though it was effectively search engine algorithms that were arguably being misled, rather than consumers. The court was concerned that consumers, finding themselves on the defendant's website after searching for the plaintiff's, might nevertheless stay on the defendant's site even after realizing it was not the plaintiff's site. According to the court, this would

[25] *Id.* at *4–5.

[26] *Id.* at 13–14.

[27] See analysis in LIPTON, *supra* note 1, at 17.

[28] *Id.*

[29] MCCARTHY ON TRADEMARKS AND UNFAIR COMPETITION, *supra* note 5, at § 23.6 (explaining genesis of "initial interest confusion" doctrine in trademark law). *See* Chapter 27 in this volume authored by Jeremey Sheff.

[30] *Brookfield Commc'ns, Inc.* v. *W. Coast Entm't Corp.*, 174 F. 3d 1036 (9th Cir. 1999).

amount to initial interest confusion for the purposes of the trademark infringement action. Even though a computer user could easily press the "back" button to search for the plaintiff's site, the concern was that many consumers might not actually do that.

There are, of course, some cases in which the possibility of a plaintiff establishing even initial interest confusion is so remote that an infringement action will be unlikely to succeed. One example was the *Panavision* v. *Toeppen* litigation,[31] discussed in the next section, where the defendant cybersquatter basically put nothing significant on its websites corresponding with the plaintiff's trademarks. Rather, he posted photographs of the town of Pana, Illinois. As a result, there was no possibility of consumer confusion, so the plaintiff markholder resorted – successfully – to a trademark dilution action.

Despite these unusual cases, most of the early cybersquatting situations that predated the UDRP and the ACPA could be handled effectively, at least from the trademark holder's viewpoint, under somewhat expanded applications of trademark infringement law. Of course, plaintiffs faced cost and jurisdictional concerns, many of which are mitigated now by the possibility of a UDRP arbitration, but the basic ability of the infringement action to address many markholders' concerns was relatively easily established in the early days of cybersquatting and similar practices.

Today there are still trademark infringement cases involving domain names, but they typically do not revolve around the "use in commerce" and "consumer confusion" issues so much as other aspects of trademark law. For example, questions arise as to whether the defendant has an available fair use defense.[32] It seems that early questions about the basic ability of a trademark infringement action to resolve a domain name dispute in principle were relatively easily resolved in favor of trademark law being an appropriate and effective avenue of regulation for these disputes.

Of course, as noted in this chapter's introduction, this point is premised on the existence of a trademark in the complainant's hands. Where the complaint about a domain name registration is based on the similarity of the domain name to, say, a personal name, or a culturally or geographically significant word or phrase that is not used as a mark, trademark law will be little help. In those cases, the UDRP and URS will also be little help as they are also premised on the protection of trademark interests. However, some UDRP/URS arbitrators have been prepared to err on the side of acknowledging unregistered trademark interests in a number of personal names, as well as some geographic and cultural indicators, presumably out of awareness that those asserting valid, legal interests in such terms have few other viable avenues of legal recourse against cybersquatters.[33]

III TRADEMARK DILUTION AND EARLY DOMAIN NAME DISPUTES

Like the trademark infringement action, the American trademark dilution action, also found in the Lanham Act, contains a use "in commerce" requirement.[34] The defendant can be liable for dilution only if it uses the plaintiff's mark in commerce. Additionally, the dilution action protects only "famous marks" as defined in the Lanham Act.[35] There is no consumer confusion requirement for a dilution action.

[31] *Panavision Int'l, LP* v. *Toeppen*, 141 F. 3d 1316 (9th Cir. 1998).
[32] *Toyota Motor Sales USA, Inc.* v. *Tabari*, 610 F.3d 1171 (9th Cir. 2010).
[33] See discussion in LIPTON, *supra* note 1, at 141–44.
[34] 15 USC § 1125(c)(1) (2018).
[35] *Id.* § 1125(c)(2)(a).

To establish dilution, the plaintiff must show that (1) it had a famous mark and (2) the defendant has used a mark or trade name that is likely to either blur or tarnish the famous mark.[36] Blurring and tarnishment are two separate sub-species of dilution.

"Blurring" refers to interfering with the distinctive qualities of the mark. Blurring can be established by reference to a statutory test which contemplates that a court will look at factors including (a) the degree of similarity between the defendant's mark or trade name and the famous mark; (b) the degree of distinctiveness of the famous mark; (c) the extent to which the owner of the famous mark is engaging in substantially exclusive use of the mark; (d) the degree of recognition of the famous mark; (e) whether the user of the mark or trade name intended to create an association with the famous mark; and (f) any actual association between the mark or trade name and the famous mark.[37]

"Tarnishment," on the other hand, simply requires a finding that the defendant's use of its mark or trade name harms the reputation of a famous mark.[38] In practice, under traditional American trademark law, the successful tarnishment cases have been those that involve harming the reputation of a famous mark through association with sexual activities or illegal drugs.[39]

Prior to the implementation of the UDRP by ICANN and the ACPA by Congress, trademark dilution was an obvious go-to action for trademark holders concerned about unauthorized uses of their marks in domain names in circumstances where they were unlikely to be able to establish a likelihood of consumer confusion for infringement purposes. In some cases, like *Planned Parenthood*, infringement and dilution were argued in the alternative.

Domestic courts hearing domain name disputes argued as trademark dilution actions treated the "in commerce" requirement similarly to courts hearing such cases as infringement actions. The typical holding has been that pretty much any activity involving registration of a domain name is sufficiently "in commerce" for the purposes of the dilution action because the Internet is a global commercial communications medium.[40] Additionally, to the extent that any defendant's website was used to promote commerce (e.g., selling a book or other product or services), this would bolster an "in commerce" holding.[41]

There has been at least one case in a domestic American court where a domain name registrant using a domain name corresponding with another's mark for purely communicative purposes (e.g., a consumer gripe site) without more was found to be a noncommercial use for trademark purposes.[42] However, the general weight of authority has been in favor of holding nearly all uses of domain names to be "in commerce" and has focused on whether the defendant's conduct is likely to confuse consumers (for trademark infringement purposes) or is likely to blur or tarnish a famous mark (for trademark dilution purposes).

In an early watershed case involving well-known cybersquatter Dennis Toeppen, the Ninth Circuit had little trouble holding a dilution cause of action to be made out where the defendant

[36] *Id.* § 1125(2)(c)(1).

[37] *Id.* § 1125(c)(2)(B).

[38] *Id.* § 1125(c)(2)(C).

[39] McCarthy on Trademarks and Unfair Competition, *supra* note 5, at § 24.89 (surveying case law decisions on tarnishment that revolve around allusions to sexual conduct and drugs).

[40] *See supra* discussion in Section I.

[41] *See, e.g.*, *People for the Ethical Treatment of Animals, Inc.* v. *Doughney*, 113 F. Supp. 2d 915 (2000) (domain name registrant linking to websites where consumers could buy fur and meat products antithetical to the plaintiff trademark holder's mission).

[42] *Bosley Med. Inst.* v. *Kremer*, 403 F. 3d 672 (2005). A similar case involving a personal name, and litigated partly under the ACPA, was the case of *Lamparello* v. *Falwell*, 420 F.3d 309 (2005). Again, the website was used for purely informational purposes.

had registered the plaintiff's (Panavision's) trademark as a domain name and simply parked the website with little content in the hope of selling it to the plaintiff.[43] The fact that Toeppen's actions took up online "space" that was, according to the court, more rightly thought to belong to the plaintiff, supported a blurring action. Additionally, the fact that Toeppen was seeking to sell the name to the plaintiff supported the finding of use "in commerce" of the mark by Toeppen.

Generally speaking, American courts have not hesitated to hold cybersquatters liable for trademark dilution. However, where a trademark is being used in the context of a purely informational website, like a consumer gripe site, dilution has not been as easy to establish. This is perhaps not a surprising result as a matter of general trademark law, where noncommercial uses of a mark are generally not a basis for a successful infringement or dilution action. Additionally, traditional trademark law (both the infringement and dilution action) has always included fair use defenses to balance the need for promoting free speech against property interests in trademarks.

IV THE ANTICYBERSQUATTING CONSUMER PROTECTION ACT

A *Substantive Cybersquatting Provisions*

The ACPA, enacted in 1999, inserted several new provisions into the Lanham Act with respect to perceived problems involving internet domain names at the time. The most significant was the substantive provision creating a new action for trademark holders concerned about cybersquatting.[44] The ACPA also inserted new *in rem* jurisdictional provisions to assist American trademark holders assert jurisdiction in cases where the defendant domain name registrants were out of the relevant jurisdiction,[45] as well as a provision about cybersquatting in relation to personal names. The latter provision was later removed from the Lanham Act, presumably because it did not require a trademark as a basis for the action. It now resides in a separate section of the US Code.[46]

The substantive cybersquatting provisions basically prohibit a defendant from registering, using, or trafficking in a domain name corresponding with another's trademark with a bad faith intent to profit from the name.[47] The statute includes a nonexclusive list of "bad faith" factors, largely derived from early cybersquatting cases, to demonstrate the kinds of issues a court might take into account in determining whether a defendant has registered, used, or trafficked in a domain name in bad faith for the purposes of the action. The list of bad faith factors invites the court to consider:

- the trademark or other intellectual property rights of the domain name registrant in the domain name;
- the extent to which the domain name consists of the legal name of the registrant or a name that is otherwise commonly used to identify that person;
- the registrant's prior use of the domain name in connection with a bona fide offering of goods or services;

[43] *Panavision Int'l, LP* v. *Toeppen*, 141 F.3d 1316 (9th Cir, 1998).
[44] 15 USC § 1125(d)(1)(a) (2018).
[45] *Id.* § 1125(d)(2).
[46] *Id.* § 8131 (2018) (entitled "Cyberpiracy Protections for Individuals").
[47] *Id.* § 1125(d)(1)(b).

- the registrant's bona fide noncommercial or fair use of the mark in a site accessible under the domain name;
- the registrant's intent to divert consumers from the mark owner's online location to a site accessible under the domain name that could harm the goodwill represented by the mark, either for commercial gain or with the intent to tarnish or disparage the mark, by creating a likelihood of confusion as to the source, sponsorship, affiliation, or endorsement of the site;
- the registrant's offer to transfer, sell, or otherwise assign the domain name to the mark owner or any third party for financial gain without having used, or having an intent to use, the domain name in the bona fide offering of any goods or services, or the person's prior conduct indicating a pattern of such conduct;
- the registrant's provision of material and misleading false contact information when applying for registration of the domain name, the registrant's intentional failure to maintain accurate contact information, or prior conduct indicating a pattern of such conduct;
- the registration or acquisition of multiple domain names which the registrant knows are identical or confusingly similar to marks of others that are distinctive at the time of registration of such domain names, or dilutive of famous marks of others that are famous at the time of registration of such domain names, without regard to the goods or services of the parties; and
- the extent to which the mark incorporated in the registrant's domain name registration is or is not distinctive and famous.[48]

The ACPA also includes a fair use defense that a domain name registrant might raise against an ACPA cybersquatting claim that "[b]ad faith intent ... shall not be found in any case in which the court determines that the [domain name registrant] believed and had reasonable grounds to believe that the use of the domain name was a fair use or otherwise lawful."[49] While the section does not define the contours of fair use in the context of an ACPA claim, one might assume that courts are intended to draw from general fair use jurisprudence in relation to trademark infringement and dilution. The kinds of uses typically protected as fair uses in trademark law relate to information, including communication, commentary, and the like. Thus, even under the ACPA, it is arguable that using domain names corresponding with others' marks for criticism and commentary would be excusable.

However, there is little actual case law on the ACPA anti-cybersquatting provisions because they were enacted at the same time as the UDRP was implemented, and the UDRP has proved much more popular as an avenue for resolving internet domain name disputes. The UDRP has the advantages of speed and low cost as well as avoiding jurisdictional questions. UDRP disputes are also heard by experienced arbitrators with expertise in the trademark/domain name space as opposed to domestic litigation where a judge assigned to a case may or may not have particular expertise with respect to trademark law generally or domain name disputes specifically. The UDRP employs similar good faith and bad faith factors to the ACPA. Coupled with the procedural advantages, the UDRP has become a much more desirable dispute resolution avenue for aggrieved trademark holders.

[48] *Id.* § 1125(d)(1)(B)(i).
[49] *Id.* § 1125(d)(1)(B)(ii).

B In Rem *Provisions*

One of the ways in which Congress attempted to address early jurisdictional concerns with respect to internet domain name disputes and the limitations of turning to trademark law was to incorporate a specific provision in the ACPA to enable proceedings to be commenced *in rem* against a domain name as a species of intangible property.[50] The objective was to avoid challenging problems that could be faced by an American trademark holder attempting to assert personal jurisdiction over an often foreign defendant.

The *in rem* provisions effectively gave a home field advantage to American plaintiffs at the time the ACPA was enacted because it not only allowed for the *in rem* action, but placed the situs of the domain name at the place of registration. At the time the law was enacted, most domain names were, in effect, registered in Herndon, Virginia (United States), because that was the location of Network Solutions, which, at the time, hosted the main domain name registry. Consequently, in cases where the *in rem* provisions applied, American plaintiffs were effectively entitled to proceed in Virginia courts. This was much easier than having to attempt to assert personal jurisdiction over far-flung defendants.

As with the substantive provisions of the ACPA, the *in rem* provisions have not been particularly well-tested in domestic courts. Not only did most internet domain name disputes go to UDRP arbitrators from 1999 onwards, but Herndon fairly quickly ceased to be the main place where domain names were registered as ICANN decentralized the registration system. Despite the congressional aims to help American trademark holders pursue claims against foreign cybersquatters, these *in rem* provisions were more or less outdated as soon as they were enacted.

C Personal Name Cyberpiracy Provisions

A final initiative in the early drafts of the ACPA was to include a provision in the Lanham Act that prohibited cybersquatting (or "cyberpiracy" as Congress labeled it) in relation to domain names corresponding with names of individual people. As noted above, many domain name disputes arise in circumstances where a cybersquatter, or other person or entity, registers a domain name corresponding with someone else's personal name, e.g., "juliaroberts.com."[51]

The personal name cyberpiracy provision was relatively quickly moved from the Lanham Act to a separate section of the United States Code because personal name protection does not truly come within the purview of trademark law, especially in cases where the personal name is not operating as a trademark. Under American trademark jurisprudence, a personal name can be protected as a trademark only where it has acquired secondary meaning.[52] This approach ensures that personal names are only protected as marks when they are truly operating as marks – this means that consumers actually do associate them with the source of a particular product or

[50] *Id.* § 1125(d)(2).

[51] See discussion in WIPO Arbitration and Mediation Center, Administrative Panel Decision, *Julia Fiona Roberts v. Russell Boyd*, No. D2000–0210 (May 29, 2000), https://wipo.int/amc/en/domains/decisions/html/2000/d2000-0210.html.

[52] McCarthy on Trademarks and Unfair Competition, *supra* note 5, at § 13.2 ("Personal names are placed by the common law into that category of noninherently distinctive terms which require proof of secondary meaning for protection. Under the traditional rule, personal names are regarded as in the same category as descriptive terms. This mans [sic] that they can be protected as trademarks only upon proof that through usage, they have acquired distinctiveness and secondary meaning").

service. Because personal fame is not the same thing as secondary meaning,[53] many individuals' names do not meet this criterion and are not protected as trademarks.

Where a personal name does operate as a trademark (i.e., it has secondary meaning), it will be protected by all of the existing trademark actions like trademark infringement, dilution (if the name qualifies as a famous mark), and the substantive cybersquatting provisions of the ACPA. Where a personal name does not operate as a trademark, the complainant cannot make use of any of these actions and must resort instead to particular laws directed at personal names.

Currently 15 USC § 8131 is the main federal law in the United States protecting personal names against cybersquatting. The statute provides that

> [a]ny person who registers a domain name that consists of the name of another living person, or a name substantially and confusingly similar thereto, without that person's consent, with the specific intent to profit from such name by selling the domain name for financial gain to that person or any third party, shall be liable in a civil action by such person.[54]

Unlike the general anti-cybersquatting prohibition in the Lanham Act, the personal name provision is limited to situations where a domain name has been *registered* with the intent to profit from selling it. The general anti-cybersquatting provision, as noted above, prohibits *registering, trafficking in, or using* a domain name *with a bad faith intent to profit*. Thus, the personal name cyberpiracy provisions are intended to be more limited in their operation than the general anti-cybersquatting provisions involving trademarks in the domain space.

The personal name cyberpiracy provision also includes a good faith defense. However, the defense is much more limited in practical terms than the general fair use defense to cybersquatting. The section 8131 defense to personal name cyberpiracy provides that:

> A person who in good faith registers a domain name consisting of the name of another living person, or a name substantially and confusingly similar thereto, shall not be liable under this paragraph if such a name is used in, affiliated with, or related to a work of authorship protected under [the Copyright Act], and if the person registering the domain name is the copyright owner or licensee of the work, the person intends to sell the domain name in conjunction with the lawful exploitation of the work, and such registration is not prohibited by a contract between the registrant and the named person.[55]

For example, if a domain name registrant is the copyright owner of an unauthorized biography of a well-known person, like Chelsea Clinton, and the domain name (say, chelseaclinton.com) resolves to a website promoting the book, that would be covered by the defense. This section goes on to make it clear that this defense is limited to actions under section 8131 and does not apply to any trademark actions or other laws.[56] Thus, if Chelsea Clinton could establish a trademark in her personal name, she could raise complaints under the Lanham Act for infringement, dilution, or potentially even cybersquatting depending on the circumstances.

Thus, unlike the general trademark cybersquatting defense, a defendant in a section 8131 action can raise the applicable statutory defense only where the domain name is used in conjunction with authorship of a copyrighted work for the specific purposes contemplated in the legislation. As with the broader ACPA provisions, the section 8131 provisions have not developed a broad American case law. The reason for this lack of decisions is probably twofold – that

[53] With secondary meaning, the name symbolizes goods or services, not the person.
[54] 15 USC §8131(1)(A) (2018).
[55] *Id.* §8131(1)(B).
[56] *Id.*

(a) many UDRP arbitrators relatively easily accept personal names as trademarks and allow personal name disputes to be heard under the UDRP even if the trademark status of the personal name is questionable and that (b) litigation in federal court is expensive for private individuals even where a cause of action like the personal name cyberpiracy provisions is available.

Thus, in the absence of a celebrity name (where the person probably has the wherewithal to fight over a domain name), most private individuals will not likely sue under section 8131 with respect to domain names corresponding with their personal names. Those who have the wherewithal to bring an action probably have names that are famous enough to convince a UDRP arbitrator that they hold a trademark in the name and can proceed under the UDRP on that basis. Because it exists outside the Lanham Act, section 8131 does not include an *in rem* procedure such as that found in the ACPA. However, as noted above, the *in rem* procedure has really outlived its usefulness in most cases due to the subsequent deregistration of domain name registry services.

V ICANN DISPUTE RESOLUTION POLICIES: THE UNIFORM DOMAIN NAME DISPUTE RESOLUTION POLICY AND THE UNIFORM RAPID SUSPENSION SYSTEM

While this chapter is predominantly about North American law on trademark/domain name disputes, it would not be complete without at least a few words about ICANN's forays into domain name dispute resolution since 1999. Most domain name disputes since the UDRP was implemented in 1999 have been arbitrated under that policy. As noted above, trademark holders typically include celebrities who are relatively easily able to convince UDRP arbitrators that they hold unregistered marks (sometimes registered marks are held) in their personal names. When the new gTLD system came online, increasing the number and type of domain name strings "to the right of the dot," ICANN also adopted the URS. The URS operates similarly to the UDRP but provides for suspension of registration of a domain name rather than cancellation or transfer.

The substantive provisions of the UDRP and URS are similar to those found in the ACPA; they favor registration and use of domain names corresponding with trademarks by valid trademark holders over "bad faith" profiteers. The advantages of the UDRP and URS over domestic legislation like the ACPA are that, being imposed by contract between a domain name registrant and the relevant registry, they allow for fast and efficient online dispute resolution per the contract terms. They avoid jurisdictional problems because domain name registrants agree contractually to submit to online arbitration. They also allow for quick and effective remedies as relevant domain name registries agree to abide by transfer, cancellation, or suspension orders granted under the respective policies, although it is worth noting that the UDRP does not preclude subsequent resort to domestic litigation under, for example, the ACPA in the United States.

Both the UDRP and the URS are premised on the complainant establishing its trademark rights or interests, and bad faith registration and use of the domain name by the registrant. One of the key differences between the two systems is that the UDRP requires only that the complainant establish a trademark interest whether registered or unregistered, whereas the URS requires the existence of a word mark (a) over which the complainant has a valid national or regional registration; (b) which has been validated by a national court; or (c) which is protected by a treaty.[57]

[57] URS, cl. 1.2.6.1.

Both systems are relatively similar in their conception of a "bad faith" use of a trademark by a domain name registrant.[58] The UDRP conception of "bad faith," closely followed by the URS, sets out the following as non-exclusive indicators of bad faith registration and use of a domain name:

(i) circumstances indicating that [the registrant] registered or acquired the domain name primarily for the purpose of selling, renting, or otherwise transferring the domain name registration to the complainant who is the owner of the trademark or service mark or to a competitor of that complainant, for valuable consideration in excess of [the registrant's] documented out-of-pocket costs directly related to the domain name;
(ii) [the registrant] has registered the domain name in order to prevent the owner of the trademark or service mark from reflecting the mark in a corresponding domain name . . . ;
(iii) [the registrant] has registered the domain name primarily for the purpose of disrupting the business of a competitor; or,
(iv) by using the domain name, [the registrant] intentionally attempted to attract, for commercial gain, Internet users to [its] web site or other on-line location, by creating a likelihood of confusion with the complainant's mark as to the source, sponsorship, affiliation, or endorsement of [the] web site or location or of a product or service on [the] web site or location.[59]

Unlike the ACPA, which requires the defendant to have registered, trafficked in, or used the domain name in bad faith, the UDRP model requires the domain name to have been *registered* in bad faith in the first place.[60] Thus, some claims where the domain name was not registered in bad faith but was later used in bad faith may not satisfy UDRP requirements, and may need to be litigated in a domestic court.[61]

Under the UDRP, a domain name registrant may rebut the bad faith claim of the trademark holder by arguing that they had a legitimate interest in the name. The URS is closely modeled on this aspect of the UDRP as well. Under the UDRP, to establish a legitimate interest in a domain name, the registrant may raise the following arguments:

(i) before any notice to [the registrant] of the dispute, [the registrant's] use of, or demonstrable preparations to use, the domain name or a name corresponding to the domain name in connection with a bona fide offering of goods or services;
(ii) [the registrant] (as an individual, business, or other organization) [has] been commonly known by the domain name, even if [it] acquired no trademark or service mark rights; or
(iii) [the registrant is] making a legitimate noncommercial or fair use of the domain name, without intent for commercial gain to misleadingly divert consumers or to tarnish the trademark or service mark at issue.[62]

[58] *Id.*, cl. 1.2.6.3; UDRP, cl. 4(b).
[59] UDRP, cl. 4(b).
[60] *Id.*, cl. 4(a)(iii).
[61] This issue can be particularly problematic in situations where the trademark owner cannot establish that its domestic trademark is well known, or known at all, by domain name registrants in foreign jurisdictions who may not have had any opportunity to come across the mark prior to registering their domain name. A recent example of this situation is found in WIPO Arbitration and Mediation Center, Administrative Panel Decision, *Zeca S.p.A. v. Whois Privacy Protection Service, Inc.*, No. D2017–0158 (Apr. 3, 2017), http://wipo.int/amc/en/domains/search/text.jsp?case=D2017-0158. In this case, the Italian trademark owner's marks were found to be unknown to the American domain name registrant, so the complainant was unable to make out the UDRP factor that requires bad faith *registration* of the name.
[62] UDRP, cl. 4(c).

Like the bad faith factors, the "legitimate use" factors are non-exclusive, so a domain name registrant may support a legitimate use claim in other ways. Most domain name disputes can be effectively resolved through ICANN processes. Therefore, there is typically little need to resort to domestic trademark law unless the trademark holder cannot establish that the registrant actually registered its domain name in bad faith (as opposed to trafficking in, or using it in bad faith), or in cases where the trademark holder seeks a remedy outside of transfer, cancellation, or suspension of the domain name. Where, for example, the trademark holder seeks damages or an order requiring a disclaimer to be added to a website, domestic litigation may be preferable.

As a procedural matter, UDRP disputes are administered by bodies that ICANN has accredited to do so. The body that handles by far the most disputes is the World Intellectual Property Organization's (WIPO) domain name dispute resolution service[63] offered by WIPO's Arbitration and Mediation Center.[64] However, ICANN has accredited other bodies to offer similar services.[65] At the time of writing, these bodies include the National Arbitration Forum,[66] the Czech Arbitration Court Arbitration Center for Internet Disputes,[67] the Asian Domain Name Dispute Resolution Centre,[68] and the Arab Center for Domain Name Dispute Resolution.[69] Historically, the UDRP procedures, regardless of the arbitration forum, have been criticized for results that typically favor trademark holders over domain name registrants. This apparent bias toward trademark holder success continues to the present day. For example, over 90 percent of UDRP disputes arbitrated through the WIPO arbitration forum result in transfer of the domain name to the complainant holder or cancellation of the domain name registration. Domain name registrants were only successful in just over 7 percent of cases arbitrated.[70]

There could be a number of valid reasons why so many disputes are decided in favor of trademark holders other than a problem with the system causing unfair bias, such as the prevalence of cybersquatting and other activities (discussed above) that may harm a trademark holder in the domain space. It is very inexpensive and easy for anyone to register a domain name that corresponds with another's trademark speculatively in the hopes of making money out of selling it. As a corollary to this point, cases are unlikely to be brought by trademark holders in bad faith. Businesses attempting to protect their goodwill likely are not easily motivated to waste resources even on relatively cheap dispute resolution processes unless they really see a need to do so. Thus, at least one plausible explanation for the tendency of UDRP disputes to favor trademark holders is that the system is doing exactly what it was intended to do – protect trademark holders against those attempting to register and use their marks online in bad faith. Regardless of the merits of the criticisms of the UDRP as being too trademark-holder-centric, it clearly is a much cheaper and easier avenue for markholders to protect their online assets than traditional domestic litigation.

63 *See Domain Name Dispute Resolution*, WIPO, http://wipo.int/amc/en/domains/.
64 *See Alternative Dispute Resolution*, WIPO, http://wipo.int/amc/en/.
65 *See List of Approved Dispute Resolution Service Providers*, ICANN, https://icann.org/resources/pages/providers-6d-2012-02-25-en.
66 *See Domain Name Disputes*, ADR Forum, http://adrforum.com/domains.
67 *See* Arbitration Center for Internet Disputes, http://adr.eu/index.php.
68 *See* Asian Domain Name Dispute Resolution Centre, https://adndrc.org/.
69 *See* Arab Center for Dispute Resolution, http://acdr.aipmas.org/default.aspx?lang=en.
70 *See Case Outcome (Consolidated) 2018*, WIPO, https://wipo.int/amc/en/domains/statistics/decision_rate.jsp?year=2018.

VI CONCLUSION

While trademark law has historically addressed claims of cybersquatting in the domain space quite effectively through infringement and dilution actions, developments from 1999 onwards by both Congress and ICANN have provided other options for trademark holders concerned about unauthorized uses of their marks in a domain space. The appropriate avenue for proceeding against a domain name registrant will likely depend on what the trademark holder actually wants: for example, a simple transfer or cancellation order can best and most effectively and cheaply be managed under the UDRP.

In cases where the trademark status of the complainant's claim is less straightforward (for example, in the case of a personal name) a complainant may prefer to resort to the UDRP than domestic litigation on the grounds that UDRP arbitrators tend to be more sympathetic than domestic courts to trademarks in personal names. Those with personal names that may not amount to trademarks may also seek to avail themselves of the personal name cyberpiracy protections in 15 USC § 8131. A personal name arbitration under the UDRP will, of course, be cheaper than domestic litigation under section 8131, but where a personal name is not sufficiently famous to satisfy a UDRP arbitrator or panel that it is operating as a trademark, domestic litigation under the cyberpiracy provisions may be the only viable option for the complainant.

24

Domain Name Dispute Resolution in Mainland China and Hong Kong

*Jyh-An Lee**

I INTRODUCTION

Domain names are internet addresses that help users identify the website operators and associated businesses.[1] In contrast to Internet Protocol (IP) addresses, which are unique strings of numbers, domain names are typically familiar strings of letters and numbers easily visualized and memorized by internet users.[2] Therefore, domain names make user navigation of the web more straightforward.

Although trademarks and domain names are distinct symbols, both are media used by business entities to communicate with their consumers,[3] and both are valuable corporate assets that protect the identity of a firm.[4] However, domain name rules are not always consistent with trademark principles. Domain names are assigned on a first come, first served basis without any inquiry into whether the names match registrants' or any third parties' trademarks. Legal issues may arise when a registered domain name is similar or identical to the trademark of another business entity.[5]

Cybersquatting has become a serious problem in China and other Asian jurisdictions.[6] In 2017, it was reported that around 10 percent of the .cn domain names were registered by cybersquatters.[7] This chapter explores the domain name dispute resolution mechanisms in mainland China and Hong Kong by illustrating how domain name disputes associated with trademarks are resolved through the implementation of Uniform Domain Name Dispute

* Associate Professor, Faculty of Law, The Chinese University of Hong Kong. The author would like to thank Irene Calboli, Jane Ginsburg, and Jacqueline Lipton for their valuable comments, and Yangzi Li and Lesley Luo Jingyu for their extraordinary research assistance. This study was supported by a grant from the Research Grants Council in Hong Kong (Project No CUHK 14612417).

1 *See, e.g.*, Mark V. B. Partridge, *Domain Names and Trademarks*, *in* Overlapping Intellectual Property Rights 298–9 (Neil Wilkof & Shamnad Basheer eds., 2012).

2 *Id.*

3 *See, e.g.*, Anan Shawqi Younes, *Trademarks and Domain Names: Exploring the Inadequacy of Existing Protection for the Economic Value of Trade Marks*, 34(12) European Intell. Prop. Rev. 847, 847 (2012).

4 *See, e.g.*, Barbara A. Solomon, *Two New Tools to Combat Cyberpiracy – A Comparison*, 90 Trademark Rep. 679, 679 (2000).

5 *See, e.g.*, Jessica Litman, *The DNS Wars: Trademarks and the Internet Domain Name System*, 4 J. Small & Emerging Bus. L. 149, 149 (2000).

6 *See, e.g.*, Loke-Khoon Tan, Trademark Law in China: Pirates in the Middle Kingdom: The New Frontier 233 (3d ed. 2017); He Fang, *China's Recent Development in Domain Name Litigation*, China Intell. Prop., Jan. 6, 2012, http://chinaipmagazine.com/en/journal-show.asp?id=776.

7 Tan, *supra* note 6, at 237.

Resolution Policy (UDRP) and litigation in these two jurisdictions. Section I of this chapter illustrates the convergence and divergence of the civil law and common law approaches to domain name dispute resolution. Section II outlines how these two jurisdictions implement the UDRP via the China International Economic and Trade Arbitration Commission (CIETAC) and the Hong Kong International Arbitration Centre (HKIAC). This section focuses particularly on the grounds for trademark owners to complain against domain names registered by other parties. Section III analyzes how parties use the court to solve domain name disputes in the two jurisdictions. Section IV probes trademark disputes and the new business models in China resulting from the introduction of new general top-level domain names (gTLDs) in 2012.

II IMPLEMENTATION OF THE UDRP IN CHINA AND HONG KONG

The UDRP was created by the Internet Corporation for Assigned Names and Numbers (ICANN)[8] to enable "an inexpensive and efficient alternative to litigation for resolving disputes between trademark owners and domain name registrants."[9] The ICANN also released the Rules for the Uniform Domain Name Dispute Resolution Policy (UDRP Rules) to facilitate the UDRP procedure.[10] The main purpose of the UDRP is to curb instances of cybersquatting in which domain name registration may infringe existing trademarks. The UDRP has been implemented in numerous jurisdictions to provide an efficient, streamlined dispute resolution process for domain name disputes associated with trademarks. Although the UDRP is implemented primarily by a chain of contracts,[11] its implementation rules in different jurisdictions might vary because of dissimilar domestic laws.[12] This part of the chapter uses mainland China and Hong Kong, respectively a civil law jurisdiction and a common law jurisdiction, to illustrate how the UDRP has been, or could be, employed in different jurisdictions.

A *Arbitration Tribunals*

As in many other jurisdictions, domain name disputes in China can be resolved via litigation or nonlitigation procedures.[13] Trademark owners can sue domain name registrants in the court or file domain name complaints in the CIETAC or the HKIAC, the two arbitration tribunals certified by the China National Network Information Center (CCNIC).[14] The CIETAC and HKIAC have jointly established the Asian Domain Name Dispute Resolution Centre (ADNDRC), which has offices in Beijing, Hong Kong, Kuala Lumpur, and Seoul.[15]

[8] *See* ICANN, Uniform Domain Name Dispute Resolution Policy (1999), http://icann.org/en/udrp/udrp-policy-24oct99.htm [hereinafter UDRP].

[9] Improvement of Technical Management of Internet Names and Addresses, 63 Fed. Reg. 8826, 8830 (Feb. 20, 1998). For a more comprehensive introduction to UDRP, *see* Chapter 23 in this volume authored by Jacqueline D. Lipton.

[10] *See* ICANN, *Rules for Uniform Domain Name Dispute Resolution Policy*, Sept. 28, 2013, https://icann.org/resources/pages/udrp-rules-2015-03-11-en [hereinafter Rules for UDRP].

[11] *See, e.g.*, Julia Hörnle, *The Uniform Domain Name Dispute Resolution Procedure: Is Too Much of a Good Thing a Bad Thing?*, 11 SMU Sci. & Tech. L. Rev. 253, 255 (2008).

[12] *See also* Ben Norton, *Note: Constitutional Internationalization of ICANN's UDRP*, 29 Ariz. J. Int'l & Comp. L. 137, 142 (2012) ("Many countries resisted the UDRP, particularly where its rules conflict with domestic law").

[13] *See, e.g.*, He, *supra* note 6; Hörnle, supra note 11, 281.

[14] *See, e.g.*, Tan, *supra* note 6, at 237.

[15] Hong Kong International Arbitration Centre (HKIAC), Guide to HKIAC Domain Name Dispute Resolution 5 (2017), http://hkiac.org/sites/default/files/ck_filebrowser/PDF/domain_name/guide_book%20_renewV4.pdf [hereinafter HKIAC]; ICANN, *ICANN Announces New Dispute Resolution Provider in the Asia Pacific Region*, Dec. 3, 2011, https://icann.org/news/announcement-2001-12-03-en.

The ADNDRC is currently one of the five UDRP service providers accredited by the ICANN.[16] It provides domain name dispute resolution services with regard to gTLDs, such as .com, .net, and .org domain names. The ADNDRC has also accepted domain name complaints regarding new gTLDs since 2014. Both the CIETAC and HKIAC provide domain name dispute services with regard to country-code top-level .cn domain name (ccTLD) domain names. The HKIAC provides the same services with regard to .hk and .香港 ccTLDs.[17]

B Dispute Resolution Rules

In particular, disputes relating to .cn and .中国[18] domain names are governed by the CNNIC Domain Name Dispute Resolution Policy (CNDRP), the Rules for the CNNIC ccTLD Domain Name Dispute Resolution Policy (CNDRP Rules), and the CIETAC Supplemental Rules to CNDRP (CIETAC Supplemental Rules).[19] Similarly, registrants of domain names with country code .hk or .香港 are contractually bound to submit to an online arbitration to the HKIAC if a third party complains about their registration or use of the domain name. The HKIAC will then resolve the dispute according to the Hong Kong Domain Name Dispute Resolution Policy (HKDRP),[20] which is the dispute resolution policy adopted by the Hong Kong Domain Name Registration Company Limited (HKDNR).[21] In addition, the HKIAC may apply the HKIAC Domain Name Dispute Supplemental Rules and the Arbitration Ordinance.[22]

Like the UDRP, the CNDRP provides an efficient mechanism for resolving domain name disputes, but it differs from the UDRP in several respects. Most notably, where Article 2 of the CNDRP stipulates that "the dispute resolution service providers do not accept the complaint regarding domain names with registration term of over two years,"[23] the UDRP allows a trademark owner to file a complaint against the domain name registrant long after the domain name registration. The trademark owner then can bring a lawsuit against the domain name registrant only under the People's Republic of China (PRC) Trademark Law or Anti-Unfair Competition Law. This time limitation was once criticized as an unreasonable obstacle for the enforcement of trademarks.[24]

The two-year limitation was lifted in the HKIAC panel's decision in *Lester Brands AV* v. *Chen Qiuheng*. The panel ruled that the transfer of a .cn domain name constituted a new registration under the CNDRP.[25] The panel opined that the transfer of a domain name was equivalent to a new registration based on the interpretation of Article 9 in the CDNRP, which is the criterion for determining bad faith registration.[26] Therefore, the transfer of a .cn domain dame will reset

[16] HKIAC, *supra* note 15.

[17] 香港 is the Chinese name of Hong Kong.

[18] 中国 is the Chinese name of China.

[19] CCNIC, *Rules for CNNIC ccTLD Domain Name Dispute Resolution Policy*, Aug. 30, 2012, https://cnnic.com.cn/PublicS/fwzxxgzcfg/201208/t20120830_35737.htm [hereinafter CDNRP].

[20] Hong Kong Internet Registration Corporation Limited (HKIRC), *Domain Name Dispute Resolution Policy for .hk and .香港 Domain Names*, Feb. 22, 2011, https://hkirc.hk/content.jsp?id=25 [hereinafter HKDRP].

[21] Kenny Wong & Alice Lee, Intellectual Property Law and Practice in Hong Kong 730 (2017).

[22] *Id.* at 733.

[23] CDNRP, *supra* note 19, art. 2.

[24] HKIAC, *supra* note 15, at 16.

[25] *Lester Brands AV* v. *Chen Qiuheng*, [2015] HKIAC Case No. DCN-1500641, http://hkiac.org/sites/default/files/ck_filebrowser/IP/cn/decision//DCN-1500641_Decision.pdf.

[26] *Id.*

the two-year limitation. The same viewpoint regarding the two-year limitation was taken in *Airbnb Inc.* v. *Guo Lanzhi*, decided by the HKIAC panel.[27]

C Grounds for Domain Name Complaints

According to UDRP, the grounds for domain name complaint include three elements: (1) the domain name is identical or confusingly similar to a trademark or service mark in which the complainant has rights; (2) the domain name registrant has no rights or legitimate interests in respect of the domain name; and (3) the domain name has been registered and is being used in bad faith.[28] Both the CDNRP and HKDRP incorporate the essence of UDRP provisions regarding the three elements of the grounds for complaining against a domain name registrant.[29] Nevertheless, the panels have developed different approaches to applying these three elements to domain name disputes associated with .cn and .hk respectively. This section will explain how the three elements are applied and developed to solve domain name disputes in these two jurisdictions.

1 *Disputes Related to Domain Name That Are Identical or Confusingly Similar to a Trademark*

Trademarks and service marks are examples of names in which the complainant has rights. Complainants occasionally claim that they have other rights against the respondent's domain name registration. For example, the complainant can file a claim based on its own earlier domain name registration against the respondent's later, similar registration.[30] The scope of "rights" differs from jurisdiction to jurisdiction. Some common law rights, such as passing off, are not protected in the same form in civil law jurisdictions. Therefore, as under the UDRP, trademark owners from one jurisdiction may enjoy a higher degree of protection than those from another jurisdiction. This difference is well illustrated in the application of CDNRP to .cn domain names and that of HKDRP to .hk domain names. Because Hong Kong is a common law jurisdiction, the application of HKDRP occasionally concerns some common law rights which do not exist in the context of CDNRP.

(I) DISPUTES RELATED TO DOMAIN NAMES WITH COUNTRY CODE .CN Both the UDRP and HKDRP require the domain name targeted by a complaint to be identical or confusingly similar to "a trademark or service mark,"[31] whereas the CDNRP requires the domain name to be identical or confusingly similar to a "name or mark."[32] Obviously the scope of "name or mark" is wider than that of "trademark or service mark."[33] Therefore, from statuary interpretation, the threshold for initiating a domain name complaint is lower in the CDNRP than in the UDRP and HKDRP. Moreover, the UDRP and HKDRP require the complainant to have a "right" in

[27] *Airbnb Inc.* v. *Guo Lanzhi*, [2017] HKIAC Case No. DCN-1700742, http://hkiac.org/sites/default/files/ck_filebrowser/IP/cn/decision//DCN-1700742_Decision.pdf.

[28] UDRP, *supra* note 8, § 4(a).

[29] CDNRP, supra note 19, art. 8; HKDRP, *supra* note 20, § 4(a).

[30] *See, e.g.*, *Sino Land Co. Ltd.* v. *Suet Chung Tsang*, [2003] ADNRC Case No. HK-0300032, https://adndrc.org/files/udrp/HK/HK-0300032_Decision.pdf.

[31] UDRP, *supra* note 8, § 4(a); HKDRP, *supra* note 20, § 4(a).

[32] Both HKIAC and CIETAC panels have linked the application of CDNRP to the PRC Anti-Unfair Competition Law. Consequently the "name" stipulated in CDNRP here is equivalent to that in the PRC Anti-Unfair Competition Law and includes personal name and trade names. *See* text accompanying note 36–49.

[33] CDNRP, *supra* note 19, art. 8.

their "mark,"[34] whereas the CDNRP requires the complainant to have a "civil right or interest" in their "name or mark."[35] Such civil rights include not only rights associated with trademark or service mark, but also rights protected by other laws, such as the PRC Copyright Law, the Anti-Unfair Competition Law, etc., of China.[36]

In particular, Article 6 of the 2017 and 2019 PRC Anti-Unfair Competition Law is frequently cited by the CDNRP panel to determine whether the complainant has a "civil right or interest" in their "name or mark":

> A business shall not commit the following acts of confusion to mislead a person into believing that a commodity is one of another person or has a particular connection with another person:
>
> (1) Using without permission a label identical or similar to the name, packaging or decoration, among others, of another person's commodity with certain influence;
> (2) Using without permission another person's name with certain influence, such as the name (including abbreviations and trade names) of an enterprise, the name (including abbreviations) of a social organization, or the name (including pseudonyms, stage names and name translations) of an individual;
> (3) Using without permission the principal part of a domain name, the name of a website, or a web page with certain influence, among others, of another person; or,
> (4) Other acts of confusion sufficient to mislead a person into believing that a commodity is one of another person or has a particular connection with another person.[37]

In *Entertainment One UK Limited* v. *Dongguan Huotu Garment Co. Ltd.* (2015), the HKIAC panel ruled for the complainant, who had used the English name "Peppa Pig" on its toy products in jurisdictions other than China, and had gained an international reputation on the basis of that name.[38] Although the complainant did not register the product name as a trademark in China, "Peppa Pig" was protected by Article 5(2) of the 1993 PRC Anti-Unfair Competition Law, which later became Article 6(1) of the 2017 and 2019 PRC Anti-Unfair Competition Law.[39] In *Airbnb Inc.* v. *Guo Lanzhi* (2017), the HKIAC panel held that although the owner of an unregistered mark may not have any legal right over the mark, he does have a legally protected "interest" in the mark if the mark has "certain influence."[40] As a result, such an owner can claim legal right over the mark against the domain name registrant. The requirement of "certain influence" in the PRC Anti-Unfair Competition Law derives from Article 32(1) of the PRC Trademark Law.[41] Therefore, what constitutes "certain influence" in PRC Anti-Unfair

[34] UDRP, *supra* note 8, § 4(a); HKDRP, *supra* note 20, § 4(a).

[35] CDNRP, *supra* note 19, art. 8.

[36] *Airbnb Inc.* v. *Guo Lanzhi, supra* note 27, at 15.

[37] Zhonghua Renmin Gongheguo Fan Buzheng Jingzheng Fa (中华人民共和国反不正当竞争法) [Anti-Unfair Competition Law] (promulgated by the Standing Comm. Nat'l People's Cong., Nov. 4, 2017, effective Jan. 1, 2018) Zhonghua Renmin Gongheguo Fan Buzheng Jingzheng Fa (中华人民共和国反不正当竞争法) [Anti-Unfair Competition Law] (promulgated by the Standing Comm. Nat'l People's Cong., Apr. 23, 2019, effective Apr. 23, 2019) [hereinafter Anti-Unfair Competition Law].

[38] *Entertainment One UK Limited* v. *Dongguan Huotu Garment Co. Ltd.*, (2015) HKIAC Case No. DCN-1500617, at 6–7, http://staging.hkiac.org/sites/default/files/ck_filebrowser/IP/cn/decision//DCN-1500617_Decision.pdf.

[39] *Id.* at 6–7. *See also Airbnb Inc.* v. *Guo Lanzhi, supra* note 27 (similarly ruling for the complainant, who did not register the "Airbnb" trademark before the subject domain name registration, based on art. 5(2) of the 1993 Anti-Unfair Competition Law).

[40] *See Airbnb Inc.* v. *Guo Lanzhi, supra* note 27, at 19.

[41] Zhonghua Renmin Gongheguo Shangbiao Fa (中华人民共和国商标法) [Trademark Law of the People's Republic of China] (2019 Amendment), art. 32(1): "No applicant for trademark application may infringe upon another person's

Competition Law would be the same as that in the PRC Trademark Law.[42] According to the Supreme People's Court, "certain influence" of a mark can be proved by showing (1) it has been used for a period of time in certain areas and reflected in sales volume and advertisement of the goods or service[43] and (2) the mark is known to the relevant public.[44]

However, not all complainants can easily claim a right over an unregistered mark against domain name registrations under the CDNRP. In 2018, the HKIAC panel ruled in *Pacific Alliance Investment Management (Hong Kong) Limited* v. *Xie Cheng Huo* that the complainant did not have any "civil right or interest" in the mark because the complainant had never used the mark "Pacific Alliance" in mainland China nor built an international reputation on its basis.[45] In *Novalash Inc.* v. *Novolash Cosmetics China* (2015), although the complainant had used the domain name "www.novolash.com" and had business franchises in more than forty jurisdictions, the company lost the case.[46] The HKIAC panel ruled that the complainant did not have any "civil right or interest" in the domain name because the complainant had never registered the Novalash trademark in China.[47] A comparison of this case with the previously mentioned *Entertainment One UK Limited* v. *Dongguan Huotu Garment Co. Ltd.* indicates that the HKIAC panel's standard for determining whether the complainant has any "civil right or interest" in the domain name is not quite consistent.[48] Different conclusions regarding a complainant's "civil right or interest" in the domain name may be reached on the basis of similar facts: in both cases, the complainant had successful businesses in other jurisdictions but lacked trademark registration in China.

(a) Complaint Based on Personal Name Article 6 of the PRC Anti-Unfair Competition Law provides a wide range of grounds for the complainant's initiation of a CDNRP procedure against

existing prior rights, nor may he, by illegitimate means, rush to register a trademark that is already in use by another person and has certain influence."

42 *See, e.g.*, *Brief Review of the Newly Revised Anti-Unfair Competition Law*, Baker & McKenzie, Mar. 8, 2018, https://globalcompliancenews.com/unfair-competition-china-20180315/.

43 *Yue Jinjun* v. *Trademark Appeal Board of the State Administration of Industry & Commerce*, (2017) Supreme People's Court, 2017 Zui Gao Fa Xin Shen No. 3107 (translation); *Wuhan Yunwu Tea Co., Ltd.* v. *Trademark Appeal Board of the State Administration of Industry & Commerce*, (2016) Supreme People's Court, 2016 Zui Gao Fa Xin Shen No. 4894; *Li Jianguo* v. *Hebei Mei Shi Lin Trading Group Co., Ltd. & Trademark Appeal Board of the State Administration of Industry & Commerce*, (2015) Supreme People's Court, Zhi Xing Zi No. 213.

44 *Yu Chunming* v. *Church & Dwight Co., Inc. & Trademark Appeal Board of the State Administration of Industry & Commerce*, (2015) Supreme People's Court, 2015 Zhi Xing Zi No. 184; *SECUREMMES.R.L Co., Ltd.* v. *Trademark Appeal Board of the State Administration of Industry & Commerce*, (2015) Supreme People's Court, 2015 Xing Ti Zi No. 6; *Kaira District Co-operative Milk Producers' Union Co., Ltd.* v. *Trademark Appeal Board of the State Administration of Industry & Commerce*, (2014) Supreme People's Court, 2014 Zhi Xing Zi No. 65. It should be noted that "certain influence" is different from "secondary meaning" stipulated in art. 11(2) of PRC Trademark Law. Although both "certain influence" and "secondary meaning" can be achieved by the use of the unregistered marks, the threshold of "secondary meaning" is higher because it requires that the mark was not distinctive before extensive use. In other words, the distinctiveness is generated through the use of the mark. By contrast, "certain influence" in art. 32 does not requires that the unregistered mark need to be indistinctive. *See, e.g.*, Trademark Law, *supra* note 41, arts. 11, 32; *Trademark Review and Adjudication Board of the State Administration for Industry and Commerce of the People's Republic of China* v. *Tencent Technology (Shenzhen) Co., Ltd.* Beijing Higher Court (2018) Jing Xing Zhong No. 3673 (北京市高级人民法院行政判决书(2018)京行终3673号).

45 *Pacific Alliance Investment Management (Hong Kong) Limited* v. *Xie Cheng Huo*, (2018) HKIAC Case No. DCN-1000406, July 28, 2018, at 5–6, http://hkiac.org/sites/default/files/ck_filebrowser/IP/cn/decision/DCN-1000406_Decision.pdf.

46 *Novalash Inc.* v. *Novolash Cosmetics China*, (2015) HKIAC Case No. DCN-1500616, Apr. 27, 2015, http://hkiac.org/sites/default/files/ck_filebrowser/IP/cn/decision//DCN-1500616_Decision.pdf.

47 *Id.*

48 *Entertainment One UK Limited* v. *Dongguan Huotu Garment Co. Ltd.*, (2015) HKIAC Case No. DCN-1500617, http://staging.hkiac.org/sites/default/files/ck_filebrowser/IP/cn/decision//DCN-1500617_Decision.pdf.

the domain name registrant. The product name, personal name, abbreviation, and trade name of an enterprise with certain influence are all protected against domain registration, even if those names are not registered as trademarks.[49] It should be noted that in China, according to the CDNRP and the PRC Anti-Unfair Competition Law, a complainant may challenge a domain name registration identical or confusingly similar to his personal name if the latter has "certain influence."

From a comparative law perspective, there is no universal approach to the relations between personal names and domain names. Personal names are thus intentionally excluded in the UDRP, because there is no harmonized protection for such rights among various jurisdictions.[50] Before the 2017 PRC Anti-Unfair Competition Law came into effect, CDNRP panels likewise ruled that even celebrities, such as Lady Gaga, could not claim the right of their personal names against domain name registration.[51] By contrast, in common law jurisdictions a celebrity needs to establish common law trademark rights in their personal name if they want to claim it in a domain name with the UDRP.[52] Nonetheless, because common law trademark rights are not available to celebrities' names (including pseudonyms) in civil law countries, it is understandable that civil law countries, such as China, have a greater need to protect such rights in their legislation. This explains why Article 6 of the 2017 and 2019 PRC Anti-Unfair Competition Law extends its protection to personal names with certain influence. This provision, together with CDNRP, has provided celebrities a legal basis to claim their name right against similar or identical domain name registrations. In other words, the Anti-Unfair Competition Law and the CDNRP in China have functioned similarly to the common law trademark protection for celebrities' personal names.

(b) Complaint Based on Another Domain Name It should also be noted that Article 6(3) of the PRC Anti-Unfair Competition Law, which was added in the 2017 legislation, will change CDNRP practice regarding complaints based on the complainant's own domain name registered in other jurisdictions. In *Google, Inc.* v. *Beijing Guowang Information Ltd.* (2003), the CIETAC panel held that although Google had owned the domain name www.google.com since 1997, this domain name was neither a "civil right" nor an "interest" protected by Chinese law.[53] Therefore, Google's complaint against the domain name www.google.com.cn was not substantiated.[54] In other words, the complainant was not allowed to argue in the CDNRP procedure based on the major part of its gTLD. Nevertheless, Article 6(3) of the 2017 and 2019 PRC Anti-Unfair Competition Law now stipulates that

> A business shall not commit the following acts of confusion to mislead a person into believing that a commodity is one of another person or has a particular connection with another person: . . .

[49] Anti-Unfair Competition Law, *supra* note 37, art. 6(1)–(2).

[50] A. Michael Froomkin, *ICANN'S "Uniform Dispute Resolution Policy" – Causes and (Partial) Cures*, 67 Brook. L. Rev. 605, 636 (2002).

[51] *See, e.g.*, Tan, *supra* note 6, at 229–30.

[52] *See, e.g.*, Tamarah L. Belczyk, *Note, Domain Names: The Special Case of Personal Names*, 82 B.U. L. Rev. 485, 513 (2002); Jacqueline D. Lipton, *Beyond Cybersquatting: Taking Domain Name Disputes Past Trademark Policy*, 40 Wake Forest L. Rev. 1361, 1415 (2005); Jacqueline D. Lipton, *Who Owns "Hillary.com"? Political Speech and the First Amendment in Cyberspace*, 49 B.C. L. Rev. 55, 67–8 (2008); Zorik Pesochinsky, *Almost Famous: Preventing Username-Squatting on Social Networking Websites*, 28 Cardozo Arts & Ent. L.J. 223, 234 (2010). *See also* Froomkin, *supra* note 50, at 699, "the right to allege a common law mark should be limited to [UDRP] complainants trading in jurisdictions which recognize such marks."

[53] *Google, Inc.* v. *Beijing Guowang Information Ltd.*, (2003) CIETAC Case No. CND-2003000065.

[54] *Id.*

3. Using without permission the principal part of a domain name, the name of a website, or a web page with certain influence, among others, of another person.

In other words, "the principal part of a domain name" now becomes a "civil right or interest" if it has "certain influence." Google would be able to win the CDNRP case based on the 2017 and 2019 PRC Anti-Unfair Competition Law.

(II) DISPUTES RELATED TO DOMAIN NAMES WITH COUNTRY CODE .HK When HKIAC panels decide cases regarding .hk domain names, the panels need to consider not only the complainant's trademark or service mark but also possible common law rights, such as passing off, because Hong Kong is a common law jurisdiction.[55] These rights are not protected in the same form in civil law jurisdictions, such as China. For example, in *Outblaze Limited* v. *Wah Cheung Leatherware Company Limited* (2001), the HKIAC panel ruled that

> there is a sufficient level of reputation in the trade and industry in Hong Kong and the region in the unregistered "OUTBLAZE" mark belonging to the Complainant as to give the Complainant a claim of passing off, and hence sufficient to constitute the Complainant's trademark rights for the purpose of paragraph 4(a) of the Policy.[56]

In common law jurisdictions, such as Hong Kong, passing off has commonly been used as a ground for domain name complaints by complainants who have used, but not registered, the name.[57] In other words, a domain name registrant is not allowed to commit passing off against recognized trade names and products. A third party possessing rights based on common law's passing off can enforce its right against the registered domain name owner. The HKIAC panel adopted the "reputation test" in the abovementioned *Outblaze* case and held that "there is a sufficient level of reputation in the trade and industry in Hong Kong and the region in the unregistered "OUTBLAZE" mark belonging to the Complainant as to give the Complainant a claim of passing off, and hence sufficient to constitute the Complainant's trademark rights for the purpose of paragraph 4(a) of the Policy."[58] Nevertheless, some HKAIC panels recognized that the respondent engaged in the acts of passing off but did not explain under what circumstances that respondent's registration and use would constitute passing off.[59]

2 *The Registrant Has No Rights or Legitimate Interests in Respect of the Domain Name.*

There is a minor difference in the second element of the HKDRP, and CDNRP. Like the UDRP, the HKDRP requires that the trademark owner shows that the registrant has no rights or

[55] As to how right of passing off is enforced in the court proceedings in Hong Kong, *see infra* text accompanying notes 139–42.

[56] *Outblaze Limited* v. *Wah Cheung Leatherware Company Ltd.*, (2001) HKIAC Case No. 0106-0001, at 5, Sept. 24, 2001, http://hkiac.org/sites/default/files/ck_filebrowser/IP/hk/decision/0106-0001.pdf.

[57] *See, e.g., Banyan Tree Limited* v. *Home Essentials (HK) Limited*, HKIAC Case No. 0207-0003, http://hkiac.org/sites/default/files/ck_filebrowser/IP/hk/decision/0207-0003.pdf.

[58] *Outblaze Limited, supra* note 56.

[59] *See, e.g., Banyan Tree Limited* v. *Home Essentials, supra* note 57 ("I do not know the trading activities or intended trading activities of the Respondent although in the light of the evidence filed by the Complainant there is at least a possibility that the Respondent's activities may constitute passing off particularly (but not necessarily) if those activities are in the same field as that of the Complainant"); *Huntsman Advanced Materials (Switzerland) GmbH* v. *Jun Wei*, HKIAC Case No. DHK-1300102, Dec. 3, 2013, http://hkiac.org/sites/default/files/ck_filebrowser/IP/hk/decision/DHK-1300102_Decision.pdf ("in the alternative, the Panel is satisfied that the Respondent has purposely engaged in the acts of passing off and or the infringement of the Complainant's products and trademark").

legitimate interests in respect of the domain name,[60] whereas the CDNRP requires a showing that the registrant has no rights or legitimate interests in respect of the domain name or "major part of the domain name."[61] Although the slight difference in language suggests that CDNRP does not require the registrant to have rights or legitimate interests in the whole domain name, this difference is not reflected obviously in the cases involving domain names with country codes .cn and .hk. Moreover, decisions regarding both .cn and .hk reveal that the best way for the registrant to prove its rights and legitimates in the domain name is to use these names.

(I) DISPUTES RELATED TO DOMAIN NAMES WITH COUNTRY CODE .CN A common distinction between trademarks and domain names is that different entities may register the same trademark in different classes of goods or services, but domain name registration is always made on a first come, first served basis.[62] In other words, if multiple companies have the same trademark in different lines of business without the likelihood of confusion, only one company can use that trademark as its domain name. Nevertheless, this does not mean that domain name disputes are unrelated to the class of goods or services for trademark registration. When the complainant and respondent register the same trademark for different classes of goods or services, the CDNRP panel has sometimes ruled that if the respondent had used the domain name to market the class of goods or services associated with their trademark registration, then the registrant has legitimate interests in respect of the domain name.[63]

In *HUGO BOSS Trade Mark Management GMBH & Co. KG* v. *Yuguo Li* (2018), the disputed domain name was "雨果.中国." Yuguo (雨果) happened to be the complainant's Chinese trademark and the respondent's first name.[64] The CIETAC panel ruled that the respondent did not have any legitimate interests in respect of his first name, which is the major part of the domain name.[65] The panel further explained that according to Chinese practice, only the combination of the first and last name can be associated with a specific individual and that the respondent's name right therefore protected only his entire name, "Yuguo Li," not his first name "Yuguo."[66] Additionally, the respondent failed to prove that he had built sufficient reputation on the basis of his first name such that the relevant public would associate the name with him.[67]

(II) DISPUTES RELATED TO DOMAIN NAMES WITH COUNTRY CODE .HK The HKAIC panels have similarly focused on a respondent's use when determining whether it "has no rights or legitimate interests in respect of the domain name." In *BABOLAT VS* v. *Guangzhousi Aotu Tiyuyongpin Co. Ltd.* (2011), the complainant, a company producing and selling sportswear and

[60] UDRP, *supra* note 8, § 4(a); HKDRP, *supra* note 20, § 4(a).

[61] CDNRP, *supra* note 19, art. 8.

[62] *See, e.g.*, TAN, *supra* note 6, at 233; G. Gervaise Davis III, *Internet Domain Names and Trademarks: Recent Developments in Domestic and International Disputes*, 21 HASTINGS COMM. & ENT L.J. 601, 608–9 (1999); Michael B. Landau, *Problems Arising out of the Use of "www.trademark.com": The Application of Principles of Trademark Law to Internet Domain Name Disputes*, 13 GA. ST. U. L. REV. 455, 484–85 (1997); Allan Lee, *Internet Domain Names and the Lanham Act's Infringement Provisions*, 12 J. CONTEMP. LEGAL ISSUES 502, 503–4 (2001).

[63] *See, e.g.*, *The Association of Charted Certified Accounts* v. *Wu Wei*, (2010) HKIAC Case No. DCN-1000391, May 21, 2010, http://hkiac.org/sites/default/files/ck_filebrowser/IP/cn/decision/DCN-1000391_Decision.pdf.

[64] *HUGO BOSS Trade Mark Management GMBH & Co. KG* v. *Yuguo Li*, (2018) CIETAC Case No. CND-2018000007, at 3–5, Apr. 18, 2018, http://dndrc.cietac.org/web/kindsDecs.action?mz15.CNEN=1&mz15.textType=5&mz07.infoType=1#.

[65] *Id.* at 7–8.

[66] *Id.* at 7.

[67] *Id.* at 7.

accessories, registered the trademark "BABOLAT" in Hong Kong in October 2008.[68] The respondent registered the domain name babolat.hk in October 2009 and had sold sportswear, shoes, and other products bearing the name or logo "Babolat" since that time.[69] The panel ruled as follows:

> This Panel recognizes that Complainant has registered its trademark/tradename "Babolat" in the category covering sportswear clothing. Therefore it may well be able to establish an excellent case of trademark infringement against Respondent were it to bring such in an appropriate court of competent jurisdiction. However, for purposes of this dispute, the fact that Respondent is in fact producing and selling clothing under the name Babolat, through its website, would, according to the Policy, seem more to establish that Respondent does have a sufficient interest in the use of the disputed name than that it does not.

According to the panel, even if the respondent's registration and use of the domain name constituted trademark infringement, it does not mean that the respondent "has no rights or legitimate interests in respect of the domain name.[70] As long as the respondent uses the domain name for its business, it has rights or legitimate interests in respect of the domain name.

3 *The Domain Name Has Been Registered and Is Being Used in Bad Faith*

The UDRP, HKDRP and CDNRP all establish criteria for determining bad faith. The criteria for bad faith determination in the UDRP and HKDRP are as follows: (1) in circumstances indicating that the registrant has registered or acquired the domain name primarily for the purpose of selling, renting, or otherwise transferring the domain name registration to the complainant who is the owner of the trademark or service mark, or to a competitor of that complainant, for valuable consideration in excess of the registrant's documented out-of-pocket costs directly related to the domain name; (2) the registrant has registered the domain name in order to prevent the owner of the trademark or service mark from reflecting the mark in a corresponding domain name, provided that the registrant has engaged in a pattern of such conduct; (3) the registrant has registered the domain name primarily for the purpose of disrupting the business of a competitor; or (4) by using the domain name, the registrant has intentionally attempted to attract, for commercial gain, internet users to the registrant's website or other online location, by creating a likelihood of confusion with the complainant's mark as to the source, sponsorship, affiliation, or endorsement of the registrant's website or location or of a product or service on the registrant's website or location.[71]

(I) DISPUTES RELATED TO DOMAIN NAMES WITH COUNTRY CODE .CN The bad faith provision in Article 9 of the CDNRP substantially resembles that in the UDRP and HKDRP. The only difference is that in the third criterion, the CDNRP includes the registrant's purpose of not only "disrupting the business of a competitor" but also "damaging the Complainant's reputation … so as to mislead the public."[72] Moreover, there is no provision in the CDNRP similar to Paragraph 4(b)(iv) of the UDRP: "by using the domain name, you have intentionally attempted to attract, for commercial gain, Internet users to your web site or other on-line location, by creating a likelihood

[68] *BABOLAT VS* v. *Guangzhousi Aotu Tiyuyongpin Co. Ltd.*, (2011) Case No. DHK-1000061, Feb 26, 2011, http://hkiac.org/sites/default/files/ck_filebrowser/IP/hk/decision/DHK-1000061_Decision.pdf.

[69] *Id.*

[70] *Id.*

[71] UDRP, *supra* note 8, § 4(b); HKDRP, *supra* note 20, § 4(b).

[72] CDNRP, *supra* note 19, art. 9.

of confusion with the complainant's mark as to the source, sponsorship, affiliation, or endorsement of your web site or location or of a product or service on your web site or location."[73] Instead of describing how the use of domain name constitutes bad faith, the fourth criterion in Article 9 provides a miscellaneous provision, stipulating that "other circumstances ... may prove the bad faith."[74] To date, the panels addressing relevant disputes have applied this miscellaneous provision in instances where the respondent registered the domain name but never used it.[75] When determining bad faith, some CIETAC panels did not apply specific provisions in Article 9 but simply explained that bad faith could be found from certain part of the fact.[76] Therefore, the CIETAC panels have rather broad discretion in the determination of bad faith.

(II) DISPUTES RELATED TO DOMAIN NAMES WITH COUNTRY CODE .HK The HKAIC has maintained a rather high standard for bad faith, consisting of the dual requirement of both "registration in bad faith" and "use in bad faith." In other words, if the complainant fails to prove one of the requirements, it will fail to win the case against the respondent. In *Specialized Bicycle Components, Inc.* v. *Specialized Hong Kong Ltd.* (2013), the panel made it quite clear that this dual requirement is higher than that in the United Kingdom and Australia:

> The Complainant here has to prove two different things: that the domain name has been registered and is being used in bad faith. Bad faith use without registration is not good enough. The Hong Kong Policy follows the position of the ICANN Policy in requiring registration to be in bad faith. Other equivalent policies elsewhere in the world, notably the UK (Nominet) and Australia, have effectively removed the dual proof requirement. Hong Kong has chosen to keep the "and" in its Policy in spite of this.[77]

If the respondent had used the domain name only for personal and noncommercial use and had not used it actively, it was essentially not "use in bad faith."[78] Nonetheless, the HKAIC panels share the viewpoint of the WIPO panels[79] that the concept of a domain name "being used in bad faith" includes inaction as well as positive action.[80] If a domain respondent has registered the complainant's trademark or trade name as a domain name but has never used it, the panel may rule that the respondent has used the domain name in bad faith. The CIETAC panels have maintained a similar viewpoint.[81] It should also be noted that the HKIAC panels may use the same fact to determine both passing off and bad faith registration. In *Shui On Construction and Materials Limited* v. *Wong Wai Chung* (2004), the panelist cancelled the domain name registration and held that

> I am satisfied that the domain name in the registered ownership of the Respondent is a registration obtained in bad faith in that it is likely to lead to deception and confusion in the market place. Visitors to the site could be misled into believing that either the Complainant or

[73] UDRP, *supra* note 8, § 4(b)(iv).
[74] CDNRP, *supra* note 19, art. 9.
[75] *See, e.g., HUGO BOSS Trade Mark Management GMBH*, *supra* note 64, at 3–5.
[76] *See, e.g., Wong To Yick Wood Lock Ointment Limited* v. *Shao Yang Lin*, (2018) CIETAC Case No. CND-201800016, *at* 9, May 24, 2018, http://dndrc.cietac.org/web/kindsDecs.action?mz15.CNEN=1&mz15.textType=5&mz07.infoType=1#.
[77] *Specialized Bicycle Components, Inc.* v. *Specialized Hong Kong Ltd.*, (2013) Case No. DHK-1300093, Apr. 21, 2013, http://hkiac.org/sites/default/files/ck_filebrowser/IP/hk/decision/DHK-1300093_Decision.pdf.
[78] *See, e.g., Expedia, Inc.* v. *Chan Chun Wai*, Case No. DHK-0500009, http://hkiac.org/sites/default/files/ck_filebrowser/IP/hk/decision/DHK-0500009%20-%20expedia.pdf.
[79] *Telstra Corporation Limited* v. *Nuclear Marshmallows*, WIPO Case No. D2000–00003 at § 7.9 (2000).
[80] *Microsoft Corporation* v. *Wong Sai Chen*, (2008) Case No. DHK-0800034, *at* 7–8, 13, Aug. 1, 2008.
[81] *See* text accompanying note 76.

> one of the other parties (see below) whose name includes Shui On is associated with the web site when no such association exists. This is a misrepresentation and could lead to passing off.[82]

In *Microsoft Corporation* v. *Wong Sai Chen*, the panelist likewise held that

> Having regard to facts set out in the preceding Paragraph hereof, and the following facts, the Panel finds that the Respondent is using the disputed domain name in bad faith: 1. The Respondent did not intend to use the domain name in the next few years; 2. taking into account all the circumstances in the case, it is not possible to conceive of any plausible actual or contemplated active use of the domain name by the Respondent that would not be illegitimate, such as by being a passing off or an infringement of the Complainant's right under the [Hong Kong] trademark law.[83]

In other words, if the domain name respondent registered the complainant's name as a domain name and thereby created confusion among consumers, such registration is very likely to indicate both bad faith and misrepresentation, which is an element of passing off.[84]

D Applicable Law

With very few substantive rules included, the UDRP and UDRP Rules primarily set forth procedural rules. Regarding the substantive rules, the UDRP Rules state that panelists should "decide a complaint on the basis of the statements and documents submitted [by the parties] and in accordance with the Policy, [the] Rules and any rules and principles of law that it deems applicable.[85] In other words, given the global nature of the UDRP procedures, the panels do not need to apply national laws from particular jurisdictions. The few substantive standards embodied in the UDRP are independent of any national law, although they sometimes look similar.[86] For example, the grounds for domain name complaint in UDRP introduced previously is one of the few substantive rules therein,[87] though there may be various options for the panelists to interpret these grounds.[88] The panels can decide cases on general principles of law or rules they deem appropriate. However, this does not mean that UDRP decisions are completely insulated from national laws. Because the complaint normally has a trademark registered and/or protection in at least one specific jurisdiction, the law of that jurisdiction is supposedly relevant.[89] Moreover, because UDRP panelists are mostly law experts from specific jurisdictions, their legal training and the development of national law will naturally influence UDRP jurisprudence.[90] CDNRP and HKDRP panels have developed different customs to

[82] *Shui On Construction and Materials Limited* v. *Wong Wai Chung*, (2004) Case No. DHK-0400001, at 4, Aug. 21, 2004, *at* http://hkiac.org/sites/default/files/ck_filebrowser/IP/hk/decision/DHK-0400001.pdf; *see also Huntsman Advanced Materials*, *supra* note 59, at 5–6 (similarly holding that the respondent's registration constituted passing off and was made in bad faith).

[83] *Microsoft Corporation* v. *Wong Sai Chen*, (2008) Case No. DHK-0800034, Aug. 1, 2008.

[84] *See, e.g.*, *Banyan Tree Limited* v. *Home Essentials (HK) Limited*, *supra* note 57; *see also* text accompanying note 139.

[85] Rules for UDRP, *supra* note 10, § 15.

[86] Graeme B. Dinwoodie, *Trademarks and Territory: Detaching Trademark Law from the Nation-State*, 41 Hous. L. Rev. 885, 937 (2004).

[87] *See* text accompanying note 28.

[88] For example, what are "rights," "legitimate interests" and "bad faith"?

[89] *See, e.g.*, Dinwoodie, *supra* note 86; Laurence R. Helfer, *Whither the UDRP: Autonomous, Americanized, or Cosmopolitan?*, 12 Cardozo J. Int'l & Comp. L. 493, 496 (2004); David A. Simon, *An Empirical Analysis of Fair Use Decisions Under the Uniform Domain-Name Dispute-Resolution Policy*, 53 B.C. L. Rev. 65, 78–9, 110 (2012).

[90] Dinwoodie, *supra* note 86, 937–38. *But see* Lisa M. Sharrock, *Note: The Future of Domain Name Disputes Resolution: Crafting Practical International Legal Solutions from Within the UDRP Framework*, 51 Duke L.J. 817, 837 (2001)

apply the substantive standard to solve domain name disputes. Although both CDNRP and HKDRP derive from the UDRP, the CDNRP panels apply domestic law to solve .cn domain name disputes much more often than the HKDRP panels dealing with issues associated with .hk domain names.

1 *Disputes Related to Domain Names with Country Code .cn*

National law plays an important role in CDNRP cases regrading .cn or .中国 domain names. As noted above, when considering whether the complainant has a civil right or interest in a name or mark, the panel inevitably applies Chinese law, such as the PRC Anti-Unfair Competition Law.[91] Because trademark is typically the main issue associated with cybersquatting, it is also common for the CDNRP panel to apply domestic trademark law. For example, in *Airbnb Inc.* v. *Guo Lanzhi* (2017), the HKIAC panel ruled that prior right, as stipulated in Article 32 of the PRC Trademark Law, should also be protected against domain name registration.[92] Such prior right includes copyright, rights of trade names, and personal names.[93]

In view of the pervasive use of UDRP or UDRP-based approaches in domain name disputes, some believe that the UDRP has internationalized and privatized the trademark law.[94] However, because of trademark's territorial nature, the implementation of the UDRP has been unavoidably localized by domestic trademark law. Therefore, a mark owner might obtain stronger protection if the law in their country specifically protects certain marks.[95]

2 *Disputes Related to Domain Names with Country Code .hk*

A casual review of HKDRP decisions regarding .hk domain names suggests that these decisions applied national law much less frequently than did CDNRP decisions regarding .cn domain names. The majority of the decisions cited previous HKDRP decisions, the HKDRP, and the UDRP,[96] whereas some decisions cited only the HKDRP or UDRP as the basis of their reasoning.[97] From 1 January 2013 to 1 October 2018, only one HKDRP decision was based on the Hong Kong Trade Mark Ordinance in addition to the HKDRP or UDRP.[98]

A possible explanation is that Hong Kong is a common law jurisdiction, where legal professionals are more comfortable using the case law approach. Commentators have argued that the

("[b]ecause international treaty standards and national laws exert only an abstract influence, and the UDRP itself articulates very general standards, arbitrators essentially exercise unfettered discretion in each case").

91 *See* text accompanying note 36–40.

92 *See Airbnb Inc. v. Guo Lanzhi*, *supra* note 27, at 18.

93 *See, e.g.*, Jyh-An Lee & Thomas Mehaffy, *Prior Rights in the Chinese Trademark Law*, 37(10) Euro. Intell. Prop. Rev. 673, 676–77 (2015).

94 Froomkin, *supra* note 50, at 612.

95 Janet Moreira, *Making an Informed Choice between Arbitration or Litigation: The Uniform Domain-Name Dispute Resolution Policy vs. the Anti-Cybersquatting Act*, 44 IDEA 147, 153–54 (2003).

96 Based on the author's empirical research, there are at least seventeen decisions in this category. *See, e.g.*, *Fareportal Inc.* v. *Zhao Ke*, (2018) HKIAC Case No. DHK-1800155, July 3, 2018, http://hkiac.org/sites/default/files/ck_filebrowser/IP/hk/decision/DHK-1800155_Decision.pdf; *Tencent Holdings Limited* v. *Million Nobel Enterprises Limited*, (2016) HKIAC Case No. DHK-1600134, Nov. 11, 2016, http://hkiac.org/sites/default/files/ck_filebrowser/IP/hk/decision/DHK-1600134_Decision.pdf; *Nike Innovate CV & Nike Hong Kong Limited* v. *UBN Limited*, HKIAC Case No. DHK-1600129, Mar. 28, 2016, http://hkiac.org/sites/default/files/ck_filebrowser/IP/hk/decision/DHK-1600129_Decision.pdf.

97 Based on the author's empirical research, there are at least twelve decisions in this category. *See, e.g.*, 1. *Alibaba Group Holding Limited & 2. Alibaba Group Services Limited* v. *Alexander Chen / Domain Network Limited*, (2017) HKIAC Case No. DHK-1700151, Dec. 7, 2017, http://hkiac.org/sites/default/files/ck_filebrowser/IP/hk/decision/DHK-1700151_Decision.pdf; *Alibaba Group Holding Limited* v. *Alexander Chen*, (2017) HKIAC Case No. DHK-1700150, Dec. 7, 2017, http://hkiac.org/sites/default/files/ck_filebrowser/IP/hk/decision/DHK-1700150_Decision.pdf.

98 *Tencent Holdings Limited* v. *T LAM*, (2017) HKIAC Case No. DHK-1700143, July 17, 2017, http://hkiac.org/sites/default/files/ck_filebrowser/IP/hk/decision/DHK-1700143_Decision.pdf.

UDRP approach resembles the common law approach in the sense that quite a few panelists have cited and relied upon previous UDRP decisions though they are not required or encouraged to do so.[99] The UDRP norms have been generated from the evolution and accumulation of panel decisions.

III DOMAIN NAME LITIGATION IN CHINA AND HONG KONG

Trademark holders typically have the option to challenge the domain name registration via UDRP procedures or in the court.[100] If the trademark owner initially decided to use UDRP or similar arbitration procedures, they can still challenge the legality of UDRP or similar arbitration decisions later in the court.[101] Alternatively, the trademark owner may sue the domain name registrant directly in the court. The court will then apply national law, instead of the UDRP, to resolve the dispute.[102] For example, a US court may apply the Anti-Cybersquatting Consumer Protection Act (ACPA) of 1999 to decide a domain name and trademark dispute,[103] whereas an English court may apply section 21 of the Trade Mark Act of 1994 in similar cases.[104] The WIPO has emphasized that national courts applying national laws will always trump UDRP rulings, and it has become important UDRP jurisprudence that a UDRP decision will never prevent the court from applying domestic law in trademark domain name disputes.[105]

This part of the chapter will analyze domain name litigation in mainland China and Hong Kong.

A *Mainland China*

Domain name cases adjudicated by the Chinese courts are not limited to those associated with .cn domain names. The courts occasionally decide cases regarding gTLDs if there is a connecting factor relevant to Chinese law. For example, the Xiamen District Court decided a case concerning the domain name thinkstockphoto.com, registered by the Chinese citizen Duan Xiangwang via a domain name registration service company in Xiamen.[106] The case began from a UDRP procedure where Getty Images, Inc., the owner of the trademark THINKSTOCK and domain name thinkstockphotos.com, filed a complaint against Duan Xiangwang in the National Arbitration Forum (NAF) in the United States, claiming that Duan Xiangwang registered the

[99] *See, e.g.*, Edward C. Anderson & Timothy S. Cole, *The UDRP – A Model for Dispute Resolution in E-Commerce?*, 6 J. Small & Emerging Bus. L. 235, 249–50 (2002); Dinwoodie, *supra* note 86, 938; David E. Sorkin, *Judicial Review of ICANN Domain Name Dispute Decisions*, 18 Santa Clara Computer & High Tech. L.J. 35, 44 (2001). *But see* Elizabeth G. Thornburg, *Fast, Cheap, and Out of Control: Lessons from the ICANN Dispute Resolution Process*, 6 J. Small & Emerging Bus. L. 191, 224 (2002) (arguing that panelists tend to decide arbitrarily since there is no review mechanism in the UDRP process).

[100] Dinwoodie, *supra* note 86, 936.

[101] *See, e.g.*, David E. Sorkin, *Judicial Review of ICANN Domain Name Dispute Decisions*, 18 Santa Clara Computer & High Tech. L.J. 35, 44–46 (2001). It should be noted however that national courts are rarely asked to review UDRP panel rulings; *see* Dinwoodie, *supra* note 86, at 938; Helfer, *supra* note 89, at 495.

[102] *See, e.g.*, Dinwoodie, *supra* note 86, at 938; Hörnle, *supra* note 13, at 281–82.

[103] *See, e.g.*, Anti-Cybersquatting Consumer Protection Act of 1999, Pub. L. No. 106-43 §§ 3(a)(2), 5, 113 Stat. 218, 220 (1999); *Barcelona.com* v. *Excelentisimo Ayuntamiento de Barcelona*, 330 F.3d 617, 626–29 (4th Cir. 2003).

[104] *See, e.g.*, *Global Projects Mgmt. Ltd* v. *Citigroup*, (2005) EWHC 2663 (Ch.) (Eng.); *Quads4Kids* v. *Campbell*, [2006] AllER (D) 162 (Eng.).

[105] WIPO, Final Report of the WIPO Internet Domain Name Process (Apr. 30, 1999), https://globalcompliancenews.com/unfair-competition-china-20180315/.

[106] *Duan Xiang* v. *Getty Images*, Xiamen District Court, 2015 Si Min Chu Zi No. 4747 ((2015)思民初字第4747號) (China).

domain name in bad faith.[107] The NAF ruled for the complainant and ordered Duan Xiangwang to transfer the domain name to Getty Images. Duan Xianwang then sued Getty Images and claimed legitimate ownership of the domain name in China.[108] Xiamen District Court eventually took this case and made a default judgment with the absence of the defendant Getty Images.[109] The court held that the plaintiff's domain name registration did not infringe the defendant's trademark because the former was registered in 2010 whereas the latter was registered in China in 2014.[110] Nevertheless, the court eventually ruled for the defendant because plaintiff's domain name thinkstockphoto.com was too similar to thinkstockphotos.com, which is registered and used earlier by the defendant.[111] Despite plaintiff not infringing defendant's trademark, the court held that his domain name registration constituted unfair competition.[112] Although the court had reached the same conclusion as the NAF, this decision subtly illustrated the tension between the UDRP procedure and Chinese court proceedings. While the NAF decision was made based on Getty Images' US trademark THINKSTOCK, the Xiamen District Court only considered Getty Images' trademark registration in China, which was granted later than the US one.[113] Had the court not further ruled for Getty Images based on Chinese unfair competition rules, the plaintiff would have taken unfair advantage of the time differences in Getty's Images' trademark registrations in the United States and China.

1 *Likelihood of Confusion*

In recent years, domain name litigation has increased in the People's Courts in Beijing, Shanghai, and other major cities in China.[114] Similar to UDRP cases, typical domain name litigation involves a trademark owner claiming its trademark against domain registration. To substantiate such a claim, the trademark holder needs to prove the likelihood of confusion between the trademark and the domain name. In *Precitec (Shanghai) Limited* v. *Kunshan Preste Laser Technology Limited*, the Suzhou Intermediate People's Court ruled that the defendant's domain name, preste.cn, was neither identical nor similar to the plaintiff's trademark, PRECITEC, and that the defendant's domain name registration therefore did not infringe the plaintiff's trademark.[115] In *Tianjin Bradi Security Equipment Co., Ltd. et al.* v. *Brady Corporation*, the Supreme People's Court held that the plaintiff's domain name registration did not result in any likelihood of confusion among the public because the defendant's trademark, BRADY, did not have any reputation in China, not to mention that it was not a well-known trademark at all.[116]

2 *Plaintiff's Rights or Interests in the Domain Name*

Most Chinese courts' decisions concerning domain names are decided according to the "Interpretation of the Supreme People's Court on Several Issues Concerning the Application of the

[107] *Id.*
[108] *Id.*
[109] *Id.*
[110] *Id.*
[111] *Id.*
[112] *Id.*
[113] *Id.*
[114] *See, e.g.*, Tan, *supra* note 6, at 237.
[115] *Precitec (Shanghai) Limited* v. *Kunshan Preste Laser Technology Limited*, Suzhou Intermediate People's Court, 2017 Su 05 Min Zhong No. 4581 ((2017)苏05民终4581号).
[116] *Tianjin Bradi Security Equipment Co., Ltd. et al.* v. *Brady Corporation*, Supreme People's Court, 2013 Min Shen Zhi Di No. 1286 ((2013)民申字第1286号).

Law to the Trial of Civil Disputes Cases Involving Computer Network Domain Names."[117] Article 4 of the Interpretation of the Supreme People's Court sets forth the criteria for a plaintiff's claim against domain name registration:

> When adjudicating cases concerning domain names, the people's court should hold that defendant's registration and/or use of a domain name constitutes infringement or unfair competition if each of the following condition is satisfied:
>
> (1) the civil right or interest for which the plaintiff seeks protection is legitimate and effective;
> (2) the defendant's domain name or its main part constitutes a copy, imitation, translation or transliteration of a well-known mark of the plaintiff, or it is identical or similar to a registered mark, domain name, etc., of the plaintiff to a degree sufficient to cause mistaken identification among the relevant public;
> (3) the defendant does not enjoy rights or interests to the domain name; and
> (4) the defendant's registration and/or use of the domain name is in "bad faith."[118]

Similar to CDNRP panels' approach to Article 8 of CDNRP, the Chinese courts frequently use Article 6 of the PRC Anti-Unfair Competition Law (or Article 5 of the 1993 PRC Anti-Unfair Competition Law) to determine whether the plaintiff (complainant) has a "civil right or interest" in the domain name.[119] For example, in *Tianjin Bradi Security Equipment Co., Ltd. et al.* v. *Brady Corporation*, the Supreme People's Court ruled that an enterprise name without certain degree of reputation or influence was not protected by the PRC Anti-Unfair Competition Law and was thus not a legitimate "civil right or interest" based on which the plaintiff could argue against the defendant.[120] Nonetheless, it should be noted that the PRC Anti-Unfair Competition Law is applied only when two parties are competing in the market. In *Guang Dong OPPO Mobile Telecommunications Corp., Ltd.* v. *Dongguan Oupo Leather Ltd.*, the Guangzhou Intellectual Property Court ruled that although the defendant's registration of the domain name oppo.so infringed the plaintiff's trademark, "oppo," this was not the venue in which to apply the PRC Anti-Unfair Competition Law, because the two parties were not competitors in the market.[121]

3 *Bad Faith*

Article 5 of the Interpretation of the Supreme People's Court establishes the criteria for bad faith:

> People's courts are to find "bad faith" exists if the defendant's conduct constitutes any of the following:
>
> (1) for commercial purposes, registering another's well-known mark as a domain name;
> (2) for commercial purposes, registering and/or using a domain name that is identical or similar to the plaintiff's registered mark, domain name, etc., and deliberately causing confusion with the products and/or services provided by the plaintiff or with the plaintiff's

[117] Zuigao Renmin, Fayuan Guanyu, Shenli Sheji, Jisuanji Wanluo, Yuming Minshi, Jiufen Anjian, Shiyung Falv, & Ruogan Wenti De Jieshi, The Interpretation of the Supreme People's Court on Several Issues Concerning the Application of the Law to the Trial of Civil Disputes Cases Involving Computer Network Domain Names (最高人民法院关于审理涉及计算机网络域名民事纠纷案件适用法律若干问题的解释) (July 24, 2001), http://zscq.court.gov.cn/sfjs/201004/t20100414_4091.html [hereinafter Interpretation of the Supreme People's Court].

[118] *Id.*, art. 4.

[119] *See* text accompanying notes 39–55.

[120] *Tianjin Bradi Security Equipment Co., Ltd. et al.*, *supra* note 116.

[121] *Guang Dong OPPO Mobile Telecommunications Corp., Ltd.* v. *Dongguan Oupo Leather Ltd.*, Guangzhou Intellectual Property Court, 2013 Yue Zhi Ha Shan Min Chu Zi No. 4 ((2015)粤知法商民初字第4号).

website in order to mislead network users into assessing one's own website or another online site;

(3) having offered to sell, lease, or otherwise transfer the domain name at a high price and obtained unfair benefits;

(4) neither using nor intending to use the domain name after registration, but intentionally preventing the registration of the domain name by the right holder; or

(5) otherwise acting in bad faith.[122]

Although the language of this article is not completely identical to that of Article 9 of the CDNRP,[123] the criteria established by these two articles overlap substantially. If the registrant has offered to sell the domain name for unfair benefit or registered the domain name for the purpose of preventing the trademark holder from using it, such registration or use of the domain name constitutes bad faith under both the CDNRP and the Interpretation of the Supreme People's Court.[124] The Interpretation of the Supreme People's Court specifically protects well-known trademark holders from cybersquatting and includes the miscellaneous provision "otherwise acting in bad faith" to cover all possible situations.

It should also be noted that even if the court finds that the domain name registration has met the requirements established in Articles 4 and 5 of the Interpretation of the Supreme People's Court, the court still needs to decide whether such registration "constitutes infringement or unfair competition."[125] In *Macy's West Stores, Inc.* v. *Beijing Guowang Information Ltd.*, the Beijing Intellectual Property Court ruled that the defendant's registration of macys.com.cn met the requirements set forth in Article 4:

(1) The plaintiff had effective registrations for trademark "Macy's" and domain name "macys.com" which were prior to defendant's domain name registration. The plaintiff had used these trademark and trade name Macy's. Therefore, the plaintiff had legitimate and effective right and interest in its trademark, trade name, and domain name;

(2) The plaintiff was the largest department store in the United States; therefore, its trademark "Macy's" had international reputation, which was also known among the general public in China. Consequently, defendant's domain name would mistakenly lead the Chinese public to believe the domain name had been registered by the plaintiff;

(3) The defendant failed to prove it had any rights or interests to the domain name; and

(4) The defendant did not use the domain name after registration, but intentionally prevented the plaintiff from registering or using it. Therefore, according to Article 5(3), the defendant's domain name was registered in "bad faith."[126]

The court also referred to Article 1(3) of the "Supreme People's Court on Several Issues Concerning the Application of the Law to the Trial of Civil Disputes Cases Involving Trademarks":

> The following acts constitute acts causing other harm to another's exclusive right to use a registered trademark as set out in Article 52(5) of the PRC Trademark Law:
>
> ... (3) registering words that are identical or similar to another's registered trademark as a domain name and using it to carry out electronic commerce business in related goods, thereby easily causing mistaken recognition on the part of the relevant public.[127]

[122] Interpretation of the Supreme People's Court, *supra* note 117, art. 5.

[123] *See* text accompanying notes 61–62.

[124] CDNRP, *supra* note 19, art. 9; Interpretation of the Supreme People's Court, *supra* note 117, art. 5.

[125] Interpretation of the Supreme People's Court, *supra* note 117, art. 4.

[126] *Macy's West Stores, Inc. v. Beijing Guowang Information Ltd.*, Beijing Intellectual Property Court, 2014 Jing Zhi Min Chu Zi No. 9 ((2014) 京知民初字第9号).

[127] Interpretation of the Supreme People's Court, *supra* note 117.

4 *Active Use of the Domain Name*

In the above *Macy's West Stores, Inc.* v. *Beijing Guowang Information Ltd.*, the Beijing Intellectual Property Court held that the defendant would infringe the plaintiff's trademark only if the former used the domain name to carry out business in related goods.[128] In this case, because the defendant never used the domain name, there was no trademark infringement.[129] Nevertheless, because the domain name was highly similar to the plaintiff's trademark and trade name and because this similarity could lead the public to believe that the domain name was registered by the plaintiff, the court opined that the defendant's domain name registration violated Article 2(2) of the PRC Anti-Unfair Competition Law: "For the purposes of this Law, 'act of unfair competition' means that in its production or distribution activities, a business disrupts the order of market competition and causes damage to the lawful rights and interests of the other businesses or consumers, in violation of this Law."[130] Therefore, the court eventually ruled that the domain name should be transferred to the plaintiff.[131]

In *Societe Civile de Chateau Lafite Rothschild* v. *Jinhongde Trade Ltd.*, the Hunan High People's Court similarly applied Article 1(3) of the "Supreme People's Court on Several Issues Concerning the Application of the Law to the Trial of Civil Disputes Cases Involving Trademarks" for the plaintiff who had registered and used the trademark "Lafite" for its wine business.[132] The court held that the defendant had infringed the plaintiff's trademark because (1) the main part of the defendant's registered domain name, lafitefamily.com, was identical to the plaintiff's trademark and (2) the fact that the defendant promoted its wine on the website could lead the relevant public to believe that the wine was produced by the plaintiff.

In sum, when adjudicating domain name cases involving trademarks, the Chinese courts adopt approaches similar to those of CDNRP panels regarding likelihood of confusion, the plaintiff's or complainant's right of interest in the disputed domain name, and bad faith. Nevertheless, the Chinese courts and the CDNRP panels have different attitudes toward the registrant's inactive use of the domain name. Like other domain name panels, the CDNRP requires that the respondent use the domain name so that it can prove its interest in the name or prove that the domain name was not registered in bad faith. By contrast, the courts take the view that the inactive use of a domain name does not constitute trademark infringement, although the registrant may be held liable for the violation of the PRC Anti-Unfair Competition Law.

B *Hong Kong*

There are significantly fewer court decisions concerning domain name disputes associated with trademarks in Hong Kong than in China. One possibility is that parties are more comfortable with the decisions made by the arbitration panel. In common law, passing off is the most

[128] *Macy's West Stores, Inc.* v. *Beijing Guowang Information Ltd.*, *supra* note 126.

[129] *Id*; the result illustrates the difference in trademark doctrines and the UDRP approach. Trademark law emphasizes more the use of trademark while inactive use of domain name may constitute bad faith in the UDRP procedure. *See* text accompanying notes 71, 81–82.

[130] *Macy's West Stores, Inc.* v. *Beijing Guowang Information Ltd.*, *supra* note 126. From a comparative law viewpoint, the United States Court of Appeals for the Second Circuit considered similar factors (similarities between the trademark and domain name, domain name registrant's failure to use the mark, and well-known status of the trademark) and likewise ruled for the trademark owner under the Anticybersquatting Consumer Protection Act (ACPA), in *Sporty's Farm LLC* v. *Sportman's Market, Inc.*, 202 F.3d 489, 498–9 (2000).

[131] *Id.*

[132] *Societe Civile de Chateau Lafite Rothschild* v. *Jinhongde Trade Ltd.*, (2011) Hunan High People's Court, 2011 Xiang Gau Fa Min San Zhong Zi No. 55 ((2011) (湘高法民三中字第55号).

common cause of action for domain name litigation.[133] In *Bios Time International Investment Ltd a.k.a.* v. *France Heson Paper (Hong Kong) Co. Ltd.*, the plaintiff's associated company registered the trademark "Biostime" in Hong Kong in 2010 and transferred the trademark to the plaintiff in 2013.[134] The defendant registered the domain name www.biostime-paper.com in 2013.[135] The High Court issued an injunction to prevent the defendant from using its website under the domain name or any domain name bearing a similarity to the plaintiff's company name[136] because such use had constituted passing off:

(1) The plaintiff enjoys a goodwill or reputation in the name "Biostime."
(2) By using a name containing the words "Biostime" on its website, the defendant has made a misrepresentation which is likely to lead members of the public to believe that the goods offered by it are goods of, or related to, the plaintiff.
(3) The plaintiff will suffer damage by reason of the erroneous belief engendered by the defendant's misrepresentation.[137]

Other similar cases include *Borri SpA* v. *Tralaco Technology Ltd.*, in which the Court of First Instance (CFI) ruled that the defendants passed themselves off as the plaintiff by registering and using the domain name borrisups.com.[138] The court held that the disputed domain name was used by the defendants as an instrument of deception and thus ordered the defendants to transfer the name to the plaintiff.[139]

IV NEW GTLDS IN CHINA

ICANN officially opened the registration for new gTLDs on 12 January 2012, before which there were only twenty-two gTLDs available, such as .com, .net, or .org.[140] When this round of registration closed on 20 April 2012, ICANN had received 1,930 applications.[141] The new gTLDs have brought about new business models and a variety of challenges for the existing trademark system. This part uses China as an example to illustrate those challenges.

A *Trademark Disputes*

The new gTLDs have created perplexing legal issues in different jurisdictions.[142] For example, trademark holders are annoyed when their marks are combined with new gTLDs that have derogatory meanings, such as .sucks or .wtf. Another problem is that a unique gTLD may indicate the registrant's identity and thus create confusion among consumers. For example, Calvin Klein Inc. filed a domain name complaint with the WIPO Arbitration and Mediation Center on 18 August 2018, requesting that the respondent transfer the domain name calvinklein.

[133] Wong & Lee, *supra* note 21, at 730, 737, 739–40.
[134] *Biostime International Investment Ltd.* v. *France Heson Paper (Hong Kong) Co. Ltd.* (23/03/2015, HCA2329/2014) [2015] 2 HKLRD 658.
[135] *Id.*
[136] *Id.* [15].
[137] *Id.* [13].
[138] *Borri SPA* v. *Tralaco Technology Ltd. and Others* (Aug. 19, 2009, HCA1170/2007).
[139] *Id.* at [85]–[86].
[140] ICANN, *About the Program*, https://newgtlds.icann.org/en/about/program.
[141] *Id.*
[142] *See, e.g.*, Chapter 23 in this volume.

wang.[143] The complainant had used the Calvin Klein trademark since 1968 and included the trademark in a number of domain names, such as calvinklein.com, calvinkleinunderwear.com, and calvinkleinfashion.com.[144] The respondent registered the domain name calvinklein.wang with Zodiac Registry Limited.[145] The panel found that the complainant's marks of Calvin Klein were well known in connection with men's and women's apparel, fragrances, accessories, and footwear products in many countries.[146] The complainant claimed that .wang did not eliminate the confusion among the public because "wang" is a transliteration of the Chinese word "网," which means website or portal.[147] The WIPO panel eventually ruled that as the gTLD, ".wang" was not a distinguishing factor and that the most prominent and distinctive part of the disputed domain name was "calvinklein," which was identical to the complainant's trademark.[148]

In *Jinbo Liu* v. *Alibab Group Holding Ltd.*, the Fujian High Court adopted an approach similar to that of the WIPO panel and ruled against the plaintiff, who registered the domain name tmall.company.[149] The court held that ".company," as the gTLD, was not a distinguishing factor and that the main part of the disputed domain name, "tmall," was identical to Alibaba's trademark "tmall" and domain name "tmall.com."[150] Therefore, the court maintained, the public could be led to mistakenly believe that the disputed domain name was associated with Alibaba.[151]

Both the WIPO panel and the Fujian High Court took the view that the new gTLDs such as .wang and .company are not the main part of domain names. Therefore, when comparing the disputed domain names with existing trademarks or domain names, the panel or the court does not need to consider the new gTLDs. Nevertheless, some commentators suggest that the court should take into consideration such source-indicating gTLDs if they create confusion among the public.[152] In other words, the court should consider the entire domain name, not just the second-level domain name (SLD). If this approach had been used in the two cases discussed above, both .wang and .company would have been included in the analysis. This approach seems the opposite of the one taken by the WIPO panel and the Fujian High Court with regard to whether the gTLD should be considered part of a disputed domain name. However, these different approaches may lead to the same conclusion, because both .wang and .company could have led consumers to believe that the disputed domain names were affiliated with the trademark holders. After all, "wang" could signal to Chinese consumers that .wang is equivalent to .net, whereas ".company" could be mistakenly understood as similar to .com.

B New Business Models

The new gTLDs have provided additional business opportunities for the online industry. For example, Dian Shang Biao (点商标), which means dot trademark, is a company that provides

[143] *Calvin Klein Trademark Trust and Calvin Klein Inc.* v. *Wang Yanchao*, WIPO Arbitration and Mediation Center, Case No. D201401413, at 1.

[144] *Id.* at 2.

[145] *Id.* at 3.

[146] *Id.* at 7.

[147] *Id.* at 2.

[148] *Id.* at 7.

[149] *Jinbo Liu* v. *Alibab Group Holding Ltd.*, (2016) Fujian High Court, 2016 Min Min Chung No. 226 ((2016) 闽民终662 号).

[150] *Id.*

[151] *Id.*

[152] Ashlie Stewart Smith, *Trademark Holders Beware: Source-Indicating gTLDs Are Here*, 57 IDEA 153.

trademark verification services. The company obtained the gTLD .商标[153] in 2014 and has marketed its registration service with .商标 to trademark owners.[154] Dian Shang Biao has emphasized that it provides professional due diligence regarding the trademark status of domain name registrants and that only the real trademark owner is eligible to register a .商标 domain name and use their trademark as an SLD. Because the gTLD .商标 is registered in Chinese, Dian Shang Biao has been targeting those who would like to use their Chinese trademark as part of the domain name. This service has attracted quite a few large companies that would like to avoid or eliminate cybersquatting and the pervasive counterfeiting of products in the online environment. Some large companies, such as Rolex, Acer, and Shiseido, have used the gTLD .商标 together with their trademark as a portal for Chinese consumers.[155]

V CONCLUSION

Domain name dispute resolution in mainland China and Hong Kong provide good examples of different approaches in civil law and common law jurisdictions. Although the UDRP was devised as an international dispute resolution mechanism, its implementation may differ from jurisdiction to jurisdiction. According to the UDRP, both the ownership of a trademark and that of a service mark are legal grounds for filing a domain name complaint. However, in China and Hong Kong, the legal grounds for domain name complaints also include legal rights other than trademark and service mark ownership. Both the CDNRP and HKAIC panels have ruled that the .cn domain name complaints were justified when based on rights or interests listed in Article 6 of the PRC Anti-Unfair Competition Law, such as an individual's or an organization's name with certain influence, the name of a website, part of an existing domain name, etc. The HKAIC panels, on the other hand, have recognized that common law passing-off rights can be a ground for .hk domain name complaints.

Active use is of great importance to both trademark owners and domain name registrants. In both mainland China and Hong Kong, if the trademark owner never uses the trademark, the panels or the court would probably rule that the trademark owner does not have any legal right or interest in the mark and that the trademark owner may therefore fail to substantiate his claim against other parties' domain name registrations.[156] If the domain name registrant never uses its domain name, the panels might hold that the name was registered in bad faith. Moreover, the fact that the domain name registrant has led consumers to believe that the domain name is associated with another mark owner may be taken to indicate both passing off and bad faith in common law jurisdictions, such as Hong Kong, where passing off is a legal ground for domain name complaint.

Although both CDNRP and HKDRP are developed based on UDRP with limited substantive rules, this chapter's comparison of CDNRP and HKDRP panel decisions regarding .cn and .hk domain names suggests that the CDNRP .cn panels apply domestic law much more frequently than do the HKDRP .hk panels. As a matter of practice, instead of referring to domestic law,

[153] 商标 means trademark in Chinese.
[154] Dian Shang Biao, *The Origin of* .商标, http://trademarkdomain.com/category/tmdomain#sbqy.
[155] Dian Shang Biao, *Cases*, http://trademarkdomain.com/category/case.
[156] It is noteworthy that unlike the United States, both mainland China and Hong Kong operate registration-based trademark systems, where trademark rights are acquired solely through first registration of the mark with the government.

such as the Hong Kong Trade Mark Ordinance, the HKDRP panels mostly decide the case based on UDRP, HKDRP, and previous decisions. This might be due to different traditions in the civil law and common law systems. Domain names with country code .hk are used in Hong Kong, a common law jurisdiction where the legal profession is arguably more familiar with the case law approach, whereas those with country code .cn are used in mainland China, a civil law jurisdiction where it is critically important to find a statutory basis for any legal claim.

IX

Overlapping Rights

25

Relationship between Trademark Law and Copyright/Design Law

Trademark Protection for Ornamental Shapes?

Estelle Derclaye and Ng-Loy Wee Loon***

I INTRODUCTION

The overlap between trademark law and copyright or design law has grown with the extension of trademark protection for subject matter that was traditionally protected only by copyright and/or design law. This extension has been triggered not only by the Trade-Related Aspects of Intellectual Property Rights (TRIPS) Agreement (Article 15(1)) but also by prior national and regional initiatives (e.g., Article 2 of the 1988 EU Trademark Directive). The overlap thus covers slogans and titles; two-dimensional artistic works (figurative marks such as color combinations, logos, graphical user interfaces, or computer visual displays); musical works (sound marks); and three-dimensional artistic works (shape marks).

This chapter concentrates only on ornamental shapes. It examines a very specific question: should there be trademark protection for an ornamental shape of a product which is also protected or had previously been protected by copyright or design law? How has this question been answered by the legislatures and/or judges in the civil law world and in the common law world?

II A PERSPECTIVE FROM THE COMMON LAW WORLD

In many common law countries, ornamental features of a product or its packaging are protectable in the design regime rather than the copyright regime. For this reason, the discussion in this section is limited to the interface between trademark law and design law.

There is, in fact, no uniformity in how common law countries approach this interface. Broadly speaking, there can be three different approaches. In the first approach – a rather outmoded one – there is an unqualified ban on trademark registration of an ornamental shape of a product: trademark protection is absolutely forbidden with no exceptions. In the second approach, there is a qualified ban on trademark registration of the shape: trademark protection is forbidden only in certain cases. In the third approach, the matter is determined solely by the distinctiveness criterion in trademark law: there is no objection to registering and protecting the shape as a trademark if the shape is distinctive of a trader's goods.

* Professor, School of Law, University of Nottingham. Section III of this chapter was prepared by Professor Derclaye.
** Professor, Faculty of Law, National University of Singapore. Section II of this chapter was prepared by Professor Ng-Loy. Please note that the position of the United States is not dealt with in this chapter, but in Chapter 26 in this volume.

The rest of this section elaborates on each of these three approaches. The countries and case law discussed in this section highlight the principal policy considerations underpinning each approach.

A An Unqualified Ban on Registering the Design as a Trademark – Absolutely No Second Bite of the Cherry, Please

At one time in various parts of the common law world, there was an absolute ban on granting trademark protection over the ornamental shape of a product or its packaging. A convenient starting point to understand the rationale for this absolute ban is the 1934 report of the Goschen Committee in the United Kingdom.[1]

The Goschen Committee was established in 1933 to review and revise the UK Trade Marks Act 1905 (UK 1905 Act). One of the proposals received by the Goschen Committee was to amend the definition of the word "mark" in the UK 1905 Act:[2] "'mark' includes a device, brand, heading, label, ticket, name, signature, word, letter, numeral, or any combination thereof." The proposal was to include in this definition, albeit non-exhaustive in scope, an explicit reference to "a container."[3] The reason for this proposal, as well as why it did not impress the Goschen Committee, is found in this passage of the committee's report:[4]

> [I]t was submitted that the shape of a container often serves to distinguish the origin of particular goods, and that in such cases the shapes and patterns of the bottles and other containers should be capable of registration as trade marks. It was not contended that the right conferred by such registration should extend beyond the mere appearance of the container, and it was admitted that it might be necessary to insert words in the existing definition to make this clear. We are unable, however, to recommend the inclusion of containers as "marks." The protection afforded by registration under the [Trade Marks] Acts may be of indefinite duration, and we think that the grant of monopolies for indefinite periods for the shape of say a bottle or jar might prove embarrassing to other traders and to the public generally. Under the Patents and Designs Acts, new designs to be applied to containers are registrable for periods of not more than fifteen years, and registration under the Trade Marks Acts might in some, cases interfere with the right of the public to use a design of which the period of protection had expired.

Two important points emerge from this passage. First, when a trader seeks and obtains design protection for an ornamental shape, it could be said that this protection is given on the premise that the shape is destined for the public domain upon the expiration of the protection period fixed by design law. There would be no quid pro quo if, at the end of this period, this trader gets further (and worse, perpetual) protection for the shape under trademark law. Second, this policy objection is so fundamental that it cannot be overcome by proof that the shape has become distinctive of this trader's goods as a result of prior use. The fact that the shape is in fact functioning as this trader's badge of origin in the marketplace is irrelevant. This remains

[1] The chairman of this committee was Viscount Goschen. The proper title of this committee is the "Department Committee on the Law and Practice Relating to Trade Marks."

[2] *See* Trade Marks Act 1905, § 3(1) (Eng.).

[3] The proposed definition was the following: "A 'mark' shall mean any sign or combination of sign including a device, brand, heading, label, wrapper, *container*, ticket, name, signature, word, letter, or numeral" (emphasis added). *See* Department Committee on the Law and Practice Relating to Trade Marks, Minutes of Evidence, 1933, § 1427 (UK). This proposal came from the British Federation of Industries (although all the members supported this proposal): *see id.* §§ 1488–9.

[4] Department Committee on the Law and Practice Relating to Trade Marks, Report, 1933, Cm. 4568, § 13 [hereinafter Report of the Department Committee].

irrelevant even if the common law action for passing off would come to the aid of this trader if others use a confusingly similar shape in relation to their goods.[5] In short, the Goschen Committee's message was this: *absolutely* no second bite of the cherry, please.

In the new law that ensued from the work of the Goschen Committee, namely, the UK Trade Marks Act 1938 (UK 1938 Act), the definition of "mark" as it appeared in the UK 1905 Act was retained.[6] This definition, it bears repeating, is non-exhaustive in scope. Therefore it was conceivably possible for a court to be persuaded that the shape of a container or an article could qualify as a "mark" under the UK 1938 Act.[7] And this was what the Coca-Cola Company sought to do in the *Coca-Cola Trademarks* case (*Coca-Cola (UK)*).[8] This is a perfect case study for our purposes because it concerned a trademark application for a shape in which design rights had expired.

The shape in question was the fluted contour shape of the Coca-Cola Company's by now iconic bottle (the Contour Bottle), which the company used as the container for its cola beverage. In the UK, the Contour Bottle had been in use since the early 1920s. The Coca-Cola Company had a design registration for the shape of the Contour Bottle,[9] which expired in 1940. Several years later, the Coca-Cola Company filed two applications[10] to register the three-dimensional shape of the Contour Bottle as a trademark under the UK 1938 Act, in respect of non-alcoholic beverages. The Coca-Cola Company tendered evidence to argue that the shape of the Contour Bottle had become distinctive of its cola beverage. It advanced the policy-based argument that was in substance the same as the one put before the Goschen Committee: the registration system was to protect distinctive trademarks and since the shape of the Contour Bottle was distinctive of its beverage, it ought to be allowed registration. The definition of "mark" in the UK 1938 Act, being non-exhaustive in scope, could accommodate shapes.

The House of Lords (now Supreme Court) was not persuaded by the distinctiveness argument. Even assuming that distinctiveness was established,[11] the court said, this was irrelevant. Instead, what was relevant was the fact the shape of the Contour Bottle had previously been protected by design rights. The court saw the Coca-Cola Company's present claim for trademark protection over this shape as an inappropriate "attempt to expand the boundaries of intellectual property and to convert [trademark law] into a source of monopoly."[12] Clearly, the Law Lords were of the same mind as the Goschen Committee.

[5] *See Reckitt & Colman Products Ltd.* v. *Borden Inc.* (No. 3) [1990] RPC 341 (HL) (the famous JIF LEMON case, involving a plastic lemon-shaped container). The House of Lords found that this container had become distinctive of the claimant's product (lemon juice) and that the defendant's container was confusingly similar to the claimant's container. The defendant was held liable for passing off.

[6] The definition of "mark" is found in Trade Marks Act 1938, 1 & 2 Geo. 6 c. 22, § 68(1) [hereinafter UK 1938 Act].

[7] Perhaps this was why the Mathys Committee (the committee established in 1972, under the chairmanship of Mr. H. R. Mathys, to review trademark law and practice under the 1938 Act) recommended that the 1938 Act should explicitly exclude the registration of the shape of goods or their container. Committee to Examine British Trade Mark Law and Practice, Report, 1972, Cm. 5601, § 64. The Mathys Committee fully endorsed the Goschen Committee's view that trademark protection for shapes was inappropriate: *see id.*, §§ 60–61.

[8] *Coca-Cola Trade Marks* [1986] RPC 421 [hereinafter *Coca-Cola (UK)*].

[9] The registration was effected under the UK Patents and Designs Act 1907, 7 Edw. 7 c. 29. This has since been repealed and replaced by the UK Registered Designs Act 1949, 12, 13 & 14 Geo. 6 c. 88.

[10] One application was filed in 1976, and one application was filed in 1980. The dispute also involved a third application filed in 1980, but this third application was to register a line drawing of the Contour Bottle as a two-dimensional trademark (that is, as a device or logo) and hence is not relevant for our purposes.

[11] *Coca-Cola (UK)*, at 457. Note that the Lords left this issue of distinctiveness undecided. The lower courts had differed in their findings: the Trade Mark Registrar and the High Court judge found that the evidence did not prove that the Contour Bottle had acquired distinctiveness, but this finding was overturned by the Court of Appeal.

[12] *Id.* at 456.

To prevent the Coca-Cola Company from having a second bite of the cherry, the House of Lords declared that the Contour Bottle was "a container not a mark."[13] Since a container was not even a "mark," the Coca-Cola Company's applications failed at the most fundamental level. This legal reasoning in effect operates as a total, unqualified bar to registration.

The impact of *Coca-Cola (UK)* reverberated through the various Commonwealth countries which had modelled their trademark legislation on the 1938 Act. Hence, at one time it was not possible to register the shape of a container or an article as a trademark in countries such as Australia,[14] New Zealand,[15] and Singapore.[16] However, not all Commonwealth countries took such an absolute stance on this issue. The positions of Canada in the late 1950s and South Africa in the 1960s are especially interesting, as discussed below.

The current position in the United Kingdom is very different, and the same can be said of the other countries mentioned in the preceding paragraph. But before looking at what their respective position currently is, let's pay a visit to Canada and South Africa.

B A Qualified Ban on Registering the Design as a Trademark – No Second Bite of the Cherry Only in Certain Cases

From the outset, policy makers in Canada accepted that the notion of a "mark" could encompass the shape of a container or an article. Its first trademark legislation after Confederation permitted the registration of "packages,"[17] and this was followed by the Unfair Competition Act 1932, which allowed the registration of a "distinguishing guise" defined to mean "a mode of shaping, moulding, wrapping or packing wares" that was adapted to distinguish the applicant's wares.[18] It was under this concept of "distinguishing guise" that the Coca-Cola Company managed to get a trademark registration for the Contour Bottle in 1952.[19] However, it should also be noted that where the shape had "any element of utility or convenience," registration would not extend trademark protection to such elements.[20]

In the late 1940s, the question that confronted the Goschen Committee came before a Canadian law reform committee: should Canada (continue to) allow registration of the shape of a container as a trademark under the concept of distinguishing guise? This law reform committee was the Fox Committee,[21] established in 1947 to review and revise the Unfair Competition Act 1932. Like the Goschen Committee, the Fox Committee was also concerned that trademark registration of a shape could harm the public interest. But unlike the Goschen

[13] *Id.* at 457.

[14] *See, e.g., Koninklijke Philips Elecs NV* v. *Remington Consumer Prods Ltd* (2000) 177 ALR 167, § 15 (Austl.), where *Cola-Cola (UK)* was cited as authority for the view that shapes were not registrable under the former Australian Trade Marks Act 1955.

[15] *See, e.g., Tot Toys Ltd.* v. *Mitchell* [1993] 1 NZLR 325 (HC) at 348, where *Cola-Cola (UK)* was cited as authority for the view that shapes were not registrable under the former New Zealand Trade Marks Act 1953.

[16] *See, e.g.*, TAN TEE JIM SC, LAW OF TRADE MARKS AND PASSING OFF IN SINGAPORE § 3.047 (3d ed. 2014) Vol. 1 at para. [3.047], where *Coca-Cola (UK)* was cited as authority for the view that shapes were not registrable under the former Singapore Trade Marks Act 1939.

[17] *See* Trade Mark and Design Act 1868, 31 Vict. c. 55, § 5 (Can.).

[18] *See* Unfair Competition Act 1932, 22 & 23 Geo. 5 c. 38, § 2(d) (Can.).

[19] COCA-COLA BOTTLE, Registration No. UCA44193 (registered on Nov. 21, 1952, in Class 32).

[20] This exclusion is found within the definition of "distinguishing guise."

[21] The proper title of this committee is "Trade-Mark Law Revision Committee." The chairman of this committee was Dr. Harold Fox, a renowned lawyer and author of various textbooks on Canadian industrial and intellectual property. One of his textbooks is *Canadian Law of Trade Marks and Unfair Competition*. The report of the Fox Committee is reproduced in the Appendix: HAROLD G. FOX, CANADIAN LAW OF TRADE MARKS AND UNFAIR COMPETITION 1142–82 (2d ed. 1956).

Committee, the Fox Committee did not think that the solution was to ban registration of shapes altogether. Instead, it recommended that the new law should have more safeguards, that is, apart from the one in the existing law which excluded protection for "an element of utility or convenience" in the shape. These safeguards were implemented in section 13 of the new law, namely, the Trade Marks Act 1953. This remains the governing trademark legislation in Canada today.[22]

The safeguard which is relevant for our purposes is the one set out in section 13(1)(b). This provision bans the registration of a shape of a container or an article (even if it has become distinctive of a trader's goods) where the registration is likely to "unreasonably [] limit the development of any art or industry." The threshold of this ban is set rather high, and the mere fact that the shape had previously enjoyed protection in the design regime would not cross this threshold. This view is borne out by what happened in *WCC Containers Sales Ltd.* v. *Haul-All Equipment Ltd.*[23] In many ways, this case is the Canadian equivalent of *Coca-Cola (UK)*. The shape in question was the configuration of a container which was designed for use as a refuse bin in public places like national parks. The company behind the creation of this container (HL) had a design registration over this shape. One year after the expiration of the design registration, HL applied for and obtained trademark registration for this shape. A rival (WCC) applied to expunge this trademark registration on various grounds. One ground was that the shape was already "dedicated to the public"[24] upon the expiration of the design registration. This is in essence the policy of no second bite of the cherry that won the debate in the United Kingdom under the stewardship of the Goschen Committee. But this policy did not find favor with the Federal Court of Canada. The court did not see section 13(1)(b) as implementing this policy. The court reasoned that if Parliament had intended to make design protection and trademark protection mutually exclusive, the limitation would have been explicit and unequivocal (as was the case with the overlap between design protection and copyright protection). Section 13(1)(b) was meant to avoid something more troubling than the prior protection of the shape in the design regime.

What is so perfect about this case is that it also illustrates what else is needed to successfully activate section 13(1)(b). As mentioned, HL's container was designed for use as a refuse bin in national parks. HL was the sole supplier of these refuse bins to the national park authorities during the years when the shape of the bin was protected by the design registration. So well-designed was this bin that when the national park authorities needed a further supply of refuse bins, their tenders specified that the bin must be shaped like HL's bin. By this time, HL's design registration had expired. Companies like HL and WCC put in bids, and even though WCC's bid was lower, the tender was awarded to HL because of HL's trademark registration for the shape of the bin. HL had even threatened to sue the national park authorities for inducing trademark infringement if they awarded the tender to any other party. These circumstances were what prompted the Federal Court to conclude that HL's trademark registration "unreasonably … limit[ed] the development of any art or industry," and accordingly to order its expungement under section 13(1)(b).

In South Africa, it has been possible to register a container as a trademark since 1963. This possibility came about as a result of a recommendation from the Chowles Committee,[25] which

22 Note, though, the potential repeal of § 13, via Economic Action Plan 2014 Act, No. 1, SC 2014, c. 20, § 16 (Can.) (which has not been brought into force).

23 *WCC Containers Sales Ltd.* v. *Haul-All Equip. Ltd.* [2003] FC 962 (Can. Fed. Ct.).

24 *Id.*, § 59.

25 The chairman of this committee was Mr. Victor Chowles, who was South Africa's Registrar of Trade Marks at the material time.

was established in 1961 to review and revise the country's first trademark legislation, the Trade Marks Act 1916. The prevailing view was that this legislation did not permit the registration of containers.[26] When considering whether this should be changed, the Chowles Committee specifically referred to the Goschen Committee's objection, noting the latter's view that trademark law should not interfere with "the right of the public to use a design"[27] once its protection under design law had expired. However, the Chowles Committee decided – just like the Fox Committee did – that the concern of overprotection of containers could be managed by having safeguards in the new law.[28] Thus, the new law, the Trade Marks Act 1963, defined the term "mark" to include "a distinctive container for goods"[29] and, at the same time, provided for the expungement of the registration where it was or had become "likely to limit the development of any art or industry."[30] Today this safeguard is found in section 10(11) of the Trade Marks Act 1993, as a ground of objection to refuse registration of a container or to expunge a registration thereof.[31]

Just like in Canada, the mere fact that the shape has previously enjoyed protection in the design regime is probably insufficient to prevent registration of the shape under this ground of objection. This appears to be the position taken in *Die Bergkelder Beperk* v. *Vredendal Koop Wynmakery*.[32] The claimant, a wine producer, had registered the shape of its wine bottle as a design. Just when the design protection was about to expire, the claimant applied for and obtained registration of its bottle as a trademark. The defendant, another wine producer, sought to expunge the trademark registration when the claimant sued for trademark infringement. The Supreme Court of Appeal was clearly not impressed with the claimant's behavior, noting at one point that the change in the law to allow registration of containers as trademarks was not meant to confer on a container "a patent-like or industrial design-like monopoly in the container itself."[33] The court ordered the expungement of the claimant's trademark registration for its bottle, but the ground for expungement was that the bottle was not distinctive of the claimant's products. No objection under section 10(11) was raised at all.

An objection under section 10(11) was raised, and successfully activated, in *Triomed (Proprietary) Ltd.* v. *Beecham Group Plc*.[34] This concerned an application to expunge the trademark registration of a particular shape of a pharmaceutical tablet. All the features in this shape mark – its elliptical shape, its curvature and thickness – had functional purposes; for example, the curvature facilitated the coating of the tablet with a polymer film, which in turn aided swallowing or controlled the release of the active ingredients in the tablet. The High Court of South

26 Patents, Designs, Trade Marks and Copyright Act 9 of 1916 (as amended up to Act No. 19 of 1947) [hereinafter Trade Marks Act 1916] defined "mark" in the same way as the UK 1938 Act. In *Cointreau et Cie* v. *Pagan International* 1991 (4) SA 706 (SCA) at 710 (S. Afr.), the Supreme Court of Appeal cited *Coca-Cola (UK)* as authority for the view that a container was not registrable under the Trade Marks Act 1916.

27 Report of the Department Committee, *supra* note 4.

28 Committee on Draft Trade Marks Bill 1961, Report, 1961, §§ 22–23. *See also* Victor Chowles, *Letter from South Africa*, 52 Trademark Rep. 992, 998–9 (1962); G. C. Webster et al., South African Law of Trade Marks, Unfair Competition, Company Names and Trading Styles 55 (3d ed. 1986).

29 *See* Trade Marks Act 1963 (Act No. 9/1963), § 2(1) (Ir.). Note that the word "distinctive" in this definition was deleted via an amendment made in 1971.

30 *See id.*, § 10(3).

31 Note that this ground of objection in § 10(11) applies not only to a container, but also to the shape, configuration, color, or pattern of goods. Note also that § 10(5) of the Trade Marks Act 1993 prohibits registration of a mark that "consists exclusively of the shape, configuration, colour of goods where such shape, configuration, colour is necessary to obtain a specific technical result, or results from the nature of the goods."

32 *Die Bergkelder Beperk* v. *Vredendal Koöp Wynmakery* 2006 (4) SA 275 (SCA) (S. Afr.).

33 *Id.*, § 11.

34 *Triomed (Propriety) Ltd.* v. *Beecham Grp. Plc* [2001] FSR 34 (SCA) (S. Afr.).

Africa expunged this registration on various grounds,[35] including the ground in section 10(11). On the latter, the High Court said:[36]

> [A] monopoly in the shape in question would clearly limit developments in the pharmaceutical industry. . . . It would grant a monopoly on the features of a shape which *give substantial value to the goods themselves*. The more functional a shape, the more likely it is or will become that a monopoly over that shape would be likely to limit the development of an industry.

Anyone familiar with the current position in the European Union (see Section III of this chapter) would immediately recognize the italicized words in this passage: this is the Substantial Value Provision in Article 3(1)(e)(iii) of the EU Trade Marks Directive. It would appear that the qualified ban in South Africa and in Canada, worded in terms of protecting "the development of any art or industry," is in effect the same as the qualified ban in the EU. It is now time to return to the United Kingdom.

The United Kingdom implemented the provisions in the EU Trade Marks Directive when it enacted the Trade Marks Act 1994 (UK 1994 Act), which repealed the UK 1938 Act. The UK 1994 Act provides that a trademark may consist inter alia of "the shape of goods or their packaging," and in so doing, abrogated the reasoning in *Coca-Cola (UK)* that a container could never qualify as a "mark." The concerns raised by the Goschen Committee are now addressed by the Substantial Value Provision, which is found in section 3(2)(c) of the UK 1994 Act.[37] The connection between this provision and design law was first made by the Court of Appeal in *Philips Electronics NV* v. *Remington Consumer Products Ltd.* when it said that section 3(2)(c) was intended to exclude "aesthetic-type shapes"[38] from the trademark regime. The court reasoned that shapes which were designed to "appeal to the eye"[39] – this is a term associated with registered design law[40] – were more properly protected as registered designs or protection of the like (in particular, copyright).

Just like in Canada and South Africa, the Substantial Value Provision in the United Kingdom does not bar the registration of a shape as a trademark merely because the shape was previously (or is still) protected by design rights. This was made clear in the UK Government's 1990 White Paper on *Reform of Trade Marks Law*:[41]

> The fact that a shape is protectable or has been protected by a registered design or by copyright does not itself mean that it should not be registrable as a trade mark (many ordinary two-dimensional marks are so protected). The question is one to be determined by the facts of the case – does the shape serve primarily to distinguish it from rival products or (to turn the question around) would the main motive of a competitor in using that shape by to mislead purchasers so to its origin.

[35] The other grounds were the following: lack of distinctiveness and the functionality objection in § 10(5) (*see Die Bergkelder Beperk* 2006 (4) SA at 275).

[36] *Triomed (Propriety) Ltd.* [2001] FSR at [83]. This ruling was upheld by the Supreme Court of Appeal: *see* [2003] FSR 27 at [30].

[37] The UK version refers to "*adds* substantial value to the goods," but this difference is immaterial.

[38] *Philips Electronics NV* v. *Remington Consumer Prods. Ltd.* [1999] RPC 809 (CA) 822.

[39] *Id.*

[40] *See* Registered Designs Act 1949, 12, 13 & 14 Geo. 6 c. 88, § 1(3) (UK) (the features of the design of the article must "appeal to and are judged solely by the eye"). Note that this is no longer a registration criterion: it was removed via the Registered Designs Regulations 2001, No. 3949 (UK).

[41] Department of Trade and Industry, Reform of Trade Mark Law, Cm. 1203, § 2.21. This White Paper examined the position under the UK 1938 Act and recommended that the law be amended to allow registration of shape marks, provided that there be safeguards like the Substantial Value Provision in the new law.

The UK courts have also adopted this approach. For example, in *Julius Sämaan Ltd* v. *Tetrosyl Ltd.* the High Court cautioned that the focus on the inquiry must not be on whether the shape was protectable by design law, but rather on whether the shape added *substantial* value to the goods.[42] In *The London Cab Corp. Ltd.* v. *Frazer-Nash Research Ltd.*, the Court of Appeal even went so far as to cast doubt on the relevance of "the presence or availability of design protection in fact" in this inquiry.[43]

The shift in position in the United Kingdom from "absolutely no second bite of the cherry" to "no second bite of the cherry only in certain cases" was followed in due course by some other common law jurisdictions. For example, when India,[44] Hong Kong,[45] and Singapore,[46] were updating their trademark legislation in the late 1990s and early 2000s, they decided to have the Substantial Value Provision in their new laws.

C No Specific Ban on Registering the Design as a Trademark – It Could Be a Different Cherry

Not all common law jurisdictions followed in the footsteps of the United Kingdom. The interesting examples in this group are Australia and New Zealand. Both these countries considered but decided against having the Substantial Value Provision.

In the case of Australia, it had for a very short period the Trade Marks Act 1994, which contained specific bans on the registration of the natural shapes of goods and functional shapes.[47] But this legislation was never brought into force. Less than a year after receiving assent, it was repealed and replaced by the Trade Marks Act 1995.[48] The specific bans in the 1994 version do not appear in the 1995 version. Their absence has been explained in this way: specific bans on the registration of the natural shapes of goods and functional shapes are

[42] *Julius Sämaan Ltd.* v. *Tetrosyl Ltd.* [2006] FSR 42 at [99]. In another part of its judgment, the High Court also noted that "merely because consumer products are designed to have an attractive appearance does not mean that their shape adds *substantial* value to the goods" (*id.* at [103]).

[43] *The London Cab Corp. Ltd.* v. *Frazer-Nash Research Ltd.* [2018] FSR 7 at [76]. The Court of Appeal made this observation in relation to the High Court's finding that the registered shape mark in question (the shape of a motor vehicle) offended the Substantial Value Provision. The High Court had taken into consideration inter alia the fact that there was a design registration for this shape (which had not expired). For the High Court's decision, *see* [2016] Eur. Trade Mark Rep. 20.

[44] Trade Marks Act, No. 47 of 1999, India Code (1999), vol. § 9(3)(c).

[45] Trade Marks Ordinance, (2003) Cap. 559, § 11(3)(c) (HK). *See Re Movado Watch Co. SA*, [2003] 2 HKC 83, where the Hong Kong Trade Mark Registry activated the Substantial Value Provision to reject an application to register the three-dimensional watch face of the MOVADO wrist watch. The design of this watch face, comprising a thick piece of metal black disc with a small concave circle in the 12 o'clock position, is part of the collection of many museums such as the Museum of Modern Art in New York.

[46] Singapore Trade Marks Act 1998, § 7(3)(c). See *Société Des Produits Nestlé SA* v. *Petra Foods Ltd.* [2014] SGHC 252, where the Substantial Value Provision was considered for the first time by a Singapore court. The shape in this case was the rectangular slab shape of the KIT KAT chocolate bar. The High Court of Singapore held that the fact that a shape added eye appeal to the product was not sufficient to bar (pun intended) the shape from registration. The Substantial Value Provision would apply only if the evidence showed that the shape was "of such appeal that it would be improper for a trader to monopolise it for an indefinite amount of time" (*id.* at [142]). Such evidence was lacking in this case. Note, though, that the High Court found that the shape of the KIT KAT chocolate bar offended the functionality prohibition in § 7(3)(b) (the shape is "necessary to obtain a technical result"), as well as lacking in distinctiveness. The trademark registration of this shape was expunged on these grounds. The High Court's findings on these two grounds were upheld by the Court of Appeal: *see* [2017] 1 SLR 35. There was no appeal on the High Court's finding on the Substantial Value Provision.

[47] Trade Marks Act 1994 (Cth) § 39 (Austl.) (No. 156 of 1994 which received Royal Assent on Dec. 13, 1994). These bans apply to shapes of goods as well as "other characteristics" of the goods.

[48] The repeal was made by Trade Marks Act 1995 (Cth) § 5 (Austl.), which came into force on Oct. 17, 1995.

"unnecessary" because these shapes would fail the distinctiveness criterion anyway.[49] Conspicuously missing from the Australian scene is the Substantial Value Provision. Clearly, the policy makers in Australia are much less (if at all) troubled by the prospect of shapes being protected first by design law and then by trademark law. They are content to leave the matter to be determined solely by the distinctiveness criterion. The Australian position may be rationalized in this way: where a shape previously protected by design law has become distinctive of the design proprietor's goods, the shape is in fact a *different* cherry from the subject matter of the design registration. Thus, granting trademark protection for this shape does not amount to giving the design proprietor a second bite of the same cherry. Rather, the proprietor is being rewarded for having created a different cherry through use and promotion of the shape.

In New Zealand's case, it decided to follow the Australian approach rather than the UK approach.[50] There are thus no specific bans on registration of shapes in the New Zealand Trade Marks Act 2002. Originally, the bill contained bans on registering natural shapes of goods, functional shapes, and shapes that add substantial value to the goods.[51] These bans were deleted on the recommendation of the Commerce Committee tasked to scrutinize the bill. Two reasons were given by this select committee: first, case law (presumably decisions from the United Kingdom and the Court of Justice of the European Union (CJEU)) has shown difficulty in the application of these bans; and second, these bans might "unduly restrict and prevent registration of shapes that are distinctive." The second reason is almost diametrically opposite from the position taken by the Goschen Committee: whereas the Goschen Committee regarded distinctiveness as irrelevant, the Commerce Committee regarded distinctiveness as the all-important consideration.

III A PERSPECTIVE FROM THE CIVIL LAW WORLD

In the civil law world, ornamental shapes can be protected by copyright and/or design rights. In France, for instance, the principle of the unity of art (*unité de l'art*) dictates this double protection.[52] A similar situation exists in the Benelux. However, there are some countries that have made it very hard to cumulate the copyright and design protection for such shapes, either by having a higher threshold of originality (e.g., Germany, Portugal, and current Italian law) or a requirement of separability (e.g., Italy before it changed its copyright law in 2001[53]). There is no uniformity in how civil law countries approach this particular interface, even in the EU, as

49 *Koninklijke Philips Elecs NV* v. *Remington Consumer Prods Ltd* (2000) 177 ALR 167, [15] (Austl.). *See also Kenman Kandy Australia Pty Ltd* v. *Registrar of Trade Marks* (2002) 122 FCR 494, [43] (Federal Court of Australia) (where the court said that these specific bans were "otiose" in the light of the distinctiveness criterion).

50 Commerce Committee, Commentary on Trade Marks Bill 2001 (142-1), 4 (NZ) ("We recommend adopting the Australian approach, which does not make any specific provision for shape trade marks, but rather relies on the general distinctiveness test").

51 *See* Trade Marks Bill 2001 (142-1), cl. 18(1) (NZ).

52 In the past, this principle meant that the cumulation was total in the sense that if the conditions of copyright were met, design protection was automatically granted and vice versa. Now cumulation only exists if the conditions of each right are met. This was stated in germ in Cour de cassation [Cass.] [supreme court for judicial matters] crim., Dec. 13, 2011, 2012 Propriété Intellectuelle Bulletin Documentaire, III, 180 (Fr.), and has been more clearly stated in Cour de cassation [Cass.] [supreme court for judicial matters] com., Mar. 29, 2017, https://legifrance.gouv.fr/affichJuriJudi.do?oldAction=rechJuriJudi&idTexte=JURITEXT000034345512&fastReqId=1171443833&fastPos=1. Thus the cumulation is full rather than total. On terminology, *see* Estelle Derclaye, *Introduction*, *in* The Copyright/Design Interface: Past, Present and Future 1 (2018).

53 *See* Decreto Legislativo 2 febbraio 2001, n. 95, art. 22, in GU Apr. 4, 2001, n. 79 (It.) (implementing Directive 98/71/EC on the Legal Protection of Designs) (entered into force on Apr. 19, 2001).

Article 17 of the Design Directive left this issue unharmonized except to say that cumulation must be possible. In September 2019, the CJEUput an end to this lack of uniformity by deciding that all works of applied art/industrial designs must gain copyright protection like other works, at the normal level of originality, which is as the author's own intellectual creation.[54] The matter is now therefore fully harmonized in the European Union.

In addition to copyright and design rights protection, it is also possible to protect some ornamental shapes by trademark law in the EU. The second approach outlined in Section II for the common law world applies; namely, there is a qualified ban on trademark registration of the shape – that is, trademark protection is forbidden only in certain cases, as will be seen below.

This section will thus examine how EU law has interpreted this rule and how some of its member states have dealt with the overlap for the area of the overlap that EU law has not harmonized. The section will envisage the two types of overlaps: concurrent (the two or three Intellectual Property (IP) rights subsist on the object they protect at the same moment in time) and subsequent (one or more IP rights "prolong" the previous IP right which has expired).

The possibility of an overlap between a trademark right and a design right (whether registered or not) and/or a copyright is easy to see because design rights and copyrights are concerned with the appearance of a product or work, be it two- or three-dimensional, and these products or works can be shape marks. In addition, in the EU, a three-dimensional work or design can be distinctive as well as original and/or novel and can have individual character.

That said, EU law has a rule (Article 4(1)(e)(iii) of the Trademark Directive (TMD) and the corresponding Article 7(1)(e)(iii) of the EU Trademark Regulation (EUTMR)) which prohibits the trademark protection of signs that consist exclusively of the shape, or another characteristic,[55] which give substantial value to the goods. The provision reads:

> Article 4 – Absolute grounds for refusal or invalidity
> 1. The following shall not be registered or, if registered, shall be liable to be declared invalid:
> (e) signs which consist exclusively of: …
> (iii) the shape, or another characteristic, which gives substantial value to the goods.

The exclusion, which applies even if the shape or other characteristic has acquired distinctiveness, regulates the trademark/copyright overlap as well as the trademark/design overlap. As the EU courts held in *Bang & Olufsen*[56] (speakers) and *Hauck*[57] (the Tripp Trapp children chair), the substantial value of a good can be its beauty, but also other aspects such as safety, comfort, and quality. In a later decision, a European Union Intellectual Property Office (EUIPO) Board found the trademark for Eames' Lounge chair invalid, stating that "[w]here an item has become a "style icon" …, it must have substantial value."[58] In a case dealing with the iconic Louboutin shoes' red soles, the CJEU held that "a sign consisting of a color applied to the sole of a high-heeled shoe, such as that at issue in the main proceedings, does not consist exclusively of a 'shape'."[59] In a later case dealing with a mark showing drawings of Manhattan registered for

[54] Case C-683/17, *Cofemel – Sociedade de Vestuário SA* v. *G-Star Raw CV* (Sept. 12, 2019). All decisions from the courts of the European Union are available at CURIA, https://curia.europa.eu.

[55] The words "or another characteristic" were added when the directive was amended in 2015. Such other characteristics can include two-dimensional aspects.

[56] Case T-508/08, *Bang & Olufsen* v. *Office for the Harmonisation in the Internal Mkt.*, 2011 ECR II-06975, [2011] Eur. Trade Mark Rep. 10, § 77.

[57] Case C-205/13, *Hauck* v. *Stokke*, 2014 EUR-Lex CELEX LEXIS 2233, §§ 29–32, 35–36 (Sept. 18, 2014).

[58] Case R-664/2011-5, *Vitra Collections* v. *European Union Intellectual Property Office*, § 42 (Mar. 18, 2015), https://euipo.europa.eu/ohimportal/en/esearch-case-law.

[59] Case C-163/16, *Christian Louboutin SAS* v. *Van Haren Schoenen BV* (June 12, 2018).

a range of goods such as napkins, bags, wallpaper, glassware, and books, the CJEU similarly held that "a sign such as that at issue in the main proceedings, consisting of two-dimensional decorative motifs, which are affixed to goods, such as fabric or paper, does not 'consist exclusively of the [sic] shape'."[60]

There has been extensive EU case law on subsection (ii) of Article 4(1)(e), which concerns signs that consist exclusively of the shape, or another characteristic, of goods that is necessary to obtain a technical result. Therefore, the shape of the Philishave three-headed electric shaver,[61] of the Lego brick,[62] and of the Rubik cube[63] have all been held unregistrable as a trademark in the EU. On the other hand, the shape of the Lego manikin was registrable.[64] Even if the feet and hands can be connected to other elements, and thus can be said to serve a technical function, they are not the essential parts of the mark, which consists of the shape of the entire manikin.[65] Whereas there has been less litigation on subsection (iii), the EU courts have nonetheless held that both indents "reflect the *legitimate aim* of not allowing individuals to use registration of a mark in order to *acquire or perpetuate* exclusive rights relating to technical solutions."[66] EU case law thus prohibits both the concurrent and the subsequent overlap.

French courts have held several shape marks valid, stating that the subsection (iii) exclusion (as implemented in the French Intellectual Property Code) did not apply. For instance, the court of appeal of Paris accepted the validity of a mark in the shape of a vine shoot for chocolate because chocolate is meant primarily to be eaten and consumers first seek the quality of the product's taste before its attractive shape.[67] The court of appeal of Bordeaux held valid a mark in the shape of a perfume bottle holding that "the shape . . . must not be 'essentially the reason of the consumer's purchase,' that in the field of perfumes, the consumer is generally first interested in the smell of the product and not in the shape of the bottle" and, in this case, the substantial value of the product "result[ed] from the properties including the colours of the product itself, not its packaging."[68]

In addition to the ban on registering signs consisting exclusively of shapes that give substantial value to the goods, the EU courts have treated shape marks, including packaging, less favorably in terms of distinctiveness because consumers do not generally perceive them as an indication of

[60] Case C-21/18, *Textilis Ltd, Ozgur Keskin* v. *Svenskt Tenn AB* (Mar. 14, 2019).

[61] Case C-299/99, *Koninklijke Philips Elecs. NV* v. *Remington Consumer Prods. Ltd.*, 2002 ECR I-05475.

[62] Case T-270/06, *Lego Juris* v. *OHMI-Mega Brands (Brique de Lego rouge)*, 2008 ECR II-03117; Case C-48/09 P, *Lego Juris A/S* v. *Office for Harmonisation in the Internal Mkt. (OHIM)*, 2010 ECR I-08403.

[63] Case C-30/15 P, *Simba Toys GmbH & Co. KG* v. *European Union Intellectual Prop. Office*, http://curia.europa.eu/juris/liste.jsf?language=en&jur=C,T,F&num=C-30/15%20P&td=ALL.

[64] Case T-395/14, *Best-Lock (Eur.) Ltd.* v. *Office for Harmonisation in the Internal Mkt.*, 2015 EUR-Lex CELEX LEXIS 380 (June 16, 2015).

[65] *Id.*, § 33.

[66] Case C-299/99, *Koninklijke Philips Elecs. NV* v. *Remington Consumer Prods. Ltd.*, 2002 ECR I-05475, § 82 (emphasis added) (shape of the three-headed Philishave electric razor). *See also* Case T-270/06, *Lego Juris* v. *OHMI-Mega Brands (Brique de Lego rouge)*, 2008 ECR II-03117; Case C-48/09 P, *Lego Juris A/S* v. *Office for Harmonisation in the Internal Mkt. (OHIM)*, 2010 ECR I-08403 (shape of the Lego brick); Case T-508/08, *Bang & Olufsen* v. *Office for the Harmonisation in the Internal Mkt.*, 2011 ECR II-06975, [2011] Eur. Trade Mark Rep. 10, §§ 64–66 (in relation to indents (ii) and (iii)); Case C-205/13, *Hauck* v. *Stokke*, 2014 EUR-Lex CELEX LEXIS 2233, § 31 (Sept. 18, 2014) (in relation to indent (iii)).

[67] Cour d'appel [CA] [regional court of appeal] Paris, Jan. 30, 2009, 07/12419, Propriété Intellectuelle Bulletin Documentaire 2009, III, 1053 (Fr.), *aff'd*, Cour de cassation [Cass.] com., Oct. 26, 2010, 2011 RTDcom 326, obs. Jacques Azéma (Fr.); Propriété Intellectuelle Bulletin Documentaire 2010, III, 823; PIDB 2011, 30, obs. Pascale Tréfigny-Goy (Fr.).

[68] Cour d'appel [CA] [regional court of appeal] Bordeaux, 1e ch., Nov. 5, 2015, 1400502 (translation by the author).

origin, and therefore the overlap is also curtailed this way.[69] In France, however, the courts are a little less strict than the EU courts on the application of this rule.[70] The overall result is that the overlap is reasonably curtailed, and some ornamental shapes are registrable but not many.

The other area harmonized at EU level concerning the overlap between trademark rights, design rights, and copyrights relates to exhaustion of the said rights. EU case law prevents the holder of a copyright and trademark on a product using copyright to block the resale of the product, the trademark right of which has been exhausted by the trademark holder's putting the product on the market. In *Dior* v. *Evora*,[71] the CJEU held that when copyright forbids the reproduction of a work "attached" to a trademarked good or service (i.e., commercialized as such by the trademark owner) but there is no trademark infringement, copyright law cannot trump the free movement of goods or services which would have prevailed if trademark law had been exclusively applicable. Accordingly, the freedom of movement of goods and services includes the freedom to resell goods but also to bring to the public's attention the further commercialization of those goods (e.g., via advertisement), unless such use of the trademark (or goods) for this purpose seriously damages the reputation of the trademark (or goods).[72] The *Dior* decision set out a rule that in this situation, copyright law must yield before the EU principle of freedom of movement of goods and services. The case involved genuine Dior perfumes bought for resale by a discount store. In order to advertise the perfumes, the discount store had to reproduce the packaging and bottles on its advertisements. The trademark right was exhausted, and Dior tried to use its copyright in the shape of the perfume bottles and their packaging to prevent the trader from reselling the perfumes. The CJEU would most likely rule the same if it was not copyright but a design right which was invoked to block the resale.

Besides these two rules, EU law does not regulate the concurrent overlap between copyright/design rights on the one hand and trademark rights on the other. So for the few ornamental shapes which can benefit from the two or three rights, most member states have no rules regulating the overlap in relation to ownership, rights, dealings, infringement, and exceptions. Thus, regime clashes occur at those levels as there is not much convergence on these points between the three intellectual property rights (IPRs). When there is no convergence, the stricter regime prevails over the other. For instance, in most countries, because the basic requirements for infringement are the same owing to international conventions and basic principles in the two rights, copyright and design law will override the limitations of trademark law (principle of specialty, use in the course of trade, and requirement of confusion in some cases) and trademark law will override the limitations of copyright and unregistered design law (requirement of copying). So, for instance, if a product is protected by both trademark and design rights, and the infringing product is not an identical or similar product, because of trademark law's principle of specialty, the trademark will not be infringed; but under design law, such principle does not apply, so the design could be infringed. Similarly, design law does not require confusion whereas trademark law does, so if the trademark is not infringed (because it is not a famous trademark, the goods or marks are not identical, and the confusion test is required), the

69 *See* Joined Cases C-53–55/01, *Linde AG, Winward Indus. & Rado Watch* v. *DPMA*, 2003 ECR I-03161. *See also* Anette Kur, *Too Common, Too Splendid, or "Just Right"? Trade Mark Protection for Product Shapes in the Light of CJEU Case Law* (Max Planck Institute for Innovation and Competition Research Paper No. 14-17, 2014); Case C-218/01, *Henkel KGaA*, 2004 ECR I-01725, § 49.

70 *See* Alain Berthet & Elisabeth Berthet, *La Marque Tridimensionnelle : Mythe ou Réalité?*, PROPRIÉTÉ INTELLECTUELLE BULLETIN DOCUMENTAIRE 413 (2016).

71 Case C-337/95, *Parfums Christian Dior SA & Parfums Christian Dior BV* v. *Evora BV*, 1997 ECR I-6013.

72 *Id.*, §§ 48, 59.

design may still be infringed as confusion is not required in the design infringement test. Trademark law does not require copying for infringement to be found, but under unregistered design law and copyright, copying is required. Private uses are not all exempted in copyright law, but they are all outside the scope of trademark law. The owner of the rights therefore gets the best of both worlds.

Similarly, in the EU and its member states, there are no exceptions in trademark law except under Articles 5(3)(a) and 10(2)(c) of the TMD (use with due cause of an identical or similar trademark with reputation on dissimilar goods and by extension on identical or similar goods[73]). Therefore, if a copyright exception applies, but the use is of an identical mark without reputation on identical goods, the trademark regime will trump the copyright regime. This has happened in France in relation to some parodies. The character Titi Fricoteur was not held to infringe the copyright in Bibi Fricotin, but was held to infringe the trademark right.[74] However, other French courts have allowed the two rights to converge in cases involving parodies. For instance, in a case parodying the ESSO trademark with the symbol "E$$O," use of the trademark was held not to infringe copyright (the parody exception was applicable) or trademark law.[75] In Germany, where there is no case law, the fundamental rights to freedom of the arts (Article 5(3) of the constitution) and freedom of speech (Article 5(1) of the constitution) are the two bases for the development of similar results in both trademark and copyright law.

As to designs, there is some convergence as both trademark and design laws allow private use/ use for non-commercial purposes. But the three other exceptions allowed under design law (acts done for experimental purposes; acts of reproduction for the purposes of making citations or of teaching; and transit of aircraft and ship equipment embodying design infringements, including importation of equipment for repairs and execution of such repairs on the equipment of such aircrafts and ships in transit) will be trumped by the trademark regime at least in double or single identity cases (i.e., cases where the trademarks and the goods of the claimant and defendant are identical, and cases when either the trademark or the goods of the defendant are identical to those of the claimant). Also, a trademark will generally be more easily infringed than a design. This is because the design law test (informed user) is stricter than the trademark law test (average consumer). The case law has interpreted the informed user as a person who is more observant than the average consumer and who will therefore pay more attention to the differences than to the similarities between designs.

For ornamental shapes which are not caught by Article 4(1)(e)(iii)'s ban, since an EU or a national trademark right is renewable ad infinitum provided it remains used and does not lose distinctiveness, a subsequent overlap subsists when the copyright or design right in the creation eventually expires. But conversely, if a trademark right expires (i.e., if it is not renewed every ten years in the EU (Article 48 of TMD) or if it has not been used for a period of five continuous years (Article 16 of TMD)) or is no longer distinctive, copyrights or registered design rights still subsist until they expire. The first scenario is more common. While the subsequent overlap is implicitly allowed, the way countries deal with it differs quite a lot.

[73] Case C-292/00, *Davidoff & Cie SA & Zino Davidoff SA* v. *Gofkid Ltd.*, 2003 ECR I-389.

[74] Cour d'appel [CA] [regional court of appeal] Paris, July 12, 1993, *cited by* VALERIE LAURE BENABOU, *Les Rapports entre Droit d'Auteur et Droit des Marques et de la Concurrence Déloyale, Rapport National, France, in* ADJUNCTS AND ALTERNATIVES TO COPYRIGHT, PROCEEDINGS OF THE ALAI CONGRESS, JUNE 13–17, 2001, NEW YORK USA 12 (Jane Ginsburg & June Besek eds., 2002).

[75] Cour d'appel [CA] [regional court of appeal] Paris, [2006] Eur. Trade Mark Rep. 53. *See also* Tribunal de grande instance [TGI] [ordinary court of original jurisdiction] Paris, Aug. 2, 2002, *aff'd*, Cour d'appel [CA] [regional court of appeal] Paris, [2003] Eur. Trade Mark Rep. 870. However, the Cour d'appel held that Greenpeace was liable in tort for denigration of the mark (because it had added a symbol of death (skull) to it).

In France and Germany, courts are divided on the issue. Some French courts allow registration of a copyright work as a trademark when the copyright has expired,[76] while some do not.[77] In the *Mona Lisa* case, the German Federal Patents Court did not allow the overlap for a famous copyright work (Leonardo da Vinci's *Mona Lisa*) because the more famous it is, the less likely it would be distinctive.[78] In the *Marlene Dietrich* case, the German Federal Court of Justice held that distinctiveness can sometimes subsist even if the person, in this case Marlene Dietrich, is famous.[79]

A decision by the Court of Justice of the European Free Trade Association States (EFTA Court) has shed some light on this issue.[80] This case concerned applications to register as trademarks the works of the Norwegian artist Gustav Vigeland. After Vigeland's works fell into the public domain in January 2014, the Municipality of Oslo filed applications for registration as trademarks of signs consisting of over one hundred visual works and sculptures by him. The Norwegian Patent Office refused most of the applications on the ground of lack of distinctiveness. The Norwegian Board of Appeal for Industrial Property Rights, before which the appeal was filed, requested an Advisory Opinion before the EFTA Court. The key question was whether a work that is in the public domain under copyright law is eligible for trademark protection. The Court recalled that Articles 4(1)(b)–(e) of the Trade Mark Directive do not entirely guarantee that a sign remains free to use, and therefore that a work remains in the public domain. However, it noted that in some cases it could be refused on the grounds of public policy set out in Article 4(1)(f) of the Trade Marks Directive. It held that it would be the case "for example, under the circumstances that its registration is regarded as a genuine and serious threat to certain fundamental values or where the need to safeguard the public domain, itself, is considered a fundamental interest of society." It added that "there would be no threat to the need to safeguard the public domain resulting from works that were primarily created to serve as signs to be registered as trade marks." On remand, the Norwegian Trademark Board of Appeal held that the works of Vigeland were not registerable because by applying to register virtually all

[76] *See* Cour de cassation [Cass.] [supreme court for judicial matters], Jan. 13, 1904, [1904] Annales de Propriété Industrielle 26, *cited by* PIERRE-YVES GAUTIER, PROPRIÉTÉ LITTÉRAIRE ET ARTISTIQUE 467 (6th ed. 2007) (a drawing or photograph can in general, even if they have fallen in the public domain as artistic works, constitute a trademark, albeit an old *obiter dictum*); Tribunal de grande instance [TGI] [ordinary court of original jurisdiction] Paris, Mar. 20, 1975, [1976] Annales de Propriété Industrielle 55; Cour d'appel [CA] [regional court of appeal] Paris, July 6, 1989, [1990] Propriété Intellectuelle Bulletin Documentaire, III, 112, *cited by* Benabou, *supra* note 74.

[77] *See* Christophe Caron, *L'Empilement des Propriétés Intellectuelles: Le Droit d'Auteur ne Chasse pas la Marque*, 6 COMMUNICATION COMMERCE ELECTRONIQUE (June 2006) (citing Cour d'appel [CA] [regional court of appeal] Besançon, June 5, 1970, 1972 Annales de Propriété Industrielle 20, obs. Dusolier (refusing the protection of an architectural work as a trademark on the basis that one should not be able to appropriate for an unlimited time a shape which belongs to the public domain or has a vocation to fall into it)) (noting that some courts including the Court of Cassation have showed some hostility to the reappropriation by trademark law of the public domain of copyright); Cour de cassation [Cass.] [supreme court for judicial matters] com., Oct. 19, 1999, [2000] *Communication Commerce Electronique* 3; Cour d'appel [CA] [regional court of appeal] Paris, 4e ch., June 25, 1997, Gaz. Pal. 1998, Somm. 63 ("[O]ne cannot, because it diverts trademark rights from their aim, protect as a trademark the arrangement and interior decoration of a shop, which cannot be protected by copyright"). However, this decision may now contradict Case C-421/13, *Apple Inc.* v. *Deutsches Patent- und Markenamt*, 2014 EUR-Lex CELEX LEXIS 2070 (July 10, 2014).

[78] Bundespatentgericht [BPatGE] [Federal Patent Court], Nov. 25, 1997, *Gewerblicher Rechtsschutz und Urheberrecht* 1021, 1998 (Ger.) (*Mona Lisa* case).

[79] Bundesgerichtshof [BGH] [Federal Court of Justice], Apr. 24, 2008, *Gewerblicher Rechtsschutz und Urheberrecht* 1093, 2008 (Ger.) (*Marlene-Dietrich-Bildnis* case).

[80] Judgment of the EFTA Court, Case E-5/16 (Apr. 6, 2017). The EFTA court is the equivalent of the CJEU for the EFTA states. It is not bound by CJEU case law but often follows it. When the EFTA court interprets EU law, its decisions are therefore relevant to the CJEU and its member states, even if not binding on them.

the works in the park, the municipality was trying to prolong the copyright in the works and not attempting to use the works as sources of origin.[81]

IV CONCLUSION

How a country should handle the overlap of trademark protection and copyright/design protection for an ornamental shape of a product is not an immediately obvious one. As the exposition in this chapter has shown, various policy concerns arise for consideration. Some would argue against this overlap on the basis that there should be no "two bites of the same cherry." On the other hand, it is also possible to argue that where the ornamental shape has been used and promoted in the course of trade to the point where it is functioning as the distinctive badge of origin of an undertaking, the proper regime for protecting this shape is that of trademark law. What this chapter also shows is that the policy choice to be made by the country on this issue is regardless of the legal tradition of a country, whether it is of the civil law or common law tradition.

[81] For a discussion, *see* Jane Ginsburg, *Intellectual Property as Seen by Barbie and Mickey: The Reciprocal Relationship of Copyright and Trademark Law*, 65 J. Copyright Soc'y USA 245 (2018).

26

Overlapping Copyright and Trademark Protection in the United States

More Protection and More Fair Use?

Jane C. Ginsburg and Irene Calboli***

I INTRODUCTION

This chapter addresses the phenomenon of overlapping rights under US law and complements Chapter 25 authored by Professors Derclay and Ng-Loy on the overlap of trademark, copyright, and design protection under several other Common Law and Civil Law jurisdictions. Because the United States does not provide *sui generis* protection for industrial design, but instead protects design through trademark law (notably by protecting trade dress) and design patents, this chapter focuses on the overlap between trademark and copyright protection.[1] The Lalique bottles created for Nina Ricci perfumes, for example, may enjoy both trademark and copyright protection in the United States.[2] Similarly, cartoon characters are components of copyrightable works (and in some jurisdictions, may be copyrightable works in their own right),[3] but many have also long been registered as trademarks for entertainment services or merchandise.[4]

* Morton L. Janklow Professor of Literary and Artistic Property Law, Columbia Law School.

** Professor of Law, Texas A&M University School of Law; Academic Fellow, School of Law, University of Geneva. This chapter adapts and partially extends the contribution that we have written as *Intellectual Property in Transition: The Several Sides of Overlapping Copyright and Trademark Protection*, in Transition and Coherence in Intellectual Property Law (Graeme Dinwoodie et al. eds., 2020), which was based on Jane Ginsburg, *Intellectual Property as Seen by Barbie and Mickey: The Reciprocal Relationship of Copyright and Trademark Law*, 65 J. Copyr. Soc. USA 245 (2018), and in part on Irene Calboli, *Overlapping Copyright and Trademark Protection: A Call for Concern and Action*, 2014 Univ. of Ill. L. Rev. Slip Ops. 25 (2014). We thank Barton Beebe and the students of the International Intellectual Property Colloquium, Spring 2020, Columbia Law School, for useful comments and discussion.

1 In this chapter we do not address the overlap between trademark and design patent protection. In this respect, *see, e.g.*, Laura A. Heymann, *Overlapping Intellectual Property Doctrines: Election of Rights versus Selection of Remedies*, 17 Stan. Tech. L. Rev. 241, 246–51 (2013).

2 The bottle designs may be protectable under copyright as "works of artistic craftsmanship," *see* Copyright Act, 17 USC § 102(a)(5) (2019) (enumerating category of pictorial, graphic and sculptural works, of which works of artistic craftsmanship are a subset), *see* § 101 (definition of "pictorial, graphic or sculptural work").

3 *See, e.g., DC Comics* v. *Towle*, 802 F.3d 1012 (9th Cir. 2015) (protecting Batmobile as a copyrighted character).

4 For example, MICKEY MOUSE (design mark of the Mickey Mouse cartoon character), Registration No. 3598848 (registered, inter alia, for audio and visual recordings, namely, animated and live action motion picture films, and prerecorded compact discs all featuring music, stories and family entertainment; computer game discs and software featuring music videos, trivia games, interactive games, activities and stories for children; consumer electronics, namely, MP3 players, computer mouse, audio speakers, microphones, headphones, and digital cameras; sunglasses); BATMAN (design mark of the Batman cartoon character), Registration No. 4871024 (registered, inter alia, for entertainment services, namely, providing a website featuring non-downloadable film clips, photographs and other multimedia materials featuring entertainment; conducting contests online); RONALD MCDONALD (design mark of the Ronald McDonald character), Registration No. 0874861 (registered, inter alia, for restaurant services, drive-in restaurant services).

Trademark and copyright protections will overlap when the same object serves to identify and distinguish one producer's goods or services and is also an original work of authorship. In theory, the regimes promote different objectives: source identification (or more abstractly, honest market information) in the case of trademarks and creativity in the case of copyright. The contours of protection differ as well. Under US law, a trademark need not be creative (though many in fact might be), but it must be "distinctive," because a sign that does not identify and distinguish goods or services does not fulfil its function of identifying products in the marketplace as originating from a single source.[5] By contrast, US copyright law covers original works of authorship; this includes a large array of creations, including pictures, architectural works, computer software, and even some works of applied art, so long as they are minimally creative. Accordingly, even though creativity is different from distinctiveness, some trademarks can be original works of authorship and some creative works can be distinctive signs.

Today, the convergence of trademark and copyright protection in the same objects may be even more prevalent, as artistic elements may enhance the attractiveness to consumers of a variety of goods and services.[6] This trend toward subject matter convergence has been further accentuated by the growth of trademark and copyright merchandising – the use of trademarks and copyrighted works on promotional and collateral products – as a common practice not only to increase revenues in building brands but also in creative industries. Intellectual property (IP) lawyers routinely advise their clients that, since trademark and copyright protections "aim to protect different subject matter and restrict different activity,"[7] it is to the advantage of IP owners "to have access to both sets of protection, whenever possible."[8]

However, when trademark and copyright subject matter protections overlap, courts need to ensure that each right remains within its proper domain: protection against only such copying as leads to confusion of source identification for trademarks, and temporally limited protection for works of authorship. Otherwise, IP owners might succeed in conferring in-gross protection on distinctive signs and perpetual protection on works of authorship. But if courts need to guard against the kind of boundary blurring of IP regimes that risks "mutant"[9] trademarks and copyrights, the convergence of trademark and copyright subject matter might also usefully facilitate the importation of limiting doctrines from copyright to trademark.

Ultimately, exploitation of the trademark/copyright overlap may herald a transition towards an integrated IP framework that reflects changes in marketing and product development and underscores the increasingly indistinct lines between distinctive signs and creative works. It also indicates how IP owners may attempt to exploit these overlaps beyond the purely national

[5] *See* Trademark Act (Lanham Act) 15 USC § 1051 (2006); *see also Abercrombie & Fitch Co.* v. *Hunting World, Inc.*, 537 F.2d 4, 9 (2d Cir. 1976) (distinguishing fanciful, arbitrary, and suggestive marks as inherently distinctive and descriptive marks as marks that required secondary meaning in order to be protected).

[6] US courts addressed the possibility of cumulating the two forms of protection on the same subject matter already in *Planters Nut & Chocolate Co.* v. *Crown Nut Co.*, 305 F.2d 916 (CCPA 1962). The Court of Customs and Patent Appeals stated that copyright and trademark protection could coexist in a "a fanciful picture of a humanized peanut … that … is also used as a design mark to identify and distinguish the source of peanuts." *See* J. Thomas McCarthy, McCarthy on Trademarks and Unfair Competition § 6:18 (5th ed. 2016). In 1979, the District Court for the Southern District of New York repeated in *Frederick Warne & Co.* v. *Book Sales, Inc.*, 481 F. Supp. 1191, 1196 (DCNY 1979), that "dual protection under copyright and trademark law is particularly appropriate for graphic representations of characters" with respect to the famous character of Peter Rabbit. *See infra* Section II.A.

[7] Craig S. Mende & Belinda Isaac, *When Copyright and Trademark Rights Overlap*, *in* Overlapping Intellectual Property Rights 137, 158 (Neil Wilkof & Shamnad Basheer eds., 2012).

[8] *Id.*

[9] *Dastar Corp.* v. *Twentieth Century Fox Film Corp.*, 539 US 23, 34 (2003).

context, but also concerning cross-border trade to control the distribution of IP protected products in separate jurisdictions. But this framework need not imply a one-way ratchet toward ever-increasing protection. Rather, as we elaborate in this chapter, the reciprocal influence of trademark and copyright protection can lead to a new balancing of trademark rights through importation of copyright limitations based on fair use and free expression, as well as through incorporation of US online service provider liability limitations from copyright into trademark. This chapter details both the instances where the trademark/copyright overlap might lead to more as well as less protection, and perhaps more laughs.

II WHEN OVERLAPPING RIGHTS MIGHT LEAD TO MORE PROTECTION

A *Trademark Protection for Creative Works: Eternal Renewal for Mickey Mouse?*

This chapter focuses primarily on overlapping protection of visual characters. Visual characters are subject matter for which trademark and copyright protection is most commonly cumulated. Moreover, the two rights are often licensed together.[10] Still, even if the subject matter of protection may merge, the nature of the rights conferred, their duration, and their rationales all diverge. Trademarks symbolize the goodwill of the producer and are largely protected only insofar as copying that sign/symbol is likely to confuse consumers as to the source or approval of the goods or services in connection with which the mark is used.[11] Thus, the object of protection is the producer's goodwill (in theory, as a proxy for consumer source identification), not (again, in theory) the mark per se. Copyright, by contrast, is a right "in gross" allowing its owner to prohibit the copying of the work without regard to source confusion.[12] Copyright protects the work of authorship itself, not the identification of that work with a single, if anonymous, source of origin.[13] Pursuant to the US constitutional grant to Congress of power to secure authors' exclusive rights "for limited times," copyright lasts for a term of years;[14] trademarks are protected as long as they are used and continue to represent a single producer's goodwill. Subject to those prerequisites, registered trademarks may be renewed indefinitely.[15]

This durational disparity prompts the question whether a trademark owner may effectively perpetuate the life of the copyright in a visual character by controlling the use of the trademark in the same image(s). For example, once the copyright in Mickey Mouse – or more accurately, in the motion picture Steamboat Willie, in which Mickey's forebear appears – expires, can Disney successfully invoke its trademark rights in various depictions of "The Mouse" to prevent third parties from exploiting the now public domain Steamboat Willie (including its depiction of Mickey's forebear)?[16]

[10] *See, e.g.*, Mende & Isaac, *supra* note 7, 158. *See also DC Comics* v. *Towle*, 802 F.3d 1012 (9th Cir. 2015), *cert. denied*, 136 S. Ct. 1390 (2016) (holding the "Batmobile" both a copyrightable character and a protected trademark).

[11] Lanham Act, 15 USC § 1114; § 1125(a) (2013). Famous marks also enjoy dilution protection under § 1125(c), which affords relief for blurring or tarnishing the distinctive character of the famous mark, even in the absence of confusion.

[12] *See* Copyright Act, 17 USC § 501 (2013) (listing the elements of an infringement claim).

[13] Aside from the narrow category of Works of Visual Art, the US Copyright Act imposes no obligation to credit the author as the creator of the work.

[14] US Constitution, art. I, § 8, cl. 8.

[15] Lanham Act, 15 USC § 1059(a) (2018). The statute imposes no limit as to the number of times the registrant may renew.

[16] *See generally* Joseph P. Liu, *The New Public Domain*, U. Ill. L. Rev. 1395, 1427–40 (2013).

Posed in these terms, this question could suggest a pernicious outcome, which has been criticized by several in the academy.[17] The Supreme Court itself expressed concerns over this outcome in *Dastar* v. *Twentieth-Century Fox* in 2003.[18] There, the Court ultimately rejected the attempt by the producer of a copyright-expired motion picture to effectively end-run the work's public domain status by seeking injunctive relief under trademark law to prevent "reverse passing off." Yet the Court did not state that the former owner of a copyright-expired original work of authorship cannot claim the work as a trademark to designate the source or sponsorship of its goods or services. Nor does *Dastar* prevent or forbid third parties from appropriating copyright-expired characters or other works as trademarks. Quite the opposite. After *Dastar*, an expired or still protected copyrighted work can be protected as a trademark as long as it can function as an indication of commercial origin of the products at issue.

A pre-*Dastar* decision, the 1979 *Frederick Warne & Co.* v. *Book Sales, Inc.*, a case involving a famous visual character, illustrates the point. In *Warne*, the court made it clear that the public domain status of the character of Peter Rabbit "should not preclude protection under the trademark laws so long as it is shown to have acquired independent trademark significance, identifying in some way the source or sponsorship of the goods,"[19] in that case, as a symbol for Frederick Warne publications. Warne's use of the Sitting Rabbit on book covers and as a colophon on pages of stories that did not feature that particular image of the Sitting Rabbit exploited the image in ways distinct from that image's role in the story from which Warne extracted it. Thus, the use signaled that this incarnation of the character was source identifying rather than narrative. The court cautioned, however, that the first publisher could not bootstrap all Peter Rabbit images to the single image used in the colophon and book covers.

If *Warne* implies that trademark rights might attach to a particular iteration of the character, leaving other visual representations in the public domain, might a trademark owner, consistent with *Dastar*, nonetheless claim trademark rights not just in one representation of the character but also in all iterations of that character? For example, if, through Disney's efforts to build brand identification in Steamboat Willie, by registering the character as a logo, and by disseminating a short video depicting Steamboat Willie morphing into Mickey Mouse, Steamboat Willie were to become a brand in its own right, could Disney successfully claim that its unlicensed appearance would confuse the public as to the source of the copies or transmissions of the work containing any incarnation of the character? But in that event, the trademark claim would clash with the public domain principle of copyright, and *Dastar* establishes that the latter prevails.[20] The public domain makes the character free for competition. Assuming the character has also served as a trademark, trademark law should enable the former copyright owner to ensure that free competition is fair competition. But remedies short of full injunctions may achieve "fairness." A court should decline to grant the trademark owner any relief other than the clear labelling of disclaimers as to the source of the competing goods.[21]

[17] *See, e.g.*, Irene Calboli, *Overlapping Rights: The Negative Effects of Trademarking Creative Works*, *in* THE EVOLUTION AND EQUILIBRIUM OF COPYRIGHT IN THE DIGITAL AGE 52 (Susy Frankel & Daniel Gervais eds., 2014); Viva R. Moffat, *Mutant Copyrights and Backdoor Patents: The Problem of Overlapping Intellectual Property Protection*, 19 BERKELEY TECH. L.J. 1473 (2004); ESTELLE DERCLAYE & MATTHIAS LEISTNER, INTELLECTUAL PROPERTY OVERLAPS: A EUROPEAN PERSPECTIVE 12–15, 47–60, 130–38, 200–05, 237–54, 290–92, 295–303, 306–33, and authorities cited therein (2011) (surveying copyright/trademark overlaps in the EU and member states).

[18] *Dastar Corp.*, 539 US 23.

[19] *Frederick Warne & Co.*, 481 F. Supp. at 1196.

[20] *Dastar Corp*, 539 US at 23.

[21] *See* Liu, *supra* note 16, at 1433 ("[A]t most the appropriate remedy would be a disclaimer, which would address the confusion without limiting the ability of a third party to use the underlying work").

However, this solution may not be so straightforward. Creative industries routinely turn to trademark rights as a complement to copyright, particularly for characters, titles, songs, and video clips. Moreover, even though the current Trademark Manual of Examining Procedures (TMEP) provides for the refusal to register a mark consisting of "the title, or a portion of a title, of a single creative work," this exclusion does not apply to titles, which have "been used on a series of creative works."[22] The TMEP imposes a higher burden for applicants seeking to register series titles as marks.[23] Still, a search in the trademark registries will reveal several marks consisting of series titles and/or visual characters that are, or were, protected under copyright.[24] Rightsholders thus seek, and will certainly continue to seek, the option to sue for both copyright and trademark infringement, or simply for the latter, even though the likelihood of success of such claims may vary.

B Copyright Protection for Distinctive Signs: Protection for Strawberry Shortcake and M&Ms as Creative Works?

Trademark and copyright protection may also converge by transforming a trademark into a copyrightable work. This commonly involves the adaptation of trademarks into the object of copyright protection through endowing trademark-protected images not only with brand significance, but also with personalities and other attributes that convert the source identifier into a literary, artistic, or audiovisual character. This strategy is the logical endpoint of the recognition since at least the late 1970s, that a trademark may be a thing of value independently of any particular goods or services with which it is associated.[25]

[22] *See* TMEP § 1202.08 (8th ed. Oct. 2018). This guideline directly addresses concerns about the copyright/trademark protection overlap: "[T]here is a compelling reason why the name or title of a book cannot be a trademark, which stems from copyright law. Unlike a copyright that has a limited term, a trademark can endure for as long as the trademark is used. Therefore, once copyright protection ends, and the work falls in the public domain, others must have the right to call the work by its name." *Id.* (*citing G. & C. Merriam Co.* v. *Syndicate Publ'g Co.*, 237 US 618, 622 (1915); *In re Cooper*, 254 F.2d at 616, 117 USPQ at 400; *Mattel Inc.* v. *Brainy Baby Co.*, 101 USPQ2d 1140, 1144 (TTAB 2011)). TMEP § 1202.08(a) and TMEP § 1202.08(b) address respectively "what constitutes" and "what does not constitute a single creative work" for the purpose of granting or refusing a trademark registration. TMEP § 1202.08(c) elaborates on what represents a "complete title of the work – evidence of a series."

[23] TMEP § 1202.08(d)(iii) ("[w]hen a mark is used merely as a *portion of the title* of a creative work, the applicant has a heavier burden in establishing that the portion for which registration is sought serves as a trademark for the goods"). According TMEP § 1202.08(d)(i) ("the mark must be used as a separate element on the specimen").

[24] *See, e.g.*, THE LORD OF THE RINGS (multiple registrations for standard character mark for a large number of goods and services); THE HOBBIT (multiple registrations for standard character mark for a large number of goods and services); HARRY POTTER (multiple registrations for standard character mark for a large number of goods and services); MICKEY MOUSE (design mark of the Mickey Mouse cartoon character), Registration No. 3598848; BATMAN (design mark of the Batman cartoon character), Registration No. 4871024; RONALD MCDONALD (design mark of the Ronald McDonald character), Registration No. 0874861; CINDERELLA (design mark of the Cinderella character), Registration No. 4874957; SNOW WHITE (design mark of the Snow White character), Registration No. 4552049; MINNE MOUSE (design mark of the Minnie Mouse character), Registration No. 3915194; DONALD DUCK (design mark of the Donald Duck cartoon character), Registration No. 1119631; PRINCESS JASMINE (design mark of the Princess Jasmine character), Registration No. 4412568; ANGRY BIRDS (design mark of the Angry Bird video game character), Serial No. 88215889; HELLO KITTY (design mark of the Hello Kitty character), Registration No. 1370105.

[25] *See, e.g.*, *Boston Prof'l. Hockey Ass'n* v. *Dallas Cap & Emblem Mfg.*, 510 F.2d 1004 (5th Cir. 1975) (acknowledging that protecting the trademark in itself – on patches to be sewn on clothing – is a shift, "[a]lthough our decision here may slightly tilt the trademark laws from the purpose of protecting the public to the protection of the business interests of plaintiffs, we think that the two become so intermeshed when viewed against the backdrop of the common law of unfair competition that both the public and plaintiffs are better served by granting the relief sought by plaintiffs"); *Panavision Int'l* v. *Toeppen*, 141 F.3d 1316 (9th Cir. 1998) ("Toeppen made a commercial use of Panavision's trademarks. It does not matter that he did not attach the marks to a product. Toeppen's commercial use was his

For example, producers of breakfast cereals and fast food chains in the United States have long exploited characters in a combination of roles – branding consumer goods or retail services as well as featuring in associated commercials, toys, and even television shows. Characters such as Strawberry Shortcake were created to serve as both trademarks and copyrighted works. More recent iterations of trademarks-as-characters differ from their predecessors in that these trademarks were not born as characters, but later received specific anthropomorphizing touches that turned uncopyrightable basic shapes into pictorial works. Consider a red circle – the well-known logo of Target, a famous chain of stores in the United States. The Supreme Court has recognized that secondary meaning can give rise to trademark protection for such a sign.[26] On the other hand, whether as an identifying indicium for shoe heels, or as the red disk of the 7-UP dot, the sign is too rudimentary to survive even a cursory examination for originality by the US Copyright Office. But accessorize the dot with arms and legs and coif it with a pair of sunglasses, and a banal form blossoms into the "Cool Spot" character.[27] Or take the rudimentary, single-colored shapes of M&Ms candies, endow them with arms and legs and a range of highly expressive (if rather gender-stereotyped) facial features, and they become "spokescandies" with prepackaged personalities and backstories.[28] Given this new life, several trademarks-as-characters have starred not only in advertising for the trademarked goods, but also in independent works such as videogames and even feature films (for example, the Lego Movie and its sequels).[29]

Yet this type of overlapping protection does not appear to pose the policy concerns articulated above regarding claims of trademark rights in works of authorship, probably because the flipside of the copyright/trademark coin does not risk compromising the public domain. In particular, the practice of converting trademarks into copyrightable works effectively protects the mark against copying that may not be source-confusing. Likewise, protection in gross for trademarks-as-characters does not raise policy concerns so long as the mark manifests sufficient authorship to qualify as a "work."[30] As mentioned in the Introduction, the influence of copyright protection over trademarks can lead to a new balancing of these rights by importing the limitations applicable in one domain to the other.

Certainly, there are several benefits to a rightholder arising from this practice. First, there is little if any downside to recasting a trademark as a copyrightable work of authorship. Copyright does not diminish the protection the characters would enjoy as a matter of trademark law. In particular, because copyright is a right in gross, it strengthens the coverage available even to trademarks that are sufficiently famous to qualify for protection against dilution. Copyright is infringed by copying; trademark infringement requires a showing that the copying causes a likelihood of confusion or (for dilution) of association that is likely to "blur" or "tarnish" a famous mark.[31] Even if it is true that US trademark law has increasingly protected brand symbols in their own right, independent of the goods or services in connection with which they initially appeared, copyright protection directly protects the work per se without the need to prove established goodwill.

attempt to sell the trademarks themselves"). For an overview of the practice of trademark merchandising, *see* Irene Calboli, *The Case for a Limited Protection of Trademark Merchandising*, 2011 U. ILL. L. REV. 865 (2011).

[26] *Mishawaka Rubber & Woolen Mfg.* v. *S. S. Kresge Co.*, 316 US 203 (1942).

[27] *7Up*, DR PEPPER SNAPPLE GROUP, https://drpeppersnapplegroup.com/brands/7up.

[28] *See generally Characters*, M&Ms, http://mms.com/en-us/experience-mms/characters (presenting the characters).

[29] *See* The Lego Movie, http://thelegomovie.net/ (presenting the various Lego movies and the characters).

[30] Some concerns in this respect have been expressed in the context of parallel imports and the application of the principle of copyright exhaustion to consumer goods. *See infra* Section II.C.

[31] Lanham Act,15 USC §§ 1114, 1125(a), 1125(c) (2012).

The US copyrights will expire ninety-five years from the first publication of the trademarks-as-works, if they are works made for hire, or seventy years after the death of their authors for other work. But during that very long stretch, the trademark owner of a work for hire will have ample time to update the work and start another copyright clock rolling.[32] The copyright lives of visual works in particular may last far longer than the copyright term of a work's initial incarnation. Many characters evolve over time, and later manifestations may depart sufficiently from the original version to qualify as copyright-protected derivative works. Take, for instance, the character of the Michelin Man, "Bibendum." First appearing in Michelin advertisements in the late nineteenth century, it has evolved from a bon vivant blob, into a still-robust but more sportif assemblage of thicker forms showing greater differentiation in torso, limbs, and especially facial characteristics. Both copyright and trademark law will protect the character in its revised instantiations.[33]

Finally, copyright offers significant remedial advantages over trademarks in the United States. The principal remedy for trademark infringement is injunctive relief.[34] Damages require a showing of actual confusion; a trademark owner would be disinclined to wait to seek relief until consumers can be shown to have been confused in fact.[35] By contrast, in copyright law, damages are a traditional remedy, and the prospect of an award of statutory damages of up to $150,000 per work willfully infringed can provide significant monetary relief.[36]

C Overlapping Rights and Parallel Imports: The Attempt to Use Copyright and Trademark Protection to Control Cross-Border Trade

IP owners in the United States have also turned to overlapping rights in an attempt to prevent parallel imports – the importation of genuine goods into the United States from foreign countries by unauthorized third parties. This has been motivated by the differences regarding the domestic rules on trademark and copyright exhaustion. These differences have changed over the years and so has the exploitation of trademark and/or copyright protection in the context of cross-border trade.[37]

In particular, the United States generally allows parallel imports of genuine goods carrying a trademark protected in the United States so long as both the foreign and US trademarks are "subjected to common ownership and control,"[38] and consumers are not confused about the origin or quality of the imported products.[39] US courts have held sections 32 and 43(a) of the Lanham Act cannot be invoked to block importation of goods manufactured by a corporate

[32] Copyright Act, 17 USC §§ 302, 304 (2019) (duration of copyright, including for works made for hire). Copyright in a derivative work extends only to the new matter, and does not affect the duration of the underlying material, § 103(b). In theory, therefore, the character as it originally appeared becomes free for unlicensed exploitation once the original copyright expires. But the original character may lack commercial value relative to its updates. So even if only the new matter added through the updates may claim copyright, the practical inextricability of the old and new content may enable copyright owners to prolong protection for the character.

[33] In the United States, Michelin may register revised Bibendums with the Patent and Trademark Office, but may also claim protection under § 43(a) of the Lanham Act for unregistered versions.

[34] Lanham Act, 15 USC § 1116 (2008); McCARTHY, *supra* note 6, § 30:1 ("A permanent injunction is the usual and normal remedy once trademark infringement has been found in a final judgment").

[35] Lanham Act, 15 USC § 1117(a) (2008) (relief for "any damages sustained" indicates that the trademark owner would in fact have had to have lost sales).

[36] Copyright Act, 17 USC § 504(b)(c) (2012). A court may award statutory damages if the work was registered with the Copyright Office before the infringement occurred, *id.* § 412.

[37] For a detailed review of overlapping rights in this context, see SHUBHA GHOSH & IRENE CALBOLI, EXHAUSTING INTELLECTUAL PROPERTY RIGHTS: A COMPARATIVE LAW AND POLICY ANALYSIS 137 (2018).

[38] *K-Mart Corp.* v. *Cartier, Inc.*, 486 US 281, 289 (1988).

[39] GHOSH & CALBOLI, *supra* note 37, at 68.

affiliate of a US trademark owner.[40] Parallel imports can be blocked only when the imported goods "differ materially" from the goods authorized for sale in the United States (referred to as the "*Lever* Rule") to prevent the quality-related confusion that could otherwise exist if two seemingly identical products of different quality are sold in the United States under the same mark.[41] As an exception to this rule under the US Customs Service Regulations,[42] parallel importers are still able to import materially different goods by affixing a disclaimer clarifying that the products are "physically and materially different" from those distributed in the United States by the trademark owners,[43] even though these disclaimers may make products more difficult to sell and do not necessarily shield domestic resellers from the liability for trademark infringement under the likelihood of confusion test.

On the other hand, for several years, US copyright law offered a convenient alternative against parallel imports. Section 109(a) of the US Copyright Act states that the owners of copyrighted works "lawfully made under this title" are entitled to be further distributed "without the authority of the copyright owner."[44] Yet section 602(a)(1) provides that the "[i]mportation into the United States" of a copyrighted work acquired outside the United States "without the authority of the [copyright] owner" is "an infringement of the exclusive right [of] distribut[ion]."[45] Reading the two provisions together, several courts concluded that section 602(a)(1) of the Act barred parallel imports.[46] Accordingly, IP owners started to claim copyright protection in the context of cross-border trade. Since consumer products usually do not qualify for copyright protection because they are frequently useful/functional products or do not meet the necessary level of originality required for copyright protection, IP owners claimed protection for non-useful decorative features (packaging, labels, tags, instructions, owner's manuals, etc.) of the products that could pass the test for copyright protection. In some cases, IP owners even registered these incidental product features with the US Copyright Office.[47]

[40] *NEC Elecs.* v. *CAL Cir. Abco*, 810 F.2d 1506, 1510 (9th Cir. 1987). Note that § 43(b) of the Lanham Act allows civil actions to enjoin importation of any goods likely to infringe or dilute registered or unregistered trademarks. *See* Lanham Act, 15 USC § 1125(b). Moreover, § 42 authorizes US Customs and Border Protection (CPB) to prevent the importation of goods that infringe registered or unregistered trademarks (15 USC § 1124).

[41] This principle follows two decisions of the DC Circuit: *Lever Bros. Co.* v. *United States*, 877 F.2d 101 (DC Cir. 1989) and *Lever Bros. Co.* v. *United States*, 981 F.2d 1330 (DC Cir. 1993).

[42] Customs Service Regulations,19 CFR § 133.23(b) (US) ("Goods determined by the Customs Service to be physically and materially different . . . shall not be detained . . . where the merchandise or its packaging bears a conspicuous and legible label designed to remain on the product until the first point of sale").

[43] *Id.* (stating that the disclaimer must be "designed to remain on the product until the first point of sale to a retail customer in the United States").

[44] Copyright Act, 17 USC § 109(a). Copyright exhaustion was created as judicial doctrine in *Bobbs-Merrill Co.* v. *Straus*, 210 US 339 (1908). In 1909, the principle was codified in the Copyright Act of 1909, Pub. L. No. 60-349, 35 Stat. 1075. *See Quality King Distribs., Inc.* v. *L'anza Research Int'l*, 523 US 135, 141–42 (1998) ("Congress subsequently codified our holding in *Bobbs-Merrill* that the exclusive right to 'vend' was limited to first sales of the work").

[45] Copyright Act, 17 USC § 602(a)(1).

[46] *See Denbicare USA Inc.* v. *Toys "R" Us, Inc.*, 84 F.3d 1143 (9th Cir. 1996); *Parfums Givenchy, Inc.* v. *Drug Emporium, Inc.*, 38 F.3d 477 (9th Cir. 1994); *BMG Music* v. *Perez*, 952 F.2d 318 (9th Cir. 1991). *Cf. Sebastian Int'l* v. *Consumer Contacts (PTY) Ltd.*, 847 F.2d 1093 (3rd Cir. 1988) (finding that parallel imports could be admitted into the US market).

[47] In one instance, this practice was found to be copyright misuse. *See Omega SA* v. *Costco Wholesale Corp.*, No. 04-05443 at 2 (CD Cal. 2011). For a comparative perspective, the claim that parallel imports of consumer goods could represent copyright infringement (in the presence of a domestic rule of national copyright exhaustion versus a rule of international trademark exhaustion) raised concerns in Australia and Canada. *See R. A. & A. Bailey & Co. Ltd.* v. *Boccaccio Pty. Ltd.* (1986) 6 IPR 279 (Austl.); *Polo/Lauren Co. LP* v. *Ziliani Holdings Pty. Ltd.* [2008] FCAFC 195 § 5 (Austl.); *Euro-Excellence Inc.* v. *Kraft Canada Inc.*, [2007] 3 SCR 20, (Can.). In Australia, this led to a revision of the Copyright Act. *See* Copyright Amendment Act (No. 1) 1998 (Cth.) (Austrl.) (amending § 10(1) and adding § 44C stating that "[t]he copyright in a work a copy of which is, or is on, or embodied in, a non-infringing accessory to an

Two out of the three cases decided by the Supreme Court on the relationship between sections 109(a) and 602(1)(a) of the US Copyright Act regarded precisely claims for copyright infringement in the context of parallel imports of commercial products with copyrighted incidental product features. In particular, *Quality King Distributors, Inc.* v. *L'anza Research International, Inc.*[48] was a case about the reimportation of shampoo bottles carrying copyrighted labels. Here, the Court found the copyright in the labels affixed to the products had been exhausted, even if the products had been imported from overseas, but only because the products had been made domestically before having been exported and later reimported into the United States.[49] Similarly, *Costco Wholesale Corporation* v. *Omega, SA*[50] was a case about Swiss-made watches carrying a small copyrighted insignia and imported into the United States without Omega's consent. In this case, an equally divided court (due to the recusal of Justice Kagan) affirmed the decision on appeal and ruled against the importers.[51]

Eventually, the Court clarified the geographical extent of copyright exhaustion in the United States in *Kirtsaeng* v. *John Wiley & Sons, Inc.* – a case about books imported from Thailand without the authorization of the publisher. Here, the Court ruled that the exhaustion principle in section 109(a) applies equally to products "lawfully made" in the United States and abroad.[52] As a result, IP owners can no longer invoke copyright law to prevent the unauthorized importation and domestic sale of "lawfully made" foreign copies of their works (including commercial products with copyrighted incidental product features). After this decision, IP owners thus went back to consider their option to block parallel imports under trademark law, notably under the *Lever* Rule that permits blocking parallel imports of materially different quality. The possibility to turn to trademark law in this context remains available even after the decision in *Dastar* discussed above.[53] *Dastar* concerned a claim of reverse passing off; trademark law claims against parallel imports invoke traditional passing off or trademark infringement.

As copyright protection can extend to incidental and ornamental features of commercial products, many copyrighted works – such as books, songs, movies, videogames, and software – carry one or more signs protected under trademark law. For example, books always carry the marks of the publishers often represented by the publishers' name, a logo, and frequently a specific color or color scheme, and design. As trademark protection extends today to non-traditional trademarks, including colors and shapes, these additional aspects of copyrighted works may also be protected under trademark law.[54] The same can be said for movies, videogames, and a variety of other works. Accordingly, the owners of these works may be able to seek all the traditional trademark remedies, including seizure of goods by agents of US Customs and Border Protection (CBP), to prevent the importation and/or domestic sale of copies that are completely lawful under copyright law.

article is not infringed by importing the accessory with the article"). *See, e.g.*, Ghosh & Calboli, *supra* note 37, at 148–52.

48 *Quality King*, 523 US at 135.

49 *Id.*, at 139.

50 *Costco Wholesale Corp.* v. *Omega SA*, 131 S. Ct. 565 (2010).

51 *Omega SA* v. *Costco Wholesale Corp.*, 541 F.3d 982 (9th Cir. 2008).

52 *Kirtsaeng* v. *John Wiley & Sons, Inc.*, 133 S. Ct. 1351, 1358 (2013) (supporting that § 109(a) also applies "where, as here, copies are manufactured abroad with the permission of the copyright owner").

53 *Dastar Corp.*, 539 US at 23.

54 For a case on point in Germany, *see* Bundesgerichtshof [BGH] [Federal Court of Justice], Sept. 18, 2014, Gewerblicher Rechtsschutz und Urheberrecht [GRUR] 581, 2015 (finding that the registration for color yellow for bilingual dictionaries in printed form could prevent Rosetta Stone's use of a similar color – yellow – for software products containing language teaching programs).

In particular, IP owners can bring a claim for trademark infringement against importers and/or resellers of parallel imports of materially different quality from the goods authorized for the United States.[55] Accordingly, courts have found material differences based on a low threshold and a variety of factors including differences in quality control, marketing methods, or differences (including very minimal) in product quality.[56] If applied to books, for example, a small difference in pagination or printing quality might be a material difference. After the decision in *Kirstsaeng*, John Wiley & Sons (the unsuccessful plaintiff) applied for *Lever* Rule protection against unauthorized importation of its textbook titles bearing the trademarks WILEY and JW & DESIGN,[57] on the ground that the imported books were materially different from those authorized for the US market.[58] The request was granted, even though the textbooks did carry a disclaimer, because it did not follow the requirements for disclaimers under the US Customs Regulations.[59]

More generally, however, parallel imports carrying a *Lever* disclaimer may be found acceptable for importation and would be unlikely to be stopped at the border under the Customs Service Regulations. These products may nonetheless infringe trademarks if IP owners successfully prove that consumers could be confused as to the products' origin and quality. Even though the finding of infringement remains based on a case-by-case analysis by the courts, scholars have noted that courts have become skeptical about the validity of disclaimers and have often found a likelihood of confusion regardless of disclaimers, including in the context of parallel imports.[60] In particular, the *Lever* disclaimer must simply state: "this product is not a product authorized by the United States trademark owner for importation and is physically and materially different from the authorized product."[61] Ultimately, as noted by scholars and several courts, this may not dispel consumer confusion as to what the differences are in practice, which could in turn lead to confusion under the test for a finding of trademark infringement.[62]

III WHEN OVERLAPPING RIGHTS MIGHT LEAD TO LESS PROTECTION (AND POSSIBLY MORE HUMOR)

In the previous section, we have seen how rightsowners may in different ways endeavor to strengthen their rights by supplementing one legal regime – trademark or copyright protection – with the other when the subject matter overlaps, or by claiming different protection for different aspects of the same product/work. But the reciprocal relationship of trademark and copyright may also import some of copyright's limiting doctrines into trademark law. We offer two examples of this phenomenon: first, the influence of copyright principles of fair use and free expression on expressive uses of trademarks; second, the recasting of trademark principles of

[55] *See, e.g.*, Mary LaFrance, *Using Trademark Law to Override Copyright's First Sale Rule for Imported Goods in the United States*, in RESEARCH HANDBOOK ON INTELLECTUAL PROPERTY EXHAUSTION AND PARALLEL IMPORTS 390 (Irene Calboli & Edward Lee eds., 2017).

[56] *Societe des Produits Nestle*, 982 F.2d at 641; *accord*, *Zino Davidoff SA* v. *CVS Corp.*, 571 F.3d 238, 243–46 (2d Cir. 2009) ("In the context of gray-market goods, . . . we apply a low threshold of materiality, requiring no more than a slight difference which consumers would likely deem relevant when considering a purchase of the product").

[57] JW & DESIGN, Registration No. 1,639,555 (Customs Recordation Number: TMK 06-01378); WILEY, Registration No. 1,003,988 (Customs Recordation No. TMK 06-01435).

[58] *General Notices*, 48 CUST. B. AND DEC., No. 7 (Feb. 19, 2014) (the differences in the products included "product construction, design, quality, appearance, market pricing, and labeling").

[59] *See id.* (noting that the books could still be imported if they satisfied the *Lever* labeling requirements).

[60] For comprehensive overview of the case law in this respect, *see* LaFrance, *supra* note 55, at 397.

[61] Customs Service Regulations, 19 CFR § 133.23(b) (2014).

[62] *See* LaFrance, *supra* note 55, at 396–99.

secondary liability in light of amendments to the copyright act to immunize online service providers from direct or secondary liability for hosting infringing content.

A *Limitations on Trademark Protection Based in Freedom of Expression*

Since the late 1980s, when works of authorship are alleged to infringe trademarks, courts in the United States have progressively imposed a free expression thumb on the scale of likelihood of confusion analysis.[63] These decisions did not always expressly cite the copyright fair use defense, but the considerations underlying the copyright doctrine ultimately informed the trademark analysis elaborated by the courts. The spillover effect of copyright doctrine into the determination of trademark infringement may indeed have been inevitable, as several of the cases in which a copyright fair use defense prevailed involved copyright/trademark overlapping subject matter, and accordingly coupled copyright and trademark claims. Thus, it is not surprising that once a court has found the use to be "transformative" and to promote speech and/or learning, and thus most often to be "fair" in the copyright sense, that court is unlikely to find the same activity to violate the copyright holder's trademark in the copied work.

In particular, even though copyright is a property "right in gross," while trademark is not (or is not supposed to be), the trademark and copyright fair use limitations have this in common: the users of the mark or of another author's work are engaged in independent economic or creative activity. They are not simply redistributing another's work of authorship or appending another's mark to the same or confusingly similar goods. Rather, at least for traditional copyright fair use, they are making a new work, or, on the trademark side, proclaiming their own goods or communicative activities. By the same token, the uses do not unfairly usurp the copyright or trademark owner's markets. A devastating review may dampen desire for the critiqued work, but that kind of harm is not cognizable in copyright. Similarly, a comparative advertisement may persuade consumers of the superior merits of the competitor's goods or services, but if the advertisement is truthful no Lanham Act claim lies.

Lawful unauthorized uses of trademarks enjoy a long pedigree. In 1924, in a case concerning the labelling of lawfully purchased and rebottled perfume, Justice Holmes famously declared: "When the mark is used in a way that does not deceive the public we see no such sanctity in the word as to prevent its being used to tell the truth. It is not taboo."[64] The Lanham Act codified part of this precept by permitting the use of descriptive terms in a registered trademark for the purpose of description, and not as a trademark.[65] For example, if TRULY BEAUTIFUL is a trademark for a fragrance, the registrant cannot prohibit a competitor from informing the public that its fragrance, call it FRANKLY GORGEOUS, will make the wearer "feel truly beautiful."[66] But the Lanham Act does not explicitly exempt a competitor's use of TRULY BEAUTIFUL to describe the competitor's product, for example, to proclaim that FRANKLY GORGEOUS will make the wearer more alluring than TRULY BEAUTIFUL. Nor does the Lanham Act explicitly allow a non-competitor, such as the (fictitious) magazine *Glamorous* to elicit its readers' perfume preferences by asking them whether TRULY BEAUTIFUL is their most or least favorite

[63] *See, e.g., Rogers* v. *Grimaldi*, 875 F.2d 994 (2d Cir. 1989).

[64] *Prestonettes, Inc.* v. *Coty*, 264 US 359, 368 (1924) (citing *Delaware & Hudson Canal Co.* v. *Clark*, 80 US 311, 327 (1871)).

[65] Lanham Act, 15 USC § 1115(b)(4) (2002).

[66] *See, e.g., United States Shoe Corp.* v. *Brown Grp.*, 740 F. Supp. 196 (SDNY 1990) (plaintiff's slogan "looks like a pump, feels like a sneaker" not infringed by advertising text stating that "when we say it feels like a sneaker, we're not just stringing you along").

fragrance. Former Ninth Circuit Judge Kozinski dubbed these latter denominations "nominative fair use," and the name has remained.[67] The nominative fair use defense to trademark infringement proceeds through an analysis of factors. As we will see, these factors complement and echo the first, third, and fourth copyright fair use factors.[68]

Nonetheless, a notable early case finding nominative fair use in trademark law (decided again by the Ninth Circuit with an opinion by Judge Kozinski) did not allege copyright infringement, though it did concern a parody. There, the song *Barbie Girl* by the Danish one-hit group Aqua in 1997 foisted on the airwaves lyrics like the following catchy refrain: "I'm a Barbie girl, in a Barbie world. Life in plastic, it's fantastic. You can brush my hair, undress me everywhere. Imagination, life is your creation ... I'm a blonde bimbo girl, in a fantasy world. Dress me up, make it tight, I'm your dolly." To which the bass in the group would interject in a froggish croak (Aqua's album was, after all, called *Aquarium*): "C'mon Barbie, let's go party!"[69]

Holding that "the trademark owner does not have the right to control public discourse whenever the public imbues his mark with a meaning beyond its source-identifying function," the Ninth Circuit rejected Mattel's claim of likelihood of confusion.[70] The court balanced the "public interest in free expression" against the "public interest in avoiding consumer confusion," and accorded the former decisive weight unless the song title's appropriation of Barbie "has no artistic relevance to the underlying work whatsoever, or, if it has some artistic relevance, unless the title explicitly misleads as to the source or the content of the work."[71] Observing that the Barbie doll was the target of the song, the court held the group was entitled to identify the butt of its joke, and had done nothing to mislead the public into thinking that Mattel authorized the song. (Ironically, Mattel subsequently licensed "Barbie Girl" for advertising Barbie dolls.[72]) In its analysis, the Ninth Circuit followed the precedent of the Second Circuit in 1989 *Rogers* v. *Grimaldi*,[73] where the court found a mark's use in an artistic context is not infringement unless it "has no artistic relevance to the underlying work whatsoever" or unless it "explicitly misleads as to the source or content of the work."[74]

Just a few months after the first Barbie case, a second Barbie case followed. This time, Mattel sought to enjoin the dissemination of the "Food Chain Barbie" series of photographs which depicted the scantily clad dolls victimized by a variety of kitchen appliances. In *Mattel, Inc.* v. *Walking Mountain Products*,[75] the claims implicated both copyright (the reproduction

[67] *See New Kids on the Block* v. *News Am. Publ'g*, 971 F.2d 302 (9th Cir. 1992); *Playboy Enter, Inc.* v. *Welles*, 279 F.3d 796 (9th Cir. 2002); *Century 21 Real Estate Corp.* v. *Lendingtree, Inc.*, 425 F.3d 211 (3d Cir. 2005) (following Ninth Circuit in adopting the doctrine but applying a different test and assigning a different conceptual role to the nominative use doctrine in trademark law); *Toyota Motor Sales, USA, Inc.* v. *Tabari*, 610 F.3d 1171 (9th Cir. 2009) (distinguishing from *New Kids on the Block* by holding that a defendant asserting a nominative fair use defense need only show that it used the mark to refer to the trademarked good, at which point the burden then reverts to the plaintiff to show a likelihood of confusion). Other circuits reach the same result through similar reasoning, albeit without applying the label "nominative fair use." *See, e.g.*, *Universal Commun. Sys.* v. *Lycos, Inc.*, 478 F.3d 413, 424–25 (1st Cir. 2007); *Swarovski Aktiengesellschaft* v. *Bldg. No. 19, Inc.*, 704 F.3d 44 (1st Cir. 2013) (refraining from endorsing any particular approach to the nominative fair use doctrine). *See generally* McCarthy, *supra* note 6, § 23:11.

[68] *See Int'l Info. Sys. Sec. Cert. Consortium, Inc.* v. *Sec. Univ. LLC*, 823 F.3d 153 (2nd Cir. 2016); *GlaxoSmithKline LLC* v. *Laclede, Inc.*, 2019 WL 293329 (SDNY, Jan. 23, 2019).

[69] Aqua, *Barbie Girl* (1997), YouTube, https://youtube.com/watch?v=ZyhrYis509A.

[70] *Mattel, Inc.* v. *Universal Music Int'l*, 296 F.3d 894, 900 (9th Cir. 2002).

[71] *Id.* at 902 (*citing Rogers* v. *Grimaldi*, 875 F.2d 994, 999 (2d Cir. 1989)).

[72] *See* Stuart Elliott, *Years Later Mattel Embraces "Barbie Girl,"* New York Times, Aug. 26, 2009, 4:30 pm, https://mediadecoder.blogs.nytimes.com/2009/08/26/years-later-mattel-embraces-barbie-girl/.

[73] *Rogers*, 875 F.2d at 994.

[74] *Id.* at 999.

[75] *Mattel, Inc.* v. *Walking Mountain Prods.*, 353 F.3d 792 (9th Cir. 2003).

right in the image of the dolls) and trademarks (use of the Barbie name in the titles of the photographs). In granting summary judgment on the copyright claim, the court (again the Ninth Circuit) ruled on the first fair use factor that the Food Chain series "parod[ies] Barbie and everything Mattel's doll has come to signify." Undoubtedly, the court continued, "one could make similar statements through other means about society, gender roles, sexuality, and perhaps even social class. But Barbie, and all the associations she has acquired through Mattel's impressive marketing success, conveys these messages in a particular way that is ripe for social comment."[76] On the third factor, the court stressed parodies need not restrict themselves "to take the absolute minimum amount of the copyrighted work possible," and thus that, in context, reproducing the entire doll did not undermine the fair use defense.[77] On the fourth factor, the court found it unlikely that Mattel would enter the market for "adult-oriented artistic photographs of Barbie."[78]

The Ninth Circuit approvingly cited another Barbie copyright parody decision, *Mattel, Inc. v. Pitt*, in which the defendant's "dungeon doll" website offered to customize Barbie dolls in a variety of dominatrix modes.[79] The differently accessorized dolls arguably violated Mattel's exclusive right to create derivative works based on Barbie and the website's photographs allegedly violated the reproduction right. Here, the Southern District of New York considered the statutory fair use factors, and ruled the defendant's use and context of Barbie sufficiently transformative and unlikely to supplant one of Mattel's markets for the work. As the district court quipped, "To the Court's knowledge, there is no Mattel line of S&M Barbie."[80] Having held defendant's use to be "fair" as a matter of copyright law, notably because of the expressive values the parody advanced, the Ninth Circuit in "Food Chain Barbie" effectively sealed the fate of the trademark claim.[81] Regarding Food Chain's incorporation of Barbie in the title of the series, the court relied on its prior decision in the Barbie Girl song case to reject a likelihood of confusion claim.[82]

Finally, the court also rejected Mattel's trade dress claim and stated:

> Forsythe used Mattel's Barbie figure and head in his works to conjure up associations of Mattel, while at the same time to identify his own work, which is a criticism and parody of Barbie. Where use of the trade dress or mark is grounded in the defendant's desire to refer to the plaintiff's product as a point of reference for defendant's own work, a use is nominative.[83]

"Conjure up," notably, is a standard formulation of the minimum extent of copying that the copyright fair use case law permits in a parody.[84] In other words, the court's analysis of the second nominative fair use factor echoed its treatment of the third copyright fair use factor.[85] By the same token, having found as a matter of copyright law that the defendant was not usurping a potential market for "adult photos" that Mattel was likely to enter, the court ruled on the third nominative fair use factor that "it is highly unlikely that any reasonable consumer would have believed that Mattel sponsored or was affiliated with [defendant's] work."[86]

76 *Id.* at 802.
77 *Id.* at 804.
78 *Id.* at 806.
79 *Mattel, Inc. v. Pitt*, 229 F. Supp. 2d 315 (SDNY 2002).
80 *Id.* at 322.
81 *Mattel, Inc. v. Walking Mountain Prods.*, 353 F.3d 792 (9th Cir. 2003).
82 *Id.* at 804.
83 *Id.* at 810.
84 *Id.* at 800 (*citing Dr. Seuss Enters, LP v. Penguin Books USA, Inc.*, 109 F.3d 1394, 1400 (9th Cir. 1997)).
85 *Id.* at 811.
86 *Id.* at 812.

B Copyright Liability for Online Service Providers and Trademark Liability for Contributory Infringement: Spillover Effects

The subject matter convergence between copyright and trademark law is also relevant in the area of contributory infringement, particularly on the Internet. Notably, a platform such as eBay, Amazon, and the like, some of whose third party vendors might offer infringing goods, could face different liability regimes for the same act of hosting if the goods are illicit copies of copyrighted works. For example, if the seller is proposing unlawfully copied items falsely labelled as branded jewelry, different standards of conduct might govern the host's exposure to injunctive or monetary relief for the two different kinds of contributory infringement.[87]

In trademark law, court decisions have traditionally referred to the test the Supreme Court articulated in *Inwood Laboratories* v. *Ives Laboratories* to assess contributory infringement. A "manufacturer or distributor" could be found liable for contributory trademark infringement if "[it] intentionally induces another to infringe a trademark, or if it continues to supply its product to one who he knows or has reason to know is engaging in trademark infringement."[88] But the Court did not further detail the meaning of "know[ing] or ha[ving] reason to know." Thus, due to the uncertainty concerning the substance and proof of actual or constructive knowledge, a few courts have adopted another assessment, in effect looking to whether intermediaries are primarily non-infringing businesses or simply "bad guys."[89] This approach recalls the Supreme Court's decision in *Sony Corp. of America* v. *Universal City Studios, Inc.*,[90] regarding copyright infringement. The court there evaluated contributory infringement in copyright law by inquiring whether the accused technology used was capable of "substantial non-infringing uses."[91]

The Second Circuit in *Tiffany* v. *eBay*[92] explicitly referenced *Sony* in its analysis. eBay runs an internet marketplace, in which third parties sell items directly to internet users, with eBay making a profit from each transaction. eBay operates several buyer protection programs in order to safeguard consumers and the legitimacy of the transactions that take place on its marketplace. It has also established a "Trust and Safety" department and a "fraud engine" to detect illegal listings as well as conducting manual reviews of listings.[93] In addition, eBay offers a "notice and take down" system by which third parties can report instances of potential infringement and eBay will remove the potentially infringing listing within twelve hours of receiving a notice.[94] Tiffany became aware that some eBay users were selling counterfeit Tiffany items and sued eBay for, inter alia, contributory trademark infringement.[95]

[87] The host would not incur this risk in the EU because the 2000 eCommerce Directive (Council Directive 2000/31, 2000 OJ (L 178) 1 (EC)) imposes a transversal liability limitation regime; in the US, these statutory liability limitations exist in the copyright act, but not in the trademark law. The EU Directive on Copyright and Related Rights in the Digital Single Market, establishing copyright liability for "Online Content Sharing Service Providers" (OCSSP), would not change the result in cases like *eBay* because Art. 2(6) of the Directive explicitly excludes online marketplaces from the definition of OCSSPs. *See* Directive (EU) 2019/790 of the European Parliament and of the Council of Apr. 17, 2019 on Copyright and Related Rights in the Digital Single Market and amending Directives 96/9/EC and 2001/29/EC, OJ (L 130) 92 (May 17, 2019).

[88] *Inwood Labs., Inc.* v. *Ives Labs., Inc.*, 456 US 844, 854 (1982).

[89] *See* Stacey L. Dogan, *"We Know It When We See It": Intermediary Trademark Liability and the Internet*, 2011 STAN. TECH. L. REV. 7 (2011) (comparing decisions in the area of secondary trademark infringement with similar cases in copyright law, including *Sony*'s progeny).

[90] *Sony Corp.* v. *Universal City Studios, Inc.*, 464 US 417 (1984).

[91] *Id.* at 442 ("The question is thus whether the Betamax is capable of commercially significant noninfringing uses").

[92] *Tiffany, Inc.* v. *eBay, Inc.*, 600 F.3d 93 (2d Cir. 2010).

[93] *Id.* at 98–99.

[94] *Id.*

[95] *Id.* at 103.

Both the Southern District of New York[96] and the Second Circuit, however, found that eBay was not liable for contributory trademark infringement.[97] In particular, the Second Circuit noted that eBay had removed many listings upon receiving take-down notices and thus it did not "continue to supply" its service to the infringers with respect to those listings.[98] The court also determined that eBay lacked sufficient knowledge to satisfy the test for contributory trademark liability with respect to the listings that it did not remove.[99] Overall, eBay had only "generalized knowledge" that counterfeit items were being sold on its website; this did not satisfy the *Inwood* test, which requires "specific knowledge."[100] The Second Circuit also acknowledged that the Supreme Court in *Inwood* did not "establish the contours of the 'knows or has reason to know' prong." The court thus evoked the Supreme Court's substantial non-infringing use standard from *Sony*,[101] concluding, "had the *Inwood* standard applied in *Sony* . . . [it] would have required knowledge by Sony of 'identified individuals' engaging in infringing conduct."[102] The court also rejected Tiffany's argument that eBay had been willfully blind and emphasized that eBay undertook significant efforts to combat the counterfeiting activities taking place on its website. Indeed, the measures eBay took in response to notices regarding eBay's sellers' infringements closely resembled the "notice and takedown" regime established under section 512(c) of the Copyright Act[103] to immunize compliant online services from direct or contributory copyright infringement.

IV CONCLUSION

In the reciprocal relationship between copyright and trademarks, we have seen how these rights can reinforce as well as limit each other. Ultimately, in an economy and society more visually-oriented than ever before, producers rely on creative and aesthetic features to differentiate their commercial products. Naturally, they seek protection for these features under multiple IP rights. This practice has increased the instances of overlapping copyright and trademark protection. Similarly, since trademark and copyright protections are enforced territorially and countries still diverge in their domestic exhaustion regimes, overlapping rights can also be used strategically by IP owners in the attempt to control international trade and ban parallel imports. Yet, in this chapter we have described how, while on one hand overlapping rights can significantly enhance the protection otherwise available under only one set of rights, on the other hand the limiting doctrines of one right, notably copyright law, can offer additional means to cabin trademark claims.

96 *Tiffany, Inc.* v. *eBay, Inc.*, 576 F. Supp. 2d 463 (SDNY 2008). The district court focused much of its analysis on eBay's efforts to suppress counterfeiting by implementing its VeRO program, fraud engine, and by conducting manual reviews of auction items. *Id.*

97 *Tiffany*, 600 F.3d at 93.

98 *Id.* at 107 ("For contributory trademark infringement liability to lie, a service provider must have more than a general knowledge or reason to know that its service is being used to sell counterfeit goods. Some contemporary knowledge of which particular listings are infringing or will infringe in the future is necessary").

99 *Id.* at 106.

100 *Id.* at 107.

101 *Sony Corp.* v. *Universal City Studios, Inc.*, 464 US 417 (1984).

102 *Tiffany*, 600 F.3d at 108 (discussing *Sony*, 464 US at 439).

103 17 USC § 512(c) (2010).

X

Theories Underlying the Standards for Trademark Infringement

27

Misappropriation-Based Trademark Liability in Comparative Perspective

*Jeremy N. Sheff**

I INTRODUCTION

The anti-misappropriation principle, at its core, is that it is wrongful and therefore actionable for a competitor to gain a commercial advantage from the efforts of another, even if that advantage does not directly harm the person whose efforts have been misappropriated. This principle appears to be a deep theoretical commitment of modern intellectual property law.[1] And nowhere in intellectual property law is the anti-misappropriation impulse more directly implicated than in the context of conspicuous consumption.

As I have written about elsewhere,[2] modern consumers engage in conspicuous consumption of branded goods to signal social affiliation and identity, and to claim their place in the socio-economic hierarchy of late capitalism. But the expressive effect of such consumption may be compromised by indiscriminate copying of the goods that serve as tokens of that expression. Protecting in-groups' tokens of social affiliation and rank against unauthorized appropriation by outsiders is therefore a necessary condition of successful conspicuous consumption. Regulation of access to such socially expressive goods – particularly fashion products – was once the function of elaborate sumptuary codes based on de jure social status.[3] Today however, conspicuously consumed signals of social identity and status are rationed through markets, aided by an unlikely legal regime: trademark law.

I say this is an unlikely role because the modern justification for trademark rights, embedded in the international standards of intellectual property law to which nearly every consumer economy on earth subscribes, is prevention of consumer confusion.[4] But the dynamics of

* Professor of Law; Faculty Director, Intellectual Property Law Center, St. John's University. I am grateful for helpful comments from both the editors of this volume and from Professor Dev Gangjee.

[1] *See generally* Wendy J. Gordon, *On Owning Information: Intellectual Property and the Restitutionary Impulse*, 78 VA. L. REV. 149 (1992); Wendy J. Gordon, *Of Harms and Benefits: Torts, Restitution, and Intellectual Property*, 21 THE JOURNAL OF LEGAL STUDIES 449 (1992).

[2] *See generally* Jeremy N. Sheff, *Veblen Brands*, 96 MINN. L. REV. 769 (2011) [hereinafter Sheff, *Veblen Brands*]; Jeremy N. Sheff, *Brand Renegades*, 1 N.Y.U. J. INTELL. PROP. & ENTM'T L. 128 (2011).

[3] *See* Barton Beebe, *Intellectual Property Law and the Sumptuary Code*, 123 HARV. L. REV. 810, 810–14 (2010).

[4] TRIPS: Agreement on Trade-Related Aspects of Intellectual Property Rights, Apr. 15, 1994, Marrakesh Agreement Establishing the World Trade Organization, Annex 1C, 1869 UNTS 299, 33 ILM 1197 (1994), art. 16.1 [hereinafter TRIPS Agreement] ("The owner of a registered trademark shall have the exclusive right to prevent all third parties not having the owner's consent from using in the course of trade identical or similar signs for goods or services which are identical or similar to those in respect of which the trademark is registered where such use would result in a likelihood of confusion").

conspicuous consumption – and especially of its most potent form, luxury consumption – have always been defined by the *admitted* replica, which members of out-groups seeking inclusion *knowingly* and enthusiastically adopt (and the existence of which social audiences generally recognize). While in-group members may complain that replication of their tokens of affiliation and status misappropriates the social expression with which the in-group had imbued those tokens, they would not seem to have any basis to complain that any of the out-group members were *confused* in doing so. Conspicuous consumption of recognized replicas thus pits two theories of trademark rights – explicit concern for consumer confusion and implicit commitments against misappropriation – directly against one another. For confusion-based trademark liability to reach the sale of such replicas to consumers who are concededly *not confused* about what they are buying has therefore required some innovative legal reasoning.

Not all legal systems have approached this challenge in the same way. A comparison of the trademark regimes of the European Union and the United States reveals different doctrinal strategies for maintaining the scarcity and discrimination necessary to support conspicuous consumption, informed by the history and culture of the two legal regimes. European law has traditionally been quite friendly to luxury-goods incumbents, and suspicious of any competitive practices that threaten the premium the incumbents' products command. American law is less overtly deferential to luxury-goods incumbents: comparative advertising laws, for example, make even referring to a luxury brand as a competitor far more chancy in Europe than in the United States.[5] But this surface dissimilarity masks a deeper convergence with respect to conspicuously consumed goods: the American system achieves similar results to the European system through convoluted reasoning regarding consumer psychology. This difference reflects a deeper philosophical rift that differentiates European from American legal culture on the relationship between misappropriation theory and competition policy.

Section II of this chapter describes how misappropriation is regulated directly in EU trademark law via the unfair advantage and double-identity bases for liability. Section III then shows how misappropriation is regulated indirectly in US trademark law by bundling it with tenuous theories of confusion, particularly through the doctrine of post-sale confusion. Section IV concludes with a critique of the American approach, and in particular its failure to own up to the way it sides with economic hierarchy over democratic egalitarianism.

II MISAPPROPRIATION IN EUROPEAN UNION TRADEMARK LAW

European doctrine has traditionally been congenial to the anti-misappropriation impulse, recognizing it as a separate and independently legitimate basis for trademark liability. While European Union courts have been known to vigorously enforce equal access and to restrict price discrimination in some areas at the interface between intellectual property and competition

[5] *See generally* Charlotte J. Romano, *Comparative Advertising in the United States and in France*, 25 Nw. J. Int'l L. & Bus. 371 (2005); *compare* Directive 2006/114/EC of the European Parliament and Council Concerning Misleading and Comparative Advertising (codification), 2006 OJ L 376/21, art. 4 (setting forth restrictive conditions on the permissibility of identifying a competitor's trademark or product in a comparative advertisement); Case C-487/07, *L'Oréal NV* v. *Bellure NV*, 2009 ECR I-5185, § 80 ("an advertiser who states explicitly or implicitly in comparative advertising that the product marketed by him is an imitation of a product bearing a well-known trade mark presents 'goods or services as imitations or replicas' … The advantage gained by the advertiser as a result of such unlawful comparative advertising must be considered to be an advantage taken unfairly of the reputation of that mark"); *with Smith* v. *Chanel*, 402 F.2d 562, 569 (9th Cir. 1968) ("in the absence of misrepresentation or confusion as to source or sponsorship a seller in promoting his own goods may use the trademark of another to identify the latter's goods").

law,[6] that impulse tends to be limited to defending the principle of the common market,[7] and generally does not extend to competitors baldly copying one another. Even where such copying does not appear to create any danger of confusion, EU authorities have responded by explicitly invoking the anti-misappropriation principle as an alternative and independent basis for liability.

Where a defendant uses a mark that is identical to a registered trademark, on goods identical to those for which the mark has been registered (the so-called double-identity standard), international and European law provide that confusion ought to be presumed.[8] But in keeping with the confusion-based justification for trademark liability, the Court of Justice of the European Union (CJEU) has insisted that double-identity cases are actionable only where the defendant's use affects the "interests [of the] proprietor of the mark, having regard to its functions," and "in particular its essential function of guaranteeing to consumers the origin of the goods."[9] Of course, where knockoffs of well-known marks are widely known to exist and are actively sought out by consumers, this "essential function" does not seem to be implicated, and the presumption of confusion seems easily rebuttable. EU authorities have responded by minimizing the relevance of confusion in such cases. They have done so by leveraging a separate basis for liability – the "unfair advantage" basis set forth in Article 10(2)(c) of the current EU Trade Marks Directive – which does not require any showing of consumer confusion or indeed of harm to the mark owner.[10]

Most notably, in *L'Oréal NV* v. *Bellure NV*[11] – a case involving comparative advertising and look-alike packaging of perfumes – the CJEU held that trademarks serve not only an "essential function" of guaranteeing the origin of a product with its manufacturer, but also as a repository of "reputation and … prestige."[12] The "prestige" of luxury goods, the court reasoned, is not something that "'downmarket' imitations"[13] may invoke by, for example, listing the luxury brands as comparable in their marketing materials, or using packaging similar to that of the luxury brand. To do so, in view of the CJEU, is unfair competition *regardless* of whether consumers are confused, because it constitutes improper misappropriation under the unfair advantage basis for liability:

> [T]he taking of unfair advantage of the distinctive character or the repute of a mark … does not require that there be a likelihood of confusion or a likelihood of detriment to the distinctive character or the repute of the mark or, more generally, to its proprietor. The advantage arising

[6] *See, e.g.*, Joined Cases C-403/08 & 429/08, *Football Ass'n Premier League Ltd.* v. *QC Leisure*, 2011 ECR I-9159.

[7] *Id.*; *cf.*, *e.g.*, Case T-359/12, *Louis Vuitton Malletier* v. *OHIM*, 2015 EURLex 62012TJ0359, EU:T:2015:215 § 84 ("It follows from the unitary character of the Community trademark that in order to be accepted for registration, a sign must have distinctive character throughout the European Union").

[8] TRIPS Agreement, *supra* note 4, art. 16.1; Directive 2015/2436/EC of the European Parliament and of the Council Approximating the Laws of the Member States Relating to Trade Marks, 2015 OJ L 336/1, art. 10(2) [hereinafter Trade Marks Directive]. This Directive replaces the earlier Trade Marks Directive, Directive 2008/95/EC of the European Parliament and of the Council to Approximate the Laws of the Member States relating to Trade Marks, 2008 OJ L 299/25, the relevant liability provisions of which are unchanged except for renumbering.

[9] Case C-206/01, *Arsenal Football Club plc* v. *Reed*, 2002 ECR I-10299, §§ 54, 51.

[10] Trade Marks Directive art. 10(2)(c) ("the proprietor of that registered trade mark shall be entitled to prevent all third parties not having his consent from using in the course of trade, in relation to goods or services, any sign where … the sign is identical with, or similar to, the trade mark irrespective of whether it is used in relation to goods or services which are identical with, similar to, or not similar to, those for which the trade mark is registered, where the latter has a reputation in the Member State and where use of that sign without due cause takes unfair advantage of, or is detrimental to, the distinctive character or the repute of the trade mark").

[11] Case C-487/07, *L'Oréal NV* v. *Bellure NV*, 2009 ECR I-5185.

[12] *Id.* § 50.

[13] *Id.* at § 46.

> from the use by a third party of a sign similar to a mark with a reputation is an advantage taken unfairly by that third party of the distinctive character or the repute of the mark where that party seeks by that use to ride on the coat-tails of the mark with a reputation in order to benefit from the power of attraction, the reputation and the prestige of that mark and to exploit, without paying any financial compensation, the marketing effort expended by the proprietor of the mark in order to create and maintain the mark's image.[14]

While *L'Oréal* discussed this "unfair advantage" basis for liability under the predecessor to Article 10(2)(c) of the current Trade Marks Directive,[15] the CJEU made clear that misappropriation-based liability is specifically available under the double-identity standard of the predecessor to Article 10(2)(a) as well.[16]

The double-identity standard, filtered through *L'Oréal*, has thus become a potent weapon in the policing of conspicuous consumption. *L'Oréal* itself – involving knockoffs of luxury perfumes – fits neatly in the conspicuous luxury consumption dynamic described in the Introduction above. Similarly, in *Arsenal Football Club plc* v. *Reed*, the CJEU applied the double-identity standard to impose liability on unauthorized branded sports merchandise – a common token of social affiliation – even where the seller prominently displayed a disclaimer that the goods were not in any way affiliated with the mark registrant.[17] In this way, the CJEU applied anti-misappropriation reasoning to conspicuous consumption that expresses not only hierarchical social status based on wealth, but also horizontal social relations based on identity and affiliation.

Of course, *L'Oréal*'s requirement that a double-identity infringement defendant derives *some* "benefit from the power of attraction, the reputation and the prestige" of the plaintiff's mark does serve as a limiting principle. In *Adam Opel AG* v. *Autec AG*,[18] the CJEU went so far as to hold that this limitation shields at least some manufacturers of replicas of branded products. But even here, the exception proves the rule that misappropriation-based liability particularly addresses socially expressive consumption. The products at issue in *Opel* were "faithful reproduction" scale model toy cars, and the Court based its opinion on a finding that

> consumer[s] will understand that the Opel logo appearing on Autec's products indicates that this is a reduced-scale reproduction of an Opel car[,] . . . that the relevant public [therefore] does not perceive the sign identical to the Opel logo appearing on the scale models marketed by Autec as an indication that those products come from Adam Opel or an undertaking economically linked to it, . . . [and] that the use at issue . . . [therefore] does not affect the *essential function* of the Opel logo as a trade mark registered for toys.[19]

Crucially, "Adam Opel does not appear to have claimed that that use affects functions of that trade mark other than its essential one."[20] Juxtaposing *Opel* with *Arsenal* and *L'Oréal* thus demonstrates the deep connection in the context of replica goods between misappropriation-

[14] *Id.* at § 50.

[15] *Id.* at §§ 41–43.

[16] *Id.* at § 65 (holding that the double-identity standard "must be interpreted as meaning that the proprietor of a registered trade mark is entitled to prevent the use by a third party . . . of a sign identical with that mark in relation to goods or services which are identical with those for which that mark was registered, even where such use is not capable of jeopardising the essential function of the mark, which is to indicate the origin of the goods or services, provided that such use affects or is liable to affect one of the other functions of the mark"); *id.* at § 63 (noting the "communication, *investment* or advertising" functions of trade marks implicated by the double-identity standard (emphasis added)).

[17] Case C-206/01, *Arsenal Football Club plc* v. *Reed*, 2002 ECR I-10299.

[18] Case C-48/05, *Adam Opel AG* v. *Autec AG*, 2007 ECR I-1034.

[19] *Id.* at §§ 23–24 (emphasis added).

[20] *Id.* at § 25.

based trademark liability and socially expressive consumption: where the latter is not implicated, neither is the former.

III MISAPPROPRIATION IN AMERICAN TRADEMARK LAW

In the United States, the anti-misappropriation impulse reached its zenith a century ago, when it formed the basis for the Supreme Court's opinion in *International News Service* v. *Associated Press* (*INS*).[21] That opinion, which rested on the principle that it is wrongful to "reap where [one] has not sown,"[22] is "no longer good law" after the abolition of federal common law in *Erie* v. *Tompkins*, though it persists as a narrowly circumscribed state common law tort.[23] And even as a matter of intellectual property law, *INS* was strictly limited in its application from soon after its inception.[24] The anti-misappropriation rationale was roundly criticized by Justice Brandeis in his dissent in *INS* as inconsistent with the principle of freedom to compete.[25] That line of criticism was implicitly adopted by a Supreme Court majority in the *Sears/Compco* cases, which purported to limit state common law misappropriation claims based on competitive copying to cases involving confusion or deception as to source.[26] Those cases and their progeny – including, notably, Lanham Act cases such as *TrafFix Devices, Inc.* v. *Marketing Displays, Inc.*[27] and *Dastar Corp.* v. *Twentieth Century Fox Film Corp.*[28] – prioritize freedom of competition over protection against misappropriation in the absence of confusion, to the point of pre-empting common law unfair competition claims that would afford broader misappropriation-based rights than patent or copyright law would permit in their respective substantive domains. Indeed, American trademark law is avowedly willing to tolerate some degree of consumer confusion in order to vindicate competitive (and expressive) freedom.[29]

Parallel developments in trademark doctrine reinforced this tendency away from the anti-misappropriation impulse. Early American federal trademark infringement law – which unlike unfair competition law applied only to "technical" or what we would today call inherently distinctive trademarks – actually *limited* liability to something approximating the "double-identity" category of conduct, though under slightly different operative language than that seen

[21] *International News Service* v. *Associated Press*, 248 US 215 (1918) (*INS*).

[22] *Id.* at 239–40.

[23] *Barclays Capital Inc.* v. *Theflyonthewall.com, Inc.*, 650 F.3d 876, 894 (2d Cir. 2011) (recognizing abrogation of *INS* under *Erie Railroad Co.* v. *Tompkins*, 304 US 64 (1938)).

[24] *See Cheney Bros.* v. *Doris Silk Corp.*, 35 F.2d 279, 280 (2d Cir. 1929) ("we think that no more was covered [in *INS* v. *AP*] than situations substantially similar to those then at bar. . . . We are to suppose that the court meant to create a sort of common-law patent or copyright for reasons of justice. Either would flagrantly conflict with the scheme which Congress has for more than a century devised to cover the subject-matter"); *but see Barclays*, 650 F.3d at 894 (recognizing that state common law torts claims for misappropriation may survive where not pre-empted by statutory intellectual property law).

[25] *INS*, 248 US at 257 (Brandeis J, dissenting) ("To appropriate and use for profit, knowledge and ideas produced by other men, without making compensation or even acknowledgment, may be inconsistent with a finer sense of propriety; but, with the exceptions indicated above [relating to trade secrecy and the right of first publication], the law has heretofore sanctioned the practice").

[26] *Sears, Roebuck & Co.* v. *Stiffel Co.*, 376 US 225, 231–32 (1964); *Compco Corp.* v. *Day-Brite Lighting, Inc.*, 376 US 234, 238 (1964); *see also Columbia Broad. Sys., Inc.* v. *DeCosta*, 377 F.2d 315, 318–19 (1st Cir. 1967) (recognizing the abrogation of *INS* under both *Erie* and *Sears/Compco*).

[27] *TrafFix Devices, Inc.*, v. *Marketing Displays, Inc.* 532 US 23 (2001).

[28] *Dastar Corp.*, v. *Twentieth Century Fox Film Corp.* 539 US 23 (2003).

[29] *See, e.g., KP Permanent Make-Up, Inc.* v. *Lasting Impression I, Inc.*, 543 US 111, 121 (2004) ("some possibility of consumer confusion must be compatible with fair use"); *Rogers* v. *Grimaldi*, 875 F.2d 994, 999 (2d Cir. 1989) ("the [Lanham] Act should be construed to apply to artistic works only where the public interest in avoiding consumer confusion outweighs the public interest in free expression").

in modern EU law.[30] Over time, however, American courts liberalized their interpretation of the applicable statutory standard to permit enforcement of trademarks against third parties using the mark on related but not directly competitive goods.[31] Today, the Lanham Act defines infringement solely by reference to confusion[32] – leaving the degree of similarity or identity of marks and goods as merely individual factors in a multifactor balancing test developed by the courts to determine liability in *all* cases.[33] Combined with the theoretical antipathy to misappropriation-based liability described above, this history means that in American trademark doctrine, anti-misappropriation thinking has always had to disguise itself in order to escape theoretical condemnation.

A Dilution

For example, the most ambitious effort to integrate the anti-misappropriation impulse into American law – Frank Schechter's famous proposal of a dilution cause of action[34] – shamelessly concealed its theoretical underpinnings in European anti-misappropriation doctrines.[35] The codification of that cause of action in the Trademark Dilution Revision Act of 2006 (TDRA)[36] likewise conspicuously fails to require, or even mention, misappropriation as an element of trademark dilution. Even so, dilution has been largely rejected by American courts – though that rejection is itself illuminating. As I discuss elsewhere,[37] from the passage of the TDRA to the time of this writing not a single US Court of Appeals has found – or affirmed a finding – that a defendant was *not* liable for infringement but *was* liable for dilution by blurring. But this is not – or not only – because American courts are skeptical of misappropriation-based liability. Rather, it

[30] Act of Feb. 20, 1905, Pub. L. No. 58-84, § 16, 33 Stat. 724, 728 (giving federal registrants the right to prevent others from "reproduc[ing], counterfeit[ing], copy[ing], or colorably imitat[ing]" their registered mark on goods of "substantially the same descriptive properties" as the goods for which the mark was registered); THOMAS MCCARTHY, MCCARTHY ON TRADEMARKS AND UNFAIR COMPETITION § 4:3–4 (5th ed. 2016) (describing the distinction between infringement of "technical" trademarks and unfair competition in the nineteenth and early twentieth centuries). On the historical distinction between trademark infringement and unfair competition (and the modern blurring of that distinction), *see generally* Mark P. McKenna, *The Normative Foundations of Trademark Law*, 82 NOTRE DAME L. REV. 1839 (2007).

[31] *See generally* Edward C. Lukens, *The Application of the Principles of Unfair Competition to Cases of Dissimilar Products*, 75 U. PA. L. REV. 197 (1927) (describing this shift).

[32] 15 USC § 1114(1) ("Any person who shall, without the consent of the registrant . . . use in commerce any reproduction, counterfeit, copy, or colorable imitation of a registered mark in connection with the sale, offering for sale, distribution, or advertising of any goods or services on or in connection with which such use is likely to cause confusion, or to cause mistake, or to deceive . . . shall be liable in a civil action by the registrant"); 15 USC § 1125(a) ("Any person who, on or in connection with any goods or services, or any container for goods, uses in commerce any word, term, name, symbol, or device, or any combination thereof . . . which . . . is likely to cause confusion, or to cause mistake, or to deceive as to the affiliation, connection, or association of such person with another person, or as to the origin, sponsorship, or approval of his or her goods, services, or commercial activities by another person . . . shall be liable in a civil action by any person who believes that he or she is or is likely to be damaged by such act").

[33] *See, e.g.*, *Polaroid Corp.* v. *Polarad Elecs. Corp.*, 287 F.2d 492, 495 (1961); *see generally* Robert G. Bone, *Taking the Confusion Out of Likelihood of Confusion: Toward a More Sensible Approach to Trademark Infringement*, 106 NW. L. REV. 1307 (2012).

[34] Frank I. Schechter, *The Rational Basis of Trademark Protection*, 40 HARV. L. REV. 813 (1927).

[35] *See generally* Barton Beebe, *The Suppressed Misappropriation Origins of Trademark Antidilution Law: The Landgericht Elberfeld's* Odol *Opinion and Frank Schechter's* The Rational Basis of Trademark Protection, *in* INTELLECTUAL PROPERTY AT THE EDGE: THE CONTESTED CONTOURS OF IP 59 (2014).

[36] Trademark Dilution Revision Act of 2006 (TDRA), Pub. L. No. 109-312, 120 Stat. 1730 (2006).

[37] Jeremy N. Sheff, *Finding Dilution*, in TRADEMARK LAW AND THEORY: REFORM OF TRADEMARK LAW (Graeme Dinwoodie & Mark Janis eds., forthcoming).

is because the equivalent of such liability has long been available through expansive – though still putatively confusion-based – theories of infringement.[38]

The Lanham Act explicitly allows liability to be imposed on the basis of confusion not only as to the source of goods or services, but also as to "affiliation, connection, ... association ... sponsorship, or approval" of those goods or services.[39] American trademark scholars have frequently critiqued such theories of confusion as "irrelevant"[40] to the legitimate functions of trademarks, and to the widely accepted economic policies underlying American trademark law – to lower consumer search costs and provide an incentive to the efficient production of quality products.[41] But this irrelevance argument rests on the assumption that American courts are serious when they condemn misappropriation-based liability as illegitimate and justify trademarks in economic terms. And the example of conspicuous consumption gives us reason to believe courts are *not* sincere in their rejection of the anti-misappropriation impulse – that in fact they have smuggled this impulse into confusion-based liability theories in disguise.

B Merchandising Rights

One such disguise has been a subtle redefinition of the concept of confusion in merchandising cases. The facts of these cases are similar to those of the *Arsenal* case in the EU: during the late twentieth century universities and sports franchises began asserting control over goods that their fans might conspicuously consume to signal horizontal identity-based affiliation – apparel, applique patches, and other merchandise bearing the name, logo, or colors of the team or school. In 1975, the Court of Appeals for the Fifth Circuit awarded that control to the National Hockey League and its franchisees, by essentially treating misappropriation as a substitute for confusion:

> The confusion question here is conceptually difficult. It can be said that the public buyer knew that the emblems portrayed the teams' symbols. Thus, it can be argued, the buyer is not confused or deceived. This argument misplaces the purpose of the confusion requirement. The confusion or deceit requirement is met by the fact that the defendant duplicated the protected trademarks and sold them to the public knowing that the public would identify them as being the teams' trademarks. The certain knowledge of the buyer that the source and origin of the trademark symbols were in plaintiffs satisfies the requirement of the act. The argument that

[38] I am aware of only one district court case – an early unpublished preliminary injunction ruling under the TDRA – that found dilution by blurring but no likelihood of confusion; this ruling was never appealed and the case settled before primary discovery. *Hershey Co. v. Art Van Furniture, Inc.*, No. 08-14463, 2008 WL 4724756 (ED Mich., Oct. 24, 2008). Similarly, a single US Trademark Trial and Appeal Board (TTAB) ruling has sustained an opposition to a trademark registration on blurring grounds while rejecting the opposition on likelihood-of-confusion grounds, *Research in Motion Ltd. v. Defining Presence Mktg. Grp. Inc.*, 102 USPQ 2d (BNA) 1187 (TTAB 2012), though that opinion could just as easily have relied on the "ornamentality" or "informational matter" exclusions for slogans appearing on apparel. TMEP §§ 1202.03(f)(i), 1202.04. In general, in the few additional instances in which US courts or the TTAB find dilution by blurring, they either *also* find likelihood of confusion, or simply do not reach the question of likelihood of confusion. *See* Sheff, *supra* note 37 (citing cases); *see also* Barton Beebe, *The Continuing Debacle of U.S. Antidilution Law: Evidence from the First Year of Trademark Dilution Revision Act Case Law*, 24 Santa Clara Computer & High Tech. L.J. 449, 459–60 (2008) (finding the federal dilution cause of action "redundant" over its first year of life because "of the[] sixty-four opinions that analyzed both an infringement and a dilution cause of action, none found dilution without also finding infringement").

[39] 15 USC § 1125(a).

[40] *See generally, e.g.*, Mark A. Lemley & Mark McKenna, *Irrelevant Confusion*, 62 Stan. L. Rev. 413 (2009).

[41] *See generally* William M. Landes & Richard A. Posner, *Trademark Law: An Economic Perspective*, 30 J. L. Econ. 265 (1987).

> confusion must be as to the source of the manufacture of the emblem itself is unpersuasive, where the trademark, originated by the team, is the triggering mechanism for the sale of the emblem.[42]

The *Boston Hockey* court's equation of "certain knowledge" with "confusion" may be a crime against the English language, but it has nevertheless become blackletter law. Similar logic has been deployed to destroy previously competitive markets for university merchandise in a series of cases that rest heavily on the assumption that fans will believe such merchandise is sponsored or approved by the referenced university,[43] even where the defendant's goods were openly critical of that university.[44] Despite the absence of evidence that any sports fan or university booster cared whether the physical token by which they expressed their affiliation was actually sold or authorized by the university or sports franchise at issue,[45] and notwithstanding the long historical tradition of third-party merchants meeting the demand for such fan merchandise with the acquiescence of the putative trademark owners,[46] courts steadily stamped out the business of those merchants by vesting universities and teams with what scholars have come to call a "merchandising right."[47] This right relies heavily on the anti-misappropriation logic of *Boston Hockey* and its odd effort to frame such misappropriation in confusion-based terms.[48]

[42] *Bos. Prof'l Hockey Ass'n* v. *Dall. Cap & Emblem Mfg.*, 510 F.2d 1004, 1012 (5th Cir. 1975).

[43] *See, e.g., Univ. of Georgia Athletic Ass'n* v. *Laite*, 756 F.2d 1535, 1547, n. 28 (11th Cir. 1985) ("at least some members of the public *do* assume that products bearing the mark of a school or a sports team are sponsored or licensed by the school or team"); *Univ. Book Store* v. *Univ. of Wisc. Bd. of Regents*, 33 USPQ 2d 1385 (TTAB 1994) ("rather than constituting uncontrolled use by opposers and third parties which resulted in the marks losing all source indicating significance, the reality of the situation which existed for many years may best be characterized as that of a royalty-free, nonexclusive, implied license to use marks which, particularly in and around the University's Madison campus, principally signified applicant in the mind of the consuming public and have continued to do so").

[44] *Bd. of Supervisors of La. State Univ.* v. *Smack Apparel Co.*, 438 F. Supp. 2d 653, 660 (ED La. 2006), *aff'd sub nom. Bd. of Supervisors for La. State Univ. Agric. & Mech. Coll.* v. *Smack Apparel Co.*, 550 F.3d 465 (5th Cir. 2008) ("Smack's use of irreverent phrases or slang comments misuses the plaintiffs' reputation and good will, which is embodied in their trademarks. Smack may not trade upon or exploit the universities' reputation and goodwill").

[45] The closest one comes to such evidence is the *Laite* court's declaration – unsupported by any evidence in the record – that, "in our view, most consumers who purchase products containing the name or emblem of their favorite school or sports team would prefer an officially sponsored or licensed product to an identical non-licensed product. Were this not true, the word 'official' would not appear in so many advertisements for such products." *Laite*, 756 F.2d at 1547 n. 28.

[46] *See, e.g., Univ. Book Store*, 33 USPQ 2d 1385 ("Insofar as use of the 'Bucky Badger' mascot on clothing is concerned, both UBS and Brown's were selling apparel which was so imprinted by the early 1950s and have continued to do so along with many other members of WMF. Marketing of such clothing by applicant [University of Wisconsin] did not occur until, at the earliest, sometime in 1983").

[47] Deven R. Desai & Spencer Waller, *Brands, Competition, and the Law*, 2010 B.Y.U. L. Rev. 1425 (2010) ("Merchandising rights cases protect a company's interest in generating and controlling consumer identity. Whether the law ought to protect these interests and, if so, how it should do so, are normative questions"). Scholars divide on the normative desirability of such a right largely along the lines of their views on the normative implications of misappropriation. *Compare, e.g.*, Stacey L. Dogan & Mark A. Lemley, *The Merchandising Right: Fragile Theory or Fait Accompli?*, 54 Emory L.J. 461 (2005) (critiquing the misappropriation-based logic of merchandising cases as inconsistent with the Lanham Act's requirement of confusion); *with* Irene Calboli, *The Case for a "Limited" Protection of Trademark Merchandising*, 2011 U. Ill. L. Rev. 865 (2011) (defending a limited merchandising right as a legitimate adjunct to the right of trademark owners to license their marks).

[48] *Smack Apparel*, 550 F.3d at 482 ("[W]hen a mark was adopted with the intent of deriving benefit from the reputation of [the mark holder] that fact alone may be sufficient to justify the inference that there is confusing similarity" (internal quotation marks and citation omitted; alteration in original)); *Laite*, 756 F.2d at 1546 ("'confusion' need not relate to the origin of the challenged product. Rather, 'confusion' may relate to the public's knowledge that the trademark, which is 'the triggering mechanism' for the sale of the product, originates with the plaintiff" (quoting *Boston Hockey*)).

C Post-Sale Confusion

Outside of the merchandising context, the key element of the courts' disguise of their anti-misappropriation impulses is the doctrine of post-sale confusion.[49] Trademark owners (and the courts that find in their favor) invoke post-sale confusion to satisfy the Lanham Act's "likelihood of confusion" standard in conspicuous consumption contexts, despite the fact that there may be *no* evidence that any consumer is (or is likely to be) confused into believing that a counterfeit product in such contexts is either genuine or authorized.[50] Post-sale confusion is an invention of the lower federal courts.[51] The Supreme Court has never endorsed the theory, nor even discussed it. But for over half a century it has been the key weapon in the arsenal of brand owners seeking to protect business models that depend on conspicuous consumption under American law. The development of post-sale confusion doctrine demonstrates how American courts smuggle misappropriation-based liability into trademark doctrine by lumping it together with other, more plausibly confusion-based, theories of liability, and blurring the distinctions between them.

1 *Status Confusion*

Before post-sale confusion even had a name, it was invoked to prevent the sale of knockoff luxury goods. In the first such case, *Mastercrafters Clock & Radio Co.* v. *Vacheron & Constantin-Le Coultre Watches, Inc.*,[52] the Second Circuit explained the theory of injury in blunt terms:

> [S]ome customers would buy [the junior user's] cheaper clock for the purpose of acquiring the prestige gained by displaying what many visitors at the customers' homes would regard as a prestigious article. [The junior user's] wrong thus consisted of the fact that such a visitor would be likely to assume that the clock was [genuine].[53]

Because it is undisputed that such purchasers of the imitation good do not think they are purchasing the genuine good, the basis for infringement liability must be confusion other than point-of-sale purchaser confusion. In *Mastercrafters*, such confusion was found not in the marketplace, but in the home, specifically when the purchaser consumes the good in view of a social audience that is led to believe the good is genuine. This theory of injury, which I refer to as "status confusion," is the historic source of what we know today as post-sale confusion.

Status confusion is the underlying theory that allows for trademark liability against manufacturers of knockoff prestige goods even where consumers know they are buying a knockoff. Such

[49] The discussion that follows is adapted from my previously published work. *See generally* Sheff, *Veblen Brands*, *supra* note 2.

[50] Proving the point, the Ninth Circuit has held that "because a defendant may violate [the federal criminal trademark counterfeiting statute] without engaging in fraudulent or deceitful conduct, a conviction under the statute cannot categorically qualify as an aggravated felony" for purposes of determining "good moral character" in immigration proceedings. *Wang* v. *Rodriguez*, 830 F.3d 958, 963 (9th Cir. 2016).

[51] Each of the Circuit Courts of Appeal has recognized the doctrine of post-sale confusion in one form or another. *See IP Lund Trading ApS* v. *Kohler Co.*, 163 F.3d 27, 44 (1st Cir. 1998); *Lois Sportswear, USA, Inc.* v. *Levi Strauss & Co.*, 799 F.2d 867, 872–3 (2d Cir. 1986); *Am. Home Prods.* v. *Barr Labs.*, 834 F.2d 368, 371 (3d Cir. 1987); *Polo Fashions, Inc.* v. *Craftex, Inc.*, 816 F.2d 145, 148 (4th Cir. 1987); *United States* v. *Yamin*, 868 F.2d 130, 132–33 (5th Cir. 1989); *Ferrari SPA Esercizio* v. *Roberts*, 944 F.2d 1235, 1245 (6th Cir. 1991); *Dorr-Oliver, Inc.* v. *Fluid-Quip, Inc.*, 94 F.3d 376, 383 (7th Cir. 1996); *Insty*Bit* v. *Poly-Tech Indus.*, 95 F.3d 663, 669–72 (8th Cir. 1996); *Levi Strauss & Co.* v. *Blue Bell, Inc.*, 632 F.2d 817, 822 (9th Cir. 1980); *Gen. Motors Corp.* v. *Urban Gorilla*, 500 F.3d 1222, 1227–28 (10th Cir. 2007); *United States* v. *Torkington*, 812 F.2d 1347, 1352–53 (11th Cir. 1987); *Payless Shoesource, Inc.* v. *Reebok Int'l Ltd.*, 998 F.2d 985, 989–90 (Fed. Cir. 1993).

[52] *Mastercrafters Clock & Radio Co.* v. *Vacheron & Constantin-LeCoulture Watches, Inc.*, 221 F.2d 464 (2d Cir. 1955).

[53] *Id.* at 466.

goods range from cigars[54] and watches[55] to handbags[56] and award statues.[57] Put simply, the cases presume that purchasers of such goods are not looking to purchase a guarantee of product quality associated with the trademark, but are rather purchasing the social status that is accorded to those who possess products bearing the trademark. This is something courts will not allow them to do (at least not without paying tribute to the trademark registrant or owner).

In the clearest statement of the theory, the Second Circuit in *Hermès International* v. *Lederer de Paris Fifth Avenue, Inc.*[58] identified two injuries flowing from status confusion. The first injury is visited not on the owner of the mark, but on its customers: "[T]he purchaser of an original is harmed by the widespread existence of knockoffs because the high value of originals, which derives in part from their scarcity, is lessened."[59] The second injury falls not on the mark owner, or even on its customers, but on the public at large: "A loss [to the public] occurs when a sophisticated buyer purchases a knockoff and passes it off to the public as the genuine article, thereby confusing the viewing public and achieving the status of owning the genuine article at a knockoff price."[60]

This logic, while it does not explicitly depend on the defendant misappropriating value that properly belongs to the plaintiff, reaches similar results to European cases that *do* depend on misappropriation. In one recent example, Judge Furman of the Southern District of New York relied heavily on *Hermès* in imposing liability in a case with facts almost identical to *L'Oréal*.[61] And, occasionally, the mask slips: Judge Simon of the Northern District of Indiana, in finding that an accused handbag counterfeiter's intent suggested a likelihood of post-sale confusion, argued: "perhaps [defendants] did not intend for anyone to think that he or she was purchasing an authentic Coach bag, but they did intend to benefit from Coach's reputation in the marketplace."[62]

There are obvious objections to treating the purported "status confusion" injuries of *Hermès* as a basis for trademark liability within the American theoretical framework. Either supposed injury would seem to be irrelevant to the economic rationale for trademark protection.[63] Neither would seem to present any possibility that a consumer would be duped into buying something they didn't want, or that a producer would lose a sale.[64] But these cases tend to avoid the

54 *Empresa Cubana del Tabaco* v. *Culbro Corp.*, 70 USPQ 2d 1650, 1689 (SDNY 2004) ("The use of an almost-identical typeface on the band only adds to the possibility that the consumer may acquire the prestige of smoking a Cuban [cigar] without actually purchasing one"), *rev'd in part on other grounds*, 399 F.3d 462 (2d Cir. 2005).

55 *Cartier, Inc.* v. *Symbolix, Inc.*, 454 F. Supp. 2d 175, 182–83 (SDNY 2006); *see also Rolex Watch USA, Inc.* v. *Michel Co.*, 179 F.3d 704, 713 (9th Cir. 1999) (finding the defendant's alterations to genuine Rolex watches "so basic that they result[ed] in different product[s]").

56 *Hermès Int'l* v. *Lederer de Paris Fifth Ave., Inc.*, 219 F.3d 104, 109 (2d Cir. 2000).

57 *Acad. of Motion Picture Arts & Sci.* v. *Creative House Promotions, Inc.*, 944 F.2d 1446, 1455–56 (9th Cir. 1991).

58 *Hermès Int'l*, 219 F.3d 104.

59 *Id.* at 108.

60 *Id.* at 109.

61 *Coty Inc.* v. *Excell Brands, LLC*, 277 F. Supp. 3d 425 (SDNY 2017). Admittedly, Judge Furman also made much of the defendant's efforts to "capitalize" on the plaintiff's goodwill by *intending to* confuse customers – a typical coded misappropriation rationale. *See id.* at 448, 454.

62 *Coach, Inc.* v. *Treasure Box, Inc.*, No. 3:11 CV 468, 2013 WL 2402922, at *9 (ND Ind., May 31, 2013).

63 *See Hermès Int'l* v. *Lederer de Paris Fifth Ave., Inc.*, 219 F.3d 104, 109 (2d Cir. 2000) and accompanying text.

64 *See* McKenna, *supra* note 30, at 1858–60 (arguing that trademark protection has traditionally been deployed to guard against diversion or loss of sales); Renée Ann Richardson Gosline, *The Real Value of Fakes: Dynamic Symbolic Boundaries in Socially Embedded Consumption* 18 (May 2009) (unpublished DBA dissertation, Harvard Business School), https://perma.cc/V57A-TDE3 (finding, based on empirical research, that "counterfeits are primarily not seen as substitutes for the authentic product"); *see generally* Lemley & McKenna, supra note 40, at 413 (arguing that trademark law should return to a focus on purchasing behavior).

European misappropriation framework as well; neither theory of injury rests liability on any gain *to the defendant* due to the labor of the plaintiff.

It is telling, however, that the status confusion rationale is invoked in exactly the same kinds of cases in which European courts give voice to the anti-misappropriation impulse. As I have pointed out in prior work, the courts' focus on the *consumers* of luxury knockoffs suggests an overarching concern with preserving the use of trademarks in Veblenian conspicuous consumption: the intentional waste of resources in view of a social audience as a signal of elevated social status. That is, American courts in status-confusion cases and European courts in misappropriation cases are policing the information that trademarks provide about the *people* who consume them, rather than about the goods to which they are affixed – a role that, as I argue elsewhere, is in tension with American First Amendment law and with democratic principles more generally.[65]

Perhaps to obscure these theoretical infirmities, status-confusion cases have been lumped together with other very different theories of injury under the overarching rubric of "post-sale confusion." The effect of this amalgam is to further obscure the connection between post-sale confusion and the anti-misappropriation impulse. And unfortunately, courts contributing to this obscurantist program create tensions and inconsistencies with other areas of trademark doctrine that do not implicate the anti-misappropriation impulse.

2 *Bystander Confusion*

One alternative theory of post-sale confusion appears consistent with the Lanham Act's stated purpose of extending infringement liability to confusion of *potential*, rather than only *actual*, purchasers.[66] In its strongest form, the theory of these cases describes an injury – referred to here as "bystander confusion" – that follows from a standard chain of events:

- The defendant sells its product – which incorporates some feature or combination of features that resembles a protectable mark of the plaintiff – to an admittedly non-confused consumer;
- The consumer uses the product in view of a *potential* purchaser of the plaintiff's product;
- The *potential* purchaser is confused as to the source of the observed product, misidentifying it as having originated with the plaintiff;
- The *potential* purchaser, observing the defendant's product in use, makes some negative evaluation about the qualities of the observed product, mistakenly ascribing that evaluation to the *plaintiff's* products;
- Under this mistaken understanding of the qualities of the *plaintiff's* products, the *potential* purchaser refrains from future purchases of the *plaintiff's* products, and potentially recommends that others do likewise.[67]

The bystander-confusion theory is entirely consistent with American justifications for trademark enforcement. Should the chain of events described above occur, consumers might rely on inaccurate information in making purchasing decisions, and honest producers of quality goods

[65] *See generally* Sheff, *Veblen Brands*, *supra* note 2.

[66] Act of Oct. 9, 1962, Pub. L. No. 87-772, 76 Stat. 769, 771, 775.; H.R. Rep. No. 87-1108, at 4, 8 (1961) ("The purpose of the proposed change is . . . to omit the word 'purchasers,' since the provision actually relates to potential purchasers as well as to actual purchasers"); S. Rep. No. 86-1685, at 4–5, 8 (1960) (same).

[67] *See, e.g.*, *CAE, Inc.* v. *Clean Air Eng'g*, 267 F.3d 660, 683 (7th Cir. 2001); *Payless Shoesource, Inc.* v. *Reebok Int'l Ltd.*, 998 F.2d 985, 989–90 (Fed. Cir. 1993); *Polo Fashions, Inc.* v. *Craftex, Inc.*, 816 F.2d 145, 148 (4th Cir. 1987).

could lose sales as a result – both injuries American trademark policy seeks to prevent. However, perhaps seeking to justify a result that is driven by anti-misappropriation impulses without using anti-misappropriation logic, courts can be sloppy in their analysis of bystander-confusion claims, extending liability to conduct that does not threaten to injure either consumers or producers.[68]

The typical path to such expansion of liability is the presumption that the entire parade of events described above will follow whenever the first of them occurs. The fact that some potential future purchaser of the plaintiff's product *could* observe a purchaser of the defendant's product, *could* misidentify the plaintiff as the source of that product, and *could* form inferences about the plaintiff's goods is supposed by some courts to establish that actionable confusion is *likely*.[69] As Professor Robert Denicola notes, "the essentially *predictive* nature of the likelihood of confusion standard permits the accommodation of interests attributable to a host of divergent social and economic prejudices."[70] Insofar as this is true even of traditional point-of-sale confusion analysis, the chain of inferences required to find bystander confusion only compounds the problem.

The danger of piling on layers of unsupported inference in bystander-confusion cases is particularly acute given that courts have made little effort to distinguish the factual predicates of a likelihood of post-sale confusion from those of a likelihood of point-of-sale confusion.[71] Thus, bystander-confusion theories are frequently found shoehorned into the analysis of a single factor in the multifactor likelihood-of-confusion balancing analysis applicable to point-of-sale confusion claims,[72] or tacked onto the end of such analysis.[73] In neither case, however,

[68] Robert G. Bone, *Hunting Goodwill: A History of the Concept of Goodwill in Trademark Law*, 86 B.U. L. Rev. 547, 608 (2006) ("In some of the broadest post-sale confusion decisions, however, there is no genuine risk that defendant's product will be perceived as inferior. In these cases, liability is difficult to square with the information transmission function of the mark, and goodwill appropriation often plays a prominent justificatory role").

[69] *See, e.g., Payless*, 998 F.2d at 989 ("Reebok contended that such confusion occurs, for example, when a consumer observes someone wearing a pair of Payless accused shoes and believes that the shoes are Reebok's. As a consequence, the consumer may attribute any perceived inferior quality of Payless shoes to Reebok, thus damaging Reebok's reputation and image ... We agree with Reebok that the district court abused its discretion in failing to adequately consider the extent of such post-sale confusion"); *Lois Sportswear USA, Inc.* v. *Levi Strauss & Co.*, 799 F.2d 867, 872–73 (2d Cir. 1986) ("post-sale confusion would involve consumers seeing appellant's jeans outside of the retail store, perhaps being worn by a passer-by. The confusion the Act seeks to prevent in this context is that a consumer seeing the familiar stitching pattern will associate the jeans with appellee and that association will influence his buying decisions"); *Levi Strauss & Co.* v. *Blue Bell, Inc.*, 632 F.2d 817, 822 (9th Cir. 1980) ("Wrangler's use of its projecting label is likely to cause confusion among *prospective* purchasers who carry even an imperfect recollection of Strauss's mark and who observe Wrangler's projecting label after the point of sale"); *Cartier* v. *Aaron Faber Inc.*, 396 F. Supp. 2d 356, 361 (SDNY 2005) ("Individuals viewing the watches on a purchaser's wrist would be misled as to the true nature of the watch's craftsmanship, and any effect such identification might have on Cartier's goodwill with the public is actionable"); *Car-Freshener Corp.* v. *Big Lots Stores, Inc.*, 314 F. Supp. 2d 145, 153 (NDNY 2004).

[70] Robert C. Denicola, *Trademarks as Speech: Constitutional Implications of the Emerging Rationales for the Protection of Trade Symbols*, 1982 Wis. L. Rev. 158, 162 n. 18 (emphasis added).

[71] *See, e.g., Gen. Motors Corp.* v. *Keystone Auto. Indus., Inc.*, 453 F.3d 351, 356–58 (6th Cir. 2006) ("To assess the likelihood of downstream confusion, we first apply the eight-factor test [used to determine point-of-sale confusion] and then discuss the potential harm from the influx of Tong Yang's grilles into the stream of commerce ... although the eight-factor test is arguably less important in assessing downstream confusion than point-of-sale confusion"); *Lois Sportswear*, 799 F.2d at 873 ("The *Polaroid* factors therefore must be applied with an eye toward post-sale confusion" (citing *Polaroid Corp.* v. *Polorad Elecs. Corp.*, 287 F.2d 492, 493 (2d Cir. 1961))).

[72] Often the factor in question is related to consumer sophistication, and the analysis amounts to little more than an excuse for refusing to hold this factor in the defendant's favor despite the admitted sophistication of the actual and potential purchasers of the plaintiff's products. *See, e.g., Acxiom Corp.* v. *Axiom, Inc.*, 27 F. Supp. 2d 478, 497 (D. Del. 1998) ("The 'sophisticated purchaser' rationale generally weighs against the likelihood of confusion. Courts, however, may consider pre-sale and post-sale confusion when evaluating [consumer sophistication]"); *Omega, S.A.* v. *S & N Jewelry Inc.*, No. 92 Civ. 3656 (PKL), 1992 WL 142746, at *5 (SDNY, June 8, 1992).

[73] E.g., *Gen. Motors Corp.*, 453 F.3d at 356.

do the courts in question discuss any facts beyond those already reviewed in the point-of-sale confusion analysis that might be probative of the likelihood of the latter links in the causal chain of the bystander-confusion injury. In short, current doctrine encourages courts to speculate about the ripples that might spread through the stream of commerce from an admittedly non-confused purchase.

Some courts, to their credit, appear to be attuned to this danger. The Seventh Circuit has found such causal speculation by a district court to be reversible error, albeit on particularly compelling facts.[74] The Ninth Circuit has reversed the award of a preliminary injunction where this kind of speculation was the basis for a finding of the irreparable harm necessary to uphold such relief.[75] The Third Circuit has affirmed the denial of injunctive relief on the basis of an uncontested district court finding that the accused goods were not of observably lower quality than the plaintiff's authentic products.[76] And some recent district court opinions are similarly circumspect.[77]

But counterexamples abound. To take one colorful example, in *Rolex Watch USA, Inc.* v. *Canner*, the court admitted that it "can only speculate as to the forms such cheapening or dilution [of the Rolex brand] might take and the injuries that might ensue," but imposed liability based precisely on such speculation, including the possibility that security guards at an airport might be "confused" should a counterfeit gold watch set off a metal detector.[78] Similarly, in *In re Artic Electronics Co.*, the Trademark Trial and Appeal Board denied a trademark registration on the theory that the registration opponent's coin and bill change machines could hypothetically malfunction at an arcade, causing children to doubt the "workmanship" of the applicant's video games bearing the same mark and therefore refuse to play them.[79] In other cases, a chain of events culminating in a trademark injury appears to be assumed *sub silentio*.[80]

74 *Dorr-Oliver, Inc.* v. *Fluid-Quip, Inc.*, 94 F.3d 376, 382 (7th Cir. 1996) ("The proper examination is not whether some people viewing clamshells in industry plants might be confused, but rather whether *consumers* in the market for clamshells are likely to be confused ... Although the district court found that plant tours were given to 'potential customers' from foreign countries, there is no evidence in the record that anyone other than the twelve domestic companies has ever purchased, or even expressed an intention to purchase, a clamshell. A determination that the market for clamshells includes these foreign visitors would be complete speculation"); *see also Perini Corp.* v. *Perini Constr., Inc.*, 915 F.2d 121, 128 (4th Cir. 1990) (reversing grant of summary judgment to the plaintiff and stating that "[i]n order for a likelihood of confusion among the public, but not typical purchasers [of the parties' construction services], to provide the basis for a trade name infringement action, it must be shown that public confusion will adversely affect the plaintiff's ability to control his reputation among its laborers, lenders, investors, or other group with whom the plaintiff interacts").

75 *Adidas Am., Inc.* v. *Skechers USA, Inc.*, 890 F.3d 747, 760–61 (9th Cir. 2018).

76 *Gucci Am., Inc.* v. *Daffy's, Inc.*, 354 F.3d 228, 234–35 (3d Cir. 2003).

77 *See, e.g., Schutte Bagclosures Inc.* v. *Kwik Lok Corp.*, 193 F. Supp. 3d 245, 278 (SDNY 2016); *Crye Precision LLC* v. *Duro Textiles, LLC*, 2016 WL 1629343, at *8 & n. 5 (SDNY, Apr. 22, 2016), *aff'd*, 689 F. App'x 104 (2d Cir. 2017); *Louis Vuitton Malletier, SA* v. *My Other Bag, Inc.*, 156 F. Supp. 3d 425, 444 (SDNY), *aff'd*, 674 F. App'x 16 (2d Cir. 2016), cert. denied, 138 S. Ct. 221, 199 L. Ed. 2d 120 (2017).

78 *Rolex Watch USA, Inc.* v. *Canner*, 645 F. Supp. 484, 493 n.3, 495 (SD Fla. 1986).

79 *In re Artic Electronics Co., Ltd.*, 220 USPQ (BNA) 836, 837–38 (TTAB 1983). That the applicant still desired the registration despite the fact that it, rather than the registration opponent, would be the party injured by this hypothesized confusion did not seem to enter into the board's analysis.

80 Typically, the analysis begins and ends with an observation that an observer might be unable to distinguish between the parties' marks in the post-sale context; what the results of this might be, and how those results might injure the plaintiff is typically left unstated – as is the factual basis for believing those results are likely to occur. *See, e.g., supra* note 69. Cases using such underdeveloped post-sale confusion theories in service of a merchandising right are also typical, though the literature on the merchandising right has addressed this issue thoroughly. *See, e.g., Au-Tomotive Gold, Inc.* v. *Volkswagen of Am., Inc.*, 457 F.3d 1062, 1077–78 (9th Cir. 2006) (granting summary judgment to automobile manufacturers in a suit against a retailer who sold car accessories adorned with manufacturers' logos). *See generally* Dogan & Lemley, *supra* note 47.

D Downstream Confusion

The third species of post-sale confusion is grounded on the theory that a defendant's (admittedly non-confused) customers might gift or resell the defendant's goods in a secondary market, in a way that will confuse purchasers or recipients of the goods in that secondary market. In some such cases, the defendant is selling admitted replicas of the plaintiff's goods;[81] in others, the defendant has acquired the genuine article and modified it in some way.[82] In either case, the injury on which liability is grounded is not directly inflicted by the defendant (who sells to a non-confused purchaser), but is rather presumed to be inflicted further down the stream of commerce by one of the defendant's customers. This theory of injury is referred to here as "downstream confusion." What is surprising about the downstream confusion cases is not that they consider confusing sales or gratuitous transfers in a secondary market harmful to the trademark owner and to the public – that much is uncontroversial. Rather, what is surprising is that these cases give almost no attention to the well-established doctrines that are addressed to such an injury: contributory infringement liability and the first-sale doctrine.

With respect to replica goods in particular, downstream confusion is in serious tension with the law of contributory liability. In *Inwood Laboratories, Inc.* v. *Ives Laboratories, Inc.*, the Supreme Court limited such liability to those cases where the defendant "intentionally induces another to infringe a trademark, or . . . continues to supply its product to one whom it knows or has reason to know is engaging in trademark infringement."[83] Recent applications of this standard reaffirm that generalized knowledge of a possibility of confusing secondary market sales is insufficient to ground a secondary infringement claim.[84] Treating downstream confusion (that is, confusion of the customers *of the defendant's customers*) as primary rather than secondary infringement eliminates this intent element of the plaintiff's case, lowering its burden merely by rephrasing the nature of its claim. It is likely that many downstream-confusion cases will include clear evidence of such intent.[85] But not all of them will, and by treating the basis for liability as "post-sale confusion" rather than secondary liability, lower courts have circumvented long-settled Supreme Court precedent in ways that can reverse adjudicative outcomes.

With respect to goods that originated with the plaintiff but are later modified and resold by the defendant (though not with respect to replicas), the first-sale doctrine would seem to be directly applicable. The American first-sale doctrine – developed in the trademark context by the

[81] *A. T. Cross Co.* v. *Jonathan Bradley Pens, Inc.*, 470 F.2d 689, 692 (2d Cir. 1972) ("The last straw was the recent mailing, as bold an attempt at persuading purchasers that their donees would think they were receiving Cross pens as could be imagined").

[82] *Cartier* v. *Aaron Faber Inc.*, 396 F. Supp. 2d 356, 361 (SDNY 2005); *Montblanc-Simplo GMBH* v. *Staples, Inc.*, 172 F. Supp. 2d 231, 233, *vacated*, 175 F. Supp. 2d 95, 95 (D. Mass. 2001); *cf. Saks & Co.* v. *Hill*, 843 F. Supp. 620, 623–24 (SD Cal. 1993) (speculating that defendant, operator of a thrift store called "Sacks Thrift Avenue," might one day resell a garment bearing plaintiff's label, thereby causing post-sale confusion).

[83] *Inwood Labs., Inc.* v. *Ives Labs., Inc.*, 456 US 844, 854 (1982).

[84] *See, e.g.*, *Tiffany (NJ) Inc.* v. *eBay Inc.*, 600 F.3d 93, 107 (2d Cir. 2010) ("For contributory trademark infringement liability to lie, a service provider must have more than a general knowledge or reason to know that its service is being used to sell counterfeit goods. Some contemporary knowledge of which particular listings are infringing or will infringe in the future is necessary"), *remanded*, No. 04 Civ. 4607 (RJS), 2010 WL 3733894 (SDNY, Sept. 13, 2010), *cert. denied*, 131 S. Ct. 647 (2010).

[85] For example, the defendant in *A. T. Cross Co.* v. *Jonathan Bradley Pens, Inc.* marketed its pens as suitable for duping donees of the defendant's customers into thinking they had received genuine Cross pens. 470 F.2d 689, 692 (2d Cir. 1972).

Supreme Court in *Prestonettes, Inc.* v. *Coty*[86] and *Champion Spark Plug Co.* v. *Sanders*[87] – holds that the resale of a genuine trademarked product by its purchaser is not trademark infringement so long as the reseller's customers are made aware that any differences in quality between the original and the resold product are attributable to the reseller[88] and the goods are not so changed from their original state "that it would be a misnomer to call the article by its original name."[89] These principles have been extensively developed in the Circuit Courts of Appeal in cases involving both new and used resale goods, whether modified, refurbished, or repackaged.[90] But the Ninth Circuit has recently decided that in case of a conflict with post-sale confusion, the first-sale doctrine must give way – despite the fact that (unlike the first-sale doctrine), it does not have a Supreme Court pedigree.[91] Perhaps unsurprisingly, the court reached this conclusion in a mixed status-confusion/downstream-confusion context,[92] where consumer concerns over quality control were largely absent. Again, the label "post-sale confusion," when deployed to achieve anti-misappropriation outcomes without admitting to anti-misappropriation reasoning, ends up doing violence to other, settled areas of American trademark doctrine.

IV CONCLUSION

The varying theoretical commitments between American and European trademark law have generated varying doctrinal solutions to the maintenance of markets for tokens of social affiliation and status (and the conspicuous consumption of those tokens). European doctrine is ostensibly more favorable to the gatekeepers of social distinction than American doctrine. But with respect to the actual sale and offering for sale of goods, while the European model – which candidly admits to enforcing the anti-misappropriation impulse – has the benefit of being relatively straightforward, the American model achieves essentially identical results. Moreover, American courts achieve those results by hiding their service of the anti-misappropriation impulse under a smokescreen of less normatively fraught doctrines – and creating inconsistencies with other areas of American trademark law in the process.

I have argued elsewhere that the peculiarities of American competition and free expression policy – the latter of constitutional dimension – suggest that using post-sale confusion liability as a tool to facilitate conspicuous consumption is unsound as a matter of doctrine, policy, and

86 *Presonettes, Inc.* v. *Coty*, 264 US 359 (1924).

87 *Champion Spark Plug Co.* v. *Sanders*, 331 US 125 (1947).

88 *Id.* at 130 ("The result is, of course, that the second-hand dealer gets some advantage from the trade mark. But under the rule of *Prestonettes* … that is wholly permissible so long as the manufacturer is not identified with the inferior qualities of the product resulting from wear and tear or the reconditioning by the dealer. Full disclosure gives the manufacturer all the protection to which he is entitled"); *Prestonettes*, 264 US at 368–69 ("The defendant of course by virtue of its ownership had a right to compound or change what it bought, to divide either the original or the modified product, and to sell it so divided. The plaintiff could not prevent or complain of its stating the nature of the component parts and the source from which they were derived if it did not use the trade mark in doing so. … If the defendant's rebottling the plaintiff's perfume deteriorates it and the public is adequately informed who does the rebottling, the public, with or without the plaintiff's assistance, is likely to find it out").

89 *Champion*, 331 U.S. at 129.

90 *See, e.g., Zino Davidoff SA* v. *CVS Corp.*, 571 F.3d 238, 243 (2d Cir. 2009); *Nitro Leisure Prods.* v. *Acushnet Co.*, 341 F.3d 1356, 1361–65 (Fed. Cir. 2003); *Davidoff & Cie, SA* v. *PLD Int'l Corp.*, 263 F.3d 1297, 1301–02 (11th Cir. 2001); *Enesco Corp.* v. *Price/Costco Inc.*, 146 F.3d 1083, 1085–86 (9th Cir. 1998); *Warner-Lambert Co.* v. *Northside Dev. Corp.*, 86 F.3d 3, 6 (2d Cir. 1996).

91 *Au-Tomotive Gold, Inc.* v. *Volkswagen of America, Inc.*, 603 F.3d 1133, 1135–39 (9th Cir. 2010).

92 The defendant had purchased auto brand emblems from authorized dealers and then incorporated them into "marquee" license plates; the defendant's product was likened to knockoff luxury products such as quartz movements encased in a genuine Rolex watch case. *Id.*

constitutional law.[93] These objections aside, bystander and downstream confusion might be rendered sound doctrinally, for example by imposing burdens of proof to inhibit undue speculation and by shifting analysis of implicated cases to more authoritative and generally applicable doctrines such as the contributory liability and first-sale doctrines. But status confusion does not seem to be susceptible to such a fix, and indeed would be directly threatened by such reforms. The lumping together of various – often superfluous – theories of liability together with status confusion under the overarching rubric of "post-sale confusion" is thus revealed for the kludgy obfuscation that it is. The need for American trademark law to resort to such doctrinal acrobatics and inconsistencies to capture conduct that the far simpler European model accommodates under the double-identity standard and the unfair advantage basis for liability shows the power of the historical pedigrees and the theoretical commitments of both systems, but it also shows the limits of those commitments. American competition law, despite its pretensions to democratic openness and egalitarianism, reveals itself in these cases to be no less solicitous of economic elites than European law. The legal systems of capitalist economies will apparently always find a way to accommodate the interests of the Veblenian leisure class – and the industries that cater to them – in conspicuous consumption.

[93] *See generally* Sheff, *Veblen Brands, supra* note 2.

28

The Doctrine of Instruments of Fraud in Historical Perspective

*Lionel Bently**

I INTRODUCTION

Jeremy Sheff's piece in this volume (Chapter 27) persuasively analyses the case law from the United States suggesting that a trader might be liable for infringement of a trademark as a result of confusion caused after an initial non-confusing sale by identifying three categories of post-sale confusion which he terms bystander confusion, status confusion and downstream confusion.[1] The latter is directed at the situation in which a non-confused purchaser resells or gives the defendant's goods (including replicas of the claimant's goods) in a secondary market in a way that will confuse purchasers or recipients of those goods. Sheff argues that to find a defendant primarily liable in such a situation creates a "serious tension with the law of contributory liability," in so far as it allows for the possibility of liability for acts that do not meet joint-tortfeasorship's intent standard.[2] In particular, he cites the US Supreme Court's decision in *Inwood Laboratories, Inc.* v. *Ives Laboratories*,[3] which predicates accessory liability either on intentional inducement or the supply of goods to a person wherethere is reason for the supplier to believe that person is engaging in trademark infringement.

While Sheff's study is not concerned with issues of sale of replicas in *primary* markets,[4] in England, similar arguments to those about legal coherence between primary and contributory liability have been raised with respect to a longstanding body of case law known as the "instruments of fraud" (or "instruments of deception") doctrine.[5] According to this doctrine, a

* Herchel Smith Professor of Intellectual Property Law, University of Cambridge.

1 Jeremy Sheff, Chapter 27 in this volume. Although twenty-five years have passed since the European Union harmonized the law of registered trade marks, it is still probably too early in the jurisprudential development of European Union trade mark law to reach a firm conclusion on the place of "status" or "bystander" confusion. Perhaps, as Sheff suggests, the rules against "free riding" offer a more coherent (if intellectually suspect) basis for what passes under the status or bystander confusion doctrines in the United States. For the position in the European Union, *see* Lionel Bently et al., Intellectual Property Law 1047–48 (5th ed. 2018).

2 As Sheff explains, "by treating the basis for liability as 'post-sale confusion' rather than secondary liability, lower courts have circumvented long-settled Supreme Court precedent in ways that can reverse adjudicative outcomes." *See* Chapter 27 in this volume.

3 456 US 844 (1982).

4 The growth of online marketplaces raises doubts about the continued sustainability of a distinction between primary and secondary markets.

5 Christopher Wadlow, The Law of Passing-Off: Unfair Competition by Misrepresentation Ch. 5, § K (5th ed. 2016); Hazel Carty, *Passing Off and Instruments of Deception*, Eur. Intell. Prop. Rev. 188 (2003).

trader may be liable for manufacturing and selling goods bearing a particular mark or get-up even where the initial recipient was not confused or deceived, because the court believes that the transaction has placed in the hands of such a purchaser a mechanism or "instrument" through which the purchasers themselves can defraud third parties. The court will not wait for the mark (or marked goods) to be used deceptively by the purchaser (typically an exporter or retailer) but will act to prevent the instrument entering into the channels of distribution. In such a situation the manufacturer is held liable even though the immediate purchaser is not deceived and even though the plaintiff may never suffer loss (e.g., lost sales) because ultimate purchasers are also not in fact deceived.[6] In recent decades, this doctrine of "instruments of fraud" has come to be regarded as suspect by commentators.[7] As with Sheff's critique of the "downstream confusion" variant of post-sale confusion, the critics challenge the instruments of fraud doctrine in the name of legal coherence:[8] in particular, they argue that it sits uncomfortably alongside current understandings of joint tortfeasance, which, like those in the United States, have scienter components. In particular, as Lord Toulson has explained:

> To establish accessory liability in tort it is not enough to show that D did acts which facilitated P's commission of the tort. D will be jointly liable with P if they combined to do or secure the doing of acts which constituted a tort. This requires proof of two elements. D must have acted in a way which furthered the commission of the tort by P; and D must have done so in pursuance of a common design to do or secure the doing of the acts which constituted the tort.[9]

In search for a legal system whose shape is determined by "principle,"[10] these critics have suggested that English courts narrow the doctrine of instruments of fraud.[11] More specifically, they seek to divide the case law into two strands: those in which use of a mark makes deception inevitable,[12] and those where the action is merely facilitative. It is only in cases where deceptive use is practically inevitable that primary liability can properly be attributed to the manufacturer under the law of passing off, given that liability for passing off is not predicated on intention. In cases where a product might – or might not – be used deceptively, liability may be attributed to the manufacture only if there was some common design or intention that the purchaser would use the product to deceive others. In such situations, the argument is made that such action should not be treated as passing off, for to so do introduces a *scienter* component that is foreign to

[6] In English law, a claimant cannot claim lost profits on sales unless they can establish that, absent the defendant's acts, the claimant would have made the sales. *See* Bently, *supra* note 1, at 1342.

[7] Wadlow, *supra* note 5.

[8] *Id.* Carty's aim is to "provide a coherent, modern framework for [the doctrine's] application." *See also* 192, advocating a "modern, coherent approach." Wadlow, *supra* note 5, at 5–140, acknowledges that he is seeking to use joint tortfeasance to provide "albeit retrospectively, a means of bringing a certain amount of coherence to the various cases not involving complete and inherently deceptive goods."

[9] *Sea Shepherd (UK)* v. *Fish & Fish* [2015] UKSC 10, [19]. Lord Toulson recognized other forms of joint liability including "procuring the commission of a tort by inducement, incitement or persuasion."

[10] Carty, *supra* note 5, at 193 ("There is a need to distinguish clearly the doctrines of instruments of deception and joint liability").

[11] *Id.*

[12] Carty, *supra* note 5; Wadlow, *supra* note 5. One might wonder whether a similar argument might justify a doctrine of "post-sale confusion" limited to situations in which resale in second-hand markets is practically certain to generate confusion – most obviously end-purchases of very good replicas.

its modern form,[13] but rather through principles of joint tortfeasance which place issues of scienter at their core.[14]

Without taking issue with the normative propositions articulated by these commentators, this chapter seeks to highlight some of the ways in which the instruments of fraud doctrine functioned historically.[15] In contrast with "post-sale confusion" in the United States, which is a relative newcomer, the doctrine of instruments of fraud has a lengthy history in England: indeed, the case law can be traced back just about as far as that protecting trade marks.[16] The prevention of downstream deception appears in the earliest cases both at common law and in equity, long before joint tortfeasance had come to be regarded as a generalized mechanism by which to attribute liability to participants for various types of tort.[17] Moreover, even if there had been clearly applicable rules of joint tortfeasance in the late nineteenth century similar to those recognized today, they would not likely have been able to provide solutions to a number of the issues confronting the courts.[18]

II THE INSTRUMENTS OF FRAUD DOCTRINE: ORIGINS

As is well known, the protection of trade marks in England developed initially in the common law courts, only later to be recognized, and then extended, through proceedings in Chancery.[19] In both contexts, the protection afforded to traders which had developed an association between the goods they sold and particular signs covered not only situations of deception of immediate consumers, but also that of deception of "downstream" consumers.

The first reported case at common law in which a claimant succeeded in establishing infringement had precisely this dimension. In *Sykes* v. *Sykes*, the plaintiff, John Sykes, was the successor to the business of his father, Thomas, of making and selling shot-belts and powder

[13] Wadlow, *supra* note 5, at para. 5-145 ("an exception to the rule that the cause of action in passing-off never depends on the defendant's state of mind. An anomaly of this magnitude is to be avoided if at all possible. It would be more logical to say that if goods are not inherently deceptive then their ultimate supplier is liable as a joint tortfeasor or not at all"); Carty, *supra* note 5, at 191 ("this lack of clarity threatens the modern framework of the tort of passing off and the certainty and limits of the doctrine of joint liability").

[14] *See Sea Shepherd (UK)* v. *Fish & Fish* [2015] UKSC 10, [41]–[44] (Lord Sumption treats the inducement/procurement and common design branches of joint tortfeasance as conditions on "common intent").

[15] Critics such as Carty, *supra* note 5, at 188, are certainly correct when they identify "the doctrine of instruments of deception (or instruments of fraud) as an area of uncertainty."

[16] *Cf.* Carty, *supra* note 5, at 191 ("The development of the doctrine of instruments of deception took place in the late nineteenth and early twentieth centuries and on the whole these early cases accepted that they were simply applying a variety of the tort of passing off"). The latter proposition is accurate; the former misunderstands the history.

[17] Jennifer Davis, *Passing Off and Joint Liability: The Rise and Fall of "Instruments of Deception,"* 33 Eur. Intell. Prop. Rev. 204–09 (2011) (describing the law of passing off as having "imported" principles of joint tortfeasance, implying some sort of universality to those principles and contingency to the rules of passing off).

[18] Carty, *supra* note 5, invokes history to characterize changes as "part of a trend" towards "expansion" of passing off, while treating her own proposals as "maintaining" a status quo. For example, Carty refers to her "crusade to maintain clear parameters for the tort of passing off," the premise being that "*in recent years* uncertainty has crept in." To make sense of Carty's appeal to history, it is important to understand that she distinguishes between "modern" and "pre-modern" versions of the law of passing off, the modern form being associated with the decisions in *Reddaway* v. *Banham* [1896] AC 199 and *Spalding* v. *Gamage* (1915) 32 RPC 273. Even so, one might reasonably question whether the law in this area has ever had "clear parameters" and when precisely the parameters of the action were distinct from judicial notions of "'unfair' or 'dishonest' commercial practice."

[19] Lionel Bently, *The Making of Modern Trade Mark Law: The Construction of the Legal Concept of Trade Mark (1860–80), in* Trade Marks and Brands: An Interdisciplinary Critique, Ch. 1, 6–7, 12–13 (Lionel Bently et al. eds., 2008).

flasks.[20] According to the plaintiff's counsel, James Scarlett KC, these were "so excellently made [that] they were used by almost all sportsmen."[21] Thomas, and then John, had stamped his goods with the mark "Sykes Patent." The defendant, William Sykes (the plaintiff's cousin) made an inferior version marked with the same terms in the same way. These were sold to retailers, who themselves sold the marked goods to customers "as and for the goods manufactured by the plaintiffs," and the plaintiffs' sales declined (he claimed by one quarter). The Court of King's Bench took the view that providing the fraudulently marked goods to a third party so that the third party could sell them as the genuine goods, was "substantially the same thing" as selling the goods directly to those customers. Bayley J, at the York Assizes, stated "whether the vendee was party to the fraud or not, and whether he was deceived or not, the injury to the plaintiff was the same."[22] The plaintiff was awarded £50 damages and £40 costs. On appeal, Abbott LCJ affirmed, rejecting an objection that facts as proved did not support the declaration, which was that the defendant had sold the goods as and for those of the plaintiff.[23] The Court held that there was nothing in this objection as it was "substantially the same thing" for a manufacturer to make and sell products, bearing a mark generally associated with the plaintiffs, to retailers all of whom knew that the products they were buying were not made by the plaintiffs, for the express purpose of being resold as goods of the plaintiff's manufacture.

Proceedings in Chancery to obtain injunctive relief in support of the common law right, resulted in a similar scope of protection. In one early case,[24] a London watchmaker, David Ralph Gout,[25] who had a reputation in Turkey (in particular Constantinople and Smyrna) for his watches, which he marked with his own name and the word PESENDADE in what the court described as "Turkish characters," obtained an injunction against Parkinson and Frodsham,[26] who had been commissioned by two other defendants, the merchants Martin Aleploghlu (of London) and Thomas Hamson (of Constantinople), to make eighteen watches.[27] Although the watches bore the name Parkinson and Frodsham, they also bore the plaintiff's name and the word PESENDEDE in Arabic lettering.[28] While the watch dealers could distinguish between the two sources, sales in Turkey were governed by the words in Turkish characters. Even though the term PESENDEDE was descriptive in Arabic, Shadwell V-C noted that Gout had acquired a reputation by virtue of long use of the word on its watches in the Turkish market, and that as the Turkish was likely the only element to which Turkish consumers would pay attention, it would be improper for the defendant to use that sign. The injunction

[20] *Sykes* v. *Sykes* (1824) 3 B. & C. 541, 107 ER 834; 3 LJKB (OS) 46–47; *Morning Chronicle*, Aug. 9, 1824, 3e; *Evening Mail*, Aug. 11, 1824, 2–3a.

[21] *Evening Mail*, Aug. 11, 1824, 2–3.

[22] "Assize Intelligence," *Morning Post*, Aug. 8, 1824, 4a.

[23] *Sykes* v. *Sykes* (1824) 3 B. & C. 541, 107 ER 834; 3 LJ KB (OS) 46–7.

[24] *David Ralph Gout* v. *Martin Aleploghlu, Mr Parkinson, James Frodsham, Thomas Hamson*, C33/842, f. 1247 r–v, Apr. 15, 1833 (V-C), The Times, Apr. 16, 1833, 6; 5 Leg. Obs. 495, 1 Chitty's Gen. Prac. 721; (1842) 5 *Beavan* 66n; C33/843, f. 1661r, Apr. 25, 1833 (MR granting Parkinson and Frodsham a further month to answer); C33/845, f. 2478v, July 25, 1833 (VC); C33/859, f. 1188v, Order, July 22, 1834 (injunction continued, with agreement that account be waived, the defendant agreeing to pay £9 plus the costs of the suit) (VC). Ludlow and Jenkyns (1879) 27 describe this as "the first clear case" of injunctive relief. For a closer look at the origins of injunctive relief, *see* Lionel Bently, *Day and Martin v. Day, Day and Martin (1816)*, *in* Landmark Cases in Intellectual Property (Jose Bellido ed., 2017).

[25] Son of the acclaimed watchmaker Ralph Gout. *See* David Buckden, *Ralph Gout, Watchmaker (1740–1828)*, Antiquarian Horology 223–36 (2016).

[26] On the partnership of William Parkinson (d. 1842) and William James Frodsham (1779–1850), *see* R. Vaudrey Mercer, The Frodshams: The Story of a Family of Chronometer Makers, Antiquarian Horological Society Monograph Ch. IV, 21, 22 (1981).

[27] *David Ralph Gout* v. *Martin Aleploghlu*, *supra* note 24, f. 1247r.

[28] *Id.*

applied both to Aleploghlu's exporting of the watches and Parkinson and Frodsham's manufacture of them.

At this stage, the intervention of Chancery was recognized as being in support of the legal right, so in cases of doubt claimants would be required to establish those rights at common law.[29] However, following *Millington* v. *Fox*, it became clear that injunctive relief would be available even where the plaintiff failed to establish that the defendant had intended to deceive.[30] During the 1860s, the courts started to explain this by appealing to an idea of property in relation to the mark (as adopted for particular goods),[31] though later the preferred account came to be that there was property in the goodwill that the mark signified.[32] It was thus established that intention to deceive was not a prerequisite for a successful action, though for some time it remained an important and relevant consideration (particularly in cases where the signs used were not identical).

The doctrine of "instruments of fraud" continued to be treated as a central part of the law of "trade marks" as it developed in the latter part of the century.[33] In two of the first tranche of trade mark cases to go before the House of Lords – *Wotherspoon* v. *Currie* and *Singer* v. *Loog* – infringement of trade marks through downstream deception was treated as a wholly unremarkable example of the wrong. We will return to both cases later, but for the moment all that matters is the fact that the court understood the circumstances covered by the doctrine as a mere application of general principles. In *Wotherspoon*,[34] Lord Hatherley LC declared "I think the principles governing these cases have been so well settled by a long series of decisions that the only difficulty which exists in a case of this kind is to apply those principles to the particular facts before us."[35] In so stating, the Lord Chancellor was echoing Vice-Chancellor Malins' observation at first instance that such cases "all proceed on the same principle [that expressed in *Croft* v. *Day*] and there is no magic in them."[36] In *Singer* v. *Hermann Loog*, having explained the downstream confusion scenario, Lord Selborne LC observed that "The principles applicable to such a case are well established and have been several times recognized and illustrated in your Lordships' House; the most recent authority in this House being *Johnston* v. *Orr Ewing*."

Even though the case law on trade marks had become quite voluminous, and texts were starting to be published on this distinct body of rules, the cases on "instruments of fraud" were not seen as a special doctrine. Indeed, the commentaries do not start to treat it as a separate body of cases until the late twentieth century.

It should be observed that, throughout the nineteenth century, the place of intention remained uncertain both in "passing off" generally, and in relation to the instruments of fraud doctrine more

[29] *Spottiswoode* v. *Clark* (1846) 1 Coop. T. Cott. 254 (Lord Cottenham LC) (dissolving injunction because of potentially serious damage to defendant were it wrongly awarded).

[30] *Millington* v. *Fox* (1838) 3 Myl. & Cr. 338; 40 ER 956. Millington was itself a case where the dispute was between two English manufacturers but related to export of the goods to foreign markets, in this case the export of bar iron to the United States. The defence offered for using the claimant's mark was that the mark in question had been understood to refer to a quality of bar iron. Accepting the fact that the defendant was unaware of the claimant when it started use of the mark, but finding the mark to belong to the claimant, the Lord Chancellor awarded injunctive relief against Fox.

[31] Lionel Bently, *From Communication to Thing, in* TRADE MARK LAW AND THEORY Ch. 1, 13–15, 20–25, (Graeme B. Dinwoodie & Mark Janis eds., 2008).

[32] *Spalding* v. *Gamage* (1915) 32 RPC 273 (HL) (Lord Parker).

[33] Bently, *supra* note 19.

[34] *Wotherspoon* v. *Currie* (1872) LR 5 App. 508.

[35] *Id.* at 512.

[36] Parl. Arch. HL/PO/JU/4/3/273, Shorthand Writer's Note of Judgment of Malins Granting Injunction, in Joint Appendix, Item 72, 144–57, 155.

specifically. If *Millington* v. *Fox* had made it clear that a demonstration of an intent to deceive was not a prerequisite to injunctive relief, it was far from established that demonstrating such intention was irrelevant, or only relevant as an evidential matter.[37] For example, in *Singer* v. *Hermann Loog*, Lord Blackburn indicated that it was well settled that:

> when any one adopted a mark so closely resembling the trade-mark of the plaintiff that it would be likely to be mistaken for it, and put it on his goods and sold them, *knowing that* though the persons to whom he sold them were well aware that they were not the plaintiff's make, yet *that they were meant to be sold to others who would see only the trade-mark, and were likely to be deceived* by its resemblance to that of the plaintiff, he might be properly found to have knowingly and fraudulently sold the goods as and for the plaintiff's goods.[38]

In part, the uncertainty over the role of knowledge and intention in the action might have reflected uncertainty over the relationship between the equitable and common law branches of the action after the Judicature Acts, as well as the continued applicability of the common law action after the Trade Mark Registration Acts of 1875–1876, which on their face seemed to indicate no such proceedings could be brought without first registering the trade mark.

The phrase "instruments of fraud" first appears in the judgment of Chitty J in *Lever* v. *Goodwin* in 1886.[39] In this case, Lever & Co, then a grocery that had just started making its own soap under the name "sunlight,"[40] brought proceedings against a competitor, alleging both infringement of its registered trade mark for the words "Self-Washer" for soap and passing off in relation to the presentation of the soap, namely, in 12-ounce tablets, wrapped in imitation parchment paper and printed in a particular way (so-called broken type), a style which Goodwin had evidently imitated. Chitty J rejected the claim based on the registered mark, finding that "Self-Washer" was not suitable for registration (which at that time was limited to "fancy words").[41] He then explained the position in relation to the get-up, as follows:

> The law applicable to the case is plain, it is founded on fraud. The simplest case is where the seller misrepresents to the buyer that the goods which are being offered for sale are the goods, not of the person who made them, but of some other manufacturer. That is a case merely between the buyer and seller. Then comes the case where the manufacturer, by devices which are to accompany the goods on their sale in the market, gets them up in such a form as to be *calculated to deceive the ultimate buyer* into the belief that the goods which he, the manufacturer, is putting on the market are the goods of some other maker. Here, generally speaking, a double fraud is committed; first, there is the fraud which is perpetrated on the ultimate buyer; and, secondly, there is a fraud perpetrated on the other manufacturer, who loses part of his trade. In this class of cases the trade is seldom deceived, the retail dealers know from whom they are buying, and if there is a fraudulent device they are rarely taken in by it. But in such a case the manufacturer puts *an instrument of fraud* into their hands. Now it has been said more than once in this case, that the manufacturer ought not to be held liable for the fraud of the ultimate

37 The evidential significance of intention has become known as the "Slazenger" principle: *Slazenger & Sons* v. *Feltham & Co.* (1889) 6 RPC 531, 538 *per* Lindley LJ ("If a defendant deliberately sought to take the benefit of the plaintiff's goodwill for himself, the court will not 'be astute to say that he cannot succeed in doing that which he is straining every nerve to do'").

38 Emphasis added.

39 *Lever* v. *Goodwin* (1886) 26 Ch. D. 1 (Chitty J). A fuller version in (1887) 4 RPC 492 includes the details of the wrappers.

40 Charles Wilson, 1 The History of Unilever: A Study in Economic Growth and Social Change 26–32 (1954).

41 *Lever* v. *Goodwin* (1887) 4 RPC 492, 498.

seller – that is, the shopkeeper or the shopkeeper's assistant; but that is not the true view of the case. The question which I have to try is whether the Defendants have or have not knowingly put into the hands of the retail dealers the means of deceiving the ultimate purchasers.[42]

Chitty J awarded not just an injunction, but also an account of profits that Goodwin had made from the sales. Goodwin appealed, arguing that the account should be determined only by reference to the sales that deceived the "ultimate consumer." Rejecting this contention, Cotton LJ explained:

> The Defendants, as I understand, do not sell anything to retail purchasers, what they sell they sell to middlemen, that is to say, to people who purchase from them as wholesale merchants, and who are going to sell it by retail; and the complaint against the Defendants is this: "You have dressed up your soap in such a dress that those middlemen to whom you sell it are enabled, by its having that deceptive dress upon it, to sell it to the ultimate purchasers as the soap of the Plaintiffs." The profit for which the Defendants must account is the profit which they have made by the sale of soap in that fraudulent dress to the middlemen. It is immaterial how the middlemen deal with it. If they find it for their benefit not to use it fraudulently, but to sell the soap to the purchasers from them as *Goodwin's*, that cannot affect the question whether the sale by the Defendants to those middlemen of this soap in a fraudulent dress was a wrongful act. It still remains a wrongful act, because *it put into the hands of the middlemen the means of committing a fraud* on the Plaintiffs by selling the soap of the Defendants as the soap of the Plaintiffs.[43]

III THE INSTRUMENT OF FRAUD DOCTRINE: FUNCTIONS

The primary function of the doctrine was to remove any possibility of a defence merely because the initial purchaser was not deceived.[44] The point was to tackle the situation where a purchaser (C) of goods from A appreciated that the goods came from A even though they bore a mark associated with B or similar to B's mark. In proceedings by B against A, A was not to be able to escape liability by arguing that C was not deceived, if as a result of the similarity between the mark applied by A and that of B, C would be able to pass off A's goods "as and for" the goods of B.

Looking at the cases, it is possible to identify four specific scenarios in which precluding A from relying on the fact that C was not deceived was of real value to B. These were: (i) where A and C were in cahoots; (ii) where A supplied goods marked as C requested, relying on C's honesty to absolve itself from further inquiries; (iii) where significant differences existed in the knowledge or understanding of different parties in the distribution chain (in particular, C versus the ultimate purchasers); (iv) and, relatedly, where the distribution chain stretched internationally.

The first and most obvious situation where the doctrine mattered because C would not be deceived was where C was "in cahoots" with A, that is where A was manufacturing goods which C could then pass off as those of B. From B's perspective, proceedings against A might be more effective in dealing with the problem at source. A related, but distinct situation was where C was a commission agent, selling A's goods and taking a commission on each unit sold.

[42] *Lever* v. *Goodwin* (1887) 36 Ch. D. 1, 2–3 (emphasis added); (1887) 4 RPC 498 (where the report is a little fuller).

[43] *Lever* v. *Goodwin* (1887) 7 RPC at 507 (emphasis added). *See also* Lindley LJ, at 8, 508, relying on *Edelsten* v. *Edelsten* (1863) 1 De G. J. & S. 185, 46 ER 72.

[44] Carty, *supra* note 5, at 189 ("In essence the doctrine avoids defences such as that (unsuccessfully) raised in *Lever* v. *Goodwin* that the middleman/retailers of the inherently deceptive products supplied by the defendant would not be deceived"). Wadlow, *supra* note 5, at para. 5-139 ("Without the doctrine of instruments of deception, the tort of passing-off goods would hardly ever be committed except by a retailer. The doctrine is therefore at the heart of almost every action brought against a manufacturer, importer or wholesale dealer in infringing goods").

If the goods as supplied by A enabled C to sell more, this would directly benefit both C and A. This was the situation in *Sykes* v. *Sykes*, where the buyers well knew the source of the powder flasks marked "Sykes Patent."[45]

The second situation was where A applied B's mark, or one highly similar to it, to goods at C's request, turning a blind eye to whether C had legitimate reasons to sell goods of A's manufacture under the mark. This was important because it was common for potential vendors in overseas markets to request manufacturers in Britain to mark goods in particular ways that would be attractive to the overseas consumers.[46] Such requests might be made with more or less specificity. Moreover, the significance of the content might not be apparent to the English manufacturer or trader. In the *Gout* case, for example, Parkinson and Frodsham had been asked to mark the watches in a particular way in Turkish characters. Moreover, in a case brought the year before, *Gout* v. *Samuel*, Samuel's defence had proceeded upon precisely this basis.[47] It did not succeed. In *Collins* v. *Reeves*, the defendant, a Birmingham manufacturer, defended itself against an application by an American company (the Collins Company of Collinsville, Connecticut) for an injunction restraining the use of its name by averring that it had relied on the respectability of the merchant ordering goods to have authority to use such name, as (it suggested) was common in the trade. As the Collins Company did not deny the existence of the custom, the judge, Stuart V-C, felt bound to refer it to the Courts of Law, the case subsequently settling.[48] The *Times* was unflinching in its condemnation of such practices,[49] but evidence shows that such practices continued for the next decades.[50] Where the practice related to marks for foreign markets, the manufacturer or shipper from Britain might well be unaware that the mark they had been asked to use would prove deceptive in the overseas market. The effect of the application of the instruments of fraud doctrine to such situations was to require manufacturers to take care – innocence being no defence to trade mark infringement (though a court would have granted only injunctive relief in a case of real innocence).

A third situation in which the doctrine played a role was where the immediate purchaser understood the term to be descriptive, though for the ultimate consumer it would be distinctive. In *Ford* v. *Foster*[51] the claimant had been using the word Eureka on the collar of the shirts it made and sold from the 1840s and advertising the shirts widely as Ford's Eureka shirts.[52] The shirts themselves were of a distinctive shape. The defendant sold similarly shaped shirts as "Foster, Porter and Company's Improved Eureka." The Court of Appeal found that the term Eureka was generic, so retailers were not misled, and thus permitted the defendant to use the term Eureka in its trade circulars, but found that Eureka remained distinctive of Ford's shirts amongst the general public. As a result, it granted an injunction prohibiting the defendant from marking its goods with the Eureka mark. This was so, even though sales would

45 *Sykes* v. *Sykes*, *Morning Chronicle*, Aug. 9, 1824, 3e ("commission merchants at 35%").

46 This practice has a longer history: John Styles, *Manufacturing, Consumption and Design in Eighteenth Century England*, *in* CONSUMPTION AND THE WORLD OF GOODS Ch. 25. 527–54, 544 (John Brewer & Roy Porter eds., 1993) (manufacturers were primarily concerned to sell to wholesalers, often making goods according to specifications provided by them).

47 *David Ralph Gout* v. *Simon Samuel*, C13/2940/3 (bill dated July 13, 1832 and answer of Nov. 2, 1832); C33/840 ff. 399r–400v, Dec. 15, 1832 (VC) (approving compromise of £30 damages, costs, and perpetual injunction, with expungement of claimant's name from watches impounded at Customs House).

48 *Collins Co.* v. *Reeves* 28 LJ Ch. 56; (1858) 6 WR 717 (Stuart V-C). For denial that there was such a custom, *see* "The Birmingham Use of Trade Marks," *The Times*, July 5, 1858, 5.

49 "Writers upon public law. . .," *The Times*, July 1, 1858, 9.

50 *R (Mishall & Co.)* v. *Joseph Henry Seed*, *Guardian*, Aug. 26, 1871, 7 (Sheffield Borough sessions).

51 *Ford* v. *Foster* (1872) 7 Ch. App. 611.

52 *See, e.g.*, *The Times*, Jan. 19, 1849, 11.

initially be to the trade and not the general public. Mellish LJ referred to the *Sykes* doctrine, explaining:

> This is a case which is exactly like *Sykes* v. *Sykes*, which is always cited as to the common law right to maintain actions of this kind, and where it was expressly held, that, although the retailer purchasing the article is not deceived, yet if a trade mark is put upon that article for the purpose of deceiving the persons who purchase from the retail dealer, an action at law will lie.[53]

The idea that passing off encompassed not just sales that deceived the immediate purchaser, but also downstream sales, radically affected the way in which deception was measured. This was because the levels of intelligence and attention of the ultimate purchaser were often assumed to be much lower than those of the immediate recipient. Frequently, the ultimate purchaser was assumed to be illiterate, whereas the middleman was more educated. The effect was that while the addition of words to packaging might be sufficient to ensure the middleman was not confused, the same could not be said of the "ultimate consumer." The doctrine of indirect infringement, in turn, operated to strengthen the independent importance of get-up and visual presentation.

Fourth, and finally, the doctrine offered a mechanism for finding liability in relation to international supply chains in circumstances where purchasers might not be deceived through sales in Britain, but those who purchased the goods abroad would be. In *Orr-Ewing* v. *Johnston*, Orr Ewing, a Glasgow firm, had shipped yarn to a consignee in Bombay bearing two labels, one of which was a green triangle with gold imagery of two elephants and a crown, as well the name "Archibald Orr-Ewing" written in Gujerati script, and the word "LEVENFIELD" and "No. 40" in Roman script.[54] The defendant, Johnston (at the request of a trader in Aden), supplied yarn to Bombay also with a green ticket, bearing its name "R. Johnston & Co.," two elephants (facing different directions and differing considerably in detail from Orr-Ewing's), as well as the image of an Indian goddess, Ganapati (a seated elephant). The House of Lords affirmed the findings of Fry J and the Court of Appeal that the defendant should be enjoined. Clearly, the Johnston & Co. consignee was not deceived, but the courts considered that purchasers further down the supply chain, in particular the weavers "up country," might well be. Key to such a conclusion was that the purchasers would not read English, and many would not read Gujerati, so would not appreciate the textual differences between the two labels. Moreover, as some purchasers would not be Hindu, the Hindu goddess would not necessarily be viewed as an important difference. Most significantly, though, was the evidence that Orr-Ewing's ticket was known in the "bazaar" as the "two elephant" ticket. The Court ordered that the defendant should not use a label that would allow its goods *to be understood* as "two elephants." The effect was close to conferring a trade mark monopoly over a concept, at least in the places where evidence showed that the ticket had come to be so understood.

IV HISTORICAL RELATIONSHIP WITH JOINT TORTFEASANCE

Critics of the current scope of the instruments of fraud doctrine – in particular Christopher Wadlow and Hazel Carty – seek to limit passing off to situations of inherent or inevitable downstream deception.[55] All other situations should be dealt with, if at all, as cases of joint

[53] *Ford* v. *Foster* (1872) 7 Ch. App. 611, 630.

[54] *Orr-Ewing* v. *Johnston* (1882) LR 7 HL 219.

[55] WADLOW, *supra* note 5; Carty *supra* note 5. The case-law on instruments of fraud also suggests that this idea of inevitably or inherently deceptive goods may not be as straightforward as the critics assume, because the meaning of a

tortfeasance. However, the idea of a branch of law – tort – that might be subject to a single set of principles was yet to emerge when the early case law, such as *Sykes* v. *Sykes*, elaborated the scope of liability for infringement of rights in trade marks.[56] As Ibbetson observes, in the early nineteenth century "tort law" in England was still "recognizably medieval" and "fragmentary."[57] When tort began to be systematized as a category in the middle of the nineteenth century,[58] commentators included trade marks within its remit (despite the now dominant role of equity), but struggled with where to place the topic within the emergent field. In his 1860 text, *Wrongs and Remedies: Being a Treatise of the Law of Torts* (1860), C. G. Addison referred to the case law on counterfeiting of trade marks in the chapter on "Fraudulent Misrepresentation and Deceit," reflecting most obviously the common law form of action with which it had been associated.[59] Arthur Underhill, in *A Summary of the Law of Torts* (1873), placed the topic in a chapter with patent and copyright, reflecting emergent ideas of a field of "intellectual property."[60] In contrast, Lewis W. Cave (1879), in a new version of Addison, treated trade mark infringement as part of "Injuries to Rights of Property," in particular property that was neither real property nor chattels.[61]

Moreover, even within the field of tort, discussions of joint tortfeasance were limited (flowing really from a reconceptualization of tort around ideas of fault). To this day there remains uncertainty as to whether principles of joint tortfeasance apply in the same manner to all torts.[62] For example, as Joachim Dietrich and Pauline Ridge explain,[63] there is not unanimity that the law contained principles of accessory liability applicable to all torts: "Accessory liability has not been widely recognised in tort law; indeed it has been questioned whether accessory liability truly exists at all . . . Accessory liability continues to be under-analysed and largely inconspicuous, a fact that is reflected in the small volume of commentary on this topic."[64] In particular, Dietrich and Ridge argue that there was no single principle as to the applicable "mental

mark can change dramatically with the context in which the goods bearing it are distributed. Indeed, the idea that marked goods are inherently deceptive is premised on an assumption of a homogeneous interpretive community (an assumption that is more plausible today than in the nineteenth century).

56 David Ibbetson, A Historical Introduction to the Law of Obligations (2001) (describing the emergence of tort from the common law "action on the case").

57 *Id.* at 169, 178.

58 Michael Lobban et al., Oxford History of the Laws of England, Part 4, § 1 (2010). The first "really scientific treatment" of principle of tort only occurred after the Common Law Procedure Act 1852. *See also* Frederick Pollock, The Law of Torts: A Treatise on the Principles of Obligation arising from Civil Wrongs in the Common Law vii (1887).

59 Charles Greenstreet Addison, Wrongs and Remedies: Being a Treatise of the Law of Torts Ch. 17, 649, 665 (1860). *See also* Melville Madison Bigelow, Elements of the Law of Torts: for the Use of Students Ch. 1, § 7 (1878) ("Of Slander of Title and Trade Marks").

60 Arthur Underhill, A Summary of the Law of Torts, or Wrongs Independent of Contract Ch. X. (1873). *See also* Sydney Hastings, A Treatise on the Law of Torts (1885) (Ch. 12 (Copyright), Ch. 13 (Patents, Designs and Trade Marks)).

61 Lewis W. Cave, Addison's Wrongs and Remedies Ch. 7 § IV (5th ed. 1879) (along with "Rights of Ferry," "Right to a Market," "Literary and Artistic Property" and "Patent Right"), an approach replicated by Horace Smith in the 6th edition (1887). Simultaneously in the United States Thomas McIntyre Cooley treated trademarks within "Injuries to Incorporeal Rights" (along with Rights of Common, Easements, Party Walls, Patents, Copyright, Letters and Goodwill). *See* Thomas McIntyre Cooley, A Treatise on the Law of Torts (1879).

62 The commentaries on instruments of deception all assume a single, coherent, body of rules of joint tortfeasance, applicable to all torts in the same manner. *See* Carty, *supra* note 5 (referring to "the doctrine of joint liability that applies to all torts"); Davis, supra note 17, at 204 ("to import the principles of joint tortfeasorship into passing off").

63 Joachim Dietrich & Pauline Ridge, Accessories in Private Law 93 (2016).

64 *Id.* at 94.

element":[65] what a person alleged to be an accessory must know will vary according to the tort in question, the facts of the case, and the extent of an alleged accessory involvement.

Wadlow himself recognizes that many of the instruments of fraud cases could not have been decided as cases of joint tortfeasance at the time. Indeed, Wadlow observes that the "invocation of the doctrine of joint tortfeasorship by the claimant is a relatively modern innovation, roughly dating from the 1970s."[66] Rather, in proposing the deployment of joint tortfeasance in the context of instruments of fraud, Wadlow admits he is explicitly trying to rationalize a body of cases.

How far could the cases in which deception was not an inevitable consequence of circulation of the marked goods in the marketplace really be reconfigured as cases of joint tortfeasance? With the exception of situations where the manufacturer and purchaser were in cahoots (and even to these where there was an international dimension), today's doctrine of joint tortfeasance would not have produced the results in many of these cases.[67]

Consider, for example, *Wotherspoon* v. *Currie*. Here claimant had established a considerable reputation for its "GLENFIELD" starch.[68] The defendant, which had a rather tenuous link with the small village of Glenfield near Paisley, sold starch bearing a label that included the word GLENFIELD, albeit surrounded with other text:

The Royal Palace
Double Refined
Patent Powder Starch

Currie & Co.
Starch and Corn Flour Manufacturers
GLENFIELD

At first instance, Malins V-C had granted a preliminary injunction,[69] stating that he had never seen a case in which the defendant had been "guilty of more reprehensible conduct," taking the view that the defendant had "a deliberate settled fraudulent intention … to use the word for the purpose of enabling him to palm off his starch as the starch of the Plaintiffs."[70] However, on appeal, the Court of Appeal in Chancery had reversed, James LJ indicating that the labels were different, so that no one who could read would be deceived, and that the reference to Glenfield was "a simple statement of an absolute and undeniable fact."[71] The House of Lords disagreed, restoring Malins V-C's conclusion. Amongst the reasons offered by Lord Hatherley LC was that by applying the labels the defendant permitted purchasers to deceive others further down the distribution chain. Having recounted evidence that Thomas Boston Fisher, Currie's agent, offered starch to William Bentley, but that there was no pretence to Bentley that this was Wotherspoon's as opposed to Currie's "'Glenfield' starch,"[72] the judge observed:

65 *Id.* at 95.

66 WADLOW, *supra* note 5, at 5–140.

67 But note *Richard Tonge* v. *Michael Ward and Samuel F. Armitage*, *The Guardian*, Nov. 9, 1869 (MR), in which Lord Romilly MR stated that "the manufacturer was responsible for the deeds of an agent in his employ."

68 It spent several thousand pounds annually on advertising. Parl. Arch., HL/PO/JU/4/3/273, Bill of Complaint, Nov. 10, 1869, Joint Appendix to the Cases of the Appellants and Respondent, Item 1, 1–9, 5, [9].

69 *Wotherspoon* v. *Currie* (1870) *The Times*, Feb. 26, 1870, 11.

70 Parl. Arch., HL/PO/JU/4/3/273, Shorthand Writer's Note of Judgment of Vice-Chancellor Malins Granting Injunction in Joint Appendix, Item 72, 144–57, 154.

71 *Wotherspoon* v. *Currie* (1870) *The Times*, July 6, 1870, 11.

72 Parl. Arch., HL/PO/JU/4/3/273, Affidavit of Thomas Boston Fisher, filed on behalf of the Defendant, Jan. 27, 1870, Item 28, 67–73, 70–71, [10]–[12]. Affidavit of William Bentley, filed Jan. 4, 1870, on behalf of Plaintiffs, *id.*, Item 4, 28–29; Affidavit of William Bentley, filed Jan. 25, 1870, on behalf of Defendant, *id.*, Item 23, 60–61.

> But the case does not rest there, because there is abundant evidence that when *Glenfield Starch* is asked for in retail shops the Respondent's goods are sold as *Glenfield Starch*, which is the designation and characteristic of the Appellants' goods. It has been long ago pointed out in decided cases that it is not upon a *mala mens* towards the first purchaser that the decision of these cases rests. The first purchaser buys the goods cheaper for the very purpose of being able to sell them as *Glenfield Starch*, the means of doing so being put in his hands by his being furnished with goods with this label – I will not say in order that he may deceive, but it is a necessary consequence that he is enabled to deceive others by this means. There is evidence that this is an article sold by retail at the same price as the Appellants' goods, although it is bought at a less price from the Respondent in order that it may be so sold. That is just the very case of all others in which the Court has constantly interfered to prevent that which is a distinct fraud.[73]

The Court was thus concerned not merely with the first purchaser but with "post-sale" confusion of those further down the chain. The injunction ordered the defendant, inter alia, not to use the word "Glenfield" in or upon any labels affixed to packets of starch manufactured by or for him.[74] This does not seem to be a case where deception was inevitable; nor does it seem to be one which can clearly be described as a situation of joint tortfeasance.

Moreover, even if a doctrine of joint tortfeasance had been established, its application to cases involving international distribution would have depended on the law of the territory in which the primary wrong took place.[75] Thus proceedings might have been impossible where the territory had no protection against misuse of foreign marks: there might simply have been no foreign wrong to be liable for procuring or assisting. The legal position in overseas markets varied widely – even after the 1886 Paris Convention began the process for an international system of accessing national trade mark laws. So, even were there potential liability, it would often have been a challenge to establish. Moreover, if the action had been brought in the English courts, the question might have arisen as to the application of the peculiar *Moçambique* and double actionability rules to acts of assisting or procuring passing off.[76] Indeed, the application of these rules to passing off was still perplexing scholars prior to their abolition.[77]

Given that Britain was for much of the nineteenth century the source of both the goods for which a reputation had been acquired and in many cases also the goods to which such traders took exception, a doctrine that could hold a British trader liable under English law for supplying goods marked in such a way that consumers abroad might be deceived short-circuited

73 *Wotherspoon* v. *Currie* (1872) LR 5 App. 508, 517–18.

74 *Id.* at 523.

75 *John Walker* v. *Henry Ost* [1970] 1 WLR 917 (Foster J) (considering liability under the instruments of fraud doctrine and on the basis of joint tortfeasance where the deception and tort occurred in Ecuador). That said, the doctrine continues to be invoked in such cases. *Modus Vivendi* v. *Keen (World Mkts.) Ltd.*, July 5, 1995, (EWHC Ch., Lightman J) (export to China).

76 The "Moçambique rule," established in *British South Africa Co.* v. *Companhia de Moçambique* (1893) AC 602 concerned actions to recover damages for trespass to immoveables situated outside England, but had been applied to patents in *Potter* v. *the Broken Hill Proprietary Co.* (1906) 3 CLR 479 and might have been thought applicable to passing off given the view expressed in *Comm'rs for the Inland Revenue* v. *Muller & Co.'s Margarine Ltd.* [1901] AC 217 that goodwill is territorial and local. The "double actionability rule" was established in *Phillips* v. *Eyre* (1870) LR 6 QB 1 and made actionability of a tort committed outside England dependent on it being both actionable under the foreign law and English law.

77 Richard Arnold, *Can One Sue in England for Infringement of Foreign Intellectual Property Rights?*, Eur. Intell. Prop. Rev. 254, 261–62 (1990) (on the application of the double actionability rule to passing off). The "double actionability" rule was abolished by the Private International Law (Miscellaneous Provisions) Act 1995, § 10. On the impact of this change, particularly for passing off, *see* Edward Bragiel, "A *Funny Thing Happened on the way to the Forum*" – *Actionability in the United Kingdom for Infringements of Intellectual Property Rights Committed Abroad*, IPQ 135 (1999).

matters significantly. Given the extent of Britain's manufacturing and trading relations, as the self-styled "workshop of the world," treating English law as applicable to transactions that had their deceptive impact in places as disparate as China, India, Morocco and South America gave British trade mark law very considerable extraterritorial effect.

Of course, applied to overseas markets, the doctrine raised some more problematic evidential questions. To begin, how was evidence of the reactions of foreign purchasers to be ascertained? In a number of cases, evidence was taken "on commission" in the overseas market. The commission would involve examination and cross-examination of various local witnesses before an independent judge, the questions and answers being transcribed, witnessed and remitted to the English (or Scottish) court. Inevitably, this made the litigation expensive and time-consuming. More importantly, what was the English tribunal to make of such evidence, in terms of its credibility and probity? By what standard was deception to be assessed? In England some courts had embraced a test of the "ordinary Englishman exhibiting ordinary prudence," but how could such a standard be applied when the court was considering marked goods circulating in a range of overseas markets?

Extending the geographical reach of English trade mark law carried with it a clear tendency to extend the breadth of protection. This was, in part, a result of sensitivity to the practices of foreign consumers, but the effect was often that the adoption of marks which would not be regarded as "deceptively similar" to English operators would be enjoined in relation to foreign markets. Sometimes evidence was produced of the methods of consumption in foreign markets, but the proceedings also betray a ready willingness on English witnesses and courts to portray some foreign purchasers as ignorant or easily beguiled. These tendencies were most evident in a series of cases, including *Johnston* v. *Orr-Ewing*, in which the defendant was found to have infringed where a feature of its mark, an elephant, meant it might be thought an exemplar of the "concept" associated with an earlier mark.

V CONCLUSION

A closer look at the history of the doctrine of instruments of fraud highlights that it developed to regulate various forms of activity, not only at a time when the doctrine of joint tortfeasance was itself only nascent, but in relation to which even a "fully developed" doctrine of joint tortfeasance would hardly have been suitable. Today, English courts can think of refashioning the doctrine of instruments of fraud, not simply because a body of principles of secondary liability is now recognized, but also because of a whole raft of other changes in the cultural, economic and legal environment in which the doctrine operates. Distribution chains and supply arrangements have altered; communities through which marked goods pass are assumed to be more homogenous; British manufacturers no longer compete to supply markets in far-flung places; those places no longer operate with peculiar or unknown laws, but fall within a partially standardized and evidently much more transparent international legal culture; and rules of private international law are increasingly simplified.

In contrast with the doctrine of "instruments of fraud" in English law, the doctrine of post-sale confusion is a relative newcomer to the law of the United States and has appeared at a time when rules of contributory liability are well-established. The question there is whether there is any good reason to extend rules of primary liability into such a space, and Sheff persuasively suggests there is none. However, the response to claims concerning "post-sale confusion" may not be resolved so easily in the European Union, where only rules of primary liability for infringement of registered trade marks have been harmonized. One lesson from the history of the doctrine of instruments of fraud is that in the absence of rules of accessory liability, courts may well be drawn to extend rules of primary liability. In the European Union, a parallel lesson is that without harmonized rules of accessory liability, the Court of Justice of the European Union is likely to extend harmonized doctrines of primary liability to breaking point.[78] If the Court is inclined to prevent downstream confusion in secondary markets, then it is likely to do so through extending the concept of damage to the functions of the mark.[79]

[78] Compare the Court of Justice of the European Union's development of the concepts of "communication to the public" and "distribution" to encompass acts that might better have been left to accessory liability. BENTLY ET AL., *supra* note 1, at 144, 150, 171, 172.

[79] The *Arsenal* case is the most likely vehicle for just such a move. Case C-206/01, *Arsenal Football Club plc* v. *Matthew Reed* [2002] ECR I-10373, [58]. For further discussion of the *Arsenal* decision and the "functions doctrine," *see* Annette Kur, *Trade Mark Functions in EU Law*, Chapter 9 in this volume, text accompanying nn. 34–41, and drawing out the relationship of the decision to post-sale confusion. *See also* Graeme B. Dinwoodie, *The Function of Trademarks in the United States*, Chapter 10 in this volume, n. 30.

XI

Trademark Dilution

29

US Anti-Dilution Law in Historical and Contemporary Context

Sandra L. Rierson[*]

I INTRODUCTION

The cause of action for dilution of a trademark seeks to prevent an inchoate harm: the watering down, or weakening, of a trademark, i.e., its dilution. Courts and commentators have employed various metaphors to define dilution, from the "gradual whittling away" of the mark's uniqueness, or "hold upon the public mind,"[1] to a "cancer"[2] or an "infection,"[3] which, left unchecked, will destroy the mark. In theory, this accretive harm stems from the use of the mark, or substantially similar variants of it, in contexts that provoke association with the targeted trademark but do not cause a likelihood of confusion, and hence do not support a claim for trademark infringement. The cause of action for trademark dilution is controversial, because it runs counter to the maxim that trademark rights in the United States are not held "in gross,"[4] and arguably extends a property right to the holder of a famous trademark.[5]

II THE ORIGINS OF THE DILUTION CAUSE OF ACTION IN THE UNITED STATES

While the claim for trademark infringement has ancient origins,[6] the cause of action for trademark dilution is of relatively recent vintage, emerging in both the United States and Europe in the 1920s. The claim for trademark dilution was proffered as a solution to the perceived "needs of modern business," which demanded more robust intellectual property protections.[7]

* Associate Professor, Thomas Jefferson School of Law.

[1] *See* Frank I. Schechter, *The Rational Basis of Trademark Protection*, 40 HARV. L. REV. 813, 825 (1927) [hereinafter Schechter, *Rational Basis*]; Frank I. Schechter, *Fog and Fiction in Trade-Mark Protection*, 36 COLUM. L. REV. 60, 65 (1935) [hereinafter Schechter, *Fog and Fiction*].

[2] *See, e.g., Sykes Lab. Inc.* v. *Kalvin*, 610 F. Supp. 849, 856 (CD Cal. 1985).

[3] Rudolf Callman, *Trade-Mark Infringement and Unfair Competition*, 14 LAW & CONTEMP. PROB. 185, 188 (1949); *see also Moseley* v. *V Secret Catalogue, Inc.*, 537 US 418, 427 (2003).

[4] *See United Drug Co.* v. *Theodore Rectanus Co.*, 248 US 90, 97 (1918).

[5] *See, e.g.*, Sandra L. Rierson, *The Moral Right of Dilution*, 11 DUKE L. & TECH. REV. 212, 234–48 (2012) (arguing that the costs of the dilution cause of action outweigh any perceived benefits); Kenneth L. Port, *The Commodification of Trademarks: Some Final Thoughts on Trademark Dilution*, 46 HOFSTRA L. REV. 669, 706 (2019) (concluding that the federal trademark statute creates trademark rights "in gross" and allows trademark holders to perceive their marks as commodities).

[6] *See* Edward S. Rogers, *Some Historical Matter Concerning Trade-Marks*, 9 MICH. L. REV. 29, 33 (1910).

[7] *See* Schechter, *Rational Basis*, *supra* note 1, at 813.

Practitioners and academics both chafed at formalistic trademark rules that seemed out of touch with the realities of twentieth-century commerce. The claim for trademark dilution was one proposed framing of the solution to problems caused by outmoded trademark rules that were embedded in both statutes and the common law.

One tenet of trademark law that caused considerable consternation in the early twentieth century was the requirement that, to prove infringement, the senior user of the trademark had to show that the junior user had placed the same or similar trademark on goods that were directly competing with the former's own.[8] Under the common law, courts often held that if two users of the same trademark (or substantially similar marks) were not directly competing with each other, there could be no unfair competition and hence no trademark infringement.[9] Similarly, the 1905 version of the federal trademark statute prohibited registration of marks that were sufficiently similar to currently registered marks as to "be likely to cause confusion or mistake in the mind of the public or to deceive purchasers," but only if the marks were placed on goods "of the same descriptive properties."[10] Many courts expressed frustration with the ambiguity of this statutory language.[11] Some courts interpreted the phrase "descriptive properties" expansively; others did not.[12] The uneven application of this rule led to unpredictable and often inequitable results.[13]

Frustration with this facet of trademark law inspired trademark scholar Frank Schechter's 1927 article in the Harvard Law Review, *The Rational Basis of Trademark Protection*.[14] In this article, Schechter advocated rejecting "old theories of trademark protection" in favor of a new paradigm in trademark law, planting a seed that came to fruition as the cause of action for trademark dilution.[15] Schechter argued that a trademark, especially a strong one, was injured by "the gradual whittling away or dispersion of the identity and hold upon the public mind of the mark" when the mark was used on non-competing goods.[16] Schechter concluded that "the preservation of the uniqueness of a trademark should constitute the only rational basis for its protection."[17]

Schechter was not an American isolationist. He supported his call for a new trademark paradigm with a German trademark opinion, which in 1924 cancelled the registration of the mark "Odol" for steel products, based on the earlier registration and use of the mark "Odol" for mouthwash.[18] The German court articulated one of the earliest justifications for anti-dilution laws, finding that the use of the Odol mark on non-competing products (steel) would reduce the

[8] *Id.* at 821–24 (critiquing this rule).

[9] *Id.* at 824 n. 52 (citing cases).

[10] Trade-Mark Act of 1905, 15 USC § 85 (1905) (repealed 1946).

[11] *See, e.g., Philco Corp.* v. *Phillips Mfg. Co.*, 133 F.2d 663, 672 (7th Cir. 1943).

[12] *Compare Rosenberg Bros. Co.* v. *Elliott*, 7 F.2d 962, 966 (3d Cir. 1925) (holding that men's suits and overcoats share the same descriptive properties as men's hats and caps, because they are worn together), *with France Milling Co.* v. *Washburn-Crosby Co.*, 7 F.2d 304, 304, 306 (2d Cir. 1925) (concluding both parties were entitled to use the mark "Gold Medal," where one applied the mark to wheat, pancake and buckwheat flour, while the other applied the mark to pure or straight wheat flour).

[13] *See B. F. Goodrich Co.* v. *Hockmeyer*, 40 F.2d 99, 101 (CCPA 1930); *see also* Schechter, *Rational Basis*, *supra* note 1, at 823–24 (comparing cases).

[14] Schechter, *Rational Basis*, *supra* note 1. For a thorough and compelling analysis of Schechter's article, *see* Robert G. Bone, *Schechter's Ideas in Historical Context and Dilution's Rocky Road*, 24 SANTA CLARA COMP. & HIGH TECH. L.J. 469 (2008).

[15] Schechter, *Rational Basis*, *supra* note 1, at 813.

[16] *Id.* at 825; *see also* Schechter, *Fog and Fiction*, *supra* note 1, at 65.

[17] Schechter, *Rational Basis*, *supra* note 1, at 831.

[18] Landgericht Elberfeld [Civil Court of Elberfeld] in (1925) 25 JURISTISCHE WOCHENSCHRIFT 502; XXV Markenshutz und Wettbewerb 264, Sept. 11, 1925; *see also* Schechter, *Rational Basis*, *supra* note 1, at 831–33 (discussing this decision); Anselm Kamperman Sanders, Chapter 30 in this volume, text accompanying notes 16–20.

trademark's selling power and thereby harm the mark owner's ability to compete with other manufacturers of mouthwash.[19] Schechter observed that, if US courts were to "squarely adopt the doctrine of the *Odol* case . . . it will not be the first time that they have gone to continental armories for the weapons with which to combat the commercial buccaneer."[20] Schechter's article likewise influenced the development of anti-dilution law in Europe, specifically the Uniform Benelux Trademarks Act introduced in 1971.[21]

One key aspect of Schechter's proposal focused on the nature of the trademark that was the target of dilution. He argued that, the stronger the mark, the greater the need for protection against dilutive harm: "The more distinctive or unique the mark, the deeper its impress upon the public consciousness, and the greater its need for protection against vitiation or dissociation from the particular product in connection with which it has been used."[22] He characterized as "entirely sound" the proposition that "arbitrary, coined or fanciful marks or names should be given a much broader degree of protection than symbols, words or phrases in common use."[23]

Although Schechter grounded his dilution claim in reasoning that emphasized the manner in which trademarks functioned in modern commerce, his creation of a higher class of protection for inherently distinctive marks – arguably recognizing a property interest in such marks – was not new. During the mid-to-late nineteenth century, *only* "technical trademarks" (primarily fanciful or arbitrary marks) were protected against trademark infringement under US common law.[24] Similarly, early trademark statutes allowed registration of only those names that qualified as technical trademarks.[25] Trade names or "non-technical trademarks," such as marks based on personal names, geographic terms, or descriptive words or phrases, could not be registered or infringed.[26] At least in theory, the degree to which a word or phrase was entitled to legal protection depended on whether it was classified as a technical trademark.[27] If the mark or name fit into this category, its owner held what many courts characterized as an exclusive property right in that trademark, creating a virtual monopoly on the part of the trademark holder.[28] As a result of the judiciary's characterization of trademarks as exclusive property, certain limitations inherent in modern trademark law did not apply to technical trademarks at the turn of the century. For example, the owner of a technical trademark did not have to show "likelihood of [consumer] confusion" to prove that a trademark had been infringed.[29]

[19] *See* Schechter, *Rational Basis*, *supra* note 1, at 832; *see also* Soyoung Yook, *Trademark Dilution in European Union*, 11 INT'L LEGAL PERSP. 223, 223 (2001).

[20] Schechter, *Rational Basis*, *supra* note 1, at 832 & n. 88 (citing cases).

[21] *See* Kamperman Sanders, *supra* note 18, at text accompanying notes 24–26.

[22] Schechter, *Rational Basis*, *supra* note 1, at 825; *see also* Schechter, *Fog and Fiction*, *supra* note 1, at 65.

[23] Schechter, *Rational Basis*, *supra* note 1, at 828–29 (citing Rolls-Royce, Aunt Jemima's, Kodak, Mazda, Corona, Nujol, and Blue Goose as examples of trademarks deserving of a broad scope of protection).

[24] *See Lawrence Mfg. Co. v. Tennessee Mfg. Co.*, 138 US 537, 547 (1891); *Canal Co. v. Clark*, 80 US 311, 323 (1871); *see generally* Deven R. Desai and Sandra L. Rierson, *Confronting the Genericism Conundrum*, 28 CARDOZO L. REV. 1789, 1811–16 (2007).

[25] Trade-Mark Act of 1905, 15 USC § 85 (1905) (repealed 1946).

[26] *Id.*

[27] *See* Daniel M. McClure, *Trademarks and Unfair Competition: A Critical History of Legal Thought*, 69 TRADEMARK REP. 305, 316–17 (1979); Milton Handler & Charles Pickett, *Trade-Marks and Trade Names – An Analysis and Synthesis: I*, 30 COLUM. L. REV. 168, 168–70 (1930); Charles Grove Haines, *Efforts to Define Unfair Competition*, 29 YALE L.J. 1, 8 (1919); JAMES LOVE HOPKINS, THE LAW OF TRADEMARKS, TRADENAMES AND UNFAIR COMPETITION § 4 (4th ed. 1924); RUDOLF CALLMAN, 2 THE LAW OF UNFAIR COMPETITION AND TRADEMARKS § 66.1 (1945).

[28] *See, e.g.*, Kenneth J. Vandevelde, *The New Property of the Nineteenth Century: The Development of the Modern Concept of Property*, 29 BUFF. L. REV. 325, 343–44 (1980); McClure, *supra* note 27, at 317–19; Grafton Dulany Cushing, *On Certain Cases Analogous to Trade-Marks*, 4 HARV. L. REV. 321, 322 (1890).

[29] *See* Milton Handler, *Unfair Competition*, 21 IOWA L. REV. 175, 183–84 (1936).

The absence of a likelihood of confusion requirement is also a hallmark of trademark anti-dilution laws, in both their original conception and in their modern-day expression.

As noted above, trade names that did not qualify as technical trademarks were granted little to no protection under the common law during this era. However, courts of equity were reluctant to allow outright deception to go undeterred and unpunished. Accordingly, courts extended protection to non-technical trademarks, or trade names, when (1) those names had acquired secondary meaning (i.e., the consuming public associated the trade name with a particular business);[30] and (2) the plaintiff could prove fraud by the defendant.[31] To establish fraud, the plaintiff had to prove that the defendant had deliberately attempted to pass off his goods as those of the plaintiff.[32] However, most courts eventually dropped the fraud requirement, so long as the plaintiff could prove actual or likely confusion on the part of the consumer.[33]

By the time Schechter wrote his *Rational Basis* article, the all-or-nothing approach to trademark law was fading, if not extinct. Courts in the US abandoned the formalist doctrine that attempted to demarcate a bright line between technical trademarks and trade names. This model was found to be simultaneously under- and over-inclusive: trade names were given too little protection, whereas trademarks received too much. As courts both expanded the protection given to trade names and limited the scope of rights afforded to technical trademarks, they gradually conflated the two categories of marks and began to treat them essentially the same.[34] Like Schechter, those who advocated in favor of this trend emphasized the need for the law to recognize and reflect the manner in which trademarks actually functioned in commerce. If a trade name and a technical trademark served the same commercial function, the law should not attempt to distinguish between them: "[t]he and lawyer and business man, unlike the grammarian, is not primarily interested in etymology for its own sake."[35]

Schechter was thus bucking the trend when he argued for a different form of trademark protection for inherently distinctive marks. Dilution is, in fact, not that different than the formalist conception of trademark law at the turn of the century. Whether a trademark is entitled to protection under the modern dilution doctrine turns on whether it is characterized as famous.[36] Once a mark is deemed famous, in practice the law does little to limit the trademark holder's ability to prevent others from using the mark. Similarly, the common law of the nineteenth century treated technical trademarks (a category that would include some but not all of today's famous trademarks) as the property of the businesses that used them and granted broad powers to restrict their use by competitors. Schechter's dilution theory, as articulated in 1927, can thus be

[30] *See* Restatement (First) of Torts: Definition of Trade Name § 716 (b) cmt. b (1938); Harry D. Nims, The Law of Unfair Competition and Trade-Marks § 50 (3d ed. 1929); *Standard Oil Co. of Maine* v. *Standard Oil Co. of N.Y.*, 45 F.2d 309, 310 (1st Cir. 1930); *Am. Waltham Watch Co.* v. *U.S. Watch Co.*, 53 NE 141, 142 (Mass. 1899).

[31] *See Weinstock, Lubin & Co.* v. *Marks*, 42 P. 142, 145, 146 (Cal. 1895); Cushing, *supra* note 28, at 332; Hopkins, *supra* note 27, at § 22; Vandevelde, *supra* note 28, at 345.

[32] *See, e.g., Hilson Co.* v. *Foster*, 80 F. 896, 897 (CCNY 1897); *Drive It Yourself Co.* v. *North*, 130 A. 57, 59 (Md. App. 1925); McClure, *supra* note 27, at 317.

[33] *See, e.g., Boice* v. *Stevenson*, 187 P.2d 648, 653 (Ariz. 1947); *see also* Handler & Pickett, *supra* note 27, at 169; Zechariah Chafee, *Unfair Competition*, 53 Harv. L. Rev. 1289, 1296–97 (1940); Callman, *supra* note 27, § 66.1; *see generally* E. H. Schloper, *Annotation, Doctrine of Secondary Meaning in the Law of Trademark and of Unfair Competition*, 150 A.L.R. 1067, 1133 (1944).

[34] *See, e.g., Church & Dwight Co.* v. *Russ*, 99 F. 276, 278 (CC Ind. 1900) (observing that "[t]he tendency of the courts at the present time seems to be to restrict the scope of the law applicable to technical trade-marks, and to extend its scope in cases of unfair competition") (citations omitted); Haines, *supra* note 27, at 21 (same); Restatement of Torts, *supra* note 30, at § 717 cmt. a; Chafee, *supra* note 33, at 1298.

[35] Handler & Pickett, *supra* note 27, at 180.

[36] 15 USC § 1125(c)(2)(A) (2006).

characterized as a proposal to re-propertize certain categories of marks.[37] The modern dilution doctrine arguably serves that same function.[38]

III THE FEDERAL CODIFICATION OF TRADEMARK LAW IN THE UNITED STATES

As discussed above, Schechter and others demanded that trademark law adapt to serve the "needs of modern business" of the twentieth century.[39] Schechter proposed the creation of an anti-dilution cause of action in an effort to accomplish that goal. When Congress enacted the Lanham Act in 1946, it modernized and expanded trademark protections in the United States. However, the cause of action at the heart of the Lanham Act was trademark infringement, not dilution. Dilution did not become a federal cause of action until Congress amended the Lanham Act to incorporate it, approximately fifty years later.

A *The 1946 Lanham Act Codifies and Unifies Trademark Law in the United States*

The 1946 Lanham Act served two functions: (1) it codified many of the prevailing, modernizing trends in the common law of trademarks, and (2) it unified and created a consistent law of trademarks that, at least as to marks used in interstate commerce, would apply throughout the United States.[40] Although Schechter most likely would have been pleased by many of the developments codified in the Lanham Act, Congress did not enact an anti-dilution statute in 1946. Instead, the Lanham Act reflected the predominant trend of treating all types of marks essentially the same. Since 1946, the Lanham Act has extended trademark registration rights and other types of protection to descriptive marks, geographic marks, and other types of marks that were not considered "trademarks" under the common law, so long as they have acquired secondary meaning, or distinctiveness.[41] The Act preserved the likelihood of confusion standard for trademark infringement of *all* types of marks (until it was amended in 1995 to include a cause of action for trademark dilution). Even today, the inherent strength of the mark, i.e., whether the mark is descriptive, suggestive, arbitrary, or fanciful,[42] remains relevant to a claim of trademark infringement, but only as a factor in the likelihood of confusion analysis.[43]

The Lanham Act also addressed Schechter's dissatisfaction with the judiciary's reluctance to find trademark infringement when the senior and junior users' goods or services were not

[37] *See, e.g.*, McClure, *supra* note 27, at 323–24.

[38] *See* Port, *supra* note 5, at 694–703.

[39] Schechter, *Rational Basis*, *supra* note 1, at 813.

[40] Prior to the Supreme Court's decision in *Erie R. R. Co.* v. *Tompkins*, 304 US 64 (1938), the federal courts followed a well-developed federal common law of trademarks. That law, however, was invalidated when the Court held that the Constitution did not permit federal courts to create substantive common law rules. *See* Edward S. Rogers, *New Concepts of Unfair Competition under the Lanham Act*, 38 Trademark Rep. 259, 263 (1948) (decrying the "chaos" created by *Erie*'s invalidation of the "great body of Federal [common] Law dealing with trade-marks and unfair competition"); *accord* Chafee, *supra* note 33, at 1299, 1300 (predicting that the valuable and "great body of federal unfair competition law" would likely be "torn into pieces" by *Erie*).

[41] *See* Lanham Act, 15 USC § 1052(f). The Lanham Act does not allow registration of generic words or phrases, regardless of whether they have acquired distinctiveness. 15 USC §1064.

[42] *See* Desai & Rierson, *supra* note 24, at 1805–10.

[43] *See, e.g.*, *AMF Inc.* v. *Sleekcraft Boats*, 599 F.2d 341, 349 (9th Cir. 1979); *see also* Barton Beebe, *An Empirical Study of the Multifactor Tests for Trademark Infringement*, 94 Cal. L. Rev. 1581, 1633–40 (2006) (discussing strength of the mark as a factor in likelihood of confusion analysis).

identical. The 1905 Trademark Act prevented registration of a mark that was likely to cause confusion with a mark that was already registered, but only if the marks were placed on goods of the "same descriptive properties" as those of the senior user.[44] The Lanham Act of 1946 eliminated this requirement.[45] As a result, courts have relegated the similarity (or lack thereof) between the types of goods or services offered by the plaintiff and defendant to a single factor in the multifactor litmus test for likelihood of confusion.[46]

The scope of rights afforded under the Lanham Act's "likelihood of confusion" standard for trademark infringement has continued to expand since 1946. In 1962, Congress deleted the reference to "purchasers" in the Lanham Act and also eliminated statutory language regarding confusion "as to the source of origin" of the plaintiff's goods or services.[47] As a result, some courts now interpret the Lanham Act as prohibiting uses of a mark that result in a likelihood of confusion by third parties rather than the purchaser (post-sale confusion)[48] and by the purchaser prior to (but not at) the point of sale (initial interest confusion).[49] The Act has also been interpreted to prohibit confusion as to sponsorship or endorsement of a good or service.[50] Schechter would scarcely recognize the likelihood of confusion standard as it exists today.

However, Schechter's cause of action did not die. Trademark anti-dilution laws materialized in state statutes as early as 1947, and many states have extant laws prohibiting trademark dilution.[51] Congress federalized anti-dilution protection when it enacted the Federal Trademark Dilution Act (FTDA) in 1995, a law that was substantially revised and expanded in 2006, when Congress passed the Trademark Dilution Revision Act (TDRA). A cause of action for trademark dilution has thus existed in the United States for over sixty years, not as a substitute for trademark infringement (as Schechter proposed), but coexistent with it.

B Congress Enacts a Law to Prohibit the Dilution of "Distinctive and Famous" Trademarks: The Federal Trademark Dilution Act (FTDA)

The federal government first protected trademarks against dilution, as opposed to infringement, many decades after Schechter published his *Rational Basis* article and the *Odol* case was decided in Germany. On the Lanham Act's fiftieth anniversary, Congress amended it to include an anti-dilution cause of action. The FTDA, enacted after a previous failed attempt,[52] was intended to provide a cause of action for trademark dilution that would be consistently applied

[44] Trade-Mark Act of 1905, 15 USC § 85 (1905) (repealed 1946).

[45] Trademark Act of 1946, 15 USC § 1125(a)(1)(A) (1946); *see also Fleischmann Distilling Corp.* v. *Maier Brewing Co.*, 314 F.2d 149, 151 (9th Cir. 1963).

[46] *See, e.g.*, *Sleekcraft*, 599 F.2d at 350; *see also* Beebe, *supra* note 43, at 1631–3 (discussing the competitive proximity factor in likelihood of confusion analysis).

[47] S. Rep. No. 87-2107, at 4 (1962), *reprinted in* 1962 USCCAN 2844, 2847.

[48] *See, e.g.*, *Ferrari SPA Esercizio* v. *Roberts*, 944 F.2d 1235, 1245 (6th Cir. 1991).

[49] *See, e.g.*, *Network Automation, Inc.* v. *Advanced Sys. Concepts, Inc.*, 638 F.3d 1137, 1147–48 (9th Cir. 2011).

[50] *See, e.g.*, *Dallas Cowboys Cheerleaders, Inc.* v. *Pussycat Cinema, Ltd.*, 604 F.2d 200, 204 (2d Cir. 1979).

[51] Massachusetts enacted the first dilution statute in 1947. Act of May 2, 1947, ch. 307, § 7a, 1947 Mass. Acts 300 (codified as amended at MASS. GEN. LAWS ANN. ch. 110H § 13 (West Supp. 2007)). New York, Illinois, and Georgia soon followed suit. *See, e.g.*, N.Y. GEN. BUS. LAW § 368-d (1961 NY Laws 1806, 1813) (recodified at N.Y. GEN. BUS. LAW § 360-*l* (McKinney 1996 & Supp. 2008)); 140 ILL. COMP. STAT. ANN. § 22 (West 1986) (superseded by 765 ILL. COMP. STAT. ANN. §§ 1036/5, 1036/65 (West 2001)); GA. CODE ANN. § 10-1-451 (2000).

[52] Congress considered adding an anti-dilution cause of action to the Lanham Act when it was amended in 1988, but the amendment was rejected due to First Amendment concerns. *See* HR Rep. No. 100–1028 (1988); *Moseley* v. *V Secret Catalogue, Inc.*, 537 US 418, 430–31 (2003).

across the United States.[53] However, the Act engendered numerous circuit splits that precluded it from fully achieving that goal.

The FTDA enabled the "owner of a famous mark" to enjoin "another person's commercial use in commerce of a mark or trade name" if such use (1) began after the mark became famous, and (2) "cause[d] dilution of the distinctive quality of the mark."[54] The Act listed eight factors for courts to consider, to determine whether a mark was "distinctive and famous."[55] The Act defined dilution as "the lessening of the capacity of a famous mark to identify and distinguish goods or services, regardless of the presence or absence of (1) competition between the owner of the famous mark and other parties, or (2) likelihood of confusion, mistake, or deception."[56] The FTDA did not delineate any factors to guide the courts' assessment of whether the use of a particular trademark diluted the distinctive qualities of that mark.

A key point of contention under the FTDA related to its definition of "distinctive and famous" trademarks. One question related to whether the Act applied to marks that were well-known within a limited geographic area or within a specific market, otherwise known as "niche fame."[57] Some courts held that "niche fame" was sufficient to enjoy protection under the FTDA; others required a showing of more widespread fame.[58] The second issue related to the distinctiveness prong of the FTDA, and whether it required marks to be inherently distinctive or also included marks with only a high degree of acquired distinctiveness.[59] The Second Circuit held that only inherently distinctive marks could be protected under the FTDA; other circuits disagreed.[60] Thus, whether a trademark satisfied the "distinctive and famous" prerequisite depended in part on where the plaintiff filed suit.

Federal courts also split on the question of whether plaintiffs claiming trademark dilution under the FTDA were required to show actual or only a likelihood of dilution, to obtain injunctive relief.[61] Trademark holders argued that a likelihood of dilution standard accorded with the FTDA's focus on injunctive relief, which is designed to prevent irreparable harm, rather than compensate for harms that have already occurred.[62] The Supreme Court temporarily resolved this dispute in *Victoria's Secret*, when it concluded that the plain language of the FTDA "unambiguously requires a showing of actual dilution, rather than a likelihood of dilution."[63] In reaching this result, the Court explained that, "at least where the marks at issue

53 *See* HR Rep. No. 104-374 at 3–4 (1995) (noting that owners of famous trademarks had to rely on a "patch-quilt system" to protect against trademark dilution, since only about half of the states had anti-dilution laws).

54 15 USC § 1125(c)(1) (1994 & Supp. 1996).

55 *Id.* § 1125(c)(1)(A)–(H).

56 *Id.* § 1127.

57 *See* Dyann L. Kostello, *Grappling with the Limits of Fame under the FTDA – Do Marks Famous Only in a Niche Market or Limited Geographic Area Qualify for Protection?*, 91 Trademark Rep. 1133 (2001); Brian A. Jacobs, *Note, Trademark Dilution on the Constitutional Edge*, 104 Colum. L. Rev. 161, 178–79 (2004).

58 *Compare Times Mirror Magazines, Inc.* v. *Las Vegas Sports News, LLC*, 212 F.3d 157, 165 (3d Cir. 2000) (holding that "a mark can be famous in a niche market where the mark has a high degree of distinctiveness within the market"), *with TCPIP Holding Co.* v. *Haar Commc'ns, Inc.*, 244 F.3d 88, 99 (2d Cir. 2001) (rejecting the concept of niche fame as inconsistent with congressional intent).

59 *See* Jacobs, *supra* note 57, at 176–78.

60 *Compare TCPIP*, 244 F.3d at 95 (FTDA protects only "marks that have a significant degree of [inherent] distinctiveness"), with *Times Mirror*, 212 F.3d at 166–67 (extending FTDA protection to a mark that lacked inherent distinctiveness but had a high degree of acquired distinctiveness).

61 *Compare Ringling Bros.-Barnum & Bailey Combined Shows* v. *Utah Div. of Travel Dev.*, 170 F.3d 449, 458 (4th Cir. 1999) (FTDA proscribes "actual, consummated dilution" only), *with Nabisco, Inc.* v. *PF Brands, Inc.*, 191 F.3d 208, 224 (2d Cir. 1999) (FTDA provides injunctive relief "to prevent the harm before it occurs").

62 *See Nabisco*, 191 F.3d at 224.

63 *Moseley* v. *V Secret Catalogue, Inc.*, 537 US 418, 433 (2003).

are not identical," a plaintiff would have to prove more than mere mental association between his famous trademark and the junior user's mark, "to establish actionable dilution."[64] Trademark holders heavily criticized the decision, in part because it required a plaintiff to suffer actionable harm before obtaining an injunction to prevent that same harm.[65]

While the Court resolved one ambiguity in the FTDA in *Victoria's Secret*, it highlighted another: whether the FTDA prohibited dilution by tarnishment. In *Victoria's Secret*, the plaintiff claimed that the reputation of the Victoria's Secret trademark had been tarnished by the name of the defendant's store (Victor's Little Secret), which sold sex toys and lingerie.[66] The legislative history of the FTDA showed that Congress intended to prohibit dilution via tarnishment.[67] However, the text of the FTDA barred only those uses of a famous trademark that lessened "the capacity of a famous mark to identify and distinguish goods or services," i.e., dilution by blurring.[68] The FTDA did not mention damage to reputation and never used the word "tarnishment." In dicta, *Victoria's Secret* cast doubt on whether the FTDA extended to cases of dilution by tarnishment, based on the plain language of the Act.[69] This omission constituted yet another ambiguity in the text of the FTDA that precluded it from having its intended effect: creating a trademark anti-dilution law that would apply consistently in all fifty states.

C Congress Clarifies and Expands Anti-Dilution Law via the Trademark Dilution Revision Act (TDRA)

The TDRA aimed to resolve many of the ambiguities that were embodied in the FTDA. Although it was initially heralded as an improvement,[70] some of the key changes in the revised version of the federal law have caused or at least permitted federal anti-dilution law to expand in ways that arguably threaten competition and raise constitutional concerns.

The TDRA answered many of the questions that were left open by the FTDA. First, it resolved the conflict over the definition of "famousness." The TDRA defines a famous mark as one that is "widely recognized by the general consuming public of the United States" as a designation of source.[71] In so doing, the TDRA implicitly rejects the concept of "niche fame," or fame within a limited geographical market or subject area.[72] Moreover, the TDRA clarified that "famous" marks need not be inherently distinctive. It did so by deleting the statutory reference to "famous and distinctive" marks, providing instead that the statute protects "famous" marks that are "distinctive, inherently *or through acquired distinctiveness*."[73] The TDRA also

[64] *Id.*

[65] *See* Trademark Dilution Revision Act of 2006: Hearing before the Subcomm. on Courts, the Internet and Intellectual Property of the Comm. on the Judiciary, 109th Cong. 6 (2005); *see also* R. Landon Dirickson, *The Trademark Dilution "Secret" Is Out: The FTDA and the Supreme Court Leave Victoria's Secret and Future Plaintiffs without a Legal or Equitable Remedy*, 40 Tulsa L. Rev. 155 (2004).

[66] *Moseley*, 537 US at 423–24 (citing complaint).

[67] *Id.* at 431–32.

[68] 15 USC § 1127.

[69] *Moseley*, 537 US at 432.

[70] *See, e.g.*, Barton Beebe, *A Defense of the New Federal Trademark Antidilution Law*, 16 Fordham Intell. Prop. Media & Ent. L.J. 1143 (2006).

[71] 15 USC § 1125(c)(2)(A).

[72] *See* David S. Welkowitz, *Famous Marks under the TDRA*, 99 Trademark Rep. 983, 989 (2009).

[73] 15 USC § 1125 (c)(1) (emphasis added).

shrinks the FTDA's eight-factor list of famousness factors to four, eliminating the statutory reference to "the degree of inherent or acquired distinctiveness of the mark."[74]

Most critically, the TDRA changed a plaintiff's burden of proof in a federal dilution case by eliminating the statutory prohibition on uses of a famous mark that "cause dilution," replacing it with a bar to uses of a famous mark that are "*likely to* cause dilution."[75] The TDRA also specifies that plaintiffs do not need to show "actual economic injury" to state an actionable dilution claim; this language did not appear in the FTDA.[76] These amendments to the Lanham Act effectively overruled the Supreme Court's decision in *Victoria's Secret*.[77]

The TDRA also clarified that federal law prohibits dilution of a famous mark both by blurring and by tarnishment. The TDRA prohibits the use of any "famous" mark that is "likely to cause dilution by blurring or dilution by tarnishment," "regardless of the presence or absence of actual or likely confusion, of competition, or of actual economic injury."[78] The TDRA's shift to a likelihood of dilution standard, under which a plaintiff has no duty to prove any actual economic harm to state an actionable claim, arguably created what many famous trademark holders had hoped to establish under the FTDA: "a genuine property right in trademarks."[79]

1 Dilution by Blurring

The claim for dilution by blurring, as codified in the TDRA, seeks to prevent the type of harm that Schechter described in 1927. The word "blurring," like the word "dilution" itself, implies an accumulative harm caused by fading or loss of distinctiveness. In theory, that loss of distinctiveness is harmful because it impairs the source-identifying function of the famous trademark and its ability to bolster economic efficiency in the marketplace.[80] The Act defines dilution by blurring as an "association arising from the similarity between a mark or trade name and a famous mark that impairs the distinctiveness of the famous mark."[81]

The TDRA directs courts to consider "all relevant factors" in assessing the likelihood that dilution by blurring will occur.[82] However, it identifies only six "relevant" factors, and in practice the vast majority of courts confine their analysis to these six factors.[83] Three of the six factors relate to the overall strength of the plaintiff's mark, and, in that sense, overlie the factors considered to determine whether the mark is famous.[84] The remaining three factors relate to (1) the degree of similarity between the marks, (2) defendant's intent to create an association with the famous mark (or lack thereof), and (3) any evidence of "actual association" between the

[74] *Id.* §§ 1125(c)(2)(A)(i)–(iv). A mark's "degree of inherent or acquired distinctiveness" is, however, still relevant under the TDRA, as it is a factor in determining whether a famous mark is likely to be diluted via blurring. *Id.* at § 1125(c)(2)(B)(ii).

[75] *Id.* § 1125(c)(1) (emphasis added).

[76] *Id.*

[77] *See Moseley* v. *V Secret Catalogue, Inc.*, 537 US 418, 433 (2003); *Starbucks Corp.* v. *Wolfe's Borough Coffee, Inc.*, 588 F.3d 97, 104 (2d Cir. 2009).

[78] 15 USC § 1125(c)(1).

[79] Eric A. Prager, *The Federal Trademark Dilution Act of 1995: Substantial Likelihood of Confusion*, 7 Fordham Intell. Prop. Media & Ent. L.J. 121, 121 (1996).

[80] *See Ty Inc.* v. *Perryman*, 306 F.3d 509, 511 (7th Cir. 2002).

[81] 15 USC § 1125(c)(2)(B).

[82] *Id.*

[83] *Id.* at §§ 1125(c)(2)(B)(i)–(vi).

[84] These factors include "[t]he degree of inherent or acquired distinctiveness of the famous mark"; "[t]he extent to which the owner of the famous mark is engaging in substantially exclusive use of the mark"; and "[t]he degree of recognition of the famous mark." 15 USC § 1125(c)(2)(B)(ii)–(iv). These factors are essentially identical to three of the "famousness" factors listed in the former version of the statute, the FTDA. *See* 15 USC §§ 1125(c)(1)(A), (F)–(G) (superseded).

marks.[85] In essence, the list of six factors in the TDRA boils down to the extent of the mark's fame, the degree of similarity between the marks, and evidence of association between them (and the intent to create such association).

Under the FTDA, many courts adopted a "substantial similarity" test for federal claims of trademark dilution. This line of cases stemmed from reasoning in *Victoria's Secret*, which held that mere association between non-identical marks was insufficient to prove dilution by blurring.[86] The FTDA, as interpreted by the Supreme Court, therefore made it more difficult for a plaintiff to prove dilution of a famous trademark in cases where the marks in question were not identical or "substantially similar," even if the plaintiff could show that consumers "associated" the defendant's mark with that of the plaintiff.[87] However, as discussed above, the impact of *Victoria's Secret* was short-lived. Congress passed the TDRA, largely in response to the *Victoria's Secret* decision, and redefined the standard of proof in these cases.[88]

Both the Second and Ninth Circuits have held that the TDRA does not require a finding of "substantial similarity" to prove dilution of a famous trademark. In *Starbucks Corporation v. Wolfe's Borough Coffee*, the district court granted summary judgment to the defendant, a small business that sold "Charbucks" coffee, largely based on its finding that Charbucks and the famous trademark Starbucks were only "minimally similar," due to the differences in the context in which they were presented to the consumer (e.g., packaging and logos).[89] Although the Second Circuit agreed with the district court's finding of minimal similarity, it reversed the court's order of summary judgment in part because it had given too much weight to the similarity factor.[90] The circuit court reasoned that if Congress had wanted to require "substantial similarity" between the competing marks to establish a dilution claim, it would have put those words in the TDRA, and it did not.[91] The Ninth Circuit has reached the same conclusion.[92]

However, when the defendant's mark is found to be "effectively identical" to the plaintiff's famous trademark, the Ninth Circuit has held that dilution by blurring is effectively presumed. In *Visa International*, the court considered whether the marks eVisa and eVisa.com were likely to dilute the famous mark Visa.[93] The Visa trademark is used to sell credit card services; the parties stipulated that it was famous.[94] The eVisa mark is shorthand for the term Ekaiwa Visa, a mark used to sell services for foreign language instruction. The Ninth Circuit upheld an order of summary judgment in favor of the *plaintiff* in this case, solely based on the strength of the Visa trademark and the degree of similarity between the marks.[95] The court disregarded evidentiary disputes regarding a survey proffered to show association between the two marks, because the evidence was superfluous: "a plaintiff seeking to establish a likelihood of dilution is not required to go to the expense of producing expert testimony or market surveys; it may rely entirely on the

[85] 15 USC §§ 1125(c)(2)(B)(i), (v)–(vi).

[86] *Moseley*, 537 US at 433; *see* discussion at notes 61–65, *supra*.

[87] *See, e.g.*, *Playtex Prods., Inc.* v. *Georgia-Pacific Corp.* 390 F.3d 158, 167 (2d Cir. 2004); *Thane Int'l, Inc.* v. *Trek Bicycle Corp.*, 305 F.3d 894, 905 (9th Cir. 2002); *Fed. Express Corp.* v. *Fed. Espresso, Inc.*, 201 F.3d 168, 176 (2d Cir. 2000).

[88] *See* text accompanying notes 75–77, *supra*.

[89] *Starbucks Corp.* v. *Wolfe's Borough Coffee, Inc.*, 588 F.3d 97, 106–07 (2d Cir. 2009).

[90] *Id.*

[91] *See id.* at 108.

[92] *See Levi Strauss & Co.* v. *Abercrombie & Fitch Trading Co.*, 633 F.3d 1158, 1172 (9th Cir. 2011).

[93] *See Visa Int'l Serv. Ass'n* v. *JSL Corp.*, 610 F.3d 1088, 1091 (9th Cir. 2010).

[94] *Id.* at 1090.

[95] *Id.* at 1091. The word "Visa" as applied to credit card services is neither fanciful nor arbitrary, given that the word was chosen to draw upon "positive mental associations with travel visas, which make potentially difficult transactions relatively simple and facilitate new opportunities and experiences." *Id.* at 1090. In this context "Visa" would at best be suggestive, which is the weakest type of inherently distinctive mark.

characteristics of the marks at issue."[96] Given that a mark must be "famous" to qualify for dilution protection at all, *Visa International* arguably suggests that a likelihood of dilution is presumed whenever the parties' marks are "essentially identical." To rebut such a presumption, the defendant needs to procure "significant evidence to show that dilution is unlikely," thereby shifting the costs of surveys and experts from the plaintiff to the defendant.[97]

In cases where the relevant trademarks are not "substantially similar" or "essentially identical," courts have tended to focus on the statutory factors of "actual association" between the two marks, and the intent of the defendant to create that association.[98] Plaintiffs traditionally prove "association" between two trademarks by introducing survey evidence intended to gauge consumer perceptions of the marks.[99] The Second Circuit has emphasized that consumer surveys have minimal probative value if they do not expose the survey participants to the marks as they are used in commerce, in the context in which consumers would likely view them.[100]

Intent to create an association with a famous trademark is typically based on testimony proffered by the defendant.[101] The district court in *Starbucks* found evidence of intent to create an association with plaintiff's mark when defendant's principal testified he adopted the name "Charbucks" for his product "to evoke associations with the sort of dark-roasted coffee purportedly favored by Starbucks' clientele."[102] Intent to create association does not require proof of "bad faith."[103] The Ninth Circuit has held that a defendant's testimony as to *lack* of intent to create association with the plaintiff's famous mark does not, by itself, rebut the presumption of a likelihood of dilution created when a strong, famous trademark is "essentially identical" to the defendant's mark.[104] However, evidence of such intent also does not, by itself, create a presumption of actual association between the relevant trademarks.[105]

In sum, the factors-based approach to dilution by blurring claims codified in the TDRA has shifted the doctrine of dilution closer to one which recognizes a property right in a "famous" trademark. The statute still defines dilution as an association between two similar trademarks that "impairs the distinctiveness of the plaintiff's famous mark."[106] However, the factors listed in the TDRA do not home in on the impairment element.[107] As a result, courts tend to presume impairment of distinctiveness based on evidence of similarity and association

[96] *Id.* at 1091.

[97] *Id.*

[98] *See* 15 USC §§ 1125(c)(2)(B)(v) (intent to create association), (vi) (actual association). A minority of courts, however, continue to require proof that "association" between marks actually impairs the distinctiveness of the famous trademark. *See, e.g., Gap, Inc.* v. *GAP Adventures Inc.*, No. 07 CIV. 9614 AKH, 2011 WL 2946384, at *16–*17 (SDNY June 24, 2011).

[99] *See, e.g., Starbucks Corp.* v. *Wolfe's Borough Coffee, Inc.*, 736 F.3d 198, 209–11 (2d Cir. 2013); *Jada Toys, Inc.* v. *Mattel, Inc.*, 518 F.3d 628, 636 (9th Cir. 2008).

[100] *See Starbucks Corp.*, 736 F.3d at 209–11.

[101] *See, e.g., Starbucks Corp.* v. *Wolfe's Borough Coffee, Inc.*, 559 F. Supp. 2d 472, 476 (SDNY 2008), *aff'd in part, vacated in part*, 588 F.3d 97 (2d Cir. 2009).

[102] *Starbucks Corp.* v. *Wolfe's Borough Coffee, Inc.*, No. 01CIV.5981(LTS)(THK), 2005 WL 3527126, at *9 (SDNY, Dec. 23, 2005), *vacated*, 477 F.3d 765 (2d Cir. 2007).

[103] *Starbucks Corp.* v. *Wolfe's Borough Coffee, Inc.*, 588 F.3d 97, 109 (2d Cir. 2009).

[104] *Visa Int'l*, 610 F.3d at 1091.

[105] *See Starbucks Corp.* v. *Wolfe's Borough Coffee, Inc.*, 736 F.3d 198, 208–09 (2d Cir. 2013).

[106] 15 USC § 1125(c)(2)(B).

[107] Professor Thomas McCarthy has characterized the six TDRA factors as "both incomplete and misleading" because none of them "directs attention to the crucial issue: is there a likelihood that this defendant's mark is likely to be a use that 'impairs the distinctiveness of the famous mark?'" J. Thomas McCarthy, 4 McCarthy on Trademarks and Unfair Competition § 24:119 (5th ed. 2011).

between the marks. When the creation of this presumption effectively requires the defendant to disprove impairment of the famous trademark, the defendant rarely prevails.

2 Dilution by Tarnishment

The TDRA also prohibits "dilution by tarnishment," defined as an "association arising from the similarity between a mark or trade name and a famous mark that harms the reputation of the famous mark."[108] As discussed *supra*, the FTDA did not explicitly prohibit dilution by tarnishment, although it was generally interpreted as having that effect.[109] Unlike a cause of action for dilution by blurring, the TDRA suggests no factors for courts to consider when determining whether dilution by tarnishment has occurred. Dilution by blurring and by tarnishment are similar in that, as to both causes of action, the plaintiff need not prove likelihood of consumer confusion, competition, or actual economic injury to state a claim.[110] Moreover, both causes of action stem from the consuming public's "association" of the junior user's mark with that of the senior user. However, in a claim for dilution by tarnishment, the association between the two marks is actionable not because it harms the mark's distinctiveness, but primarily because, in theory, it harms the mark owner's goodwill. The concept of dilution by tarnishment has more intuitive appeal than the claim of dilution by blurring but it remains controversial, largely because it may restrict critical speech and thereby raises First Amendment concerns.[111]

To suffer dilution via tarnishment, a famous trademark must sustain reputational harm even though the consumer is not likely to believe that the defendant's product or service is produced or endorsed by the holder of the famous mark. Unlike the injury suffered by a mark holder in a case of trademark infringement, the alleged injury to goodwill triggered by tarnishment is indirect, due to the lack of consumer confusion. In theory, even though the consumers are unlikely to think that the trademark holder is the source of the junior user's unsavory or inferior product or service, they will nonetheless have negative associations with the original trademark as a result of their exposure to the tarnishing use.[112] In a case of tarnishment, the consumer's distaste for the unsavory or inferior product has "rubbed off" on the famous trademark, thereby damaging it. Whether this phenomenon actually occurs in practice is debatable. Recent empirical research suggests that it does not.[113]

As with dilution by blurring, proving that "association" with defendant's mark is likely to harm the reputation of plaintiff's famous trademark can be difficult. To measure impact on reputation directly, a party would have to hire an expert to conduct polling and/or a survey to assess consumer opinion re plaintiff's famous trademark, both before and after exposure to defendant's unsavory mark. However, even more so than in dilution by blurring cases, courts have found dilution by tarnishment absent this type of direct proof.

In practice, courts have rarely required trademark holders to prove reputational harm to sustain a claim of dilution by tarnishment in cases involving the use of marks relating to sex or

108 15 USC § 1125(c)(2)(C).

109 *See, e.g.*, *Kraft Foods Holdings, Inc.* v. *Helm*, 205 F. Supp. 2d 942, 948–50 (ND Ill. 2002); Prager, *supra* note 79, at 124; *see* discussion at notes 66–69, *supra*.

110 15 USC § 1125(c)(1).

111 *See, e.g.*, Michael Handler, *What Can Harm the Reputation of a Trademark? A Critical Re-evaluation of Dilution by Tarnishment*, 106 Trademark Rep. 639 (2016); *see also* notes 140–41, *infra*.

112 *See Ty Inc.* v. *Perryman*, 306 F.3d 509, 511 (7th Cir. 2002).

113 *See* Christopher Buccafusco, Paul J. Heald & Wen Bu, *Testing Tarnishment in Trademark and Copyright Law: The Effect of Pornographic Versions of Protected Marks and Works*, 94 Wash. U.L. Rev. 341 (2016); *see also* Handler, *supra* note 111, at 672–83.

the use of illegal drugs, even prior to the enactment of the TDRA. Courts have adopted a virtual per se rule regarding uses of trademarks in contexts involving pornography, finding almost uniformly that such uses tarnish the image of the mark holder.[114] On the other hand, when the allegedly tarnishing use is a non-vulgar parody or generally does not relate to sex or the illegal use of drugs, the dilution plaintiff has been less likely to prevail.[115]

Since anti-dilution law has been codified in the TDRA, courts have tended to focus their analysis in tarnishment cases on the similarity and association between the relevant trademarks, conflating the two when the defendant's mark is sex-related. The Sixth Circuit has held that, when plaintiff can show a "clear semantic association" between a new mark that is used to sell "sex-related products" and the famous one, this association creates "a kind of rebuttable presumption, or at least a very strong inference" that the new mark is likely to tarnish the famous one.[116] If the presumption is established, the owner of the new mark has "the burden of coming forward with evidence that there is *no* likelihood or probability of tarnishment," such as "expert testimony or surveys or polls or customer testimony."[117] Because of this burden-shifting, the court in *Victoria's Secret* found a likelihood of dilution by tarnishment, even though it also found that the tarnishing effect on plaintiff's famous trademark was "somewhat speculative."[118]

As illustrated by *Victoria's Secret* and *Visa International*, courts in cases involving dilution by tarnishment and by blurring tend to presume a likelihood of dilution if defendant's mark is highly similar to plaintiff's famous one; the presumption of tarnishment also effectively requires that defendant's mark be sex-related. By creating this presumption, these courts have placed the burden of proof on dilution defendants to disprove harm. Plaintiffs tend to prevail when the burden of proof is shifted in this manner, given that defendants often lack the resources to *disprove* dilution, either by blurring or by tarnishment.[119]

3 *Affirmative Defenses to Federal Trademark Dilution Claims*

The TDRA codifies three affirmative defenses that are designed to protect First Amendment and competitive interests that might otherwise be threatened by the broad protections embodied in the statute: (1) fair use, including comparative advertising and criticism, commentary or parodies, (2) news reporting, and (3) noncommercial use.[120] Most of the litigation surrounding these defenses has focused on fair use. Unlike the FTDA,[121] the TDRA specifies that parodies or

[114] *See, e.g., Dallas Cowboys Cheerleaders, Inc.* v. *Pussycat Cinemas, Ltd.*, 604 F.2d 200, 204 (2d Cir. 1979); *Pillsbury Co.* v. *Milky Way Prods., Inc.*, 215 USPQ 125, 126, 134 (ND Ga. 1981); *but see Burnett* v. *Twentieth Century Fox Film Corp.*, 491 F. Supp. 2d 962, 972 (CD Cal. 2007).

[115] *See, e.g., Hormel Foods Corp.* v. *Jim Henson Prods., Inc.*, 73 F.3d 497, 506, 508 (2d Cir. 1996) (defendant's use of wild boar puppet named "Spa'am" in the movie *Muppett Treasure Island* did not dilute or tarnish the SPAM trademark (for lunch meat)); *see also Louis Vuitton Malletier SA* v. *Haute Diggity Dog, LLC*, 507 F.3d 252 (4th Cir. 2007) (defendant's Chewy Vuitton dog toys did not dilute plaintiff's famous fashion trademark in part because they were a successful parody).

[116] *V Secret Catalogue, Inc.* v. *Moseley*, 605 F.3d 382, 388 (6th Cir. 2010).

[117] *Id.* at 388–89.

[118] *Id.* at 389.

[119] This type of evidence is notoriously costly. *See, e.g., Lon Tai Shing Co., Ltd.* v. *Koch & Lowy*, 19 USPQ 2d 1081, 1095 (SDNY June 20, 1991) (estimating the cost of conducting a consumer survey in a trademark case at approximately $100,000).

[120] 15 USC § 1125(c)(3).

[121] The FTDA definition of fair use was limited to "use of a famous mark by another person in comparative commercial advertising or promotion to identify the competing goods or services of the owner of the famous mark." 15 USC §1125(c)(4)(A). The FTDA also contained a general exemption for "noncommercial uses" of a mark, which is identical to the language in the TDRA. *Id.* at (c)(2)(C).

criticism of a famous trademark fall within its definition of "fair use."[122] However, the TDRA excludes from fair use protection any use of a mark that serves as a "designation of source" for the defendant's "own goods or services."[123] As a result of that exemption and the constrictive interpretation of fair use by many courts,[124] the fair use defense under the TDRA remains inadequate to insulate from liability many uses of a famous trademark that should not be actionable.[125]

Parodies are often a controversial form of trademark fair use. In the context of trademark law, courts have defined "parody" as "a simple form of entertainment conveyed by juxtaposing the irreverent representation of the trademark with the idealized image created by the mark's owner."[126] Simply stated, parodies use trademarks (often famous ones) to mock the companies that "own" those marks and may profit from them to an enormous degree. Historically, trademark holders have not appreciated this type of humor and have sued to enjoin it, often on the grounds that the "joke" constitutes dilution by tarnishment.[127] At least to some degree, however, the First Amendment to the US Constitution protects "successful" parodies.[128]

To be considered "successful" and hence not actionable as trademark infringement or dilution, a parody must copy the original trademark only so much as is necessary to communicate to the public that it is making fun of the trademark (and/or its owner) and does not originate from the trademark holder itself. "Thus, '[a] parody relies upon a difference from the original mark, presumably a humorous difference, in order to produce its desired effect.'"[129] For example, the Fourth Circuit held that Haute Diggity Dog's use of the mark "Chewy Vuitton" for its own brand of dog toys was a successful parody of the famous trademark held by Louis Vuitton, maker of luxury handbags.[130] The court concluded that Haute Diggity Dog's parody of Louis Vuitton succeeded because it "undoubtedly and deliberately conjures up the famous [Louis Vuitton] marks and trade dress, but at the same time, it communicates that it is not the [Louis Vuitton] product."[131] Even though the parody was "successful," however, the statutory language designed to protect parodies did not apply.

A finding of a successful parody does not guarantee immunity from liability under the TDRA, which by its plain language does not apply when defendant's mark is being used as a designation of source for its goods, as in this case.[132] The *Louis Vuitton* opinion does not address the First Amendment in its analysis of the defendant's parodic use of the Louis Vuitton trademark. Rather, the court considered the parodic nature of Haute Diggity Dog's use of the Louis Vuitton mark in balancing the statutory factors for dilution by blurring.[133] Although the court in *Louis Vuitton* ultimately concluded that the Chewy Vuitton parody would neither "impair the distinctiveness" of the famous trademark nor harm its reputation, that result was not a foregone conclusion.

[122] *Id.* at § 1125(c)(3)(A)(ii).
[123] *Id.* at § 1125(c)(3)(A).
[124] *See* text at notes 133–38, *infra*.
[125] *See* Handler, *supra* note 111, at 687.
[126] *Louis Vuitton Malletier SA* v. *Haute Diggity Dog, LLC*, 507 F.3d 252, 260 (4th Cir. 2007).
[127] *See, e.g.*, *Mattel, Inc.* v. *MCA Records, Inc.*, 296 F.3d 894, 902–03 (9th Cir. 2002); *Jordache Enterprises, Inc.* v. *Hogg Wyld, Ltd.*, 828 F.2d 1482, 1486 (10th Cir. 1987); *see also* Stacey L. Dogan & Mark A. Lemley, *Parody as Brand*, 47 U.C. Davis L. Rev. 473, 484–85 (2013) (listing cases).
[128] *See Mattel*, 296 F.3d at 902–07.
[129] *Haute Diggity Dog*, 507 F.3d at 260.
[130] *Id.*
[131] *Id.*
[132] *Id.* at 266; *see also* Dogan & Lemley, *supra* note 127, at 488.
[133] *Haute Diggity Dog*, 507 F.3d at 267.

Moreover, subtle yet humorous references to a famous trademark are not likely to be considered successful parodies. For example, in *Starbucks*, the Second Circuit found that the defendant's reference to the Starbucks trademark via the "Charbucks" brand was at best a "subtle satire" and therefore too indirect to be considered a parody.[134] Under the specific language of the Act, the business owner who wishes to choose a trademark that parodies but does not dilute is therefore faced with a difficult task. A parody, by its very nature, evidences an "intent to associate" with a famous trademark.[135] That intent to associate, however, is one of the factors that tends to show a likelihood of dilution by blurring.[136] If the parody is ultimately deemed unsuccessful, efforts to associate with the mark owner will constitute evidence of dilution, as it did in this case.

The statute's fair use exemption for comparative advertising[137] likewise does not appreciate subtlety. Comparative advertising has long been considered a fair use defense to a claim alleging misuse of a trademark, both in the infringement and dilution contexts.[138] However, if the comparative advertising is not stated in an obvious way, the defense will not apply. The *Starbucks* case illustrates this principle as well. Defendant's parody defense, as noted above, was rejected in part because the reference that it made to the Starbucks trademark was too subtle and indirect. The court also rejected the parody claim because it effectively interpreted defendant's message, as communicated via the Charbucks marks, as one of comparative advertising (casting Starbucks in a positive rather than a negative light) rather than humor. The court described the Charbucks logo as a "beacon to identify Charbucks as a coffee that competes at the same level and quality as Starbucks in producing dark-roasted coffees."[139] If the defendant had made this statement directly – "this coffee competes at the same level and quality as Starbucks in producing dark-roasted coffees" – rather than using the Charbucks marks as a "beacon" to convey the same message, its use would have been protected from a dilution claim as a matter of law.

Concerns about the First Amendment implications of anti-dilution laws have persisted, despite the TDRA's inclusion of the affirmative defenses described above.[140] First Amendment objections to the scope and implementation of the TDRA have increased since the Supreme Court invalidated the Lanham Act's section 2(a) bar to the registration of "disparaging" and "scandalous" marks on First Amendment grounds, in *Matal* v. *Tam* and *Iancu* v. *Brunetti*.[141] Dilution by tarnishment raises particular First Amendment concerns, because it regulates speech – based on the perceived impact of that speech on plaintiff's reputation – without requiring the plaintiff to show any "actual economic harm" as a result of that speech. The

[134] *Starbucks Corp.* v. *Wolfe's Borough Coffee, Inc.*, 588 F.3d 97, 113 (2d Cir. 2009).

[135] *See Haute Diggity Dog*, 507 F.3d at 260 ("A parody must convey two simultaneous – and contradictory – messages: that it is the original, but also that it is not the original and is instead a parody") (citations omitted).

[136] 15 USC § 1125(c)(2)(B)(v); *see* Dogan & Lemley, *supra* note 127, at 488.

[137] 15 USC § 1125 (c)(3)(A)(i) (exempting from liability any "advertising or promotion that permits consumers to compare goods or services").

[138] *See, e.g.*, *Smith* v. *Chanel, Inc.*, 402 F.2d 526, 565–66 (9th Cir. 1968).

[139] *Starbucks Corp.*, 588 F.3d at 113.

[140] *See, e.g.*, Rierson, *supra* note 5, at 292–97; Lisa P. Ramsey, *Increasing First Amendment Scrutiny of Trademark Law*, 61 S.M.U. L. Rev. 381, 438–47 (2008); Mary LaFrance, *No Reason to Live: Dilution Laws as Unconstitutional Restrictions on Commercial Speech*, 58 S.C.L. Rev. 709 (2007).

[141] *See Matal* v. *Tam*, 137 S. Ct. 1744 (2017); *Iancu* v. *Brunetti*, 139 S.Ct. 2294 (2019). Several commentators have argued that these decisions should result in the invalidation of trademark anti-dilution law under the First Amendment. *See, e.g.*, Sara Gold, *Does Dilution "Dilute" the First Amendment? Trademark Dilution and the Right to Free Speech after Tam and Brunetti*, 59 IDEA: L. Rev. Franklin Pierce Ctr. for Intell. Prop. 483 (2019); Lisa P. Ramsey, *Free Speech Challenges to Trademark Law after Matal v. Tam*, 56 Hous. L. Rev. 401 (2018).

breadth of the dilution cause of action, in its modern conception, increases the likelihood that it will impinge upon the rights of others to speak and to compete.

IV CONCLUSION

In sum, anti-dilution law in the United States today – as it has been codified in the FTDA, later revised in the TDRA, and interpreted by federal courts – has drifted ever closer towards extending a property right in a trademark to the person or entity who uses it and registers it. Although the TDRA defines dilution as an association between two similar marks that impairs the distinctiveness of the plaintiff's famous mark, courts have tended to ignore the element of impairment because it is not reflected in a statutory factor. As a result, holders of famous trademarks can effectively enjoin the use of any highly similar mark, unless the user of that mark can disprove dilutive effect. Trademark holders' need for this broad, property-like form of protection is dubious, especially given that the modern likelihood of confusion standard for trademark infringement prohibits much of the same conduct originally targeted by anti-dilution laws. Congress, however, has shown little interest in scaling back the scope of trademark protections. Whether the TDRA will ultimately withstand constitutional scrutiny, particularly under the Court's recent First Amendment jurisprudence, remains to be seen.

30

Dilution and Damage beyond Confusion in the European Union

*Anselm Kamperman Sanders**

I INTRODUCTION

Dilution is commonly defined as the "gradual whittling away of the distinctive character of a trademark." An action against dilution is relevant in cases where the consumer is not confused as to the commercial origin of goods or services and where the same or similar sign is used in relation to dissimilar goods or services for which the claimant's mark is registered. Yet the original concept articulated in the first case considering protection of a trademark beyond the notion of confusion and similarity of goods, the 1924 *Odol* decision of the Landgericht at Elberfeld in Germany, speaks of damage to the drawing or selling power of a mark leading to the lessening of the mark's significance in its own market, even if the goods to which the defendant applies the same sign are not in competition with the plaintiff's goods. This contribution assesses whether the common definition of dilution fully encompasses the type of damage that goes beyond confusing uses. The contribution also addresses the question of whether from an international and domestic European Union perspective the protection of reputational value of a trademark is commensurate to the protection of the "interest of the owner" the Trade Related Aspects to Intellectual Property Rights (TRIPS) Agreement of the World Trade Organization (WTO) defines as a minimum standard in the context of protection of well-known marks under 6*bis* of the Paris Convention for the Protection of Industrial Property (Paris Convention).

II THE INTERNATIONAL FRAMEWORK

The protection of trademarks has traditionally been confined to the protection of signs used to distinguish the goods of one trade from that of another from confusion in trade. For this purpose, trademarks need to be capable of conferring a commercial origin.[1] This means the scope of protection for trademarks has traditionally been confined to address the use in the course of trade of identical or similar signs used in relation to identical or similar goods or services for which the

* Professor of Intellectual Property Law, Director of the Advanced Masters Intellectual Property Law and Knowledge Management (IPKM LLM/MSc), and Academic Director of the Institute for Globalization and International Regulation (IGIR) at Maastricht University, the Netherlands; Deputy Judge, Court of Appeal The Hague.

[1] Agreement on Trade-Related Aspects of Intellectual Property Rights, Apr. 15, 1994, Marrakesh Agreement Establishing the World Trade Organization, Annex 1C, 1869 UNTS 299, 33 ILM 1197, art. 15 (1994) [hereinafter TRIPS Agreement].

trademark has been registered, where such use results in the likelihood of confusion.[2] In cases of double identity, confusion will be presumed.

In the context of the Paris Convention, trademark registrations are, in principle, subject to domestic law.[3] Article 6*bis* of the Paris Convention,[4] introduced in the 1925 Hague revision of the Convention, offers holders of marks that are well-known in the respective member state the enhanced protection of the Paris Union, even if the mark in question is unregistered. Article 6*bis* Paris Convention has a number of shortcomings in that it extends only to the use of identical or similar goods (not services) and most countries limit the scope to marks that are famous in the jurisdiction itself.[5]

The Hague revision Conference of the Paris Convention also introduced an obligation to establish safeguards against practices of unfair competition. Article 10*bis* of the Paris Convention obligates the member states to enact a general clause against *any act of competition contrary to honest practices in industrial or commercial matters*.[6] This was a rather bold move that, to this day, has not resulted in a uniform implementation, let alone interpretation of what protection against unfair competition actually entails.[7] Britain especially is still reluctant to engage with a general concept of unfair competition,[8] and the statement: "To draw a line between fair and unfair competition, between what is reasonable and unreasonable, passes the

[2] *Id.* at art. 16.1: "The owner of a registered trademark shall have the exclusive right to prevent all third parties not having the owner's consent from using in the course of trade identical or similar signs for goods or services which are identical or similar to those in respect of which the trademark is registered where such use would result in a likelihood of confusion. In case of the use of an identical sign for identical goods or services, a likelihood of confusion shall be presumed. The rights described above shall not prejudice any existing prior rights, nor shall they affect the possibility of Members making rights available on the basis of use."

[3] Paris Convention for the Protection of Industrial Property, Mar. 20, 1888, as revised at the Stockholm Revision Conference, July 14, 1967, 21 UST 1538, TIAS No. 6903, 828 UNTS 305 [hereinafter Paris Convention].

[4] *Id.* at art. 6*bis* : "The countries of the Union undertake, *ex officio* if their legislation so permits, or at the request of an interested party, to refuse or to cancel the registration, and to prohibit the use, of a trademark which constitutes a reproduction, an imitation, or a translation, liable to create confusion, of a mark considered by the competent authority of the country of registration or use to be well known in that country as being already the mark of a person entitled to the benefits of this Convention and used for identical or similar goods. These provisions shall also apply when the essential part of the mark constitutes a reproduction of any such well-known mark or an imitation liable to create confusion therewith."

[5] Anette Kur, *Well-Known Marks, Highly Renowned Marks and Marks Having a Reputation – What's It All About*, 23 INT'L REV. OF INTELL. PROP. AND COMPETITION L. (2018).

[6] Paris Convention, *supra* note 3, art. 10*bis* PC:

> (1) The countries of the Union are bound to assure to nationals of such countries effective protection against unfair competition. (2) Any act of competition contrary to honest practices in industrial or commercial matters constitutes an act of unfair competition. (3) The following in particular shall be prohibited:
>
> 1 all acts of such a nature as to create confusion by any means whatever with the establishment, the goods, or the industrial or commercial activities, of a competitor;
> 2 false allegations in the course of trade of such a nature as to discredit the establishment, the goods, or the industrial or commercial activities, of a competitor;
> 3 indications or allegations the use of which in the course of trade is liable to mislead the public as to the nature, the manufacturing process, the characteristics, the suitability for their purpose, or the quantity, of the goods.

[7] *See* DAS RECHT DES UNLAUTEREN WETTBEWERBS IN DEN MITGLIESTAATEN DER EUROPÄISCHEN WIRTSCHAFTSGEMEINSHAFT vol. 1–6 (Eugen Ulmer ed., 1965–1981); on the lack of progress in harmonization, *see* Gerhard Schricker, *European Harmonisation of Unfair Competition Law – A Futile Venture?*, 22 INT'L REV. OF INTELL. PROP. AND COMPETITION L. 788 (1991); Gerhard Schricker, 25 *Years of Protection Against Unfair Competition*, 26 INT'L REV. OF INTELL. PROP. AND COMPETITION L. 782 (1995).

[8] *Hodgkinson & Corby Ltd and Roho Inc.* v. *Wards Mobility Services Ltd* [1995] FSR. 169: "There is no tort of copying. There is no tort of taking a man's market or customers. Neither the market nor the customers are the plaintiffs to own. There is no tort of making use of another's goodwill as such. There is no tort of competition."

power of the courts"[9] is still relied upon.[10] In other European jurisdictions, most notably in the Benelux countries, the law against unfair competition served as an underpinning for the development of the trademark dilution concept.[11]

As one of the WTO Agreements, the TRIPS Agreement requires its members (customs territories as well as states) to adhere to the principles of the Paris Convention and in section 2 (Articles 15–21) also provides for minimum standards that are relevant to the protection of trademarks.[12] Articles 16.2 and 16.3 of TRIPS provide clarification with respect to Article 6*bis* of the Paris Convention. First of all, service marks are to receive the same protection under Article 6*bis* PC as trademarks for goods.[13] Furthermore, "[i]n determining whether a trade mark is well-known, account shall be taken of the knowledge of the trademark in the relevant sector of the public, including knowledge in the Member concerned which has been obtained as a result of the promotion of the trademark." This wording under Article 16.2 of TRIPS is generally understood to mean that a mark can be well-known without actual use in the member where protection is sought. The wording would supposedly allow promotion in another country to be sufficient, provided some form of international or cross-border renown has extended to the public in the member where protection is sought.

Article 16.3 of TRIPS provides a rather confusing clarification to Article 6*bis* of the Paris Convention, in that it protects well-known marks in relation to use to goods or services that are dissimilar to those of a *registered* well-known mark, if such use would indicate a connection between those goods or services and the owner of the registered trademark and provided that the interests of the owner of the registered trademark are likely to be damaged by such use.[14] To discuss "registered trademarks" in the context of Article 6*bis* PC is peculiar, as this provision clearly applies in case a well-known mark is *not* registered, but where nevertheless it is a well-known mark recognized as being the mark of a person entitled to the benefits.

If we simply consider the intent and purpose of this provision, it is to enlarge the scope or protection of well-known and famous marks beyond that of confusion of the public as to origin and allocation of the product or service and to protect against dilution.

Although we can simply put this matter aside as an error in drafting with respect to well-known marks that have not yet been registered, it nevertheless raises the question which registry, if any, needs to be consulted in order to determine (dis)similarity of goods or services, whether

[9] *Mogul Steamship Co.* v. *McGregor, Gow and Co.*, 23 QBD 598, 615 (1889).

[10] *See Hodgkinson*, *supra* note 8: "At the heart of passing off lies deception or its likelihood, deception of the ultimate consumer in particular . . . Never has the tort shown even a slight tendency to stray beyond classes of deception. Were it to do so it would enter the field of honest competition, declared unlawful for some reason other than deceptiveness. Why there should be any such reason I cannot imagine. It would serve only to stifle competition." *See also Erven Warnink* v. *Townend* [1980] RPC 31; *Reckitt & Colman* v. *Borden* [1990] 1 WLR 491; *Cadbury Schweppes* v. *Pub Squash* [1981] 1 WLR 193; *Taittinger* v. *Allbev* [1993] FSR 641.

[11] For an overview, *see* Anselm Kamperman Sanders, Unfair Competition Law – The Protection of Intellectual and Industrial Creativity (1997).

[12] TRIPS Agreement, *supra* note 1, at art. 2.1.

[13] *Id.* at art. 16.2: art. 6*bis* of the Paris Convention (1967) shall apply, *mutatis mutandis*, to services. In determining whether a trademark is well-known, members shall take account of the knowledge of the trademark in the relevant sector of the public, including knowledge in the member concerned which has been obtained as a result of the promotion of the trademark.

[14] *Id.* at art. 16.3 TRIPS: Article 6*bis* of the Paris Convention (1967) shall apply, *mutatis mutandis*, to goods or services which are not similar to those in respect of which a trademark is registered, provided that use of that trademark in relation to those goods or services would indicate a connection between those goods or services and the owner of the registered trademark and provided that the interests of the owner of the registered trademark are likely to be damaged by such use.

there is a likely connection, what the interests of the "owner" are, and whether these interests are likely to be damaged.

III DILUTION – A CONCEPT WITH WATERY ORIGINS[15]

The concept of dilution, however, predates the TRIPS Agreement and even the Hague revision of the Paris Convention. Its origins can be traced to a German court decision by the Landgericht at Elberfeld of 1924.[16] The case involves the registered trademark "Odol" for mouthwash. This mouthwash was first marketed in 1892 by the Dresdner Chemisches Laboratorium Lingner, which developed the mouthwash and came up with the name by combining the Greek words odus (tooth) and oleum (oil). Due to the antibacterial properties of Odol, it became a huge success, establishing mouthwash as a prime hygiene product and the mark Odol as a household name. On 5 March 1895, the Dresden company registered the mark with the German trademark office as a tooth-and-mouth cleaning product/product for oral hygiene.

In 1924, Dresdner Chemisches Laboratorium Lingner discovered that another firm intended to use the same trademark in relation to steel railroad ties. The German trademark act of the time provided grounds for opposition or infringement only if a likelihood of public confusion could be shown.[17] Furthermore, the scope of protection was usually limited to similarity of goods. Only if the public was led to believe that the goods came from the same source could the scope of trademark protection be extended to non-competing goods. This can be seen as the use of a mark that gives rise to a likelihood of confusion "in a wider sense." Nevertheless, confusion as to the source remained a necessary prerequisite for opposition and infringement proceedings and this prevented Odol mouthwash from bringing a successful action against the steel company's application for Odol. It was held the public was unlikely to believe that *Odol* steel would come from the company producing *Odol* mouthwash. The trial court at Elberfeld, however, came up with an alternative to those of source confusion and introduced a new doctrine, now known as trademark dilution. In order to break through the barrier of the requirement for a likelihood of confusion, the court relied on general principles of tort enshrined in the German civil code, which later served as an example for the general clause in the German Law against Unfair Competition (UWG).[18] The German Civil Code (BGB), which entered into force on 1 January 1900, contained two general clauses in sections 138 and 826 BGB, which referred to actions that could be deemed tortious because they would contravene "guten Sitten," or good morals.[19] With roots in the Roman legal principle of "boni mores," these general clauses were included to allow judges to deal with new and unforeseen legal developments. In short, these general clauses allow for the creation of judge-made law. The court held the following:

> To be sure, the parties, on account of the wholly different goods put out by them are not in actual competition. That, however, is beside the point. The complainant has created a demand for its goods, while employing thereon a word having attractive power, for only through the year-long activity of the complainant was its selling power acquired. … Complainant's ability to

[15] Contains an adapted passage from Anselm Kamperman Sanders, *Odol: The Introduction of a Watery Concept with Steeled Resilience, in* LANDMARK INTELLECTUAL PROPERTY CASES AND THEIR LEGACY 51–62 (Christopher Heath & Anselm Kamperman Sanders eds., 2011).

[16] Landgericht Elberfeld [Civil Court of Elberfeld] in (1925) 25 JURISTISCHE WOCHENSCHRIFT 502.

[17] Markenschutzgesetz, German Trademark Statute of May 12, 1894.

[18] Gesetz gegen den unlauteren Wettbewerb (UWG), German Anti-competition Statute of Mar. 7, 2004.

[19] Bürgerliche Gesetzbuch (BGB) (Civil Code), §§ 138, 826 *translation at* https://bmjv.de/SharedDocs/Gesetzgebungsverfahren/DE/Berufsanerkennungsrichtlinie.html.

compete with other manufacturers of mouth wash will be impaired if the significance of its mark is lessened.[20]

The decision lay dormant in Germany for many years and the concept of dilution was not revisited in Germany until the 1980s, when the German Supreme Court (BGH) was able to finalize the application of the general clause of the German Law against Unfair Competition[21] in deciding a number of comparable cases involving well-known trademarks.[22] Similarly, elsewhere in Europe, claims for trademark dilution were treated as claims in unfair competition and the classical notion of trademark infringement continued to revolve around the notion of confusion as to trade origin. This continued until new types of trademark damage were introduced in the Benelux countries in 1971.

A *Reintroduction of Dilution in Europe*

In the context of the Benelux customs union, Belgium, the Netherlands and Luxemburg replaced their national variants of the old French trademark law of 1811 with one single legal instrument – the Uniform Benelux Trademarks Act that entered into force on 1 January 1971. The Benelux countries decided to base their uniform laws on the most "modern" thinking on trademark law at the time, taking into account changes to business practices and marketing. A key role in this process of adopting the concept of dilution was taken by negotiating Dutch civil servant Georg Bodenhausen, who became the director of the United International Bureaux for the Protection of Intellectual Property (BIRPI) from 1963 to 1970, and the first director-general of the World Intellectual Property Organization (WIPO) from 1970 to 1973. He was the author of the leading book on the Paris Convention at the time, and was very much involved in articulating the shortcomings of Article 6*bis* of the Paris Convention, leading much later to the enhancements contained in Article 16 of TRIPS.[23]

Due in part to Bodenhausen's vision, the Uniform Benelux Trademarks Act was greatly influenced by Schechter's article "Rational Basis of Trademark Protection"[24] and the further systematic exposé of the dilution doctrine by Rudolf Callmann. Callmann was a Jewish German refugee who had written extensively on the German law against unfair competition before fleeing to the United States.[25] He systematically captured Schechter's arguments and those expressed in the *Odol* decision in the context of trademark law, thereby providing the theoretical underpinnings for the action against dilution as a form of trademark infringement. From the first

[20] (1925) XXV Markenschutz und Wettbewerb 264 – "Odol"; [1924] Gewerblicher Rechtsschutz und Urheberrecht (GRUR) 204; Sanders, *supra* note 15, at 51–62.

[21] *See* Dietrich C. Ohlgart, *Gebrauch der Marke eines Dritten ohne Verwechslungsgefahr, in* Gewerblicher Rechtsschutz und Urheberrecht, Internationaler Teil 211 (1989); Ansgar Ohly, Richterrecht und Generalklausel im Recht des unlauteren Wettbewerbs 268–314 (1995).

[22] Bundesgerichtshof [BGH] [Federal Court of Justice] 1983, Gewerblicher Rechtsschutz und Urheberrecht 247 – "Rolls Royce /Dimple" (Ger.); Bundesgerichtshof [BGH] [Federal Court of Justice] 1985, Gewerblicher Rechtsschutz und Urheberrecht 876 – "Tchibo/Rolex" (Ger.); Bundesgerichtshof [BGH] [Federal Court of Justice] 1986, Gewerblicher Rechtsschutz und Urheberrecht, 759 (Ger.); Bundesgerichtshof [BGH] [Federal Court of Justice] 1987, Gewerblicher Rechtsschutz und Urheberrecht, 711 (Ger.); Bundesgerichtshof [BGH] [Federal Court of Justice] 1991, Gewerblicher Rechtsschutz und Urheberrecht, 465 (Ger.).

[23] G. H. C. Bodenhausen, Guide to the Application of the Paris Convention for the Protection of Industrial Property as Revised at Stockholm in 1967 (1968)).

[24] Frank Schechter, *Rational Basis of Trademark Protection*, 40 Harv. L. Rev. 813 (1927).

[25] Rudolf Callmann, Der Unlautere Wettbewerb – Kommentar zum Gesetz gegen den unlauteren Wettbewerb und zu den materiell-rechtlichen Vorschriften des Gesetzes zum Schutze der Warenbezeichnungen (1929).

edition of Callmann's influential treatise on *The Law of Unfair Competition and Trade-Marks* in 1945, he advocated for the incorporation of protecting the advertising value of the trademark in trademark law, actually coining the term "dilution," and describing it as follows:

> The injury [from dilution] differs materially from that arising out of confusion. ... [C]onfusion leads to immediate injury, while dilution is the infection, which, if allowed to spread, will inevitably destroy the advertising value of the mark. ... It should be recognized therefore that dilution gives rise to a cause of action and should not be relegated to the status of a test of infringement.[26]

From its inception, the Uniform Benelux Trademarks Act sought to provide relief for use in the course of trade of signs corresponding with marks with a reputation in relation to goods or services dissimilar to those for which the trademark had been registered.

The 1971 Benelux Act's rules for trademark infringement were set out in Article 13A and read:

> Without prejudice to the application of ordinary civil law in matters of tort, the proprietor of a trade mark may, by virtue of his exclusive right, oppose:
>
> 1 any use of the mark or similar sign for the goods or services in respect of which the mark is registered, or for similar goods or services;
> 2 any other use, made without a valid reason in the course of trade of the mark or of a similar sign, likely to cause the proprietor of the mark damage.

Crucial to the application in practice, however, is the notion that there is a commensurate relationship between the strength and notoriety of the mark and the scope of protection entitled to the owner.[27] The strength of the mark may be the result of its use, but investments in advertising and thus the importance of the practice of "branding" is also recognized. This means that where goods or services are similar or dissimilar, a claim for dilution was possible in both cases, as it was included in the definition of damage. The seminal decision of the Benelux Court of Justice in *Colgate-Palmolive/Bols*,[28] confirms this advertising function.[29] In this case, Colgate-Palmolive marketed a detergent under the mark "Klarein." This mark was phonetically similar to a well-known mark of a Dutch gin "Claeryn." In the assessment of damage, the court asked whether there was "a likelihood of association" between the registered mark and the sign used. It held that the use of a similar sign on a detergent would negatively affect the persuasive (advertising) power of the mark for gin, as the consumer would no longer have the unique association between the mark Claeryn and gin. Viewed from an almost palpable perspective, the consumer

[26] Rudolf Callmann, The Law of Unfair Competition and Trademarks § 84.2 (1945).

[27] Benelux Court, Decision of Oct. 5, 1981, Nederlandse Jurisprudentie 71 (1984), holding that the lower the distinctive character of the mark, the greater the need for similarity, impacting the scope of protection. *See also* Case C-408/01, *Adidas-Salomon AG and Adidas Benelux BV* v. *Fitnessworld Trading Ltd.*, 2003 ECR I-582, where the court also developed the concept of a "link" between an earlier well-known mark and the later sign, stating that "the existence of a link must be assessed globally, taking in to account all the factors relevant to the case at issue." In particular, the factors to be taken into account are:

1 The degree of similarity between the trademarks.
2 The nature of the products or services for which the trademarks have been respectively registered, including the degree of proximity or dissimilarity between these products or services, as well as of the relevant public.
3 The level of notoriety of the earlier trademark.
4 The distinctive character of the earlier trademark, whether it is inherent or acquired due to use.
5 The existence of a risk of confusion in the mind of the public.

[28] Benelux Court, Decision of Mar. 1, 1975, Nederlandse Jurisprudentie 472 (1975).

[29] Anselm Kamperman Sanders & Spyros Maniatis, *A Consumer Trade Mark – Protection Based on Origin and Quality*, 11 Eur. Intell. Prop. Rev. 406 (1993).

should not get the taste of soap in the mouth when drinking or thinking of Claeryn. The damage that may arise in this respect was categorized as the loss of attractive, or "appetite for purchase," power of the mark, and the loss of exclusivity. It is not necessary to find additional factors, such as the use of the alleged infringing sign results in a lessening of the distinctive character of the mark, confusion, taking unfair advantage of the notoriety of the mark, or that the mark is famous. However, finding a combination of these factors would strengthen the position of the rightsholder. In listing these forms of damages in the context of the case at hand, the Benelux Court of Justice provided an almost full catalogue of damaging uses that may give rise to liability.[30]

A common misunderstanding is that the broad scope of trademark protection led to an avalanche of cases decided in favor of trademark proprietors in the absence of confusion. The threshold for likelihood of damages was quite substantial, especially in cases of use on dissimilar goods or services. In *Jeep for motor vehicles* v. *Jeep for Clothing*, for example, the Court of Appeal Amsterdam[31] held that loss of uniqueness and associative power is inherent in the mere fact of the use of that same mark "Jeep" for dissimilar goods and is not sufficient grounds to accept damages in the given case. Since the markets were very distant from each other, damages were held to be unlikely. Looking back, it is important to realize Jeep was not a widely established name in the consumer automotive market at the time. Its use was restricted to rather specialty terrain vehicles and therefore was not well-known.

Finally, it is relevant to point out that the drafting of the Benelux provision enables the rightsholder to address uses other than those for the purposes of distinguishing goods or services. This resulted in decisions of damaging use in the course of trade, even though classical "trademark use"[32] was absent. The cases often revolve around derogatory or unsavory presentations of the complainant's trademark,[33] where there is still a form of commercial gain.[34]

The Benelux legislation was, like all EU member states' trademark instruments, superseded in 1991 by harmonizing effects of the First Trade Mark Directive[35] and augmented by the Community Trade Mark Regulation (European Union Trade Mark – EUTM) that came into force on 15 March 1994.[36]

B EU Harmonization and a Unitary Title for EU Trade Marks

The idea of providing protection beyond the scope of confusion found its way into the First Trade Mark Directive and subsequently the EU Trade Mark Regulation. These instruments

30 *See also* Benelux Court, Decision of May 22, 1985, NEDERLANDSE JURISPRUDENTIE 770 (1985).

31 Court of Appeal Amsterdam, Decision of May 22, 1980, BIJBLAD INDUSTRIËLE EIGENDOM 1981, 324.

32 For later discussions in the EU on this issue, *see* Case C-206/01, *Arsenal Football Club Plc* v. *Matthew Reed*, 2003 ETMR 19; *But see* Case C-48/05, *Adam Opel AG* v. *Autec AG*, 2007 ECR I-55.

33 *See, e.g.*, Court of Appeal Amsterdam, Decision of Dec. 18, 1977, NEDERLANDSE JURISPRUDENTIE 59 (1977), involving the display and use of a Coca-Cola bottle in a sex scene in a film called *Alicia*; President District Court Amsterdam, Decision of Dec. 18, 1981, BIJBLAD INDUSTRIËLE EIGENDOM 1982, 41, holding as unnecessarily damaging the depiction of the Philips logo in which the stars were replaced by swastikas on the cover of a periodical news magazine to highlight a story with the headline "Eindhoven 1920–1940 – The Terror of the Philips Police"; President Commercial Court Brussels, Decision of Feb. 24, 1987, Guerlain, BIJBLAD INDUSTRIËLE EIGENDOM 1988, 158, involving the use of the trademark in a sex comic.

34 Benelux Court, Decision of July 9, 1984, NEDERLANDSE JURISPRUDENTIE 101 (1985).

35 First Council Directive 89/104 1988 OJ (L 040) 1–7, to approximate the laws of the member states relating to trademarks. Its provisions were required to be introduced into national law by Dec. 29, 1991. Later amended by Directive 2008/95/, 2008 OJ (L 299) 25 (EC). The current version is Directive 2015/2436, 2015 OJ (L 336) 1–26 (EC) to approximate the laws of the member states relating to trademarks.

36 Council Regulation 40/94 1 (OJ (L 11) 1 (EC). Amended inter alia by Council Regulation 207/2009 OJ (L 78) 1 (EC). The current version is Regulation 2017/1001 OJ (L 154) 1–99 (EC).

offered protection for marks with a reputation against use on dissimilar goods or services as "taking unfair advantage of, or causing detriment to, the distinctive character or the repute of the trademark."[37] In fact, the Benelux countries had requested such a provision to be included in Article 5(2) of the Directive:[38]

> Any Member State may also provide that the proprietor [of a registered trademark] shall be entitled to prevent all third parties not having his consent from using in the course of trade any sign which is identical with, or similar to, the trademark in relation to goods or services which are not similar to those for which the trade mark is registered, where the latter has a reputation in the Member State and where use of that sign without due cause takes unfair advantage of, or is detrimental to, the distinctive character or the repute of the trademark.

Curiously, protection against use in relation to the same or similar goods was covered by a more nebulously drafted criterion of "confusion, which includes the likelihood of association." In the English decision *Wagamama* v. *City Centre Restaurants*,[39] Laddie J dismissed the association criterion as a tautology, citing it as "repetitive" or "unnecessary," leading to a debate on the question whether damages were limited to confusion or whether damages to the reputation or drawing power of the plaintiff's mark would be actionable under this heading.[40]

The Court of Justice of the European Union (CJEU) at first appeared to follow the English vision in the landmark 1997 case *Sabel* v. *Puma*, rejecting the view that "likelihood of association" means that the accused mark merely "calls to mind" the senior mark and that "the concept of likelihood of association is not an alternative to that of likelihood of confusion but serves to define its scope."[41] In the 2003 case *Davidoff* v. *Gofkid*,[42] however, the CJEU held that there is a lacuna in protection against forms of damages to the distinctive character or reputation of the mark in the absence of confusion in the case of use on similar goods or services. The court noted that member states would therefore be free to fill this lacuna by allowing mark holders to initiate actions based on national law (e.g. in unfair competition) against competitors for causing "detriment to, or taking unfair advantage of, the distinctive character or repute of a trademark." This lacuna was filled in updates to the trademark Directive and EU Trade Mark Regulation (EUTMR), so that damage to the distinctive character or reputation of a trademark may be actionable irrespective of whether the same or similar sign is used in connection to the same, similar, or dissimilar goods or services. Article 9(2) EUTMR now reads:

> Without prejudice to the rights of proprietors acquired before the filing date or the priority date of the EU trademark, the proprietor of that EU trademark shall be entitled to prevent all third

[37] Art. 5(2) of the Directive rather provides: "Any Member State may also provide that the proprietor [of a registered trademark] shall be entitled to prevent all third parties not having his consent from using in the course of trade any sign which is identical with, or similar to, the trade mark in relation to goods or services which are not similar to those for which the trade mark is registered, where the latter has a reputation in the Member State and where use of that sign without due cause takes unfair advantage of, or is detrimental to, the distinctive character or the repute of the trade mark."

[38] Case C-375/97, *Gen. Motors* v. *Yplon* [1999] ECR I-408, and the Opinion by A. G. Jacobs, § 28: "[I]n the course of negotiations in the Council, a provision protecting marks 'with a reputation' was included at the request of the Benelux countries, and became Article 5(2) of the Directive."

[39] *Wagamama* v. *City Ctr. Restaurants* [1955] FSR 713.

[40] *See* Anselm Kamperman Sanders, *The Wagamama Decision: Back to the Dark Ages of Trade Mark Law*, 1 Eur. Intell. Prop. Rev. 3 (1996); Peter Prescott, *Think before You Waga Finger*, 6 Eur. Intell. Prop. Rev. 317 (1996); Anselm Kamperman Sanders, *The Return to Wagamama*, 10 Eur. Intell. Prop. Rev. 521 (1996); Peter Prescott, *Has the Benelux Trade Mark Law Been Written into the Directive?*, 3 Eur. Intell. Prop. Rev. 99 (1997).

[41] Case C-251/95, *SABEL* v. *Puma*, 1997 ECR I-528, I-6224, § 18; *see also* Case C-39/97, *Canon* v. *Metro-Goldwyn-Mayer, Inc.*, 1998 ECR I-442.

[42] Case C-292/00, *Davidoff* v. *Gofkid Ltd.*, 2003 ECR I-9.

parties not having his consent from using in the course of trade, in relation to goods or services, any sign where:

(a) . . .
(b) . . .
(c) the sign is identical with, or similar to, the EU trade mark irrespective of whether it is used in relation to goods or services which are identical with, similar to or not similar to those for which the EU trade mark is registered, where the latter has a reputation in the Union and where use of that sign without due cause takes unfair advantage of, or is detrimental to, the distinctive character or the repute of the EU trade mark.

The Harmonization Directive has a similar provision in Article 10, but also has a paragraph 6 indicating that harmonization leaves unaffected provisions in any member state relating to protection against the use of a sign other than use for the purposes of distinguishing goods or services, where use of that sign without due cause takes unfair advantage of, or is detrimental to, the distinctive character or the repute of the trademark. This option has been taken up only by the Benelux member states that did not want to undo the harmonizing effect of the more broadly worded use provision contained in the 1971 Uniform Benelux Trade Mark Act.[43]

In order to benefit from protection against uses that take unfair advantage of, or are detrimental to, the distinctive character or the repute of the trademark, a reputation[44] must be demonstrated in the member state, or with respect to an EUTM in a substantial part of the territory of the EU.[45] In interpreting the elements of unfair advantage or detriment to the distinctive character or the repute of the trademark, the CJEU placed considerable restrictions on its application in *Intel & Intelmark*, where the semiconductor manufacturer sought the revocation of a UK company's registration of "Intelmark" for marketing and telemarketing services.[46]

In this context, the CJEU held that the following factors are not sufficient to prove there is a "link" as established in *Adidas-Salomon AG*, and/or unfair advantage, and/or detriment: (a) the reputation of the earlier mark for products or services which are dissimilar to the goods or services for which the later mark has been registered; (b) the earlier mark is unique with respect to any goods or services; (c) the earlier mark would be brought to mind by the average consumer when they encounter the later mark used for the services of the later mark.[47]

Rather different factors should be taken into account, being: (a) whether, having regard to the nature of the goods or services for which the later mark is used, the average consumer would consider there is an economic connection between the owners of the two marks; (b) whether the distinctive character or repute of the earlier mark for the goods or services for which it is

[43] *See supra* note 33.

[44] For the required levels of proof of reputation see Case C-375/97, *Gen. Motors Corp.* v. *Yplon, SA*, 1999 ECR I-5421, 1999 ETMR 950, § 27: "The existence of repute must be assessed by taking into consideration all the relevant factors of the case, that is to say, in particular, the market share held by the trade mark, the intensity, geographical extent and duration of its use, and the size of the investment made by the undertaking in promoting it"; *see also* Case T-62/16, *EUIPO* v. *Puma SE*, EU:T:2018:509, on admissibility of earlier decisions holding that a mark has a reputation.

[45] With respect to the geographical extent of the reputation required, *see* Case C-301/07, *PAGO Int'l GmbH* v. *Tirolmilch registrierte Genossenschaft mbH* 2009 ECR I-611: "[A] Community trade mark must be known by a significant part of the public concerned by the products or services covered by that trade mark, in a substantial part of the territory of the European Community, and that, in view of the facts of the main proceedings, the territory of the Member State in question may be considered to constitute a substantial part of the territory of the Community."

[46] Case C-252/07, *Intel* v. *CPM UK Ltd*, 2008 ECR I-655.

[47] Case C-408/01, *Adidas-Salomon AG and Adidas Benelux BV* v. *Fitnessworld Trading Ltd.*, 2003 ECR I-582 (on the concept of a "link" between an earlier well-known mark and the later sign, where the CJEU held that: "the existence of a link must be assessed globally, taking in to account all the factors relevant to the case at issue").

registered is really likely to be affected if the later mark is used for the specific goods or services covered by its registration.

The CJEU then attempted to articulate a more objective test to assess whether there is tangible and real detriment to the distinctive character of the trademark. After all, there was no evidence of consumer confusion between the marks of both companies, but this is not necessary for finding detriment to the distinctive character of the mark when:

> [S]uch detriment is caused when that mark's ability to identify the goods or services for which it is registered and used as coming from the proprietor of that mark is weakened, since use of the later mark leads to dispersion of the identity and hold upon the public mind of the earlier mark. That is notably the case when the earlier mark, which used to arouse immediate association with the goods and services for which it is registered, is no longer capable of doing so.[48]

In order to prove detriment to the distinctive character of the mark with a reputation, the proprietor must present evidence of a change in economic behavior[49] of the average consumer of the earlier goods or services as a consequence of the use of the later mark or a likelihood that such a change will occur in the future. Vice versa, when seeking to argue that unfair advantage has been taken of the reputation of the mark, a change in consumer behavior or a likelihood thereof must be shown in the defendant's market. The factors to consider are: (1) there is a real risk that the use of the later mark for its specific goods or services would affect the "pulling power" of the earlier mark for its specific goods or services; (2) there is a real risk the owner of the later mark is likely to obtain a real commercial advantage from its use by reason of the repute of the earlier mark; (3) if the earlier mark is unique, it is used for goods or services different from those the later trademark is registered for; (4) where a later mark is not the same as the earlier mark, whether there are changes in the behavior of the average consumer, particularly whether the earlier mark is merely evoked in the mind of the average consumer; (5) whether the economic behavior of the average consumer in relation to the earlier mark when used for its goods or services is likely to be affected; (6) how inherently distinctive the earlier mark is; and (7) how strong the reputation of the earlier mark is for its good or services.

The criteria have been reaffirmed inter alia in a number of cases in relation to EUTM oppositions and revocations.[50] In the context of comparative advertising, however, the CJEU has employed a broader notion of trademark infringement in the absence of confusion in relation to the referencing of L'Oréal marks on comparison lists for traders in an attempt to market smell-alike perfumes.[51] In establishing there is a connection between trademark law and the law on comparative advertising, meaning the norms expressed in the two instruments are the expression of the same basic principle, the ECJ held that:

[48] Case C-375/97, *Gen. Motors Corp.* v. *Yplon, SA*, 1999 ECR I-5421, 1999 ETMR 950, § 29.

[49] Jukka Palm, *The ECJ's Puzzling Concept of a "Change in Economic Behaviour,"* Brands in the Boardroom (2009), https://iam-media.com/litigation/ecjs-puzzling-concept-change-economic-behaviour.

[50] Case CT-369/10, *You-Q BV, formerly Handicare Holding BV* v. *OHIM and Apple Corps Ltd.*, 2012 EGC I-177, in which the EU General Court held that "The Beatles" is a mark with a strong reputation, meaning that use the later mark "Beatle" on dissimilar goods and services would have resulted in an unfair advantage. *See also* Case T-201/14, *EGC Monopole SpA* v. *OHIM*, 2007 ECLI:EU:T:2007:93; Case T-47/06, *Antartica Srl* v. *OHIM, The Nasdaq Stock Market Inc.*, 2007 ECR 00 I-146. *See also* the possibility to argue likelihood of dilution in opposition or cancellation proceedings in the USA in *NASDAQ Stock Market, Inc.* v. *Antarctica, Srl*, 69 USPQ 2d 1718, 1735 (TTAB 2003); for "unfair advantage" in relation to the collective mark Darjeeling and the use on lingerie, *see* Case C-673/15, *The Tea Board* v. *EUIPO – Delta Lingerie* 2017 ECLI:EU:C:2017:702; and on the use of one's own first name, *see* C-85/15P, *Kenzo Tsuijmoto* v. *EUIPO – Kenzo*, 2018 ECLI:EU:C:2018:349.

[51] Case C-487/07, *L'Oréal SA, Lancôme parfums et beauté & Cie SNC en Laboratoire Garnier & Cie* v. *Bellure NV, Malaika Inv. Ltd. and Starion Int'l Ltd.* 2009 EWCA I-378.

> Since, under Directive 84/450, comparative advertising which presents the advertiser's products as an imitation of a product bearing a trademark is inconsistent with fair competition and thus unlawful, any advantage gained by the advertiser through such advertising will have been achieved as the result of unfair competition and must, accordingly, be regarded as taking unfair advantage of the reputation of that mark.[52]

The case highlights the role the CJEU sees for itself in harmonization not only in relation to trademark law, but also in relation to the law against unfair competition.[53] For this purpose, it is clearly willing to broaden its competence to cover the regulatory distance between trademark and comparative advertising instruments by applying the law against unfair competition.

IV ANALYSIS AND CONCLUSION

The concept of protection beyond confusion, including "dilution," employed in the European Union is much wider in scope compared to the protection of well-known trademarks articulated in the peculiarly worded Article 16.3 of the TRIPS Agreement. Rather than focusing on the ability of the trademark proprietor to address issues where the distinctive character of the trademark itself is at stake, EU law focuses on a negative impact on the "pulling power" of the earlier trademark. In this context, the mark need not be well-known, but should rather have a reputation in its relevant market. This reputation can be negatively affected as this "pulling power" is diminished in the market where the rightsowner is active. This is the classic dilution case where the distinctive character of the trademark is gradually whittled away and the business of the rightsowner is ultimately negatively affected due to the fact that consumers' behavior is no longer positively driven by the trademark's reputation.

The "pulling power" of the trademark is also a pivotal concept in that others can be deemed to take unfair advantage of the repute of the mark to further their own commercial activities. Following *Intel* v. *CPM*, the significant challenge for the rightsowner wishing to oppose an alleged taking advantage of the repute of the registered trademark is to establish that the alleged infringer has enjoyed a tangible and real benefit.[54] Whether the goods or services in relation to which the contentious sign is used are similar or dissimilar, however, is no longer a consideration, as the rightsowner can bring an action for the reasons mentioned above in both cases, even in the absence of confusion.

As is increasingly the case in other jurisdictions, protection of trademarks in the EU is not confined to safeguarding the market against trademark confusion, or even trademark dilution in the classical sense of protection of the distinctive character. The CJEU has consistently used its mandate based on the trademark Directive and the EUTMR to harmonize the law against unfair competition under the guise of trademark law. In doing so, the CJEU has provided protection for trademarks to safeguard functions that lie in advertising efforts, investments in market positions, or even sweat of the brow.[55] In straying so far from the basic function of a trademark, namely that of conferring a commercial origin in trade, EU trademark law has become rather

[52] *Id.* at § 79.

[53] Darren Meale & Joel Smith, *Enforcing a Trade Mark When Nobody's Confused: Where the Law Stands after L'Oreal and Intel*, 2 J. INTELL. PROP. L. & PRAC. 96 (2010).

[54] Case C-252/07, *Intel* v. *CPM UK Ltd*, 2008 ECR I-655.

[55] For an overview of such cases, *see* Anselm Kamperman Sanders, *Unfair Competition: Complementary or Alternative to Intellectual Property in the EU?*, *in* CONSTRUCTING EUROPEAN INTELLECTUAL PROPERTY 329–39 (Christophe Geiger ed., 2013).

difficult to understand.[56] With every new function of the trademark the CJEU comes up with and deems worthy of protection, it becomes increasingly difficult to see where the limits of protection of trademark rights lie and where unfair competition law begins.[57] What is worrying in this regard is that the law against unfair competition, although not harmonized and subject to national law in the EU member states,[58] is often subject to very different policy considerations that find justification in the preservation of a competitive market as a whole, rather than the protection of individual trader's interests.[59]

[56] Meale & Smith, *supra* note 53; Mats Björkenfeldt, *The Genie Is out of the Bottle: The ECJ's Decision in L'Oréal v. Bellure*, 2 J. Intell. Prop. L.& Prac. 105 (2010).

[57] For a rather bizarre, and from a trademark perspective unjustifiable, decision on debranding, *see* Case C-129/17, *Mitsubishi Shoji Ltd.* v. *Duma Forklifts NV*, ECLI:EU:C:2018:594, significantly broadening the concept of infringing trademark use based on the advertisement and investment functions of trademarks to protect the trademark owners' interest in "undistorted competition" (§ 35) in controlling the first placing on the market of goods in the European Economic Area (EEA).

[58] *See* Case C-6/81, *IDG* v. *Beele* 1982, ECR I-72, holding that as long as the national rules on unfair competition are applied equally to domestic and imported product alike, any impact on the free movement of goods that may occur, but equally the possible disparity between national legislations and their different application, is covered by the exemption to the EU's free movement principle provided for in art. 34 of the Treaty on the Function of the European Union. At para. 9:

> National case-law prohibiting the precise imitation of someone else's product which is likely to cause confusion may indeed protect consumers and promote fair trading; these are general interests which, according to the decisions of the court cited above, may justify the existence of obstacles to movement within the community resulting from disparities between national laws relating to the marketing of products. That such a rule does meet mandatory requirements is moreover borne out by the fact that it accords with the principle underlying article 10 bis of the Paris Convention for the protection of industrial property, as last revised on 14 July 1967 at Stockholm, which prohibits inter alia all acts of such a nature as to create confusion with the goods of a competitor, and by the fact that this rule is recognized in principle in the case-law of most member states.

[59] *See* Callmann, *supra* note 25; Stephen P. Ladas, Patents, Trademarks, and Related Rights 1675–42, 1677 (1975): "[T]he law of unfair competition ... is an ordering of interests, individual and public, growing out of the relationship of competitors among themselves and with the general public, in an effort to reconcile and satisfy these interests with the least sacrifice of any of them."

XII

Secondary Trademark Liability

31

Approaches to Secondary Liability for Trademark Infringement

Common Law Evolution

*Stacey Dogan**

I INTRODUCTION

How does the law decide when a party should face trademark liability for infringement committed by someone else? The law of secondary trademark liability addresses that question. It offers trademark law's perspective on what the US Supreme Court has described as the "problem of identifying the circumstances in which it is just to hold one individual accountable for the actions of another."[1] This apparently straightforward question masks a complex set of underlying issues, including a surprisingly tricky one: what *is* direct trademark infringement? In other words, what distinguishes principal from secondary liability in trademark law? Only after defining primary infringement can the law resolve the topic of this chapter: how to define the liability of individuals who have not themselves infringed, but nonetheless should be held to account for another's infringement.

In the United States, both of these issues – the line between primary and secondary infringement, and the standard for secondary liability – have been resolved primarily through judge-made common law. For most of trademark law's history, the first issue received virtually no attention. Courts appeared to assume a common understanding of direct infringers as those who offered products under an infringing mark; they invented secondary liability as a tool for reaching culpable parties that did not "use" trademarks in this way.[2] Contributory trademark infringement, the principal such doctrine,[3] applies to parties who knowingly facilitate another party's infringement.[4]

* Associate Dean for Academic Affairs, Professor & Law Alumni Scholar, Boston University School of Law. Thanks to Mark Lemley, Graeme Dinwoodie, Mark Janis, and Mark McKenna for decades of constructive debate about these issues, and to Tanner Cooper for excellent research assistance. This chapter focuses on the common law development of secondary liability standards in the United States. For an excellent discussion of common law approaches in other jurisdictions, *see* Irene Calboli, *Reading the Tea Leaves in Singapore: Who Will Be Left Holding the Bag for Secondary Trademark Infringement on the Internet?*, 37 Columbia Journal of Law & the Arts 593, 593–607 (2014).

1 *Sony Corp.* v. *Universal City Studios, Inc.*, 464 US 417, 435 (1984).

2 *See* Stacey Dogan & Mark Lemley, *Grounding Trademark Law Through Trademark Use*, 92 Iowa L. Rev. 1669 (2007), reprinted in 98 Trademark Rep. 1345 (2008), and in Beijing Priv. L. Rev. (2014) (Chinese translation).

3 A few courts have also recognized vicarious trademark liability, based on an agency theory, but it is a rarely invoked and narrow doctrine. *See, e.g., AT&T Co.* v. *Winback & Conserve Program, Inc.*, 42 F.3d 1421, 1433–34 (3d Cir. 1994) (recognizing vicarious liability as a viable trademark claim); *cf. Mini Maid Servs. Co.* v. *Maid Brigade Sys.*, 967 F. 2d 1516 (11th Cir. 1992) (rejecting secondary liability in franchise context).

4 *Inwood Labs., Inc.* v. *Ives Labs., Inc.*, 456 US 844, 855 (1982).

The Internet, however, blurred the distinction between those who "use" trademarks to infringe and those who may enable such infringement. Search engines, auction sites, and other indexing tools "use" marks in new ways, sometimes pointing consumers to competing or complementary products against the will of the trademark holder. These intermediaries are not themselves selling products bearing the mark, but they are "using" the mark to call attention to products offered by their advertisers, subscribers, or other third parties. Recent decades have seen an explosion of trademark claims based on these new uses of trademarks online. While some plaintiffs allege contributory infringement, others contend that the intermediaries' direct engagement with trademarks justifies treating them as direct infringers.

The courts' resolution of these lawsuits bears the hallmarks of case-by-case common law evolution. Early decisions came sporadically and reflected not only variability in outcomes, but frequent confusion about both doctrinal and normative questions. Much of this confusion has cleared up over time, but the threshold question – how to distinguish primary from secondary liability – remains muddled.[5] As a practical matter, this blurry line has given courts discretion to impose direct liability against defendants that they perceive as wrongdoers, even if the defendant fits neither the traditional direct-infringer model nor the doctrinal requirements for contributory infringement.[6]

For intermediaries who are not perceived as direct wrongdoers, trademark's common law treatment mirrors copyright's statutory approach. In particular, for parties who do not themselves infringe, the core principles of secondary liability in trademark law have come to resemble the ones that Congress applied to copyright through the 1998 Digital Millennium Copyright Act.[7] In both regimes, liability turns on whether the defendant continued to enable infringement after receiving knowledge of specific infringing individuals or acts.

This chapter describes the US experience in shaping secondary trademark liability through a common law approach.[8] It begins with a brief history of secondary liability in a pre-internet world, and then turns to recent case law. In particular, it explains the recent common law treatment of the two questions at the heart of secondary liability analysis: the line between primary and secondary infringement, and the standard for deciding whether those who have not directly infringed should nonetheless be liable for someone else's infringement.

II SECONDARY TRADEMARK INFRINGEMENT BEFORE THE INTERNET

Before the end of the twentieth century, a survey of US law on secondary trademark liability would be short and straightforward.[9] Direct infringers offered products to the public under an infringing trademark; those who induced or facilitated such behavior were liable, if at all, as contributory infringers. Although courts rarely focused on the line between direct and secondary infringement, they presumed its existence, and so did plaintiffs. Before the Internet, trademark holders simply did not sue for direct trademark infringement unless the defendant was selling

[5] *See* Stacey L. Dogan, *Principled Standards vs. Boundless Discretion: A Tale of Two Approaches to Intermediary Trademark Liability Online*, 37 COLUM. J. L. & ARTS 503, 519 (2014) ("Unlike the carefully calibrated balance in contributory infringement doctrine, direct infringement claims against intermediaries lack the normative coherence that might both justify them and define their limits").

[6] *See id.*

[7] 17 USC § 512.

[8] Of course, trademark law in the United States is governed by a federal statute, the Lanham Act. 15 USC §§ 1127 et seq. That statute, however, does not explicitly address the question of secondary liability, leaving courts to resolve its existence and scope as a matter of common law. *See Inwood Labs.* v. *Ives Labs.*, 456 US 844, 855 (1982).

[9] *See* Dogan & Lemley, *supra* note 2, at 1675–82.

or offering products under plaintiff's mark. The standard for secondary infringement developed against that accepted notion of primary liability. As summarized by the Supreme Court in *Inwood* v. *Ives*:[10]

> Even if a manufacturer does not directly control others in the chain of distribution, it can be held responsible for their infringing activities under certain circumstances. Thus, if a manufacturer or distributor [1] *intentionally induces* another to infringe a trademark, or if it [2] *continues to supply its product to one whom it knows or has reason to know* is engaging in trademark infringement, the manufacturer or distributor is contributorily responsible for any harm done as a result of the deceit.[11]

Early cases of contributory infringement often involved manufacturers of liquids – such as spirits, pharmaceutical products, and soft drinks – who sold their product to retailers with the knowledge or intent that the retailer would pour it into containers labeled with someone else's trademark and sell it under that name.[12] In *Warner* v. *Eli Lilly*, for example, a low-cost seller of chocolate quinine marketed its product to pharmacists who then passed it off to the public under the plaintiff's well-known mark. While recognizing that the manufacturer was not directly infringing because *its* customers (the retailers) knew exactly what they were buying, the Court nonetheless found the manufacturer liable for the druggists' direct infringement. "The wrong," the Court held, "was in designedly enabling the dealers to palm off the preparation as that of the respondent. … One who induces another to commit a fraud and furnishes the means of consummating it is equally guilty and liable for the injury."[13]

Later opinions applied contributory infringement in different factual contexts, but their focus remained on the defendant's knowing complicity in the direct infringer's acts.[14] Courts in these cases emphasized the importance of a defendant's *knowledge* of the direct infringer's fraud, paired with a deliberate decision to help make it happen. Absent such evidence of culpability, courts hesitated to hold parties responsible for another party's wrongdoing. In *Mini Maid Services Co.* v. *Maid Brigade Systems*,[15] for example, the Eleventh Circuit rejected an attempt to hold a franchisor liable for a franchisee's alleged infringement based on a failure to supervise. Following *Inwood*, the court held "that liability for trademark infringement can extend beyond those entities that actually perform the acts of infringement, but only under certain circumstances. With respect to a franchisor's liability for the independent infringing acts of its franchisees, we hold that a franchisor may be held accountable only if it intentionally induced its franchisees to infringe another's trademark or if it knowingly participated in a scheme of trademark infringement carried out by its franchisees."[16]

The emphasis on culpability was not accidental. The common law principle of secondary trademark liability mirrors other doctrines that assign blame to parties one step removed from active wrongdoing. In crafting these doctrines, courts recognize that overly broad liability could chill behavior that may enable the wrongdoing, but also have innocent – and socially valuable – effects. As the Supreme Court has emphasized in the copyright context, secondary "liability is

[10] *Inwood Labs.* v. *Ives Labs.*, 456 US 844, 855 (1982).

[11] Dogan & Lemley, *supra* note 2, at 1679 (emphasis added).

[12] *See, e.g.*, *Hostetter Co.* v. *Brueggeman-Reinert Distilling Co.*, 46 F. 188, 189 (CCED Mo. 1891); *William R. Warner & Co.* v. *Eli Lilly & Co.*, 265 US 526, 530 (1924).

[13] *Eli Lilly*, 265 US at 530–31 (internal citations omitted).

[14] *See, e.g.*, *David Berg & Co.* v. *Gatto Intern. Trading Co.*, 884 F.2d 306, 311 (7th Cir. 1989) ("The determination of contributory infringement depends on a defendant's intent and its knowledge of the wrongful acts of its distributors").

[15] *Mini Maid Servs. Co.* v. *Maid Brigade Sys.*, 967 F. 2d 1516 (11th Cir. 1992).

[16] *Id.* at 1522.

imposed in virtually all areas of the law, and the concept of contributory infringement is merely a species of the broader problem of identifying the circumstances in which it is just to hold one individual accountable for the actions of another."[17] Such liability is often necessary to provide "effective – not merely symbolic – protection" of intellectual property rights; at the same time, however, courts must balance that interest against "the rights of others freely to engage in substantially unrelated areas of commerce."[18] Trademark law guards this interest by limiting secondary liability to those with a knowing and deliberate relationship to another party's infringement. The Supreme Court has described the trademark standard as "narrow[er]" than copyright's, applying only to parties that "intentionally induce" infringement or "supply [their] products to *identified individuals* known by [them] to be engaging in continuing infringement."[19]

By the late 1990s, then, the common law of secondary trademark liability had been in place for almost a century, and it turned on proof of two conditions:

- A principal infringer offered a product to the public under an infringing mark; and
- The defendant's relationship to that infringer justified imputing culpability to it, either because it *induced* the individual defendant, or because it *knew* of a particular party's infringement and deliberately played a supporting role.

III SECONDARY LIABILITY IN THE INTERNET AGE

The advent of the Internet wreaked havoc across numerous areas of law, and trademark law was no exception. Mark Lemley and I have written about the early mistakes that courts made in trademark suits against online intermediaries, conflating primary and secondary liability and neglecting inquiries into culpability and knowledge.[20] Some of these mistakes have been corrected over time, while others remain. Unlike pre-internet cases, which assumed a primary/secondary liability distinction and grappled with how to define the culpability of secondary actors, the online cases introduced new uncertainty over the very definition of direct infringement. For the first time, parties that did not offer products under a trademark faced a risk of liability for direct infringement, based on an imprecise and subjective definition of the doctrine. On the other hand, for parties that managed to escape a finding of direct infringement, courts applied the same narrow approach to secondary liability that prevailed in the pre-internet era. The result is a system in which legal obligations and liability can turn on courts' initial, impressionistic assessment of the legitimacy of the defendant's engagement with the plaintiff's trademark.[21]

A *Defining Direct Infringers*

The challenge of distinguishing between direct and contributory infringement in the online context results from the Internet's transformation of the ways in which buyers, sellers, and intermediaries transfer information. Network platforms including search engines, auction sites, and other technologies empower product sellers and content distributors to reach their audiences in new ways. And people sometimes use these platforms to commit trademark and

[17] *Sony Corp.* v. *Universal City Studios, Inc.*, 464 US 417, 435 (1984).
[18] *Id.* at 442.
[19] *Id.* at 439 & n. 19 (emphasis added).
[20] *See, e.g.*, Stacey L. Dogan & Mark A. Lemley, *Trademarks and Consumer Search Costs on the Internet*, 44 HOUSTON L. REV. 777 (2004); Dogan & Lemley, *supra* note 2.
[21] *See* Dogan, *supra* note 5; *see also* Stacey L. Dogan, *"We Know It When We See It": Intermediary Trademark Liability and the Internet*, 2011 STAN. TECH. L.J. 7.

copyright infringement. Just as the mid-1990s brought lawsuits alleging direct copyright infringement by online service providers based on their storage of content at the direction of users,[22] so the turn of the century brought trademark suits against search engines and other intermediaries based on their role in enabling third parties' online advertising and sales.[23] Whereas Congress responded to the copyright crisis by giving intermediaries limited safe-harbor protection through the Digital Millennium Copyright Act,[24] it left the resolution of trademark law's quandary to the courts.

The Ninth Circuit Court of Appeals issued the first major appellate decision on intermediary trademark liability in *Playboy* v. *Netscape* in 2004.[25] *Playboy* v. *Netscape* involved claims by the famous purveyor of sexual content against a search engine that allowed Playboy's competitors to place advertisements keyed to its protected marks. When a consumer entered "Playboy" into the search engine, Netscape would generate ads for non-Playboy products along with ordinary search results. The ads, according to Playboy, were "often graphic in nature and … confusingly labeled or not labeled at all."[26] Netscape, moreover, *required* all "adult-oriented companies to link their ads" to a package of keywords that included "playboy" and "playmate," both protected marks of the plaintiff.[27] Playboy alleged that such ads would confuse consumers, and that Netscape should face both direct and contributory liability for such confusion.

The district court rejected Playboy's claims, concluding that trademark infringement does not apply to a defendant who "does not use the plaintiff's mark *as its trademark*."[28] Netscape could not have infringed, in other words, because it "d[id] not 'use' [Playboy's] trademarks *qua* trademarks."[29] The unpublished opinion does not elaborate, so it's difficult to discern whether the court saw online, keyword-based advertising as categorically immune from liability, or whether it based its decision on the fact that *Netscape*, as a search engine, had not adopted Playboy's trademarks *as its mark*. Regardless, the Ninth Circuit disagreed, and reversed the district court's grant of summary judgment.

Because the district court in *Playboy* v. *Netscape* had based its decision on the defendant's failure to use the marks in a trademark sense, the briefing on appeal focused largely on that issue. As the Ninth Circuit put it, "the parties dispute whether a direct or a contributory theory of liability applies to the defendants' actions."[30] Rather than resolving that "tricky question,"[31] however, the Ninth Circuit decided that it "need not decide" it. Concluding that Netscape was "*either* directly or contributorily liable," the court found it unnecessary to choose between the theories of liability for purposes of summary judgment.[32] Instead, the court found evidence

[22] *See, e.g., Playboy Enters., Inc.* v. *Frena*, 839 F. Supp. 1552 (MD Fla. 1993) (finding direct copyright infringement liability against bulletin-board-service operator based on material posted by its users); *Sega Enterprises Ltd.* v. *MAPHIA*, 857 F. Supp. 679 (ND Cal. 1994) (same). Compare *Religious Tech. Ctr.* v. *Netcom On-Line Commc'n Services, Inc.*, 907 F. Supp. 1361 (ND Cal. 1995) (rejecting direct infringement claims against online service provider, but remanding for evaluation of contributory and vicarious liability).

[23] *E.g., Playboy Enters., Inc.* v. *Netscape Commc'ns Corp.*, 354 F.3d 1020 (9th Cir. 2004); *see generally, Playboy Enters., Inc.* v. *Webbworld, Inc.*, 991 F. Supp. 543 (ND Tex. 1997).

[24] 17 USC § 512.

[25] *Playboy*, 354 F.3d 1020.

[26] *Id.* at 1023.

[27] *Id.*

[28] *Playboy Enters., Inc.* v. *Netscape Commc'ns Corp.*, 2000 WL 1308815, at *1 (CD Cal., Sept. 13, 2000) (granting summary judgment for defendant), *rev'd*, 354 F.3d 1020 (9th Cir. 2004).

[29] *Id.*

[30] *Playboy Enters., Inc.* v. *Netscape Commc'ns Corp.*, 354 F.3d 1020, 1024 (9th Cir. 2004).

[31] *Id.*

[32] *Id.*

that consumers may well be confused by the use of Playboy marks to generate ads, and that Netscape, "in conjunction with advertisers," was responsible for that confusion.[33] It thus reversed the district court's grant of summary judgment and remanded for further proceedings.

The *Playboy* v. *Netscape* opinion included a number of dubious conclusions about trademark law that have been explored in other work.[34] For present purposes, the opinion is significant because it injected uncertainty into the distinction between direct and contributory infringement. For the first time, a court suggested that even parties outside the chain of distribution – parties whose "use" of the mark involved assisting someone else's product promotion and sale – could face liability as a direct infringer. While this may appear to be a distinction without a difference – and the opinion supports this view by dodging the direct/contributory question – in fact, it reflects a dramatic change in trademark law. In particular, because direct infringement turns only on the likelihood of consumer confusion and does not require knowledge or intent, critics worried that defendants could face liability for enabling confusion that they neither intended nor knowingly brought about.[35] If a search engine's sale of keyword-based advertising constitutes a "use" of a trademark for purposes of direct infringement, in other words, then the search engine could be liable when its *advertisers* misuse the platform and place confusing ads, regardless of the search engine's knowledge or intent. This approach could impose substantial costs on intermediaries by requiring them to police their users' behavior ex ante, thus potentially chilling all sorts of legitimate, pro-competitive uses of trademarks.[36] Significantly, the acceptance of direct trademark infringement claims against intermediaries moves internet trademark law in a different direction than copyright, where both Congress and the courts opted against strict liability for online intermediaries out of concern about creating "a serious chilling effect on what some say may turn out to be the best public forum for free speech yet."[37]

Beyond these normative concerns about direct infringement claims against intermediaries, *Playboy* v. *Netscape* results in a bizarre mismatch between doctrine and facts. The core doctrinal standard in direct infringement claims turns on the likelihood that consumers will be confused as to the source, sponsorship, or affiliation of the allegedly infringing product.[38] To determine whether a defendant has infringed, the fact finder weighs a series of factors designed to assess the "likelihood of confusion" among consumers. These factors include a comparison between the plaintiff's and defendant's products, trademarks, marketing channels, and advertising practices – all of which presume that the two parties are offering products or services under

[33] *Id.* at 1025.

[34] Among other things, the court adopted a broad view of "initial interest confusion" that threatened legitimate uses of trademarks to call attention to competing products. *See* Dogan & Lemley, *supra* note 20, at 813–31.

[35] *See id.* at 831–37; Margreth Barrett, *Internet Trademark Suits and the Demise of "Trademark Use,"* 39 U.C. Davis L. Rev. 371 (2006). Intent is a factor in a trademark's likelihood of confusion analysis, but it is not dispositive. *See* J. Thomas McCarthy, McCarthy on Trademarks and Unfair Competition, Vol. IV § 23:106 (5th ed. 2017) ("Only the rare maverick decision in modern times clings to the archaic notion that a wrongful intent is necessary or must be presumed from a finding of actual or likely confusion").

[36] Keyword-based advertising enables competitors, resellers, and vendors of complementary products to reach customers seeking the trademark holder. These uses promote consumer choice and facilitate competitive markets. *See generally*, Dogan & Lemley, *supra* note 2, at 1678–79.

[37] *See Religious Tech. Ctr.* v. *Netcom On-Line Commc'n Servs., Inc.*, 907 F. Supp. 1361 (ND Cal. 1995) (rejecting direct infringement claims against online service provider, but remanding for evaluation of contributory and vicarious liability); *see also* 17 USC § 512 (providing limited immunity from copyright liability for online intermediaries).

[38] The details of the likelihood of confusion standard vary from one federal circuit to another, but the basic inquiry is quite similar. *See, e.g.*, *Polaroid Corp.* v. *Polarad Elecs. Corp.*, 287 F.2d 492, 495 (2d Cir.), *cert. denied*, 368 US 820 (1961) (listing Second Circuit's "Polaroid factors"); *AMF Inc.* v. *Sleekcraft Boats*, 599 F.2d 341 (9th Cir. 1979) (Ninth Circuit "Sleekcraft factors").

the mark. It makes no sense to analyze these factors in a suit against intermediaries based on their general policies that play a role in third parties' sales or promotional efforts.[39]

Because the *Playboy* court never chose between direct and contributory theories of liability, the opinion left much uncertainty about the relationship between the two doctrines. In particular, the court failed to address whether any meaningful distinction remained in the online context between direct infringers and those whose "use" of a mark enables *others* to infringe.[40] The opinions since *Playboy* have done little to resolve this uncertainty. On the one hand, a handful of courts have embraced the prospect of direct infringement by intermediaries, even in the absence of their use of the marks to sell their own products. On the other hand, "direct infringement" by intermediaries appears to mean something different than "direct infringement" as historically understood. Rather than a product- and mark-based inquiry into likelihood of confusion, this new form of direct infringement resembles a "roving unfair competition law" designed to protect consumers against suspect practices that happen to involve trademarks.[41] For the few courts that have invoked it, direct infringement appears to serve as a blunt tool to ferret out perceived bad actors.

The first appellate decision to suggest this shift came five years after *Playboy*, in *Rescuecom v. Google* in the Second Circuit.[42] The plaintiff alleged that Google infringed its trademark rights by allowing competitors to place ads in response to user searches for the Rescuecom mark. According to the allegations, Google's practice sowed confusion by failing to differentiate these ads from the organic search results generated by Google's search algorithm. Google defended by arguing that it had never "used" Rescuecom's mark in the sale or marketing of its own goods or services, and therefore could not have directly infringed. Google's position found support in the historical distinction between direct and contributory infringement, as well as a Second Circuit decision that appeared to embrace a "trademark use" requirement for direct infringement claims.[43] The trial court dismissed Rescuecom's claims based on Google's lack of trademark use,[44] but the Second Circuit reversed.[45]

Because the district court had dismissed based on the threshold question of trademark use, the court of appeals addressed only that issue. The court cautioned that it was not concluding that Google had in fact infringed, but only that Google's "use" of the Rescuecom mark was of the sort that *could* – if confusing – constitute direct infringement.[46] At a glance, this ruling appeared to fuel the worst fears of critics who worried that, without a trademark use requirement, even innocuous uses of trademarks by intermediaries could subject them to strict liability for subsequent misdeeds by third parties.[47] Further scrutiny, however, reveals a more limited holding. The plaintiff did not allege – and the court thus did not contemplate – that Google's mere act of selling "Rescuecom" as a keyword made it legally responsible for any subsequent confusion. Instead, the plaintiff alleged that Google itself confused consumers by presenting resulting ads

[39] *See* Dogan & Lemley, *supra* note 20, at 831–37.
[40] *See Inwood Labs., Inc.* v. *Ives Labs., Inc.*, 456 US 844, 855 (1982).
[41] Dogan, *supra* note 21, at 503.
[42] *Rescuecom Corp.* v. *Google Inc.*, 562 F.3d 123 (2d Cir. 2009).
[43] *See 1-800 Contacts, Inc.* v. *WhenU.Com, Inc.*, 414 F.3d 400 (2d Cir. 2005).
[44] *Rescuecom Corp.* v. *Google, Inc.*, 456 F. Supp. 393, 403 (NDNY 2006) ("in the absence of allegations that defendant placed plaintiff's trademark on any goods, displays, containers, or advertisements, or used plaintiff's trademark in any way that indicates source or origin, plaintiff can prove no facts in support of its claim which would demonstrate trademark use").
[45] *Rescuecom Corp.* v. *Google, Inc.*, 562 F.3d 123 (2d Cir. 2009).
[46] *Id.*
[47] *See, e.g.*, Stacey Dogan, *Beyond Trademark Use*, 8 J. on Telecom. & High Tech. L. 135, 149–50 (2010).

in a way that blurred the line between them and organic search results. This allegedly deceptive ad placement was central to the court's conclusion that Google's "use" could constitute infringement:

> What Rescuecom alleges is that *by the manner of Google's display* of sponsored links of competing brands in response to a search for Rescuecom's brand name (which fails adequately to identify the sponsored link as an advertisement, rather than a relevant search result), Google creates a likelihood of consumer confusion as to trademarks. If the searcher sees a different brand name as the top entry in response to the search for "Rescuecom," the searcher is likely to believe mistakenly that the different name which appears is affiliated with the brand name sought in the search and will not suspect, *because the fact is not adequately signaled by Google's presentation*, that this is not the most relevant response to the search.[48]

The emphasis on Google's own behavior – as distinguished from the actions of its advertisers – suggests, at the very least, that this odd form of direct infringement requires some level of individual culpability beyond providing a neutral tool that others may use to infringe. Indeed, the court's reinterpretation of direct infringement appears motivated by worry that a narrower standard might insulate unscrupulous intermediaries who were deliberately deceiving consumers.[49] In classic common law fashion, the court reshaped trademark doctrine to address this concern. Yet the court did not anticipate the downsides of using direct infringement doctrine to address general problems with search engine integrity. If search engines are deceiving consumers about the difference between paid ads and search results, their behavior may constitute an unfair trade practice under state and federal law.[50] Calling it direct trademark infringement, however, not only distorts that doctrine, but risks over-deterring behavior that may confuse some consumers, but have net positive effects. This risk was borne out three years later, in *Rosetta Stone* v. *Google*.[51]

The plaintiff in *Rosetta Stone* asserted a direct infringement claim based on Google's 2009 decision to allow the use of trademarks in the text of keyword-generated ads.[52] The evidence suggested that, at the time of this policy change, Google knew that confusion could

48 *Rescuecom*, 562 F.3d at 131 (emphasis added).

49 *Id.* at 130 ("If we were to adopt Google and its amici's argument, the operators of search engines would be free to use trademarks in ways *designed to* deceive and cause consumer confusion . . . This is surely neither within the intention nor the letter of the Lanham Act") (emphasis added). Similar concerns led some leading scholars to support the possibility of direct infringement claims against intermediaries. *See, e.g.*, Graeme B. Dinwoodie & Mark D. Janis, *Confusion over Use: Contextualism in Trademark Law*, 92 Iowa L. Rev. 1597, 1605 (2007) (suggesting that rejecting direct infringement claims against those who facilitated infringement would result in "immunity" for search engines and other online intermediaries).

50 The Federal Trade Commission has recognized that deceptively blending ads and search results would likely violate the Federal Trade Commission Act. *See* Letter from Heather Hippsley, Acting Associate Director of Division of Advertising Practices, Federal Trade Commission, to Gary Ruskin, Executive Director of Commercial Alert (June 27, 2002), https://ftc.gov/sites/default/files/documents/closing_letters/commercial-alert-response-letter/commercialalertletter.pdf (responding to complaint by Commercial Alert about search engine practices, and noting "the need for clear and conspicuous disclosures of paid placement, and in some instances paid inclusion, so that businesses may avoid possible future Commission action"). State laws – which often allow consumers standing to sue – provide additional alternatives. *See Heller* v. *Lexton-Ancira Real Estate Fund, Ltd.*, 809 P.2d 1016, 1022 (Colo. App. 1990); *cf.* D. Wes Sullenger, *Only We Can Save You: When and Why Non-Consumer Businesses Have Standing to Sue Business Competitors under the Tennessee Consumer Protection Act*, 35 U. Mem. L. Rev. 485, 492 (2005).

51 *Rosetta Stone Ltd.* v. *Google, Inc.*, 676 F.3d 144 (4th Cir. 2012). This section borrows substantially from Dogan, *supra* note 5, at 520–22.

52 *Id.* at 151–52. From 2004 until 2009, Google allowed keyword-based advertising but prohibited the unauthorized use of trademarks in ads themselves. Before 2004, Google's policy "precluded both the use of trademarks in the text of an advertisement and the use of trademarks as keywords upon the request of the trademark holder." *Id.*

result from the use of trademarks in ads.[53] In fact, a number of counterfeiters had misused the policy to advertise counterfeit Rosetta Stone software.[54] Yet undoubtedly the policy change also enabled perfectly lawful and informative ads, such as advertisements for used versions of the expensive software.[55] Google's new policy, in other words, was a classic example of a "staple" tool that does not infringe on its own, but can be put to both infringing and non-infringing use.[56] As such, Google should be analyzed under standards of secondary trademark liability. Under *Rescuecom*, however, the plaintiff could plausibly allege direct infringement by arguing that the new policy (and thus Google's own action) would increase the risk of confusion for some consumers, even if it improved the utility of consumers as a whole.

Indeed, the Fourth Circuit adopted this broad notion of direct infringement, based on a truncated analysis of the "likelihood of confusion" factors used to determine infringement.[57] Most of these factors, of course, made no sense in a suit against a search engine. Google's use of the Rosetta Stone mark, as the court found, was largely "nominative," in the sense that it used the mark to refer to Rosetta Stone itself, rather than as a trademark for some third party's products.[58] The court acknowledged that, given the nominative nature of Google's use, factors such as the strength of the plaintiff's trademark and similarity between the marks were "clearly of limited value."[59] Moreover, because Google did not itself offer products or services under the mark, several additional factors, including similarity in products or services, quality of products, and similarities in sales channels and advertising, were also irrelevant.[60] This left the court with intent, actual confusion, and consumer sophistication. On intent, the court concluded that since Google stood to profit from the keyword-based ads, a reasonable fact-finder could decide that it had "*intended to cause confusion* in that it acted with the knowledge that confusion was very likely to result from its use of the marks."[61] This is like saying that a reasonable fact-finder could conclude that the maker of the VCR had *intended to cause* copyright infringement because it knew that some home tapers would use its machine to infringe – an argument explicitly precluded by Supreme Court doctrine.[62] Google's knowledge went to *risk* of confusion, not certainty; both *Sony* and *Inwood* proscribe liability under those circumstances.[63] In its analysis of actual confusion, the court did not look at Google's ad policy across the board to determine whether Google's policy – allowing trademarks in ad text – consistently caused confusion. Instead, the court looked only at counterfeit ads, and thus attributed to Google the confusion created by counterfeit sellers, who were acting in violation of Google's policy.[64]

[53] *See id.* at 156.

[54] *Id.* at 152.

[55] *See Champion Spark Plug Co.* v. *Sanders*, 331 US 125, 128–29 (1947) (allowing use of original manufacturer's trademarks in connection with the sale of used or reconditioned goods). Google's policy specifically allowed the use of trademarks in the text of ads in four contexts: "(1) the sponsor is a reseller of a genuine trademarked product; (2) the sponsor makes or sells component parts for a trademarked product; (3) the sponsor offers compatible parts or goods for use with the trademarked product; or (4) the sponsor provides information about or reviews a trademarked product." *Rosetta Stone*, 676 F.3d at 151–52. All of these, of course, constitute lawful uses of third-party marks.

[56] *Cf. Sony Corp. of Am.* v. *Universal City Studios, Inc.*, 464 US 417, 442 (1984).

[57] *Rosetta Stone Ltd.* v. *Google, Inc.*, 676 F.3d 144, 154–56 (4th Cir. 2012).

[58] *See, e.g.*, *Toyota Motor Sales Inc.* v. *Tabari*, 610 F.3d 1171, 1177–80 (9th Cir. 2010).

[59] *Rosetta Stone*, 676 F.3d at 154.

[60] *Id.* at 155.

[61] *Id.* at 156 (emphasis added).

[62] *Sony Corp. of Am.* v. *Universal City Studios, Inc.*, 464 US 417, 442 (1984).

[63] *Id.* at 439–42 (1984); *Inwood Labs., Inc.* v. *Ives Labs., Inc.*, 456 US 844, 855 (1982).

[64] The evidence of actual confusion consisted of: (1) consumer testimony; (2) an expert report; (3) Google documents; and (4) testimony suggesting that Google's own employees could not tell the difference between ads for genuine and for counterfeit Rosetta Stone products. *See Rosetta Stone Ltd.*, 676 F.3d at 156–59.

Again, Google's ad policy may well have created a *risk* that this wrongdoing would occur, but it was the ads – not the policy – that led to deception of consumers.

That is not to suggest that Google should be immune from liability for confusion caused by advertisements for counterfeit products. If Google knows of a particular advertisement that is hawking counterfeit goods, it has an obligation to disable access to that ad. More generally, as discussed below, the willful blindness doctrine requires Google to keep its eyes open to evidence of actual counterfeit advertisements and sales.[65] Yet these obligations go to its responsibility to help police another party's wrongdoing; they have nothing to do with whether Google committed an act of direct infringement by allowing advertisers to use trademarks in the text of ads. By holding that a jury could find that Google intentionally created confusion through its policy, the court conflated questions of risk and wrongdoing, and threatened the values that compel a distinction between secondary and primary infringement.

Both *Rescuecom* and *Rosetta Stone* demonstrate the power of perceived equities in shaping the common law. Both courts appeared troubled by a business model that uses trademarks to connect consumers to information that they might find confusing.[66] That intuition led the courts to stretch direct infringement doctrine to address the perceived wrong, but the doctrine they created lacks principled limits and threatens core values that underlie the more nuanced rules of secondary liability. Such is the way with the common law: idiosyncratic case-specific concerns can lead courts to shape doctrines in ways that can have unanticipated costs. With any luck, a future case will demonstrate these costs in a way that some future court will find compelling, and the court will discipline the doctrine accordingly. Until then, courts confronted with parties whose online practices involve trademarks may well continue to use direct infringement as a flexible tool to target behavior that may mislead in some way. In other words, in cases involving perceived bad actors, direct infringement doctrine can serve as a substitute for secondary liability's more rigorous standard – even when the defendant is really a secondary player in someone else's infringing advertising and sales.

B The Standard for Contributory Infringement

Although *Rescuecom* and its progeny establish direct infringement as a viable claim against some online intermediaries, contributory infringement remains the principal method for evaluating the liability of secondary actors – i.e., parties one step removed from use of marks in the "chain of distribution" of products.[67] In contrast to the nebulous form of direct infringement that has emerged in the online cases, contributory infringement has greater coherence in both normative foundations and doctrinal shape. This relative clarity undoubtedly owes in part to the fact that contributory infringement – unlike the new species of direct infringement – has had over a century to settle and mature through common law evolution. During this time, the law has evolved in a way that balances the need to protect against consumer deception against the importance of allowing access to trademarks for pro-competitive, information-facilitating use.

As discussed above, the Supreme Court in *Inwood* defined contributory infringement to include (1) inducement of third-party infringement, and (2) continuing to provide products to other parties with knowledge that they will be used to infringe.[68] In the years since *Inwood*,

65 *See infra* text at notes 86–88.

66 *See also* Dinwoodie & Janis, *supra* note 49 (advocating the possibility of direct infringement claims against parties whose business practices generate confusion).

67 *Inwood*, 456 US at 855.

68 *Id.*

the lower courts have developed a sparse, but increasingly coherent, approach to contributory infringement claims under both the "inducement" and the "continuing to provide" prongs.

To satisfy the "inducement" requirement, a party must encourage the infringement and specifically intend it to occur. Post-*Inwood* courts have focused on the context of the relationship between the direct and contributory infringer, to "decide whether or not the [defendant] explicitly or implicitly encouraged the trademark violations."[69] But inducement does not apply to a mere failure to take precautions to ward off infringement before it occurs. The Supreme Court rejected a "reasonable anticipation" standard for contributory infringement in *Inwood*,[70] and courts have consistently required both intent and "affirmative acts" before imposing liability for inducement.[71]

Despite its demanding standard, this form of liability could well apply to some of the hypothetical behavior that led the *Rescuecom* and *Rosetta Stone* courts to redefine direct infringement. Suppose, for example, that a search engine adopted a business model with the intent of supporting its advertisers in selling counterfeits to consumers.[72] In such circumstances, a court could conclude that the search engine's deliberate behavior rose to the level of inducement.[73] The court could first analyze whether direct infringement was occurring by considering whether the ads presented to consumers created a likelihood of confusion over the source of the advertisers' goods. After resolving that question, it could then turn to the intermediary's culpability in promoting that infringement. As distinguished from *Rosetta Stone*'s version of direct infringement, the inducement approach not only preserves the coherence of the likelihood-of-confusion test, but it allows a more thorough inquiry into the broader context of the intermediary's business model and commercial goals. Because inducement considers whether the defendant has a *purpose* to promote infringement, rather than mere knowledge of

[69] *Mini Maid Servs. Co.* v. *Maid Brigade Sys. Inc.*, 967 F.2d 1516, 1522 (11th Cir. 1992).

[70] *Inwood*, 456 US at 854 n. 13.

[71] See *Perfect 10, Inc.* v. *Visa Int'l Serv. Ass'n*, 494 F.3d 788, 807 (9th Cir. 2007) (dismissing contributory trademark infringement claims when plaintiff's "allegations ... cite no affirmative acts by Defendants suggesting that third parties infringe [plaintiff's] mark, much less induce them to do so"); *Hard Rock Cafe Licensing Corp.* v. *Concession Servs., Inc.*, 955 F.2d 1143, 1149 (7th Cir. 1992) (contributory infringement requires more than a "failure to take precautions against counterfeiting"); *Mini Maid*, 967 F.2d at 1522 ("In making these determinations of intent and knowledge, a district court should consider the nature and extent of the communication between [the defendant and the direct infringer] regarding the infringing acts; specifically, the court should decide whether or not the [defendant] explicitly or implicitly encouraged the trademark violations"); *Optimum Techs., Inc.* v. *Henkel Consumer Adhesives, Inc.*, 496 F.3d 1231, 1243–44 (11th Cir. 2007) (noting absence of evidence of intentional inducement, and countervailing evidence that the defendant had taken steps to prevent infringement from occurring).

[72] *Rescuecom Corp.* v. *Google Inc.*, 562 F.3d 123, 130 (2d Cir. 2009) (expressing concern about leaving search engines "free to use trademarks in ways designed to deceive and cause consumer confusion"). As Eric Goldman has pointed out, such a business model would probably not serve the search engine well over the long run, because customers and advertisers would look to more accurate and better-matched alternatives. *See* Eric Goldman, *Deregulating Relevancy in Internet Trademark Law*, 54 EMORY L.J. 507, 536–37 (2005).

[73] In *Mini Maid*, for example, the court instructed the district court to consider the underlying facts to decide whether the defendant intended to participate in the primary party's infringement:

> In making these determinations of intent and knowledge, a district court should consider the nature and extent of communications between a franchisor and its franchisees regarding the infringing acts; specifically, the court should decide whether or not the franchisor explicitly or implicitly encouraged the trademark violations. In addition, the court may wish to consider the extent and nature of the violations being committed. If the infringement is serious and widespread, it is more likely that the franchisor knows about and condones the acts of its franchisees. (967 F.2d at 1522; citations omitted)

Of course, the relationship between a franchisor and franchisee is more direct and intimate than that between a search engine and its advertisers, making the attribution of knowledge and intent more likely in the former case. But it's not inconceivable that a search engine could have the motive and means to promote passing off by advertisers in certain circumstances.

its risk,[74] it better promotes the core insight of *Inwood* and *Sony* that secondary liability should not reach parties whose behavior has substantial non-infringing purpose and effect.[75]

While inducement focuses on purposeful behavior by a defendant, the second form of *Inwood* liability applies to parties who continue to support another's infringement after learning of its existence. The Supreme Court addressed one variant of this behavior – a party's "continu[ing] to supply its product to one whom it knows or has reason to know is engaging in trademark infringement."[76] Subsequent courts have extended the Court's reasoning to other circumstances in which a defendant knowingly contributed to another's infringement. Thus, in *Hard Rock Café* v. *Concession Services*,[77] the court held that a party that continues to provide services to sellers with knowledge of their infringement can satisfy the *Inwood* standard.[78] This reasoning applies to online intermediaries that fail to cut off advertisers, vendors, or other affiliates after learning of their infringement. But the knowledge must be specific and substantial; mere generalized knowledge of the potentially infringing use of a service cannot justify a contributory infringement claim.[79]

Tiffany (NJ) Inc. v. *eBay Inc.* is the seminal online example.[80] Tiffany sued eBay for its failure to stop the widespread counterfeit sales of Tiffany jewelry on eBay's auction site. Tiffany's theory was contributory infringement, i.e., that eBay either knew or should have known "that counterfeit Tiffany goods were being sold ubiquitously on its website," but nonetheless "continued to make its services available to infringing sellers."[81] eBay, in turn, pointed to its elaborate system for receiving and responding to notices of counterfeit goods sold on its service.[82] In eBay's view, *Inwood* limited liability to those who knowingly facilitated *particular instances* of infringement.[83] Because eBay took swift action upon receiving specific knowledge of counterfeit auctions, such a standard would preclude liability against it.

Both the district court and the Second Circuit agreed with eBay's interpretation of *Inwood* and its application to the facts of that case.[84] In particular, the court of appeals held that, for liability to apply, eBay must have specific knowledge of particular acts of infringement and fail to act on that knowledge. Put differently, an intermediary's duty to police infringement arises only after it receives particularized knowledge of infringement; it has no general obligation to prevent misuse of its service by third parties. In this way, the common law standard resembles the "notice and takedown" regime that the US Congress adopted for copyright law in the Digital Millennium Copyright Act.[85]

74 *Cf. MGM Studios, Inc.* v. *Grokster, Ltd.*, 545 US 913 (2005).

75 *Sony Corp. of Am.* v. *Universal City Studios, Inc.*, 464 US 417, 442 (1984).

76 *Inwood Labs., Inc.* v. *Ives Labs., Inc.*, 456 US 844, 854 (1982).

77 *Hard Rock Cafe Licensing Corp.* v. *Concession Servs., Inc.*, 955 F.2d 1143, 1149 (7th Cir. 1992).

78 955 F.2d at 1149; *accord Fonovisa, Inc.* v. *Cherry Auction, Inc.*, 76 F.3d 259, 265 (9th Cir. 1996) (swap-meet operator who had actual knowledge of counterfeit sales on its premises could face contributory trademark liability; "a swap meet can not [sic] disregard its vendors' blatant trademark infringements with impunity").

79 *See Tiffany (NJ) Inc.* v. *eBay, Inc.*, 576 F. Supp. 2d 463, 510 (SDNY 2008); *Gucci Am., Inc.* v. *Hall & Assocs.*, 135 F. Supp. 2d 409, 420 (SDNY 2001) ("plaintiffs bear a high burden in establishing 'knowledge' of contributory infringement"); *Lockheed Martin Corp.* v. *Network Solutions, Inc.*, 985 F. Supp. 949, 962 (CD Cal. 1997) (requiring "unequivocal knowledge" of primary infringement, in case where defendant's involvement with the infringing acts was remote); *cf. Inwood*, 456 US at 861 (White J, concurring) ("The mere fact that a generic drug company can anticipate that some illegal substitution will occur to some unspecified extent, and by some unknown pharmacists, should not by itself be a predicate for contributory liability").

80 *Tiffany (NJ) Inc.* v. *eBay, Inc.*, 600 F.3d 93 (2d Cir. 2010). This discussion borrows from Dogan, *supra* note 5, at 515–16.

81 *Tiffany*, 600 F.3d. at 106.

82 *Id.* at 109.

83 *Id.*

84 *Id.* at 107; *see also Tiffany (NJ) Inc.* v. *eBay, Inc.*, 576 F. Supp. 2d 463, 511 (SDNY 2008).

85 17 USC § 512.

While this "specific knowledge" standard may appear to give broad immunity to intermediaries, the full opinion reveals a more contextual analysis that requires intermediaries to act reasonably in cooperating with trademark holders.[86] The court indicated that defendants who turn a blind eye to infringement may face liability under the "willful blindness" doctrine, a doctrine that finds its roots in the fault-based foundations of secondary trademark liability.[87] By limiting enforcement responsibilities to known instances of infringement, the opinion allows resellers and others to make legal, information-disseminating uses of marks,[88] but leaves open the possibility of liability against intermediaries who deliberately enable another party's infringement. Other opinions follow a similar contextual analysis of contributory infringement, refusing to find liability that might interfere with legitimate operations but imposing it against parties that appear eager to promote or ignore infringement.[89]

Together, these cases reveal contributory infringement as a flexible doctrine designed to promote the core principles of secondary liability. Its inducement branch assures liability for culpable parties. For others – those whose acts create a risk of wrongdoing but are not wrong in themselves – the doctrine takes a contextualized approach to determining what they knew and what they could do with their knowledge. The contributory infringement standard in *Inwood*, complemented by a robust doctrine of willful blindness, thus offers a balanced and normatively grounded approach to intermediary liability online.

IV CONCLUSION

The US experience with secondary trademark liability typifies the common law approach to lawmaking. Over the long run, the law evolves to promote a set of normative objectives that themselves adapt in response to social norms and commercial context. While disruptions like the Internet sometimes cause short-term uncertainties and doctrinal mistakes, the common law offers the possibility of correction. The standards for secondary trademark infringement are no different: after some fits, starts, and missteps, courts will likely restore the principled distinction between primary and secondary liability, and thus restore the balance between trademark holders and people who have, at best, an indirect relationship to some other party's infringement.

86 For elaboration, *see* Dogan, *supra* note 5, at 515–17.

87 *Tiffany*, 600 F.3d at 109–10 (suggesting that if eBay had "intentionally shielded itself from discovering the offending listings or the identity of the sellers behind them, eBay might very well have been charged with knowledge").

88 *Cf. Tiffany*, 600 F.3d at 103 (in discussing direct infringement claims against eBay, finding no liability because "eBay used the [Tiffany] mark to describe accurately the genuine Tiffany goods offered for sale on its website").

89 *See, e.g.*, *Tiffany (NJ) LLC* v. *Dong*, No. 11 Civ. 2183(GBD)(FM), 2013 WL 4046380, at *7 (SDNY, Aug. 9, 2013) (finding contributory liability against a credit card company that, after receiving a copy of a legal complaint of counterfeiting, continued to provide credit card services to the counterfeiter; concluding that the defendant "had knowledge that [their clients] traded in counterfeit products, or was willfully blind to that fact"); *see also Gucci*, 721 F. Supp. 2d at 249; *Rosetta Stone Ltd.* v. *Google, Inc.*, 676 F.3d 144, 163–65 (4th Cir. 2012) (reversing summary judgment for Google, based on evidence that the search engine had allowed "known infringers and counterfeiters" to continue to use its keyword-based advertising service); *Car-Freshner Corp.* v. *Getty Images, Inc.*, 822 F. Supp. 2d 167, 180 (NDNY 2011); *cf. 1-800 Contacts, Inc.* v. *Lens.com, Inc.*, 722 F.3d 1229 (10th Cir. 2013) (suggesting that party may have obligation to respond to a known instance of infringement by member of its affiliate network, even if affiliate's specific identity is unknown); *see generally* Dogan, *supra* note 5, at 517–19. *Compare Sellify, Inc.* v. *Amazon.com, Inc.*, No. 09 Civ. 10268, 2010 WL 4455830, at *4 (SDNY, Nov. 4, 2010) (rejecting contributory infringement claim against party that had "specifically sought to bar" the defendant from infringing, and had "promptly initiated enforcement action against [the direct infringer] and eventually terminated its contractual relationship with the company in large part because it continued to infringe on plaintiff's mark").

32

Approaches to Secondary Liability for Trademark Infringement

A Limited Harmonization under European Union Law

*Miquel Peguera**

I INTRODUCTION

European Union trademark law is essentially laid down in two statutory instruments, namely, (i) the EU Trade Mark Regulation (EUTMR), which governs EU-wide trademarks and is directly applicable to all EU member states;[1] and (ii) the Trade Mark Directive (TMD), which harmonizes member states' national marks.[2] Both statutes confer on the trademark owner the exclusive right to prevent some third-party uses of a sign identical or similar to the registered trademark. Those uses encroach directly upon the proprietor's exclusive rights and thus constitute a primary trademark infringement.

In contrast, with the exception of some preparatory acts,[3] third-party activities that contribute to, or take advantage of, someone else's primary infringement, are not dealt with by the EUTMR or by the TMD. The *secondary* liability that may arise from those activities is essentially left to member states' national laws,[4] although crucially conditioned by EU law in some respects. Such liability may hinge upon specific, non-harmonized provisions included in domestic trademark laws or derive more generally from member states' legal doctrines and traditions in the field of tort law, which is not harmonized at the EU level either.[5]

This results in a patchwork of different regimes, where there is not even a common notion of trademark secondary liability, let alone a unified terminology to refer to it.[6] For the purposes of this chapter, we may group under the term of "secondary liability" the situations where liability – including injunctive relief – is imposed on a person who does not infringe the

* Associate Professor of Law. Universitat Oberta de Catalunya, Barcelona, Spain.

[1] Regulation (EU) 2017/1001 of the European Parliament and of the Council of June 14, 2017 on the European Union trademark (codification), OJ L 154, June 16, 2017.

[2] Directive (EU) 2015/2436 of the European Parliament and of the Council of Dec. 16, 2015 to approximate the laws of the member states relating to trademarks (recast), OJ L 336, Dec. 23, 2015.

[3] Both the EUTMR (art. 10) and the TDM (art. 11) now grant the trademark owner the right to prohibit some preparatory acts in relation to packaging, labels, tags or other items to which the trademark is affixed, where there is a risk that they could be used in relation to goods or services and that use would constitute a primary infringement. *See* Martin Senftleben, *Rights Conferred*, *in* EUROPEAN TRADE MARK LAW: A COMMENTARY 269, 390 (Annette Kur & Martin Senftleben eds., 2017).

[4] *See* Martin Leistner, *Structural Aspects of Secondary (Provider) Liability in Europe*, 9 J. INTELL. PROP. L. & PRAC. 75, 76 (2014).

[5] *See* Annette Kur, *Secondary Liability for Trademark Infringement on the Internet: The Situation in Germany and throughout the EU*, 37 COLUMBIA J.L. & ARTS 525, 525 (2014).

[6] *Id.* at 529.

trademark owner's rights, i.e., does not engage in a primary infringement but nonetheless plays a role in someone else's actual or potential violation of those rights. That role may be in the form of encouraging the infringement, facilitating it, contributing to it, or otherwise benefiting from it. The liability that may arise under national law may be termed as secondary, indirect, accessory or derivative liability – or even constitute *direct* tortious liability.[7]

As noted, although trademark secondary liability ultimately depends on national law, it is nonetheless conditioned by EU law in several respects. In this vein, some degree of harmonization at EU level regarding trademark secondary liability does exist.[8]

Firstly, the notion of primary infringement, which is harmonized by the EUTMR and the TMD – as construed by the Court of Justice of the EU (CJEU) – is key to drawing a line between primary and secondary infringement. It is essential to ascertain whether the conduct under examination might be categorized as a direct violation of trademark rights, or rather may only be deemed a secondary infringement. In addition, finding that a primary infringement has occurred – or is likely to occur – is generally required to impose secondary liability on someone else.[9]

Secondly, when it comes to internet intermediaries, the E-Commerce Directive (ECD) sets some limits on the liability that may be imposed under national law, thus affecting secondary liability. When the conditions are met, the service provider is excluded from any liability regarding the intermediated content. Such an exclusion, however, does not affect the possibility of injunctions against the intermediary – although the ECD also restricts the reach of eventual injunctions by prohibiting the imposition of general monitoring obligations on those providers.

Thirdly, the Intellectual Property Enforcement Directive (IPRED),[10] obliges member states to provide for the possibility of issuing injunctions against intermediaries that are not engaging in a direct infringement but whose services are being used by a third party to infringe intellectual property rights. This applies to intermediaries of any kind, whether online or offline. As a result, some sort of secondary liability – although limited to injunctive relief – is in fact imposed by EU law.[11]

To be sure, the procedures and conditions of such injunctions are left to national laws.[12] Nonetheless, EU law establishes both a minimal floor and a maximal ceiling for the scope of injunctive relief. On the one hand, national law may not provide a protection which falls short of that intended by the IPRED – again, as interpreted by the CJEU. On the other hand, injunctions may not go beyond the general limits set by the IPRED, or beyond what is reasonable and proportionate in view of the concurring rights recognized under the Charter of Fundamental Rights of the EU. Moreover, as noted, when directed against internet intermediaries, injunctions must respect the ECD prohibition on establishing general monitoring obligations – a limit that may arguably extend also to other scenarios, as will be discussed below.

[7] *See* Graeme Dinwoodie, *A Comparative Analysis of the Secondary Liability of Online Service Providers*, *in* Secondary Liability of Internet Service Providers 1, 12 (Graeme Dinwoodie ed., 2017).

[8] *See* Opinion of Advocate General Jääskinen in Case C-324/09, *L'Oréal* v. *eBay*, Dec. 9, 2010, ECLI:EU:C:2010:757, para. 55 [hereinafter AG Opinion in *L'Oréal* v. *eBay*].

[9] *See, e.g.*, Kur, *supra* note 5, at 536.

[10] Directive (2004/48/EC) of the European Parliament and of the Council of Apr. 29, 2004 on the enforcement of intellectual property rights OJ L 157, Apr. 30, 2004 (Corrigendum, OJ L 195, June 2, 2004).

[11] *See* Leistner, *supra* note 4, at 76.

[12] *See* Recital 23 IPRED, and Recital 59 of Directive 2001/29/EC of the European Parliament and of the Council of May 22, 2001 on the harmonization of certain aspects of copyright and related rights in the information society, OJ L 167, June 22, 2001, 10–19 [hereinafter InfoSoc Directive].

A detailed analysis of the mosaic of national regimes and case law would exceed the scope and length of this chapter; it will focus instead on the common elements of EU law referred to above, which directly affect the national approaches. This chapter will first consider the boundaries of primary infringement. Then it will briefly consider the main grounds used in national law to impose secondary liability on uses that cannot be deemed primary infringements. Next, it will turn to the liability limitations laid down by the ECD safe harbours. Finally, the chapter will deal with injunctive relief required by the IPRED.

II THE BOUNDARIES OF PRIMARY TRADEMARK INFRINGEMENT

The exclusive rights conferred by a trademark do not grant the proprietor an absolute monopoly over the sign of which the mark consists. Rather, the owner's right to prohibit third-party uses of an identical or similar sign is limited to what is necessary to protect the functions of a trademark – in particular its essential function of indicating the commercial origin of the goods or services offered under the mark. Accordingly, the unconsented third-party uses a trademark owner has the right to prevent under the EUTMR or the TMD must fulfil some specific conditions. Those include the general threshold requirements of being a use made (i) in the course of trade, (ii) in relation to goods or services, and (iii) for the purpose of distinguishing goods or services – a requirement the CJEU has changed into a more general condition of being liable to have an adverse effect on one or more functions of the trademark.[13] Those threshold requirements are in turn based on the premise that the concerned use constitutes an actual "use" for the purposes of the relevant EUTMR and TMD provisions.[14]

The underlying notion of "use" under those provisions, and the general conditions a challenged use must meet, have been examined by the CJEU in a series of cases involving both an alleged direct infringer and a third-party providing services that facilitate the claimed infringement. The Court analysed whether the service provider's conduct may constitute a direct infringement in itself – that is, a use of the sign the trademark owner is entitled to prevent based on the exclusive rights conferred by the trademark. If that were the case, the right owner would benefit from the harmonized legal framework governing primary infringement, which greatly facilitates a uniform enforcement throughout the EU. In contrast, if the service provider's activity would not constitute a "use," would not meet the threshold conditions, or otherwise would not amount to a direct infringement, it should be examined under rules other than those premised on the realization of a primary violation. In such a case, the essentially non-harmonized national rules on secondary liability would come into play.

In *Google France*,[15] the CJEU considered Google's role as a provider of the "Adwords" paid referencing service (currently Google Ads), which allows advertisers to select one or more keywords and, subject to some conditions, have an ad displayed along with the natural results when a user enters one of the selected keywords as a search term on Google's search engine. The conflict concerned the "use" – both by the advertiser and by Google – of registered trademarks as keywords in the context of the referencing service. Regarding the advertiser, the Court held that by purchasing the service and choosing as a keyword a word identical with someone else's

[13] On the trademark functions debate, *see* Senftleben, *supra* note 3, at 6.

[14] Art. 9 EUTMR 2017/1001; art. 10 TMD 2015/2436 (formerly art. 5 TMD 2008/95/EC).

[15] *See* Joined Cases C-236, 237 & 238/08, *Google France SARL* v. *Louis Vuitton Malletier SA*, Judgment of Mar. 23, 2010, EU:C:2010:159 (*Google France*).

trademark, the advertiser makes a "use" of that mark in the course of trade – a use that will constitute a primary infringement if the rest of conditions are met.

Regarding Google's participation, however, the Court noted that "[t]he fact of creating the technical conditions necessary for the use of a sign and being paid for that service does not mean that the party offering the service itself *uses* the sign."[16] It held that for the purposes of finding an infringement "the use, by a third party, of a sign identical with, or similar to, the proprietor's trade mark implies, at the very least, that that third party uses the sign *in its own commercial communication*."[17] Hence, the Court held that while Google provides the referencing service in the course of trade, allows advertisers to select words identical to registered trademarks, stores those keywords and displays the ads on the basis of the keywords, it does not make a *use* of the mark for the purposes of the EUTMR or the TMD. Thus, according to the Court, a referencing service provider "allows its clients to use signs ... *without itself using those signs*."[18] In such a scenario, the service provider does not engage in a direct infringement, and its liability, if any, for having "permitted its client to make such a use of the sign"[19] may only arise under national law provisions dealing with secondary liability.

Lack of "use" was similarly found by the CJEU in *L'Oréal* v. *eBay*,[20] a case regarding offers for sale displayed on eBay's website. The operator of an online marketplace shows on its website the offers posted by its customer-sellers, which include the display of the goods' trademarks. However, the CJEU found, the operator does not "use" those marks within the meaning of TMD and EUTMR, because it does not use the signs for its own commercial communication. Rather, the relevant use for the purposes of the infringement provisions "is made by the sellers who are customers of the operator of that marketplace and not by that operator itself."[21] As a consequence, the Court noted, the role of the online marketplace operator should be assessed from the point of view of other rules of law, particularly under the safe harbours provisions set out in the ECD.[22]

The CJEU examined again the notion of use in *Winters* v. *Red Bull*,[23] a case not related to internet services but concerning a service provided by Frisdranken Industrie Winters BV ("Winters"), consisting of filling cans with energizing drinks. The underlying question was whether Winters' activity should be categorized as direct infringement, or rather may only give rise to secondary liability. Acting on the instructions of Smart Drinks Ltd., a competitor of Red Bull GmbH, Winters filled cans bearing signs allegedly similar to Red Bull's famous marks. Smart Drinks supplied Winters with the empty cans already bearing the sings. The extract contained in the fizzy drinks was also provided by Smart Drinks. Following Smart Drinks' instructions, Winters filled the cans and placed them at the disposal of Smart Drinks, who then exported the cans to countries outside the Benelux, the jurisdiction where the filling of the cans took place. Winters did not send the cans to Smart Drinks, or sell them to any third party. Red Bull sued Winters, arguing that, by filling the cans bearing the signs, Winters infringed Red Bull's trademark rights.

[16] *Id.*, at para. 57 (emphasis added).
[17] *Id.*, at para. 56 (emphasis added).
[18] *Id.* (emphasis added).
[19] *Id.*, at para. 57.
[20] CJEU, Case C-324/09, *L'Oréal* v. *eBay*, Judgment of July 12, 2011, ECLI:EU:C:2011:474 (*L'Oréal* v. *eBay*).
[21] *Id.*, at para. 103.
[22] *Id.*, at para. 104.
[23] CJEU, Case C-119/10, *Frisdranken Industrie Winters* v. *Red Bull*, Judgment of Dec. 15, 2011, ECLI:EU:C:2011:837 (*Winters* v. *Red Bull*).

It must be noted that after establishing the conditions for there to be a trademark infringement the TMD offers some examples of specific uses that may be prevented by the proprietor – provided that the conditions for the infringement are met. One of such specific use is that of "affixing the sign to the goods or to the packaging thereof."[24] Red Bull claimed that Winters had indeed affixed the sign to the goods by filling the cans bearing the sign. The CJEU, however, held that the question of whether the filling of the cans amounts to affixing the sign to the goods was irrelevant because there was no "use" of the signs by Winters in the first place.[25]

Referring to *Google France*, the Court noted that creating the technical conditions for the use of a sign does not necessarily mean that the service provider itself uses that sign. In this vein, it held that

> a service provider who, in circumstances such as those in the main action, merely fills, under an order from and on the instructions of another person, cans already bearing signs similar to trade marks and therefore *merely executes a technical part of the production process of the final product* without having any interest in the external presentation of those cans and in particular in the signs thereon, *does not itself "use" those signs* within the meaning of Article 5 of Directive 89/104, *but only creates the technical conditions necessary for the other person to use them.*[26]

Moreover, the Court noted that such use would not meet in any event the threshold requirement of being made in relation to goods or services identical with, or similar to, those for which the trademark was registered. Indeed, the Court interprets requirement of being a use made in relation to goods or services as meaning, generally, a use for goods or services *of* the third party making such use – which would not be the case of Winters, as the filled cans were the property of its customer, Smart Drinks.[27]

The CJEU stressed that holding that the owner is not entitled to prohibit conduct like that of Winters under the TMD does not imply that trademark protection can be easily circumvented by dividing the production process by resorting to third-party service providers. The Court dismissed such a concern, noting that "those services may be attributed to the customer who therefore remains liable under that directive."[28]

On a different note, the Court did not consider expanding the notion of infringing use to include the activities of service providers that may have constructive knowledge about the direct infringement carried out by their customers. In fact, the CJEU did not discuss whether Winters knew or should have known about the possible infringement made by Smart Drinks, or whether such a knowledge might play a role in characterizing Winters' conduct as infringing. In this way, the Court seems to follow the advice of the Advocate General Kokott, who warned against such an expansion, cautioning that it would expose service providers to disproportionate risks, as "[i]t is practically impossible for them to ensure that the signs chosen by the client do not infringe

[24] Art. 5(3)(a) TMD 2008/95/EC (currently, art. 10(3)(a) TMD 2015/2436).

[25] *Winters* v. *Red Bull*, at para. 34.

[26] *Id.*, at para. 30 (emphasis added).

[27] *See id.*, at para. 31 and the case law cited therein. As an exception to that general understanding, the CJEU accepts that a broker who uses the sign to promote its customer's goods – instead of its own – may also be deemed to use the sign "in relation to goods or services," as long as a link can be established between the sign and the service provided by the broker. *See* CJEU, Case C-62/08, *UDV North America Inc.* v. *Brandtraders NV*, Order of Feb. 19, 2009, ECLI:EU:C:2009:111, paras. 43–51 (*UDV* v. *Brandtraders*). However, the service provided by Winters was not similar to that of a broker, as Winters' activity was not apparent to the consumer. *See Winters* v. *Red Bull*, at para. 33.

[28] *Winters* v. *Red Bull*, at para. 36. The Court does not refer in this ruling to the possibility of considering a service provider such as Winters an intermediary whose services are used by a third party to infringe an intellectual property right, and thus subject to injunctions under art. 11 IPRED.

marks belonging to another,"[29] and noting also that subjective elements of knowledge cannot be decisive to find an infringement, "as the infringement of the rights associated with a mark does not depend on the manifestation of any bad faith."[30]

As shown in those cases, defining what may or may not constitute a primary infringement is of utmost importance for dealing with secondary liability. To be sure, this is also the case in the field of copyright, where secondary liability is likewise left to national law.[31] The CJEU might be tempted to assuage the enforcement difficulties arising from the lack of harmonization by expanding the notion of primary infringement so as to cover a wider range of uses. In fact, when it comes to copyright, and specifically regarding the characterization of hyperlinks as acts of communication to the public, the CJEU has embarked in an enlargement of the notion of primary copyright violation so as to include instances which could be best described as indirect or contributory infringements.[32] With such an approach, the CJEU arguably engages in an indirect harmonization of copyright secondary liability regarding the provision of hyperlinks pointing to protected content.[33] This indirect harmonization, however, seems for now confined to that particular area within the field of copyright law, with no signs of being adopted with regard to trademark secondary liability.[34]

III A MOSAIC OF NATIONAL APPROACHES

In addition to specific provisions dealing with instances of secondary liability in some national trademark laws,[35] or in other national norms such as those on unfair competition law, member states generally approach indirect liability through some form of tort law.[36]

An example of this approach may be France, where trademark secondary liability is addressed under the general rules on non-contractual liability, particularly those establishing liability based on the defendant's fault or negligence and causation.[37] While this may be understood as a form of secondary liability in relation to the direct trademark infringement, in terms of tort liability the defendant is made directly liable because of its own fault.[38] In a series of cases against eBay, the Cour de cassation upheld the lower courts' findings that eBay's role was not neutral enough for the safe harbours of the ECD to apply, and holding eBay liable for damages regarding the

[29] *See* Opinion of Advocate General Kokott in Case C-119/10, *Winters* v. *Red Bull*, Apr. 14, 2011, ECLI:EU:C:2011:258, para 33 [hereinafter AG Opinion in *Winters* v. *Red Bull*].

[30] *See id.* at para. 32.

[31] Christina Angelopoulos, European Intermediary Liability in Copyright: A Tort-Based Analysis 3 (2016).

[32] *See* CJEU, Case C-160/15, *GS Media BV* v. *Sanoma Media Netherlands BV*, Judgment of Sept. 8, 2016, ECLI:EU:C:2016:644; CJEU, Case C-527/15, *Stichting Brein* v. Jack Frederik Wullems, Judgment of Apr. 26, 2017, ECLI:EU:C:2017:300 (*Filmspeler*); CJEU, Case C-610/15, *Stichting Brein* v. *Ziggo BV*, *XS4ALL Internet BV*, Judgment of June 14, 2017, ECLI:EU:C:2017:456 (*Ziggo*). *See* Jane C. Ginsburg & Luke Ali Budiardjo, *Liability for Providing Hyperlinks to Copyright-Infringing Content: International and Comparative Law Perspectives*, 41 Columbia J.L. & Arts 153, 167 (2018); Miquel Peguera, *Hyperlinking under the Lens of the Revamped Right of Communication to the Public*, 34 Computer Law & Security Review 1099, 1106 (2018).

[33] *See* Angelopoulos, *supra* note 31, at 66.

[34] Nonetheless, as Husovec notes, accepting injunctions that entail a full restriction of conduct would amount to expanding the scope of the exclusive rights. *See* Martin Husovec, Injunctions against Intermediaries in the European Union: Accountable but Not Liable? 108 (2017).

[35] *See, e.g.*, art. 14(4) German Trade Mark Act; art. 10(5) UK Trade Marks Act of 1994.

[36] *See* Kur, *supra* note 5, at 525; Leistner, *supra* note 4, at 75.

[37] Those rules have been traditionally embodied in arts. 1382 and 1383 of the *Code Civil*, which in 2016 were renumbered as arts. 1240 and 1241.

[38] *See* Angelopoulos, *supra* note 31, at 205–06. There are also norms establishing liability for the acts of others, but they require a special relationship between the defendant and the third party. *See* art. 1242 *Code Civil*.

trademark infringements that occurred on its website.[39] It was held that eBay has a duty of ensuring that its activity does not generate illicit acts, and thus a duty to prevent trademark infringements on its site. The basis for the liability was eBay's own fault for failing to comply with that duty. In particular, the court of appeals noted that eBay failed to implement effective measures to comply with its obligation to ensure that the goods on sale did not infringe the plaintiffs' rights. In addition, the court argued that eBay had not removed the suspicious offers as required by the plaintiffs, even though some of them were clearly signalling the counterfeit nature of the goods. The court concluded that these faults triggered eBay's liability under the general rules of non-contractual liability.[40]

A different approach is followed in England, where accessory liability for trademark infringement is governed by the common law, particularly under the law as to joint tortfeasorship.[41] A defendant may be found to be a joint tortfeasor where it has acted in concert with the primary infringer, participating in a common design, that is, combining to secure the doing of acts which proved to be infringements.[42] A defendant may also be liable as joint tortfeasor where it procures a primary infringement by inducement, incitement or persuasion. Such procurement must be by a defendant to an individual infringer and must relate to a particular infringement.[43] Both categories of joint tortfeasorship, namely *participation in a common* design and *procurement* of primary infringements, may of course overlap as some cases may qualify under both heads.[44] On the other hand, the mere facilitation of infringements with the knowledge that infringements are likely to occur does not amount to joint tortfeasorship.[45] In the UK case *L'Oréal* v. *eBay*, Justice Arnold held that eBay was not liable as a joint tortfeasor. He noted that as a matter of common law eBay does not have a legal duty to prevent infringement. In addition, while admitting that eBay facilitates third-party trademark infringements, knows that such infringements have occurred or are likely to occur, and profits from them, Justice Arnold held that this is not enough to make eBay a joint tortfeasor.[46] Nonetheless, not being liable as a joint tortfeasor does not exclude the possibility of injunctions. Indeed, UK case law provides examples of injunctions against innocent intermediaries, including website blocking orders on internet access providers to prevent trademark infringements.[47]

In Germany, the liability of those participating in someone else's primary infringement, both in copyright and trademark law, particularly when it comes to internet platforms, is usually approached under a concept of German private law called *Störerhaftung* or "interferer liability."[48] This traditional notion, derived by analogy from a provision of the German Civil Code dealing with the prejudice suffered by proprietors because of a third-party interference,[49] only provides for injunctive relief.[50] It does not allow damages to be claimed. Damages may be

[39] *See* Cour de cassation, Chambre commerciale, financière et économique, Judgments of May 3, 2012: *eBay Inc., eBay Int'l* v. *Christian Dior Couture; eBay Inc., eBay Int'l* v. *Louis Vuitton Malletier; eBay Inc., eBay Int'l* v. *LVMH.*

[40] *See* Cour d'appel de Paris, Pôle 5, chambre 2, Judgment of Sept. 3, 2010, *eBay Inc., eBay Int'l* v. *Christian Dior Couture.*

[41] *See L'Oréal* v. *eBay* [2009] EWHC 1904 (Ch.), para. 346.

[42] *Id.* at para. 360.

[43] *Id.* at para. 359 (quoting *CBS Songs Ltd.* v. *Amstrad Consumer Elecs. PLC* [1988] UKHL 15).

[44] *Id.* at para. 349 (quoting *Unilever Plc.* v. *Gillette Ltd.* [1989] RPC 583, 608–09).

[45] *See id.* at para 367.

[46] *Id.* at paras. 381–82.

[47] *See Cartier Int'l AG* v. *British Telecomms. PLC* [2018] UKSC 28, para. 39 (holding that that the ISP's reasonable costs of complying with the website blocking order must be indemnified by the claimants).

[48] *See* Leistner, *supra* note 4, at 78.

[49] *See* Kur, *supra* note 5, at 532. *See* § 1004 German Civil Code (BGB).

[50] *See* Leistner, *supra* note 4, at 79.

claimed in case of tortious liability, which requires intent and is thus difficult to establish.[51] In order to find *Störerhaftung*, the interferer, who is not tortiously liable, must have made an adequate casual contribution to the third-party infringement and be legally and factually able to prevent the infringement. In addition, and most importantly, courts require a breach by the interferer of a reasonable duty of care to prevent the infringement.[52]

The injunctive relief stemming from *Störerhaftung* may consist of orders aimed not only at putting the infringement to an end but also at *preventing future infringements of the same kind* by adopting reasonable *preventive measures* – normally by means of some kind of filtering when it comes to internet intermediaries.[53] What may constitute a reasonable measure is determined by courts on a case-by-case basis.[54] The broad reach of those preventive measures is one of the more debated aspects regarding the application of *Störerhaftung*, particularly regarding internet intermediaries due to the prohibition of general monitoring obligations established the ECD.[55]

IV THE E-COMMERCE DIRECTIVE SAFE HARBOURS

When it comes to online infringements – an extremely relevant area for trademark secondary liability – EU law sets important limits to the liability member states may impose on internet intermediaries providing mere conduit, caching or hosting services.[56] The E-Commerce Directive provides for a series of liability exemptions, or "safe harbours," ordering member states to ensure that those intermediary service providers are not liable for the information they transmit or store at the request of their users, provided that some conditions are met. The exclusions are very broad, covering all kinds of liability – civil, criminal and administrative[57] – although they do not prevent injunctive relief. They "shall not affect the possibility for a court or administrative authority, in accordance with Member States' legal systems, of requiring the service provider to terminate or prevent an infringement."[58]

The ECD safe harbours apply horizontally to any type of illicit third-party content,[59] thus including content that constitutes or involves trademark infringement. Most importantly, the safe harbours are not meant to *attribute* liability on intermediaries who fail to meet their conditions. Rather, they exclusively establish some specific situations where liability *may not*

[51] *Id.* at 78; Husovec, *supra* note 34, at 164.

[52] *See* Leistner, *supra* note 4, at 78–79.

[53] *See* the three seminal judgments from the Federal Court of Justice (BGH) regarding auction platforms: *Internet-Versteigerung I* (BGH, I ZR 304/01, Mar. 11, 2004, GRUR 2004, 860); *Internet-Versteigerung II* (BGH, I ZR 35/04, Apr. 19, 2007, GRUR 2007, 708); *Internet-Versteigerung III* (BGH, I ZR 73/05, Apr. 30, 2008, GRUR 2008, 702). *See also*, more recently, *Kinderhochstühle im Internet III* (BGH, I ZR 240 12, Feb. 5, 2015, GRUR 2015, 485).

[54] Leistner, *supra* note 4, at 79. Failure to comply with the injunction may lead to administrative sanctions. Only in rare cases of persistently ignoring the injunction order, and on the condition of specific knowledge about the direct infringer, the lack of compliance might lead to contributory tortious liability, and thus damages. I am grateful to Professor Leistner for providing me with this information.

[55] Husovec, *supra* note 34, at 170.

[56] *See* arts. 12–15 ECD. Unlike the US Digital Millennium Copyright Act of 1998 (DMCA), the ECD does not grant safe harbour for the provision of hyperlinks and information location tools. Some member states have nonetheless introduced such a safe harbour in their national law.

[57] See EU Commission, First Report on the application of Directive 2000/31/EC, COM (2003) 702 final, Nov. 21, 2003, at 12 [hereinafter First Report].

[58] *See* arts. 12(3), 13(2) and 14(3) ECD. Injunctions, however, may not entail a general obligation to monitor the information they transmit or store, or actively to seek facts or circumstances indicating illegal activity (art. 15 ECD).

[59] *See* First Report, *supra* note 57, at 12. This is one of the most notable differences between the ECD and the DMCA, which deals exclusively with liability arising from copyright infringement. *See* Miquel Peguera, *The DMCA Safe Harbors and Their European Counterparts: A Comparative Analysis of Some Common Problems*, 32 Columbia J.L. & Arts 481, 482 (2009).

be imposed on those intermediaries.[60] In this vein, although only in the merely negative sense of prohibiting the attribution of liability, the ECD safe harbours also provide for some level of harmonization regarding trademark secondary liability in relation to internet intermediaries.

Therefore, when analysing the potential secondary liability of intermediaries, it must be examined whether they can benefit from the safe harbours. Hence, both in *Google France* and in *L'Oréal/eBay*, the CJEU explicitly noted that the eventual liability of Google and eBay for enabling the infringing use made by its customers should be assessed under the ECD safe harbour provisions.[61]

National courts must thus examine, on a case-by-case basis, whether the safe harbours' conditions are met. Among those conditions, the concerned service must constitute an "information society service," and therefore a service "normally provided for remuneration."[62] While this is not meant to exclude services provided for free, it does require the service to constitute an economic activity.[63] In addition, the information must have been provided by a third party–a recipient of the service.[64] The hosting safe harbour adds the requirement that the recipient providing the information is not acting under the authority or control of the service provider.[65]

Regarding particularly the hosting safe harbour – the one that might apply in the case of the services provided by Google or eBay in the CJEU cases referred to above – it has been hotly discussed whether activities going beyond pure hosting may still fall under the exemption's scope.[66] Since *Google France*, this is normally assessed under the neutrality test provided by the CJEU. In that case, the Court held that, in light of recital 42 of the ECD, the safe harbours – including that of hosting – apply only where the service provider "has not played an active role of such a kind as to give it knowledge of, or control over, the data stored."[67] The CJEU has consistently followed this interpretation,[68] even though it seems safe to assume that recital 42 ECD does not cover hosting, but only mere conduit and caching,[69] and although a test

60 *See Google France*, at para. 107; Kur, *supra* note 5, at 526; ANGELOPOULOS, *supra* note 31, at 5–6.

61 *See Google France*, at para. 57; *L'Oréal* v. *eBay*, C-324/09, at para. 104. The Court stated this after holding that neither Google nor eBay was using the trademark for the purposes of the TMD or the EUTMR and thus did not engage in a primary infringement. However, this does not mean that the safe harbours would only exclude secondary liability. In fact, primary liability would also be excluded in the event all the safe harbours conditions are met. *See* ANGELOPOULOS, *supra* note 31, at 68.

62 *See* art. 1(1)(b) of Directive (EU) 2015/1535 laying down a procedure for the provision of information in the field of technical regulations and of rules on information society services (OJ 2015 L 241). This Directive replaced Directive 98/34 (OJ 1998 L 204), which, as amended by Directive 98/48/EC (OJ 1998 L 217), provided the same definition.

63 Recital 18 ECD; CJEU, Case C-291/13, *Sotiris Papasavvas* v. *O. Fileleftheros Dimosia Etairia Ltd.*, EU:C:2014:2209, paras. 26–30. The CJEU has confirmed the applicability of the safe harbours to economic services not remunerated by the users. *See* CJEU, Case C-484/14, *Tobias McFadden* v. *Sony Music Entm't Ger. GmbH*, EU:C:2016:689, paras. 34–43 (*McFadden*).

64 *See* arts. 12(1), 13(1), 14(1) ECD.

65 Art. 14(2) EDC. Arguably, this condition may also be considered a prerequisite for the mere conduit and caching safe harbours. Indeed, if the recipient acts under the authority or control of the provider, the information would not have been provided by a truly third party, and thus the provider's activity could hardly be considered an intermediary service.

66 National case law has been wrestling with this issue over the years when analysing claims against video-sharing platforms, electronic marketplaces, or news portals hosting users' comments. *See* Patrick Van Eecke, *Online Service Providers and Liability: A Plea for a Balanced Approach*, 48 COMMON MARKET L. REV. 1455, 1457 (2011).

67 *See Google France*, at paras. 113–14.

68 *See McFadden*, at paras. 61–62, arguing that recital 42 of the eCommerce Directive also covers web hosting providers. More recently, *see* CJEU, Case C-521/17, *Coöperatieve Vereniging SNB-REACT UA* v. *Deepak Mehta*, Judgment of Aug. 7, 2018, ECLI:EU:C:2018:639, paras. 46–50 (*SNB-REACT*).

69 This seems clear from the language of the recital, which exclusively considers the "cases where the activity of the information society service provider is limited to the technical process of operating and giving access to a communication network over which information made available by third parties is transmitted or temporarily stored, for the sole

hardly comports with the wording of Article 14 ECD, which admits that the provider may obtain knowledge of the content. Moreover, the neutrality test seems difficult to apply in practice as the CJEU has offered little guidance to national courts, mentioning only, as examples of lack of neutrality, the fact of "optimizing" or "promoting" the content stored.[70] In any event, the court noted in *L'Oréal* v. *eBay* that the absence of neutrality regarding specific data hosted would only disqualify the provider in relation to the concerned data.[71]

If the service provider is considered neutral enough, then it must be assessed whether it has complied with the specific conditions of the relevant safe harbour. The bulk of the discussion has focused on the hosting exemption requirements, namely, that

(a) the provider does not have actual knowledge of illegal activity or information and, as regards claims for damages, is not aware of facts or circumstances from which the illegal activity or information is apparent; or

(b) the provider, upon obtaining such knowledge or awareness, acts expeditiously to remove or to disable access to the information.[72]

The ECD does not define such actual knowledge or awareness.[73] Regarding the later standard, the CJEU holds that it is sufficient that the provider becomes aware "of facts or circumstances on the basis of which a diligent economic operator should have identified the illegality in question."[74] Such awareness may be obtained by any means.[75] The fact that the provider is notified of the existence of the activity or information, however, does not automatically bring about the said awareness, though such notification must be taken into account by the national court, as a general rule, when determining whether the provider obtained such awareness.[76] The Directive does not provide for notice-and-take-down procedural rules,[77] and thus it does not determine the minimum requirements for notices of illegal material.[78]

As noted, the exclusions from liability do not affect the possibility of injunctions.[79] However, they may not encroach upon the prohibition, set out in Article 15 ECD, of imposing on those intermediaries a general obligation to monitor the information they transmit or store, or actively

purpose of making the transmission more efficient." Advocate General Jääskinen stressed this point in his Opinion in the *L'Oréal* v. *eBay* case (*see* AG Opinion in *L'Oréal* v. *eBay*, at paras. 138–42). *See also* Van Eecke, *supra* note 66, at 1481–84.

70 *L'Oréal* v. *eBay*, at para. 116.

71 *Id.*

72 Art. 14.1 ECD.

73 The former entails probably a higher degree of knowledge than the latter. While the lack of actual knowledge is enough to be free from criminal liability, when it comes to damages a lack of awareness of facts or circumstances indicating illegality is also required. *See* Emmanuel Crabit, *La Directive Sur le Commerce Électronique: Le Projet Méditerranée*, Revue du Droit de l'Union Européenne 749, 811–12 (2000) (noting that the two standards correspond to the distinction between criminal and civil liability).

74 *L'Oréal* v. *eBay*, at para. 120.

75 *Id.* at para. 121.

76 *Id.* at paras. 121–22.

77 A Memorandum of Understanding promoted by the EU Commission was concluded in 2011 and revised in 2016. It brings together some major internet platforms and trademark owners and facilitates a voluntary procedure of notice and action. *See* EU Commission, Overview of the Functioning of the Memorandum of Understanding on the Sale of Counterfeit Goods Via the Internet, SWD (2017) 430 final, Nov. 29, 2017.

78 Some national courts, dealing with copyright infringement, have concluded that, as a consequence of the prohibition of general monitoring obligations, notices must identify precisely the allegedly illegal content, for instance, by mentioning its URL. *See, e.g.*, *Telecinco* v. *YouTube*, Madrid Court of Appeals, Jan. 14, 2014; *RTI* v. *Yahoo Italia*, Milano Court of Appeals, Jan. 7, 2015. But holding otherwise, *see, e.g.*, *RTI* v. *Break Media*, Tribunale di Roma (first instance), Apr. 27, 2016.

79 *See, e.g.*, *SNB-REACT*, at para. 51.

to seek facts or circumstances indicating illegal activity.[80] The scope of the admissible injunction relief against intermediaries, both online and offline, is addressed in the following section.

V INJUNCTIVE RELIEF AGAINST ONLINE AND OFFLINE INTERMEDIARIES

A person may contribute to someone else's primary trademark infringement by providing a service which is used by the third party to commit the infringement. As seen above, however, the performance of the service is not likely to constitute a direct trademark infringement, though it may give rise to secondary liability under national law. Such liability may consist of different sanctions and remedies, including damages. The service provider may also be ordered, by means of an injunction, to carry out a particular task or to stop performing a specific conduct. In a broad sense, this may also be regarded as a form of liability.[81] In any event, injunctions are not necessarily premised on a finding that the addressee has violated the law; they may rather be based on other rationales, such as the mere fact that the service provider is in a better position to stop or prevent someone else's infringement.[82]

Injunctive relief is of great importance for trademark owners, particularly when it comes to intermediary service providers, whether online or offline, as from an enforcement standpoint it may be more effective than going against primary infringers. EU law obliges member states to provide for the availability of injunctions against intermediaries whose services are used by third parties to infringe intellectual property rights. This obligation was first laid down in Article 8(3) of the InfoSoc Directive, in 2001, regarding infringements of copyright and related rights. In 2004, it was established more broadly in Article 11 IPRED, covering any intellectual property right. The third sentence of Article 11 IPRED obliges member states to "ensure that rightholders are in a position to apply for an injunction against intermediaries whose services are used by a third party to infringe an intellectual property right."[83] Such an obligation provides for some harmonization with regard to injunctive relief against those who play an intermediary role on a third-party infringement.

The CJEU has clarified that the third sentence of Article 11 IPRED applies both to online and offline service providers. In *Tommy Hilfiger*, the Court considered the role played by Delta Center, a tenant of a marketplace in Prague, that would sublet physical sales areas to market traders.[84] Some of the market traders used the sales points to offer counterfeit branded goods. The Court held that IPRED's scope is not limited to electronic commerce and that its objective of ensuring a high and homogeneous level of protection would be substantially weakened if an operator of a physical marketplace could not be subject to the injunctions referred to in Article 11, third sentence.[85]

[80] Art. 15, ECD.

[81] *See* the so-called interferer liability in Germany, *supra* Section III.

[82] *See* Recital 59 Infosoc Directive.

[83] Art. 11 IPRED. This Directive also provides for interlocutory injunctions against intermediaries (art. 9). It also establishes information duties on, among others, those "found to be providing on a commercial scale services used in infringing activities" (art. 8). In *Coty Germany*, a case regarding the sale of counterfeit goods in an online platform where the claimant sought to know the identity of the holder of a bank account, the Court held that a national law that allows, unconditionally, a banking institution to refuse to provide that information would be precluded by art. 8 IPRED. *See* CJEU, Case C-580/13, *Coty Germ. GmbH* v. *Stadtsparkasse Magdeburg*, Judgment of July 16, 2015, ECLI:EU:C:2015:485 (*Coty Germany*).

[84] CJEU, Case C-494/15, Tommy Hilfiger Licensing, Judgment of July 7, 2016, ECLI:EU:C:2016:528 (*Tommy Hilfiger*).

[85] Id. at para. 29.

In addition, the Court interprets the notion of "intermediary" in a very broad way, holding that it is not even necessary that the service provider maintains a specific relationship with the person or persons who use its services to infringe. This was first held by the CJEU in *UPC Telekabel Wien*,[86] a case concerning an internet access provider. It held that the concept of "intermediary" in Article 8(3) InfoSoc encompasses any provider that transmits copyright infringing content supplied by a third party. Therefore, an internet access provider which allows its users to access infringing content made available on the Internet by a third party fits into the notion of intermediary, even though that third party lacks a contractual relationship with the access provider.[87] While this case concerned specifically Article 8(3) InfoSoc, the Court accepts the same reasoning when it comes to Article 11 IPRED.[88]

The CJEU has also held that member states must make those injunctions available against intermediaries regardless of any liability of their own.[89] Thus, it is not a condition that they are considered secondary infringers under national law. Crucially, the Court holds that injunctions against intermediaries may consist not only of measures aimed at bringing infringements committed by their users to an end but also at preventing further infringements of that kind.[90] Nonetheless, when devising injunctions to prevent future infringements – and, for that matter, any other type of injunction – due account must be taken of the limits EU law imposes. Indeed, as noted, EU law sets a maximal ceiling for injunctive relief, regardless of how national law characterizes the provider's conduct in terms of liability.

In this vein, Article 3 IPRED requires that the measures, procedures and remedies provided for by member states to ensure the enforcement of intellectual property rights must (i) be fair and equitable; (ii) not be unnecessarily complicated or costly, or entail unreasonable time limits or unwarranted delays; (iii) be effective, proportionate and dissuasive; (iv) not create barriers to legitimate trade;[91] and (v) provide for safeguards against their abuse. Based on these limitations, the CJEU held in *L'Oréal* v. *eBay* that an injunction against the operator of the marketplace "cannot have *as its object or effect* a general and permanent prohibition on the selling, on that marketplace, of goods bearing [the concerned] trade marks."[92]

In addition, Article 15 ECD prohibition of imposing general monitoring obligations must be respected when it comes to providers of mere conduit, caching and hosting services. In fact, injunctions entailing general monitoring obligations – at least very broad ones – are likely to be prevented by EU law also regarding other types of intermediaries. In this sense, the CJEU has considered that a broad general monitoring obligation, such as unlimited filtering, would also be incompatible with Article 3 IPRED;[93] it would constitute a serious infringement of the

86 CJEU, Case C-314/12, *UPC Telekabel Wien*, Judgment of Mar. 27, 2014, ECLI:EU:C:2014:192 (*UPC Telekabel*).

87 Id. at para. 32.

88 *See Tommy Hilfiger*, at para. 23. Similarly, in the *Winters* v. *Red Bull* case, Advocate General Kokott suggested that Winters might be the subject of injunctions stemming from art. 11 IPRED as an intermediary whose services are used by a third party to infringe an intellectual property right. *See* AG Opinion in *Winters* v. *Red Bull*, at paras. 36–39.

89 *See* CJEU, Case C-70/10, *Scarlet Extended SA* v. *SABAM*, Judgment of Nov. 24, 2011, ECLI:EU:C:2011:771, para. 31 (*Scarlet Extended*); *L'Oréal* v. *eBay*, at paras. 127–34; *Tommy Hilfiger*, at para. 22.

90 *L'Oréal* v. *eBay*, at paras. 131, 144; *Scarlet Extended*, at para. 31; CJEU, Case C-360/10, *SABAM* v. *Netlog NV*, Judgment of Feb. 16, 2012, ECLI:EU:C:2012:85, para. 29 (*Sabam* v. *Netlog*).

91 Avoiding interference with legitimate commerce is a shared concern in other jurisdictions regarding secondary liability. *See* Stacey Dogan, *Principled Standards vs. Boundless Discretion: A Tale of Two Approaches to Intermediary Trademark Liability Online*, 37 Columbia J.L. & Arts 503, 505 (2014).

92 *L'Oréal* v. *eBay*, at para. 140.

93 *See id.*, at para. 139; *Scarlet Extended*, at paras. 36, 48. *See* Husovec, *supra* note 34, at 118 (noting that, as a result, the prohibition of general monitoring obligations applies as well to offline intermediaries).

provider's freedom to conduct business;[94] and it may infringe a user's right to personal data protection and freedom to receive or impart information.[95] Such a prohibition is especially relevant when dealing with injunctions to prevent future infringements, as those injunctions may easily amount to a general monitoring obligation. For now, the CJEU has accepted as compatible with Article 15 ECD that the intermediary is ordered "to take measures which contribute to avoiding new infringements of the same nature by the same market-trader from taking place."[96] It has also accepted orders to block access to a specific website.[97]

A last group of limitations for injunctive relief is based in EU primary law. Since any injunction against intermediaries will ultimately be an implementation of EU law, the limits stemming from the Charter of Fundamentals Rights of the EU apply.[98] As a consequence, according to Article 52(1) of the Charter, whenever the injunction may entail an interference against another fundamental right, it must (i) be provided by law and (ii) respect the essence of the affected rights and freedoms. In addition, it must be proportionate, in the sense that (i) it is necessary; (ii) it genuinely meets objectives of general interest recognized by the Union or the need to protect the rights and freedoms of others; and (iii) it respects the proportionality test *stricto sensu*, i.e., it is the least onerous measure among those available, and the harm is proportionate to the aims pursued.[99] The CJEU has rejected different kinds of injunctions aiming at filtering all the contents transmitted or stored by the intermediary as failing to meet the proportionality principle.[100]

VI CONCLUSION

Secondary trademark liability in the EU remains an issue for national law, thus hinging on the peculiarities of member states' legal traditions, particularly on their approach to tort law. Nonetheless, regarding those who are more likely to be involved in secondary liability claims, i.e., different kinds of intermediaries, EU law sets forth a decisive body of harmonizing elements. These encompass both the exemptions of liability for internet intermediary service providers and a harmonized minimal floor and maximal ceiling for injunctive relief. The evolving case law of the CJEU plays a crucial role in defining the precise boundaries of those elements, which are not always easy to draw.

94 *See Scarlet Extended*, at para. 48; *Sabam* v. *Netlog*, at para. 46.

95 *See Sabam* v. *Netlog*, at para. 48.

96 *Tommy Hilfiger*, at para. 34; *L'Oréal* v. *eBay*, at para. 141. The AG in the *L'Oréal* v. *eBay* case had suggested that a limit for the scope of injunctions may be that of a double requirement of identity, i.e., preventing future infringements from the same user regarding the same trademark. *See* AG Opinion in *L'Oréal* v. *eBay* at para. 182.

97 *See UPC Telekabel*. In this case, Advocate General Villalón had expressed the view that the blocking of a specific website would not infringe art. 15(1) ECD. *See* Opinion of Advocate General Villalón in Case C-314/12, *UPC Telekabel*, Nov., 2013, ECLI:EU:C:2013:781, at para. 78 [hereinafter AG Opinion in *UPC Telekabel*]. However, some ways of carrying out the blockade may arguably entail general filtering.

98 *See* Martin Husovec & Miquel Peguera, *Much Ado about Little: Privately Litigated Internet Disconnection Injunctions*, 46 INT'L REV. INTELL. PROP. & COMPETITION L. 10, 18 (2015). According to art. 51(1) of the Charter, the Charter's provisions apply to member states only when they are implementing Union law.

99 *See* AG Opinion in *UPC Telekabel*, at para. 103. *See also* ECJ, Case C-375/96, *Galileo Zaninotto & Ispettorato Centrale Repressione Frodi*, Judgment of Oct. 29, 1998, ECLI:EU:C:1998:517, para. 63.

100 *See Scarlet Extended*; *Sabam* v. *Netlog*.

XIII

Trademark Defenses

33

Valuing the Freedom of Speech and the Freedom to Compete in Defenses to Trademark and Related Claims in the United States

*Jennifer E. Rothman**

I INTRODUCTION

Trademark and related unfair competition laws promote fair competition and protect goodwill but do not do so by providing broad monopoly rights. Instead, rights to a particular mark are limited to leave room for competitors, the dissemination of information, and the production of creative expression and commentary. This latitude is protected in part by limits on the scope of the rights afforded, but also by defenses to these claims. This chapter primarily considers affirmative defenses to trademark infringement, trademark dilution, and false endorsement claims, focusing on defenses that serve the goals of free expression and fair competition. These free-speech-based defenses should be of particular interest to comparative law scholars and non-US practitioners because of their unique and elevated status in US law. The First Amendment to the US Constitution expressly prohibits Congress (and by extension states) from making or enforcing laws that "abridg[e] the freedom of speech." This foundational aspect of US law has influenced the development of and the interpretation of speech-based defenses to trademark and related claims.[1]

Federal and state laws both provide trademark, unfair competition, and false endorsement laws, as well as defenses to those claims. This chapter focuses on the federal regime under the Lanham Act, but the analysis here also applies to most state laws.[2] The chapter covers the defenses of genericism, functionality, descriptive and nominative fair use, the *Rogers* test, statutory exemptions to dilution claims, and the questions of whether and how an independent First Amendment defense applies. The chapter does not address other defense strategies, such as challenges to the validity of the underlying mark or to the likelihood of confusion (both parts of the prima facie case), even though they too are often guided by the values of promoting free speech and protecting the freedom to compete.[3]

Before turning to the specifics of each defense, several overarching observations can be made about these speech and competition-related defenses. First, the speech or competition values asserted by the defendants influence the likely success of the claims. Defenses are more

* William G. Coskran Professor of Law, Loyola Law School, Loyola Marymount University.

[1] U.S. CONST. amend. I; *see also Gitlow* v. *New York*, 268 US 652, 666–67 (1925) (noting the extension of the First Amendment to the states through the Fourteenth Amendment).

[2] The governing federal Lanham Act is codified in 15 USC § 1051 (2012) *et seq.*

[3] The chapter also does not consider affirmative defenses not rooted in free speech concerns, such as abandonment, misuse, antitrust violations, and various equitable defenses. *See, e.g.*, Lanham Act § 33(b), 15 USC § 1115(b) (2012).

successful when the uses are in creative or artistic works, convey relevant information to potential consumers (even in advertising), or are deemed a commercial necessity.

A second and related observation is that the perceived "reasonableness" of the defendant's use will determine the likely success of the asserted defense. This is true even when the particular defense does not explicitly include such a consideration. Courts want to provide breathing room for expression, fair competition, and the provision of information, but do not want to give refuge to those who are unreasonably exploiting and profiting from someone else's mark. This particular instinct likely explains courts' disfavoring of uses in merchandise.

Third, these defenses serve as a counterbalance to the broad scope of today's trademark law, which has expanded dramatically over the last century, particularly in the last few decades with the addition of dilution claims to the federal regime. Trademark law has moved away from a tort-based framework rooted in fraud and unfair competition claims, toward an intellectual property framework more similar to the monopolistic copyright and patent regimes with which it has long been contrasted. Originally, US trademark law limited liability to instances in which there was likely confusion as to the origin of competing goods. Beginning in the late 1920s, it expanded to consider likely confusion as to related goods, then, in the 1960s, to consider potential (as well as actual) purchasers, and then once again, in the 1980s, to explicitly recognize confusion as to sponsorship and affiliation, as well as of origin. There can also be liability without regard to confusion, either under dilution laws (first added to federal law in 1996), or a misapplication of the initial interest confusion doctrine (that sometimes has allowed liability for simply attracting customers to a competing product or service without regard to likely confusion). Some of these expansions of the law are appropriate and uncontroversial, such as allowing claims based on consumer confusion as to sponsorship or in the context of related goods, but in combination these expansions mean that trademark law today can potentially limit far more speech than it used to. Accordingly, the speech-related defenses discussed in this chapter provide increasingly important limits on trademark claims.[4]

II GENERICISM AND GENERICIDE

As part of the prima facie case for trademark infringement or dilution, a plaintiff needs to establish that it has a source-identifying mark that is being used in commerce to distinguish its services or products. If the mark ceases to identify the source of the product or service and has instead become a generic name for that particular product, then courts will not provide trademark protection. Famous examples of what is sometimes described as "genericide" are "aspirin," "yo-yo," and "escalator," which all began their lives as source-identifying trade names for these items, but over time became the terms used to refer to the products themselves, rather than to their source.[5]

[4] *See, e.g.*, Trademark Dilution Revision Act of 2006, Pub. L. No. 109-312, 120 Stat. 1730; Federal Trademark Dilution Act of 1995, Pub. L. No. 104-98, 109 Stat. 985 (1996); Trademark Law Revision Act of 1988, Pub. L. No. 100-667, 102 Stat. 3935, 3946 § 132 (1988); Pub. L. No. 87-772, 76 Stat. 769 (1962); *Control Components, Inc.* v. *Valtek, Inc.*, 609 F.2d 763, 770 (5th Cir. 1980); *Yale Elec. Corp.* v. *Robertson*, 26 F.2d 972 (2d Cir. 1928); *Aunt Jemima Mills Co.* v. *Rigney & Co.*, 247 F. 407 (2d Cir. 1917); S. Rep. No. 1333, at 3 (1946) (noting that "Trade-marks are not monopolistic grants like patents and copyrights) (citing *Prestonettes* v. *Coty*, 264 US 359, 368 (1924) and *United Drug Co.* v. *Theodore Rectanus Co.*, 284 US 90, 97–98 (1918)). For critiques of some aspects of this trend see Jennifer E. Rothman, *Initial Interest Confusion: Standing at the Crossroads of Trademark Law*, 27 Cardozo L. Rev. 105 (2005); Barton Beebe, *The Semiotic Analysis of Trademark Law*, 51 UCLA L. Rev. 621 (2004); Mark A. Lemley, *The Modern Lanham Act and the Death of Common Sense*, 108 Yale L.J. 1687 (1999); Jessica Litman, *Breakfast with Batman: The Public Interest in the Advertising Age*, 108 Yale L.J. 1717 (1999); Rochelle Cooper Dreyfuss, *Expressive Genericity: Trademarks as Language in the Pepsi Generation*, 65 Notre Dame L. Rev. 297 (1990).

[5] *Bayer Co.* v. *United Drug Co.*, 272 F. 505 (SDNY 1921); *Donald F. Duncan, Inc.* v. *Royal Tops Mfg.*, 343 F.2d 655 (7th Cir. 1965); *Haughton Elevator Company* v. *Seeberger (Otis Elevator Co.)*, 85 USPQ 80 (Dec. Comm'r Pat. 1950).

The denial of trademark protection to generic terms is driven in part by the doctrinal requirement that trademark protection be granted only to words, designs, or symbols that serve a source-identifying function, something that generic words and symbols cannot do. But the genericism doctrine also has an underlying speech-protective and competition-promoting impulse. Consumers and competitors need to be able to adequately describe their products in the marketplace. The defense of genericism arises when there are no equally good substitutes for the claimed mark to describe a particular product. In such circumstances, others need to be able to use the term to accurately convey information about what the product is — a First Amendment value, and also something necessary to compete in the marketplace.[6]

A *The Right to Use a Term by Which a Product is Known*

The central concern for evaluating a genericism defense is whether taking a word out of circulation (at least in the context of a particular category of products) will prevent competition and obstruct the provision of information to the public. One of the best-known cases to apply this doctrine is the 1938 US Supreme Court decision in *Kellogg Co.* v. *National Biscuit Co.*[7] This case involved an unfair competition claim brought by the National Biscuit Company against the Kellogg Company. National Biscuit objected to Kellogg calling its breakfast cereal "Shredded Wheat," and selling the cereal in a "pillow shape." National Biscuit claimed to have trademarks in both the name and shape of shredded wheat (tracing back to the inventor of shredded wheat, Henry D. Perky). Perky had obtained utility patents for the process and machinery used to produce the "pillow-shaped" whole-wheat biscuits. There was also an issued design patent for the shape. All of the patents had expired by the time of Kellogg's use.[8]

The Supreme Court held that "Shredded Wheat" was a generic term, and therefore Kellogg could continue to use it for its own version of the breakfast cereal. The Court concluded that consumers understood "shredded wheat" to refer to the *product itself*, rather than to the *source* of the product. The Court highlighted that there was no other term that consumers or competitors could use to refer to the product. The public and competitors needed an equally good term to describe the particular product, and in the absence of one, the term "shredded wheat" could not be monopolized by National Biscuit.[9]

B *Overlapping Intellectual Property and the Public Domain*

The *Kellogg* case provides several other more general insights about defenses to trademark-based claims. The case involved the interaction of trademark law with other IP laws, and the need to balance these overlapping laws to protect breathing room for invention, creativity, and communication. Although not a formal defense, courts resist (and for good reason) allowing trademark law to obstruct uses of works, inventions, or designs that were once protected by patent or copyright laws but have since entered the public domain. This issue arose in the *Kellogg* case

6 *See* Pierre N. Leval, *Trademark: Champion of Free Speech*, 27 Colum. J.L. & Arts 187, 189–192 (2004); *see also Cent. Hudson Gas & Elec. Corp.* v. *Pub. Serv. Comm'n of New York*, 447 US 557, 562–63 (1980); Eugene Volokh, *Speech as Conduct: Generally Applicable Laws, Illegal Courses of Conduct, "Situation-Altering Utterances," and the Uncharted Zones*, 90 Cornell L. Rev. 1277, 1304 (2005); *cf.* Thomas I. Emerson, *Toward a General Theory of the First Amendment*, 72 Yale L.J. 877, 878–79, 881–84 (1963) (the free speech values of truth-seeking and informed decision-making turn on the conveyance of information).

7 *Kellogg Co.* v. *Nat'l Biscuit Co.*, 305 US 111 (1938).

8 *Id.* at 113–20. The design patent had been invalidated prior to its expiration. *Id.* at 119 n. 4.

9 *Id.* at 116–17.

because the shredded wheat patents had expired. The Supreme Court noted in its holding that "shredded wheat" was generic in part because the patent claims had not provided an alternative term for describing the invention. Accordingly, the name, as well as the invention, entered the public domain "upon the expiration of the patent." Trademark law could not take away with one hand what patent law had granted to the public domain with the other.[10]

C Toleration of Confusion and the "Reasonable Precaution" Standard

The *Kellogg* decision highlights another issue in speech-related defenses to trademark claims – which is the need to tolerate some degree of likely consumer confusion as to source, sponsorship, or affiliation to provide room for the dissemination of information and creative expression. In the context of shredded wheat, the Court recognized that some confusion might occur if more than one company sold shredded wheat, particularly since the National Biscuit Company (and its predecessors) for many years had been the only seller of the product (given its patents on the process, machinery, and design). Nevertheless, the Court rejected National Biscuit's contention that Kellogg had an obligation to remove "*all* possibility of deception or confusion."[11] Instead, Kellogg only needed to act reasonably and fairly. It could use the term shredded wheat both as the name for the product and to describe it, as long as it took "*reasonable precaution* to prevent confusion or the practice of deception in the sale of its product."[12] Kellogg met this standard – the Court noted that there was no evidence that it tried to deceive consumers or pass off its product as that of National Biscuit.[13]

The *Kellogg* opinion highlights an important guiding principle that applies across trademark law's speech-related defenses – competitors are free to profit from goodwill created by others, as long as they do so reasonably and fairly. As the Court explained:

> Kellogg Company is undoubtedly sharing in the goodwill of the article known as "Shredded Wheat"; and thus is sharing in a market which was created by the skill and judgment of plaintiff's predecessor and has been widely extended by vast expenditures in advertising persistently made. But that is not unfair. Sharing in the goodwill of an article unprotected by patent or trade-mark is the exercise of a right possessed by all – and in the free exercise of which the consuming public is deeply interested.[14]

Even though there is no explicit requirement today that a defendant take "reasonable precautions" to dispel confusion, the analysis from *Kellogg* illuminates what remains true today – courts are heavily influenced by whether a defendant acted in good faith. When faced with potential confusion, defendants that make reasonable efforts to dispel such confusion will fare better.[15]

[10] *Id.* at 117–18; *cf. Dastar Corp.* v. *Twentieth Century Fox Film Corp.*, 539 US 23 (2003) (limiting the application of the Lanham Act in the context of a public domain work to avoid a "conflict with the law of copyright" and to prevent the creation of "a species of mutant copyright law that limits the public's federal right to copy and to use expired copyrights") (citations and internal quotations omitted).

[11] *Kellogg Co.*, 305 US 121 (emphasis added).

[12] *Id.* at 122 (emphasis added).

[13] *Id.*

[14] *Id.*

[15] *Cf.* Barton Beebe, *An Empirical Study of the Multifactor Tests for Trademark Infringement*, 94 Calif. L. Rev. 1581, 1610, 1620–21, 1626–31 (2006) ("[A] finding of bad faith intent creates … a nearly un-rebuttable presumption of a likelihood of confusion").

D Expressive Genericity

In part because of the genericism doctrine's free speech motivations, some have advocated for a broadening out of the doctrine to cover expressive uses of marks that rely on a mark's symbolic or cultural meaning, rather than on its source-identifying function. Most notably, Rochelle Dreyfuss in her influential 1990 article, *Expressive Genericity: Trademarks as Language in the Pepsi Generation*, contends that the defense of "genericity" should apply when a word or symbol is not substitutable, and is being used in an expressive context. Dreyfuss proposes that courts should

> first decide whether there is an expressive component to the challenged use and then consider how central the trademark is to the usage. If the mark is found to be rhetorically unique within its context, it would be considered expressively – but not necessarily competitively – generic, and the trademark owner would not be permitted to suppress its utilization in that [expressive] context.[16]

Although courts have not explicitly adopted the proposed "expressive genericity" approach, they have incorporated its spirit in the context of other defenses (particularly nominative fair use analysis) – often allowing uses of marks in expressive works when the references are symbolic, rather than source-identifying.[17]

III FUNCTIONALITY

The functionality defense serves similar goals to those of genericism. If the claimed product feature is functional in nature and the very reason a product works, it cannot be protected. One reason functional features are not protected is because they are not source-identifying – consumers will read the claimed feature not as telling them whose product it is, but instead as an aspect of the product itself. The doctrine also ensures fair competition, and in some instances protects free speech. Monopolizing a particular product feature may lock others out of the marketplace, and unduly limit expression.[18] The functionality defense often arises in the context of trade dress. Trade dress encompasses the design of a product, its packaging, and its overall image and appearance.[19]

Courts have held that a product feature is functional under three circumstances: if the product feature is "essential to the use or purpose of the article"; if the feature "affects the cost or quality of the article"; or if the "exclusive use" of the feature would "put competitors at a significant non-reputation related disadvantage."[20] In its 2001 decision in *TrafFix Devices, Inc.* v. *Marketing Displays, Inc.*, the Supreme Court focused on the first of these inquiries – is the claimed feature essential to the use or purpose of the product? In *TrafFix*, the trade dress at issue

[16] Dreyfuss, *supra* note 4, at 397, 418 & *passim*.

[17] *See* discussion *infra* Section IV.B.

[18] *Cf.* Dan Burk, *Patents and the First Amendment*, 96 WASH. U.L. REV. 197 (2018); Tun-Jen Chiang, *Patents and Free Speech*, 107 GEO. L.J. 309 (2019).

[19] In the context of unregistered trade dress, a plaintiff must establish (as part of the prima facie case) that the trade dress is *not* functional. In the context of *registered* trade dress, however, nonfunctionality is presumed, and a defendant has the burden to establish that a claimed feature is functional. Lanham Act §§ 2(e)(5), 33(b)(8), 43(a)(3), 15 USC §§ 1052(e)(5), 1115(b)(8), 1125(a)(3) (2012).

[20] *TrafFix Devices, Inc.* v. *Mktg. Displays, Inc.*, 532 US 23, 32 (2001) (quoting *Qualitex Co.* v. *Jacobson Prod. Co.*, 514 US 159, 165 (1995)); *Inwood Labs., Inc.* v. *Ives Labs., Inc.*, 456 US 844, 850 n. 10 (1982).

was a dual-spring design for road signs. The claimed trade dress was the central subject of an expired utility patent, and the patent specifically included the dual-spring system in its claims as a mechanism to prevent the sign from blowing over in the wind. The plaintiff, Marketing Displays (MDI), identified no purely ornamental features as part of the claimed trade dress. Accordingly, the Court concluded that the claimed design was functional and could not serve as a protectable mark. The design was the "reason the device work[ed]" – not a source-identifier.[21]

A Functionality and the Role of Alternative Designs

The Supreme Court in *TrafFix* suggested that courts should not consider alternative designs when a product feature is "essential to the use or purpose of the article."[22] In such instances, the feature is what makes the product work, and others are free to use that feature, even if there are other possible designs that could work as well for a similar cost. Most courts, however, even after *TrafFix*, continue to consider alternative designs. This is not surprising because in the absence of a particular feature being identified as functional in a utility patent, looking at alternative designs may be the best way to determine whether a feature is essential to the product's functioning. As the Ninth Circuit Court of Appeals has explained, "the existence of alternative designs cannot negate a trademark's functionality, but may indicate whether the trademark itself embodies functional or merely ornamental aspects of the product."[23]

B Aesthetic Functionality

The third inquiry in functionality determinations turns not on whether a particular feature is essential for the product to work, nor on whether the feature affects the cost or quality of the product, but instead on whether the inability to use a particular feature would put competitors at a significant disadvantage in the marketplace for other reasons. This basis for finding a feature functional often arises in the context of *aesthetic functionality* – functionality derived from the appearance of a product. The Supreme Court has endorsed the doctrine of aesthetic functionality, and the notion that the appearance of a product can sometimes be essential to the appeal and usefulness of a product.[24]

The doctrine of aesthetic functionality furthers consumers' interests in getting relevant and sometimes important information about products and services. Consider the use of blue for sleep aids. Blue is a color that signals nighttime and sleep, and is recognized as such by consumers, so the use of blue for sleep aids, like Tylenol PM and Unisom, is aesthetically functional – meaning that no one company can lock up the use of blue for this category of products. The use of similar shapes and colors may be especially important when it comes to generic versus brand-name versions of prescription medications.[25]

The doctrine of aesthetic functionality sweeps more broadly than the appearance of prescription or over-the-counter medication. For example, the Seventh Circuit has held that the use of a

[21] *TrafFix Devices*, 532 US at 24, 29–30, 34–35.

[22] *Id.* at 35.

[23] *Moldex-Metric, Inc.* v. *McKeon Prods., Inc.*, 891 F.3d 878, 884–85 (9th Cir. 2018) (quoting *Au-Tomotive Gold, Inc.* v. *Volkswagen of Am., Inc.*, 457 F.3d 1062, 1072 n. 8 (9th Cir. 2006)). Courts have adopted a variety of factors to evaluate functionality. *See, e.g., Moldex-Metric, Inc.*, 891 F.3d at 880 n. 2, 882.

[24] *Qualitex Co.*, 514 US at 169–70.

[25] *Inwood Labs*, 456 US at 861–62 (White J, concurring); *see also Qualitex Co.*, 514 US at 165, 169–70; RESTATEMENT (THIRD) OF UNFAIR COMPETITION § 17, cmt. c (AM. LAW INST. 1995).

circular shape for a beach towel is aesthetically functional, and a "basic design" that cannot be locked up by a single producer.[26] The Eleventh Circuit has held that certain colors of ice cream are functional for particular ice cream flavors, such as pink for strawberry, white for vanilla, and brown for chocolate.[27] And other courts have held functional the use of various colors in contexts in which the matching of colors is important, such as with furniture or farm equipment.[28]

In addition to promoting the dissemination of information and providing room for competition when consumers care about the appearance of products, the aesthetic functionality doctrine also provides room for expressive communication. For example, Christian Louboutin's eponymous company has claimed that it has a protectable mark in the color red when used on the soles of shoes. The company sued Yves Saint Laurent (YSL) for using red on the soles of some of its shoes. YSL claimed that using red on the soles of shoes is aesthetically functional. The district court agreed and suggested that the use of colors in the context of fashion is presumptively functional.[29]

On appeal, however, the Second Circuit rejected such a sweeping conclusion. The appellate court avoided deciding the question of aesthetic functionality by concluding that Christian Louboutin's red soles were not source-identifying in the context of an all-red shoe – which is what YSL was selling – and therefore no claim could proceed.[30] Despite the court's dodge of the aesthetic functionality question, there are good reasons why courts should consider the use of red soles on shoes as functional. Louboutin has said that he adopted the enameled red color for use on the soles because red is the color of attraction and sex, and using the color on the soles functions like a matador using a red cape to attract a bull (here the shoes are supposedly attracting potential mates). No other color can serve this function as well according to Louboutin.[31] Nevertheless, not everyone agrees that the use is aesthetically functional. Some have suggested that because consumers now associate the red soles with Louboutin's shoes, his company should reap the rewards of that association.[32]

C *Expressive Functionality?*

Jessica Litman has analogized the danger of locking up the symbolic meaning of marks to the dangers of locking up essential *functional* features of a product. She notes that "it has long been the rule that functional product features may not be protected, because they have too

[26] *Jay Franco & Sons, Inc.* v. *Franek*, 615 F.3d 855, 860–61 (7th Cir. 2010).

[27] *Dippin' Dots, Inc.* v. *Frosty Bites Distrib.*, 369 F.3d 1197, 1202–06, 1203 n. 7, 1205 nn. 8–9 (11th Cir. 2004).

[28] *See, e.g., Deere & Co.* v. *Farmland, Inc.*, 560 F. Supp. 85, 98 (SD Iowa 1982), *aff'd*, 721 F.2d 253 (8th Cir. 1983).

[29] *Christian Louboutin SA* v. *Yves Saint Laurent Am., Inc.*, 778 F. Supp. 2d 445, 449–50 (SDNY 2011), *aff'd in part, rev'd in part and remanded sub nom. Christian Louboutin SA* v. *Yves Saint Laurent Am. Holding, Inc.*, 696 F.3d 206 (2d Cir. 2012).

[30] *Christian Louboutin SA* v. *Yves Saint Laurent Am. Holding, Inc.*, 696 F.3d 206, 228 (2d Cir. 2012). Litigation about the validity of Christian Louboutin's claimed mark in its red-soled shoes has spanned the globe. For a survey of some of the European decisions on the issue see Carina Gommers & Eva De Pauw, *"Red Sole Diaries": A Tale on the Enforcement of Louboutin's Position Mark*, 11 J. Intell. Prop. L & Prac. 258 (2016).

[31] *Louboutin's Hot High Heels* (ABC television broadcast Nov. 18, 2011), https://abcnews.go.com/Nightline/video/louboutins-hot-high-heels-14987574.

[32] *See, e.g.*, Theodore C. Max, *Coloring Outside the Lines in the Name of Aesthetic Functionality: Qualitex, Louboutin, and How the Second Circuit Saved Color Marks for Fashion*, 102 Trademark Rep. 1081, 1094 (2012). For a detailed examination and critique of the current aesthetic functionality analysis see Justin Hughes, *Cognitive and Aesthetic Functionality in Trademark Law*, 36 Cardozo L. Rev. 1227 (2015); *cf.* Barton Beebe, *Intellectual Property Law and the Sumptuary Code*, 123 Harv. L. Rev. 809 (2010) (discussing the communicative function of fashion).

much value, not too little."[33] When the motivation for the defendant's use is based on conveying an expressive message, such as allegiance to or enthusiasm for a particular team, celebrity, or brand, some have suggested that a functionality defense is appropriate. Stacey Dogan and Mark Lemley contend that the functionality doctrine should protect uses of others' marks on merchandise, at least when there is no confusion as to official endorsement.[34]

The answer to whether aesthetic functionality (or other doctrines, such as fair use) should apply in the context of merchandise largely turns on the answer to the question of who should reap the rewards of what some describe as the "surplus value" of marks – the value that comes not from the source-identifying function of the mark, but from the cultural and expressive value of the mark. Markholders, whether the University of Kansas, the San Francisco Giants, Taylor Swift, or J. K. Rowling and Warner Brothers (with regard to the Harry Potter franchise), often contend that they should have the exclusive right to use their names, emblems, images, logos, and other symbols on merchandise even when consumers are not confused as to whether they are getting an official product from the sports team, recording artist, or author/film studio. So far, most courts have agreed with the markholders, no matter what defense is asserted, concluding that the markholders or celebrities should reap the value of the use of their marks or identities, even in the absence of confusion.[35]

In the context of uses of marks on merchandise and clothing, most courts have therefore rejected functionality defenses.[36] The Fifth Circuit, for example, rejected an aesthetic functionality defense in *Boston Professional Hockey Association* v. *Dallas Cap & Emblem Manufacturing*. The court held that the Boston Bruins and other NHL teams could stop others from making and selling team emblems.[37] The primary exception to this treatment is the Ninth Circuit's 1980 decision in *International Order of Job's Daughters* v. *Lindeburg and Co.* In that case, the International Order of Job's Daughters, a young women's fraternal organization, sued a jewelry company for trademark infringement when it sold jewelry with the organization's insignia. The Ninth Circuit concluded that the uses by the defendant were aesthetically functional – used to signal support for the organization—rather than to indicate source or sponsorship.[38]

Despite the potential breadth of the analysis in *Job's Daughters*, other courts have not adopted such an approach, and the Ninth Circuit has limited the scope of that decision. In its 2006 decision *Au-Tomotive Gold* v. *Volkswagen of America*, the circuit rejected an aesthetic functionality defense when a defendant used Volkswagen's and Audi's marks on key chains and license plate covers. The court concluded that in such an instance the "alleged aesthetic function is indistinguishable from and tied to the mark's source-identifying nature ... [C]onsumers want 'Audi' and 'Volkswagen' accessories, not beautiful accessories ... Any disadvantage Auto Gold claims in not being able to sell Volkswagen or Audi marked goods is tied to

[33] Litman, *supra* note 4, at 1728.

[34] Stacey L. Dogan & Mark A. Lemley, *The Merchandising Right: Fragile Theory or Fait Accompli?*, 54 Emory L.J. 461, 502–05 (2005); *see also Savannah Coll. of Arts & Design, Inc.* v. *Sportswear*, 872 F. 3d 1256, 1260–67 (11th Cir. 2017).

[35] For a defense of such decisions, see Irene Calboli, *The Case for a Limited Protection of Trademark Merchandising*, 2011 U. Ill. L. Rev. 865. For a recent critique of this trend see Madhavi Sunder, *Intellectual Property in Experience*, 117 Mich. L. Rev. 197 (2018); *see also* Hughes, *supra* note 32, at 1230 (discussing shift to "valorization" of marks as "objects of value in and of themselves," rather than as source indicators).

[36] *See, e.g., Bd. of Supervisors for Louisiana State Univ. Agric. & Mech. Coll.* v. *Smack Apparel Co.*, 550 F.3d 465, 486–89 (5th Cir. 2008); *Au-Tomotive Gold, Inc.* v. *Volkswagen of Am., Inc.*, 457 F.3d 1062, 1072–74 (9th Cir. 2006); *Bos. Prof'l Hockey Ass'n.* v. *Dall. Cap & Emblem Mfg., Inc.*, 510 F.2d 1004, 1013 (5th Cir. 1975).

[37] *Bos. Prof'l Hockey Ass'n*, 510 F.2d at 1013–14.

[38] *Int'l Order of Job's Daughters v. Lindeburg & Co.*, 633 F.2d 912, 914, 918–20 (9th Cir. 1980).

the reputation and association with Volkswagen and Audi."[39] Accordingly, the defendant, Auto-Gold, was put at a *reputation*-related disadvantage, rather than a *non-reputation*-related one.[40]

IV FAIR USE DEFENSES

The fair use defenses to trademark claims provide room for businesses to compete in the marketplace, ensure that consumers get the information they need to make informed choices, and provide breathing room for free expression. Fair use in trademark law is substantively different from copyright's better-known fair use doctrine. Nevertheless, despite their doctrinal differences both share similar underlying motivations. Both are driven by a concern that if unbounded, these IP regimes could shut down important commentary and expression, and undermine the very basis for providing the IP protections in the first place. If trademark and related laws deny consumers useful information, and shut out legitimate competition, then they are working at cross-purposes with some of trademark law's intended objectives.

There are two distinct fair use defenses in the context of trademark law. The first is the defense of *descriptive fair use* – which focuses on the use of another's mark (or something similar) to describe qualities of a defendant's *own* product or services. This is sometimes referred to as "classic" fair use. The second type of fair use in trademark cases is *nominative* or *referential fair use* – which focuses on the use of *another's mark* to refer to and often comment on that mark (or associated product, service, or company). Each of these defenses will be considered in turn.

A *Descriptive Fair Use*

Descriptive fair use has long been allowed by the common law, and is also codified. Section 33(b)(4) of the Lanham Act provides a defense when the "use of the name, term, or device charged to be an infringement is a use, otherwise than as a mark," and the use is in a "descriptive" manner "*fairly and in good faith* only to describe the goods or services of such party, or their geographic origin."[41] Descriptive fair use is also expressly provided as a defense to federal trademark dilution claims.[42] To be considered a fair use, the use must be in "good faith," and not to trade off the goodwill of a plaintiff's mark. Instead, the primary motive to use the particular term or symbol must be to accurately describe the defendant's *own* product or service. The defense applies only if the use is *not* as a mark for the defendant's products or services.[43]

One recent example of this defense is the Sixth Circuit's decision in *Sazerac Brands v. Peristyle*. The court allowed a competitor in the bourbon market to accurately refer to its plan to make bourbon at the famous Old Taylor Distillery in Kentucky, under the brand name CASTLE & KEY. This use was allowed even though another company sells bourbon under

[39] *Au-Tomotive Gold*, 457 F.3d at 1074. *see also LTTB, LLC v. Redbubble, Inc.*, 385 F. Supp.3d 916, 921–22 (ND Cal. 2019) (citing *Job's Daughters* with approval and distinguishing *Au-Tomotive Gold* in context of witty pun printed on T-shirt), *appeal docketed*, No. 19-16464 (9th Cir. July 25, 2019).

[40] *Id.* at 1064, 1073–74.

[41] Lanham Act § 33(b)(4), 15 USC § 1115(b)(4) (2012) (emphasis added).

[42] *Id.* at § 43(c)(3)(A), § 1125(c)(3)(A). This provision was added as part of the Trademark Dilution Revision Act of 2006, Pub. L. No. 109-312, 120 Stat. 1730 (Oct. 6, 2005).

[43] This longstanding defense and requirement that the use not be as a mark indicates that liability can exist for nontrademark uses of marks. In part because of this, as well as the argument's limited success in court, the possibility that a defense exists when a defendant does not use a plaintiff's mark as a mark for the defendant's own products or services is not addressed here. For those interested in this issue, *compare* Stacey L. Dogan & Mark A. Lemley, *Grounding Trademark Law through Trademark Use*, 92 Iowa L. Rev. 1669 (2007), *with* Graeme B. Dinwoodie & Mark D. Janis, *Confusion over Use: Contextualism in Trademark Law*, 92 Iowa L. Rev. 1597 (2007).

the label OLD TAYLOR and COLONEL E. H. TAYLOR. The use of the accurate geographic information about the location of the defendant's distillery could not be barred by the plaintiff despite its claim to the use of the Old Taylor name as a mark in the whiskey market. Free speech values and the promotion of fair competition both support the dissemination of this truthful and useful information to the public.[44]

Descriptive fair use is not limited to uses of geographic terms or product ingredients; it can also apply to descriptions of broader qualities or features of products. For example, in *US Shoe Corp.* v. *Brown Group*, a court held that describing women's dress shoes as feeling like "sneakers" was a fair use. The case involved two competitors. Both companies touted the comfortable fit of their women's pumps. The plaintiff, US Shoe, sold shoes under the brand name EASY SPIRIT. It claimed trademark protection for its ad slogan: "LOOKS LIKE A PUMP, FEELS LIKE A SNEAKER." US Shoe claimed that the defendant Brown Group's use of phrases in its ad campaign referring to "sneakers" infringed its mark. Brown's advertisements for its pumps included the headline, "Think Of It As A Sneaker With No Strings Attached," and the phrase, "when we say it feels like a sneaker, we're not just stringing you along."[45] In allowing the defendant's uses, the court explained the heart of the descriptive fair use defense:

> A user of a descriptive word may acquire the exclusive right to use that descriptive word *as an identifier* of the product or source. This, however, does not justify barring others from using the words in good faith *for descriptive purposes* pertinent to their products … The purpose of [the descriptive fair use] provision is to ensure that the according of monopoly trademark rights over descriptive marks … will not over-broadly deprive society of the use of those terms in their descriptive sense in commercial communication.[46]

Brown designed its pumps specifically to provide "the comfort of athletic shoes." The best way to inform consumers of that feature is to say that they feel like sneakers. The court therefore concluded that no company should be able to lock up the word "sneakers," or the useful information it conveys to consumers making selections in the marketplace.[47]

Although descriptive fair use often arises in the context of word marks, it can apply to any type of mark. One court, for example, held that the use of a pine-tree-shaped air freshener with a pine-tree scent was descriptive of the product. The plaintiff which sold all of its air fresheners (regardless of scent) in the shape of pine trees could therefore not stop others from using the shape of a pine tree when the scent of the freshener being sold was pine. The pine-tree shape signals to consumers the scent of the product – crucial information for their purchasing decision.[48]

Some confusion as to source or sponsorship must be tolerated in descriptive fair use cases. If this were not the case, the likelihood of confusion analysis would make the defense irrelevant. Nevertheless, several courts have suggested that there may be some tipping point at which confusion can defeat the defense. If a defendant intentionally misleads consumers, then it has acted in bad faith, and cannot benefit from the defense. Short of this, however, it is not clear

[44] *Sazerac Brands LLC* v. *Peristyle LLC*, 892 F.3d 853, 855, 857–59 (6th Cir. 2018).

[45] *US Shoe Corp.* v. *Brown Grp., Inc.*, 740 F. Supp. 196, 196–97 (SDNY 1990) (emphasis in original), *aff'd*, 923 F.2d 844 (2d Cir. 1990).

[46] *Id.* at 197–99.

[47] *Id.* at 197–200.

[48] *Car-Freshner Corp.* v. *S. C. Johnson & Son, Inc.*, 70 F.3d 267, 270 (2d Cir. 1995).

when, or if, some high likelihood of confusion – or evidence of actual confusion by a substantial number of consumers – could defeat the defense even if a defendant acts in good faith.

There was hope that the Supreme Court might answer this question in its 2004 decision in *KP Permanent Make-Up* v. *Lasting Impression*. In that decision, the Court clarified that a defendant asserting a descriptive fair use defense does not have to establish the negative proposition that consumers are *not* likely to be confused. Instead, the plaintiff retains the burden to show a likelihood of confusion as part of the prima facie case. The Court noted that some level of confusion must be tolerated when a descriptive fair use has been made, but left open the question of whether there was some tipping point at which there was so much confusion that it could defeat the defense.[49]

Considering the case on remand, the Ninth Circuit concluded that "the degree of customer confusion remains a factor in evaluating fair use." The court denied summary judgment to the defendant on its fair use defense for using the term "micro colors" in the context of permanent make-up. The appellate court instructed the jury to consider the fairness of the defendant's use, taking into consideration a number of factors, including the likely confusion caused by the use.[50] Accordingly, there remains uncertainty about when likely (or actual) confusion can defeat a fair use defense.

B Nominative or Referential Fair Use

Trademarks and celebrities are part of our culture and therefore reference to them is often crucial for communication and artistic expression. To participate in the world around us we need to be able to refer to others' marks. These sorts of referential uses further fair competition, inform consumers, and promote the interests of free speech and free expression. Some courts have interpreted descriptive fair use to include references to *another's* products or services; for example, in comparative advertising, or to describe the content of expressive works that include marks, or a person's likeness or name.[51] Many courts, however, evaluate these referential uses under a distinct fair use doctrine known as *nominative fair use*.

The nominative fair use defense is thought to originate with the Ninth Circuit's 1992 decision in *New Kids on the Block* v. *News America Publishing*. This case involved a lawsuit brought by the then hit boy band, New Kids on the Block. The New Kids objected to the use of their names and images by two newspapers that used them in the context of telephone-based polls that asked their readers to vote either for their favorite member of the band, or the sexiest. The newspapers advertised for the polls in their pages, and charged for the phone calls. Because the newspapers used the New Kids' mark to refer to the band, rather than to the papers' own products, the court concluded that the descriptive fair use defense did not apply.[52]

Nevertheless, the Ninth Circuit still held the use fair. The court emphasized the importance of being able to refer to another's mark for purposes of communication and comparison. How could the papers conduct a poll about the New Kids without being able to refer to the band or its members? To establish the fairness of such referential uses the court held that a defendant must prove: (1) "the product or service in question must be one not readily identifiable without use of

[49] *KP Permanent Make-Up, Inc.* v *Lasting Impression I, Inc.*, 543 US 111, 121–24 (2004).

[50] *KP Permanent Make-Up, Inc.* v. *Lasting Impression I, Inc.*, 408 F.3d 596, 609 (9th Cir. 2005); *see also Marketquest Grp., Inc.* v. *BIC Corp.*, 862 F.3d 927, 935–38 (9th Cir. 2017) (emphasizing "that the degree of consumer confusion is a *factor* in the fair use analysis, not an *element* of fair use"), *cert denied*, 138 S. Ct. 1988 (2018).

[51] *See, e.g.*, *ETW Corp.* v. *Jireh Publ'g, Inc.*, 332 F.3d 915, 918, 920–21 (6th Cir. 2003).

[52] *New Kids on the Block* v. *News Am. Publ'g*, 971 F.2d 302, 304, 308 (9th Cir. 1992).

the trademark"; (2) "only so much of the mark or marks may be used as is reasonably necessary to identify the product or service"; and (3) the defendant "must do nothing … [to] suggest sponsorship or endorsement by the trademark holder."[53] Applying these elements to the polls and announcements, the court held the newspapers' uses fair. The court rejected the New Kids' contention that only the band should profit from its fame: "trademark laws do not give the New Kids the right to channel their fans' enthusiasm (and dollars) only into items licensed or authorized by them."[54]

Not all courts have agreed on this last point, even if they generally have welcomed and sometimes adopted the nominative fair use defense. In the context of merchandise, courts have been hesitant to extend the nominative fair use defense to uses of recording artists', celebrities', and sports teams' marks and identities on apparel and other merchandise. Although nominative fair use often fails as a defense in merchandise cases, it has usually been successful in the context of uses in more traditional artistic works, or in accurate descriptions of the lawful sale or repair of products. The DC Circuit has described the "prototypical example of nominative fair use" as

> an automobile repair shop specializing in foreign vehicles run[ning] an advertisement using the trademarked names of various makes and models to highlight the kind of cars it repairs. Permitting such use accommodates situations where it would be virtually impossible to refer to a particular product for purposes of comparison, criticism, point of reference or any other such purpose without using the mark.[55]

Many federal circuits (though not all) have embraced the nominative fair use doctrine. Congress also has endorsed the doctrine by explicitly including such a defense in the 2006 Trademark Dilution Revision Act.[56] As with the descriptive fair use defense, there remains an open question of how much confusion will be tolerated. Part of the problem is the ambiguity contained within the third element of the nominative fair use defense – the one that requires that the user "do nothing that would, in conjunction with the mark, suggest sponsorship or endorsement by the trademark holder."[57] Read one way, this could simply conflate with a likelihood of confusion analysis, but the doctrine makes sense only if interpreted to require some affirmative action to mislead or confuse consumers; otherwise, the likelihood of confusion analysis would be determinative and the defense irrelevant.[58] Nevertheless, some courts have suggested that a showing of likely confusion defeats a nominative fair use defense.[59]

The second element of the defense is also sometimes challenging to determine. What is "reasonably necessary" to identify a product or service? Perhaps this inquiry is best understood as an evaluation of whether the use was unreasonably excessive in the context of an otherwise legitimate use. The Ninth Circuit, for example, rejected Terri Welles's nominative fair use defense on this basis. Welles, a former Playboy Playmate of the Year, was allowed to refer to Playboy and to having been the Playmate of the Year, but could not repeatedly and excessively use PMOY '81 (short for "Playmate of the Year 1981") as the wallpaper/background for her website.[60]

[53] *Id.* at 306, 308.
[54] *Id.* at 309.
[55] *Am. Soc'y for Testing and Materials* v. *Public.Resource.Org, Inc.*, 896 F.3d 437, 456 (DC Cir. 2018) (internal quotations and citations omitted); *see also Toyota Motor Sales, USA, Inc.* v. *Tabari*, 610 F.3d 1171, 1175–83 (9th Cir. 2010).
[56] Trademark Dilution Revision Act of 2006, Pub. L. No. 109-312, 120 Stat. 1730, 1730–32 (2006), codified at 15 USC § 1125(c)(3)(A) (2012).
[57] *New Kids*, 971 F.2d at 308.
[58] *See Cairns* v. *Franklin Mint Co.*, 292 F.3d 1139, 1152–56 (9th Cir. 2002).
[59] *International Info. Sys.* v. *Security Univ., LLC*, 823 F.3d 153, 165–69 (2d Cir. 2016).
[60] *Playboy Enters., Inc.* v. *Welles*, 279 F.3d 796, 804–05 (9th Cir. 2002).

V THE *ROGERS* TEST AND USES IN EXPRESSIVE WORKS

Some of the preceding defenses have been applied in the context of expressive works, but most often courts apply what is known as the *Rogers* test in such contexts. Courts have recognized that there are significant free speech concerns with using trademark and false endorsement laws to limit artistic expression, particularly in movies, songs, books, and other works of art. To address this concern the Second Circuit Court of Appeals developed what is known as the *Rogers* test, in which courts look at whether the allegedly infringing use is artistically relevant, and not explicitly misleading as to source or sponsorship.

The Second Circuit adopted this approach in *Rogers* v. *Grimaldi*, a case involving a claim that the movie title *Fred & Ginger* constituted a false endorsement by famed screen star Ginger Rogers.[61] The movie was written and directed by acclaimed Italian director Federico Fellini, and told the story of Italy's "Fred and Ginger" (in reference to the Hollywood duo Fred Astaire and Ginger Rogers). The court rejected Rogers's suit warning of the dire consequences if artistic expression could be limited by claims like hers. In doing so, the court set forth the analysis now known as the *Rogers* test:

> [The Lanham Act] should be construed to apply to artistic works only where the public interest in avoiding consumer confusion outweighs the public interest in free expression. In the context of allegedly misleading titles using a celebrity's name, that balance will normally not support application of the Act unless the title has no artistic relevance to the underlying work whatsoever, or, if it has some artistic relevance, unless the title explicitly misleads as to the source or the content of the work.[62]

The *Rogers* test has been widely adopted in the context of artistic works, and applied beyond uses in titles. The test is considered a First Amendment analysis, rather than a doctrine internal to trademark law.[63] The Sixth Circuit applied the *Rogers* test as one of several bases for rejecting trademark and false endorsement claims brought by Tiger Woods arising out of the use of his name and image in an artist's painting (and prints) that showed Woods winning the Masters tournament. The court concluded that the uses of Woods's image and name were artistically relevant, and that the artist had done nothing affirmatively to suggest that Woods had endorsed or was affiliated with the work or its sale.[64] The *Rogers* test has also insulated from liability uses of company names in video games and television shows, and of Mattel's Barbie dolls in various works of art.[65]

While the artistic relevance bar is supposed to be low, some courts have rejected uses as not sufficiently relevant. A recent Ninth Circuit decision, applying the *Rogers* test, concluded that uses of a social media sensation's catchphrases (such as "Honey Badger Don't Care") on greeting

[61] *Rogers* v. *Grimaldi*, 875 F.2d 994 (2d Cir. 1989).

[62] *Id.* at 999. In addition to her Lanham Act claims, Rogers brought state right of publicity and false light claims, which were also rejected by the court. *Id.* at 1002–05. In the context of false endorsement claims, state-based right of publicity claims can often be brought on the same set of facts. These right of publicity claims sometimes survive First Amendment review even when a Lanham Act claim does not. *Compare In re NCAA Student-Athlete Name & Likeness Licensing Litig.*, 724 F.3d 1268 (9th Cir. 2013), and *Davis* v. *Elec. Arts Inc.*, 775 F.3d 1172 (9th Cir. 2015), with *Brown* v. *Elec. Arts Inc.*, 724 F.3d 1235 (9th Cir. 2013); *see also* JENNIFER E. ROTHMAN, THE RIGHT OF PUBLICITY: PRIVACY REIMAGINED FOR A PUBLIC WORLD 157–59 (2018).

[63] *Rogers*, 875 F.2d at 997–1002.

[64] *ETW Corp.* v. *Jireh Publ'g, Inc.*, 332 F.3d 915, 937 (6th Cir. 2003).

[65] *Twentieth Century Fox Television* v. *Empire Dist., Inc.*, 875 F.3d 1192, 1197–99 (9th Cir. 2017); *ESS Entm't 2000, Inc.* v. *Rock Star Videos, Inc.*, 547 F.3d 1095, 1100–01 (9th Cir. 2008); *Mattel, Inc.* v. *Walking Mountain Prods.*, 353 F.3d 792, 807 (9th Cir. 2003); *Mattel, Inc.* v. *MCA Records, Inc.*, 296 F.3d 894, 902 (9th Cir. 2002).

cards was not artistically relevant under the *Rogers* analysis. The court so concluded because the defendant did not add its own artistic expression, but merely appropriated the goodwill of the plaintiff.[66] More controversially, the Sixth Circuit held in *Parks* v. *LaFace Records* that the hip-hop group Outkast's use of "Rosa Parks" as the title for one of its songs was not artistically relevant as a matter of law, and that the case could proceed to trial on that issue.[67] The court so concluded even though the song repeated the refrain "everybody move to the back of the bus," a clear reference to Parks, a civil rights icon who is best known for her refusal to move to the back of a segregated bus. The appellate court's questionable reversal highlights the challenge of determining what is artistically relevant. The district court in the case had concluded that the artistic relevance of Park to the song was patently "obvious."[68]

While the *Rogers* test has often been a successful defense in the context of artistic works, it has fared less well when uses are in the context of merchandise. The Eleventh Circuit, for example, accepted the *Rogers*-test-based First Amendment defense in the context of paintings, prints, and calendars that used the University of Alabama's uniforms, but declined to apply the defense in the context of "mugs and other 'mundane products,'" such as flags, towels, and t-shirts – even though the same images appeared in both the artistic works and the "mundane products." Although the court concluded that the appellant, New Life Art, did not preserve the First Amendment and fair use defenses in the context of the mundane products, the court's division of the categories and differential treatment was not required, and the court left in place the district court's rejection of those defenses in the context of uses on merchandise (with the exception of the uses on calendars).[69]

Although the *Rogers* test has been widely adopted, at least some courts and scholars contend that the test is largely superfluous because the Lanham Act should not apply to most uses in expressive works other than advertising for such works. This view rests on the contention that the Lanham Act applies only to commercial speech (loosely defined either as commercial advertising or other speech directed primarily at selling products or services).[70] Many courts, however, have concluded (or presumed) that the Lanham Act does apply to noncommercial speech, including to expressive works.[71] As I discussed in *Commercial Speech, Commercial Use, and the Intellectual Property Quagmire*, this is a reasonable reading of the statute, and supported by the policy behind the legislation.[72] As the Second Circuit in *Rogers* explains:

> Movies, plays, books, and songs are all indisputably works of artistic expression and deserve protection. Nonetheless, they are also sold in the commercial marketplace like other more

66 *Gordon* v. *Drape Creative, Inc.*, 897 F.3d 1184, 1195–96 (9th Cir. 2018).

67 *Parks* v. *LaFace Records*, 329 F.3d 437, 442, 452–59 (6th Cir. 2003).

68 *Parks* v. *LaFace Records*, 76 F. Supp. 2d 775, 780 (ED Mich. 1999), *aff'd in part, rev'd in part and remanded*, 329 F.3d 437 (6th Cir. 2003); *see also* Rothman, *supra* note 62, at 149–51.

69 *Univ. of Alabama Bd. of Trustees* v. *New Life Art, Inc.*, 683 F.3d 1266, 1278–80 (11th Cir. 2012); *Univ. of Alabama Bd. of Trustees* v. *New Life Art, Inc.*, 677 F. Supp. 2d 1238, 1250–51, 1258–59 (ND Ala. 2009); *cf.* Rothman, *supra* note 62, at 170–75 (discussing the different treatment of merchandise in right of publicity cases).

70 *See, e.g.*, *Farah* v. *Esquire Magazine*, 736 F.3d 528, 541 (DC Cir. 2013); *Taubman Co.* v. *Webfeats*, 319 F.3d 770, 774 (6th Cir. 2003); Rebecca Tushnet, *Trademark Law as Commercial Speech Regulation*, 58 S.C. L. Rev. 737, 738–39 (2007). The widespread confusion and disagreement among the courts about these issues is discussed in Jennifer E. Rothman, *Commercial Speech, Commercial Use, and the Intellectual Property Quagmire*, 101 Va. L. Rev. 1929 (2015); *see also* Lisa P. Ramsey, *Increasing First Amendment Scrutiny of Trademark Law*, 61 SMU L. Rev. 381, 403–04 (2008).

71 *See, e.g.*, *Westchester Media* v. *PRL USA Holdings, Inc.*, 214 F.3d 658, 672 (5th Cir. 2000); *Dr. Seuss Enterprises, LP* v. *Penguin Books USA, Inc.*, 109 F.3d 1394, 1403–07 (9th Cir. 1997); *Anheuser-Busch, Inc.* v. *Balducci Publ'ns*, 28 F.3d 769, 776–78 (8th Cir. 1994); *Browne* v. *McCain*, 611 F. Supp.2d 1073, 1079 (CD Cal. 2009). For more examples, see Rothman, *supra* note 70, at 1937–46 & accompanying notes.

72 Rothman, *supra* note 70, at 1937–46, 1988–92.

> utilitarian products making the danger of consumer deception a legitimate concern that warrants some government regulation. Poetic license is not without limits. The purchaser of a book, like the purchaser of a can of peas, has a right to not be mislead as to the source of the product.[73]

If the Lanham Act applies to expressive works, which it likely does, liability should nevertheless be rare when the uses are in the body of these works, rather than in the titles or advertisements for those works. Uses within the expressive works themselves are not likely to signal sponsorship or source, and therefore should not give rise to an infringement claim. For example, the fact that a character has a Louis Vuitton bag (or a knock-off version of one) in a scene in a movie should not be an actionable infringement of any Louis Vuitton mark because no viewer would think the bag was there to indicate source, sponsorship, or affiliation by that company.[74]

VI STATUTORY EXEMPTIONS FROM DILUTION CLAIMS

In addition to providing for nominative and descriptive fair use defenses, the Lanham Act's dilution provision also contains specific exemptions for uses of marks in "news reporting and news commentary," and for "[a]ny noncommercial use of a mark."[75] Although the exemption for news is relatively straightforward, it is not clear exactly what is meant by a "noncommercial use" of a mark.[76] The statute does not define the term. An accompanying congressional report to the Federal Trademark Dilution Act of 1995 suggests that the term means *not* "commercial speech," and "expressly incorporates the concept of 'commercial' speech from the 'commercial speech' doctrine, and proscribes dilution actions that seek to enjoin use of famous marks in 'non-commercial' uses (such as consumer product reviews)."[77] The report also indicates that Congress wanted to exempt news reporting from liability for dilution, and perhaps exempt media more broadly (such as entertainment companies).[78] Given that both news and the entertainment industry are most often for-profit enterprises, this goal can make sense only if the language is interpreted as exempting uses that are not commercial speech. This interpretation has been the one followed by most (though not all) courts.[79]

[73] *Rogers* v. *Grimaldi*, 875 F.2d 994, 997–98 (2d Cir. 1989) (internal quotations and citations omitted); Rothman, *supra* note 70, at 1991.

[74] *Louis Vuitton Malletier SA* v. *Warner Bros. Entm't Inc.*, 868 F. Supp. 2d 172, 177–84 (SDNY 2012). This should be true even if some film studios routinely license trademarked products that appear in movies. *See* Jennifer E. Rothman, *The Questionable Use of Custom in Intellectual Property*, 93 VA. L. REV. 1899, 1912–16 (2007).

[75] Lanham Act § 43(c)(3), 15 USC § 1125(c)(3) (2012).

[76] Rothman, *supra* note 70, at 1942–44.

[77] H.R. REP. NO. 104-374, at 8 (1995), *reprinted in* 1996 USCCAN 1029, 1035.

[78] *Id.*; *see also* 141 CONG. REC. H14317–01 (daily ed. Dec. 12, 1995) (statement of Rep. Moorhead).

[79] *See, e.g.*, *Radiance Found., Inc.* v. *NAACP*, 786 F.3d 316, 323–24 (4th Cir. 2015); *Mattel, Inc.* v. *MCA Records Inc.*, 296 F.3d 894, 904–07 (9th Cir. 2002); *but see Hershey Co.* v. *Friends of Steve Hershey*, No. CIV. WDQ-14-1825, 2015 WL 795841, at *5–6 (D. Md. Feb. 24, 2015); *Kraft Foods Holdings, Inc.* v. *Helm*, 205 F. Supp. 2d 942, 952–55 (ND Ill. 2002); *Films of Distinction, Inc.* v. *Allegro Film Prods.*, Inc., 12 F. Supp. 2d 1068, 1078–79 (CD Cal. 1998). Some state dilution claims also have been allowed in the context of noncommercial speech. *See, e.g.*, *Anheuser-Busch, Inc.* v. *Balducci Publ'ns*, 28 F.3d 769, 777–78 (8th Cir. 1994). For further discussion of this issue see Rothman, *supra* note 70, at 1947–78; *see also* Lee Ann W. Lockridge, *When Is a Use in Commerce a Noncommercial Use?*, 37 FLA. ST. U. L. REV. 337, 338 (2010).

VII INDEPENDENT FIRST AMENDMENT REVIEW

With the exception of the *Rogers* test, which is understood as a particular analysis applying the First Amendment, the other speech-protective doctrines discussed in this chapter are internal to trademark law. Other than the *Rogers* test, courts usually do not engage in additional independent First Amendment review in trademark cases. Even though intellectual property laws limit speech and do so on the basis of the content of that speech – something that is usually disfavored and presumptively unconstitutional – intellectual property laws have not been subject to the same level of scrutiny as other laws.[80]

In the context of copyright law, for example, the Supreme Court has suggested that the First Amendment will rarely (if ever) apply independently as a defense to copyright infringement claims because of copyright's internal speech restrictions, including its fair use defense and its exclusion of ideas and facts.[81] This analysis suggests that courts might find trademark's internal limits on scope, combined with its fair use and other defenses, adequately speech protective, without need for further First Amendment analysis.[82] Even if courts can consider independent First Amendment analysis in trademark cases, they may rarely do so – preferring to apply defenses internal to trademark law under the doctrine of constitutional avoidance.[83] To the extent that courts do consider First Amendment defenses, such defenses will likely be less successful in the context of uses in commercial speech. If the commercial speech at issue is false or misleading, then there is no First Amendment protection available.[84]

Despite these hurdles to First Amendment review in trademark cases, two recent decisions have raised the possibility that the First Amendment may start to play a bigger role. In *Matal* v. *Tam*, the Supreme Court struck down the Lanham Act's prohibition on the registration of marks that may "disparage ... or bring ... into contempt or disrepute" "persons, living or dead, institutions, beliefs, or national symbols."[85] The Court held that the provision violated the First Amendment because it is a content-based speech restriction that discriminates on the basis of the speaker's viewpoint. *Tam* involved the US Patent and Trademark Office's (PTO's) refusal to register the mark, THE SLANTS, for a rock band with Asian-American members who sought to reclaim the racial slur and defuse its negative connotations. The Supreme Court held that the PTO could not refuse to register negative terms for Asian people, while registering positive ones.[86]

On the basis of *Tam*, the Federal Circuit in *In re Brunetti* struck down a similar provision barring the registration of "immoral ... or scandalous matter." The appellate court held that the PTO's refusal to register the term "FUCT" for apparel was unconstitutional even if viewpoint-neutral. In reviewing this decision, the Supreme Court in *Iancu* v. *Brunetti* agreed that the bar was facially unconstitutional, but on a different basis – that it too discriminated on the basis of

80 *Reed* v. *Town of Gilbert*, 135 S. Ct. 2218, 2226 (2015) (indicating that "[c]ontent-based laws ... are presumptively unconstitutional and may be justified only if the government proves that they are narrowly tailored to serve compelling state interests"); *see also* ROTHMAN, *supra* note 62, at 143–45; Jennifer E. Rothman, *The Right of Publicity's Intellectual Property Turn*, 42 COLUMBIA J. L. & ARTS 277, 312–14 (2019).

81 *Eldred* v. *Ashcroft*, 537 US 186, 218–21 (2003); *see also* ROTHMAN, *supra* note 62, at 143–45; Jennifer E. Rothman, *Liberating Copyright: Thinking beyond Free Speech*, 95 CORNELL L. REV. 463, 476–92 (2010).

82 *See, e.g.*, *Westchester Media* v. *PRL USA Holdings, Inc.*, 214 F.3d 658, 672 (5th Cir. 2000); *Mutual of Omaha Ins. Co.* v. *Novak*, 836 F.2d 397, 402 (8th Cir. 1987); *cf. Anheuser-Busch*, 28 F.3d at 775–78; *Hershey Co.* v. *Friends of Steve Hershey*, 33 F. Supp. 3d 588, 594–95 (D. Md. 2014).

83 Leval, *supra* note 6, at 209.

84 *See Central Hudson Gas & Elec.* v. *Pub. Serv. Comm'n*, 447 US 557, 563 (1980).

85 *Matal* v. *Tam*, 137 S. Ct. 1744 (2017); *see also* 15 USC § 1052(a) (Lanham Act § 2(a)).

86 *Tam*, 137 S. Ct. at 1747, 1751.

viewpoint, the same basis for the Court's holding in *Tam*.[87] The Court held that the immoral and scandalous bar was impermissible because the provision "permits registration of marks that champion society's sense of rectitude and morality, but not marks that denigrate those concepts." For example, "the PTO has refused to register marks communicating 'immoral or scandalous' views about (among other things) drug use, religion, and terrorism," but has "approved marks expressing more accepted views on the same topics."[88]

Although a majority of the Court struck down the bar as facially unconstitutional, four justices suggested that a narrower bar on the registration of marks – limited to those that are obscene, profane, or vulgar – could be constitutional. The majority did not opine on the constitutionality of such a provision, but it is possible that if Congress were to pass a more limited ban on the registration of these types of marks, it might survive constitutional review.[89]

It would be a mistake to think that *Tam* and *Brunetti* set the stage for a host of other challenges to the underlying constitutionality of trademark laws, or for increased First Amendment review in infringement and dilution claims. *Tam* and *Brunetti* both involved challenges to the denial of the benefits that registration provides to markholders, rather than challenges to the enforcement of markholders' rights. This makes these precedents less likely to be influential when asserted by defendants.

Although *Tam* and *Brunetti* are not likely to produce a massive shift in infringement and false endorsement analysis, they might fuel challenges to dilution claims, particularly viewpoint-based determinations of tarnishment. Some scholars even before these cases questioned the constitutionality of dilution laws because dilution claims do not require a showing that consumers are likely to be confused.[90] Several Supreme Court decisions, however, suggest that dilution laws are likely to withstand a direct constitutional challenge even after *Tam* and *Brunetti*. Although the Supreme Court's 2012 decision in *United States* v. *Alvarez* struck down as unconstitutional the Stolen Valor Act, a law that made it a crime to falsely claim to have received a military or Congressional Medal of Honor, a majority of justices in the case concluded that false speech could be penalized under some circumstances.[91] And of particular relevance, both the concurrence and dissent pointed to trademark law as an example of a constitutional law that can restrict speech even when it is not false, but instead is only misleading or merely diluting.[92]

Further support for the broad constitutionality of dilution law is the Supreme Court's decision in *San Francisco Arts & Athletics* v. *US Olympic Committee* (SFAA). This 1987 case involved the application of a quasi-trademark statute that prohibited the use of the word "Olympics" and related marks without the authorization of the United States Olympic Committee (USOC). The Court held the statute constitutional even when applied to uses that were not confusing and that were not commercial speech, such as sporting events and theatrical works:

> The mere fact that the SFAA claims an expressive, as opposed to a purely commercial, purpose does not give it a First Amendment right to "appropriat[e] to itself the harvest of those who

[87] *Iancu* v. *Brunetti*, 139 S. Ct. 2294 (2019); *In re Brunetti*, 877 F.3d 1330 (Fed. Cir. 2017).

[88] *Brunetti*, 139 S. Ct. at 2300.

[89] *Id.* at 2301–02; *id.* at 2303 (Alito J, concurring); *id.* at 2303–04 (Roberts J, concurring in part); *id.* at 2304, 2306–08 (Breyer J, concurring in part); *id.* at 2308–19 (Sotomayor J, concurring in part).

[90] *See, e.g.*, Eugene Volokh, *Freedom of Speech and Intellectual Property: Some Thoughts after Eldred, 44 Liquormart, and Bartnicki*, 40 Hous. L. Rev. 697, 732–39 (2003); *see also* Lisa P. Ramsey, *Free Speech Challenges to Trademark Law after Matal v. Tam*, 56 Hous. L. Rev. 401 (2018).

[91] *United States* v. *Alvarez*, 567 US 709, 721 (2012).

[92] *Id.* at 729–37 (Breyer J, concurring); *id.* at 738–53 (Alito J, dissenting); *see also Brunetti*, 139 at 2305 (Breyer J, concurring in part).

> have sown." The USOC's right to prohibit use of the word "Olympic" in the promotion of athletic events is at the core of its legitimate property right.[93]

There is much to criticize in the Supreme Court's analysis in *SFAA*, and its unconvincing claim that there are adequate alternatives to the use of the word "Olympics." The "Gay Olympics" – the use SFAA wanted to make – has a very different meaning from the "Gay Games," and in other contexts First Amendment analysis has held that such differences matter; for example, that "Fuck the Draft" is not the same as "Stop the Draft."[94] Yet the *SFAA* decision remains good law, and continues to be cited favorably by the Court.[95]

Despite the likely constitutionality of dilution law generally, the decisions in *Tam* and *Brunetti* suggest that the First Amendment may come into play if trademark laws are being applied in ways that discriminate on the basis of a speaker's viewpoint, or if they rest solely on causing offense. Some dilution claims based on tarnishment might therefore be ruled unconstitutional. In particular, the frequent conclusion that associations with sex presumptively tarnish a mark are constitutionally suspect after *Tam* and *Brunetti*.[96]

The Sixth Circuit's decision in *V Secret Catalogue, Inc.* v. *Moseley* seems unsupportable in light of these Supreme Court decisions.[97] In *V Secret*, Victor Moseley, the defendant, ran an adult sex-themed shop that he named "Victor's Little Secret." The store sold lingerie and sex toys, among other items. The plaintiff, owner of the famous Victoria's Secret stores and marks, sued, contending that Moseley's use caused dilution by tarnishment. The Sixth Circuit held that the use of a similar mark to that of Victoria's Secret's – in the context of a "sex related product" – created a "rebuttable presumption" that it was tarnishing, a seemingly insurmountable hurdle for any defendant.[98] This viewpoint-based conclusion (anti-sex) should not survive First Amendment review after *Tam* and *Brunetti*. The Sixth Circuit's conclusion that the use tarnished the famous lingerie chain's VICTORIA'S SECRET mark by associating it with sex was particularly absurd given the company's longstanding advertising campaigns that explicitly use the term "sexy" and show models in suggestive poses wearing only lingerie to promote sales of lingerie (which itself could be considered sex-themed).[99] By holding that Moseley's use was tarnishing in this context, the Sixth Circuit weighed in not only on what it thought was broadly

[93] *SF Arts & Athletics, Inc.* v. *US Olympic Comm.*, 483 US 522, 525, 541 (1987) (quoting *Int'l News Serv.* v. *Associated Press*, 248 US 215, 239–40 (1918)) (alteration in original); *see also* 36 USC § 220506 (2012) (granting by statute exclusive right to use the word "Olympic" and other related terms).

[94] *Cohen* v. *California*, 403 US 15 (1971); Dreyfuss, *supra* note 4, at 398–99, 410–21; Rothman, *supra* note 81, at 489; *but see Iancu* v. *Brunetti*, 139 S. Ct. 2294, 2314–15 (2019) (Sotomayor J, concurring in part) (distinguishing *Cohen* on the grounds that it was a criminal case).

[95] *See, e.g.*, *Matal* v. *Tam*, 137 S. Ct. 1744, 1752 (2017); *Alvarez*, 567 US at 723, 736 (Breyer J, concurring); *Eldred* v. *Ashcroft*, 537 US 186, 221 (2003).

[96] For a discussion of such sex exceptionalism in IP cases, *see* Jennifer E. Rothman, *Sex Exceptionalism in Intellectual Property*, 23 STAN. L. & POL'Y REV. 119 (2012).

[97] *V. Secret Catalogue, Inc.* v. *Moseley*, 605 F.3d 382 (6th Cir. 2010). The case was resurrected after a prior Supreme Court decision had thrown out Victoria's Secret's dilution claim on the basis that there was no evidence of actual dilution. After the decision, Congress amended the dilution provision to allow for liability on the basis of a likelihood of dilution, enabling the claim to proceed. *See Moseley* v. *V. Secret Catalogue, Inc.*, 537 US 418, 432–34 (2003), *abrogated* by Congress in the Trademark Dilution Revision Act of 2006 (codified at Lanham Act § 43(c)(1), 15 USC § 1125(c)(1) (2012)).

[98] *V. Secret*, 605 F.3d. at 384–85, 388.

[99] *See id.* at 391 (Moore J, dissenting); *Victoria's Secret "Very Sexy 2013" Campaign*, HYPEBEAST (Apr. 16, 2013), https://hypebeast.com/2013/4/victorias-secret-very-sexy-2013-campaign-directed-by-michael-bay.

tarnishing – references to sex – but also expressed a view about what vision of sex is a good one. This conclusion is not constitutionally sound after *Tam* and *Brunetti*.[100]

VIII CONCLUSION

The defenses highlighted in this chapter provide a powerful antidote to the potential for trademark and related laws to shut down speech and unduly limit competition. Defendants are more likely to prevail when they can make a convincing case that their uses further free speech values. When defendants use others' marks (or something similar) to provide consumers with information, or to express themselves, particularly in a non-advertising, artistic context, the uses will likely be protected by one of the defenses discussed.

In contrast, when courts think the uses are exploiting a plaintiff's mark, trade dress, or identity for financial benefit without a corresponding free speech benefit of providing commentary, comparison, or original expression, these defenses are likely to fail. This evaluation will turn in part on the necessity and reasonableness of the uses given the articulated speech objectives, and the demands of competing in the marketplace. Speech-related defenses are less likely to prevail if a use conveys false or misleading information because such uses deceive rather than inform the public. Similarly, when a use provides no additional commentary on the underlying mark, or original expression, courts will often view the use as a subterfuge for the defendant's exploitation of another's goodwill, rather than as a use in furtherance of free expression.

The First Amendment and its speech-protective penumbras incorporated into trademark law provide latitude to use others' marks both in commercial and noncommercial speech, but this protection is not without limits. When a use exceeds what is appropriate under the circumstances, and is perceived as primarily profiting from another's goodwill without a corresponding speech benefit, these defenses are unlikely to provide protective shade.

100 *But see Iancu* v. *Brunetti*, 139 S.Ct. 2294, 2313 (2019) (Sotomayor J, concurring in part) (discussing that regulations on pornography are constitutional even though they may regulate the expression of views on "sexual liberation").

34

Limitations to Trademark Protection as Defences to Infringement

*Jennifer Davis**

I INTRODUCTION

True to its free market origins, the EU Trade Mark Directive (TMD)[1] allows any sign to be registered as long as it is acting as a badge of origin and as long as it does not fall into one of the absolute grounds for refusal of registration. Some bars to registration cannot be overcome, such as those prohibiting the registration of functional shapes or signs that offend against public morality. However, other signs, which are descriptive, non-distinctive or generic, while disallowed from immediate registration, can subsequently be registered provided they have acquired distinctiveness through use. The EU trademark regime thus allows for the registration of signs that under previous laws of member states might have been denied registration in the public interest. For instance, in the United Kingdom and in Germany, this category included signs that were distinctive but, the courts held, should be left free for others to use, such as geographical names.[2] For the same reason, under its 1938 Trade Marks Act, the UK courts would not allow the registration of functional and non-functional shape marks even with acquired distinctiveness.[3] Given its overwhelmingly laissez-faire attitude toward the determination of which marks are registerable, it is all the more important that the TMD provides limitations to the rights afforded by registration. These limitations would allow use of the registered mark or an identical or similar sign by a third party in certain defined circumstances and would thus provide a defence to infringement. It is these limitations that delineate, in large measure, the boundaries to trademark protection.

The Preamble to the TMD, as amended in 2015 with entry into force in 2016 (2015 TMD), at paragraph 27 introduces the principle of limitations. It states: "The exclusive rights conferred by a trade mark should not entitle the proprietor to prohibit the use of signs or indications by third parties which are used fairly and thus in accordance with honest practices in industrial and

* Emeritus Fellow, Wolfson College, Cambridge; Member, Centre for Intellectual Property and Information Law, University of Cambridge.

[1] Council Directive 2015/2436/EU to approximate the laws of member states relating to trademarks (hereinafter 2015 TMD); Directive 89/104/EEC (hereinafter 1989 TMD) codified as Directive 2008/95 EC (hereinafter 2008 TMD). EU trademarks are currently regulated by Regulation (EU) 2017/1001.

[2] For a UK example, *see Yorkshire Copper Works LTD's Application for a Trade Mark, in* Reports of Patent Design & Trade Mark Cases vol. 70, 1–9 (1953), https://academic.oup.com/rpc/article/70/1/1/1584465; the equivalent in Germany was the doctrine of "Freihaltedurfnis." *See* Jennifer Davis, *Protecting the Common: Delineating a Public Domain in Trade Mark Law, in* Trade Mark Law and Theory: A Handbook of Contemporary Research 345 (Graeme. B. Dinwoodie & Mark. D. Janis eds., 2008).

[3] Coca Cola Trade Mark, 1985 FSR 315.

commercial matters."[4] These "fair" uses are then set out in Article14(1) of the 2015 TMD, entitled: "Limitations on the effects of a trade mark." They are: the use of the name or address of the third party, where that third party is a natural person;[5] the use of signs or indications that are not distinctive or that concern the kind, quality, quantity, intended purpose, value, geographical origin, the time of production of goods or of rendering of the service, or other characteristics of goods or services;[6] and the use of the trademark for the purpose of identifying or referring to goods or services as those of the proprietor of that trademark, especially where the use of the trademark is necessary to indicate the intended purpose of a product or service, in particular as accessories or spare parts.[7] Echoing the Preamble, Article 14(2) states that these limitations will apply only if the third party's use of the registered mark or its equivalent "is in accordance with honest practices in industrial or commercial matters."[8]

Returning to the Preamble, three additional "limitations" are identified. At paragraph 20, the Preamble makes clear that the use of a registered trademark in comparative advertising is non-infringing unless it is contrary to the 2006 EU Comparative Advertising Directive (2006 CAD).[9] And returning to paragraph 27, the Preamble identifies the right for third parties to use the registered mark for the reselling of the goods of the proprietor. Finally, and perhaps most notably, use of a trademark for the "purpose of artistic expression" is non-infringing. The paragraph concludes: "this Directive should be applied in a way that ensures full respect for fundamental rights and freedoms, and in particular the freedom of expression."[10]

The broad principle behind these limitations was summarized by the Court of Justice of the European Union (CJEU) in the early case of *BMW* v. *Deenik* when it noted about the 1989 TMD: "Art. 6[11] seeks to reconcile the fundamental interests of trade-mark protection with those of the free movement of goods and freedom to provide services in the common market in such a way that trade mark rights are able to fulfill their essential role in the system of undistorted competition."[12]

This chapter will be concerned with these limitations. It will look at each in turn and it will examine how the courts have interpreted limitations in order to balance the interests of market actors in trademark infringement actions. But first, because it is necessary for the third party to act "in accordance with honest practices in industrial or commercial matters" in order to rely on any of these limitations,[13] this chapter will look at how this caveat is understood to apply. The chapter will conclude by returning to limitations set out in paragraph 27 of the Preamble and

[4] This paragraph was not included in the preamble to the earlier directives. However, it reflects the legal principles that have emerged through subsequent CJEU decisions.

[5] 2015 TMD, art. 14(1)(a).

[6] *Id.*, art. 14(1)(b).

[7] *Id.*, art. 14(1)(c).

[8] Art. 14(3) adds a further limitation: "a trade mark shall not entitle the proprietor to prohibit a third party from using, in the course of trade, an earlier right which applies in a particular locality, only if that right is recognised by the law of the Member State in question and the use of that right is within the limits of the territory in which it is recognised." In the UK, this would apply to marks protected under passing off. *See* 2015 TMD, art. 14(3).

[9] Council Directive 2006/114/EC concerning misleading and comparative advertising (hereinafter 2006 CAD).

[10] The reference is to the Charter of Fundamental Rights of the European Union, including most notably art. 11, freedom of expression, art. 12, the freedom to conduct business, and art. 13, the right to property. *See* European Parliament et al., *Charter of Fundamental Rights of the European Union*, 2012/C 326/02 Official Journal of the European Union (2012).

[11] The equivalent of art. 14 under the 2015 TMD.

[12] Case C-63/97, *Bayerische Motorenwerke AG (BMW)* v. *Ronald Karel Deenik*, 1999 ECR I-905, EU:C2003:145, § 62.

[13] Preamble, 2015 TMD, § 27.

ask whether the concern to protect expressive uses of registered marks, explicitly recognized for the first time in the 2015 TMD, the newly adopted Trade Mark Directive, will likely impact the protection afforded to registered marks in the future.

II HONEST PRACTICES

The necessity to act in accordance with honest practices in industrial or commercial matters qualifies all the limitations set out in Article 14 of the 2015 TMD. In *BMW* v. *Deenik*, a case relating to the advertising of spare parts, the CJEU held that "honest practices" constituted "a duty to act fairly in relation to the legitimate interests of the trade mark owner."[14] This condition has also been described as a tool for the "balancing or reconciliation of potentially conflicting interests between the trade mark proprietor and third parties."[15] In the leading case of *Celine Sarl* v. *Celine* SA, which involved an "own name" defence, the CJEU considered what constitutes honest practices.[16] It held that in assessing whether use is honest, account should be taken first of the extent to which the mark is understood by the relevant public, or a significant section of it, as indicating a link between the third party's goods or services and those of the trademark proprietor and, second, the extent to which the third party ought to be aware that a link is being made. A third factor to be taken into account is whether the trademark concerned enjoys a reputation in the member state in which it is registered and from which the third party might profit. In other words, does the third party's use of the mark lead to its dilution or tarnishment, or to the taking of unfair advantage? Elsewhere, it was held that the possibility of a measure of confusion does not preclude the use of these defences.[17]

Such an assessment was carried out by the UK Court of Appeal in *Roger Maier* v. *ASOS*. The claimants had a European Trade Mark (EUTM) for ASSOS for clothing. It sold high-end cycling gear and did not sell online. The defendant ran a successful online fashion shop named "ASOS." Both had been trading for some years. In 2011, ASSOS brought infringement proceedings against ASOS. ASOS mounted an own name defence. In the Court of Appeal, Kitchin LJ, for the majority, found for ASOS and in doing so assessed whether it had acted according to honest practices. Among the factors taken into account were the following: that the name was adopted independently; that ASOS had no intention of damaging the claimant's business; and that even though ASOS failed to conduct a trademark search before adopting the trading name ASOS, had it done so ASOS would not have believed its business would impact the defendant's business. Interestingly, Sales LJ, dissenting, held that ASOS's failure to conduct a trademark search did not constitute honest practice.[18] It is possible to take from this finding not only the breadth of considerations that might be applied in deciding whether the defendant has acted in accordance with honest practices, but also their subjectivity. Indeed, it would seem that courts will have relatively wide discretion to decide whether the actions of the defendant, claiming one of these limitations in its defence, are fair and hence contribute to the optimum balance of interests among market actors.

[14] Case C-63/97, *BMW* v. *Deenik*, § 61.

[15] Case A3/2014/0619, *Roger Maier Assos of Switzerland SA* v. *ASOS plc ASOS.com Ltd*, 2015 EWCA Civ. 22, at 147.

[16] Case C-17/06, *Celine Sarl* v. *Celine SA*, 2007 ECR I-7041.

[17] Case C-100/02, *Gerolsteiner Brunnen GmbH & Co.* v. *Putsch GmbH*, 2004 ECR I-691, EU:C:2004:11, at 25–26.

[18] Case A3/2014/0619, *Maier* v. *ASOS*, § 245.

III USE OF OWN NAME

While a finding of honest practices allows for a wide-ranging assessment by the courts, the same is not now true for the "own name" defence. As the courts previously interpreted the 1989 and 2008 TMDs, the own name defence was available both to companies and to natural persons.[19] Under the 2015 TMD it is now available only to natural persons. This new, more limited, protection follows advice given in the study by the Max Planck Institute (MPI Study), which was tasked with surveying the workings of the 2008 TMD and suggesting reforms. The concern expressed in the study was that under this provision, unregistered trade names were often given protection against registered, but younger marks. As a result, allowing the defence to apply to companies upsets the principle engraved in trademark law that conflicts between registered marks and signs should be resolved on the basis of priority. It followed that this limitation should be applied only if it were based "on the legitimate interest of the owner to use his own personal name in commerce in order to designate his business."[20]

In a recent case in the Chancery Division of the United Kingdom, *Sky* v. *Skykick*,[21] the defendant argued that removing the own name defence from companies would infringe its rights under the Charter of Fundamental Rights of the EU, in particular its right to free expression and freedom to conduct business.[22] Arnold J agreed that the change was in conflict with these rights.[23] However, applying the proportionality principle as set out in Article 52 of the Charter, Arnold J (as he then was) held the measure was "justified by legitimate objectives and was not manifestly inappropriate."[24] Its purpose was to protect intellectual property as set out in Article 17 of the Charter, guaranteeing the right to property. He explained that legal persons, unlike natural persons, could choose their own names; that the change had been a legitimate policy choice as advocated in the MPI Study; and that acting on a case-by-case basis in relation to legal persons could produce uncertainty.[25] Interestingly, returning to the *Maier* case, at the time of the judgment, ASOS's online business was valued at over £2 billion and the UK Court of Appeal concluded the claimant would not be damaged if ASOS continued to trade under that name. Yet under the new regime, the damage to ASOS's business would have been substantial and it is difficult to see to what end. Conversely, it is possible to ask how likely it is for natural persons to offer such a defence if challenged by a wealthy company.

IV USE OF SIGNS THAT ARE NON-DISTINCTIVE OR DESCRIPTIVE

This is perhaps the most important limitation under Article 14 of the 2015 TMD. It allows the use of "signs or indications which are not distinctive or which concern kind, quality, quantity, intended purpose, value, geographical origin or other characteristics of goods or services."[26]

19 Case C-245/02, *Anheuser-Busch* v. *Budejovicky Budvar, Narodni Podnik*, 2005 ETMR 27, §§ 81–85. This had not been the intention of the framers of the Directive, i.e. the EU Council and Commission. *See* MAX PLANCK INSTITUTE FOR INTELLECTUAL PROPERTY AND COMPETITION LAW (MPI), STUDY ON THE OVERALL FUNCTIONING OF THE EUROPEAN TRADE MARK SYSTEM, 117 (2011) (hereinafter MPI Study), § 2.240.

20 MPI Study, *supra* note 19, 70-121, § 2.25–2.255.

21 Case HC/2016/001587, *Sky plc* v. *Skykick UK Ltd*, 2018 EWHC 155 (Ch.), 2018 ETMR.

22 *See* arts. 11–13, *supra* note 10.

23 Case HC/2016/001587, *Sky* v. *Skykick*, § 354. *See also Sky* v. *Skykick* [2020] EUECJ C-371/18. In *Sky* v. *Skykick* 2020 WL 02047926, Lord Arnold reaffirmed his earlier approach to the own name defence.

24 *Id.*, § 351, citing Case C-447/14, *Pillbox 38 (UK) Ltd* v. *Sec'y of State for Health*, EU:C:2016:324, at 49.

25 Case HC/2016/001587, *Sky* v. *Skykick*, § 354.

26 Art. 14(1)(b), Directive (EU) 2015/2436 of the European Parliament and of the Council of Dec. 16, 2015.

If the stated purpose of these limitations is to balance the interests of market actors and to strengthen freedom to trade within the common market, then it is easy to see how the monopoly of any of the signs identified in Article 14(1)(b) by a single commercial entity might undermine both. We have seen how, in the United Kingdom under previous trademark law, many descriptive words would not be registered even if they were distinctive. A prominent example arose when an application was made to register the geographical name "York" for tractor trailers manufactured in York, Ontario. The application was rejected. According to Lord Wilberforce in the House of Lords, referring to laudatory epithets and geographical names, "traders could not obtain a monopoly of the use of such words (however distinctive) to the detriment of members of the public who, in the future, and in connection with other goods, might desire to use them."[27] Under EU trademark law the decision in this case would have immediately been weighted in favour of the applicant for the mark as it had acquired distinctiveness. Hence the importance of Article 14(1)(b), in the current 2015 TMD, as a means of protecting a domain of signs that other traders might wish to use.[28]

In the course of a number of CJEU decisions interpreting the 1989 and 2008 TMDs, the precise relationship between infringement and this specific defence became obfuscated.[29] The CJEU held, over a number of cases, that the use of an identical sign on identical goods, even if it were not trademark use, would be infringing if it affected any of the "functions" of a registered trademark rather than just its "essential" origin function.[30] These other functions identified by the CJEU are guaranteeing the quality of the goods or services, communication, investment, and advertising.[31] *Arsenal* v. *Reed* was the first case in which the CJEU explicitly raised the idea that even non-trademark use might infringe, if it affects the functions of a trademark.[32] In later cases, the CJEU took a restrictive approach to finding that the functions of a registered trademark had been affected, frequently balancing the interests of the proprietor of the registered mark against those of the defendant. Thus in *Opel* v. *Autec*,[33] Opel manufactured cars but had a trademark, inter alia, for toys. Autec manufactured scale model toy cars, one of which was an Opel carrying the Opel trademark. Here the use of the mark on the model car was held not to be protected as an indication of the characteristics of the product. But it was also held not to have affected the functions of the registered mark, in particular the origin function. The average consumer would understand the use of the mark by the defendants to be indicating that theirs was a scale model of the Opel car. As a result, there would be no infringement. In *Google* v. *Louis Vuitton*[34] the CJEU held that forcing a trademark proprietor to pay a higher price to ensure their mark came above its use by others as a Google Adword did not constitute an adverse effect on the advertising function of the mark. While in *Marks & Spencer* v. *Interflora*[35] the CJEU defined the investment function as using the mark to acquire or preserve a reputation

27 York Trade Mark, 1984 FP 231, at 254.

28 Previously 1989 TMD and 2008 TMD, art. 6(6)(b).

29 For an account of this development, *see* Annette Kur, *Trade Marks Function Don't They? CJEU and Unfair Competition Practices*, 45 Int'l Rev. Intell. Prop. & Competition L. 434 (2014).

30 For an illuminating account of the relationship between "functions theory" and freedom of expression, *see* Lukasz Zelechowski, *Invoking Freedom of Expression and Freedom of Competition in Trade Mark Infringement Disputes: Legal Mechanisms for Striking a Balance* (Feb. 21, 2018), 115, https://ssrn.com/abstract=3129655.

31 Case C-324/09, *L'Oréal SA* v. *Bellure NV*, 2011 ETMR 52, § 58.

32 Case C-206/01, *Arsenal Football Club plc* v. *Reed*, 2003 ECR I-10273. Arguably, though, the idea was not fully tested in *Arsenal* because the CJEU held there could be infringement of the origin function leading to customer confusion.

33 Case C-48/05, *Adam Opel AG* v. *Autec AG*, 2007 ECR I-1017.

34 Case C-238/08, *Google France Sarl* v. *Louis Vuitton Malletier SA*, 2010 ECR I-2417.

35 Case C-323/09, *Interflora Inc.* v. *Marks & Spencer Plc*, 2012 ETMR 1.

capable of attracting consumers and retaining their loyalty. But it also held that even if such use by the third party obliged the proprietor to adapt its efforts to gain consumer loyalty and to protect its reputation, the investment function would not be affected.

In the case of *Opel,* as we have seen, the fact that the CJEU could determine there had been no damage to the functions of the registered mark allowed it to find for the defendant even though the limitation to trademark infringement, under the general rubric "descriptive use," did not apply. The same argument might possibly apply to *Google* and *Interflora.*[36] The 2015 TMD addressed the uncertainty that arose when a concern with a trademark's other functions, and not just its origin function, was injected into double-identity infringement actions in two ways. It states that in such cases the guarantee of the sign as an indication origin should be absolute;[37] and that an infringement of a trademark can be established only if the later mark or sign is used in the course of trade for the purpose of distinguishing goods and services.[38] It goes on: "use of a sign for purposes other than for distinguishing goods and services should be subject to the provisions of national law." This would appear to erase the possibility that a mark being used purely descriptively can infringe. But also suggests it is still possible for a national court, perhaps applying unfair competition law, to make a different finding.

By contrast, in a number of cases concerned with "double identity" infringement, the CJEU gave examples of purely descriptive use; that is where the sign was not used as a trademark and there would be no question of any of the functions of the registered mark being affected. The leading case is undoubtedly *Michael Holterhoff* v. *Ulrich Freiesleben.*[39] In this case, Freisleben was the proprietor of two trademarks, "Spirit Sun" and "Context Cut," for precious stones of a particular cut. Holterhoff also dealt in precious stones, and sold two garnets identified in the course of oral negotiations with the purchaser as "Spirit Sun" and "Context Cut," while the order was for two stones in the "Spirit Sun cut." The CJEU held that the trademark had been used by the defendant purely descriptively in order to reveal the characteristics of the products offered for sale and not to indicate their origin. Interestingly, in the recent US case *Tiffany* v. *Costco*, the New York Southern District Court came to an opposite conclusion on similar facts.[40] The plaintiff had the registered trademark "Tiffany" for jewelry. The defendant used the word "Tiffany" to describe the appearance of a diamond ring sold instore. The defendant argued, inter alia, that such descriptive use was compatible with the registered mark maintaining its distinctive character. In contrast to the CJEU judgment in *Freiesleben*, the US court dismissed the notion that there could be such "dual use" of a registered mark. *Holterhoff* was later distinguished by the CJEU in *Arsenal*, where it was held that the defendant, Reed, was not using the Arsenal mark, "for purely descriptive purposes." However, another oft-cited case, which is concerned with the geographical origin of goods, *Gerolsteiner* v. *Putsch*, appears to contradict the distinction made in *Arsenal.*[41] In *Gerolsteiner*, the claimant had a registered mark, "Gerri," for soft drinks and the defendant was selling sparkling water under the name "Kerry Gold," originating from Kerry, Ireland. The CJEU held that although there might be

[36] Porangaba argues that the functions theory allows the court to find there has been no infringement even with trademark use to decide such cases in light of market realities. *See* Luis H. Porangaba, A *Contextual Account of the Trade Mark Functions Theory, in* Intell. Prop. Q. 230 (2018).

[37] Preamble, 2015 TMD, § 16.

[38] *Id.*, § 18.

[39] Case C-2/00, *Holterfoff (Michael)* v. *Ulrich Freiesleben*, 2002 ECR I-4187.

[40] *Tiffany and Co.* v. *Costco Wholesale Corp.*, 127 F. Supp. 3d 241 (SDNY 2015).

[41] Case C-100/02, *Gerolsteiner* v. *Putsch.*

some confusion if a registered mark and a mark indicating the geographical origin of the goods were used together, the registered mark holder could not prevent such use by the defendant if it was in accordance with honest practices.

It is possible to find other cases at the national and EU level where courts engaged with delineating the scope of these particular limitations. But they are surprisingly few. Two reasons may be suggested for this. First, as was pointed out in the MPI Study,[42] these limitations are of course also reasons to deny registration to trademarks in the first instance. And there are many more reported cases where such battles are fought at the point of registration. Second, it is possible to argue that once a non-distinctive mark or a descriptive mark is registered it becomes much more difficult to prove that use by the defendant is non-infringing. For example, in *Gerolsteiner*, the registered trademark was not itself a mark that had a descriptive meaning before registration. The same might be said for *Holterhoff*. By contrast, where an applicant can prove that its non-distinctive or descriptive mark has acquired distinctiveness and is legitimately registered, then it is difficult to see how its use by a third party, even if it is meant to be descriptive use, will not be infringing.

A case that illustrates these potential limits of the descriptive use defence is *Windsurfing* v. *Walter Huber*,[43] an infringement action and an important judgment in establishing the registrability of descriptive signs in the EU. In this case, the claimant had a number of German-registered graphic marks for clothing that incorporated the word "Chiemsee," which is a lake and a tourist attraction in Germany. Windsurfing sold its clothes by the lake although they were made elsewhere. The defendant also sold clothes marked "Chiemsee" in a different graphic form, in proximity to the lake. The question for the CJEU was whether a descriptive term such as "Chiemsee" could be a registered trademark as it was a mark other traders might wish to use. The court answered, inter alia, that once a descriptive mark had acquired distinctiveness through use – that is, it had become a badge of origin for the relevant consumers – it could be registered. It is submitted that it is difficult to see how "Chiemsee" can now be used descriptively by a third party in a way which will not also be seen as trademark use. In other words, it is submitted that "Chiemsee" has been robbed of its descriptive character, as far as its market use is concerned. It is also interesting to note that in *Windsurfing*, the defendant, rather than relying for its defence on the available limitation, sought to argue that the earlier mark had been wrongly registered under Article 3(1)(c) of the 2008 TMD and should be declared invalid. This strategy, too, is not uncommon, thus further undermining the extent to which these limitations – supposedly designed to protect the use of registered trademarks by third parties in ways other than as a badge of origin – have proved a particularly useful tool in balancing market interests.[44]

[42] MPI Study, *supra* note 19, 121, § 2.257.

[43] Case C-108/97, *Windsurfing Chiemsee Produktions-und Vertriebs GmBH* v. *Boots- und Segelzubehor Walter Huber*, 1999 ECR I-2779, § 37.

[44] For an example of a leading CJEU infringement case where the defendant argued that the claimant's colour mark was invalidly registered as lacking distinctiveness, *see* Case C-217, *Oberbank AG* v. *Deutscher Sparkassen- und Giroverband eV Banco Santander SA*, 2014 WLR 274, EU:C:2014:2012. In relation to distinctiveness and shapes, *see* Case C-299/99, *Koninklijke Philips Electronics NV* v. *Remington Consumer Products Ltd*, 2012 ECR I-5475. *See also* Jennifer Davis, *Promoting the Public Interest and the European Trade Mark Directive: A Contradictory Approach*, ERA Forum 14, 117–29 (2013).

V USE OF THE REGISTERED MARK TO IDENTIFY GOODS OR SERVICES AS FUNCTIONING WITH THOSE OF THE PROPRIETOR, OR FOR THE RESELLING OF THE PROPRIETOR'S GOODS

It is useful to consider these two defences together: use to indicate the intended purpose of a product and use by a third party in reselling goods. They both allow traders to refer to a registered trademark in order to indicate the nature of the goods and services that they offer to the public, for example if their business is to repair or supply spare parts for the proprietor's goods or if they are reselling the proprietor's goods. Their purpose is to ensure that competition to supply spare parts and other goods, which might be identified by reference to a registered trademark, is not inhibited by the threat of an infringement action. The scope of the "spare parts defence" (or use to indicate the intended purpose of a product) was first considered by the CJEU in *BMW* v. *Deenik*.[45] The defendant, who was not an authorized BMW dealer, advertised that he sold and repaired second-hand BMWs. BMW sued Deenik for trademark infringement, and defendant raised the defence of intended purpose. The CJEU gave guidance as to when the defence might succeed. It held that use must be "necessary" to indicate the intended purpose of the goods or services. It also made clear that the defence fails if the mark is used in such a way "that may create the impression that there is a commercial connection between the other undertaking and the trade mark proprietor, and in particular that the reseller's business is affiliated to the trademark proprietor's distribution network or that there is a special relationship between the two undertakings."[46]

Inevitably, the CJEU was later called upon to define what constitutes "necessity" and what constitutes fair use of the registered trademark. It did so in *Gillette* v. *LA-Laboratories Ltd Oy*.[47] The claimant marketed razors in Finland, including replaceable blades, under the registered marks "Gillette" and "Sensor." LA manufactured razors and replaceable blades similar to the claimant's products under a different mark, "Parason Flexor." Although it used this different mark, LA fixed a sticker to their packaging bearing the words "all Parason Flexor and Gillette Sensor handles are compatible with this blade." Gillette sued for trademark infringement and LA claimed a defence under Article 6(1)(c) of the 2008 TMD. The questions for the CJEU, inter alia, were whether a trader may refer to the third-party mark only if it is strictly necessary, even if such a prohibition puts the consumer at a disadvantage and, second, what constitutes honest practices. According to the CJEU, use of a trademark by a third party is necessary if that is "the only means of providing the public with comprehensible and complete information on that intended purpose in order to preserve the undistorted system of competition in the market for that product." In determining whether it is necessary, account must be taken of the nature of the public for which the product marketed by the third party is intended.[48] As to the further question of what constitutes honest use, the CJEU held that it would not be compatible with "honest practices" if there is an impression that there is a commercial connection with the proprietor; that it takes unfair advantage of the distinctiveness or repute of the mark; or if it denigrates the mark. Furthermore, the third party cannot present its product as an imitation or replica of the product bearing the trademark.[49] The CJEU also held that it is for the national court to determine whether the third party has met these criteria and, in doing so, account should be taken of the overall presentation of the product as marketed by the third party, including the

45 Case C-63/97, *BMW* v. *Deenik*.
46 *Id.*, § 64.
47 Case C-228/03, *Gillette Co.* v. *LA-Labs. Ltd Oy*, 2005 ECR I-2337.
48 *Id.*, § 39.
49 *See* Case C-323/09, *Interflora* v. *Marks & Spencer*.

distinction made between use of the registered trademark and the mark or sign of the third party, and the effort made by that third party to ensure that consumers can distinguish its products from those of the trademark owner. Finally, the CJEU held that to indicate the intended purpose of a product by using the proprietor's mark does not have to mean the third party's product is of an equivalent quality.[50]

Turning to the second defence, the use of a registered trademark by a third party in reselling goods, arguably the courts have taken a more restrictive approach than the one taken in interpreting the "spare parts defence." This might be explained by the fact that the leading case relating to the reselling of goods arose in the course of e-commerce. In *Portakabin* v. *Primakabin*,[51] the CJEU looked at the defence provided by Article 6(1)(c) 2008 TMD when the trademark at issue is used as a keyword on the Internet by resellers of the trademark proprietor's goods. In this case, the "Portakabin" trademark was used by a company selling second-hand Portakabin products. In its judgment, the CJEU looked at the meaning of "honest practices." It held that an advertiser cannot, in general, rely on the exception for "intended use" in order to avoid liability for infringement. The CJEU noted that it is the advertiser that is acquainted with the particular market in which it operates who chooses the keyword that corresponds to another person's trademark, designs the advertisement alone or with the service provider, and therefore decides how the goods should be presented. As a result, if the advertisement leaves a significant number of consumers assuming the trademark proprietor had authorized the use of its mark or makes it difficult for the average internet user to ascertain who is supplying the goods, there would not be honest practices in industrial or commercial matters. It follows that despite the inclusion of reselling as a limitation to infringement in the preamble to the 2015 TMD, it may prove difficult, if not impossible, for a third party to make use of keyword advertising on the Internet where it is selling second-hand goods or spare parts that relate to that keyword (assuming it is a registered trademark).

VI COMPARATIVE ADVERTISING

The other circumstances where there is a defence to trademark infringement, where a third party uses a registered sign on the same or similar goods, is if it is used in the course of comparative advertising and so long as it does not contravene the 2006 CAD. In the recent case of *Carrefour* v. *ITM*,[52] the CJEU described the rationale behind this limitation:

> [S]ince comparative advertising contributes to demonstrating, in an objective manner, the advantages of various comparable goods and thus to stimulating competition between suppliers of goods and services to the consumer's advantage, the conditions to be met for such advertising must be interpreted in the sense most favourable to that advertising, while ensuring at the same time that comparative advertising is not used anti-competitively and unfairly or in a manner which affects adversely the interests of consumers.

According to Article 4 of the 2006 CAD, comparative advertising is permitted when it is not misleading; does not create confusion between the advertiser's trademark and those of a

[50] A recent UK Court of Appeal case involving the "spare parts" defence is *Bayerische* v. *Technosport*. *See Bayerische Motoren Werke AG* v. *Technosport London Ltd*, 2017 EWCA Civ. 779, 2018 RTR 1. Interestingly, there was no suggestion in the judgment that *BMW* v. *Deenik* is no longer authoritative.

[51] Case C-558/08, *Portakabin Ltd* v. *Primakabin BV*, 2010 ETMR 52.

[52] Case C-562/15, *Carrefour Hypermarches SAS* v. *ITM Alimentaire International SASU*, 2017 EU:C:2017:95, 3 CMLR 1, § 21.

competitor or take unfair advantage of the reputation of a trademark, trade name, or other distinguishing marks; and it does not present the goods or services as imitations or replicas of goods or services bearing a protected trademark or trade name. In essence, the defence of comparative advertising allows the use of the registered mark by a third party in a way which would not infringe that mark under the terms of the TMD.

A leading case establishing the link between comparative advertising, trademark use and CAD is *O2 Holdings* v. *Hutchison*.[53] The claimant, O2, had various registered trademarks including one for "O2" and another for bubbles used in relation to, inter alia, telecommunications apparatus and telecommunications services. The defendant, H3G, also a mobile phone service provider, launched an advertising campaign comparing its services to other providers, including O2. In the case of O2, it used as a reference both the trademark "O2" and bubbles, which were similar but not identical to the bubbles registered by O2. O2 did not contest the accuracy of the comparison but alleged infringement of its trademark, through use of a similar mark on identical goods.[54] The case eventually reached the CJEU. The CJEU held that a comparative advertisement will not satisfy Article 3a(1) of CAD[55] if such use presents a risk of origin confusion because of the way the comparative advertiser deploys the competitor's mark.[56] Rather, such use will be infringing use. On the facts of this case, the CJEU held that H3G's use of the bubbles would not cause confusion or suggest a link with O2.[57]

With its decision in O2, the CJEU made clear that if a comparative advertisement causes customer confusion, it is infringing. *L'Oréal* v. *Bellure* was also a case of comparative advertising. In this case, the defendants advertised their cheap perfumes as smelling like the claimant's expensive perfumes, using the claimant's registered trademarks as a reference. There was no allegation by the claimant that consumers would be confused by the use of its marks in the defendant's advertisements. Rather, the defendant was alleged to have taken unfair advantage of the claimant's trademarks.[58] The CJEU was asked about the relationship between infringement under the 2008 TMD and CAD. The CJEU held that under CAD, a comparative advertisement that presents the advertiser's products as an imitation of a product bearing a trademark is inconsistent with fair competition and thus unlawful. As a result, any advantage gained by the advertiser through such advertising will have been achieved as the result of unfair competition and must, accordingly, be regarded as taking unfair advantage of the reputation of that mark.[59]

The decision in *L'Oréal* is controversial. When the case returned to the UK Court of Appeal, Jacob LJ reluctantly found for the claimant but expressed his concern that the CJEU's approach placed a limit on free speech, preventing traders from making "honest statements about their products."[60] In this case, defendant Bellure was simply stating that it supplied smell-alike perfumes to those marketed by L'Oréal at a cheaper price, to the benefit of consumers who did not wish to pay the brand premium placed on L'Oréal's perfumes. A more general question, following *L'Oréal* v. *Bellure*, is whether it is more important for competitors to have the opportunity to give consumers relevant information about two competing products than it is to protect the "reputation" of the trademark with which comparisons are to be made. In *L'Oréal*,

[53] Case C-533/06, *O2 Holdings Ltd* v. *Hutchison 3G UK Ltd*, 2008 E.C.R I-4231, 2007, 2 CMLR 15.

[54] 2008 TMD, art. 4(1)(b); 2015 TMD, art. 5(1)(b).

[55] Article 3(1) here is from Council Directive 97/55/EC concerning misleading advertising so as to include comparative advertising (hereinafter CAD). Art. 3(1) of this directive is equivalent to art. 4 in the 2006 CAD.

[56] Case C-533/06, *O2* v. *Hutchinson*, § 44.

[57] *Id.*, § 63.

[58] 2008 TMD, art. 5(2); 2015 TMD, art. 10(1)(c).

[59] Case C-324/09, *L'Oréal* v. *Bellure*, § 69.

[60] Case C-487/07, *L'Oréal SA* v. *Bellure*, 2010 EWCA Civ. 535, § 8.

the CJEU expressed the view that the law should be interpreted in a way most favourable to comparative advertising, so long as the advertisements were not infringing. Brand holders may well disagree, holding that any use of their marks in comparative advertising is in effect taking advantage of their attractiveness. By contrast, it has been suggested that perhaps using registered trademarks in a referential manner (that is, not as a badge of origin), even if done in a commercial context, should have general and explicit protection.[61]

VII TRADEMARKS AND FREEDOM OF EXPRESSION AS A DEFENCE TO INFRINGEMENT

Thus far this chapter has addressed specific situations where the 2015 TMD offers, through a series of limitations, a defence for a third party that uses a registered trademark in the course of trade. There are of course many other defences available to one accused of infringing a trademark, including a claim of honest concurrent use or that the rights of the trademark proprietor have been exhausted for a variety of reasons.[62] It is also open to a defendant to claim that the mark should not have been registered in the first instance because it falls within one of the absolute grounds for refusal of registration and so should be revoked; or that the registered trademark should be declared invalid because, for example, during the period of its use it has become generic. But at the start of this chapter we also pointed out that, according to the Preamble to the 2016 Directive, the rights of a trademark proprietor to bring an infringement action should be limited to allow for "artistic expression" and that trademark law should be applied so as to respect fundamental rights, in particular freedom of expression.

In the period before the adoption of the 2015 TMD there was considerable lobbying from academics and others to ensure that it would stress the importance of the principles of freedom of expression and undistorted competition, including weighing up the interests of competitors as well as consumers.[63] We have seen how the Directive did indeed mirror some of these concerns, although not a request that the Directive contain "an open-ended clause" to the limitations that would allow courts to "develop appropriate new defences on a case-by-case basis" where the fundamental principles of the Directive should permit third party use.[64] No doubt, at least some of those lobbying for this change of emphasis had in mind prominent US actions that have helped draw the boundaries between trademark protection and free speech in that country. Two of the most prominent are undoubtedly *Mattel* v. *MCA Records*[65] and *Rogers* v. *Grimaldi*,[66] the latter producing the widely used "Rogers test" for balancing expressive use with trademark protection.[67] Most recently the Supreme Court decision in *Matal* v. *Tam*[68] held that the disparagement clause in the Lanham Act was unconstitutional.

[61] *See* Nari Lee, *Public Domain at the Interface of Trade Mark and Unfair Competition Law: The Case of Referential Use of Trade Marks*, in INTELL. PROP., UNFAIR COMPETITION AND PUBLICITY: CONVERGENCES AND DEVELOPMENT, 334–38 (Nari Lee, Guido Westkamp, Annette Kur, & Ansgar Ohly eds., 2014).

[62] Martin Senftleben et al., *The Recommendation on Measures to Safeguard Freedom of Expression and Undistorted Competition: Guiding Principles for the Future Development of EU Trade Mark Law*, 37(6) EUROPEAN INTELL. PROP. REV. 337 (2015).

[63] *Id.* at 339.

[64] *Id.* at 342.

[65] *Mattel* v. *MCA Records*, 296 F.3d 894 (9th Cir. 2002).

[66] *Rogers* v. *Grimaldi*, 875 F.2d 994 (2d Cir. 1989).

[67] For a detailed discussion of these cases, see Chapter 33 in this volume.

[68] *Matal* v. *Tam*, 137 US 1744 (2017).

What is remarkable, however, is, until very recently, how little authoritative case law there is, certainly at the European level, addressing similar concerns. We have already seen that the interpretation of specific limitations, such as what constitutes descriptive use or what falls within the "spare parts" defence, has advanced very little from the early days of the first Directive. And, in the case of descriptive use, once a descriptive word has become distinctive, it is difficult to see how a defence of descriptive use by a third party would succeed in any event. As for cases concerned with freedom of expression, there have been, since the Directive, instances in member states where the courts have been asked to choose between free political speech and trademark protection, but again they are surprisingly few.[69] This may change following the CJEU decision in *Constantin Film Produktion v. EUIPO*,[70] where the Court essentially held that that EU trade mark law should be interpreted in a way that will ensure full respect for fundamental rights and freedoms, in particular freedom of expression. Interestingly, to date in the EU, perhaps the most prominent case in which claimants argued, albeit unsuccessfully, that their rights to exploit their trademarks were being truncated was not an infringement action at all; instead it was the claim by the tobacco companies that plain packaging interfered with their right to property.[71] In sum, there has not been demonstrated, across the period of both directives, a pressing concern with the issue of freedom of speech among parties to trademark infringement actions. Furthermore, to take the United Kingdom as an example, it is interesting that where the balance between trademark protection and freedom of expression has been at issue, it has largely been part of a dispute between two, often weighty, commercial enterprises.[72]

VIII CONCLUSION

This chapter has sought to describe the limitations to infringement that allow referential use of a registered trademark; to show how these limitations have been applied; and to assess their significance as a means of protecting competition within the common market and the right to freedom of expression. We have noted that while the limitations have been accorded considerable importance in the 2016 Directive, they have not had commensurate importance in case law, at least so far. Ostensibly then, the EU serves as a contrast to the United States, where limitations to trademark infringement have been viewed as important for protecting a public domain of free speech. For example, while the *Tam* case led to a finding that the morality clause of the Lanham Act was unconstitutional, the MPI Study did not refer to the equivalent clause in the Directive, despite its concern for the protection of freedom of expression.[73] And in *Constantin v. EUIPO*, the CJEU did not question the existence of the 'morality clause'; stating only that its application should be compatible with freedom of expression. One can only speculate why the balance

[69] *See* Case C-04/12417, *Esso Plc* v. *Greenpeace France*, 2006 ETMR 53; *see also Societe des Participants du Commissariat a l'Energie Atomique SA* v. *Greenpeace France*, 2005 ETMR 78.

[70] Case C-240/18 *Constantin Film Produktion GmbH v. EUIPO*, 2020, EU:C:2020:118; *see also Casado Coca v Spain (A/285)*, 1994, 18 E.H.R.R. 1.

[71] Case C-220/17, *PlanTabak-Manufaktur Dr Manfred Obermann GmBH* v. *Land Berli*, 2019, WLR 28. For the United Kingdom seee *Regina (British American Tobacco) and others* v. *Secretary of State for Health*, 2016, EWCA Civ. 1182.

[72] *See* Case HC/2016/001587, *Sky* v. *Skykick*. *See also Boehringer Ingelheim Ltd* v. *VetPlus Ltd*, 2007 EWCA Civ. 583 (holding that the granting of an interim injunction in trademark cases must be compatible with freedom of expression under the Human Rights Act 1998 § 12(3), and granted only if the claimant is more than likely to succeed at trial).

[73] The equivalent morality clause in the 2008 TMD is art. 3(1)(f), and in the 2015 TMD is art. 4(1)(f). A recent case at the General Court of the EU was a failed attempt to register "laMafia" for, inter alia, restaurants. The applicant argued the sign was meant to parody *The Godfather* films. The Court found it offended against public morality. *See La Mafia Franchises SL* v. *European Union Intellectual Prop. Office*, 2018 ECLI:EU:T:2018:146. *See also Constantin Film Produktion v. EUIPO*.

between trademark protection and freedom of expression in the EU has been raised in relatively few cases, and these few have been cases primarily concerned with referential, commercial use. Perhaps this is because when there is a danger that trademark protection might inhibit free speech, it is generally the case that the mark at issue is a well-known one – in other words, that it would embody meanings beyond its basic one as a badge of origin. For it is precisely these additional meanings that might be parodied or used in other expressive ways, perhaps to make a political point. And it might also be posited that when such use is made of a powerful mark, it is a matter of "brand" protection not to take those concerned to court, but instead to seek other ways to protect the "brand."[74] Nike is a case in point. Although its name and its distinctive "swoosh" have been widely parodied and reproduced by critics of its labour practices, its response has not been litigation but, rather, a public commitment to improving conditions amongst those who are employed to produce its products. Recently, a leading business website was able to headline its article about Nike, "How Nike shed its sweatshop image to dominate the shoe industry."[75] In other words, if the limitations to trademark infringement have had any effect, it has been to help balance the interests of (often powerful) competitors rather than to create a protected public domain for freedom of expression.

[74] A relatively rare example of an EU-registered design proprietor taking a private individual to court is *Plesner Joensen* v. *Louis Vuitton*, where Plesner displayed a painting with a starving child holding a bag incorporating the claimant's design. LV sued Plesner for infringement, and the Dutch District court held that Plesner's right to freedom of expression under art. 10 of the European Convention on Human Rights trumped Louis Vuitton's right to property under art. 1. Although, arguably LV had grounds for appeal, it chose not to proceed further. *See* Case 389526/KG ZA 11-294, *Nadia Plesner Joensen* v. *Louis Vuitton Malletier SA*, 2011 ZA 11-294.

[75] Ashley Lutz, *How Nike Shed Its Sweatshop Image to Dominate the Shoe Industry*, Business Insider (June 6, 2015), https://businessinsider.com/how-nike-fixed-its-sweatshop-image-2015-6?r=UK&IR=T.

XIV

The Principle of Exhaustion of Trademark Rights

35

Common Law and Civil Law Approaches to Trademark Exhaustion in Europe

The Distribution Function of Trademarks

Apostolos G. Chronopoulos and Spyros M. Maniatis***

I INTRODUCTION

This chapter examines the exceptions to the so-called principle of exhaustion pursuant to which a trademark proprietor has no authority to control by virtue of their exclusive right the further commercialization of trademarked goods already placed on the market with their consent. The chapter focuses on German and UK law as they stood before the harmonization of trademark laws in Europe to juxtapose the civil and the common law approaches to the same legal problem. In particular, it examines the circumstances under which the exclusive right in a trademark may be relied upon to exercise control over the distribution channels that carry the product to the ultimate consumer. It then turns to appreciate the role of trademark rights in safeguarding the integrity of distribution networks. In that regard, it will focus on the exceptions to the principle of exhaustion as these apply under the current legal framework of the European Union trademark system. A more detailed review of the principle of trademark exhaustion in the EU is provided by Irene Calboli in her corresponding chapter on the exhaustion doctrine (Chapter 36). Calboli also discusses trademark exhaustion in the United States and other selected jurisdictions to highlight the relationship between trademark exhaustion and free movement of goods in the context of cross-border trade.

II DISTRIBUTION RESTRAINTS AND TRADEMARK RIGHTS UNDER THE TRADITIONAL COMMON LAW APPROACH IN THE UNITED KINGDOM

A The Doctrine of Implied License

Originally, trademarks had been protected in England through an action at law based on the tort of passing off, which allowed traders to recover damages for loss of custom and damage to reputation.[1] Preventive justice in the form of injunctive relief was available through the Courts of Equity whose jurisdiction included the protection of legal rights such as any trader's "right to have a particular trade mark to designate a commodity" as pointed out in the case of *Farina*.[2] In this context, the use of a source identifier for a specific trade constituted the essence of the

* Senior Lecturer in Intellectual Property Law, Centre for Commercial Law Studies, Queen Mary University of London.
** Director, British Institute of International and Comparative Law; Honorary Professor of Intellectual Property Law, Queen Mary University of London.

[1] Duncan M. Kerly, The Law of Trade Marks, Trade Name and Merchandise Marks 1–5 (1894).

[2] *Farina* v. *Silverlock* (1856) 6 De. G. M. & G. 214, 222, 43 Eng. Rep. 1214, 1218 (Ch.).

property right. There was no property in the mark distinct from its use. Hence, infringement would only occur if a third party used the same mark as a source designator for the same class of goods for which that mark had already been used by the plaintiff.[3] An infringing use would thus involve a defendant that had used the earlier trademark to designate their own goods in such a way as to cause the public to believe that the goods originated from the plaintiff.[4] Conversely, there could be no infringement if the earlier trademark was used in connection with goods that were unrelated to the plaintiff's trade. And, importantly, no liability would attach if the mark had been used in connection with genuine goods of the plaintiff because such use was unlikely to deceive as to the commercial origin. *Farina* was about the denial to an injunction against a third party that created imitations of the labels attached to the bottles of the plaintiff's eau de cologne. An injunction was denied because the labels printed by the defendant were most likely to be put to a lawful use as it was very common back then for retailers to replace soiled or worn-out labels of products they had in stock with new ones. The junior use was not bound to cause deception because the plaintiff's mark would be most likely used in connection with genuine goods.[5] A junior user trading on genuine goods could not escape liability, though, if they had somehow adulterated plaintiff's products.[6]

Those principles remained intact even after the introduction of laws for the protection of registered trademarks relieving traders from the burden of establishing their right in the use of a specific mark each time they filed suit for passing off. The Registration Acts of 1875 and 1883 as well as the Trade Marks Act of 1905 did not confer upon the proprietor of a registered trademark any rights additional to the right to use a source identifier for specific goods and the right to exclude others from using the same mark for the same class of goods in the case of actual deception or likelihood thereof. By its very nature, this right did not carry with it the authority to condition or restrict the sale of, or any other dealing with, genuine goods bearing the protected trademark. In other words, the authority to control dealings with genuine goods was deemed to lie outside the scope of the statutory right unless, of course, the goods had been adulterated. It was therefore not necessary for the British courts to formulate an independent "first sale doctrine" at that time. Importantly, it was immaterial for the application of this rule whether the trademark proprietor had placed the goods on the domestic or any other international market. The leading case had been *Champagne Heidsieck* v. *Buxton*.[7]

The plaintiffs were champagne producers in France selling their product in bottles with a label containing the words "Champagne Dry Monopole." At some point, they started differentiating their beverage to match diverse consumer preferences in the various export markets. To distinguish the wine meant for consumption in France, which was of a sweeter quality, the plaintiffs placed the word "Brut" in red writing across their standard label. The bottles containing the version targeting the British consumers, which bore a label that was nearly identical to the original label used in France, were distinguished through an additional label with the indication "Reserved for England." The plaintiffs had obtained registered trademark rights in the United Kingdom for the lettering and the design of the standard label. Moreover, the words "Registered Trade Mark" were included in the main label to inform third parties about the

[3] Kerly, *supra* note 1 at 307–08.
[4] *Farina* v. *Silverlock*, 1216.
[5] *Id.* at 1217–18 (an injunction would suppress legitimate uses to exclude the theoretical possibility of unlawful ones).
[6] Kerly, *supra* note 1 at 310.
[7] *Champagne Heidsieck et Cie Monopole Societe Anonyme* v. *Buxton* [1930] 1 Ch. 330. Similar issues had arisen before in *Apollinaris Co.* v. *Snook* [1891] 8 RPC 166 (CA) but they were not resolved because the crucial UK registration had to be cancelled.

plaintiffs' registration. The plaintiffs were not successful in raising obstacles to the importation of Brut wine in England. No trademark infringement was found because the defendant importers had used the earlier trademark in connection with genuine goods. They had not suggested that Brut wine was the product of someone other than the plaintiffs. To reach this conclusion, the court relied on the principles established by *Farina*.[8]

Traders were free, however, to impose restrictions on the distribution of the goods bearing their marks as long as the underlying contract was lawful. In other words, the legality of such restrictions was not assessed under trademark law. It was thus possible to devise business strategies that would involve the marketing of an identical product or different versions of the same good at different prices in the various targeted foreign markets and enforce them contractually. UK trademark rights could then be relied upon to prevent the unauthorized importation of contracted products. To achieve that aim, traders would often organize their activities through a network of local subsidiaries owning national trademark rights. In *Dunlop* v. *Booth*, the plaintiff, the English Dunlop Company, was successful in enjoining a parallel importer from marketing tyres of the French Dunlop Company in the United Kingdom on trademark infringement grounds.[9] The plaintiff could not, however, oppose the reimportation of the tyres already sold in the United Kingdom. Dunlop's distribution system implemented a price differential strategy charging a lower price in the French market. The underlying contractual arrangements and the separate ownership of the national trademarks by distinct legal entities distinguished *Dunlop*[10] from *Heidsieck*.[11]

Failure to act proactively to maintain the integrity of such distribution systems would trigger the application of the default rule, which would deprive the trademark proprietor of any authority to control the further commercialization of their products regardless of whether they had placed the goods in the domestic or an international market. The possibility of reserving the right to oppose specific subsequent dealings with the contracted goods allowed traders to enforce restrictions such as resale price maintenance or sales prohibitions that are immanent in sole or exclusive distributorship schemes through the enforcement of IP rights.[12] Those agreements were held to constitute a "reasonable restraint of trade" because they were deemed to improve distribution to the benefit of both the parties to the contract and the consumers.[13] In the course of time, the legality of conditions restricting the commercialization of goods after their first sale fell within the ambit of (European) competition law, which eventually curbed those practices to a significant extent.[14]

The common law roots of the default rule have been traced to the old case of *Betts* v. *Wilmott*.[15] There, the court held that any unqualified sale of a patented article comes along with an implied licence authorizing the buyer to use or to alienate the acquired item at will. The doctrine of implied licence reflects the notion of a seller being able to impose restrictions to the further commercialization of the good sold provided there is a relevant contractual stipulation which does not violate any other laws. On the other hand, the very nature of trademark rights as

[8] *Champagne Heidsieck*, 334–35.

[9] *Dunlop Rubber Company Ltd* v A. A. *Booth & Co. Ltd* [1926] 43 RPC 139.

[10] *Id.*

[11] *Champagne Heidsieck*, [1930] 1 Ch. 330.

[12] William R. Cornish, Intellectual Property: Patents, Copyright, Trade Marks and Allied Rights 41 (4th ed. 1999); Alan W. White, *Sunglasses: A Benefit to Health?*, 21 Eur. Intell. Prop. Rev. 176, 178–79 (1999).

[13] John Dyson Heydon, The Restraint of Trade Doctrine 205–39 (1971); Simon Horner, Parallel Imports 20–25 (1987).

[14] *See generally*, Alexandra Kamerling & Chris Goodwill, Restrictive Covenants under Common and Competition Law (6th ed. 2010).

[15] *Betts* v. *Wilmott* [1871] LR Ch. App. 239.

rights meant to combat consumer deception suggested that the trademark proprietor should not impede the trade of genuine goods bearing their mark by virtue of their exclusive right alone. The traditional common law approach recognizes the need to avoid the absurdities that would ensue if a licence had to be obtained each time a trademarked good was about to be resold.

B Trademarks and Free Trade under the Trade Marks Act of 1938

It was with the Trade Marks Act of 1938 (the 1938 Act) that the principle holding that the scope of trademark rights does not include the authority to impose restrictions to trade on genuine goods found explicit statutory recognition. The 1938 Act introduced new infringing uses not requiring the use of an earlier mark as a trademark.[16] In particular, section 4(2)(b) of the 1938 Act gave authority to the rights holder to enjoin third-party uses in the course of trade likely to be perceived as "importing a reference" to the trademark proprietor or their goods. This was meant to combat practices such as using an earlier trademark while promoting one's own products with comparison lists to retailers. Such a practice had been considered as a mischief by the legislator back then.[17] Hence, the freedom to use earlier trademarks on genuine goods could no longer be justified on the grounds of such use not being deceptive.[18] For this reason, the 1938 Act provided explicitly in section 4(3)(a) that "[t]he right to the use of a trade mark given by registration shall not be deemed to be infringed" by a junior user if the following requirements were met: (1) the earlier trademark must have been used "in relation to goods connected in the course of trade with the proprietor or a registered user"; and (2) either (a) the mark has been applied to those goods by the proprietor – or the registered user – without having been subsequently removed or obliterated by them; or (b) the proprietor or the registered user has consented to the use of the mark. Where the goods have been lawfully adapted, third parties may use the earlier mark if reasonably necessary to convey that the goods have been so adapted.

The concept of genuine goods presupposes that the mark has been applied to the goods by the proprietor or an authorized party. This requirement has been interpreted in light of the territoriality principle. Accordingly, the proprietor of a trademark registered in the United Kingdom could only be deemed to have applied the mark within the meaning of section 4(3)(a) of the 1938 Act if that mark has been used within the UK jurisdiction. Hence, for the national rights of the trademark proprietor to be implicated by the parallel importation of goods that were marketed outside the United Kingdom first, the trademark proprietor must have applied the mark to goods with a view to marketing them in the United Kingdom at some point.[19] In other words, unless there is some intention of marketing the trademarked good in the UK market, the trademark proprietor is exercising foreign trademark rights in placing the trademarked goods on a market abroad. As a result thereof, the marketing of goods outside the United Kingdom does not normally qualify as an exercise of the right to apply the mark to the goods within the jurisdiction of registration. In a legal order where restrictions to parallel imports are not categorically excluded

[16] On the importance of use as a factor determining whether infringement has taken place under the 1938 and the 1994 Act, *see* Spyros M. Maniatis, *Aspects of Trade Mark Use and Misuse*, *in* TRADE MARKS RETROSPECTIVE (Norma Dawson & Alison Firth eds., 2000).

[17] *Bismag Ltd* v. *Amblins (Chemists) Ltd* [1940] 57 RPC 209; *Chanel Ltd* v. *Triton Packaging Ltd (formerly l'Arome (UK) Ltd)* [1993] RPC 32.

[18] T. A. BLANCO WHITE & ROBIN JACOB, KERLY'S LAW OF TRADE MARKS AND TRADE NAMES 278 (12th ed. 1986).

[19] *Colgate-Palmolive Ltd. and Another* v. *Markwell Finance Ltd. and Another* [1989] RPC 497, 522, 533–34. Section 68(1) of the 1938 Act defined a "trade mark" as "a mark used or proposed to be used" as source designator by the trademark proprietor. This was understood to mean that the mark should be used or proposed to be used in the United Kingdom since the 1938 Act did not purport to provide for extraterritorial rights or redress extraterritorial infringement.

there could be no place for a rule resulting in an automatic "exhaustion" of trademark rights once a product bearing the relevant mark is placed on the market somewhere in the world.

In similar vein, there is no per se prohibition on dividing markets by assigning the national trademark rights to a subsidiary or a distributor in the United Kingdom. Courts have accordingly shown reluctance to lift the corporate veil so that a company established to serve the purpose of holding property assets, such as trade mark registrations in the United Kingdom, could not be deemed to have applied the mark in the jurisdiction simply because the mark has been used in some part of the world by the parent company or one of its other subsidiaries unless the existence of separate corporate entities could be said to constitute a "mere facade."[20] Rather than reflecting a formalistic approach in applying the law, the interpretation of section 4(3)(a) by the courts had been aimed at effectively implementing the traditional common law approach to the treatment of parallel imports in an era of statutes.[21]

All this did not mean, however, that traders were simply able to rely on the UK registration to oppose undesired parallel imports. In the absence of specific contractual stipulations to the contrary, the default rule would apply, treating the unqualified sale of goods as the grant of a consent to their further commercialization by the trademark registrant. In effect, the courts have interpreted the provision in a manner that shifts the determinative part of the analysis to the assessment of the consent requirement, thereby implementing the traditional common law approach which hinged upon whether the trademark proprietor has taken appropriate steps to ensure that subsequent buyers are bound by contractual terms restricting the sale of the trademarked good. Importantly, the conditions imposed on the buyer did not run with the goods. Due to the privity of contract, subsequent buyers would not be bound by the conditions accompanying the initial sale, unless the trademark proprietor took measures to ensure continued compliance of third parties with these terms. This would normally happen through the affixation of relevant notice upon the goods or by requiring the buyer to impose the same restrictions on subsequent buyers.

In the context of assessing whether there has been (implied) consent for the marketing in the United Kingdom of goods placed into circulation abroad pursuant to section 4(3)(a) of the 1938 Act, the corporate structure within which the owner of the UK registration operated did matter. UK courts would take into account the commercial realities of globalized trade characterized by economic operators organized as multinational concerns to rationalize their functions in order to exploit international markets. Where someone trades internationally using a web of legal entities whose operation is controlled by them, then the unqualified sale of an article by a member of the group within the UK jurisdiction counts as a use of the mark that is consented to by that trader, who is actually the "puppeteer" of the group, regardless of who is the owner of the domestic registration.[22] This pragmatic approach was sensible because it protected the legitimate

[20] *Id.* at 523; *Revlon Inc. and Others* v. *Cripps & Lee Ltd and Others* [1980] FSR 85; Buckley LJ noted that while the acts of a subsidiary could be attributed to the parent, the opposite, namely to attribute the parent's act to the subsidiary, could not hold true because the subsidiary is not the controlling party. *Id.* at 107. Templeman LJ was of a different view, arguing that legal technicalities should not lead us to distinguish between the case where the national trademarks are owned by the same company and the case where those IP rights are owned by separate legal entities belonging to the same group. *Id.* at 116. In the end, Buckley LJ explicitly preferred to base his decision on the existence of consent and Templeman LJ, recognizing the ambivalence of the matter, noted that he would alternatively rule for the defendant on the same ground. *Id.* at 107 and 117.

[21] *See* also Graeme B. Dinwoodie, *The Common Law and Trade Marks in an Age of Statutes*, *in* THE COMMON LAW OF INTELLECTUAL PROPERTY – ESSAYS IN HONOUR OF PROFESSOR DAVID VAVER 331, 341 (Catherine W. Ng, Lionel Bently, & Giuseppina D'Agostino eds., 2010) (explaining how the sufficiently open-ended language of trademark statutes allows courts to reach conclusions they would have likely reached relying on the common law principles of trademark law).

[22] *Revlon* v. *Cripps*, 107–08 (Buckley LJ); *see also id.* at 117 (Templeman LJ).

expectations of those with awareness of the fact that a mark may point to a group of companies as the source of goods marketed internationally, while leaving it open for the trademark proprietor to impose restrictions on the further commercialization of the goods it has marketed. It recognized "the legal and factual position resulting from the mutual relationship of the various companies" without actually piercing the corporate veil.[23]

In *Revlon*[24] the plaintiff company, an established manufacturer of cosmetics and toiletries, extended its product line to market an anti-dandruff version of the shampoo it had been successfully selling for quite a while in the United States. Unhappy with the project's performance, the plaintiff decided to withdraw the product and dispose of the remaining stock. Some of those bottles ended up with the defendants, who sought to import them into the United Kingdom. Although the goods were indeed associated in the course of trade with the plaintiff, it was not certain whether the trademark proprietor had consented to the use of the mark when the goods were first marketed. This was because the party actually owning the registrations of the marks "REVLON" and "REVLON FLEX" was not the plaintiff but a Swiss subsidiary. Sensibly, the High Court ruled that the plaintiff should be treated as the proprietor within the meaning of section 4(3)(a) of the 1938 Act for the purpose of assessing whether the junior use has been consented to because it had the authority to control every aspect related to the operation of its subsidiaries and was itself actually the party to which the benefit of the trademark inured.[25] Furthermore, quality control over the product was exercised by the plaintiff alone. All surrounding circumstances suggested that the plaintiff implicitly provided its consent to the further commercialization of the goods. Importantly, Revlon had not sold any of its products subject to an export ban.[26]

In contrast, the trademark proprietor was able to prevail in *Castrol*.[27] Burmah Oil Co. marketed motor oil under the mark "GASTROL GTX" through its wholly owned subsidiaries. Burmah-Castrol Canada was manufacturing and selling its product under a licence restricted to Canada whereas Castrol was responsible for the UK market, owning the respective national registrations. The mark's use in Canada was held not to constitute an application of the mark in the United Kingdom. Moreover, the importation could be enjoined since the licence agreement clearly indicated there was no consent to the use of the marks outside Canada. Purchasers were notified about this restriction through a notice affixed to the containers sold in Canada.

In *Colgate-Palmolive* v. *Markwell*, the local subsidiary was licensed to use various COLGATE trademarks in Brazil to market toothpaste made from cheaper raw materials available there.[28] Those products were inferior to the brands marketed in the United Kingdom. It was held that by marketing Brazilian toothpaste in the United Kingdom, the defendants made themselves liable for passing off by falsely representing to the consumers that the imported goods were in terms of their quality equal to the product they were familiar with already.[29] As regarding the claim based on trademark infringement, the Court of Appeal noted that the sale of Colgate toothpaste in Brazil did not involve the use of the UK trademarks and, in any event, the agreement with the

[23] *Id.* at 105 (Buckley LJ).

[24] *Id.* at 85.

[25] *Id.* at 105–08 (Buckley LJ); *see also id.* at 117 (Templeman LJ).

[26] *Id.* at 104. There was also no misrepresentation as to the origin of the goods. The shampoos were branded as "REVLON New York-Paris-London." In addition, all the companies involved pursued common marketing policies acting jointly worldwide as the "Revlon Group." As a result thereof, consumers viewed all products bearing the mark as stemming from the REVLON group and not from one of its members (*see id.* at 103).

[27] *Castrol Ltd* v. *Auto. Oil Supplies Ltd* [1983] RPC 315.

[28] *Colgate-Palmolive* [1989] RPC 497.

[29] *Id.* at 508–17 (Slade LJ); *see also id.* at 529–31 (Lloyd LJ).

Brazilian subsidiary provided for an obligation to refrain from exporting the goods marketed under licence to countries where Colgate subsidiaries existed.[30] *Colgate* and *Castrol* were distinguished from *Revlon* on the grounds that such contractual restrictions were in place.[31] Notably, the courts did not seek to provide an answer to the legal problem of parallel imports by simply focusing on the source-identifying function of trademarks. Even in cases where the public would attribute the parallel imported goods to a group of companies to which the proprietor of the UK registration belonged, the courts would strive to give effect to lawful contracts regulating the distribution of the relevant goods.

The decision of the Court of Appeal in *Colgate* added a significant qualification to the general principle established in *Champagne Heidsieck*. No consent to the parallel importation of an article put into circulation in another country could be implied when a trader had adopted a vertical differentiation strategy marketing different versions – in terms of quality – of the same product with a view to better matching diverse consumer preferences in international markets the importation of which would give rise to a misrepresentation to consumers regarding the quality of the goods. In essence, the court modified the default rule to consider trader interests it deemed worthy of protection.[32] Similarly, in *Castrol* the court held that Burmah Oil Co. had not consented to the importation of the goods given that the motor oil marketed in Canada differed in viscosity from the product meant for UK consumption.[33] Importantly, the court stressed that the outcome was justified by the need to protect the quality function of the trademark.[34] Rather than justifying the outcome purely in terms of the need to avoid damage to reputation resulting from attribution of lower quality to the trademark proprietor, the reference to the quality function of trademarks indicates that the court invoked the interests of the consuming public as a legitimizing ground for trademark protection standing on equal footing with trader interests. At the same time, the court addressed concerns about the fairness of competition, which were previously the exclusive domain of the cause of action based on passing off.[35]

C *Appraisal of the Common Law Approach*

The focus of the common law approach in the United Kingdom has been to formulate the optimal default rule. Freedom of trade was set as the default rule and it applied regardless of whether the initial act of commercialization took place within the jurisdiction or abroad. The opposite would not only have been absurd but also totally inefficient to contract around. In any event, the distribution of the goods, and consequently parallel imports, could be controlled through contractual arrangements whose legality had to be ascertained pursuant to legal rules other than those of trademark law. While trademark rights did not, by their nature, confer upon the proprietor any right to control distribution, the exclusive right vested in a registered UK trademark could be relied upon in practice to enforce contractual terms prohibiting parallel imports and restrictions imposed on registered users. The registration of a registered user agreement pursuant section 28(4)(c) of the 1938 Act required the proprietor to furnish the details

30 *Id.* at 520–29 (Slade LJ); *see also id.* at 532–36 (Lloyd LJ).

31 *Colgate-Palmolive*, 526–27 (Slade LJ); *Castrol*, 324. *See also* Helen Norman, *Parallel Imports from Non-EEA Member States: The Vision Remains Unclear*, 22 Eur. Intell. Prop. Rev. 159, 160 (2000).

32 Daniel Alexander, *Colgate-Palmolive v. Markwell Finance – The Carving Knife Sharpened*, 12 Eur. Intell. Prop. Rev. 456, 459 (1989).

33 *Castrol*, 324–25.

34 *Id.*

35 On this point, *see* Anselm Kamperman Sanders & Spyros M. Maniatis, *A Consumer Trade Mark: Protection Based on Origin and Quality*, 11 Eur. Intell. Prop. Rev. 406 (1993).

of any conditions or restrictions proposed with respect to the characteristics of the goods, to the mode or place of permitted use, or to any other matter. Failure to observe the conditions stipulated in a registered agreement on behalf of a registered user amounted to trademark infringement.[36] The liberal approach of the common law, which retained its vitality until the implementation of the Trade Marks Directive in the United Kingdom, rested on the premise that distribution controlled through lawful private contracts is more efficient than a radical "first sale" rule that would categorically eradicate the possibility of any such restrictions.[37] In developing a functional approach, after having derived the basic principle from an analogy to existing precedent, the judicial opinions took into account all the interests at stake, those of trademark proprietors, competitors, parallel importers, and the consuming public.

III THE DOCTRINE OF EXHAUSTION IN GERMAN TRADEMARK LAW

A *The Rejection of the Implied Licence Doctrine and the Birth of the Exhaustion Doctrine*

The Germans were very sceptical about the implied licence theory.[38] If, for instance, it were necessary for sub-purchasers other than the original buyer to obtain consent from the patentee to use a patented article, the concern was that then patentees would have the possibility of inhibiting competition or reducing the flow of distribution channels towards private consumers by imposing *erga omnes* restrictions to the further commercialization of products. In the quest of an alternative theory, Josef Kohler formulated the so-called theory of cohesion between the various forms of commercial use with respect to a patented article (*Lehre vom Zusammenhang der Benutzungsarten*).[39] According to this theory, which views all subsequent uses of a specific patented article by its various buyers as one single use in legal terms, the use of a patented article by a sub-purchaser constitutes simply a continuation of the use to which the original buyer was entitled. The patentee could not, therefore, impose restrictions on sales to third parties because those were deemed to simply continue a lawful use that the patentee had already authorized after selling the article for the first time. Apparently, the theory operated independently from the will of the patentee, who was unable to circumvent it. The latter point marks the fundamental difference between the traditional UK approach, which is characterized by the prevalence of contract, and the traditional German approach, under which IP laws themselves prohibit rights holders from controlling the distribution channels of goods they have already sold.[40]

As German courts started to refine the principle, after applying it in contexts involving different types of IP rights, the doctrine of trademark exhaustion emerged. German and British courts were, in any event, unanimous that trademark rights do not themselves confer upon their

[36] WHITE & JACOB, *supra* note 18 at 257, 288–91.

[37] According to European law, implied consent could not be inferred by the fact that the trademark proprietor has not imposed any contractual reservations pertaining to the further commercialization of the goods that were first marketed outside the EEA. *See* Joined Cases C-414/99 to C-416/99, *Zino Davidoff SA* v. *A&G Imports Ltd*, *Levi Strauss & Co.* v. *Tesco Stores Ltd* and *Levi Strauss (UK) Ltd* v. *Costco Wholesale UK Ltd*, ECLI:EU:C:2001:617.

[38] For a concise overview of the historical development of the law in Germany, *see* Henning Harte-Bavendamm & Eva Scheller, *Die Auswirkungen der Markenrechtsrichtlinie auf die Lehre von der internationalen Erschöpfung*, 40 WRP 571, 573–74 (1994).

[39] JOSEF KOHLER, DEUTSCHES PATENTRECHT 452–59 (1900). *See also* Friedrich-Karl Beier, *Zur Zulässigkeit von Parallelimporten patentierter Erzeugnisse*, 45 GRUR INT. 1, 3 (1996).

[40] Christopher Heath, *Parallel Imports and International Trade*, 28 INT'L REV. INTELL. PROP. & COMPETITION L. 623, 624–26 (1997); Jens Schovsbo, *The Exhaustion of Rights and Common Principles of European Intellectual Property Law*, *in* COMMON PRINCIPLES OF EUROPEAN INTELLECTUAL PROPERTY LAW 169, 171–72 (Ansgar Ohly ed., 2012).

proprietor any authority to control distribution. What made things a bit more complicated was the fact that the scope of the statutory right provided for in paragraph 12 of the Warenbezeichnungsgestz of 1894, the German trademark statute of that time, included the authority to market goods bearing the mark registered. At first glance, this could have been taken to suggest that the trademark proprietor could assert the right to control the distribution channels of goods bearing their mark.

In 1902, the Imperial Court of Justice (Reichsgericht) provided a solution to this legal problem by creating the doctrine of exhaustion.[41] The court ruled that the right to market goods under a registered trademark is "consumed" at the very moment the trademark proprietor places goods into circulation bearing that mark with the consequence that this particular right can no longer be asserted with respect to those specific goods.[42] The exhaustion doctrine was derived from the legal nature of the registration right, which, as a matter of positive law, protected trademarks only as source identifiers. Pursuant to paragraph 1 of the Warenbezeichnungsgestz, anyone who wishes to use a sign to distinguish their goods from the goods of other traders could apply to register it as a trademark. A trader of mineral water was accordingly not able to rely on its registered trademark rights in the mark "Kölnisch Wasser" to prevent the sale of its own products at a price lower than the resale price contractually imposed on those who directly bought the product from its commercial source. Apart from the fact that the trademark rights involved had been exhausted, the plaintiff was also not able to prevail because, as the court noted, the contractual terms imposing resale price maintenance on the first buyers could not have any binding effect on those who are not parties to the contract. Notably, trademark law did not have any effect on the legality of distribution restrictions.[43] In any event, the lack of remedies in contract could not be compensated by the assertion of trademark rights. In view of their legal nature as exclusive rights in a source identifier, those rights could not serve the additional function of protecting the interest position of a trademark proprietor who had entered into such contracts.[44]

B The Principle of Universality as Justification for a Rule of International Exhaustion

Within the same year, the Reichsgericht was called upon to decide whether the principle established in the *Kölnisch Wasser* case could be invoked to deny the proprietor of a German trademark any authority to prevent the parallel importation of goods branded with the same mark by the party who owned the registration in a foreign jurisdiction.[45] In particular, a French manufacturer who marketed a health beverage labelled as "Vin Mariani" had obtained registrations for the sign "Mariani" in France and the sign "V. Mariani" in Germany. Eventually, the rights of use associated with the German registration were transferred to a local company which was set up by a third party who had agreed to act as the exclusive distributor of the beverage in Germany for a certain period of time. That company filed suit for trademark infringement against another trader who was selling bottles of Vin Mariani, which had been originally marketed in France, to German consumers.

41 RGZ 50, 229 – *Kölnisch Wasser* (Ger.).

42 *Id.* at 231.

43 Adolf Baumbach & Wolfgang Hefermehl, Warenzeichenrecht § 15 Rn. 47, 668 (12th ed. 1985); Dietrich Reimer, *Der Erschöpfungsgrundsatz im Urheberrecht und gewerblichen Rechtsschutz unter Berücksichtigung der Rechtsprechung des Europäischen Gerichtshofs*, 21 Grur Int. 221, 223 (1972).

44 *Kölnisch Wasser*, 232.

45 RGZ 51, 263 – *Mariani* (Ger.).

In the context of patent law, German courts had already held that the parallel importation of goods lawfully acquired in the land of exportation could not be deemed as continuation of a single lawful use within the jurisdiction of importation because it was not derived by the domestic patent. In light of the principle of territoriality, the theory of cohesion between the various types of commercial use was held inapplicable to cases involving independent national patents regardless of whether they were owned by the same legal or natural person.[46]

In *Mariani*, the Reichsgericht had to rule upon whether those principles developed in the field of patent law were also applicable to trademarks. The court answered in the negative.[47] In contrast to patents, trademarks were, in the view of the court, universal and not national rights since they were recognized throughout the world (principle of universality).[48] Accordingly, the right in a trademark is first established in some home jurisdiction and then extended to other countries (principle of unity). The protection afforded in other jurisdictions is accessory to that granted in the home jurisdiction (principle of uniformity).

The plaintiff sought to rely on the fact that the French retailers were bound by contract not to export the goods in Germany. Given the accessorial nature of the protection granted to a universal trademark and given that, according to French law, the trademark proprietor could rely on their exclusive right in the mark to enforce distribution restraints provided for in contracts with retailers against third parties who had knowledge of those contractual terms, the court should, in the plaintiff's view, provide the same protection in Germany.[49] The Reichsgericht, however, did not accept that argument. As the court noted, the principle of accessory protection does not require the domestic jurisdiction to apply the rules on the legality of trademark transactions of the country in which the universal trademark was originally established. It simply secured protection of the same subject matter in the domestic jurisdiction. According to German law, which was applicable, trademark rights could not be asserted against third parties to implement contractual terms agreed upon between the proprietor and those who directly bought the trademarked good from them.[50]

The principle of universality was derived from a broader theory, which viewed the protection of personality rights as the actual justification for protecting trademarks.[51] Hence, trademark protection extended across the world just like the protection of personality rights but it was only available, of course, if the party seeking protection had obtained a registration and/or exercised commercial activity in the jurisdiction where protection was sought.

C International Exhaustion under the Principle of Territoriality

In the early days of trademark protection in Germany, traders had to rely on the criminal sanctions available against fraud and falsification.[52] The next step was for the legislator to introduce a specific criminal offence targeting trademark misuse.[53] Consumer deception and

46 *Id.* at 266–67.
47 *Id.* at 267–68.
48 *See generally* Hans Peter Kunz, Die Verletzung Des Markenrechts Durch Unerwünschte Importe von Originalwaren 5–6 (1966).
49 *Mariani*, 268.
50 *Id.*
51 Ulrich Loewenheim, *Nationale und internationale Erschöpfung von Schutzrechten im Wandel der Zeiten*, 45 GRUR Int. 307, 308 (1996).
52 Josef Kohler, Das Recht des Markenshutzes 39 et seq. (1884).
53 Elmar Wadle, Fabrikenzeichenschutz und Markenrecht, Historisch-Dogmatische Grundlinien des Markenschutzes 280 et seq. (1983).

economic loss were required for criminal liability to attach. Due to their exclusive focus on consumer deception as opposed to confusion in the modern sense, those criminal law rules were not capable of providing optimal protection for trademarks because they did not take due account of the interest position of traders. It was thus necessary to provide for subjective rights of individuals in trademarks. The first German trademark statute (Gesetz über Markenschutz) entered into force in 1874. Several doctrinal issues remained unresolved at that point, however, the most important one being the exact locus of the newly introduced trademark statute within the legal order. Subsuming a statute under a broader set of rules sharing a common regulatory goal was very important for the application of the law. It facilitated the derivation of those teleological and systematic legal arguments that a judge should resort to in order to adjudicate issues not explicitly addressed by the legislator. Josef Kohler contributed his theory suggesting that trademark protection was meant to enhance personality rights, which led to the adoption by the courts of the principle of universality as discussed above.[54]

This derivation of legal rules from principles pervading statutory law, rather than precedent, is generally speaking one of the typical features of the civil law approach.[55] Principles would often be dethroned, however, when it turns out they do not really conform with what may be clearly ascertained as positive law at a later stage. While developing the principles further, the courts adopt a functional approach.

In 1927 the Reichsgericht explicitly rejected the universality principle mainly because it was incompatible with the system of protection established by the Paris Convention and the Madrid Agreement.[56] For a while it remained uncertain whether the rule of international exhaustion established in *Mariani*, whereby exhaustion of IP rights is triggered by sales in any part of the world, would retain its vitality under the new governing legal principle. It was in 1964 that the German Federal Supreme Court of Justice (Bundesgerichtshof) had the opportunity to rule on this issue of law.[57] A Spanish company marketed soap internationally under the mark "Maja." It had obtained registrations in Spain, Germany and other countries. Later on, that company engaged an exclusive distributor in Germany to which the use of the respective national trademarks was licensed. Trademark infringement proceedings were initiated by the distributor against the marketing of genuine goods, which had been originally placed on the market in Spain by the owner of the national registration.

At the core of the court's analysis lies the observation that the principle of territoriality does not necessarily imply that uses occurring abroad bear no effect upon the legal position of the trademark proprietor in the jurisdiction.[58] Whether the sale of the goods abroad would qualify as an "application" of the national mark to the goods or constitute "marketing" of the goods under the mark leading to the exhaustion of the respective national rights, was essentially a matter of interpretation of the applicable German statute. According to the court, the principle of territoriality did not necessarily imply the owner of a national registration would, without more, be in a position to prevent parallel imports.[59]

To ascertain the meaning of the law, the court fell back on the method of interest balancing, which had been the driving force for the development of unfair competition law.[60] Courts

[54] Kohler, *supra* note 52 at 73 et seq.; Josef Kohler, Warenzeichenrecht 62 et seq. (1910).

[55] *See generally*, Rudolf B. Schlesinger, Comparative Law: Cases–Text–Materials 275–78 (1960).

[56] RGZ 118, 76, 81–82 – *Hengstenberg* (Ger.). *See also* Kunz, *supra* note 48 at 8–9 (1966).

[57] BGH [Bundesgerichtshof], 66 Grur Int. 372 – *Maja*.

[58] *Id.* at 374. *See also* Gerhard Riehle, Markenrecht und Parallelimport 78–81 (1968).

[59] *Id.* at 374–75.

[60] *See generally* Alfons Kraft, Interessenabwagung und Gute Sitten im Wettbewerbsrecht (1963).

would rely on this method to administer the general clause contained in the unfair competition statute of 1909, which prohibited those competitive acts that contravened good morals. Along with trader interests, the courts would consider the interests of competitors and consumers as well as the broader public interest in an undistorted competition.[61] By means of this method, courts were able to apply the law to unprecedented circumstances and assess the legality of previously unknown means for obtaining a competitive advantage. Its application in the area of trademark law could also be doctrinally justified by the fact that courts and commentators had, in the meantime, explicitly recognized the systematic adherence of trademark law to the broader field of competition law.[62]

The court started its analysis by determining the trademark proprietor's interest position, which it sought to derive from the legal nature of trademark rights as this was inferred from the provisions of the trademark statute. By their nature as source identifiers, trademark rights are neither meant to control the distribution of the trademarked good nor supposed to ensure the observance of contractual terms imposed by the trademark proprietor.[63] In the view of the court, the interest of a trader in setting up separate distribution schemes for individual countries was not an interest protectable under the trademark statute.[64] Holding the opposite would, in the court's view, undermine the welfare effects of free trade.[65] The flow of commerce would be unduly inhibited if purchasers were required to examine whether trademarked goods had been put into circulation abroad before. In an era where national economies were gradually getting more and more intertwined, it would not make sense, in the view of the court, to have a legal perception of the market for a specific good as being confined to the geographical boundaries of a national territory.[66] Were the capacity to partition national markets to be treated as part of the bundle of authorities reserved for the rights holder, the latter could then maintain high prices and artificially determine the estuaries of distribution channels without it being possible to object to those practices on the grounds of competition law.[67]

Seemingly, the BGH was calling for an approach based on legal realism following its own perception of commercial reality. The court was concerned with the optimal scope of the property right because there was no way for competition law to prevent the exercise of IP rights. According to the then prevalent "content theory"[68] ("Inhaltstheorie"), antitrust law could not intervene to deprive the owner of IP rights of authorities that formed the subject matter of the legal exclusivity. Moreover, it was considered preferable, for practical reasons, to regulate the legality of restraints to distribution through other areas of law.[69]

[61] On those concepts *see generally* Frauke Henning-Bodewig, *Unfair Competition Law – An Introduction to a Complex Topic, in* INTERNATIONAL HANDBOOK ON UNFAIR COMPETITION 1–8 (Frauke Henning Bodewig ed., 2012).

[62] On this development and its implications, *see* Friedrich-Karl Beier & Annette Kur, *Das Verhältnis von Markenrecht und Recht des unlauteren Wettbewerbs im Wandel der Zeiten, in* FESTSCHRIFT FÜR WOLFGANG FIKENTSCHER ZUM 70. GEBURTSTAG 478–93 (Bernhard Grossfield, Rolf Sack, Thomas M. J. Mollers, Josef Drexl & Andreas Heinemann eds., 1998).

[63] *Maja*, 374–75.

[64] *Id.* at 375.

[65] *Id.*

[66] *Id.*

[67] *Id.*

[68] *See generally*, Josef Drexl, *Intellectual Property Rights as Constituent Elements of a Competition-based Market Economy, in* INTELLECTUAL PROPERTY AND MARKET POWER – ATRIP PAPERS 2006–2007, 167–78 (Gustavo Ghidini & Luis Mariano Genovesi eds., 2008) (contrasting the "content theory" with the theory of complementarity); WOLFGANG FIKENSCHER, WETTBEWERB UND GEWERBLICHER RECHTSSCHUTZ – DIE STELLUNG DES RECHTS DER WETTBEWERBSBESCHRÄNKUNGEN IN DER RECHTSORDNUNG 284–85 (1958).

[69] Friedrich-Karl Beier, *Territoriality of Trademark Law and International Trade*, 1 INT'L REV. INTELL. PROP. & COMPETITION L. 48, 71 (1970).

In technical terms, the court justified the outcome by referring to the origin and quality function as the only functions of trademarks that enjoyed legal recognition.[70] Trademark rights were not absolute but rather qualified property rights with their scope being dependent upon which trademark functions, or aspects thereof, positive law protects.[71] With its *Maja* decision, the BGH firmly established the doctrine of international exhaustion of trademark rights in Germany.[72]

Cinzano[73] was the next important decision that came to elaborate upon the principles established by the BGH in *Maja*. The case concerned an Italian vermouth brand. In Italy, the product was marketed by the parent company, which owned the national registration. The Italian product was imported into Germany by a subsidiary. A series of nearly identical CINZANO marks were registered in Germany. Some of those registrations were owned by the parent company while others were owned by the German subsidiary. Different versions of the product were marketed in France and Spain to match the diverse preferences of local consumers. The Spanish subsidiary and the French licensee manufactured the national version, using some local wine as a basis. Quality control was exercised by the Italian company. The German subsidiary sued for trademark infringement a trader who had imported bottles of CINZANO originally marketed in France and Spain. All imported goods bore labels that identified those products as "French" and "Spanish" vermouth respectively.

In the court's view, the fact that the national registrations implicated in the case were owned by separate legal entities was irrelevant to the application of the exhaustion principle, as this was established in *Maja* where the marks were owned by the same company.[74] In contrast to the United Kingdom approach, the BGH gave absolute prominence to the freedom of trade over the interests of traders whose distribution policies relied on partitioning national markets. Those traders could not partition the German market by assigning the national trademark rights to a separate legal entity and designing contractual terms that would prevent parallel imports into Germany. In fact, the essential function of trademarks was expanded to include, apart from an identification of a particular commercial source, the indication of common origin from a group of companies that are trading at an international level.[75]

The opinion of the court reflects a conscious balance of interests which took into consideration the concerns of traders in avoiding damage to reputation that would accrue if a product version of lower quality meant for distribution in foreign markets was imported into Germany, where traders had sought to acquire reputation with products that are differentiated to match diverse consumer preferences within the various national markets.[76] Such interest was not protectable under German trademark law which did not recognize the "guarantee function" of trademarks as a legally protected function. Trademarks do not provide the consumers with any guarantee of constant quality but with an instrument of control allowing them to punish low quality. It is only that latter aspect of the quality function that is legally protected.

[70] *Maja*, 374–75.

[71] *See generally*, REINHOLD EMMERT, DIE STELLUNG DER MARKENLIZENZ IM DEUTSCHEN PRIVATRECHT 37–49 (2001) (noting how the focus on the trademark functions ensures that the trademark proprietor does not obtain a right to control all possible uses of the mark); RUPERT SCHREINER, DIE DIENSTLEISTUNGSMARKE: TYPUS, RECHTSSCHUTZ UND FUNKTION 415–35 (1983).

[72] KARL-HEINZ FEZER, MARKENRECHT, § 24 Rn. 7–8 (4th ed. 2009) (explaining how the exhaustion doctrine was derived from the origin function of trademarks).

[73] BGH, 75 GRUR, 468 (1973) – *Cinzano* (Ger.).

[74] *Id.* at 470.

[75] BAUMBACH & HEFERMEHL, *supra* note 43, § 15 Rn. 55 at 673–74; *see also* Beier, *supra* note 69 at 71.

[76] *Cinzano*, 470–71.

The court noted that trademark proprietors in the position of the parent company could protect their interests by making use of labels that would inform the consumers about the attributes of their goods.[77]

D Appraisal of the German Approach

In contrast to the approach taken by the British Court of Appeal in *Colgate*, the BGH declined to extend the exclusionary scope of trademark rights to protect interests other than those associated with the avoidance of confusion as to source.[78] This has to be attributed partly to a competition ideal that was characterized by the goal to confine IP rights to the narrowest scope possible and partly to the conviction that trademark law is not the right instrument to protect those other interests. The strong adherence to the protection of the origin function reflects a policy decision not to allow proprietors to exercise any control whatsoever over the commercialization of their trademarked goods at any stage of the distribution channels that lead to the final consumer by virtue of their exclusive rights. Accordingly, the German trademark statute, the Warenzeichengesetz of 1936, contained no provision analogous to section 28(4)(c) of the UK Trade Marks Act 1938, which would render the violation of some licensing terms that are key to the administration of an effective distribution system an infringing act. Violations of terms stipulated in a trademark licence would only result in contractual remedies.[79]

This marks a significant difference between the UK approach, which recognizes that trademark rights do not create distribution monopolies but may be relied upon to implement lawful contracts containing resale restrictions on registered users and prohibitions on parallel imports, and the German approach, which rejects the notion of contractual resale restraints being enforced through the assertion of trademark rights.

German trademark law came to recognize the important role of trademark enforcement in maintaining the integrity of distribution systems when the Markengesetz of 1994 came into force implementing the First Trade Mark Directive (TMD).[80] In paragraph 30, the Markengesetz provides that the violation of specific contractual terms on behalf of the licensee amounts to trademark infringement. The grave practical significance of this rule is that the action for trademark infringement may be directed against third parties who market an infringing product.[81] Exhaustion of rights is precluded due to the licensee's intervening act of infringement.

IV THE DISTRIBUTION FUNCTION OF TRADEMARKS AS AN ELEMENT OF HARMONIZED EUROPEAN TRADEMARK LAW

In light of the above, it seems that any divergence between a UK approach stemming from traditional common law principles and the continental European approaches to the same issue

[77] The court also held that the labels indicating the geographical origin of the goods were sufficient to exclude deception as to the quality (taste) of the product because consumers were aware of the fact that goods stemming from one undertaking may feature differences attributed to their geographical origin or other market conditions in the country of manufacture. Hence, the claim based on unfair competition was rejected as well. *Id.* at 471.

[78] BAUMBACH & HEFERMEHL, *supra* note 43, § 15 Rn. 56 at 674–75 (reviewing the antithetical lines of argumentation adopted by various scholars).

[79] *Id.* at 672–73. *See also* RUDOLF BUSSE, WARENZEICHENGESETZ 298 (1960).

[80] First Council Directive 89/104/EEC of Dec. 21, 1988 to approximate the laws of the member states relating to trademarks, [1989] OJ L040/1 (EC) [hereinafter TMD].

[81] See also FEZER, *supra* note 72 at § 30 Rn. 28–31 (drawing a comparison to the law as it stood under the Warenzeichengesetz of 1936).

are primarily attributable to the different trade and competition policies that separate jurisdictions wished to pursue as a matter of national policy rather than to the particularities of their individual methods of ascertaining the law. It is indicative that, prior to the harmonization of national trademark laws in Europe, some civil law jurisdictions adhered to the principle of international exhaustion while others recognized the authority of the trademark proprietor to enjoin undesired parallel imports.[82] Eventually, as Irene Calboli further elucidates in her corresponding chapter on trademark exhaustion (Chapter 36), harmonized European law opted for a system of regional exhaustion[83] with a view to promoting the integration of the single market and the competitiveness of European traders. Economic operators may not partition the internal market by assigning or licensing national rights to subsidiaries or other economically affiliated entities.[84] While European courts have been unanimous all along that there is nothing in the nature of trademark rights suggesting that they confer upon their proprietors the authority to control the distribution of trademarked goods already placed on the market with their consent, trademarks have come to play an important role in maintaining the integrity of distribution systems.

In the case of *Copad*, the CJEU highlighted the role modern trademark rights may play in securing the effectiveness of established distribution systems.[85] Where a licensee contravenes provisions of the licensing contract imposing marketing obligations to maintain the trademark's prestige, such as prohibitions on sales to discount stores, the trademark proprietor can assert their rights against that licensee on the grounds of the latter violating a contractual term that refers to the quality of the licensed goods or services pursuant to Article 8(2) TMD (Article 25(2) of Directive 2015).[86] For the trademark proprietor to be successful in this claim, they must establish that the defendant's acts are indeed likely to damage "the allure and prestigious image, which bestows upon the goods an aura of luxury."[87] Notably, the trademark proprietor can assert their right against third parties to enjoin such harmful resales. Since the licensing contract was breached, any sales of the licensed goods by the licensee were not commenced with the consent of the rights holder. Hence, no exhaustion of rights took place. The practical significance of that case is grave. As long as a trader imposes licensing terms that establish marketing obligations towards the maintenance of brand image that are lawful, they could rely on their trademark

[82] For an overview of the rules adopted in the various national jurisdictions in Europe before the First Trade Mark Directive, *see* Friedrich-Karl Beier & Alexander von Mühlendahl, *Der Grundsatz der internationalen Erschöpfung des Markenrechts in den Mitgliedstaaten der EG und ausgeqählten Drittstaaten*, 71 MITT. D. PATENTANWÄLTE 101 (1980); KUNZ, *supra* note 48 at 25–47; RIEHLE, *supra* note 58 at 250–62. Under the traditional approach in Italy, for instance, trademark rights could be relied upon to oppose parallel imports as long as the trademark registration in the state of export was owned by a different party. This rule applied even when the proprietor of the Italian trademark was a subsidiary or a licensee of the party that owned the foreign registration. Furthermore, an exclusive distributor could rely on its trademark rights to prevent parallel imports despite the fact that both the national and the foreign registration were owned by the principal. In most national jurisdictions of Europe, important legal issues related to parallel imports had not been conclusively addressed by the courts at the time trademark laws in Europe had to be harmonized.

[83] Case C-355/96, *Silhouette Int'l Schmied GmbH & Co. KG* v. *Hartlauer Handelsgesellschaft mbH*, ECLI:EU:C:1998:374.

[84] Joined Cases 56 and 58–64, *Établissements Consten SàRL and Grundig-Verkaufs-GmbH* v. *Comm'n. of the Eur. Econ. Cmty.*, ECLI:EU:C:1966:41; Case C-9/93, *IHT Internationale Heiztechnik GmbH and Uwe Danzinger* v. *Ideal-Standard GmbH and Wabco Standard GmbH*, ECLI:EU:C:1994:261; Case C-291/16, *Schweppes SA* v. *Red Paralela SL and Red Paralela BCN SL*, ECLI:EU:C:2017:990.

[85] Case C-59/08, *Copad SA* v. *Christian Dior couture SA, Vincent Gladel and Société industrielle lingerie (SIL)*, ECLI:EU:C:2009:260.

[86] Directive 2015/2436, of the European Parliament and of the Council of Dec. 16, 2015 to approximate the laws of the member states relating to trademarks, 2015 OJ (L336/1) [hereinafter Directive 2015].

[87] *Copad*, 37.

rights to enjoin unauthorized harmful uses by third parties bound to undermine the integrity and the effectiveness of their distribution system. Recently, the CJEU ruled that even online sales bans may be justified as a means to maintain brand image from a competition law perspective, provided also that the general requirements for the legality of selective distribution systems are met.[88] This further suggests that trademark proprietors will often be able to control some important aspects of the commercialization of their products in online markets as well.

Despite the robust policy in favour of parallel trade, there are quite a few instances where the trademark proprietor has indeed the opportunity to exercise a significant degree of control over the distribution channels of the trademarked good. As has always been the case, the trademark proprietor would be in a position to prevent the marketing of goods they have volitionally put into circulation, where their distribution involves dealings with them that adversely affect their original condition.[89]

National registrations provide their owners with substantial leeway for implementing marketing strategies involving the use of different packaging or even different trademarks within the internal market. Specifically, the CJEU has ruled that the trademark proprietor may oppose the importation of trademarked goods placed on the internal market with their consent in cases where a product is being imported into a member state after being repackaged, relabelled, reboxed, overstickered or rebranded. The rights holder has legitimate reasons to oppose the importation within the meaning of Article 15(2) Directive 2015 (Article 7(2) TMD) because the aforementioned activities of the parallel importer are liable to imperil the origin function of the mark.[90] It is no longer possible for the mark to offer to the consumers a guarantee that the trademarked good has not been subject at a previous stage of marketing to interference by a third person without the authorization of the trademark owner in such a way as to affect the original condition of the product.

There are, of course, limits to this exception to the principle of free movement of goods, which aims to protect proprietary interests in national trademark registrations. The assertion of trademark rights should not give rise to an artificial partitioning of the internal market. Accordingly, repackaging, relabelling, reboxing, overstickering and rebranding may be objectively necessary to ensure effective access to the market of a member state or a substantial part thereof.[91] Such necessity may exist, for instance, with regard to pharmaceutical products when national regulation or rules related to the reimbursement of health expenses require the product to be packaged in a specific way[92] or in cases where there is a strong resistance from a significant part of the consuming public to relabelled pharmaceutical products.[93]

Even in those cases of necessity, the trademark proprietor may still be able to prevail if some requirements are not met which have been established to safeguard their legitimate interests.[94]

88 Case C-230/16, *Coty Germany GmbH* v. *Parfümerie Akzente GmbH*, ECLI:EU:C:2017:941.

89 Art. 7(2) TMD (art. 15(2) Directive 2015).

90 Joined Cases C-427/93, C-429/93 and C-436/93, *Bristol-Myers Squibb* v. *Paranova A/S and C. H. Boehringer Sohn, Boehringer Ingelheim KG and Boehringer Ingelheim A/S* v. *Paranova A/S* and *Bayer Aktiengesellschaft and Bayer Danmark A/S* v. *Paranova A/S*, ECLI:EU:C:1996:282, [43]–[51]. Case C-379/97, *Pharmacia & Upjohn SA* v. *Paranova A/S*, ECLI:EU:C:1999:494, 31–32; Case C-143/00, *Boehringer Ingelheim KG, Boehringer Ingelheim Pharma KG, Glaxo Group Ltd., The Wellcome Foundation Ltd, SmithKline Beecham plc, Beecham Group plc, SmithKline & French Laboratories Ltd and Eli Lilly and Co.* v. *Swingward Ltd and Dowelhurst Ltd*, ECLI:EU:C:2002:246, 34–35 [hereinafter *Boehringer I*]; Case C-348/04, *Boehringer Ingelheim KG and Others* v. *Swingward Ltd and Dowelhurst Ltd*, ECLI:EU:C:2007:249, 32 [hereinafter *Boehringer II*].

91 *Bristol-Myers*, 52–57; *Pharmacia & Upjohn*, 46; *Boehringer I*, 50.

92 *Bristol-Myers*, 53.

93 *Boehringer I*, 51–52.

94 *Bristol-Myers*, 67–79.

Among others, the parallel importer must give the trademark proprietor advance notice of the trademarked good being put on sale. The requirement of advance notice facilitates the efforts of brand owners to combat counterfeiting.[95] Most importantly, the presentation of the product must not be such as to be liable to damage the reputation of the mark and its owner.[96] Untidy or poor-quality packaging of pharmaceuticals is bound to cause such harm, especially when those products target the ultimate consumer and not professionals.[97] The trademark proprietor would be able to enforce their rights against the parallel importer on the same reputational grounds even when there is nothing wrong with the quality of the new packaging itself. When luxury goods, for instance, are resold or advertised under circumstances that do not correspond to their perceived image of luxury and exclusivity, the trademark proprietor has the authority to oppose the further commercialization of goods they placed on the market with their consent provided that the alleged harm to their reputational interests is serious.[98] Depending on the circumstances, de-branding and co-branding may be deemed as detrimental to the trademark's reputation.[99]

Repackaging and rebranding would be deemed unnecessary, and therefore illegal, if they are explicable solely by the parallel importer's attempt to secure a commercial advantage.[100] This requirement may be relied upon to address free-rider problems within distribution networks.

Finally, yet importantly, the trademark proprietor would be able to successfully assert their rights against a parallel importer who has removed the products' identification numbers provided that this would not give rise to an artificial portioning of the internal market.[101] Identifiers of that kind may be necessary to promote legitimate purposes such as the compliance with legal obligations related to product identification, the recall of faulty products and the implementation of measures to combat counterfeiting.

V CONCLUSION

On that note, it is fair to say that, at least from the perspective of harmonized European trademark law, trademark rights also have an evolving "distribution function."[102] The rule of regional exhaustion allows for the implementation of distribution strategies that rely on the absence of undesired parallel imports into EU's internal market.[103] Nowadays, trademark rights play a significant role in safeguarding the integrity of distribution systems and the maintenance of brand image while the trademarked good is still in circulation and has not reached the ultimate consumer yet.

[95] *Id.* at 78.
[96] *Id.* at 75; *Boehringer II*, 40–44.
[97] *Bristol-Myers*, 77.
[98] Case C-337/95, *Parfums Christian Dior SA and Parfums Christian Dior BV* v. *Evora BV*, ECLI:EU:C:1997:517, 48. See also Case C-324/09, *L'Oréal SA* v. *eBay International AG*, ECLI:EU:C:2011:474, 83.
[99] *Boehringer II*, 45–47.
[100] *Pharmacia & Upjohn*, 44; *see also Boehringer II*, 37.
[101] Case C-349/95, *Frits Loendersloot* v. *George Ballantine & Son Ltd and Others*, ECLI:EU:C:1997:530, 39–43. *See also* FEZER, *supra* note 72 at § 24 Rn. 167–69 (noting the importance of that aspect of trademark protection for the protection of selective distribution systems).
[102] FEZER, *supra* note 72 at Einl D Rn. 12–17. This distribution function partly overlaps with the broad advertising function encompassing the trademark proprietor's reputational interests, which the CJEU circumscribed in *Parfums Christian Dior SA and Parfums Christian Dior BV*, 39–48.
[103] *See, e.g.*, Case C-535/13, *Honda Giken Kogyo Kabushiki Kaisha* v. *Maria Patmanidi AE*, ECLI:EU:C:2014:2123; Case C-129/17, *Mitsubishi Shoji Kaisha Ltd. and Mitsubishi Caterpillar Forklift Europe BV* v. *Duma Forklifts NV and G. S. Int'l BVBA*, ECLI:EU:C:2018:594.

36

The Relationship between Trademark Exhaustion and Free Movement of Goods

A Review of Selected Jurisdictions and Regional Organizations

*Irene Calboli**

I INTRODUCTION

This chapter complements the chapter authored by Professors Chronopoulos and Maniatis (Chapter 35) and focuses on the relationship between the principle of exhaustion in trademark law and the free movement of goods in the context of cross-border trade and parallel imports – imports of genuine goods that are not authorized by trademark owners. In particular, this chapter reviews the national and regional policies on trademark exhaustion in selected jurisdictions, namely: the European Union (intended as a group of sovereign countries applying a harmonized trademark law); the United States, Canada, and Mexico, as the three nation members of the North American Free Trade Agreement (NAFTA, soon to be renamed the United States, Mexico, and Canada agreement, USMCA); the members of the Association of South East Asian Nations (ASEAN); the People's Republic of China; and India.

As a result of this survey, this chapter highlights how different countries or regional organizations follow different policies regarding the regulation of trademark exhaustion based on a variety of national economic and trade-related interests. For example, small economies which are often importers of Intellectual Property (IP) protected goods and user-based economies, seem to follow a more liberal approach towards trademark exhaustion, as these countries are interested in increasing competition and product availability in their national markets through trade policies that favour international trade and parallel imports. To the contrary, larger economies which frequently house IP-intensive industries tend to favour a more protectionist approach to promote their national industries and shield them from the additional competition of parallel imports.[1]

* Professor of Law, Texas A&M University School of Law; Academic Fellow, School of Law, University of Geneva. This chapter is based on my previous research which has been published most recently in the monograph SHUBHA GHOSH & IRENE CALBOLI, EXHAUSTING INTELLECTUAL PROPERTY RIGHTS: A COMPARATIVE LAW AND POLICY ANALYSIS (2018). I thank Jane Ginsburg for comments on previous drafts, and Lee Chedister and Victoria Gonzales for research and editorial assistance.

[1] *See, e.g.*, the contributions in IRENE CALBOLI & EDWARD LEE (EDS.), RESEARCH HANDBOOK ON INTELLECTUAL PROPERTY EXHAUSTION AND PARALLEL IMPORTS (2016). *See also* Christopher Heath, *Parallel Imports and International Trade*, 28 I.I.C. 623 (1997); Herman Cohen Jehoram, *International Exhaustion versus Importation Right: A Murky Area of Intellectual Property Law*, 4 G.R.U.R. INT'L 280 (1996); John C. Hilke, *Free Trading or Free-Riding: An Examination of the Theories and Available Empirical Evidence on Gray Market Imports*, 31 WORLD COMPETITION L. & ECON. REV. 75 (1988).

In particular, this chapter shows that today a considerable number of countries, including IP-producing countries, seem to accept parallel imports into their jurisdictions provided the owners of the marks affixed to the imported products are the same in the domestic and foreign markets (the so called common origin principle) so the marks can continue to perform their traditional function of indicators of commercial origin. However, several countries prohibit these imports when the imported products "differ materially" from the goods authorized for sale in the domestic market, unless specific labels are applied to the goods disclosing these differences, and thus preventing consumer confusion. This approach reflects an interpretation favouring parallel imports so long as trademarks continue to perform their function of indicators of the products' quality and characteristics and consumers are not confused in this respect.

This chapter limits its analysis to the free movement of physical goods (sold through traditional bricks-and-mortar channels and online) and does not include analysis of the exhaustion of trademark rights related to digital goods. This chapter also does not elaborate on how contractual clauses (primarily in licensing and other distribution agreements) can be used to limit the resale of products in foreign markets, how these clauses may impact the application of domestic policies on trademark exhaustion even though the validity of these clauses is not accepted uniformly, and how several jurisdictions accept parallel imports even when the goods have been imported in breach of foreign contractual clauses. Last, this chapter does not address the competition-related aspects of these contracts, which could potentially represent anticompetitive practices.[2]

II A BRIEF REVIEW OF THE RELATIONSHIP BETWEEN TRADEMARK EXHAUSTION AND FREE MOVEMENT OF GOODS

Trademark rights grant owners the right to exclude third parties from using signs identical or similar to those registered and/or using them for identical or similar products, when such use could lead to a likelihood of confusion for the public.[3] For the owners of famous marks, this right extends to the ability to exclude third parties from using identical or similar signs when these signs are used on non-similar products where such use is likely to take unfair advantage of, or damage, the marks' distinctiveness or reputation – the so-called protection of famous trademarks against "trademark dilution."[4] Whether confusion-based or fame-based, trademark protection encounters the shared limiting principle of exhaustion. This principle, also referred to as "trademark first sale" in the United States, provides that the right "to control distribution of [] trademarked product does not extend beyond the first sale of the product"[5] and that "[the]

[2] For a detailed review of these aspects, *see* Shubha Ghosh & Irene Calboli, Exhausting Intellectual Property Rights: A Comparative Law and Policy Analysis (2018).

[3] *See* William M. Landes & Richard A. Posner, *Trademark Law: An Economic Perspective*, 30 J.L. & Econ. 265, 265–66 (1987); Nicholas S. Economides, *The Economics of Trademarks*, 78 Trademark Rep. 523, 526 (1988); William P. Kratzke, *Normative Economic Analysis of Trademark Law*, 21 Mem. St. U. L. Rev. 199, 205 (1991).

[4] *See* Frank I. Schechter, *The Rational Basis of Trademark Protection*, 40 Harv. L. Rev. 813, 818 (1927) ("The true functions of the trademark are, then, to identify a product as satisfactory and thereby to stimulate further purchases by the consuming public"). For a critical analysis of anti-dilution laws in the United States and Europe, *see* Chapters 29 and 30 in this volume.

[5] *Sebastian Int'l, Inc. v. Longs Drug Stores Corp.*, 53 F.3d 1073, 1074 (9th Cir. 1995).

resale by the first purchaser of the original article under the producer's trademark is neither trademark infringement nor unfair competition."[6]

As Professors Chronopoulos and Maniatis have explained in detail in their chapter, trademark exhaustion finds its rationale in the principle that trademarks must not be used as a tool to control market distribution or as a means of market division beyond trademarks' protected function as indicators of commercial origin and guarantors of consistent product quality.[7] In principle, once goods have been lawfully distributed into the market, the act of reselling the same goods does not create consumer confusion regardless of whether these subsequent acts of product distribution are performed by third parties instead of trademark owners or their authorized distributors. More specifically, regardless of who is performing these subsequent distribution acts, the marks affixed to these products continue to perform their original function of indicating to the public the actual commercial origin and quality of the products (at least so long as there are no undisclosed material differences in the domestic and imported goods).[8]

The origin of this principle dates back to the late nineteenth century, a period of profound change in product manufacturing and distribution. During this time, new layers of intermediaries were added to the traditional channels of product marketing. This, in turn, led to attempts by manufacturers to control product distribution after they introduced goods into the market. Yet courts generally disfavour trademark owners' use of trademark rights to bind the buyers of their goods – retailers and consumers – to arbitrary terms of subsequent sale, for example, by fixing prices for retailers or preventing secondary markets for used goods. As courts in North America explain it, this position was necessary to create a "demarcation line between two colliding properties: the intellectual property right of the producer and the common proprietary right of the owner of [the] product he has bought."[9] In other words, the product's proprietary owner "should remain free to enjoy the specific privileges of traditional ownership: he should be free to resell or otherwise dispose of his property."[10]

Still, as I have explained in detail before, while this principle has been generally accepted regarding the distribution of products originating within national markets, national legislators "have struggled with the question whether [trademark owners] ought to be able to block" the importation of genuine products originating outside the national markets – so-called parallel imports.[11] This struggle is directly reflected in the lack of any international provision on the issue. Instead, Article 6 of the Agreement on Trade-Related Aspects of Intellectual Property Rights (TRIPS) famously states that "[n]othing in this Agreement shall be used to address the issue of the exhaustion of intellectual property rights."[12] In the absence of any international guideline on the issue, nation

[6] *Id.* at 1074.

[7] *See* Chapter 35 in this volume. *See also*, Ghosh & Calboli, *supra* note 2, at 65.

[8] *See Yamaha Corp. of Am. v. United States*, 961 F.2d 245, 248 n. 2 (DC Cir. 1992) ("'Genuine' goods are goods that are in fact manufactured by the same manufacturer that supplies the U.S. trademark holder… [T]hey *are* the genuine article, although they may not have been intended for distribution in the U.S. market").

[9] Cohen Jehoram, *supra* note 1, at 280.

[10] *Id.*

[11] *See* Irene Calboli, *Trademark Exhaustion in the European Union: Community-Wide or International? The Saga Continues*, 6 Marq. Intell. Prop. L. Rev. 47, 53–59 (2002) [hereinafter Calboli, *Trademark Exhaustion in the EU*]; Irene Calboli, *Reviewing the (Shrinking) Principle of Trademark Exhaustion in the European Union (Ten Years Later)*, 16 Marq. Intell. Prop. L. Rev. 257 (2012) [hereinafter Calboli, *Reviewing Trademark Exhaustion*]; Timothy H. Hiebert, Parallel Importation in U.S. Trademark Law 1 (1994).

[12] Agreement on Trade-Related Aspects of Intellectual Property Rights, Apr. 15, 1994, Marrakesh Agreement Establishing the World Trade Organization, Annex 1C, Legal Instrument – Result of the Uruguay Rounds Vol. 31, 33 ILM 83, 1869 UNTS 299 (1994), art. 6 [hereinafter TRIPS]. On the drafting of art. 6 of TRIPS, *see* Herman Cohen Jehoram,

states have adopted different approaches regarding the geographical extent of their national regimes of trademark exhaustion. These approaches can be grouped into three categories: national exhaustion, international exhaustion, and regional exhaustion.

Notably, the principle of *national exhaustion* provides that trademark rights are considered exhausted only when products have been distributed for sale into the domestic territory by the mark's owners, or with their consent, by, for example, an affiliated company, a licensee, distributor, or agent.[13] Under this principle, trademarkowners can oppose the importation (or reimportation) into the domestic market of genuine goods bearing their trademark (of the same or different quality) that are imported from a foreign country without their consent, even when the national trademark owner authorized the use of the mark on the goods for foreign markets.[14] Trademark owners have traditionally favoured this principle because it affords them the ability to price differentiate and control product distribution across different jurisdictions.[15]

At the opposite end of the spectrum, under the principle of *international exhaustion*, trademark rights are considered exhausted after the mark's owner, or someone authorized by them, has sold the goods anywhere in the world.[16] International exhaustion, however, does not apply if the goods imported under the mark are not the same, either because the goods have been altered without the domestic trademark owner's consent,[17] or, in some jurisdictions, because the goods, although genuine, are of materially different quality than the products distributed under authorization by trademark owners in the national market.[18] In both instances, these differences in the goods or their quality could lead to consumer confusion.

Last, a hybrid solution has emerged as a compromise between national and international exhaustion – *regional exhaustion*. Under this principle, national trademark rights granted by each member of a regional agreement are exhausted after the trademark owner places the goods on the market in any of the national territories of the members of the agreement.[19] Yet while trademark owners cannot object to the further circulation of those goods within the boundaries of the regional free trade area,[20] they can still oppose the importation of goods first sold outside the national territories of the members of that region.[21]

Prohibition of Parallel Imports through Intellectual Property Rights, 30 I.I.C. 495, 508 (1999) (noting that this provision represents a compromise between two opposite approaches: "[t]he US Proposal [to introduce its own national system,] national exhaustion[,] and the [pleas of] developing countries . . . for the opposite," international exhaustion); Stanislaw Soltysinsky, *International Exhaustion of Intellectual Property Rights under the TRIPS, the EC Law and the Europe Agreements*, 4 G.R.U.R. Int'l 316, 317–20 (1996).

13 To date, national exhaustion with respect to trademark rights seem to be a less frequent choice among World Trade Organization (WTO) members, even though most members practise national exhaustion with respect to patents and copyrights. *See* International Trademark Association (INTA), *Position Paper on Parallel Imports*, July 2007, http://inta.org/Advocacy/Documents/INTAParallelImports2007.pdf at 5.

14 *See generally* Jesper Rasmussen, *The Principle of Exhaustion of Trade Mark Rights Pursuant to Directive 89/104 (and Regulation 40/94)*, 4 E.I.P.R. 174 (1995) (describing the effects of the different types of trademark exhaustion).

15 INTA, *supra* note 13, at 5.

16 *See, e.g.*, S. K. Verma, *Exhaustion of Intellectual Property Rights and Free Trade – Article 6 of the TRIPS Agreements*, 29 I.I.C. 534, 539 (1998).

17 *See* TRIPS, *supra* note 12, art. 16 (providing the general principle against trademark infringement that member countries have to follow).

18 Hiebert, *supra* note 11, at 153.

19 *See* Rasmussen, *supra* note 14, at 174.

20 *Id.*

21 *See* discussion *infra* Section III. To date, the other example of regional exhaustion for IP rights, including trademarks, is the *Organisation Africaine de la Propriété Intellectuelle* (OAPI), the regional organization for French-speaking countries in Africa.

III TRADEMARK EXHAUSTION IN THE EUROPEAN UNION/EUROPEAN ECONOMIC AREA: FORTRESS EUROPE AND CROSS-BORDER TRADE

As many of the chapters in this book have highlighted, trademark law has been harmonized throughout the EU member states since the adoption of the First Council Directive 89/104/EEC. This Directive was later replaced by Directive 2008/95, and more recently by Directive 2015/2436.[22] As part of this process, EU member states also harmonized the treatment of trademark exhaustion across the EU. In particular, Directive 89/104/EEC established the principle of Community-wide exhaustion as the general rule for all EU member states.[23] Until the adoption of this principle, individual EU member states followed separate national approaches, with some countries like the United Kingdom and Germany adopting international exhaustion, and others like Italy and France adopting national exhaustion.[24] Yet individual and diverging positions on trademark exhaustion could not continue, as one of the EU's fundamental objectives was to promote the free movement of goods within the territory of the EU member states.[25] The adoption of a common rule on trademark exhaustion (and IP exhaustion in general) was crucial to achieve this purpose.

In particular, first Article 7(1) of Directive 89/104/EEC and today Article 15(1) of the 2015 Directive prescribe that trademark rights "shall not entitle the proprietor to prohibit its use in relation to goods which have been put on the market in the Community under that trade mark by the proprietor or with his consent."[26] In the 1990s, soon after the adoption of Directive 89/104/EEC, some EU member states (notably the United Kingdom and Germany) tried to argue that this principle was only a minimum standard and that countries with a more liberal approach – i.e. international trademark exhaustion – could retain their previous regimes. However, the Court of Justice of the European Union (CJEU or, as referred to then, the European Court of Justice, ECJ) clarified that Community-wide exhaustion was the *only* applicable criterion and national rules providing different exhaustion regimes needed to be amended.[27] This position was necessary, the ECJ ruled, because any national variation from a common principle would have resulted in having the equivalent effect of a barrier to EU-wide trade.[28] The same principle was introduced verbatim in the language of Council Regulation EC/40/94, which created a supranational EU right, and was later replaced by Council Regulation 207/2009 (Community Trademark Regulation), and now has been replaced by

[22] Council Directive 89/104, 1989 OJ (L 40) 1 (EC), replaced by European Parliament and Council Directive 2008/95, 2008 OJ (L 299) 25 (EC) [hereinafter Trademark Directive], and repealed by European Parliament and Council Directive 2015/2436, 2015 OJ L336/1 (EU) [hereinafter 2015 Directive].

[23] Trademark Directive, art. 7(1), replaced by art. 15 of the 2015 Directive starting in January 2019.

[24] *See, e.g.*, Friedrich-Karl Beier, *Industrial Property and the Free Movement of Goods in the Internal European Market*, 21(4) I.I.C. 131 (1990).

[25] Consolidated Version of the Treaty on the Functioning of the European Union, Mar. 30, 2010, 2010 OJ (C 83) [hereinafter TFEU] as amended following the entering into force of the Treaty of Lisbon on Dec. 1, 2009. Treaty of Lisbon, Dec. 13, 2007, 2007 OJ (C 306).

[26] Trademark Directive, art. 7(1), replaced by art. 15 of the 2015 Directive starting in January 2019.

[27] Case C-355/96, *Silhouette Int'l Schmied* v. *Hartlauer Handelsgesellschaft*, 30 INT'L REV. INTELL. PROP. & COMP. L. 920 (1998); Case C-173/98, *Sebago Inc. & Ancienne Maison Dubois et Fils AS* v. *GB-Unic SA*, 1999 CMLR 1317; Joined Cases C-414/99–C-416/99, *Zino Davidoff SA* v. *A & G Imports Ltd*; *Levi Strauss & Co.* v. *Tesco Stores Ltd*; *Levi Strauss & Co.* v. *Costco Wholesale UK Ltd*, 2001 ECR I-8691; C-324/08, *Makro Zelfbedieningsgroothandel CV*, *Metro Cash & Carry BV*, *Remo Zaandam BV* v. Diesel SpA, 2009 ECR I-10019. *But see* Case C-306/96, *Javico Int'l & Javico AG* v. *Yves Saint Laurent Parfums SA*, 1998 ECR I-1983 and *Mag Instrument Inc.* v. *California Trading Co.*, 29 INT'L REV. INTELL. PROP. & COMP. L. 316 (EFTA 1998).

[28] *See* the analysis elaborated in the decisions in note 27.

EU Trademark Regulation 2017/1001 (EU Trademark Regulation).[29] The adoption of the Agreement for the European Economic Area (EEA) of 2 May 1992, extended this principle to the European Free Trade Agreement (EFTA) countries joining the EEA (Norway, Iceland, and Liechtenstein).[30] Accordingly, trademark rights are exhausted in the EU/EEA only when the goods are put into the market in an EU/EEA member state while genuine goods coming from outside "Fortress Europe" can be legally stopped at the will of IP owners as IP infringements.[31]

The importance of the free movement of goods within the EU was such that, in the early years of the European Economic Community, the ECJ promoted free movement of goods by applying the competition law provisions of the Treaty on the Functioning of the European Union (TFEU) – then the Treaty Establishing the European Economic Community (EEC Treaty).[32] In subsequent years, the ECJ turned to Articles 34 and 36 of the EEC Treaty, which entered into force a few decades after the adoption of the EEC Treaty and specifically provide rules to promote free movement. In particular, Article 34 prohibits quantitative restrictions on imports within the member states and other measures having "equivalent effect,"[33] while Article 36 prohibits "arbitrary discrimination or a disguised restriction of trade between Member States."[34] The ECJ applied these provisions in the context of trademark exhaustion, on the ground that there was no reason to prevent the free circulation of goods within the EU when the goods were identified by marks controlled by the same companies in the member states at issue.[35] The ECJ clarified that trademark owners could block parallel imports within the EU only when the marks affixed on the products did not share a common origin,[36] or when the products had been altered without the trademark owners' consent.[37]

In 1979, the ECJ also developed the principle of "mutual recognition" in the case *Cassis de Dijon*. Here, the ECJ stated that EU member states could not "prohibit the sale in [their] territory of a product lawfully produced and marketed in another Member ... even if the product is produced according to technical or quality requirements which differ from those imposed on its domestic products."[38] Following this ruling, European legislators undertook the harmonization of existing national technical standards to promote further integration within the EU market. In 1985, the European Council adopted the New Approach to Technical

[29] Council Regulation 40/94 of Dec. 20, 1993, on the Community Trade Mark, 1994 OJ (L 011) 1 (EC), replaced by Council Regulation 207/2009, 2009 OJ (L 78) 1 (EC), and now replaced by EU Trademark Regulation (EU) 2017/1001 of the European Parliament and of the Council of June 14, 2017 on the EU trademark, 2017 OJ L 154/1 (EC).

[30] Protocol to the Agreement on the European Economic Area on Jan. 3, 1994, 1994 OJ (L 1) Annex XVII, art. 2(1) extended the effect of art. 7 of the Trademark Directive to the EEA from Jan. 1, 1994.

[31] *See, e.g.*, Carl Steele, *"Fortress Europe" for Trademark Owners*, 1998 Trademark World 14 (Aug. 1998).

[32] *See* TFEU, arts. 101–02; Joined Cases 56 & 58/64, *Costen & Grunding* v. *EC Comm'n*, 1966 ECR 299; Case 24/67, *Parke Davis* v. *Centrafarm*, 1968 ECR 55; Case 40/70, *Sirena* v. *Eda*, 1971 ECR 69.

[33] TFEU, art. 34.

[34] TFEU, art. 36.

[35] Case 78/70, *Deutsche Grammophon Gesellschaft mbH* v. *Metro-SB-Grossmarket GmbH*, 1971 ECR 487; Case 16/74, *Centrafarm BV* v. *Winthrop BV*, 1974 ECR 1183, 1194; Case 3/78, *Centrafarm BV* v. *Am. Home Prods. Corp.*, 1978 ECR 183; Case 1/81, *Pfizer Inc.* v. *Eurim-Pharm GmbH*, 1981 ECR 2913.

[36] *Compare* Case 192/73, *Van Zuylen Freres* v. *Hag AG*, 1974 ECR 731 *with* Case 119/75, *Terrapin Ltd* v. *Terranova Industrie CA Kapferer & Co.*, 1976 ECR 1039 and Case C-10/89, *CNL-Sucal* v. *Hag AG*, 1990 ECR I-3711; *see also IHT Internationale Heiztechnik GmbH* v. *Ideal-Standard GmbH* 1994 ECR I-2782.

[37] Case 102/77, *Hoffmann-La Roche & Co.* v. *Centrafarm Vertriebsgesellschaft Pharmazeutischer Erzeugnisse mbH*, 1978 ECR 1139, 1164–65.

[38] The ECJ developed the principle of "mutual recognition" in Case 120/78, *Rewe-Zentral AG* v. *Bundesmonopolverwaltung fur Branntwein*, 1979 ECR 649 (*Cassis de Dijon*). *See also* Commission Communication No. C 256/2, 1980 OJ (C 256) 2, 2–3 (EC).

Harmonization and Standards,[39] under which independent European standards organizations would develop the actual technical standards complying with these requirements.[40] In the following decades, EU/EEA member states continued to increase compliance with European standards to promote product uniformity within the EU as part of a new legislative framework.[41] Member states also continued, and continue, to be subject to the principle of mutual recognition.[42]

Still, some exceptions apply to the principle of Community-wide trademark exhaustion. Article 7(2) of Directive 89/104/EEC, now Article 15(1) of the 2015 Directive, state that trademark proprietors could "oppose further commercialization of the goods" when these present "legitimate reasons" such as "where the condition of the goods is changed or impaired after they have been put on the market."[43] The ECJ/CJEU has clarified the meaning of what constitutes a "legitimate reason"[44] in several decisions. For example, it held the unauthorized repackaging and relabelling of genuine products can constitute a "legitimate reason" when this may lead to consumer confusion or provoke unfair detriment to the reputation of a mark.[45] The most problematic decision in this respect was *Copad SA* v. *Christian Dior Couture*,[46] issued a decade ago. Notably, the CJEU stated that a breach of contract – a clause expressly prohibiting sales to discount stores in order to "maintain the repute and prestige" of the mark – could fall within the reasons to deny "trademark owners' consent" under Article 7(1), and at the same time could represent a "legitimate reason" to oppose a product's further distribution in the EEA under Article 7(2).[47] As I have critically observed in the past, this decision considerably limited the application of trademark exhaustion to parallel imports of luxury goods within the EU/EEA.[48]

IV TRADEMARK EXHAUSTION IN THE UNITED STATES, CANADA, AND MEXICO: THE LAISSEZ FAIRE APPROACH OF THE NORTH AMERICAN FREE TRADE AREA

Unlike the EU, the members of NAFTA–the United States, Canada, and Mexico–do not adopt a common policy on trademark exhaustion. All the members follow, however, a system of international exhaustion. This position is unchanged in the new agreement, the United States–Mexico–Canada Agreement (USMCA), recently signed to replace NAFTA.[49]

39 Council Resolution of 7 May 1985 on a new approach to technical harmonization and standards, 1985 OJ (C 136) 1 (EC).
40 European Commission, Enterprise Directorate General, Vademecum on European Standardisation (2004).
41 *See* Ghosh & Calboli, *supra* note 2, at 72.
42 Council Resolution of Oct. 28, 1999 on mutual recognition, 2000 OJ (C141/2).
43 Trademark Directive, art. 7(2); 2015 Directive, art. 15.
44 Case C-349/95, *Loendersloot* v. *Ballantine & Son Ltd*, 1997 ECR I-6227; Case C-337/95, *Parfums Christian Dior SA* v. *Evora BV*, 1997 ECR I-6013; Case C-59/08, *Copad SA* v. *Christian Dior Couture SA & ors.*, 2009 ECR I-3421.
45 *Copad*, 2009 ECR I-3421; Case C-558/08, *Portakabin Ltd, Portakabin BV* v. *Primakabin BV*, 2010 ECR I-0000; Case C-127/09, *Coty Prestige Lancaster Grp. GmbH* v. *Simex Trading AG*, 2010 ECR I-0000.
46 *Copad*, 2009 ECR I-3421.
47 *Id.*
48 Calboli, *Reviewing Trademark Exhaustion*, *supra* note 11, at 264.
49 *See* United States–Mexico–Canada Agreement (USMCA) (signed Nov. 30, 2018), art. 20.11 ("Exhaustion of Intellectual Property Rights: nothing in this Agreement prevents a Party from determining whether or under what conditions the exhaustion of intellectual property rights applies under its legal system"), https://ustr.gov/trade-agreements/free-trade-agreements/united-states-mexico-canada-agreement/agreement-between.

In general, the United States has traditionally allowed parallel imports of genuine goods carrying a trademark protected in the United States provided consumers are not confused on the origin or quality of the imported products.[50] The justification for this approach of international exhaustion derives from the principle that the public should be allowed to benefit from the lower prices usually accompanying parallel imports as long as consumers are not confused, and that trademark owners should not be allowed to control downstream distribution after the products have been legitimately sold in the marketplace, even if the sale takes place outside of the United States. Moreover, US law explicitly allows parallel imports when "both the foreign and the U.S. trademark are owned by the same person or business entity" or the owners of these marks are "parent and subsidiary companies or otherwise subjected to common ownership and control."[51] In this respect, US courts have held that sections 32 and 43(a) of the Lanham Act – respectively the infringement provisions for registered and unregistered trademarks – cannot be invoked to block importation of goods manufactured by a corporate affiliate of a US trademark owner.[52]

On the other hand, US courts have prohibited the importation of genuine products first marketed outside the United States when the imported goods "differ materially" from the goods authorized for sale in the domestic market.[53] This rule was first adopted in *Lever Brothers* and seeks to prevent the product quality-related confusion that could otherwise exist if two seemingly identical products of different quality are sold in the United States under the same mark.[54] In the past decade, US courts found a likelihood of confusion in several instances of imported products carrying "material differences,"[55] including in the case of "subtle differences."[56] Yet under the US Customs Service Regulations, materially different products can still be lawfully imported when importers properly label the goods to avoid confusion.[57] Notably, parallel importers can overcome the ban on the importation of genuine but materially different goods by affixing a prominent disclaimer on the goods stating: "This product is not a product authorized by the United States trademark owner for importation and is physically and materially different from the authorized product." The disclaimer must be "designed to remain on the product until the first point of sale to a retail customer in the United States."[58] In other words, proper labelling seems to be able to cure the likelihood of consumer confusion as to the quality of the goods,

[50] *See* Ghosh & Calboli, *supra* note 2, at 68.

[51] *K-Mart Corp.* v. *Cartier, Inc.*, 486 US 281, 289 (1988).

[52] *NEC Elecs.* v. *CAL Cir. Abco*, 810 F.2d 1506, 1510 (9th Cir. 1987). Note that § 43(b) of the Lanham Act allows civil actions to enjoin importation of any goods likely to infringe or dilute registered or unregistered trademarks (15 USC § 1125(b)). Moreover, § 42 authorizes US Customs and Border Protection (CPB) to prevent the importation of goods that infringe registered or unregistered trademarks (15 USC § 1124.). *But see infra* the exception provided by the US Customs Service Regulations (19 CFR § 133.23(b) (US)).

[53] This principle follows two decisions of the DC Circuit: *Lever Bros. Co.* v. *United States*, 877 F.2d 101 (DC Cir. 1989) and *Lever Bros. Co.* v. *United States*, 981 F.2d 1330 (DC Cir. 1993).

[54] *Id.*

[55] Mary LaFrance, *Wag the Dog: Using Incidental Intellectual Property Rights to Block Parallel Imports*, 20 Mich. Telecomm. & Tech. L. Rev. 45 (2013).

[56] *Societe des Produits Nestle, SA* v. *Casa Helvetia, Inc.*, 982 F.2d 633, 641 (1st Cir. 1992); *accord*, *Zino Davidoff SA* v. *CVS Corp.*, 571 F.3d 238, 243, 246 (2d Cir. 2009). *See* Mary LaFrance, *supra* note 55, at 53 (describing that material differences have been found in cases including: different product warranties; dolls with non-English-language accessories; soaps with different ingredients; candies produced in different size and with different calorie count; chocolates in different shapes; products whose quality control protocols were different; products whose packaging or labelling were different; and event products that were advertised and marketed differently).

[57] 19 CFR § 133.23(b) (US) ("Goods determined by the Customs Service to be physically and materially different … shall not be detained … where the merchandise or its packaging bears a conspicuous and legible label designed to remain on the product until the first point of sale").

[58] 19 CFR § 133.23(b).

and guarantees that marks continue to serve the function of indicating to consumers the origin of the products.

Like the United States, Canada has traditionally adopted a system of international trademark exhaustion since the late 1880s.[59] In particular, Canada's trademark statutes do not provide an exclusive importation right and courts have generally ruled that once products have entered the stream of trade anywhere in the world, their importation into the national territory is permitted and does not constitute trademark infringement when the same or affiliated owners control the marks both inside and outside Canada (common origin marks).[60] In other words, trademark owners cannot successfully turn to trademark or unfair competition law to block the importation and sale of goods manufactured overseas either by the Canadian trademark owner or by one of its affiliates or licensees.[61] Instead, Canadian trademark owners can oppose only the importation of products bearing marks identical or similar to marks in the instance where: (1) these marks are already in use in the national territory; (2) the marks are not owned or controlled by the same entity; and (3) the imported goods could create a likelihood of consumer confusion.[62]

But like the United States, Canadian courts have occasionally objected to the importation of goods carrying common origin marks when these goods were materially different from the products already sold directly or under the authorization of the trademark owners on the Canadian market and when these differences could create confusion for the public. However, judicial decisions in this respect have been inconsistent, even though the courts have generally found the imports unlawful when: the goods had been damaged and the distributor had replaced the original labels placed on the goods[63] or when the formulation of the imported goods was different than the products sold nationally.[64] Canadian courts have also carefully scrutinized the importation of products that required compliance with technical standards and only allowed their sale if importers disclosed to the public any differences regarding product standards.[65] Still, Canadian courts have been generally sympathetic toward unauthorized parallel importers. Moreover, where the goods differ in quality, proper labelling may preclude liability in Canada.[66] In particular, it seems that courts rarely prohibit the importation of genuine goods when the importers use labels to disclose that the goods are imported and may be of different quality.[67]

Finally, Mexico also adopts a system of international trademark exhaustion. According to Article 92(II) of the Mexican Industrial Property Law,[68] the registration of a mark cannot be used against "any person who markets, distributes, acquires or uses the product to which the

[59] *Condy* v. *Taylor*, [1887] 56 LTR 891 (Can.) (stating that no trademark infringement occurs when the goods are genuine goods manufactured by trademark owners).

[60] *Wilkinson Sword (Can.) Ltd* v. *Juda*, [1966] 51 CPR 55 (Can.); *Wella Canada Inc.* v. *Pearlon Prods. Ltd*, [1984] 4 CPR 3d 287 (Can. Ont. HCJ); *Coca-Cola Ltd* v. *Pardham*, [1999] 85 CPR 3d 489 (Can. FCA).

[61] *Consumers Distrib. Co.* v. *Seiko Time Canada*, [1984] 1 SCR 583; *Sony du Canada Ltée* v. *Impact Électronique* (1991), 39 CPR (3d) 414 (Que. SC); *Sony du Canada Ltée* v. *Multitronic Stéréo Inc.* (1991), 42 CPR (3d) 53 (Que. CA.); *Sharp Elecs. of Can. Ltd* v. *Cont'l Elec. Info. Inc.* (1988), 23 CPR (3d) 330 (BCSC); *Nestlé Enters. Ltd* v. *Edan Food Sales Inc.* (1991), 37 CPR (3d) 480 (FCTD).

[62] *Consumers Distrib. Co.* v. *Seiko Time Canada Ltd*, [1984] 1 CPR 3d 1, 13–14 (Can. SCC). This decision was codified in the Canadian Trade-marks Act of 1985, SC 1952–53, c. 49, *as amended*, RSC 1985, c. T-10 (Can).

[63] *Dupont of Canada Ltd* v. *Nomad Trading Co.*, [1968] 55 CPR 97 (Can. Que. SC).

[64] *See H. J. Heinz Co. of Canada* v. *Edan Foods Sales Inc.*, [1991] 35 CPR 3d 213 (Can. FCTD).

[65] *Consumers Distributing*, 1 CPR 3d 1. *But see Sharp Elec. of Canada Ltd* v. *Cont'l Elec. Info. Inc.*, [1988] 23 CPR 3d 330 (Can. BCSC).

[66] *Nestlé Enters. Ltd*, 37 CPR (3d) 480 (FCTD).

[67] *Consumers Distributing*, 1 CPR 3d at 24–25. *See also Nestle Enters. Ltd*, 37 CPR 3d 480 (Can. FCA).

[68] Ley de Fomento y Protección de la Propiedad Industrial [Mexican Industrial Property Law], Diario Oficial de la Federación [DOF], June 27, 1991, *as amended* Diario Oficial de la Federación [DOF], Aug. 2, 1994 (Mex.) [hereinafter Mexican Industrial Property Law].

trademark is applied for after the said product has been lawfully introduced on the market by the owner of the registered mark or his licensee."[69] Specifically, "[t]his case shall include the import of legitimate products to which the registered mark is applied, carried out by any person for their use, distribution or marketing in Mexico."[70] Even though the Mexican Industrial Property Law does not specify the geographical extent of the wording "the market" in Article 92, the Mexican Industrial Property Law Regulations clarify the issue. The Regulations deem parallel imports "legitimate" based upon two conditions: (a) that the goods are introduced into the market of the country from which they are imported by the "owner or licensee of the registered mark"; and (b) that the owner of the mark inside and outside Mexico is "the same person or members of the same joint economic interest group, or their licensees or sublicensees."[71]

As in Canada and the United States, Mexican trademark law prohibits the circulation of trademarked goods when unauthorized third-party importers have altered their quality,[72] have altered the mark or removed the mark altogether.[73] However, the Mexican Industrial Property Regulations do not prevent the importation of materially different genuine grey market goods and do not require special labelling for those goods to be admitted and lawfully circulate in the Mexican territory.[74] Moreover, to date, Mexican courts do not seem to have halted or expressed concern for consumer confusion in the case of importation into Mexico of materially different parallel imports.

In summary, the rules on trademark exhaustion are similar within the three members of NAFTA, and soon to be USMCA. This means trademark owners are generally unable to control further distribution of their products within NAFTA (and later USMCA), subject to the possibility of preventing the importation of goods of materially different quality. In all three countries, appropriate labelling can cure the existence of material differences between the imported products and the products sold nationally. However, unlike the EU/EEA, this similarity is based on individual national policies and subsequent judicial decisions, and does not respond to a specific design to harmonize national laws and promote free movement of goods within the trade area. Similar to TRIPS, NAFTA, and the USMCA, leave the countries free to adopt their preferred position on the geographic extent of their national rules on IP exhaustion.[75] Moreover, the United States, Canada, and Mexico do not follow a principle equivalent to the EU principle of mutual recognition, nor are they pursuing the harmonization of national technical standards to further facilitate trade within the trade area.[76]

V TRADEMARK EXHAUSTION IN SOUTH EAST ASIA: THE "WAIT AND SEE APPROACH" OF ASEAN

ASEAN was established in 1967 with the aim of integrating the ASEAN members into a regional economic organization.[77] However, unlike the EU, ASEAN members follow the principle of

[69] *Id.*, art. 92(II).
[70] *Id.*
[71] Reglamento de la Ley de la Propiedad Industrial [Regulation on the Industrial Property Law], Diario Oficial de la Federación [DOF], Nov. 18, 1994, art. 54 (Mex.) [hereinafter Mexican Industrial Property Regulation].
[72] Mexican Industrial Property Law, art. 213(XX).
[73] *Id.*, art. 213(XXI).
[74] Mexican Industrial Property Regulations, art. 54. The Mexican Industrial Property Regulations are also silent as to the case of imports concerning repackaged or relabelled goods.
[75] *See* North American Free Trade Agreement, Can.–Mex.–U.S., Dec. 17, 1992, 32 ILM 289 [hereinafter NAFTA], art. 714; *see also* USMCA, art. 20.11.
[76] *See* NAFTA, ch. 7B on sanitary and phytosanitary measures (SPS), and ch. 9 on technical barriers to trade (TBT).
[77] The ASEAN Declaration (Bangkok Declaration), Bangkok, Thailand, ASEAN, Aug. 8, 1967, https://asean.org/the-asean-declaration-bangkok-declaration-bangkok-8-august-1967/.

non-interference with national policies.[78] In addition, ASEAN never established regional institutions in charge of developing, administering, or ruling on issues related to ASEAN-focused policies. In 2003, the ASEAN members resolved to establish an ASEAN Community and, in 2007, adopted the ASEAN Charter.[79] One of the pillars of the ASEAN Community was the creation of the ASEAN Economic Community (AEC), launched in 2015[80] and aiming to create a single market that comprises the free movement of goods, services, investment, capital, and skilled labour.[81] The foundation of the ASEAN market can be traced to the Declaration on the ASEAN Economic Community Blueprint.[82] In 1992, ASEAN members signed an Agreement on the Common Effective Preferential Tariff Scheme for the ASEAN Free Trade Area[83] (AFTA) in order to foster regional economic integration and eliminate tariff and non-tariff barriers.[84]

As part of the process of integration, in 1995 ASEAN members adopted the ASEAN Framework Agreement on Intellectual Property Cooperation[85] aiming at establishing cooperation in several IP-related areas.[86] Based on the general principle of non-interference, ASEAN adopted "a more flexible IP cooperation model" which "enables its members to move forward collectively, but at varying paces in accordance with their developmental level and capacity."[87] To date, this cooperation has focused primarily on administrative matters, such as interoperability between and assistance with domestic procedures adopted for patent and trademark searches and the creation of regional databases.[88] Generally, IP laws of ASEAN members are already largely harmonized, as all ASEAN members are part of the World Trade Organization (WTO) and accordingly have to follow the principles set by TRIPS, as well as they are member of several of the international agreements administered by the World Intellectual Property Organization (WIPO).[89]

78 Treaty of Amity and Cooperation in Southeast Asia, Indonesia, ASEAN, Feb. 24, 1976, 2012 OJ (L 154) 6.

79 Declaration of ASEAN Concord II (Bali Concord II), ASEAN, Oct. 7, 2003, https://asean.org/?static_post=declaration-of-asean-concord-ii-bali-concord-ii; The ASEAN Charter, ASEAN, Nov. 20, 2007, https://asean.org/asean/asean-charter/charter-of-the-association-of-southeast-asian-nations/.

80 ASEAN members committed to accelerate the establishment of the ASEAN Economic Community in the Cebu Declaration on the Acceleration of the Establishment of an ASEAN Community by 2015.

81 For a detailed analysis of the creation of the AEC, *see* Stefano Inama & Edmund W. Sim, An Institutional and Legal Profile (2015).

82 ASEAN, Declaration on the ASEAN Economic Community Blueprint, § 11, 13, & 14, 2008, https://asean.org/?static_post=declaration-on-the-asean-economic-community-blueprint.

83 Agreement on the Common Effective Preferential Tariff (CEPT) Scheme for the ASEAN Free Trade Area (AFTA), art. 5, Jan. 28, 1992, WIPO Lex. No. TRT/AFTA/001 [hereinafter CEPT-AFTA], https://asean.org/?static_post=agreement-on-the-common-effective-preferential-tariff-cept-scheme-for-the-asean-free-trade-area-afta.

84 ASEAN Trade in Goods Agreement (ATIGA), art. 8(d), Feb. 26, 2009, WIPO Lex. NO. TRT ASEAN/001, http://investasean.asean.org/files/upload/Doc%2002%20-%20ATIGA.pdf.

85 ASEAN Framework Agreement on Intellectual Property Cooperation, Dec. 15, 1995, WIPO Lex. No. TRT/ASEAN-IP/001, https://asean.org/?static_post=asean-framework-agreement-on-intellectual-property-cooperation-bangkok-thailand-15-december-1995.

86 *Id.* at art. 3(1).

87 Elizabeth Siew-Kuan Ng, *ASEAN IP Harmonization: Striking the Delicate Balance*, 25 Pace Int'l L. Rev. 129 (2013).

88 *See* ASEAN, Hanoi Plan of Action, 1997, https://asean.org/?static_post=hanoi-plan-of-action; Intellectual Property Rights Action Plan 2004–2010, https://asean.org/?static_post=asean-intellectual-property-right-action-plan-2004-2010; ASEAN Secretariat, Work Plan for ASEAN Cooperation on Copyright, 2006; ASEAN Secretariat, Intellectual Property Rights Action Plan 2011–2015, https://asean.org/wp-content/uploads/images/2012/Economic/sectoral_aem/service/agreement/ASEAN%20IPR%20Action%20Plan%202011-2015.pdf; ASEAN Working Group on Intellectual Property Cooperation (AWGIPC), Intellectual Property Rights Action Plan 2016-2025, https://aseanip.org/Portals/0/ASEAN%20IPR%20ACTION%20PLAN%202016-2025%20(for%20public%20use).pdf?ver=2017-12-05-095916-273.

89 With the exception of Myanmar, all ASEAN members are signatories to the Paris Convention for the Protection of Industrial Property and to the Berne Convention for the Protection of Literary and Artistic Works, the two most relevant international agreements harmonizing national IP laws pre-TRIPS, which have also considerably harmonized substantive laws on IP across all members. *See* Paris Convention for the Protection of Industrial Property,

No common position has been adopted regarding the national treatment of trademark exhaustion, however, and ASEAN members remain free to decide their preferred national policies also based on the silence of TRIPS on this topic. In particular, ASEAN members can be divided into several separate groups: Singapore, Vietnam, Malaysia, the Philippines, Thailand, and Myanmar follow a system of international trademark exhaustion through legislative provisions or case law; Cambodia and Lao PDR follow a system of national exhaustion based on legislative provisions that have not yet been applied by the courts; Indonesia and Brunei do not have a specific rule on exhaustion.

Notably, in Singapore, the Trade Marks Act[90] excludes trademark infringement for goods distributed in the market "whether in Singapore or outside Singapore" with the "express or implied consent (conditional or otherwise)" of the trademark owners in Article 29(1).[91] The exception to this rule applies when "the condition of the goods has been changed or impaired after they have been put on the market" or "the use of the registered trade mark in relation to those goods has caused dilution in an unfair manner of the distinctive character of the registered trade mark."[92]

Similarly, in Vietnam, Article 125 (2)(b) of the Intellectual Property Law[93] provides statutory support for the principle of international trademark exhaustion.[94] Remarkably, the provision does not address the issue of products of different quality but states that the following does not constitute infringement: "circulating, importing, exploiting utilities of products having been lawfully put on the market, including overseas markets, except for products put on the overseas markets not by the mark owners or their licensees."[95]

In Malaysia, the Trade Marks Act provides a statutory exception to infringement for the imports of genuine goods.[96] In particular, section 40(1)(d) provides that it does not constitute infringement to use a mark (protected in Malaysia) with respect to products "connected in the course of trade" with the trademark owners as long as the trademark "has not subsequently removed or obliterated it."[97] The judiciary in Malaysia has embraced the application of the principle of international trademark exhaustion in the *Panadol* case,[98] where the court held that the parallel imports of goods sharing a common origin should be allowed.[99] Nevertheless, the court did not address the parallel importation of goods of different origins or with materially different qualities.[100]

Last, Myanmar did not have a law on trademarks and thus did not regulate the issue of exhaustion until very recently. However, a new trademark law draft was adopted in December 2018 and enacted in early 2019. As reported by the International Trademark Association (INTA), Article 41 of the new Myanmar Trademark Law adopts the principle of international

Mar. 20, 1883, *as revised* July 14, 1967, 21 UST 1583, 828 UNTS 305; The Berne Convention for the Protection of Literary and Artistic Works, Sept. 9, 1886, *as revised* July 24, 1971, and *as amended* Sept. 28, 1979, 102 Stat. 2853, 1161 UNTS 3.

90 Trade Marks Act, ch. 332 (2005) (Sing.).

91 *Id.*, § 29(1).

92 Trade Marks Act, *supra* note 90, at § 29; *see also* NG-LOY WEE LOON, INTELLECTUAL PROPERTY LAW OF SINGAPORE, 401–02 (2d ed. 2014).

93 Law No. 50/2005/QH11 of 2005, on Intellectual Property (Nov. 29, 2005) (Viet.).

94 *Id.*, art. 125(2)(b).

95 *Id.*

96 Trade Marks Act 1976, Act 175 (June 21, 1976) (amended by ACT A1138 OF 2002) (Malay.).

97 *Id.*, § 40(1)(d).

98 *Winthrop Prods. Inc. & Anor* v. *Sun Ocean (M) Sdn Bhd & Anor*, 2 MLJ 317 (1988).

99 *Id.*

100 LAZAROS G. GRIGORIADIS, TRADE MARKS AND FREE TRADE: A GLOBAL ANALYSIS 483 (2014).

exhaustion while Article 42 "prevents the importation of goods which have been altered after their initial sale."[101]

In contrast, the Philippines Intellectual Property Code does not explicitly include a provision on exhaustion.[102] According to Article 166, importation of an article into the Philippines which copies or simulates a mark registered in the Philippines is an infringement.[103] Since parallel imports involve genuine products – while the provision refers to counterfeits or infringing products – one may suppose that the principle of international exhaustion applies to the importation of genuine goods, even though the term is not explicitly mentioned. In addition, neither the Intellectual Property Code of the Philippines nor the Philippine courts have addressed the issues thus far relating to goods of materially different qualities for different markets.

Similarly, Thailand also has no express legislation regarding the exhaustion of trademark rights.[104] Nevertheless, the Thai Central Intellectual Property and International Trade Court[105] and the Thai Supreme Court have embraced international trademark exhaustion in their decisions.[106] In particular, a 1999 decision of the Thai Central Intellectual Property and International Trade Court allowed the parallel import of genuine goods bearing the same mark from Singapore to Thailand, stating that trademark rights are internationally exhausted because trademark owners have already fairly received rewards from the first sale of the goods. This decision was affirmed by the Supreme People's Court of Thailand in 2000.[107]

On the other hand, Cambodia and Lao PDR both adopted a system of national trademark exhaustion. Article 11(c) of the Cambodian Law[108] provides that "[t]he rights conferred by registration of a mark shall not extend to acts with respect to articles which have been put on the market in the Kingdom of Cambodia by the registered owner or with his consent."[109] Similarly, Lao PDR's Law on Intellectual Property states[110] in Article 57 (as revised) that "A trademark owner has the following rights: ... (2) to prevent the sale or advertising of goods bearing the mark or the use of the mark in connection with services, and the importation or export of goods bearing such a mark."[111] Based on the language of this provision, Lao PDR also seem to forbid parallel imports.

Finally, Indonesia[112] and Brunei Darussalam[113] do not seem to have adopted any relevant statutory provision to date on trademark exhaustion and no judicial decision on the issue can be found so far in either country.

101 International Trademark Association, Comments by the International Trademark Association on the Myanmar Draft Trademark Law, https://perma.cc/QJ8A-GAJN.

102 Intellectual Property Code of the Philippines, Rep. Act No. 8293 (June 6, 1997) (Phil.) *as amended by* Implementing Rules and Regulations of the Rep. Act No. 9502 of 2008 (July 4, 2008) (Phil.) *as amended by* Rep. Act No. 10372 (Feb. 28, 2013) (Phil.).

103 *Id.*, art. 166.

104 Trademark Act BE 2543, § 44 (1991) (consolidated as of 2000) *as amended* up to Trademark Act (No. 3) BE 2559 (2016) (Thai.). *See* Vichai Ariyanuntaka, *Exhaustion and Parallel Imports in Thailand, in* Parallel Imports in Asia 98–100 (Christopher Heath ed., 2004).

105 Thailand Central Intellectual Property and International Trade Court Decision, No. 16/2542 (1999).

106 Thailand Supreme Court Decision, No. 2817/2543 (2000).

107 Thailand Supreme Court Decision affirmed Decision No. 16/2542 (1999) in decision No. 2817/2543 (2000).

108 Law Concerning Marks, Trade Names and Acts of Unfair Competition of the Kingdom of Cambodia, WIPO Lex No. KH001 (2002) (Cambodia).

109 Grigoriadis, *supra* note 100, at 488.

110 Lao People's Democratic Republic Intellectual Property Laws, Law No. 01/NA (Dec. 20, 2011) (Lao).

111 *Id.*, art. 57(2).

112 Law on Trade Marks and Geographical Indications, Law No. 20 (2016) (Indon.).

113 Trade Marks Act, ch. 98 (2000), https://jpo.go.jp/e/system/laws/gaikoku/document/index/brunei-e_trademarks_law.pdf (Brunei).

VI TRADEMARK EXHAUSTION IN THE PEOPLE'S REPUBLIC OF CHINA AND INDIA

To date, the treatment of trademark exhaustion does not seem to have been addressed explicitly in the People's Republic of China (PRC).[114] In particular, Article 57 of the Trademark Law of the PRC, as last amended in 2013, provides that

> Any of the following constitutes an infringement of the exclusive right to use a registered trademark: (1) Using a trademark that is identical with a registered trademark in connection with the same goods without the authorization of the owner of the registered trademark; ... (3) Selling goods that violate the exclusive right to use a registered trademark; ... (5) Altering another party's registered trademark without authorization and selling goods bearing such an altered trademark ... (7) Otherwise causing prejudice to another party's exclusive right to use its registered trademark.[115]

However, the provision does not mention the right to prevent the importation of trademark goods nor does it indicate that the rights of trademark owners are exhausted once the products are placed in the market, whether national or international markets. This could be interpreted as prohibiting parallel importations of good carrying nationally registered trademarks. Article 57 also does not define the wording "exclusive right to use its registered trademark." In turn, one might contend that this exclusive right does not necessarily refer to the right to prohibit the importation of genuine trademark goods and that the provision seems too vague to prescribe either the permission or the prohibition of parallel imports into the PRC.[116]

Hence, the existing case law seem to support courts in favouring an interpretation of Article 57 of the Trademark Law of the PRC as not prohibiting parallel imports. In particular, five well-known decision were issued on trademark exhaustion by courts in the PRC in this area:[117] the 1999 *Lihua* v. *Business Trading Co. (Lux* case),[118] in which the court ultimately avoided a ruling on the issue of exhaustion and found, instead, the imported products to be counterfeited products because defendant could not prove the goods were genuine; the 2003 *An'ge* case,[119] in which the court stated, for the first time in China, that grey market goods could be permitted as lawful as long as they are not substantively different from the goods bearing the same trademark sold in China by an authorized dealer; the 2009 *Michelin Tyres* case,[120] in which the court turned to technical standard requirements, rather than the issue of exhaustion per se, to decide the case and ruled that the parallel imported tyres were not allowed into China because they had not obtained a Chinese compulsory product certification and consumers would attribute the lack of certification to Michelin and thereby damage Michelin's reputation in China; the 2013 *Absolut Vodka* case,[121] in which the court ruled in favour of plaintiff because defendant had altered the quality of the

[114] Daniel Chow, *Exhaustion of Trademarks and Parallel Imports in China*, 51 SANTA CLARA L. REV. 1283 (2011); Andrea Zappalaglio, *The Exhaustion of Trademarks in the PRC Compared with the US and EU Experience: A Dilemma That Still Needs an Answer*, EUR. INTELL. PROP. REV. 610 (2015).

[115] Trademark Law of the People's Republic of China (as amended up to Decision of Aug. 30, 2013, of the Standing Committee of National People's Congress on Amendments to the Trademark Law of the People's Republic of China), art. 57.

[116] Zappalaglio, *supra* note 114, at 614.

[117] *Id.* at 614–15.

[118] *Shanghai Unilever Co.* v. *Com. Import and Export Trading Co. of Guangzhou Econ. Tech. Developing Dist.*, Guangzhou Interm. People's Ct. (1999).

[119] *Fahuayilin Inc.* v. *Shijihengyuan Inc. & Taipingyang Dept. Store*, Beijing No. 2 Interm. People's Ct. (2003).

[120] *Michelin Grp.* v. *Tan Guoquiang & Ou Can*, Changsha Interm. People's Ct. (2009).

[121] *Pernod Ricard China (Trading) Co.* v *unknown* (Suzhou Interm. Ct., Oct. 8, 2013 unreported). The case is summarized by Zappalaglio, *supra* note 114, at 618.

goods by removing the quality identifier code from the goods and found that defendant's acts constitute infringement as proscribed by Article 52.5 of the Trademark Law; and the 2013 *Victoria's Secret* case, or *Victoria's Secret* v. *Jintian Ltd*,[122] in which the court ruled in favour of defendant on the issue of parallel imports resold online, but found defendant liable under unfair competition and false advertising law.

In summary, while the survey of existing decisions tends to indicate that these courts do not exclude the legality of parallel imports, these decisions also do not provide a clear acceptance of this practice. They also remain a handful of decisions, all by lower-intermediate courts in various Chinese provinces, in a very large judicial system. Certainly, however, these decisions indicate a consistent concern about the relationship between parallel imports and product quality as the products whose quality and/or other characteristics had been altered by importers were not allowed into the market.

By contrast, the Trade Marks Act of India of 1999 explicitly addresses the principle of trademark exhaustion.[123] The relevant provision is Section 30 of the Trademarks Act, which provides, in section 30(3), that trademark owners cannot control the further circulation of trademarked products once they have been distributed in the market by the "proprietor or with his consent."[124] Yet, section 30(4) of the Trademarks Act also provides that trademark owners may have "legitimate reasons" to oppose parallel importation of goods bearing the trademark, especially where the condition of the goods has been changed or impaired after they have been put on the market.[125] However, section 30 does not define, in the provision itself, the geographical extent of the word "market," a task that has been left to the judiciary.

At first, courts seemed to be sceptical of parallel imports, in particular when grey market products were of different quality or had minor differences compared to the products distributed nationally. In 2006, in *Cisco Technologies* v. *Shrikanth*,[126] the Delhi High Court restrained the defendant from importing CISCO computer hardware and hardware components because non-authorized products could lead to confusion and create problems for consumers. Moreover, the court instructed Customs that third-party consignments should not be permitted to enter the Indian territory. The same year, in *Samsung Electronics Co. Ltd* v. *Mr G. Choudhary* the Delhi High Court rendered a second and similar decision on the topic.[127] The court there blocked the imports of parallel-imported ink cartridges and toners because the products did not conform to Indian laws and regulations.

More recently, however, Indian courts seem to have shifted away from only national exhaustion. In 2013, in *Kapil Wadhva* v. *Samsung Electronics*,[128] the Delhi High Court interpreted the term "market" in section 30 of the Trademarks Act as referring to the global market. The court cited the legislative history of the Trademarks Act to confirm its interpretation of the provision favouring international exhaustion.[129] Yet the court added that trademark owners may still have "legitimate reasons" to oppose the parallel imports, especially where the condition of the goods

[122] *Victoria's Secret Stores Brand Mgmt., Inc.* v. *Shanghai Jintian Clothing Ltd* (Shanghai No. 2 Interm. People's Ct. 2013).

[123] The Trade Marks Act, No. 47 of 1999 (India) [hereinafter Indian Trade Marks Act].

[124] Indian Trade Marks Act, § 30(3).

[125] *Id.*, § 30(4).

[126] *Cisco Techs.* v. *Shrikanth*, (2006) 31 PTC 538 (India).

[127] *Samsung Elecs. Co.* v. *Mr G. Choudhary*, (2006) 33 PTC 425 (India).

[128] *Kapil Wadhva* v. *Samsung Elecs.*, (2013) 53 PTC 112 (India). The full text of the decision is available at https://indiankanoon.org/doc/86466712/.

[129] For a commentary of the decision, *see* Sai Vinod, *Breaking News: Delhi High Court Recognizes International Exhaustion under Indian Trademark Law*, Spicy IP, Oct. 4, 2012, https://spicyip.com/2012/10/breaking-news-delhi-high-court.html.

has been changed or impaired after they have been put on the market.[130] These reasons may include the alteration of the following details: services and warranties; advertising and promotional efforts; packaging; quality control, pricing and presentation; and the language of the product literature. Still, the court ruled that unauthorized dealers and parallel importers may avoid liability when they use specific disclaimers stating the products have been imported, and that dealers or parallel importers are, for example, the providers of the related warranty and aftercare services instead of the trademark owners. In the case at issue, the court ordered the products carry the sign: "Samsung/SAMSUNG Products sold are imported into India and SAMSUNG (KOREA) does not warranty the quality of the goods nor provide any after sales service for the goods. We warranty the quality of the goods and shall provide after sales service for the goods."[131]

Nevertheless, trademark owners can continue to prohibit the importation and subsequent distribution of goods that either have not been lawfully acquired or were changed or materially altered after their acquisition. In 2014, in *Microsoft Corporation & Anr* v. *Jayesh & Anr*,[132] the court found that defendant had infringed plaintiff's mark because it had sold grey market/unauthorized importations of the XBOX gaming consoles, which had been tampered with to enable users, inter alia, to run counterfeited/pirated XBOX games on the console. Moreover, the XBOX gaming consoles were not eligible for warranty support by the manufacturer. Similarly, in 2014, in *Philip Morris Products SA* v. *Sameer*,[133] the Delhi High Court held in favour of plaintiff because the importer could not show the goods had been lawfully acquired outside India. In general, the court stated that an importer, its representative or a subsequent purchaser of parallel imported goods is not be liable for infringement under section 29 of the Trademark Act provided the imports comply with the condition of section 30(3). However, these parties need to prove the imported goods were placed on a worldwide market by the trademark owner or with its consent, and thereafter that the party lawfully acquired them.

VII CONCLUSION

The principle of trademark exhaustion is based on the premise that trademark rights should not be used to control the distribution of goods after their first release into the market. The geographic scope of the "market," however, differs by jurisdiction. With respect to cross-border trade, the key inquiry remains whether trademark rights exhaust only with respect to goods distributed in the national market or also in foreign markets, as long as the goods are genuine.

The above survey of selected jurisdictions highlights how individual countries or a regional organization like the EU address the treatment of trademark exhaustion subject to national or regional trade interests. These interests include: the extent of current imports and exports, including parallel trade, of a country, with particular attention to which countries represent the primary trading partners; the importance of IP protection for particular sectors of the national economy; existing price differences for IP protected goods sold in a country; the amount and impact of transaction costs such as shipping and other distribution-related costs on the final costs of consumer goods; existing trade barriers; and vertical constraints that

[130] *Kapil Wadhva*, (2013) 53 PTC 112, §§ 72–75.
[131] *Id.* at § 75.
[132] *Microsoft Corp. & Anr* v. *Jayesh & Anr*, Feb. 21, 2014, https://indiankanoon.org/doc/107721244/ (India).
[133] *Philip Morris Prods. SA* v. *Sameer*, (2014) 209 DLT 1 (India).

(otherwise) affect the IP owners' ability to price discriminate in a country or region.[134] For all these reasons, choosing a national or regional policy on exhaustion remains a sensitive topic, as reflected in the silence of TRIPS on the issue.

Hence, the above survey indicates that a considerable number of jurisdictions today follow a system of international exhaustion, either explicitly in their legislation or by judicial interpretation. This system encounters exceptions, such as the EU, which follows Community-wide exhaustion, and individual countries, such as Cambodia or Laos in ASEAN, which adopt a system of national exhaustion. Moreover, most countries do not permit parallel imports materially different from the goods sold in the national market. Still, several countries allow importers and/or national distributors to cure these differences by affixing disclaimers to the goods clearly notifying that these goods have been imported by third parties and may be of a different quality. These outcomes support the conclusion that today a relevant number of jurisdictions favour parallel imports, and thus international trade and open markets. Of course, this may be subject to additional factors such as the existence of contractual limitations that may interfere, in practice, with the application of the principle of exhaustion and possibly nullify the impact of a system of international exhaustion.[135]

[134] National Economic Research Associates (NERA), *The Economic Consequences of the Choice of Regime in the Area of Trademarks: Final Report for DG XV of the European Commission* 108–22 (1999).

[135] Even though this chapter did not elaborate on these limitations, several of the decisions cited here indicate that national judges frequently do not favour these clauses.

XV

Trademark Transactions

37

Trademark Transactions in Common Law Countries

Liberalisation and Its Limits

Robert Burrell and Michael Handler***

I INTRODUCTION

Historically, common law countries took a restrictive approach to transactions involving trademarks. This restrictive approach was said to flow from the reasons for granting protection for trademarks in the first place. If a trademark communicates information to consumers as to the origin and quality of a particular trader's goods or services, it was thought that any dealing with a trademark, such as an assignment or the grant of a licence to a third party, would disrupt the source and quality guarantee functions of the mark and potentially cause confusion among consumers. In other words, the very reasons that a trademark receives legal protection were thought to justify constraining an owner's ability to deal with the mark (in contrast with other personal property, such as an unencumbered chattel or a patent). Initially, these sorts of concerns were highly influential, and the law either proscribed or imposed strict limitations on the exploitation of trademarks. However, over the course of the last century there was a gradual liberalisation of these rules. Consequently, in most common law countries, we have now reached a position where the law recognises registered trademarks to be personal property, which can be exploited with fewer restrictions than in the past. This liberalisation has to a large extent reflected changes in business practices, as brands have come to be recognised as valuable commodities in their own right and as trademark licensing, merchandising and franchising have become large and lucrative industries. Notwithstanding this, the tension between the idea of the mark as "property" and the mark as a badge of origin remains. This tension is reflected in the fact that the law retains restrictions on trademark transactions in cases where marks have been or might be used in such a way as to deceive consumers. Working out when a badge of origin can be transferred to an unrelated third party whilst not falling into the category of a "deceptive transaction" remains difficult.

II TRADEMARK ASSIGNMENTS

Restrictions on the assignment of trademarks in the British Commonwealth can be traced back to the 1860s, that is, to the point when a law of trademarks recognisable as such to modern eyes first emerged. By the mid-1860s, Chancery courts had come to the conclusion that trademarks

* Professor of Intellectual Property and Information Technology Law, Faculty of Law, University of Oxford; and Professor, Melbourne Law School.

** Professor, Faculty of Law, University of New South Wales.

were a species of property. However, it was also clear that trademarks could not be freely assigned to third parties; they could not be dealt with "in gross." In particular, in the 1865 decision of the House of Lords in *Leather Cloth Co. Ltd* v. *American Leather Cloth Co.* it was held that a trademark could be assigned only "upon a sale and transfer of the manufactory of goods on which the mark has been used."[1] The first British Commonwealth trademarks statutes followed the courts' lead in providing that a registered mark could be assigned only in conjunction with the goodwill of the owner's business.[2] The rationale for this limitation, as at common law, was to prevent the public from being deceived by a break in the link between the mark and the provider of the goods.[3]

However, over the course of the twentieth century, restrictions on the assignment of registered trademarks came to be challenged. Most notably, brand owners pressed for a more permissive approach in the course of public enquiries into the state of trademark law.[4] Over time these efforts bore fruit and it began to be accepted that the very restrictive approach rested on a narrow conception of the trademark as an indicator of a specific, known source of goods, rather than a guarantee of consistent quality provided by a potentially unknown source.[5] British Commonwealth legislation was therefore amended in the mid-twentieth century to permit the assignment of registered marks without goodwill.[6] Certain restrictions and conditions were, however, retained. For example, under both the UK Trade Marks Act of 1938 and Australia's Trade Marks Act of 1955 an assignment without goodwill could be invalidated if the continued use by the assignor in relation to the specified goods or services resulted in public deception or confusion.[7]

A further round of liberalisation occurred from the mid-1990s, when Commonwealth countries began to pass new trademark statutes in the post-TRIPS period. It is now the case that the modern laws of the United Kingdom, Australia and New Zealand do not set out specific grounds on which an assignment without goodwill might be invalidated.[8] However, this does not mean that such assignments, and the continued presence of assigned marks on the register, cannot be challenged. As will be seen below, in each case the legislation leaves open the possibility that such an assignment can result in registration of the mark being cancelled, on the grounds that the use of the mark has become deceptive.

Rules governing the assignment of trademarks in the United States follow a somewhat similar arc. By the start of the twentieth century, courts had held that a trademark could not be assigned

[1] *Leather Cloth Co. Ltd* v. *Am. Leather Cloth Co.*, (1865) 11 HL Cas. 523, 534 (Lord Cranworth) (appeal taken from Eng.).

[2] *See, e.g.*, Trade Marks Registration Act, 1875, 38 & 39 Vict., c. 91, § 2 (UK); Patents, Designs, and Trade-Marks Act 1889, § 77 (NZ); Trade Marks Act 1905 (Cth) § 58 (Austl.).

[3] *See, e.g.*, *Pinto* v. *Badman*, (1891) 8 RPC 181 (CA) (Eng.).

[4] In the United Kingdom, see REPORT OF THE DEPARTMENTAL COMMITTEE ON THE LAW AND PRACTICE RELATING TO TRADE MARKS, Cmd 4568 (1934) (hereinafter, Goschen Committee Report). In Australia, see REPORT OF COMMITTEE APPOINTED DURING 1938 BY THE THEN ATTORNEY-GENERAL TO CONSIDER WHAT ALTERATIONS ARE DESIRABLE IN THE TRADE MARKS LAW OF THE COMMONWEALTH (1954) (hereinafter Knowles Committee Report); REPORT OF COMMITTEE APPOINTED TO CONSIDER WHAT ALTERATIONS ARE DESIRABLE IN THE TRADE MARKS LAW OF THE COMMONWEALTH (1954) (hereinafter Dean Committee Report).

[5] *See, e.g.*, Knowles Committee Report, *supra* note 4, at [69]–[71].

[6] *See, e.g.*, Trade Marks Act, 1938, 1 & 2 Geo. 6, c. 22, § 22(1) (UK); Trade Marks Act 1953, § 31(1) (NZ); Trade Marks Act 1955 (Cth) § 82(1) (Austl.). It remains the law that an unregistered trademark cannot be assigned separately from the underlying goodwill of the business. *See, e.g.*, *Kraft Foods Group Brands LLC* v. *Bega Cheese Ltd* [2020] FCAFC 65 (Austl.).

[7] Trade Marks Act, 1938, 1 & 2 Geo. 6, c. 22, § 22(4) (UK); Trade Marks Act 1955 (Cth) § 82(2)(b) (Austl.). *See also* Trade Marks Act 1953, § 31(4) (NZ).

[8] Trade Marks Act, 1994, c. 26, § 24(1) (UK); Trade Marks Act 1995 (Cth) § 106(3) (Austl.); Trade Marks Act 2002, § 10(1)(c) (NZ).

"except as incidental to a transfer of the business or property in connection with which it has been used."[9] Congress preserved this approach in the Trademark Act of 1905.[10] The Lanham Act of 1946 retained a prohibition on assignments in gross, but did not expressly require the transfer of the underlying business: the focus was solely on the question of whether the goodwill associated with the mark had also been assigned.[11] Irene Calboli has demonstrated that the change in legislative language allowed courts to shift the inquiry to the question of whether the assignee's goods were sufficiently similar to those of the assignor such that consumer interests would not be harmed.[12] Unlike in British Commonwealth countries, there was no further round of legislative liberalisation in the 1990s, despite repeated lobbying by brand owners for the removal of the prohibition on assignments in gross under the Lanham Act. As a consequence, it is often said that the continued presence of the prohibition marks out the United States as different from other common law countries.[13] However, what tends to be overlooked is that whether there are, in practice, differences between the position in the United States and elsewhere depends on how the general prohibitions on "deceptive transactions" in other countries are interpreted.

III TRADEMARK LICENSING

For much the same reasons as those raised against the assignment of marks in gross, British Commonwealth courts were initially unreceptive to the idea that the use of a trademark could be "licensed" to a third party. In the early twentieth century, it was thought that the inevitable result of licensing would be the deception of the public, since the mark's function as a badge of origin would be compromised if the mark were used on goods provided by a party other than the trademark owner.[14] Later in the century this view came to be challenged as failing to reflect emerging business practices and consumer perceptions that marks functioned to indicate the company with overarching control and hence to guarantee the quality of goods, rather than to indicate a specific site of production.[15] This led to the United Kingdom introducing provisions allowing for third-party "registered users" of registered trademarks.[16] Similar provisions were subsequently incorporated into legislation in other Commonwealth countries.[17] These provisions allowed a licensee of a registered mark to be registered if the Registrar was satisfied as to the "degree of control" that the owner exercised over the permitted use of the mark, such that the registration would not facilitate so-called trafficking in the mark.[18]

[9] *MacMahan Pharmacal Co.* v. *Denver Chem. Mfg. Co.*, 113 F. 468, 474–75 (8th Cir. 1901).

[10] Trademark Act of 1905 § 10 (repealed 1946).

[11] Trademark Act of 1946 § 10, 15 USC § 1060 (2016).

[12] Irene Calboli, *Trademark Assignment "With Goodwill": A Concept Whose Time Has Gone*, 57 FLA. L. REV. 771, 790 (2005). For detailed consideration of when the differences between the assignor and assignee's goods are substantial enough to result in the assignment being in gross, *see, e.g.*, *Clark & Freeman Corp.* v. *Heartland Co. Ltd*, 811 F. Supp. 137, 139–41 (SDNY 1993).

[13] *See, e.g.*, J. THOMAS MCCARTHY, 3 MCCARTHY ON TRADEMARKS AND UNFAIR COMPETITION, § 18:10 (5th ed. 2018).

[14] The House of Lords' decision in *Bowden Wire Ltd* v. *Bowden Brake Co. Ltd*, (1914) 31 RPC 385 (appeal taken from Eng.) was often used as authority for this view, although the case arguably only went as far as deciding that if a registered trademark were licensed it could become invalid if it ceased to show a connection in the course of trade with the registered proprietor or otherwise became deceptive. This latter view came to find favour with UK courts.

[15] *See* Goschen Committee Report, *supra* note 4, at [118].

[16] Trade Marks Act, 1938, 1 & 2 Geo. 6, c. 22, § 28 (UK).

[17] Trade Marks Amendment Act 1948 (Cth) (Austl.); Trade Marks Act 1953, § 37 (NZ). *See also* Sam Ricketson, *The Licensing of Trade Marks and the Operation of Section 103 of the Trade Marks Act 1955 (Cth): Some Aspects of the Pioneer Case*, 14 U. W. AUSTL. L. REV. 30 (1979).

[18] *See, e.g.*, Trade Marks Act, 1938, 1 & 2 Geo. 6, c. 22, § 28(6) (UK); Trade Marks Act 1953, § 37(6) (NZ); Trade Marks Act 1955 (Cth) § 74 (Austl.). This practice was described by the House of Lords as "dealing in a trade mark primarily as

Perhaps the most important development in the period following the adoption of the registered user scheme was the acceptance by courts that registration was not, in fact, mandatory for licensees. That is, it was considered that *any* licensing arrangement could preserve the validity of a registered mark, provided that the conditions of control imposed by the owner over the licensee's use were sufficient to prevent the public from being deceived. For example, in Australia, Aickin J in *Pioneer Kabushiki Kaisha* v. *Registrar of Trade Marks* held:

> the essential requirement for the maintenance of the validity of a trade mark is that *it must indicate a connexion in the course of trade with the registered proprietor*, even though the connexion may be slight, such as selection or quality control or control of the user in the sense in which a parent company controls a subsidiary. Use by either the registered proprietor or a licensee (whether registered *or otherwise*) will protect the mark from attack on the ground of non-user, but it is essential both that the user maintains the connexion of the registered proprietor with the goods and that the use of the mark does not become otherwise deceptive.[19]

The "registered user" schemes in place under mid-twentieth-century British Commonwealth legislation have not been retained. Instead, modern legislation builds on the more liberal views of licensing taken in cases such as *Pioneer*, with registries having no ongoing role in overseeing licensing arrangements. However, much as with assignments, there are still mechanisms by which uncontrolled licensing might be able to be challenged, primarily through revocation of trademark registrations.

The US law on trademark licensing, again, followed a similar path. At the start of the twentieth century, licensing was understood to be antithetical to the function of a mark as a badge of origin, such that courts dismissed trademark licensing as an impossibility.[20] However, as early as 1909, some courts were prepared to accept that there might be forms of acceptable licensing, provided always that the trademark owner retained a degree of control over the quality of the goods produced by the licensee.[21] The Lanham Act confirmed that licensing with quality control was permissible,[22] a point affirmed by the well-known decision in *Dawn Donut Co.* v. *Hart's Food Stores, Inc.*[23] The modern law remains essentially unaltered: licensing with control is unobjectionable, whereas licensing without control will result in the cancellation of the registration. The question we explore in the final section of this chapter is the extent to which the US rule and the rules found in other common law countries achieve a common end.

IV RESTRICTIONS ON EXPLOITATION: DECEPTION AND NON-USE

Having set out a brief history of how the restrictions on the assignment and licensing of trademarks came to be loosened in common law countries, we now turn to look at the restrictions the law continues to impose on the freedom of trademark owners to deal with their marks. Specifically, this section focuses on the restrictions that arise from a desire to prevent

a commodity in its own right and not primarily for the purpose of identifying or promoting the merchandise in which the proprietor of the mark is interested": *HOLLY HOBBIE Trade Mark*, [1984] RPC 329, 356 (Lord Brightman) (appeal taken from Eng.). Importantly, in this case, the trafficking provision was used to invalidate a trademark that had been licensed in an uncontrolled manner (for character merchandise).

19 *Pioneer Kabushiki Kaisha* v. *Registrar of Trade Marks* (1977) 137 CLR 670, 683 (our emphases). To similar effect in English cases, see *BOSTITCH Trade Mark*, [1963] RPC 183 (Ch.); *GE Trade Mark*, [1969] RPC 418 (Ch.), *aff'd* [1970] RPC 339 (CA).

20 *See* McCarthy, *supra* note 13, at § 18:39.

21 *Nelson* v. *J. H. Winchell & Co.*, 89 NE 180, 183 (Mass. 1909).

22 Trademark Act of 1946 §§ 5, 45 (definition of "related company"), 15 USC §§ 1055, 1127 (2016).

23 *Dawn Donut Co.* v. *Hart's Food Stores, Inc.*, 267 F. 2d 358, 367 (2d Cir. 1959).

consumer confusion – that is, the restrictions that might continue to embody the common law's traditional concerns about the possibility of consumers being deceived. Consequently, we do not consider restrictions aimed at protecting other traders from predatory behaviour of the type found in antitrust law and in codes regulating franchising agreements.[24]

A *Assignments in Gross*

Continued restrictions on the freedom to assign trademarks in British Commonwealth countries are found in provisions that make registered trademarks vulnerable to revocation or cancellation where use of the mark is likely to deceive or cause confusion.[25] These provisions are of continued significance where there has been an assignment in gross.[26] Indeed, there is a significant tension within Commonwealth statutes which, on the one hand, accept that a registered trademark can be assigned without goodwill while, on the other hand, allowing for an assignment to be set aside and a mark revoked on the ground that use of the mark would be confusing or deceptive.[27] This tension can be illustrated by reference to three scenarios.

The first scenario is unique to Australia. However, it provides a good starting point as an illustration of the degree of uncertainty that attaches to the relationship between assignment provisions that are obviously intended to liberalise trademark transactions and cancellation provisions that apply to marks whose use has become deceptive. The background is that Australia has long had a policy of facilitating parallel importation. However, the relevant provision in the Trade Marks Act of 1995 was, until August 2018, worded in such a way that parallel importation was possible only where the owner of the Australian trademark consented to the application of the trademark to the imported goods.[28] Ownership in this context was strictly construed, such that even where a trademark was owned by another company within the same corporate group as the company that consented to the application of the mark, the parallel importation provisions did not apply. As a consequence, foreign trademark owners entered into assignments in order to place the ownership of the mark in the hands of an Australian licensee or a shell company, thereby circumventing the effect of the parallel importation defence to infringement.[29] From a policy perspective, this was clearly undesirable. Notably, a compelling argument was made (but never tested in court) that since the marked goods were still clearly those of the foreign owner, produced without any meaningful control by the Australian assignee, the assignment of the mark would have confused consumers, leaving the registration of the mark vulnerable to cancellation under section 88(2)(c) of the Australian Act.[30]

[24] *See generally* Robert Burrell & Michael Handler, Australian Trade Mark Law 589–91, 596–603 (2d ed. 2016).

[25] *See, e.g.*, Trade Marks Act, 1994, c. 26, § 46(1)(d) (UK); Trade Marks Act 1995 (Cth) § 88(2)(c) (Austl.); Trade Marks Act 2002, § 66(1)(e) (NZ).

[26] *See, e.g.*, Trade Marks Act, 1994, c. 26, § 24(1) (UK); Trade Marks Act 1995 (Cth), § 106(3) (Austl.)); Trade Marks Act 2002, § 10(1)(c) (NZ). Such statutes do not contain a requirement similar to that contained in § 82(5) of the Trade Marks Act 1955 (Cth) (Austl.), under which an assignment was not able to be invalidated after three years.

[27] *See also* David Keeling et al., Kerly's Law of Trade Marks and Trade Names § 15-048 (16th ed. 2017), referring to the 1994 UK Act and stating "[t]he important question which requires an answer is how far the permissive nature of s. 24 can be pressed before the tension with s. 46 becomes unbearable."

[28] Trade Marks Act 1995 (Cth) § 123(1) (Austl.) (in force from Jan. 1, 1996 until its repeal by the Intellectual Property Laws Amendment (Productivity Commission Response Part 1 and Other Measures) Act 2018 (Cth) sch. 1, item 4 (Austl.), with effect from Aug. 25, 2018. The former § 123(1) still applies in relation to actions for trademark infringement commenced before that date).

[29] *See, e.g.*, *Transp. Tyre Sales Pty Ltd* v. *Mont. Tyres Rims & Tubes Pty Ltd* (1999) 93 FCR 421 (Full Fed. Ct.) (Austl.).

[30] James W. Dwyer & David L. Yates, *The Montana Case on Appeal – Dealing with "Parallel Importers,"* 10 Austl. Intell. Prop. J. 111, 122–23 (1999).

That the above argument was even open remains instructive. Consumers would indeed, in some sense, be confused as to the "trade origin" of the goods in the above scenario: following the assignment, consumers would understand the goods to be produced by someone other than the trademark owner. Judged as an infringement matter, there could be no question that this type of response would be sufficient to result in a finding that consumers were being confused. But if this analysis were applied universally, then assignments in gross would never be possible. This first scenario therefore illustrates three key issues:

(i) Although we tend to assume that assignments in gross are vulnerable to challenge only where they lead to some more profound degree of consumer confusion (in particular, where consumers are likely to be confused as to the quality of the goods), there is nothing in the Australian Act, or indeed in the legislation of other British Commonwealth countries, that confines the operation of the cancellation provisions to this scenario.

(ii) Insofar as infringement analysis remains a touchstone for the operation of the cancellation ground, our analysis suffers from the fact that we have no clearly articulated understanding of when a degree of consumer confusion is to be tolerated in order to facilitate other desirable ends.[31]

(iii) It is unclear whether the operation of a cancellation ground ostensibly designed to deal with consumer confusion can also be informed by other public policy concerns, such as the preservation of a clear and longstanding policy to allow parallel importation.

The second scenario we wish to explore is the more commonly recognised problem of the extent to which a ground of cancellation might arise because, following an assignment in gross, the assignee's goods are of different quality. In some such scenarios, it must be the case that cancellation would sometimes be warranted. As yet, however, we have very little guidance in British Commonwealth case law as to when this would be so.[32] As the current editors of *Kerly's Law of Trade Marks and Trade Names* have suggested (and as our parallel importation example illustrates), some temporary confusion is *always* likely in the period immediately after a mark is assigned.[33] However, as they go on to suggest, where the legislation countenances the possibility of assignments in gross, some degree of confusion will be tolerated.[34] It should also be kept in mind that an assignee has a significant commercial incentive to maintain quality standards, such that we ought not to imagine that cancellation would be warranted in more than a small proportion of cases. Nevertheless, there is a clear need for further guidance as to the steps that an assignee can legitimately be expected to take to ensure a consistent consumer experience and hence the validity of the mark.

Here we suggest that there might be scope for British Commonwealth countries to draw on US jurisprudence. The US experience is helpful because there is a consensus that the prohibition on

[31] *See* Burrell & Handler, *supra* note 24, at 375–87 (discussing consumer confusion and policy factors in the context of the Australian infringement provisions).

[32] *See, e.g.*, *Scandecor Devs. AB* v. *Scandecor Mktg. AV*, [2001] UKHL 21, [44] (Lord Nicholls) (appeal taken from Eng.). *See also Heintzman* v. *751056 Ontario Ltd* (1990), 34 CPR 3d 1 (Can. Fed. Ct.).

[33] Keeling et al., *supra* note 27, at § 15-058.

[34] *Id.* The willingness of courts in Commonwealth countries to overlook some limited degree of confusion can be illustrated by the decision of the Full Federal Court in *Kraft Foods Group Brands LLC* v. *Bega Cheese Ltd* [2020] FCAFC 65 (Austl.). In that case, the court had little difficulty in dismissing an argument that an assignee and purchaser of a business that ran an advertising campaign that emphasised the continutity of its business with that of the assignor had not engaged in misleading or deceptive conduct under the Australian Consumer Law (Competition and Consumer Act 2010 (Cth) sch. 2 (Austl.)).

assignments in gross means that the assignee must take steps to maintain quality control – even accepting this as a single touchstone for the analysis would mark an improvement on the current Commonwealth position. Moreover, it is also clear in the United States that maintenance of quality control per se is not sufficient: the requirement is of *continuity* of quality control. As Neal Platt explains, "[i]t is insufficient (perhaps even irrelevant) for the purchaser to show that for some time after the closing the purchaser exercised quality control that was 'good' or even 'excellent'; the purchaser's burden, rather, is to show that for such period her quality control remained essentially the same as the seller's."[35] A body of case law provides guidance as to the sorts of steps that assignees should undertake. For example, in the case of a mark for retail services, ensuring continuity of managerial control, employee numbers, range and depth of inventory, return policies, and employee attire may all help establish the requisite consistency.[36] Admittedly, in US commentaries it is often noted that a degree of uncertainty can remain as to whether the assignee has done enough to overcome the prohibition on assignments in gross, but this is largely because of the fact-specific nature of the inquiry. Even if there are elements of the current US position that might be improved, there is certainly no reason why British Commonwealth courts ought not to draw upon the US experience. A shared understanding of when a trademark assignment is vulnerable is particularly valuable given that assignments of the same mark might take place in more than one jurisdiction more or less simultaneously.

The third scenario is where the mark contains an explicit reference to a particular individual or organisation as being the provider of the specified goods or services. For example, if a compound mark (such as a label on a bottle of spirits) contains a statement that the goods are produced by a specific party, then, following an assignment of that mark by that party, even with the transfer of the underlying business, there has to be a strong case that the assignee's use of that mark would cause confusion.[37] This conclusion receives strong support from the House of Lords' decision in *Scandecor Developments AB* v. *Scandecor Marketing AV*, where Lord Nicholls gave the example of "an artist's mark on his own artistic works" as the sort of mark that is unassignable because it "connotes a personal connection between the original owner of the mark and the goods in respect of which it is used."[38] The question in this type of case, therefore, is not so much when the assignment might be prohibited, but when it might be allowed.

A useful case through which to explore the issue of when an assignment of a mark containing a personal reference might be allowed is *Elizabeth Emanuel* v. *Continental Shelf 128 Ltd.*[39] The background to that case was that a fashion designer, Elizabeth Emanuel, sold her wedding dress business and assigned the registered trademark ELIZABETH EMANUEL to an unrelated third party, who continued to provide wedding dresses under the mark. The Court of Justice of the European Communities held that, in the circumstances, the registration could not be revoked.[40] An important consideration was that the transfer of the underlying business meant that the same

[35] Neal R. Platt, *Good Will Enduring: How to Ensure that Trademark Priority Will Not Be Destroyed by the Sale of a Business*, 99 TRADEMARK REP. 788, 797 (2009).

[36] *Id.* at 803.

[37] *See Heublein Inc.* v. *Cont'l Liqueurs Pty Ltd* (1959) 103 CLR 435 (Austl.), where the compound mark contained the statement "Prepared and Bottled by Ste Pierre Smirnoff Fls Inc. Hartford Conn. U.S.A." and the mark had been assigned from Ste Pierre Smirnoff to Heublein in 1954. Kitto J thought that it was "obvious that if the mark be applied to liquor manufactured since 1954 it must convey false information": *id.* at 440.

[38] *Scandecor Devs. AB* v. *Scandecor Mktg. AV*, [2001] UKHL 21, [20] (appeal taken from Eng.).

[39] Case C-259/04, *Emanuel* v. *Cont'l Shelf 128 Ltd*, 2006 ECR I-3089.

[40] *Id.* at [51].

designs were being produced, in the same workshops, by the same employees.[41] Interestingly, therefore, the Court of Justice seems to have accepted that consistency of quality was the overarching consideration. The outcome is not, however, unproblematic. As the Court itself noted, "the average consumer might be influenced in his act of purchasing a garment bearing the trade mark ELIZABETH EMANUEL by imagining that [Ms Emanuel] was involved in the design of that garment."[42] It therefore seems to us that the outcome is open to debate, and even if the case is rightly decided it must very much be regarded as a case at the margins of what ought to be permissible.

This is not to say that marks containing personal names should never be assignable. In many industries, consumers would not expect that the presence of an individual's name in the mark means that the individual is personally involved in the production of the goods or services. And once a person whose name appears in the mark has died, concerns about consumer confusion would tend to fall by the wayside.[43] There are, however, some industries (high-end fashion strikes us as being a particularly good example) where it must be that in many cases consumers would expect that goods bearing the name of a living person have been made by that person or with that person's input or imprimatur, which must then impact on how those marks are dealt with.

B Licensing: Consequences of Lack of "Control"

Unconstrained licensing must, at least in principle, also be capable of triggering cancellation on the ground that the mark has become deceptive. This was certainly the case under former British Commonwealth law. For example, in *McGREGOR Trade Mark*[44] Whitford J in the English High Court held that "uncontrolled" or "bare" licences were inherently deceptive. The difficulty, much as with assignments in gross, is working out how and why the current position is different – modern Commonwealth legislation seeks to make licensing easier, but provides no guidance as to how the cancellation provision is to be applied under a more liberal regime. Importantly, moreover, there are signs that Commonwealth courts may be diverging on this issue.

The leading case in the United Kingdom remains the 2002 decision of the House of Lords in *Scandecor*, which we also discussed in the previous section. Lord Nicholls held that the 1994 UK Act took a different approach to trademark licensing, such that the approach adopted in cases like *McGREGOR* had to be set aside. More specifically, Lord Nicholls noted that the legislative definition no longer referred to a trademark as a sign used to indicate a "connection in the course of trade" with the proprietor, but rather to a sign "capable of distinguishing goods or services of one undertaking from those of other undertakings." His Lordship concluded that this change in statutory language had brought about a fundamental change in the law.[45] Under the 1994 Act, an exclusive bare licensee's use of a mark could not be said to be deceptive because such use would still indicate that the goods came from a single source (namely, the licensee,

[41] *Id.* at [45].

[42] *Id. at* [48]. *See also* Ron Moscona, *What Really Matters? The Designer's Name or the Name on the Label?*, 29 Eur. Intell. Prop. Rev. 152 (2007).

[43] Of course, it might be said that consumers may not know about the death of a designer or other prominent individual (or at least not immediately). However, this goes to the broader point that some degree of consumer confusion may always attach to trademark transactions. The question is when a degree of confusion is to be tolerated in order to facilitate market transactions.

[44] McGREGOR Trade Mark, [1979] RPC 36 (Ch.).

[45] *Scandecor Devs. AB* v. *Scandecor Mktg. AV*, [2001] UKHL 21, [33] (appeal taken from Eng.).

rather than the licensor). His Lordship went on to note that, as a practical matter, an owner would impose "suitable terms" on a licensee to ensure that the mark did not become devalued.[46] But it was held that "[c]ustomers are not to be taken to rely on the protection supposedly afforded by a legal requirement that the proprietor must always retain and exercise an inherently imprecise degree of control over the licensee's activities."[47]

The advantage of the *Scandecor* approach is that it pays deference to the legislature's desire to make licensing easier. This decision does not, however, mean that uncontrolled licensing could never give rise to a ground of cancellation. The possibility of cancellation on the ground that the mark has become deceptive remains. What is missing from *Scandecor* is any sense of when harm to consumers might rise to such a level as to justify cancellation. The disadvantage of *Scandecor* is that it would seem in every case to require a fact-intensive enquiry into the nature of consumer expectations and the extent to which those expectations have been disappointed.[48] It is arguable that an approach that focuses on the question of whether the licensor exercised real and effective control over the licensee's activities is a much less unwieldy enquiry. It is an enquiry that courts are in a much better position to undertake. Of course, if it can be demonstrated that consumer expectations have indeed been disappointed then an action for cancellation ought always to arise. Our point is that lack of control provides a useful proxy for the types of situation where consumer expectations are most likely not to have been met, and one that allows courts to sidestep a more difficult enquiry in the majority of cases.

Significantly, other common law countries have maintained a much greater focus on control than the United Kingdom. This is true, for example, in the United States, where it has been held that licensing without control (often referred to as "naked licensing" in American legal parlance) is inherently deceptive and amounts to "abandonment" of the mark.[49] This also represents the position in Australia, although the mechanism by which uncontrolled use leads to marks being expunged from the Register is not immediately obvious from a review of cases dealing with the deceptiveness ground of cancellation under Australian law, that is, section 88(2)(c) of the Trade Marks Act of 1995. The principal case to deal with this point is *Health World Ltd* v. *Shin-Sun Australia Pty Ltd*, a 2008 first instance decision of the Federal Court.[50] That case concerned the registered mark "HealthPlus" for pharmaceuticals. This mark was owned by Shin-Sun, but had been used exclusively by an associated family business, Nature's Hive. Shin-Sun and Nature's Hive had a common general manager (the daughter of the directors of Shin-Sun), who was also the majority shareholder of Nature's Hive, and a common place of business.[51] Notwithstanding these links, Jacobson J considered that there was no evidence that Shin-Sun exercised a "legally enforceable power of control" over Nature's Hive, with the consequence that his Honour

[46] *Id.* at [39].

[47] *Id.*

[48] That a fact-intensive inquiry might justify cancellation is implicit in some aspects of Lord Nicholls' decision: *id.* at [44].

[49] *See Eva's Bridal Ltd* v. *Halanick Enters., Inc.*, 639 F. 3d 788 (7th Cir. 2011); *FreecycleSunnyvale* v. *Freecycle Network*, 626 F. 3d 509 (9th Cir. 2010); *Barcamerica Int'l USA Trust* v. *Tyfield Importers, Inc.*, 289 F. 3d 589 (9th Cir. 2002). *See generally* McCarthy, *supra* note 13, at § 18:48; Irene Calboli, *The Sunset of "Quality Control" in Modern Trademark Licensing*, 57 Am. U. L. Rev. 341 (2007). Moreover, it might be noted that as a matter of US law, in the absence of control by the licensor it is more likely that goodwill will be attributed to the licensee rather than the licensor.

[50] *Health World Ltd* v. *Shin-Sun Austl. Pty Ltd* (2008) 75 IPR 478 (Fed. Ct.) (Austl.).

[51] *Id.* at 487. By the time of the hearing, the directors of Shin-Sun had also become the directors of Nature's Hive. Jacobson J considered that this was not evidence of Shin-Sun's control over Nature's Hive's activities on the basis that the daughter, being the majority shareholder of Nature's Hive, retained the power to remove her parents as directors: *id.* at 501. In any event, as the change in directorship took place after the rectification proceedings were commenced, this issue could not have been taken into account for the purposes of § 88(2)(c).

ordered cancellation of the mark under section 88(2)(c).[52] One complicating factor is that the case concerned a mark for pharmaceuticals. Nature's Hive was listed as the party with obligations to maintain the quality of the goods under the Therapeutic Goods Act of 1989 and this weighed heavily against the argument that Shin-Sun had exercised de facto control. However, as argued in detail elsewhere, *Health World* should not be read as turning on the Therapeutic Goods Act point.[53] The better reading of the case is that it stands for the broader proposition that licensing without control can always give rise to cancellation. This comes across most clearly from Jacobson J's focus on the absence of a written agreement between the family entities, which meant that there was no legally enforceable power of control, such that cancellation was justified.[54]

In any event, moreover, licensing without control in Australia can always lead to the mark being expunged from the register not by virtue of section 88(2)(c), but rather because of the way the removal for non-use provisions operate. Under section 92(4)(b) of the Trade Marks Act of 1995 a mark is vulnerable to removal if it has not been used by the owner in the preceding three years. Use by a licensee can inure to the benefit of the owner, but only to the extent that the licensee's use is *authorised.* Authorised use is defined in section 8 of the 1995 Act as being use "under the control" of the owner of the mark. This includes, but is not limited to, use in circumstances where the owner exercises "quality control" over the goods or services or "financial control" over the operations of the licensee, as provided for by sub-sections 8(3) and (4) respectively.[55] The question with which the courts have struggled is whether owners are required to demonstrate that they have in fact exercised control or whether it is sufficient for them to point to a legally enforceable right of control.

In early cases under the 1995 Act, the Federal Court adopted a permissive interpretation of the authorised user provisions. Under this approach it was sufficient for the licensee's use to demonstrate a "slight connection" with the trademark owner. In practice, this meant an owner could resist removal for non-use merely by pointing to a contract that gave it a right to exercise a degree of control over the activities of the licensee. The permissive approach is best illustrated by *Yau's Entertainment Pty Ltd* v. *Asia Television Ltd.*[56] The mark owner was a Hong Kong television broadcaster that had entered into an agreement with Yau's, an Australian distributor, under which the broadcaster supplied Yau's with master tapes of programmes bearing the registered mark to be copied and distributed by Yau's in Australia. The Full Federal Court held that the owner's contractual right to veto the selection of television programmes released on video in Australia by Yau's amounted to a sufficient degree of control under section 8 so as to make Yau's an authorised user.[57] This was so even though there was no evidence of this power ever having been exercised. The result in *Yau's* is consistent with how Aickin J's decision in *Pioneer* (a decision under the 1955 Act, noted above) had come to be interpreted. The reasoning in *Yau's* is, however, problematic, not least because sub-sections 8(3) and (4) apply only where the owner *exercises* quality or financial control.

[52] *Id.* at 500–01.

[53] Burrell & Handler, *supra* note 24, at 583, 587.

[54] *Health World*, 75 IPR at 500–01.

[55] A further factor is that the authorised use must be use "as a trade mark." For recent consideration, *see Dunlop Aircraft Tyres Ltd* v. *The Goodyear Tire & Rubber Co.* (2018) 262 FCR 76 (Fed. Ct.) (Austl.).

[56] *Yau's Ent. Pty Ltd* v. *Asia Television Ltd* (2002) 54 IPR 1 (Full Fed. Ct.) (Austl.).

[57] *Id.* at 16 (Hely J, with whose reasons Sundberg and Finkelstein JJ agreed).

The breadth of *Yau's*, and its inconsistency with the statutory language, was recognised in *Skyy Spirits LLC* v. *Lodestar Anstalt*, a first instance decision of Perram J.[58] The plaintiff, a manufacturer of bourbon, had agreed to settle a dispute with a small winemaker using a similar unregistered mark on the basis that the plaintiff could seek to register the mark and that it would, in return, license the winemaker to use the mark. The licence fee was $1 and, although the licence agreement contained quality control provisions, there was no evidence that these were ever exercised. Indeed, Perram J went as far as saying that there was "a total lack of control or interest in the marks beyond the most formalistic recognition of the licence agreement," and that the owner's "ability to control the quality of the wine was entirely theoretical and had no footing in reality."[59] His Honour considered that he was bound to follow *Yau's* in finding that the winemaker's use was nevertheless "under the control" of the owner and thus not liable to be removed for non-use, but was highly critical of *Yau's*.[60] These criticisms have significant force and, on appeal, in *Lodestar Anstalt* v. *Campari America LLC*, an enlarged five-judge Full Bench of the Federal Court held that the exercise of control is central to the notion of authorised use.[61] In finding that there had been no authorised use of the mark by the winemaker, the court emphasised that "control in section 8 means actual control in relation to the use of the trade mark and it means actual control in relation to the trade mark from time to time."[62] It also noted that this result was consistent with the legislative history, and that attempts to read *Pioneer* as supporting the more permissive approach were inconsistent with the overall tenor of that judgment.[63] Interestingly, the Full Court was directed to the decision of the House of Lords in *Scandecor*, but held that this case had no applicability in Australia, as English and Australian law "have taken different paths."[64]

Australian law has thus returned to being closer to the historical position at common law, and to the position that pertains in the United States. Although this approach may look dated to a UK audience, it is one that adheres more closely to the historical function of trademarks as badges of origin. Trademarks are neither free-floating signifiers nor mere receptacles for brand value. This is recognised in Article 19(2) of the TRIPS Agreement, which provides "[w]hen subject to the control of its owner, use of a trade mark by another person shall be recognised as use of a trade

[58] *Skyy Spirits LLC* v. *Lodestar Anstalt* (2015) 112 IPR 328 (Fed. Ct.) (Austl.).

[59] *Id.* at 337–38. This has strong similarities with the facts of *Barcamerica Int'l USA Trust* v. *Tyfield Importers, Inc.*, 289 F. 3d 589 (9th Cir. 2002).

[60] *Skyy Spirits*, 112 IPR at 339–40, 342.

[61] *Lodestar Anstalt* v. *Campari Am. LLC* (2016) 244 FCR 557, 581 (Besanko J, with whose reasons Allsop CJ and Greenwood J agreed), 585 (Nicholas J, with whose reasons Allsop CJ agreed), 598 (Katzmann J). In doing so, four of the judges interpreted *Yau's* as not in fact turning on the point that mere theoretical control was sufficient to amount to authorised use: *id.* at 580 (Besanko J), 594 (Katzmann J). *See generally* Anna Harley, *Keeping the Faith: Is There a Standard of Sufficient "Use" of a Trade Mark in Australia?*, 111 INTELL. PROP. F. 25 (2018).

[62] *Lodestar*, 244 FCR at 581 (Besanko J). His Honour noted that "actual control will be a question of fact and degree," and that the nature of the agreement between the parties "may be such that it is not necessary for the registered owner to give directions or instructions from time to time": *id. See, e.g.*, *Trident Seafoods Corp.* v. *Trident Foods Pty Ltd* (2019) 143 IPR 1 (Full Fed. Ct.) (Austl.), where it was held that a parent company's use of a mark was under the control of its wholly owned subsidiary that owned the mark, even though the subsidiary could not point to an illustration of conduct amounting to actual control. It was thought to be sufficient that the companies had common directors and "operated with a unity of purpose . . . to maximise sales and to enhance the value of the brand": *id.* at 14. The court did not, however, express any disagreement with the approach taken in *Health World Ltd* v. *Shin-Sun Austl. Pty Ltd* (2008) 75 IPR 478 (Fed. Ct.) (Austl.), discussed *supra* notes 50–54 and accompanying text.

[63] *Lodestar*, 244 FCR at 574–76, 580 (Besanko J), 585 (Nicholas J), 596–98 (Katzmann J).

[64] *Id.* at 581 (Besanko J).

mark for the purpose of maintaining the registration."[65] The Full Federal Court in *Lodestar* cited this provision as a reason for rejecting the more permissive approach to licensing.[66]

There is one final issue that is worthy of consideration. This is when a licensed mark might be vulnerable to being expunged from the Register even though the requirement of control would appear to be satisfied. As noted above when considering Lord Nicholls' approach to naked licensing in *Scandecor*, we believe that there are good reasons for regarding control as a necessary condition, but that it ought not to be treated as a sufficient condition in every case. Most obviously, this would arise where there is reason to believe on the face of the mark that consumer expectations are not going to be met. For example, this might occur where a feature of a compound mark indicates that the goods are manufactured by a specific party, but the goods in question are produced by the licensee (even under the licensor's control).[67] More controversially, there is a live question, at least in Australia, about when an apparent exercise of actual control is to be disregarded as being merely "colorable," or use other than in good faith. This possibility was raised by Nicholas J in *Lodestar*.[68] Section 92(4)(b) of the Australian Act is worded in such a way that this possibility must remain open, but identifying the boundary between merely colourable control and genuine control undertaken partly with an eye to preserving the registration is difficult, as Nicholas J himself recognised.

V CONCLUSION

Among the trademark community it is generally understood that the United States continues to impose more onerous restrictions on the assignment and licensing of trademarks than many other countries. In European commentaries, including those produced by UK authors, this tends to be treated as another example of American trademark exceptionalism. On this account, restrictions on trademark transactions sit alongside the maintenance of a use-based model of registration and infringement,[69] the requirement of proof of use on renewal,[70] and the concept of incontestability.[71] However, from an Australian perspective at least, the US law on trademark transactions remains instantly recognisable. Indeed, it might provide useful guidance, particularly on when an assignee of a trademark should be deemed to have done enough to ensure that its use of the mark has not become deceptive (an issue that remains largely unlitigated and under-theorised outside the United States). Viewed from Australia, it is the United Kingdom where the law on trademark transactions, particularly licensing, has moved furthest from the

[65] Agreement on Trade-Related Aspects of Intellectual Property Rights, art 19(2), Apr. 15, 1994, Marrakesh Agreement Establishing the World Trade Organization, Annex 1C, 1869 UNTS 299, 33 ILM 1197.

[66] *Lodestar*, 244 FCR at 575 (Besanko J).

[67] *Cf.* the facts of *Heublein Inc. v. Cont'l Liquers Pty Ltd* (1959) 103 CLR 435 (Austl.), discussed *supra* note 37.

[68] *Lodestar*, 244 FCR at 587–88 (Nicholas J).

[69] *See generally* Graeme B. Dinwoodie & Mark D. Janis, *Use, Intent to Use, and Registration in the USA*, *in* Trade Mark Use 313 (Jeremy Phillips & Ilanah Simon eds., 2005); Rebecca L. Tushnet, *Registering Disagreement: Registration in Modern American Trademark Law*, 130 Harv. L. Rev. 867 (2017); Jane C. Ginsburg, *Euro-Yearnings? Moving toward a "Substantive" Registration-Based Trademark Regime*, 130 Harv. L. Rev. F. 95 (2017).

[70] Trademark Act of 1946 § 8(a)(2), 15 USC § 1058(a)(2) (2016). This provision is often singled out, not least because there is a strong argument that it puts the United States in breach of art. 3(1)(a)(xvii) and 3(6) of the Trademark Law Treaty and of art. 3(1)(a)(xvi) and 3(3) of the Singapore Treaty on the Law of Trademarks. *See* Burrell & Handler, *supra* note 24, at 366.

[71] Trademark Act of 1946 § 15, 15 USC § 1065 (2016). *See generally* Rebecca Tushnet, *Fixing Incontestability: The Next Frontier?*, 23 B.U. J. Sci. & Tech. L. 434 (2017); Kenneth L. Port, *The Illegitimacy of Trademark Incontestability*, 26 Ind. L. Rev. 519 (1993).

common law fold. But as we have tried to demonstrate, there must remain circumstances in the United Kingdom in which uncontrolled transactions can give rise to cancellation of the mark. Knowledge of the more restrictive approach that continues to apply in other common law countries might help sharpen understanding of when cancellation might be justified, even after the more liberal approach adopted by the House of Lords in *Scandecor*.

38

Civil Law Perspectives on Trademark Transactions

*Nicolas Binctin**

I INTRODUCTION

This chapter focuses on the analysis of trademark transactions from a civil law perspective, principally within the main EU jurisdictions. At the outset, it is important to observe that even though trademark law currently follows the general principles set forth by a harmonized EU trademark law, contract law largely remains the province of national legislation.[1] Therefore, presenting a civil law perspective on trademark transactions can be difficult in a legal environment that is less and less national regarding substantive trademark norms, but is still largely national regarding contract law.

More specifically, EU trademark law establishes the general principles that a trademark can be assigned or licensed, yet the legal conditions under which trademarks are assigned or licensed are not directly established by EU law.[2] Of course, any assignment or licensing agreement has to be in compliance with EU competition law, but the substantive conditions of these agreements continue to be regulated under the national law on contracts of each EU member state.[3] In practice, any of the three principal types of trademark transactions (i.e. the assignment, the licence, and the use of the intellectual property as collateral) is designed by the parties based on the circumstances of each individual case, ranging from a very simple assignment or licence to a very complex operation, such as using the mark as security or collateral for securing financing or venture capital. This chapter specifically refers to each of these transactions and addresses their complexities from a civil law perspective.

As a matter of general principle, the civil law model is built with a double system of codified regimes and contractual freedom and offers both generalized rules and supplemental legal regimes that can be applied to specific transactions. The supplemental effect of the civil law means that the law is applicable in the absence of other legal or conventional provisions. Moreover, even if the law provides some model agreements, parties are not bound by them and can draft their own contract terms, thus developing different and alternative models. These

* Professor, Faculty of Law, Université de Poitiers.

[1] Annette Kur & Thomas Dreier, European Intellectual Property Law 238 (2013).

[2] Regulation 2015/2424 of the European Parliament and of the Council of Dec. 16, 2015, amending Council Regulation No. 207/2009 on the Community trademark and Commission Regulation No. 2868/95, implementing Council Regulation No. 40/94 on the Community trademark (EC).

[3] Consolidated Version of the Treaty on the Functioning of the European Union, 2010 OJ (C 83) 47, art. 81 [hereinafter TFEU]; *see also* TFEU, art. 102; *see also* Jacques Raynard, *Aspects Civilistes des Contrats de Transfert de Technique, in* Les Contrats de la Propriété Intellectuelle 9 (Jean-Michel Bruguière ed., 2013).

principles are followed in the majority of civil law countries, including EU countries such as Germany[4] and France,[5] as well as in other civil law countries such as Brazil[6] and Japan.[7]

Accordingly, as is elaborated in this chapter, presenting the civil law perspectives on trademark transactions ultimately results in presenting the interaction and relationship between the general common principles of civil contract law as well as those of trademark law. As noted before, the long-awaited adoption of common principles of EU contract law could later impact, if and when it happens, all contractual transactions of intellectual property-related products in the EU.[8]

II TRADEMARK ASSIGNMENT

With respect to trademark assignment, under the civil law system, an assignment is perfected and the ownership of a trademark is transferred when the parties agree on the property (in this instance the trademark) to be transferred and the price to be paid for it. The assignment occurs even if the property has not yet been delivered and the price has not yet been paid. The only specific civil law requirement is that the agreement at issue must be done in writing.[9] Furthermore, the price has either to be determined and stated in the contract or needs to be determinable, meaning the price has to be comparable to the value of the trademark and more than just a symbolic gesture.[10] For example, a trademark's value can be set to be one euro, but if the real value of the trademark is higher (as it most likely will be), the symbolic amount of one euro can become the reason to invalidate the agreement or requalify it, primarily for tax purposes, as a donation. There are several known examples of trademark agreements being structured as donations for corporate management reasons or similar.[11]

As mentioned in the Introduction, the general provisions of contract law apply directly to the contract of trademark assignment. This means that the assignment of a trademark is treated like an ordinary transfer of ownership. The parties to the agreement must have the legal capacity to enter into contracts and to be able to sell the property at issue.[12] If there is joint ownership of the property (the trademark) by more than one party, the legal capacity of the individual

[4] Axel Nordemann & Christian Czychowski, *Trademark Transaction in Germany: A Continental European System Moves towards Common Understanding with the EU*, *in* The Law and Practice of Trademark Transaction 387 (Irene Calboli & Jacques de Werra eds., 2016).

[5] Nicolas Binctin, *French Perspectives on Trademark Transactions: From the Civil Code to the Business Law*, *in* The Law and Practice of Trademark Transaction 410 (Irene Calboli & Jacques de Werra eds., 2016).

[6] Jose Carlos Vaz e Dias, *New Dress Code for Business Transaction in Brazil: Essentials and Peculiarities of Trademarks in the Spotlight*, *in* The Law and Practice of Trademark Transaction 462 (Irene Calboli & Jacques de Werra eds., 2016).

[7] Shinto Teramoto, *Japanese Perspectives on Trademark Transactions: Is Expansive Trademark Practice Prevailing over the Conservative Stoicism?*, *in* The Law and Practice of Trademark Transaction 511 (Irene Calboli & Jacques de Werra eds., 2016).

[8] Nicolas Binctin, *Le Droit Européen de la Vente et la Propriété Intellectuelle*, *in* Les Contrats de la Propriété Intellectuelle 101 (Jean-Michel Bruguière ed., 2013).

[9] *See, e.g.*, according to French law, the written form can be required as a proof according to Code Civil, art. 1173 (Fr.); for the validity of the agreement in the case of trademark assignment, *see* Code de la Propriété Intellectuelle [CPI] [Intellectual Property Code], art. L. 714-1.

[10] In the French Civil Code, the agreement can be cancelled if the price is not a real counterpart. *See* Code Civil, art. 1168, 1169, 1108 (Fr.).

[11] Charlotte Urman, *Licences intragroupes, avez-vous anticipé les risques fiscaux? En savoir plus sur*, Village de la Justice, https://village-justice.com/articles/Licences-intragroupes-Avez-vous,20014.html#i1Qjc355sT8ztYwb.99.

[12] The application of these two criteria can be adapted if a party is a natural body or a legal body. In case of a legal body, the legal representative can have limited power and not be able to sell some important assets as the trademarks.

parties has to be established according to the general principles of civil law[13] or based on an undivided ownership agreement.[14] The co-ownership of trademarks is not subject to specific rules, but to the general rules governing undivided ownership. In this regard, it is important to distinguish between the assignment of a trademark, which is a classic trademark transfer of ownership, and the sale of a part of the undivided ownership which is an adaptation of the undivided ownership. Only the assignment part of the transaction needs to follow the principles provided by trademark law. This means, for example, that trademark law does not apply to the assignment if the assignment only modifies the structure of an undivided ownership without an actual transfer of the trademark. For example, since the civil law accepts that the transfer of a part of an undivided ownership can be done without written form, trademark law has no impact on the validity of the agreement. But, nevertheless, the civil law requires that there must be publication of any changes related to the undivided ownership with a specific form, not for the validity of the agreement, but as notice to third parties.

It should also be noted that a trademark assignment does not implicitly include the transfer of the six-month priority period granted under the Paris Convention for the protection of industrial property.[15] Instead, the transfer of the priority right has to be included in the assignment agreement explicitly or it could be assigned on its own. Take an international company, for example. We can imagine that, for strategic reasons, the company could transfer to a specific subsidiary, based anywhere in the world, the priority right of a specific trademark so that the subsidiary would be able to secure the rights in the trademark all around the world, except in the initial country where the mark was first registered. Instead, in the absence of a specific indication in this regard the seller continues to own the priority right. Similarly, if there is a coexistence agreement between the owner of the mark and third parties, the coexistence agreement has to be included in the conditions of the assignment to remain in force after the assignment is perfected. This requirement is very important, as it could be possible that, absent the transfer of the coexistence agreement as part of the trademark assignment, the validity of the mark itself could be jeopardized. Moreover, the transfer of a coexistence agreement requires the consent of the third party, which is part of the coexistence agreement.[16] Lastly, if the assigned trademark was involved in an infringement proceeding, the assignment can include the transfer of the judicial action. Still, this has to be explicitly mentioned in the agreement.

Inconsistencies across civil law countries still remain regarding the *numerus clausus* doctrine for ownership in cases of dismemberment of property.[17] For example, the French Court of

[13] *See, e.g.*, in the case of French law, according to art. 815 et seq. Code Civil.The question can be complex if one considers an EU trademark which is undivided, and which is owned by two persons and thus attached to two different applicable laws.

[14] The undivided ownership agreement can organize the representation of the undivided ownership to an assignment. *Cf.* Code Civil, art. 815-3 (Fr.); Frédéric Pollaud-Dulian, *La Propriété Industrielle*, 1612 Economica 936 (2011); Jacques Raynard, Emmanuel Py & Pascale Tréfigny, Droit de la Propriété Industrielle 244 (2016).

[15] Paris Convention for the Protection of Industrial Property, Mar. 20, 1883, *as revised* July 14, 1967, 21 UST 1583, 828 UNTS 305, art. 4A(1) [hereinafter Paris Convention].

[16] *See, e.g.*, in the French Law, the conditions of a transfer of an agreement are exposed in arts. 1216 et seq. Code Civil. François Terré, Philippe Simler, Yves Lequette & François Chénedé, Les Obligations 1736 (12th ed. 2019); Philippe Malaurie, Laurent Aynès & Philippe Stoffel-Munck, Droit des Obligations 475 (10th ed. 2018).

[17] The *numerus clausus* is a concept of property law which limits the number of types of rights that the courts will acknowledge as having the character of "property." Several consequences follow from a right having the nature of property, as opposed to being a personal right, like a contract or obligation to pay compensation. Under English law today, there are fourteen property rights in the *numerus clausus*. In German law, the *numerus clausus* principle has a constitutional foundation and limits property rights in their number (*Typenzwang*) and content (*Typenfixierung*). *See* Thomas Merrill & Henry Smith, *Optimal Standardization in the Law of Property: The Numerus Clausus Principle*, 110

Cassation gave up the *numerus clausus* doctrine, which applied to real property rights.[18] Thus, based on the principle of contractual freedom, it is possible to sell any kind of right *in rem* on a trademark and to enter into any kind of division or subdivision of the right of ownership on a given trademark. Moreover, one can not only transfer the full ownership, but also some isolated elements of a trademark. For example, one can transfer the right – "droit réel démembré" – in a mark only with respect to some, but not all, of the goods and services for which the trademark is registered. In such instances, the subject matter of the agreement is the conventional property right in the mark. The agreement and the transfer can be either temporary or permanent.[19] All in all, the conditions set by the parties in these agreements can be an important area of contractual creativity.[20] For example, it is possible to divide the trademark into different utilities and give a *jus in re* for each utility to the user. This would not result in a simple right to use the trademark. The legal nature of this right is different to the one the user has with a licence (which is the right to use the mark under certain conditions)[21] and different of a division of a single ownership in two or more autonomus ownership rights.

For any assignment, the price stipulated between the parties can be an inclusive price, which can be paid in a lump sum or in several instalments, or the price can also be a fully proportional price, meaning the price will be paid according to the exploitation of the sign during a contractual duration.[22] It can also be both (that is, part of the price is an inclusive price and the other one is proportional). In the case of a proportional price, the assignment agreement has to define the base and the rate to calculate this part of the price.[23]

For warranties, the general provisions are set forth in the national Civil Codes. When the assignment agreement is stipulated amongst professionals (as opposed to consumers and non-professional organizations), warranties can be excluded.[24] A deal is done by professionals when it involves persons acting in their professional capacity.[25] If there are only business entities in the agreement, the agreement is always the result of a professional operation. To the contrary, if there is even a single individual as a party to the agreement, the purpose of the agreement needs to be determined to ensure that the agreement is not a consumer agreement or a non-professional act.[26]

As indicated above, a trademark can be sold independently, but typically the trademark is transferred with the *company assets*, or part of it. According to civil law, the main issue is to

YALE L.J. 1 (2000); Henry Hansmann & Reinier Kraakman, *Property, Contract and Verification: The Numerus Clausus Problem and the Divisibility of Rights*, 31 J. OF LEGAL STUD. 373 (2003).

[18] Anna di Robilant, *Property and Deliberation. The Numerus Clausus Principle, New Property Forms and New Property Values*, AMER. J. COMP. L. 7 (2014); *see also* Cour de Cassation [Cass.] [Federal Supreme Court] req., Feb. 13, 1834 S. Jur. 1 (Fr.).

[19] R. Charles Henn Jr. et al., *Trademark Licensing Basics, Intellectual Property Desk Reference*, Kilpatrick Stockton LLP, 69, https://extranet.kilpatricktownsend.com/IPDeskReference/Documents/Articles%20-%20Copyright%20and%20Trademark.pdf.

[20] Louis d'Avout, *Démembrement de Propriété, Perpétuité et Liberté*, 29 RECUEIL DALLOZ, 1934 (2012); Thierry Revet, *Propriété et Drois Réels*, 3 REVUE TRIMESTRIELLE DE DROIT CIVIL 2012, 549 (2012); William Dross, *La Perpétuité des Droits Réels Sui Generis*, LA SEMAINE JURIDIQUE EDITION GÉNÉRALE 930 (2012); Frédéric Danos, *Perpétuité, Droits Réels sur la Chose d'Autrui et Droit de Superficie*, RÉPERTOIRE DEFRÉNOIS 1067 (2012); Louis d'Avout & Blandine Mallet-Bricout, *La Liberté de Création des Droits Réels Aujourd'hui*, 1 RECUEIL DALLOZ 53 (2012).

[21] For the reception of such legal organization, *see* Council Regulation 2017/1001 of the European Parliament and of the Council of June 14, 2017 on the European Union trademark, 2017 OJ (L 154), art. 26.

[22] Henn Jr. et al., *supra* note 19.

[23] *Id.*

[24] TERRÉ ET AL., *supra* note 16, at 944.

[25] Eloise Roca et al., *No-Warranty Clauses in Europe*, ASSOCIATION OF CORPORATE COUNSEL (Mar. 25, 2013), https://acc.com/resource-library/no-warranty-clauses-europe#.

[26] The trademark can be owned by a non-professional association or a physical body that is not directly using the trademark. It is a common situation.

determine whether a transfer of the company or a transfer of part of it has occurred, because the two are not the same. The transfer of a company is a stock transfer and includes the company debts (i.e. share deal). The transfer of *company assets* includes the transfer of tangible and intangible assets and excludes the buildings and debts (i.e. asset deal). It is possible to sell the *company assets* without some of its elements if that is explicitly mentioned in the sale agreement.[27] In this way, it is possible to have a trademark transfer that includes the value of the brand image and the accessories of the trademark.[28] Likewise, the *company assets* can be primarily composed of trademarks.

The link between the sale of a trademark and the *company assets* transfer is important. For example, in France, case law considers that if the sale of the trademark transfers the seller's customers to the buyer, such an operation is a *company assets* transfer, even if the sale object is a trademark only. Such a characterization is important because the legal procedure to sell *company assets* is different from the one relating to selling a trademark. The consequence regarding the definition of the transaction's legal nature is not only a tax effect question[29] but also a question of the characterization of the agreement, formalities, and possibly the notice and publication of the agreement with the national intellectual property office and/or, where applicable, with the national company register which is used by any EU member state and is interconnected.[30] The Code de Commerce provides an extensive and special procedure for *company assets* transfers to protect the creditors. The legal nature of the trademark transfer has to be clarified before the execution of the transfer. A guide for defining the legal nature of the transaction determines that an unused trademark can be sold directly (i.e. out of a company assets procedure). If the trademark is used, it is necessary to check whether the seller's customers are willing to follow the trademark and become clients of the trademark's new owner. While this is the case for a significant trademark, it may not be the case for a secondary trademark. In particular, regarding the division of *company assets*, it does not seem to be efficient to sell different elements of it through two agreements as the judges can requalify the agreement.[31]

The law related to any type of trademark transaction asks, however, for a formal obligation, that is the publication of the operation for an *erga omnes* opposability.

III TRADEMARK LICENSING

A similar approach to the one described for trademark assignments is followed for trademark licensing. A trademark licensing agreement is similar to a rental agreement – that is, a lease on intangible property.[32] In the absence of specific provisions under civil law, the general principles that apply to leasing can be found in any national Civil Code. The general principles of civil lease law are similar to the general principles of civil sale law.[33]

[27] For Germany, *see* Nordemann & Czychowski, *supra* note 4, at § 16.58 et seq.

[28] Priority right, coexistence agreements, judicial procedures, etc.

[29] On tax, *see* Teramoto, *supra* note 7, at § 21.39.

[30] Council Directive 2017/1132 of the European Parliament and of the Council of June 14, 2017 relating to certain aspects of company law, 2017 OJ (L 169), 46–127, https://e-justice.europa.eu/content_business_registers_at_european_level-105-fr.do.

[31] *See, e.g.*, a company sells its goods in one agreement and its trademark in another one; such a deal has to be qualified as a *company assets* transfer even for the isolated trademark, i.e. Cass. Com., Oct. 23, 2007, Bulletin 2007, IV, No. 222.

[32] For Germany, *see* Nordemann & Czychowski, *supra* note 4, at § 16.36 et seq.; for Japan, see Teramoto, *supra* note 7, at § 21.12.

[33] *See, supra*, Section II. *See also* NICOLAS BINCTIN, DROIT DE LA PROPRIÉTÉ INTELLECTUELLE 711 (5th ed. 2018).

The main difference between the two principles is that there is no ownership transfer involved in a trademark licensing agreement. This means that at the end of the licence, any trademark goodwill earned by the licensee is legally attributed to the licensor. And, in terms of determining contractual capacity and undivided ownership, the rules for licensing are the same as the sale rules. In the case of a sub-licence, the licensor can be a tenant. The general rules of civil law contracts leave the possibility of sub-licence agreements to be determined by the parties during negotiations. The licensor can either agree or prohibit the licensee from granting sub-licences. If the licensor allows the licensee to sub-licence, the sub-licence is limited to the terms and scope of the original licence agreement.[34] The influence of EU regulations is limited even with respect to the licence. The only common provisions in the UETMR (Article 22) concern basic rules. According to those provisions, licences can be exclusive or non-exclusive, and can be granted for all or part of the listed goods and services, and for the whole or part of the territory for which it is owned. This means that there is no possibility of conflict between EUTMR rules and general civil law contract rules because EUTMR rules are limited and need general civil law contract rules to be applied.

The licensing agreement can cover either all or only some of the economic uses of a trademark, and, similarly, the licence can cover one or several territories. Furthermore, the licence can be granted for either a limited or unlimited duration,[35] which is an important distinction because the duration of the licence agreement influences the termination conditions. The only exclusion in the civil law is a perpetual agreement, but unlimited and perpetual are not the same. An unlimited agreement can be stopped at any moment. The licence agreement can include or exclude any element and/or economic use depending on the licensee's interests and the licensor's strategy.

One of the main questions involved in a licensing agreement is exclusivity. Civil law allows the parties freedom to negotiate a licence agreement with territorial and/or product exclusivity. The legality of exclusivity is a question of competition law rather than contract law. The Court of Justice of the EU (CJUE) assessed the exclusivity of a licensing agreement under provisions of the Treaty on the Functioning of the European Union.[36]

The licensing agreement can be for free or can include royalty payments to the licensor. The royalties are defined broadly as either a fixed or proportional rate, meaning that the royalty is proportional to any element of the business as defined in the licensing agreement.[37] Moreover, the rate can be adjusted and the agreement can include a minimum amount guaranteed.[38] According to the CJUE case law, the basis of the rate has to be in accordance with the use of the trademark.[39] However, the royalties are based on the existence of the trademark, so if the trademark enters the public domain, the licensing agreement is no longer valid because the trademark is no longer owned by the licensor. But the parties can include in the licence agreement a provision relating to the payment of royalties after the trademark has entered

34 Henn Jr. et al., *supra* note 19.

35 Marie-Elodie Ancel, *La Clause de Durée dans les Contrats de Licence de Marque*, COMMUNICATION COMMERCE ELECTRONIQUE 9 (2012).

36 Case C-403/08 and C-429/08, *Football Ass'n Premier League and Others* v. *QC Leisure and Others*, 2011 ECR I-09083; *see also* Consolidated Version of the Treaty on the Functioning of the European Union, art. 101, 2012 OJ (C 326) 47 (EN).

37 Henn Jr. et al., *supra* note 19.

38 *Id.*

39 Case C-193/83, *Windsurfing Int'l Inc.* v. *Comm.*, 1986 ECR 611. For observations on the case, *see* Georges Bonet, *Propriétés intellectuelles*, *in* REVUE TRIMESTRIELLE DE DROIT EUROPÉEN 313 (1987).

the public domain.[40] In the event the trademark enters the public domain – for example because the mark has become generic or has been abandoned – as the royalty payments began prior to the trademark entering the public domain and were based on the use of the trademark, the royalty payments will continue until the date specified in the agreement. The agreement must specify the payment terms and conditions, the necessary amount of control exercised by the licensor over the licensee's use of the trademark, and all the technical dispositions of the licence.[41]

The warranties included in the licence agreement are similar to the ones included in the sales contract for the existence of the good, the existence of the ownership, and the qualities of the trademark.[42] The existence of the ownership can be warranted not only on the date of the contract but also during all the agreement effect. We could imagine that a mark which entered the public domain because of the owner's inactivity could be a breach of warranty. Some special warranties may be added in a licence agreement. Many licence agreements include a warranty covering the mismanagement of the trademark by the licensor. For example, the licensor warrants to pay all the taxes necessary to maintain the trademark in the licence area. If the licensor does not comply with this warranty, the licensor has to cover the licensee's damages.

The relationship between a licence transfer and the licensed trademark is an important question under the civil law. The licensor can assign the licensed trademark to a trademark buyer without being in conflict with a civil code. The transfer of the trademark is possible after the parties have fulfilled their obligations under the agreement. The trademark buyer must respect the finalized licence agreement before the transfer and perform all the obligations of the licensor under the agreement. The trademark buyer also has to respect the licensee's position under the agreement. But if the licence agreement provides for certain personal obligations (*intuitus personae*) of the licensor, the transfer of the licensed trademark can be limited. If those commitments are not *intuitus personae* – for example, to pay the taxes – the trademark buyer has to perform them. But if there are some *intuitus personae* obligations in the licence agreement – for example, to transfer special knowledge about the trademark to the buyer – the licensor cannot transfer the ownership of the trademark unless the licensor has received prior authorization from the licensee. In general, the transfer of the trademark licence can be achieved in the civil law system as a kind of sale; the buyer is taking the contractual place of the seller. To secure such a transaction, it is best to explicitly include a provision in the licence agreement regarding the possible sale of the trademark.

Under a trademark licence, the licensor is liable for any defective goods in the market bearing the trademark, and remains involved in the liability for defective goods under the EU Product Liability Directive.[43] The licensor is identified as the producer of the goods associated with the trademark according to the Product Liability Directive because the trademark is used to

40 By analogy, *see* the ECJ solution for a patent: Case C-567/14, *Genentech Inc.* v. *Hoechst*, 2016 EUR-Lex ECLI:EU:C:2016:526, comm. 220, note Georges Decocq; Axel Reidlinger, Diana Ionescu & Thomas Kustor, *The CJEU's Genentech Judgment of 7 July 2016 (C-567/14): Lessons for the Review of Arbitration Awards on EU Competition Law by State Courts*, 9(3) Global Competition Lit. Rev. 109 (2016); Laurence Idot, *Accord de Licence et Paiement de Redevances*, 10 Europe 28 (2016); Jérôme Passa, *Les Redevances de Licence dues Après l'Annulation du Brevet en Droit de la Concurrence*, 19 Prop. Indust. (2016); Jacques Raynard, *L'Obligation Contractuelle de Payer des Redevances au Titre d'une Exploitation qui n'est pas Couverte par le Brevet*, 23 Prop. Indust. (2016).

41 *See generally*, Henn Jr. et al., *supra* note 19.

42 Yan Basire, *Les Clauses de Non-garantie Dans les Contrats de Licence de Brevet, in* Propriété Industrielle (2012).

43 Council Directive 85/374/EEC, on the Approximation of the Laws, Regulations and Administrative Provisions of the Member States Concerning Liability for Defective Products, 1985 OJ (L 210) (EC). The liability is applied in case of exploitation of a product; the licence is a kind of exploitation.

identify the producer of the goods,[44] and, thus, the licence makes the trademark owner liable on this basis. The parties can derogate from the licensor's liability by contract, thus making the licensee liable for defects in goods that it produces but the derogation cannot be opposed to any corporal damages.[45]

The licensee also has to perform obligations under the agreement.[46] Particularly, the licensee has to use the licensed trademark.[47] The use of the trademark is a condition for the continued ownership of the trademark. If the licensee does not use the trademark in the course of business, the licensor may lose the trademark as a result. The obligation on the licensee to use the trademark in the course of business is not an obligation to use the trademark with success, but simply to use the trademark. This requirement is included to protect the licensor from losing ownership over the trademark because of the licensee's failure to use it. According to CJEU case law, the licensee has to use the trademark in accordance with the business habits. The licensee's obligation to use the trademark is also in line with a proportional royalty scheme if the licence is negotiated and agreed on such a business model. When the royalty is proportional to the use of the trademark, the licensee has the obligation to use the trademark.

For the use of a trademark as an "in kind" contribution to incorporate or to secure collateral for loans, there is no legal limit under civil law.[48] The incorporation act can be structured as a sale or a licence, for a long or short period, and with or without exclusivity. The incorporation act can be done under any kind of contractual operation, like a trademark assignment or a licensing agreement. The incorporation act exchanges money for a counterpart of stock. If there is an ownership transfer through the incorporation, the company becomes the owner of the trademark. In the case of incorporation that is limited to a licence, the licensor – not the company – remains the owner of the trademark, and a standard licence agreement, as discussed above, between the licensor and the company has to be concluded.[49] If the incorporation is for a short or limited period, such as two years, the company no longer has the right to use the trademark after the term of the licence agreement has expired, but the trademark owner-partner remains a stockholder in the company.

Different types of trademark transactions can be involved in such agreements according to civil contract law. Of course, a national trademark can be the object of sale, assignment, or licensing agreement, but any EU trademark can also be the subject of a trademark transaction. In addition to national and EU trademarks, any trademark in the world can be the subject of a trademark transaction that is governed by civil law. The contractual freedom of the parties to negotiate and determine the governing law of the agreement is important to expressly include in the agreement, especially if elements of the agreement can create conflicts in different countries. For example, any trademark transaction can be governed by national law, but any national trademark can also be the subject of a foreign trademark transaction and subject to foreign laws. It will be the same question for the issue of jurisdiction (judicial competence). Contracting

[44] *Id.*; *see also* CODE CIVIL [C. CIV.][CIVIL CODE], art. 1245-5 (Fr.).

[45] For a general presentation of this specific regime to the trademark, *see* BINCTIN, *supra* note 33, at No. 1116 et seq., p. 719 et seq.

[46] Martin Senftleben, *Trademark Transaction in EU Law: Refining the Approach to Selective Distribution Networks and National Unfair Competition Law*, *in* THE LAW AND PRACTICE OF TRADEMARK TRANSACTION 327 (Irene Calboli & Jacques de Werra eds., 2016).

[47] DENISE BAUMANN, L'OBLIGATION D'EXPLOITER LES MARQUES EN DROIT FRANÇAIS ET ALLEMAND – ÉTUDE COMPARATIVE 14 (1978).

[48] About the incorporation of intellectual goods in the French law, for a global study, *see* NICOLAS BINCTIN, LE CAPITAL INTELLECTUAL (2007).

[49] Henn Jr. et al., *supra* note 19, at 69.

parties may designate a national court or foreign one for a national or EU trademark transaction. They can also consider an arbitral jurisdiction. The only limit to the jurisdiction of a foreign court or an arbitral jurisdiction for a trademark generally lies in disputes concerning the validity of the trademark. For this type of dispute, the jurisdiction of a foreign court or of an arbitral jurisdiction can be excluded.[50]

The law related to any type of trademark licence asks for a formal obligation, that is the publication of the operation at the IP office for an *erga omnes* opposability.

IV TRADEMARKS AND SECURITIES

Trademarks can also be used as collateral in financial transactions.[51] According to civil law provisions, a trademark can be used as collateral per se without the need to include tangible assets as part of the security interests that are generally used to protect investors. In the context of trademark securities, the intellectual property provisions focus on and require the publication of the agreement that stipulates the security interest between the parties, whereas general civil law provisions regarding securities apply to the type of agreement entered into by the parties. A trademark, which is considered an asset belonging to a specific person, can thus become the element of the general pledge of the creditors.[52] In turn, a security can be requested by any creditor on a trademark, even though it is more likely that creditors request that the security interest includes the goods displaying the trademark.[53] As a trademark is an intangible asset, one has to distinguish between the security that can be granted on the trademark per se and the one that can be granted on the trademark receivables or goods.

In the former case, a security on a trademark is a security on an intangible property, either present or future, that is used to secure the loan and also ensures repayment of the loan. The security on a trademark can be executed by agreement or by a court decision. The civil law defines few principles for the security on intangible products. The principles applicable to intangible products are similar to those principles applicable to tangible products. Intellectual property law requires only the publication of the security for notice purposes for third parties. For the perfection of the security, the agreement must be in writing, has to identify the debt, and has to describe the trademark given as a pledge. The debtor (i.e. the trademark owner) must preserve the quality and reputation of the marks – that is, of the products that are identified by it. In the event that the trademark owner breaches the obligation to preserve the trademark, the creditor can ask for a close-out netting provision or for a complementary security.[54] In practice, this means that the trademark owner has to continue to pay the IP office taxes to maintain the trademark right and that the trademark owner has to use the trademark in the course of trade. The trademark owner cannot abandon an application or a registration for all or part of the goods

[50] On trademarks and arbitration, *see* Dario Moura Vicente, *Arbitrability of Intellectual Property Disputes: A Comparative Survey*, 31 Arb. Int'l 151 (2015). On trademarks and judicial competence, *see* Chapter 7 in this volume, by Edouard Treppoz and Jane C. Ginsburg.

[51] Brian W. Jacobs, *Using Intellectual Property to Secure Financing after the Worst Financial Crisis since the Great Depression*, 15 Marq. Intell. Prop. L. Rev. 449, 457–58 (2011); in Germany, *see* Nordemann & Czychowski, *supra* note 4, at § 16.61 et seq.; in Brazil, *see* Vaz e Dias, *supra* note 6, at No. 19.35 et seq.; in Japan, *see* Teramoto, *supra* note 7, at § 21.53 et seq.

[52] *See* Nathalie Martial, Droit des sûretés réelles sur propriétés intellectuelles (2007).

[53] Nicolas Borga, *Pour un renouveau des garanties conventionnelles sur droits de propriété intellectuelle*, *in* Les contrats de la propriété intellectuelle 117 (Jean-Michel Bruguière ed., 2013).

[54] *See generally* David Mengle, *ISDA Research Notes, The Importance of Close-Out Netting*, International Swaps and Derivatives Association (2010), https://isda.org/a/USiDE/netting-isdaresearchnotes-1-2010.pdf.

or services to which the mark applies without previous authorization from the creditor. If the owner does not pay the debt for which the mark was used as collateral, the creditor can request from a court the sale of the trademark or the transfer of the trademark ownership to the creditor. In the event that ownership is transferred, the valuation of the trademark must be done by an expert on the day of the transfer.[55]

In addition to national trademarks, EU trademarks (EUTMs) can also be used as collateral. In these instances, however, the transaction is governed by national laws regarding securities because, at this time, EU law does not include provisions relating to the regulation of EUTMs as a security. Still, when a EUTM is used as a security,[56] the transaction must be published.[57] Therefore, a national civil law can be designated as the applicable law for the transaction if the parties so determine.

As mentioned above, a security can also be created on trademark receivables.[58] A security on receivables is typically used more often than a security on intangibles only, and is easier to organize. The security on trademark receivables does not need to comply with the specific provisions of trademark law because it is governed only by the general civil security law. A security can also be created based on universality, or an assignment patrimony such as assets allocated or a trust.[59]

In general, a security on a trademark is long and expensive to set up. On one hand, the security can be based only on a national trademark, but this security is limited in scope. On the other hand, the security can include trademarks registered in various countries, but the establishment of this bundle of transactions is complex and expensive. Moreover, its practical effects can be different from one country to another. Furthermore, the security could be quite complex and quite expensive to enforce in the various countries at issue. In this case, all the elements of the *universality* (that is, all the registrations and related rights regarding a specific trademark) could be covered by the security agreement, especially when the security agreement explicitly states that all trademarks, registered either in France or in foreign countries, included in the *universality* are covered by the security agreement.[60] In such an agreement, a broad security is formed, which includes fewer national administrative procedures. In practice, when a trademark is used as a security, the creditor checks that there are no other securities on the trademark. Then, the creditor requests a security on the *universality* explicitly including all the rights related to the trademark. The trademark or the trademark receivables can also be transferred to a security trust.[61]

[55] For a global study, *see* Michel Sejean & Nicolas Binctin, *French Security Rights on Intellectual Property*, *in* SECURITY RIGHTS IN INTELLECTUAL PROPERTY (Eva-Maria Kieninger ed., 2019); KATHARINA BOELE-WOELKI & DIEGO FERNANDEZ ARROYO, EDS., IUS COMPARATUM – GLOBAL STUDIES IN COMPARATIVE LAW (2019).

[56] Council Regulation No. 2015/2424, *supra* note 2.

[57] *Id.* at art. 33.

[58] The European Legal Alliance, *Taking Effective Security in European Jurisdictions*, 6 FIELD FISHER WATERHOUSE (Nov. 2005).

[59] The universality can be universality of law or universality of fact. The first is an aggregate of assets and debts forming a whole, i.e. patrimony. The second is an aggregate of things forming a collection or a complex legal entity (i.e. business) considered overall as a single thing and subject to a specific legal regime. *See* DICTIONARY OF THE CIVIL CODE (Alain Levasseur & Marie-Eugenie Laporte-Legeais transl., 2014).

[60] DOMINIQUE LEGEAIS, DROIT COMMERCIAL ET DES AFFAIRES 152 (2019).

[61] CODE CIVIL [C. CIV.][CIVIL CODE], art. 2372-1 (Fr.); *see also* V. FRANÇOIS BARRIÈRE, LA FIDUCIE-SÛRETÉ (2015).

In some more complex agreements, trademark receivables can be used in a securitization agreement in civil law countries.[62] For example, the securitization of intellectual property assets was introduced in France in 1998.[63] This legal framework changed in 2008[64] in order to harmonize the law with the EU Directive on Reinsurance.[65] According to the Monetary and Financial Code, the first purpose of securitization structures is to be aware of the risks associated with the securitization of intellectual property assets. These risks include insurance risks from the acquisitions of receivables, from the finalization of agreements that secure future financing, and from insurance transfer risks. The second purpose is to fully finance or cover these risks by issuing shares, units, or debt securities through securitization funds or securitization companies.[66] The Monetary and Financial Code adds that the nature and characteristics of trademark receivables for securitization may be established by decree. The decree has a major importance for intellectual property securitization in the French law system: receivables alone, and not the trademark itself, can be included in securitization structures, irrespective of the receivable's origin.[67]

The French regulation is different, for example, from that of Luxemburg, as in Luxemburg securitization can be done with any asset, including trademarks, and not just debt.[68] However, the legal restrictions on securitization under French law do not exclude intellectual property securitization. Any kind of receivables can be included in a securitization transaction, among them trademark receivables/products (e.g. receivables of trademark licences, especially long-term trademark licences). Under French intellectual property law and French securitization law such a transaction can be considered a valid transaction. The main question in this regard concerns the debt repayment for securities in the event the trademark is cancelled. Two elements should be considered regarding the possibility of the cancellation of a mark: (1) the fact that cancellations are specific to intellectual property rights (trademarks in this instance) and only a small number of intellectual property rights are cancelled every year; thus, if there are intellectual property rights in the securitization transaction, the risk of trademark cancellation remains low; and (2) in any securitization transaction, the risks associated with the underlying asset or underlying contract must always be assessed before concluding the transactions. When drafting a security agreement, it is thus advisable to include a specific provision to cover the protection against the possibility of the cancellation of the mark that is the subject of the security.

At this time, there has been no pure trademark securitization development in Europe, so the legal solutions and protections for trademark securitizations are unclear.[69] If the securitization is based on a trademark receivable model, the original company maintains ownership of the trademark, but it must continue to use the trademark. The success of the securitization is the result of the use of the trademark in the market. The securitization agreement must be

[62] Christophe Caron, *Quelques Observations sur les Montages Contractuels en droit de la Propriété Intellectuelles*, RDC 1001 (2007); *see also* Nora Wouters, *IP Securitization – The Belgium Case*, Intellectual Property Expert Group, https://ipeg.com/ip-securitization-the-case-for-belgium/.

[63] Alexandre Quiquerez, La Titrisation des Actifs Intellectuels (2013).

[64] European Parliament and Council Directive 2005/68/EC of Nov. 16, 2005, on Reinsurance and Amending Council Directives 73/239/EEC, 92/49/EEC and Directives 98/78/EC and 2002/83/EC (text with EEA relevance) 2005 OJ (L 323) 1.

[65] *Id.*

[66] *Id.*

[67] Decree No. 2008-711, July 17, 2008 Reforming the Legal Framework of the UCITS, Journal Officiel de la République Française 11554 (July 19, 2008), http://legifrance.gouv.fr/eli/decret/2008/7/17/2008-711/jo/texte.

[68] Alexandre Quiquerez, Droit et techniques internationales de la titrisation (2018).

[69] Alexandre Quiquerez, La titrisation des actifs intellectuels: au prisme du droit luxembourgeois (Collection de la Faculté de Droit, d'Économie et de Finance de l'Université du Luxembourg) (2013).

precise concerning this use obligation and can include economic sanctions if there are not sufficient revenues.

Despite the limits of French law, national trademarks in France can be involved in a securitization deal entered into in another European country, for example, Luxemburg. For these reasons, it appears that securitization of trademarks seems available in France, beyond French securitization law. Here again, the security agreement should be published for an *erga omnes* opposability. The publication may be double, according to the trademark system and according to the security one if the security law asks for it or if the company register publishes such operation on company assets.

V SPECIFIC PROVISIONS RELATED TO TRADEMARK TRANSACTIONS

Contractual freedom for trademark transactions is subject to some limits under civil law. These limits are typical formal requirements that the transaction has to satisfy to be valid. For example, the agreement has to be written, has to be made public, has to expressly state who has the right to initiate an infringement suit against third parties (opposability of the trademark), and state who has the right to use the trademark.[70]

The type of agreement determines what kind of writing requirement is necessary for the agreement to be valid. For example, if the transaction is a transfer of trademark ownership (trademark assignment), a written agreement is required to prove the validity of the transfer. If the transaction grants exclusive rights to the trademark (trademark licence), again, a written agreement is necessary. However, for a non-exclusive licence, French law upholds the validity of the licence with or without an accompanying written agreement. This policy of not requiring a written agreement for non-exclusive licensing agreements is based on the view that the law does not require publicity when the agreement relates to a non-exclusive licence. This policy is interesting in practice because generally any trademark licence is executed by a written agreement. The exception, however, is used only in the case where a conflict arises to justify the use of a trademark without any written authorization. In any case, the written form can be an authentic act[71] or a private agreement.[72]

The publication of the specific trademark agreement at issue is required to ensure that third parties and the public are made aware of the transaction.[73] In other words, the agreement has to be known by everyone and this is a legal requirement for the validity of the agreement.[74] Registration of the transaction is required to maintain public notice of the agreement.[75] If the transaction is not registered, the agreement is not known to the public, but is only known by the parties involved in the agreement. Some mandatory information, however, is accessible to third parties, such as the new owner's or licensee's name, the licensee's business nature, the licensor, and the licensor's address. But even if such information is not mandatory, the lack of

[70] *See* Henn Jr. et al., *supra* note 19.

[71] An authentic act executed or drawn by a competent public legal officer and according to the formalities required is valid and is absolute, proof by itself until it is challenged as a forgery; *see* Dictionary of the Civil Code, *supra* note 59.

[72] Jérôme Passa, Droit de la Propriété Industrielle Vol. I, 561 (2009); *see also* Annette Kur & Thomas Dreier, Eur. Intell. Prop. L. 238, §4.6 (2013).

[73] *See, e.g.*, in Brazil, Vaz e Dias, *supra* note 6, at § 19.46; *see also* Regulation (EU) 2017/1001 of the European Parliament and of the Council of June 14, 2017 on the European Union trademark, OJ (L 154), art. 27 (EC).

[74] It is the same for a national trademark or an EU trademark.

[75] *See* Regulation (EU) 2017/1001 of the European Parliament and of the Council of June 14, 2017 on the European Union trademark, OJ (L 154), art. 111 et seq. (EC).

additional information can lead to some difficulties, such as missing a new address. Typically, the interested party initiates the registration process and the registration can be recorded at any time after the agreement is executed. The registration does not ensure the existence or the quality of the trademark, but only provides the identity of the present owner and of the licensees. An uninterrupted chain of registration, however, is not necessary to achieve this goal. For a third party, the possession and the appearance theory should allow third parties to identify the owner of the trademark.[76] If the register is not up to date, but someone knows that a trademark is owned by a company, this appearance may affect the capacity of the company owner to use its trademark.

However, if the trademark is not registered, the owner or the licensee of a trademark can directly provide the proof of trademark ownership to any third party through a notification. The owner or the licensee can show legal power and rights associated with the trademark and warn third parties of potential infringement by showing this document.

The effective date agreement that is published in the official intellectual property journal is the constructive date for public knowledge. The registration has no retroactive effect regarding public knowledge and therefore the date of public knowledge is not the date of the agreement, but the date of the publication of the registration. A licensee or a new owner cannot claim damages in an infringement case during the administration procedure period, but the licensee or the new owner can directly communicate proof of its power on the trademark and show standing to sue the infringer. Whatever the importance of the registration, this procedure remains optimal for the trademark owner, without affecting the validity of the agreement.[77] In 2008, the French regulator[78] limited the effect of the lack of public knowledge for trademark transactions.[79] Even if the licence, simple or with exclusivity, was not registered with the national register, the licensee can be a party to an infringement action initiated by the trademark owner. In this action, the licensee could claim damages for its own prejudice. The consequence of the non-opposability is, therefore, limited to the inability of the licensee to sue the infringer independently.

To initiate the registration, the parties must provide the national trademark offices or the EU IP office, if applicable, with a document explaining the nature of the trademark transaction. If the owner is a legal entity, it is not necessary to mention the legal form of the legal entity (i.e. the corporate name is sufficient) in the document. If the legal entity is in the process of incorporation without legal personality or its own assets, it cannot be the owner and cannot be registered as such. In that case, the registration has to be made in the name of another person and mention that this person is acting for the company that will be incorporated. After the incorporation, it will be possible to modify the registration.[80]

[76] Judge-made theory, according to which the mere appearance suffices to have effects vis-à-vis third parties that, as a result of a legitimate error, have taken no notice of the reality of the things.

[77] Heloise Deliquiet, *L'incidence de la publicité des contrats sur l'action en contrefaçon*, *in* Les contrats de la propriété intellectuelle 19 (Jean-Michel Bruguière ed., 2013).

[78] In France, Loi 2008-776 du 4 août 2008 de Modernisation de l'Économie, OJ of the French Republic no. 0181 of Aug. 5, 2008, p. 12471.

[79] *See* in the ECJ approach, by analogy, Case C-419/15, *Thomas Philipps GmbH & Co. v. Grüne Welle Vertriebs GmbH*, (2016) EURLex 62015CJ0419; Laure Marino, *Coup de Pouce de la CJUE pour l'Action en Contrefaçon du Licencié de Dessin et Modèle*, 37 Gaz Pal. 25 (2016); Laure Marino, Prop. Indust. 2016, comm. 63. *See also*, Case C-163/15, Feb. 4, 2016, aff., *Prop. Indust.* 2016, comm. 18, note Antoine Folliard-Monguiral.

[80] Michel Germain & Véronique Magnier, Les sociétés commerciales – Traité de droit des affaires – Ripert et Roblot 63 (22d ed., 2017).

To fulfil the registration requirements, the applicant has to pay taxes[81] for the procedure. The registration is usually published within six to eight months after the registration has begun. It is possible to ask for a quicker procedure. However, this requires additional taxes to be paid. In a single registration procedure, it is possible to ask for multiple registrations for the same category of IP rights, such as trademarks, and for the same nature of operations, sales or licences, or pledges.

If the request is accepted, the registration is recorded on the national register. The national IP office sends the party that initiated the procedure a document with the identification number and the date of the registration.[82] The office then proceeds with the publication.[83] Any person interested in the procedure/transaction can send a request to the office to obtain an excerpt from the register with the registration.[84]

VI CONCLUSION

The civil law framework for trademark transactions accepts a broad contractual freedom approach. Trademark owners, licensors, licensees, and any parties in a trademark transaction can, for the most part, decide the contractual conditions that apply to their specific agreement. The law related to any type of trademark transaction asks, however, for a formal obligation for the validity of these agreements. This obligation is that the transaction should be in writing and be published so that any interested party may be informed and, if required, formally file an opposition (*erga omnes* opposability). As a result of this contractual freedom, considerable legal creativity has been developed in this area of law in order to permit the parties to maximize their options regarding the transaction at issue and, with it, the value that can be granted to the mark. As important company assets, trademarks can be involved in all above-mentioned transactions. Moreover, as established under civil law principles, a mark, including its registration for specific and separate goods and services, can be assigned or licensed "in gross" (or without any business-related assets). This affords trademark owners additional options for how to structure trademark transactions, especially for securities, as part of their company strategies and business development.

[81] The taxes are called "fees" in the official IP office documents, but to be more precise on the nature of the payment, we prefer using the term "tax." The IP offices are state organizations which collect taxes on ownership.

[82] *See* Regulation 2017/1001 of the European Parliament and of the Council of June 14, 2017 on the European Union trade mark, OJ (L 154), art. 43, § 7; art. 54, art. 55 (EC).

[83] *Id.* at art. 44.

[84] *Id.* at art. 114.

Index

www.ingramcontent.com/pod-product-compliance
Ingram Content Group UK Ltd.
Pitfield, Milton Keynes, MK11 3LW, UK
UKHW050055090825
461487UK00036B/1739
* 9 7 8 1 0 0 9 2 9 3 1 3 6 *